organisational behaviour

on the Pacific Rim

The McGraw·Hill Companies

National Library of Australia Cataloguing-in-Publication Data

McShane, Steven Lattimore.

Title: Organisational Behaviour on the Pacific Rim / Steven McShane, Tony Travaglione, Mara Olekalns.

Edition: 3e

ISBN: 9780070140271 (pbk.)

Subjects: Organizational behavior—Pacific Area

Other Authors/Contributors: Travaglione, A. Olekalns, Mara.

Dewey Number: 302.35091823

Published in Australia by
McGraw-Hill Australia Pty Ltd
Level 2, 82 Waterloo Road, North Ryde NSW 2113
Publisher: Ailsa Brackleydubois
Development Editor: Stephanie Erb
Production Editor: Michael McGrath
Editor: Emma Driver
Permissions Editor: Haidi Bernhardt
Art Director: Astred Hicks
Internal design: David Rosemeyer
Cover design: Lee Stephens
Proofreaders: Victoria Fisher and Karen Jayne
Indexer: Shelly Barons
Typeset in Scala 9.5 pt by diacriTech
Printed in China on 70 gsm matt art by iBook Printing Ltd.

Steven McShane
University of Western Australia

Mara Olekalns
Melbourne Business School

Tony Travaglione
Curtin University of Technology

organisational behaviour
on the Pacific Rim

3rd EDITION

The McGraw·Hill Companies

Sydney New York San Francisco Auckland
Bangkok Bogotá Caracas Hong Kong
Kuala Lumpur Lisbon London Madrid
Mexico City Milan New Delhi San Juan
Seoul Singapore Taipei Toronto

Preface

Welcome to the emerging knowledge and practice of organisational behaviour! Social networks and virtual teams are replacing committee meetings. Knowledge is replacing infrastructure. Values and self-leadership are replacing command-and-control management. Companies are looking for employees with emotional intelligence and team competencies, not just technical smarts. Globalisation is the new mantra of corporate survival. Co-workers aren't down the hall; they're at the other end of an internet connection located somewhere else on the planet.

Organisational Behaviour on the Pacific Rim, 3rd edition, is written in the context of these emerging workplace realities. It prepares students for this new era by discussing the latest OB concepts and practices, such as self-concept, four-drive theory, appreciative inquiry, Schwartz's values model, social networking, learning orientation and employee engagement.

Active learning, critical thinking and outcomes-based teaching have become important foundations of classroom learning. *Organisational Behaviour on the Pacific Rim* sets the standard of support by providing dozens of cases, team exercises, self-assessments, video programs and online support materials. Dismissing the traditional model that OB is for managers alone, this book also pioneers the more realistic view that OB is for everyone who works in and around organisations.

Contents *in brief*

Contents

Chapter 3 Perception and learning in organisations 86

Chapter 4 Workplace emotions, attitudes and stress 120

Chapter 5 Foundations of employee motivation 166

Chapter 6 Applied performance practices 204

Chapter 7 Decision making and creativity 240

Team Processes 297

Chapter 8 Team dynamics 298

Chapter 9 Communicating in teams and organisations 342

Chapter 10 Power and influence in the workplace 380

Chapter 11 Conflict and negotiation in the workplace 412

Chapter 12 Leadership in organisational settings 454

Part 4 Organisational Processes 499

Chapter 13 Organisational structure 500

Chapter 14 Organisational culture 536

Chapter 15 Organisational change 570

Additional case studies 614

Video case studies 636

Text *at a glance*

Organisational Behaviour on the Pacific Rim 3e is a pedagogically rich learning resource. The features laid out on these pages are specifically designed to enhance your learning experience and help you gain a deeper understanding of the concepts this text examines.

Chapter Material

Chapter openers with learning objectives

Every chapter opens with a series of learning objectives that outline the skills that you should have attained upon completing each chapter. Each learning objective is repeated in the margin of the main text where the relevant material is covered.

Opening vignettes

Each chapter opens with an introductory vignette. These stories will help you place the concepts covered in the chapter into the context of a real organisation.

Ergon Energy's emphasis on teamwork is one of the reasons why it was able to successfully integrate six regional Queensland electricity distributors a decade ago to become one of the state's most respected companies. Other organisations around the Pacific Rim and globally have also embraced teamwork as their operational model. New Zealand Post's largest delivery branch in Marua Road, Auckland, was the poorest performing branch in the country until employees were reorganised into teams. Now, it is the company's model operation in terms of performance and morale. Hong Kong–based Regal Printing relies on advanced technology to print up to 40 000 softcover books per day, but it also created a special team of 20 staff members to handle urgent jobs. Rackspace Hosting, Inc. physically organises most of its 1900 employees into teams of 14 to 20 people. The world's largest provider of enterprise-level Web infrastructure assigns every customer to one of these dedicated teams, which provides around-the-clock service.[2]

This chapter begins by defining *teams* and examining the reasons why organisations rely on teams, and why people join informal groups in organisational settings. A large segment of this chapter examines a model of team effectiveness, which includes organisational and team environment; team design; and the team processes of development, norms, cohesion and trust. We then turn our attention to two specific types of teams: self-directed and virtual teams. The final section of this chapter looks at the challenges making better decisions in teams.

OB windows

Each chapter contains a range of captioned photographs which provide quick insights into OB in action. The organisations that appear in this feature provide examples of workplaces both from the Pacific Rim and around the globe.

KEY TERMS

absorptive capacity, p. 12
corporate social responsibility (CSR), p. 16
counterproductive work behaviours (CWBs), p. 18
deep-level diversity, p. 21
ethics, p. 15
evidence-based management, p. 25
globalisation, p. 21
high-performance work practices (HPWP), p. 13
human capital, p. 12
intellectual capital, p. 12
lean management, p. 9
open systems, p. 8
organisational behaviour (OB), p. 4
organisational citizenship behaviours (OCBs), p. 17
organisational effectiveness, p. 7
organisational efficiency, p. 9
organisational learning, p. 10
organisational memory, p. 12
organisations, p. 4
stakeholders, p. 14
surface-level diversity, p. 21
values, p. 15
virtual work, p. 23
work-life balance, p. 23

Key terms

The field of organisational behaviour has its own unique terminology. Key terms are printed in bold text throughout the text and defined in the margin to help you learn the language of OB. You will also find a list of key terms at the end of each chapter, which will be useful for revision.

Text *at a glance* *(continued)*

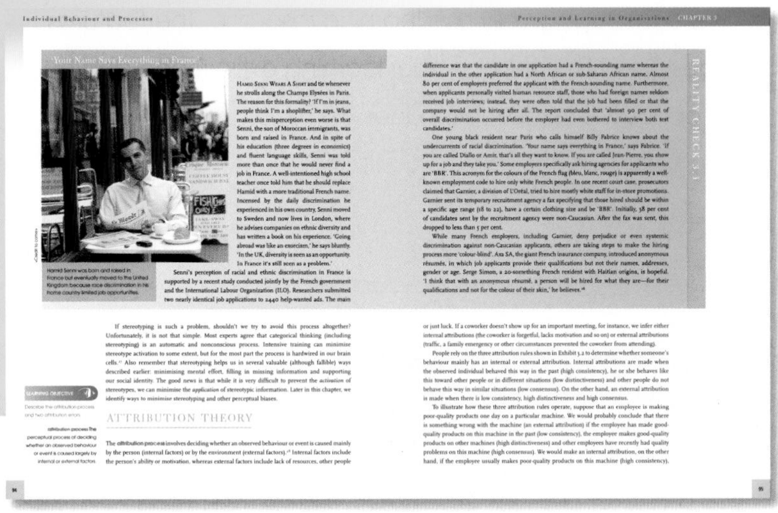

Individual Behaviour and Processes

Perception and Learning in Organisations CHAPTER 3

'Your Name Says Everything in France'

HAMID SENNI WEARS A SHIRT and tie whenever he strolls along the Champs Elysées in Paris. The reason for this formality? 'If I'm in jeans, people think I'm a shoplifter,' he says. What makes this misperception even worse is that Senni, the son of Moroccan immigrants, was born and raised in France. And in spite of his education (three degrees in economics) and fluent language skills, Senni was told more than once that he would never find a job in France. A well-intentioned high school teacher once told him that he should replace Hamid with a more traditional French name. Incensed by the daily discrimination he experienced in his own country, Senni moved to Sweden and now lives in London, where he advises companies on ethnic diversity and has written a book on his experience. 'Going abroad was like an exorcism,' he says bluntly. 'In the UK, diversity is seen as an opportunity. In France it's still seen as a problem.'

Hamid Senni was born and raised in France but eventually moved to the United Kingdom because race discrimination in his home country limited job opportunities.

Senni's perception of racial and ethnic discrimination in France is supported by a recent study conducted jointly by the French government and the International Labour Organization (ILO). Researchers submitted two nearly identical job applications to 2440 help-wanted ads. The main difference was that the candidate in one application had a French-sounding name whereas the individual in the other application had a North African or sub-Saharan African name. Almost 80 per cent of employers preferred the applicant with the French-sounding name. Furthermore, when applicants personally visited human resource staff, those who had foreign names seldom received job interviews; instead, they were often told that the job had been filled or that the company would not be hiring after all. The report concluded that 'almost 90 per cent of overall discrimination occurred before the employer had even bothered to interview both test candidates.'

One young black resident near Paris who calls himself Billy Fabrice knows about the undercurrents of racial discrimination. 'Your name says everything in France,' says Fabrice. 'If you are called Diallo or Amir, that's all they want to know. If you are called Jean-Pierre, you show up for a job and they take you.' Some employers specifically ask hiring agencies for applicants who are 'BBR'. This acronym for the colours of the French flag (bleu, blanc, rouge) is apparently a well-known employment code to hire only white French people. In one recent court case, prosecutors claimed that Garnier, a division of L'Oréal, tried to hire mostly white staff for in-store promotions. Garnier sent its temporary recruitment agency a fax specifying that those hired should be within a specific age range (18 to 22), have a certain clothing size and be 'BBR'. Initially, 38 per cent of candidates sent by the recruitment agency were non-Caucasian. After the fax was sent, this dropped to less than 5 per cent.

While many French employers, including Garnier, deny prejudice or even systemic discrimination against non-Caucasian applicants, others are taking steps to make the hiring process more 'colour-blind'. Axa SA, the giant French insurance company, introduced anonymous résumés, in which job applicants provide their qualifications but not their names, addresses, gender or age. Serge Simon, a 20-something French resident with Haitian origins, is hopeful. 'I think that with an anonymous résumé, a person will be hired for what they are—for their qualifications and not for the colour of their skin,' he believes.[16]

REALITY CHECK 3.1

If stereotyping is such a problem, shouldn't we try to avoid this process altogether? Unfortunately, it is not that simple. Most experts agree that categorical thinking (including stereotyping) is an automatic and nonconscious process. Intensive training can minimise stereotype activation to some extent, but for the most part the process is hardwired in our brain cells.[17] Also remember that stereotyping helps us in several valuable (although fallible) ways described earlier: minimising mental effort, filling in missing information and supporting our social identity. The good news is that while it is very difficult to prevent the *activation* of stereotypes, we can minimise the *application* of stereotypic information. Later in this chapter, we identify ways to minimise stereotyping and other perceptual biases.

LEARNING OBJECTIVE

Describe the attribution process and two attribution errors.

ATTRIBUTION THEORY

attribution process The perceptual process of deciding whether an observed behaviour or event is caused largely by internal or external factors.

The **attribution process** involves deciding whether an observed behaviour or event is caused mainly by the person (internal factors) or by the environment (external factors).[18] Internal factors include the person's ability or motivation, whereas external factors include lack of resources, other people or just luck. If a coworker doesn't show up for an important meeting, for instance, we infer either internal attributions (the coworker is forgetful, lacks motivation and so on) or external attributions (traffic, a family emergency or other circumstances prevented the coworker from attending).

People rely on the three attribution rules shown in Exhibit 3.2 to determine whether someone's behaviour mainly has an internal or external attribution. Internal attributions are made when the observed individual behaved this way in the past (high consistency), he or she behaves like this toward other people or in different situations (low distinctiveness) and other people do not behave this way in similar situations (low consensus). On the other hand, an external attribution is made when there is low consistency, high distinctiveness and high consensus.

To illustrate how these three attribution rules operate, suppose that an employee is making poor-quality products one day on a particular machine. We would probably conclude that there is something wrong with the machine (an external attribution) if the employee has made good-quality products on this machine in the past (low consistency), the employee makes good-quality products on other machines (high distinctiveness) and other employees have recently had quality problems on this machine (high consensus). We would make an internal attribution, on the other hand, if the employee usually makes poor-quality products on this machine (high consistency),

94 95

Reality checks

The best way to understand a theory is to see it in action in a real-life situation. These short cases illustrate a particular concept that is discussed in the text, helping you learn how a theory is put into practice.

End-of-Chapter Material

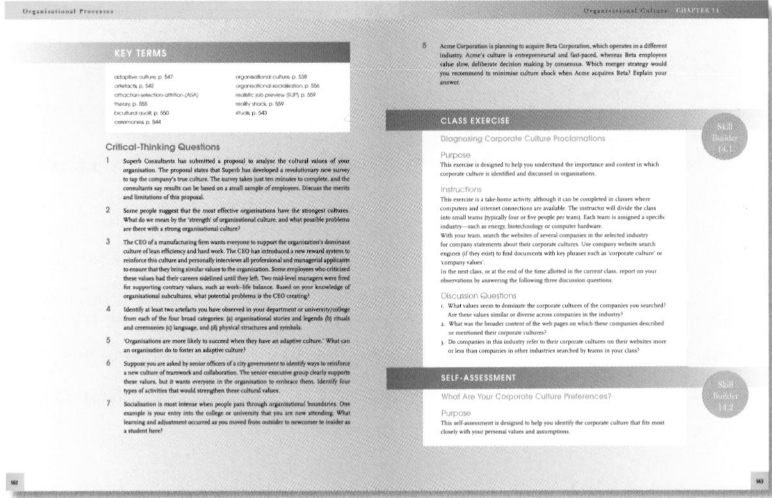

Organisational Processes

Organisational Culture CHAPTER 14

KEY TERMS

adaptive culture, p. 547
artefacts, p. 542
attraction-selection-attrition (ASA) theory, p. 555
bicultural audit, p. 550
ceremonies, p. 544
organisational culture, p. 538
organisational socialisation, p. 556
realistic job preview (RJP), p. 559
reality shock, p. 559
rituals, p. 543

Critical-Thinking Questions

1 Superb Consultants has submitted a proposal to analyse the cultural values of your organisation. The proposal states that Superb has developed a revolutionary new survey to tap the company's true culture. The survey takes just ten minutes to complete, and the consultants say results can be based on a small sample of employees. Discuss the merits and limitations of this proposal.

2 Some people suggest that the most effective organisations have the strongest cultures. What do we mean by the 'strength' of organisational culture, and what possible problems are there with a strong organisational culture?

3 The CEO of a manufacturing firm wants everyone to support the organisation's dominant culture of lean efficiency and hard work. The CEO has introduced a new reward system to reinforce this culture and personally interviews all professional and managerial applicants to ensure that they bring similar values to the organisation. Some employees who criticised these values had their careers sidelined until they left. Two mid-level managers were fired for supporting contrary values, such as work–life balance. Based on your knowledge of organisational subcultures, what potential problems is the CEO creating?

4 Identify at least two artefacts you have observed in your department or university/college from each of the four broad categories: (a) organisational stories and legends (b) rituals and ceremonies (c) language, and (d) physical structures and symbols.

5 'Organisations are more likely to succeed when they have an adaptive culture.' What can an organisation do to foster an adaptive culture?

6 Suppose you are asked by senior officers of a city government to identify ways to reinforce a new culture of teamwork and collaboration. The senior executive group clearly supports these values, but it wants everyone in the organisation to embrace them. Identify four types of activities that would strengthen these cultural values.

7 Socialisation is most intense when people pass through organisational boundaries. One example is your entry into the college or university that you are now attending. What learning and adjustment occurred as you moved from outsider to newcomer to insider as a student here?

8 Acme Corporation is planning to acquire Beta Corporation, which operates in a different industry. Acme's culture is entrepreneurial and fast-paced, whereas Beta employees value slow, deliberate decision making by consensus. Which merger strategy would you recommend to minimise culture shock when Acme acquires Beta? Explain your answer.

CLASS EXERCISE

Skill Builder 14.1

Diagnosing Corporate Culture Proclamations

Purpose

This exercise is designed to help you understand the importance and context in which corporate culture is identified and discussed in organisations.

Instructions

This exercise is a take-home activity, although it can be completed in classes where computers and internet connections are available. The instructor will divide the class into small teams (typically four or five people per team). Each team is assigned a specific industry—such as energy, biotechnology or computer hardware.

With your team, search the websites of several companies in the selected industry for company statements about their corporate cultures. Use company website search engines (if they exist) to find documents with key phrases such as 'corporate culture' or 'company values'.

In the next class, or at the end of the time allotted in the current class, report on your observations by answering the following three discussion questions.

Discussion Questions

1. What values seem to dominate the corporate cultures of the companies you searched? Are these values similar or diverse across companies in the industry?
2. What was the broader content of the web pages on which these companies described or mentioned their corporate cultures?
3. Do companies in this industry refer to their corporate cultures on their websites more or less than companies in other industries searched by teams in your class?

SELF-ASSESSMENT

Skill Builder 14.2

What Are Your Corporate Culture Preferences?

Purpose

This self-assessment is designed to help you identify the corporate culture that fits most closely with your personal values and assumptions.

562 563

Team and class exercises

The end-of-chapter material provides a broad range of exercises to help further develop your skills. Enjoy working with your peers on the team and class exercises, which will not only help you understand the content of the chapter, but will also improve your communication skills.

Self-assessment exercises

These exercises are designed with personal reflection in mind and allow you to actively link OB concepts to your own attitudes and behaviours. You will find more of these exercises on the Online Learning Centre that accompanies the text.

Critical thinking questions

These short answer questions provide you with the opportunity to revisit, discuss and critically engage with concepts and scenarios that relate to the chapter you've just read.

End-of-Part Material

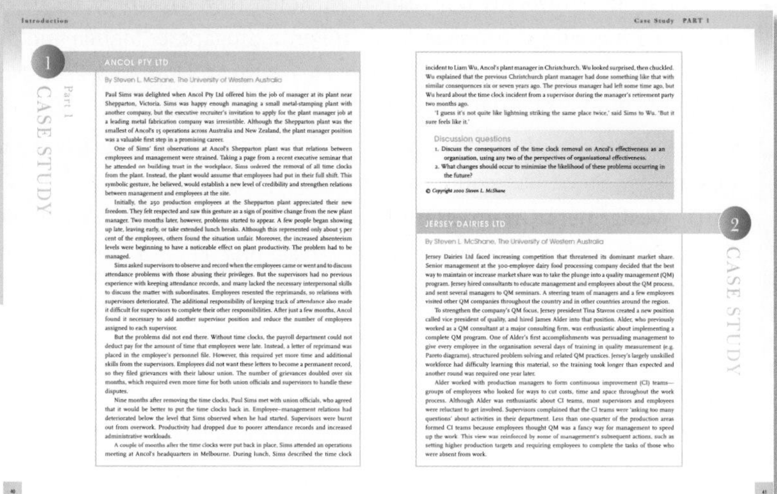

Introduction

Part 1 CASE STUDY

1 ANCOL PTY LTD

By Steven L. McShane, The University of Western Australia

Paul Sims was delighted when Ancol Pty Ltd offered him the job of manager at its plant near Shepparton, Victoria. Sims was happy enough managing a small metal-stamping plant with another company, but the executive recruiter's invitation to apply for the plant manager job at a leading metal fabrication company was irresistible. Although the Shepparton plant was the smallest of Ancol's 15 operations across Australia and New Zealand, the plant manager position was a valuable first step in a promising career.

One of Sims' first observations at Ancol's Shepparton plant was that relations between employees and management were strained. Taking a page from a recent executive seminar that he attended on building trust in the workplace, Sims ordered the removal of all time clocks from the plant. Instead, the plant would assume that employees had put in their full shift. This symbolic gesture, he believed, would establish a new level of credibility and strengthen relations between management and employees at the site.

Initially, the 250 production employees at the Shepparton plant appreciated their new freedom. They felt respected and saw this gesture as a sign of positive change from the new plant manager. Two months later, however, problems started to appear. A few people began showing up late, leaving early, or take extended lunch breaks. Although this represented only about 5 per cent of the employees, others found the situation unfair. Moreover, the increased absenteeism levels were beginning to have a noticeable effect on plant productivity. The problem had to be managed.

Sims asked supervisors to observe and record when the employees came or went and to discuss attendance problems with those abusing their privileges. But the supervisors had no previous experience with keeping attendance records, and many lacked the necessary interpersonal skills to discuss the matter with subordinates. Employees resented the reprimands, so relations with supervisors deteriorated. The additional responsibility of keeping track of attendance also made it difficult for supervisors to complete their other responsibilities. After just a few months, Ancol found it necessary to add another supervisor position and reduce the number of employees assigned to each supervisor.

But the problems did not end there. Without time clocks, the payroll department could not deduct pay for the amount of time that employees were late. Instead, a letter of reprimand was placed in the employee's personnel file. However, this required yet more time and additional skills from the supervisors. Employees did not want these letters to become a permanent record, so they filed grievances with their labour union. The number of grievances doubled over six months, which required even more time for both union officials and supervisors to handle these disputes.

Nine months after removing the time clocks, Paul Sims met with union officials, who agreed that it would be better to put the time clocks back in. Employee–management relations had deteriorated below the level that Sims observed when he had started. Supervisors were burnt out from overwork. Productivity had dropped due to poorer attendance records and increased administrative workloads.

A couple of months after the time clocks were put back in place, Sims attended an operations meeting at Ancol's headquarters in Melbourne. During lunch, Sims described the time clock

40

Case Study PART 1

incident to Liam Wu, Ancol's plant manager in Christchurch. Wu looked surprised, then chuckled. Wu explained that the previous Christchurch plant manager had done something like that with similar consequences six or seven years ago. The previous manager had left some time ago, but Wu heard about the time clock incident from a supervisor during the manager's retirement party two months ago.

'I guess it's not quite like lightning striking the same place twice,' said Sims to Wu. 'But it sure feels like it.'

Discussion questions

1. Discuss the consequences of the time clock removal on Ancol's effectiveness as an organisation, using any two of the perspectives of organisational effectiveness.
2. What changes should occur to minimise the likelihood of these problems occurring in the future?

© *Copyright 2000 Steven L. McShane*

2 JERSEY DAIRIES LTD

CASE STUDY

By Steven L. McShane, The University of Western Australia

Jersey Dairies Ltd faced increasing competition that threatened its dominant market share. Senior management at the 300-employee dairy food processing company decided that the best way to maintain or increase market share was to take the plunge into a quality management (QM) program. Jersey hired consultants to educate management and employees about the QM process, and sent several managers to QM seminars. A steering team of managers and a few employees visited other QM companies throughout the country and in other countries around the region.

To strengthen the company's QM focus, Jersey president Tina Stavros created a new position called vice president of quality, and hired James Alder into that position. Alder, who previously worked as a QM consultant at a major consulting firm, was enthusiastic about implementing a complete QM program. One of Alder's first accomplishments was persuading management to give every employee in the organisation several days of training in quality measurement (e.g. Pareto diagrams), structured problem solving and related QM practices. Jersey's largely unskilled workforce had difficulty learning this material, so the training took longer than expected and another round was required one year later.

Alder worked with production managers to form continuous improvement (CI) teams—groups of employees who looked for ways to cut costs, time and space throughout the work process. Although Alder was enthusiastic about CI teams, most supervisors and employees were reluctant to get involved. Supervisors complained that the CI teams were 'asking too many questions' about activities in their department. Less than one-quarter of the production areas formed CI teams because employees thought QM was a fancy way for management to speed up the work. This view was reinforced by some of management's subsequent actions, such as setting higher production targets and requiring employees to complete the tasks of those who were absent from work.

41

End-of-part case studies

These cases present key concepts from real-life situations to help you develop relevant diagnostic skills. The accompanying questions prompt you to practise the analytical skills required in the workplace.

End-of-Book Material

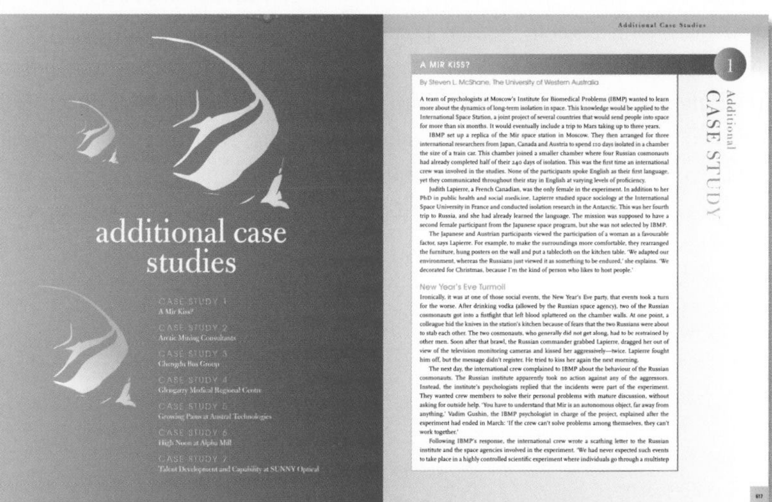

additional case studies

CASE STUDY 1
A Mir Kiss?

CASE STUDY 2
Arctic Mining Consultants

CASE STUDY 3
Chengdu Bus Group

CASE STUDY 4
Glengarry Medical Regional Centre

CASE STUDY 5
Growing Pains at Austral Technologies

CASE STUDY 6
High Noon at Alpha Mill

CASE STUDY 7
Talent Development and Capability at SUNNY Optical

Additional Case Studies

1 A MIR KISS?

Additional CASE STUDY

By Steven L. McShane, The University of Western Australia

A team of psychologists at Moscow's Institute for Biomedical Problems (IBMP) wanted to learn more about the dynamics of long-term isolation in space. This knowledge would be applied to the International Space Station, a joint project of several countries that would send people into space for more than six months. It would eventually include a trip to Mars taking up to three years.

IBMP set up a replica of the Mir space station in Moscow. They then arranged for three international researchers from Japan, Canada and Austria to spend 110 days isolated in a chamber the size of a train car. This chamber joined a smaller chamber where four Russian cosmonauts had already completed half of their 240 days of isolation. This was the first time an international crew was involved in the studies. None of the participants spoke English as their first language, yet they communicated throughout their stay in English at varying levels of proficiency.

Judith Lapierre, a French Canadian, was the only female in the experiment. In addition to her PhD in public health and social medicine, Lapierre studied space sociology at the International Space University in France and conducted isolation research in the Antarctic. This was her fourth trip to Russia, and she had already learned the language. The mission was supposed to have a second female participant from the Japanese space program, but she was not selected by IBMP.

The Japanese and Austrian participants viewed the participation of a woman as a favourable factor, says Lapierre. For example, to make the surroundings more comfortable, they rearranged the furniture, hung posters on the wall and put a tablecloth on the kitchen table. 'We adapted our environment, whereas the Russians just viewed it as something to be endured,' she explains. 'We decorated for Christmas, because I'm the kind of person who likes to host people.'

New Year's Eve Turmoil

Ironically, it was at one of those social events, the New Year's Eve party, that events took a turn for the worse. After drinking vodka (allowed by the Russian space agency), two of the Russian cosmonauts got into a fistfight that left blood splattered on the chamber walls. At one point, a colleague hid the knives in the station's kitchen because of fears that the two Russians were about to stab each other. The two cosmonauts, who generally did not get along, had to be restrained by other men. Soon after that brawl, the Russian commander grabbed Lapierre, dragged her out of view of the television monitoring cameras and kissed her aggressively—twice. Lapierre fought him off, but the message didn't register. He tried to kiss her again the next morning.

The next day, the international crew complained to IBMP about the behaviour of the Russian cosmonauts. The Russian institute apparently took no action against any of the aggressors. Instead, the institute's psychologists replied that the incidents were part of the experiment. They wanted crew members to solve their personal problems with mature discussion, without asking for outside help. 'You have to understand that Mir is an autonomous object, far away from anything,' Vadim Gushin, the IBMP psychologist in charge of the project, explained after the experiment had ended in March: 'If the crew can't solve problems among themselves, they can't work together.'

Following IBMP's response, the international crew wrote a scathing letter to the Russian institute and the space agencies involved in the experiment. 'We had never expected such events to take place in a highly controlled scientific experiment where individuals go through a multistep

617

Additional case studies

Additional case studies appear at the end of the book. These can be used to diagnose OB issues and apply ideas presented throughout the book. They are a mixture of new cases to this edition and proven classics from local and international OB scholars.

Video case study notes

Video case study notes are provided for each part of the text. These include summaries of the video footage that you will find on the Online Learning Centre that accompanies this book. The discussion questions included for each video case explore the themes and issues that relate to that video clip.

About *the authors*

Steven L. McShane

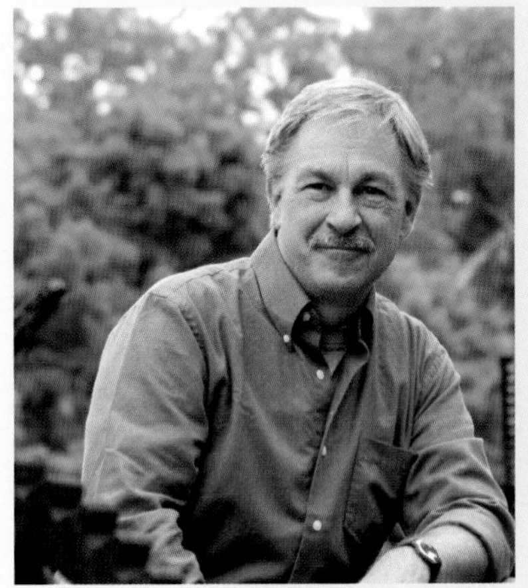

Steven L McShane is Winthrop Professor of Management in the Business School at the University of Western Australia (UWA), where he receives high teaching ratings from students in Perth, Singapore, Manila and other cities where UWA offers its programs. He is also an Honorary Professor at Universiti Tunku Abdul Rahman (UTAR) in Malaysia and previously taught in the business faculties at Simon Fraser University and Queen's University in Canada. Steve has conducted executive programs with Nokia, TÜV-SÜD, Wesfarmers Group, Main Roads WA, McGraw-Hill, ALCOA World Alumina Australia and many other organisations. He is a popular visiting speaker, having given presentations to faculty and students in almost a dozen countries over the past four years.

Steve earned his Ph.D. from Michigan State University in organisational behaviour, human resource management and labour relations. He also holds a Master of Industrial Relations from the University of Toronto and an undergraduate degree from Queen's University in Canada. Steve has served as President of the Administrative Sciences Association of Canada (the Canadian equivalent of the Academy of Management and ANZAM) and Director of Graduate Programs in the business faculty at Simon Fraser University.

Along with co-authoring *Organisational Behaviour on the Pacific Rim, Third Edition,* Steve is co-author with Mary Ann von Glinow (Florida International University) of *Organizational Behavior, Fifth Edition* (2010) and *Organizational Behavior: Essentials, Second Edition* (2009). He is also the co-author with Sandra Steen (University of Regina) of *Canadian Organizational Behaviour, Seventh Edition* (2009) and with Charles Hill (University of Washington) of *Principles of Management, First Edition* (2008). Steve has co-authored of editions or translations of his organisational behaviour book in China, India, Quebec and Taiwan. He has published several dozen articles and conference papers on workplace values, training transfer, organizational learning, exit-voice-loyalty, employee socialisation, wrongful dismissal, media bias in business magazines and other diverse topics.

Steve enjoys spending his leisure time swimming, body board surfing, canoeing, skiing and travelling with his wife and two daughters.

Mara Olekalns

Mara Olekalns is a Professor of Management (Negotiations) at the Melbourne Business School, University of Melbourne, where she teaches Negotiation Strategy and Processes in the MBA programme. She also teaches negotiations within Executive Development programmes and conducts workshops on negotiation skills for women. Before joining MBS, Mara taught organisational behaviour for the Department of Management at Melbourne University, and for the Department of Psychology at the University of Otago. She is the recipient of *Universitas 21* Teaching Fellowship from the University of Melbourne.

Mara's research focuses on the relationships between how individuals think about negotiation, what they do and say during the negotiation, and their outcomes. Her particular interests are in trust and trust-building, deception and how gender shapes the interpretation of and reaction to negotiators' strategic choices. Mara's research has been published in leading, international journals. She has served on the Editorial Boards of the *International Journal of Conflict Management and Journal of Organisational Behaviour*; she is currently a Division Editor for *Group Decision and Negotiation* and from 2010 she will co-edit *Negotiation and Conflict Management Research.* Mara is a past President of the International Association for Conflict Management.

In a previous life, Mara worked for Department of Employment, Education & Training (Staff Training, Equal Opportunity, Organisation Development, Resources); Public Service Board (Project Officer for Regional Director) and National Police Research Unit (research on recruitment, training, stress, domestic violence).

Outside of work, her energy is channelled into travelling, cooking, wine tasting and her loved one—husband Philip—and cats, Muddy Waters and Otis Rush.

Tony Travaglione

Tony Travaglione is Head of the School of Management at Curtin Business School, Curtin University of Technology. Over the course of his career, Tony has held a number of senior leadership roles including Professor and Dean of the Adelaide Graduate School of Business and Professor and Head of the Newcastle Graduate School of Business. He has also held the position of Visiting Professor at the Stanford University Graduate School of Business.

Tony holds a Doctor of Philosophy degree from the University of Western Australia. He is recognised internationally as an expert in the area of leadership. He has developed numerous leadership development programs for both public and private sector organisations. He is skilled in the delivery and feedback of a number of assessment instruments, ranging from staff attitudes to leadership-style inventories. Tony is currently working on an Australian Research Council (ARC) grant in collaboration with Main Roads Western Australia on developing a new approach to values-driven leadership.

Tony has been active in the area of consulting in Australia and overseas. In Australia, his clients have included the ANZ Bank, QANTAS, Main Roads Western Australia, Westrail, Hunter Area Health and Centrelink. His consultancy work has appeared in prestigious and rigorously refereed international journals including the *International Journal of Human Resource Management* (UK), *Personnel Review* (UK), *Journal of Managerial Psychology* (USA), *Journal of Strategic Change* (UK) and the *Journal of Business and Leadership* (USA). Tony has always enjoyed his spare time by the beach and walking. In more recent years he has developed a keen interest in cooking traditional Italian and Greek dishes.

Case and Vignette *Matrix*

	PART 1	PART 2					
Chapters	**1**	**2**	**3**	**4**	**5**	**6**	**7**
Opening Vignette	Wesfarmers (Australia), p. 3	Johnson & Johnson (India), p. 45	IBM (New Zealand), p. 87	NAB's Clydesdale Bank & Bank of New Zealand (UK, New Zealand), p. 121	Standard Chartered Bank (Asia, India), p. 167	Factory workers in China's Pearl River Delta, p. 205	Google (Australia), p. 241
Reality Checks	**Reality Check 1.1** Hospitals Take the Lean Journey to Efficiency (UK, Australia), p. 10–11	**Reality check 2.1** Feeling valued adds value (Canada, USA, Australia), p. 56–57 **Reality check 2.2** Infosys Australia bridges the cross-cultural divide (Australia, India), p. 64–65	**Reality check 3.1** "Your name says everything in France", p. 94–95	**Reality check 4.1** Fun in the workplace (global), p. 126–127 **Reality check 4.2** GM Holden revs up emotional intelligence (Australia), p. 132–133	**Reality check 5.1** Shining the spotlight on employee recognition (global), p. 174–175	**Reality check 6.1** Nucor rewards the team (USA), p. 210–211 **Reality check 6.2** When rewards go wrong (global), p. 214–215	**Reality check 7.1** Famous missed opportunities (USA), p. 246–247
End-of-part case studies	**Case study 1:** Ancol Pty Ltd. , p. 40 **Case study 2:** Jersey Dairies Ltd., p. 41	**Case study 1:** Bust Up, p. 282 **Case study 2:** Fran Hayden Joins Dairy Engineering, p. 283 **Case study 3:** Hy Dairies, Inc., p. 287 **Case study 4:** Keeping Suzanne Chalmers, p. 288 **Case study 5:** The Regency Grand Hotel, p. 290 **Case study 6:** SK Telecom Goes Egalitarian, p. 292 **Case study 7:** Vêtements Ltée, p. 294 **Case study 8:** YakkaTech Pty Ltd., p. 295					
Video case studies	**Video case study 1:** Yahoo!7 Part 1, p. 636 **Video case study 2:** Wal-Mart's Public Image Campaign, p. 636 **Video case study 3:** Good Business Deeds, p. 636	**Video case study 1:** Yahoo!7 Part 2, p. 637 **Video case study 2:** Clockless Office: Best Buy's ROWE Program, p. 637 **Video case study 3:** Employee Loyalty, p. 638 **Video case study 4:** Johnson & Johnson, p. 638 **Video case study 5:** Pike Place Fish Market, p. 638 **Video case study 6:** Stress in Japan, p. 639					
Additional case studies	**Case study 1:** A Mir Kiss? p. 615	**Case study 2:** Arctic Mining Consultants, p. 616	**Case study 3:** Chengdu Bus Group, p. 619	**Case study 4:** Glengarry Medical Regional Centre, p. 621	**Case study 5:** Growing Pains at Austral Technologies, p. 627	**Case study 6:** High Noon at Alpha Mills, p. 630	**Case study 7:** Talent Development and Capability in SUNNY Optical, p. 633

E-student

Online LearningCentre

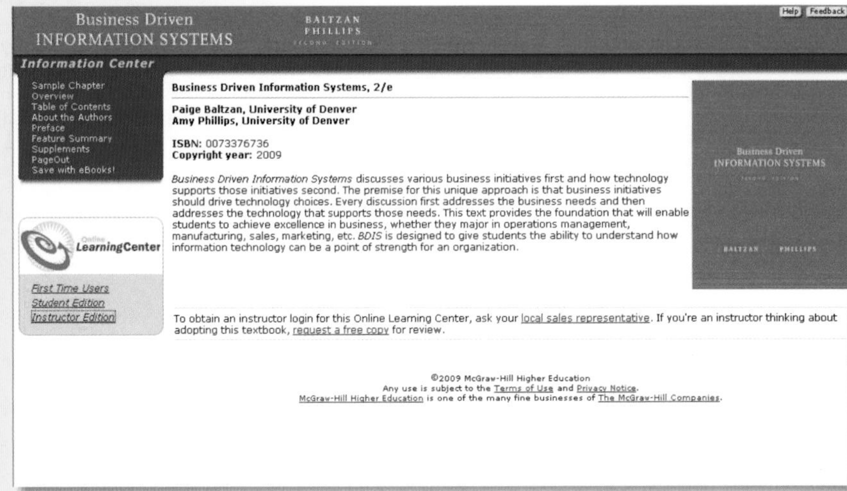

The Online Learning Centre that accompanies this text is designed to help students and lecturers get the most from their course. It provides a powerful learning experience beyond the printed page. Students can access the premium content areas by registering the code at the front of this book. After registration, you will have seamless access to the online revision program: a unique self-paced assessment tool that is ideal for revision and exam preparation.

What are Organisations?

Groups of people who work interdependently toward some purpose

- Structured patterns of interaction
- Coordinated tasks
- Work toward some purpose

Courtesy of Westpac Banking Corporation

Copyright © 2010 McGraw-Hill Australia Pty Ltd
PPTs t/a *Organisational Behaviour on the Pacific Rim 3e* by Steven McShane and Tony Travaglione
Slides prepared by Steven McShane

1-3

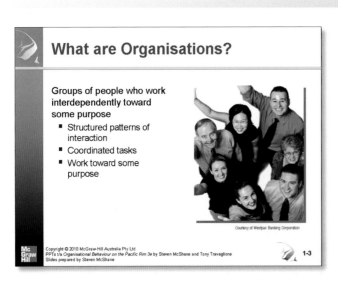

PowerPoint® slides

PowerPoint slides summarise the key points of each chapter. They can be downloaded as a valuable revision aid.

www.mhhe.com/au/mcshane3e

Student revision questions

Students can test their knowledge using our online quizzes. Each chapter contains a range of multiple-choice questions to help students review and retain the concepts explored throughout the text. Answers to the questions are supplied immediately, along with page references to relevant sections of the book.

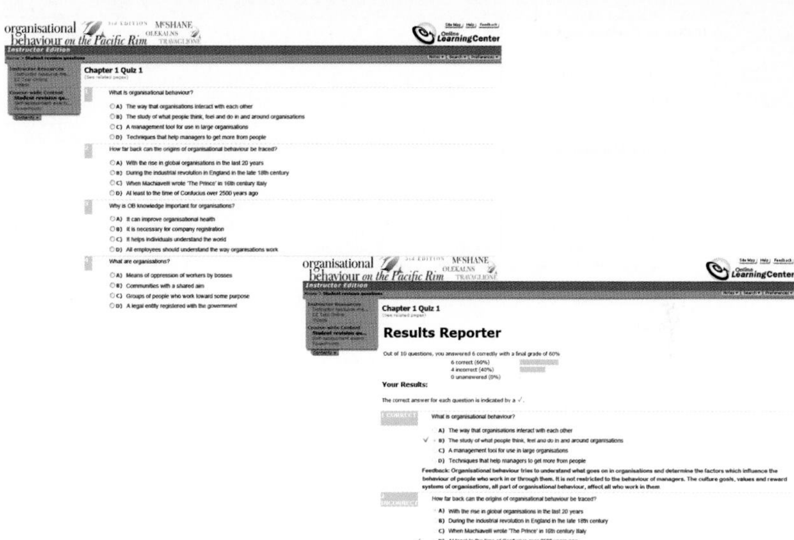

Self-assessment exercises

The Online Learning Centre provides numerous interactive self-assessment exercises to help students personalise the meaning of specific organisational behaviour concepts. These self-scoring exercises provide detailed feedback as well as allowing students to probe their own attitudes, beliefs and personalities in relation to the OB topics discussed in this book. These self-scoring exercises allow students to probe their own attitudes, beliefs and personalities in relation to OB topics discussed in the text, and provide detailed feedback.

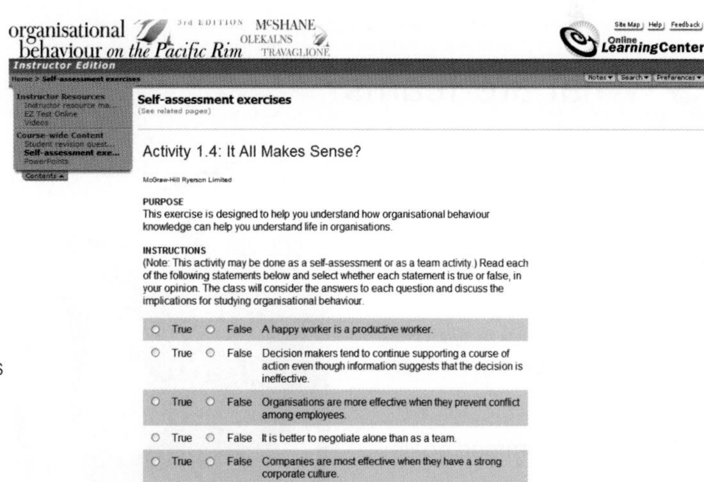

eBook
Be eSmart.

McGraw-Hill eBooks offer students new choices in the format of their textbook content and considerable savings on the price of the traditional printed book! They are engaging and efficient, with a powerful search engine that allows students to find topics easily. Students can download the eBook, print what they need, highlight specific content, take notes and share notes with others.

E-instructor

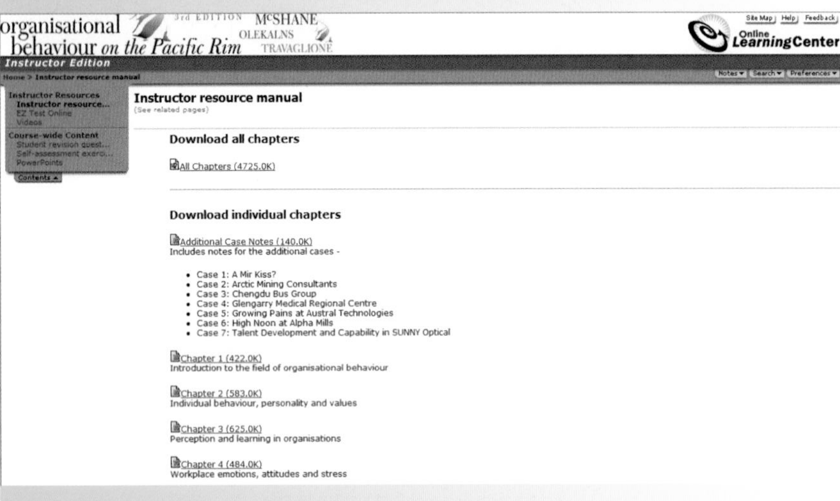

Instructor resource manual

Steven McShane wrote the instructor resource manual. It features lecture outlines that correspond with PowerPoint® slides, teaching notes, solutions to Critical thinking questions and case study discussion questions. It also provides additional cases and class exercises to enrich your learning program.

What are Teams?

- Groups of two or more people
- Exist to fulfil a purpose
- Interdependent -- interact and influence each other
- Mutually accountable for achieving common goals
- Perceive themselves as a social entity

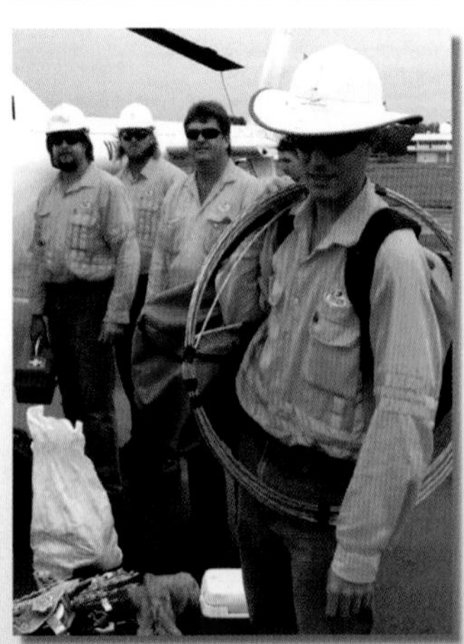

McShane-Olekalns-Travaglione OB Pacific Rim 3e 3 © 2010 The McGraw-Hill Companies, Inc. All rights reserved

PowerPoint® slides

PowerPoint slides can be downloaded and adapted to suit a lecturer's requirements. These slides are also provided on the student section of the website.

EZ Test Online

EZ Test is a flexible and easy-to-use testing program. It generates tests that can be exported to other course management systems (such as WebCT and Blackboard) and can be used to create hard-copy tests. Questions can be selected from a number of test-banks, and more than a dozen question types are supported. You can scramble questions, create algorithmic questions, and create multiple versions of the same test.

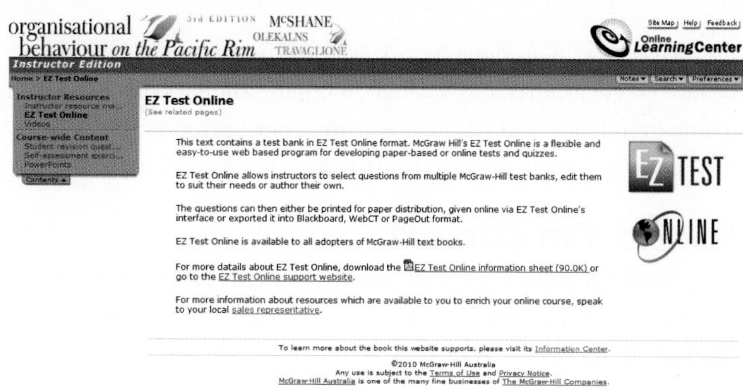

Video case studies

The various video case studies that accompany the book can be accessed via the instructor Online Learning Centre. These video cases explore how organisational behaviour theories and concepts are put into practice in real-life workplace settings. Each clip is supported by corresponding video case study notes, including discussion questions.

Learning Management System

McGraw-Hill can provide the online material to accompany this book in a format to suit your learning-management system, including Blackboard, WebCT and PageOut. With these systems, lecturers can deliver and manage a course via the internet, employing useful resources such as discussion boards and calendars. Please see your McGraw-Hill representative for details. We help you teach your course, your way.

About *the book*

Organisational Behaviour on the Pacific Rim, 3rd edition, is written around three important philosophies that we believe create a refreshing change in organisational behaviour reading: (1) Pacific Rim context; (2) contemporary theory foundation and (3) active learning. Furthermore, this book is written with the view that everyone who works in and around organisations needs to understand and make use of organisational behaviour knowledge.

Pacific Rim context

Organisational Behaviour on the Pacific Rim, 3rd edition, is written completely in the Pacific Rim region by authors who live and work here. This Pacific Rim orientation is most apparent in the numerous real-life anecdotes spread throughout this book. For example, the book describes how Air New Zealand CEO Rob Fyfe relies on a hands-on approach to improve his and others' perceptions, how Ergon Energy in Queensland is the ultimate team-based organisation, how a young executive at Hoppy fought resistance to change to bring new life to the Tokyo beverage company and how those who participate and thrive in Australia's Antarctic expeditions have a unique personality to support those conditions. The Pacific Rim focus also comes through in the many case studies about companies in this region.

Without losing its Pacific Rim focus, *Organisational Behaviour on the Pacific Rim*, 3rd edition, also serves up plenty of examples from around the planet. For instance, readers will learn how the California operations of Rolls Royce Engine Services encourages shared leadership, how employees at engineering consultancy Mott Macdonald experience positive emotions through desert safaris in Abu Dhabi, how stories of Cirque du Soleil's origins help the entertainment company to maintain a strong organisational culture, how American electronics retailer Best Buy improves employee role perceptions during its busiest shopping day and how Sweden's Svenska Handelsbanken relies on employee empowerment and organisational rewards rather than centralised budgets to remain competitive and serve customers better.

Contemporary theory foundation

Vivid real-world examples and practices are only valuable if they are connected to good theory. *Organisational Behaviour on the Pacific Rim* has developed a reputation for its solid foundation of contemporary and classic research and writing. You can see this in the references. Each chapter is based on dozens of articles, books and other sources. The most recent literature receives thorough coverage, resulting in what we believe is the most up-to-date organisational behaviour textbook available. These references also reveal that we reach out to marketing, information management, human resource management and other disciplines for new ideas. At the same time, this textbook is written for students, not the scholars whose work is cited. So, although this book provides new knowledge and its practical implications, it rarely names researchers and their university affiliations. It focuses on organisational behaviour knowledge rather than 'who's-who' in the field.

One of the driving forces for writing *Organisational Behaviour on the Pacific Rim* was to provide a conduit whereby emerging OB knowledge more quickly reaches students, practitioners and fellow scholars. To its credit, *Organisational Behaviour on the Pacific Rim* is the first textbook to discuss workplace emotions, social identity theory, four-drive theory, appreciative inquiry, affective events theory (but without the jargon), somatic marker theory (also without the jargon), virtual teams, future search events, Schwartz's values model, resilience, employee engagement, learning orientation, workaholism and several other groundbreaking topics. This edition introduces several other emerging OB knowledge and practices, including social networking communication, the competencies of effective team members, exceptions to media richness theory, the importance of self-concept in organizational behaviour, the globally-integrated enterprise, global mindset and strengths-based feedback.

Active learning

We teach organisational behaviour, so we understand how important it is to use a textbook that supports active learning and critical thinking. *Organisational Behaviour on the Pacific Rim*, 3rd edition, offers valuable resources to aid student learning. The book offers more than two dozen case studies, including several comprehensive cases, that challenge students to diagnose issues and apply organisational behaviour concepts. Many of these cases are written by instructors around the Pacific Rim and relate to companies in this region.

Along with case studies, Organisational Behaviour on the Pacific Rim, 3rd edition, supports active learning with one or two engaging team, web or class activities in every chapter. Many of these learning activities are not available in other organisational behaviour textbooks, such as: Test Your Knowledge of Personality (Chapter 2), Where in the World are We? (Chapter 6) and the Cross-Cultural Communication Game (Chapter 9). This edition also has three dozen self-assessments. Self-assessments personalise the meaning of organisational behaviour concepts, such as introversion-extroversion personality, corporate culture preferences, need for social approval, preferred influence tactics, self-leadership and creative disposition.

We also have a strong commitment to the philosophy of linking theory with practice, which is essential for active learning. By connecting concepts with real-life examples, students are more likely to remember the content and see how it relates to them in the workplace. And, quite frankly, these examples make the content even more interesting, thereby motivating students to read on. This engaging approach is further strengthened through several video segments which highlight specific organisations on a variety of organisational behaviour topics.

Acknowledgments

Have you ever worked on a high-performance team where everything just seems to 'click'? We have—on this third edition of *Organisational Behaviour on the Pacific Rim*! Although we spend considerable time alone writing and researching for this book, it never ceases to amaze how teamwork really does make a difference. Several people provided valued expertise to smooth out the rough spots of writing, search out the most challenging photos, create a fantastic design, develop the various forms of student and instructor support and pull together these many pieces into a comprehensive textbook. This teamwork is even more amazing when you consider that the authors and other team members live in several locations around Australia.

Publisher Ailsa Brackley du Bois led the way with unwavering support, along with the strong endorsement from McGraw-Hill Australia Managing Director Murray St Leger. Developmental editor Stephanie Erb demonstrated superhuman skills at coordinating the volumes of emails and files from the three authors and other team members who produced this edition. Our copy editor, Emma Driver, caught the most subtle errors and improved the authors' writing. Michael McGrath, our senior production editor, is another true professional as he guided the book through its production schedule. Photo researcher Danielle Townsend met the challenge of finding the best photos. Natalie Winter created the elegant cover and David Rosemeyer the striking interior design that represent the philosophy and style of this book, under the thoughtful art direction of Astred Hicks. Finally, marketing manager Jared Dunn created high-quality marketing materials to help McGraw-Hill's superb sales team. These professionals help instructors to discover that this book really does deliver the content and support needed for an excellent learning experience. Thanks to all of you. This has been an exceptional team effort!

Several lecturers provided reviews that helped shape *Organisational Behaviour on the Pacific Rim*, 3rd edition. Their compliments were energising and their suggestions significantly improved this edition. We extend our special thanks to:

- Melanie Bryant, Monash University
- Alan Coetzer, Massey University
- Melissa Edwards, University of Technology, Sydney
- Richard Hall, University of Sydney
- Andrew Noblet, Deakin University
- Megan Paull, Murdoch University
- Soma Pillay, Swinburne University of Technology
- Lesley Treleaven, University of Sydney
- Lucy Taksa, University of New South Wales

We also thank more than 100 university and college lecturers in the United States and Canada who reviewed one or more chapters of the American and Canadian editions of this book over the past three years. Their suggestions also strengthened the quality of this Pacific Rim edition.

Organisational Behaviour on the Pacific Rim, 3rd edition, includes dozens of cases, exercises and self-assessments to support active learning and critical thinking in the classroom. We would like to thank the following people whose cases and exercises appear in this edition:

- Terrance Bogyo, WorkSafeBC
- Joe Bovell, Optima Agriculture
- Gerard A. Callanan, West Chester University of Pennsylvania
- Sharon Card
- David J. Cherrington, Brigham Young University
- Julia Connell, University of Technology, Sydney
- Kandy Dayaram, Curtin University of Technology
- Mary Gander, Winona State University

- Cheryl Harvey, Wilfrid Laurier University
- Arif Hassan, International Islamic University Malaysia
- Elizabeth Ho, Prada Singapore
- Runtian Jing, The University of Electronic Science and Technology of China
- Glyn Jones, University of Waikato
- Peter Lok, University of Sydney
- Kim Morouney, Wilfrid Laurier University
- Tim Neale
- Trevor Overton, Austral Technologies
- David F. Perri, West Chester University of Pennsylvania
- David Pick, Curtin University of Technology
- Jo Rhodes, Macquarie University
- Joseph C. Santora, Essex County College and TSTDCG, Inc.
- James C. Sarros, Monash University
- Brenda Scott-Ladd, Curtin University of Technology
- Roy Smollan, Auckland University of Technology
- William Todorovic, Indiana-Purdue University, Fort Wayne
- Thivagar Velayutham, International Islamic University Malaysia

Along with the reviewers, contributors and editorial team, Steve extends his gratitude to his coauthors—Mara Olekalns and Tony Travaglione—for their exceptional work on this book. Steve is also honoured to work with co-authors on other editions and translations of this book, including Professor Mary Ann Von Glinow at Florida International University (American editions), Sandra Steen at the University of Regina (Canadian edition), Professor Radha Sharma at MDI (Indian edition), Professor Runtian Jing at UESTC (Chinese edition), and Professor Charles Benabou at UQAM (Quebec French edition). Steve would also like to thank his students in Perth, Singapore and Manila, for sharing their learning experiences and for assisting with the development of *Organisational Behaviour on the Pacific Rim* as well as with the other editions of this book. But, more than anything else, Steve is forever indebted to his wife Donna McClement and to their wonderful daughters, Bryton and Madison. Their love and support give special meaning to his life.

Mara was delighted to contribute to this edition of *Organisational Behaviour on the Pacific Rim*. Her chapters benefited from discussions with her students, who always remind her that great ideas are even better when they have practical applications. She was grateful for the support from Steve and the editorial team at McGraw-Hill, which made the writing process highly enjoyable. Most of all, Mara appreciated the unquestioning support of her family: her husband Philip, who asks "Are you sure you want to do this?" then unfailingly encourages her in every and any project she undertakes and her fur kids, Muddy and Otis, who unerringly find the sunny places and remind her to take time out to enjoy the sunshine with them. *Wear your ruby shoes when you're far away, so you'll always stay home in your heart.* (Rhodes & Harris)

Tony would like to thank all of his academic colleagues who have supported him over his 20-year career as an academic. Tony is especially grateful to Professor David Plowman from the University of Western Australia. A special thanks also to his three fantastic daughters Natalie, Michelle and Annalise who have provided wonderful support to him over many years.

Steve McShane
University of Western Australia
Mara Olekalns
Melbourne Business School
Tony Travaglione
Curtin University of Technology

PART 1
introduction

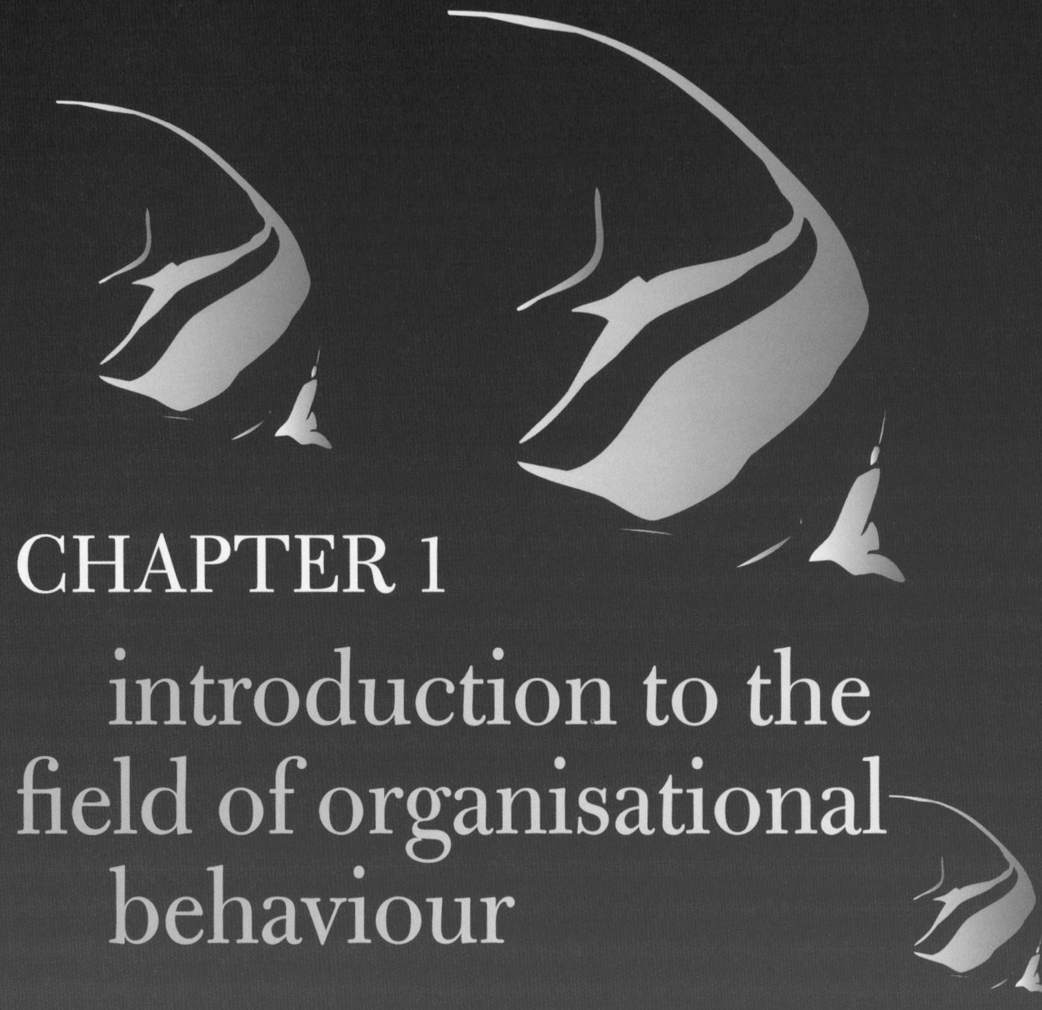

CHAPTER 1

introduction to the field of organisational behaviour

LEARNING OBJECTIVES

After reading this chapter, you should be able to:

- define *organisational behaviour* and *organisations* and discuss the importance of this field of inquiry
- diagram an organisation from an open-systems perspective
- define *intellectual capital* and describe the organisational learning perspective of organisational effectiveness
- diagnose the extent to which an organisation or one of its work units applies high-performance work practices
- explain how the stakeholder perspective emphasises the importance of values, ethics and corporate social responsibility
- summarise the five types of individual behaviour in organisations
- debate the organisational opportunities and challenges of globalisation, workforce diversity and virtual work
- discuss the anchors on which organisational behaviour knowledge is based.

Soon after the announcement that Wesfarmers Limited had acquired beleaguered retailer Coles Group, chief executive Richard Goyder arranged a video hook-up so he could speak from Wesfarmers' head office in Perth to about 200 Coles senior managers in Melbourne. Before Goyder could say a word, the Coles staff stood up and greeted their new boss with enthusiastic applause. The standing ovation symbolised that Coles staff wanted new leadership and believed that Wesfarmers could return Coles to its previous glory as a premier retailer.

Wesfarmers

By adopting many organisational behaviour practices, Wesfarmers has become the largest private-sector employer in Australia and one of the most admired companies in the region.

From its humble foundations a century ago as a farmers' cooperative, Wesfarmers has grown to become Australia's largest private-sector employer. It is one of Australia's most admired companies and recognised as the best managed large business in the region (including Asia). Besides operating a stable of retail brands (Bunnings, Coles, Officeworks, Kmart, Target and others), Wesfarmers has sizeable businesses in chemicals/fertilisers (e.g. SCBP, Australian Vinyls), coal mines (e.g. Curragh, Premier Coal), insurance (e.g. WFI, Lumley), energy (e.g. Coregas), and industrial and safety consumables (e.g. Blackwoods, NZ Safety).

What makes Wesfarmers so successful? CEO Richard Goyder points to human capital as the answer. When asked to list the five key factors for business success, he quickly and decisively answered: people, people, people, people and people. 'The greatest challenge facing Australian public companies in the years ahead is the recruitment, development and retention of high-quality employees,' he suggests. Goyder adds that the company's culture is another competitive advantage. 'One of the very significant things that Wesfarmers brings [to Coles] is a very strong performance culture,' he says.

Along with its focus on human capital, Wesfarmers tries to serve stakeholders beyond shareholders and employees. For example, Bunnings employees provide services to the community, such as installing a water tank for a primary school, while Bunnings stores offer non-profit groups facilities to make money through sausage sizzles. Wesfarmers is active in reducing environmental waste through recycling and energy reduction. Its energy businesses have programs to reduce greenhouse gas emissions.

Of course, no organisation is a perfect specimen. Transforming Coles has proven to be a tough challenge. Bunnings' New Zealand staff were recently outraged to discover that they earn significantly less than Australian employees performing the same jobs. And there have been public concerns about the large pay cheques of Wesfarmers' executives. Still, Wesfarmers' success has become the benchmark for other companies in Australia, New Zealand and Asia.[1]

Leadership, organisational culture, human capital, stakeholders—these are some of the organisational behaviour concepts behind the success of Wesfarmers and other companies. They are also some of the topics featured in this book. Our main objective is to help you understand behaviour in organisations and to work more effectively in organisational settings.

We begin in this chapter by introducing the field of organisational behaviour, and explaining why knowledge of this field is important to organisations as well as to your career. Next, the chapter describes the four main perspectives on organisational effectiveness, which is considered the 'ultimate dependent variable' in organisational behaviour. This is followed by an overview of the five main types of individual behaviour in organisations.

This chapter also describes three challenges facing organisations—globalisation, increasing workforce diversity and emerging employment relationships—and highlights the anchors that guide knowledge development in the field of organisational behaviour. The chapter closes by describing the four main anchors of this field.

Define *organisational behaviour* and *organisations* and discuss the importance of this field of inquiry.

THE FIELD OF ORGANISATIONAL BEHAVIOUR

organisational behaviour (OB) The study of what people think, feel and do in and around organisations.

Organisational behaviour (OB) is the study of what people think, feel and do in and around organisations. It looks at employee behaviour, decisions, perceptions and emotional responses. It examines how individuals and teams in organisations relate to each other and to their counterparts in other organisations. OB also encompasses the study of how organisations interact with their external environments, particularly in the context of employee behaviour and decisions. OB researchers systematically study these topics at multiple levels of analysis, namely, the individual, team (including interpersonal) and organisation levels.[2]

organisations Groups of people who work interdependently toward some purpose.

The definition of organisational behaviour begs the question: what are organisations? **Organisations** are groups of people who work interdependently toward some purpose.[3] Notice that organisations are not buildings or government-registered entities. In fact, many organisations exist without either physical walls or government documentation to confer their legal status. Organisations have existed for as long as people have worked together.[4] Massive temples dating back to 3500 BC were constructed through the organised actions of multitudes of people. Craftspeople and merchants in ancient Rome formed guilds, complete with elected managers. More than 1000 years ago, Chinese factories were producing some 125 000 tonnes of iron each year. Throughout history, organisations have consisted of people who communicate, coordinate and collaborate with each other to achieve common objectives.

One key feature of organisations is that they are collective entities. They consist of human beings (typically, but not necessarily, employees) and these people interact with each other in an *organised* way. This organised relationship requires some minimal level of communication, coordination and collaboration to achieve organisational objectives. As such, all organisational members have degrees of interdependence with each other; they accomplish goals by sharing materials, information or expertise with coworkers.

A second key feature of organisations is that their members have a collective sense of purpose. There is some debate among OB experts about whether all organisations really have a collective sense of purpose. The collective purpose isn't always well defined or agreed on.

Furthermore, although most companies have vision and mission statements, these documents are sometimes out of date or don't describe what employees and leaders try to achieve in reality. These arguments may be true, but imagine an organisation without goals: it would consist of a mass of people wandering around aimlessly without any sense of direction. So, whether it's selling fresh food at Coles or constructing the mammoth Angel Platform on Australia's north-west coast, people working in organisations do have some sense of collective purpose. 'A business is just a registered name on a piece of paper,' explains Grahame Maher, the Australian executive who revived Vodafone's operations in both New Zealand and Australia and now leads Vodafone in Qatar. 'It's nothing more than that unless there's a group of people who care about a common purpose for why they are, where they are going, how they are going to be when they are there.'[5]

Historical Foundations of Organisational Behaviour

Organisational behaviour emerged as a distinct field around the 1940s, but organisations have been studied by experts in other fields for many centuries.[6] For example, the Greek philosopher Plato wrote about the essence of leadership. Around the same time, the Chinese philosopher Confucius extolled the virtues of ethics and leadership. In 1776, Adam Smith advocated a new form of organisational structure based on the division of labour. One hundred years later, German sociologist Max Weber wrote about rational organisations, the work ethic and charismatic leadership. Soon after, industrial engineer Frederick Winslow Taylor proposed new ways to organise employees and motivate them through goal setting and rewards.

In the 1920s, Australian-born Harvard professor Elton Mayo and his colleagues established the 'human relations' school of management, which developed the study of employee attitudes and informal group dynamics in the workplace. Around that same time, Mary Parker Follett pioneered new ways of thinking about several OB topics, including constructive conflict, team dynamics, organisational democracy, power and leadership. A decade later, Chester Barnard wrote insightful views regarding individual behaviour, motivation, communication, leadership and authority, and team dynamics in organisational settings. This brief historical tour indicates

Founding a New Discipline

Getty Images

Elton Mayo was a pioneer of organisational behaviour thinking almost two decades before OB became a distinct field of inquiry. Born and educated in Australia, Mayo accepted a position at Harvard Business School, where he became a founding scholar of the 'human relations' school of management. At a time when organisational research focused on work efficiency and functionality, Mayo and several colleagues concentrated their research around employee attitudes, interpersonal relations and informal group dynamics. Their studies of Western Electric Hawthorne Works employees from 1928 to 1933 laid the foundation for the emerging view that employee morale and productivity will improve when companies pay more attention to employee needs and the social system. Historians suggest that Mayo's human relations school of management laid the foundation for the field of organisational behaviour in the 1940s.[7]

that OB has been around for a long time; it just wasn't organised into a unified discipline until after World War II.

Why Study Organisational Behaviour?

Organisational behaviour lecturers face a challenge: Students who have not yet begun their careers tend to value courses related to specific jobs, such as accounting and marketing.[8] However, OB doesn't have a specific career path—there is no 'vice president of OB'—so students sometimes have difficulty recognising the value that OB knowledge can offer to their future. Meanwhile, students with several years of work experience place OB near the top of their list of important courses. Why? Because they have directly observed that OB *does make a difference* to their career success. To begin with, OB theories help people to make sense of the workplace. These theories also give them the opportunity to question and rebuild the personal mental models that they have developed through observation and experience. Thus, OB is important because it helps to fulfil the need to understand and predict the world in which we live.[9]

But the main reason why people with work experience value OB knowledge is that they have discovered how it helps them to get things done in organisations. This practical side of organisational behaviour is, according to some experts, a critical feature of the best OB theories.[10] Everyone in the organisation needs to work with other people, and OB provides the knowledge and tools for working with and through others. Building a high-performance team, motivating coworkers, handling workplace conflicts, influencing your boss and changing employee behaviour are just a few of the areas of knowledge and skills offered in organisational behaviour. No matter what career path you choose, you'll find that OB concepts play an important role in performing your job and working more effectively within organisations.

Organisational Behaviour is for Everyone

Our explanation of why organisational behaviour is important for your career success does not assume that you are, or intend to be, a manager. In fact, this book pioneered the notion that OB knowledge is for everyone. Whether you are a geologist, financial analyst, customer service representative or chief executive officer, you need to understand and apply the many organisational behaviour topics that are discussed in this book. Yes, organisations will continue to have managers, but their roles have changed and the rest of us are increasingly expected to manage ourselves in the workplace. In the words of one forward-thinking OB writer many years ago: everyone is a manager.[11]

OB and the Bottom Line

Up to this point, our answer to the question 'Why study OB?' has focused on how organisational behaviour knowledge benefits you as an individual. However, OB knowledge is just as important for the organisation's financial health. Wesfarmers, described at the beginning of this chapter, has flourished because of its emphasis on employee performance and wellbeing. This competitive advantage was apparent several years ago when Bunnings (a division of Wesfarmers) battled with BBC Hardwarehouse for dominance of the retail home-improvement business. Both companies built big-box stores in strategic locations, but Bunnings consistently delivered higher returns and customer satisfaction because it outshone BBC in the talent and commitment of its staff and management. Bunnings eventually acquired its rival.[12]

Several studies report that a company's performance increases with employee involvement, training and development, performance-based rewards, high-quality leadership, employee communication and other OB practices.[13] For example, one investigation found that hospitals with higher levels of specific OB activities (e.g. training, staff involvement, reward and recognition) have lower patient mortality rates. Another study found that companies receiving 'the best place to work' awards have significantly higher financial and long-term stock market performance.

The bottom-line value of organisational behaviour is also supported by investment portfolio studies. These investigations suggest that specific OB characteristics (employee attitudes, work–life balance, performance-based rewards, leadership, employee training and development, and so on) are important 'positive screens' for selecting companies with the best long-term share appreciation. For instance, Sydney-based AMP Capital estimates that three-quarters of the value of a typical Australian company comes from its intangible assets, which includes the ability to manage and retain employees. 'The best companies are the ones that see their human resources as a competitive advantage,' concludes Mike Murray, senior portfolio manager of AMP Capital's Sustainable Alpha Team.[14]

PERSPECTIVES OF ORGANISATIONAL EFFECTIVENESS

Almost all organisational behaviour theories have the implicit or explicit objective of making organisations more effective.[15] Indeed, organisational effectiveness is considered the 'ultimate dependent variable' in organisational behaviour.[16] The first challenge, however, is to define **organisational effectiveness**. Experts agree that this topic is burdened with too many labels—organisational performance, success, goodness, health, competitiveness, excellence and so on—with no consensus on the meaning of each label.

organisational effectiveness A broad concept represented by several perspectives, including the organisation's fit with the external environment, internal-subsystems configuration for high performance, emphasis on organisational learning and ability to satisfy the needs of key stakeholders.

Long ago, organisational effectiveness was defined as the extent to which an organisation achieved its stated goals.[17] According to this view, Wesfarmers is effective because it achieves its stated objectives, such as achieving specific weekly sales targets at Coles or coal production output at Curragh Queensland Mining. The goal-attainment view is no longer accepted, however, because a company can be considered effective simply by establishing easily achievable goals. Also, some goals—such as social responsibility to the community—are so abstract that it is difficult to know how well the organisation has achieved them. A third flaw with the goal-attainment definition is that a company's stated objectives might threaten its long-term survival. For example, some corporate leaders receive incentives (such as stock options) to maximise short-term profits. Some accomplish this objective by slashing expenditures, including funds for marketing and product development. The result is often a lack of new products and deterioration in the company's brand value in the long run. In extreme cases, the company achieves its short-term profitability targets but eventually goes out of business.

How is organisational effectiveness defined today? The answer is that there are several perspectives of effectiveness, so this concept is defined by *all of these perspectives together*.[18] Organisations are considered effective when they have a good fit with their external environment, when their internal subsystems are efficient and effective (i.e. high-performance work practices), when they are learning organisations and when they satisfy the needs of key stakeholders. Over the next few pages, we will discuss each of these four perspectives of organisational effectiveness in some detail.

LEARNING OBJECTIVE 

Diagram an organisation from an open-systems perspective.

open systems A perspective which holds that organisations depend on the external environment for resources, affect that environment through their output and consist of internal subsystems that transform inputs to outputs.

Open-Systems Perspective

The **open-systems** perspective of organisational effectiveness is one of the earliest and deeply entrenched ways of thinking about organisations. Indeed, the other major perspectives on organisational effectiveness might be considered detailed extensions of the open-systems model.[19] As depicted in Exhibit 1.1, the open-systems perspective views organisations as complex organisms that 'live' within an external environment. The word *open* describes this permeable relationship, whereas *closed* systems can exist without dependence on an external environment.

As open systems, organisations depend on the external environment for resources, including raw materials, employees, financial resources, information and equipment. Wesfarmers and other companies could not survive without employees, raw materials, knowledge and so forth. The open-systems perspective also describes numerous subsystems within the organisation, such as processes (communication and reward systems), work units (production, marketing) and social dynamics (informal networks, power relationships). With the aid of technology (such as equipment, work methods and information), these subsystems transform inputs into various outputs. Some outputs (e.g. products and services) may be valued by the external environment, whereas other outputs (e.g. employee layoffs, pollution) have adverse effects. The organisation receives feedback from the external environment regarding the value of its outputs and the availability of future inputs.

According to the open-systems perspective, successful organisations monitor their environments and are able to maintain a close fit with changing conditions.[20] One way they do this is by finding new opportunities to secure essential inputs. For instance, many fast-food restaurants struggle to find enough employees, but McDonald's Restaurants has identified several ways to

Exhibit 1.1 *Open-systems Perspective of Organisations*

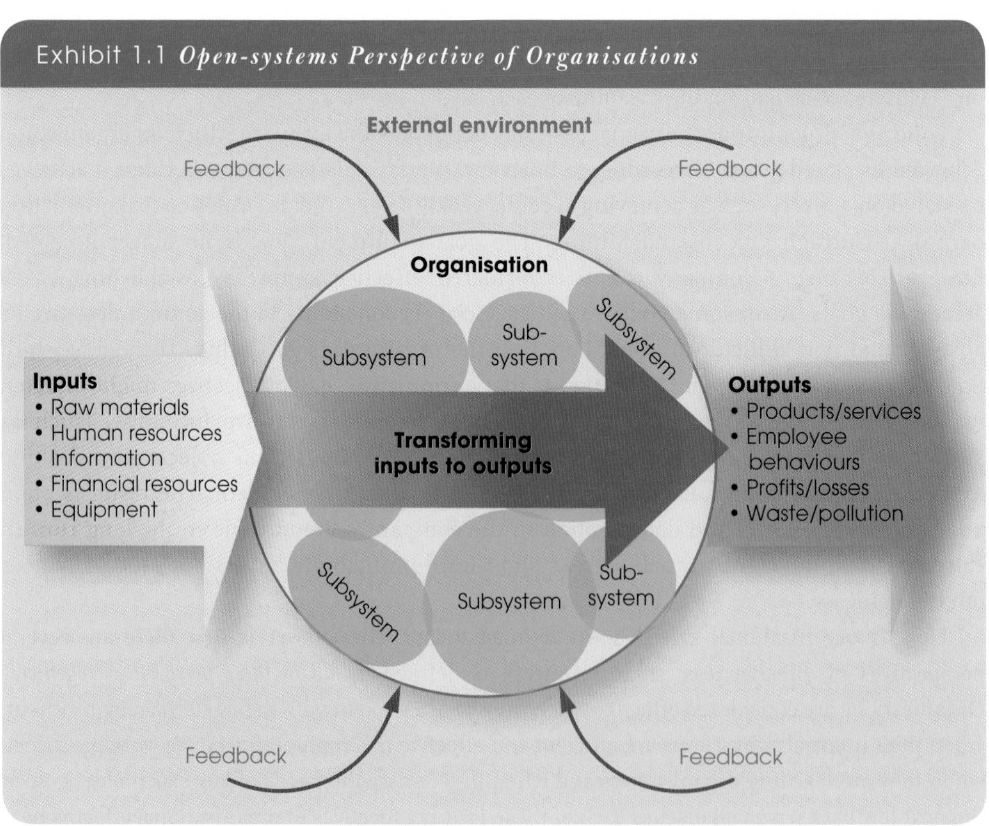

ensure that it has enough qualified staff. It was among the first to recruit retirees. McDonald's UK introduced the 'family contract', which allows members of the employee's family (spouses, grandparents and children over the age of 16) to swap shifts without notifying management.[21] Successful organisations also redesign outputs so that they remain compatible with demands from the external environment. For example, sensing a need for environmental responsibility, Bunnings was one of the first companies in this region to discourage use of plastic bags. Similarly, in response to consumer demand and government requirements, car manufacturers have been scrambling to design models that are more fuel-efficient or rely on different energy sources. This open-systems view is reflected in the words of Huh Chang-soo, chairman of Korean conglomerate GS Group: 'Customer needs are changing fast. If we do not detect the changes, and act on them in a timely way, such as by making investments, we will fail.'[22]

Internal-Subsystems Effectiveness

The open-systems perspective considers more than an organisation's fit with the external environment. It also examines how well the organisation operates internally, that is, how well it transforms inputs into outputs. The most common indicator of this internal transformation process is **organisational efficiency** (also called *productivity*), which is the amount of outputs relative to inputs.[23] Companies that produce more goods or services with less labour, materials and energy are more efficient.

organisational efficiency The amount of outputs relative to inputs in the organisation's transformation process.

A popular strategy for improving efficiency in the transformation process is **lean management**.[24] Based on practices developed by the Toyota Motor Company, lean management involves continuously reducing waste, unevenness and overburden in the production process. Waste (called *muda*) takes many forms, such as excess travel of the product or service through the production process, too much time during which the work is sitting idle (waiting for the next step in production), too much inventory, too much physical movement of employees and too much finished product without a buyer. Lean management also involves minimising situations in which people and equipment are overloaded (too much demand per unit time) and smoothing out the production process (e.g. reducing bottlenecks). The 'lean' movement originated in manufacturing, but it is now being adopted by hospitals, governments, accounting firms and other service providers.[25] Reality Check 1.1 describes how British and Australian hospitals have improved efficiency and effectiveness through various lean practices.

lean management A cluster of practices to improve organisational efficiency by continuously reducing waste, unevenness and overburden in the production process.

Keep in mind that efficiency does not necessarily translate into effectiveness. Efficiency is about *doings things right*, whereas effectiveness is about *doing the right things*. A company might be highly efficient at making a product or providing a service, but it will be ineffective if no one wants that product or service, for example. Also, efficiency often requires standardisation, whereas companies operating in rapidly changing environments need to remain nimble and responsive. Organisations often need more *adaptive* and *innovative* transformation processes, not just more efficient ones. For example, German engineering conglomerate Siemens AG has an effective transformation process because its subsystems are innovative and responsive, not necessarily the most efficient. 'Whether I have additional costs or not doesn't matter as much as the speed to market and the quality of the design,' says a Siemens executive. 'We're not talking about a pure cost game.'[27]

Another important issue in the transformation process is how well the organisation's subsystems coordinate with each other. The more each subsystem depends on other subsystems, the higher the risk of problems that undermine the transformation process.[28] Information gets

Hospitals Take the Lean Journey to Efficiency

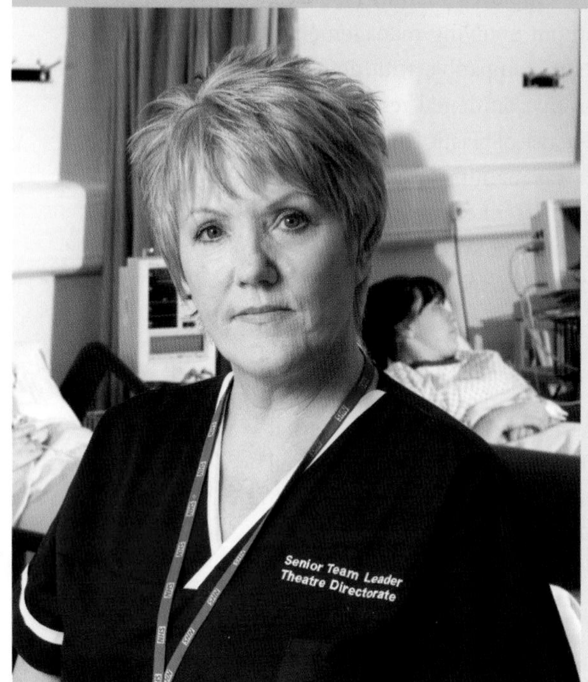

Photo: Jim Varney

Sunderland Royal Hospital learned from the nearby Nissan factory how to implement lean management in its new day-surgery unit.

How is serving surgical patients similar to manufacturing a car? The answer is clear to staff at Sunderland Royal Hospital. The health facility in northern England recently borrowed several lean management ideas from the nearby Nissan factory, one of the most efficient car plants in Europe, to improve its day-surgery unit. 'We took [Sunderland hospital staff] on a tour of our plant, showing them a variety of lean processes in action, and let them decide which ones could be applied back at the hospital,' says a training manager at Nissan's factory in Sunderland.

Sunderland's day-surgery staff members were actively involved in applying lean management to their work unit. After attending Nissan's two-day workshop on lean thinking, they mapped out the work processes, questioned assumptions about the value or relevance of some activities and discovered ways to reduce the lengthy patient wait times (which were up to three hours). Some staff members were initially resistant and sceptical, but the hospital's day surgery soon realised significant improvements in efficiency and service quality.

'By working with Nissan's staff, we have streamlined the patient pathway from twenty-nine to eleven discrete stages,' says Anne Fleming (shown in

lost, ideas are not shared, materials are hoarded, communication messages are misinterpreted, resources and rewards are distributed unfairly, and so forth. These coordination challenges are amplified as organisations grow, such as when employees are clustered into several departments and when departments are clustered into several organisational divisions. That is why even the best-laid plans produce unintended consequences. A slight change in work practices in one subsystem may ripple through the organisation and affect other subsystems in adverse ways. For example, an adjustment in accounting procedures might have the unintended effect of motivating sales staff to sell more products with a lower profit margin, or discouraging administrative staff from accurately completing documents that are vital for executive decisions.

Organisational Learning Perspective

organisational learning
A perspective which holds that organisational effectiveness depends on the organisation's capacity to acquire, share, use and store valuable knowledge.

The open-systems perspective has traditionally focused on physical resources that enter the organisation and are processed into physical goods (outputs). This was representative of the industrial economy but not the 'new economy', in which the most valued input is knowledge. Accordingly, knowledge is the driver of competitive advantage in the **organisational learning** perspective (also called *knowledge management*). Through this lens, organisational effectiveness depends on the organisation's capacity to acquire, share, use and store valuable knowledge.[29]

REALITY CHECK 1.1

photo), who oversees Sunderland's 32-bed day-case unit and its 54 employees. 'We have done this by reducing duplication, halving the time that patients spend in the unit to three hours by giving them individual appointment times, and introducing the just-in-time approach to the patient pathway.' Fleming also reports that Sunderland's operating rooms are now much more efficient.

Flinders Medical Centre in South Australia has also adopted lean management practices to improve work efficiency. Flinders experienced severe congestion of patients in its emergency department, so it mapped out the steps in the patient journey through the department. Staff immediately realised that the process was chaotic and inefficient. In particular, the work unit created confusion by rating patients on the severity of their ailments, and then bumping lower rated patients further down the wait list as new high-priority patients arrived. This ongoing bumping process confused staff members regarding who had priority, and created stress for patients who were being bumped down the queue.

Flinders staff relied on lean principles to create a simpler system. Now, incoming emergency patients are immediately streamed to one of two emergency teams—those who will be treated and sent home, and those who will be treated and admitted to hospital. Patients are seen in order of their arrival; only those with life-threatening ailments are given priority. This change immediately improved efficiency and the quality of patient care. The percentage of patients leaving without receiving treatment (i.e. deciding not to wait any longer) dropped from 7 per cent to about 3 per cent. Within the first year, the average time patients spent in the emergency department fell from 5.7 hours to 5 hours. Soon after, Western Hospital in Melbourne adopted Flinders' emergency department process. They also reported significantly reduced wait times and half the previous number of ambulance bypass episodes (where ambulances are requested to send patients, except those in a critical condition, elsewhere).[26]

To understand knowledge acquisition, sharing and use, consider how Google engages in organisational learning. *Knowledge acquisition* occurs when information is brought into the organisation from the external environment. Google acquires knowledge by hiring the best talent and buying entire companies (such as Keyhole, Inc., whose knowledge created Google Earth). Knowledge acquisition also includes the process of creative insight—experimenting and discovering new ideas.[30] Google encourages this by allowing engineering staff to allocate 20 per cent of their time to discovering new knowledge of their choosing.

Knowledge sharing refers to the distribution of knowledge throughout the organisation. Google encourages knowledge sharing by organising employees into teams so they share information as part of their job. Its campus-like environments (called Googleplexes) increase the chance that employees from different parts of the organisation will mingle and casually share information, whether dining at the company's subsidised gourmet restaurant or playing a game of volleyball in the sports area. Google also relies on sophisticated information technologies—wikis, blogs and intranet repositories—to support knowledge sharing.

Knowledge use is the application of knowledge in ways that improve the organisation's effectiveness. Google encourages knowledge use by giving employees the freedom to apply their new-found knowledge and encouraging them to experiment with that knowledge. 'Google is truly a learning organisation,' says Google's chief financial officer, George Reyes.[31]

absorptive capacity The ability to recognise the value of new information, assimilate it and use it for value-added activities.

An interesting dilemma in organisational learning is that the ability to acquire, share and use new knowledge is limited by the company's existing body of knowledge. To recognise the value of new information, assimilate it and use it for value-added activities, organisations require sufficient **absorptive capacity**.[32] For example, many companies were slow to develop online marketing practices because no one in the organisation had enough knowledge about the internet to fathom its potential or apply that knowledge to the company's business. In some cases, companies had to acquire entire teams of people with the requisite knowledge to realise the potential of this marketing channel. Entire countries also suffer from a lack of absorptive capacity. Without sufficient knowledge, a society is slow or completely unable to adopt new information that may improve social and economic conditions.[33]

LEARNING OBJECTIVE 

Define *intellectual capital* and describe the organisational learning perspective of organisational effectiveness.

intellectual capital A company's stock of knowledge, including human capital, structural capital and relationship capital.

human capital The stock of knowledge, skills and abilities among employees that provides economic value to the organisation.

Intellectual Capital: The Stock of Organisational Knowledge

Knowledge acquisition, sharing and use represent the flow of knowledge. The organisational learning perspective also considers the company's stock of knowledge, called its **intellectual capital**.[34] The most obvious form of intellectual capital is **human capital**—the knowledge, skills and abilities that employees carry around in their heads. This is an important part of a company's stock of knowledge, and it is a huge risk in companies where knowledge is the main competitive advantage. When key people leave, they take with them some of the knowledge that makes the company effective.

Even if every employee left the organisation, intellectual capital would still remain as *structural capital*. This includes the knowledge captured and retained in an organisation's systems and structures, such as the documentation of work procedures and the physical layout of the production line. Structural capital also includes the organisation's finished products because knowledge can be extracted by taking them apart to discover how they work and are constructed (i.e. reverse engineering). Finally, intellectual capital includes *relationship capital*, which is the value derived from an organisation's relationships with customers, suppliers and others who provide added mutual value for the organisation.

organisational memory The storage and preservation of intellectual capital.

Organisational Memory and Unlearning

Corporate leaders need to recognise that they are the keepers of an **organisational memory**.[35] This unusual metaphor refers to the storage and preservation of intellectual capital. It includes knowledge that employees possess as well as knowledge embedded in the organisation's systems and structures. It includes documents, objects and anything else that provides meaningful information about how the organisation should operate.

How do organisations retain intellectual capital? One way is by keeping good employees. Progressive companies achieve this by adapting their employment practices to become more compatible with emerging workforce expectations, including work–life balance, an egalitarian hierarchy and a workspace that generates more fun. A second organisational memory strategy is to systematically transfer knowledge to other employees. This occurs when newcomers apprentice with skilled employees, thereby acquiring knowledge that is not documented. A third strategy is to transfer knowledge into structural capital. This includes bringing out hidden knowledge, organising it and putting it in a form that can be available to others. Reliance Industries, India's largest business enterprise, applies this strategy by encouraging employees to document their successes and failures through a special intranet knowledge portal. One of these reports alone provided information that allowed others to prevent a costly plant shutdown.[36]

The organisational learning perspective states not only that effective organisations learn, but also that they unlearn routines and patterns of behaviour that are no longer appropriate.[37] Unlearning removes knowledge that no longer adds value and, in fact, may undermine the organisation's effectiveness. Some forms of unlearning involve replacing dysfunctional policies, procedures and routines. Other forms of unlearning erase attitudes, beliefs and assumptions. For instance, employees may rethink the 'best way' to perform a task and how to serve clients.

High-Performance Work Practices Perspective

LEARNING OBJECTIVE 

Diagnose the extent to which an organisation or one of its work units applies high-performance work practices.

The open-systems perspective states that successful companies are good at transforming inputs into outputs. However, it does not identify the most important subsystem characteristics of effective organisations. Consequently, an entire field of research has blossomed around the objective of determining specific 'bundles' of organisational practices that offer competitive advantage. This research has had various labels over the years, but it is now most commonly known as **high-performance work practices (HPWP)**.[38]

high-performance work practices (HPWP) A perspective which holds that effective organisations incorporate several workplace practices that leverage the potential of human capital.

The HPWP perspective begins with the idea that *human capital*—the knowledge, skills and abilities that employees possess—is an important source of competitive advantage for organisations.[39] Human capital helps the organisation realise opportunities or minimise threats in the external environment. Furthermore, human capital is neither widely available nor easily duplicated. For instance, a new company cannot quickly acquire a workforce with the same capabilities as those of the workforce at an established company. Nor can technology replace the capabilities that employees bring to the workplace. In short, human capital is valuable, rare, difficult to imitate and nonsubstitutable.[40] Therefore, organisations excel by introducing a bundle of systems and structures that leverage the potential of their workforce.

Many high-performance work practices have been studied over the years.[41] Four practices with strong research support are employee involvement, job autonomy, employee competence, and performance and/or skill-based rewards. As you will learn later in this book, employee involvement and job autonomy tend to strengthen employee motivation as well as improve decision making, organisational responsiveness and commitment to change.

Another key variable in the HPWP model is employee competence. Specifically, organisations are more effective when they recruit and select people with relevant skills, knowledge, values and other personal characteristics. Furthermore, successful companies invest in their employees by supporting further competency development (see Chapter 2). A fourth characteristic of high-performance organisations is that they link performance and skill development to various forms of financial and nonfinancial rewards valued by employees. We discuss reward systems in Chapter 6 as one of several practices to improve employee performance.

The HPWP perspective is currently popular among OB experts and practitioners, but it also has its share of critics. One concern is that many studies try to find out which practices predict organisational performance without understanding *why* those practices should have this effect.[42] In other words, some of the practices identified as HPWPs lack theoretical foundation; the causal connection between work practices and organisational effectiveness is missing. Without this explanation, it is difficult to be confident that the practice will be valuable in the future and in other situations.

A second concern with the HPWP perspective is that it may satisfy shareholder and customer needs at the expense of employee wellbeing.[43] Some experts point out that HPWPs increase work stress and that management is reluctant to delegate power or share the financial benefits of productivity improvements. If high-performance work practices improve organisational performance at a cost to employee wellbeing, then this perspective (along with the open-systems and organisational learning perspectives) offers an incomplete picture of organisational effectiveness. The remaining gaps are mostly filled by the stakeholder perspective of organisational effectiveness.

Explain how the stakeholder perspective emphasises the importance of values, ethics and corporate social responsibility.

stakeholders Individuals, organisations and other entities who affect, or are affected by, the organisation's objectives and actions.

Stakeholder Perspective

The three organisational effectiveness perspectives described so far mainly consider processes and resources, yet they only minimally recognise the importance of relations with **stakeholders**. Stakeholders include individuals, organisations and other entities that affect, or are affected by, the organisation's objectives and actions. They include anyone with a stake in the company—employees, shareholders, suppliers, labour unions, governments, communities, consumer and environmental interest groups, and so on. The essence of the stakeholder perspective is that companies must take into account how their actions affect others, and this requires that they understand, manage and satisfy the interests of their stakeholders.[44] The stakeholder perspective personalises the open-systems perspective; it identifies specific people and social entities in the external and internal environment. It also recognises that stakeholder relations are dynamic; they can be negotiated and managed, not just taken as a fixed condition.[45]

Consider the troubles that Wal-Mart has faced in recent years.[46] For decades, the world's largest retailer concentrated on customers by providing the lowest possible prices, and on shareholders by generating healthy financial returns. Yet emphasising these two stakeholders exposed the company to increasing hostility from other groups in society. Some interest groups accused Wal-Mart of destroying America's manufacturing base and tacitly allowing unethical business practices (such as child labour) in countries where it purchased goods. Other groups pointed out that Wal-Mart had a poor record of environmental and social responsibility. Still other groups lobbied to keep Wal-Mart out of their communities because the giant retailer typically builds in outlying suburbs where land is cheap, thereby fading the vibrancy of the community's downtown area. These stakeholder pressure points existed for some time, but Wal-Mart mostly ignored them until they became serious threats. In fact, Wal-Mart recently created the position 'senior director of stakeholder engagement' to ensure that it pays more attention to most stakeholders and to proactively manage stakeholder relationships.

Understanding, managing and satisfying the interests of stakeholders is more challenging than it sounds because stakeholders have conflicting interests and organisations don't have the resources to satisfy every stakeholder to the fullest. Therefore, organisational leaders need to decide how much priority to give to each group. One commonly cited factor is to favour the stakeholders with the most power.[47] This makes sense when one considers that the most powerful stakeholders present the greatest threat and opportunity to the company's survival. Yet stakeholder power should not be the only criterion for determining organisational strategy and resource allocation. Ignoring less powerful stakeholders might motivate them to become more powerful by forming coalitions or seeking government support. It might also irritate more powerful stakeholders if ignoring weaker interests violates the norms and standards of society.

Values, Ethics and Corporate Social Responsibility

This brings us to one of the key strengths of the stakeholder perspective, namely, that it incorporates values, ethics and corporate social responsibility into the organisational effectiveness equation.[48]

The stakeholder perspective states that to manage the interests of diverse stakeholders, leaders ultimately need to rely on their personal and organisational values for guidance. **Values** are relatively stable, evaluative beliefs that guide our preferences for outcomes or courses of action in a variety of situations.[49] Values help us to know what is right or wrong, or good or bad, in the world. Chapter 2 explains how values are an important part of our self-concept and, as such, motivate our actions. Although values exist within individuals, groups of people often hold similar values, so we tend to ascribe these *shared values* to the team, department, organisation, profession or entire society. For example, Chapter 14 discusses the importance and dynamics of organisational culture, which includes shared values across the company or within subsystems.

values Relatively stable, evaluative beliefs that guide a person's preferences for outcomes or courses of action in a variety of situations.

Values have become a popular topic in corporate boardrooms because leaders are discovering that the values-driven organisational approach to guiding employee behaviour is potentially more effective, as well as more popular, than the old command-and-control approach (i.e. top-down decisions with close supervision of employees). For example, governments in Australia, New Zealand, the United Kingdom, Canada and several other countries have made values the foundation of employee decisions and behaviour. As one New Zealand government report proclaimed: 'Values are essentially the link between the daily work of public servants and the broad aims of democratic governance.'[50] In a recent global survey of MBA students (one-fifth of whom were from Asia), almost 80 per cent felt that a well-run company operates according to its values and code of ethics.[51]

By incorporating values into organisational effectiveness, the stakeholder perspective also provides the strongest case for ethics and corporate social responsibility. In fact, the stakeholder perspective emerged out of earlier writing on ethics and corporate social responsibility. **Ethics** refers to the study of moral principles or values that determine whether actions are right or

ethics The study of moral principles or values that determine whether actions are right or wrong and outcomes are good or bad.

Aviva's CSR Way of Life

While most business leaders are still figuring out how to implement corporate social responsibility (CSR), Aviva has already made it a corporate lifestyle. In fact, the world's fifth-largest insurer has won several CSR awards and is the only UK-listed insurer included in the Dow Jones Sustainability World Index. Aviva was the first insurer to carbon-neutralise its worldwide operations. More than half of its electricity now comes from zero emissions sources. Aviva Hong Kong sponsors energy research and uses its ship (the *Aviva Junk*) as a test site. 'Aviva Hong Kong's CSR focuses on battling air pollution,' says Shaun Meadows, Aviva's CEO for Hong Kong, Singapore and the Middle East. Meadows is shown at right in this photo with two dozen Aviva Hong Kong staff in another CSR initiative—planting trees. Aviva actively involves staff in CSR initiatives. For example, nominated managers from around the world congregate at Aviva's annual CSR conference to discuss objectives and set targets. 'CSR only becomes truly embedded into the company culture when there is employee involvement,' says Meadows. 'Only when the employees are engaged to the cause, do they become advocates.'[52]

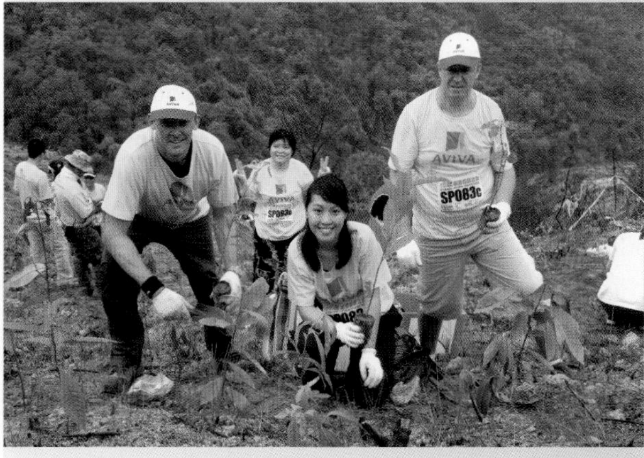

Courtesy of Aviva

wrong and outcomes are good or bad. We rely on our ethical values to determine 'the right thing to do'. Ethical behaviour is driven by the moral principles we use to make decisions. These moral principles represent fundamental values. Chapter 2 provides more detail about ethical principles and related influences on moral reasoning.

corporate social responsibility (CSR) Organisational activities intended to benefit society and the environment beyond the firm's immediate financial interests or legal obligations.

Corporate social responsibility (CSR) consists of organisational activities intended to benefit society and the environment beyond the firm's immediate financial interests or legal obligations.[53] It is the view that companies have a contract with society, in which they must serve stakeholders beyond shareholders and customers. In some situations, the interests of the firm's shareholders should be secondary to those of other stakeholders.[54] As part of CSR, many companies have adopted the triple-bottom-line philosophy: they try to support or 'earn positive returns' in the economic, social and environmental spheres of sustainability. Firms that adopt the triple bottom line aim to survive and be profitable in the marketplace (economic), but they also intend to maintain or improve conditions for society (social) as well as the physical environment.[55]

Not everyone agrees with the idea that organisations are more effective when they cater to a wide variety of stakeholders. More than thirty years ago, economist Milton Friedman pronounced that 'there is one and only one social responsibility of business—to use its resources and engage in activities designed to increase its profits.' Although few writers take this extreme view today, some point out that companies can benefit other stakeholders only if those with financial interests in the company receive first priority. Yet four out of five people in an American survey said that a company's commitment to a social issue is an important factor in deciding whether to work for the company and whether to buy its products or services. In another survey, more than two-thirds of North American students said they would not apply for a job if the company was considered irresponsible. Most American and European MBA students also claim they would accept lower financial rewards to work for an organisation with a better ethical/CSR reputation. However, a recent global survey indicated that while most MBA students believe socially responsible companies have a better reputation, less than half of these respondents believe CSR improves revenue, employee loyalty, customer satisfaction, community wellbeing or the company's long-term viability.[56]

Capgemini, a Netherlands-based information technology (IT) consulting firm, discovered the importance of corporate social responsibility when it tried to fill 800 IT and management consulting positions in that country. Rather than offering a T-shirt for completing the thirty-minute online survey on recruitment issues, Capgemini advised respondents (IT and management consultants) that for each completed survey it would provide funding for a homeless child in Kolkata, India, to have one week of schooling and accommodation. The survey included an option for respondents to find out more about employment with the consulting firm. Far beyond its expectations, Capgemini received more than 10 000 completed surveys and 2000 job inquiries from qualified respondents. The company filled its 800 jobs and developed a waiting list of future prospects. Furthermore, media attention about this initiative raised Capgemini's brand reputation for corporate social responsibility. The consulting firm supported 10 400 weeks of housing and education for children in Kolkata.[57]

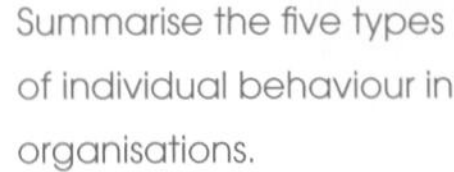

Summarise the five types of individual behaviour in organisations.

TYPES OF INDIVIDUAL BEHAVIOUR

The four perspectives described over the past few pages—open systems, organisational learning, high-performance work practices and stakeholder—provide a multidimensional view of what makes companies effective. Within these models, however, are individual behaviours that enable companies to interact with their environments; acquire, share and use knowledge to the best advantage; process inputs to outputs efficiently and responsively; and satisfy the needs of various groups in society. While organisational effectiveness is the ultimate dependent variable, the behaviours described here are the individual-level dependent variables found in most OB research. Exhibit 1.2 highlights the five types of behaviour discussed most often in the organisational behaviour literature: task performance, organisational citizenship, counterproductive work behaviours, joining and staying with the organisation, and work attendance.

Task Performance

Task performance refers to goal-directed behaviours under the individual's control that support organisational objectives. Task performance behaviours transform raw materials into goods and services, or support and maintain technical activities.[58] For example, foreign exchange traders at the Bank of New Zealand make decisions and take actions to exchange currencies. Employees in most jobs have more than one performance dimension. Foreign exchange traders must be able to identify profitable trades, work cooperatively with clients and coworkers in a stressful environment, assist in training new staff and work on special telecommunications equipment without error. Some of these performance dimensions are more important than others, but only by considering all of them can we fully evaluate an employee's contribution to the organisation.

Organisational Citizenship

Companies could not effectively compete, transform resources or serve the needs of their stakeholders if employees performed only their formal job duties. Employees also need to engage in **organisational citizenship behaviours (OCBs)**—various forms of cooperation and helpfulness to others that support the organisation's social and psychological context.[60] In other words, companies require contextual performance (i.e. OCBs) along with task performance.

organisational citizenship behaviours (OCBs) Various forms of cooperation and helpfulness to others that support the organisation's social and psychological context.

Exhibit 1.2 *Types of Work-Related Behaviour*

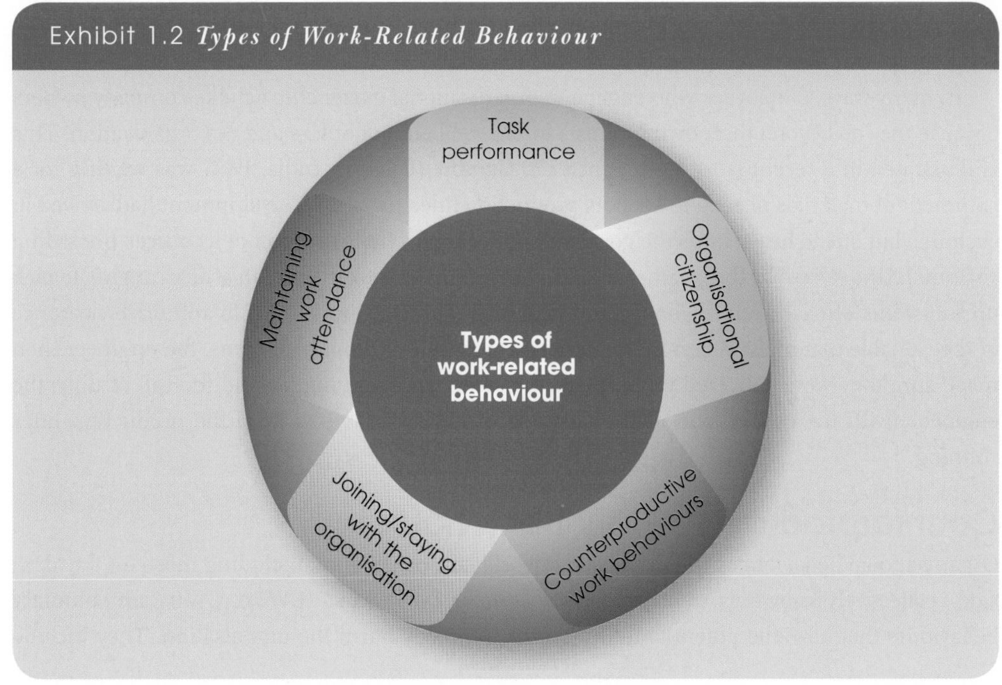

Australia Post Superstar Performance

Australia Post's Dandenong Letters Centre is the largest mail-processing facility in the Southern Hemisphere. Fifteen hundred employees work across seven shifts, processing more than 7 million separate mail articles each day. During Christmas season, daily production jumps to 12 or 13 million items. Computerised equipment processes most letters, directing them to regions and specific delivery routes. Each day thousands of documents aren't readable by machine, so the computer scans them and sends the image to human 'video coders' who view the image and type in the correct postcode. The performance of these video coders is staggering. One video coder named Edna routinely processes 5000 addresses per hour, even while carrying on a conversation. 'She can sit there and just talk; she's just got such a light touch,' says supervisor Michelle D'Rozario, who calls Edna her 'superstar'.[59]

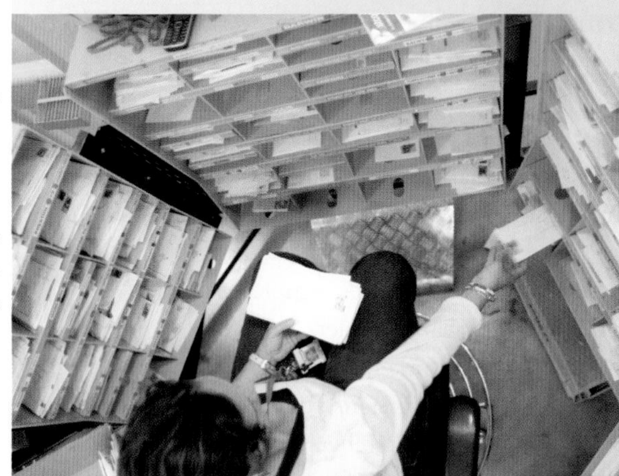
Jason Edwards/Oakleigh Springvale Dandenong Leader

Organisational citizenship behaviours take many forms.[61] Some are directed toward individuals, such as assisting coworkers with their work problems, adjusting your work schedule to accommodate coworkers, showing genuine courtesy toward coworkers and sharing your work resources (supplies, technology, staff). Other OCBs represent cooperation and helpfulness toward the organisation in general. These include supporting the company's public image, taking discretionary action to help the organisation avoid potential problems, offering ideas beyond those required for your own job, attending voluntary functions that support the organisation and keeping up with new developments in the organisation.

In many ways, employees who engage in organisational citizenship act like company owners because they go beyond their own interests to the wellbeing of others and the organisation. This is illustrated in a recent story from Procter & Gamble (P&G) in India. P&G was waiting for a shipment of materials needed to keep its production lines running. The shipment had arrived in customs, but due to heavy rains the government declared a holiday for all of its offices (including customs). Undeterred by the weather, a P&G plant engineer took the initiative of arranging to pick up a customs official from his house and take him to the customs office to authorise clearance of the valuable materials. When the materials were cleared through customs, the engineer then made sure they were delivered to the plant the same day. By going beyond the call of duty, the engineer (with the cooperation of the customs officer) was able to keep the production lines running.[62]

Counterproductive Work Behaviours

counterproductive work behaviours (CWBs) Voluntary behaviours that have the potential to directly or indirectly harm the organisation.

Organisational behaviour is interested in all workplace behaviours, including those on the 'dark side', collectively known as **counterproductive work behaviours (CWBs)**. CWBs are voluntary behaviours that have the potential to directly or indirectly harm the organisation. They include abuse of others (e.g. insults and nasty comments), threats (threatening harm), work avoidance (e.g. tardiness), work sabotage (doing work incorrectly) and overt acts (theft). CWBs are not minor concerns. One Australian study found that units of a fast-food restaurant chain with higher CWBs had a significantly worse performance, whereas organisational citizenship had a relatively minor benefit.[63]

Joining and Staying with the Organisation

Task performance, organisational citizenship and the lack of counterproductive work behaviours are obviously important, but if qualified people don't join and stay with the organisation, none of these performance-related behaviours will occur. Although staff shortages vary as the economy rises and falls, it appears that some employers never seem to get enough qualified staff. During the most recent economic recession, for example, one Australian newspaper published stories of employers who didn't have any qualified applicants in spite of rising unemployment. (Most employers filled their vacancies after the stories were reported.) The effects of staff shortages are apparent in Wittlesea, Victoria, where a chronic shortage of paramedics has resulted in cancellation of some ambulance services. The shortage has also placed a heavy strain on existing staff, some of whom are regularly (and reluctantly) working fourteen-hour days without a lunch break, and also covering other shifts on their days off. 'The paramedics are exhausted and each patient is then forced to wait longer for treatment,' says the union representing paramedics.[64]

Companies survive and thrive not just by hiring people with talent or potential; they also need to ensure that these employees stay with the company. Companies with high turnover suffer because of the high cost of replacing people who leave. More important, as mentioned earlier in this chapter, much of an organisation's intellectual capital is the knowledge carried around in employees' heads. When people leave, some of this vital knowledge is lost, often resulting in inefficiencies, inferior customer service and so forth. This threat is not trivial: One large-scale survey revealed that nearly two-thirds of Indonesian employees plan to move to a different employer even though the position, area of work and remuneration are the same. During the recent mining boom, a survey of thirteen mining operations across Australia reported an average turnover rate of 24 per cent, with some mining sites experiencing annual employee turnover approaching 60 per cent.[65]

Maintaining Work Attendance

Along with attracting and retaining employees, organisations need everyone to show up for work at scheduled times. Situational factors—such as severe weather or car breakdown—explain some work absences. Motivation is another factor. Employees who experience job dissatisfaction or work-related stress are more likely to be absent or late for work because taking time off is a way to temporarily withdraw from stressful or dissatisfying conditions. Absenteeism is also higher in organisations with generous sick leave because this benefit limits the negative financial impact of taking time away from work. Studies have found that absenteeism is also higher in teams with strong absence norms, meaning that team members tolerate and even expect coworkers to take time off. One study of Queensland government employees discovered that absenteeism rates changed over time, and that these changing absence levels may be due to changing norms about how much unscheduled time off team members should take.[67]

Google Attracts and Keeps Talent through 'Cool' Campuses

Courtesy of Camenzind Evolution

Google is ranked by university students in many countries as one of the top ten places to work. One reason why the internet technology company is able to attract so many applicants is that its workplaces look like every student's dream of a university campus. Google's headquarters (called Googleplex) in Mountain View, California, is outfitted with lava lamps, exercise balls, casual sofas, foosball, pool tables, workout rooms, video games, slides and a restaurant with free gourmet meals. Google's new EMEA engineering hub in Zurich, Switzerland, also boasts a fun, campus-like environment. These photos show a few areas of Google's offices in Zurich, including private temporary workspaces in beehives and ski gondolas. Google's offices are so comfortable that executives occasionally remind staff of building code regulations against making the offices their permanent home.[66]

LEARNING OBJECTIVE

Debate the organisational opportunities and challenges of globalisation, workforce diversity and virtual work.

CONTEMPORARY CHALLENGES FOR ORGANISATIONS

A message threaded throughout the earlier organisational effectiveness discussion is that organisations are deeply affected by the external environment. They need to maintain a good fit with their external environment by continuously monitoring and adjusting to changes in that environment. This external environment is continuously changing, but some changes, over the past decade and in the decade to come, are more profound than others. These changes require that corporate leaders and all other employees adjust to new realities. In this section, we highlight three of the major challenges facing organisations: globalisation, increasing workforce diversity and emerging employment relationships.

Globalisation

Most people in the world have not heard of Fonterra, but chances are they have recently purchased or eaten one of its products. The New Zealand–based company is the world's largest dairy exporting business and the world's lowest cost producer of dairy ingredients. It operates in 140 countries, employs 20 000 people (including 2000 in Australia and 2500 in Asia) and represents 40 per cent of the global dairy trade. In many countries, it forms joint partnerships, such as those with the Dairy Farmers of America, SanCor in Argentina and Aria in Europe.

Fonterra's current position on the world stage is quite different from the situation a decade ago, when three New Zealand dairy companies joined forces. They realised that forming a global enterprise was essential to their survival. The merged company was so globally focused from the outset that it was temporarily called GlobalCo until the name Fonterra was chosen. Fonterra's adjustment to a global operation was not easy, however. Executives were replaced as the company needed to adopt a different mindset. 'A lot of people in the [pre-merger companies] were very New Zealand–centric and culturally did not understand the global challenges of the teams offshore and the different operating companies,' acknowledges a Fonterra executive.[68]

Fonterra is a rich example of the globalisation of business over the past few decades. **Globalisation** refers to economic, social and cultural connectivity with people in other parts of the world. Fonterra and other organisations globalise when they actively participate in other countries and cultures. Although businesses have traded goods across borders for centuries, the degree of globalisation today is unprecedented because information technology and transportation systems allow a much more intense level of connectivity and interdependence across the planet.[69]

globalisation Economic, social and cultural connectivity with people in other parts of the world.

Globalisation offers numerous benefits to organisations in terms of larger markets, lower costs, and greater access to knowledge and innovation. At the same time, there is considerable debate about whether globalisation benefits developing nations, and whether it is primarily responsible for increasing work intensification, as well as reducing job security and work–life balance in developed countries.[70] Globalisation is now well entrenched, so the real issue in organisational behaviour is how corporate leaders and employees alike can lead and work effectively in this emerging reality.[71] OB researchers are turning their attention to this topic. In Project GLOBE, for example, dozens of experts are studying leadership and organisational practices worldwide.[72]

Increasing Workforce Diversity

Walk into the country headquarters of HSBC Bank in Sydney, London or elsewhere and you might think you have entered a United Nations building. The London-based financial institution has dramatically embraced diversity over the past decade. 'In a world where homogeneity and standardisation dominate, HSBC is building a business in the belief that different people from different cultures and different walks of life create value,' says HSBC Australia's head of marketing. Margaret Leung, located in Hong Kong as HSBC's global cohead of commercial banking, echoes this sentiment. 'We want to attract the best people and we want the best to rise to the top. The wider you cast the net, the better the chance of catching the top performers,' she says.[73]

HSBC Bank is a reflection of the increasing diversity of people in many countries. This description of HSBC's diversity refers to **surface-level diversity**—the observable demographic and other overt differences in people, such as their race, ethnicity, gender, age and physical capabilities. Surface-level diversity has changed considerably in Australia, New Zealand and many parts of Asia over the past few decades. For example, during the late 1960s, more than half of Australia's immigrants came from the United Kingdom and Ireland. Today, these countries represent only 15 per cent of immigrants, whereas more than 25 per cent are from various parts of Asia.[74] Even in countries with less diversity, globalisation puts employees in more contact with people with diverse backgrounds. Hong Kong is about 95 per cent Chinese, but many Hong Kong employees do business daily with suppliers and customers from every possible ethnic and cultural background elsewhere in the world.

surface-level diversity The observable demographic or physiological differences in people, such as their race, ethnicity, gender, age and physical disabilities.

deep-level diversity Differences in the psychological characteristics of employees, including personalities, beliefs, values and attitudes.

Diversity also includes differences in the psychological characteristics of employees, including personalities, beliefs, values and attitudes.[75] This **deep-level diversity** isn't as visible as surface-level diversity, but it is evident in a person's decisions, statements and actions. One illustration of deep-level diversity is the different attitudes and expectations held by employees across generational cohorts.[76] *Baby boomers*—people born between 1946 and 1964—seem to expect and desire more job security and are more intent on improving their economic and social status. In contrast, *Generation-X* employees—those born between 1965 and 1979—expect less job security and are motivated more by workplace flexibility, the opportunity to learn (particularly new technology), and egalitarian and 'fun' organisations. Meanwhile, some observers suggest that *Generation-Y* employees (those born after 1979) are noticeably self-confident, optimistic, multitasking and more independent than even their Gen-X coworkers. These statements certainly don't apply to everyone in each cohort, but they do reflect the dynamics of deep-level diversity, and shifting values and expectations across generations.

Consequences of Diversity

Diversity presents both opportunities and challenges in organisations.[77] In some circumstances and to some degree, diversity can become a competitive advantage by improving decision making and team performance on complex tasks. Studies suggest that teams with some forms of diversity (particularly occupational diversity) make better decisions on complex problems than do teams whose members have similar backgrounds. A few studies also report that companies that win diversity awards have higher financial returns, at least in the short run.[78]

The evidence supporting diversity is consistent with anecdotal evidence that having a diverse workforce improves customer service, creativity and employee retention. For instance, Mt Albert PAK'nSAVE in New Zealand employs 300 people from fourteen cultures around the world. Brian Carran, who owns the PAK'nSAVE franchise, actively supports this diversity. Employees are encouraged to display their national flags on their name badges, making it easier for customers to find a staff member who speaks their language. By recognising and supporting each employee's ethnic origins, the Mt Albert PAK'nSAVE enjoys a much lower employee turnover rate than other supermarkets and (based on revenue) has become the fifth-largest supermarket in New Zealand.

Overall, the popular refrain is that workforce diversity is a sound business proposition. Unfortunately, the effect of diversity on organisations is much more complex. There is growing evidence that most forms of diversity creates challenges as well as the aforementioned benefits.[79] Teams with diverse employees usually take longer to perform effectively. Diversity brings numerous communication problems as well as 'faultlines' in informal group dynamics. Diversity is also a source of conflict, which can lead to lack of information sharing and, in extreme cases, morale problems and higher turnover.

Workforce diversity is likely to be much more of a business advantage than a liability, but aside from that debate companies need to make it a priority on purely ethical grounds. Surface-level diversity is a moral and legal imperative. Companies that offer an inclusive workplace are, in essence, making fair and just decisions regarding employment, promotions, rewards and so on. This fairness is valuable in its own right (as a moral imperative) and because fairness is a well-established influence on employee loyalty and satisfaction.

Emerging Employment Relationships

Combine globalisation with emerging workforce diversity, and add in new information technology. The resulting concoction has created incredible changes in employment relationships. A few decades ago, most (although not all) employees in Australia, New Zealand and similar cultures would finish their workday after eight or nine hours and could separate their personal time from the workday. There were no Blackberrys and no internet connections to keep staff tethered to work on a 24/7 schedule. Even business travel was more of an exception due to its high cost. Most competitors were located in the same country, so they had similar work practices and labour costs. Today, work hours are longer (although arguably less than they were 100 years ago), employees experience more work-related stress, and there is growing evidence that family and personal relations are suffering. Little wonder that one of the emerging issues in this new century is for more **work-life balance**—minimising conflict between work and nonwork demands.[80]

work-life balance The degree to which a person minimises conflict between work and nonwork demands.

virtual work Work performed away from the traditional physical workplace by means of information technology.

Another employment relationship trend is **virtual work**, in which employees use information technology to perform their jobs away from the traditional physical workplace. The most common form of virtual work, called *telecommuting* or *teleworking*, involves working at home rather than commuting to the office. In another form of virtual work, employees are connected to the office while on the road or at clients' offices. Various surveys estimate that between 15 and 25 per cent of Australian employees (excluding owners and self-employed) telework some of the time, and that two-thirds of large Australian companies offer eligible staff the opportunity to telework. Studies in the United States indicate that around 20 per cent of employees in that country work at home at least one day each month. More than 10 per cent of Japanese employees telework at

Welcome to My Office

When someone calls Kelvin Brown's office in Sydney, chances are that the KPMG senior manager will answer the phone. Nothing unusual there, except that Brown isn't in Sydney very often. Instead, the call relays to his 200-hectare farm in the small town of Harden, NSW, a four-hour drive away. Brown is an extreme teleworker. 'Most mornings I'll get up about six, go out and check the stock, be back here by eight o'clock, take the kids up to the bus, then I start the day's work,' he explains. 'If I've got a truckload of hay coming, I just send my boss in Sydney an email to say I'm ducking out for an hour and a half to unload a truck.' Twice each month, Brown meets with clients around Australia, with each trip lasting about three days. Otherwise, he does his work from home. 'The real benefit of this to me—and this is what I sell to KPMG—is the fact that I'm more productive when I can have time away from everybody else,' says Brown, who complains that he can't concentrate in the increasingly common open-office work environment.[82]

Andrew Sheargold/*Sydney Morning Herald*

least one day each week, a figure that the Japanese government wants to double within the next few years.[81]

Some research suggests that virtual work, particularly teleworking, potentially reduces employee stress by offering better work–life balance and dramatically reducing time lost through commuting to the office.[83] For example, NRMA Insurance employee Loveena Sharma enjoys teleworking to avoid the stress of commuting. '[Commuting] affected me physically, because I was very tired with all the driving,' she recalls. Under some circumstances, telework arrangements also increase productivity and job satisfaction. Genpact, the India-based information technology services company, plans to have more than 5000 teleworking employees within the next couple of years because executives noticed that this arrangement increased employee satisfaction and reduced turnover. Another benefit, at least for companies, is reduced office costs. For instance, more than 40 per cent of IBM's 330 000 employees work on the road, from home, or at a client location, which IBM estimates saves the company about US $100 million annually.

Against these potential benefits, virtual workers face a number of real or potential challenges. Family relations may suffer rather than improve if employees lack sufficient space and resources for a home office. Some virtual workers complain of social isolation and reduced promotion opportunities. Managers at IBM Australia introduced ways to reduce this sense of isolation by motivating its teleworkers to visit the office once or twice each week. 'It is all about getting [teleworkers] back to the office, for social reasons, or encouraging people to come into the office and have those face-to-face meetings,' says IBM's manager of diversity in Australia.[84] Virtual work is clearly better suited to people who are self-motivated and organised, can work effectively with contemporary information technologies and have sufficient fulfilment of social needs elsewhere in their life. It also works better in organisations that evaluate employees by their performance outcomes rather than 'face time'.[85]

Discuss the anchors on which organisational behaviour knowledge is based.

ANCHORS OF ORGANISATIONAL BEHAVIOUR KNOWLEDGE

Globalisation, increasing workforce diversity and emerging employment relationships are just a few of the trends that challenge organisations and make OB knowledge more relevant than ever before. To understand these and other topics, the field of organisational behaviour relies on a set of basic beliefs or knowledge structures (see Exhibit 1.3). These conceptual anchors represent the principles on which OB knowledge is developed and refined.

The Multidisciplinary Anchor

Organisational behaviour is anchored around the idea that the field should develop from knowledge in other disciplines, not just from its own isolated research base. For instance, psychological research has aided our understanding of individual and interpersonal behaviour. Sociologists have contributed to our knowledge of team dynamics, organisational socialisation, organisational power and other aspects of the social system. OB knowledge has also benefited from knowledge in emerging fields such as communications, marketing and information systems. Some OB

Exhibit 1.3 *Anchors of Organisational Behaviour Knowledge*

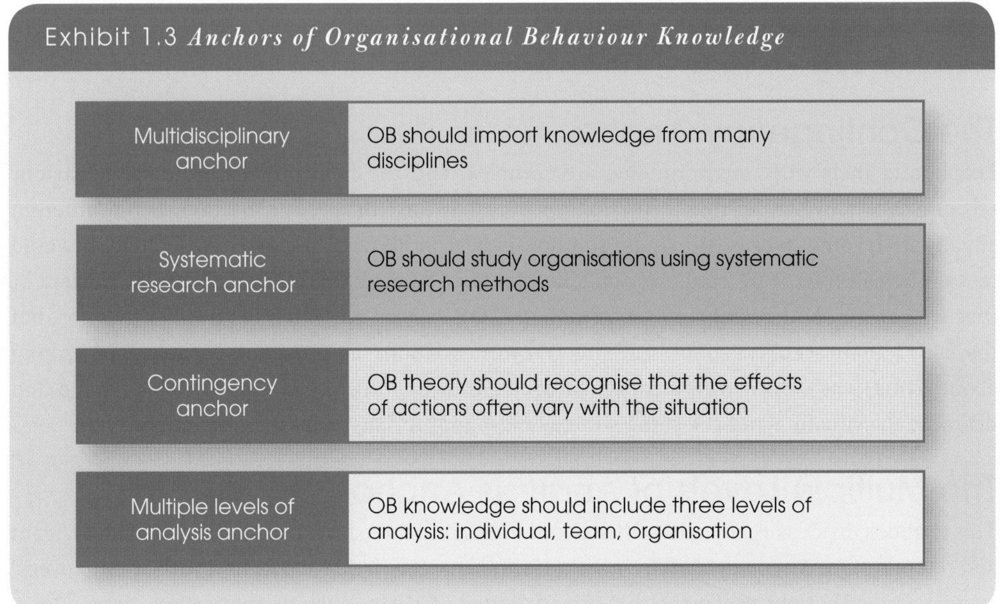
Multidisciplinary anchor
OB should import knowledge from many disciplines
Systematic research anchor
OB should study organisations using systematic research methods
Contingency anchor
OB theory should recognise that the effects of actions often vary with the situation
Multiple levels of analysis anchor
OB knowledge should include three levels of analysis: individual, team, organisation

experts have recently argued that the field suffers from a 'trade deficit'—importing far more knowledge from other disciplines than it exports to other disciplines. Although this may be a concern, organisational behaviour has thrived through the diversity of knowledge it has gleaned from other fields of study.[86]

The Systematic Research Anchor

A critical feature of OB knowledge is that it should be based on *systematic research*, which typically involves forming research questions, systematically collecting data and testing hypotheses against those data. Appendix A at the end of this book details some of the features of the systematic research process, including hypotheses, sampling, research design and qualitative methods research. When research is founded on theory and conducted systematically, we can be more confident that the results are meaningful and useful for practice. This is known as **evidence-based management**—making decisions and taking actions based on research evidence.

evidence-based management The practice of making decisions and taking actions based on research evidence.

Evidence-based management makes sense, yet OB experts are often amazed at how frequently corporate leaders embrace fads, consulting models and their own pet beliefs without bothering to find out if they actually work![87] There are many reasons why people have difficulty applying evidence-based management. One explanation is that corporate decision makers are bombarded with so many ideas from newspapers, books, consultant reports and other sources that they have difficulty figuring out which ones are based on good evidence. Another reason why people ignore evidence and embrace fads is that good OB research is necessarily generic; it is rarely described in the context of a specific problem in a specific organisation. Managers therefore have the difficult task of figuring out which theories are relevant to their unique situation. A third reason is that many consultants and popular book writers are rewarded for marketing their concepts and theories, not for testing to see if they actually work. Indeed, some management concepts have become popular (and are even found in some OB textbooks!) because of heavy marketing, not because of any evidence that they are valid. Finally, as you will learn in Chapter 3, people form perceptions and beliefs quickly and tend to ignore evidence that their beliefs are inaccurate.

The Contingency Anchor

People and their work environments are complex, and the field of organisational behaviour recognises this by stating that a particular action may have different consequences in different situations. In other words, no single solution is best in all circumstances. Of course, it would be so much simpler if we could rely on 'one best way' theories, in which a particular concept or practice has the same results in every situation.[88] OB experts do search for simpler theories, but they also remain sceptical about 'sure-fire' recommendations; an exception is likely to be lurking about. Thus, when faced with a particular problem or opportunity, we need to understand and diagnose the situation and select the strategy most appropriate *under those conditions*.[89]

The Multiple Levels of Analysis Anchor

This textbook divides organisational behaviour topics into three levels of analysis: individual, team and organisation. The *individual level* includes the characteristics and behaviours of employees, as well as the thought processes that are attributed to them, such as motivation, perceptions, personalities, attitudes and values. The *team level* of analysis looks at the way people interact. This includes team dynamics, communication, power, organisational politics, conflict and leadership. At the *organisational level*, we focus on how people structure their working relationships and how organisations interact with their environments.

Although an OB topic is typically pegged into one level of analysis, it usually relates to multiple levels.[90] For instance, communication is located in this book as a team (interpersonal) process, but we also recognise that it includes individual and organisational processes. Therefore, you should try to think about each OB topic at the individual, team and organisational levels, not just at one of these levels.

CHAPTER SUMMARY

Organisational behaviour is the study of what people think, feel and do in and around organisations. Organisations are groups of people who work interdependently toward some purpose. Although OB doesn't have a specific career path, it offers knowledge and skills that are vitally important to anyone who works in organisations. OB knowledge also has a significant effect on the success of organisations. This book takes the view that OB is for everyone, not just managers.

Organisational effectiveness is a multidimensional concept represented by four perspectives: the open-systems, organisational learning, high-performance work practices and stakeholder perspectives. The open-systems perspective says that organisations need to adapt to their external environment and configure their internal subsystems to maximise efficiency and responsiveness. For the most part, the other perspectives of organisational effectiveness are detailed extensions of the open-systems model. The organisational learning perspective states that organisational effectiveness depends on the organisation's capacity to acquire, share, use and store valuable knowledge. Intellectual capital is knowledge that resides in an organisation, including its human capital, structural capital and relationship capital. Effective organisations also 'unlearn', meaning that they remove knowledge that no longer adds value.

The high-performance work practices (HPWP) perspective states that effective organisations leverage the human capital potential of their employees. Specific HPWPs have been identified, and experts in this field suggest that they need to be bundled together for maximum benefit. The stakeholder perspective states that effective organisations take into account how their actions affect others, and this requires them to understand, manage and satisfy the interests of their stakeholders. This perspective incorporates values, ethics and corporate social responsibility into the organisational effectiveness equation.

The five main types of workplace behaviour are task performance, organisational citizenship, counterproductive work behaviours, joining and staying with the organisation, and work attendance. These represent the individual-level dependent variables found in most OB research.

Three environmental shifts challenging organisations include globalisation, increasing workforce diversity and emerging employment relationships. Globalisation refers to economic, social and cultural connectivity with people in other parts of the world. Workforce diversity includes both surface-level and deep-level diversity. Two emerging employment relationship changes are: demands for work–life balance and virtual work.

Several conceptual anchors represent the principles on which OB knowledge is developed and refined. These anchors include beliefs that OB knowledge should be multidisciplinary and based on systematic research, that organisational events usually have contingencies and that organisational behaviour can be viewed from three levels of analysis (individual, team and organisation).

KEY TERMS

absorptive capacity, p. 12
corporate social responsibility (CSR), p. 16
counterproductive work behaviours (CWBs), p. 18
deep-level diversity, p. 21
ethics, p. 15
evidence-based management, p. 25
globalisation, p. 21
high-performance work practices (HPWP), p. 13
human capital, p. 12
intellectual capital, p. 12
lean management, p. 9
open systems, p. 8
organisational behaviour (OB), p. 4
organisational citizenship behaviours (OCBs), p. 17
organisational effectiveness, p. 7
organisational efficiency, p. 9
organisational learning, p. 10
organisational memory, p. 12
organisations, p. 4
stakeholders, p. 14
surface-level diversity, p. 21
values, p. 15
virtual work, p. 23
work–life balance, p. 23

Critical Thinking Questions

1 A friend suggests that organisational behaviour courses are useful only to people who will enter management careers. Discuss the accuracy of your friend's statement.

2 A number of years ago, employees in a city water distribution department were put into teams and encouraged to find ways to improve efficiency. The teams boldly crossed departmental boundaries and areas of management discretion in search of problems. Employees working in other parts of the city began to complain about these intrusions. Moreover, when some team ideas were implemented, the city managers discovered that a dollar saved in the water distribution unit may have cost the organisation two dollars in higher costs elsewhere. Use the open-systems perspective to explain what happened here.

3 After hearing a seminar on organisational learning, a mining company executive argues that this perspective ignores the fact that mining companies cannot rely on knowledge alone to stay in business. They also need physical capital (such as digging and ore-processing equipment) and land (where the minerals are located). In fact, the executive argues, these two resources may be more important than the knowledge that employees carry around in their heads. Evaluate the mining executive's comments.

4 A common refrain among executives is 'People are our most important asset.' Relate this statement to any two of the four perspectives of organisational effectiveness presented in this chapter. Does this statement apply better to some perspectives than to others? Why or why not?

5 Corporate social responsibility is one of the hottest issues in corporate boardrooms these days, partly because it is becoming increasingly important to employees and other stakeholders. In your opinion, why have stakeholders given CSR more attention recently?

Does abiding by CSR standards potentially cause companies to have conflicting objectives with some stakeholders in some situations?

6 Look through the list of chapters in this textbook, and discuss how globalisation could influence each organisational behaviour topic.

7 'Organisational theories should follow the contingency approach.' Comment on the accuracy of this statement.

8 What does *evidence-based management* mean? Describe situations you have heard about in which companies have practised evidence-based management, as well as situations in which companies have relied on fads that lacked sufficient evidence of their worth.

TEAM EXERCISE

Skill Builder 1.1

Human Checkers

Purpose

This exercise is designed to help you understand the importance and application of organisational behaviour concepts.

Materials

None, but the instructor has more information about the team's task.

Instructions

1. Form teams with eight students. If possible, each team should have a private location where team members can plan and practise the required task without being observed or heard by other teams.
2. All teams receive special instructions in class about their assigned task. All teams have the same task and the same amount of time to plan and practise the task. At the end of this planning and practice, each team will be timed while completing the task in class. The team that completes the task in the least time wins.
3. No special materials are required or allowed (see rules below) for this exercise. Although the task is not described here, the following rules for planning and implementing the task apply:
    a. You cannot use any written form of communication or any props to assist in the planning or implementation of this task.
    b. You may speak to other students in your team at any time during the planning and implementation of this task.
    c. When performing the task, you can move only forward, not backward. (You are not allowed to turn around.)
    d. When performing the task, you can move forward to the next space, but only if it is vacant. In Exhibit 1 (see page 30), the individual (dark circle) can move directly into an empty space (light circle).
    e. When performing the task, you can move forward two spaces if that space is vacant. In other words, you can move around a person who is one space in

front of you to the next space if that space is vacant. (In Exhibit 2, two people occupy the blue dots, and the white dot is an empty space. A person can move around the person in front to the empty space.)

4. When all teams have completed their task, the class will discuss the implications of this exercise for organisational behaviour.

Discussion Questions

1. Identify organisational behaviour concepts that the team applied to complete this task.
2. What personal theories of people and work teams were applied to complete this task?
3. What organisational behaviour problems occurred, and what actions were (or should have been) taken to solve them?

Skill Builder 1.2

WEB EXERCISE

Diagnosing Organisational Stakeholders

Purpose

This exercise is designed to help you understand how stakeholders influence organisations as part of the open-systems perspective of organisational effectiveness.

Materials

You need to select a company and, prior to class, retrieve and analyse publicly available information over the past year or two about that company. This may include annual reports, which are usually found on the websites of publicly traded companies. Where possible, you should also scan full-text newspaper and magazine databases for articles published over the previous year about the company.

Instructions

(*Note*: Your instructor may require you to work alone or in groups for this activity.) Select a company and investigate the relevance and influence of various stakeholder groups on the organisation. Stakeholders can be identified from annual reports, newspaper articles, website statements and other available sources. Organise the stakeholders in rank order in terms of their perceived importance to the organisation. You should be prepared to present or discuss your rank ordering of the organisation's stakeholders, and include evidence for this ordering.

Discussion Questions

1. What are the main reasons why some stakeholders are more important than others for this organisation?
2. On the basis of your knowledge of the organisation's environmental situation, is this rank order of stakeholders in the organisation's best interest, or should other stakeholders be given higher priority?
3. What societal groups, if any, are not mentioned as stakeholders by the organisation? Does this lack of reference to these unmentioned groups make sense?

SELF-ASSESSMENT

Skill Builder 1.3

It All Makes Sense?

Purpose

This exercise is designed to help you comprehend how organisational behaviour knowledge can help you to understand life in organisations.

Instructions

(*Note*: Your instructor might conduct this activity as a self-assessment or as a team activity.)

Read each of the statements below and circle whether each statement is true or false, in your opinion. The class will consider the answers to each question and discuss the implications for studying organisational behaviour.

Due to the nature of this activity, the instructor will provide the answers to these questions. There is no scoring key in Appendix B.

1.	❑ True	❑ False	A happy worker is a productive worker.
2.	❑ True	❑ False	Decision makers tend to continue supporting a course of action even though information suggests that the decision is ineffective.
3.	❑ True	❑ False	Organisations are more effective when they prevent conflict among employees.
4.	❑ True	❑ False	It is better to negotiate alone than as a team.
5.	❑ True	❑ False	Companies are more successful when they have strong corporate cultures.
6.	❑ True	❑ False	Employees perform better without stress.
7.	❑ True	❑ False	The best way to change people and organisations is by pinpointing the source of their current problems.
8.	❑ True	❑ False	Female leaders involve employees in decisions to a greater degree than do male leaders.
9.	❑ True	❑ False	The best decisions are made without emotion.
10.	❑ True	❑ False	If employees feel they are paid unfairly, nothing other than changing their pay will reduce their feelings of injustice.

Skill Builder 1.4

Available online

SELF-ASSESSMENT

Is Telecommuting For You?

Some employees adapt better than others to telecommuting (also called *teleworking*) and other forms of virtual work. This self-assessment measures personal characteristics that seem to relate to telecommuting, and therefore it provides a rough indication of how well you would adapt to telework. The instrument asks you to indicate how much you agree or disagree with each of the statements provided. You need to be honest with yourself to get a reasonable estimate of your telework disposition. Please keep in mind that this scale considers only your personal characteristics. Other factors, such as organisational, family and technological systems support, must also be taken into account.

Endnotes

1 'Asia's Best-Managed Companies', *Asiamoney*, 28 December 2007; C. Bolt, 'Goyder Backs His Ability to the Hilt', *West Australian*, 17 November 2007, 81; R. Urban, 'Out in the Coles', *The Bulletin*, 2 October 2007; B. Atkinson, 'Cultural Change May Finally Occur at Coles', *Inside Retailing*, 18 February 2008; B. Speedy, 'Wesfarmers Hires Foster's HR Boss and Searches for New Coles Chief', *The Australian*, 24 January 2008, 23.

2 M. Warner, 'Organizational Behavior Revisited', *Human Relations* 47 (October 1994): 1151–1166; R. Westwood and S. Clegg, 'The Discourse of Organization Studies: Dissensus, Politics, and Paradigms', in *Debating Organization: Point-Counterpoint in Organization Studies*, ed. R. Westwood and S. Clegg (Malden, MA: Blackwood, 2003), 1–42.

3 D. Katz and R. L. Kahn, *The Social Psychology of Organizations* (New York: Wiley, 1966), ch. 2; R. N. Stern and S. R. Barley, 'Organizations as Social Systems: Organization Theory's Neglected Mandate', *Administrative Science Quarterly* 41 (1996): 146–162.

4 L. E. Greiner, 'A Recent History of Organizational Behavior', in *Organizational Behaviour*, ed. S. Kerr (Columbus, OH: Grid, 1979), 3–14; J. Micklethwait and A. Wooldridge, *The Company: A Short History of a Revolutionary Idea* (New York: Random House, 2003).

5 N. Hooper, 'Call Me Irresistable', *Australian Financial Review*, 5 December 2003, 38

6 Some of the historical bases of OB mentioned in this paragraph are described in J. A. Conger, 'Max Weber's Conceptualization of Charismatic Authority: Its Influence on Organizational Research', *The Leadership Quarterly* 4, no. 3–4 (1993): 277–288; R. Kanigel, *The One Best Way: Frederick Winslow Taylor and the Enigma of Efficiency* (New York: Viking, 1997); J. H. Smith, 'The Enduring Legacy of Elton Mayo', *Human Relations* 51, no. 3 (1998): 221–249; T. Takala, 'Plato on Leadership', *Journal of Business Ethics* 17 (May 1998): 785–798; J. A. Fernandez, 'The Gentleman's Code of Confucius: Leadership by Values', *Organizational Dynamics* 33, no. 1 (2004): 21–31.

7 C. D. Wrege, 'Solving Mayo's Mystery: The First Complete Account of the Origin of the Hawthorne Studies—The Forgotten Contributions of C. E. Snow and H. Hibarger' in *Academy of Management Proceedings* (1976): 12–16; J. A. Sonnenfeld, 'Shedding Light on the Hawthorne Studies', *Journal of Occupational Behaviour* 6, no. 2 (1985): 111–130; E. O'Connor, 'Minding the Workers: The Meaning of "Human" and "Human Relations" in Elton Mayo', *Organization* 6, no. 2 (1999): 223–246; 'A Field Is Born', *Harvard Business Review* 86, no. 7/8 (2008): 164.

8 S. L. Rynes *et al.*, 'Behavioral Coursework in Business Education: Growing Evidence of a Legitimacy Crisis', *Academy of Management Learning & Education* 2, no. 3 (2003): 269–283; R. P. Singh and A. G. Schick, 'Organizational Behavior: Where Does It Fit in Today's Management Curriculum?', *Journal of Education for Business* 82, no. 6 (2007): 349.

9 P. R. Lawrence and N. Nohria, *Driven: How Human Nature Shapes Our Choices* (San Francisco: Jossey-Bass, 2002), ch. 6.

10 P. R. Lawrence 'Historical Development of Organizational Behavior', in *Handbook of Organizational Behavior*, ed. L. W. Lorsch (Englewood Cliffs, NJ: Prentice Hall, 1987),

1–9; S. A. Mohrman, C. B. Gibson and A. M. Mohrman Jr, 'Doing Research That Is Useful to Practice: A Model and Empirical Exploration', *Academy of Management Journal* 44 (April 2001): 357–375. For a contrary view, see A. P. Brief and J. M. Dukerich, 'Theory in Organizational Behavior: Can It Be Useful?', *Research in Organizational Behavior* 13 (1991): 327–352.

11 M. S. Myers, *Every Employee a Manager* (New York: McGraw Hill, 1970).

12 T. Lee, 'The Three I's of Leadership—Integrity, Inspiration, Implementation', *Management Today*, May 2003, 20–22.

13 B. N. Pfau and I. T. Kay, *The Human Capital Edge* (New York: McGraw-Hill, 2002); I. S. Fulmer, B. Gerhart and K. S. Scott, 'Are the 100 Best Better? An Empirical Investigation of the Relationship between Being a "Great Place to Work" and Firm Performance', *Personnel Psychology* 56, no. 4 (2003): 965–993; Y.-H. Ling and B.-S. Jaw, 'The Influence of International Human Capital on Global Initiatives and Financial Performance', *The International Journal of Human Resource Management* 17, no. 3 (2006): 379–398; M. A. West *et al.*, 'Reducing Patient Mortality in Hospitals: The Role of Human Resource Management', *Journal of Organizational Behavior* 27, no. 7 (2006): 983–1002. However, one recent study warns about the direction of causation. Although OB practices seem to predict subsequent firm performance, firm performance also seems to predict the presence of OB practices (such as employee involvement, training and pay-for-performance). See P. M. Wright *et al.*, 'The Relationship between HR Practices and Firm Performance: Examining Causal Order', *Personnel Psychology* 58, no. 2 (2005): 409–446.

14 F. Smith, 'Shareholders New Force in Employee Rights', *Australian Financial Review*, 29 May 2007. For a sample of specific studies on OB practices and share performance, see Deloitte & Touche, *Human Capital Roi Study: Creating Shareholder Value through People* (Toronto: Deloitte & Touche, 2002); D. Wheeler and J. Thomson, *Human Capital Based Investment Criteria for Total Shareholder Returns: A Canadian and International Perspective* (Toronto: Schulich School of Business, York University, 2004).

15 Mohrman, Gibson and Mohrman Jr, 'Doing Research That Is Useful to Practice: A Model and Empirical Exploration'; J. P. Walsh *et al.*, 'On the Relationship between Research and Practice: Debate and Reflections', *Journal of Management Inquiry* 16, no. 2 (June 2007): 128–154. Similarly, in 1961, Harvard business professor Fritz Roethlisberger proposed that the field of OB is concerned with human behaviour 'from the points of view of both (a) its determination ... and (b) its improvement.' See P. B. Vaill, 'F. J. Roethlisberger and the Elusive Phenomena of Organizational Behavior', *Journal of Management Education* 31, no. 3 (June 2007): 321–338.

16 R. H. Hall, 'Effectiveness Theory and Organizational Effectiveness', *Journal of Applied Behavioral Science* 16, no. 4 (1980): 536–545; K. Cameron, 'Organizational Effectiveness: Its Demise and Re-Emergence through Positive Organizational Scholarship', in *Great Minds in Management*, ed. K. G. Smith and M. A. Hitt (New York: Oxford University Press, 2005), 304–330.

17 J. L. Price, 'The Study of Organizational Effectiveness', *The Sociological Quarterly* 13 (1972): 3–15.

18 S. C. Selden and J. E. Sowa, 'Testing a Multi-Dimensional Model of Organizational Performance: Prospects and Problems', *Journal of Public Administration Research and Theory* 14, no. 3 (2004): 395–416.

19 F. E. Kast and J. E. Rosenweig, 'General Systems Theory: Applications for Organization and Management', *Academy of Management Journal* (1972): 447–465; P. M. Senge, *The Fifth Discipline: The Art and Practice of the Learning Organization* (New York: Doubleday Currency, 1990); A. De Geus, *The Living Company* (Boston: Harvard Business School Press, 1997); R. T. Pascale, M. Millemann and L. Gioja, *Surfing on the Edge of Chaos* (London: Texere, 2000).

20 V. P. Rindova and S. Kotha, 'Continuous "Morphing": Competing through Dynamic Capabilities, Form, and Function', *Academy of Management Journal* 44 (2001): 1263–1280; J. McCann, 'Organizational Effectiveness: Changing Concepts for Changing Environments', *Human Resource Planning* 27, no. 1 (2004): 42–50.

21 J. Arlidge, 'McJobs That All the Family Can Share', *Daily Telegraph (London)*, 26 January 2006, 1.

22 'Business Leaders Take Fighting Spirit into 2008', *Korea Herald*, 3 January 2008.

23 C. Ostroff and N. Schmitt, 'Configurations of Organizational Effectiveness and Efficiency', *Academy of Management Journal* 36, no. 6 (1993): 1345. There are different ways of defining efficiency, as well as some disagreement as to whether work efficiency and productivity are the same thing.

24 J. P. Womack and D. T. Jones, *Lean Thinking*, 2nd edn (New York: Free Press, 2003); J. K. Liker, *The Toyota Way* (New York: McGraw-Hill, 2004); T. Melton, 'The Benefits of Lean Manufacturing: What Lean Thinking Has to Offer the Process Industries', *Chemical Engineering Research and Design* 83, no. 6 (2005): 662–673.

25 F. A. Kennedy and S. K. Widener, 'A Control Framework: Insights from Evidence on Lean Accounting', *Management Accounting Research* 19, no. 4 (December 2008): 301–323.

26 D. Jones and A. Mitchell, *Lean Thinking for the NHS* (London: NHS Confederation, 2006); M. McCarthy, 'Can Car Manufacturing Techniques Reform Health Care?', *Lancet* 367, no. 9507 (28 January 2006): 290–291; 'Nissan "Shot in the Arm" for Healthcare Sector', *Newcarinfo.co.uk*,

13 February 2007; D. I. Ben-Tovim *et al.*, 'Lean Thinking across a Hospital: Redesigning Care at the Flinders Medical Centre', *Australian Health Review* 31, no. 1 (2007): 10–15; I. Green, 'Drive for Success', *Nursing Standard* 21, no. 38 (30 May 2007): 62–63; A.-M. Kelly *et al.*, 'Improving Emergency Department Efficiency by Patient Streaming to Outcomes-Based Teams', *Australian Health Review* 31, no. 1 (2007): 16–21.

27 P. S. Adler *et al.*, 'Performance Improvement Capability: Keys to Accelerating Performance Improvement in Hospitals', *California Management Review* 45, no. 2 (2003): 12–33; J. Jamrog, M. Vickers and D. Bear, 'Building and Sustaining a Culture That Supports Innovation', *Human Resource Planning* 29, no. 3 (2006): 9–19. The Siemens quotation is from 'Siemens CEO Klaus Kleinfeld: "Nobody's Perfect, but a Team Can Be"', *Knowledge@Wharton*, 19 April 2006.

28 K. E. Weick, *The Social Psychology of Organizing* (Reading, MA: Addison-Wesley, 1979); S. Brusoni and A. Prencipe, 'Managing Knowledge in Loosely Coupled Networks: Exploring the Links between Product and Knowledge Dynamics', *Journal of Management Studies* 38, no. 7 (2001): 1019–1035; D. Pinelle and C. Gutwin, 'Loose Coupling and Healthcare Organizations: Deployment Strategies for Groupware', *Computer Supported Cooperative Work* 15, no. 5/6 (2006): 537–572.

29 G. Huber, 'Organizational Learning: The Contributing Processes and Literature', *Organizational Science* 2 (1991): 88–115; D. A. Garvin, *Learning in Action: A Guide to Putting the Learning Organization to Work* (Boston: Harvard Business School Press, 2000); H. Shipton, 'Cohesion or Confusion? Towards a Typology for Organizational Learning Research', *International Journal of Management Reviews* 8, no. 4 (2006): 233–252.

30 W. C. Bogner and P. Bansal, 'Knowledge Management as the Basis of Sustained High Performance', *Journal of Management Studies* 44, no. 1 (2007): 165–188; D. Jiménez-Jiménez and J. G. Cegarra-Navarro, 'The Performance Effect of Organizational Learning and Market Orientation', *Industrial Marketing Management* 36, no. 6 (2007): 694–708.

31 M. Liedtke, 'Google vs. Yahoo: Heavyweights Attack from Different Angles', *Associated Press Newswires*, 18 December 2004; R. Basch, 'Doing Well by Doing Good', *Searcher Magazine*, January 2005, 18–28; A. Ignatius and L. A. Locke, 'In Search of the Real Google', *Time*, 20 February 2006, 36.

32 W. Cohen and D. Levinthal, 'Absorptive Capacity: A New Perspective on Learning and Innovation', *Administrative Science Quarterly* 35 (1990): 128–152; G. Todorova and B. Durisin, 'Absorptive Capacity: Valuing a Reconceptualization', *Academy of Management Review* 32, no. 3 (2007): 774–786.

33 M. Rogers, 'Absorptive Capacity and Economic Growth: How Do Countries Catch Up?', *Cambridge Journal of Economics* 28, no. 4 (2004): 577–596.

34 T. A. Stewart, *Intellectual Capital: The New Wealth of Organizations* (New York: Currency/Doubleday, 1997); H. Saint-Onge and D. Wallace, *Leveraging Communities of Practice for Strategic Advantage* (Boston: Butterworth–Heinemann, 2003), 9–10; J.-A. Johannessen, B. Olsen and J. Olaisen, 'Intellectual Capital as a Holistic Management Philosophy: A Theoretical Perspective', *International Journal of Information Management* 25, no. 2 (2005): 151–171.

35 M. N. Wexler, 'Organizational Memory and Intellectual Capital', *Journal of Intellectual Capital* 3, no. 4 (2002): 393–414.

36 'A Cornerstone for Learning', *T&D*, October 2008, 66–89.

37 M. E. McGill and J. W. Slocum Jr., 'Unlearn the Organization', *Organizational Dynamics* 22, no. 2 (1993): 67–79; A. E. Akgün, G. S. Lynn and J. C. Byrne, 'Antecedents and Consequences of Unlearning in New Product Development Teams', *Journal of Product Innovation Management* 23 (2006): 73–88.

38 J. Pfeffer, *The Human Equation: Building Profits by Putting People First* (Boston: Harvard University Press, 1998); E. Appelbaum et al., *Manufacturing Advantage: Why High-Performance Work Systems Pay Off* (Ithaca, NY: Cornell University Press, 2000); G. S. Benson, S. M. Young and E. E. Lawler III, 'High-Involvement Work Practices and Analysts' Forecasts of Corporate Earnings', *Human Resource Management* 45, no. 4 (2006): 519–537; L. Sels et al., 'Unravelling the HRM-Performance Link: Value-Creating and Cost-Increasing Effects of Small Business HRM', *Journal of Management Studies* 43, no. 2 (2006): 319–342.

39 M. A. Huselid, 'The Impact of Human Resource Management Practices on Turnover, Productivity, and Corporate Financial Performance', *Academy of Management Journal* 38, no. 3 (1995): 635; B. E. Becker and M. A. Huselid, 'Strategic Human Resources Management: Where Do We Go from Here?', *Journal of Management* 32, no. 6 (2006): 898–925; J. Combs *et al.*, 'How Much Do High-Performance Work Practices Matter? A Meta-Analysis of Their Effects on Organizational Performance', *Personnel Psychology* 59, no. 3 (2006): 501–528.

40 J. Barney, 'Firm Resources and Sustained Competitive Advantage', *Journal of Management* 17, no. 1 (1991): 99–120.

41 E. E. Lawler III, S. A. Mohrman and G. E. Ledford Jr., *Strategies for High Performance Organizations* (San Francisco: Jossey-Bass, 1998); S. H. Wagner, C. P. Parker and D. Neil, 'Employees That Think and Act Like

Owners: Effects of Ownership Beliefs and Behaviors on Organizational Effectiveness', *Personnel Psychology* 56, no. 4 (2003): 847–871; P. J. Gollan, 'High Involvement Management and Human Resource Sustainability: The Challenges and Opportunities', *Asia Pacific Journal of Human Resources* 43, no. 1 (2005): 18–33; Y. Liu *et al.*, 'The Value of Human Resource Management for Organizational Performance', *Business Horizons* 50 (2007): 503–511; P. Tharenou, A. M. Saks and C. Moore, 'A Review and Critique of Research on Training and Organizational-Level Outcomes', *Human Resource Management Review* 17, no. 3 (2007): 251–273.

42 S. Fleetwood and A. Hesketh, 'HRM-Performance Research: Under-Theorized and Lacking Explanatory Power', *International Journal of Human Resource Management* 17, no. 12 (2006): 1977–1993.

43 J. Godard, 'High Performance and the Transformation of Work? The Implications of Alternative Work Practices for the Experience and Outcomes of Work', *Industrial and Labor Relations Review* 54, no. 4 (2001): 776–805; G. Murray *et al.*, eds., *Work and Employment Relations in the High-Performance Workplace* (London: Continuum, 2002); B. Harley, 'Hope or Hype? High Performance Work Systems', in *Participation and Democracy at Work: Essays in Honour of Harvie Ramsay*, ed. B. Harley, J. Hyman and P. Thompson (Houndsmills, UK: Palgrave Macmillan, 2005), 38–54.

44 A. L. Friedman and S. Miles, *Stakeholders: Theory and Practice* (New York: Oxford University Press, 2006); M. L. Barnett, 'Stakeholder Influence Capacity and the Variability of Financial Returns to Corporate Social Responsibility', *Academy of Management Review* 32, no. 3 (2007): 794–816; R. E. Freeman, J. S. Harrison and A. C. Wicks, *Managing for Stakeholders: Survival, Reputation, and Success* (New Haven, CT: Yale University Press, 2007).

45 C. Eden and F. Ackerman, *Making Strategy: The Journey of Strategic Management* (London: Sage, 1998).

46 T. A. Hemphill, 'Rejuvenating Wal-Mart's Reputation', *Business Horizons* 48, no. 1 (2005): 11–21; A. Bianco, *The Bully of Bentonville: How the High Cost of Wal-Mart's Everyday Low Prices Is Hurting America* (New York: Random House, 2006); C. Fishman, *The Wal-Mart Effect* (New York: Penguin, 2006). For a description of Wal-Mart's recent corrective actions on environmentalism, see E. L. Plambeck and L. Denend, 'Wal-Mart', *Stanford Social Innovation Review* 6, no. 2 (2008): 53–59.

47 G. R. Salancik and J. Pfeffer, *The External Control of Organizations: A Resource Dependence Perspective* (New York: Harper & Row, 1978); T. Casciaro and M. J. Piskorski, 'Power Imbalance, Mutual Dependence, and Constraint Absorption: A Closer Look at Dependence Theory', *Administrative Science Quarterly* 50 (2005): 167–199; N. Roome and F. Wijen, 'Stakeholder Power and Organizational Learning in Corporate Environmental Management', *Organization Studies* 27, no. 2 (2005): 235–263.

48 R. E. Freeman, A. C. Wicks and B. Parmar, 'Stakeholder Theory and "The Corporate Objective Revisited"', *Organization Science* 15, no. 3 (2004): 364–369; D. Balser and J. McClusky, 'Managing Stakeholder Relationships and Nonprofit Organization Effectiveness', *Nonprofit Management & Leadership* 15, no. 3 (Spring 2005): 295–315; Friedman and Miles, *Stakeholders: Theory and Practice*, ch. 3.

49 B. M. Meglino and E. C. Ravlin, 'Individual Values in Organizations: Concepts, Controversies, and Research', *Journal of Management* 24, no. 3 (1998): 351–389; B. R. Agle and C. B. Caldwell, 'Understanding Research on Values in Business', *Business and Society* 38, no. 3 (1999): 326–387; A. Bardi and S. H. Schwartz, 'Values and Behavior: Strength and Structure of Relations', *Personality and Social Psychology Bulletin* 29, no. 10 (2003): 1207–1220; S. Hitlin and J. A. Pilavin, 'Values: Reviving a Dormant Concept', *Annual Review of Sociology* 30 (2004): 359–393.

50 K. Kernaghan, 'Integrating Values into Public Service: The Values Statement as Centrepiece', *Public Administration Review* 63, no. 6 (2003): 711–719. Some popular books that emphasise the importance of values include J. C. Collins and J. I. Porras, *Built to Last: Successful Habits of Visionary Companies* (London: Century, 1995); C. A. O'Reilly III and J. Pfeffer, *Hidden Value* (Cambridge, MA: Harvard Business School Press, 2000); R. Barrett, *Building a Values-Driven Organization: A Whole System Approach to Cultural Transformation* (Burlington, MA: Butterworth-Heinemann, 2006); J. M. Kouzes and B. Z. Posner, *The Leadership Challenge*, 4th edn (San Francisco: Jossey-Bass, 2007).

51 Aspen Institute, *Where Will They Lead? MBA Student Attitudes About Business & Society* (Washington, D.C.: Aspen Institute, April 2008).

52 'Seeing Green', *Business Times Singapore*, 5 May 2008; N. Harrison, 'Make a Difference: Aviva—Perfect Match', *Human Resources*, September 2008, 38–40.

53 M. van Marrewijk, 'Concepts and Definitions of CSR and Corporate Sustainability: Between Agency and Communion', *Journal of Business Ethics* 44, no. 2/3 (2003): 95–105; Barnett, 'Stakeholder Influence Capacity and the Variability of Financial Returns to Corporate Social Responsibility'.

54 L. S. Paine, *Value Shift* (New York: McGraw-Hill, 2003); A. Mackey, T. B. Mackey and J. B. Barney, 'Corporate Social Responsibility and Firm Performance: Investor Preferences and Corporate Strategies', *Academy of Management Review* 32, no. 3 (2007): 817–835

55 S. Zadek, *The Civil Corporation: The New Economy of Corporate Citizenship* (London: Earthscan, 2001); S. Hart and M. Milstein, 'Creating Sustainable Value', *Academy of Management Executive* 17, no. 2 (2003): 56–69.

56 'Canadians Inclined to Punish Companies Deemed Socially Irresponsible, Study Suggests', *Canadian Press*, 23 April 2005; M. Johne, 'Show Us the Green, Workers Say', *Globe & Mail*, 10 October 2007, C1; Aspen Institute, *Where Will They Lead? MBA Student Attitudes About Business & Society.*

57 A. Fox, 'Corporate Social Responsibility Pays Off', *HRMagazine*, August 2007, 42–47.

58 J. P. Campbell, 'The Definition and Measurement of Performance in the New Age', in *The Changing Nature of Performance: Implications for Staffing, Motivation, and Development*, ed. D. R. Ilgen and E. D. Pulakos (San Francisco: Jossey-Bass, 1999), 399–429; R. D. Hackett, 'Understanding and Predicting Work Performance in the Canadian Military', *Canadian Journal of Behavioural Science* 34, no. 2 (2002): 131–140.

59 A. Ballantyne, 'At the Heart and Soul of Snail Mail', *Oakleigh Springvale Dandenong Leader*, 26 November 2008

60 D. W. Organ, 'Organizational Citizenship Behavior: It's Construct Clean-up Time', *Human Performance* 10 (1997): 85–97; S. J. Motowidlo, 'Some Basic Issues Related to Contextual Performance and Organizational Citizenship Behavior in Human Resource Management', *Human Resource Management Review* 10, no. 1 (2000): 115–126; J. A. LePine, A. Erez, and D. E. Johnson, 'The Nature and Dimensionality of Organizational Citizenship Behavior: A Critical Review and Meta-Analysis', *Journal of Applied Psychology* 87, no. 1 (2002): 52–65.

61 K. Lee and N. J. Allen, 'Organizational Citizenship Behavior and Workplace Deviance: The Role of Affect and Cognitions', *Journal of Applied Psychology* 87, no. 1 (2002): 131–142.

62 S. Majumdar, 'Meaningful Engagement', *Business Standard (India)*, 5 March 2009, 8.

63 M. Rotundo and P. Sackett, 'The Relative Importance of Task, Citizenship, and Counterproductive Performance to Global Ratings of Job Performance: A Policy-Capturing Approach', *Journal of Applied Psychology* 87, no. 1 (2002): 66–80; P. D. Dunlop and K. Lee, 'Workplace Deviance, Organizational Citizenship Behaviour, and Business Unit Performance: The Bad Apples Do Spoil the Whole Barrel', *Journal of Organizational Behavior* 25 (2004): 67–80. For discussion of various counterproductive workplace issues, see J. Langan-Fox, C. L. Cooper and R. J. Klimoski, eds., *Research Companion to the Dysfunctional Workplace* (Cheltenham, UK: Edward Elgar, 2007).

64 M. Smith, 'Whittlesea Ambos Struggle to Fill Shifts', *Whittlesea Leader*, 2 December 2008.

65 Watson Wyatt, 'Watson Wyatt Announces Findings of Indonesian Employee Attitude Survey', news release, (Jakarta, 30 November 2004); 'Research Highlights Mine Industry Worker Turnover', *ABC News Online*, 14 November 2005.

66 Basch, 'Doing Well by Doing Good'; K. Coughlin, 'Goooood Move', *Star-Ledger (Newark, NJ)*, 5 June 2005, 1.

67 D. A. Harrison and J. J. Martocchio, 'Time for Absenteeism: A 20-Year Review of Origins, Offshoots, and Outcomes', *Journal of Management* 24 (Spring 1998): 305–350; C. M. Mason and M. A. Griffin, 'Group Absenteeism and Positive Affective Tone: A Longitudinal Study', *Journal of Organizational Behavior* 24 (2003): 667–687; A. Vaananen *et al.*, 'Job Characteristics, Physical and Psychological Symptoms, and Social Support as Antecedents of Sickness Absence among Men and Women in the Private Industrial Sector', *Social Science & Medicine* 57, no. 5 (2003): 807–824.

68 '"Huge Responsibility" on Globalco to Perform', *New Zealand Herald*, 18 June 2001; 'A Major Player on the World Milk Stage', *Weekly Times (Sydney)*, 8 September 2004, 91; K. Newman, 'Greener Pastures', *MIS New Zealand*, September 2004, 18; D. Blayney *et al.*, *U.S. Dairy at a Global Crossroads* (Washington, D.C.: Economic Research Service, United States Department of Agriculture, November 2006).

69 S. Fischer, 'Globalization and Its Challenges', *American Economic Review* (May 2003): 1–29. For discussion of the diverse meanings of 'globalisation', see M. F. Guillén, 'Is Globalization Civilizing, Destructive or Feeble? A Critique of Five Key Debates in the Social Science Literature', *Annual Review of Sociology* 27 (2001): 235–260.

70 The ongoing debate regarding the advantages and disadvantages of globalisation are discussed in Guillén, 'Is Globalization Civilizing, Destructive or Feeble?'; D. Doane, 'Can Globalization Be Fixed?', *Business Strategy Review* 13, no. 2 (2002): 51–58; J. Bhagwati, *In Defense of Globalization* (New York: Oxford University Press, 2004); M. Wolf, *Why Globalization Works* (New Haven, CT: Yale University Press, 2004).

71 K. Ohmae, *The Next Global Stage* (Philadelphia: Wharton School Publishing, 2005).

72 R. House, M. Javidan and P. Dorfman, 'Project GLOBE: An Introduction', *Applied Psychology: An International Journal* 50, no. 4 (2001): 489–505; M. M. Javidan *et al.*, 'In the Eye of the Beholder: Cross Cultural Lessons in Leadership from Project GLOBE', *Academy of Management Perspectives* 20, no. 1 (2006): 67–90.

73 R. Autherson, 'Embracing Diversity', *South China Morning Post (Hong Kong)*, 12 March 2005, 10; HSBC Australia, 'HSBC's Largest Australian Advertising Campaign', news release (Sydney, 13 October 2005).

74 Australian Government Department of Immigration and Multicultural and Indigenous Affairs (DIMIA), *Immigration Update 2004–2005* (Canberra: DIMIA, December 2005).

75 D. A. Harrison *et al.*, 'Time, Teams, and Task Performance: Changing Effects of Surface- and Deep-Level Diversity on Group Functioning', *Academy of Management Journal* 45, no. 5 (2002): 1029–1046.

76 R. Zemke, C. Raines and B. Filipczak, *Generations at Work: Managing the Clash of Veterans, Boomers, Xers, and Nexters in Your Workplace* (New York: Amacom, 2000); M. R. Muetzel, *They're Not Aloof, Just Generation X* (Shreveport, LA: Steel Bay, 2003); S. H. Applebaum, M. Serena and B. T. Shapiro, 'Generation X and the Boomers: Organizational Myths and Literary Realities', *Management Research News* 27, no. 11/12 (2004): 1–28; N. Howe and W. Strauss, 'The Next 20 Years: How Customer and Workforce Attitudes Will Evolve', *Harvard Business Review* 85, no. 7/8 (2007): 41–52.

77 O. C. Richard, 'Racial Diversity, Business Strategy, and Firm Performance: A Resource-Based View', *Academy of Management Journal* 43 (2000): 164–177; D. D. Frink *et al.*, 'Gender Demography and Organization Performance: A Two-Study Investigation with Convergence', *Group & Organization Management* 28 (March 2003): 127–147; T. Kochan *et al.*, 'The Effects of Diversity on Business Performance: Report of the Diversity Research Network', *Human Resource Management* 42 (2003): 3–21; R. J. Burke and E. Ng, 'The Changing Nature of Work and Organizations: Implications for Human Resource Management', *Human Resource Management Review* 16, no. 2 (2006): 86–94.

78 D. Porras, D. Psihountas and M. Griswold, 'The Long-Term Performance of Diverse Firms', *International Journal of Diversity* 6, no. 1 (2006): 25–34; R. A. Weigand, 'Organizational Diversity, Profits and Returns in U.S. Firms', *Problems and Perspectives in Management*, no. 3 (2007): 69–83.

79 R. J. Ely and D. A. Thomas, 'Cultural Diversity at Work: The Effects of Diversity Perspectives on Work Group Processes and Outcomes', *Administrative Science Quarterly* 46 (June 2001): 229–273; Kochan *et al.*, 'The Effects of Diversity on Business Performance: Report of the Diversity Research Network'; D. van Knippenberg and S. A. Haslam, 'Realizing the Diversity Dividend: Exploring the Subtle Interplay between Identity, Ideology and Reality', in *Social Identity at Work: Developing Theory for Organizational Practice*, ed. S. A. Haslam *et al.* (New York: Taylor and Francis, 2003), 61–80; D. van Knippenberg, C. K. W. De Dreu and A. C. Homan, 'Work Group Diversity and Group Performance: An Integrative Model and Research Agenda', *Journal of Applied Psychology* 89, no. 6 (2004): 1008–1022; E. Molleman, 'Diversity in Demographic Characteristics, Abilities and Personality Traits: Do Faultlines Affect Team Functioning?', *Group Decision and Negotiation* 14, no. 3 (2005): 173–193.

80 W. G. Bennis and R. J. Thomas, *Geeks and Geezers* (Boston: Harvard Business School Press, 2002), 74–79; E. D. Y. Greenblatt, 'Work/Life Balance: Wisdom or Whining', *Organizational Dynamics* 31, no. 2 (2002): 177–193.

81 Australian Telework Advisory Committee (ATAC), *Telework in Australia (Paper II)*, (Canberra: Australian Government Department of Communications, Information Technology and the Arts, March 2005); Australian Telework Advisory Committee (ATAC), *Telework—International Developments (Paper III)* (Canberra: Australian Government Department of Communications, Information Technology and the Arts, March 2005); Telework Advisory Group for World at Work, *Exploring Telework as a Business Continuity Strategy: A Guide to Getting Started* (Scottsdale, AZ: WorldatWork, 2005); 'Japan Aims to Double Number of Teleworkers', *Agence France Presse*, 29 May 2007; Sensis, *The Sensis Business Index: Teleworking* (Melbourne: Sensis, July 2007).

82 'Telecommuters Tap into Office Work Revolution', *Agence France Presse*, 1 June 2007.

83 S. Raghuram and B. Wiesenfeld, 'Work-Nonwork Conflict and Job Stress among Virtual Workers', *Human Resource Management* 43, no. 2/3 (2004): 259–277; R. King, 'Working From Home: It's in the Details', *BusinessWeek*, 12 February 2007, 9; D. Cullen, 'Home and Work Mix Well', *The Australian*, 7 February 2009, 1; T. Shekhawat and V. Markandeya, 'Send Workers Home ...' *Business Today (India)*, 25 January 2009.

84 F. Smith, 'Teleworkers—So Near and Yet So Far', *Australian Financial Review*, 6 September 2005, 58.

85 D. E. Bailey and N. B. Kurland, 'A Review of Telework Research: Findings, New Directions, and Lessons for the Study of Modern Work', *Journal of Organizational Behavior* 23, no. 4 (2002): 383–400; D. W. McCloskey and M. Igbaria, 'Does "Out of Sight" Mean "Out of Mind"? An Empirical Investigation of the Career Advancement Prospects of Telecommuters', *Information Resources Management Journal* 16, no. 2 (2003): 19–34; Sensis, *Sensis Insights Report: Teleworking* (Melbourne: Sensis, June 2005).

86 M. N. Zald, 'More Fragmentation? Unfinished Business in Linking the Social Sciences and the Humanities', *Administrative Science Quarterly* 41 (1996): 251–261. Concerns about the 'trade deficit' in OB are raised in C. Heath and S. B. Sitkin, 'Big-B Versus Big-O: What Is Organizational About Organizational Behavior?', *Journal of Organizational Behavior* 22, no. 1 (2001): 43–58.

87 J. Pfeffer and R. I. Sutton, *Hard Facts, Dangerous Half-Truths, and Total Nonsense* (Boston: Harvard Business

School Press, 2006); D. M. Rousseau and S. McCarthy, 'Educating Managers from an Evidence-Based Perspective', *Academy of Management Learning & Education* 6, no. 1 (2007): 84–101.

88 C. M. Christensen and M. E. Raynor, 'Why Hard-Nosed Executives Should Care about Management Theory', *Harvard Business Review* 81, no. 9 (2003): 66–74. For an excellent critique of the 'one best way' approach in early management scholarship, see P. F. Drucker, 'Management's New Paradigms', *Forbes*, 5 October 1998, 152–177.

89 H. L. Tosi and J. W. Slocum Jr, 'Contingency Theory: Some Suggested Directions', *Journal of Management* 10 (1984): 9–26.

90 D. M. Rousseau and R. J. House, 'Meso Organizational Behavior: Avoiding Three Fundamental Biases', in *Trends in Organizational Behavior*, vol. 1, ed. C. L. Cooper and D. M. Rousseau (Chichester, UK: Wiley, 1994), 13–30.

Part 1 CASE STUDY

1 ANCOL PTY LTD

By Steven L. McShane, The University of Western Australia

Paul Sims was delighted when Ancol Pty Ltd offered him the job of manager at its plant near Shepparton, Victoria. Sims was happy enough managing a small metal-stamping plant with another company, but the executive recruiter's invitation to apply for the plant manager job at a leading metal fabrication company was irresistible. Although the Shepparton plant was the smallest of Ancol's 15 operations across Australia and New Zealand, the plant manager position was a valuable first step in a promising career.

One of Sims' first observations at Ancol's Shepparton plant was that relations between employees and management were strained. Taking a page from a recent executive seminar that he attended on building trust in the workplace, Sims ordered the removal of all time clocks from the plant. Instead, the plant would assume that employees had put in their full shift. This symbolic gesture, he believed, would establish a new level of credibility and strengthen relations between management and employees at the site.

Initially, the 250 production employees at the Shepparton plant appreciated their new freedom. They felt respected and saw this gesture as a sign of positive change from the new plant manager. Two months later, however, problems started to appear. A few people began showing up late, leaving early or taking extended lunch breaks. Although this represented only about 5 per cent of the employees, others found the situation unfair. Moreover, the increased absenteeism levels were beginning to have a noticeable effect on plant productivity. The problem had to be managed.

Sims asked supervisors to observe and record when the employees came or went and to discuss attendance problems with those abusing their privileges. But the supervisors had no previous experience with keeping attendance records, and many lacked the necessary interpersonal skills to discuss the matter with subordinates. Employees resented the reprimands, so relations with supervisors deteriorated. The additional responsibility of keeping track of attendance also made it difficult for supervisors to complete their other responsibilities. After just a few months, Ancol found it necessary to add another supervisor position and reduce the number of employees assigned to each supervisor.

But the problems did not end there. Without time clocks, the payroll department could not deduct pay for the amount of time that employees were late. Instead, a letter of reprimand was placed in the employee's personnel file. However, this required yet more time and additional skills from the supervisors. Employees did not want these letters to become a permanent record, so they filed grievances with their labour union. The number of grievances doubled over six months, which required even more time for both union officials and supervisors to handle these disputes.

Nine months after removing the time clocks, Paul Sims met with union officials, who agreed that it would be better to put the time clocks back in. Employee–management relations had deteriorated below the level that Sims observed when he had started. Supervisors were burnt out from overwork. Productivity had dropped due to poorer attendance records and increased administrative workloads.

A couple of months after the time clocks were put back in place, Sims attended an operations meeting at Ancol's headquarters in Melbourne. During lunch, Sims described the time clock incident to Liam Wu, Ancol's plant manager in Christchurch. Wu looked surprised, then chuckled. Wu explained that the previous Christchurch plant manager had done something like that with similar consequences six or seven years ago. The previous manager had left some time ago, but Wu heard about the time clock incident from a supervisor during the manager's retirement party two months ago.

'I guess it's not quite like lightning striking the same place twice,' said Sims to Wu. 'But it sure feels like it.'

Discussion questions

1. Discuss the consequences of the time clock removal on Ancol's effectiveness as an organisation, using any two of the perspectives of organisational effectiveness.
2. What changes should occur to minimise the likelihood of these problems occurring in the future?

CASE STUDY 2

JERSEY DAIRIES LTD

By Steven L. McShane, The University of Western Australia

Jersey Dairies Ltd faced increasing competition that threatened its dominant market share. Senior management at the 300-employee dairy food processing company decided that the best way to maintain or increase market share was to take the plunge into a quality management (QM) program. Jersey hired consultants to educate management and employees about the QM process, and sent several managers to QM seminars. A steering team of managers and a few employees visited other QM companies throughout the country and in other countries around the region.

To strengthen the company's QM focus, Jersey president Tina Stavros created a new position called vice president of quality, and hired James Alder into that position. Alder, who previously worked as a QM consultant at a major consulting firm, was enthusiastic about implementing a complete QM program. One of Alder's first accomplishments was persuading management to give every employee in the organisation several days of training in quality measurement (e.g. Pareto diagrams), structured problem solving and related QM practices. Jersey's largely unskilled workforce had difficulty learning this material, so the training took longer than expected and another round was required one year later.

Alder worked with production managers to form continuous improvement (CI) teams—groups of employees who looked for ways to cut costs, time and space throughout the work process. Although Alder was enthusiastic about CI teams, most supervisors and employees were reluctant to get involved. Supervisors complained that the CI teams were 'asking too many questions' about activities in their department. Less than one-quarter of the production areas formed CI teams because employees thought QM was a fancy way for management to speed up the work. This view was reinforced by some of management's subsequent actions, such as setting higher production targets and requiring employees to complete the tasks of those who were absent from work.

To gain more support for QM, Jersey president Tina Stavros spoke regularly to employees and supervisors about how QM was their answer to beating the competition and saving jobs. Although these talks took her away from other duties, she wanted every employee to know that their primary objective was to improve customer service and production efficiency in the company. To encourage more involvement in the CI teams, Stavros and Alder warned employees that they must support the QM program to save their jobs. To further emphasise this message, the company placed large signs throughout the company's production facilities that said, 'Our Jobs Depend on Satisfied Customers' and 'Quality Management: Our Competitive Advantage'.

Alder and Stavros agreed that Jersey's suppliers must have a strong commitment toward the QM philosophy, so Jersey's purchasing manager was told to get suppliers 'on board' or find alternative sources. Unfortunately, the purchasing manager preferred a more collegial and passive involvement with suppliers, so he was replaced a few months later. The new purchasing manager informed suppliers that they should begin a QM program immediately because Jersey would negotiate for lower prices in the next contracts and would evaluate their bids partly based on their QM programs.

Twenty months after Jersey Dairies began its QM journey, Tina Stavros accepted a lucrative job offer from a large food products company in Europe. Jersey Dairies promoted its vice president of finance, Thomas Cheun, to the president's job. The board of directors was concerned about Jersey's falling profits over the previous couple of years and wanted Cheun to strengthen the bottom line. Although some CI teams did find cost savings, these were mostly offset by higher expenses. The company had nearly tripled its training budget and had significantly higher costs in paid time off costs as employees took these courses. A considerable sum was spent on customer surveys and focus groups. Employee turnover was higher, mainly due to dissatisfaction with the QM program. Just before Stavros left the company, she received word that many employees were joining the union, whereas few had been members previously.

A group of suppliers asked for a confidential meeting in which they told Cheun to reconsider the QM demands on them. They complained that their long-term relationships with Jersey were being damaged and that other dairies were being more realistic about price, quality and delivery requirements. Two major suppliers bluntly stated that they might decide to end their contracts with Jersey rather than agree to Jersey's demands.

Almost two years after Jersey Dairies began QM, Thomas Cheun announced that James Alder was leaving Jersey Dairies, that the position of vice president of quality would no longer exist, and that the company would end several QM initiatives begun over the previous two years. Instead, Jersey Dairies Ltd would use better marketing strategies and introduce new technologies to improve its competitive position in the marketplace.

Discussion questions

1. What perspective of organisational effectiveness did Tina Stavros and James Alder attempt to apply in this case? Describe how specific elements of that perspective related to their interventions.
2. Explain what went wrong in this case, using one or more of the other perspectives of organisational effectiveness.

PART 2

individual behaviour and processes

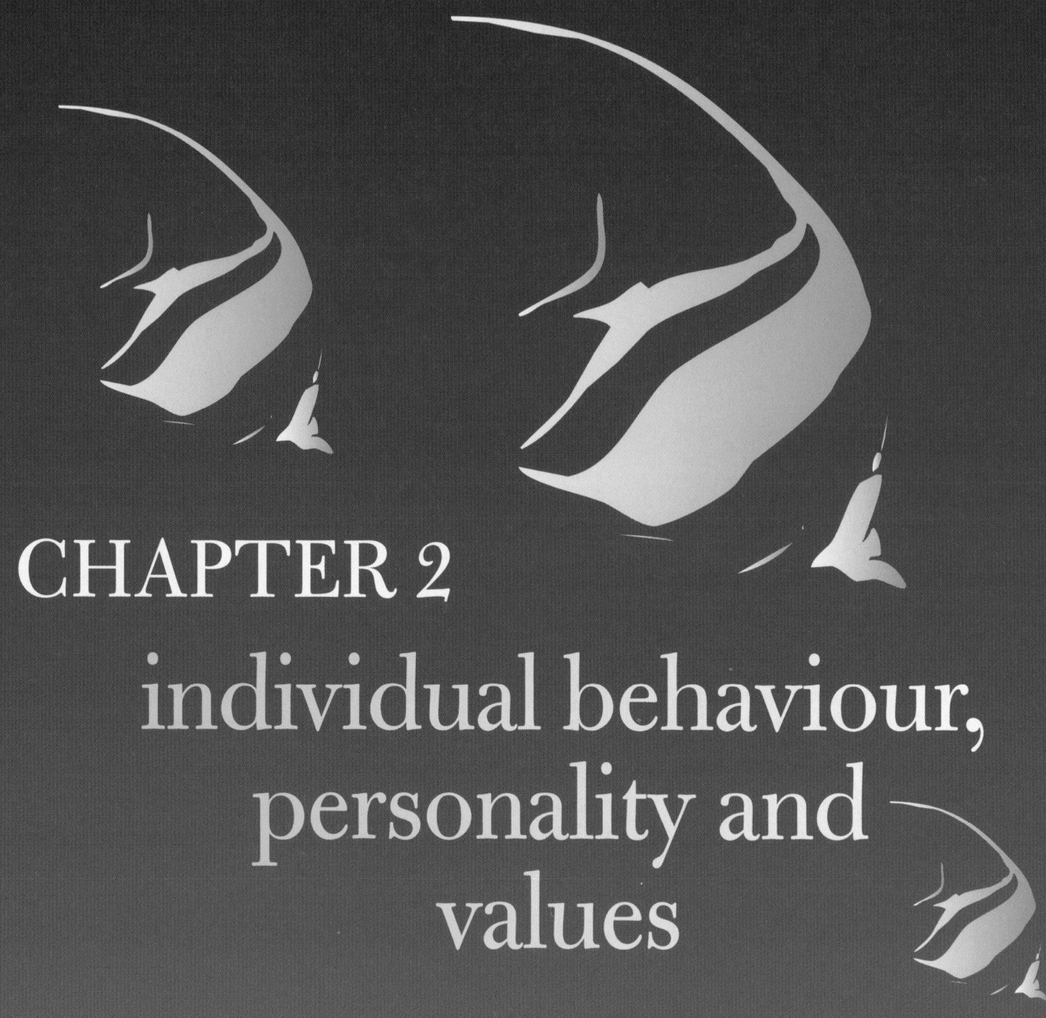

CHAPTER 2

individual behaviour, personality and values

LEARNING OBJECTIVES

After reading this chapter, you should be able to:

- describe the four factors that directly influence voluntary individual behaviour and performance
- define *personality* and discuss what determines an individual's personality characteristics
- summarise the 'Big Five' personality traits in the five-factor model and discuss their influence on organisational behaviour
- describe self-concept in terms of self-enhancement, self-verification and self-evaluation
- explain how social identity theory relates to a person's self-concept
- distinguish personal, shared, espoused and enacted values, and explain why value congruence is important
- summarise five values commonly studied across cultures
- explain how moral intensity, ethical sensitivity and the situation influence ethical behaviour.

The India Today Group

Johnson & Johnson is one of the world's most respected employers because it strengthens employee performance and wellbeing by valuing employees and ensuring that their personal values are aligned with the company's values. 'We make them feel the company belongs to them,' says Narendra Ambwani (shown here), the company's managing director in India.

Every Saturday, Vikas Shirodkar takes his daughter to dance lessons and pops into his office at Johnson & Johnson (J&J) India's headquarters in Mumbai, which is located next door to the dance class. Doing work at the office saves Shirodkar the trouble of driving home and back again to pick up his daughter after class. After three weeks, Shirodkar received a phone call during a weekday from J&J India's managing director, Narendra Ambwani, asking if he was overburdened and needed additional staff. Shirodkar was surprised by the question, until Ambwani explained that he noticed the executive's name on the register every Saturday and was concerned about his workload.

The managing director's phone call was a defining moment for Shirodkar because it illustrated how much J&J values its employees. The company's credo, written in 1943, says that J&J's first responsibility is to the people who use its products, then to its employees, followed by communities and the environment, and finally its shareholders. It states that every employee 'must be considered as an individual' and the company 'must respect [employees'] dignity and recognise their merit'. Narendra Ambwani applies the credo by ensuring that employees feel valued and have meaningful involvement in the organisation. 'We make them feel the company belongs to them,' says Ambwani.

J&J's Pacific operations, headquartered in Sydney, also ensures that job applicants learn about the credo, particularly the company's emphasis on customers and social responsibilities. J&J Pacific president Max Johnson explains that describing the company's values to job applicants is an important part of the induction and interview process, 'making it very clear to people this is the sort of organisation we are and letting people have the opportunity to decide whether that's the sort of organisation they want to join.' The result, he says, is a workforce whose personal values are more closely aligned with the company's values.[1]

What makes Johnson & Johnson a successful company in India, Australia and elsewhere in the world? Some people point to the company's credo, while others mention its decentralised structure, which encourages entrepreneurial empowerment. But as this opening story reveals, the company's success also comes from treating employees as valued stakeholders, and recognising that they are ultimately individuals with personal values, personalities and self-concepts that require dignity, nurturing and recognition.

This chapter concentrates our attention on the role of the individual in organisations. We begin by presenting the MARS model, which outlines the four direct drivers of individual behaviour and results. Next, we introduce the most stable aspect of individuals—personality—including personality development, personality traits and how personality relates to organisational behaviour. We then look at the individual's self-concept, including self-enhancement, self-verification, self-evaluation and social identity. The latter part of this chapter examines another relatively stable characteristic of individuals: their personal values. We look at types of values, issues of value congruence in organisations, cross-cultural values, and ethical values and practices.

LEARNING OBJECTIVE 

Describe the four factors that directly influence voluntary individual behaviour and performance.

MARS MODEL OF INDIVIDUAL BEHAVIOUR AND PERFORMANCE

For most of the past century, experts in psychology, sociology and, more recently, organisational behaviour have investigated the direct predictors of individual behaviour and performance.[2] One of the earliest formulas was *performance* = *person* × *situation*, where *person* includes individual characteristics and *situation* represents external influences on the individual's behaviour. Another frequently mentioned formula is *performance* = *ability* × *motivation*. Sometimes known as the 'skill-and-will' model, this formula elaborates two specific characteristics within the person that influence individual performance. Ability, motivation and situation are by far the most commonly mentioned direct predictors of individual behaviour and performance, but in the 1960s researchers identified a fourth key factor: role perceptions (the individual's expected role obligations).[3]

Exhibit 2.1 illustrates these four variables—motivation, ability, role perceptions and situational factors—which are represented by the acronym *MARS*.[4] All four factors are critical influences on an individual's voluntary behaviour and performance; if any one of them is low in a given situation, the employee would perform the task poorly. For example, motivated salespeople with clear role perceptions and sufficient resources (situational factors) will not perform their jobs as well if they lack sales skills and related knowledge (ability). Let's look at each of these four factors in more detail.

Employee Motivation

motivation The forces within a person that affect his or her direction, intensity and persistence of voluntary behaviour.

Motivation represents the forces within a person that affect his or her direction, intensity and persistence of voluntary behaviour.[5] *Direction* refers to the path along which people engage their effort. People have choices about where they put their effort; they have a sense of what they are trying to achieve and at what level of quality, quantity and so forth. In other words, motivation is goal-directed, not random. People are motivated to arrive at work on time, finish a project a few hours early, or aim for many other targets. The second element of motivation, called *intensity*, is the amount of effort allocated to the goal. Intensity is all about how much

Exhibit 2.1 *MARS Model of Individual Behaviour and Results*

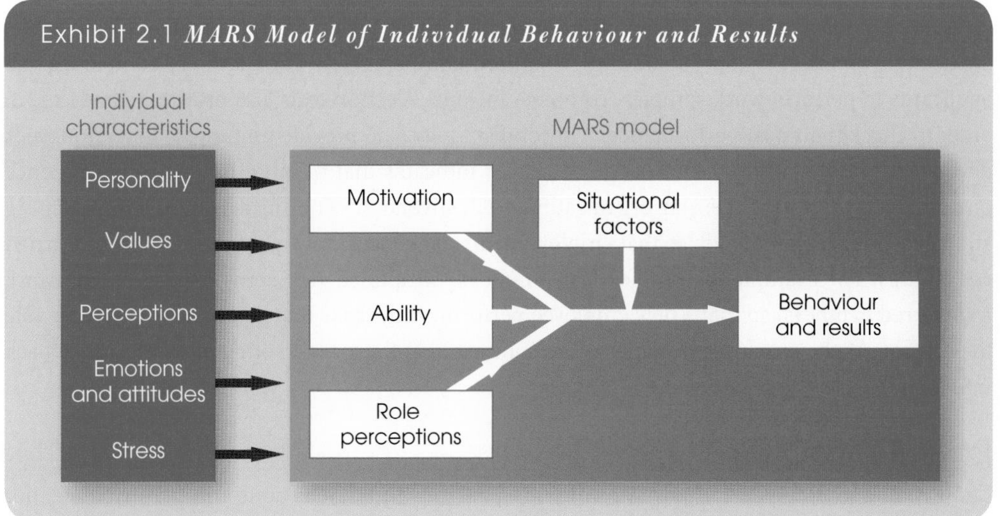

people push themselves to complete a task. For example, two employees might be motivated to finish their project a few hours early (direction), but only one of them puts forth enough effort (intensity) to achieve this goal.

Finally, motivation involves varying levels of *persistence*, that is, continuing the effort for a certain amount of time. Employees sustain their effort until they reach their goal or give up beforehand. Remember that motivation exists within individuals; it is not their actual behaviour. Thus, direction, intensity and persistence are cognitive (thoughts) and emotional conditions that directly cause us to move.

Ability

Employee abilities also make a difference in behaviour and task performance. **Ability** includes both the natural aptitudes and the learned capabilities required to successfully complete a task. *Aptitudes* are the natural talents that help employees learn specific tasks more quickly and perform them better. There are many physical and mental aptitudes, and our ability to acquire skills is affected by these aptitudes. For example, finger dexterity is an aptitude by which individuals learn more quickly and potentially achieve higher performance at picking up and handling small objects with their fingers. Employees with high finger dexterity are not necessarily better than others at first; rather, their learning tends to be faster and performance potential tends to be higher. Learned *capabilities* are the skills and knowledge that you currently possess. These capabilities include the physical and mental skills and knowledge you have acquired. Learned capabilities tend to wane over time when not in use.

ability The natural aptitudes and learned capabilities required to successfully complete a task.

Aptitudes and learned capabilities are closely related to *competencies*, which has become a frequently used term in business. **Competencies** are characteristics of a person that result in superior performance.[6] Many experts describe these characteristics as personal traits (i.e. knowledge, skills, aptitudes, personality, self-concept, values). Others suggest that competencies represent actions produced by a person's traits, such as serving customers, coping with heavy workloads and providing creative ideas. With either definition, the challenge is to match a person's competencies with the job's task requirements. A good person–job match not only produces higher performance, but also tends to increase the employee's wellbeing.

competencies Skills, knowledge, aptitudes and other personal characteristics that lead to superior performance.

One way to match a person's competencies with the job's task requirements is to select applicants who already demonstrate the required competencies. For example, companies ask applicants to perform work samples, complete various selection tests and provide references, in order to check their past performance. A second strategy is to provide training so that employees develop required skills and knowledge. Research indicates that training has a strong influence on individual performance and organisational effectiveness.[7] The third person–job matching strategy is to redesign the job so that employees are given tasks only within their current learned capabilities. For example, a complex task might be simplified (i.e. some aspects of the work transferred to others) so that a new employee performs only tasks that he or she is currently able to perform. As the employee becomes more competent at these tasks, other tasks are added back into the job.

Role Perceptions

role perceptions The extent to which people understand the job duties (roles) assigned to or expected of them.

Motivation and ability are important influences on individual behaviour and performance, but employees also require accurate **role perceptions** to perform their jobs well. Role perceptions are the extent to which people understand the job duties (roles) assigned to them or expected of them. These perceptions are critical because they guide the employee's direction of effort and improve coordination with coworkers, suppliers and other stakeholders. Unfortunately, many employees do not have clear role perceptions. According to one large-scale survey, most

Best Buy Sorts Out Role Perceptions for Black Friday

It's 5 am on 'Black Friday'—the Friday after Thanksgiving in the United States and one of the busiest shopping days of the year—and hundreds of eager shoppers are pouring through the doors of the Best Buy retail outlet in Columbia, Maryland, to grab up the advertised bargains. Fortunately, the electronic retailer's 225 employees in Columbia know what is expected of them on this extremely busy day. A huge floor plan in the back office has colour-coded stickers marking where every staff member will be located; six green dots indicate where employees will stand outside to monitor and support customers who have lined up for hours. Many Best Buy stores held special rehearsals—complete with acting customers—during the week before Black Friday to help employees understand their roles and hone their customer service skills. For example, this photo shows customer assistance supervisor Aaron Sanford orchestrating a Black Friday practice run at a Best Buy store in Denver. 'If you do it right, you're very profitable,' advises Kevin McGrath, Best Buy's store manager in Columbia. McGrath explains that clear role perceptions are just as important for a retail outlet as for a winning sports team. 'The (Baltimore) Ravens are successful because (the players) know what is expected of them,' he says.[9]

Rocky Mountain News

employees understand their organisation's business goals, but only 39 per cent know what to do in their own jobs to achieve those goals.[8]

There are three components to role perceptions. First, employees have accurate role perceptions when they understand the specific tasks assigned to them—that is, when they know the specific duties or consequences for which they are accountable. This may seem obvious, but employees have been (unjustly) fired for failing to perform tasks that they didn't even know were part of their job duties. Second, people have accurate role perceptions when they understand the priority of their various tasks and performance expectations. This includes the quantity versus quality dilemma, such as how many customers to serve in an hour (quantity) versus how well the employee should serve each customer (quality). It also refers to properly allocating time and resources to various tasks, such as how much time a manager should spend coaching employees in a typical week. The third component of role perceptions is understanding the preferred behaviours or procedures for accomplishing the assigned tasks. This refers to situations in which more than one method could be followed to perform the work. Employees with clear role perceptions know which of these methods is preferred by the organisation.

Situational Factors

Employees' behaviour and performance also depend on how much the situation supports or interferes with their task goals. Situational factors include conditions beyond the employee's immediate control that constrain or facilitate behaviour and performance.[10] Some situational characteristics—such as consumer preferences and economic conditions—originate from the external environment and, consequently, are beyond the control of the employee and the organisation. However, other situational factors—such as time, people, budget and physical work facilities—are controlled by people within the organisation. Therefore, corporate leaders need to carefully arrange these conditions so that employees can achieve their performance potential.

The four elements of the MARS model—motivation, ability, role perceptions and situational factors—affect all voluntary workplace behaviours and their performance outcomes. These elements are themselves influenced by other individual differences. In the remainder of this chapter, we introduce three of the most stable individual characteristics: personality, self-concept and values.

PERSONALITY IN ORGANISATIONS

Define *personality* and discuss what determines an individual's personality characteristics.

Qantas, Jetstar and Air New Zealand, among other airlines, carefully screen job applicants to find those who will perform well and fit into the company's culture. They conduct reference checks and job interviews, and have applicants complete a battery of tests. Some of these assessments are personality tests. For example, Air New Zealand discovered which personality traits predicted high-performing staff in various job functions. 'We sampled a high-performing group of cabin crew, call centre agents and corporate Air NZers,' explains Simon Pomeroy, Air New Zealand's head of recruitment. 'That gave us a group of items that created a model Air NZer.' Pomeroy emphasises that the personality test does not screen out applicants. Instead, it helps to identify questions that the applicant would be asked in the job interview. He also suggests that the test results help applicants to decide whether the company fits their work preferences or not.[11]

personality The relatively enduring pattern of thoughts, emotions and behaviours that characterise a person, along with the psychological processes behind those characteristics.

Personality is an important individual characteristic, which explains why many airlines and numerous other organisations try to estimate the personality profiles of job applicants and employees. **Personality** is the relatively enduring pattern of thoughts, emotions and behaviours that characterise a person, along with the psychological processes behind those characteristics.[12] It is, in essence, the bundle of characteristics that make us similar to or different from other people. We estimate an individual's personality by what they say and do, and we infer the person's internal states—including thoughts and emotions—from these observable behaviours.

A basic premise of personality theory is that people have inherent characteristics or traits that can be identified by the consistency or stability of their behaviour across time and situations.[13] For example, you probably have some friends who are more talkative than others. You might know some people who like to take risks and others who are risk-averse. This consistency is an essential requirement for personality theory because it attributes a person's behaviour to something within them—the individual's personality—rather than to purely environmental influences.

Of course, people do not act the same way in all situations; in fact, such consistency would be considered abnormal because it indicates a person's insensitivity to social norms, reward systems and other external conditions.[14] People vary their behaviour to suit the situation, even if the behaviour is at odds with their personality. For example, talkative people remain relatively quiet in a library where 'no talking' rules are explicit and strictly enforced.

People typically exhibit a wide range of behaviours, yet within that variety are discernible patterns that we refer to as *personality traits*. Traits are broad concepts that allow us to label and understand individual differences. Furthermore, traits predict an individual's behaviour far into the future. For example, studies report that an individual's personality in childhood predicts various behaviours and outcomes in adulthood, including educational attainment, employment success, marital relationships, illegal activities and health-risk behaviours.[15]

Personality Determinants: Nature versus Nurture

What determines an individual's personality? Most experts now agree that personality is shaped by both nature and nurture, although the relative importance of each continues to be debated and studied. *Nature* refers to our genetic or hereditary origins—the genes that we inherit from our parents. Studies of identical twins, particularly those separated at birth, reveal that heredity has a very large effect on personality; up to 50 per cent of variation in behaviour and 30 per cent of temperament preferences can be attributed to a person's genetic characteristics.[16] In other words, genetic code not only determines our eye colour, skin tone and physical shape but also has a significant effect on our attitudes, decisions and behaviour.

Some similarities of identical twins raised apart are surreal. Consider Jim Springer and Jim Lewis, twins who were separated when only four weeks old and didn't meet each other until age 39. In spite of being raised in different families and communities in Ohio, the 'Jim twins' held similar jobs, smoked the same type of cigarettes, drove the same make and colour of car, spent their vacations on the same Florida beach, had the same woodworking hobby, gave their first sons almost identical names and had been married twice. Both their first and second wives also had the same first names![17]

Although personality is heavily influenced by heredity, it is also affected to some degree by *nurture*—the person's socialisation, life experiences and other forms of interaction with the environment. Studies have found that the stability of an individual's personality increases up to at least age 30 and possibly to age 50, indicating that some personality development and change occurs when people are young.[18] The main explanation of why personality becomes more stable over time is that people form clearer and more rigid self-concepts as they get older. The executive function—the part of the brain that manages goal-directed behaviour—tries to keep our behaviour consistent with our self-concept.[19] As self-concept becomes clearer and more stable with age, behaviour and personality therefore also become more stable and consistent. We discuss self-concept in more detail later in this chapter. The main point here is that personality is not completely determined by heredity; life experiences, particularly early in life, also shape each individual's personality traits.

Five-Factor Model of Personality

LEARNING OBJECTIVE

Summarise the 'Big Five' personality traits in the five-factor model and discuss their influence on organisational behaviour.

One of the most important elements of personality theory is that people possess specific personality traits. Traits such as sociable, depressed, cautious and talkative represent clusters of thoughts, feelings and behaviours that allow us to identify, differentiate and understand people.[20] The most widely respected model of personality traits is the **five-factor model (FFM)**. Several decades ago, personality experts identified more than 17 000 words in *Roget's Thesaurus* and *Webster's Dictionary* that describe an individual's personality. These words were aggregated into 171 clusters and then further reduced to five abstract personality dimensions. Using more sophisticated techniques, recent investigations identified the same five personality dimensions. Analyses of trait words in several other languages have produced strikingly similar results, although they also lend support for the notion of six or possibly seven dimensions of personality. Generally, though, the five-factor model is fairly robust across cultures.[21] These 'Big Five' dimensions, represented by the handy acronym *CANOE*, are outlined in Exhibit 2.2 and described below:

five-factor model (FFM) The five abstract dimensions representing most personality traits: conscientiousness, emotional stability, openness to experience, agreeableness and extroversion.

Exhibit 2.2 *The Five-Factor Model's 'Big Five' Personality Dimensions*

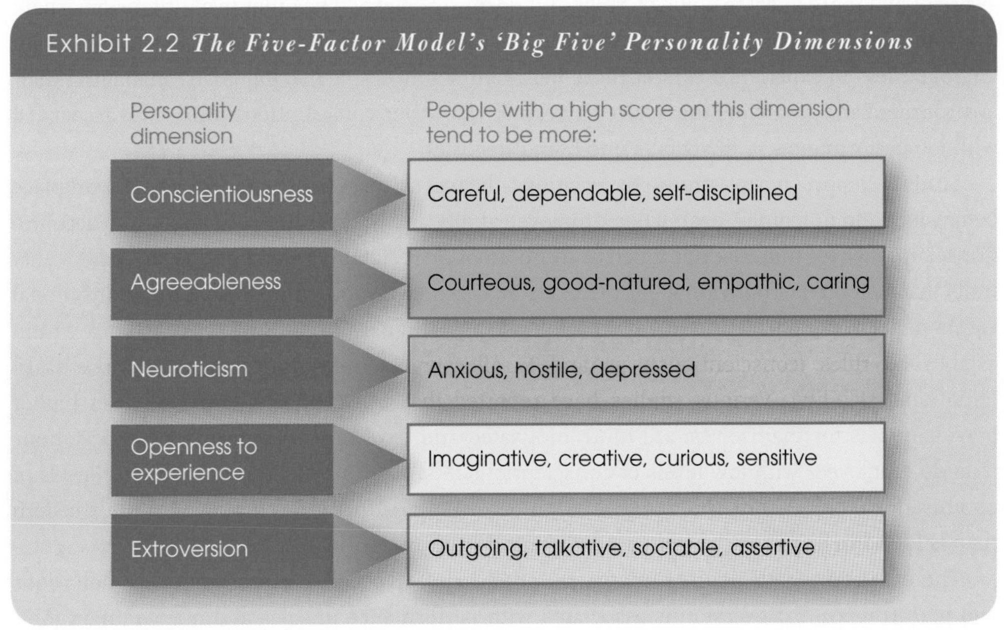

conscientiousness A personality dimension describing people who are careful, dependable and self-disciplined.

- **Conscientiousness** characterises people who are careful, dependable and self-disciplined. Some scholars argue that this dimension also includes the will to achieve. People with low conscientiousness tend to be careless, less thorough, more disorganised, and irresponsible.
- Agreeableness—This dimension includes the traits of being courteous, good-natured, empathic and caring. Some scholars prefer the label 'friendly compliance' for this dimension, with its opposite being 'hostile noncompliance'. People with low agreeableness tend to be uncooperative, short-tempered and irritable.

neuroticism A personality dimension describing people with high levels of anxiety, hostility, depression and self-consciousness.

- **Neuroticism** characterises people with high levels of anxiety, hostility, depression and self-consciousness. In contrast, people with low neuroticism (high emotional stability) are poised, secure and calm.
- Openness to experience—This dimension is the most complex and is the least agreed-upon among scholars. It generally refers to the extent to which people are imaginative, creative, curious and aesthetically sensitive. Those who score low on this dimension tend to be more resistant to change, less open to new ideas, and more conventional and fixed in their ways.

extroversion A personality dimension describing people who are outgoing, talkative, sociable and assertive.

- **Extroversion** characterises people who are outgoing, talkative, sociable and assertive. The opposite is *introversion*, which characterises those who are quiet, shy and cautious. Extroverts get their energy from the outer world (people and things around them), whereas introverts get their energy from the internal world, such as personal reflection on concepts and ideas. Introverts do not necessarily lack social skills. Rather, they are more inclined to direct their interests to ideas than to social events. Introverts feel quite comfortable being alone, whereas extroverts do not.

These five personality dimensions are not independent of each other. Some experts suggest that conscientiousness, agreeableness and low neuroticism (high emotional stability) represent a common underlying characteristic broadly described as 'getting along'; people with these traits are aware of and more likely to abide by rules and norms of society. The other two dimensions share the common underlying factor called 'getting ahead'; people with high scores on extroversion and openness to experience exhibit more behaviours aimed at achieving goals, managing their environment and advancing themselves in teams.[22] However, conscientiousness is also associated with job performance, so likely falls into both categories.

Studies report fairly strong associations between personality and several workplace behaviours and outcomes, even when employee ability and other factors are taken into account. Conscientiousness and low neuroticism (high emotional stability) stand out as the personality traits that best predict individual performance in almost every job group.[23] Both are motivational components of personality because they energise a willingness to fulfil work obligations within established rules (conscientiousness) and to allocate resources to accomplish those tasks (emotional stability). Various studies have reported that conscientious employees set higher personal goals for themselves, are more motivated and have higher performance expectations than do employees with low levels of conscientiousness. They also tend to have higher levels of organisational citizenship and work better in organisations that give employees more freedom than is found in traditional command-and-control workplaces.[24]

The other three personality dimensions predict more specific types of employee behaviour and performance. Extroversion is associated with performance in sales and management jobs, where employees must interact with and influence people. Agreeableness is associated with performance in jobs where employees are expected to be cooperative and helpful, such as working in teams, customer relations and other conflict-handling situations. People high on the openness-to-experience personality dimension tend to be more creative and adaptable to change. Finally, personality influences employee wellbeing in various ways. Studies report that personality influences a person's general emotional reactions to his or her job, how well the person copes with stress and what type of career paths make that person happiest.[25]

The Right Personality for the Antarctic

Australia's Antarctic stations attract and possibly require people who are curious, adventurous, poised and calm. Scientific studies report that, compared to the general population, Australia's Antarctic expeditioners have significantly higher levels of the openness to experience personality trait (i.e. they are curious and adventurous). Those with higher levels of this trait are also more inclined to believe they work well at these stations. Australia's Antarctic expeditioners also have lower levels of neuroticism than the general population (i.e. they are more poised and calm). People with high levels of neuroticism are likely to be screened out during the selection process. However, some self-selection also occurs; those with higher neuroticism are less willing and less likely to return to the Antarctic after their first tour of duty.

Other research has similarly found that Norwegian and British Antarctic expeditioners score higher in the openness to experience dimension and lower in neuroticism compared to the general population.[26]

Lee Sice/Australian Antarctic Division

Jungian Personality Theory and the Myers-Briggs Type Indicator

The five-factor model of personality is the most respected and supported in research, but it is not the most popular in practice. That distinction goes to Jungian personality theory, which is measured through the **Myers-Briggs Type Indicator (MBTI)**. Nearly a century ago, Swiss psychiatrist Carl Jung proposed that personality is primarily represented by the individual's preferences regarding perceiving and judging information.[27] Jung explained that perceiving, which involves how people prefer to gather information or perceive the world around them, occurs through two competing orientations: *sensing (S)* and *intuition (N)*. Sensing involves perceiving information directly through the five senses; it relies on an organised structure to acquire factual and preferably quantitative details. Intuition, on the other hand, relies more on insight and subjective experience to see relationships among variables. Sensing types focus on the here and now, whereas intuitive types focus more on future possibilities.

Myers-Briggs Type Indicator (MBTI) An instrument designed to measure the elements of Jungian personality theory, particularly preferences regarding perceiving and judging information.

Jung also proposed that judging—how people process information or make decisions based on what they have perceived—consists of two competing processes: *thinking (T)* and *feeling (F)*. People with a thinking orientation rely on rational cause–effect logic and systematic data collection to make decisions. Those with a strong feeling orientation, on the other hand, rely on their emotional responses to the options presented, as well as to how those choices affect others. Jung noted that along with differing in the four core processes of sensing, intuition, thinking and feeling, people also differ in their degrees of extroversion and introversion, which was introduced earlier as one of the Big Five personality traits.

In addition to measuring the personality traits identified by Jung, the MBTI measures Jung's broader categories of *perceiving* and *judging*. People with a perceiving orientation are open, curious and flexible, prefer to adapt spontaneously to events as they unfold and prefer to keep their options open. Judging types prefer order and structure and want to resolve problems quickly.

The MBTI is one of the most widely used personality tests in work settings as well as in career counselling and executive coaching.[28] For example, Indonesian state-owned construction company PT Wijaya Karya uses the MBTI to identify the best career paths for employees. At the New Zealand operations of CanTeen, a support organisation for young people living with cancer, senior staff and some regional offices completed this instrument to help them work better together and improve their self-awareness. Southwest Airlines in the United States also relies on the MBTI to help staff understand and respect coworkers' different personalities and thinking styles. 'You can walk by and see someone's four-letter [MBTI type] posted up in their cube,' says Elizabeth Bryant, Southwest's director of leadership development.[29]

In spite of this popularity, evidence regarding the effectiveness of the MBTI and Jung's psychological types is mixed.[30] On the one hand, the MBTI does a reasonably good job of measuring Jung's psychological types and seems to improve self-awareness for career development and mutual understanding. On the other hand, it poorly predicts job performance and is generally not recommended for employment selection or promotion decisions. Furthermore, the MBTI overlaps with the five-factor personality model, yet it does so less satisfactorily than existing measures of the Big Five personality dimensions.[31]

Caveats about Personality Testing in Organisations

Personality is clearly an important concept for understanding, predicting and changing behaviour in organisational settings. However, there are a few problems that continue to hound personality testing.[32] One concern is that most tests are self-report scales, which allow applicants or employees to fake their answers. Rather than measuring a person's personality, many test results might identify the traits that people believe the company values. This concern is compounded by the fact that test takers often don't know what personality traits the company is looking for and may not know which statements are relevant to each trait. Thus, the test scores might not represent the individual's personality or anything else meaningful.

A second issue is that personality is a relatively weak predictor of a person's performance. Some experts point to strong associations between a few personality traits and specific types of performance, but personality generally doesn't predict a person's behaviour and performance as well as more immediate indicators (such as recent past performance). Thus, personality testing could cause companies to wrongly reject applicants who would have performed well. Finally, some companies have discovered that personality testing does not convey a favourable image of the company. For example, the British operations of PricewaterhouseCoopers (PwC) required that applicants complete an online personality test early in the selection process. The accounting firm learned that the test discouraged female applicants from applying because the process was impersonal and the test could be faked. 'Our personality test was seen to alienate women and so we had to respond to that,' said PwC's head of diversity.[33] Overall, we need to understand personality in the workplace but also to be cautious about measuring and applying it too precisely.

SELF-CONCEPT: THE 'I' IN ORGANISATIONAL BEHAVIOUR

LEARNING OBJECTIVE 

Describe self-concept in terms of self-enhancement, self-verification and self-evaluation.

self-concept An individual's self-beliefs and self-evaluations.

Self-concept refers to an individual's self-beliefs and self-evaluations. It is the 'Who am I?' and 'How do I feel about myself?' questions that people ask themselves and that guide their decisions and actions. Self-concept has not received much attention in organisational behaviour research, but scholars in psychology, social psychology and other disciplines have discovered that it is critically important for understanding individual perceptions, attitudes, decisions and behaviour.

People do not have a unitary self-concept.[34] Rather, they think of themselves in several ways in various situations. For example, you might think of yourself as a creative employee, a health-conscious vegetarian and an aggressive skier. A person's self-concept has higher *complexity* when it consists of many categories. As well as varying in complexity, self-concept varies in the degree of its *consistency*. People have high consistency when similar personality traits and values are required across all aspects of self-concept. Low consistency occurs when some aspects of self require personal characteristics that conflict with the characteristics required for other aspects of self. A third structural feature of self-concept is *clarity*, that is, the degree to which a person's self-conceptions are clearly and confidently described, internally consistent and stable across time. A clear self-concept necessarily requires a consistent self-concept. Generally, people develop a clearer self-concept as they get older.

These three structural dimensions of self-concept—complexity, consistency and clarity—influence an individual's adaptability and wellbeing. People function better when their self-concept has many elements (high complexity) that are compatible with each other (high consistency) and are relatively clear. In contrast, people are more rigid and inflexible, and therefore less adaptable, when their self-view consists of only a few similar characteristics (low complexity). People also have poorer psychological adjustment when their self-concept is less clear and includes conflicting elements.

Self-Enhancement

A key ingredient in self-concept is the desire to feel valued. People are inherently motivated to promote and protect a self-view of being competent, attractive, lucky, ethical and important.[35] This *self-enhancement* is observed in many ways. Individuals tend to rate themselves above average, selectively recall positive feedback while forgetting negative feedback, attribute their successes to personal motivation or ability while blaming the situation for their mistakes, and believe that they have a better than average probability of success. People don't see themselves as above average in all circumstances. Rather, self-enhancement occurs more for everyday events than for unique incidents.[36]

Feeling Valued Adds Value

Nathan Denette/National Post

YASMEEN YOUSSEF'S SELF-CONFIDENCE WAS a bit shaky when she and her husband moved from Egypt to Canada a few years ago. 'I was worried no one would take a chance on me, would believe in me,' she recalls. But any self-doubts slowly disappeared after taking an entry-level job with Fairmont Hotels & Resorts corporate offices in Toronto. 'Everything changed when I started working at Fairmont,' says Youssef, who is now on Fairmont's human resource team and recently trained new staff in Cairo. 'I can't believe the amount of value, care, respect everyone has extended to me.'

As North America's largest luxury hotel operator, Fairmont discovered long ago that one of the secret ingredients for employee

Fairmont Hotels has excelled as North America's largest luxury hotel operator by hiring people such as Yasmeen Youssef (shown here) with the right values and personality, and then nurturing their self-concept and cross-cultural competencies.

Self-enhancement has both positive and negative consequences in organisational settings.[37] On the positive side, research has found that individuals have better personal adjustment and experience better mental and physical health when they view their self-concept in a positive light. On the negative side, self-enhancement can result in bad decisions. For example, studies report that self-enhancement causes managers to overestimate the probability of success in investment decisions.[38] Generally, though, successful companies strive to help employees feel that they are valued and integral members of the organisation. Reality Check 2.1 describes how companies build employee motivation and loyalty by supporting their self-concept.

Self-Verification

Along with being motivated by self-enhancement, people are motivated to verify and maintain their existing self-concept.[40] *Self-verification* stabilises an individual's self-concept, which, in turn, provides an important anchor that guides his or her thoughts and actions. Self-verification differs from self-enhancement because people usually prefer feedback that is consistent with their self-concept even when that feedback is unflattering. Self-verification has several implications for organisational behaviour.[41] First, it affects the perceptual process because employees are more likely to remember information that is consistent with their self-concept. Second, the more confident employees are in their self-concept, the less they will accept feedback—positive or negative—that is at odds with their self-concept. Third, employees are motivated to interact with others who affirm their self-concept, and this affects how well they get along with their boss and with coworkers in teams.

REALITY CHECK 2.1

performance and wellbeing is supporting the individual's self-concept. 'People want to feel valued and they stay where they feel valued,' says Carolyn Clark, Fairmont's senior vice president of human resources.

ING Direct also motivates and builds loyalty in employees by nurturing their self-concept. Michelle Little is a case in point. The IT project officer, who has been with ING Direct in Sydney for more than a dozen years, values the company's formal practice of personally recognising her contribution and value to the organisation. For example, after her fifth and tenth year of service, ING Direct held a barbecue and gave her a gift certificate. The chief executive also wrote a personal letter thanking Little for her work. 'It was really nice to get because it was specific to me', says Little. She was particularly touched that the CEO mentioned previous occasions when they had met.

Building a person's self-concept is particularly important in the fast-food business, which is not known for the high status of its jobs. McDonald's Restaurants of Australia offsets its public image with plenty of support and reminders that its staff play important roles in a major business. 'When training, we make our managers feel important,' explains a McDonald's operations manager in Adelaide. 'When they say they're "just" a manager, we quickly correct them by pointing out that they're running a multimillion-dollar business. From then on they stand tall and feel appreciated and respected in their leadership roles.'[39]

Self-Evaluation

Almost everyone strives to have a positive self-concept, but some people have a more positive evaluation of themselves than do others. This self-evaluation is mostly defined by three concepts: self-esteem, self-efficacy and locus of control.[42]

Self-Esteem

Self-esteem—the extent to which people like, respect and are satisfied with themselves—represents a global self-evaluation. People with high self-esteem are less influenced by others, tend to persist in spite of failure and think more rationally. Self-esteem regarding specific aspects of self (e.g. a good student, a good driver, a good parent) predicts specific thoughts and behaviours, whereas a person's overall self-esteem predicts only large bundles of thoughts and behaviours.[43]

Self-Efficacy

self-efficacy A person's belief that he or she has the ability, motivation, correct role perceptions and favourable situation to complete a task successfully.

Self-efficacy refers to a person's belief that he or she can successfully complete a task.[44] Those with high self-efficacy have a 'can do' attitude. They believe they possess the energy (motivation), resources (situational factors), understanding of the correct course of action (role perceptions) and competencies (ability) to perform the task. In other words, self-efficacy is an individual's perception regarding the MARS model in a specific situation. Although originally defined in terms of specific tasks, self-efficacy is also a general trait related to self-concept.[45] General self-efficacy is a perception of one's competence to perform across a variety of situations. The higher the person's general self-efficacy, the higher is his or her overall self-evaluation.

Locus of Control

locus of control A person's general belief about the amount of control he or she has over personal life events.

Locus of control, the third concept related to self-evaluation, is defined as a person's general belief about the amount of control he or she has over personal life events. Individuals with more of an internal locus of control believe that their personal characteristics (i.e. motivation and competencies) mainly influence life's outcomes. Those with more of an external locus of control believe that events in their life are due mainly to fate, luck or conditions in the external environment. Locus of control is a generalised belief, so people with an external locus can feel in control in familiar situations (such as performing common tasks). However, their underlying locus of control would be apparent in new situations in which control over events is uncertain.

People with a more internal locus of control have a more positive self-evaluation. They also tend to perform better in most employment situations, are more successful in their careers, earn more money and are better suited for leadership positions. Internals are also more satisfied with their jobs, cope better in stressful situations and are more motivated by performance-based reward systems.[46]

LEARNING OBJECTIVE

Explain how social identity theory relates to a person's self-concept.

The Social Self

A person's self-concept can be organised into two fairly distinct categories: personal identity characteristics and social identity characteristics.[47] *Personal identity* consists of characteristics that make us unique and distinct from people in the social groups to which we have a connection. For instance, an unusual achievement that distinguishes you from other people typically becomes a personal identity characteristic. Personal identity refers to something about you as an individual without reference to a larger group. At the same time, human beings are social animals; they have an inherent drive to be associated with others and to be recognised as part of social communities. This drive to belong is reflected in self-concept by the fact that all individuals define themselves to some degree by their association with others.[48]

social identity theory A theory that explains self-concept in terms of the person's unique characteristics (personal identity) and membership in various social groups (social identity).

This social element of self-concept is described by **social identity theory**. According to social identity theory, people define themselves by the groups to which they belong or have an emotional attachment. For instance, someone might have a social identity as an Australian, a graduate of the University of Tasmania and an employee at Rio Tinto (see Exhibit 2.3). Social identity is a complex combination of many memberships arranged in a hierarchy of importance. One factor determining importance is how easily we are identified as a member of the reference group, such as by our gender, age and ethnicity. It is difficult to ignore your gender in a class where most other students are the opposite gender, for example. In that context, gender tends to become a stronger defining feature of your social identity than it is in social settings where there are many people of the same gender.

Along with our demographic characteristics, a group's status is typically an important influence on whether we include the group in our social identity. We identify with groups that have high status or respect because this aids the self-enhancement of our self-concept. Medical doctors usually define themselves by their profession because of its high status, whereas people in low-status jobs tend to define themselves by nonjob groups. Some people define themselves in terms of where they work because their employer has a positive reputation in the community. In contrast, other people never mention where they work because their employer is noted for poor relations with employees or has a poor reputation in the community.[49]

Exhibit 2.3 *Social Identity Theory Example*

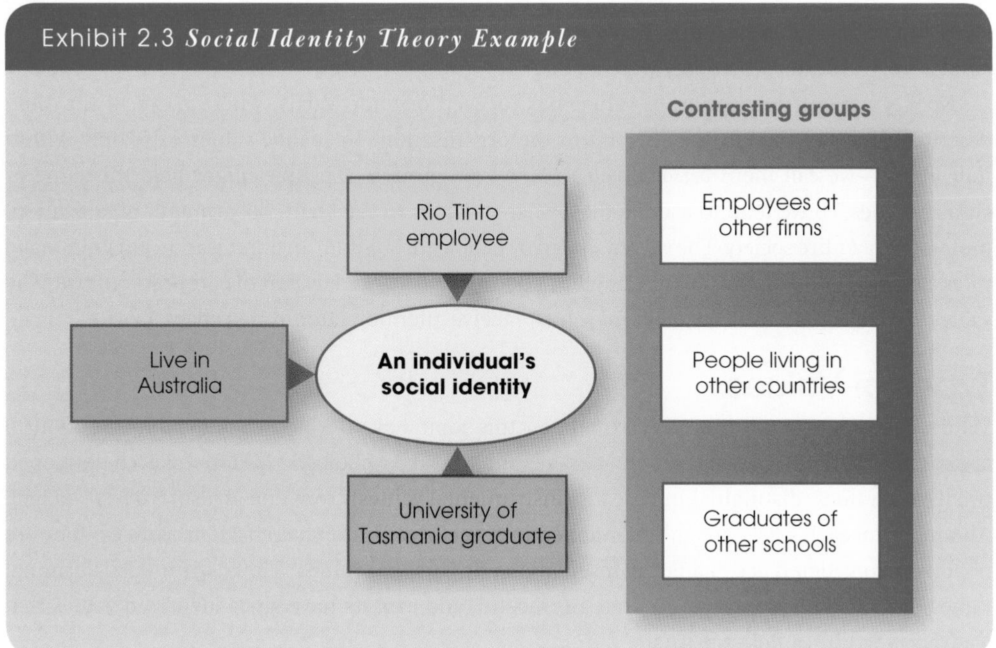

Self-Concept and Organisational Behaviour

We began this section by stating that self-concept is an important topic for understanding individual perceptions, attitudes, decisions and behaviour. In fact, self-concept may eventually be recognised as one of the more useful ways to understand and improve an employee's performance and wellbeing. Some aspects of self-concept, such as self-efficacy and locus of control, are already known to have powerful influences on job performance. Self-concept also affects how people select and interpret information, as well as their biases in judgments (such as probability of success). Furthermore, as you will learn in future chapters, the social identity component of self-concept influences team dynamics, organisational commitment and other OB concepts.

VALUES IN THE WORKPLACE

LEARNING OBJECTIVE

Distinguish personal, shared, espoused and enacted values, and explain why value congruence is important.

Related to self-concept are the individual's personal values.[50] *Values* are stable, evaluative beliefs that guide our preferences for outcomes or courses of action in a variety of situations. They are perceptions about what is good or bad, right or wrong. Values tell us what we 'ought' to do. They serve as a moral compass that directs our motivation and, potentially, our decisions and actions. Values are related to self-concept because they partly define who we are as individuals and as members of groups with similar values.

People arrange values into a hierarchy of preferences, called a *value system*. Some individuals value new challenges more than they value conformity. Others value generosity more than frugality. Each person's unique value system is developed and reinforced through socialisation from parents, religious institutions, friends, personal experiences and the society in which he or she lives. As such, a person's hierarchy of values is stable and long-lasting. For example, one study found that value systems of a sample of intellectually gifted adolescents were remarkably similar 20 years later when they were adults.[51]

Notice that our description of values has focused on individuals, whereas executives often describe values as though they belong to the organisation. In reality, values exist only within individuals—we call them *personal values*. However, groups of people might hold the same or similar values, so we tend to ascribe these shared values to the team, department, organisation, profession or entire society. The values shared by people throughout an organisation (*organisational values*) receive fuller discussion in Chapter 14 because they are a key part of corporate culture. The values shared across a society (*cultural values*) receive attention later in this chapter.

Types of Values

Values come in many forms, and experts on this topic have devoted considerable attention to organising them into clusters. Several decades ago, social psychologist Milton Rokeach developed two lists of values, distinguishing means (instrumental values) from end goals (terminal values). Although Rokeach's lists are still mentioned in some organisational behaviour sources, they are no longer considered acceptable representations of personal values. The instrumental/terminal values distinction was neither accurate nor useful, and experts have since identified values that were excluded from Rokeach's lists.

Today, by far the most respected and widely studied set of values is the model developed and tested by social psychologist Shalom Schwartz and his colleagues.[52] Schwartz's list of 57 values builds on Rokeach's earlier work but does not distinguish instrumental from terminal values. Instead, through painstaking empirical research, Schwartz reported that human values are organised into the circular model (circumplex) shown in Exhibit 2.4.[53] The model organises values into ten broad categories, each representing several specific values. For example, conformity consists of four values: politeness, honouring parents, self-discipline and obedience.

These ten categories of values are further reduced to two bipolar dimensions. One dimension has the opposing value domains of openness to change, and conservation. *Openness to change* refers to the extent to which a person is motivated to pursue innovative ways. It includes the value domains of self-direction (creativity, independent thought) and stimulation (excitement and challenge). *Conservation* is the extent to which a person is motivated to preserve the status quo. This dimension includes the value clusters of conformity (adherence to social norms and expectations), security (safety and stability) and tradition (moderation and preservation of the status quo).

The other bipolar dimension in Schwartz's model has the opposing value domains of self-enhancement and self-transcendence. *Self-enhancement*—how much a person is motivated by self-interest—includes the value categories of achievement (pursuit of personal success) and power (dominance over others). The opposite of self-enhancement is *self-transcendence*, which refers to motivation to promote the welfare of others and nature. Self-transcendence includes the values of benevolence (concern for others in one's life) and universalism (concern for the welfare of all people and nature).

Values and Individual Behaviour

Personal values guide our decisions and actions to some extent, but this connection isn't always as strong as some would like to believe. Habitual behaviour tends to be consistent with our values, but our everyday conscious decisions and actions apply our values much less consistently. The main reason for the 'disconnect' between personal values and individual behaviour is that values are abstract concepts that sound good in theory but are less easily followed in practice.

Exhibit 2.4 *Schwartz's Values Circumplex*

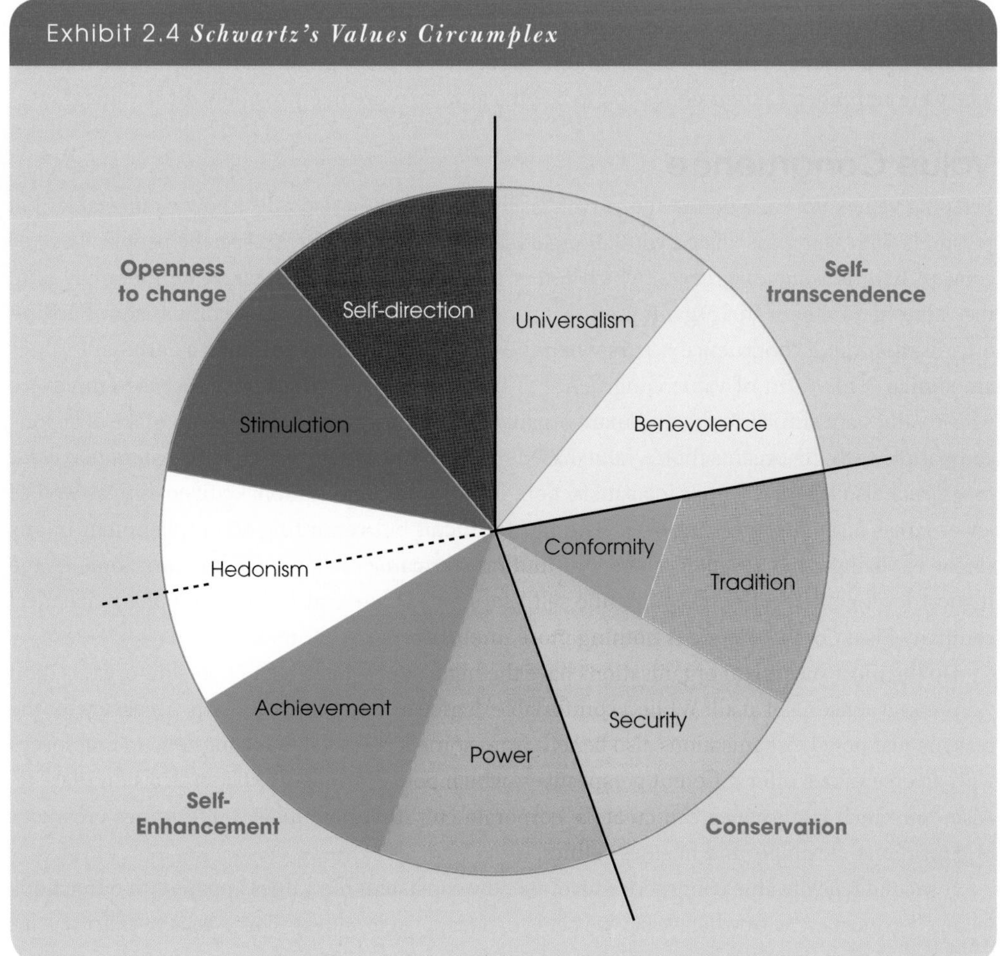

Sources: S. H. Schwartz, 'Universals in the Content and Structure of Values: Theoretical Advances and Empirical Tests in 20 Countries', *Advances in Experimental Social Psychology*, 25 (1992): 1–65; S. H. Schwartz and G. Sagie, 'Value Consensus and Importance: A Cross-National Study', *Journal of Cross-Cultural Psychology*, 31 (July 2000): 465–497.

Three conditions strengthen the linkage between personal values and behaviour.[54] First, we tend to apply our values only when we can think of specific reasons for doing so. In other words, we need logical reasons for applying a specific value in a specific situation. Second, we tend to apply our values in situations that facilitate doing so. Work environments shape our behaviour, at least in the short term, so they necessarily encourage or discourage value-consistent behaviour.

Third, we are more likely to apply values when we are reminded of them. This effect is illustrated in the following study. Students were given a mathematics test in which they were paid for each correct answer. It wasn't possible to cheat under one condition (the results were scored by the experimenter) but under another condition, where students kept their results and told the experimenter how well they scored, it was possible to cheat. Students did cheat under this second condition. However, the experimenters also created a third condition where cheating was possible but the test form had the following statement at the top of the page: 'I understand that this short survey falls under [the university's] honour system.' The university had no such honour code, but students who received that version of the test were required to sign their name to the pledge. The researchers found that none of the students who received the honour system form cheated on the test. Similar results were reported in another study in which some students were asked to list as many of the Ten Commandments as they could remember. In each study, students who were reminded of their obligation to be ethical were more likely to apply those values.[55]

Value Congruence

Personal values not only define the person's self-concept; they also affect how comfortable that person is with being associated with an organisation and working with specific people. The key concept here is *value congruence*, which refers to how similar a person's value hierarchy is to the value hierarchy of the organisation, a coworker or another source of comparison. Person–organisation value congruence occurs when the employee's and organisation's dominant values are similar. This form of value congruence is important for organisations because employees whose values are similar to the dominant organisational values are more likely to make decisions compatible with the organisation's value-based mission and objectives. *Person–organisation value congruence* also leads to higher job satisfaction, loyalty and organisational citizenship, as well as lower stress and employee turnover. 'The most difficult but rewarding accomplishment in any career is "living true" to your values and finding companies where you can contribute at the highest level while being your authentic self,' says an executive at Japanese biopharmaceutical company Eisai Co. Ltd. 'There is nothing more important in my estimation.'[56]

Do the most successful organisations have the highest possible levels of person–organisation value congruence? Not at all! While a comfortable degree of value congruence is necessary for the reasons just noted, organisations also benefit from some level of value incongruence. Employees with diverse values offer different perspectives, which potentially lead to better decision making. Also, too much congruence can create a 'corporate cult' that potentially undermines creativity, organisational flexibility and business ethics.

A second type of value congruence involves how consistent the values apparent in our actions (enacted values) are with what we say we believe in (espoused values). This *espoused–enacted value congruence* is especially important for people in leadership positions because any obvious gap between espoused and enacted values undermines their perceived integrity—a critical feature of effective leaders. One global survey reported recently that 55 per cent of employees believe senior managers behave consistently with the company's core values.[57] Some companies try to maintain high levels of espoused–enacted value congruence by surveying subordinates and peers about whether managers' decisions and actions are consistent with the company's espoused values.

A third type of value congruence involves the compatibility of an organisation's dominant values with the prevailing values of the community or society in which it conducts business.[58] For example, an organisation headquartered in one country that tries to impose its value system on employees and other stakeholders located in another culture may experience higher employee turnover and have more difficult relations with the communities in which the company operates. SC Johnson was aware of this need for alignment in its Australian business. The American healthcare products company has strong paternalistic values in its home country. 'It's a family company with family values,' says an SC Johnson Australia executive. But many Australians would rather keep their work lives separate from their personal lives, so SC Johnson tweaked its values somewhat. 'You can't sell that family company idea in Australia, so we position it as family values with work–life balance,' explains the Australian executive. Rather than hearing that they are part of the SC Johnson 'family', the company's Australian employees learn about work–life balance and the company's social responsibility.[59] Thus, globalisation calls for a delicate balancing act: companies depend on shared values to maintain consistent standards and behaviours, yet they need to operate within the values of different cultures around the world. Let's look more closely at how values vary across cultures.

VALUES ACROSS CULTURES

LEARNING OBJECTIVE

Summarise five values commonly studied across cultures.

Sean Billing had been working as director of rooms at Fairmont Hotels in Chicago when he casually asked his boss whether the hotel chain could use his skills and knowledge elsewhere. Soon after, the economics graduate was offered a position in Kenya, bringing Fairmont's new properties in the African country up to world-class standards through training and technology, but without losing the distinctive Kenyan character. Billing jumped at the opportunity, but he also soon discovered the challenge of inculcating Fairmont's deep values of customer service, environmentalism and empowerment into another culture. 'It's a little bit of hotel culture shock ... things are quite different here,' admits Billing.[60]

Fairmont Hotels & Resorts operates world-class hotels in several countries and is eager to help Sean Billing and other employees to strengthen their cross-cultural competence. As Billing learned, people think and act differently across cultures, and these differences are due to unique norms of behaviour as well as emphasis on different values. As Reality Check 2.2 describes, Infosys Australia also wants its employees to be prepared for cross-cultural encounters, particularly as its employees in Australia interact with coworkers in India. The next few pages describe the five values most widely studied across cultures.

Individualism and Collectivism

Many values have been studied in the context of cross-cultural differences, but the two most commonly mentioned are *individualism* and *collectivism*. **Individualism** is the extent to which we value independence and personal uniqueness. People with high individualism value personal freedom, self-sufficiency, control over their own lives and appreciation of the unique qualities that distinguish them from others. As shown in Exhibit 2.5, Australians and Italians generally

individualism A cross-cultural value describing the degree to which people in a culture emphasise independence and personal uniqueness.

Exhibit 2.5 ***Five Cross-Cultural Values in Selected Countries***

Country	Individualism	Collectivism	Power distance	Uncertainty avoidance	Achievement orientation
Australia	High	Low	Medium low	Medium	Medium high
Denmark	Medium	Medium low	Low	Low	Low
India	Medium high	Medium	High	Medium low	Medium high
Italy	High	High	Medium	High	High
Japan	Medium high	Low	Medium	High	High
New Zealand	High	Low	Low	Medium low	Medium high
Taiwan	Low	High	Medium	High	Medium

Sources: Individualism and collectivism results are from the meta-analysis reported in D. Oyserman, H. M. Coon and M. Kemmelmeier, 'Rethinking Individualism and Collectivism: Evaluation of Theoretical Assumptions and Meta-Analyses', *Psychological Bulletin*, 128, no. 1 (2002): 3–72. The other results are from G. Hofstede, *Culture's Consequences: Comparing Values, Behaviors, Institutions, and Organizations across Nations*, 2nd edn (Thousand Oaks, CA: Sage, 2001).

Infosys Australia Bridges the Cross-Cultural Divide

Shutterstock

INFOSYS TECHNOLOGIES, a computer systems design firm from India, was prepared for cross-cultural differences when it acquired an Australian company to create Infosys Australia. Sean Fernando, Infosys Australia general manager of human resources, provides a vivid example of one of these cultural differences: when asked to travel on business, Infosys employees in India would pack their bags without hesitation and be ready to go even though

Infosys Australia and its parent company in India are training their managers to be aware of cross-cultural differences between the two countries.

collectivism A cross-cultural value describing the degree to which people in a culture emphasise duty to groups they belong to and to group harmony.

exhibit high individualism, whereas Taiwanese tend to have low individualism. **Collectivism** is the extent to which we value our duty to groups to which we belong and to group harmony. Highly collectivist people define themselves by their group memberships and value harmonious relationships within those groups.[62] New Zealanders and Australians generally have low collectivism, whereas Italians and Taiwanese have relatively high collectivism.

Contrary to popular belief, individualism is not the opposite of collectivism. In fact, an analysis of previous studies reports that the two concepts are unrelated.[63] Some cultures that highly value duty to one's group do not necessarily give a low priority to personal freedom and self-sufficiency. The distinction between individualism and collectivism makes sense when we realise that people across all cultures define themselves by both their uniqueness (personal identity) and their relationship to others (social identity). Some cultures clearly emphasise one more than the other, but both have a place in a person's values and self-concept.

Power Distance

As a senior manager throughout Asia, Stephen Roberts rarely received questions or critiques from staff about his proposals or ideas. 'I spent nine years in Asia and managing in Asia was a relatively easy process because no one pushed back,' he recalls. The high power distance in Asian countries motivated staff to defer to Roberts' judgment. In contrast, Roberts experienced very low power distance when he transferred to Australia. Even though he was now a chief executive officer at Citibank, his ideas were quickly, and sometimes brutally, questioned. 'I remember arriving in Australia and I was asked to present to an executive committee of our equities team, and it felt like a medical examination,' recalls Roberts, who was born and raised in Australia. 'I walked out battered and bruised. So to be pushed, challenged all the time, is more Australian than most other [cultures].'[64]

power distance A cross-cultural value describing the degree to which people in a culture accept unequal distribution of power in a society.

The Citibank Australia executive experienced profound differences in **power distance** between staff in Australia and in the Asian countries where he previously worked. Power distance refers to the extent to which people accept unequal distribution of power in a society.[65] On average, employees in Thailand, Malaysia and most (but not all) other Asian countries they lacked details about the trip. Australian staff, on the other hand, wanted to know about the accommodation, allowances and project specifics before they felt at ease. In other words, employees from India had noticeably lower levels of uncertainty avoidance.

Another difference was that staff in India expect the boss to give them instructions on what to do, whereas Australian employees expect to be consulted. In other words, Australian employees have much lower power distance. Fernando recalls an incident where an Australian project manager met with a project team from India. He described the project, then suggested that they share ideas about how to successfully complete the project. 'They didn't know what he meant,' says Fernando. 'Then one of the people just said: "We were wondering when you are going to tell us what the plan was."'

To minimise cross-cultural conflict, Infosys Australia holds a three-hour session in which employees from both countries learn about each other's cultures and discuss how they can manage employees with these different values.[61]

REALITY CHECK 2.2

have high power distance. They accept and value unequal power. They also value obedience to authority and are comfortable receiving commands from their superiors without consultation or debate. They prefer to resolve differences indirectly through formal procedures rather than directly.

In contrast, the Citibank executive observed low power distance in Australia. His Australian staff expected relatively equal power sharing. They viewed the relationship with their boss as one of interdependence, not dependence; that is, they believed their boss was also dependent on them, so they expected power sharing and consultation before decisions affecting them were made. Along with Australians and New Zealanders, people in Denmark and the United States tend to have low power distance.

Uncertainty Avoidance

Uncertainty avoidance is the degree to which people tolerate ambiguity (low uncertainty avoidance) or feel threatened by ambiguity and uncertainty (high uncertainty avoidance). Employees with high uncertainty avoidance value structured situations in which rules of conduct and decision making are clearly documented. They usually prefer direct rather than indirect or ambiguous communications. Uncertainty avoidance tends to be high among people in Italy and Taiwan and very high in Japan. This cross-cultural value tends to be very low in Singapore and Jamaica and moderately low in Malaysia, Hong Kong and China. Australians, New Zealanders and Americans have similar scores around the middle of the range.

uncertainty avoidance A cross-cultural value describing the degree to which people in a culture tolerate ambiguity (low uncertainty avoidance) or feel threatened by ambiguity and uncertainty (high uncertainty avoidance).

Achievement–Nurturing Orientation

Achievement–nurturing orientation reflects a competitive versus cooperative view of relations with other people.[66] People with a high achievement orientation value assertiveness, competitiveness and materialism. They appreciate people who are tough, and they favour the acquisition of money and material goods. In contrast, people in nurturing-oriented cultures emphasise relationships and the wellbeing of others. They focus on human interaction and caring rather than competition and personal success. People in Sweden, Norway and Denmark

achievement–nurturing orientation A cross-cultural value describing the degree to which people in a culture emphasise competitive versus cooperative relations with other people.

score very low on achievement orientation (i.e. they have a high nurturing orientation). In contrast, very high achievement orientation scores have been reported in Japan and Hungary. Achievement orientation scores hover around the middle of the range in most Asian countries (other than Japan and Thailand) as well as New Zealand and Australia.

Before leaving this topic, we need to point out two concerns about this information on cross-cultural values.[67] One concern is that country scores on power distance, uncertainty avoidance and achievement–nurturing orientation are based on a survey of IBM staff worldwide more than a quarter of a century ago. More than 100 000 IBM employees in dozens of countries completed that survey, but IBM employees might not represent the general population. Indeed, there is evidence that values have since changed considerably in some countries. For example, studies report that value systems are converging across Asia as people in these countries interact more frequently with each other and as globalisation results in more standardised business practices at both the corporate and national levels.[68]

A second concern is the assumption that everyone in a society has similar cultural values. This may be true in a few countries, but *multiculturalism*—in which several microcultures coexist in the same country—is becoming the more common trend. For example, one study reported significantly different values amongst Javanese, Batik and Chinese Indonesians, yet cross-cultural studies tend to lump these diverse groups together into one culture. By attributing specific values to an entire society, we are engaging in a form of stereotyping that limits our ability to understand the more complex reality of that society.[69]

ETHICAL VALUES AND BEHAVIOUR

When Australian healthcare workers were asked what conditions would motivate them to stay with their current employer, the top considerations were more pay, quality of management, workplace environment and work hours. But also significant among the top five factors was good company ethics. Several other studies report that honesty/ethics is the most important characteristic that employees look for in a leader.[70] *Ethics* refers to the study of moral principles or values that determine whether actions are right or wrong and outcomes are good or bad. People rely on their ethical values to determine 'the right thing to do'.

According to recent survey results, New Zealand, Denmark and Sweden were perceived to be the least corrupt countries among the 180 countries surveyed. Singapore (4th) and Australia (9th) follow closely behind. Yet these countries and others in the region have their share of business scandals.[71] Amcor and Visy, two of the largest packaging companies in the region, colluded for many years to fix corrugated box prices. Qantas (along with several other airlines) was also recently found guilty of fixing prices in a cartel that controlled the cargo market in the United States. A former Qantas executive was jailed for the wrongdoing. Executives at Bridgecorp face criminal charges of misrepresenting the company's financial status (making false statements in its prospectus). Bridgecorp, which experienced phenomenal growth to become one of New Zealand's largest nonbank finance companies, is now in receivership. Likely one of the most serious cases of corruption in Australian history is the Australian Wheat Board's payment of kickbacks to the former regime of Saddam Hussein in Iraq. Some claim that this corruption was known at the highest levels of the Australian government, but no one attempted to stop the wrongdoing until it was revealed in a United Nations report.[72]

Three Ethical Principles

To better understand business ethics, we need to consider three distinct types of ethical principles: utilitarianism, individual rights and distributive justice.[73] While you might prefer one principle more than the others on the basis of your personal values, all three should be actively considered to put important ethical issues to the test.

UTILITARIANISM This principle advises us to seek the greatest good for the greatest number of people. In other words, we should choose the option that provides the highest degree of satisfaction to those affected. This is sometimes known as a consequential principle because it focuses on the consequences of our actions, not on how we achieve those consequences. One problem with utilitarianism is that it is almost impossible to evaluate the benefits or costs of many decisions, particularly when many stakeholders have wide-ranging needs and values. Another problem is that most of us are uncomfortable engaging in behaviours that seem unethical to attain results that are ethical.

INDIVIDUAL RIGHTS This principle reflects the belief that all people have entitlements that allow them to act in a certain way. Some of the most widely cited rights are freedom of movement, physical security, freedom of speech, fair trial and freedom from torture. The individual-rights principle includes more than legal rights; it also includes human rights that everyone is granted as a moral norm of society. One problem with individual rights is that certain individual rights may conflict with others. The shareholders' right to be informed about corporate activities may ultimately conflict with an executive's right to privacy, for example.

DISTRIBUTIVE JUSTICE This principle suggests that people who are similar to each other should receive similar benefits and burdens; those who are dissimilar should receive different benefits and burdens in proportion to their dissimilarity. For example, we expect that two employees who contribute equally in their work should receive similar rewards, whereas those who make a lesser contribution should receive less. A variation of the distributive justice principle says that inequalities are acceptable when they benefit the least well-off in society. Thus, employees in risky jobs should be paid more if their work benefits others who are less well-off. One problem with the distributive justice principle is that it is difficult to agree on who is 'similar' and what factors are 'relevant'.

Moral Intensity, Ethical Sensitivity and Situational Influences

LEARNING OBJECTIVE 

Explain how moral intensity, ethical sensitivity and the situation influence ethical behaviour.

Along with ethical principles and their underlying values, three other factors influence ethical conduct in the workplace: the moral intensity of the issue, the individual's ethical sensitivity and situational factors. **Moral intensity** is the degree to which an issue demands the application of ethical principles. Decisions with high moral intensity are more important, so the decision maker needs to more carefully apply ethical principles to resolve them. Several factors influence the moral intensity of an issue, including those listed in Exhibit 2.6. Keep in mind that this list represents the factors people tend to think about; some of them might not be considered morally acceptable when people are formally making ethical decisions.[74]

moral intensity The degree to which an issue demands the application of ethical principles.

Exhibit 2.6 ***Factors Influencing Perceived Moral Intensity****

Moral intensity factor	**Moral intensity question**	**Moral intensity is higher when:**
Magnitude of consequences	How much harm or benefit will occur to others as a result of this action?	The harm or benefit is larger.
Social consensus	How many other people agree that this action is ethically good or bad?	Many people agree.
Probability of effect	1. What is the chance that this action will actually occur? 2. What is the chance that this action will actually cause good or bad consequences?	The probability is higher.
Temporal immediacy	How long after the action will the consequences occur?	The time delay is shorter.
Proximity	How socially, culturally, psychologically and/or physically close to me are the people affected by this decision?	Those affected are close rather than distant.
Concentration of effect	1. How many people are affected by this action? 2. Are the people affected by this action easily identifiable as a group?	Many people are affected. Those affected are easily identifiable as a group.

*These are factors people tend to ask themselves about when determining the moral intensity of an issue. Whether some of these questions *should* be relevant is itself an ethical question.

Source: Based on information in T. J. Jones, 'Ethical Decision Making by Individuals in Organisations: An Issue Contingent Model', *Academy of Management Review* 16 (1991): 366–395.

ethical sensitivity A personal characteristic that enables people to recognise the presence of an ethical issue and determine its relative importance.

Even if an issue has high moral intensity, some employees might not recognise its ethical importance because they have low **ethical sensitivity**. Ethical sensitivity is a personal characteristic that enables people to recognise the presence of an ethical issue and determine its relative importance.[75] Ethically sensitive people are not necessarily more ethical. Rather, they are more likely to sense whether an issue requires ethical consideration; that is, they can more accurately estimate the moral intensity of the issue. Ethically sensitive people tend to have higher empathy. They also have more information about the specific situation. For example, accountants would be more ethically sensitive regarding the appropriateness of specific accounting procedures than would someone who has not received training in this profession.

The third important factor explaining why good people engage in unethical decision making and behaviour is the situation in which the conduct occurs. Employees say they regularly experience pressure from top management that motivates them to lie to customers, breach regulations or otherwise act unethically. According to a global survey of managers and human resource managers, pressure from top management or the board to meet unrealistic deadlines and business objectives is the leading cause of unethical corporate behaviour.[76] Situational factors do not justify unethical conduct. Rather, we need to be aware of these factors so that organisations can reduce their influence in the future.

Supporting Ethical Behaviour

Most corporate leaders would agree that ethics is important, yet few firms in the Asia-Pacific region seem to be systematically developing or monitoring ethical values in their employees. One of the most basic steps in this direction is to develop a code of ethical conduct. Almost all Fortune 500 companies in the United States and the majority of the 500 largest UK companies now have codes of ethics. These statements communicate the organisation's ethical standards and signal to employees that the company takes ethical conduct seriously. However, critics point out that ethics codes alone do little to reduce unethical conduct. After all, Enron had a well-developed code of ethics, but that document didn't prevent senior executives from engaging in wholesale accounting fraud, resulting in the energy company's bankruptcy.[77]

To supplement ethics codes, many firms provide ethics training. At Texas Instruments, employees learn to ask the following questions as their moral compass: 'Is the action legal? Does it comply with our values? If you do it, will you feel bad? How would it look in the newspaper? If you know it's wrong, don't do it! If you're not sure, ask. Keep asking until you get an answer.' Molson Coors developed an award-winning online training program set up as an expedition: employees must resolve ethics violations at each 'camp' as they ascend a mountain. The first few camps present real scenarios with fairly clear ethical violations of the company's ethics code; later camps present much fuzzier dilemmas requiring more careful thought about the company's underlying values.[78]

Some companies have also introduced procedures whereby employees can communicate possible ethical violations in confidence. Through its parent company in the United States, Australian consulting engineering firm Maunsell AECOM has a 24-hour ethics hotline, where employees can report wrongdoing or ask about ethical concerns. The hotline assures confidentiality by using a third-party organisation. Food manufacturer H. J. Heinz Co. also has

Protecting E&Y's Brand with Values-Based Ethics Training

As a leading accounting and professional services firm, Ernst & Young (E&Y) has a lot at stake in maintaining its reputation for ethical conduct. 'We can't ever be in a position to have our ethics challenged,' says E&Y human resource executive Michael Hamilton. Although the financial world has become very rule-based, the rules still leave gaps where ethical missteps can occur. To minimise this risk, E&Y invests heavily in values-based ethics training. 'Ethics training and value training are about providing all of our people with a clear message and some guiding principles about what to do when the rules don't address a situation or area,' Hamilton explains.

All E&Y staff members are required to complete a two-hour web-based ethics course called 'Living Our Core Values' in which they learn about the company's values and ethical principles, followed by analysis of several specific case situations. Ethical topics are also being integrated throughout E&Y's professional development courses. 'We're trying to bake ethics training into all of our curriculum,' says Jeffrey Hoops, an E&Y ethics and compliance officer. 'It's about continually reminding people that doing the right thing and speaking up when you see the wrong thing is not just accepted—it is the expected way we do things at Ernst & Young.'[80]

James Leynse/Corbis

an ethics hotline that operates around the clock and in 150 languages for its global workforce. Heinz's director of ethics says that the hotline 'has provided an early warning signal of problems we were not aware of.'[79]

These additional measures support ethical conduct to some extent, but the most powerful foundation is a set of shared values that reinforce ethical conduct. 'If you don't have a culture of ethical decision making to begin with, all the controls and compliance regulations you care to deploy won't necessarily prevent ethical misconduct,' warns a senior executive at British communications giant Vodafone. This culture is supported by the ethical conduct and vigilance of corporate leaders. By acting with the highest standards of moral conduct, leaders not only gain support and trust from followers; they provide a role model for the ethical standards that employees are more likely to follow.[81]

CHAPTER SUMMARY

Individual behaviour is influenced by motivation, ability, role perceptions and situational factors (MARS). Motivation consists of internal forces that affect the direction, intensity and persistence of a person's voluntary choice of behaviour. Ability includes both the natural aptitudes and the learned capabilities required to successfully complete a task. Role perceptions are a person's beliefs about what behaviours are appropriate or necessary in a particular situation. Situational factors are environmental conditions that constrain or facilitate employee behaviour and performance.

Personality is the relatively enduring pattern of thoughts, emotions and behaviours that characterise a person, along with the psychological processes behind those characteristics. Most experts now agree that personality is shaped by both nature and nurture. Most personality traits are represented within the five-factor model, which includes conscientiousness, agreeableness, neuroticism, openness to experience and extroversion.

Another set of traits, measured by the Myers-Briggs Type Indicator, represents how people prefer to perceive and judge information. Conscientiousness and low neuroticism (high emotional stability) stand out as the personality traits that best predict individual performance in almost every job group. The other three personality dimensions predict more specific types of employee behaviour and performance.

Self-concept includes an individual's self-beliefs and self-evaluations. It has three structural dimensions: complexity, consistency and clarity. People are inherently motivated to promote and protect their self-concept; this is self-enhancement. At the same time, people are motivated to verify and maintain their existing self-concept; this is self-verification.

Self-evaluation, an important aspect of self-concept, consists of self-esteem, self-efficacy and locus of control. Self-esteem is the extent to which people like, respect and are satisfied with themselves. Self-efficacy is a person's belief that he or she has the ability, motivation, correct role perceptions and favourable situation to complete a task successfully; general self-efficacy is a perception of one's competence to perform across a variety of situations. Locus of control is defined as a person's general belief about the amount of control he or she has over personal life events. Self-concept consists of both personal identity and social identity. Social identity theory explains how people define themselves in terms of the groups to which they belong or have an emotional attachment.

Values are stable, evaluative beliefs that guide our preferences for outcomes or courses of action in a variety of situations. People arrange values into a hierarchy of preferences, called a *value system*. Espoused values—what we say and think we use as values—are different from enacted values, which are values evident from our actions. Values have been organised into a circle with ten clusters. Value congruence is the similarity of value systems between two entities.

Five values that differ across cultures are: individualism, collectivism, power distance, uncertainty avoidance and achievement–nurturing orientation. Three values that guide ethical conduct are utilitarianism, individual rights and distributive justice. Three factors that influence ethical conduct are the extent to which an issue demands ethical principles (moral intensity), the person's ethical sensitivity to the presence and importance of an ethical dilemma, and situational factors that cause people to deviate from their moral values. Companies improve ethical conduct through a code of ethics, ethics training, ethics hotlines and by providing role models in the conduct of corporate leaders.

KEY TERMS

ability, p. 47
achievement–nurturing orientation, p. 65
collectivism, p. 64
competencies, p. 47
conscientiousness, p. 52
ethical sensitivity, p. 68
extroversion, p. 52
five-factor model (FFM), p. 51
individualism, p. 63
locus of control, p. 58
moral intensity, p. 67
motivation, p. 46
Myers-Briggs Type Indicator (MBTI), p. 53
neuroticism, p. 52
personality, p. 50
power distance, p. 64
role perceptions, p. 48
self-concept, p. 55
self-efficacy, p. 57
social identity theory, p. 58
uncertainty avoidance, p. 65

Critical Thinking Questions

1 An insurance company has high levels of absenteeism among its office staff. The head of office administration argues that employees are misusing the company's sick leave benefits. However, some of the mostly female staff members have explained that family responsibilities interfere with work. Using the MARS model, as well as your knowledge of absenteeism behaviour, discuss some of the possible reasons for absenteeism here and how it might be reduced.

2 As the district manager responsible for six stores in a large electronics retail chain, you have had difficulty with the performance of some sales employees. Although they are initially motivated and generally have good interpersonal skills, many have difficulty with the complex knowledge of the wide variety of store products, ranging from computers to high-fidelity sound systems. Describe three strategies you might apply to improve the match between the competencies of new sales employees and the job requirements.

3 Studies report that heredity has a strong influence on an individual's personality. What are the implications of this in organisational settings?

4 Suppose that you give all candidates applying for a management trainee position a personality test that measures the five dimensions in the five-factor model. Which personality traits would you consider to be the most important for this type of job? Explain your answer.

5 An important aspect of self-concept is the idea that almost everyone engages in self-enhancement. What problems tend to occur in organisations as a result of the self-enhancement phenomenon? What can organisational leaders do to make use of a person's inherent drive for self-enhancement?

6 This chapter discussed value congruence mostly in the context of an employee's personal values versus the organisation's values. But value congruence also relates to the

juxtaposition of other pairs of value systems. Explain how value congruence is relevant with respect to organisational versus professional values (i.e. the values of professional occupations, such as medical practitioners, accountants and pharmacists).

7 People in a particular South American country have high power distance and high collectivism. What does this mean, and what are the implications of this information for a senior executive who is visiting employees working for his or her company in that country?

8 'All decisions are ethical decisions.' Comment on this statement, particularly by referring to the concepts of moral intensity and ethical sensitivity.

CLASS EXERCISE

Skill Builder 2.1

Test Your Knowledge of Personality

Purpose

This exercise is designed to help you think about and understand the effects of the Big Five personality dimensions on individual preferences and outcomes.

Instructions (Large Class)

Below are several questions relating to the Big Five personality dimensions and various preferences or outcomes. Answer each of these questions, relying on your personal experience or best guess. Later, the instructor will show you the answers based on scholarly results. You will *not* be graded on this exercise, but it may help you to better understand the effect of personality on human behaviour and preferences.

Instructions (Small Class)

1. The instructor will organise you into teams. Work together with your team members to answer each of the questions below relating to the Big Five personality dimensions and various preferences or outcomes.
2. The instructor will reveal the answers based on scholarly results. (*Note*: The instructor might create a competition to see which team has the most answers correct.)

Personality and Preferences Questions

1. Which two Big Five personality dimensions are positively associated with enjoyment of workplace humour?

   ____

   ____

2. Listed on page 74 are several jobs. Please check no more than two personality dimensions that you believe are positively associated with preferences for each occupation.

Personality Dimension					
Job	Extroversion	Conscien-tiousness	Agreeableness	Neuroticism	Openness to experience
Budget analyst	❑	❑	❑	❑	❑
Corporate executive	❑	❑	❑	❑	❑
Engineer	❑	❑	❑	❑	❑
Journalist	❑	❑	❑	❑	❑
Life insurance agent	❑	❑	❑	❑	❑
Nurse	❑	❑	❑	❑	❑
Medical practitioner	❑	❑	❑	❑	❑
Production supervisor	❑	❑	❑	❑	❑
Public relations director	❑	❑	❑	❑	❑
Research analyst	❑	❑	❑	❑	❑
Schoolteacher	❑	❑	❑	❑	❑
Sculptor	❑	❑	❑	❑	❑

3. Rank order (1 = highest, 5 = lowest) the Big Five personality dimensions in terms of how much you think they predict a person's degree of life satisfaction. (Note: You are ranking these personality dimensions by their absolute effect, regardless of whether their impact on life satisfaction is positive or negative.)
   — Conscientiousness
   — Agreeableness
   — Neuroticism
   — Openness to experience
   — Extroversion

Skill Builder 2.2

TEAM EXERCISE

Comparing Cultural Values

Purpose

This exercise is designed to help you determine the extent to which you and your class members hold similar assumptions about the values that dominate in other countries.

Instructions (Small Class)

The terms in the left column represent labels that a major consulting project identified with businesspeople in a particular country, based on its national culture and values. These terms appear in alphabetical order. In the right column are the names of countries, also in alphabetical order, corresponding to the labels in the left column.

1. Working alone, connect the labels with the countries by relying on your perceptions of these countries. Each label is associated with only one country, so each label should be connected to only one country, and vice versa. Draw a line to connect the pairs, or put the label number beside the country name.

2. The instructor will form teams of four or five members. Members of each team will compare their results and try to reach consensus on a common set of connecting pairs.
3. Teams or the instructor will post the results so that all can see the extent to which your class members hold common opinions about businesspeople in other cultures. Class discussion can then consider the reasons why the results are so similar or different, as well as the implications of these results for working in a global work environment.

Instructions (Large Class)

1. Working alone, connect the labels with the countries by relying on your perceptions of these countries. Each label is associated with only one country, so each label should be connected to only one country, and vice versa. Draw a line to connect the pairs, or put the label number beside the country name.
2. Asking for a show of hands, the instructor will find out which country is identified by most of your class members with each label. The instructor will then post the correct answers.

Values Labels and Country Names

Values label (alphabetical)	Country name (alphabetical)
Affable humanists	Australia
Ancient modernisers	Brazil
Commercial catalysts	Canada
Conceptual strategists	China
Efficient manufacturers	France
Ethical statesmen	Germany
Informal egalitarians	India
Modernising traditionalists	Netherlands
Optimistic entrepreneurs	New Zealand
Quality perfectionists	Singapore
Rugged individualists	Taiwan
Serving merchants	United Kingdom
Tolerant traders	United States

Source: Based on R. Rosen *et al.*, *Global Literacies* (New York: Simon & Schuster, 2000).

SELF-ASSESSMENT

Skill Builder 2.3

Ethics Dilemmas

Purpose

This exercise is designed to make you aware of the ethical dilemmas people face in various business situations, as well as the competing principles and values that operate in these situations.

Instructions (Small Class)

The instructor will form teams of four or five students. In your team, you will read each case below and discuss the extent to which the company's action in each case was ethical. Teams should be prepared to justify their evaluation using ethics principles and the perceived moral intensity of each incident.

Instructions (Large Class)

Working alone, read each case below and determine the extent to which the company's action in each case was ethical. Your instructor will use a show of hands to determine the extent to which students believe the case represents an ethical dilemma (high or low moral intensity) and the extent to which the main people or company in each incident acted ethically.

Case 1

An employee who worked full-time at a café owned by a large restaurant chain wrote a weblog (blog). In one of his writings, the employee complained that his boss wouldn't let him go home when he felt sick and that his district manager refused to promote him because of his dreadlocks. His blog named the employer, but the employee didn't use his real name. Although all blogs are on the internet, the employee claims that his was low profile and that it didn't show up in a Google search of his name or the company. Still, the employer somehow discovered the blog, figured out the employee's real name and fired him for 'speaking ill-will of the company in a public domain'.

Case 2

Computer printer manufacturers usually sell printers at a low margin over cost, and generate much more income from subsequent sales of the high-margin ink cartridges required for each printer. One global printer manufacturer now designs its printers so that they work only with ink cartridges made in the same region. Ink cartridges purchased in the United States will not work with the same printer model sold in Europe, for example. This 'region coding' of ink cartridges does not improve performance. Rather, it prevents consumers and grey marketers from buying the product at a lower price in another region. The company says this policy allows it to maintain stable prices within a region rather than continually changing prices due to currency fluctuations.

Case 3

For the past few years, the design department of a small (40-employee) company has been using a particular software program, but the three employees who use the software have been complaining for more than a year that the software is out of date and is slowing down their performance. The department agreed to switch to a competing software program, costing several thousand dollars. However, the next version won't be released for six months and buying the current version will not allow much discount on the next version. The company has put in advance orders for the next version. Meanwhile, one employee was able to get a copy of the current version of the software from a friend in the industry. The company has allowed the three employees to use this current version of the software even though they did not pay for it.

Case 4

Judy Ho is a popular talk-show radio personality and opinionated commentator on the morning phone-in show of a radio station. Ms Ho is married to John Ho, a lawyer who was recently elected for the first time to government. He also became minister for the environment in the newly formed government. The radio station's board of directors is very concerned that the station's perceived objectivity will be compromised if Ms Ho remains on air as a commentator and talk-show host while her husband holds such a public position. For example, the managing director believes that Ms Ho recently gave minimal attention to the environment ministry's slow response to concerns about the nation's water quality. Ms Ho denied that her views are biased, and argued that the incident didn't merit as much attention as other issues on that particular day. To ease the board's concerns, the managing director has transferred Ms Ho from her position as talk-show host and commentator to the hourly news reporting position, where most of her scripts are edited by others. Although technically a lower position, Ms Ho's total salary package remains the same. Ms Ho is now seeking professional advice to determine whether the radio station's action represents a form of discrimination on the basis of marital status.

Case 5

A large European bank requires all employees to open a bank account with that bank. The bank deposits employee pay cheques to those accounts. The bank explains that this is a formal policy which all employees agree to at the time of hire. Furthermore, the bank argues that an employee's failure to have an account with the bank shows disloyalty, which could limit career advancement opportunities with the bank. Until recently, the bank has reluctantly agreed to deposit pay cheques to accounts at other banks for a small percentage of employees. Now, bank executives want to reinforce the policy. They announced that employees have three months to open an account with the bank or face disciplinary action.

SELF-ASSESSMENT

Skill Builder 2.4

Are You Introverted or Extroverted?

Purpose

This self-assessment is designed to help you estimate the extent to which you are introverted or extroverted.

Instructions

The statements in the scale below refer to personal characteristics that might or might not be characteristic of you. Mark the box indicating the extent to which the statement accurately or inaccurately describes you. Then use the scoring key in Appendix B at the end of this book to calculate your results. This exercise should be completed alone so that you can assess yourself honestly without concerns of social comparison. Class discussion will focus on the meaning and implications of extroversion and introversion in organisations.

International Personality Item Pool (IPIP) Introversion–Extroversion Scale

	How accurately does each of the statements listed below describe you?	Very accurate description of me	Moderately accurate	Neither accurate nor inaccurate	Moderately inaccurate	Very inaccurate description of me
1.	I feel comfortable around people.	❑	❑	❑	❑	❑
2.	I make friends easily.	❑	❑	❑	❑	❑
3.	I keep in the background.	❑	❑	❑	❑	❑
4.	I don't talk a lot.	❑	❑	❑	❑	❑
5.	I would describe my experiences as somewhat dull.	❑	❑	❑	❑	❑
6.	I know how to captivate people.	❑	❑	❑	❑	❑
7.	I don't like to draw attention to myself.	❑	❑	❑	❑	❑
8.	I am the life of the party.	❑	❑	❑	❑	❑
9.	I am skilled in handling social situations.	❑	❑	❑	❑	❑
10.	I have little to say.	❑	❑	❑	❑	❑

Source: Adapted from instruments described and/or presented in L. R. Goldberg *et al.*, 'The International Personality Item Pool and the Future of Public-Domain Personality Measures', *Journal of Research in Personality* 40 (2006): 84–96.

Skill Builder 2.5

Available online

SELF-ASSESSMENT

What are Your Dominant Values?

Values have taken centre stage in organisational behaviour. Increasingly, OB experts are realising that our personal values influence our motivation, decisions and attitudes. This self-assessment is designed to help you estimate your personal values and value system. The instrument consists of several words and phrases, and you are asked to indicate whether each word or phrase is highly opposite or highly similar to your personal values, or is at some point between these two extremes. As with all self-assessments, you need to be honest with yourself when completing this activity in order to get the most accurate results.

SELF-ASSESSMENT

Individualism-Collectivism Scale

Skill Builder 2.6

Available online

Two of the most important concepts in cross-cultural organisational behaviour are individualism and collectivism. This self-assessment measures your levels of individualism and collectivism with one of the most widely adopted measures. The scale consists of several statements, and you are asked to indicate how well each statement describes you. You need to be honest with yourself to receive a reasonable estimate of your level of individualism and collectivism.

SELF-ASSESSMENT

Estimating Your Locus of Control

Skill Builder 2.7

Available online

This self-assessment is designed to help you estimate the extent to which you have an internal or external locus-of-control personality. The instrument asks you to indicate the degree to which you agree or disagree with each of the statements provided. As with all self-assessments, you need to be honest with yourself when completing this activity to get the most accurate results. The results show your relative position on the internal–external locus continuum and the general meaning of this score.

SELF-ASSESSMENT

Identifying Your General Self-Efficacy

Skill Builder 2.8

Available online

Self-efficacy refers to a person's belief that he or she has the ability, motivation and resources to complete a task successfully. Self-efficacy is usually conceptualised as a situation-specific belief: you may believe that you can perform a certain task in one situation but may be less confident with that task in another situation. However, there is evidence that people develop a more general self-efficacy. This exercise helps you estimate your general self-efficacy. Read each of the statements in this self-assessment and select the response that best fits your personal belief. This self-assessment should be completed alone so that you rate yourself honestly without concerns of social comparison. Class discussion will focus on the meaning and importance of self-efficacy in the workplace.

Endnotes

1 S. Lath, 'Johnson & Johnson: Living by Its Credo', *Business Today (India)*, 5 November 2006, 126–129; V. Reiner, 'A Fit Like a Glove Is Good', *The Australian*, 17 May 2008, 13.

2 L. L. Thurstone, 'Ability, Motivation, and Speed', *Psychometrika* 2, no. 4 (1937): 249–254; N. R. F. Maier, *Psychology in Industry*, 2nd edn (Boston: Houghton Mifflin, 1955); V. H. Vroom, *Work and Motivation* (New York: Wiley, 1964); J. P. Campbell *et al.*, *Managerial Behavior, Performance, and Effectiveness* (New York: McGraw-Hill, 1970).

3 E. E. I. Lawler and L. W. Porter, 'Antecedent Attitudes of Effective Managerial Performance', *Organizational Behavior and Human Performance* 2 (1967): 122–142; M. A. Griffin, A. Neal and S. K. Parker, 'A New Model of Work Role Performance: Positive Behavior in Uncertain and Interdependent Contexts', *Academy of Management Journal* 50, no. 2 (2007): 327–347.

4 Only a few literature reviews have included all four factors. These include J. P. Campbell and R. D. Pritchard, 'Motivation Theory in Industrial and Organizational Psychology', in *Handbook of Industrial and Organizational Psychology*, ed. M. D. Dunnette (Chicago: Rand McNally, 1976), 62–130; T. R. Mitchell, 'Motivation: New Directions for Theory, Research, and Practice', *Academy of Management Review* 7, no. 1 (1982): 80–88; G. A. J. Churchill *et al.*, 'The Determinants of Salesperson Performance: A Meta-Analysis', *Journal of Marketing Research* 22, no. 2 (1985): 103–118; R. E. Plank and D. A. Reid, 'The Mediating Role of Sales Behaviors: An Alternative Perspective of Sales Performance and Effectiveness', *Journal of Personal Selling & Sales Management* 14, no. 3 (1994): 43–56. The *MARS* acronym was coined by senior officers in the Singapore armed forces. Chris Perryer at the University of Western Australia suggests the full model should be called the 'MARS BAR' because the outcomes might be labelled 'behaviour and results'!

5 C. C. Pinder, *Work Motivation in Organizational Behavior* (Upper Saddle River, NJ: Prentice-Hall, 1998); G. P. Latham and C. C. Pinder, 'Work Motivation Theory and Research at the Dawn of the Twenty-First Century', *Annual Review of Psychology* 56 (2005): 485–516.

6 L. M. Spencer and S. M. Spencer, *Competence at Work: Models for Superior Performance* (New York: Wiley, 1993); R. Kurz and D. Bartram, 'Competency and Individual Performance: Modelling the World of Work', in *Organizational Effectiveness: The Role of Psychology*, ed. I. T. Robertson, M. Callinan and D. Bartram (Chichester, UK: Wiley, 2002), 227–258; D. Bartram, 'The Great Eight Competencies: A Criterion-Centric Approach to Validation', *Journal of Applied Psychology* 90, no. 6 (2005): 1185–1203; H. Heinsman *et al.*, 'Competencies through the Eyes of Psychologists: A Closer Look at Assessing Competencies', *International Journal of Selection and Assessment* 15, no. 4 (2007): 412–427.

7 P. Tharenou, A. M. Saks and C. Moore, 'A Review and Critique of Research on Training and Organizational-Level Outcomes', *Human Resource Management Review* 17, no. 3 (2007): 251–273; T. W. H. Ng and D. C. Feldman, 'How Broadly Does Education Contribute to Job Performance?', *Personnel Psychology* 62, no. 1 (2009): 89–134.

8 Canada Newswire, 'Canadian Organizations Must Work Harder to Productively Engage Employees', news release (25 January 2005).

9 H. Cho, 'Super Bowl of Retail Days', *Baltimore Sun*, 23 November 2006; A. Cheng, 'Black Friday Kicks Off Retailers' Biggest Selling Season', *Dow Jones Business News*, 24 November 2007; J. Davis, 'Training Helps Sales Staff Cope with Black Friday', *Rocky Mountain News (Denver)*, 20 November 2007, Bus3. Black Friday is so-called because it apparently marks the first day of the year when many retailers become profitable—i.e. their books go 'in the black'.

10 K. F. Kane, 'Special Issue: Situational Constraints and Work Performance', *Human Resource Management Review* 3 (Summer 1993): 83–175; S. B. Bacharach and P. Bamberger, 'Beyond Situational Constraints: Job Resources Inadequacy and Individual Performance at Work', *Human Resource Management Review* 5, no. 2 (1995): 79–102; G. Johns, 'Commentary: In Praise of Context', *Journal of Organizational Behavior* 22 (2001): 31–42.

11 H. Tatham, 'Conforming or Conscientious?', *New Zealand Management*, May 2008, 60–65.

12 Personality researchers agree on one point about the definition of personality: it is difficult to pin down. A definition necessarily captures one perspective of the topic more than others, and the concept of personality is itself very broad. The definition presented here is based on C. S. Carver and M. F. Scheier, *Perspectives on Personality*, 6th edn (Boston: Allyn & Bacon, 2007); D. C. Funder, *The Personality Puzzle*, 4th edn (New York: W. W. Norton & Company, 2007).

13 D. P. McAdams and J. L. Pals, 'A New Big Five: Fundamental Principles for an Integrative Science of Personality', *American Psychologist* 61, no. 3 (2006): 204–217.

14 B. Reynolds and K. Karraker, 'A Big Five Model of Disposition and Situation Interaction: Why a "Helpful" Person May Not Always Behave Helpfully', *New Ideas*

in Psychology 21, no. 1 (2003): 1–13; W. Mischel, 'Toward an Integrative Science of the Person', *Annual Review of Psychology* 55 (2004): 1–22.

15 B. W. Roberts and A. Caspi, 'Personality Development and the Person-Situation Debate: It's Déjà Vu All over Again', *Psychological Inquiry* 12, no. 2 (2001): 104–109.

16 K. L. Jang, W. J. Livesley and P. A. Vernon, 'Heritability of the Big Five Personality Dimensions and their Facets: A Twin Study', *Journal of Personality* 64, no. 3 (1996): 577–591; N. L. Segal, *Entwined Lives: Twins and What They Tell Us about Human Behavior* (New York: Plume, 2000); T. Bouchard and J. Loehlin, 'Genes, Evolution, and Personality', *Behavior Genetics* 31, no. 3 (2001): 243–273; G. Lensvelt-Mulders and J. Hettema, 'Analysis of Genetic Influences on the Consistency and Variability of the Big Five across Different Stressful Situations', *European Journal of Personality* 15, no. 5 (2001): 355–371; P. Borkenau *et al.*, 'Genetic and Environmental Influences on Person X Situation Profiles', *Journal of Personality* 74, no. 5 (2006): 1451–1480.

17 Segal, *Entwined Lives*, 116–118. For critiques of the genetics perspective of personality, see J. Joseph, 'Separated Twins and the Genetics of Personality Differences: A Critique', *American Journal of Psychology* 114, no. 1 (2001): 1–30; P. Ehrlich and M. W. Feldman, 'Genes, Environments & Behaviors', *Daedalus* 136, no. 2 (2007): 5–12.

18 B. W. Roberts and W. F. DelVecchio, 'The Rank-Order Consistency of Personality Traits from Childhood to Old Age: A Quantitative Review of Longitudinal Studies', *Psychological Bulletin* 126, no. 1 (2000): 3–25; A. Terracciano, P. T. Costa and R. R. McCrae, 'Personality Plasticity after Age 30', *Personality and Social Psychology Bulletin* 32, no. 8 (2006): 999–1009.

19 M. Jurado and M. Rosselli, 'The Elusive Nature of Executive Functions: A Review of Our Current Understanding', *Neuropsychology Review* 17, no. 3 (2007): 213–233.

20 B. W. Roberts and E. M. Pomerantz, 'On Traits, Situations, and Their Integration: A Developmental Perspective', *Personality & Social Psychology Review* 8, no. 4 (2004): 402–416; W. Fleeson, 'Situation-Based Contingencies Underlying Trait-Content Manifestation in Behavior', *Journal of Personality* 75, no. 4 (2007): 825–862.

21 J. M. Digman, 'Personality Structure: Emergence of the Five-Factor Model', *Annual Review of Psychology* 41 (1990): 417–440; O. P. John and S. Srivastava, 'The Big Five Trait Taxonomy: History, Measurement, and Theoretical Perspectives', in *Handbook of Personality: Theory and Research*, ed. L. A. Pervin and O. P. John (New York: Guilford Press, 1999), 102–138; A. Caspi, B. W. Roberts and R. L. Shiner, 'Personality Development: Stability and Change', *Annual Review of Psychology* 56, no. 1 (2005): 453–484; McAdams and Pals, 'A New Big Five: Fundamental Principles for an Integrative Science of Personality'.

22 J. Hogan and B. Holland, 'Using Theory to Evaluate Personality and Job-Performance Relations: A Socioanalytic Perspective', *Journal of Applied Psychology* 88, no. 1 (2003): 100–112; D. S. Ones, C. Viswesvaran and S. Dilchert, 'Personality at Work: Raising Awareness and Correcting Misconceptions', *Human Performance* 18, no. 4 (2005): 389–404.

23 M. R. Barrick and M. K. Mount, 'Yes, Personality Matters: Moving on to More Important Matters', *Human Performance* 18, no. 4 (2005): 359–372.

24 M. R. Barrick, M. K. Mount and T. A. Judge, 'Personality and Performance at the Beginning of the New Millennium: What Do We Know and Where Do We Go Next?', *International Journal of Selection and Assessment* 9, no. 1/2 (2001): 9–30; T. A. Judge and R. Ilies, 'Relationship of Personality to Performance Motivation: A Meta-Analytic Review', *Journal of Applied Psychology* 87, no. 4 (2002): 797–807; A. Witt, L. A. Burke and M. R. Barrick, 'The Interactive Effects of Conscientiousness and Agreeableness on Job Performance', *Journal of Applied Psychology* 87, no. 1 (2002): 164–169; J. Moutafi, A. Furnham and J. Crump, 'Is Managerial Level Related to Personality?', *British Journal of Management* 18, no. 3 (2007): 272–280.

25 K. M. DeNeve and H. Cooper, 'The Happy Personality: A Meta-Analysis of 137 Personality Traits and Subjective Well-Being', *Psychological Bulletin* 124, no. 2 (1998): 197–229; R. Ilies, M. W. Gerhardt and H. Le, 'Individual Differences in Leadership Emergence: Integrating Meta-Analytic Findings and Behavioral Genetics Estimates', *International Journal of Selection and Assessment* 12, no. 3 (2004): 207–219; B. Kozak, J. Strelau and J. N. V. Miles, 'Genetic Determinants of Individual Differences in Coping Styles', *Anxiety, Stress & Coping* 18, no. 1 (2005): 1–15.

26 D. M. Musson *et al.*, 'Personality Testing in Antarctic Expeditioners; Cross Cultural Comparisons and Evidence for Generalizability', paper presented at 53rd International Astronautical Congress, The World Space Congress, Houston, 10–19 October 2002; D. M. Musson and R. L. Helmreich, 'Personality Determinants of Professional Culture in Astronauts and Analogue Populations', paper presented at Bioastronautics Investigators' Workshop, Behavioral Health and Performance Poster Session, Galveston, Texas, 10–12 January 2005; A. Sarris, 'Personality, Culture Fit, and Job Outcomes on Australian Antarctic Stations', *Environment and Behavior* 38, no. 3 (2006): 356–372.

27 C. G. Jung, *Psychological Types*, trans. H. G. Baynes (Princeton, NJ: Princeton University Press, 1971); I. B. Myers, *The Myers-Briggs Type Indicator* (Palo Alto, CA: Consulting Psychologists Press, 1987).

28 M. Gladwell, 'Personality Plus', *New Yorker*, 20 September 2004, 42–48; R. B. Kennedy and D. A. Kennedy, 'Using the Myers-Briggs Type Indicator in Career Counseling', *Journal of Employment Counseling* 41, no. 1 (March 2004): 38–44.

29 *CanTeen National Magazine*, Winter 2007, 7, 12; K. M. Butler, 'Using Positive Four-Letter Words', *Employee Benefit News*, April 2007; R. Abdullah, 'Companies Apply Various Methods to Develop Leaders', *Jakarta Post*, 6 August 2008, 16; M. Weinstein, 'Personality Assessment Soars at Southwest', *Training*, 3 January 2008.

30 W. L. Johnson *et al.*, 'A Higher Order Analysis of the Factor Structure of the Myers-Briggs Type Indicator', *Measurement and Evaluation in Counseling and Development* 34 (July 2001): 96–108; R. M. Capraro and M. M. Capraro, 'Myers-Briggs Type Indicator Score Reliability across Studies: A Meta-Analytic Reliability Generalization Study', *Educational and Psychological Measurement* 62, no. 4 (2002): 590–602; J. Michael, 'Using the Myers-Briggs Type Indicator as a Tool for Leadership Development? Apply with Caution', *Journal of Leadership & Organizational Studies* 10, no. 1 (2003): 68–81.

31 R. R. McCrae and P. T. Costa, 'Reinterpreting the Myers-Briggs Type Indicators From the Perspective of the Five-Factor Model of Personality', *Journal of Personality* 57 (1989): 17–40; A. Furnham, 'The Big Five Versus the Big Four: The Relationship between the Myers-Briggs Type Indicator (MBTI) and NEO-PI Five Factor Model of Personality', *Personality and Individual Differences* 21, no. 2 (1996): 303–307.

32 R. Hogan, 'In Defense of Personality Measurement: New Wine for Old Whiners', *Human Performance* 18, no. 4 (2005): 331–334; K. Murphy and J. L. Dzieweczynski, 'Why Don't Measures of Broad Dimensions of Personality Perform Better as Predictors of Job Performance?', *Human Performance* 18, no. 4 (2005): 343–357; F. P. Morgeson *et al.*, 'Reconsidering the Use of Personality Tests in Personnel Selection Contexts', *Personnel Psychology* 60, no. 3 (2007): 683–729; R. P. Tett and N. D. Christiansen, 'Personality Tests at the Crossroads: A Response to Morgeson, Campion, Dipboye, Hollenbeck, Murphy, and Schmitt (2007)', *Personnel Psychology* 60, no. 4 (2007): 967–993.

33 V. Baker, 'Why Men Can't Manage Women', *The Guardian*, 14 April 2007, 1.

34 J. D. Campbell, S. Assanand and A. Di Paula, 'The Structure of the Self-Concept and Its Relation to Psychological Adjustment', *Journal of Personality* 71, no. 1 (2003): 115–140; M. J. Constantino *et al.*, 'The Direct and Stress-Buffering Effects of Self-Organization on Psychological Adjustment', *Journal of Social and Clinical Psychology* 25, no. 3 (2006): 333–360.

35 C. Sedikides and A. P. Gregg, 'Portraits of the Self', in *The Sage Handbook of Social Psychology*, ed. M. A. Hogg and J. Cooper (London: Sage Publications, 2003), 110–138; M. R. Leary, 'Motivational and Emotional Aspects of the Self', *Annual Review of Psychology* 58, no. 1 (2007): 317–344.

36 D. A. Moore, 'Not So above Average after All: When People Believe They Are Worse Than Average and Its Implications for Theories of Bias in Social Comparison', *Organizational Behavior and Human Decision Processes* 102, no. 1 (2007): 42–58.

37 D. A. Moore and P. J. Healy, 'The Trouble with Overconfidence', *Psychological Review* 115, no. 2 (2008): 502–517.

38 N. J. Hiller and D. C. Hambrick, 'Conceptualizing Executive Hubris: The Role of (Hyper-)Core Self-Evaluations in Strategic Decision-Making', *Strategic Management Journal* 26, no. 4 (2005): 297–319; U. Malmendier and G. Tate, 'CEO Overconfidence and Corporate Investment', *The Journal of Finance* 60, no. 6 (2005): 2661–2700; J. A. Doukas and D. Petmezas, 'Acquisitions, Overconfident Managers and Self-Attribution Bias', *European Financial Management* 13, no. 3 (2007): 531–577.

39 R. Langlois, 'Fairmont Hotels: Business Strategy Starts with People', *Canadian HR Reporter*, 5 November 2001, 19; T. McPherson, 'A Winning Time on the Mac Team', *The Advertiser (Adelaide)*, 3 December 2005, E03; M. T. Bitti, 'Rewards of Hard Work', *National Post (Canada)*, 17 October 2007, WK2; H. Budd, 'Workin' Nine to Five, It's So Nice to Feel Appreciated', *Daily Telegraph (Sydney)*, 20 September 2008, 1.

40 W. B. Swann Jr, 'To Be Adored or to Be Known? The Interplay of Self-Enhancement and Self-Verification', in *Handbook of Motivation and Cognition: Foundations of Social Behavior*, vol. 2, ed. R. M. Sorrentino and E. T. Higgins (New York: Guilford, 1990), 408–448; W. B. Swann Jr, P. J. Rentfrow and J. S. Guinn, 'Self-Verification: The Search for Coherence', in *Handbook of Self and Identity*, ed. M. R. Leary and J. Tagney (New York: Guilford, 2002), 367–383.

41 Leary, 'Motivational and Emotional Aspects of the Self'.

42 T. A. Judge and J. E. Bono, 'Relationship of Core Self-Evaluations Traits—Self-Esteem, Generalized Self-Efficacy, Locus of Control, and Emotional Stability—with Job Satisfaction and Job Performance: A Meta-Analysis', *Journal of Applied Psychology* 86, no. 1 (2001): 80–92; T. A. Judge and C. Hurst, 'Capitalizing on One's Advantages: Role of Core Self-Evaluations', *Journal of Applied Psychology* 92, no. 5 (2007): 1212–1227. We have described the three most commonly noted components of self-evaluation. The full model also includes emotional stability (low neuroticism). However, the core self-evaluation model has received limited research and its

dimensions are being debated. For example, see R. E. Johnson, C. C. Rosen and P. E. Levy, 'Getting to the Core of Core Self-Evaluation: A Review and Recommendations', *Journal of Organizational Behavior* 29 (2008): 391–413.

43 W. B. Swann Jr, C. Chang-Schneider and K. L. McClarty, 'Do People's Self-Views Matter?: Self-Concept and Self-Esteem in Everyday Life', *American Psychologist* 62, no. 2 (2007): 84–94.

44 A. Bandura, *Self-Efficacy: The Exercise of Control* (New York: W. H. Freeman, 1997).

45 G. Chen, S. M. Gully and D. Eden, 'Validation of a New General Self-Efficacy Scale', *Organizational Research Methods* 4, no. 1 (2001): 62–83.

46 P. E. Spector, 'Behavior in Organizations as a Function of Employees' Locus of Control', *Psychological Bulletin* 91, no. 3 (1982): 482–497; K. Hattrup, M. S. O'Connell and J. R. Labrador, 'Incremental Validity of Locus of Control after Controlling for Cognitive Ability and Conscientiousness', *Journal of Business and Psychology* 19, no. 4 (2005): 461–481; T. W. H. Ng, K. L. Sorensen and L. T. Eby, 'Locus of Control at Work: A Meta-Analysis', *Journal of Organizational Behavior* 27 (2006): 1057–1087.

47 H. Tajfel, *Social Identity and Intergroup Relations* (Cambridge, UK: Cambridge University Press, 1982); B. E. Ashforth and F. Mael, 'Social Identity Theory and the Organization', *Academy of Management Review* 14 (1989): 20–39; M. A. Hogg and D. J. Terry, 'Social Identity and Self-Categorization Processes in Organizational Contexts', *Academy of Management Review* 25 (January 2000): 121–140; S. A. Haslam, R. A. Eggins and K. J. Reynolds, 'The ASPIRe Model: Actualizing Social and Personal Identity Resources to Enhance Organizational Outcomes', *Journal of Occupational and Organizational Psychology* 76, no. 1 (2003): 83–113.

48 Sedikides and Gregg, 'Portraits of the Self'. The history of the social self in human beings is described in M. R. Leary and N. R. Buttermore, 'The Evolution of the Human Self: Tracing the Natural History of Self-Awareness', *Journal for the Theory of Social Behaviour* 33, no. 4 (2003): 365–404.

49 M. R. Edwards, 'Organizational Identification: A Conceptual and Operational Review', *International Journal of Management Reviews* 7, no. 4 (2005): 207–230; D. A. Whetten, 'Albert and Whetten Revisited: Strengthening the Concept of Organizational Identity', *Journal of Management Inquiry* 15, no. 3 (September 2006): 219–234.

50 B. M. Meglino and E. C. Ravlin, 'Individual Values in Organizations: Concepts, Controversies, and Research', *Journal of Management* 24, no. 3 (1998): 351–389; B. R. Agle and C. B. Caldwell, 'Understanding Research on Values in Business', *Business and Society* 38, no. 3 (1999): 326–387; S. Hitlin and J. A. Pilavin, 'Values: Reviving a Dormant Concept', *Annual Review of Sociology* 30 (2004): 359–393.

51 D. Lubinski, D. B. Schmidt and C. P. Benbow, 'A 20-Year Stability Analysis of the Study of Values for Intellectually Gifted Individuals from Adolescence to Adulthood', *Journal of Applied Psychology* 81, no. 4 (1996): 443–451.

52 Hitlin and Pilavin, 'Values: Reviving a Dormant Concept'; A. Pakizeh, J. E. Gebauer and G. R. Maio, 'Basic Human Values: Inter-Value Structure in Memory', *Journal of Experimental Social Psychology* 43, no. 3 (2007): 458–465.

53 S. H. Schwartz, 'Universals in the Content and Structure of Values: Theoretical Advances and Empirical Tests in 20 Countries', *Advances in Experimental Social Psychology* 25 (1992): 1–65; S. H. Schwartz, 'Are There Universal Aspects in the Structure and Contents of Human Values?', *Journal of Social Issues* 50, no. 4 (1994): 19–45; D. Spini, 'Measurement Equivalence of 10 Value Types from the Schwartz Value Survey across 21 Countries', *Journal of Cross-Cultural Psychology* 34, no. 1 (2003): 3–23; S. H. Schwartz and K. Boehnke, 'Evaluating the Structure of Human Values with Confirmatory Factor Analysis', *Journal of Research in Personality* 38, no. 3 (2004): 230–255.

54 G. R. Maio and J. M. Olson, 'Values as Truisms: Evidence and Implications', *Journal of Personality and Social Psychology* 74, no. 2 (1998): 294–311; G. R. Maio *et al.*, 'Addressing Discrepancies between Values and Behavior: The Motivating Effect of Reasons', *Journal of Experimental Social Psychology* 37, no. 2 (2001): 104–117; B. Verplanken and R. W. Holland, 'Motivated Decision Making: Effects of Activation and Self-Centrality of Values on Choices and Behavior', *Journal of Personality and Social Psychology* 82, no. 3 (2002): 434–447; A. Bardi and S. H. Schwartz, 'Values and Behavior: Strength and Structure of Relations', *Personality and Social Psychology Bulletin* 29, no. 10 (2003): 1207–1220; M. M. Bernard and G. R. Maio, 'Effects of Introspection about Reasons for Values: Extending Research on Values-as-Truisms', *Social Cognition* 21, no. 1 (2003): 1–25.

55 N. Mazar, O. Amir and D. Ariely, 'The Dishonesty of Honest People: A Theory of Self-Concept Maintenance', *Journal of Marketing Research* 45 (December 2008): 633–644.

56 K. Hornyak, 'Upward Move: Cynthia Schwalm', *Medical Marketing & Media*, June 2008, 69. For research on the consequences on value congruence, see A. L. Kristof, 'Person-Organization Fit: An Integrative Review of Its Conceptualizations, Measurement, and Implications', *Personnel Psychology* 49, no. 1 (1996): 1–49; M. L. Verquer, T. A. Beehr and S. H. Wagner, 'A Meta-Analysis of Relations between Person-Organization Fit and Work Attitudes', *Journal of Vocational Behavior* 63 (2003): 473–489; J. W. Westerman and L. A. Cyr, 'An Integrative Analysis of Person-Organization Fit Theories', *International*

Journal of Selection and Assessment 12, no. 3 (2004): 252–261; D. Bouckenooghe *et al.*, 'The Prediction of Stress by Values and Value Conflict', *Journal of Psychology* 139, no. 4 (2005): 369–382.

57 T. Simons, 'Behavioral Integrity: The Perceived Alignment between Managers' Words and Deeds as a Research Focus', *Organization Science* 13, no. 1 (2002): 18–35; Watson Wyatt, 'Employee Ratings of Senior Management Dip, Watson Wyatt Survey Finds', news release (New York, 4 January 2007).

58 T. A. Joiner, 'The Influence of National Culture and Organizational Culture Alignment on Job Stress and Performance: Evidence from Greece', *Journal of Managerial Psychology* 16 (2001): 229–242; Z. Aycan, R. N. Kanungo and J. B. P. Sinha, 'Organizational Culture and Human Resource Management Practices: The Model of Culture Fit', *Journal of Cross-Cultural Psychology* 30 (July 1999): 501–526.

59 C. Fox, 'Firms Go Warm and Fuzzy to Lure Staff', *Australian Financial Review*, 15 May 2001, 58.

60 V. Galt, 'A World of Opportunity for Those in Mid-Career', *Globe & Mail* (Toronto), 7 June 2006, C1.

61 L. Gettler, 'The New Global Manager Needs to Understand Different Work Cultures', *The Age*, 6 February 2008, 12.

62 D. Oyserman, H. M. Coon and M. Kemmelmeier, 'Rethinking Individualism and Collectivism: Evaluation of Theoretical Assumptions and Meta-Analyses', *Psychological Bulletin* 128, no. 1 (2002): 3–72; C. P. Earley and C. B. Gibson, 'Taking Stock in Our Progress on Individualism-Collectivism: 100 Years of Solidarity and Community', *Journal of Management* 24 (May 1998): 265–304; F. S. Niles, 'Individualism-Collectivism Revisited', *Cross-Cultural Research* 32 (November 1998): 315–341.

63 Oyserman, Coon and Kemmelmeier, 'Rethinking Individualism and Collectivism: Evaluation of Theoretical Assumptions and Meta-Analyses'. Also see F. Li and L. Aksoy, 'Dimensionality of Individualism–Collectivism and Measurement Equivalence of Triandis and Gelfand's Scale', *Journal of Business and Psychology* 21, no. 3 (2007): 313–329. The relationship between individualism and collectivism is still being debated, but most experts now agree that there are problems with the conceptualisation and measurement of individualism and collectivism.

64 H. Trinca, 'It's about Soul but Don't Get Too Soft', *Australian Financial Review*, 12 August 2005, 56.

65 G. Hofstede, *Culture's Consequences: Comparing Values, Behaviors, Institutions, and Organizations across Nations*, 2nd edn (Thousand Oaks, CA: Sage, 2001).

66 Hofstede, *Culture's Consequences*. Hofstede used the terms *masculinity* and *femininity* for *achievement* and *nurturing orientation*, respectively. We (along with other writers) have adopted the latter two terms to minimise the sexist perspective of these concepts.

67 M. Voronov and J. A. Singer, 'The Myth of Individualism-Collectivism: A Critical Review', *Journal of Social Psychology* 142 (August 2002): 461–480; N. Jacob, 'Cross-Cultural Investigations: Emerging Concepts', *Journal of Organizational Change Management* 18, no. 5 (2005): 514–528.

68 W. K. W. Choy, A. B. E. Lee and P. Ramburuth, 'Multinationalism in the Workplace: A Myriad of Values in a Singaporean Firm', *Singapore Management Review* 31, no. 1 (2009).

69 J. S. Osland *et al.*, 'Beyond Sophisticated Stereotyping: Cultural Sensemaking in Context', *Academy of Management Executive* 14 (February 2000): 65–79; S. S. Sarwono and R. W. Armstrong, 'Microcultural Differences and Perceived Ethical Problems: An International Business Perspective', *Journal of Business Ethics* 30, no. 1 (2001): 41–56.

70 C. Savoye, 'Workers Say Honesty Is Best Company Policy', *Christian Science Monitor*, 15 June 2000; J. M. Kouzes and B. Z. Posner, *The Leadership Challenge*, 3rd edn (San Francisco: Jossey-Bass, 2002); J. Schettler, 'Leadership in Corporate America', *Training & Development*, September 2002, 66–73; SEEK Ltd, 'Healthcare Workers Sick of Stress', news release (Melbourne, 18 February 2009).

71 Transparency International, *Transparency International Corruption Perceptions Index 2008* (Berlin: Transparency International, October 2008).

72 S. Tedmanson, 'BA and Qantas Fined Millions for Price-Fixing', *The Times* (London), 28 October 2008; L. Wood, 'How a Cartel's Wheels Fell Off', *The Age* (Melbourne), 13 September 2008, 1; C. Harris, 'Lessons Learnt from Bridgecorp', *Dominion Post* (Wellington, NZ), 31 January 2009, 1; D. Marr, 'Calling the Shots', *Sydney Morning Herald*, 7 March 2009, 1.

73 P. L. Schumann, 'A Moral Principles Framework for Human Resource Management Ethics', *Human Resource Management Review* 11 (Spring/Summer 2001): 93–111; J. Boss, *Analyzing Moral Issues*, 3rd edn (New York: McGraw-Hill, 2005), ch. 1; M. G. Velasquez, *Business Ethics: Concepts and Cases*, 6th edn (Upper Saddle River, NJ: Prentice Hall, 2006), ch. 2.

74 T. J. Jones, 'Ethical Decision Making by Individuals in Organizations: An Issue Contingent Model', *Academy of Management Review* 16 (1991): 366–395; B. H. Frey, 'The Impact of Moral Intensity on Decision Making in a Business Context', *Journal of Business Ethics* 26, no. 3 (2000): 181–195; D. R. May and K. P. Pauli, 'The Role of Moral Intensity in Ethical Decision Making', *Business and Society* 41 (March 2002): 84–117.

75 J. R. Sparks and S. D. Hunt, 'Marketing Researcher Ethical Sensitivity: Conceptualization, Measurement, and Exploratory Investigation', *Journal of Marketing* 62 (April 1998): 92–109.

76 K. F. Alam, 'Business Ethics in New Zealand Organizations: Views from the Middle and Lower Level Managers', *Journal of Business Ethics* 22, no. 2 (1999): 145–153; Human Resource Institute, *The Ethical Enterprise: State-of-the-Art* (St. Petersburg, FL: Human Resource Institute, January 2006).

77 B. Farrell, D. M. Cobbin and H. M. Farrell, 'Codes of Ethics: Their Evolution, Development and Other Controversies', *Journal of Management Development* 21, no. 2 (2002): 152–163; G. Wood and M. Rimmer, 'Codes of Ethics: What Are They Really and What Should They Be?', *International Journal of Value-Based Management* 16, no. 2 (2003): 181.

78 S. Greengard, 'Golden Values', *Workforce Management*, March 2005, 52–53; K. Tyler, 'Do the Right Thing', *HRMagazine*, February 2005, 99–102.

79 T. F. Lindeman, 'A Matter of Choice', *Pittsburgh Post-Gazette*, 30 March 2004; AECOM Technology Corporation, *AECOM Code of Conduct* (Los Angeles: AECOM, May 2005).

80 K. Whitney, 'Ernst & Young Ethics Training: Part of the Company Fabric', *Chief Learning Officer*, July 2007, 32.

81 E. Aronson, 'Integrating Leadership Styles and Ethical Perspectives', *Canadian Journal of Administrative Sciences* 18 (December 2001): 266–276; D. R. May *et al.*, 'Developing the Moral Component of Authentic Leadership', *Organizational Dynamics* 32 (2003): 247–260. The Vodafone director quotation is from R. Van Lee, L. Fabish and N. McGaw, 'The Value of Corporate Values', *strategy+business*, 23 May 2005, 1–13.

CHAPTER 3

perception and learning in organisations

LEARNING OBJECTIVES

After reading this chapter, you should be able to:

- outline the perceptual process
- explain how social identity and stereotyping influence the perceptual process
- describe the attribution process and two attribution errors
- summarise the self-fulfilling-prophecy process
- explain how halo, primacy, recency and false-consensus effects bias our perceptions
- discuss three ways to improve social perception, with specific application to organisational situations
- describe the A-B-C model of behaviour modification and the four contingencies of reinforcement
- describe the three features of social learning theory
- outline the elements of organisational learning and ways to improve each element.

Tanzania is a long way from Wellington, New Zealand, but even this reality didn't prepare Mike Goddard for his month-long working visit to the African country. The Wellington-based IBM information technology architect was teamed up with a dozen other IBM-ers from Italy, Japan and other countries to assist local Tanzanian projects, such as more effectively distributing pumps to farmers. Goddard welcomed the opportunity to 'experience a new culture, meet new people and be exposed to different ways of thinking.'

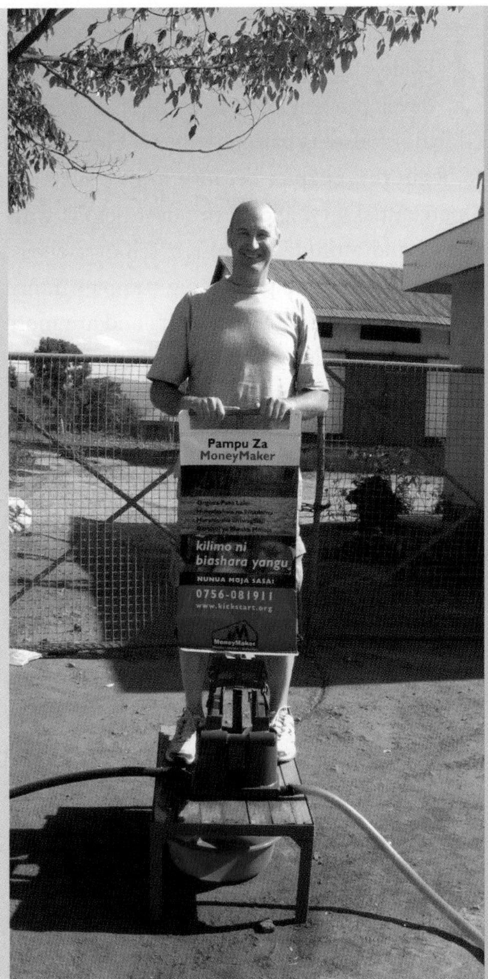

Courtesy IBM

Mike Goddard and other employees at IBM are developing their empathy, cultural sensitivity and cosmopolitan perceptions of the world by working on community development projects in Tanzania and other developing nations.

But Goddard underestimated the extent to which the trip would improve his perceptions of himself and others. First, he quickly learned that his usual way of getting the job done wouldn't work in Tanzania. 'We came in with these expectations of what we'd achieve if we were at home,' admits Goddard, referring particularly to extremely slow and intermittent internet services. 'We take it for granted, but in Tanzania you can't get to it. We had to think of other ways of working.' Goddard also discovered how often people interpret conversations differently. 'Just hearing what the client was saying within the room, I'd interpret it one way, Sara [another IBM team member] from Italy would interpret it another way.'

Goddard's third epiphany from the trip to Tanzanian was that he and other Westerners focus too much on the work rather than the relationship. 'Perhaps we do charge around too much and lose sight; the task becomes more important than the person,' he suggests. 'Over there [in Tanzania] it's very much the person, and the interaction with the people is still more important than the job.' Goddard explains that 'rushing into a meeting—"Hi I want to know this, let's go, bang"—is very offensive' in Tanzania.

If Mike Goddard's experience in Tanzania is any gauge, IBM's practice of sending employees to developing countries is having the intended effect—to develop their perceptual capabilities and global mindset. IBM CEO Sam Palmisano explains that participants 'work in these other kinds of environments, so they can get a perspective and learn ... how to think about problems from another perspective, from another point of view.' Ernst & Young has a similar program with a similar purpose. 'We need people with a global mindset, and what better way to develop a global mindset, and what more realistic way, than for somebody to have an immersion experience with just enough safety net,' says Deborah K. Holmes, an Ernst & Young executive responsible for corporate responsibility.[1]

global mindset The capacity for complex perceiving and thinking characterised by superior awareness of and openness to different ways that others perceive their environment.

International corporate volunteering programs have become a key component of global leadership development because they nurture a **global mindset**.[2] They help employees develop a superior awareness of and openness to different cultures and environments. Global mindset is gaining interest among organisational behaviour experts and is a fitting topic to begin this chapter because it encompasses the dynamics of perceptions and learning. From a perceptual view, global mindset begins with self-awareness—understanding our own beliefs, values and attitudes. Through self-awareness, we are more open-minded and nonjudgmental when receiving and processing complex information. A global mindset also occurs when people have better perceptions of others and are more open to different points of view. From a learning perspective, a global mindset occurs when people are able to quickly absorb large volumes of information in diverse environments. Furthermore, people with a global mindset have a strong learning orientation. They welcome new situations as learning opportunities rather than view them as threats, and they continually question rather than quickly confirm what they know.

This chapter describes these two related topics of perceptions and learning in organisations. We begin by describing the perceptual process, that is, the dynamics of selecting, organising and interpreting external stimuli. Next, we examine the perceptual processes of social identity and stereotyping, attribution and self-fulfilling prophecy, including biases created within these processes. Four other perceptual biases—halo, primacy, recency and false consensus—are also briefly introduced. We then identify potentially effective ways to improve perceptions, including practices similar to corporate volunteering. The latter part of this chapter looks at three perspectives of learning: behaviour modification, social learning theory and experiential learning, followed by the key elements in organisational learning.

LEARNING OBJECTIVE

Outline the perceptual process.

THE PERCEPTUAL PROCESS

perception The process of receiving information about and making sense of the world around us.

Perception is the process of receiving information about and making sense of the world around us. It entails determining which information to notice, how to categorise this information and how to interpret it within the framework of our existing knowledge. This perceptual process is far from perfect, as you will learn in this chapter, but it generally follows the steps shown in Exhibit 3.1.

Selective Attention

Perception begins when environmental stimuli are received through our senses. Most stimuli that bombard our senses are screened out; the rest are organised and interpreted. The process of attending to some information received by our senses and ignoring other information is called **selective attention**. Selective attention is influenced by characteristics of the person or object being perceived, particularly size, intensity, motion, repetition and novelty. For example, a small, flashing red light on a nurse station console is immediately noticed because it is bright (intensity), flashing (motion), a rare event (novelty) and has symbolic meaning (i.e. that a patient's vital signs are failing). Notice that selective attention is also influenced by the context in which the target is perceived. The selective attention process is triggered by things or people who might be out of context, such as hearing someone with a foreign accent in a setting where most people have Australian accents.

selective attention The process of attending to some information received by our senses and ignoring other information.

Characteristics of the perceiver play an important role in selective attention, much of it without the perceiver's awareness.[3] When information is received through the senses, our brain quickly and nonconsciously assesses whether it is relevant or irrelevant to us and then attaches emotional

Exhibit 3.1 *Model of the Perceptual Process*

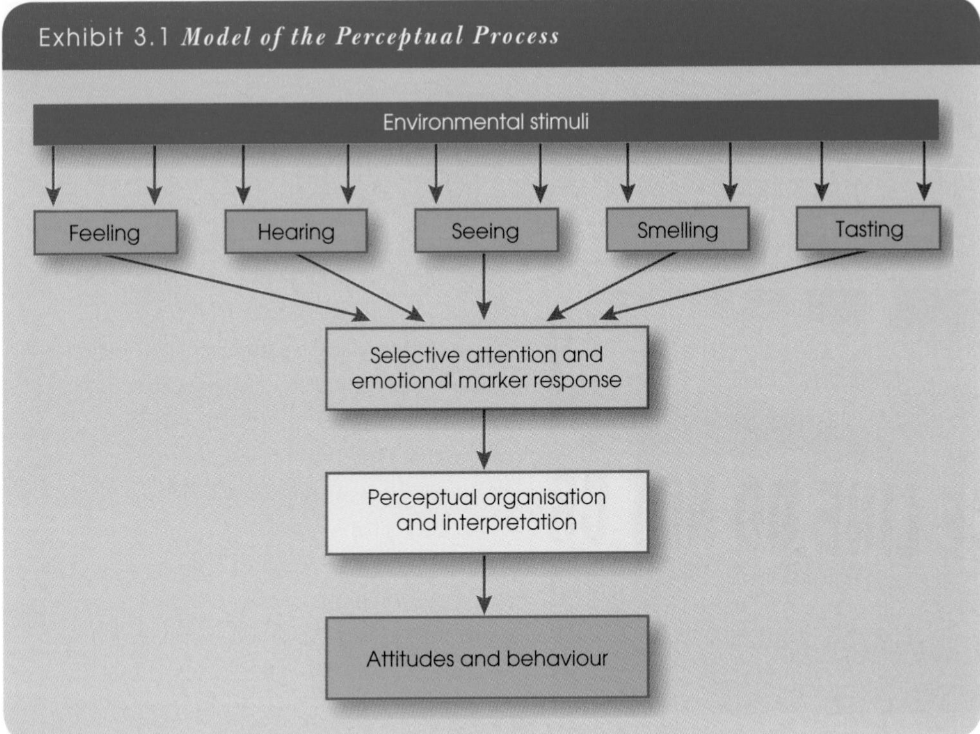

markers (e.g. worry, happiness, boredom) to that information. The emotional markers help us to store information in memory; they also reproduce the same emotions when we are subsequently thinking about this information.[4]

The selective attention process is far from perfect. As mentioned in Chapter 2, we have a natural tendency to seek out information that supports our self-concept or puts us in a favourable light, and to ignore or undervalue information that is contrary to our self-concept. This *confirmation bias* also screens out information that is contrary to our values and assumptions.[5] Several studies have found that people fail to perceive (or soon forget) statements and events that undermine the political parties they support. One Australian study examined how people perceived and accepted stories during the first weeks of the Iraq War that were subsequently retracted (acknowledged by the media as false stories). The investigation found that most of the Germans and Australians surveyed dismissed the retracted events, whereas a significantly large percentage of Americans continued to believe these false stories, even though many of them recalled that the stories had been retracted by the media. In essence, people in the American sample were reluctant to reject and forget about information that supported their beliefs about the Iraq War.[6]

Finally, selective attention is influenced by our assumptions and conscious anticipation of future events. You are more likely to notice a coworker's email among the daily bombardment of messages when you expect to receive that email (particularly when it is important to you). Unfortunately, expectations and assumptions also cause us to screen out potentially important information. In one study, students were asked to watch a 30-second video clip in which several people passed around two basketballs. Students who were asked just to watch the video clip easily noticed someone dressed in a gorilla suit walking among the players for 9 seconds and stopping to thump its chest. But only half of the students who were asked to carefully count the number of times one basketball was passed around noticed the intruding gorilla.[7]

Detectives Avoid Tunnel Vision

Successful detectives don't test their theories about a crime. Instead, they *avoid* forming any theories too early in the investigation. 'We're very careful to let the evidence drive the investigation, not theories,' explains US Federal Bureau of Investigation (FBI) special agent Mark MacKizer when discussing the case of a family murdered in Virginia. 'All the investigators on this case are cognisant of not having tunnel vision.' Similarly, when four prostitutes were murdered in just three days in Hong Kong, Senior Superintendent Steve Li Wing-Hong said: 'We are keeping an open mind and looking into all possible clues.' Researchers have found that wrongful convictions often occur because investigators form theories and filter evidence around those theories. 'At times investigators may close their minds to other possibilities once they've developed a theory,' explains Vernon Geberth, retired lieutenant commander of the New York City police department's homicide division. 'Then they begin to try to make the evidence fit their theory instead of allowing the evidence to lead you to the suspect.'[9]

Shutterstock

This perceptual blindness also occurs when we form an opinion or theory about something, such as a consumer trend or an employee's potential. The preconception causes us to select information that is consistent with the theory and to ignore contrary or seemingly irrelevant information. Studies have reported that this faulty selective attention occurs when police detectives and other forensic experts quickly form theories about what happened in a particular case.[8] These experts are now increasingly aware of the need to avoid selective attention traps by keeping an open mind, absorbing as much information as possible and avoiding theories too early in the investigation.

Perceptual Organisation and Interpretation

categorical thinking Organising people and objects into preconceived categories that are stored in our long-term memory.

People make sense of information even before they become aware of it. This sense making partly includes **categorical thinking**—the mostly nonconscious process of organising people and objects into preconceived categories that are stored in our long-term memory.[10] Categorical thinking relies on a variety of automatic perceptual grouping principles. Things are often grouped together on the basis of their similarity or proximity to others. If you notice that a group of similar-looking people includes several professors, for instance, you will likely assume that others in group are also professors. Another form of perceptual grouping is based on the need for cognitive closure, such as filling in missing information about what happened at a meeting that you didn't attend (e.g. who was there, where it was held). A third form of grouping occurs when we think we see trends in otherwise ambiguous information. Several studies have found that people have a natural tendency to see patterns that really are random events, such as presumed winning streaks among sports stars or in gambling.[11]

The process of 'making sense' of the world around us also involves interpreting incoming information. This occurs as quickly as selection and organisation because the previously mentioned emotional markers are tagged to incoming stimuli, which are essentially quick judgments about whether that information is good or bad for us. To give you an idea of how quickly and systematically this nonconscious perceptual interpretation process occurs, consider the following study.[12] After viewing video clips of university instructors teaching an undergraduate class, eight observers rated the instructors on several personal characteristics (optimism, likeability, anxiety, activeness and so on). The observers, who had never seen the instructors before, were similar to each other in their ratings of the instructors, even though they completed their ratings alone. Equally important, these ratings were very similar to the ratings completed by students who attended the actual class.

These results may be interesting, but they become extraordinary when you realise that the observers formed their perceptions from as little as *six seconds* of video—three segments of two seconds each selected randomly from the one-hour class! Furthermore, the video didn't have any sound. In other words, people form similar perceptions and judgments on the basis of very thin slices of information. Other studies have reported similar findings for observations of high school teachers, courtroom judges and medical practitioners. Collectively, these 'thin slice' studies reveal that selective attention, as well as perceptual organisation and interpretation, operates very quickly and, to a large extent, without our awareness.

Mental Models

To achieve our goals with some degree of predictability and sanity, we need road maps of the environments in which we live. These road maps, called **mental models**, are internal representations of the external world.[13] They consist of visual or relational images in our mind, such as what the classroom looks like or, conceptually, what happens when we submit an assignment late. We rely on mental models to make sense of our environment through perceptual grouping; the models fill in the missing pieces, including the causal connection among events. For example, you have a mental model about attending a class lecture or seminar, including assumptions or expectations about where the instructor and students seat themselves in the room, how they ask and answer questions, and so forth. We can create a mental image of a class in progress.

mental models Visual or relational images in our mind that represent the external world.

Mental models play an important role in sense making, yet they also make it difficult to see the world in different ways. For example, accounting professionals tend to see corporate problems in terms of accounting solutions, whereas marketing professionals see the same problems from a marketing perspective. Mental models also block our recognition of new opportunities. How do we change mental models? That's a tough challenge. After all, we developed models from several years of experience and reinforcement. The most important way to minimise the perceptual problems with mental models is to constantly question them. We need to ask ourselves about the assumptions we make. Working with people from diverse backgrounds is another way to break out of existing mental models. Colleagues from different cultures and areas of expertise tend to have different mental models, so working with them makes our own assumptions more obvious.

SOCIAL IDENTITY AND STEREOTYPING

LEARNING OBJECTIVE 

Explain how social identity and stereotyping influence the perceptual process.

In the previous chapter, you learned that social identity is an important component of a person's self-concept. We define ourselves to a large extent by the groups to which we belong or have an emotional attachment. Along with shaping our self-concept, social identity theory explains the dynamics of *social perception*—how we perceive others.[14] Social perception is influenced by three activities in the process of forming and maintaining our social identity: categorisation, homogenisation and differentiation.

CATEGORISATION Social identity is a comparative process, and the comparison begins by categorising people into distinct groups. By viewing someone (including yourself) as an Australian, for example, you remove that person's individuality and, instead, see them as a prototypical representative of the group 'Australians'. This categorisation then allows you to distinguish Australians from people who live in New Zealand, Hong Kong and other countries in this region.

HOMOGENISATION To simplify the comparison process, we tend to think that people within each group are very similar to each other. For instance, we think Australians collectively have similar attitudes and characteristics, whereas, say, Malaysians collectively have their own set of characteristics. Of course, every individual is unique, but we tend to lose sight of this fact when thinking about our social identity and how we compare to people in other social groups.

DIFFERENTIATION Social identity fulfils our inherent need to have a distinct and positive self-concept. To achieve this, we do more than categorise people and homogenise them; we also differentiate groups by assigning more favourable characteristics to people in our groups than to people in other groups. This differentiation is often subtle, but it can escalate into a 'good-guy–bad-guy' contrast when groups are in conflict with each other.[15]

Stereotyping in Organisations

stereotyping The process of assigning traits to people on the basis of their membership in a social category.

Stereotyping is an extension of social identity theory and a product of our natural process of organising information through categorical thinking.[16] Stereotyping has three elements. First, we develop social categories and assign traits that are difficult to observe. For instance, students might form the stereotype that professors are both intelligent and absentminded. Personal experiences shape stereotypes to some extent, but stereotypes are mainly provided to us through cultural upbringing and media images (e.g. movie characters). Second, we assign people to one or more social categories on the basis of easily observable information about them, such as their gender, appearance or physical location. Third, people who seem to belong to the stereotyped group are assigned nonobservable traits associated with the group. For example, if we learn that someone is a professor, we might implicitly assume that the person is also intelligent and absentminded.

One reason why people engage in stereotyping is that, as a form of categorical thinking, it is a natural and mostly nonconscious 'energy-saving' process that simplifies our understanding of the world. It is easier to remember features of a stereotype than the constellation of characteristics unique to everyone we meet.[17] A second reason is that we have an innate need to understand and anticipate how others will behave. We don't have much information when first meeting someone, so we rely heavily on stereotypes to fill in the missing pieces. People with a strong need for cognitive closure have a higher tendency to rely on stereotypes. A third reason is that stereotyping enhances our self-concept. As mentioned earlier, the social identity process includes differentiation—we have more favourable views of members of our own groups than we do of people in other groups. When out-group members threaten our self-concept, we are particularly motivated (often without our awareness) to assign negative stereotypes to them.[18]

Problems with Stereotyping

Stereotypes are not completely fictional, but neither do they accurately describe every person in a social category. For instance, the widespread 'bean counter' stereotype of accountants views people in this profession as 'single-mindedly preoccupied with precision and form, methodical and conservative' and possessing 'a boring joyless character'.[19] Although this may be true of some accountants, it is certainly not characteristic of all—or even most—people in this profession. Even so, once we categorise someone as an accountant, the features of accountants in general rather than the features of the specific person get recalled, even when the person does not possess many of the stereotypic traits.

Another problem with stereotyping is that it lays the foundation for discriminatory attitudes and behaviour. Most of this perceptual bias occurs as *unintentional (systemic) discrimination*, whereby decision makers rely on stereotypes to establish notions of the 'ideal' person in specific roles. A person who doesn't fit the ideal tends to receive a less favourable evaluation. This subtle discrimination often shows up in age discrimination claims, such as the case in which Ryanair's recruitment advertising said it was looking for 'young dynamic' employees. Recruiters at the Irish discount airline probably didn't intentionally discriminate against older people, but the tribunal concluded that systemic discrimination did occur because none of the job applicants were over 40 years old.[20]

The more serious form of stereotype bias is *intentional discrimination* or *prejudice*, in which people hold unfounded negative attitudes toward people belonging to a particular stereotyped group.[21] Consider the following example. Two decades ago, investigators mailed several hundred letters of employment enquiry to companies in Victoria, Australia, that had advertised job openings. The letters were identical except for the applicant's addresses (which were in similar neighbourhoods) and their names; some applicants had British names, whereas others had Vietnamese or Greek family names. The study reported that the applicants with British-sounding names were seven times more likely than those with Vietnamese names, and three times more likely than those with Greek names, to be offered an interview.[22]

Is overt prejudice less common today? Perhaps, but there is still evidence that it exists. For example, a classroom experiment recently found that Executive MBA and senior undergraduate students in New Zealand were more likely to select job applicants with European rather than Indian or Chinese names and/or ethnicity, even though the applicants had the same qualifications.[23] A Victorian government report recently cited numerous incidents in which people with ethnic backgrounds experienced discrimination in job hiring and promotions. Intentional discrimination is also apparent elsewhere. More than one-quarter of Americans say they have overheard racial slurs in the workplace.[24] Three female advisers in California successfully sued their employer, Smith Barney, on the grounds that their male coworkers were deliberately assigned more lucrative clients (and therefore received higher pay) and more administrative support. A tribunal in Quebec, Canada, was recently shocked to discover that one of Canada's largest vegetable farms required black employees to eat in a 'blacks only' eating area that lacked heat, running water, proper toilets and refrigeration.[25] As Reality Check 3.1 describes, France is also coming to terms with both intentional and unintentional discrimination against non-Caucasian job applicants.

'Your Name Says Everything in France'

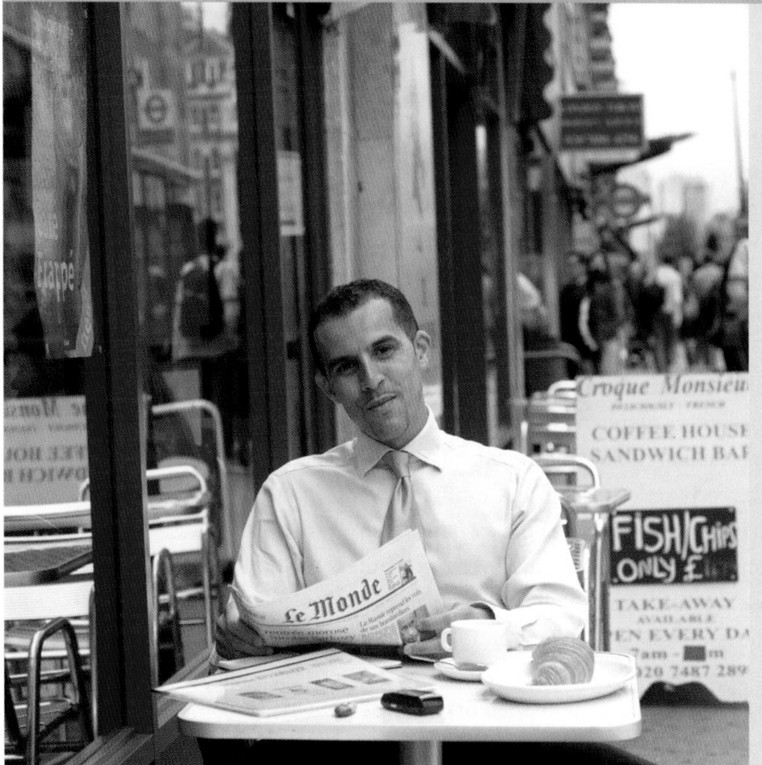

John Anderson

Hamid Senni was born and raised in France but eventually moved to the United Kingdom because race discrimination in his home country limited job opportunities.

Hamid Senni Wears A Shirt and tie whenever he strolls along the Champs Elysées in Paris. The reason for this formality? 'If I'm in jeans, people think I'm a shoplifter,' he says. What makes this misperception even worse is that Senni, the son of Moroccan immigrants, was born and raised in France. And in spite of his education (three degrees in economics) and fluent language skills, Senni was told more than once that he would never find a job in France. A well-intentioned high school teacher once told him that he should replace Hamid with a more traditional French name. Incensed by the daily discrimination he experienced in his own country, Senni moved to Sweden and now lives in London, where he advises companies on ethnic diversity and has written a book on his experience. 'Going abroad was like an exorcism,' he says bluntly. 'In the UK, diversity is seen as an opportunity. In France it's still seen as a problem.'

Senni's perception of racial and ethnic discrimination in France is supported by a recent study conducted jointly by the French government and the International Labour Organization (ILO). Researchers submitted two nearly identical job applications to 2440 help-wanted ads. The main

If stereotyping is such a problem, shouldn't we try to avoid this process altogether? Unfortunately, it is not that simple. Most experts agree that categorical thinking (including stereotyping) is an automatic and nonconscious process. Intensive training can minimise stereotype activation to some extent, but for the most part the process is hardwired in our brain cells.[27] Also remember that stereotyping helps us in several valuable (although fallible) ways described earlier: minimising mental effort, filling in missing information and supporting our social identity. The good news is that while it is very difficult to prevent the *activation* of stereotypes, we can minimise the *application* of stereotypic information. Later in this chapter, we identify ways to minimise stereotyping and other perceptual biases.

LEARNING OBJECTIVE

Describe the attribution process and two attribution errors.

ATTRIBUTION THEORY

attribution process The perceptual process of deciding whether an observed behaviour or event is caused largely by internal or external factors.

The **attribution process** involves deciding whether an observed behaviour or event is caused mainly by the person (internal factors) or by the environment (external factors).[28] Internal factors include the person's ability or motivation, whereas external factors include lack of resources,

REALITY CHECK 3.1

difference was that the candidate in one application had a French-sounding name whereas the individual in the other application had a North African or sub-Saharan African name. Almost 80 per cent of employers preferred the applicant with the French-sounding name. Furthermore, when applicants personally visited human resource staff, those who had foreign names seldom received job interviews; instead, they were often told that the job had been filled or that the company would not be hiring after all. The report concluded that 'almost 90 per cent of overall discrimination occurred before the employer had even bothered to interview both test candidates.'

One young black resident near Paris who calls himself Billy Fabrice knows about the undercurrents of racial discrimination. 'Your name says everything in France,' says Fabrice. 'If you are called Diallo or Amir, that's all they want to know. If you are called Jean-Pierre, you show up for a job and they take you.' Some employers specifically ask hiring agencies for applicants who are 'BBR'. This acronym for the colours of the French flag (bleu, blanc, rouge) is apparently a well-known employment code to hire only white French people. In one recent court case, prosecutors claimed that Garnier, a division of L'Oréal, tried to hire mostly white staff for in-store promotions. Garnier sent its temporary recruitment agency a fax specifying that those hired should be within a specific age range (18 to 22), have a certain clothing size and be 'BBR'. Initially, 38 per cent of candidates sent by the recruitment agency were non-Caucasian. After the fax was sent, this dropped to less than 5 per cent.

While many French employers, including Garnier, deny prejudice or even systemic discrimination against non-Caucasian applicants, others are taking steps to make the hiring process more 'colour-blind'. Axa SA, the giant French insurance company, introduced anonymous résumés, in which job applicants provide their qualifications but not their names, addresses, gender or age. Serge Simon, a 20-something French resident with Haitian origins, is hopeful. 'I think that with an anonymous résumé, a person will be hired for what they are—for their qualifications and not for the colour of their skin,' he believes.[26]

other people or just luck. If a coworker doesn't show up for an important meeting, for instance, we infer either internal attributions (the coworker is forgetful, lacks motivation and so on) or external attributions (traffic, a family emergency or other circumstances prevented the coworker from attending).

People rely on the three attribution rules shown in Exhibit 3.2 to determine whether someone's behaviour mainly has an internal or external attribution. Internal attributions are made when the observed individual behaved this way in the past (high consistency), he or she behaves like this toward other people or in different situations (low distinctiveness) and other people do not behave this way in similar situations (low consensus). On the other hand, an external attribution is made when there is low consistency, high distinctiveness and high consensus.

To illustrate how these three attribution rules operate, suppose that an employee is making poor-quality products one day on a particular machine. We would probably conclude that there is something wrong with the machine (an external attribution) if the employee has made good-quality products on this machine in the past (low consistency), the employee makes good-quality products on other machines (high distinctiveness) and other employees have recently had quality problems on this machine (high consensus). We would make an internal attribution, on the other

Exhibit 3.2 *Rules of Attribution*

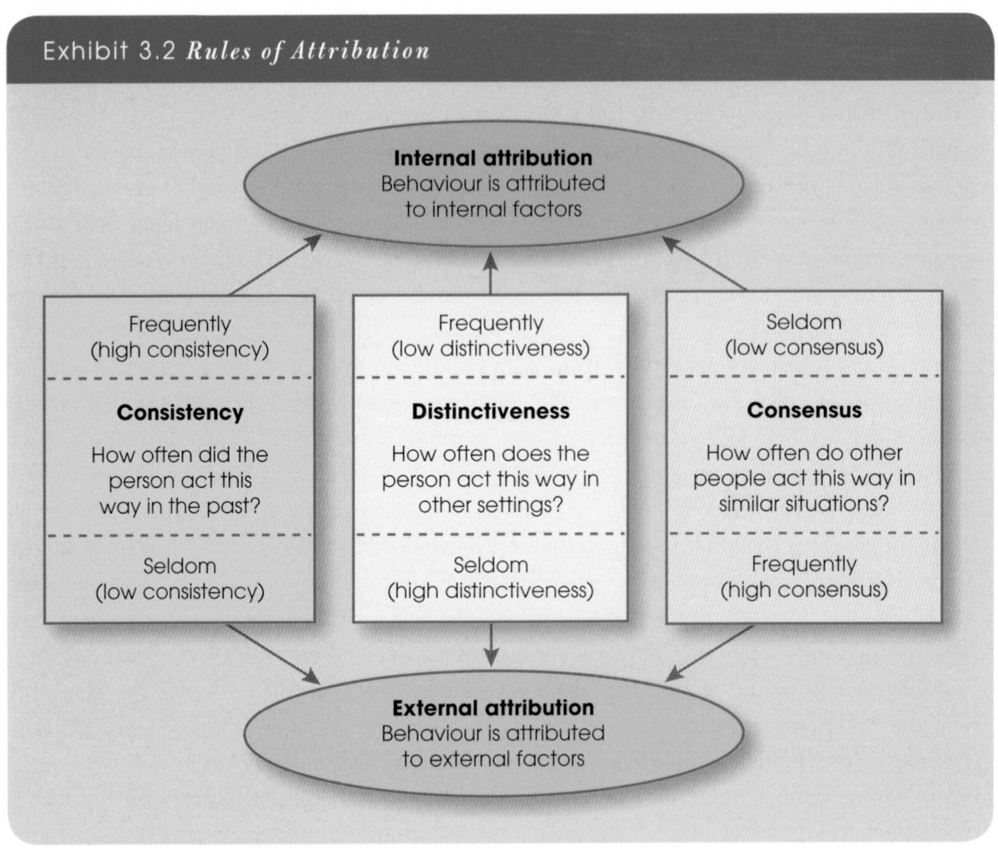
Internal attribution
Behaviour is attributed to internal factors
Frequently (high consistency)
Consistency
How often did the person act this way in the past?
Seldom (low consistency)
Frequently (low distinctiveness)
Distinctiveness
How often does the person act this way in other settings?
Seldom (high distinctiveness)
Seldom (low consensus)
Consensus
How often do other people act this way in similar situations?
Frequently (high consensus)
External attribution
Behaviour is attributed to external factors

hand, if the employee usually makes poor-quality products on this machine (high consistency), other employees produce good-quality products on this machine (low consensus) and the employee also makes poor-quality products on other machines (low distinctiveness).[29]

Attribution is an essential perceptual process because it forms cause–effect relationships, which, in turn, affect how we respond to others' behaviour and how we act in the future. How we react to a coworker's poor performance depends on our internal or external attribution of that performance. Students who make internal attributions about their poor performance are more likely to drop out of their courses, for instance.[30]

Attribution Errors

fundamental attribution error The tendency to see the person rather than the situation as the main cause of that person's behaviour.

People are far from perfect when making attributions. One bias, called **fundamental attribution error**, refers to our tendency to see the person rather than the situation as the main cause of that person's behaviour.[31] If an employee is late for work, observers are more likely to conclude that the person is lazy than to realise that external factors may have caused this behaviour. Fundamental attribution error occurs because observers can't easily see the external factors that constrain the person's behaviour. We didn't see the traffic jam that caused the person to be late, for instance. Research suggests that fundamental attribution error is more common in Western countries than in Asian cultures, where people are taught from an early age to pay attention to the context in interpersonal relations and to see everything as being connected in a holistic way.[32]

self-serving bias The tendency to attribute our favourable outcomes to internal factors and our failures to external factors.

Another attribution error, known as **self-serving bias**, is the tendency to attribute our favourable outcomes to internal factors and our failures to external factors. Simply put, we take credit for our successes and blame others or the situation for our mistakes. Self-serving bias is one of several related biases that maintain a positive self-concept, particularly engaging in self-enhancement to maintain a positive self-evaluation. It is evident in many aspects of work life. In annual reports, for example, executives mainly refer to their personal qualities as reasons for the company's successes and to external factors as reasons for the company's failures. Similarly, a New Zealand study found that 90 per cent of employees in a government organisation who received lower-than-expected performance ratings blamed their supervisor, the organisation, the appraisal system or other external causes for their performance problems. Only a handful blamed themselves for the unexpected results.[33]

SELF-FULFILLING PROPHECY

LEARNING OBJECTIVE 

Summarise the self-fulfilling-prophecy process.

self-fulfilling prophecy The perceptual process in which our expectations about another person cause that person to act in a way that is consistent with those expectations.

Self-fulfilling prophecy occurs when our expectations about another person cause that person to act in a way that is consistent with those expectations. In other words, our perceptions can influence reality. Exhibit 3.3 illustrates the four steps in the self-fulfilling-prophecy process using the example of a supervisor and a subordinate.[34] The process begins when the supervisor forms expectations about the employee's future behaviour and performance. These expectations are sometimes inaccurate, because first impressions are usually formed from limited information. The supervisor's expectations influence his or her treatment of employees. Specifically, high-expectancy employees (those expected to do well) receive more emotional support through nonverbal cues (e.g. more smiling and eye contact), more frequent and valuable feedback and reinforcement, more challenging goals, better training and more opportunities to demonstrate good performance.

The third step in self-fulfilling prophecy includes two effects of the supervisor's behaviour on the employee. First, through better training and more practice opportunities, a high-expectancy employee learns more skills and knowledge than a low-expectancy employee.

Exhibit 3.3 *The Self-Fulfilling-Prophecy Cycle*

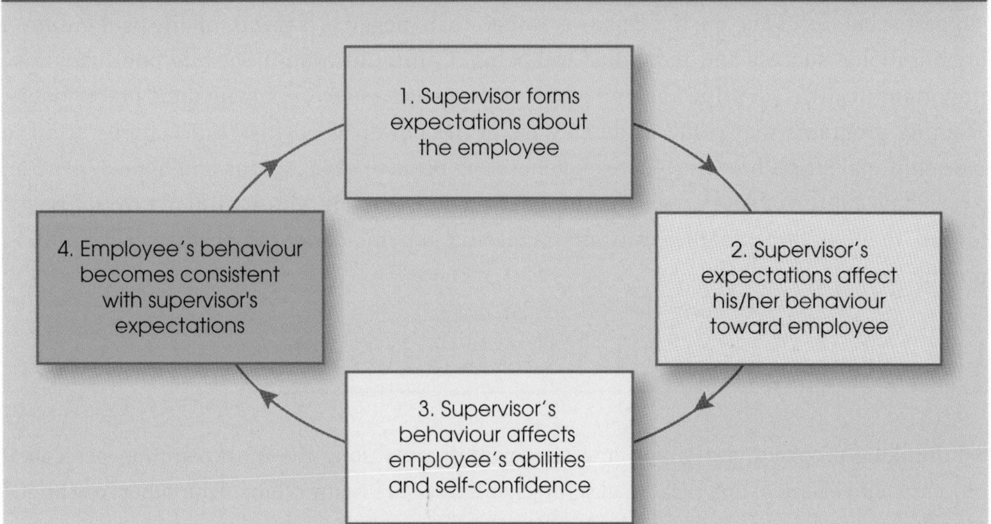

1. Supervisor forms expectations about the employee
2. Supervisor's expectations affect his/her behaviour toward employee
3. Supervisor's behaviour affects employee's abilities and self-confidence
4. Employee's behaviour becomes consistent with supervisor's expectations

Second, the employee becomes more self-confident, which results in higher motivation and willingness to set more challenging goals.[35] In the final step, high-expectancy employees have higher motivation and better skills, resulting in better performance, while the opposite is true of low-expectancy employees.

There are many examples of self-fulfilling prophecies in work and school settings.[36] Research has found that women perform less well on maths tests after being informed that men tend to perform better on them. Women perform better on these tests when they are not exposed to this negative self-fulfilling prophecy. Similarly, people over 65 years of age receive lower results on memory tests after hearing that mental ability declines with age. Another study reported that the performance of Israeli Defence Force trainees was influenced by their instructor's expectations regarding the trainee's potential in the program. Self-fulfilling prophecy was at work here because the instructor's expectations were based on a list provided by researchers showing which recruits had high and low potential, even though the researchers had actually listed these trainees randomly.

Contingencies of Self-Fulfilling Prophecy

Self-fulfilling prophecies are more powerful under some conditions than others. The self-fulfilling-prophecy effect is stronger at the beginning of a relationship, such as when employees are first hired. It is also stronger when several people (rather than just one person) hold the same expectations of the individual. In other words, we might be able to ignore one person's doubts about our potential but not the collective doubts of several people. The self-fulfilling-prophecy effect is also stronger among people with a history of low achievement. High achievers can draw on their past successes to offset low expectations, whereas low achievers do not have past successes to support their self-confidence. Fortunately, the opposite is also true. Low achievers respond more favourably than high achievers to positive self-fulfilling prophecy; they don't receive this positive encouragement very often, so it probably has a stronger effect on their motivation to excel.[37]

The main lesson from the self-fulfilling-prophecy literature is that leaders need to develop and maintain a positive yet realistic expectation toward all employees. This recommendation is consistent with the emerging philosophy of **positive organisational behaviour**, which suggests that focusing on the positive rather than negative aspects of life will improve organisational success and individual wellbeing. Communicating hope and optimism is so important that it is identified as one of the critical success factors for medical practitioners. Training programs that make leaders aware of the power of positive expectations seem to have minimal effect, however. Instead, generating positive expectations and hope depend on a corporate culture of support and learning. Hiring supervisors who are inherently optimistic toward their staff is another way of increasing the incidence of positive self-fulfilling prophecies.

positive organisational behaviour A perspective of organisational behaviour that focuses on building positive qualities and traits within individuals or institutions as opposed to focusing on what is wrong with them.

OTHER PERCEPTUAL ERRORS

LEARNING OBJECTIVE

Explain how halo, primacy, recency and false-consensus effects bias our perceptions.

Self-fulfilling prophecy, attribution and stereotyping are among the most common perceptual processes and biases in organisational settings, but there are many others. Four others are briefly described below because they can also bias our perception of the world around us.

HALO EFFECT The **halo effect** occurs when our general impression of a person, usually based on one prominent characteristic, distorts our perception of other characteristics of that person.[38] If a supervisor who values punctuality notices that an employee is sometimes late for work, the supervisor might form a negative image of the employee and evaluate that person's other traits unfavourably as well. The halo effect is most likely to occur when concrete information about the perceived target is missing or we are not sufficiently motivated to search for it. Instead, we use our general impression of the person to fill in the missing information.

halo effect A perceptual error whereby our general impression of a person, usually based on one prominent characteristic, colours our perception of other characteristics of that person.

PRIMACY EFFECT The **primacy effect** is our tendency to quickly form an opinion of people on the basis of the first information we receive about them.[39] This rapid perceptual organisation and interpretation occurs because we need to make sense of the world around us. The problem is that first impressions—particularly negative first impressions—are difficult to change. After categorising someone, we tend to select subsequent information that supports our first impression and screen out information that opposes that impression.

primacy effect A perceptual error in which we quickly form an opinion of people on the basis of the first information we receive about them.

RECENCY EFFECT The **recency effect** occurs when the most recent information dominates our perceptions.[40] This perceptual bias is most common when people (especially those with limited experience) are making an evaluation involving complex information. For instance, auditors must digest large volumes of information in their judgements about financial documents, and the most recent information received prior to the decision tends to be weighted more heavily than information received at the beginning of the audit. Similarly, when supervisors evaluate the performance of employees over the previous year, the most recent performance information dominates the evaluation because it is the most easily recalled.

recency effect A perceptual error in which the most recent information dominates our perception of others.

FALSE-CONSENSUS EFFECT Sometimes called the *similar-to-me effect*, the **false-consensus effect** is a widely observed bias in which we overestimate the extent to which others have beliefs and characteristics similar to our own.[41] Employees who are thinking of quitting their jobs believe that a large percentage of their coworkers are also thinking about quitting. This bias occurs to some extent because we associate with others who are similar to us, and we selectively remember information that is consistent with our own views. We also believe 'everyone does it' to reinforce our self-concept regarding behaviours that do not have a positive image (quitting, parking illegally and so on).

false-consensus effect A perceptual error in which we overestimate the extent to which others have beliefs and characteristics similar to our own.

IMPROVING PERCEPTIONS

We can't bypass the perceptual process, but we should make every attempt to minimise perceptual biases and distortions. Three potentially effective ways to improve perceptions include awareness of perceptual biases, self-awareness and meaningful interaction.

Awareness of Perceptual Biases

LEARNING OBJECTIVE 

Discuss three ways to improve social perception, with specific application to organisational situations.

One of the most obvious and widely practised ways to reduce perceptual biases is by knowing that they exist. For example, diversity awareness training tries to minimise discrimination by making people aware of systemic discrimination as well as prejudices that occur through stereotyping. This training also attempts to dispel myths about people from various cultural and demographic groups. Awareness of perceptual biases can reduce these biases to some extent by making people more mindful of their thoughts and actions. However, awareness has only a limited effect.[42] For example, trying to correct misinformation about demographic groups has little effect on people with deeply held prejudices against those groups. Also, self-fulfilling-prophecy training informs managers about this perceptual bias and encourages them to engage in more positive rather than negative self-fulfilling prophecies, yet research has found that managers continue to engage in negative self-fulfilling prophecies after they complete the training program.

Improving Self-Awareness

A more powerful way to minimise perceptual biases is to help people become more aware of biases in their own decisions and behaviour.[43] As mentioned at the beginning of this chapter, self-awareness is a critical foundation for developing a global mindset. We need to understand our beliefs, values and attitudes to be more open-minded and nonjudgmental toward others. Self-awareness is equally important in other ways. The emerging concept of authentic leadership, for instance, emphasises self-awareness as the first step in a person's ability to effectively lead others (see Chapter 12).[44]

But how do we become more self-aware? One formal procedure, called the Implicit Association Test (IAT), detects subtle race, age and gender bias by associating positive and negative words with specific demographic groups.[45] Many people are much more cautious about their stereotypes and prejudices after discovering that their test results show a personal bias against older people or individuals from different ethnic backgrounds. For example, Jennifer Smith-Holladay was surprised to learn after taking the IAT that she is biased in favour of white people, a group to which she belongs, and in favour of heterosexuals, a group to which she does not belong. 'I discovered that I not only have some in-group favouritism lurking in my subconscious, but also possess some internalised oppression in terms of my sexuality,' says Smith-Holladay. She adds that the IAT results will make her more aware of personal biases and help her to minimise their application in decision making. 'In the case of my own subconscious in-group favouritism for white people, for example, my charge is to be colour conscious, not colour blind, and to always explicitly consider how race may affect behaviours and decisions.'[46]

Johari Window A model of mutual understanding that encourages disclosure and feedback to increase our own open area and reduce the blind, hidden and unknown areas.

Another way to increase self-awareness (and thereby reduce perceptual biases) is by applying the **Johari Window**.[47] Developed by Joseph Luft and Harry Ingram (hence the name 'Johari'), this model of self-awareness and mutual understanding divides information about you into four 'windows'—open, blind, hidden and unknown—based on whether your own values, beliefs and experiences are known to you and to others (see Exhibit 3.4). The *open area* includes information about you that is known to you and to others. The *blind area* refers to information that is known to others but not to you. For example, your colleagues might notice that you are self-conscious and awkward when meeting the company chief executive, but you are unaware of this fact. Information known to you but unknown to others is found in the *hidden area*. Finally, the *unknown area* includes your values, beliefs and experiences that aren't known to you or others.

The main objective of the Johari Window is to increase the size of the open area so that both you and colleagues are aware of your perceptual limitations. This is partly accomplished by reducing the hidden area through *disclosure*—informing others of your beliefs, feelings and experiences that may influence the work relationship.[48] The open area also increases through *feedback* from others about your behaviour. This information helps you to reduce your blind area, because coworkers often see things in you that you do not see. Finally, the combination of disclosure and feedback occasionally produces revelations about information in the unknown area.

Exhibit 3.4 *The Johari Window Model of Self-Awareness and Mutual Understanding*

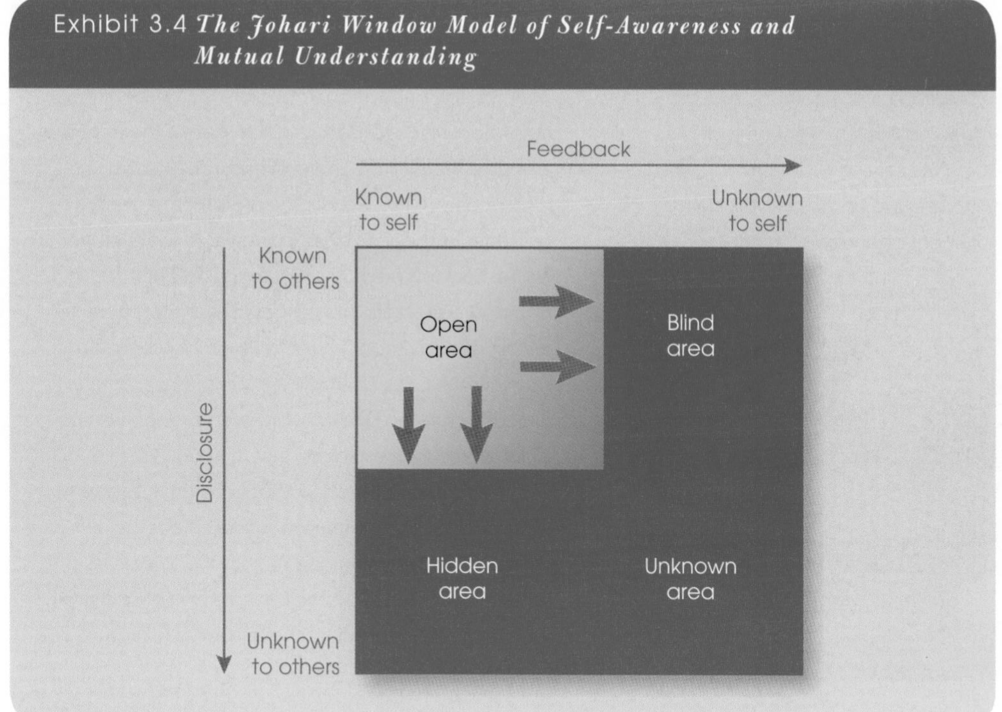

Source: Based on J. Luft, *Group Processes: An Introduction to Group Dynamics* (Palo Alto, CA: Mayfield, 1984).

Meaningful Interaction

While the Johari Window relies on dialogue, our self-awareness and mutual understanding can also improve through *meaningful interaction*.[49] This statement is based on the **contact hypothesis**, which states that, under certain conditions, people who interact with each other will be less prejudiced or perceptually biased against each other. Simply spending time with members of other groups can improve your understanding and opinion of those persons to some extent. 'I've learned that the more you get to know someone on a personal level, the easier it is to overcome time zones and differences—and work together,' says Jennifer Vickery, an IBM employee who worked in Romania for a month on the same program described at the beginning of this chapter.[50] In other words, through direct interaction with her IBM colleagues during the community work assignment in Romania, Vickery was able to develop more accurate perceptions of these people, and improve her understanding of them.

contact hypothesis A theory stating that the more we interact with someone, the less prejudiced or perceptually biased we will be against that person.

The contact hypothesis effect is strongest when people have close and frequent interaction with each other, in which they work toward a shared goal and need to rely on each other (i.e. cooperate rather than compete). Everyone should have equal status in that context and should be engaged in a meaningful task. IBM's month-long community project work is an ideal example of this setting. In these programs, professionals from developed countries work alongside people from developing countries. Although the volunteers have expertise (and therefore status), they often perform work outside that expertise and in unfamiliar environments that require the expertise of people in the local community.

Another potential application of the contact hypothesis occurs when senior executives and other staff from headquarters work in front-line jobs frequently or for an extended time. Every month, Air New Zealand executives work on the front lines to maintain a better perspective of operational

Air New Zealand Executives Get Meaningful Interaction

If the meal service seems a bit slower than usual on your next Air New Zealand flight, it might be that CEO Rob Fyfe is doing the serving while chatting with passengers. Every month, Fyfe and his top executive team fill the roster as flight attendants, check-in counter staff or baggage handlers. (The executives had to pass tests to work as cabin crew.) The front-line jobs give the Air New Zealand executives a regular reality check while working alongside employees, and offer employees an opportunity to see that the airline's leaders are human beings who care about staff and customers. The process is also somewhat reversed; every month one staff member spends a day with the CEO. 'That will include sitting in on an executive briefing and possibly even a lunch with a politician,' Fyfe explains. 'They go everywhere with me for the entire day.' That program has been extended to other senior executives. The result of this meaningful interaction and many other initiatives to support employees is that morale and customer service at Air New Zealand have soared in recent years.[51]

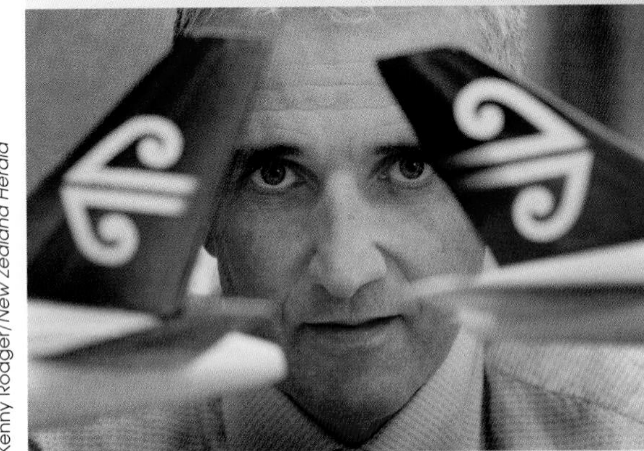

Kenny Rodger/New Zealand Herald

issues. Everyone at Domino's Pizza head office in Ann Arbor, Michigan, attends Pizza Prep School, where they learn how to make pizzas and run a pizza store. Every new hire at 1-800-GOT-JUNK? (North America's largest rubbish removal company) spends an entire week on a junk removal truck to better understand how the business works. 'How can you possibly empathise with someone out in the field unless you've been on the truck yourself?' asks CEO and founder Brian Scudamore.[52]

empathy A person's understanding of and sensitivity to the feelings, thoughts and situations of others.

Meaningful interaction does more than reduce our reliance on stereotypes. It also potentially improves **empathy**, that is, the extent to which we understand and are sensitive to the feelings, thoughts and situations of others.[53] You have empathy when actively visualising the other person's situation and feeling their emotions in that situation. Empathising with others improves our sensitivity to the external causes of another person's performance and behaviour, thereby reducing fundamental attribution error. A supervisor who imagines what it's like to be a single mother, for example, would become more sensitive to the external causes of lateness and other events among such employees.

The perceptual process represents the filter through which information passes from the external environment to our memory. As such, it is really the beginning of the learning process, which we discuss next.

LEARNING IN ORGANISATIONS

learning A relatively permanent change in behaviour (or behavioural tendency) that occurs as a result of a person's interaction with the environment.

Learning is a relatively permanent change in behaviour (or behavioural tendency) that occurs as a result of a person's interaction with the environment. Learning occurs when the learner behaves differently. For example, you have 'learned' computer skills when you operate the keyboard and software more quickly than before. Learning occurs when interaction with the environment leads to behaviour change. This means that we learn through our senses, such as through study, observation and experience.

Some of what we learn is *explicit knowledge,* such as reading information in this book. However, explicit knowledge is really only the tip of the knowledge iceberg. Most of what we know is **tacit knowledge.**[54] Tacit knowledge is not documented; rather, it is acquired through observation and direct experience. For example, airline pilots learn to operate commercial jets more by watching experts and practising on flight simulators than by attending lectures. They acquire tacit knowledge by directly experiencing the complex interaction of behaviour with the machine's response.

tacit knowledge Knowledge that is embedded in our actions and ways of thinking, and is transmitted only through observation and experience.

Three perspectives of learning tacit and explicit knowledge are reinforcement, social learning and direct experience. Each perspective offers a different angle for understanding the dynamics of learning.

Behaviour Modification: Learning through Reinforcement

One of the oldest perspectives on learning, called **behaviour modification** (also known as *operant conditioning* and *reinforcement theory*), takes the rather extreme view that learning is completely dependent on the environment. Behaviour modification does not question the notion that thinking is part of the learning process, but it views human thoughts as unimportant, intermediate stages between behaviour and the environment. The environment teaches us to alter our behaviours so that we maximise positive consequences and minimise adverse consequences.[55]

behaviour modification A theory that explains learning in terms of the antecedents and consequences of behaviour.

A-B-Cs of Behaviour Modification

LEARNING OBJECTIVE 

Describe the A-B-C model of behaviour modification and the four contingencies of reinforcement.

The central objective of behaviour modification is to change behaviour (B) by managing its antecedents (A) and consequences (C). This process is nicely illustrated in the A-B-C model of behaviour modification, shown in Exhibit 3.5.[56]

Antecedents are events preceding the behaviour, informing employees that certain behaviours will have particular consequences. An antecedent may be a sound from your computer signalling that an email has arrived, or a request from your supervisor asking you to complete a specific

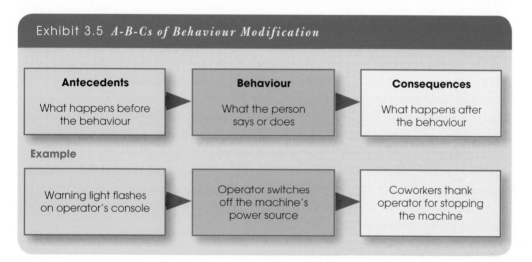

Exhibit 3.5 ***A-B-Cs of Behaviour Modification***

Antecedents	**Behaviour**	**Consequences**
What happens before the behaviour	What the person says or does	What happens after the behaviour
Example		
Warning light flashes on operator's console	Operator switches off the machine's power source	Coworkers thank operator for stopping the machine

Sources: Adapted from T. K. Connellan, *How to Improve Human Performance: Behaviorism in Business and Industry* (New York: Harper & Row, 1978), 50; F. Luthans and R. Kreitner, *Organizational Behavior Modification and Beyond: An Operant and Social Learning Approach* (Glenview, IL: Scott Foresman, 1985), 85–88.

task by tomorrow. Notice that antecedents do not cause behaviours. The computer sound doesn't cause us to open our email; rather, the sound is a cue telling us that certain consequences are likely to occur if we engage in certain behaviours. In behaviour modification, *consequences* are events following a particular behaviour that influence its future occurrence. Generally speaking, people tend to repeat behaviours that are followed by pleasant consequences and are less likely to repeat behaviours that are followed by unpleasant consequences or no consequences at all.

Contingencies of Reinforcement

Behaviour modification identifies four types of consequences, called the *contingencies of reinforcement,* that increase, maintain or reduce the probability that behaviour will be repeated.[57]

POSITIVE REINFORCEMENT occurs when the *introduction* of a consequence *increases or maintains* the frequency or future probability of a specific behaviour. Receiving a bonus after successfully completing an important project is considered positive reinforcement because it typically increases the probability that you will use that behaviour in the future.

PUNISHMENT occurs when a consequence decreases the frequency or future probability of a behaviour. This consequence typically involves introducing something that employees try to avoid. For instance, most of us would consider being demoted or being ostracised by our coworkers as forms of punishment.[58]

NEGATIVE REINFORCEMENT occurs when the removal or avoidance of a consequence increases or maintains the frequency or future probability of a specific behaviour. Supervisors apply negative reinforcement when they stop criticising employees whose substandard performance has improved. When the criticism is withheld, employees are more likely to repeat behaviours that improved their performance. Notice that negative reinforcement is not punishment. Whereas punishment extinguishes behaviour by introducing a negative consequence, negative reinforcement actually reinforces behaviour by removing the negative consequence.

EXTINCTION occurs when the target behaviour decreases because no consequence follows it. In this respect, extinction is a do-nothing strategy. Generally, behaviour that is no longer reinforced tends to disappear; it becomes extinct. For instance, research suggests that performance tends to decline when managers stop congratulating employees for their good work.[59]

Which contingency of reinforcement should be used in the learning process? In most situations, positive reinforcement should follow desired behaviours, and extinction (do nothing) should follow undesirable behaviours. This approach is preferred because punishment and negative reinforcement generate negative emotions and attitudes toward the punisher (e.g. supervisor) and organisation. However, some form of punishment (such as dismissal, suspension or demotion) may be necessary for extreme behaviours, such as deliberately hurting a coworker or stealing inventory. Indeed, research suggests that, under certain conditions, punishment maintains a sense of fairness.[60]

Schedules of Reinforcement

Along with the types of reinforcement, the frequency and timing of the reinforcers also influence employee behaviours.[61] These reinforcement schedules can be continuous or intermittent. The most effective reinforcement schedule for learning new tasks is *continuous reinforcement*—providing positive reinforcement after every occurrence of the desired behaviour. Employees learn desired behaviours quickly, and when the reinforcer is removed, extinction also occurs very quickly.

The best schedule for reinforcing learned behaviour is a *variable ratio schedule* in which employee behaviour is reinforced after a variable number of times. Salespeople experience variable ratio reinforcement because they make a successful sale (the reinforcer) after a varying number of client calls. They might make four unsuccessful calls before receiving an order on the fifth one, then make ten more calls before receiving the next order and so on. The variable ratio schedule makes behaviour highly resistant to extinction because the reinforcer is never expected at a particular time or after a fixed number of accomplishments.

Behaviour Modification in Practice

Everyone practises behaviour modification in one form or another. We thank people for a job well done, are silent when displeased and sometimes try to punish those who go against our wishes. Behaviour modification also occurs in various formal programs to reduce absenteeism, improve task performance, encourage safe work behaviours and have a healthier lifestyle.[62] For instance, the Australian arm of Michelin Tyres has an incentive plan in which tyre resellers earn one credit per tyre purchased, and a bonus if the reseller exceeds its monthly target. The highest credit earners are sent on a trip. Crown Casino in Melbourne reinforces good attendance by giving staff with fewer than six days' sick leave a 1 per cent wage bonus. ExxonMobil's Fawley refinery in the

Reinforcing the Long (and Healthy) Walk

Courtesy of Stoke-on-Trent City Council

Walking to work is starting to look much more appealing to city employees in Stoke-on-Trent, Staffordshire. The British municipality issued pedometers to its staff (see photo) and encouraged them to develop a regimen of daily walking. The goal is to get sedentary employees walking at least 10 000 steps each day for five days a week. The pedometers provide instant feedback, thereby reinforcing longer walks.

The city also introduced support groups to further encourage people to walk regularly. American health insurance company Humana, Inc., developed the Stoke-on-Trent program and has a similar program of its own. Humana employees use a pedometer to count the number of steps, and the results are uploaded from the pedometer to a website. The more steps taken, the higher the rewards in the form of cash cards that can be used at popular retail stores. 'This program has changed the culture within Humana,' says Phil Smeltzer, Humana's wellness strategy leader. 'People have started paying attention to how many steps they are taking. When it gets late in the day and they haven't walked enough, they take the long way to their car.'[64]

United Kingdom introduced a 'Behave Safely Challenge' program in which supervisors rewarded employees and contractors on the spot when they exhibited good safety behaviour or intervened to ensure the safe behaviour of coworkers. These rewards were a form of positive reinforcement using a variable ratio schedule (safe work behaviours were reinforced after a variable number of occurrences).[63]

Although a natural part of human interaction, behaviour modification has a number of limitations when applied strategically in organisational settings. One limitation is 'reward inflation', in which the reinforcer is eventually considered an entitlement. For this reason, most behaviour modification programs must run infrequently and for a short duration. Another concern is that the variable ratio schedule of reinforcement tends to create a lottery-style reward system, which is unpopular with people who dislike gambling. Probably the most significant problem is behaviour modification's radical view that behaviour is learned only through personal interaction with the environment.[65] This view is no longer accepted; instead, learning experts recognise that people also learn by observing others and thinking logically about possible consequences. This learning-through-observation process is explained by social learning theory.

LEARNING OBJECTIVE 

Describe the three features of social learning theory.

Social Learning Theory: Learning by Observing

social learning theory A theory stating that much learning occurs by observing others, then modelling the behaviours that lead to favourable outcomes and avoiding behaviours that lead to punishing consequences.

Social learning theory states that much learning occurs by observing others, then modelling the behaviours that lead to favourable outcomes and avoiding behaviours that lead to punishing consequences.[66] This form of learning occurs in three ways: behaviour modelling, learning behaviour consequences and self-reinforcement.

BEHAVIOUR MODELLING People learn by observing the behaviours of a role model on a critical task, remembering the important elements of the observed behaviours and then practising those behaviours.[67] This is a valuable form of learning because tacit knowledge and skills are mainly acquired through observation and practice. As an example, it is difficult to document or explain in a conversation all the steps necessary to bake professional-quality bread. Student chefs also need to observe the master baker's subtle behaviours. Behavioural modelling also increases self-efficacy because people gain more self-confidence after seeing someone else perform the task. This is particularly true when observers identify with the model, such as someone who is similar in age, experience, gender and related features.

LEARNING BEHAVIOUR CONSEQUENCES People learn the consequences of behaviour through logic and observation, not just through direct experience. They logically anticipate consequences after completing a task well or poorly. They also learn behavioural consequences by observing the experiences of other people. Consider the employee who observes a coworker receiving a stern warning for working in an unsafe manner. This event would reduce the observer's likelihood of engaging in unsafe behaviours because he or she has learned to anticipate a similar reprimand following those behaviours.[68]

self-reinforcement Reinforcement that occurs when an employee has control over a reinforcer but doesn't 'take' it until completing a self-set goal.

SELF-REINFORCEMENT **Self-reinforcement** occurs whenever an employee has control over a reinforcer but doesn't 'take' it until completing a self-set goal.[69] For example, you might be thinking about having a snack after you finish reading the rest of this chapter. Raiding the refrigerator is a form of self-induced positive reinforcement for completing this reading assignment. Self-reinforcement takes many forms, such as taking a short walk, watching a movie, or simply congratulating yourself for completing a task.

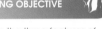

Learning from Near Misses

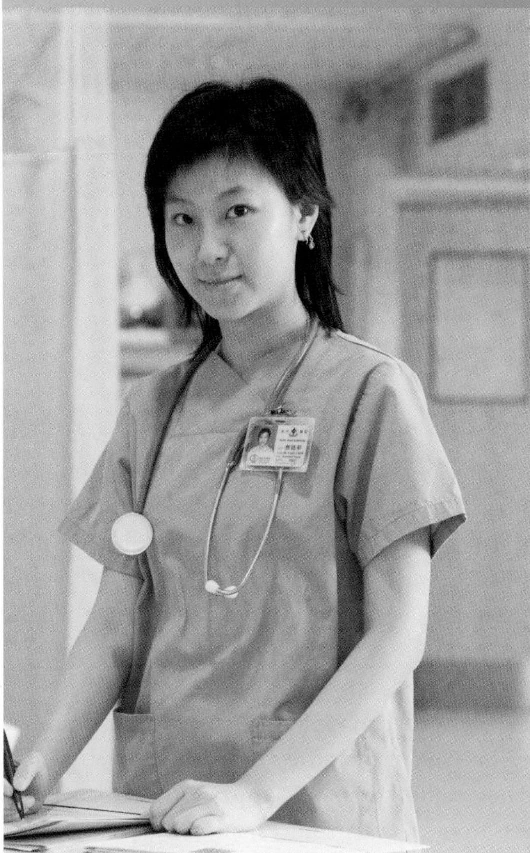

Ken Chernus/The Image Bank/Getty Images

If there is one thing more serious than making mistakes in a hospital setting, it would be failing to report and learn from those mistakes. With that idea in mind, Osaka University Hospital in Japan has developed a 'no-blame' web-based system whereby staff can anonymously report 'near-miss' incidents, thereby enabling the hospital to quickly identify practices that most urgently require better procedures or training. For example, when the reporting system identified medication ordering and dispensing as the most common near misses, staff developed new procedures to reduce those errors. Canossa Hospital in Hong Kong also encourages staff to speak up about near misses so that everyone can improve the quality of hospital care. 'The hospital believes through staff's alertness of potential risk and early reporting of near misses, both quality and safety of the hospital could be improved,' explains Terence Chow, Canossa Hospital's physiotherapy department manager. 'The training program also serves to help employees cultivate a positive attitude towards learning from mistakes.'[73]

Learning through Experience

Along with behaviour modification and social learning, another way that employees learn is through direct experience. In fact, most tacit knowledge and skills are acquired through experience as well as observation. Generally, experiential learning begins when we engage with the environment; then we reflect on that experience and form theories about how the world around us works. This is followed by experimentation, in which we find out how well the newly formed theories work.[70] Experiential learning requires all these steps, although people tend to prefer one step more than the others.

One of the most important ingredients for learning through experience is a strong **learning orientation** within the organisation and its employees.[71] As mentioned at the beginning of this chapter, people with a global mindset have a strong learning orientation, meaning that they welcome new learning opportunities, actively experiment with new ideas and practices, view reasonable mistakes as a natural part of the learning process and continuously question past practices. This individual orientation becomes part of the organisation's culture when it is held by many people throughout the organisation.

learning orientation An individual attitude and organisational culture in which people welcome new learning opportunities, actively experiment with new ideas and practices, view reasonable mistakes as a natural part of the learning process and continuously question past practices.

Organisations develop and maintain learning-orientation cultures by supporting experimentation, acknowledging reasonable mistakes without penalty and supporting the mindset that employees should engage in continuous learning. They encourage employees to question long-held assumptions or mental models and to actively 'unlearn' practices that are no longer ideal. Without a learning orientation, mistakes are hidden and problems are more likely to escalate or re-emerge later. It's not surprising, then, that one of the most frequently mentioned lessons from the best-performing manufacturers is to expect mistakes. 'At CIMB we have learnt to admit our mistakes openly,' says Datuk Nazir Razak, chief executive of CIMB Group, Malaysia's second-largest financial services company. 'Some of these mistakes cost us a lot of money,' he adds, but 'each mistake is a learning opportunity.'[72]

LEARNING OBJECTIVE 

Outline the elements of organisational learning and ways to improve each element.

FROM INDIVIDUAL TO ORGANISATIONAL LEARNING

One of the most popular contemporary perspectives of organisational effectiveness is *organisational learning,* which was defined in Chapter 1 as any structured activity that improves an organisation's capacity to acquire, share and use knowledge in ways that improve its survival and success. Organisational learning is heavily dependent on individual learning, but companies should establish systems, structures and organisational values that support the process of knowledge management. These three processes are knowledge acquisition, knowledge sharing and knowledge use.[74]

KNOWLEDGE ACQUISITION This includes extracting information and ideas from the external environment as well as through insight. One of the fastest and most powerful ways to acquire knowledge is by hiring individuals or acquiring entire companies. Knowledge also enters the organisation when employees learn from external sources, such as by discovering new resources from suppliers or becoming aware of new trends from clients. A third knowledge acquisition strategy is experimentation. Companies receive knowledge through insight as a result of research and other creative processes.

KNOWLEDGE SHARING This aspect of organisational learning involves distributing knowledge to others across the organisation. Although typically associated with computer intranets and digital repositories of knowledge, knowledge sharing also occurs through informal online or face-to-face communication.[75] Most social learning (such as behavioural modelling) and experiential learning are forms of knowledge sharing because the learning is transferred from one employee to another.

KNOWLEDGE USE The competitive advantage of knowledge comes from applying it in ways that add value to the organisation and its stakeholders. To do this, employees must realise that the knowledge is available and that they have enough freedom to apply it. This requires a culture that supports the learning process.

This chapter has introduced two fundamental activities in human behaviour in the workplace: perceptions and learning. These activities involve receiving information from the environment, organising it and acting on it as a learning process. Our knowledge about perceptions and learning in the workplace lays the foundation for the next chapter, which looks at workplace emotions and attitudes.

CHAPTER SUMMARY

Perception involves selecting, organising and interpreting information to make sense of the world around us. Perceptual organisation engages categorical thinking—the mostly nonconscious process of organising people and objects into preconceived categories that are stored in our long-term memory. Mental models—internal representations of the external world—also help us to make sense of incoming stimuli.

Social identity theory explains how we perceive people through categorisation, homogenisation and differentiation. Stereotyping is a derivative of social identity theory, in which people assign traits to others based on their membership of a social category. Stereotyping economises mental effort, fills in missing information, and enhances our self-perception and social identity. However, it also lays the foundation for prejudice and systemic discrimination.

The attribution process involves deciding whether an observed behaviour or event is caused mainly by the person (internal factors) or the environment (external factors). Attributions are decided by perceived consistency, distinctiveness and consensus of the behaviour. This process helps us to link together the various pieces of our world in cause–effect relationships, but it is also subject to attribution errors, including fundamental attribution error and self-serving bias.

Self-fulfilling prophecy occurs when our expectations about another person cause that person to act in a way that is consistent with those expectations. Essentially, our expectations affect our behaviour toward the target person, which then affects that person's opportunities and attitudes, which then influences his or her behaviour. Self-fulfilling prophecies tend to be stronger when the relationship begins (such as when employees first join a department), when several people hold the same expectations of the employee and when the employee has a history of low achievement.

Four other perceptual errors commonly noted in organisations are the halo effect, primacy effect, recency effect and false-consensus effect. We can minimise these and other perceptual problems through awareness of perceptual bias, self-awareness and meaningful interaction.

Learning is a relatively permanent change in behaviour (or behaviour tendency) that occurs as a result of a person's interaction with the environment. Much of what we learn is tacit knowledge, which is embedded in our actions without conscious awareness.

The behaviour-modification perspective of learning states that behaviour change occurs by altering the antecedents and consequences of behaviour. Antecedents are environmental stimuli that provoke (not necessarily cause) behaviour. Consequences are events that follow behaviour and influence its future occurrence. Consequences include: positive reinforcement, punishment, negative reinforcement and extinction. The schedules of reinforcement also influence behaviour.

Social learning theory states that much learning occurs by observing others, then modelling the behaviours that seem to lead to favourable outcomes and avoiding behaviours that lead to punishing consequences. It also recognises that we often engage in self-reinforcement. Behaviour modelling is effective because it transfers tacit knowledge and enhances the observer's confidence in performing a task.

Many companies now use experiential learning because employees do not acquire tacit knowledge through formal classroom instruction. Experiential learning begins with concrete experience, and is then followed by reflection on that experience, formation of a theory from that experience and testing of that theory in the environment.

Organisational learning is any structured activity that improves an organisation's capacity to acquire, share and use knowledge in ways that improve its survival and success. Organisations acquire knowledge through the learning and experimentation of individuals. Knowledge sharing occurs mainly through various forms of communication and training. Knowledge use occurs when employees realise that the knowledge is available and that they have enough freedom to apply it.

KEY TERMS

attribution process, p. 94
behaviour modification, p. 103
categorical thinking, p. 90
contact hypothesis, p. 101
empathy, p. 102
false-consensus effect, p. 99
fundamental attribution error, p. 96
global mindset, p. 88
halo effect, p. 99
Johari Window, p. 100
learning, p. 102
learning orientation, p. 107
mental models, p. 91
perception, p. 88
positive organisational behaviour, p. 98
primacy effect, p. 99
recency effect, p. 99
selective attention, p. 88
self-fulfilling prophecy, p. 97
self-reinforcement, p. 106
self-serving bias, p. 96
social learning theory, p. 106
stereotyping, p. 92
tacit knowledge, p. 103

Critical Thinking Questions

1 Several years ago, senior executives at energy company CanOil wanted to acquire an exploration company (HBOG) that was owned by another energy company, AmOil. Rather than face a hostile takeover and unfavourable tax implications, CanOil's two top executives met with the CEO of AmOil to discuss a friendly exchange of stock to carry out the transaction. AmOil's chief executive was previously unaware of CanOil's plans, and as the meeting began, the AmOil executive warned that he was there merely to listen. The CanOil executives were confident that AmOil wanted to sell HBOG because energy legislation at the time made HBOG a poor investment for AmOil. AmOil's CEO remained silent for most of the meeting, which CanOil executives interpreted as an implied agreement to proceed to buy AmOil stock on the market. But when CanOil launched the stock purchase a month later, AmOil's CEO was both surprised and outraged. He thought he had given the CanOil executives the cold shoulder, remaining silent to show his disinterest in the deal. The misunderstanding nearly bankrupted CanOil because AmOil reacted by protecting its stock. What perceptual problem(s) likely occurred that led to this misunderstanding?

2 What mental models do you have about attending a university or college lecture? Are these mental models helpful? Could any of these mental models hold you back from achieving the full benefit of the lecture?

3 Do you define yourself in terms of the university or college you attend? Why or why not? What are the implications of your answer for your university?

4 During a diversity management session, a manager suggests that stereotypes are a necessary part of working with others. 'I have to make assumptions about what's in the other person's head, and stereotypes help me do that,' she explains. 'It's better to rely on stereotypes than to enter a working relationship with someone from another culture without any idea of what they believe in!' Discuss the merits of and problems with the manager's statement.

5 Describe how a manager or coach could use the process of self-fulfilling prophecy to enhance an individual's performance.

6 Describe a situation in which you used behaviour modification to influence someone's behaviour. What specifically did you do? What was the result?

7 Why are organisations moving toward the use of experiential approaches to learning? What conditions are required for success?

8 BusNews Pty Ltd is the leading stock market and business news service. Over the past two years, BusNews has experienced increased competition from other news providers. These competitors have brought in internet and other emerging computer technologies to link customers with information more quickly. There is little knowledge within BusNews about how to use these computer technologies. On the basis of the knowledge acquisition processes for knowledge management, explain how BusNews might gain the intellectual capital necessary to become more competitive in this respect.

CLASS EXERCISE

Skill Builder 3.1

The Learning Exercise

Purpose

This exercise is designed to help you understand how the contingencies of reinforcement in behaviour modification affect learning.

Materials

Any objects normally available in a classroom will be acceptable for this activity.

Instructions

The instructor will ask for three volunteers, who are then briefed outside the classroom. The instructor will spend a few minutes briefing the remaining students in the class about their duties. Then, one of the three volunteers will enter the room to participate in the exercise. When completed, the second volunteer enters the room and participates in the exercise. When completed, the third volunteer enters the class and participates in the exercise.

For you to gain the full benefit of this exercise, no other information will be provided here. However, the instructor will have more details at the beginning of this fun activity.

Skill Builder 3.2

CLASS EXERCISE

Stereotyping in Corporate Annual Reports

Purpose

This exercise is designed to help you diagnose evidence of stereotyping and identify corporate role models that minimise stereotyping in corporate annual reports.

Materials

You need to complete your research for this activity prior to class, including selecting a publicly traded company and downloading the past four or more years of its fully illustrated annual reports.

Instructions

The instructor may have you work alone or in groups for this activity. You will select a company that is publicly traded and posts its annual reports on the company website. Ideally, annual reports for at least the past four years should be available, and these reports should be presented in their final illustrated format (typically PDF replicas of the original hard-copy report).

You will then closely examine images in the selected company's recent annual reports in terms of how women, visible minorities, and older employees and clients are presented. Specifically, you should be prepared to discuss and provide the following details.

1. What percentage of images show (i.e. visually represent) women, visible minorities, and older workers and clients? You should also be sensitive to the size and placement of these images on the page and throughout the annual report.
2. In what roles are women, visible minorities, and older workers and clients depicted? For example, are women shown more in traditional or nontraditional occupations and nonwork roles in these annual reports?

If several years of annual reports are available, pick one that is a decade or more old and compare its visual representation/role depiction of women, visible minorities, and older employees and clients.

If possible, pick one of the most blatantly stereotypic illustrations you can find in these annual reports to show in class, either as a hard-copy printout or as a digital projection.

Skill Builder 3.3

SELF-ASSESSMENT

How Much Perceptual Structure Do you Need?

Purpose

This self-assessment is designed to help you estimate your personal need for perceptual structure.

Instructions

Read each of the statements below and decide how much you agree with each according to your attitudes, beliefs and experiences. Then use the scoring key in Appendix B at the end of this book to calculate your results. It is important for you to realise that there are no right or wrong answers to these questions. This self-assessment should be completed alone so that you can rate yourself honestly without concerns of social comparison. Class discussion will focus on the meaning of need for structure, as well as how this need influences the perceptual process at work and in other settings.

Personal Need for Structure Scale

To what extent do you agree or disagree with each of these statements about yourself?	Strongly agree	Moderately agree	Slightly agree	Slightly disagree	Moderately disagree	Strongly disagree
1. It upsets me to go into a situation without knowing what I can expect from it.	❑	❑	❑	❑	❑	❑
2. I'm not bothered by things that interrupt my daily routine.	❑	❑	❑	❑	❑	❑
3. I enjoy being spontaneous.	❑	❑	❑	❑	❑	❑
4. I find that a well-ordered life with regular hours makes my life tedious.	❑	❑	❑	❑	❑	❑
5. I find that a consistent routine enables me to enjoy life more.	❑	❑	❑	❑	❑	❑
6. I enjoy having a clear and structured mode of life.	❑	❑	❑	❑	❑	❑
7. I like to have a place for everything and everything in its place.	❑	❑	❑	❑	❑	❑
8. I don't like situations that are uncertain.	❑	❑	❑	❑	❑	❑
9. I hate to change my plans at the last minute.	❑	❑	❑	❑	❑	❑
10. I hate to be with people who are unpredictable.	❑	❑	❑	❑	❑	❑
11. I enjoy the exhilaration of being in unpredictable situations.	❑	❑	❑	❑	❑	❑
12. I become uncomfortable when the rules in a situation are not clear.	❑	❑	❑	❑	❑	❑

Source: M. M. Thompson, M. E. Naccarato, K. H. Parker and G. B. Moskowitz (Ed.), 'The Personal Need for Structure (PNS) and Personal Fear of Invalidity (PFI) Scales: Historical Perspectives, Present Applications and Future Directions.' *Cognitive Social Psychology: On the Tenure and Future of Social Cognition* (New York: Erlbaum), pp. 19–40, (2001)

Skill Builder 3.4

Available online

SELF-ASSESSMENT

Assessing Your Perspective Taking (Cognitive Empathy)

Empathy is an important perceptual ability in social relations, but the degree to which people empathise varies considerably. This self-assessment provides an estimate of one form of empathy, known as *cognitive empathy* or *perspective taking*. That is, it measures the level of your cognitive awareness of another person's situational and individual circumstances. To complete this scale, indicate the degree to which each of the statements presented does or does not describe you very well. You need to be honest with yourself to obtain a reasonable estimate of your level of perspective taking. The results show your relative position along the perspective-taking continuum and the general meaning of this score.

Skill Builder 3.5

Available online

SELF-ASSESSMENT

Assessing Your Emotional Empathy

Empathy is an important perceptual ability in social relations, but the degree to which people empathise varies considerably. This self-assessment provides an estimate of one form of empathy, known as *emotional empathy*—the extent that you are able to experience the emotions or feelings of another person. To complete this scale, indicate the degree to which each of the statements presented does or does not describe you very well. You need to be honest with yourself to obtain a reasonable estimate of your level of emotional empathy. The results show your relative position along the emotional empathy continuum and the general meaning of this score.

Endnotes

1 G. Hills and A. Mahmud, *Volunteering for Impact: Best Practices in International Corporate Volunteering* (Boston: FSG Social Impact Advisors, September 2007); IBM, *Sam Palmisano Discusses IBM's New Corporate Service Corps* (Armonk, NY: IBM, 25 July 2007); IBM, 'IBM's Corporate Service Corps Heading to Six Emerging Countries to Spark Socio-Economic Growth While Developing Global Leaders', news release (Armonk, NY, 26 March 2008); A. Campbell, 'Global Volunteers Do the Business', *New Zealand Herald*, 25 October 2008, F1; M. Jackson, 'Corporate Volunteers Reaching Worldwide', *Boston Globe*, 4 May 2008, 3; U. Hedquist, 'Kiwi Volunteer in Tanzania Project Receives Lessons in Life', *Computerworld (NZ)*, 22 January 2009.

2 J. S. Black, 'The Mindset of Global Leaders: Inquisitiveness and Duality', in *Advances in Global Leadership*, vol. 4, ed. W. H. Mobley and E. Weldon (Bingley, UK: Emerald, 2006), 181–200; O. Levy *et al.*, 'What We Talk About When We Talk About "Global Mindset": Managerial Cognition in Multinational Corporations', *Journal of International Business Studies* 38, no. 2 (2007): 231–258; S. Beechler and D. Baltzley, 'Creating a Global Mindset', *Chief Learning Officer* 7, no. 6 (2008): 40–45.

3 The effect of the target in selective attention is known as 'bottom-up selection'; the effect of the perceiver's psychodynamics on this process is known as 'top-down

selection'. See C. E. Connor, H. E. Egeth and S. Yantis, 'Visual Attention: Bottom-up Versus Top-Down', *Current Biology* 14, no. 19 (2004): R850–R852; E. I. Knudsen, 'Fundamental Components of Attention', *Annual Review of Neuroscience* 30, no. 1 (2007): 57–78.

4 A. Mack *et al.*, 'Perceptual Organization and Attention', *Cognitive Psychology* 24, no. 4 (1992): 475–501; A. R. Damasio, *Descartes' Error: Emotion, Reason, and the Human Brain* (New York: Putnam's Sons, 1994); C. Frith, 'A Framework for Studying the Neural Basis of Attention', *Neuropsychologia* 39, no. 12 (2001): 1367–1371; N. Lavie, 'Distracted and Confused?: Selective Attention under Load', *Trends in Cognitive Sciences* 9, no. 2 (2005): 75–82; M. Shermer, 'The Political Brain', *Scientific American* 295, no. 1 (2006): 36; D. Westen, *The Political Brain: The Role of Emotion in Deciding the Fate of the Nation* (Cambridge, MA: PublicAffairs, 2007).

5 Confirmation bias is defined as 'unwitting selectivity in the acquisition and use of evidence'. R. S. Nickerson, 'Confirmation Bias: A Ubiquitous Phenomenon in Many Guises', *Review of General Psychology* 2, no. 2 (1998): 175–220. This occurs in a variety of ways, including overweighting positive information, perceiving only positive information and restricting cognitive attention to a favoured hypothesis. Research has found that confirmation bias is typically nonconscious and driven by emotions.

6 S. Lewandowsky *et al.*, 'Memory for Fact, Fiction, and Misinformation. The Iraq War 2003', *Psychological Science* 16, no. 3 (2005): 190–195.

7 D. J. Simons and C. F. Chabris, 'Gorillas in Our Midst: Sustained Inattentional Blindness for Dynamic Events', *Perception* 28 (1999): 1059–1074.

8 K. A. Lane, J. Kang and M. R. Banaji, 'Implicit Social Cognition and Law', *Annual Review of Law and Social Science* 3, no. 1 (2007).

9 K. A. Findley and M. Scott, 'The Multiple Dimensions of Tunnel Vision in Criminal Cases', *Wisconsin Law Review* 2 (2006): 291–397; V. Geberth, '10 Most Common Errors in Death Investigations: Part 1', *Law & Order* 55, no. 11 (2007): 84–89; M. Allen, 'Unsolved Killings', *Roanoke Times (Virginia)*, 10 August 2008; C. Lo, A. Lamand and J. But, 'Police Step up Hunt after Fourth Prostitute Found Dead in City', *South China Morning Post* (Hong Kong), 18 March 2008.

10 C. N. Macrae and G. V. Bodenhausen, 'Social Cognition: Thinking Categorically about Others', *Annual Review of Psychology* 51 (2000): 93–120. For literature on the automaticity of the perceptual organisation and interpretation process, see J. A. Bargh, 'The Cognitive Monster: The Case against the Controllability of Automatic Stereotype Effects', in *Dual Process Theories in Social Psychology*, ed. S. Chaiken and Y. Trope (New York: Guilford, 1999), 361–382; J. A. Bargh and M. J. Ferguson, 'Beyond Behaviorism: On the Automaticity of Higher Mental Processes', *Psychological Bulletin* 126, no. 6 (2000): 925–945; M. Gladwell, *Blink: The Power of Thinking without Thinking* (New York: Little, Brown, 2005).

11 E. M. Altmann and B. D. Burns, 'Streak Biases in Decision Making: Data and a Memory Model', *Cognitive Systems Research* 6, no. 1 (2005): 5–16. For a discussion of cognitive closure and perception, see A. W. Kruglanski, *The Psychology of Closed Mindedness* (New York: Psychology Press, 2004).

12 N. Ambady and R. Rosenthal, 'Half a Minute: Predicting Teacher Evaluations from Thin Slices of Nonverbal Behavior and Physical Attractiveness', *Journal of Personality and Social Psychology* 64, no. 3 (1993): 431–441. For other research on thin slices, see N. Ambady and R. Rosenthal, 'Thin Slices of Expressive Behavior as Predictors of Interpersonal Consequences: A Meta-Analysis', *Psychological Bulletin* 111, no. 2 (1992): 256–274; N. Ambady *et al.*, 'Surgeons' Tone of Voice: A Clue to Malpractice History', *Surgery* 132, no. 1 (2002): 5–9.

13 P. M. Senge, *The Fifth Discipline: The Art and Practice of the Learning Organization* (New York: Doubleday Currency, 1990), ch. 10; P. N. Johnson-Laird, 'Mental Models and Deduction', *Trends in Cognitive Sciences* 5, no. 10 (2001): 434–442; A. B. Markman and D. Gentner, 'Thinking', *Annual Review of Psychology* 52 (2001): 223–247; T. J. Chermack, 'Mental Models in Decision Making and Implications for Human Resource Development', *Advances in Developing Human Resources* 5, no. 4 (2003): 408–422.

14 M. A. Hogg *et al.*, 'The Social Identity Perspective: Intergroup Relations, Self-Conception, and Small Groups', *Small Group Research* 35, no. 3 (2004): 246–276; J. Jetten, R. Spears and T. Postmes, 'Intergroup Distinctiveness and Differentiation: A Meta-Analytic Integration', *Journal of Personality and Social Psychology* 86, no. 6 (2004): 862–879.

15 J. W. Jackson and E. R. Smith, 'Conceptualizing Social Identity: A New Framework and Evidence for the Impact of Different Dimensions', *Personality and Social Psychology Bulletin* 25 (January 1999): 120–135.

16 L. Falkenberg, 'Improving the Accuracy of Stereotypes within the Workplace', *Journal of Management* 16 (1990): 107–118; S. T. Fiske, 'Stereotyping, Prejudice, and Discrimination', in *Handbook of Social Psychology*, ed. D. T. Gilbert, S. T. Fiske and G. Lindzey, 4th edn (New York: McGraw-Hill, 1998), 357–411; Macrae and Bodenhausen, 'Social Cognition: Thinking Categorically about Others'.

17 C. N. Macrae, A. B. Milne and G. V. Bodenhausen, 'Stereotypes as Energy-Saving Devices: A Peek inside

the Cognitive Toolbox', *Journal of Personality and Social Psychology* 66, no. 1 (1994): 37–47; J. W. Sherman *et al.*, 'Stereotype Efficiency Reconsidered: Encoding Flexibility under Cognitive Load', *Journal of Personality and Social Psychology* 75, no. 3 (1998): 589–606; Macrae and Bodenhausen, 'Social Cognition: Thinking Categorically about Others'.

18 L. Sinclair and Z. Kunda, 'Motivated Stereotyping of Women: She's Fine If She Praised Me but Incompetent If She Criticized Me', *Personality and Social Psychology Bulletin* 26 (November 2000): 1329–1342; J. C. Turner and S. A. Haslam, 'Social Identity, Organizations, and Leadership', in *Groups at Work: Theory and Research*, ed. M. E. Turner (Mahwah, NJ: Lawrence Erlbaum Associates, 2001), 25–65.

19 A. L. Friedman and S. R. Lyne, 'The Beancounter Stereotype: Towards a General Model of Stereotype Generation', *Critical Perspectives on Accounting* 12, no. 4 (2001): 423–451.

20 'Employers Face New Danger: Accidental Age Bias', *Omaha World-Herald*, 10 October 2005, D1; 'Tiptoeing through the Employment Minefield of Race, Sex, and Religion? Here's Another One', *North West Business Insider (Manchester, UK)*, February 2006.

21 S. O. Gaines and E. S. Reed, 'Prejudice: From Allport to Dubois', *American Psychologist* 50 (February 1995): 96–103; Fiske, 'Stereotyping, Prejudice, and Discrimination'; M. Hewstone, M. Rubin and H. Willis, 'Intergroup Bias', *Annual Review of Psychology* 53 (2002): 575–604.

22 P. A. Riach and J. Rich, 'Testing for Racial Discrimination in the Labour Market', *Cambridge Journal of Economics* 15 (1991): 239–256.

23 M. G. Wilson *et al.*, 'A Rose by Any Other Name: The Effect of Ethnicity and Name on Access to Employment', *University of Auckland Business Review* 7, no. 2 (2005): 65–72. One review of these studies concluded that employment discrimination against non-whites and women has been persistent and pervasive across time. See P. A. Riach and J. Rich, 'Field Experiments of Discrimination in the Market Place', *The Economic Journal* 112, no. 483 (2002): F480–F518.

24 M. Weinstein, 'Racism, Sexism, Ageism: Workplace Not Getting Any Friendlier', *Training*, May 2006, 11.

25 M. Patriquin, 'Quebec Farm Segregated Black Workers', *Globe & Mail* (Toronto), 30 April 2005, A1; S. Foley, 'The Women Who Took on a Banking Giant and Won a $33m Sexism Case', *The Independent* (London), 5 April 2008.

26 P. Ford, 'Next French Revolution: A Less Colorblind Society', *Christian Science Monitor*, 14 November 2005, 1; J. W. Anderson, 'French Firm Tests Colorblind Hiring', *Washington Post*, 29 January 2006, A20; L. Ash, 'Escaping France's Ghettoes', *BBC Radio: Crossing Continents (London)*, 29 March 2007; P. Gumbel, 'The French Exodus', *Time International*, 16 April 2007, 18; A. Sage, 'L'Oréal Accused of Discrimination in "All-White" Campaign', *The Times (London)*, 16 May 2007, 57; D. Vidal, 'Affirmative Action Bypasses Those at the Bottom of the Pile', *Le Monde Diplomatique*, May 2007. In an interesting twist, L'Oréal now lists Hamid Senni as one of its consultants on workplace diversity.

27 J. A. Bargh and T. L. Chartrand, 'The Unbearable Automaticity of Being', *American Psychologist* 54, no. 7 (1999): 462–479; S. T. Fiske, 'What We Know Now about Bias and Intergroup Conflict, the Problem of the Century', *Current Directions in Psychological Science* 11, no. 4 (2002): 123–128. For recent evidence that shows that intensive training can minimise stereotype activation, see K. Kawakami *et al.*, 'Just Say No (to Stereotyping): Effects of Training in the Negation of Stereotypic Associations on Stereotype Activation', *Journal of Personality and Social Psychology* 78, no. 5 (2000): 871–888; E. A. Plant, B. M. Peruche and D. A. Butz, 'Eliminating Automatic Racial Bias: Making Race Non-Diagnostic for Responses to Criminal Suspects', *Journal of Experimental Social Psychology* 41, no. 2 (2005): 141.

28 H. H. Kelley, *Attribution in Social Interaction* (Morristown, NJ: General Learning Press, 1971).

29 J. M. Feldman, 'Beyond Attribution Theory: Cognitive Processes in Performance Appraisal', *Journal of Applied Psychology* 66, no. 2 (1981): 127–148.

30 J. M. Crant and T. S. Bateman, 'Assignment of Credit and Blame for Performance Outcomes', *Academy of Management Journal* 36 (1993): 7–27; B. Weiner, 'Intrapersonal and Interpersonal Theories of Motivation from an Attributional Perspective', *Educational Psychology Review* 12 (2000): 1–14; N. Bacon and P. Blyton, 'Worker Responses to Teamworking: Exploring Employee Attributions of Managerial Motives', *International Journal of Human Resource Management* 16, no. 2 (2005): 238–255.

31 Fundamental attribution error is part of a larger phenomenon known as *correspondence bias*. See D. T. Gilbert and P. S. Malone, 'The Correspondence Bias', *Psychological Bulletin* 117, no. 1 (1995): 21–38.

32 I. Choi, R. E. Nisbett and A. Norenzayan, 'Causal Attribution across Cultures: Variation and Universality', *Psychological Bulletin* 125, no. 1 (1999): 47–63; D. S. Krull *et al.*, 'The Fundamental Fundamental Attribution Error: Correspondence Bias in Individualist and Collectivist Cultures', *Personality and Social Psychology Bulletin* 25, no. 10 (1999): 1208–1219; R. E. Nisbett, *The Geography of Thought: How Asians and Westerners Think Differently—and Why* (New York: Free Press, 2003), ch. 5.

33 P. J. Taylor and J. L. Pierce, 'Effects of Introducing a Performance Management System on Employees' Subsequent Attitudes and Effort', *Public Personnel Management* 28 (Fall 1999): 423–452; F. Lee and L. Z. Tiedens, 'Who's Being Served? "Self-Serving" Attributions in Social Hierarchies', *Organizational Behavior and Human Decision Processes* 84, no. 2 (2001): 254–287; E. W. K. Tsang, 'Self-Serving Attributions in Corporate Annual Reports: A Replicated Study', *Journal of Management Studies* 39, no. 1 (2002): 51–65; N. J. Roese and J. M. Olson, 'Better, Stronger, Faster: Self-Serving Judgment, Affect Regulation, and the Optimal Vigilance Hypothesis', *Perspectives on Psychological Science* 2, no. 2 (2007): 124–141.

34 Similar models are presented in D. Eden, 'Self-Fulfilling Prophecy as a Management Tool: Harnessing Pygmalion', *Academy of Management Review* 9 (1984): 64–73; R. H. G. Field and D. A. Van Seters, 'Management by Expectations (MBE): The Power of Positive Prophecy', *Journal of General Management* 14 (Winter 1988): 19–33; D. O. Trouilloud *et al.*, 'The Influence of Teacher Expectations on Student Achievement in Physical Education Classes: Pygmalion Revisited', *European Journal of Social Psychology* 32 (2002): 591–607.

35 D. Eden, 'Interpersonal Expectations in Organizations', in *Interpersonal Expectations: Theory, Research, and Applications*, ed. P. D. Blanck (Cambridge, UK: Cambridge University Press, 1993), 154–178.

36 D. Eden, 'Pygmalion Goes to Boot Camp: Expectancy, Leadership, and Trainee Performance', *Journal of Applied Psychology* 67, no. 2 (1982): 194–199; R. P. Brown and E. C. Pinel, 'Stigma on My Mind: Individual Differences in the Experience of Stereotype Threat', *Journal of Experimental Social Psychology* 39, no. 6 (2003): 626–633.

37 S. Madon, L. Jussim and J. Eccles, 'In Search of the Powerful Self-Fulfilling Prophecy', *Journal of Personality and Social Psychology* 72, no. 4 (1997): 791–809; A. E. Smith, L. Jussim and J. Eccles, 'Do Self-Fulfilling Prophecies Accumulate, Dissipate, or Remain Stable over Time?', *Journal of Personality and Social Psychology* 77, no. 3 (1999): 548–565; S. Madon *et al.*, 'Self-Fulfilling Prophecies: The Synergistic Accumulative Effect of Parents' Beliefs on Children's Drinking Behavior', *Psychological Science* 15, no. 12 (2005): 837–845.

38 W. H. Cooper, 'Ubiquitous Halo', *Psychological Bulletin* 90, no. 2 (1981): 218–244; K. R. Murphy, R. A. Jako and R. L. Anhalt, 'Nature and Consequences of Halo Error: A Critical Analysis', *Journal of Applied Psychology* 78, no. 2 (1993): 218–225; T. H. Feeley, 'Comment on Halo Effects in Rating and Evaluation Research', *Human Communication Research* 28, no. 4 (2002): 578–586. For a variation of the classic halo effect in business settings, see P. Rosenzweig, *The Halo Effect ... And the Eight Other Business Delusions that Deceive Managers* (New York: Free Press, 2007).

39 C. L. Kleinke, *First Impressions: The Psychology of Encountering Others* (Englewood Cliffs, NJ: Prentice Hall, 1975); E. A. Lind, L. Kray and L. Thompson, 'Primacy Effects in Justice Judgments: Testing Predictions from Fairness Heuristic Theory', *Organizational Behavior and Human Decision Processes* 85 (July 2001): 189–210; O. Ybarra, 'When First Impressions Don't Last: The Role of Isolation and Adaptation Processes in the Revision of Evaluative Impressions', *Social Cognition* 19 (October 2001): 491–520; S. D. Bond *et al.*, 'Information Distortion in the Evaluation of a Single Option', *Organizational Behavior and Human Decision Processes* 102, no. 2 (2007): 240–254.

40 D. D. Steiner and J. S. Rain, 'Immediate and Delayed Primacy and Recency Effects in Performance Evaluation', *Journal of Applied Psychology* 74, no. 1 (1989): 136–142; K. T. Trotman, 'Order Effects and Recency: Where Do We Go from Here?', *Accounting & Finance* 40 (2000): 169–182; W. Green, 'Impact of the Timing of an Inherited Explanation on Auditors' Analytical Procedures Judgements', *Accounting & Finance* 44 (2004): 369–392.

41 R. W. Clement and J. Krueger, 'The Primacy of Self-Referent Information in Perceptions of Social Consensus', *British Journal of Social Psychology* 39 (2000): 279–299; R. L. Gross and S. E. Brodt, 'How Assumptions of Consensus Undermine Decision Making', *MIT Sloan Management Review*, January 2001, 86–94; J. Oliver *et al.*, 'Projection of Own on Others' Job Characteristics: Evidence for the False Consensus Effect in Job Characteristics Information', *International Journal of Selection and Assessment* 13, no. 1 (2005): 63–74.

42 D. Eden *et al.*, 'Implanting Pygmalion Leadership Style through Workshop Training: Seven Field Experiments', *Leadership Quarterly* 11, no. 2 (2000): 171–210; S. S. White and E. A. Locke, 'Problems with the Pygmalion Effect and Some Proposed Solutions', *Leadership Quarterly* 11 (Autumn 2000): 389–415; M. Bendick, M. L. Egan and S. M. Lofhjelm, 'Workforce Diversity Training: From Anti-Discrimination Compliance to Organizational Development HR', *Human Resource Planning* 24 (2001): 10–25; L. Roberson, C. T. Kulik and M. B. Pepper, 'Using Needs Assessment to Resolve Controversies in Diversity Training Design', *Group & Organization Management* 28, no. 1 (2003): 148–174; D. E. Hogan and M. Mallott, 'Changing Racial Prejudice through Diversity Education', *Journal of College Student Development* 46, no. 2 (2005): 115–125.

43 T. W. Costello and S. S. Zalkind, *Psychology in Administration: A Research Orientation* (Englewood Cliffs,

NJ: Prentice Hall, 1963), 45–46; J. M. Kouzes and B. Z. Posner, *The Leadership Challenge*, 4th edn (San Francisco: Jossey-Bass, 2007), ch. 3.

44 B. George, *Authentic Leadership: Rediscovering the Secrets to Creating Lasting Value* (San Francisco: Jossey-Bass, 2004); W. L. Gardner *et al.*, '"Can You See the Real Me?" A Self-Based Model of Authentic Leader and Follower Development', *Leadership Quarterly* 16, no. 3 (2005): 343–372; B. George, *True North: Discover Your Authentic Leadership* (San Francisco: Jossey-Bass, 2007).

45 For a discussion of the Implicit Association Test, including critique, see H. Blanton *et al.*, 'Decoding the Implicit Association Test: Implications for Criterion Prediction', *Journal of Experimental Social Psychology* 42, no. 2 (2006): 192–212; A. G. Greenwald, B. A. Nosek and N. Sriram, 'Consequential Validity of the Implicit Association Test: Comment on Blanton and Jaccard (2006)', *American Psychologist* 61, no. 1 (2006): 56–61; W. Hofmann *et al.*, 'Implicit and Explicit Attitudes and Interracial Interaction: The Moderating Role of Situationally Available Control Resources', *Group Processes Intergroup Relations* 11, no. 1 (2008): 69–87.

46 P. Babcock, 'Detecting Hidden Bias', *HRMagazine*, February 2006, 50.

47 J. Luft, *Group Processes: An Introduction to Group Dynamics* (Palo Alto, CA: Mayfield, 1984). For a variation of this model, see J. Hall, 'Communication Revisited', *California Management Review* 15 (Spring 1973): 56–67.

48 L. C. Miller and D. A. Kenny, 'Reciprocity of Self-Disclosure at the Individual and Dyadic Levels: A Social Relations Analysis', *Journal of Personality and Social Psychology* 50, no. 4 (1986): 713–719.

49 J. Dixon and K. Durrheim, 'Contact and the Ecology of Racial Division: Some Varieties of Informal Segregation', *British Journal of Social Psychology* 42, no. 1 (2003): 1–23; P. J. Henry and C. D. Hardin, 'The Contact Hypothesis Revisited: Status Bias in the Reduction of Implicit Prejudice in the United States and Lebanon', *Psychological Science* 17, no. 10 (2006): 862–868; T. F. Pettigrew and L. R. Tropp, 'A Meta-Analytic Test of Intergroup Contact Theory', *Journal of Personality and Social Psychology* 90, no. 5 (2006): 751–783; C. Tredoux and G. Finchilescu, 'The Contact Hypothesis and Intergroup Relations 50 Years On: Introduction to the Special Issue', *South African Journal of Psychology* 37, no. 4 (2007): 667–678; T. F. Pettigrew, 'Future Directions for Intergroup Contact Theory and Research', *International Journal of Intercultural Relations* 32, no. 3 (2008): 187–199.

50 C. Hymowitz, 'IBM Combines Volunteer Service, Teamwork to Cultivate Emerging Markets', *Wall Street Journal*, 4 August 2008, B6.

51 W. Frey, 'Rubbish Boy Doing Well as Junk Man', *Metro-Vancouver*, 25 April 2005, 11; PR Newswire, 'Domino's Pizza Named One of Michigan's "Cool Places to Work"', news release (Ann Arbor, 10 September 2007).

52 G. Thomas, 'Fyfe Rewrites the Tune at ANZ', *Air Transport World*, September 2007, 61.

53 W. G. Stephen and K. A. Finlay, 'The Role of Empathy in Improving Intergroup Relations', *Journal of Social Issues* 55 (Winter 1999): 729–743; S. K. Parker and C. M. Axtell, 'Seeing Another Viewpoint: Antecedents and Outcomes of Employee Perspective Taking', *Academy of Management Journal* 44 (December 2001): 1085–1100; G. J. Vreeke and I. L. van der Mark, 'Empathy, an Integrative Model', *New Ideas in Psychology* 21, no. 3 (2003): 177–207.

54 I. Nonaka and H. Takeuchi, *The Knowledge-Creating Company: How Japanese Companies Create the Dynamics of Innovation* (New York: Oxford University Press, 1995); P. Duguid, '"The Art of Knowing": Social and Tacit Dimensions of Knowledge and the Limits of the Community of Practice', *The Information Society* 21 (2005): 109–118.

55 B. F. Skinner, *About Behaviorism* (New York: Alfred A. Knopf, 1974); J. Komaki, T. Coombs and S. Schepman, 'Motivational Implications of Reinforcement Theory', in *Motivation and Leadership at Work*, ed. R. M. Steers, L. W. Porter and G. A. Bigley (New York: McGraw-Hill, 1996), 34–52; R. G. Miltenberger, *Behavior Modification: Principles and Procedures* (Pacific Grove, CA: Brooks/Cole, 1997).

56 T. K. Connellan, *How to Improve Human Performance: Behaviorism in Business and Industry* (New York: Harper & Row, 1978), 48–57; F. Luthans and R. Kreitner, *Organizational Behavior Modification and Beyond: An Operant and Social Learning Approach* (Glenview, IL: Scott Foresman, 1985), 85–88.

57 Miltenberger, *Behavior Modification: Principles and Procedures*, chs 4–6.

58 Punishment can also include removing a pleasant consequence, such as when employees must switch from business-class to economy-class flying when their sales fall below the threshold for top-tier sales 'stars'.

59 T. R. Hinkin and C. A. Schriesheim, '"If You Don't Hear from Me You Know You Are Doing Fine"', *Cornell Hotel & Restaurant Administration Quarterly* 45, no. 4 (2004): 362–372.

60 L. K. Trevino, 'The Social Effects of Punishment in Organizations: A Justice Perspective', *Academy of Management Review* 17 (1992): 647–676; L. E. Atwater *et al.*, 'Recipient and Observer Reactions to Discipline: Are Managers Experiencing Wishful Thinking?', *Journal of Organizational Behavior* 22, no. 3 (2001): 249–270.

61 G. P. Latham and V. L. Huber, 'Schedules of Reinforcement: Lessons from the Past and Issues for the Future', *Journal of Organizational Behavior Management* 13 (1992): 125–149; B. A. Williams, 'Challenges to Timing-Based Theories of Operant Behavior', *Behavioural Processes* 62 (April 2003): 115–123.

62 S. Overman, 'Many Offer Basic Wellness Initiatives, Few Track Results', *Employee Benefit News*, 15 April 2006; H. Wecsler, 'Sick Day Incentive Plan Favored by NLR Board', *Arkansas Democrat Gazette*, 17 February 2006, 14.

63 ExxonMobil, *UK and Ireland Corporate Citizenship* (ExxonMobil, August 2004); J. Masanauskas, 'Unions in Sick Leave Tussle', *Herald-Sun (Melbourne)*, 7 July 2006, 7; A. Tilbury, 'Offer Incentives and Staff Will Never Tyre', *Courier-Mail (Brisbane)*, 15 December 2008, 54.

64 D. Gibson, 'Investing in Employees' Health', *Lane Report (Kentucky)*, December 2007, 28; '10,000 Steps in the Right Direction', *Our City (Stoke-on-Trent)*, no. 8, January 2009, 11; D. Blackhurst, '£1m Bill to Get Council and NHS Staff Walking', *The Sentinel (Staffordshire)*, 2 February 2009, 13}.

65 Bargh and Ferguson, 'Beyond Behaviorism'. Some writers argue that behaviourists long ago accepted the relevance of cognitive processes in behaviour modification. See I. Kirsch *et al.*, 'The Role of Cognition in Classical and Operant Conditioning', *Journal of Clinical Psychology* 60, no. 4 (2004): 369–392.

66 A. Bandura, *Social Foundations of Thought and Action: A Social Cognitive Theory* (Englewood Cliffs, NJ: Prentice Hall, 1986).

67 A. Pescuric and W. C. Byham, 'The New Look of Behavior Modeling', *Training & Development* 50 (July 1996): 24–30.

68 M. E. Schnake, 'Vicarious Punishment in a Work Setting', *Journal of Applied Psychology* 71, no. 2 (1986): 343–345; Trevino, 'The Social Effects of Punishment in Organizations: A Justice Perspective'; J. B. DeConinck, 'The Effect of Punishment on Sales Managers' Outcome Expectancies and Responses to Unethical Sales Force Behavior', *American Business Review* 21, no. 2 (2003): 135–140.

69 A. Bandura, 'Self-Reinforcement: Theoretical and Methodological Considerations', *Behaviorism* 4 (1976): 135–155; C. A. Frayne and J. M. Geringer, 'Self-Management Training for Improving Job Performance: A Field Experiment Involving Salespeople', *Journal of Applied Psychology* 85, no. 3 (2000): 361–372; J. B. Vancouver and D. V. Day, 'Industrial and Organisation Research on Self-Regulation: From Constructs to Applications', *Applied Psychology: An International Journal* 54, no. 2 (2005): 155–185.

70 D. A. Kolb, *Experiential Learning* (Englewood Cliffs, NJ: Prentice-Hall, 1984); S. Gherardi, D. Nicolini and F. Odella, 'Toward a Social Understanding of How People Learn in Organizations', *Management Learning* 29 (September 1998): 273–297; D. A. Kolb, R. E. Boyatzis and C. Mainemelis, 'Experiential Learning Theory: Previous Research and New Directions', in *Perspectives on Thinking, Learning, and Cognitive Styles*, ed. R. J. Sternberg and L.F. Zhang (Mahwah, NJ: Lawrence Erlbaum, 2001), 227–248.

71 W. E. Baker and J. M. Sinkula, 'The Synergistic Effect of Market Orientation and Learning Orientation on Organizational Performance', *Academy of Marketing Science Journal* 27, no. 4 (1999): 411–427; Z. Emden, A. Yaprak and S. T. Cavusgil, 'Learning from Experience in International Alliances: Antecedents and Firm Performance Implications', *Journal of Business Research* 58, no. 7 (2005): 883–892.

72 R. Farson and R. Keyes, 'The Failure-Tolerant Leader', *Harvard Business Review* 80 (August 2002): 64–71; T. C. Li, 'Loyalty Pays Off for Chief of Malaysia's CIMB', *Wall Street Journal Asia*, 23 June 2008, 36.

73 M. Cheong, 'Risk Awareness on the Table', *South China Morning Post (Hong Kong)*, 10 June 2008, 10; H. Takeda, 'Medical Risk and Quality Management through Informatics', Paper presented at Saudi e-Health Conference, Riyadh, 19 March 2008.

74 H. Shipton, 'Cohesion or Confusion? Towards a Typology for Organizational Learning Research', *International Journal of Management Reviews* 8, no. 4 (2006): 233–252; D. Jiménez-Jiménez and J. G. Cegarra-Navarro, 'The Performance Effect of Organizational Learning and Market Orientation', *Industrial Marketing Management* 36, no. 6 (2007): 694–708.

75 R. Garud and A. Kumaraswamy, 'Vicious and Virtuous Circles in the Management of Knowledge: The Case of Infosys Technologies', *MIS Quarterly* 29, no. 1 (2005): 9–33.

CHAPTER 4 workplace emotions, attitudes and stress

LEARNING OBJECTIVES

After reading this chapter, you should be able to:

- explain how emotions and cognition (conscious reasoning) influence attitudes and behaviour
- identify the conditions that require, and the problems associated with, emotional labour
- describe the four dimensions of emotional intelligence
- summarise the consequences of job dissatisfaction in terms of the exit-voice-loyalty-neglect model
- discuss the effects of job satisfaction on job performance and customer service
- distinguish organisational (affective) and continuance commitment, and discuss their influences on employee behaviour
- describe five strategies for increasing organisational (affective) commitment
- define *stress* and describe the stress experience
- explain why the same stressor might produce different stress levels in two people
- identify five ways to manage workplace stress.

Clydesdale Bank

By giving its contact centre employees more positive experiences at work, Clydesdale Bank (a division of National Australia Bank) has reduced absenteeism and turnover while significantly improving customer satisfaction.

Contact centre employees at Clydesdale Bank—a Scottish subsidiary of National Australia Bank (NAB)—were not very happy a few years ago. Up to 12 per cent of the 300 staff were absent each day. Employee turnover was so high—around 65 per cent—that managers spent much of their time hiring and inducting replacements for those who quit. Kevin Page, head of Clydesdale's contact centre at the time, quipped: 'We were a professional recruitment and training company.' Customer service suffered, operating costs were 25 per cent above the industry average in Europe and employee productivity was substantially below average.

Two years later, Clydesdale's contact centre had become a global role model. Job satisfaction and commitment improved substantially. Absenteeism dropped to four per cent each day; employee turnover was cut in half. Customers were much more satisfied with their contact centre calls. Due to this dramatic improvement, Clydesdale Bank won a Best Contact Centre award for its region (including Europe, the Middle East and Africa). A few months later, it was named the best large contact centre in the world, beating 1000 entrants across all industries.

How did NAB's Clydesdale Bank achieve this amazing turnaround? According to Kevin Page, now Clydesdale Bank's operations director, the answer is treating employees well so that they treat customers well. Page and his management team listened to and acted on employee concerns, spruced up the work environment, introduced career development programs, provided better coaching and gave staff more freedom to decide how to serve clients. 'Our staff started to treat their jobs more seriously,' says Page. 'They felt their role was important and felt better about themselves.'

Around the same time as Clydesdale's contact centre overhaul, the Bank of New Zealand (BNZ), another National Australia Bank subsidiary, also changed its contact centres for the better. 'Our centres were not attractive places to work,' recalls Susan Basile, BNZ's managing director of direct sales and service. To improve morale and performance, BNZ established better work shifts, raised the importance of call centres to the organisation and developed better career pathways to management positions. The company also encouraged employees to have 'great conversations' with customers rather than focus on completing as many calls as possible. As a result, BNZ recently won a Best in Customer Service award for a contact centre in the Asia-Pacific region across all industries. It was also rated as the top customer contact centre in New Zealand against all industries for three consecutive years.[1]

Clydesdale Bank, Bank of New Zealand and other National Australia Bank subsidiaries are discovering that emotions and attitudes make a difference in individual behaviour and wellbeing, as well as in the organisation's performance and customer service. Over the past decade, the field of organisational behaviour has experienced a sea change in thinking about workplace emotions, so this chapter begins by introducing the concept and explaining why researchers are so eager to discover how emotions influence attitudes and behaviour. Next, we consider the dynamics of emotional labour, followed by the popular topic of emotional intelligence. The specific work attitudes of job satisfaction and organisational commitment are then discussed, including their association with various employee behaviours and work performance. The final section looks at work-related stress, including the stress experience, three prominent stressors, individual differences in stress and ways to combat excessive stress.

EMOTIONS IN THE WORKPLACE

LEARNING OBJECTIVE 

Explain how emotions and cognition (conscious reasoning) influence attitudes and behaviour.

Emotions influence almost everything we do in the workplace. This is a strong statement, and one that you would rarely find a decade ago in organisational behaviour research or textbooks. Until recently, OB experts assumed that a person's thoughts and actions were governed primarily by conscious reasoning (called *cognition*). Yet groundbreaking discoveries in neuroscience have revealed that our perceptions, attitudes, decisions and behaviour are influenced by both cognition and emotion.[2] In fact, emotions may have a greater influence because emotional processes often occur before cognitive processes and, consequently, influence the latter. By ignoring emotionality, many theories have overlooked a large piece of the puzzle about human behaviour in the workplace.

emotions Physiological, behavioural and psychological episodes experienced toward an object, person or event that create a state of readiness.

Emotions are physiological, behavioural and psychological episodes experienced toward an object, person or event that create a state of readiness.[3] These 'episodes' are very brief events that typically subside or occur in waves lasting from milliseconds to a few minutes. Emotions are directed toward someone or something. For example, we experience joy, fear, anger and other emotional episodes toward tasks, customers or a software program we are using. This differs from *moods*, which are less intense, longer-term emotional states that are not directed toward anything in particular.[4]

Emotions are experiences. They represent changes in our physiological state (e.g. blood pressure, heart rate), psychological state (e.g. ability to think clearly) and behaviour (e.g. facial expression). Most of these emotional reactions are subtle and occur without our awareness. This is a particularly important point because people often think about 'getting emotional' when the subject of emotions is mentioned. In reality, you experience emotions every minute but aren't even aware of most of them. Finally, emotions put us in a state of readiness. When we get worried, for example, our heart rate and blood pressure increase to make our body better prepared to engage in 'fight or flight'. Strong emotions also trigger our conscious awareness of a threat or opportunity in the external environment.[5]

Types of Emotions

People experience many emotions as well as various combinations of emotions, but all of them have two common features. First, emotions generate a global evaluation (called *core affect*) that something is good or bad, helpful or harmful, to be approached or to be avoided. Second, all emotions produce some level of activation. However, they vary considerably in this activation, that is, in how much they demand our attention and motivate us to act. These two dimensions of emotions are the foundation of the circumplex model shown in Exhibit 4.1.[6] 'Distressed' is a negative emotion that generates a high level of activation, whereas 'relaxed' is a pleasant emotion that has fairly low activation.

Emotions, Attitudes and Behaviour

To understand how emotions influence our thoughts and behaviour in the workplace, we first need to know about attitudes. **Attitudes** represent the cluster of beliefs, assessed feelings and behavioural intentions toward a person, object or event (called an *attitude object*).[7] Attitudes are *judgements*, whereas emotions are *experiences*. In other words, attitudes involve conscious logical reasoning, whereas emotions operate as events, usually without our awareness. We also experience most emotions briefly, whereas our attitude toward someone or something is more stable over time.

attitudes The cluster of beliefs, assessed feelings and behavioural intentions toward a person, object or event (called an *attitude object*).

Until recently, experts believed that attitudes could be understood just by the three cognitive components illustrated on the left side of Exhibit 4.2: beliefs, feelings and behavioural intentions. Now evidence suggests that a parallel emotional process is also at work, shown on the right

Exhibit 4.1 *Circumplex Model of Emotions*

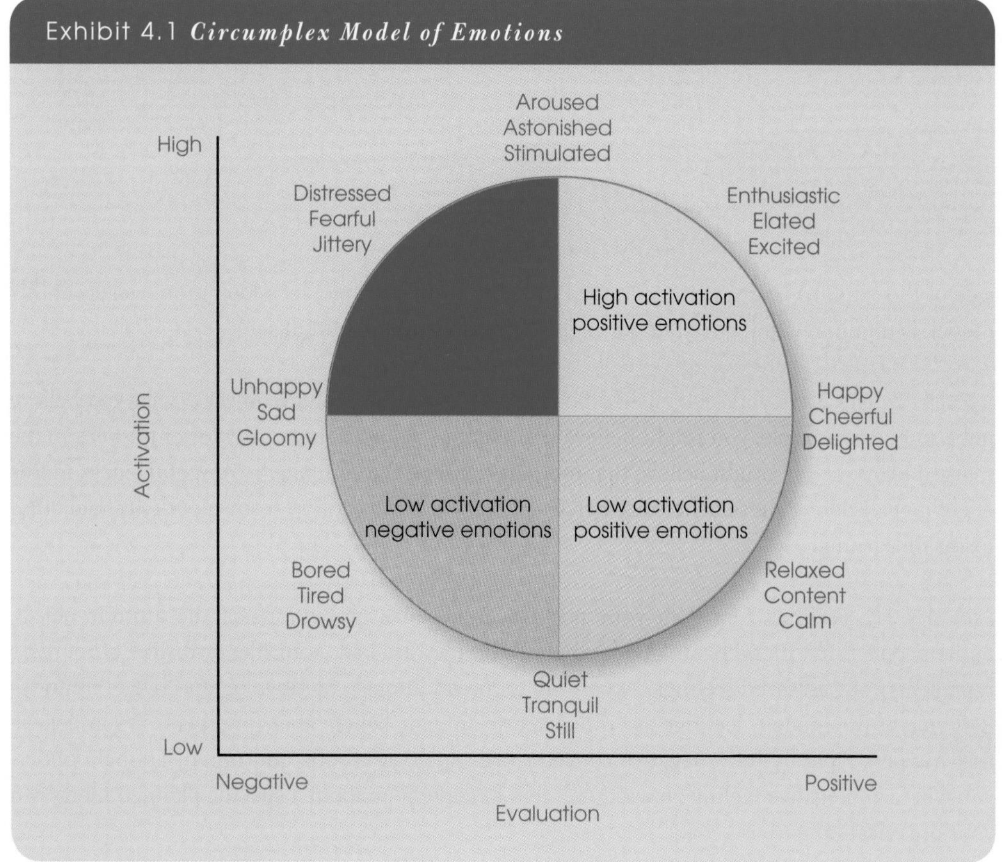

Sources: Adapted from J. Larson, E. Diener and R. E. Lucas, 'Emotion: Models, Measures, and Differences', in *Emotions in the Workplace*, ed. R. G. Lord, R. J. Klimoski and R. Kanfer (San Francisco: Jossey-Bass, 2002), 64–113; J. A. Russell, 'Core Affect and the Psychological Construction of Emotion', *Psychological Review* 110, no. 1 (2003): 145–172.

Exhibit 4.2 *Model of Emotions, Attitudes and Behaviour*

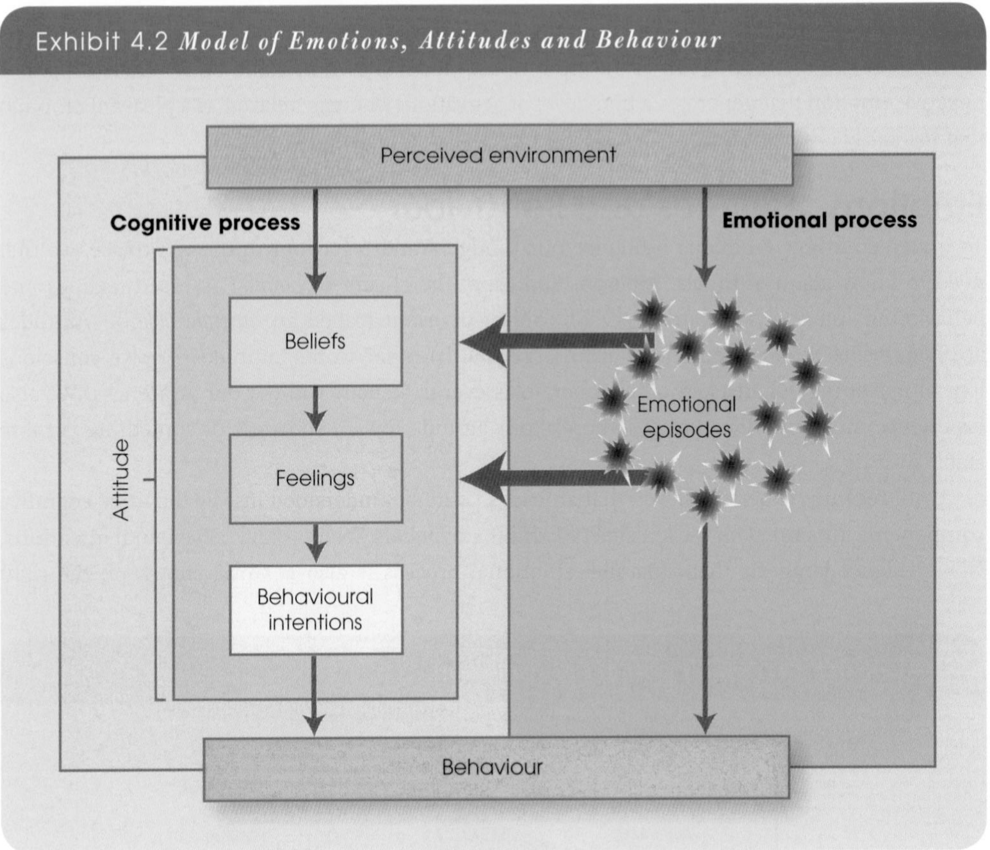

side of the exhibit.[8] Using attitude toward mergers as an example, let's look more closely at this model, beginning with the traditional cognitive perspective of attitudes.

BELIEFS These are your established perceptions about the attitude object—what you believe to be true. For example, you might believe that mergers reduce job security for employees in the merged firms, or you might believe that mergers increase the company's competitiveness in this era of globalisation. These beliefs are perceived facts that you acquire from experience and other forms of learning.

FEELINGS Feelings represent your positive or negative evaluations of the attitude object. Some people think mergers are good; others think they are bad. Your like or dislike of mergers represents your assessed feelings. According to the traditional cognitive perspective of attitudes (left side of the model), feelings are calculated from your beliefs about mergers. If you believe that mergers typically have negative consequences such as lay-offs and organisational politics, you will form negative feelings toward mergers in general or about a specific planned merger in your organisation.

BEHAVIOURAL INTENTIONS Intentions represent your motivation to engage in a particular behaviour regarding the attitude object.[9] Upon hearing that the company will merge with another organisation, you might become motivated to look for a job elsewhere or possibly to complain to management about the merger decision. Your feelings toward mergers motivate your behavioural intentions, and which actions you choose depends on your past experience, self-concept (values, personality) and social norms of appropriate behaviour.

Exhibit 4.2 also illustrates that behavioural intentions directly predict behaviour. However, whether your intentions translate into behaviour depends on all four elements of the MARS model, such as opportunity and ability to act. Attitudes are also more likely to influence behaviour when they are strong, meaning that they are anchored by strong emotions.

How Emotions Influence Attitudes and Behaviour

As we mentioned, emotions play a central role in forming and changing employee attitudes.[10] The right side of Exhibit 4.2 illustrates this process, which (like the cognitive process) also begins with perceptions of the world around us. The emotional centres of our brain quickly and imprecisely tag emotional markers onto incoming sensory information, triggered by whether that information supports or threatens our innate drives. These markers are not calculated feelings; they are automatic and nonconscious emotional responses based on very thin slices of sensory information.[11]

Returning to the example of your attitude toward mergers, you might experience worry, nervousness or relief upon learning that your company intends to merge with a competitor. The large dots on the right side of Exhibit 4.2 illustrate the numerous emotional episodes you experience upon hearing the merger announcement, subsequently thinking about the merger, discussing the merger with coworkers and so on. These emotions are transmitted to the reasoning process, where they are logically analysed along with other information about the attitude object.[12] Thus, while you are consciously evaluating whether the merger is good or bad, your emotions have already formed an opinion, which then sways your conscious evaluation. In fact, we often deliberately 'listen in' on our emotions to help us consciously decide whether to support or oppose something.[13] While thinking about what it will be like to work in the merged organisation, you might become aware of your emotional reaction to the proposed merger. The positive or negative emotions you experience are then incorporated into your logical reasoning regarding your attitude toward the merger.

This dual cognitive–emotional attitude process explains why companies are trying to inject more positive experiences in the workplace. Work attitudes are shaped by the almost continuous bombardment of emotional experiences people have at work. Those who experience more positive emotions tend to have more favourable attitudes toward their jobs and organisations, even when they aren't consciously aware of many of these emotional experiences. And when they do think about how they feel about their jobs, they listen in on the emotions regenerated from positive or negative events they have experienced in the workplace. Reality Check 4.1 describes some of the ways that organisations develop positive attitudes by generating positive emotions in the workplace.

The influence of both cognitive reasoning and emotions on attitudes is most apparent when they disagree with each other. People occasionally experience this mental tug-of-war, sensing that something isn't right even though they can't think of any logical reason to be concerned. This conflicting experience indicates that the person's logical analysis of the situation (left side of Exhibit 4.2) can't identify reasons to support the automatic emotional reaction (right side of Exhibit 4.2).[15]

Should we pay attention to our emotional response or our logical analysis? This question is not easy to answer, but some studies indicate that while executives tend to make quick decisions based on their gut feelings (emotional response), the best decisions usually occur when executives spend time logically evaluating the situation.[16] Thus, we should pay attention

Fun in the Workplace

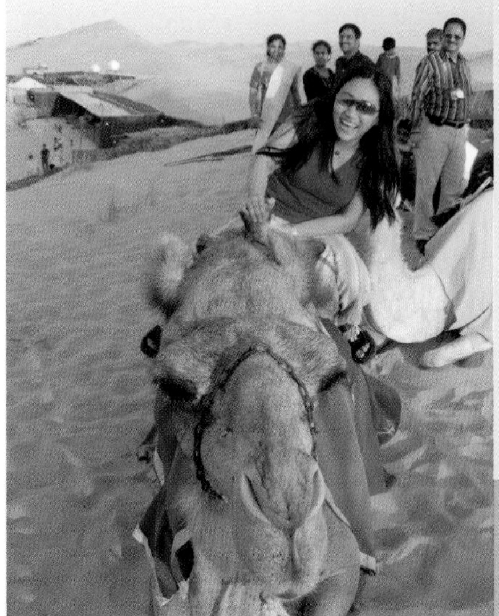

Mott Macdonald/*Meridian* 2006–7

YOU KNOW THE FUN is about to begin at ING Direct Australia when the financial institution announces its annual 'WOW' day. 'WOW is always a surprise for staff and is top secret until the day itself,' says ING Direct Australia's executive director of human resources, Sharyn Schultz. One year, staff had a choice of seven activities, such as taking hip-hop dance lessons or learning how to trapeze. Another year, ING Direct's 750 employees were flown from Sydney (in groups of 150 over five days) for one day of fun at Dreamworld in Brisbane. 'Our main goal is to celebrate the company's success and thank staff for all their last year's efforts,' explains Schultz. 'Of course it's also a perfect opportunity to have some fun away from the office.'

Having fun is part of the culture at Mott MacDonald. This photo shows a Mott employee during the Abu Dhabi oil and gas team's annual desert safari for staff and families.

to both the cognitive and emotional sides of the attitude model, and hope they agree with each other most of the time!

One last comment about Exhibit 4.2: notice the arrow from the emotional episodes to behaviour. It indicates that emotions directly (without conscious thinking) influence a person's behaviour. This occurs when we jump suddenly if someone sneaks up on us. It also occurs in everyday situations because even low-intensity emotions automatically change our facial expressions. These actions are not carefully thought out. They are automatic emotional responses that are learned or hardwired by heredity for particular situations.[17]

Cognitive Dissonance

cognitive dissonance A condition that occurs when we perceive an inconsistency between our beliefs, feelings and behaviour.

Emotions and attitudes usually lead to behaviour, but the opposite sometimes occurs through the process of **cognitive dissonance**.[18] Cognitive dissonance occurs when we perceive an inconsistency between our beliefs, feelings and behaviour. When this inconsistency violates our self-concept, it generates emotions that motivate us to change one or more of these elements. For example, let's say that you agreed to accept a foreign posting, even though it didn't interest you, because you believed it might be necessary for promotion into senior management. However, you later learn that many people become senior managers in the firm without spending any time on foreign assignment. In this situation, you will likely experience cognitive dissonance because of the inconsistency between your beliefs and feelings (dislike foreign assignments) and behaviour (accepted a foreign posting).

Behaviour is usually more difficult to change than beliefs and feelings. This is particularly true when the dissonant behaviour has been observed by others, was done voluntarily and can't be undone. In the foreign assignment example, you experience cognitive dissonance because others know that you accepted the assignment, it was accepted voluntarily (e.g. you weren't threatened with dismissal if you refused the assignment) and working overseas can't be undone

REALITY CHECK 4.1

Fun at work? It sounds like an oxymoron. But to attract and keep talented employees, companies are finding creative ways to generate positive emotions in the workplace. AstraZeneca's 'Fun Department' in the United States set up a mock doctor's office where employees with 'terminal seriousness' receive 'prescriptions to play'. The pharmaceutical company is also known for fun pranks, such as surprising one employee on his birthday with a cubicle filled to the brim with colourful peanut-shaped packing material. Employees at Mott MacDonald, a United Kingdom-based global management, engineering and development consulting firm, also have plenty of fun. For example, the Abu Dhabi oil and gas team has an annual desert safari, complete with camel rides (shown in photo).

Another company that generates plenty of fun is Razer in Singapore. The gaming peripherals company's casually dressed 85 employees zoom around on scooters and pit their gaming skills against each other on the state-of-the-art online gaming console set up for ten people. Razer's chief executive Tan Min-Liang wants staff to enjoy themselves as long as the work gets done on time. 'We're a gaming company; play is part of work for us,' Tan explains. Tammy Tang says her work experience at Razer hardly seems like work. 'Sometimes I can't believe that I have been here for seven months already,' Tang admits. 'I guess you don't feel the time passing when you are having so much fun.'[14]

(although you might be able to change your mind beforehand). Thus, people usually change their beliefs and feelings to reduce the inconsistency. For example, you might convince yourself that the foreign posting is not so bad after all because it will develop your management skills. Alternatively, you might downplay the features that previously made the foreign posting less desirable. Over time, a somewhat negative attitude toward foreign assignments becomes a more favourable one.

Emotions and Personality

Our coverage of the dynamics of workplace emotions wouldn't be complete unless we mentioned that emotions are also partly determined by a person's personality, not just workplace experiences.[19] Some people experience positive emotions as a natural trait. These people are generally extroverted—outgoing, talkative, sociable and assertive (see Chapter 2). In contrast, other people have a personality with a tendency to experience more negative emotions. Positive and negative emotional traits affect a person's attendance, turnover and long-term work attitudes. According to several studies, people with a personality that produces more negative emotions have lower levels of job satisfaction and higher levels of job burnout.[20] While positive and negative personality traits have some effect, other research concludes that the actual situation in which people work has a noticeably stronger influence on their attitudes and behaviour.[21]

Emotional Labour: Managing Emotions at Work

LEARNING OBJECTIVE

Identify the conditions that require, and the problems associated with, emotional labour.

The Elbow Room Café is packed and noisy on this Saturday morning. A customer at the restaurant in Vancouver, Canada, half shouts across the room for more coffee. A passing waiter scoffs: 'You want more coffee, get it yourself!' The customer only laughs. Another diner complains loudly that he and his party are running late and need their food. This time, restaurant manager Patrick

Savoie speaks up: 'If you're in a hurry, you should have gone to McDonald's.' The diner and his companions chuckle. To the uninitiated, the Elbow Room Café is an emotional basket case, where staff turn rudeness into a fine art. But it's all a performance—a place where guests can enjoy good food and play out their emotions about dreadful customer service. 'It's almost like coming to a theatre,' says Savoie, who spends much of his time inventing new ways to insult the clientele.[22]

Whether giving the most insulting service at Elbow Room Café in Vancouver or the friendliest service at a Bank of New Zealand contact centre, people are expected to manage their emotions in the workplace. They must conceal their frustration when serving an irritating customer, display compassion to an ill patient and hide their boredom in a long meeting with senior management. These are all forms of **emotional labour**—the effort, planning and control needed to express organisationally desired emotions during interpersonal transactions.[23] Almost everyone is expected to abide by *display rules*—norms requiring us to display specific emotions and to hide other emotions.

emotional labour The effort, planning and control needed to express organisationally desired emotions during interpersonal transactions.

Emotional labour is higher in jobs requiring a variety of emotions (e.g. anger as well as joy) and more intense emotions (e.g. showing delight rather than smiling weakly), as well as in jobs where interaction with clients is frequent and has a longer duration. Emotional labour also increases when employees must precisely rather than casually abide by the display rules.[24] This particularly occurs in the service industries, where employees have frequent face-to-face interaction with clients. For instance, the Ritz-Carlton Hotel Company's motto is 'Smile—we are on stage'. To ensure that this standard is maintained at the dozens of properties it manages around the world, the Ritz developed a detailed training program that teaches staff how to look

Learning to Show Correct Emotions at Malaysia Airlines

Newspix

Malaysia Airlines flight attendants receive extensive training on the essentials of safety and medical emergencies, but they also learn how to remain composed and pleasant even in difficult conditions. 'Are they presentable? Respectable? Do they make you feel comfortable? Do they seem approachable?' asks Madam Choong Lee Fong, Malaysia Airlines' cabin crew training and standards manager. Students at the Malaysia Airlines Academy in Petaling Jaya learn the fine art of smiling, making eye contact and keeping their chin up at a level that displays confidence without arrogance. The academy even has mirrors on every wall so students constantly see how their facial expressions appear to others. Students receive training in voice enrichment and public speaking. They also learn about personal grooming as well as the different formalities of behaviour in countries where the airline flies.[26]

pleasant in front of guests. Its orientation manual even includes two pages on phrases to use and to avoid saying, such as 'My pleasure' rather than 'OK, sure'.[25]

Emotional Display Norms across Cultures

How much we are expected to hide or reveal our true emotions in public depends to some extent on the culture in which we live. Cultural values in some countries—particularly Ethiopia, Korea, Japan and Austria—expect people to subdue their emotional expression and minimise physical contact with others. Even voice intonation tends to be monotonic. In other countries—notably Kuwait, Egypt, Spain and Russia—cultural values allow or encourage open display of one's true emotions. People are expected to be transparent in revealing their thoughts and feelings, dramatic in their conversational tones and animated in their use of nonverbal behaviours to get their message across.

These cultural variations in emotional display can be quite noticeable. One survey reported that 83 per cent of Japanese believe it is inappropriate to get emotional in a business context, compared with 40 per cent of Americans, 34 per cent of French and only 29 per cent of Italians. In other words, Italians are more likely to accept or tolerate people who display their true emotions at work, whereas emotional behaviour would be considered rude or embarrassing in Japan.[27] Even so, governments and business leaders encourage employees to practise more emotional labour by being pleasant. For example, Berliners are accustomed to the city's 'Berliner Schnauze' culture of gruffness and cheerlessness, but the city has initiated a 'friendliness offensive' in the hope that smiling will become more of the norm. A campaign two years earlier also encouraged Berliners to smile more often during the World Cup soccer finals. 'Smiles create more smiles, and in this city we need a bit more smiling,' said Klaus Böger, Berlin's senator for education and sport.[28]

Emotional Dissonance

Emotional labour can be challenging for most of us because it is difficult to conceal true emotions and to display the emotions required by our jobs. Joy, sadness, worry and other emotions automatically activate a complex set of facial muscles that are difficult to prevent and equally difficult to fake. Pretending to be cheerful or concerned requires adjustment and coordination of several specific facial muscles and body positions. Meanwhile, our true emotions tend to reveal themselves as subtle gestures, usually without our awareness. More often than not, observers see when we are faking and sense that we feel a different emotion.[29]

Emotional labour also creates conflict between required and true emotions, which is called **emotional dissonance**. The larger the gap between the required and true emotions, the more employees tend to experience stress, job burnout and psychological separation from self.[30] Hiring people with a natural tendency to display the emotions required for the job can minimise emotional dissonance. For example, Container Store in the United States expects employees to display positive emotions on the job, so its unofficial motto is 'Grouchy People Need Not Apply'. St. Wilfred's Hospice in Chichester, England, takes a similar view. 'We have standards of behaviour,' says chief executive Alison Moorey. 'We expect anyone who comes into the hospice to be treated with smiles and courtesy.'[31]

emotional dissonance The conflict between required and true emotions.

Emotional dissonance is also minimised through deep acting rather than surface acting.[32] People engage in *surface acting* when they try to modify their behaviour to be consistent with required emotions but continue to hold different internal feelings. For instance, we force a smile while greeting a customer whom we consider rude. *Deep acting* involves changing true emotions to match the required emotions. Rather than feeling irritated by a rude customer, you might view your next interaction with that person as an opportunity to test your sales skills. This change in perspective can potentially generate more positive emotions next time you meet that difficult customer, thereby producing friendlier displays of emotion. However, deep acting also requires considerable emotional intelligence, which we discuss next.

LEARNING OBJECTIVE 

Describe the four dimensions of emotional intelligence.

EMOTIONAL INTELLIGENCE

Exactech, Inc., is growing quickly, so the orthopaedic device manufacturer in Gainesville, Florida, introduced a program to develop future leaders. Two dozen high-potential employees were identified among the staff of 260 and then given intensive, year-long training. This program didn't focus completely on technical skill development. Rather, participants learned how to improve their self-awareness and interaction with other staff members. 'Especially as people rise to higher levels in organisations, their ability to do their job effectively depends on emotional intelligence qualities more than technical qualities,' explains Exactech cofounder Bill Petty.[33]

emotional intelligence (EI) A set of abilities to perceive and express emotion, assimilate emotion in thought, understand and reason with emotion, and regulate emotion in oneself and others.

Exactech is one of many organisations discovering that **emotional intelligence (EI)** can significantly improve individual, team and organisational effectiveness. Emotional intelligence includes a set of *abilities* to perceive and express emotion, assimilate emotion in thought, understand and reason with emotion, and regulate emotion in oneself and others.[34] One popular model, shown in Exhibit 4.3, organises EI into four dimensions representing the recognition of emotions in ourselves and in others, as well as the regulation of emotions in ourselves and in others.[35] These four dimensions are also found in other models of EI, but experts disagree on the definitive list of abilities representing EI. For example, the authors of the model shown here include a list of 'abilities' for each cell, but others warn that the list includes personality traits and personal values (e.g. achievement, optimism) as well as task outcomes (e.g. teamwork, inspirational leadership).[36]

Exhibit 4.3 ***Dimensions of Emotional Intelligence***

	Yourself	Other people
Recognition of emotions	Self-awareness	Social awareness
Regulation of emotions	Self-management	Relationship management

Source: D. Goleman, R. Boyatzis and A. McKee, *Primal Leadership: Realizing the Power of Emotional Intelligence* (Boston: Harvard Business School Press, 2002), chap. 3; D. Goleman, 'An EI-Based Theory of Performance', in *The Emotionally Intelligent Workplace*, ed. C. Cherniss and D. Goleman (San Francisco: Jossey-Bass, 2001), 28.

SELF-AWARENESS Self-awareness is the ability to perceive and understand the meaning of your own emotions. If you are self-aware, you are more sensitive to your subtle emotional responses to events and understand their message. Self-aware people are better able to eavesdrop on their emotional responses to specific situations and to use this awareness as conscious information.[37]

SELF-MANAGEMENT Self-management is the ability to manage your own emotions, something that we all do to some extent. We keep disruptive impulses in check. We try not to feel angry or frustrated when events go against us. We try to feel and express joy and happiness toward others when the occasion calls for these emotional displays. We try to create a second wind of motivation later in the workday. Notice that self-management goes beyond displaying behaviours that represent desired emotions in a particular situation; it includes generating or suppressing emotions. In other words, the deep acting described earlier requires high levels of the self-management component of emotional intelligence.

SOCIAL AWARENESS Social awareness is the ability to perceive and understand the emotions of other people. To a large extent, this ability is represented by *empathy*—having an understanding of and sensitivity to the feelings, thoughts and situations of others (see Chapter 3). This includes understanding another person's situation, experiencing the other person's emotions and knowing his or her needs even though unstated. Social awareness extends beyond empathy to include being organisationally aware, which includes sensing office politics and understanding social networks.

RELATIONSHIP MANAGEMENT This dimension of EI involves managing other people's emotions. This includes consoling people who feel sad, emotionally inspiring your team members to complete a class project on time, getting strangers to feel comfortable working with you and managing dysfunctional emotions among staff who experience conflict with customers or other employees. Some emotional intelligence experts link this component of EI to a wide variety of interpersonal activities, but here we will restrict relationship management to managing other people's emotions, whereas working effectively with other people extends to other competencies.

These four dimensions of emotional intelligence form a hierarchy.[38] Self-awareness is the lowest level of EI because it is a prerequisite for the other three dimensions but does not require the other dimensions. Self-management and social awareness are necessarily above self-awareness in the EI hierarchy. You can't manage your own emotions (self-management) if you aren't good at knowing your own emotions (self-awareness). Relationship management is the highest level of EI because it requires all three other dimensions. In other words, we require a high degree of emotional intelligence to master relationship management because this set of competencies requires sufficiently high levels of self-awareness, self-management and social awareness.

Most jobs involve social interaction with coworkers or external stakeholders, so employees need emotional intelligence to work effectively. Emotional intelligence is particularly important for managers because their work requires management of their own emotions and the emotions of others. 'Managers need higher EQ [emotional intelligence] to deal with the increased ambiguity engendered in various aspects of their work, such as strategic decision making and managing interpersonal relationships,' says Amy Choi, director of sales and distribution of Citibank Global

Consumer Group in Hong Kong. Elaine Luey Kit-ling, Greater China regional director for Marriott International, agrees: '[Managers] need to use EQ to influence and convince their peers to foster effective collaboration.'[39]

Research indicates that people with high EI are better at interpersonal relations, perform better in jobs requiring emotional labour, are superior leaders, make better decisions involving social exchanges, are more successful in many aspects of job interviews and are better at organisational learning activities. Teams whose members have high emotional intelligence initially perform better than teams with low EI.[40] However, emotional intelligence does not improve some forms of performance, such as tasks that require minimal social interaction.[41]

Improving Emotional Intelligence

Emotional intelligence is associated with some personality traits, as well as with the emotional intelligence of one's parents. For this reason, some companies have attempted to test the levels of EI in applicants. For example, all new pilots at Air Canada receive EI testing. Pilots are team leaders of the on-board crew and need to work effectively with staff on the ground, so they must have the ability to understand and manage their own emotions as well as the emotions of others. 'If you have to interact well with other people, these [emotional intelligence tests] are instruments that we can use during the selection process to identify people who have these enhanced skills,' says Captain Dave Legge, vice president of Air Canada flight operations. 'At the end of the day, we want to have a better idea of who we're hiring.'[42]

Emotional intelligence is not completely innate, however. It can also be learned, which is why Exactech invests in developing EI skills in its future leaders.[43] Sony Europe also incorporates EI training in its executive development program, including an exercise in which leaders keep a journal of their emotional experiences throughout a week of work. One study reported that business students scored higher on emotional intelligence after taking an undergraduate interpersonal skills course.[44] As Reality Check 4.2 describes, employees at GM Holden in Australia also improved their interpersonal relations after completing an emotional intelligence training program. Personal coaching, plenty of practice and frequent feedback are particularly effective at developing EI. Emotional intelligence also increases with age; it is part of the process

GM Holden Revs Up Emotional Intelligence

GM Corp

GM HOLDEN CAREFULLY SELECTED staff for its new production facility at Port Melbourne, Australia. It wasn't long, however, before the project unravelled due to infighting and interpersonal tensions. Consultants called in to analyse the problems offered the following solution: employees needed to improve their emotional intelligence. With this advice, the 30 plant

Emotional intelligence training helped employees at GM Holden, the Australian division of General Motors, to get along better.

called maturity. Overall, emotional intelligence offers considerable potential, but we also have a lot to learn about its measurement and effects on people in the workplace.

So far, this chapter has introduced the model of emotions and attitudes, as well as emotional intelligence as the means by which we manage emotions in the workplace. The next two sections of this chapter introduce the topics of job satisfaction and organisational commitment. These two attitudes are so important in our understanding of workplace behaviour that some experts suggest that together they should be called 'overall job attitude'.[45]

JOB SATISFACTION

job satisfaction A person's evaluation of his or her job and work context.

Job satisfaction, a person's evaluation of his or her job and work context, is probably the most studied attitude in organisational behaviour.[47] It is an *appraisal* of the perceived job characteristics, work environment and emotional experiences at work. Satisfied employees have a favourable evaluation of their jobs, based on their observations and emotional experiences. Job satisfaction is best viewed as a collection of attitudes about different aspects of the job and work context. You might like your coworkers but be less satisfied with your workload, for instance.

How satisfied are employees at work? The answer depends on the person, the workplace and the country. Global surveys indicate with some consistency that job satisfaction tends to be highest in the Nordic countries (Denmark, Sweden, Norway and Finland) as well as in India and the United States. The lowest levels of overall job satisfaction are usually recorded in Hungary and several Asian countries (e.g. mainland China, Hong Kong and South Korea). One annual survey reports that more than 85 per cent of Americans say they are moderately or very satisfied with their jobs, a level that has been consistent for the past three decades. Another recent survey reports that employees in India are, on average, happier than employees in other parts of Asia on every aspect of the job measured in that study: pay, supervision, working conditions, communication and teamwork. One recent survey of more than 10 000 Australians found that 48 per cent of employees are unhappy in their current work role, yet a survey of the Australian public service recently reported that 81 per cent of these employees are satisfied with their jobs.[48]

REALITY CHECK 4.2

design team members and more than 300 other employees completed a detailed assessment of their emotional intelligence. The company then introduced a variety of training modules targeting different aspects of emotional intelligence, such as effective self-expression, understanding others and controlling emotions.

Some staff were sceptical about these 'touchy-feely' seminars, so GM Holden evaluated the program to see whether employee scores improved and behaviour changed. The company discovered that employee scores on the emotional intelligence test improved by almost 50 per cent and that employees became much more cooperative and diplomatic in their behaviour. 'It has greatly improved communication within the team and with other teams outside the plant,' says GM Holden quality systems engineer Vesselka Vassileva. Some employees also note that it has improved their interpersonal behaviour outside the workplace. 'I'm not so aggressive or assertive,' says manufacturing engineer Alf Moore. 'I feel better and it's helped me at home.'[46]

It's probably fair to conclude that employees in India and Australia are more satisfied with their jobs than those in some other parts of the world, but we also need to be somewhat cautious about these and other job satisfaction surveys. One problem is that surveys often use a single direct question, such as 'How satisfied are you with your job?' Many dissatisfied employees are reluctant to reveal their feelings in a direct question because this is tantamount to admitting that they made a poor job choice and are not enjoying life. For instance, one survey found that although most employees in Malaysia say they are satisfied with their job and work environment, only 55 per cent would recommend their company to others and less than half would stay if a comparable job were available in another company.[49]

A second problem is that cultural values make it difficult to compare job satisfaction across countries. People in China, South Korea and Japan tend to subdue their emotions in public, so they probably avoid extreme survey ratings such as 'very satisfied'. A third problem is that job satisfaction changes with economic conditions. Employees with the highest job satisfaction in this survey tend to be in countries whose economies were booming at the time of the survey.[50]

LEARNING OBJECTIVE

Summarise the consequences of job dissatisfaction in terms of the exit-voice-loyalty-neglect model.

Job Satisfaction and Work Behaviour

Brad Bird pays a lot of attention to job satisfaction. 'In my experience, the thing that has the most significant impact on a budget—but never shows up in a budget—is morale,' advises Bird, who directed *Ratatouille* and other award-winning films at Pixar Animation Studios. 'If you have low morale, for every dollar you spend, you get 25 cents of value. If you have high morale, for every dollar you spend, you get about three dollars of value.'[51]

Brad Bird's opinion about the importance of job satisfaction is consistently reflected in the actions of leaders in many companies, who carefully monitor job satisfaction and related employee attitudes every year. An added incentive is the increasing competition to win awards for their workplaces. In some firms, executive bonuses depend partly on employee satisfaction ratings. The reason for this attention is simple: job satisfaction affects many of the individual behaviours introduced in Chapter 1. A useful template for organising and understanding the consequences of job dissatisfaction is the **exit-voice-loyalty-neglect (EVLN) model**. As the name suggests, the EVLN model identifies four ways that employees respond to dissatisfaction:[52]

exit-voice-loyalty-neglect (EVLN) model The four ways, as indicated in the name, that employees respond to job dissatisfaction.

- Exit includes leaving the organisation, transferring to another work unit, or at least trying to get away from the unsatisfactory situation. The general theory is that job dissatisfaction builds over time and is eventually strong enough to motivate employees to search for better work opportunities elsewhere. This is likely true to some extent, but the most recent opinion is that specific 'shock events' quickly energise employees to think about and engage in exit behaviour. For example, the emotional reaction you experience to an unfair management decision or a conflict episode with a coworker motivates you to look at job ads and speak to friends about job opportunities where they work. This begins the process of realigning your self-concept more with another company than with your current employer.[53]
- Voice is any attempt to change, rather than escape from, the unsatisfactory situation. Voice can be a constructive response, such as recommending ways for management to improve the situation, or it can be more confrontational, such as filing formal grievances or forming a coalition to oppose a decision.[54] In extreme cases, some employees might engage in counterproductive behaviours to get attention and force changes in the organisation.

- In the original version of the EVLN model, loyalty was not an outcome of dissatisfaction. Rather, it determined whether people chose exit or voice (i.e. high loyalty resulted in voice; low loyalty produced exit).[55] More recent writers describe loyalty as an outcome, but in various and somewhat unclear ways. Generally, they suggest that 'loyalists' are employees who respond to dissatisfaction by patiently waiting—some say they 'suffer in silence'—for the problem to work itself out or be resolved by others.[56]
- Neglect includes reducing work effort, paying less attention to quality, and increasing absenteeism and lateness. It is generally considered a passive activity that has negative consequences for the organisation.

Which of the four EVLN alternatives do employees use? It depends on the person and situation.[57] One determining factor is the person's self-concept. Some people avoid the self-image of being a complainer, whereas others view themselves very much as taking action when they dislike a work situation. Self-concept relates to personal and cultural values as well as personality. For example, people with a high-conscientiousness personality are less likely to engage in neglect and more likely to engage in voice. Past experience also influences which EVLN action is applied. Employees who were unsuccessful with voice in the past are more likely to engage in exit or neglect when experiencing job dissatisfaction in the future. Another factor is loyalty, as it was originally intended in the EVLN model. Specifically, employees are more likely to quit when they have low loyalty to the company, and they are more likely to engage in voice when they have high loyalty. Finally, the response to dissatisfaction depends on the situation. Employees are less likely to use the exit option when there are few alternative job prospects, for example.

Job Satisfaction and Performance

LEARNING OBJECTIVE

Discuss the effects of job satisfaction on job performance and customer service.

Is a happy worker a more productive worker? Stuart Wilson, the chief executive of the Australian Shareholders Association, thinks so. 'Clearly, the performance of a company is impacted by the morale of the staff,' he says.[58] Yet, for most of the past century, organisational behaviour scholars have challenged this belief, concluding that job satisfaction minimally affects job performance. Now the evidence suggests that the popular saying may be correct after all: there is a *moderate* relationship between job satisfaction and job performance. In other words, happy workers really are more productive workers *to some extent*.[59]

Even with a moderate association between job satisfaction and performance, there are a few underlying reasons why the relationship isn't stronger. One argument is that general attitudes (such as job satisfaction) don't predict specific behaviours very well. As we learned with the EVLN model, job dissatisfaction can lead to a variety of outcomes other than lower job performance (neglect). Some employees continue to work productively while they complain (voice), look for another job (exit), or patiently wait for the problem to be fixed (loyalty). A second explanation is that job performance leads to job satisfaction (rather than vice versa), but only when performance is linked to valued rewards. Higher performers receive more rewards and, consequently, are more satisfied than low-performing employees who receive fewer rewards. The connection between job satisfaction and performance isn't stronger because many organisations do not reward good performance. The third explanation is that job satisfaction influences employee motivation but doesn't affect performance in jobs where employees have little control over their job output (such as assembly-line work).

Job Satisfaction and Customer Satisfaction

Another popular belief is that happy customers are the result of happy employees. This view is clearly held by Kevin Page, the Clydesdale Bank manager described in the opening story of this chapter. Page improved customer satisfaction levels by ensuring that the bank's contact centre employees were satisfied and felt valued. This philosophy also explains how the Bank of New Zealand (BNZ), another National Australia Bank subsidiary, improved customer attitudes towards its contact centres. 'We made a philosophical decision based on the service/profit chain,' explains Shona Bishop, BNZ's general manager of sales and service. 'Happy staff means happy customers, which means shareholders are also happy.' Ralph Norris, the CEO of the Commonwealth Bank of Australia and previously CEO of Air New Zealand, is another executive who applies the view that happy employees result in happy customers (and shareholders). 'I'm not primarily interested in shareholder returns,' says Norris. 'If we look after and inspire the staff, they will look after the customers and that will take care of shareholder returns.'[60]

These executives are referring to the *service profit chain model*, which proposes that increasing employee satisfaction and loyalty results in higher customer perceptions of value, thereby improving the company's profitability. In other words, job satisfaction has a positive effect on customer service, which flows on to shareholder financial returns.[62] There are two main reasons why job satisfaction should predict customer satisfaction. First, employees are usually in a more positive mood when they feel satisfied with their jobs and working conditions. Employees in a good mood display friendliness and positive emotions more naturally and frequently, and this causes customers to experience positive emotions. Second, satisfied employees are less likely to quit their jobs, so they have better knowledge and skills to serve clients. Lower turnover also enables customers to have the same employees serve them, so there is more consistent service. Some evidence indicates that customers build their loyalty to specific employees, not to the organisation, so keeping employee turnover low tends to build customer loyalty.[63]

Employees First, Customers Second

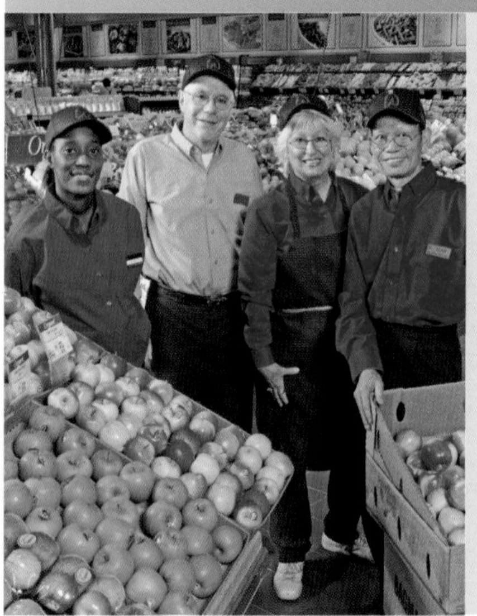

Courtesy of Wegmans

Wegmans Food Markets has an unusual motto: 'Employees first, customers second'. The grocery chain definitely puts its 33 000 employees in New York and four nearby states on top of the stakeholder list. They enjoy above-average pay, health benefits and other perks, resulting in labour costs of about 16 per cent of sales compared to 12 per cent at most supermarkets. Perhaps more important is that employees feel welcome and valued. 'You're not part of a company, you're part of a family,' says Katie Southard, who works in customer service at a Wegmans' store in Rochester, New York. 'You're treated as an individual, not just one of the 350 persons in the store.' Why don't customers come first? Wegmans' rationale is that you can't have happy customers if employees have low morale. The theory seems to work: Wegmans enjoys one of the highest levels of customer loyalty and lowest levels of employee turnover in the industry.[61]

Job Satisfaction and Business Ethics

Before leaving the topic of job satisfaction, we should mention that job satisfaction does more than improve work behaviours and customer satisfaction. Job satisfaction is also an ethical issue that influences the organisation's reputation in the community. People spend a large portion of their time working in organisations, and many societies now expect companies to provide work environments that are safe and enjoyable. Indeed, employees in several countries closely monitor ratings of the best companies to work for, an indication that employee satisfaction is a virtue worth considerable goodwill to employers. This virtue is apparent when an organisation has low job satisfaction. The company tries to hide this fact, but when morale problems become public, corporate leaders are usually quick to improve the situation.

ORGANISATIONAL COMMITMENT

LEARNING OBJECTIVE 

Distinguish organisational (affective) and continuance commitment, and discuss their influences on employee behaviour.

Along with studying job satisfaction, OB researchers have been very interested in an attitude called organisational commitment. **Organisational commitment** is the employee's emotional attachment to, identification with and involvement in a particular organisation.[64] This definition pertains specifically to *affective commitment* because it is an emotional attachment—our feelings of loyalty—to the organisation. Organisational (affective) commitment differs from **continuance commitment**, which is a calculative attachment.[65] Employees have high continuance commitment when they do not particularly identify with the organisation where they work but feel bound to remain there because it would be too costly to quit. In other words, they choose to stay because the calculated (typically financial) value of staying is higher than the value of working somewhere else. You can tell an employee has high calculative commitment when he or she says: 'I hate this place but can't afford to quit!' This reluctance to quit occurs when employees forfeit a large bonus as a result of quitting or when they are well established in the community where they work.[66]

organisational (affective) commitment The employee's emotional attachment to, identification with and involvement in a particular organisation.

continuance commitment An employee's calculative attachment to the organisation, whereby the employee is motivated to stay only because leaving would be costly.

Consequences of Organisational Commitment

Organisational (affective) commitment can be a significant competitive advantage.[67] Loyal employees are less likely to quit their jobs and be absent from work. They also have higher work motivation and organisational citizenship, as well as somewhat higher job performance. Organisational commitment also improves customer satisfaction because long-tenure employees have better knowledge of work practices and because clients like to do business with the same employees. One warning is that employees with very high loyalty tend to have high conformity, which results in lower creativity. There are also cases of dedicated employees who have violated laws to defend the organisation. However, most companies suffer from too little rather than too much employee loyalty.

While affective commitment is beneficial, research suggests that continuance commitment can be dysfunctional. In fact, employees with high levels of continuance commitment tend to have *lower* performance ratings and are *less* likely to engage in organisational citizenship behaviours. Furthermore, unionised employees with high continuance commitment are more likely to use formal grievances, whereas employees with high affective commitment engage in more constructive problem solving when their relations with employers sour.[68] Although some level of financial connection may be necessary, employers should not confuse continuance commitment with employee loyalty. Employers still need to win employees' hearts (affective commitment) beyond tying them financially to the organisation (continuance commitment).

LEARNING OBJECTIVE

Describe five strategies for increasing organisational (affective) commitment.

Building Organisational Commitment

There are almost as many ways to build organisational loyalty as there are topics in this textbook, but the following strategies are most prominent in the literature.

- Justice and support—Affective commitment is higher in organisations that fulfil their obligations to employees and abide by humanitarian values, such as fairness, courtesy, forgiveness and moral integrity. These values relate to the concept of organisational justice, which we discuss in the next chapter. Similarly, organisations that support employee wellbeing tend to cultivate higher levels of loyalty in return.[69]
- Shared values—The definition of affective commitment refers to a person's identification with the organisation, and that identification is highest when employees believe their values are congruent with the organisation's dominant values. Also, employees experience more comfort and predictability when they agree with the values underlying corporate decisions. This comfort increases their motivation to stay with the organisation.[70]
- **Trust** refers to positive expectations one person has toward another person or group in situations involving risk.[71] Trust means putting faith in the other person or group. It is also a reciprocal activity: to receive trust, you must demonstrate trust. Employees identify with and feel obliged to work for an organisation only when they trust its leaders. This explains why lay-offs are one of the greatest blows to employee loyalty. By reducing job security, companies reduce the trust employees have in their employer and the employment relationship.[72]
- Organisational comprehension refers to how well employees understand the organisation, including its strategic direction, social dynamics and physical layout. This awareness is a necessary prerequisite to affective commitment because it is difficult to identify with something that you don't know very well. The practical implication here is to ensure that employees are able to develop a reasonably clear and complete mental picture of the organisation. This occurs by giving staff information and opportunities to keep up to date about organisational events, interact with coworkers, discover what goes on in different parts of the organisation, and learn about the organisation's history and future plans.[73]
- Employee involvement increases affective commitment by strengthening the employee's social identity with the organisation. Employees feel that they are part of the organisation when they participate in decisions that guide the organisation's future. Employee involvement also builds loyalty because giving this power is a demonstration of the company's trust in its employees.

trust refers to positive expectations one person has toward another person or group in situations involving risk.

Organisational commitment and job satisfaction are two of the most often studied and discussed attitudes in the workplace. Each is linked to emotional episodes and cognitive judgements about the workplace, and to an employee's relationship with the company. Emotions also play an important role in another concept that is on everyone's mind these days: stress. The final section of this chapter provides an overview of work-related stress and how it can be managed.

WORK-RELATED STRESS AND ITS MANAGEMENT

LEARNING OBJECTIVE

Define stress and describe the stress experience.

Rural doctors around Australia are so busy attending to patients that some observers worry the practitioners themselves may be candidates for medical attention. Due to a chronic shortage of doctors in the bush, many of these professionals are stressed out from overwork and lack of resources to perform their jobs. 'We often hear from doctors who feel like they are up to their eyeballs in work and can't provide the quality of care that they would like,' says Steve Sant, chief executive officer of the Rural Doctors Association of Australia. 'When you have to work long hours and you can't fulfil the needs of your patients you're going to get stressed.' Two recent surveys support this assessment, each reporting that many rural doctors are ready to leave their practices, or plan to retire early due to stress and the need to preserve their health.[74]

Experts have trouble defining **stress**, but it is most often described as an adaptive response to a situation that is perceived as challenging or threatening to the person's wellbeing.[75] Stress is a physiological and psychological condition that prepares us to adapt to hostile or noxious environmental conditions. Our heart rate increases, muscles tighten, breathing speeds up and perspiration increases. Our body also moves more blood to the brain, releases adrenaline and other hormones, fuels its systems by releasing more glucose and fatty acids, activates systems that sharpen our senses and conserves resources by shutting down our immune system. One school of thought suggests that stress is a negative evaluation of the external environment. However, critics of this cognitive appraisal perspective point out that the stress experience is an emotional experience, which may occur before or after a conscious evaluation of the situation.[76]

stress An adaptive response to a situation that is perceived as challenging or threatening to a person's wellbeing.

Whether stress is a complex emotion or a cognitive evaluation of the environment, it has become a pervasive experience in the daily lives of most people. Research by Medibank Private Health reported that 53 per cent of Australian employees across all occupations feel under pressure a significant amount of the time. A major global study reports that three out of four Australians (and a similar percentage of people in Germany, Canada, the United States and the United Kingdom) say they frequently or sometimes feel stress in their daily lives. Approximately one in every four employees in the United Kingdom feels 'very or extremely stressed', and this condition has become the top cause of absenteeism there. More than one-quarter of Canadians say they experience high levels of stress each day. A survey of 4700 people across Asia reported that one-third were feeling more stress than they had in the recent past. The percentage of people reporting stress was highest in Taiwan and lowest in Thailand. The Japanese government, which tracks work-related stress every five years, has found that the percentage of Japanese employees who feel 'strong worry, anxiety or stress at work or in daily working life' has increased from 51 per cent in 1982 to almost two-thirds of the population today.[77]

As these surveys imply, stress is typically described as a negative experience. This is known as *distress*—the degree of physiological, psychological and behavioural deviation from healthy functioning. However, some level of stress—called *eustress*—is a necessary part of life because it activates and motivates people to achieve goals, change their environments and succeed in life's challenges.[78] Our focus is on the causes and management of distress, because it has become a chronic problem in many societies.

General Adaptation Syndrome

More than 500 years ago, people began using the word *stress* to describe the human response to harsh environmental conditions. However, it wasn't until the 1930s that Hans Selye (often described as the father of stress research) first documented the stress experience, called the **general adaptation syndrome**. Selye determined (initially by studying rats) that people have a fairly consistent and automatic physiological response to stressful situations, which helps them to cope with environmental demands.

general adaptation syndrome A model of the stress experience, consisting of three stages: alarm reaction, resistance and exhaustion.

The general adaptation syndrome consists of the three stages shown in Exhibit 4.4.[79] The *alarm reaction* stage occurs when a threat or challenge activates the physiological stress responses that were noted above. The individual's energy level and coping effectiveness decrease in response to the initial shock. The second stage, *resistance*, activates various biochemical, psychological and behavioural mechanisms that give the individual more energy and engage coping mechanisms to overcome or remove the source of stress. To focus energy on the source of the stress, the body reduces resources to the immune system during this stage. This explains why people are more likely to catch a cold or some other illness when they experience prolonged stress. People have a limited resistance capacity, and if the source of stress persists, the individual will eventually move into the third stage, *exhaustion*. Most of us are able to remove the source of stress or remove ourselves from that source before becoming too exhausted. However, people who frequently reach exhaustion have increased risk of long-term physiological and psychological damage.[80]

Consequences of Distress

Stress takes its toll on the human body.[81] Many people experience tension headaches, muscle pain and related problems mainly due to muscle contractions from the stress response. Studies have found that high stress levels also contribute to cardiovascular disease, including heart attacks and strokes, and may be associated with some forms of cancer. Stress also produces various psychological consequences, such as job dissatisfaction, moodiness, depression and

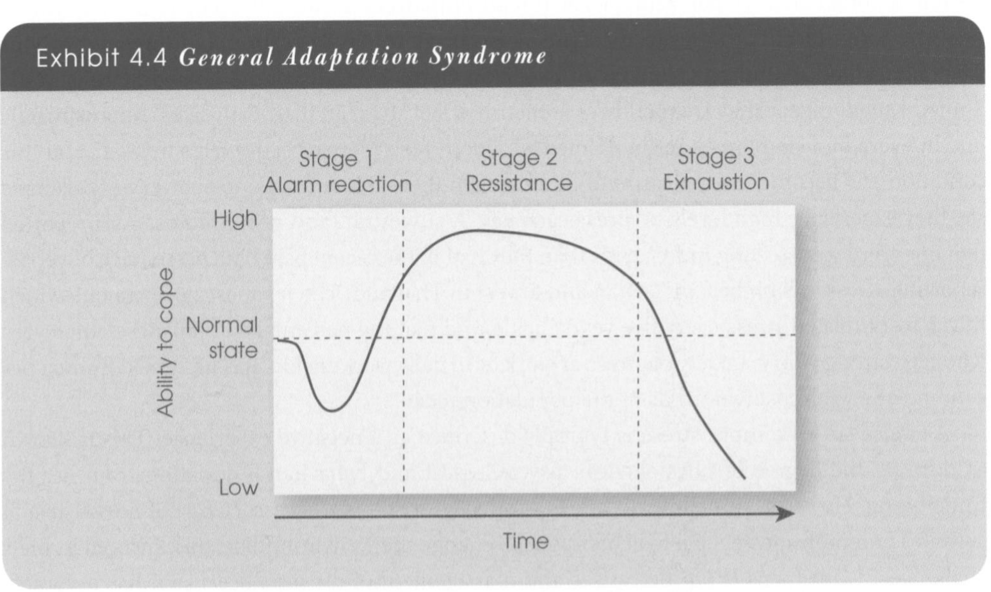

Source: Adapted from H. Selye, *The Stress of Life* (New York: McGraw-Hill, 1956).

lower organisational commitment. Furthermore, various behavioural outcomes have been linked to high or persistent stress, including lower job performance, poor decision making, and increased workplace accidents and aggressive behaviour. Most people react to stress through 'fight or flight', so increased absenteeism is another outcome because it is a form of flight.[82]

Job Burnout

Job burnout is a particular stress consequence that refers to the process of emotional exhaustion, cynicism and reduced feelings of personal accomplishment.[83] *Emotional exhaustion*, the first stage, is characterised by a lack of energy, tiredness and a feeling that one's emotional resources are depleted. This is followed by *cynicism* (also called *depersonalisation*), which is characterised by an indifferent attitude toward work, emotional detachment from clients, a cynical view of the organisation, and a tendency to strictly follow rules and regulations rather than adapt to the needs of others. The final stage of burnout, called *reduced personal accomplishment*, entails feelings of diminished confidence in one's ability to perform the job well. In such situations, employees no longer believe that their efforts make a difference.

job burnout The process of emotional exhaustion, cynicism and reduced personal accomplishment that results from prolonged exposure to stressors.

Stressors: The Causes of Stress

Before identifying ways to manage work-related stress, we must first understand its causes, known as stressors. **Stressors** include any environmental conditions that place a physical or emotional demand on a person.[84] There are numerous stressors in the workplace and in life in general. In this section, we will highlight three of the most common workplace stressors: harassment, workload and lack of task control.

stressors Any environmental conditions that place a physical or emotional demand on a person.

Harassment

One of the fastest-growing sources of workplace stress is **psychological harassment**. Psychological harassment includes repeated hostile or unwanted conduct, verbal comments, actions and gestures that undermine an employee's dignity, or their psychological or physical integrity. This covers a broad landscape of behaviours, from threats and bullying to subtle yet persistent forms of incivility.[85] Psychological harassment permeates many workplaces. A New South Wales Law Society survey reported that more than half of the 1800 lawyers polled have been bullied or intimidated. Three separate studies estimate that between 15 and 26 per cent of government employees in Tasmania, Victoria and South Australia experience harassment each year from their managers, fellow employees or clients. Half of the junior doctors at Auckland City Hospital say they have been bullied by nurses or more senior doctors. A survey of more than 100 000 employees in Asia reported that between 19 per cent (China) and 46 per cent (Korea) of employees experience incivility monthly or more often. Two-thirds of Americans think people are less civil today than 20 years ago; 10 per cent say they witness incivility daily in their workplaces and are targets of that abuse at least once each week.[86]

psychological harassment Repeated and hostile or unwanted conduct, verbal comments, actions or gestures that affect an employee's dignity or psychological or physical integrity.

Sexual harassment is a type of harassment in which a person's employment or job performance is conditional and depends on unwanted sexual relations (called *quid pro quo* harassment) and/or the person experiences sexual conduct from others (such as posting pornographic material) that unreasonably interferes with work performance or creates an intimidating, hostile or offensive working environment (called *hostile work environment* harassment).[87] Victims of sexual harassment experience trauma (especially from sexual abuse) or must endure tense coworker relations in a hostile work environment. Moreover, they are

sexual harassment Unwelcome conduct of a sexual nature that detrimentally affects the work environment or leads to adverse job-related consequences for its victims.

expected to endure more stress while these incidents are investigated. This is particularly true in countries where women who complain of harassment are sometimes stigmatised by friends and coworkers.

Work Overload

A half century ago, social scientists predicted that technology would allow employees to enjoy a 15-hour work week at full pay by 2030.[88] So far, it hasn't turned out that way. As described at the beginning of this section on workplace stress, rural doctors in Australia are experiencing stress due to *work overload*—working more hours, and more intensely during those hours, than they can reasonably manage. Work overload extends beyond the medical profession. One recent survey that tracked 8000 Australians over five years found that the average employee works more than 44 hours per week, far in excess of the maximum regular weekly hours stated in employment regulations (typically 38 hours). Surveys by the Families and Work Institute report that 44 per cent of Americans say they are overworked, up from 28 per cent who felt this way a few years earlier. Almost 25 per cent of Canadian employees work more than 50 hours per week, compared with only 10 per cent a decade ago. Work overload is an important predictor of job burnout. It is also a major cause of work–family conflicts, because overworked employees have insufficient time to satisfy their nonwork roles of being parents, spouses and so forth.[89]

Why do employees work such long hours? One explanation is the combined effect of technology and globalisation. 'Everyone in this industry is working harder now because of email, wireless access, and globalisation,' says Christopher Lochhead, chief marketing officer of Mercury Interactive, a California-based consulting firm. 'You can't even get a rest on the weekend.'[90] A second cause, according to an Australian study, is that many people are caught up in consumerism; they want to buy more goods and services, and doing so requires more income through longer work hours. A third reason, called the 'ideal worker norm', is that professionals expect themselves and others to work longer hours. For many, toiling away far beyond the normal work week is a badge of honour, a symbol of their superhuman capacity to perform above others.[91] This badge of honour is particularly serious in several (but not all) Asian countries, to the point where 'death from overwork' is now part of the common language (*karoshi* in Japanese and *guolaosi* in Chinese).

Low Task Control

An increasingly popular model of job burnout suggests that emotional exhaustion depends on both job demands and job resources.[93] *Job demands* are aspects of work that require sustained physical or psychological effort. High workload is one of the more significant job demands in the contemporary workplace. At the same time, the effect of job demands on burnout (or stress in general) depends on the individual's job resources. *Job resources* represent aspects of the job that help employees to achieve work goals, reduce job demands, and/or stimulate personal growth and development.

An important job resource is autonomy or control over the pace of work. Low task control increases employee exposure to the risk of burnout because they face high workloads without the ability to adjust the pace of the load to their own energy, attention span and other resources. Furthermore, the degree to which low task control is a stressor increases with the burden of responsibility the employee must carry.[94] Assembly-line workers have low task control, but their stress can be fairly low if their level of responsibility is also low. In contrast, sports coaches are under immense pressure to win games (high responsibility), yet they have little control over what happens on the playing field (low task control).

Japanese Professionals are Dying to Get Ahead

Kenichi Uchino (left in photo) worked long hours as a Toyota quality control inspector in Japan. After each regular shift, he would stay to complete paperwork, perform unpaid 'voluntary' activities such as leading quality circle meetings and complete additional administrative duties. After about fourteen hours at the Toyota plant, Uchino would go home, sleep for a few hours, then return to work. At 4:20 am one morning, after working for thirteen hours, Uchino collapsed and died on the factory floor from sudden heart failure. He was just 30 years old. Uchino was a victim of *karoshi*—death from overwork. The Japanese government recognises about 300 cases of karoshi each year, including cases of suicide from overwork (*karo-jisatsu*). However, this number only counts cases in which family members claimed and received compensation. Experts say the karoshi death toll in Japan is probably closer to 10 000. According to the Japanese government, employees who work more than eighty hours of overtime per month have a significantly higher risk of karoshi. Currently, more than 20 per cent of male Japanese employees exceed that level of overtime.[92]

National Labor Committee

Individual Differences in Stress

LEARNING OBJECTIVE

Explain why the same stressor might produce different stress levels in two people.

Because of unique personal characteristics, people have different stress experiences when exposed to the same stressor. One reason for this is that people have different threshold levels of resistance to the stressor. Those who exercise and have healthy lifestyles have a larger store of energy to cope with high stress levels. A second reason for different stress responses is that people use different coping strategies, some of which are more effective than others. Research suggests that employees who try to ignore or deny the existence of a stressor suffer more in the long run than those who try to find ways to weaken the stressor and seek social support.[95]

A third reason why some people experience less stress than others is that some have higher resilience.[96] **Resilience** is the capability of individuals to cope successfully in the face of significant change, adversity or risk. Those with high resilience are able to withstand adversity as well as recover more quickly from it. Resilient people possess personality traits (such as high extroversion and low neuroticism) that generate more optimism, confidence and positive emotions. Resilience also involves specific competencies and behaviours for responding and adapting more effectively to stressors. Research indicates that resilient people have higher emotional intelligence and good problem-solving skills. They also apply productive coping strategies, such as analysing the sources of stress and finding ways to neutralise these problems.[97]

resilience The capability of individuals to cope successfully in the face of significant change, adversity or risk.

While resilience helps people to withstand stress, another personal characteristic—workaholism—attracts more stressors and weakens the capacity to cope with them. The classic **workaholic** (also called *work addict*) is highly involved in work, feels compelled or driven to work because of inner pressures and has a low enjoyment of work. Workaholics are compulsive and preoccupied with work, often to the exclusion and detriment of personal health, intimate relationships and family.[98] Classic workaholics are more prone to job stress and have significantly higher scores on depression, anxiety and anger.[99]

workaholic A person who is highly involved in work, feels compelled to work and has a low enjoyment of work.

LEARNING OBJECTIVE 

Identify five ways to manage workplace stress.

Managing Work-Related Stress

A few years ago, Koh Ching Hong would dutifully arrive at work around 7.30 am and stay until 10 pm. The managing director of Fuji Xerox in Singapore would continue working at home for a few more hours, sending off emails listing tasks to be completed by employees 'first thing in the morning'. Eventually, Koh realised that the relentless pace was defeating a higher purpose. 'It came to a point that the people whom I worked so hard to provide for, my family, weren't getting to see me,' says the father of three children. Today, Koh is out of the office by 6.30 pm and shoos his staff out at the same time. Fuji Xerox also gives staff the opportunity to work from home as well as flexibility regarding when they want to begin and end their workday.[100]

Koh Ching Hong was fortunate. He was able to change his work habits and improve conditions for his 500 employees before matters got worse. Unfortunately, many people deny the existence of their stress until it has more serious outcomes. This avoidance strategy creates a vicious cycle because the failure to cope with stress becomes another stressor on top of the one that created the stress in the first place. To prevent this vicious cycle, employers and employees need to apply one or more of the stress-management strategies described below: remove the stressor, withdraw from the stressor, change stress perceptions, control stress consequences and/or receive social support.[101]

Remove the Stressor

Removing the stressor usually begins by identifying areas of high stress and determining their main causes. By identifying the specific stressors that adversely affect specific areas of the organisation, such 'stress audits' recognise that a one-size-fits-all approach to stress management is ineffective. For example, Unisys Asia-Pacific conducted this diagnosis through a survey in which employees were asked where they were struggling with work, and how well they took care of their physical and mental health. These results gave the information technology services company some direction on how to help combat employee stress. In particular, the company introduced a health and wellbeing program called 'Living Wellness@Unisys'. Unisys Asia-Pacific estimates that employee stress fell by 11 per cent and employee health levels improved significantly.[102]

There are many ways to remove the stressor, but some of the more common actions involve assigning employees to jobs that match their skills and preferences, reducing excessive workplace noise, having a complaint system and taking corrective action against harassment, and giving employees more control over the work process. Another important way that companies can remove stressors is by facilitating better work–life balance. Work–life balance initiatives minimise conflict between the employee's work and nonwork demands. Five of the most common work–life balance initiatives are flexible and limited work time, job sharing, teleworking, personal leave and child care support.[103]

- Flexible and limited work time—An important way to improve work–life balance is limiting the number of hours that employees are expected to work and giving them flexibility in scheduling those hours. Propaganda Games stands out in the overworked electronic games industry because it keeps work hours within reasonable limits. American electronics retailer Best Buy has become a role model in work–life balance by giving employees very flexible work hours.
- Job sharing splits a career position between two people so that they experience less time-based stress between work and family. They typically work different parts of the week, with

Getting a Life at McGraw-Hill

Publishing is a fast-paced business with tight deadlines. Even so, The McGraw-Hill Companies minimise the impact of these stressors by encouraging work-life balance through flexible work arrangements, including telecommuting, flexible hours, part-time employment, compressed work weeks, job sharing and several forms of personal leave. These initiatives have earned McGraw-Hill several awards and have significantly improved the work-life balance of many staff.

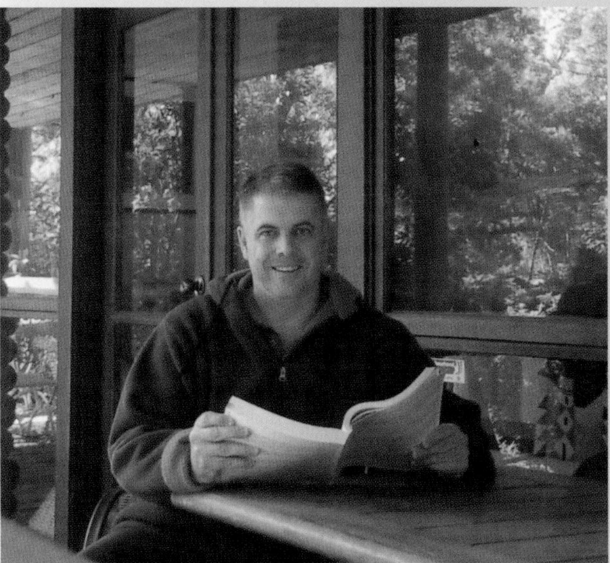

Matthew Coxhill is a case in point. Coxhill works part time (about three days a week) as a publisher in McGraw-Hill Australia's higher education group. He conducts most of this business from his home in regional Australia rather than from McGraw-Hill's Sydney offices. This arrangement allows Coxhill to enjoy semi-rural life and continue his other vocations as a professional trainer and mediator. 'With telecommuting and part-time flexible work hours, I am able to offer McGraw-Hill effective management of some key higher education lists. McGraw-Hill offers me the opportunity to participate in the other aspects of education and training I am interested in,' explains Coxhill.[104]

some overlapping work time in the weekly schedule to coordinate activities. This strategy gives employees the ability to work part-time in jobs that are naturally designed for full-time responsibilities.

- Teleworking, which was described in Chapter 1, reduces the time and stress of commuting to work and makes it easier to fulfil family obligations, such as temporarily leaving the home office to pick up the kids from school. Research suggests that teleworkers tend to experience better work–life balance.[105] However, teleworking may increase stress for those who crave social interaction, and who lack the space and privacy necessary to work at home.
- Personal leave—Employers with strong work–life values offer extended maternity, paternity and personal leave for employees to care for a new family or take advantage of a personal experience. Most countries provide 12 to 16 weeks of paid leave, with some offering one year or more of fully or partially paid maternity leave. Australia, New Zealand and the United States stand out as high-income countries without legislated paid maternity leave, although one-third of large and medium-sized firms in Australia offer paid maternity leave.[106]
- Child care support—According to one estimate, almost one-quarter of large American organisations provide on-site or subsidised child care facilities. Child care support reduces stress because employees are less rushed to drop off children and less worried during the day about their children's welfare.[107]

Withdraw from the Stressor

Removing the stressor may be the ideal solution, but it is often not feasible. An alternative strategy is to permanently or temporarily remove employees from the stressor. Permanent withdrawal occurs when employees are transferred to jobs that better fit their competencies and values. Temporarily withdrawing from stressors is the most frequent way that employees manage stress. Holidays are important opportunities for employees to recover from stress and reenergise for future challenges. Australia is one of the few countries with legislation that provides long-service leave. Generally, Australians receive two or three months of paid leave after ten or fifteen years of service. IBM, Colliers International and a few other firms in Australia and New Zealand offer unpaid leave, also known as sabbaticals. 'Sabbaticals result in happier, healthier employees,' says Colliers managing director Mark Synnott, who has taken four sabbaticals during his career. 'People recharge their batteries and come back clear-headed and motivated.'[108]

Some companies have innovative ways to help employees withdraw from stressful work throughout the day. SAS Institute employees in Cary, North Carolina, enjoy live piano recitals at lunchtime. Consulting firms Segal Co. in New York and Vielife in London have nap rooms where staff can recover with a few winks of sleep. Dixon Schwabl, a small marketing and public relations firm, has a 'scream room' where employees can privately verbalise their daily frustrations. Liggett-Stashower, Inc., the Cleveland-based creative agency, has three theme rooms, including a karaoke room where employees can sing away their stress. 'The higher the stress level, the more singing there is going on,' says the company's art director.[109]

Change Stress Perceptions

Earlier, we learned that employees experience different stress levels because they have different levels of resilience, including self-confidence and optimism. Consequently, another way to manage stress is to help employees improve their self-concept so that job challenges are not perceived as threatening. One study reported that personal goal setting and self-reinforcement can also reduce the stress that people experience when they enter new work settings. Other research suggests that some (but not all) forms of humour can improve optimism and create positive emotions by taking some psychological weight off the situation.[110]

Control Stress Consequences

Coping with workplace stress also involves controlling its consequences. For this reason, many companies have fitness centres or subsidise the cost of membership at off-site centres. Research indicates that physical exercise reduces the physiological consequences of stress by helping employees moderate their breathing and heart rate, muscle tension and stomach acidity.[111] A few firms, such as AstraZeneca, encourage employees to practise relaxation and meditation techniques during the workday. Research has found that various forms of meditation decrease anxiety, reduce blood pressure and muscle tension, and moderate breathing and heart rate.[112]

Along with fitness and relaxation/meditation, wellness programs can also help control the consequences of stress. These programs educate and support employees in regard to better nutrition and fitness, regular sleep and other good health habits. Many large employers offer *employee assistance programs (EAPs)*—counselling services that help employees resolve marital, financial or work-related troubles.

Receive Social Support

Social support occurs when coworkers, supervisors, family members, friends and others provide emotional and/or informational support to buffer an individual's stress experience. It potentially improves the person's resilience (particularly optimism and self-confidence) because support makes people feel valued and worthy. Social support also provides information to help the person interpret, comprehend and possibly remove the stressor. For instance, to reduce a new employee's stress, coworkers could describe ways to handle difficult customers. Seeking social support is called a 'tend and befriend' response to stress, and research suggests that women often follow this route rather than the 'fight-or-flight' response mentioned earlier.[113]

Employee emotions, attitudes and stress influence employee behaviour mainly through motivation. Recall, for instance, that behavioural intentions are judgements or expectations about the motivation to engage in a particular behaviour. The next chapter introduces the prominent theories of employee motivation.

CHAPTER SUMMARY

Emotions are physiological, behavioural and psychological episodes experienced toward an object, person or event that create a state of readiness. Emotions differ from attitudes, which represent a cluster of beliefs, feelings and behavioural intentions toward a person, object or event. Beliefs are a person's established perceptions about the attitude object. Feelings are positive or negative evaluations of the attitude object. Behavioural intentions represent a motivation to engage in a particular behaviour toward the target.

Attitudes have traditionally been described as a purely rational process in which beliefs predict feelings, which predict behavioural intentions, which predict behaviour. We now know that emotions have an influence on behaviour that is equal to or greater than that of cognition. This dual process is apparent when we internally experience a conflict between what logically seems good or bad and what we emotionally feel is good or bad in a situation. Emotions also affect behaviour directly. Behaviour sometimes influences our subsequent attitudes through cognitive dissonance, which occurs when we perceive an inconsistency between our beliefs, feelings and behaviour.

Emotional labour consists of the effort, planning and control needed to express organisationally desired emotions during interpersonal transactions. It is more common in jobs requiring a variety of emotions and more intense emotions, as well as in jobs where interaction with clients is frequent and has a long duration. Cultures also differ on the norms of displaying or concealing a person's true emotions. Emotional dissonance occurs when required and true emotions are incompatible with each other. Deep acting can minimise this dissonance, as can the practice of hiring people with a natural tendency to display desired emotions.

Emotional intelligence is the ability to perceive and express emotion, assimilate emotion in thought, understand and reason with emotion, and regulate emotion in oneself and others. This concept includes four components arranged in a hierarchy: self-awareness, self-management, social awareness and relationship management. Emotional intelligence can be learned to some extent, particularly through personal coaching.

Job satisfaction represents a person's evaluation of his or her job and work context. The exit-voice-loyalty-neglect (EVLN) model outlines four possible consequences of job dissatisfaction. Job satisfaction has a moderate relationship with job performance and with customer satisfaction. Affective organisational commitment (loyalty) is the employee's emotional attachment to, identification with and involvement in a particular organisation. This contrasts with continuance commitment, which is a calculative bond with the organisation. Companies build loyalty through justice and support, shared values, trust, organisational comprehension and employee involvement.

Stress is an adaptive response to a situation that is perceived as challenging or threatening to a person's wellbeing. The stress experience, also called the general adaptation syndrome, involves moving through three stages: alarm reaction, resistance and exhaustion. The causes of stress are called stressors; these include any environmental conditions that place a physical or emotional demand on a person. Three stressors that have received considerable attention are harassment and incivility, work overload and low task control.

Two people exposed to the same stressor may experience different stress levels. Many interventions are available to manage work-related stress, including removing the stressor, withdrawing from the stressor, changing stress perceptions, controlling stress consequences and receiving social support.

KEY TERMS

attitudes, p. 123
cognitive dissonance, p. 126
continuance commitment, p. 137
emotional dissonance, p. 129
emotional intelligence (EI), p. 130
emotional labour, p. 128
emotions, p. 122
exit-voice-loyalty-neglect (EVLN) model, p. 134
general adaptation syndrome, p. 140
job burnout, p. 141
job satisfaction, p. 133
organisational (affective) commitment, p. 137
psychological harassment, p. 141
resilience, p. 143
sexual harassment, p. 141
stress, p. 139
stressors, p. 141
trust, p. 138
workaholic, p. 143

Critical Thinking Questions

1. A recent study reported that university instructors are frequently required to engage in emotional labour. Identify the situations in which emotional labour is required for this job. In your opinion, is emotional labour more troublesome for university instructors or for telephone operators working at an emergency service?
2. 'Emotional intelligence is more important than cognitive intelligence in influencing an individual's success.' Do you agree or disagree with this statement? Support your perspective.
3. Describe a time when you effectively managed someone's emotions. What happened? What was the result?
4. 'Happy employees create happy customers.' Explain why this statement might be true and identify conditions in which it might not be true.
5. What factors influence an employee's organisational loyalty?
6. Is being a full-time university or college student a stressful role? Why or why not? Contrast your response with other students' perspectives.
7. Two university graduates recently joined the same major newspaper as journalists. Both work long hours and have tight deadlines for completing their stories. They are under

constant pressure to scout out new leads and be the first to report new controversies. One journalist is increasingly fatigued and despondent and has taken several days of sick leave. The other is getting the work done and seems to enjoy the challenges. Use your knowledge of stress to explain why these two journalists are reacting differently to their jobs.

8 A senior official of a labour union stated: 'All stress management does is help people cope with poor management. [Employers] should really be into stress reduction.' Discuss the accuracy of this statement.

Skill Builder 4.1

CLASS EXERCISE

Strengths-Based Coaching

Purpose

To help students practise a form of interpersonal development built on the dynamics of positive emotions.

Background

Several chapters in this book introduce and apply the emerging philosophy of *positive organisational behaviour*, which suggests that focusing on the positive rather than negative aspects of life will improve organisational success and individual wellbeing. An application of positive OB is strength-based or appreciative coaching, in which the coach focuses on the person's strengths rather than weaknesses, and helps to realise the person's potential. As part of any coaching process, the coach listens to the employee's story and uses questions and suggestions to help that person redefine her or his self-concept and perceptions of the environment. Two important skills in effective coaching are active listening and probing for information (rather than telling the person a solution or direction). The instructions below identify specific information and issues that the coach and coachee will discuss.

Instructions

1. Form teams of four people. One team can have six people if the class does not have multiples of four. For odd-numbered class sizes, one person may be an observer. Divide into pairs in which one person is coach and the other coachee. Ideally for this exercise, the coach and coachee should have *little* knowledge of each other.
2. Coachees will describe something about themselves in which they excel and for which they like to be recognised. This competency might be work-related, but not necessarily. It should be a personal achievement or ability that is close to their self-concept (how they define themselves). The coach mostly listens, but also prompts more details from the coachee using 'probe' questions (e.g. 'Tell me more about that.' 'What did you do next?' 'Could you explain that further, please?' 'What else can you remember about that event?'). As the coachee's story develops, the coach will guide the coachee to identify ways to leverage this strength. For example, the pair would explore situational barriers

to practising the coachee's strength as well as aspects of this strength that require further development. The strength may also be discussed as a foundation for the coachee to develop strengths in other related ways. The session should end with some discussion of the coachee's goals and action plans. The first coaching session can be any length of time specified by the instructor, but 15 to 25 minutes is typical for each coaching session.

3. After completing the first coaching session, regroup so that each pair consists of different partners than those in the first pair (i.e. if pairs were A-B and C-D in session 1, pairs are A-C and B-D in session 2). The coaches become coachees to their new partners in session 2.
4. The class will debrief regarding the emotional experience of discussing personal strengths, the role of self-concept in emotions and attitudes, the role of managers and coworkers in building positive emotions in people, and the value and limitations of strength-based coaching.

Note: For further information about strength-based coaching, see S. L. Orem, J. Binkert and A. L. Clancy, *Appreciative Coaching: A Positive Process for Change* (San Francisco: Jossey-Bass, 2007); M. Buckingham and C. Coffman, *First, Break All the Rules: What the World's Greatest Managers Do Differently* (New York: Simon & Schuster, 1999).

TEAM EXERCISE

Skill Builder 4.2

Ranking Jobs on Their Emotional Labour

Purpose

This exercise is designed to help you understand the jobs in which people tend to experience higher or lower degrees of emotional labour.

Instructions

1. Individually rank-order the extent that the jobs listed below require emotional labour. In other words, assign a '1' to the job you believe requires the most effort, planning and control to express the emotions desired by the organisation during interpersonal transactions. Assign a '10' to the job you believe requires the least amount of emotional labour. Mark your rankings in column 1.
2. The instructor will form teams of four or five members and each team will rank-order the items on the basis of consensus (not simply averaging the individual rankings). These results are placed in column 2.
3. The instructor will provide expert ranking information. This information should be written in column 3. Then you can calculate the differences in columns 4 and 5.
4. The class will compare the results and discuss the features of jobs with high emotional labour.

Occupational Emotional Labour Scoring Sheet

Occupation	1. Individual ranking	2. Team ranking	3. Expert ranking	4. Absolute difference of 1 and 3	5. Absolute difference of 2 and 3
Bartender					
Cashier					
Dental hygienist					
Insurance adjuster					
Lawyer					
Librarian					
Postal clerk					
Registered nurse					
Social worker					
Television announcer					
			TOTAL		
				Your score	Team score

(The lower the score, the better.)

Skill Builder 4.3

TEAM EXERCISE

Stage Fright!

Purpose

This exercise is designed to help you diagnose a common stressful situation and determine how stress management practices apply to this situation.

Background

Stage fright—including the fear of public speaking—is one of the most stressful experiences many people have in everyday life. According to some estimates, nearly three-quarters of us frequently get stage fright, even when speaking or acting in front of a small audience. Stage fright is an excellent topic for this team activity on stress management because the psychological and physiological symptoms of stage fright are really symptoms of stress. In other words, stage fright is the stress experience in a specific context involving a public audience. On the basis of the personal experiences of team members, your team will be asked to identify the symptoms of stage fright and to determine specific stress management activities that effectively combat it.

Instructions

1. The instructor will organise your class into teams, typically four to six students per team. Ideally, each team should have one or more people who acknowledge that they have experienced stage fright.

2. Each team's first task is to identify the symptoms of stage fright. The best way to organise these symptoms is to look at the three categories of stress outcomes described earlier in this chapter: physiological, psychological and behavioural. The specific stage fright symptoms may be different from the stress outcomes described in the chapter, but the three broad categories are relevant. Your team should be prepared to identify several symptoms and to present one or two specific examples of stage fright symptoms based on personal experiences of team members. (Individual students are *not* required to describe their experiences to the entire class.)
3. Each team's second task is to identify specific strategies people could or have applied to minimise stage fright. (The five categories of stress management presented in the chapter will likely provide a useful template for categorising these specific activities for managing stage fright.) In your team, document several strategies for minimising stage fright, and prepare to present one or two specific examples to the class to illustrate some of these strategies.
4. The class will congregate to hear each team's analysis of symptoms of and solutions to stage fright. This information will then be compared to the stress experience and stress management practices, respectively.

SELF-ASSESSMENT

Skill Builder 4.4

University Commitment Scale

Purpose

This self-assessment is designed to help you understand the concept of organisational commitment and to assess your commitment to the university you currently attend.

Overview

The concept of commitment is as relevant to students enrolled in university courses as it is to employees working in various organisations. This self-assessment adapts a popular organisational commitment instrument so that it refers to your commitment as a student to the educational institution you attend.

Instructions

Read each of the statements below and circle the response that best fits your personal belief. Then use the scoring key in Appendix B at the end of this book to calculate your results. This self-assessment should be completed alone so that you can rate yourself honestly without concerns of social comparison. Class discussion will focus on the meaning of the different types of organisational commitment and how well this scale applies to the commitment of students toward the university they attend.

University Commitment Scale

To what extent do you agree or disagree with each of these statements about yourself?	Strongly agree	Moderately agree	Slightly agree	Neutral	Slightly disagree	Moderately disagree	Strongly disagree
1. I would be very happy to complete the rest of my education at this university.	❑	❑	❑	❑	❑	❑	❑
2. One of the difficulties of leaving this university is that there are few alternatives.	❑	❑	❑	❑	❑	❑	❑
3. I really feel as if this university's problems are my own.	❑	❑	❑	❑	❑	❑	❑
4. Right now, staying enrolled at this university is a matter of necessity as much as desire.	❑	❑	❑	❑	❑	❑	❑
5. I do not feel a strong sense of belonging to this university.	❑	❑	❑	❑	❑	❑	❑
6. It would be very hard for me to leave this university right now even if I wanted to.	❑	❑	❑	❑	❑	❑	❑
7. I do not feel emotionally attached to this university.	❑	❑	❑	❑	❑	❑	❑
8. Too much of my life would be disrupted if I decided to move to a different university now.	❑	❑	❑	❑	❑	❑	❑
9. I do not feel like part of the 'family' at this university.	❑	❑	❑	❑	❑	❑	❑
10. I feel that I have too few options to consider leaving this university.	❑	❑	❑	❑	❑	❑	❑
11. This university has a great deal of personal meaning for me.	❑	❑	❑	❑	❑	❑	❑
12. If I had not already put so much of myself into this university, I might consider completing my education elsewhere.	❑	❑	❑	❑	❑	❑	❑

Source: Adapted from: J. P. Meyer, N. J. Allen and C. A. Smith, 'Commitment to Organisations and Occupations: Extension and Test of a Three-Component Model', *Journal of Applied Psychology*, 78 (1993): 538–551.

SELF-ASSESSMENT

Skill Builder 4.5

Available online

Dispositional Mood Scale

This self-assessment is designed to help you understand mood states or personality traits of emotions and to assess your own mood or emotional personality. This self-assessment consists of several words representing various emotions that you might have experienced. For each word presented, indicate the extent to which you have felt this way generally across all situations *over the past six months*. You need to be honest with yourself to receive a reasonable estimate of your mood state or personality trait on these scales. The results provide an estimate of your level on two emotional personality scales. This instrument is widely used in research, but it is only an estimate. You should not assume that the results are accurate without a more complete assessment by a trained professional.

SELF-ASSESSMENT

Skill Builder 4.6

Available online

Work Addiction Risk Test

This self-assessment is designed to help you identify the extent to which you are a workaholic. This instrument presents several statements and asks you to indicate the extent to which each statement is true of your work habits. You need to be honest with yourself for a reasonable estimate of your level of workaholism.

SELF-ASSESSMENT

Skill Builder 4.7

Available online

Perceived Stress Scale

This self-assessment is designed to help you estimate your perceived general level of stress. The items in this scale ask you about your feelings and thoughts during the last month. In each case, please indicate how often you felt or thought a certain way. You need to be honest with yourself for a reasonable estimate of your general level of stress.

SELF-ASSESSMENT

Skill Builder 4.8

Available online

Stress Coping Preference Scale

This self-assessment is designed to help you identify the type of coping strategy you prefer to use in stressful situations. This scale lists a variety of things you might do when faced with a stressful situation. You are asked how often you tend to react in these ways. You need to be honest with yourself for a reasonable estimate of your preferred coping strategy.

Endnotes

1 Customer Contact Management Association, 'CCW-Update', news release (Melbourne, 7 December 2007); E. G. Brown and J. Lubahn, 'We Need "To Talk"', *Bank Marketing* 39, no. 7 (2007): 32–36; J. Penman, 'Clydesdale Rings the Changes', *Sunday Times (London)*, 4 February 2007, 13; T. Russell, 'Centres of Excellence', *Personnel Today*, 23 January 2007, 24–25.

2 The centrality of emotions in economics, sociology and marketing is discussed in G. Loewenstein, 'Emotions in Economic Theory and Economic Behavior', *American Economic Review* 90, no. 2 (2000): 426–432; D. S. Massey, 'A Brief History of Human Society: The Origin and Role of Emotion in Social Life', *American Sociological Review* 67 (February 2002): 1–29; J. O'Shaughnessy and N. J. O'Shaughnessy, *The Marketing Power of Emotion* (New York: Oxford University Press, 2003).

3 The definition presented here is constructed from the following sources: N. M. Ashkanasy, W. J. Zerbe and C. E. J. Härtel, 'Introduction: Managing Emotions in a Changing Workplace', in *Managing Emotions in the Workplace*, ed. N. M. Ashkanasy, W. J. Zerbe and C. E. J. Härtel (Armonk, NY: M. E. Sharpe, 2002), 3–18; H. M. Weiss, 'Conceptual and Empirical Foundations for the Study of Affect at Work', in *Emotions in the Workplace* ed. R. G. Lord, R. J. Klimoski and R. Kanfer (San Francisco: Jossey-Bass, 2002), 20–63. However, the meaning of emotions is still being debated. See, for example, M. Cabanac, 'What Is Emotion?', *Behavioral Processes* 60 (2002): 69–83.

4 R. Kanfer and R. J. Klimoski, 'Affect and Work: Looking Back to the Future', in *Emotions in the Workplace*, ed. R. G. Lord, R. J. Klimoski and R. Kanfer (San Francisco: Jossey-Bass, 2002), 473–490; J. A. Russell, 'Core Affect and the Psychological Construction of Emotion', *Psychological Review* 110, no. 1 (2003): 145–172.

5 R. B. Zajonc, 'Emotions', in *Handbook of Social Psychology*, ed. D. T. Gilbert, S. T. Fiske and L. Gardner (New York: Oxford University Press, 1998), 591–634.

6 N. A. Remington, L. R. Fabrigar and P. S. Visser, 'Reexamining the Circumplex Model of Affect', *Journal of Personality and Social Psychology* 79, no. 2 (2000): 286–300; R. J. Larson, E. Diener and R. E. Lucas, 'Emotion: Models, Measures, and Differences', in *Emotions in the Workplace*, ed. R. G. Lord, R. J. Klimoski and R. Kanfer (San Francisco: Jossey-Bass, 2002), 64–113; L. F. Barrett *et al.*, 'The Experience of Emotion', *Annual Review of Psychology* 58, no. 1 (2007): 373–403.

7 A. H. Eagly and S. Chaiken, *The Psychology of Attitudes* (Orlando, FL: Harcourt Brace Jovanovich, 1993); A. P. Brief, *Attitudes in and around Organizations* (Thousand Oaks, CA: Sage, 1998). There is an amazing lack of consensus on the definition of attitudes. This book adopts the three-component model, whereas some experts define attitude as only the 'feelings' component, with 'beliefs' as a predictor and 'intentions' as an outcome. Some writers specifically define attitudes as an 'evaluation' of an attitude object, whereas others distinguish attitudes from evaluations of an attitude object. For some of these definitional variations, see I. Ajzen, 'Nature and Operation of Attitudes', *Annual Review of Psychology* 52 (2001): 27–58; D. Albarracín *et al.*, 'Attitudes: Introduction and Scope', in *The Handbook of Attitudes*, ed. D. Albarracín, B. T. Johnson and M. P. Zanna (Mahwah, NJ: Lawrence Erlbaum, 2005), 3–20; W. A. Cunningham and P. D. Zelazo, 'Attitudes and Evaluations: A Social Cognitive Neuroscience Perspective', *Trends in Cognitive Sciences* 11, no. 3 (2007): 97–104.

8 C. D. Fisher, 'Mood and Emotions While Working: Missing Pieces of Job Satisfaction?', *Journal of Organizational Behavior* 21 (2000): 185–202; Cunningham and Zelazo, 'Attitudes and Evaluations'; M. D. Lieberman, 'Social Cognitive Neuroscience: A Review of Core Processes', *Annual Review of Psychology* 58, no. 1 (2007): 259–289.

9 S. Orbell, 'Intention-Behavior Relations: A Self-Regulation Perspective', in *Contemporary Perspectives on the Psychology of Attitudes*, ed. G. Haddock and G. R. Maio (East Sussex, UK: Psychology Press, 2004), 145–168.

10 H. M. Weiss and R. Cropanzano, 'Affective Events Theory: A Theoretical Discussion of the Structure, Causes, and Consequences of Affective Experiences at Work', *Research in Organizational Behavior* 18 (1996): 1–74; J. Wegge *et al.*, 'A Test of Basic Assumptions of Affective Events Theory (AET) in Call Centre Work', *British Journal of Management* 17 (2006): 237–254.

11 J. A. Bargh and M. J. Ferguson, 'Beyond Behaviorism: On the Automaticity of Higher Mental Processes', *Psychological Bulletin* 126, no. 6 (2000): 925–945; R. H. Fazio, 'On the Automatic Activation of Associated Evaluations: An Overview', *Cognition and Emotion* 15, no. 2 (2001): 115–141; M. Gladwell, *Blink: The Power of Thinking without Thinking* (New York: Little, Brown, 2005).

12 A. R. Damasio, *Descartes' Error: Emotion, Reason, and the Human Brain* (New York: Putnam Sons, 1994); A. Damasio, *The Feeling of What Happens: Body and Emotion in the Making of Consciousness* (New York: Harcourt Brace and Co., 1999); P. Ekman, 'Basic Emotions', in *Handbook of Cognition and Emotion*, ed. T. Dalgleish and M. Power (San Francisco: Jossey-Bass, 1999), 45–60; J. E. LeDoux, 'Emotion Circuits in the Brain', *Annual*

Review of Neuroscience 23 (2000): 155–184; R. J. Dolan, 'Emotion, Cognition, and Behavior', *Science* 298, no. 5596 (2002): 1191–1194.

13 N. Schwarz, 'Emotion, Cognition, and Decision Making', *Cognition and Emotion* 14, no. 4 (2000): 433–440; M. T. Pham, 'The Logic of Feeling', *Journal of Consumer Psychology* 14, no. 4 (2004): 360–369.

14 M. Labash, 'Are We Having Fun Yet?', *Weekly Standard,* 17 September 2007; Mott MacDonald, *Meridian: Mott MacDonald Annual Review 2006–2007,* (Croydon, UK: Mott MacDonald, 2007); 'A Little Mystery ...', *Motivation,* October–November 2008; H. Budd, 'Workin' Nine to Five, It's So Nice to Feel Appreciated', *Daily Telegraph (Sydney),* 20 September 2008, 1; S. Davies, 'Razer Employees Wear Shorts, T-Shirts and Flip-Flops to Work', *Straits Times (Singapore),* 10 May 2008; L. Lister, 'Holding on to the Good People', *B&T Magazine* 58, no. 2668 (2008), 6; Mott MacDonald, *Meridian: Mott MacDonald Annual Review 2007–2008* (Croydon, UK: Mott MacDonald, 2008).

15 G. R. Maio, V. M. Esses and D. W. Bell, 'Examining Conflict between Components of Attitudes: Ambivalence and Inconsistency are Distinct Constructs', *Canadian Journal of Behavioural Science* 32, no. 2 (2000): 71–83.

16 P. C. Nutt, *Why Decisions Fail* (San Francisco: Berrett-Koehler, 2002); S. Finkelstein, *Why Smart Executives Fail* (New York: Viking, 2003); P. C. Nutt, 'Search During Decision Making', *European Journal of Operational Research* 160 (2005): 851–876.

17 Weiss and Cropanzano, 'Affective Events Theory'.

18 L. Festinger, *A Theory of Cognitive Dissonance* (Evanston, IL: Row, Peterson, 1957); G. R. Salancik, 'Commitment and the Control of Organizational Behavior and Belief', in *New Directions in Organizational Behavior,* ed. B. M. Staw and G. R. Salancik (Chicago: St. Clair, 1977), 1–54; A. D. Galinsky, J. Stone and J. Cooper, 'The Reinstatement of Dissonance and Psychological Discomfort Following Failed Affirmation', *European Journal of Social Psychology* 30, no. 1 (2000): 123–147.

19 T. A. Judge, E. A. Locke and C. C. Durham, 'The Dispositional Causes of Job Satisfaction: A Core Evaluations Approach', *Research in Organizational Behavior* 19 (1997): 151–188; Massey, 'A Brief History of Human Society'.

20 C. M. Brotheridge and A. A. Grandey, 'Emotional Labor and Burnout: Comparing Two Perspectives of "People Work"', *Journal of Vocational Behavior* 60 (2002): 17–39; P. G. Irving, D. F. Coleman and D. R. Bobocel, 'The Moderating Effect of Negative Affectivity in the Procedural Justice-Job Satisfaction Relation', *Canadian Journal of Behavioural Science* 37, no. 1 (2005): 20–32.

21 J. Schaubroeck, D. C. Ganster and B. Kemmerer, 'Does Trait Affect Promote Job Attitude Stability?', *Journal of Organizational Behavior* 17 (1996): 191–196; C. Dormann and D. Zapf, 'Job Satisfaction: A Meta-Analysis of Stabilities', *Journal of Organizational Behavior* 22 (2001): 483–504.

22 R. Corelli, 'Dishing out Rudeness', *Maclean's,* 11 January 1999, 44–47; D. Matheson, 'A Vancouver Cafe Where Rudeness Is Welcomed', *Canada AM,* CTV Television (11 January 2000).

23 B. E. Ashforth and R. H. Humphrey, 'Emotional Labor in Service Roles: The Influence of Identity', *Academy of Management Review* 18 (1993): 88–115. For a more recent review of the emotional labour concept, see T. M. Glomb and M. J. Tews, 'Emotional Labor: A Conceptualization and Scale Development', *Journal of Vocational Behavior* 64, no. 1 (2004): 1–23.

24 J. A. Morris and D. C. Feldman, 'The Dimensions, Antecedents, and Consequences of Emotional Labor', *Academy of Management Review* 21 (1996): 986–1010; D. Zapf, 'Emotion Work and Psychological Well-Being: A Review of the Literature and Some Conceptual Considerations', *Human Resource Management Review* 12 (2002): 237–268.

25 K. B. Mathis, 'Puttin' on the Ritz', *Florida Times-Union (Jacksonville),* 22 January 2006, G1.

26 'Reach for the Sky', *New Sunday Times (Kuala Lumpur),* 16 November 2008, 4; C. Platt, 'Inside Flight Attendant School', *WA Today (Perth),* 24 February 2009.

27 E. Forman, '"Diversity Concerns Grow as Companies Head Overseas", Consultant Says', *Sun-Sentinel (Fort Lauderdale, FL),* 26 June 1995. Cultural differences in emotional expression are discussed in F. Trompenaars, 'Resolving International Conflict: Culture and Business Strategy', *Business Strategy Review* 7, no. 3 (1996): 51–68; F. Trompenaars and C. Hampden-Turner, *Riding the Waves of Culture: Understanding Cultural Diversity in Business,* 2nd edn (New York: McGraw-Hill, 1998), ch. 6; A. E. Raz and A. Rafaeli, 'Emotion Management in Cross-Cultural Perspective: "Smile Training" in Japanese and North American Service Organizations', *Research on Emotion in Organizations* 3 (2007): 199–220.

28 S. Dowling, 'Teaching Berlin How to Smile', *Spiegel Online,* 11 January 2006; 'Teaching Berlin to Be Nice', *Spiegel Online,* 10 March 2009.

29 This relates to the automaticity of emotion, which is summarised in P. Winkielman and K. C. Berridge, 'Unconscious Emotion', *Current Directions in Psychological Science* 13, no. 3 (2004): 120–123; K. N. Ochsner and J. J. Gross, 'The Cognitive Control of Emotions', *Trends in Cognitive Sciences* 9, no. 5 (2005): 242–249.

30 W. J. Zerbe, 'Emotional Dissonance and Employee Well-Being', in *Managing Emotions in the Workplace*, ed. N. M. Ashkanasy, W. J. Zerbe and C. E. J. Härtel (Armonk, NY: M. E. Sharpe, 2002), 189–214; R. Cropanzano, H. M. Weiss and S. M. Elias, 'The Impact of Display Rules and Emotional Labor on Psychological Well-Being at Work', *Research in Occupational Stress and Well Being* 3 (2003): 45–89.

31 J. Verdon, 'They Can Hardly Contain Themselves', *The Record (Bergen, NJ)*, 21 April 2007, A15; S. Leonard and M. Clayton, 'Long Hours Hurt Business and Families', *Sunday Times (Best Companies Guide 2009) (London)*, 29 June 2008, 12.

32 Brotheridge and Grandey, 'Emotional Labor and Burnout'; Zapf, 'Emotion Work and Psychological Well-Being'; J. M. Diefendorff, M. H. Croyle and R. H. Gosserand, 'The Dimensionality and Antecedents of Emotional Labor Strategies', *Journal of Vocational Behavior* 66, no. 2 (2005): 339–357.

33 K. K. Spors, 'Top Small Workplaces 2007', *Wall Street Journal*, 1 October 2007, R1.

34 J. D. Mayer, P. Salovey and D. R. Caruso, 'Models of Emotional Intelligence', in *Handbook of Human Intelligence*, ed. R. J. Sternberg, 2nd edn (New York: Cambridge University Press, 2000), 396–420. This definition is also recognised in C. Cherniss, 'Emotional Intelligence and Organizational Effectiveness', in *The Emotionally Intelligent Workplace*, ed. C. Cherniss and D. Goleman (San Francisco: Jossey-Bass, 2001), 3–12; M. Zeidner, G. Matthews and R. D. Roberts, 'Emotional Intelligence in the Workplace: A Critical Review', *Applied Psychology: An International Review* 53, no. 3 (2004): 371–399.

35 These four dimensions of emotional intelligence are discussed in detail in D. Goleman, R. Boyatzis and A. McKee, *Primal Leadership: Realizing the Power of Emotional Intelligence* (Boston: Harvard Business School Press, 2002), ch. 3. Slight variations of this model are presented in R. Boyatzis, D. Goleman and K. S. Rhee, 'Clustering Competence in Emotional Intelligence', in *The Handbook of Emotional Intelligence*, ed. R. Bar-On and J. D. A. Parker (San Francisco: Jossey-Bass, 2000), 343–362; D. Goleman, 'An EI-Based Theory of Performance', in *The Emotionally Intelligent Workplace*, ed. C. Cherniss and D. Goleman (San Francisco: Jossey-Bass, 2001), 27–44.

36 Which model best represents EI and its abilities is debated in several sources, including several chapters in K. R. Murphy, ed., *A Critique of Emotional Intelligence: What Are the Problems and How Can They Be Fixed?* (Mahwah, NJ: Lawrence Erlbaum, 2006).

37 H. A. Elfenbein and N. Ambady, 'Predicting Workplace Outcomes from the Ability to Eavesdrop on Feelings', *Journal of Applied Psychology* 87, no. 5 (2002): 963–971.

38 The hierarchical nature of the four EI dimensions is discussed by Goleman, but it is more explicit in the Salovey and Mayer model. See D. R. Caruso and P. Salovey, *The Emotionally Intelligent Manager* (San Francisco: Jossey-Bass, 2004).

39 W. Lau, 'Staff with High EQ Help Motivate Team Members Events Watch', *South China Morning Post (Hong Kong)*, 23 August 2008, 22.

40 P. N. Lopes *et al.*, 'Emotional Intelligence and Social Interaction', *Personality and Social Psychology Bulletin* 30, no. 8 (2004): 1018–1034; C. S. Daus and N. M. Ashkanasy, 'The Case for the Ability-Based Model of Emotional Intelligence in Organizational Behavior', *Journal of Organizational Behavior* 26 (2005): 453–466; J. E. Barbuto Jr and M. E. Burbach, 'The Emotional Intelligence of Transformational Leaders: A Field Study of Elected Officials', *Journal of Social Psychology* 146, no. 1 (2006): 51–64; M. A. Brackett *et al.*, 'Relating Emotional Abilities to Social Functioning: A Comparison of Self-Report and Performance Measures of Emotional Intelligence', *Journal of Personality and Social Psychology* 91, no. 4 (2006): 780–795; D. L. Reis *et al.*, 'Emotional Intelligence Predicts Individual Differences in Social Exchange Reasoning', *NeuroImage* 35, no. 3 (2007): 1385–1391; S. K. Singh, 'Role of Emotional Intelligence in Organisational Learning: An Empirical Study', *Singapore Management Review* 29, no. 2 (2007): 55–74.

41 Some studies have reported situations in which EI has a limited effect on individual performance. For example, see A. L. Day and S. A. Carroll, 'Using an Ability-Based Measure of Emotional Intelligence to Predict Individual Performance, Group Performance, and Group Citizenship Behaviors', *Personality and Individual Differences* 36 (2004): 1443–1458; Z. Ivcevic, M. A. Brackett and J. D. Mayer, 'Emotional Intelligence and Emotional Creativity', *Journal of Personality* 75, no. 2 (2007): 199–236; J. C. Rode *et al.*, 'Emotional Intelligence and Individual Performance: Evidence of Direct and Moderated Effects', *Journal of Organizational Behavior* 28, no. 4 (2007): 399–421.

42 D. McGinn, 'The Emotional Workplace', *National Post*, 18 August 2007, FW3.

43 Goleman, Boyatzis and McKee, *Primal Leadership*; S. C. Clark, R. Callister and R. Wallace, 'Undergraduate Management Skills Courses and Students' Emotional Intelligence', *Journal of Management Education* 27, no. 1 (2003): 3–23; Lopes *et al.*, 'Emotional Intelligence and Social Interaction'; H. A. Elfenbein, 'Learning in Emotion Judgements: Training and the Cross-Cultural

Understanding of Facial Expressions', *Journal of Nonverbal Behavior* 30, no. 1 (2006): 21–36; C.-S. Wong *et al.*, 'The Feasibility of Training and Development of EI: An Exploratory Study in Singapore, Hong Kong and Taiwan', *Intelligence* 35, no. 2 (2007): 141–150.

44 R. Johnson, 'Can You Feel It?', *People Management*, 23 August 2007, 34–37.

45 D. A. Harrison, D. A. Newman and P. L. Roth, 'How Important are Job Attitudes? Meta-Analytic Comparisons of Integrative Behavioral Outcomes and Time Sequences', *Academy of Management Journal* 49, no. 2 (2006): 305–325.

46 C. Fox, 'Shifting Gears', *Australian Financial Review*, 13 August 2004, 28; J. Thomson, 'True Team Spirit', *Business Review Weekly*, 18 March 2004, 92.

47 E. A. Locke, 'The Nature and Causes of Job Satisfaction', in *Handbook of Industrial and Organizational Psychology*, ed. M. Dunnette (Chicago: Rand McNally, 1976), 1297–1350; H. M. Weiss, 'Deconstructing Job Satisfaction: Separating Evaluations, Beliefs and Affective Experiences', *Human Resource Management Review*, no. 12 (2002): 173–194. Some definitions still include emotion as an element of job satisfaction, whereas the definition presented in this book views emotion as a cause of job satisfaction. Also, this definition views job satisfaction as a 'collection of attitudes', because each source produces a different attitude (e.g. coworker satisfaction, pay satisfaction).

48 Ipsos-Reid, 'Ipsos-Reid Global Poll Finds Major Differences in Employee Satisfaction around the World', news release (Toronto, 8 January 2001); International Survey Research, *Employee Satisfaction in the World's 10 Largest Economies: Globalization or Diversity?* (Chicago: International Survey Research, 2002); Watson Wyatt Worldwide, 'Malaysian Workers More Satisfied with Their Jobs Than Their Companies' Leadership and Supervision Practices', news release (Kuala Lumpur, 30 November 2004); Kelly Global Workforce Index, *American Workers are Happy with Their Jobs and Their Bosses* (Troy, MI: Kelly Services, November 2006); T. W. Smith, *Job Satisfaction in America: Trends and Socio-Demographic Correlates* (Chicago: National Opinion Research Center/University of Chicago, August 2007); L. Briggs, 'APS in Good Shape but More Remains to Be', *Canberra Times*, 5 February 2008, 8; Watson Wyatt Worldwide, 'Worker Bees Buzz Happily, but Want More Honey', news release (Singapore, 2008); SEEK Limited, 'Teachers among Australia's Happiest Employees', news release (Melbourne, 18 February 2009).

49 Watson Wyatt Worldwide, 'Malaysian Workers More Satisfied with Their Jobs'.

50 The problems with measuring attitudes and values across cultures is discussed in G. Law, 'If You're Happy & You Know It, Tick the Box', *Management (Auckland)* 45 (March 1998): 34–37; P. E. Spector *et. al.*, 'Do National Levels of Individualism and Internal Locus of Control Relate to Well-Being: An Ecological Level International Study', *Journal of Organizational Behavior*, no. 22 (2001): 815–832; L. Saari and T. A. Judge, 'Employee Attitudes and Job Satisfaction', *Human Resource Management* 43, no. 4 (2004): 395–407.

51 H. Rao and R. I. Sutton, 'Innovation Lessons from Pixar: An Interview with Oscar-Winning Director Brad Bird', *McKinsey Quarterly* (April 2008): 1–9.

52 M. J. Withey and W. H. Cooper, 'Predicting Exit, Voice, Loyalty, and Neglect', *Administrative Science Quarterly*, no. 34 (1989): 521–539; W. H. Turnley and D. C. Feldman, 'The Impact of Psychological Contract Violations on Exit, Voice, Loyalty, and Neglect', *Human Relations* 52 (July 1999): 895–922. Subdimensions of 'silence' and 'voice' also exist. See L. van Dyne, S. Ang and I. C. Botero, 'Conceptualizing Employee Silence and Employee Voice as Multidimensional Constructs', *Journal of Management Studies* 40, no. 6 (2003): 1359–1392.

53 T. R. Mitchell, B. C. Holtom and T. W. Lee, 'How to Keep Your Best Employees: Developing an Effective Retention Policy', *Academy of Management Executive* 15 (November 2001): 96–108; C. P. Maertz and M. A. Campion, 'Profiles of Quitting: Integrating Process and Content Turnover Theory', *Academy of Management Journal* 47, no. 4 (2004): 566–582; K. Morrell, J. Loan-Clarke and A. Wilkinson, 'The Role of Shocks in Employee Turnover', *British Journal of Management* 15 (2004): 335–349; B. C. Holtom, T. R. Mitchell and T. W. Lee, 'Increasing Human and Social Capital by Applying Job Embeddedness Theory', *Organizational Dynamics* 35, no. 4 (2006): 316–331.

54 A. A. Luchak, 'What Kind of Voice Do Loyal Employees Use?', *British Journal of Industrial Relations* 41 (March 2003): 115–134.

55 A. O. Hirschman, *Exit, Voice, and Loyalty: Responses to Decline in Firms, Organizations, and States* (Cambridge, MA: Harvard University Press, 1970); E. A. Hoffmann, 'Exit and Voice: Organizational Loyalty and Dispute Resolution Strategies', *Social Forces* 84, no. 4 (2006): 2313–2330.

56 J. D. Hibbard, N. Kumar and L. W. Stern, 'Examining the Impact of Destructive Acts in Marketing Channel Relationships', *Journal of Marketing Research* 38 (February 2001): 45–61; J. Zhou and J. M. George, 'When Job Dissatisfaction Leads to Creativity: Encouraging the Expression of Voice', *Academy of Management Journal* 44 (August 2001): 682–696.

57 M. J. Withey and I. R. Gellatly, 'Situational and Dispositional Determinants of Exit, Voice, Loyalty and Neglect', *Proceedings of the Administrative Sciences Association of Canada, Organizational Behaviour Division* (June 1998); D. C. Thomas and K. Au, 'The Effect of

Cultural Differences on Behavioral Responses to Low Job Satisfaction', *Journal of International Business Studies* 33, no. 2 (2002): 309–326; S. F. Premeaux and A. G. Bedeian, 'Breaking the Silence: The Moderating Effects of Self-Monitoring in Predicting Speaking up in the Workplace', *Journal of Management Studies* 40, no. 6 (2003): 1537–1562.

58 F. Smith, 'Shareholders New Force in Employee Rights', *Australian Financial Review*, 29 May 2007.

59 T. A. Judge *et al.*, 'The Job Satisfaction-Job Performance Relationship: A Qualitative and Quantitative Review', *Psychological Bulletin* 127, no. 3 (2001): 376–407; Saari and Judge, 'Employee Attitudes and Job Satisfaction'. Other studies report stronger correlations with job performance when both the belief and feeling components of job satisfaction are consistent with each other and when overall job attitude (satisfaction and commitment combined) is being measured. See D. J. Schleicher, J. D. Watt and G. J. Greguras, 'Reexamining the Job Satisfaction-Performance Relationship: The Complexity of Attitudes', *Journal of Applied Psychology* 89, no. 1 (2004): 165–177; Harrison, Newman and Roth, 'How Important Are Job Attitudes?'. The positive relationship between job satisfaction and employee performance is also consistent with emerging research on the outcomes of positive organisational behaviour. For example, see J. R. Sunil, 'Enhancing Employee Performance through Positive Organizational Behavior', *Journal of Applied Social Psychology* 38, no. 6 (2008): 1580–1600.

60 EEO Trust, 'Fixed Shifts Key to Customer Service at BNZ Call Centres', *EEO Trust Work & Life Bulletin*, June 2005, 3; G. Thomas, 'Air NZ Execs Switch Roles to Embrace Change', *The Australian*, 17 August 2007, 35.

61 F. Bilovsky, 'Wegmans Is Named America's No. 1 Employer', *Democrat & Chronicle (Rochester, NY)*, 11 January 2005; M. Boyle, 'The Wegmans Way', *Fortune*, 24 January 2005, 62; S. R. Ezzedeen, C. M. Hyde and K. R. Laurin, 'Is Strategic Human Resource Management Socially Responsible? The Case of Wegman's Food Markets, Inc.', *Employee Rights and Responsibilities Journal* 18 (2007): 295–307.

62 J. I. Heskett, W. E. Sasser and L. A. Schlesinger, *The Service Profit Chain* (New York: Free Press, 1997); D. J. Koys, 'The Effects of Employee Satisfaction, Organizational Citizenship Behavior, and Turnover on Organizational Effectiveness: A Unit-Level, Longitudinal Study', *Personnel Psychology* 54 (April 2001): 101–114; W.-C. Tsai and Y.-M. Huang, 'Mechanisms Linking Employee Affective Delivery and Customer Behavioral Intentions', *Journal of Applied Psychology* 87, no. 5 (2002): 1001–1008; T. DeCotiis *et al.*, 'How Outback Steakhouse Created a Great Place to Work, Have Fun, and Make Money', *Journal of Organizational Excellence* 23, no. 4 (2004): 23–33; G. A. Gelade and S. Young, 'Test of a Service Profit Chain Model in the Retail Banking Sector', *Journal of Occupational and Organizational Psychology* 78 (2005): 1–22.

63 P. Guenzi and O. Pelloni, 'The Impact of Interpersonal Relationships on Customer Satisfaction and Loyalty to the Service Provider', *International Journal of Service Industry Management* 15, no. 3–4 (2004): 365–384; S. J. Bell, S. Auh and K. Smalley, 'Customer Relationship Dynamics: Service Quality and Customer Loyalty in the Context of Varying Levels of Customer Expertise and Switching Costs', *Journal of the Academy of Marketing Science* 33, no. 2 (2005): 169–183; P. B. Barger and A. A. Grandey, 'Service with a Smile and Encounter Satisfaction: Emotional Contagion and Appraisal Mechanisms', *Academy of Management Journal* 49, no. 6 (2006): 1229–1238.

64 R. T. Mowday, L. W. Porter and R. M. Steers, *Employee Organization Linkages: The Psychology of Commitment, Absenteeism, and Turnover* (New York: Academic Press, 1982).

65 J. P. Meyer, 'Organizational Commitment', *International Review of Industrial and Organizational Psychology* 12 (1997): 175–228. Along with affective and continuance commitment, Meyer identifies 'normative commitment', which refers to employee feelings of obligation to remain with the organisation. This commitment has been excluded so we can focus on the two most common perspectives of commitment.

66 R. D. Hackett, P. Bycio and P. A. Hausdorf, 'Further Assessments of Meyer and Allen's (1991) Three-Component Model of Organizational Commitment', *Journal of Applied Psychology* 79, no. 1 (1994): 15–23.

67 J. P. Meyer *et al.*, 'Affective, Continuance, and Normative Commitment to the Organization: A Meta-Analysis of Antecedents, Correlates, and Consequences', *Journal of Vocational Behavior* 61 (2002): 20–52; M. Riketta, 'Attitudinal Organizational Commitment and Job Performance: A Meta-Analysis', *Journal of Organizational Behavior* 23 (2002): 257–266.

68 J. P. Meyer *et al.*, 'Organizational Commitment and Job Performance: It's the Nature of the Commitment That Counts', *Journal of Applied Psychology* 74, no. 1 (1989): 152–156; A. A. Luchak and I. R. Gellatly, 'What Kind of Commitment Does a Final-Earnings Pension Plan Elicit?', *Relations Industrielles* 56 (Spring 2001): 394–417; Z. X. Chen and A. M. Francesco, 'The Relationship between the Three Components of Commitment and Employee Performance in China', *Journal of Vocational Behavior* 62, no. 3 (2003): 490–510; D. M. Powell and J. P. Meyer, 'Side-Bet Theory and the Three-Component Model of Organizational Commitment', *Journal of Vocational Behavior* 65, no. 1 (2004): 157–177.

69 E. W. Morrison and S. L. Robinson, 'When Employees Feel Betrayed: A Model of How Psychological Contract Violation Develops', *Academy of Management Review* 22 (1997): 226–256; J. E. Finegan, 'The Impact of Person and Organizational Values on Organizational Commitment', *Journal of Occupational and Organizational Psychology* 73 (June 2000): 149–169.

70 D. M. Cable and T. A. Judge, 'Person-Organization Fit, Job Choice Decisions, and Organizational Entry', *Organizational Behavior and Human Decision Processes* 67, no. 3 (1996): 294–311; T. J. Kalliath, A. C. Bluedorn and M. J. Strube, 'A Test of Value Congruence Effects', *Journal of Organizational Behavior* 20, no. 7 (1999): 1175–1198; J. W. Westerman and L. A. Cyr, 'An Integrative Analysis of Person-Organization Fit Theories', *International Journal of Selection and Assessment* 12, no. 3 (2004): 252–261.

71 D. M. Rousseau *et al.*, 'Not So Different after All: A Cross-Discipline View of Trust', *Academy of Management Review* 23 (1998): 393–404.

72 S. Ashford, C. Lee and P. Bobko, 'Content, Causes, and Consequences of Job Insecurity: A Theory-Based Measure and Substantive Test', *Academy of Management Journal* 32 (1989): 803–829; C. Hendry and R. Jenkins, 'Psychological Contracts and New Deals', *Human Resource Management Journal* 7 (1997): 38–44.

73 T. S. Heffner and J. R. Rentsch, 'Organizational Commitment and Social Interaction: A Multiple Constituencies Approach', *Journal of Vocational Behavior* 59 (2001): 471–490.

74 'AMA Survey Shows Rural Doctors "Really Neglected"', *ABC News*, 2 May 2007; T. Shepherd, 'Rural GPs Want to Quit', *The Advertiser (Adelaide)*, 21 November 2007, 5; L. Hoffman, 'Rewards of Rural Practice', *The Australian*, 19 April 2008, 9.

75 J. C. Quick *et al.*, *Preventive Stress Management in Organizations* (Washington, D.C.: American Psychological Association, 1997), 3–4; R. S. DeFrank and J. M. Ivancevich, 'Stress on the Job: An Executive Update', *Academy of Management Executive* 12 (August 1998): 55–66; A. L. Dougall and A. Baum, 'Stress, Coping, and Immune Function', in *Handbook of Psychology*, vol. 3, ed. M. Gallagher and R. J. Nelson (Hoboken, NJ: Wiley, 2003), 441–455. There are at least three schools of thought regarding the meaning of stress, and some reviews of the stress literature describe these schools without pointing to any one as the preferred definition. One reviewer concluded that the stress concept is so broad that it should be considered an umbrella concept, capturing a broad array of phenomena and providing a simple term for the public to use. See T. A. Day, 'Defining Stress as a Prelude to Mapping Its Neurocircuitry: No Help from Allostasis', *Progress in Neuro-Psychopharmacology and Biological Psychiatry* 29, no. 8 (2005): 1195–1200; R. Cropanzano and A. Li, 'Organizational Politics and Workplace Stress', in *Handbook of Organizational Politics*, ed. E. Vigoda-Gadot and A. Drory (Cheltenham, UK: Edward Elgar, 2006), 139–160; R. L. Woolfolk, P. M. Lehrer and L. A. Allen, 'Conceptual Issues Underlying Stress Management', in *Principles and Practice of Stress Management*, ed. P. M. Lehrer, R. L. Woolfolk and W. E. Sime (New York: Guilford Press, 2007), 3–15.

76 Finegan, 'The Impact of Person and Organizational Values on Organizational Commitment'; Dougall and Baum, 'Stress, Coping, and Immune Function'; R. S. Lazarus, *Stress and Emotion: A New Synthesis* (New York: Springer Publishing, 2006); L. W. Hunter and S. M. B. Thatcher, 'Feeling the Heat: Effects of Stress, Commitment, and Job Experience on Job Performance', *Academy of Management Journal* 50, no. 4 (2007): 953–968.

77 T. Haratani, 'Job Stress Trends in Japan', in *Job Stress Trends in East Asia (Proceedings of the First East-Asia Job Stress Meeting)*, ed. A. Tsutsumi (Tokyo: Waseda University, 8 January 2000), 4–10; PR Newswire, 'New Survey: Americans Stressed More Than Ever', news release (26 June 2003); Mind (National Association for Mental Health), *Stress and Mental Health in the Workplace*, (London: Mind, 2005); D. Passmore, 'We're All Sick of Work', *Sunday Mail (Brisbane)*, 27 November 2005, 45; M. Shields, 'Stress and Depression in the Employed Population', *Health Reports (Statistics Canada)* 17, no. 4 (October 2006): 11–32; W. Lester, 'A World of Stress', *Daily News (South Africa)*, 6 February 2007.

78 Quick *et al.*, *Preventive Stress Management in Organizations*, 5–6; B. L. Simmons and D. L. Nelson, 'Eustress at Work: The Relationship between Hope and Health in Hospital Nurses', *Health Care Management Review* 26, no. 4 (October 2001): 7–18.

79 H. Selye, 'A Syndrome Produced by Diverse Nocuous Agents', *Nature* 138, no. 1 (4 July 1936): 32; H. Selye, *Stress without Distress* (Philadelphia: J. B. Lippincott, 1974). The earliest use of the word *stress*, over 500 years ago, is reported in R. M. K. Keil, 'Coping and Stress: A Conceptual Analysis', *Journal of Advanced Nursing* 45, no. 6 (2004): 659–665.

80 S. E. Taylor, R. L. Repetti and T. Seeman, 'Health Psychology: What Is an Unhealthy Environment and How Does It Get under the Skin?', *Annual Review of Psychology* 48 (1997): 411–447.

81 D. Ganster, M. Fox and D. Dwyer, 'Explaining Employees' Health Care Costs: A Prospective Examination of Stressful Job Demands, Personal Control, and Physiological Reactivity', *Journal of Applied Psychology* 86, no. 5 (2001): 954–964;

M. K ivimaki *et al.*, 'Work Stress and Risk of Cardiovascular Mortality: Prospective Cohort Study of Industrial Employees', *British Medical Journal* 325 (19 October 2002): 857–860; S. Andrew and S. Ayers, 'Stress, Health, and Illness', in *The Sage Handbook of Health Psychology*, ed. S. Sutton, A. Baum and M. Johnston (London: Sage, 2004), 169–196; A. Rosengren *et al.*, 'Association of Psychosocial Risk Factors with Risk of Acute Myocardial Infarction in 11 119 Cases and 13 648 Controls from 52 Countries (The Interheart Study): Case-Control Study', *Lancet* 364, no. 9438 (11 September 2004): 953–962.

82 R. C. Kessler, 'The Effects of Stressful Life Events on Depression', *Annual Review of Psychology* 48 (1997): 191–214; L. Greenburg and J. Barling, 'Predicting Employee Aggression against Coworkers, Subordinates and Supervisors: The Roles of Person Behaviors and Perceived Workplace Factors', *Journal of Organizational Behavior* 20 (1999): 897–913; M. Jamal and V. V. Baba, 'Job Stress and Burnout among Canadian Managers and Nurses: An Empirical Examination', *Canadian Journal of Public Health* 91, no. 6 (November–December 2000): 454–458; L. Tourigny, V. V. Baba and T. R. Lituchy, 'Job Burnout among Airline Employees in Japan: A Study of the Buffering Effects of Absence and Supervisory Support', *International Journal of Cross Cultural Management* 5, no. 1 (April 2005): 67–85; M. S. Hershcovis *et al.*, 'Predicting Workplace Aggression: A Meta-Analysis', *Journal of Applied Psychology* 92, no. 1 (2007): 228–238.

83 C. Maslach, W. B. Schaufeli and M. P. Leiter, 'Job Burnout', *Annual Review of Psychology* 52 (2001): 397–422; J. R. B. Halbesleben and M. R. Buckley, 'Burnout in Organizational Life', *Journal of Management* 30, no. 6 (2004): 859–879.

84 K. Danna and R. W. Griffin, 'Health and Well-Being in the Workplace: A Review and Synthesis of the Literature', *Journal of Management* (Spring 1999): 357–384.

85 This is a slight variation of the definition in the Quebec antiharassment legislation. See www.cnt.gouv.qc.ca. For related definitions and discussion of workplace incivility, see H. Cowie *et. al.*, 'Measuring Workplace Bullying', *Aggression and Violent Behavior* 7, no. 1 (2002): 33–51; C. M. Pearson and C. L. Porath, 'On the Nature, Consequences and Remedies of Workplace Incivility: No Time for "Nice"? Think Again', *Academy of Management Executive* 19, no. 1 (February 2005): 7–18.

86 Pearson and Porath, 'On the Nature, Consequences and Remedies of Workplace Incivility'; S. Toomey, 'Bullying Alive and Kicking', *The Australian*, 16 July 2005, 9; J. Scott, C. Blanshard and S. Child, 'Workplace Bullying of Junior Doctors: A Cross-Sectional Questionnaire Survey', *New Zealand Medical Journal* 121, no. 1282 (19 September 2008): 10–14; A. Yeung and B. Griffin, 'Workplace Incivility: Does It Matter in Asia?', *People & Strategy* 31, no. 1 (December 2008): 14–19.

87 For a legal discussion of types of sexual harassment, see: B. Lindemann and D. D. Kadue, *Sexual Harassment in Employment Law* (Washington: BNA Books, 1999), pp. 7–9.

88 Past predictions of future work hours are described in B. K. Hunnicutt, *Kellogg's Six-Hour Day* (Philadelphia: Temple University Press, 1996).

89 B. van Wanrooy *et al.*, *Working Lives: Statistics and Stories* (Sydney: Workplace Research Centre, University of Sydney, October 2008); E. Galinsky *et al.*, *Overwork in America: When the Way We Work Becomes Too Much* (New York: Families and Work Institute, March 2005); J. MacBride-King, *Wrestling with Workload: Organizational Strategies for Success* (Ottawa: Conference Board of Canada, 2005); R. G. Netemeyer, J. G. Maxham III and C. Pullig, 'Conflicts in the Work-Family Interface: Links to Job Stress, Customer Service Employee Performance, and Customer Purchase Intent', *Journal of Marketing* 69 (April 2005): 130–145.

90 R. Konrad, 'For Some Techies, an Interminable Workday,' *Associated Press*, 10 May 2005.

91 R. Drago, D. Black and M. Wooden, *The Persistence of Long Work Hours*, Melbourne Institute Working Paper Series (Melbourne: Melbourne Institute of Applied Economic and Social Research, University of Melbourne, August 2005).

92 C. B. Meek, 'The Dark Side of Japanese Management in the 1990s: Karoshi and Ijime in the Japanese Workplace', *Journal of Managerial Psychology* 19, no. 3 (2004): 312–331; 'Nagoya Court Rules Toyota Employee Died from Overwork', *Japan Times*, 1 December 2007; Y. Kageyama, 'Questions Rise About Temps, Overwork at Toyota', *Associated Press Newswires*, 10 September 2008; Y. Kawanishi, 'On Karo-Jisatsu (Suicide by Overwork)', *International Journal of Mental Health* 37, no. 1 (Spring 2008): 61–74; P. Novotny, 'Overwork a Silent Killer in Japan', *Agence France Presse*, 11 January 2009.

93 A. Bakker, E. Demerouti and W. Verbeke, 'Using the Job Demands-Resources Model to Predict Burnout and Performance', *Human Resources Management* 43, no. 1 (2004): 83–104; W. B. Schaufeli, 'Job Demands, Job Resources, and Their Relationship with Burnout and Engagement: A Multisample Study', *Journal of Organizational Behavior* 25 (2004): 293–315; A. Bakker and E. Demerouti, 'The Job Demands-Resources Model: State of the Art', *Journal of Managerial Psychology* 22, no. 3 (2007): 309.

94 R. Karasek and T. Theorell, *Healthy Work: Stress, Productivity, and the Reconstruction of Working Life* (New York: Basic Books, 1990); N. Turner, N. Chmiel and M. Walls, 'Railing for Safety: Job Demands, Job Control, and Safety Citizenship Role Definition', *Journal of Occupational Health Psychology* 10, no. 4 (2005): 504–512.

95 S. J. Havlovic and J. P. Keenan, 'Coping with Work Stress: The Influence of Individual Differences', *Journal of Social Behavior and Personality* 6 (1991): 199–212.

96 S. S. Luthar, D. Cicchetti and B. Becker, 'The Construct of Resilience: A Critical Evaluation and Guidelines for Future Work', *Child Development* 71, no. 3 (May–June 2000): 543–562; F. Luthans, 'The Need for and Meaning of Positive Organizational Behavior', *Journal of Organizational Behavior* 23 (2002): 695–706; G. A. Bonanno, 'Loss, Trauma, and Human Resilience: Have We Underestimated the Human Capacity to Thrive after Extremely Aversive Events?', *American Psychologist* 59, no. 1 (2004): 20–28.

97 M. Beasley, T. Thompson and J. Davidson, 'Resilience in Response to Life Stress: The Effects of Coping Style and Cognitive Hardiness', *Personality and Individual Differences* 34, no. 1 (2003): 77–95; M. M. Tugade, B. L. Fredrickson and L. Feldman Barrett, 'Psychological Resilience and Positive Emotional Granularity: Examining the Benefits of Positive Emotions on Coping and Health', *Journal of Personality* 72, no. 6 (2004): 1161–1190; I. Tsaousis and I. Nikolaou, 'Exploring the Relationship of Emotional Intelligence with Physical and Psychological Health Functioning', *Stress and Health* 21, no. 2 (2005): 77–86; L. Campbell-Sills, S. L. Cohan and M. B. Stein, 'Relationship of Resilience to Personality, Coping, and Psychiatric Symptoms in Young Adults', *Behaviour Research and Therapy* 44, no. 4 (April 2006): 585–599.

98 J. T. Spence and A. S. Robbins, 'Workaholism: Definition, Measurement and Preliminary Results', *Journal of Personality Assessment* 58 (1992): 160–178; R. J. Burke, 'Workaholism in Organizations: Psychological and Physical Well-Being Consequences', *Stress Medicine* 16, no. 1 (2000): 11–16; I. Harpaz and R. Snir, 'Workaholism: Its Definition and Nature', *Human Relations* 56 (2003): 291–319; R. J. Burke, A. M. Richardson and M. Martinussen, 'Workaholism among Norwegian Senior Managers: New Research Directions', *International Journal of Management* 21, no. 4 (December 2004): 415–426.

99 R. J. Burke and G. MacDermid, 'Are Workaholics Job Satisfied and Successful in Their Careers?', *Career Development International* 4 (1999): 277–282; R. J. Burke and S. Matthiesen, 'Short Communication: Workaholism among Norwegian Journalists: Antecedents and Consequences', *Stress and Health* 20, no. 5 (2004): 301–308.

100 S.-A. Chia and E. Toh, 'Give Employees a Break', *Straits Times (Singapore)*, 23 July 2005.

101 M. Siegall and L. L. Cummings, 'Stress and Organizational Role Conflict', *Genetic, Social, and General Psychology Monographs* 12 (1995): 65–95.

102 'Workaholics Anonymous', *Human Capital Magazine*, 26 November 2008; 'What Is HR's Greatest Downfall?', *Human Resources Leader*, 25 November 2008.

103 'How Flexible Work Arrangement were Implemented at McGraw-Hill,' *Managing Benefits Plans*, July 2006, pp. 1–2; 'How Research and Education Led to Flex Work Success,' *HR Focus*, Vol. 84 (2) (2007), pp. 6–8; 'Working Mother: Top 10,' *Working Mother*, Vol. 31 (7) (2008), pp. 58–60. Information about Matthew Coxhill is from personal correspondence.

104 N. Davidson, 'Vancouver Developer Looks to Make Video Games without Burning out Staff', *Canadian Press*, 21 February 2006. Some quotations are from Propaganda's website: propagandagames.go.com.

105 S. R. Madsen, 'The Effects of Home-Based Teleworking on Work-Family Conflict', *Human Resource Development Quarterly* 14, no. 1 (2003): 35–58.

106 K. Hansen, 'Mum's the Word', *Intheblack*, June 2005, 32–36; Organisation for Economic Cooperation and Development, *Babies and Bosses: Reconciling Work and Family Life*, vol. 4 (Canada, Finland, Sweden and the United Kingdom) (Paris: OECD Publishing, 2005); B. Pettit and J. Hook, 'The Structure of Women's Employment in Comparative Perspective', *Social Forces* 84, no. 2 (December 2005): 779–801; J. Heymann *et al.*, *The Work, Family, and Equity Index: How Does the United States Measure Up?*, Project on Global Working Families (Montreal: Institute for Health and Social Policy, June 2007).

107 M. Secret, 'Parenting in the Workplace: Child Care Options for Consideration', *Journal of Applied Behavioral Science* 41, no. 3 (September 2005): 326–347.

108 V. Bland, 'Sabbaticals Ideal Refresher', *New Zealand Herald*, 31 August 2005; A. E. Carr and T. L.-P. Tang, 'Sabbaticals and Empoyee Motivation: Benefits, Concerns, and Implications', *Journal of Education for Business* 80, no. 3 (January–February 2005): 160–164; R. Schwarz, 'Keeping the Workers Happy', *Dominion Post (Auckland)*, 4 April 2005, 10; S. Overman, 'Sabbaticals Benefit Companies as Well as Employees', *Employee Benefit News*, 15 April 2006.

109 S. Moreland, 'Strike up Creativity', *Crain's Cleveland Business*, 14 April 2003, 3; J. Saranow, 'Anybody Want to Take a Nap?', *Wall Street Journal*, 24 January 2005, R5.

110 M. Waung, 'The Effects of Self-Regulatory Coping Orientation on Newcomer Adjustment and Job Survival', *Personnel Psychology* 48 (1995): 633–650; M. H. Abel, 'Humor, Stress, and Coping Strategies', *Humor: International Journal of Humor Research* 15, no. 4 (2002): 365–381; N. A. Kuiper *et al.*, 'Humor Is Not Always the Best Medicine: Specific Components of Sense of Humor

and Psychological Well-Being', *Humor: International Journal of Humor Research* 17, no. 1/2 (2004): 135–168; E. J. Romero and K. W. Cruthirds, 'The Use of Humor in the Workplace', *Academy of Management Perspectives* 20, no. 2 (2006): 58–69; M. McCreaddie and S. Wiggins, 'The Purpose and Function of Humor in Health, Health Care and Nursing: A Narrative Review', *Journal of Advanced Nursing* 61, no. 6 (2008): 584–595.

111 W. M. Ensel and N. Lin, 'Physical Fitness and the Stress Process', *Journal of Community Psychology* 32, no. 1 (January 2004): 81–101.

112 S. Armour, 'Rising Job Stress Could Affect Bottom Line', *USA Today*, 29 July 2003; V. A. Barnes, F. A. Treiber and M. H. Johnson, 'Impact of Transcendental Meditation on Ambulatory Blood Pressure in African-American Adolescents', *American Journal of Hypertension* 17, no. 4 (2004): 366–369; P. Manikonda *et al.*, 'Influence of Non-Pharmacological Treatment (Contemplative Meditation and Breathing Technique) on Stress Induced Hypertension—A Randomized Controlled Study', *American Journal of Hypertension* 18, no. 5, Supplement 1 (2005): A89–A90.

113 S. E. Taylor *et al.*, 'Biobehavioral Responses to Stress in Females: Tend-and-Befriend, Not Fight-or-Flight', *Psychological Review* 107, no. 3 (July 2000): 411–429; R. Eisler and D. S. Levine, 'Nurture, Nature, and Caring: We Are Not Prisoners of Our Genes', *Brain and Mind* 3 (2002): 9–52.

CHAPTER 5

foundations of employee motivation

LEARNING OBJECTIVES

After reading this chapter, you should be able to:

- diagram and discuss the relationship between human drives, needs and behaviour
- summarise Maslow's needs hierarchy and discuss Maslow's contribution to the field of motivation
- summarise McClelland's learned needs theory, including the three needs he studied
- describe four-drive theory and discuss its implications for motivating employees
- diagram the expectancy theory model and discuss its practical implications for motivating employees
- describe the characteristics of effective goal setting and feedback
- summarise equity theory and describe how to improve procedural justice
- identify the factors that influence procedural justice, as well as the consequences of procedural justice.

Courtesy Standard Chartered

Through goal setting, strengths-based feedback, community involvement and fun activities in the workplace, Standard Chartered Bank has significantly improved employee engagement and motivation throughout its operations, most of which are in Asia and India.

Standard Chartered Bank's operations in Hong Kong recently won the Gallup Great Workplace Award for two consecutive years and was named Employer of Choice at the Hong Kong HR Awards. The company's businesses in India (Scope International-India) and Korea (First Bank Korea Ltd) were also recognised as two of the top-rated employers in those countries. These major achievements are outcomes of a journey that began eight years ago to improve employee engagement and motivation. Employee engagement scores among Standard Chartered employees worldwide (75 per cent of whom work in Asia and India) have more than doubled over this time. Almost half of the bank's employees are now highly engaged, whereas at most large organisations only 25–30 per cent are highly engaged.

How has Standard Chartered boosted employee engagement and motivation? First, managers receive training to establish clear key performance indicators (KPIs) for teams and individuals, coach employees frequently and provide constructive feedback regarding those goals. Employees also receive several days of training and development each year. As a result, almost all the bank's employees say they understand their role and have confidence in performing those objectives. Second, the bank rewards performance, particularly through career development opportunities, and offers a share ownership program so that employees can benefit from the company's financial performance. Third, Standard Chartered supports fun activities in the workplace and encourages employees to be involved in community events.

Finally, Standard Chartered focuses on its employees' strengths, rather than what's wrong with them. 'We deliberately build on strengths to help people understand their talents, how to develop these into strengths and how to work around what they are not so good at,' explains Laura Wilson, Standard Chartered's project lead and manager of performance and engagement. Dustin Woods describes how the strengths-based approach motivates employees. 'It's all in the dialogue,' says Woods, who is Standard Chartered's organisational learning manager in Pakistan. 'Through sharing stories of "Me at My Best", individuals build a common understanding of what they want from the workplace.'

'Using this focus [employee engagement], we have seen spectacular results,' says Tim Miller, Standard Chartered's director of people, property and assurance and non-executive chairman of the company's operations in Korea [SC First Bank]. 'Our most engaged bank branches [have] significantly higher deposit growth, better cost income ratios and lower employee attrition than less engaged branches.'[1]

Goal setting, strengths-based feedback, rewards and various social bonding events are designed to maintain and improve employee motivation at Standard Chartered Bank in Hong Kong and other countries. This motivation has catapulted the company's performance over the past decade and raised its employer brand, making it easier to attract top-quality talent. Recall from Chapter 2 that **motivation** refers to the forces within a person that affect the direction, intensity and persistence of voluntary behaviour.[2] Motivated employees are willing to exert a particular level of effort (intensity), for a certain amount of time (persistence), toward a particular goal (direction). Motivation is one of the four essential drivers of individual behaviour and performance.

motivation The forces within a person that affect his or her direction, intensity and persistence of voluntary behaviour.

This chapter introduces the core theories of employee motivation. We begin by introducing employee engagement, an increasingly popular concept associated with motivation. Next, we distinguish drives and needs and explain how needs are shaped through the individual's self-concept and other personal factors. Three theories that focus on drives and needs—Maslow's needs hierarchy, McClelland's learned needs theory and four-drive theory—are introduced and evaluated. Next, we turn our attention to the popular rational decision model of employee motivation: expectancy theory. This is followed by a discussion of the key elements of goal setting and feedback. In the final section, we look at organisational justice, including the dimensions and dynamics of equity theory and procedural justice.

EMPLOYEE ENGAGEMENT

When executives at Standard Chartered discuss employee motivation, they are just as likely to use the phrase *employee engagement*. This concept, which is closely connected to employee motivation, has become so popular in everyday language that we introduce it here. Employee engagement's popularity far exceeds its conceptual development; its definition varies across studies, and it is unclear how it differs from job satisfaction, organisational commitment and other known organisational behaviour variables.[3] Even so, there is enough similarity across studies that we can cautiously define **employee engagement** as the employee's emotional and cognitive motivation, self-efficacy to perform the job, perceived clarity of the organisation's vision and his or her specific role in that vision, and belief that he or she has the resources to get the job done.[4] This definition relates to the four cornerstones of individual behaviour and performance identified in the MARS model (see Chapter 2): motivation, ability, role perceptions and situational factors. Employee engagement encompasses the employee's beliefs about and emotional responses to these conditions, as well as the employee's perceived alignment with the organisation's values. Additionally, employee engagement includes a high level of absorption in the work—the experience of 'getting carried away' while working.

employee engagement The employee's emotional and cognitive motivation, self-efficacy to perform the job, perceived clarity of the organisation's vision and his or her specific role in that vision, and belief that he or she has the resources to get the job done.

Employee engagement is a hot topic among executives and consultants. One report estimates that one in every four large organisations has a formal employee engagement program and three out of five intend to develop plans to improve employee engagement.[5] Some companies even have employee engagement departments or managers. The popularity of employee engagement is partly due to preliminary evidence that it improves organisational effectiveness. Standard Chartered Bank estimates that branches with highly engaged employees produce 20 per cent higher returns than branches with lower engagement scores. British retailer Marks & Spencer claims that a 1 per cent improvement in the engagement levels of its workforce produces a 2.9 percent increase in sales per square foot. American electronics retailer Best Buy reports that a 0.1 increase (on a 5.0 point scale) in a store's engagement score is associated with a

Getting Engaged at JCPenney

In the hyper-competitive retail industry, the number-one ingredient for winning the hearts and wallets of customers is the quality, style and price of the merchandise. What's the second most important ingredient? It's employee engagement, according to executives at JCPenney. 'We feel strongly there's a correlation between engaged associates and store profitability,' says Myron 'Mike' Ullman, CEO of the Plano, Texas, retailer. In fact, the company's internal research revealed that stores with the top-quartile engagement scores generate about 10 per cent more in sales per square foot and 36 per cent greater operating income than similar-sized stores in the lowest quartile. A few years ago, about two-thirds of JCPenney associates were 'engaged'. Thanks to improved training, career development and other management practices, more than three-quarters of employees are now engaged. Per-share earnings have more than doubled since JCPenney management focused on improving employee engagement. 'We see a 200 basis-point (increase in) profit when we engage the associates,' Ullman claims. 'This isn't just warm, fuzzy stuff. It's solid business logic.'[7]

Matt York/AP Images

$100 000 increase in that store's profitability for the year. Other research indicates that employee engagement is associated with higher organisational citizenship and lower turnover intentions. Unfortunately, it isn't clear whether employee engagement makes companies more successful, or whether company success makes employees more engaged. However, the interventions at Standard Chartered, Best Buy and some other companies suggest that employee engagement scores cause the company outcomes more than vice versa.[6]

The challenge facing organisational leaders is that most employees aren't very engaged. The numbers vary from one study to the next due to inconsistent measures and definitions, but generally only about 15–20 per cent of employees in Australia and New Zealand are highly engaged, about 60 per cent are somewhat engaged, and approximately 20 per cent have low engagement or are actively disengaged. Actively disengaged employees tend to be disruptive at work, not just disconnected from work. Employees in several Asian countries (notably Japan, China and South Korea) and a few European countries (notably Italy, Netherlands and France) have the lowest levels of employee engagement, whereas the highest scores are usually found in the United States, Brazil and India. Furthermore, one study recently reported that younger employees are significantly less engaged than are baby boomers.[8]

Why is it so difficult to engage and motivate employees? Some writers suggest that globalisation, information technology, corporate restructuring and other changes have potentially undermined the levels of trust and commitment necessary to motivate employees beyond minimum standards.[9] Others point out that companies have not adjusted to the changing needs and expectations of new workforce entrants, which would explain why younger employees seem less engaged and motivated.[10] Overall, these reports of low employee engagement imply that many employees are not very motivated to perform their jobs. To create a more motivated workforce, we first need to understand employee drives and needs, and how these concepts relate to individual goals and behaviour.

LEARNING OBJECTIVE

Diagram and discuss the relationship between human drives, needs and behaviour.

drives Hardwired characteristics of the brain that correct deficiencies or maintain an internal equilibrium by producing emotions to energise individuals.

needs Goal-directed forces that people experience.

EMPLOYEE DRIVES AND NEEDS

To figure out how to create a more engaged and motivated workforce, we first need to understand the motivational 'forces' within people. Unfortunately, writing about the prime movers of employee behaviour has produced a stream of confusing phrases such as *innate drives, learned needs, motivations, instincts, secondary drives* and *primary needs*.[11] We define **drives** (also called *primary needs* or *innate motives*) as hardwired characteristics of the brain that correct deficiencies or maintain an internal equilibrium by producing emotions that energise individuals to act on their environment.[12] Drives are the 'prime movers' of behaviour because they generate emotions, and these emotions put people in a state of readiness to change their situation (see Chapter 4). Although typically overlooked in organisational behaviour, emotions play a central role in motivation.[13] In fact, both words (*emotion* and *motivation*) are derivations of the same Latin word, *movere*, which means 'to move'. Although there is no clear list of human drives, several are consistently identified in research, such as the drives for social interaction, understanding of the environment, competence or status, and defending oneself against physiological and psychological harm.[14]

As Exhibit 5.1 illustrates, drives (and, in particular, the emotions produced by these drives) create human needs. We define **needs** as goal-directed forces that people experience. They are the motivational forces of emotions channelled toward particular goals to correct deficiencies or imbalances. Consider the following example: suppose that you arrive at work to discover a stranger sitting at your desk. Seeing this situation produces emotions that motivate you to act. You channel these emotions toward specific goals, such as finding out who that person is, and possibly engaging in behaviours to protect your job (in case the stranger's presence threatens your job security). Notice from this example that the emotional reaction you experience to seeing the stranger sitting at your desk represents the force that moves you, whereas the direction of your actions is guided by the needs produced by those emotions. This example illustrates how drives produce immediate needs; however, the frequent generation of nonconscious emotions produces longer-term needs, such as the need for more challenging work.

Individual Differences in Needs

Everyone has the same drives; they are hardwired in us through evolution. However, people have different emotional responses (such as loneliness, curiosity or anger) and resulting needs in the same situation. Exhibit 5.1 explains why this difference occurs. The left side of the model

Exhibit 5.1 *Drives, Needs and Behaviour*

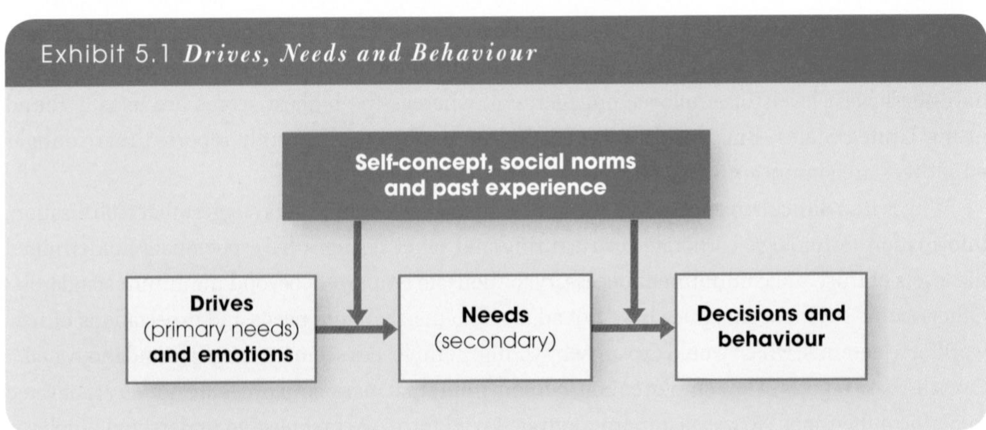

shows that the individual's self-concept (including personality and values), social norms and past experience amplify or suppress drive-based emotions, thereby resulting in stronger or weaker needs.[15] People who define themselves as very sociable typically experience a strong need for social interaction if alone for a while, whereas people who view themselves as less sociable would experience a less intense need to socialise over that time. These individual differences also explain, as will be discussed later in this chapter, why needs can be 'learned' to some extent. Socialisation and reinforcement may cause people to alter their self-concept somewhat, resulting in a stronger or weaker need for social interaction, achievement and so on.

Self-concept, social norms and past experience do more than adjust the emotions generated by our built-in drives. The right side of Exhibit 5.1 shows that these individual characteristics also regulate a person's motivated decisions and behaviour. Consider the earlier example of the stranger sitting at your desk. Even if you feel some anger that someone has taken your work space, you probably wouldn't walk up to the person and demand that they leave immediately; this action is contrary to social norms of behaviour in most (but not all) cultures. Some people might approach the stranger and politely (but maybe with firmness in their voice) ask what they are doing in that office; other people wouldn't even approach the stranger until they had asked coworkers about this unusual situation. These decisions and actions vary from one individual to the next because people regulate their goals and behaviour on the basis of social and cultural norms, their self-concept and reinforcement (or observation of others) in previous situations. Employees who view themselves as being forthright would be more likely to approach the stranger directly, whereas those who have a different self-concept or have misinterpreted similar situations in the past might gather information from coworkers first.

We have presented this detail about needs and drives for a few reasons.[16] First, as mentioned, motivation theories use the terms *needs, drives* and *motivations* so loosely that they make it difficult to compare theories, so it is important to settle this confusion at the outset. Second, the field of organisational behaviour has been woefully slow to acknowledge the central role of emotions in employee motivation, as will be apparent when we review most motivation theories in this chapter. Third, Exhibit 5.1 provides a useful template for understanding various motivation theories. In fact, you will see pieces of this template when we discuss four-drive theory, expectancy theory, goal setting and other concepts in this chapter. The remainder of this section describes theories that try to explain the dynamics of drives and needs. Later in this chapter, we will discuss theories that explain how experiences—such as expectancies, feedback and work experiences—influence the motivation process.

Maslow's Needs Hierarchy Theory

LEARNING OBJECTIVE 

Summarise Maslow's needs hierarchy and discuss Maslow's contribution to the field of motivation.

By far, the most widely known theory of human motivation is **Maslow's needs hierarchy theory** (see Exhibit 5.2). Developed by psychologist Abraham Maslow in the 1940s, the model condenses and integrates the long list of needs that had been studied previously into a hierarchy of five basic categories (from lowest to highest):[17]

Maslow's needs hierarchy theory A motivation theory of needs arranged in a hierarchy, whereby people are motivated to fulfil a higher need as a lower one becomes gratified.

PHYSIOLOGICAL the need for food, air, water, shelter and the like

SAFETY the need for a secure and stable environment and the absence of pain, threat or illness

BELONGINGNESS/LOVE the need for love, affection and interaction with other people

Exhibit 5.2 *Maslow's Needs Hierarchy*

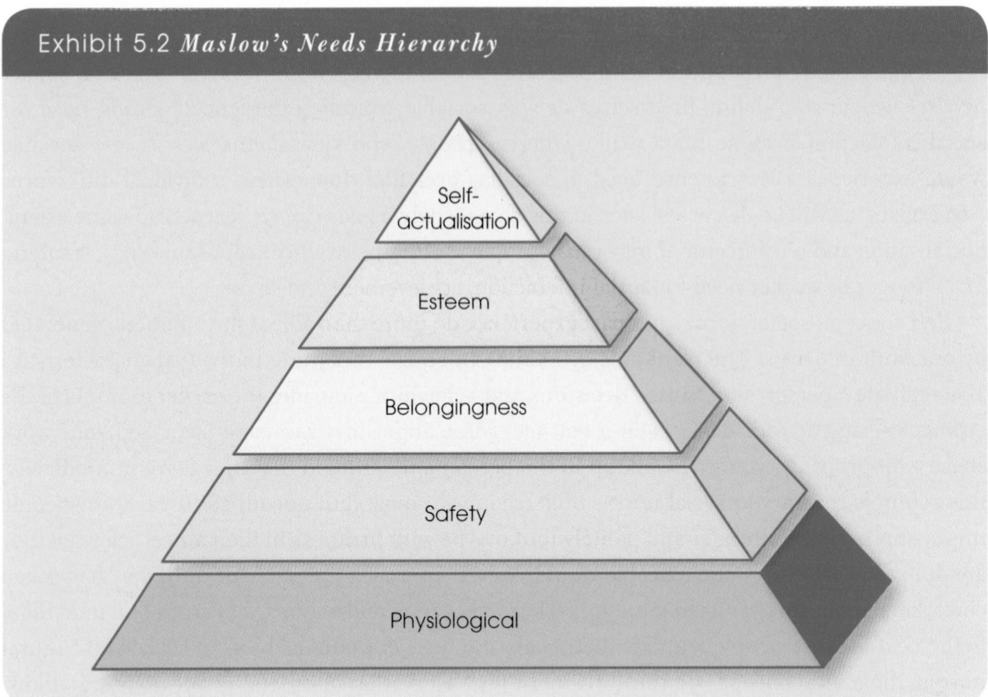

Source: Based on information in A. H. Maslow, 'A Theory of Human Motivation', *Psychological Review* 50 (1943): 370–396.

ESTEEM the need for self-esteem through personal achievement, as well as social esteem through recognition and respect from others

SELF-ACTUALISATION the need for self-fulfilment, realisation of one's potential.

Along with developing these five categories, Maslow identified the desire to know and the desire for aesthetic beauty as two innate drives that do not fit within the hierarchy.

Maslow's list represents drives (primary needs) because they are described as innate and universal. According to Maslow, we are motivated simultaneously by several needs but the strongest source is the lowest unsatisfied need at the time. As the person satisfies a lower level need, the next higher need in the hierarchy becomes the primary motivator and remains so even if never satisfied. Physiological needs are initially the most important, and people are motivated to satisfy them first. As they become gratified, the desire for safety emerges as the strongest motivator. As safety needs are satisfied, belongingness needs become most important, and so forth. The exception to this need fulfilment process is self-actualisation; as people experience self-actualisation, they desire more rather than less of this need. Thus, while the bottom four groups are *deficiency needs* because they become activated when unfulfilled, self-actualisation is known as a *growth need* because it continues to develop even when fulfilled.

Limitations and Contributions of Maslow's Work

In spite of its popularity, Maslow's needs hierarchy theory has been dismissed by most motivation experts.[18] Maslow developed the theory from only his professional observations, and he was later surprised that it was so widely accepted before anyone tested it. Empirical studies have concluded that people do not progress through the hierarchy as the theory predicts. For example, some people strive more for self-esteem before their belongingness needs have been satisfied. The theory also assumes that needs priorities shift over a long time, whereas needs priorities rise and fall far more frequently with the situation. A person's needs for status, food, social interaction and so forth change daily or weekly, not every few years. As Reality Check 5.1 describes, companies around the world routinely motivate all staff through recognition. These examples illustrate that people regularly need—and are motivated to receive—respect and belongingness in the workplace.

Although needs hierarchy theory has failed the reality test, Maslow deserves credit for bringing a more holistic, humanistic and positive approach to the study of human motivation.[20] First, Maslow brought a more holistic perspective by explaining that needs and drives should be studied together because human behaviour is typically initiated by more than one of them at the same time. Previously, motivation experts had splintered needs or drives into dozens of categories, each studied in isolation.[21]

Second, Maslow brought a more humanistic perspective to the study of motivation. In particular, he suggested that higher order needs are influenced by personal and social influences, not just instincts. In other words, he was among the first to recognise that human thoughts (including self-concept, social norms and past experience) play a role in motivation. Previous motivation experts had focused almost entirely on human instincts without considering that motivation could be shaped by human thought.

Third, Maslow brought a more positive perspective of employee motivation by focusing on need gratification rather than only need deprivation. In particular, he popularised the previously developed concept of *self-actualisation*, suggesting that people are naturally motivated to reach their potential, and that organisations and societies need to be structured to help people continue and develop this motivation.[22] Due to his writing on self-actualisation and the power of need gratification, Maslow was a pioneer in *positive organisational behaviour*. As discussed in Chapter 3, positive OB says that focusing on the positive rather than negative aspects of life will improve organisational success and individual wellbeing. In other words, this approach advocates building positive qualities and traits within individuals or institutions as opposed to focusing on trying to fix what might be wrong with them.[23]

What's Wrong with Needs Hierarchy Models?

Maslow's theory is not the only attempt to map employee needs onto a single hierarchy. Another hierarchy model, called **ERG theory**, reorganises Maslow's five groups into three—existence, relatedness and growth.[24] Unlike Maslow's theory, which only explained how people progress up the hierarchy, ERG theory also describes how people regress down the hierarchy when they fail to fulfil higher needs. ERG theory seems to explain human motivation somewhat better than Maslow's needs hierarchy, but that is mainly because it is easier to cluster human needs around ERG's three categories than Maslow's five categories. Otherwise, research studies have found that ERG theory only marginally improves our understanding of human needs.[25]

ERG theory A needs hierarchy theory consisting of three fundamental needs—existence, relatedness and growth.

Why have Maslow's needs hierarchy theory, ERG theory and other needs hierarchies largely failed to explain the dynamics of employee needs? The most glaring explanation is that people don't fit into a single needs hierarchy. Some people place social status at the top of their personal hierarchy; others consider personal development and growth an ongoing priority over social relations or status. There is increasing evidence that needs hierarchies are unique to each

Shining the Spotlight on Employee Recognition

Courtesy of Sarova Panafric Hotel

David Gachuru (left in this photo) motivates staff at Sarova Panafric Hotel in Nairobi, Kenya, through plenty of praise and recognition.

David Gachuru lives by a motto that motivates employees with much more than money: 'If an employee's work calls for a thumbs-up, I will appreciate him or her as many times as possible.' Translating this advice into practice is a daily event for the general manager of Sarova Panafric Hotel in Nairobi, Kenya. Along with thanking staff personally and through emails, Gachuru holds twice-monthly meetings at which top-performing employees are congratulated and receive paid holidays with their families. Employee achievements are also celebrated in the hotel's newsletter, which is distributed to guests as well as to employees.

Sarova Panafric Hotel and other firms are returning to good old-fashioned praise and recognition to regularly motivate staff. Good thing, because recent surveys in several countries identify lack of praise, recognition or appreciation as a major reason why employees are demotivated and disengaged, and decide to find work elsewhere. For instance, only 39 per cent of Australian public service employees say they feel valued for their contribution. Similarly,

person and are not universal, because needs are strongly influenced by each individual's self-concept, including personal values and social identity. If your most important values lean toward stimulation and self-direction, you probably pay more attention to self-actualisation needs. If power and achievement are at the top of your value system, status needs will likely be at the top of your needs hierarchy. This connection between values and needs suggests that each person has a unique needs hierarchy and can possibly change over time, just as values change over a lifetime.[26]

LEARNING OBJECTIVE

Summarise McClelland's learned needs theory, including the three needs he studied.

Learned Needs Theory

Earlier in this chapter we said that drives (primary needs) are innate whereas needs are shaped, amplified or suppressed through self-concept, social norms and past experience. Maslow noted that individual characteristics influence the strength of higher order needs, such as the need to belong. Psychologist David McClelland further investigated the idea that the strength of needs can be altered through social influences. In particular, he recognised that a person's needs can be strengthened through reinforcement, learning and social conditions. McClelland examined three 'learned' needs: achievement, affiliation and power.[27]

Need for Achievement

need for achievement (nAch) A need in which people want to accomplish reasonably challenging goals, and desire unambiguous feedback and recognition for their success.

People with a strong **need for achievement (nAch)** want to accomplish reasonably challenging goals through their own effort. They prefer working alone rather than in teams, and they choose tasks with a moderate degree of risk (i.e. neither too easy nor impossible to complete). High-nAch people also desire unambiguous feedback and recognition for their success. Money is a weak motivator, except when it provides feedback and recognition.[28] In contrast, employees with a low nAch perform their work better when money is used as an incentive. Successful entrepreneurs

REALITY CHECK 5.1

when Ireland's Small Firms Association (SMA) recently examined information from 1000 exit interviews, they found that lack of recognition was a top reason why employees in that country quit their jobs. 'Increasingly people need to feel that their contribution is valued,' suggests SMA director Patricia Callan. 'If people do not feel important, they are not motivated to stay.'

The challenge of recognition is to 'catch' employees doing extraordinary work or showing organisational citizenship. Yum Brands Inc. found one solution from its Australian KFC operations. The KFC managers created a peer recognition system in which coworkers give each other 'Champs' cards when they are observed doing something beyond the call of duty that is consistent with the company's values. Champs is an acronym for KFC's values (cleanliness, hospitality and so on). In addition to recognition, the cards have reward value because they are entered into draws for prizes. Yum Brands has since rolled out this peer recognition activity worldwide and to its other restaurant groups (including Taco Bell and Pizza Hut).

The Ritz Carlton Hotel in Kuala Lumpur applies a similar peer recognition process using First Class Cards. An executive at Ritz Carlton Kuala Lumpur explains that 'congratulatory messages or words of appreciation are written down by any member of the team to another and even as far as from the hotel and corporate senior leaders. This serves as a motivational aspect of the work environment.'[19]

tend to have a high nAch, possibly because they establish challenging goals for themselves and thrive on competition.[29]

Need for Affiliation

Need for affiliation (nAff) refers to a desire to seek approval from others, conform to their wishes and expectations, and avoid conflict and confrontation. People with a strong nAff try to project a favourable image of themselves. They tend to actively support others and try to smooth out workplace conflicts. High-nAff employees generally work well in coordinating roles to mediate conflicts and in sales positions where the main task is cultivating long-term relations. However, they tend to be less effective at allocating scarce resources and making other decisions that potentially generate conflict. People in decision-making positions must have a relatively low need for affiliation so that their choices and actions are not biased by a personal need for approval.[30]

need for affiliation (nAff) A need in which people seek approval from others, conform to their wishes and expectations, and avoid conflict and confrontation.

Need for Power

People with a high **need for power (nPow)** want to exercise control over others and are concerned about maintaining their leadership positions. They frequently rely on persuasive communication, make more suggestions in meetings and tend to publicly evaluate situations more frequently. McClelland pointed out that there are two types of nPow. Individuals who enjoy their power for its own sake, use it to advance personal interests and wear their power as a status symbol have *personalised power*. Others mainly have a high need for *socialised power* because they desire power as a means to help others.[31] McClelland argues that effective leaders should have a high need for socialised rather than personalised power. They must have a high degree of altruism and social responsibility, and be concerned about the consequences of their own actions on others.

need for power (nPow) A need in which people want to control their environment, including people and material resources, to benefit either themselves (personalised power) or others (socialised power).

Learning Needs

McClelland's research supported his theory that needs can be learned (more accurately, strengthened or weakened), so he developed training programs for this purpose. In his achievement-motivation program, trainees write achievement-oriented stories and practise achievement-oriented behaviours in business games. They also complete a detailed achievement plan for the next two years and form a reference group with other trainees to maintain their new-found achievement motivation style.[32] These programs seem to work. Participants attending a need-for-achievement course in India subsequently started more new businesses, had greater community involvement, invested more in expanding their businesses and employed twice as many people as non-participants did. Research on similar achievement motivation courses for US small-business owners reported dramatic increases in the profitability of the participants' businesses. In essence, these programs attempt to alter the individual's self-concept or experiences such that they amplify or suppress emotions generated by innate drives.

LEARNING OBJECTIVE

Describe four-drive theory and discuss its implications for motivating employees.

Four-Drive Theory

One of the central messages of this chapter is that emotions play a significant role in employee motivation. This view is supported by a groundswell of research in neuroscience, but it is almost completely absent from contemporary motivation theories in organisational behaviour. Also, social scientists in several fields (psychology, anthropology and so on) increasingly agree that human beings have several hardwired drives, including social interaction, learning and dominance. One of the few theories to apply this emerging knowledge is **four-drive theory**.[33] Developed by Harvard Business School professors Paul Lawrence and Nitin Nohria, four-drive theory states that everyone has the drive to acquire, bond, learn and defend.

four-drive theory A motivation theory that is based on the innate drives to acquire, bond, learn and defend, and that incorporates both emotions and rationality.

DRIVE TO ACQUIRE This is the drive to seek, take, control and retain objects and personal experiences. The drive to acquire extends beyond basic food and water; it includes enhancing one's self-concept through relative status and recognition in society.[34] Thus, it is the foundation of competition and the basis of our need for esteem. Four-drive theory states that the drive to acquire is insatiable because the purpose of human motivation is to achieve a higher position than others, not just to fulfil one's physiological needs.

DRIVE TO BOND This is the drive to form social relationships and develop mutual caring commitments with others. It explains why people form social identities by aligning their self-concept with various social groups (see Chapter 2). It may also explain why people who lack social contact are more prone to serious health problems.[35] The drive to bond motivates people to cooperate and, consequently, is a fundamental ingredient in the success of organisations and the development of societies.

DRIVE TO LEARN This is the drive to satisfy our curiosity, and to know and understand ourselves and the environment around us.[36] When observing something that is inconsistent with or beyond our current knowledge, we experience a tension that motivates us to close that information gap. In fact, studies have revealed that people who are removed from any novel information will crave even boring information; the drive to learn generated such strong emotions that the participants in one study eventually craved month-old stock reports![37] The drive to learn is related to the higher order needs of growth and self-actualisation described earlier.

DRIVE TO DEFEND This is the drive to protect ourselves physically and socially. Probably the first drive to develop, it creates a 'fight-or-flight' response in the face of personal danger. The drive to defend goes beyond protecting our physical self. It includes defending our relationships, our acquisitions and our belief systems.

These four drives are innate and universal, meaning that they are hardwired in our brains and are found in all human beings. They are also independent of each other. There is no hierarchy of drives, so one drive is neither dependent on nor inherently inferior or superior to another drive. Four-drive theory also states that these four drives are a complete set—there are no fundamental drives excluded from the model. Another key feature is that three of the four drives are proactive—we regularly try to fulfil them. Only the drive to defend is reactive—it is triggered by threat. Thus, any notion of fulfilling drives is temporary, at best.

How Drives Influence Employee Motivation

Four-drive theory draws from current neuroscience knowledge to explain how drives translate into goal-directed effort. To begin with, recall from previous chapters that the information we receive is quickly and nonconsciously tagged with emotional markers that subsequently shape our logical analysis of a situation.[38] According to four-drive theory, the four drives determine which emotions are tagged to incoming stimuli. If you arrive at work one day to see a stranger sitting in your office chair, you might quickly experience worry or curiosity—or both. These emotions are automatically created by one or more of the four drives. In this example, the emotions produced are likely strong enough to demand your attention and motivate you to act on this observation.

Most of the time, we aren't aware of our emotional experiences because they are subtle and fleeting. However, emotions do become conscious experiences when they are sufficiently strong or when we experience conflicting emotions. Under these circumstances, our mental skill set relies on social norms, past experience and personal values to direct the motivational force of our emotions to useful and acceptable goals that address the source of those emotions (see Exhibit 5.3).

Exhibit 5.3 *Four-Drive Theory of Motivation*

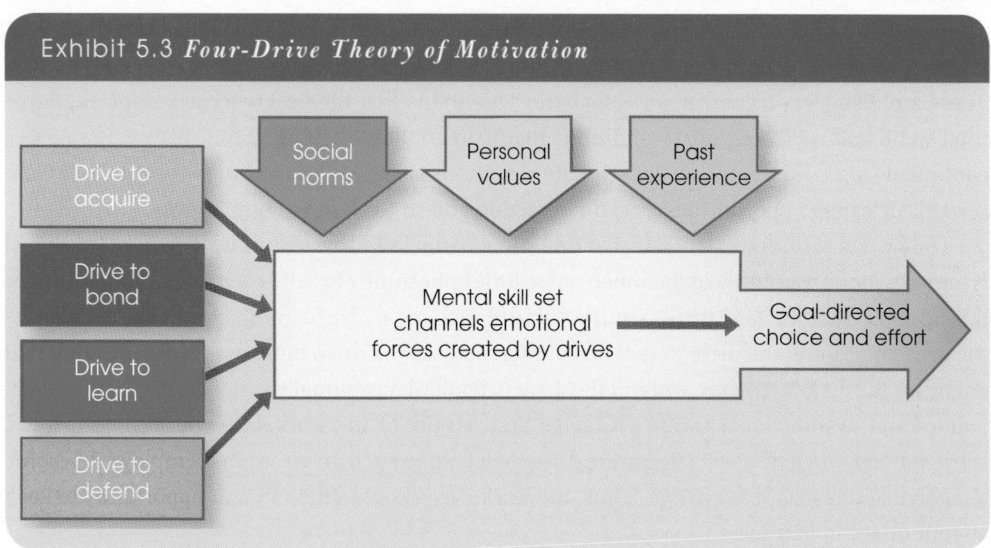

Source: Based on information in P. R. Lawrence and N. Nohria, *Driven: How Human Nature Shapes Our Choices* (San Francisco: Jossey-Bass, 2002).

In other words, the emotions generated by the four drives motivate us to act, and our mental skill set chooses courses of action that are acceptable to society and our own moral compass.[39] This is the process described at the beginning of this chapter: drives produce emotions; our self-concept, social norms and past experience translate these emotions into goal-directed needs; and these individual characteristics also translate needs into decisions and behaviour.

Evaluating Four-Drive Theory

Although four-drive theory was introduced very recently, it is based on a deep foundation of research that dates back more than three decades. The drives have been identified from psychological and anthropological studies. The translation of drives into goal-directed behaviour originates from considerable research on emotions and neural processes. The theory avoids the assumption that everyone has the same needs hierarchy, and it explains why needs vary from one person to the next. Notice, too, that four-drive theory is both holistic (it relates to all drives, not just one or two) and humanistic (it acknowledges the role of human thought and social influences, not just instinct). Maslow had identified these two principles as important features of an effective motivation theory. Four-drive theory also provides a much clearer understanding of the role of emotional intelligence in employee motivation and behaviour. Employees with high emotional intelligence are more sensitive to competing demands from the four drives, are better able to avoid impulsive behaviour from those drives, and can judge the best way to act to fulfil those drive demands in a social context.

Even with its well-researched foundations, however, four-drive theory is far from complete. First, most experts would argue that one or two other drives exist that should be included. Second, social norms, personal values and past experience probably don't represent the full set of individual characteristics that translate emotions into goal-directed effort. For example, other elements of self-concept beyond personal values, such as personality and social identity, likely play a significant role in translating drives into needs, and needs into decisions and behaviour.

Practical Implications of Four-Drive Theory

The main recommendation from four-drive theory is to ensure that individual jobs and workplaces provide a balanced opportunity to fulfil the drives to acquire, bond, learn and defend.[40] There are really two recommendations here. The first is that the best workplaces for employee motivation and wellbeing offer conditions that help employees fulfil all four drives. Employees continually seek fulfilment of their innate drives, so successful companies provide sufficient rewards, learning opportunities, social interaction and so forth for all employees.

The second recommendation is that fulfilment of the four drives must be kept in balance; that is, organisations should avoid too much or too little opportunity to fulfil each drive. The reason for this advice is that the four drives counterbalance each other. The drive to bond counterbalances the drive to acquire; the drive to defend counterbalances the drive to learn. An organisation that energises the drive to acquire without the drive to bond may eventually suffer from organisational politics and dysfunctional conflict. Change and novelty in the workplace will aid the drive to learn, but too much of it will trigger the drive to defend to such an extent that employees become territorial and resistant to change. Thus, the workplace should offer enough opportunity to keep all four drives in balance.

These recommendations help explain why Standard Chartered Bank, described at the beginning of this chapter, has a motivated workforce and is rated as one of the best places to work in Asia and India. The company encourages staff to be courageous and creative, yet balances those values with a nurturing environment that emphasises employee strengths rather than faults. The company probably also minimises the drive to defend because it strives to distribute rewards and resources equitably, and offers generous benefits to all staff.

EXPECTANCY THEORY OF MOTIVATION

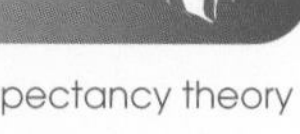

Diagram the expectancy theory model and discuss its practical implications for motivating employees.

expectancy theory A motivation theory based on the idea that work effort is directed toward behaviours that people believe will lead to desired outcomes.

The theories described so far mainly explain the internal origins of employee motivation. But how do these drives and needs translate into specific effort and behaviour? Four-drive theory recognises that social norms, personal values and past experience direct our effort, but it doesn't offer any more detail. **Expectancy theory**, on the other hand, offers an elegant model based on rational logic to predict the chosen direction, level and persistence of motivation. Essentially, the theory states that work effort is directed toward behaviours that people believe will lead to desired outcomes. In other words, we are motivated to achieve the goals with the highest expected pay-off. As illustrated in Exhibit 5.4, an individual's effort level depends on three factors: effort-to-performance (E-to-P) expectancy, performance-to-outcome (P-to-O) expectancy and outcome valences. Employee motivation is influenced by all three components of the expectancy theory model. If any component weakens, motivation weakens.[41]

E-TO-P EXPECTANCY This is the individual's perception that his or her effort will result in a particular level of performance. In some situations, employees may believe that they can unquestionably accomplish the task (a probability of 1.0). In other situations, they expect that even their highest level of effort will not result in the desired performance level (a probability of 0.0). In most cases, the E-to-P expectancy falls somewhere between these two extremes.

P-TO-O EXPECTANCY This is the perceived probability that a specific behaviour or performance level will lead to a particular outcome. In extreme cases, employees may believe that accomplishing a particular task (performance) will definitely result in a particular outcome (a probability of 1.0), or they may believe that successful performance will have no effect on this outcome (a probability of 0.0). More often, the P-to-O expectancy falls somewhere between these two extremes.

Exhibit 5.4 *Expectancy Theory of Motivation*

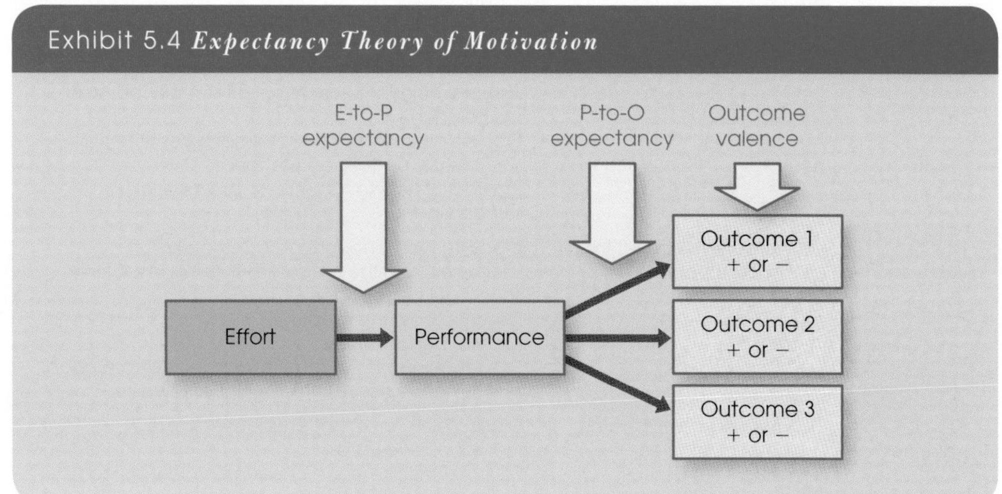

OUTCOME VALENCES A *valence* is the anticipated satisfaction or dissatisfaction that an individual feels toward an outcome. It ranges from negative to positive. (The actual range doesn't matter; it may be from −1 to +1 or from −100 to +100.) An outcome valence represents a person's anticipated satisfaction with the outcome.[42] Outcomes have a positive valence when they are consistent with our values and satisfy our needs; they have a negative valence when they oppose our values and inhibit need fulfilment.

Expectancy Theory in Practice

One of the appealing characteristics of expectancy theory is that it provides clear guidelines for increasing employee motivation.[43] Several practical applications of expectancy theory are listed in Exhibit 5.5 and described below.

Increasing E-to-P Expectancies

E-to-P expectancies are influenced by the individual's belief that he or she can successfully complete the task. Some companies increase this can-do attitude by assuring employees that they have the necessary competencies, clear role perceptions and necessary resources to reach the desired levels of performance. An important part of this process involves matching employees' competencies to job requirements and clearly communicating the tasks required for the job. Similarly, E-to-P expectancies are learned, so behavioural modelling and supportive feedback (positive reinforcement) typically strengthen the individual's belief that he or she is able to perform the task.

Increasing P-to-O Expectancies

The most obvious ways to improve P-to-O expectancies are to measure employee performance accurately and distribute more valued rewards to those with higher job performance. P-to-O

Exhibit 5.5 *Practical Applications of Expectancy Theory*

Expectancy theory component	Objective	Applications
E→P expectancies	To increase the belief that employees are capable of performing the job successfully	• Select people with the required skills and knowledge. • Provide required training and clarify job requirements. • Provide sufficient time and resources. • Assign simpler or fewer tasks until employees can master them. • Provide examples of similar employees who have successfully performed the task. • Provide coaching to employees who lack self-confidence.
P→O expectancies	To increase the belief that good performance will result in certain (valued) outcomes	• Measure job performance accurately. • Clearly explain the outcomes that will result from successful performance. • Describe how the employee's rewards were based on past performance. • Provide examples of other employees whose good performance has resulted in higher rewards.
Outcome valences	To increase the expected value of outcomes resulting from desired performance	• Distribute rewards that employees value. • Individualise rewards. • Minimise the presence of countervalent outcomes.

expectancies are perceptions, so employees need to know that higher performance will result in higher rewards, and they need to know how that connection occurs. Companies satisfy these needs by explaining how specific rewards are connected to specific past performance, and by using examples, anecdotes and public ceremonies to illustrate when behaviour has been rewarded.

Many companies claim they provide higher rewards to people with higher performance, yet employees typically believe the performance-to-outcome linkage is ambiguous or non-existent. Less than half of the 6000 employees surveyed in one study said they know how to increase their base pay or cash bonuses. Another poll reported that only 32 per cent of employees believe that people at their company are paid more for doing a better job. Less than half of employees in a large-scale Malaysian survey said they believe their company rewards high performance or deals appropriately with poor performers. Only one-quarter of 10 000 Canadian employees recently surveyed said they regularly receive rewards for a job well done. This is consistent with another survey which reported that only 27 per cent of Canadian employees say there is a clear link between their job performance and pay.[44]

Increasing Outcome Valences

Everyone has unique values and experiences which translate into different needs at different times. Consequently, individualising rather than standardising rewards and other performance outcomes is an important ingredient in employee motivation. At the same time, leaders need to watch for countervalent outcomes—consequences with negative valences that reduce rather than enhance employee motivation. For example, peer pressure may cause some employees to perform their jobs at the minimum standard even though formal rewards and the job itself would otherwise motivate them to perform at higher levels.

Overall, expectancy theory is a useful model that explains how people rationally figure out the best direction, intensity and persistence of their efforts. It has been tested in a variety of situations and predicts employee motivation in different cultures.[45] However, critics have a number of concerns with how the theory has been tested. Another concern is that expectancy theory ignores the central role of emotion in employee effort and behaviour. The valence element of expectancy theory captures some of this emotional process, but only peripherally.[46]

GOAL SETTING AND FEEDBACK

LEARNING OBJECTIVE

Describe the characteristics of effective goal setting and feedback.

Walk into almost any customer contact centre (i.e. call centre)—whether it is BNZ's contact centre in Auckland, or Dell's contact centre in Quezon City in the Philippines—and you will notice that work activities are dominated by goal setting and plenty of feedback.[47] Contact-centre performance is judged on several *key performance indicators (KPIs)*, such as average time to answer the call, length of time per call and abandon rates (customers who hang up before the call is handled by a customer service representative). Some contact centres have large electronic boards showing how many customers are waiting, the average time they have been waiting and the average time before someone talks to them. A few even have 'emotion detection' software, which translates words and voice intonation into a measure of the customer's level of happiness or anger during the telephone conversation.[48]

goal setting The process of motivating employees and clarifying their role perceptions by establishing performance objectives.

Goal setting is the process of motivating employees and clarifying their role perceptions by establishing performance objectives. It potentially improves employee performance in two ways: (1) by amplifying the intensity and persistence of effort and (2) by giving employees clearer role perceptions so that their effort is channelled toward behaviours that will improve work performance. Goal setting is more complex than simply telling someone to 'do your best'. It requires several specific characteristics. Some consultants refer to these as 'SMART goals', but the acronym doesn't quite capture all the key ingredients identified by goal-setting research. The six key characteristics are specific goals, relevant goals, challenging goals, goal commitment, participation in goal formation (sometimes) and goal feedback.[49]

SPECIFIC GOALS Employees put more effort into a task when they work toward specific goals rather than 'do your best' targets. Specific goals have measurable levels of change over a specific and relatively short time frame, such as 'reduce patient wait time by 25 per cent over the next six months'. Specific goals communicate more precise performance expectations, so employees can direct their effort more efficiently and reliably.

RELEVANT GOALS Goals must also be relevant to the individual's job and be within his or her control. For example, a goal to reduce waste materials would have little value if employees don't have much control over waste in the production process.

CHALLENGING GOALS Challenging goals (rather than easy ones) cause people to raise the intensity and persistence of their work effort and to think through information more actively. They also fulfil a person's achievement or growth needs when the goal is achieved. General Electric, Goldman Sachs and many other organisations challenge employees with *stretch goals*. These goals don't just stretch a person's abilities and motivation; they are goals that people don't even know how to reach, so they need to be creative to achieve them.

GOAL COMMITMENT Ideally goals should be challenging without being so difficult that employees lose their motivation to achieve them.[50] This is the same as the E-to-P expectancy that was discussed in the section on expectancy theory. The lower the E-to-P expectancy that the goal can be accomplished, the less committed (motivated) the employee is to the goal.

GOAL PARTICIPATION (SOMETIMES) Goal setting is usually (but not always) more effective when employees participate in setting the goals.[51] Participation potentially creates a higher level of goal commitment than is found when goals are set alone by the supervisor. Participation may also improve goal quality, because employees have valuable information and knowledge that may not be known to those who initially formed the goal.

GOAL FEEDBACK Feedback is another necessary condition for effective goal setting.[52] Feedback is any information that lets us know whether we have achieved the goal or are properly directing our effort toward it. Feedback redirects our effort, but it potentially also fulfils our growth needs.

balanced scorecard (BSC) A goal-setting and reward system that translates the organisation's vision and mission into specific, measurable performance goals related to financial, customer, internal and learning/growth (i.e. human capital) processes.

Balanced Scorecard

Balanced scorecard (BSC) represents an organisation-level form of goal setting that attempts to represent objectives across various stakeholders and processes. Although popular among large companies worldwide, one study estimates that only about one-fifth of Australian companies use a BSC.[53] The balanced scorecard translates the organisation's vision and mission into specific, measurable performance goals related to financial, customer, internal and learning/growth

Trouble Keeping Score

Martin Sykes/New Zealand Herald

In 2000, the New Zealand government adopted a balanced scorecard to measure and improve the performance of public hospitals and related services. The original model, which was managed by the country's twenty-one district health boards, divided the scorecard into four quadrants: clinical quality, delivery quality, productivity and financial. Many of the specific performance indicators were reported monthly. Although the BSC system is well established in other industries, some public health staff experienced philosophical and practical problems with this process. For example, the mental health service in one South Island district discovered difficulties in prioritising the various performance indicators and in ensuring the data were sufficiently accurate. As members of a caring profession, some employees also felt uncomfortable quantifying the performance of a service that cannot be easily measured. In 2006, the New Zealand government transformed the BSC indicators into benchmarks and revised these criteria to represent a more patient-centred view of hospital performance.[54]

(i.e. human capital) processes. The objective of a BSC is to ensure that the full range of organisational performance is captured in the goal-setting process. Each dimension includes several goals related to specific operations within the organisation, thereby connecting each work unit to the overall corporate objectives. For example, an airline might include on-time performance as one of its customer process goals, and number of hours of safety training per employee as a learning and growth process goal. These specific goals are often weighted and scored to create a composite measure of achievement across the organisation each year.

Western Water, a water utility in Victoria, Australia, introduced a balanced scorecard to monitor progress towards its purpose 'to contribute to healthy communities by meeting their current and future water service needs'. Western Water's balanced scorecard model includes measures in five key areas—customer, stakeholder, financial, sustainable internal processes and people. For example, Western Water has goals to achieve 100 per cent recycled water, implement a new trade waste system and implement mobile computing technology. Each month, a team of managers across the utility's six functional units meets to monitor progress toward specific goals in those five areas. Employees also receive the monthly scorecard results. Since introducing the BSC, Western Water's performance has soared. It has also received CPA Australia's award for public sector organisation of the year, and is one of the few companies from Australia to be inducted into the Balanced Scorecard Hall of Fame.[55]

Characteristics of Effective Feedback

A major component of Lenovo's talent management process is its 'caring manager' philosophy. 'A caring manager is essentially one who actively delivers on the following: giving and receiving feedback, people coaching, being a role model for integrity and championing a work–life balance,' explains David Miller, Asia-Pacific president of the Chinese-based computer maker.[56] Executives at Lenovo are discovering that feedback is an important practice in employee motivation and performance. Along with clarifying role perceptions and improving employee skills and knowledge, feedback motivates when it is constructive and when employees have strong self-efficacy.[57]

As with goal setting, feedback should be *specific* and *relevant*. In other words, the information should refer to specific metrics (e.g. sales increased by 5 per cent last month) and to the individual's behaviour or outcomes within his or her control. Feedback should also be *timely*; the information should be available soon after the behaviour or results occur so that employees see a clear association between their actions and the consequences. Effective feedback is also *credible*. Employees are more likely to accept feedback from trustworthy and credible sources.

The final characteristic of effective feedback is that it should be *sufficiently frequent*. How frequent is 'sufficiently'? The answer depends on at least two things. One consideration is the employee's knowledge and experience with the task. Feedback is a form of reinforcement, so employees working on new tasks should receive more frequent feedback because they require more direction regarding work behaviours (see Chapter 3). Employees who perform repetitive or familiar tasks can receive less frequent feedback. The second factor is how long it takes to complete the task. Feedback is necessarily less frequent in jobs with a long cycle time (e.g. executives and scientists) than in jobs with a short cycle time (e.g. grocery store cashiers).

Feedback through Strength-Based Coaching

Forty years ago, Peter Drucker recognised that leaders are more effective when they focus on strengths rather than weaknesses. 'The effective executive builds on strengths—their own strengths, the strengths of superiors, colleagues, subordinates; and on the strength of the situation,' wrote the late management guru.[58] Standard Chartered Bank, which was described at the beginning of this chapter, has adopted this positive OB approach. It gives employees opportunities to develop their strengths rather than requiring them to focus on areas where they have limited interest or talent. This is the essence of **strength-based coaching** (also known as *appreciative coaching*)—maximising employee potential by focusing on their strengths rather than weaknesses.[59] In strength-based coaching, the employee describes areas of work in which they excel or demonstrate potential. The coach guides this discussion by asking exploratory questions and by helping the employee to discover ways of leveraging this strength. For example, the pair would discuss how to further build and apply the coachee's strengths, as well as identify barriers that might interfere with the development of those strengths.

strength-based coaching A positive organisational behaviour approach to coaching and feedback that focuses on building and leveraging the employee's strengths rather than trying to correct his or her weaknesses.

Strength-based coaching is logical because people inherently seek feedback about their strengths, not their flaws. Recall from Chapter 2 that people engage in self-enhancement, at least for those domains of self that are most important. Strength-based coaching also makes sense

Sony Europe Builds on Strengths

When competition from Korea and China threatened Sony Europe's market position, the electronics and music company decided that its competitive advantage would be to leverage the power of strengths rather than battle against weaknesses. Employees were asked to identify activities in which they excel, enjoy the work and feel at ease. On the basis of this information, Sony Europe designed jobs around these strengths, instead of moulding people to fit into existing, rigid job structures. For example, the performance of a Sony Europe employee dropped after he moved to another sales position. Rather than pushing the employee to deliver higher performance in the new job, Sony compared the individual's strengths against the job requirements. The company learned that the employee's strength was in face-to-face communication, whereas his new job required very little social interaction. Sony created a new role for the employee that leveraged his strengths. Within a year, the employee's team had delivered record sales and increased profits at a lower cost. Strength-based coaching 'ensures that everybody in Sony is focusing on what they do best,' says Ray White, Sony Europe's vice president of human resources. 'They're aligning their "A" talents to make their best contribution to the business and their best contributions are outstanding.'[60]

Getty Images

because personality becomes quite stable early in the employee's career, which makes it more difficult to change his or her interests, preferences and competencies.[61] In spite of these research observations, most companies focus goal setting and feedback on tasks that employees are performing poorly. After the initial polite compliments, many coaching or performance feedback sessions analyse the employee's weaknesses, including determining what went wrong and what the employee needs to do to improve. These inquisitions sometimes produce so much negative feedback that employees become defensive; they can also undermine self-efficacy, thereby making the employee's performance worse rather than better. By focusing on weaknesses, companies fail to realise the full potential of the employee's strengths. One survey reports that only 20 per cent of employees in large organisations believe they are given the opportunity to perform tasks that leverage their strengths.[62]

Sources of Feedback

Feedback can originate from nonsocial or social sources. Nonsocial sources provide feedback without someone communicating that information. Employees at contact centres view electronic displays showing how many callers are waiting and the average time they have been waiting. Nova Chemicals operators receive feedback from a computer screen that monitors in real time the plant's operational capacity, depicted as a gently flowing green line, and actual production output, shown as a red squiggly line. Soon after Nova installed the feedback system, employees engaged in friendly bouts of rivalry to determine who could keep the actual production output as close as possible to the plant's maximum capacity.[63]

Corporate intranets allow many executives to receive feedback instantaneously on their computer, usually in the form of graphic output on an executive dashboard. Almost half of Microsoft's employees use a dashboard to monitor project deadlines, sales and other metrics. Microsoft CEO Steve Ballmer regularly reviews dashboard results in one-on-one meetings with his division leaders. 'Every time I go to see Ballmer, it's an expectation that I bring my dashboard with me,' says the head of the Microsoft Office division.[64]

Multisource (360-Degree) Feedback

Standard Chartered Bank improved employee engagement by creating an effective and culturally sensitive performance review and coaching process. The London-based financial institution maintains cultural sensitivity by giving its managers the freedom to choose how feedback information is collected. 'We give the managers appraisal tools such as 180-degree or 360-degree feedback,' explains Tim Miller, Standard Chartered's director of people, property and assurance and nonexecutive chairman of the company's operations in Korea (SC First Bank). 'Our African businesses like the 360-degree, team-based approach. In China, they are more reticent about it and prefer 180-degree feedback. But it's up to the local manager what they choose.'[65]

multisource (360-degree) feedback Information about an employee's performance collected from a full circle of people, including subordinates, peers, supervisors and customers.

Standard Chartered Bank relies on variations of **multisource (360-degree) feedback** to provide meaningful feedback to employees. As the name implies, multisource feedback is information about an employee's performance collected from a full circle of people, including subordinates, peers, supervisors and customers. Almost all the Fortune 500 companies use multisource feedback, typically for managers rather than nonmanagement employees.[66] Multisource feedback tends to provide more complete and accurate information than feedback from a supervisor alone. It is particularly useful when the supervisor is unable to observe the employee's behaviour or performance throughout the year. Lower-level employees also feel a greater sense of fairness and open communication when they are able to provide upward feedback about their boss's performance.[67]

However, multisource feedback also creates challenges. Having several people review so many other people can be expensive and time-consuming. With multiple opinions, the 360-degree process can also produce ambiguous and conflicting feedback, so employees may require guidance to interpret the results. A third concern is that peers may provide inflated rather than accurate feedback to avoid conflicts during the forthcoming year. A final concern is that employees experience a stronger emotional reaction when they receive critical feedback from many people rather than from just one person (such as the boss). 'Initially you do take it personally,' admits a manager at software maker Autodesk. '[360-degree feedback] is meant to be constructive, but you have to internally battle that.'[68]

Choosing Feedback Sources

With so many sources of feedback—multisource feedback, executive dashboards, customer surveys, equipment gauges, nonverbal communication from your boss—which one works best under which conditions? The preferred feedback source depends on the purpose of the information. To learn about their progress toward goal accomplishment, employees usually prefer nonsocial feedback sources, such as computer printouts or feedback directly from the job. This is because information from nonsocial sources is considered more accurate than information from social sources. Feedback from nonsocial sources is also less damaging to self-esteem. In contrast, social sources tend to delay negative information, leave some of it out and distort the bad news in a positive way.[69] When employees want to improve their self-image, they seek out positive feedback from social sources. It feels better to have coworkers say that you are performing the job well than to discover this from a computer screen.

Evaluating Goal Setting and Feedback

Goal setting represents one of the 'tried-and-true' theories in organisational behaviour, so much so that scholars consider it to be one of the top OB theories in terms of validity and usefulness.[70] In partnership with goal setting, feedback also has an excellent reputation for improving employee motivation and performance. At the same time, putting goal setting into practice can create problems.[71] One concern is that goal setting tends to focus employees on a narrow subset of measurable performance indicators while ignoring aspects of job performance that are difficult to measure. The saying 'What gets measured, gets done' applies here. A second problem is that when goal achievement is tied to financial rewards, many employees are motivated to set easy goals (while making the boss think they are difficult) so that they have a higher probability of the bonus or pay increase. As a former chief executive at Ford once quipped: 'At Ford, we hire very smart people. They quickly learn how to make relatively easy goals look difficult!'[72] A third problem is that setting performance goals is effective in established jobs but seems to interfere with the learning process in new, complex jobs. Thus, we need to be careful not to apply goal setting where an intense learning process is occurring.

ORGANISATIONAL JUSTICE

The government of Tasmania, Australia, recently bought the unfinished Bell Bay power station when the original owners (Babcock & Brown) experienced financial problems. United Group, the construction company hired to finish building the electricity generation station, brought in crews from other states to work alongside the Tasmanian workers at the site. It wasn't long before the Tasmanian workers discovered a huge gap in pay rates. The new interstate workers were being paid $31.50 per hour, whereas the Tasmanian workers were paid $22 for doing the same job at the same work site. 'The situation is basically unfair and the Tasmanian workers are very angry,' said the local labour union leader.[73]

Most organisational leaders know that treating employees fairly is both morally correct and good for employee motivation, loyalty and wellbeing. Yet the feelings of injustice that the Tasmanian workers at the Bell Bay power station site experienced are regular occurrences in the workplace. To minimise these incidents, we need to first understand that there are two forms of organisational justice: distributive justice and procedural justice.[74] **Distributive justice** refers to perceived fairness in the outcomes we receive, compared to our contributions and the outcomes and contributions of others. **Procedural justice**, on the other hand, refers to fairness of the procedures used to decide the distribution of resources. The Tasmanian workers experienced distributive injustice because coworkers from other parts of Australia earned much bigger pay cheques for doing the same work. Depending on how this pay gap was determined and how the employer, United Group, addresses these grievances, the workers might also experience procedural injustice.

distributive justice Perceived fairness in the individual's ratio of outcomes to contributions compared with a comparison other's ratio of outcomes to contributions.

procedural justice Perceived fairness of the procedures used to decide the distribution of resources.

LEARNING OBJECTIVE 

Summarise equity theory and describe how to improve procedural justice.

Equity Theory

The first thing we usually think about and experience in situations of injustice is distributive injustice—the belief (and its emotional response) that the pay and other outcomes we receive in the exchange relationship are unfair. What is considered 'fair' varies with each person and situation. We apply an *equality principle* when we believe that everyone in the group should receive the same outcomes, such as when everyone gets subsidised meals in the company cafeteria. The *need principle* is applied when we believe that those with the greatest need should receive greater outcomes than others with less need. The *equity principle* infers that people should be paid in proportion to their contribution. The equity principle is the most common distributive justice rule in organisational settings, so let's look at it in more detail.

equity theory A theory explaining how people develop perceptions of fairness in the distribution and exchange of resources.

To explain how the equity principle operates, OB scholars developed **equity theory**, which says that employees determine feelings of equity by comparing their own outcome/input ratio to the outcome/input ratio of some other person.[75] The *outcome/input ratio* is the value of the outcomes you receive divided by the value of the inputs you provide in the exchange relationship. Inputs include such things as skill, effort, reputation, performance, experience and hours worked. Outcomes are what employees receive from the organisation in exchange for the inputs, such as pay, promotions, recognition, preferential treatment or preferred jobs in the future. In our example, the Tasmanian workers likely believed that, collectively, all the workers on the site provided the same skills, effort and hours of work, but the interstate workers received much more favourable outcomes—that is, bigger pay cheques.

Equity theory states that we compare our outcome/input ratio with that of a comparison other.[76] In our example, the Tasmanian workers compared themselves to other employees in the same job, namely, the interstate workers at the same work site. In other situations, the comparison other might be another person or group of people in other jobs (e.g. comparing your pay with the CEO's pay) or another organisation. Some research suggests that employees frequently collect information on several other people to form a 'generalised' comparison other.[77] For the most part, however, the comparison other varies from one person to the next and is not easily identifiable.

People develop feelings of equity or inequity by comparing their own outcome/input ratio with the comparison other's ratio. Exhibit 5.6 diagrams the three equity evaluations. In the underreward inequity situation—which the Tasmanian workers experienced—people believe their outcome/input ratio is lower than the comparison other's ratio. In the equity condition, people believe that their outcome/input ratio is similar to the ratio of the comparison other. In the overreward inequity condition, people believe their ratio of outcomes/inputs is

Exhibit 5.6 ***Equity Theory Model***

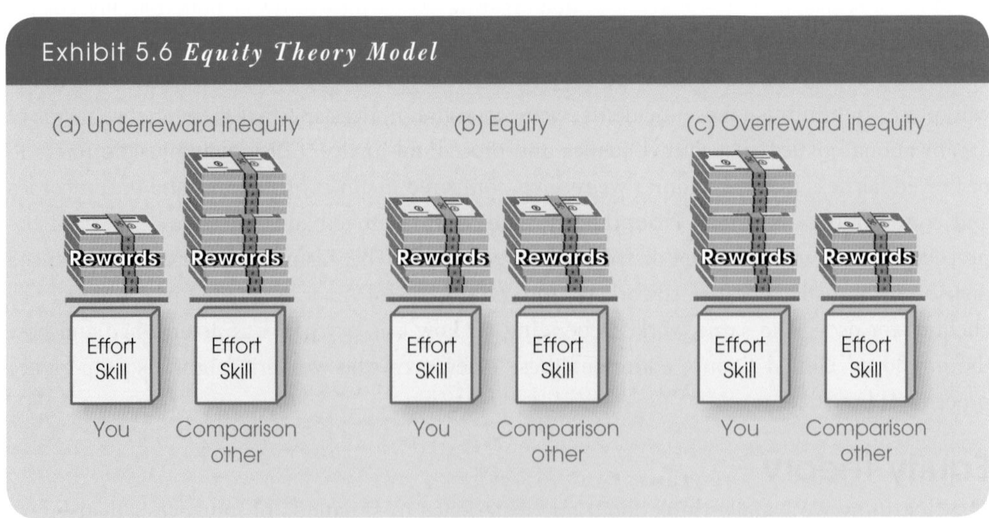

higher than the comparison other's ratio. However, overreward inequity isn't as common as underreward inequity because people often change their perceptions to justify the favourable outcomes.

Inequity and Employee Motivation

How does the equity evaluation relate to employee motivation? The answer is that feelings of inequity generate negative emotions, and, as we have pointed out throughout this chapter, emotions are the engines of motivation. In the case of inequity, people are motivated to reduce the emotional tension. Consider the plight of the underpaid Tasmanian workers at the Bell Bay power station construction site. These individuals experienced anger and frustration when they discovered how much less they earned than coworkers who came in from other places in Australia. These emotions motivated the workers to contact their labour union to correct the problem. There are many other ways that people respond to feelings of underreward inequity. The most common responses (some of which are unethical) include the following:[78]

- *Reduce our inputs.* Perform the work more slowly, give fewer helpful suggestions, engage in less organisational citizenship behaviour.
- *Increase our outcomes.* Ask for a pay increase directly or through a labour union, make unauthorised use of company resources.
- *Increase the comparison other's inputs.* Subtly ask the better-off coworker to do a larger share of the work to justify his or her higher pay or other outcomes.
- *Reduce the comparison other's outcomes.* Ask the company to reduce the coworker's pay.
- *Change our perceptions.* Believe that the coworker really is doing more (e.g. working longer hours) or that the higher outcomes (e.g. better office) he or she receives really aren't so much better than what you get.
- *Change the comparison other.* Compare yourself to someone else closer to your situation (job duties, pay scale).
- *Leave the field.* Avoid thinking about the inequity by keeping away from the work site where the overpaid coworker is located, taking more sick leave, moving to another department or quitting your job.

Although the seven responses to inequity remain the same, people who feel overreward inequity would, of course, act differently. Some overrewarded employees reduce their feelings of inequity by working harder. 'What helps motivate me is that I look around the office and I see people who are working as hard or harder than I am. You feel guilty if you're not pulling your weight,' says an American accountant. However, many overrewarded employees don't work harder. Some might encourage the underrewarded coworker to work at a more leisurely pace. A common reaction, however, is that the overrewarded employee changes his or her perceptions to justify the more favourable outcomes. As author Pierre Burton once said: 'I was underpaid for the first half of my life. I don't mind being overpaid for the second half.'[79]

Individual Differences: Equity Sensitivity

Thus far, we have described equity theory as though everyone has the same feelings of inequity in a particular situation. The reality, however, is that people vary in their **equity sensitivity**, that is, their outcome/input preferences and reaction to various outcome/input ratios.[80] At one end

equity sensitivity An individual's outcome/input preferences and reaction to various outcome/input ratios.

Costco Wholesale CEO Keeps Executive Pay Equitable

John Pierpont Morgan, who in the 1800s founded the financial giant now called JPMorgan Chase, warned that no CEO should earn more than 20 times an average worker's pay. That advice didn't stop James L. Dimon from earning an average of US $40 million in total compensation for each of his first two years as the CEO of JPMorgan Chase. Dimon took home more than 1200 times the pay of the average employee in the United States. Costco Wholesale chief executive Jim Sinegal (shown in photo) thinks such a large wage gap is blatantly unfair and can lead to long-term employee motivation problems. 'Having an individual who is making 100 or 200 or 300 times more than the average person working on the floor is wrong,' says Sinegal, who cofounded the Issaquah, Washington, company. Even though Costco is one of the world's largest retailers, Sinegal's annual salary and bonus usually amount to less than US $600 000. Stock options raised his latest total compensation to $3.2 million, which was much less than Costco's board wanted to pay him. Sinegal explained that receiving higher pay would not affect his motivation and performance. At the same time, Costco employees enjoy some of the highest pay rates in the American retail industry (averaging US $17 per hour).[82]

Chris Mueller/Redux Pictures

of the equity sensitivity continuum are the 'benevolents'—people who are tolerant of situations in which they are underrewarded. They might still prefer equal outcome/input ratios, but they don't mind if others receive more than they do for the same inputs. In the middle are people who fit the standard equity theory model. These 'equity sensitives' want their outcome/input ratio to be equal to the outcome/input ratio of the comparison other. Equity sensitives feel increasing inequity as the ratios become different. At the other end are the 'entitleds'. These people feel more comfortable in situations where they receive proportionately more than others. They might accept having the same outcome/input ratio as others, but they would prefer to receive more than others performing the same work.

Evaluating Equity Theory

Equity theory is widely studied and quite successful at predicting various situations involving feelings of workplace injustice.[81] However, equity theory isn't so easy to put into practice because it doesn't identify the comparison other and doesn't indicate which inputs or outcomes are most valuable to each employee. The best solution here is for leaders to know their employees well enough to minimise the risk of inequity feelings. Open communication is also a key, enabling employees to let decision makers know when they feel decisions are unfair. A second problem is that equity theory accounts for only some of our feelings of fairness or justice in the workplace. Experts now say that procedural justice is at least as important as distributive justice.

Procedural Justice

LEARNING OBJECTIVE 

Identify the factors that influence procedural justice, as well as the consequences of procedural justice.

As mentioned earlier, *procedural justice* refers to the fairness of the procedures used to decide the distribution of resources. How do companies improve procedural justice?[83] A good way to start is by giving employees 'voice' in the process; encourage them to present their facts and perspectives on the issue. Voice also provides a 'value-expressive' function; employees tend to feel better after having an opportunity to speak their mind. Procedural justice is also higher when the decision maker is perceived as unbiased, relies on complete and accurate information, applies existing policies consistently and has listened to all sides of the dispute. If employees still feel unfairness in the allocation of resources, their feelings tend to weaken if they given the opportunity to appeal the decision to a higher authority.

Finally, people usually feel less inequity when they are given a full explanation of the decision and when their concerns are treated with respect. Managers who refuse to explain the logic behind their decision might further inflame inequity feelings among employees who believe the decision was unfair. For instance, one study found that nonwhite nurses who experienced racism tended to file grievances only after experiencing disrespectful treatment in their attempt to resolve the racist situation. Another study reported that employees with repetitive strain injuries were more likely to file workers' compensation claims after experiencing disrespectful behaviour from management. A third recent study noted that employees have stronger feelings of injustice when the manager has a reputation of treating people unfairly most of the time.[84]

Consequences of Procedural Injustice

Procedural justice has a strong influence on a person's emotions and motivation. Employees tend to experience anger toward the source of the injustice, which generates various response behaviours that scholars categorise as either withdrawal or aggression.[85] Notice how these response behaviours are similar to the fight-or-flight responses described earlier in the chapter regarding situations that activate our drive to defend. Research suggests that being treated unfairly threatens our self-concept and social status, particularly when others see that we have been unjustly treated. Employees retaliate to restore their self-concept, and reinstate their status and power in the relationship with the perpetrator of the injustice. Employees also engage in these counterproductive behaviours to educate the decision maker, thereby trying to minimise the likelihood of future injustices.[86]

CHAPTER SUMMARY

Motivation consists of the forces within a person that affect his or her direction, intensity and persistence of voluntary behaviour in the workplace. Drives (also called primary needs) are neural states that energise individuals to correct deficiencies or maintain an internal equilibrium. They are the 'prime movers' of behaviour, activating emotions that put us in a state of readiness to act. Needs—goal-directed forces that people experience—are shaped by the individual's self-concept (including personality and values), social norms and past experience.

Maslow's needs hierarchy organises needs into five levels, and states that the lowest needs are initially most important but higher needs become more important as the lower ones are satisfied. Although very popular, the theory lacks research support, as does ERG theory, which attempted to overcome some of the limitations in Maslow's needs hierarchy. Both models assume that everyone has the same hierarchy, whereas the emerging evidence suggests that needs hierarchies vary from one person to the next according to their personal values.

McClelland's learned needs theory argues that needs can be strengthened through learning. The three needs studied in this respect have been need for achievement, need for power and need for affiliation. Four-drive theory states that everyone has four innate drives—the drives to acquire, bond, learn and defend. These drives activate emotions that we regulate through a skill set that considers social norms, past experience and personal values. The main recommendation from four-drive theory is to ensure that individual jobs and workplaces provide a balanced opportunity to fulfil the four drives.

Expectancy theory states that work effort is determined by the perception that effort will result in a particular level of performance (E-to-P expectancy), the perception that a specific behaviour or performance level will lead to specific outcomes (P-to-O expectancy) and the valences that the person feels for those outcomes. The E-to-P expectancy increases by improving the employee's ability and confidence to perform the job. The P-to-O expectancy increases by measuring performance accurately, distributing higher rewards to better performers and showing employees that rewards are performance-based. Outcome valences increase by finding out what employees want and using these resources as rewards.

Goal setting is the process of motivating employees and clarifying their role perceptions by establishing performance objectives. Goals are more effective when they are specific, relevant and challenging; have employee commitment; and are accompanied by meaningful feedback. Participative goal setting is important in some situations. Effective feedback is specific, relevant, timely, credible and sufficiently frequent.

Organisational justice consists of distributive justice (perceived fairness in the outcomes we receive relative to our contributions, and the outcomes and contributions of others) and procedural justice (fairness of the procedures used to decide the distribution of resources). Equity theory has four elements: outcome/input ratio, comparison other, equity evaluation and consequences of inequity. The theory also explains what people are motivated to do when they feel inequitably treated. Companies need to consider not only equity in the distribution of resources but also fairness in the process of making resource allocation decisions.

KEY TERMS

balanced scorecard (BSC), p. 182
distributive justice, p. 187
drives, p. 170
employee engagement, p. 168
equity sensitivity, p. 189
equity theory, p. 188
ERG theory, p. 173
expectancy theory, p. 179
four-drive theory, p. 176
goal setting, p. 181
Maslow's needs hierarchy theory, p. 171
motivation, p.168
multisource (360-degree) feedback, p. 186
need for achievement (nAch), p. 174
need for affiliation (nAff), p. 175
need for power (nPow), p. 175
needs, p. 170
procedural justice, p. 187
strength-based coaching, p. 184

Critical Thinking Questions

1 Four-drive theory is conceptually different from Maslow's needs hierarchy (as well as ERG theory) in several ways. Describe these differences. At the same time, needs are based on drives, so the four drives should parallel the seven needs that Maslow identified (five in the hierarchy and two additional needs). Map Maslow's needs onto the four drives in four-drive theory.

2 Learned needs theory states that needs can be strengthened or weakened. How might a company strengthen the achievement needs of its management team?

3 Exhibit 5.1 illustrates how a person's drives and needs result in decisions and behaviour. Explain where the expectancy theory of motivation fits into this model.

4 Use all three components of expectancy theory to explain why some employees are motivated to show up for work during a severe storm whereas others make no effort to leave their home.

5 Two friends who have just completed an organisational behaviour course at another university or college inform you that employees must fulfil their need for self-esteem and social esteem before they can reach their full potential through self-actualisation. What theory are these friends referring to? How does their statement differ from what you have learned about that theory in this chapter?

6 Using your knowledge of the characteristics of effective goals, establish two meaningful goals related to your performance in this class.

7 Several service representatives are upset that the newly hired representative with no previous experience will be paid $3000 a year above the usual starting salary in the pay range. The department manager explained that the new hire would not accept the entry-level rate, so the company raised the offer by $3000. All five reps currently earn salaries

near the top of the scale ($15 000 higher than the new recruit), although they all started at the minimum starting salary a few years earlier. Use equity theory to explain why the five service representatives feel inequity in this situation.

8 Organisational injustice can occur in the classroom as well as in the workplace. Identify classroom situations in which you experienced feelings of injustice. What can instructors do to maintain an environment that fosters both distributive and procedural justice?

Skill Builder 5.1

CLASS EXERCISE

Needs Priority Exercise

Purpose

This class exercise is designed to help you understand the characteristics and contingencies of employee needs in the workplace.

Instructions (Large Class)

STEP 1 The table on page 195 lists, in alphabetical order, fourteen characteristics of the job or work environment. Working alone, use the far-left column to rank-order these characteristics in terms of how important they are to you personally. Write in '1' beside the most important characteristic, '2' for the second most important, and so on through to '14' for the least important characteristic on this list.

STEP 2 In the second column, rank-order these characteristics in the order that you think human resource managers believe they are important for their employees.

STEP 3 The instructor will ask your class, by a show of hands (or use of classroom technology), to identify the top-ranked options.

STEP 4 The instructor will provide results of a recent large-scale survey of employees. When these results are presented, identify the reasons for any noticeable differences. Relate the differences to your understanding of the emerging view of employee needs and drives in work settings.

Instructions (Small Class)

STEP 1 AND STEP 2 Same as above.

STEP 3 The instructor will assign you to a team, in which you compare your rank-order results and explain your ranking. The rationale for different rankings should be noted and discussed with the entire class. Pay close attention to different needs, self-concepts and various forms of diversity (culture, profession, age and so on) to identify possible explanations for any variation of results across the class.

STEP 4 Same as above.

Importance to *you*	What HR managers believe are important to employees	Job or work environment characteristics
_______	_______	Autonomy and independence
_______	_______	Benefits (health care, dental, etc.)
_______	_______	Career development opportunities
_______	_______	Communication between employees and senior management
_______	_______	Compensation/pay
_______	_______	Feeling safe in the work environment
_______	_______	Flexibility to balance work–life issues
_______	_______	Job security
_______	_______	Job-specific training
_______	_______	Management recognition of employee job performance
_______	_______	Opportunities to use skills and abilities
_______	_______	Organisation's commitment to professional development
_______	_______	Relationship with immediate supervisor
_______	_______	The work itself

TEAM EXERCISE

Skill Builder 5.2

A Question of Feedback

Purpose

This exercise is designed to help you understand the importance of feedback, including problems that occur with imperfect communication in the feedback process.

Materials

After organising the class into pairs, the instructor will distribute a few pages of exhibits to one person in each pair. The other students will require a pencil, eraser and blank paper. Moveable chairs and tables in a large area are helpful.

Instructions (Small Class)

STEP 1 The class is divided into pairs of students. Each pair is ideally located in a private area, where they are away from other students and one person can write. One student is given the pages of exhibits from the instructor. The other student in each pair is not allowed to see these exhibits.

STEP 2 The student holding the materials will describe each of the exhibits and the other student's task is to accurately replicate each exhibit. You can compare the replication with the original at the end of each drawing. You may also switch roles for each exhibit, if you wish. If roles are switched, the instructor must distribute exhibits separately to each student so that they are not seen by the other person. Each exhibit has a different set of limitations, as described below.

EXHIBIT 1 The student describing the exhibit cannot look at the other student, or at his or her diagram. The student drawing the exhibit cannot speak or otherwise communicate with the person describing the exhibit.

EXHIBIT 2 The student describing the exhibit may look at the other student's diagram. However, he or she may say only 'yes' or 'no' when the student drawing the diagram asks a specific question. In other words, the person presenting the information can use only these words for feedback and can use them only when asked a question by the student doing the drawing.

EXHIBIT 3 (optional, if time permits). The student describing the exhibit may look at the other student's diagram and may provide any feedback at any time to the person replicating the exhibit.

STEP 3 The class will gather to analyse this exercise. This may include discussion on the importance of feedback, and the characteristics of effective feedback for individual motivation and learning.

Instructions (Large Class)

Some parts of this exercise are possible in large classes. Here is one variation:

STEP 1 Students are asked to prepare for the exercise by having a pencil and paper ready.

STEP 2 One student volunteers to provide instructions from the front of the class regarding Exhibit 1. The volunteer receives the first exhibit and describes it to the class, while other students try to replicate the exhibit. When finished, the exhibit is shown to the class on a transparency or computer projection.

STEP 3 For Exhibit 2, one student volunteers to provide instructions and a few other students serve as feedback helpers. The helpers have a copy of Exhibit 2, which they may view, but it cannot be shown to students doing the drawing. The helpers are dispersed to various parts of the room to provide feedback to a group of students under their care (if the class has 100 students, the exercise might have five helpers, each responsible for feedback to twenty students). Helpers can say only 'yes' or 'no', but they may point to specific locations of the student's drawing when uttering these words (because these helpers provide feedback to many students). Throughout this activity, the student describing the exhibit must *not* stop his or her description. After the speaker has finished and the drawings are completed, the helpers might be asked to select the most accurate drawing among those within their domain. The students who drew the accurate depictions might be asked to discuss their experience with feedback.

SELF-ASSESSMENT

Skill Builder 5.3

Need-Strength Questionnaire

Although everyone has the same innate drives, our secondary or learned needs vary on the basis of our self-concept. This self-assessment provides an estimate of your need strength on selected secondary needs. Read each of the statements below and check the response that you believe best reflects your position regarding each statement. Then use the scoring key in Appendix B at the end of the book to calculate your results. To receive a meaningful estimate of your need strength, you need to answer each item honestly and with reflection on your personal experiences. Class discussion will focus on the meaning of the needs measured in this self-assessment as well as their relevance in the workplace.

Personal Needs Questionnaire

How accurately do each of the following statements describe you?	Very accurate description of me	Moderately accurate	Neither accurate nor inaccurate	Moderately inaccurate	Very inaccurate description of me
1. I would rather be myself than be well thought of.	☐	☐	☐	☐	☐
2. I'm the type of person who never gives up.	☐	☐	☐	☐	☐
3. When the opportunity occurs, I want to be in charge.	☐	☐	☐	☐	☐
4. I try not to say things that others don't like to hear.	☐	☐	☐	☐	☐
5. I find it difficult to talk about my ideas if they are contrary to group opinion.	☐	☐	☐	☐	☐
6. I tend to take control of things.	☐	☐	☐	☐	☐
7. I am not highly motivated to succeed.	☐	☐	☐	☐	☐
8. I usually disagree with others only if I know my friends will back me up.	☐	☐	☐	☐	☐
9. I try to be the very best at what I do.	☐	☐	☐	☐	☐
10. I seldom make excuses or apologise for my behaviour.	☐	☐	☐	☐	☐
11. If anyone criticises me, I can take it.	☐	☐	☐	☐	☐
12. I try to outdo others.	☐	☐	☐	☐	☐
13. I seldom change my opinion when people disagree with me.	☐	☐	☐	☐	☐
14. I try to achieve more than what others have accomplished.	☐	☐	☐	☐	☐
15. To get along and be liked, I tend to be what people expect me to be.	☐	☐	☐	☐	☐

Sources: Adapted from instruments described and/or presented in L. R. Goldberg *et al.*, 'The International Personality Item Pool and the Future of Public-Domain Personality Measures', *Journal of Research in Personality* 40 (2006): 84–96; H. J. Martin, 'A Revised Measure of Approval Motivation and Its Relationship to Social Desirability', *Journal of Personality Assessment* 48 (1984): 508–519.

Skill Builder 5.4

Available online

SELF-ASSESSMENT

Measuring Your Growth-Need Strength

Abraham Maslow's needs hierarchy theory distinguished between deficiency needs and growth needs. Deficiency needs become activated when unfulfilled, such as the need for food or belongingness. Growth needs, on the other hand, continue to develop even when temporarily fulfilled. Maslow identified self-actualisation as the only category of growth needs. Research has found that Maslow's needs hierarchy theory overall doesn't fit reality but that specific elements, such as the concept of growth needs, remain valid. This self-assessment is designed to estimate your level of growth-need strength. This instrument asks you to consider what it is about a job that is most important to you. Please indicate which of the two jobs you personally would prefer if you had to make a choice between them. In answering each question, assume that everything else about the jobs is the same. Pay attention only to the characteristics actually listed.

Skill Builder 5.5

Available online

SELF-ASSESSMENT

Your Equity Sensitivity

Some people experience stronger or weaker feelings of unfairness in specific situations. This self-assessment estimates your level of equity sensitivity. Read each of the statements in this questionnaire, and indicate the response that you believe best reflects your position regarding each statement. This exercise should be completed alone so that you can assess yourself honestly, without concerns of social comparison. Class discussion will focus on equity theory and the effect of equity sensitivity on perceptions of fairness in the workplace.

Endnotes

1 Corporate Research Forum, *Workshop Review: Using Strengths-Based Approaches to Improve Individual and Organisational Performance* (London: Corporate Research Forum, 10 July 2007); H. Syedain, 'A Talent for Numbers', *People Management*, 14 June 2007; P. Flade, 'Employee Engagement Drives Shareholder Value', *Director of Finance Online*, 13 February 2008; Standard Chartered, *Sustainability Review 2007: Leading the Way in Asia, Africa, and the Middle East* (London: Standard Chartered Bank, 17 March 2008).

2 C. C. Pinder, *Work Motivation in Organizational Behavior* (Upper Saddle River, NJ: Prentice Hall, 1998); R. M. Steers, R. T. Mowday and D. L. Shapiro, 'The Future of Work Motivation Theory', *Academy of Management Review* 29 (2004): 379–387.

3 A. B. Bakker and W. B. Schaufeli, 'Positive Organizational Behavior: Engaged Employees in Flourishing Organizations', *Journal of Organizational Behavior* 29, no. 2 (2008): 147–154; W. H. Macey and B. Schneider, 'The Meaning of Employee Engagement', *Industrial and Organizational Psychology* 1 (2008): 3–30.

4 N. P. Rothbard, 'Enriching or Depleting? The Dynamics of Engagement in Work and Family Roles', *Administrative Science Quarterly* 46, no. 4 (2001): 655–684; R. Baumruk, 'The Missing Link: The Role of Employee Engagement

in Business Success', *Workspan*, November 2004, 48; F. D. Frank, R. P. Finnegan and C. R. Taylor, 'The Race for Talent: Retaining and Engaging Workers in the 21st Century', *Human Resource Planning* 27, no. 3 (2004): 12; D. R. May, R. L. Gilson and L. M. Harter, 'The Psychological Conditions of Meaningfulness, Safety and Availability and the Engagement of the Human Spirit at Work', *Journal of Occupational and Organizational Psychology* 77 (March 2004): 11–37; A. M. Saks, 'Antecedents and Consequences of Employee Engagement', *Journal of Managerial Psychology* 21, no. 7 (2006): 600–619; F. Catteeuw, E. Flynn and J. Vonderhorst, 'Employee Engagement: Boosting Productivity in Turbulent Times', *Organization Development Journal* 25, no. 2 (2007): P151–P157.

5 G. Ginsberg, ed., *Essential Techniques for Employee Engagement, The Practitioner's Guide To ...* (London: Melcrum Publishing, 2007).

6 M. Millar, 'Getting the Measure of Its People', *Personnel Today*, 14 December 2004, 6; K. Ockenden, 'Inside Story', *Utility Week*, 28 January 2005, 26; Saks, 'Antecedents and Consequences of Employee Engagement'; Scottish Executive Social Research, *Employee Engagement in the Public Sector: A Review of the Literature* (Edinburgh: Scottish Executive Social Research, May 2007).

7 Voxant Fair Disclosure Wire, 'Event Brief of Q2 2006 JCPenney Earnings Conference Call', news release, 10 August 2006; S. Edelson, 'The Penney Program', *Women's Wear Daily*, 12 February 2007, 1; J. Engen, 'Are Your Employees Truly Engaged?', *Chief Executive*, March 2008, 42.

8 Gallup Study: Feeling Good Matters in the Workplace', *Gallup Management Journal*, 12 January 2006; 'Few Workers Are "Engaged" at Work and Most Want More from Execs', *Dow Jones Business News (San Francisco)*, 22 October 2007; M. Weinstein, 'The Young and the Engage-Less', *Training*, October 2008, 6; BlessingWhite, *The State of Employee Engagement 2008: Asia Pacific Overview* (Princeton, NJ: BlessingWhite, 3 March 2009); Gallup Consulting, *The Gallup Q12-Employee Engagement-Poll 2008 Results* (Washington, D.C.: Gallup Consulting, February 2009).

9 Business Wire, 'Towers Perrin Study Finds, Despite Layoffs and Slow Economy, a New, More Complex Power Game is Emerging between Employers and Employees', news release (New York: 30 August 2001); K. V. Rondeau and T. H. Wagar, 'Downsizing and Organizational Restructuring: What is the Impact on Hospital Performance?', *International Journal of Public Administration* 26 (2003): 1647–1668.

10 C. Lachnit, 'The Young and the Dispirited', *Workforce* 81 (August 2002): 18; S. H. Applebaum, M. Serena and B. T. Shapiro, 'Generation X and the Boomers: Organizational Myths and Literary Realities', *Management Research News* 27, no. 11/12 (2004): 1–28. Motivation and needs across generations are also discussed in R. Zemke and B. Filipczak, *Generations at Work: Managing the Clash of Veterans, Boomers, Xers, and Nexters in Your Workplace* (New York: AMACOM, 2000).

11 The confusing array of definitions about drives and needs has been the subject of criticism for a half century. See, for example, R. S. Peters, 'Motives and Motivation', *Philosophy* 31 (1956): 117–130; H. Cantril, 'Sentio, Ergo Sum: "Motivation" Reconsidered', *Journal of Psychology* 65, no. 1 (1967): 91–107; G. R. Salancik and J. Pfeffer, 'An Examination of Need-Satisfaction Models of Job Attitudes', *Administrative Science Quarterly* 22, no. 3 (1977): 427–456.

12 A. Blasi, 'Emotions and Moral Motivation', *Journal for the Theory of Social Behaviour* 29, no. 1 (1999): 1–19; D. W. Pfaff, *Drive: Neurobiological and Molecular Mechanisms of Sexual Motivation* (Cambridge, MA: MIT Press, 1999); T. V. Sewards and M. A. Sewards, 'Fear and Power-Dominance Drive Motivation: Neural Representations and Pathways Mediating Sensory and Mnemonic Inputs, and Outputs to Premotor Structures', *Neuroscience and Biobehavioral Reviews* 26 (2002): 553–579; K. C. Berridge, 'Motivation Concepts in Behavioral Neuroscience', *Physiology & Behavior* 81, no. 2 (2004): 179–209. We distinguish drives from emotions, but future research may find that the two concepts are not so different as is stated here.

13 K. Passyn and M. Sujan, 'Self-Accountability Emotions and Fear Appeals: Motivating Behavior', *Journal of Consumer Research* 32, no. 4 (2006): 583–589; S. G. Barsade and D. E. Gibson, 'Why Does Affect Matter in Organizations?', *Academy of Management Perspectives* 21, no. 2 (2007): 36–59.

14 G. Loewenstein, 'The Psychology of Curiosity: A Review and Reinterpretation', *Psychological Bulletin* 116, no. 1 (1994): 75–98; R. E. Baumeister and M. R. Leary, 'The Need to Belong: Desire for Interpersonal Attachments as a Fundamental Human Motivation', *Psychological Bulletin* 117, no. 3 (1995): 497–529; A. E. Kelley, 'Neurochemical Networks Encoding Emotion and Motivation: An Evolutionary Perspective', in *Who Needs Emotions? The Brain Meets the Robot*, ed. J.M. Fellous and M. A. Arbib (New York: Oxford University Press, 2005), 29–78.

15 S. Hitlin, 'Values as the Core of Personal Identity: Drawing Links between Two Theories of Self', *Social Psychology Quarterly* 66, no. 2 (2003): 118–137; D. D. Knoch and E. E. Fehr, 'Resisting the Power of Temptations: The Right Prefrontal Cortex and Self-Control', *Annals of the New York Academy of Sciences* 1104, no. 1 (2007): 123; B. Monin, D. A. Pizarro and J. S. Beer, 'Deciding Versus Reacting: Conceptions of Moral Judgment and the Reason-Affect Debate', *Review of General Psychology* 11, no. 2 (2007): 99–111.

16 N. M. Ashkanasy, W. J. Zerbe and C. E. J. Härtel, 'A Bounded Emotionality Perspective on the Individual in the Organization', in *Emotions in Organizational Behavior*, ed. C. E. J. Härtel, W. J. Zerbe and N. M. Ashkanasy (Mahwah, NJ: Lawrence Erlbaum, 2005), 113–117.

17 A. H. Maslow, 'A Theory of Human Motivation', *Psychological Review* 50 (1943): 370–396; A. H. Maslow, *Motivation and Personality* (New York: Harper & Row, 1954).

18 D. T. Hall and K. E. Nougaim, 'An Examination of Maslow's Need Hierarchy in an Organizational Setting', *Organizational Behavior and Human Performance* 3, no. 1 (1968): 12; M. A. Wahba and L. G. Bridwell, 'Maslow Reconsidered: A Review of Research on the Need Hierarchy Theory', *Organizational Behavior and Human Performance* 15 (1976): 212–240; E. L. Betz, 'Two Tests of Maslow's Theory of Need Fulfillment', *Journal of Vocational Behavior* 24, no. 2 (1984): 204–220; P. A. Corning, 'Biological Adaptation in Human Societies: A "Basic Needs" Approach', *Journal of Bioeconomics* 2, no. 1 (2000): 41–86.

19 W. L. Lee, 'Net Value: That Loving Feeling', *The Edge Financial Daily (Malaysia)*, 25 April 2005; N. Mwaura, 'Honour Staff for Good Work', *Daily Nation (Nairobi, Kenya)*, 27 September 2005; E. White, 'Praise from Peers Goes a Long Way', *Wall Street Journal*, 19 December 2005, B3; 'Firms Told to Buy Loyalty and Not Time', *The Kingdom (Killarney, Ireland)*, 10 January 2008; L. Briggs, 'APS in Good Shape but More Remains to Be', *Canberra Times*, 5 February 2008, 8.

20 K. Dye, A. J. Mills and T. G. Weatherbee, 'Maslow: Man Interrupted—Reading Management Theory in Context', *Management Decision* 43, no. 10 (2005): 1375–1395.

21 A. H. Maslow, 'A Preface to Motivation Theory', *Psychosomatic Medicine* 5 (1943): 85–92.

22 A. H. Maslow, *Maslow on Management* (New York: Wiley, 1998).

23 F. F. Luthans, 'Positive Organizational Behavior: Developing and Managing Psychological Strengths', *The Academy of Management Executive* 16, no. 1 (2002): 57–72; S. L. Gable and J. Haidt, 'What (and Why) Is Positive Psychology?', *Review of General Psychology* 9, no. 2 (2005): 103–110; M. E. P. Seligman *et al.*, 'Positive Psychology Progress: Empirical Validation of Interventions', *American Psychologist* 60, no. 5 (2005): 410–421.

24 C. P. Alderfer, *Existence, Relatedness, and Growth* (New York: Free Press, 1972).

25 J. Rauschenberger, N. Schmitt and J. E. Hunter, 'A Test of the Need Hierarchy Concept by a Markov Model of Change in Need Strength', *Administrative Science Quarterly* 25, no. 4 (1980): 654–670; J. P. Wanous and A. A. Zwany, 'A Cross-Sectional Test of Need Hierarchy Theory', *Organizational Behavior and Human Performance* 18 (1977): 78–97.

26 B. A. Agle and C. B. Caldwell, 'Understanding Research on Values in Business', *Business and Society* 38 (September 1999): 326–387; B. Verplanken and R. W. Holland, 'Motivated Decision Making: Effects of Activation and Self-Centrality of Values on Choices and Behavior', *Journal of Personality and Social Psychology* 82, no. 3 (2002): 434–447; S. Hitlin and J. A. Pilavin, 'Values: Reviving a Dormant Concept', *Annual Review of Sociology* 30 (2004): 359–393.

27 D. C. McClelland, *The Achieving Society* (New York: Van Nostrand Reinhold, 1961); D. C. McClelland and D. H. Burnham, 'Power Is the Great Motivator', *Harvard Business Review* 73 (January–February 1995): 126–139; D. Vredenburgh and Y. Brender, 'The Hierarchical Abuse of Power in Work Organizations', *Journal of Business Ethics* 17 (September 1998): 1337–1347; S. Shane, E. A. Locke and C. J. Collins, 'Entrepreneurial Motivation', *Human Resource Management Review* 13, no. 2 (2003): 257–279.

28 McClelland, *The Achieving Society*.

29 Shane, Locke and Collins, 'Entrepreneurial Motivation'.

30 McClelland and Burnham, 'Power Is the Great Motivator'; J. L. Thomas, M. W. Dickson and P. D. Bliese, 'Values Predicting Leader Performance in the U.S. Army Reserve Officer Training Corps Assessment Center: Evidence for a Personality-Mediated Model', *The Leadership Quarterly* 12, no. 2 (2001): 181–196.

31 Vredenburgh and Brender, 'The Hierarchical Abuse of Power in Work Organizations'.

32 D. Miron and D. C. McClelland, 'The Impact of Achievement Motivation Training on Small Business', *California Management Review* 21 (1979): 13–28.

33 P. R. Lawrence and N. Nohria, *Driven: How Human Nature Shapes Our Choices* (San Francisco: Jossey-Bass, 2002).

34 L. Gaertner *et al.*, 'The "I", the "We", and the "When": A Meta-Analysis of Motivational Primacy in Self-Definition', *Journal of Personality and Social Psychology* 83, no. 3 (2002): 574–591; M. R. Leary, 'Motivational and Emotional Aspects of the Self', *Annual Review of Psychology* 58, no. 1 (2007): 317–344.

35 Baumeister and Leary, 'The Need to Belong'.

36 J. Litman, 'Curiosity and the Pleasures of Learning: Wanting and Liking New Information', *Cognition and Emotion* 19, no. 6 (2005): 793–814; T. G. Reio Jr *et al.*, 'The Measurement and Conceptualization of Curiosity', *Journal of Genetic Psychology* 167, no. 2 (2006): 117–135.

37 W. H. Bexton, W. Heron and T. H. Scott, 'Effects of Decreased Variation in the Sensory Environment', *Canadian Journal of Psychology* 8 (1954): 70–76; Loewenstein, 'The Psychology of Curiosity: A Review and Reinterpretation'.

38 A. R. Damasio, *Descartes' Error: Emotion, Reason, and the Human Brain* (New York: Putnam Sons, 1994); J. E. LeDoux, 'Emotion Circuits in the Brain', *Annual Review of Neuroscience* 23 (2000): 155–184; P. Winkielman and K. Berridge, 'Unconscious Emotion', *Current Directions in Psychological Science* 13, no. 3 (2004): 120–123.

39 Lawrence and Nohria, *Driven: How Human Nature Shapes Our Choices*, 145–147.

40 Lawrence and Nohria, *Driven: How Human Nature Shapes Our Choices*, ch. 11.

41 Expectancy theory of motivation in work settings originated in V. H. Vroom, *Work and Motivation* (New York: Wiley, 1964). The version of expectancy theory presented here was developed by Edward Lawler. Lawler's model provides a clearer presentation of the model's three components. P-to-O expectancy is similar to 'instrumentality' in Vroom's original expectancy theory model. The difference is that instrumentality is a correlation whereas P-to-O expectancy is a probability. See J. P. Campbell *et al.*, *Managerial Behavior, Performance, and Effectiveness* (New York: McGraw-Hill, 1970); E. E. Lawler III, *Motivation in Work Organizations* (Monterey, CA: Brooks-Cole, 1973); D. A. Nadler and E. E. Lawler, 'Motivation: A Diagnostic Approach', in *Perspectives on Behavior in Organizations*, ed. J. R. Hackman, E. E. Lawler III and L. W. Porter, 2nd edn (New York: McGraw-Hill, 1983), 67–78.

42 M. Zeelenberg *et al.*, 'Emotional Reactions to the Outcomes of Decisions: The Role of Counterfactual Thought in the Experience of Regret and Disappointment', *Organizational Behavior and Human Decision Processes* 75, no. 2 (1998): 117–141; B. A. Mellers, 'Choice and the Relative Pleasure of Consequences', *Psychological Bulletin* 126, no. 6 (2000): 910–924; R. P. Bagozzi, U. M. Dholakia and S. Basuroy, 'How Effortful Decisions Get Enacted: The Motivating Role of Decision Processes, Desires, and Anticipated Emotions', *Journal of Behavioral Decision Making* 16, no. 4 (2003): 273–295.

43 Nadler and Lawler, 'Motivation: A Diagnostic Approach'.

44 P. W. Mulvey et al., *The Knowledge of Pay Study: E-Mails from the Frontline* (Scottsdale, AZ: WorldatWork, 2002); Watson Wyatt, *WorkMalaysia* (Kuala Lumpur: Watson Wyatt, November 2004); Watson Wyatt, *WorkCanada 2004/2005—Pursuing Productive Engagement* (Toronto: Watson Wyatt, January 2005); Kelly Services, 'Majority of Canada's Workers Happy, Bosses among Best in World', news release (Toronto: 28 November 2006); Hudson, *Rising above the Average: 2007 Compensation and Benefits Report* (New York: June 2007).

45 T. Matsui and T. Terai, 'A Cross-Cultural Study of the Validity of the Expectancy Theory of Motivation', *Journal of Applied Psychology* 60, no. 2 (1975): 263–265; D. H. B. Welsh, F. Luthans and S. M. Sommer, 'Managing Russion Factory Workers: The Impact of U.S.-Based Behavioral and Participative Techniques', *Academy of Management Journal* 36 (1993): 58–79.

46 This limitation was recently acknowledged by Victor Vroom, who had introduced expectancy theory in his 1964 book. See G. P. Latham, *Work Motivation: History, Theory, Research, and Practice* (Thousand Oaks, CA: Sage, 2007), 47–48.

47 S. Zeller, 'Good Calls', *Government Executive*, 15 May 2005; C. Bailor, 'Checking the Pulse of the Contact Center', *Customer Relationship Management*, November 2007, 24–29.

48 A. Shin, 'What Customers Say and How They Say It', *Washington Post*, 18 October 2006, D01; D. Ververidis and C. Kotropoulos, 'Emotional Speech Recognition: Resources, Features, and Methods', *Speech Communication* 48, no. 9 (2006): 1162–1181.

49 G. P. Latham, 'Goal Setting: A Five-Step Approach to Behavior Change', *Organizational Dynamics* 32, no. 3 (2003): 309–318; E. A. Locke and G. P. Latham, *A Theory of Goal Setting and Task Performance* (Englewood Cliffs, NJ: Prentice Hall, 1990). The acronym 'SMART' refers to goals that are specific, measurable, acceptable, relevant and timely. However, this list duplicates some characteristics (e.g. specific goals are by definition measurable) and overlooks challenging and feedback-related dimensions of goals.

50 A. Li and A. B. Butler, 'The Effects of Participation in Goal Setting and Goal Rationales on Goal Commitment: An Exploration of Justice Mediators', *Journal of Business and Psychology* 19, no. 1 (2004): 37–51.

51 Locke and Latham, *A Theory of Goal Setting and Task Performance*, chs 6–7; J. Wegge, 'Participation in Group Goal Setting: Some Novel Findings and a Comprehensive Model as a New Ending to an Old Story', *Applied Psychology: An International Review* 49 (2000): 498–516.

52 M. London, E. M. Mone and J. C. Scott, 'Performance Management and Assessment: Methods for Improved Rater Accuracy and Employee Goal Setting', *Human Resource Management* 43, no. 4 (2004): 319–336; G. P. Latham and C. C. Pinder, 'Work Motivation Theory and Research at the Dawn of the Twenty-First Century', *Annual Review of Psychology* 56 (2005): 485–516.

53 D. Brown *et al.*, *The Balanced Scorecard in Australia* (Melbourne: CPA Australia, September 2006).

54 C. F. Coop, 'Balancing the Balanced Scorecard for a New Zealand Mental Health Service', *Australian Health Review* 30, no. 2 (2006): 174–180; L. Walton and N. J. Goodwin, 'Public Hospital Benchmarking', *Health Policy Monitor*, October 2007; New Zealand Ministry of Health, *Toward*

Clinical Excellence: An Introduction to Clinical Audit, Peer Review and Other Clinical Practice Improvement Activities (Wellington, NZ: Ministry of Health, 2009).

55 E. Charles, 'Final Score', *Australian CPA*, July 2003, 30; Western Water, *Water Plan 2008–2013* (Sunbury, VIC: Western Water, 2008); Western Water, *Western Water Annual Report 2007/08* (Sunbury, VIC: Western Water, 2009).

56 K. James, 'Making Talent Count', *Business Times Singapore*, 18 August 2008.

57 S. P. Brown, S. Ganesan and G. Challagalla, 'Self-Efficacy as a Moderator of Information-Seeking Effectiveness', *Journal of Applied Psychology* 86, no. 5 (2001): 1043–1051; P. A. Heslin and G. P. Latham, 'The Effect of Upward Feedback on Managerial Behaviour', *Applied Psychology: An International Review* 53, no. 1 (2004): 23–37; D. Van-Dijk and A. N. Kluger, 'Feedback Sign Effect on Motivation: Is It Moderated by Regulatory Focus?', *Applied Psychology: An International Review* 53, no. 1 (2004): 113–135; J. E. Bono and A. E. Colbert, 'Understanding Responses to Multi-Source Feedback: The Role of Core Self-Evaluations', *Personnel Psychology* 58, no. 1 (2005): 171–203.

58 P. Drucker, *The Effective Executive* (Oxford: Butterworth-Heinemann, 2007), p.22.

59 M. Buckingham, *Go Put Your Strengths to Work* (New York: Free Press, 2007); S. L. Orem, J. Binkert and A. L. Clancy, *Appreciative Coaching: A Positive Process for Change* (San Francisco: Jossey-Bass, 2007); S. Gordon, 'Appreciative Inquiry Coaching', *International Coaching Psychology Review* 3, no. 2 (2008): 19–31.

60 R. White, 'Building on Employee Strengths at Sony Europe', *Strategic HR Review* 5, no. 5 (2006): 28–31.

61 A. Terracciano, P. T. Costa and R. R. McCrae, 'Personality Plasticity after Age 30', *Personality and Social Psychology Bulletin* 32, no. 8 (2006): 999–1009; Leary, 'Motivational and Emotional Aspects of the Self'.

62 M. Buckingham and D. O. Clifton, *Now, Discover Your Strengths* (New York: Free Press, 2001).

63 D. Hendry, 'Game-Playing: The Latest Business Tool', *Globe & Mail (Toronto)*, 17 November 2006, C11.

64 L. Hollman, 'Seeing the Writing on the Wall', *Call Center Magazine*, August 2002, 37; S. E. Ante, 'Giving the Boss the Big Picture', *BusinessWeek*, 13 February 2006, 48.

65 Syedain, 'A Talent for Numbers'.

66 S. Brutus and M. Derayeh, 'Multisource Assessment Programs in Organizations: An Insider's Perspective', *Human Resource Development Quarterly* 13 (July 2002): 187–202.

67 F. P. Morgeson, T. V. Mumford and M. A. Campion, 'Coming Full Circle: Using Research and Practice to Address 27 Questions about 360-Degree Feedback Programs', *Consulting Psychology Journal* 57, no. 3 (2005): 196–209; J. W. Smither, M. London and R. R. Reilly, 'Does Performance Improve Following Multisource Feedback? A Theoretical Model, Meta-Analysis, and Review of Empirical Findings', *Personnel Psychology* 58, no. 1 (2005): 33–66; L. E. Atwater, J. F. Brett and A. C. Charles, 'Multisource Feedback: Lessons Learned and Implications for Practice', *Human Resource Management* 46, no. 2 (2007): 285–307.

68 A. S. DeNisi and A. N. Kluger, 'Feedback Effectiveness: Can 360-Degree Appraisals Be Improved?', *Academy of Management Executive* 14 (February 2000): 129–139; M. A. Peiperl, 'Getting 360 Degree Feedback Right', *Harvard Business Review* 79 (January 2001): 142–147; M.-G. Seo, L. F. Barrett and J. M. Bartunek, 'The Role of Affective Experience in Work Motivation', *Academy of Management Review* 29 (2004): 423–449.

69 S. J. Ashford and G. B. Northcraft, 'Conveying More (or Less) Than We Realize: The Role of Impression Management in Feedback Seeking', *Organizational Behavior and Human Decision Processes* 53 (1992): 310–334; J. R. Williams *et al.*, 'Increasing Feedback Seeking in Public Contexts: It Takes Two (or More) to Tango', *Journal of Applied Psychology* 84, no. 6 (1999): 969–976.

70 J. B. Miner, 'The Rated Importance, Scientific Validity, and Practical Usefulness of Organizational Behavior Theories: A Quantitative Review', *Academy of Management Learning and Education* 2, no. 3 (2003): 250–268. Also see C. C. Pinder, *Work Motivation in Organizational Behavior* (Upper Saddle River, NJ: Prentice Hall, 1997), p. 384.

71 P. M. Wright, 'Goal Setting and Monetary Incentives: Motivational Tools That Can Work Too Well', *Compensation and Benefits Review* 26 (May–June 1994): 41–49; E. A. Locke and G. P. Latham, 'Building a Practically Useful Theory of Goal Setting and Task Motivation: A 35-Year Odyssey', *American Psychologist* 57, no. 9 (2002): 705–717.

72 Latham, *Work Motivation*, 188.

73 Power Station Workers Upset over "Unfair" Pay', *Hobart Mercury*, 26 September 2008.

74 J. Greenberg and E. A. Lind, 'The Pursuit of Organizational Justice: From Conceptualization to Implication to Application', in *Industrial and Organizational Psychology: Linking Theory with Practice*, ed. C. L. Cooper and E. A. Locke (London: Blackwell, 2000), 72–108; R. Cropanzano and M. Schminke, 'Using Social Justice to Build Effective Work Groups', in *Groups at Work: Theory and Research*, ed. M. E. Turner (Mahwah, NJ: Lawrence Erlbaum, 2001), 143–171; D. T. Miller,

'Disrespect and the Experience of Injustice', *Annual Review of Psychology* 52 (2001): 527–553.

75 J. S. Adams, 'Toward an Understanding of Inequity', *Journal of Abnormal and Social Psychology* 67 (1963): 422– 436; R. T. Mowday, 'Equity Theory Predictions of Behavior in Organizations', in *Motivation and Work Behavior*, ed. L. W. Porter and R. M. Steers, 5th edn (New York: McGraw-Hill, 1991), 111–131; R. Cropanzano and J. Greenberg, 'Progress in Organizational Justice: Tunneling through the Maze', in *International Review of Industrial and Organizational Psychology*, ed. C. L. Cooper and I. T. Robertson (New York: Wiley, 1997), 317–372; L. A. Powell, 'Justice Judgments as Complex Psychocultural Constructions: An Equity-Based Heuristic for Mapping Two- and Three-Dimensional Fairness Representations in Perceptual Space', *Journal of Cross-Cultural Psychology* 36, no. 1 (2005): 48–73.

76 C. T. Kulik and M. L. Ambrose, 'Personal and Situational Determinants of Referent Choice', *Academy of Management Review* 17 (1992): 212–237; G. Blau, 'Testing the Effect of Level and Importance of Pay Referents on Pay Level Satisfaction', *Human Relations* 47 (1994): 1251–1268.

77 T. P. Summers and A. S. DeNisi, 'In Search of Adams' Other: Reexamination of Referents Used in the Evaluation of Pay', *Human Relations* 43 (1990): 497–511.

78 Y. Cohen-Charash and P. E. Spector, 'The Role of Justice in Organizations: A Meta-Analysis', *Organizational Behavior and Human Decision Processes* 86 (November 2001): 278–321.

79 Canadian Press, 'Pierre Berton, Canadian Cultural Icon, Enjoyed Long and Colourful Career', *Times Colonist (Victoria, BC)*, 30 November 2004.

80 K. S. Sauleya and A. G. Bedeian, 'Equity Sensitivity: Construction of a Measure and Examination of Its Psychometric Properties', *Journal of Management* 26 (September 2000): 885–910; G. Blakely, M. Andrews and R. Moorman, 'The Moderating Effects of Equity Sensitivity on the Relationship between Organizational Justice and Organizational Citizenship Behaviors', *Journal of Business and Psychology* 20, no. 2 (2005): 259–273.

81 M. Ezzamel and R. Watson, 'Pay Comparability across and within UK Boards: An Empirical Analysis of the Cash Pay Awards to CEOs and Other Board Members', *Journal of Management Studies* 39, no. 2 (2002): 207–232; J. Fizel, A. C. Krautman and L. Hadley, 'Equity and Arbitration in Major League Baseball', *Managerial and Decision Economics* 23, no. 7 (2002): 427–435.

82 B. Murphy, 'Rising Fortunes', *Milwaukee Journal Sentinel*, 10 October 2004, 1; S. Greenhouse, 'How Costco Became the Anti-Wal-Mart', *New York Times*, 17 July 2005, BU1; '#19 James Dimon', *Forbes*, 3 May 2007; R. Wartzman, 'Put a Cap on CEO Pay', *BusinessWeek*, 12 September 2008.

83 Greenberg and Lind, 'The Pursuit of Organizational Justice: From Conceptualization to Implication to Application'; K. Roberts and K. S. Markel, 'Claiming in the Name of Fairness: Organizational Justice and the Decision to File for Workplace Injury Compensation', *Journal of Occupational Health Psychology* 6 (October 2001): 332–347; J. B. Olson-Buchanan and W. R. Boswell, 'The Role of Employee Loyalty and Formality in Voicing Discontent', *Journal of Applied Psychology* 87, no. 6 (2002): 1167–1174.

84 R. Hagey et al., 'Immigrant Nurses' Experience of Racism', *Journal of Nursing Scholarship* 33, no. 4 (2001): 389–395; Roberts and Markel, 'Claiming in the Name of Fairness: Organizational Justice and the Decision to File for Workplace Injury Compensation'; D. A. Jones and D. P. Skarlicki, 'The Effects of Overhearing Peers Discuss an Authority's Fairness Reputation on Reactions to Subsequent Treatment', *Journal of Applied Psychology* 90, no. 2 (2005): 363–372.

85 Miller, 'Disrespect and the Experience of Injustice'.

86 M. L. Ambrose, M. A. Seabright and M. Schminke, 'Sabotage in the Workplace: The Role of Organizational Injustice', *Organizational Behavior and Human Decision Processes* 89, no. 1 (2002): 947–965.

CHAPTER 6 applied performance practices

LEARNING OBJECTIVES

After reading this chapter, you should be able to:

- discuss the advantages and disadvantages of the four reward objectives
- identify several performance-based rewards at the team level and the organisational level
- describe five ways to improve reward effectiveness
- discuss the advantages and disadvantages of job specialisation
- diagram the job characteristics model of job design
- identify three strategies for improving employee motivation through job design
- define *empowerment* and identify strategies that support empowerment
- describe the five elements of self-leadership
- identify specific personal and work-environment influences on self-leadership.

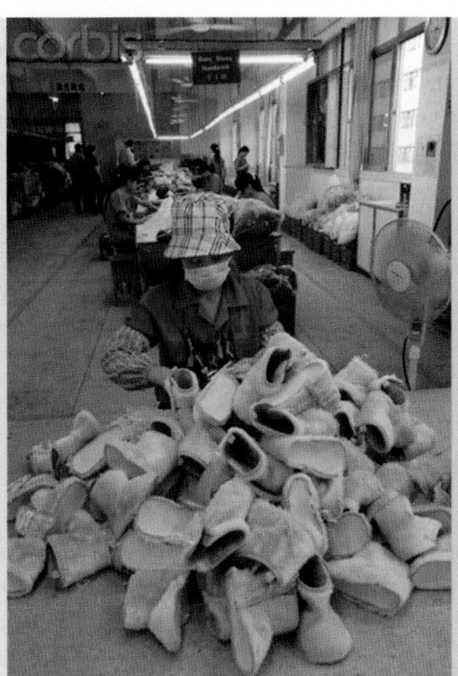

Bobby Yip/Reuters

Most factory workers in China's Pearl River Delta are paid for the number of units they produce. Most work is highly repetitive, cycling several thousand times each day.

China's Pearl River Delta is home to 60 million people and 100 000 manufacturing plants. Many factory employees in this sprawling area north of Hong Kong work by piece rate; the more they produce, the more they earn. Employees at Shenzhen Rishen Cashmere Textile factory apparently earn (all figures in US currency) 17 cents for each garment sewed—about $240 per month for the fastest employees and little more than $100 for the slowest. Other factories pay a flat amount for reaching the production quota and a bonus based on output beyond the quota. Most factories also use financial disincentives. Employees are docked pay for being late for work, losing their ID cards, talking with coworkers, walking on the grass and producing less than the production quota.

Many factories in the Pearl River Delta require employees to work overtime. Work shifts often violate China's regulations, but many employees accept the long hours because of the pay-for-performance rewards. 'I always wanted to work overtime because we got paid more if we exceeded our daily quota of pillows,' says Wang, who works at a pillow factory. Unfortunately, the long hours also cause fatigue. Wang mangled his right hand on a machine while working overtime. 'I'd been working eleven hours straight and was tired,' he explains.

Most factory work is tedious. Li Mei's first job at a toy factory in the Pearl River Delta involved using four pens to paint the eyes on dolls. The 18-year-old was given exactly 7.2 seconds to paint each doll—about 4000 every day. Eventually, the paint fumes made Li Mei too faint to work, so she was moved to another department that stamped out plastic doll parts. Again, the work was repetitive: open the machine, insert the plastic, press the machine, remove the plastic. Li Mei repeated this cycle 3000 times each day. After several months of this work, Li Mei is exhausted and disillusioned. 'I'm tired to death and I don't earn much,' she says despondently. 'It makes everything meaningless.'[1]

This opening vignette is not a good news story about rewards and job design, but it does illustrate the importance of pay and job duties in motivating and demotivating employees. This chapter looks at both of these topics, as well as two other applied performance practices: empowerment and self-leadership. The chapter begins by examining the meaning of money. This is followed by an overview of financial reward practices, including the different types of rewards and how to implement rewards effectively. Next, we look at the dynamics of job design, including specific job design strategies for motivating employees. We then consider the elements of empowerment, as well as conditions that support empowerment. The final part of the chapter explains how employees manage their own performance through self-leadership.

THE MEANING OF MONEY IN THE WORKPLACE

Rewarding people with money is one of the oldest and certainly the most widespread applied performance practices. At the most basic level, money and other financial rewards represent a form of exchange; employees provide their labour, skill and knowledge in return for money and benefits from the organisation. From this perspective, money and related rewards align employee goals with organisational goals. This concept of economic exchange can be found across cultures. The word for *pay* in Malaysian and Slovak means 'to replace a loss'; in Hebrew and Swedish it means 'making equal'.[2]

However, money is much more than an object of compensation for an employee's contribution to organisational objectives. Money relates to our needs, our emotions and our self-concept. It is a symbol of achievement and status, a reinforcer and motivator, and a source of enhanced or reduced anxiety.[3] According to one source, 'Money is probably the most emotionally meaningful object in contemporary life: only food and sex are its close competitors as common carriers of such strong and diverse feelings, significance and strivings.'[4]

The meaning of money varies considerably from one person to the next.[5] Studies report that money is viewed as a symbol of status and prestige, as a source of security, as a source of evil, or as a source of anxiety or feelings of inadequacy. It is considered a 'taboo' topic in many social settings. It has been described both as a 'tool' (i.e. money is valued because it is an instrument for acquiring other things of value) and as a 'drug' (i.e. money is an object of addictive value in itself). One large-scale study revealed that money generates a variety of emotions, most of which are negative, such as anxiety, depression, anger and helplessness.[6] A widely studied model of money attitudes suggests that people have a strong 'money ethic' when they believe that money is not evil; they view it as a symbol of achievement, respect and power; and they believe that it should be budgeted carefully. These attitudes toward money influence an individual's ethical conduct, organisational citizenship, and many other behaviours and attitudes.[7]

The meaning of money seems to differ between men and women. One large-scale survey revealed that in almost all 43 countries studied men attached more importance or value to money than do women. Men particularly tend to view money as a symbol of power and status.[8] Personal and cultural values influence the meaning of money. People in countries with high power distance (such as China and Japan) tend to have a high respect and priority for money, whereas people in countries with a strong egalitarian culture (such as Denmark, Austria and Israel) are discouraged from openly talking about money or displaying their personal wealth. One study suggests that Swiss culture values saving money whereas Italian culture places more value on spending it.[9]

Many experts now believe that money is a much more important motivator than was previously thought, more because of its inherent or symbolic value than because of what it can buy.[10] Philosopher John Stuart Mill made this observation 150 years ago when he wrote: 'The love of money is not only one of the strongest moving forces of human life, but money is, in many cases, desired in and for itself.'[11] One recent study found that people who are more highly paid have higher job performance because the higher pay cheque makes them feel more valued in the organisation (i.e. they have a more positive self-concept). Others have pointed out that the symbolic value of money and other rewards is particularly motivational when few people receive this reward. In these situations, the reward gives beneficiaries a degree of social distinction, which is consistent with the drive to acquire, introduced in Chapter 5.

Overall, current organisational behaviour knowledge indicates that money is much more than a means of exchange between employer and employee. It fulfils a variety of needs, influences emotions, and shapes or represents a person's self-concept. This is important to remember when the employer is distributing financial rewards in the workplace. Over the next few pages, we look at various reward practices and how to improve the implementation of performance-based rewards.

FINANCIAL REWARD PRACTICES

LEARNING OBJECTIVE

Discuss the advantages and disadvantages of the four reward objectives.

Financial rewards comes in many forms, which can be organised into the four specific objectives identified in Exhibit 6.1: membership/seniority, job status, competencies and task performance.

Exhibit 6.1 *Reward Objectives, Advantages and Disadvantages*

Reward objective	Sample rewards	Advantages	Disadvantages
Membership/ seniority	• Fixed pay • Most employee benefits • Paid time off	• May attract applicants • Minimises stress of insecurity • Reduces turnover	• Doesn't directly motivate performance • May discourage poor performers from leaving • 'Golden handcuffs' may undermine performance
Job status	• Promotion-based pay increase • Status-based benefits	• Tries to maintain internal equity • Minimises pay discrimination • Motivates employees to compete for promotions	• Encourages hierarchy, which may increase costs and reduce responsiveness • Reinforces status differences • Motivates job competition and exaggerated job worth
Competencies	• Pay increase based on competency • Skill-based pay	• Improves workforce flexibility • Tends to improve quality • Is consistent with employability	• Relies on subjective measurement of competencies • Skill-based pay plans are expensive
Task performance	• Commissions • Merit pay • Gainsharing • Profit sharing • Share options	• Motivates task performance • Attracts performance-oriented applicants • Organisational rewards create an ownership culture • Pay variability may avoid lay-offs during downturns	• May weaken job content motivation • May distance reward giver from receiver • May discourage creativity • Tends to address symptoms, not underlying causes of behaviour

Membership- and Seniority-Based Rewards

Membership-based and seniority-based rewards (sometimes called 'pay for pulse') represent the largest part of most pay cheques. Some employee benefits, such as free or discounted meals in the company cafeteria, remain the same for everyone, whereas others increase with seniority. For example, Solid Energy in New Zealand reportedly has a 'loyalty bonus', which pays $5000 to employees who stay with the company for two years of continuous work. Many Asian companies distribute a 'thirteenth month' bonus, which every employee expects to receive each year no matter how well the company performed over the previous year. Although many Japanese firms have shifted to performance-based pay, others have retained or returned to wage scales based on the employee's age. 'Even during that period [when the employee's performance is below expectations], we raise salaries according to their age,' says the president of Tokai Rubber Industries Ltd., which returned to age-based salaries after discarding a short-lived performance-based pay plan.[12]

These membership- and seniority-based rewards potentially attract job applicants (particularly those who desire predictable income) and reduce turnover. However, they do not directly motivate job performance; on the contrary, they discourage poor performers from seeking work better suited to their abilities. Instead, the good performers are lured to better paying jobs. Some of these rewards are also 'golden handcuffs'—they discourage employees from quitting because of deferred bonuses or generous benefits that are not available elsewhere. However, golden handcuffs potentially weaken job performance because they generate continuance rather than affective commitment (see Chapter 4).

Job Status–Based Rewards

job evaluation Systematically rating the worth of jobs within an organisation by measuring their required skill, effort, responsibility and working conditions.

Almost every organisation rewards employees to some extent on the basis of the status or worth of the jobs they occupy. In some parts of the world, companies measure job worth through **job evaluation**. Most job evaluation methods give higher value to jobs that require more skill and effort, have more responsibility and have more difficult working conditions.[13] The more values assigned to a job, the higher the minimum and maximum pay for people in that job. As well as receiving higher pay, employees with more valued jobs sometimes receive larger offices, company-paid vehicles and other perks.

Rewards based on job status try to improve feelings of fairness, such as that people in higher-valued jobs should get higher pay. These rewards also motivate employees to compete for promotions. However, at a time when companies are trying to be more cost-efficient and responsive to the external environment, job-status–based rewards potentially do the opposite by encouraging a bureaucratic hierarchy. These rewards also reinforce a status mentality, whereas Generation-X and Generation-Y employees expect a more egalitarian workplace. Furthermore, status-based pay potentially motivates employees to compete with each other for higher status jobs, and to raise the value of their own jobs by exaggerating job duties and hoarding resources.[14]

Competency-Based Rewards

Over the past two decades, many companies have shifted reward priorities from job status to skills, knowledge and other competencies that lead to superior performance. The most common competency-based reward practices identify a set of competencies (adaptability, team orientation, technical expertise, leadership and so on) relevant to all jobs within a broad pay group, and give employees within each group higher pay rates as they improve those competencies.[15] In other words, rather than paying people for the specific jobs that they perform, competency-based plans pay people for their assessed skills and knowledge, whether they currently use those competencies in their job duties or not. Job-status-based pay has not been completely abandoned, because the broad pay groups reflect job status (the technical staff pay range is lower than the senior executive pay range, for example). Within those pay groups, however, employees are rewarded for skills, knowledge and other competencies. This reward system is sometimes known as *broadbanding* because several jobs with narrow pay ranges are grouped together into a much broader pay range.

Skill-based pay plans are a more specific variation of competency-based rewards in which people receive higher pay based on their mastery of measurable skills. For example, Sutton Tools in Australia, and its subsidiary Patience and Nicholson in New Zealand, pay production employees based on the number of skill blocks they have mastered. Employees at the precision cutting tools company (which produces drill bits, jigsaw blades and so on) receive higher pay rates as they learn to operate different machines and pass industry standards tests.[16]

Competency-based rewards motivate employees to learn new skills.[17] This tends to improve organisational effectiveness by creating a more flexible workforce; more employees are multiskilled for performing a variety of jobs, and they can more easily adapt to new practices in a dynamic environment. Product or service quality also tends to improve because employees with multiple skills are more likely to understand the work process and know how to improve it. However, competency-based pay plans have not always worked out as well as promised by their advocates. They are often overdesigned, making them difficult to communicate to employees. Competency definitions are often vague, which raises questions about fairness when employers are relying on these definitions to award pay increases. Skill-based pay systems measure specific skills, so they are usually more objective. However, they are expensive because employees spend more time learning new tasks.[18]

Performance-Based Rewards

Identify several performance-based rewards at the team level and organisational level.

Performance-based rewards have existed since ancient Babylonian days 4000 years ago, but their popularity has increased dramatically over the past couple of decades.[19] Here is an overview of some of the most popular individual, team and organisational performance-based rewards.

Individual Rewards

Individual performance rewards are fairly common throughout the Pacific rim. The opening vignette to this chapter describes how most factory workers in China are on a piece rate pay system in which they earn money for each product they complete. Housekeeping staff in some British hotels also earn a piece rate for each room they clean (about $3 per room). Real estate agents and other salespeople typically earn *commissions*, in which their pay increases with sales volume. Many employees receive individual bonuses or awards for accomplishing a specific task or exceeding annual performance goals. For example, a dozen top performing managers at Stefan hair salons, Queensland's largest hairstylist company, were awarded a free trip to Paris and given the keys to a fleet of luxury cars.[20]

Team Rewards

As organisations have shifted their focus from individuals to teams, they have also introduced more team-based rewards to support a team environment. Forward Media is a case in point.

Nucor Rewards the Team

Will Crockett/Shoot Smarter

Nucor's high-performance culture is fuelled by team and organisational rewards representing up to two-thirds of annual pay.

TWO DECADES AGO, NUCOR was an upstart in an industry dominated by Bethlehem Steel, National Steel and other mega-firms. Today, battered by global competition, two-thirds of American steel companies have disappeared or are under bankruptcy protection. Nucor, on the other hand, has become the largest steel company in America and the tenth largest in the world. Although it now employs more than 12 000 people (most in the United States), Nucor remains nimble, highly competitive and profitable.

What's Nucor's secret to success? One of the most important factors is its performance-based reward system. In recent years, the average Nucor steelworker has annually earned more than $80 000 (all figures in US currency), but most of that pay is variable—it depends on team and organisation performance. 'We pay a real low base wage, but high bonuses on a weekly basis,' explains a Nucor

'We have seen individual incentive programs fail,' says James Ward, who cofounded the enterprise software consulting firm, based in Sydney, a decade ago with his wife, Nadia. 'We set a group revenue target for each team, then give people a bonus according to the profit their team achieves.'[21] One of the most successful companies to apply team (as well as organisational) rewards is Nucor, Inc. As Reality Check 6.1 describes, America's largest steelmaker rewards teams for higher output and applies financial penalties if their output falls below satisfactory quality.

gainsharing plans Team-based rewards that calculate bonuses from the work unit's cost savings and productivity improvement.

Gainsharing plans are a form of team-based compensation that calculates bonuses from the work unit's cost savings and productivity improvement. Whole Foods Market uses this form of team incentive. The American food retailer assigns a monthly payroll budget to teams operating various departments within a store. If payroll money is unspent at the end of the month, the surplus is divided among members of that team.[23] American hospitals have cautiously introduced a form of gainsharing whereby medical practitioners and other hospital staff within a particular unit (cardiology, orthopaedics, and so on) are collectively rewarded for cost reductions in surgery and patient care. One recent study found that introduction of gainsharing in six hospital cardiology units reduced costs per patient by more than 7 per cent. Almost all of this cost reduction occurred through lower prices (likely due to standardised purchasing) rather than reduced use of supplies.[24] More generally, gainsharing plans tend to improve team dynamics, knowledge sharing and pay satisfaction. They also create a reasonably strong link between effort and performance because much of the cost reduction and labour efficiency is within the team's control.[25]

REALITY CHECK 6.1

executive. 'The bonuses are based on the quality and tons produced and shipped through a team. The average base pay is about $9 to $10 an hour, but they could get an additional $15 to $20 an hour for bonuses.' These bonuses are paid to everyone on the team, which might include 12 to 20 people. Nucor does not limit the amount of bonus a team can receive, but it is usually equal or double the base pay.

Nucor's team bonus system relies on quality of output, not just quantity. If employees catch a bad batch of steel before it leaves their work area, that tonnage of product is subtracted from the team's weekly bonus calculation. If the bad batch makes its way to the next internal customer or shipping department within the mini-mill, two times the tonnage of bad product is subtracted from the team's bonus. And if the bad product makes its way to the customer, the team loses a bonus amount equal to three times that amount of product.

Production employees have the highest variable pay, but Nucor's professional and administrative employees also earn bonuses, representing about one-third of their salary, that are based on their division's performance. In addition to these team and division rewards, Nucor employees receive an annual profit-sharing bonus representing 10 per cent of the company's operating profit. This has been as much as $18 000 per employee in some recent years.[22]

Organisational Rewards

Along with using individual and team-based rewards, many firms rely on organisational-level rewards to motivate employees. Some firms reward all staff members for achieving challenging sales goals or other indicators of organisational performance. **Employee share ownership plans (ESOPs)** encourage employees to buy company shares, usually at a discounted price or through a no-interest loan. The financial incentive takes the form of dividends and market appreciation of the stock. Only about 4 per cent of the Australian workforce holds shares through these plans, although this is as high as 22 per cent of employees in manufacturing and 19 per cent in finance and insurance. Fosters Group and Lend Lease are among the Australian companies with broad-based ESOPs (available to most or all employees). Beca, the New Zealand-based engineering and related services company, is owned entirely by its 1500 employees located in two dozen countries.[26]

employee share ownership plans (ESOPs) Reward systems that encourage employees to buy company shares.

While ESOPs involve purchasing company shares, **share options** give employees the right to purchase shares from the company at a future date at a predetermined price, up to a fixed expiration date. For example, an employer might offer employees the right to purchase 100 shares at $50 at any time in the next two to six years. If the share price is, say, $60 two years later, employees could earn $10 from these options, or they could wait up to six years for the share price to rise further. If shares never rise above $50 during that time, they are 'out of the money' and employees would just let the options expire. The intention of share options is to motivate employees to make the company more profitable, thereby

share options Reward systems that give employees the right to purchase company shares at a future date at a predetermined price.

raising the company's share price and enabling them to reap the value above the exercise price of the share options.

profit-sharing plan A reward system that pays bonuses to employees on the basis of the previous year's level of corporate profits.

Profit-sharing plans, a third organisational-level reward, calculate bonuses from the previous year's level of corporate profits. REDARC Electronics, the South Australian electronic voltage converter manufacturer, pays all employees the same size of bonus calculated from the company's profits each year.[27] As mentioned earlier in Reality Check 6.1, Nucor employees earn a profit-sharing bonus on top of their fixed pay and team bonuses. Each year, the steelmaker distributes 10 per cent of its earnings before taxes to employees, a percentage that recently amounted to more than $18 000 per employee.

Evaluating Organisational-Level Rewards

How effective are organisational-level rewards? Research indicates that ESOPs and share options tend to create an 'ownership culture' in which employees feel aligned with the organisation's success.[28] Profit sharing tends to create less ownership culture, but it has the advantage of automatically adjusting employee compensation with the firm's prosperity, thereby reducing the need for lay-offs or negotiated pay reductions during recessions.

The main problem with ESOPs, share options and profit sharing is that employees often perceive a weak connection between individual effort and corporate profits or the value of company shares. Even in small firms, the company's stock price or profitability is influenced by economic conditions, competition and other factors beyond the employee's immediate control. This low individual performance-to-outcome expectancy (see Chapter 5) weakens employee motivation. Another concern is that some companies, notably in the United States, use ESOPs as a replacement for employee superannuation (pension) plans. This is a risky strategy because the superannuation funds lack diversification. If the company goes bankrupt, employees lose both their jobs and a large portion of their retirement nest egg.[29]

Describe five ways to improve reward effectiveness.

Improving Reward Effectiveness

Performance-based rewards have come under attack over the years for discouraging creativity, distancing management from employees, distracting employees from the meaningfulness of the work itself and being quick fixes that ignore the true causes of poor performance. While these issues have kernels of truth under specific circumstances, they do not necessarily mean that we should abandon performance-based pay. On the contrary, as the high-performance work practices perspective of organisational effectiveness advises (see Chapter 1), top-performing companies are more likely to have performance-based rewards.[30] Reward systems do motivate most employees, but only under the right conditions. Here are some of the more important strategies for improving reward effectiveness.

Link Rewards to Performance

Behaviour modification theory (Chapter 3) and expectancy theory (Chapter 5) both recommend that employees with better performance should be rewarded more than those with poorer performance. Unfortunately, as was mentioned in Chapter 5, this simple principle seems to be unusually difficult to apply. Few employees see a relationship between job performance and the amount of pay they and coworkers receive. Employees get particularly ruffled by the subjectivity and bias in annual performance appraisals. 'After the last one I was spitting,' recalls an IT employee in New Zealand. 'I was getting graded on projects and activities I hadn't even agreed to take on!'[31]

How can companies improve the pay–performance linkage? Inconsistencies and bias can be minimised by introducing gainsharing, ESOPs and other plans that use objective performance measures. Where subjective measures of performance are necessary, companies should rely on multiple sources of information. Companies also need to apply rewards soon after the performance occurs, and in a large-enough dose (such as a bonus rather than a pay increase), so that employees experience positive emotions when they receive the reward.[32]

Ensure that Rewards are Relevant

Companies need to align rewards with performance that is within the employee's control. The more employees see a 'line of sight' between their daily actions and the reward, the more they are motivated to improve performance. BHP Billiton applies this principle by awarding bonuses to top executives based on the company's overall performance, whereas front-line mining staff earn bonuses based on the production output, safety performance and other local indicators. Reward systems also need to correct for situational factors. Salespeople in one region may have higher sales because the economy is stronger there than elsewhere, so sales bonuses need to be adjusted for such economic factors.

Use Team Rewards for Interdependent Jobs

Team rewards should be used rather than individual rewards when employees work in highly interdependent jobs because it is difficult to measure individual performance in these situations. Nucor relies on team-based bonuses for this reason; steelmaking is a team effort, so employees earn bonuses based on team performance. Team rewards also encourage cooperation, which is more important when work is highly interdependent. A third benefit of team rewards is that they tend to support employee preferences for team-based work. One concern, however, is that employees (particularly the most productive employees) in Australia, New Zealand and many other low-collectivism cultures prefer rewards based on their individual performance rather than team performance.[33]

Ensure That Rewards Are Valued

It seems obvious that rewards work best when they are valued. Yet companies sometimes make false assumptions about what employees want, with unfortunate consequences. The solution, of course, is to ask employees what they value. The Campbell Soup Company did this a few years ago at its distribution centres in Canada. Executives thought the employees would ask for more money in a special team reward program. Instead, distribution staff said the most valued reward was a leather jacket with the Campbell Soup logo on the back. The leather jackets cost much less yet were worth much more than the financial bonus the company had intended to distribute.[34]

Watch Out for Unintended Consequences

Performance-based reward systems sometimes have an unexpected—and undesirable—effect on employee behaviours. Consider the pizza company that decided to reward its drivers for on-time delivery. The plan got more hot pizzas to customers on time, but it also increased the accident rates of the company's drivers because the incentive motivated them to drive recklessly.[35] Reality Check 6.2 describes a few other examples in which reward systems had unintended consequences. The solution here is to carefully think through the consequences of rewards and, where possible, test incentives in a pilot project before applying them across the organisation.

When Rewards Go Wrong

Getty

UBS suffered a $37 *billion* loss in one year because its bonus system rewarded staff for short-term revenue without imposing any penalties for buying high-risk securities to generate that revenue.

THERE IS AN OLD saying that 'what gets rewarded gets done'. But what companies reward isn't always what they had intended their employees to do. Here are a few dramatic examples of how performance-based rewards produce unintended consequences:

- UBS AG, Switzerland's largest bank, recently lost more than $37 billion (yes, *billion*) in one year because of its exposure to high-risk mortgage securities. The massive loss forced the bank to lay off staff, close down a hedge fund business, borrow from foreign governments and suffer an exodus of clients. Many financial institutions suffered horrendous losses (and a few went bankrupt) during this subprime mortgage crisis, but UBS openly acknowledged that a faulty reward system was partly responsible. Specifically, its bonus plan motivated its traders to generate short-term revenue without penalising them for exposing the bank to high-risk investments. 'Essentially, bonuses were measured against gross revenue with no formal account taken of the quality or sustainability of those earnings,' says a UBS report submitted to the Swiss banking regulator.[36]
- Most bus drivers in Santiago, Chile, are paid by the number of paying passengers rather than by the hours worked. This incentive system motivates drivers to begin their route on time, take shorter breaks and drive efficiently. Unfortunately, it also has several undesirable consequences. To collect more passengers, these drivers often stop abruptly and drive away

Financial rewards come in many forms and, as mentioned at the outset of this section, influence employees in complex ways. But money isn't the only thing that motivates people to join an organisation and perform effectively. 'At the end of the year [employees] see the benefits by way of their incentive or gainshare bonus, but incentives alone are not enough,' advises John Gomersall, chief executive of Pretoria Portland Cement in South Africa. Along with revising rewards, Pretoria Cement transformed jobs so employees have more autonomy and interesting work. 'Through the process, the lives of all of our employees both at work and at home have been enriched,' says Gomersall.[41] In other words, companies motivate employees mainly by designing interesting and challenging jobs, the topic we discuss next.

JOB DESIGN PRACTICES

How do you build a better job? That question has challenged organisational behaviour experts, psychologists, engineers and economists for a few centuries. Some jobs have very few tasks and usually require very little skill. Other jobs are immensely complex and require years of experience

REALITY CHECK 6.2

before passengers have safely departed or stepped on board, causing thousands of injuries each year. Some drivers will drive past a stop altogether if there is only one passenger waiting. Drivers routinely leave the doors open to save time, which causes a quarter of passenger accidents and deaths. One study found that Santiago bus drivers who are paid per passenger cause twice as many traffic accidents as drivers paid per hour.[37]

- Share options are supposed to motivate executives to improve corporate performance. Instead, they seem to motivate some leaders to distort or misrepresent the company's performance through dodgy accounting practices. One recent study found that financial misrepresentation was associated with executive share options but not with bonuses or other forms of executive compensation. Another report estimated that for every 25 per cent increase in share options awarded to executives, the risk of fraud rises by 68 per cent. Companies with the largest corporate frauds in recent years have, on average, eight times as many share options as similar companies that did not experience fraud.[38]
- Integrated steel companies often rewarded managers for increased labour efficiency. The lower the labour hours required to produce a tonne of steel, the larger the manager's bonus. Unfortunately, steel firms usually didn't count the work of outside contractors in the formula, so the reward system motivated managers to hire expensive contractors in the production process. By employing more contractors, the true cost of production increased, not decreased.[39]
- Toyota rewards its dealerships on the basis of customer satisfaction surveys, not just car sales. What Toyota discovered, however, is that this motivates dealers to increase satisfaction scores, not customer satisfaction. One Toyota dealership received high ratings because it offered free detailing to every customer who returned a 'Very Satisfied' survey. The dealership even had a special copy of the survey showing clients which boxes to check off. This increased customer ratings, but not customer satisfaction.[40]

and learning to master them. From one extreme to the other, jobs have different effects on work efficiency and employee motivation. The challenge, at least from the organisation's perspective, is to find the right combination so that work is performed efficiently but employees are motivated and engaged.[42] This challenge requires careful **job design**—the process of assigning tasks to a job, including the interdependency of those tasks with other jobs. A *job* is a set of tasks performed by one person. To understand this issue more fully, let's begin by describing early job design efforts aimed at increasing work efficiency through job specialisation.

job design The process of assigning tasks to a job, including the interdependency of those tasks with other jobs.

Job Design and Work Efficiency

LEARNING OBJECTIVE 

Discuss the advantages and disadvantages of job specialisation.

The opening vignette to this chapter not only described how factory workers in China are paid; it also highlighted how much of the work they produce is tedious and repetitive. For example, recall Li Mei, who painted the eyes on 4000 dolls every day. Even white-collar jobs (whether in China or elsewhere) can be highly repetitive. For instance, Melody Zou earns close to $600 per month as an accountant for a media company in Shanghai, but the novelty of her work wore off after the first six months. 'I do the same thing day by day, month by month, year by year,' complains Zou.[43]

job specialisation The result of a division of labour where work is subdivided into separate jobs and assigned to different people.

These employees perform jobs with a high degree of **job specialisation**. Job specialisation occurs when the work required to make a toy—or any other product or service—is subdivided into separate jobs assigned to different people. Each resulting job includes a narrow subset of tasks, usually completed in a short cycle time. *Cycle time* is the time required to complete the task before starting over with a new work unit. Li Mei had an average cycle time of 7.2 seconds, which means she repeated the same set of tasks at least 450 times each hour.

Why would companies divide work into such tiny bits? The simple answer is that job specialisation improves work efficiency. One reason that efficiency is higher is that employees have fewer tasks to juggle and therefore spend less time changing activities. They also require fewer physical and mental skills to accomplish the assigned work, so less time and resources are needed for training. A third reason is that shorter work cycles allow employees to practise their tasks more frequently, so jobs are mastered quickly. A fourth reason why work efficiency increases is that employees with specific aptitudes or skills can be matched more precisely to the jobs for which they are best suited.[44]

The efficiency of job specialisation was noted more than 2300 years ago by the Chinese philosopher Mencius and the Greek philosopher Plato. In the 1400s and 1500s, the Arsenal of Venice employed up to 4000 people in specialised jobs (caulkers, paymasters, division managers, carpenters, iron workers, warehouse supervisors, and so on) to build ships and many accessories such as cannons, ropes, oars and armour. The state-owned organisation became so efficient that in 1570 it built 100 ships in two months. After construction, the galleons travelled along a waterway where workers apportioned food, ammunition, cordage and other supplies from specially designed warehouses. This assembly line could outfit 10 galleons in just six hours.[45]

Scottish economist Adam Smith wrote 250 years ago about the advantages of job specialisation. Smith described a small factory where 10 pin makers collectively produced as many as 48 000 pins per day because they performed specialised tasks, such as straightening, cutting, sharpening, grinding and whitening the pins. In contrast, Smith explained that if these 10 people worked alone producing complete pins, they would collectively manufacture no more than 200 pins per day.[46]

Scientific Management

scientific management The practice of systematically partitioning work into its smallest elements and standardising tasks to achieve maximum efficiency.

One of the strongest advocates of job specialisation was Frederick Winslow Taylor, an American industrial engineer who introduced the principles of **scientific management** in the early 1900s.[47] Scientific management consists of a toolkit of activities. Some of these interventions—training, goal setting and work incentives—are common today but were rare until Taylor popularised them. However, scientific management is mainly associated with high levels of job specialisation and standardisation of tasks to achieve maximum efficiency.

According to Taylor, the most effective companies have detailed procedures and work practices developed by engineers, enforced by supervisors and executed by employees. Even the supervisor's tasks should be divided: one person manages operational efficiency, another manages inspection and another is the disciplinarian. Taylor and other industrial engineers demonstrated that scientific management significantly improves work efficiency. There is no doubt that some of the increased productivity can be credited to the training, goal setting and work incentives, but job specialisation quickly became popular in its own right.

Problems with Job Specialisation

Frederick Taylor and his contemporaries focused on how job specialisation reduces labour 'waste' by improving the mechanical efficiency of work (i.e. matching skills, faster learning, less switchover time). Yet they didn't seem to notice how this extreme job specialisation adversely affects employee attitudes and motivation. Some jobs—such as painting eyes on dolls—are so specialised that they soon become tedious, trivial and socially isolating. (Recall Li Mei's statement that her work situation 'makes everything meaningless'.) Employee turnover and absenteeism tend to be higher in specialised jobs with very short time cycles. Companies sometimes have to pay higher wages to attract job applicants to this dissatisfying, narrowly defined work.[48]

Job specialisation often reduces work quality because employees see only a small part of the process. As one observer of an automobile assembly line reports: 'Often [employees] did not know how their jobs related to the total picture. Not knowing, there was no incentive to strive for quality—what did quality even mean as it related to a bracket whose function you did not understand?'[49]

Equally important, job specialisation can undermine the motivational potential of jobs. As work becomes specialised, it tends to become easier to perform but less interesting. As jobs become more complex, work motivation increases but the ability to master the job decreases. Maximum job performance occurs somewhere between these two extremes, where most people can eventually perform the job tasks efficiently yet the work remains interesting.

Job Design and Work Motivation

LEARNING OBJECTIVE

Diagram the job characteristics model of job design.

Industrial engineers may have overlooked the motivational effect of job characteristics, but it is now the central focus of many job design changes. Organisational behaviour scholar Frederick Herzberg is credited with shifting the spotlight when he introduced **motivator-hygiene theory** in the 1950s.[50] Motivator-hygiene theory proposes that employees experience job satisfaction when they fulfil growth and esteem needs (called *motivators*), and experience dissatisfaction when they have poor working conditions, job security and other factors categorised as lower order needs (called *hygienes*). Herzberg argued that only characteristics of the job itself motivate employees, whereas the hygiene factors merely prevent dissatisfaction. It might seem obvious to us today that the job itself is a source of motivation, but the concept was radical when Herzberg proposed the idea.

motivator-hygiene theory Herzberg's theory stating that employees are primarily motivated by growth and esteem needs, not by lower level needs.

Motivator-hygiene theory has been soundly rejected due to lack of research support, but Herzberg's ideas generated new thinking about the motivational potential of the job itself.[51] Out of subsequent research emerged the **job characteristics model**, shown in Exhibit 6.2. The job characteristics model identifies five core job dimensions that produce three psychological states. Employees who experience these psychological states tend to have higher levels of internal work motivation (motivation from the work itself), job satisfaction (particularly satisfaction with the work itself) and work effectiveness.[52]

job characteristics model A job design model that relates the motivational properties of jobs to specific personal and organisational consequences of those properties.

Core Job Characteristics

The job characteristics model identifies five core job characteristics. Under the right conditions, employees are more motivated and satisfied when jobs have higher levels of these characteristics.

Exhibit 6.2 *The Job Characteristics Model*

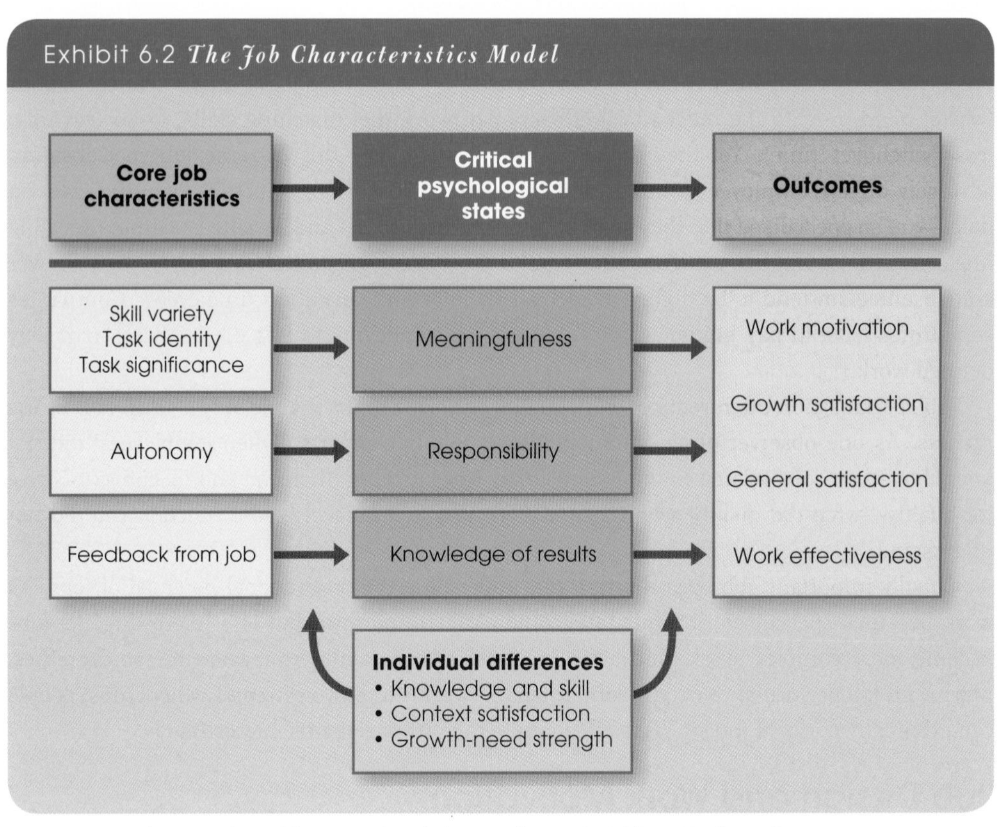

Source: J. R. Hackman and G. Oldham, *Work Redesign* (Reading, MA: Addison-Wesley, 1980), 90.

skill variety The extent to which employees must use different skills and talents to perform tasks within their jobs.

task identity The degree to which a job requires completion of a whole or an identifiable piece of work.

task significance The degree to which a job has a substantial impact on the organisation and/or larger society.

autonomy The degree to which a job gives employees the freedom, independence and discretion to schedule their work, and to determine the procedures used in completing it.

SKILL VARIETY **Skill variety** refers to the use of different skills and talents to complete a variety of work activities. For example, retail salespeople who normally only serve customers might be assigned the additional duties of stocking inventory and changing shopfront displays.

TASK IDENTITY **Task identity** is the degree to which a job requires completion of a whole or identifiable piece of work, such as assembling an entire broadband modem rather than just soldering in the circuitry.

TASK SIGNIFICANCE **Task significance** is the degree to which the job affects the organisation and/or larger society. For instance, to make employees more aware of the task significance of their jobs, Rolls Royce Engine Services in Oakland, California invited customer representatives to talk to production staff about why the quality of these engines is important to them. '[This program] gives employees with relatively repetitive jobs the sense that they're not just working on a part but rather are key in keeping people safe,' explains a Rolls Royce Engine Services executive.[53]

AUTONOMY Jobs with high levels of **autonomy** provide freedom, independence and discretion in scheduling the work and determining the procedures to be used to complete the work. In autonomous jobs, employees make their own decisions rather than relying on detailed instructions from supervisors or procedure manuals.

Camera-Ready Job Enlargement (and Enrichment)

Television networks usually require several people to prepare a news feature: a reporter, camera operator, sound operator, video editor, and often a lighting person and on-site producer. Australian network SBS threw out that production model a decade ago for its popular news program *Dateline*. Instead, *Dateline* relies on individual video journalists (VJs) to perform most or all of these jobs. This extreme job enlargement not only lowers production costs, but also allows the journalists access to places that would be prohibited to a large news crew. Award-winning *Dateline* video journalist Mark Davis says the video journalist job offers much more personal control and freedom. 'I find video journalism more personal and I like the ability to bring spontaneity to reporting,' says Davis, shown here on location in East Timor. 'The real advantage to being on my own is that you make your own decisions.'[57]

The Age

job satisfaction and work motivation, along with lower absenteeism and turnover. Productivity is also higher when task identity and job feedback are improved. Product and service quality tend to improve because job enrichment increases the jobholder's felt responsibility and sense of ownership over the product or service.[59]

One way to increase job enrichment is by combining highly interdependent tasks into one job. This *natural grouping* approach is reflected in the video journalist job. This was earlier described as an enlarged job, but it is also an example of job enrichment because it naturally groups tasks together to complete an entire product (i.e. a news story). By forming natural work units, jobholders have stronger feelings of responsibility for an identifiable body of work. They feel a sense of ownership, which tends to increase job quality. Forming natural work units increases task identity and task significance because employees perform a complete service or create a complete product, and can more readily see how their work affects others.

A second job enrichment strategy, called *establishing client relationships*, involves putting employees in direct contact with their clients rather than using the supervisor as a go-between. By being directly responsible for specific clients, employees have more information and can make decisions affecting those clients.[60] Establishing client relationships also increases task significance because employees see a line-of-sight connection between their work and consequences for customers. City Telecom in Hong Kong redesigned customer service jobs around customers for this reason. 'We introduced a one-stop service for our customers,' explains Ellis Ng, City Telecom's head of learning and development. 'Each of our staff in the special duty unit (SDU) can handle all inquiries including sales, customer service and simple troubleshooting. They are divided into small working units and serve a set number of customers so they have the chance to build a rapport and create a personalised service.'[61]

Forming natural task groups and establishing client relationships are common ways to enrich jobs, but the heart of the job enrichment philosophy is to give employees more autonomy over their work. This basic idea is at the core of one of the most widely mentioned—and often misunderstood—practices, known as empowerment.

EMPOWERMENT PRACTICES

LEARNING OBJECTIVE

Define *empowerment* and identify strategies that support empowerment.

'Can an organisation let people do what they want, when they want, and how they want?' asks Ricardo Semler, CEO of Semco Corporation, SA in Sao Paulo, Brazil. The answer appears to be 'Yes'. Today, the industrial manufacturing and services company has 3000 employees who work in teams of 6 to 10 people. Employees choose their objectives, hire coworkers, calculate budgets, set their own salaries, decide when to come to work and elect their own bosses. The only policy manual is a comic book that introduces newcomers to Semco's democratic culture. 'Treating employees like two-year-olds is a comfortable norm for too many businesses. Perpetuating this behaviour will deal the killing blow to any organisation,' Semler warns. 'Treating employees like intelligent adults and allowing them to manage themselves is a business model that worked at Semco.'[62]

Semco Corporation might be considered the ultimate organisation of employee **empowerment**. *Empowerment* is a term that has been loosely tossed around in corporate circles and has been the subject of considerable debate among academics. However, the most widely accepted definition is that empowerment is a psychological concept represented by four dimensions: self-determination, meaning, competence and impact of the individual's role in the organisation. If any dimension weakens, the employee's sense of empowerment will weaken.[63]

empowerment A psychological concept in which people experience more self-determination, meaning, competence and impact regarding their role in the organisation.

SELF-DETERMINATION Empowered employees feel that they have freedom, independence and discretion over their work activities.

MEANING Employees who feel empowered care about their work and believe that what they do is important.

COMPETENCE Empowered people are confident about their ability to perform the work well and have a capacity to grow with new challenges.

IMPACT Empowered employees view themselves as active participants in the organisation; that is, their decisions and actions have an influence on the company's success.

Supporting Empowerment

Chances are that you have heard leaders say they are 'empowering' the workforce. Yet empowerment is a state of mind, so what these executives really mean is that they are changing the work environment to support the feeling of empowerment.[64] Numerous individual, job design and organisational or work-context factors support empowerment. At the individual level, employees must possess the necessary competencies to be able to perform the work as well as handle the additional decision-making requirements.[65] Job characteristics clearly influence the degree to which people feel empowered.[66] Employees are much more likely to experience self-determination when working in jobs with a high degree of autonomy and

Empowering Handelsbanken

Corbis

One of Europe's most successful banks doesn't believe in budgets or centralised financial targets. Executives at Svenska Handelsbanken AB learned decades ago that these costly controls from the head office stifle rather than motivate employees. Instead, the Swedish bank gives its 10 000 employees and managers across 450 branches in 21 countries (mostly Nordic countries and Britain) considerable autonomy to run the local branches as their own businesses. Branches have the freedom to prepare their own action plans as well as decide how to advertise products, how much to pay for property leases, how many staff to hire and so forth. 'The culture of our company is based on entrusting employees and allowing those who are closest to the customer and who know the customer best to take decisions,' says a Handelsbanken executive in Northern Britain. 'Being empowered and having this trust leads to better decisions and higher satisfaction.'[67]

minimal bureaucratic control. They experience more meaningfulness when working in jobs with high levels of task identity and task significance. They experience more self-confidence when working in jobs that allow them to receive feedback about their performance and accomplishments.

Several organisational and work-context factors also influence empowerment. Employees experience more empowerment in organisations where information and other resources are easily accessible. Empowerment also requires a learning orientation culture. In other words, empowerment flourishes in organisations that appreciate the value of employee learning and that accept reasonable mistakes as a natural part of the learning process. Furthermore, as mentioned above in describing Handelsbanken, empowerment requires corporate leaders who trust employees and are willing to take the risks that empowerment creates.[68]

With the right individuals, job characteristics and organisational environment, empowerment can substantially improve motivation and performance. For instance, a study of bank employees concluded that empowerment improved customer service and tended to reduce conflict between employees and their supervisors. A study of nurses reported that empowerment is associated with higher trust in management, which ultimately influences job satisfaction, belief and acceptance of organisational goals and values, and effective organisational commitment. Empowerment also tends to increase personal initiative because employees identify with and assume more psychological ownership of their work.[69]

LEARNING OBJECTIVE 

Describe the five elements of self-leadership.

SELF-LEADERSHIP PRACTICES

What is the most important characteristic that companies look for in their employees? Leadership potential, ability to work in a team and good communication skills are important, but a survey of 800 British employers concludes that they don't top the list. Instead, the most important employee characteristic is self-motivation. Nick Crosby can identify with these survey results. The manager at Bayer CropScience, a division of Germany-based conglomerate Bayer AG, is continually looking for job applicants who can lead themselves. 'We're not in the game these days of just getting people who can read, write and shovel stuff around,' Crosby insists. 'We need self-motivated people who work well with empowered teams—people who can think for themselves, do basic diagnosis, and keep the plants operating at an optimum.'[70]

Most of the concepts introduced in this chapter and in Chapter 5 have assumed that leaders do things to motivate employees. Certainly, these theories and practices are valuable, but they overlook the fact that the most successful employees ultimately motivate and manage themselves.

Self-Leadership Puts Accountant in Fast Forward

Angela Brkic

At 24, Katarina Vicelik is already a senior tax consultant with PricewaterhouseCoopers in Sydney and is working towards becoming a chartered accountant. Vicelik plans to take a master's degree after completing her CA, is looking at work opportunities in Europe, and wants to reach managerial level within three years. Vicelik regularly sets goals for herself, and reflects on where her future should be headed. In other words, she has moved well along in her career by practising self-leadership. 'If you want to make the most out of your career, anywhere, you've got to be self-motivated,' she advises. 'That's the only way you're going to get ahead.'[72]

In other words, they engage in self-leadership. **Self-leadership** refers to the process of influencing oneself to establish the self-direction and self-motivation needed to perform a task.[71] This concept includes a toolkit of behavioural activities borrowed from social learning theory and goal setting. It also includes constructive thought processes that have been extensively studied in sports psychology. Overall, self-leadership suggests that individuals mostly regulate their own actions through these behavioural and cognitive (thought) activities.

self-leadership The process of influencing oneself to establish the self-direction and self-motivation needed to perform a task.

Self-Leadership Strategies

Although self-leadership consists of several processes, the five main activities are identified in Exhibit 6.4. These elements, which generally follow each other in a sequence, are personal goal setting, constructive thought patterns, designing natural rewards, self-monitoring and self reinforcement.[73]

Personal Goal Setting

The first step in self-leadership is to set goals for your own work effort. This applies the ideas learned in Chapter 5 on goal setting, such as identifying goals that are specific, relevant and challenging. The main difference is that self-leadership involves setting goals alone, rather than having them assigned by or jointly decided with a supervisor. Research suggests that employees are more focused and perform better when they set their own goals, particularly in combination with other self-leadership practices.[74] Personal goal setting also requires a high degree of self-awareness, because people need to understand their current behaviour and performance before establishing meaningful goals for personal development.

Constructive Thought Patterns

Before beginning a task and while performing it, employees should engage in positive (constructive) thoughts about that work and its accomplishment. In particular, employees are more motivated and better prepared to accomplish a task after they have engaged in positive self-talk and mental imagery.

POSITIVE SELF-TALK Do you ever talk to yourself? Most of us do, according to a major study of university students.[75] **Self-talk** refers to any situation in which we talk to ourselves about our own thoughts or actions. Some of this internal communication assists the decision-making process, such as weighing the advantages of a particular choice. Self-leadership is mostly interested in evaluative self-talk, in which you evaluate your capabilities and accomplishments.

self-talk The process of talking to ourselves about our own thoughts or actions.

Exhibit 6.4 *Elements of Self-Leadership*

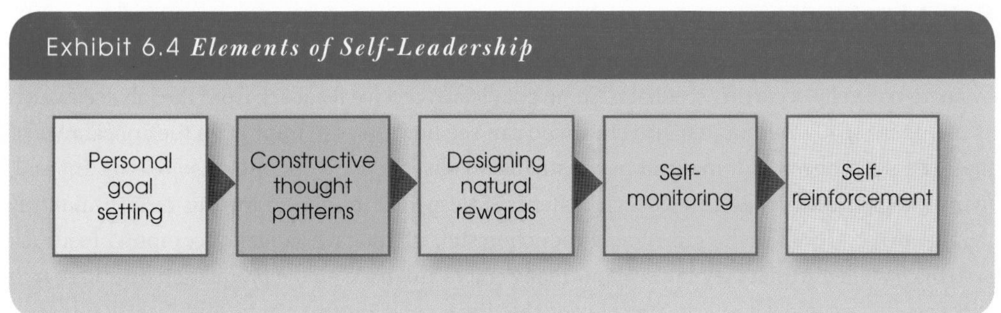

The problem is that most evaluative self-talk is negative; we criticise much more than encourage or congratulate ourselves. Negative self-talk undermines our confidence and potential to perform a particular task. In contrast, positive self-talk creates a 'can-do' belief and thereby increases motivation by raising our effort-to-performance expectancy. We often hear that professional athletes 'psych' themselves up before an important event. They tell themselves that they can achieve their goal and that they have practised enough to reach that goal. They are motivating themselves through self-talk.

mental imagery Mentally practising a task and visualising its successful completion.

MENTAL IMAGERY You've probably heard the phrase 'I'll cross that bridge when I come to it!' Self-leadership takes the opposite view. It suggests that we need to mentally practise a task and imagine successfully performing it beforehand. This process, known as **mental imagery**, has two parts. One part involves mentally practising the task, anticipating obstacles to goal accomplishment and working out solutions to those obstacles before they occur. By mentally walking through the activities required to accomplish the task, we begin to see problems that may occur. We can then imagine what responses would be best for each contingency.[76]

While one part of mental imagery helps us to anticipate things that could go wrong, the other part involves visualising successful completion of the task. You might imagine the experience of completing the task and the positive results that follow, such as being promoted, receiving a prestigious award or taking time off work. This visualisation increases goal commitment and motivates people to complete the task effectively. This is the strategy that salesperson Tony Wang applies to motivate himself. 'Since I am in sales, I think about the reward I get for closing new business—the commission cheque—and the things it will allow me to do that I really enjoy,' explains Wang. 'Or I think about the feeling I get when I am successful at something and how it makes me feel good, and use that to get me going.'[77]

Designing Natural Rewards

Self-leadership recognises that employees actively craft their jobs. To varying degrees, they can alter tasks and work relationships to make the work more motivating.[78] One way to build natural rewards into the job is to alter the way a task is accomplished. People often have enough discretion in their jobs to make slight changes to suit their needs and preferences. 'In 28 years I do not think I have ever had a bad job—it is about the attitude that you bring to your work,' says Steve Collier, National Australia Bank's general manager of sales and distribution services. 'Self motivation has meant that even in tough times I have changed the job or changed the way I did it.' Collier's approach seems to work; he was recently awarded top honours for best contact centre leader in the world.[79]

Self-Monitoring

Self-monitoring is the process of keeping track at regular intervals of one's progress toward a goal by using naturally occurring feedback. Some people can receive feedback from the job itself, such as members of a lawn maintenance crew who can see how they are improving the appearance of their client's property. But many of us are unable to observe our work output so readily. Instead, many people need to design feedback systems. Salespeople might arrange to receive monthly reports on sales levels in their territory. Production staff might have gauges or computer feedback systems installed so that they can see how many errors are made on the production line. Research suggests that people who have control over the timing of performance feedback carry out their tasks better than do those with feedback assigned by others.[80]

Self-Reinforcement

Self-leadership includes the social learning theory concept of self-reinforcement (see Chapter 3). Self-reinforcement occurs whenever an employee has control over a reinforcer but doesn't 'take' the reinforcer until completing a self-set goal.[81] A common example is taking a break after reaching a predetermined stage of your work. The work break is a self-induced form of positive reinforcement. Self-reinforcement also occurs when you decide to do a more enjoyable task after completing a task that you dislike. For example, after slogging through a difficult report, you might decide to spend time doing a more pleasant task, such as catching up on industry news by scanning websites.

Effectiveness of Self-Leadership

Self-leadership is shaping up to be a valuable applied performance practice in organisational settings. A respectable body of research shows consistent support for most elements of self-leadership. Self-set goals and self-monitoring increased the frequency of wearing safety equipment among employees in a mining operation. Airline employees who received constructive thought training experienced better mental performance, enthusiasm and job satisfaction than coworkers who did not receive this training. Mental imagery helped supervisors and process engineers in a pulp-and-paper mill to transfer what they learned in an interpersonal communication skills class back to the job.[82] Studies also indicate that constructive thought processes improve individual performance in cycling, hockey goalkeeping, ice skating, soccer and other sports. Indeed, studies show that almost all Olympic athletes rely on mental rehearsal and positive self-talk to achieve their performance goals.[83]

Self-Leadership Contingencies

Identify specific personal and work-environment influences on self-leadership.

As with most other forms of organisational behaviour, self-leadership is more or less likely to occur depending on the person and the situation. With respect to individual differences, preliminary research suggests that self-leadership behaviours are more frequently found in people with higher levels of conscientiousness and extroversion. Some writers also suggest that people with a positive self-evaluation (i.e. self-esteem, self-efficacy and internal locus of control) are more likely to apply self-leadership strategies.[84]

Although the research is still very sparse, the work environment also seems to influence the extent to which employees engage in self-leadership strategies. In particular, employees require some degree of autonomy to engage in some or most aspects of self-leadership. They probably also feel more confident with self-leadership when their boss is empowering rather than controlling, and where there is a high degree of trust between them. Employees are also more likely to engage in self-monitoring in companies that emphasise continuous measurement of performance.[85] Overall, self-leadership promises to be an important concept and practice for improving employee motivation and performance.

CHAPTER SUMMARY

Money and other financial rewards are a fundamental part of the employment relationship, but their value and meaning varies from one person to the next. Organisations reward employees for their membership and seniority, job status, competencies and performance. Membership-based rewards may attract job applicants and seniority-based rewards reduce turnover, but these reward objectives tend to discourage turnover among those with the lowest performance. Rewards based on job status try to maintain internal equity and motivate employees to compete for promotions. However, they tend to encourage a bureaucratic hierarchy, support status differences, and motivate employees to compete and hoard resources. Competency-based rewards are becoming increasingly popular because they improve workforce flexibility and are consistent with the emerging idea of employability. However, they tend to be subjectively measured and can result in higher costs as employees spend more time learning new skills.

Awards and bonuses, commissions and other individual performance-based rewards have existed for centuries and are widely used. Many companies are shifting to team-based rewards such as gainsharing plans, and to organisational rewards such as employee share ownership plans (ESOPs), share options and profit sharing. ESOPs and share options create an ownership culture, but employees often perceive a weak connection between individual performance and the organisational reward.

Financial rewards have a number of limitations, but reward effectiveness can be improved in several ways. Organisational leaders should ensure that rewards are linked to work performance, rewards are aligned with performance within the employee's control, team rewards are used where jobs are interdependent, rewards are valued by employees and rewards have no unintended consequences.

Job design is the process of assigning tasks to a job, including the interdependency of those tasks with other jobs. Job specialisation subdivides work into separate jobs for different people. This increases work efficiency because employees master the tasks quickly, spend less time changing tasks, require less training and can be matched more closely with the jobs best suited to their skills. However, job specialisation may reduce work motivation; create mental health problems; lower product or service quality; and increase costs through discontentment, absenteeism and turnover.

Contemporary job design strategies reverse job specialisation through job rotation, job enlargement and job enrichment. The job characteristics model is a template for job redesign that specifies core job dimensions, psychological states and individual differences. Organisations introduce job rotation to reduce job boredom, develop a more flexible workforce and reduce the incidence of repetitive strain injuries. Two ways to enrich jobs are clustering tasks into natural groups and establishing client relationships.

Empowerment is a psychological concept represented by four dimensions: self-determination, meaning, competence, and the impact of the individual's role in the organisation. Individual characteristics seem to have a minor influence on empowerment. Job design is a major influence, particularly autonomy, task identity, task significance and job feedback. Empowerment is also supported at the organisational level through a learning orientation culture, sufficient information and resources, and corporate leaders who trust employees.

Self-leadership is the process of influencing ourselves to establish the self-direction and self-motivation needed to perform a task. This includes personal goal setting, constructive thought patterns, designing natural rewards, self-monitoring and self-reinforcement. Constructive thought patterns include self-talk and mental imagery. Self-talk occurs in any situation in which we talk to ourselves about our own thoughts or actions. Mental imagery involves mentally practising a task and imagining successfully performing it beforehand.

KEY TERMS

autonomy, p. 218
employee share ownership plans (ESOPs), p. 211
empowerment, p. 222
gainsharing plans, p. 210
job characteristics model, p. 217
job design, p. 215
job enlargement, p. 220
job enrichment, p. 220
job evaluation, p. 224
job rotation, p. 219
job specialisation, p. 216
mental imagery, p. 226
motivator-hygiene theory, p. 217
profit-sharing plans, p. 212
scientific management, p. 216
self-leadership, p. 225
self-talk, p. 225
share options, p. 211
skill variety, p. 218
task identity, p. 218
task significance, p. 218

Critical Thinking Questions

1 As a consultant, you have been asked to recommend either a gainsharing plan or a profit-sharing plan for employees who work in the four regional distribution and warehousing facilities of a large retail organisation. Which reward system would you recommend? Explain your answer.

2 You are a member of a team responsible for developing a reward system for your university faculty unit. Assume that the faculty is nonprofit, so profit sharing is not an option. What other team- or organisation-level rewards might work in this situation? Describe specific measures that could be used to calculate the amount of bonus.

3 Rotorua Tyre Corporation redesigned its production facilities around a team-based system. However, the company president believes that employees will not be motivated unless they receive incentives based on their individual performance. Give three reasons why Rotorua Tyre should introduce team-based rather than individual rewards in this setting.

4 What can organisations do to increase the effectiveness of financial rewards?

5 Most of us have watched pizzas being made while waiting in a pizzeria. What level of job specialisation do you usually notice in these operations? Why does this high or low level of specialisation exist? If some pizzerias have different levels of specialisation than others, identify the contingencies that might explain these differences.

6 Can a manager or supervisor 'empower' an employee? Discuss fully.

7 Describe a time when you practised self-leadership to successfully perform a task. With reference to each step in the self-leadership process, describe what you did to achieve this success.

8 Can self-leadership replace formal leadership in an organisational setting?

TEAM EXERCISE

Skill Builder 6.1

Is Student Work Enriched?

Purpose

This exercise is designed to help you learn how to measure the motivational potential of jobs and evaluate the extent that jobs should be further enriched.

Instructions (Small Class)

Being a student is like working in a job in several ways. You have tasks to perform, and someone (such as your instructor) oversees your work. Although few people want to be students for most of their lives (the pay rate is too low!), it may be interesting to determine how enriched your job is as a student.

1. The instructor will place you in teams (preferably four or five people).
2. Working alone, complete both sets of measures in this exercise. Then, using the guidelines below, individually calculate the score for the five core job characteristics, as well as the overall motivating-potential score for the job.
3. Compare your individual results within your team. Your group should identify differences of opinion for each core job characteristic. You should also note which core job characteristics have the lowest scores and recommend how these scores could be increased.
4. The entire class will then meet to discuss the results of the exercise. The instructor may ask some teams to present their comparisons and recommendations for a particular core job characteristic.

Instructions (Large Class)

1. Working alone, complete both sets of measures in this exercise. Then, using the guidelines below, individually calculate the score for the five core job characteristics, as well as the overall motivating-potential score for the job.
2. Using a show of hands or classroom technology, the instructor will ask you to indicate your results for each core job characteristic, asking for results for several bands across the range of the scales. Alternatively, you can complete this activity prior to class and submit your results through online classroom technology. Later,

the instructor will provide feedback to the class showing the collective results (i.e. distribution of results across the range of scores).

3. Where possible, the instructor might ask class members with very high or very low results to discuss their views with the class.

Job Diagnostic Survey

Circle the number on the right that best describes student work.	Very Little			Moderately			Very Much
1. To what extent does student work permit you to decide on your own how to go about doing the work?	1	2	3	4	5	6	7
2. To what extent does student work involve doing a whole or identifiable piece of work, rather than a small portion of the overall work process?	1	2	3	4	5	6	7
3. To what extent does student work require you to do many different things, using a variety of your skills and talents?	1	2	3	4	5	6	7
4. To what extent are the results of your work as a student likely to significantly affect the lives and wellbeing of other people (e.g. within your school, your family, society)?	1	2	3	4	5	6	7
5. To what extent does working on student activities provide information about your performance?	1	2	3	4	5	6	7
6. Being a student requires me to use a number of complex and high-level skills.	1	2	3	4	5	6	7
7. Student work is arranged so that I do not have the chance to do an entire piece of work from beginning to end.	7	6	5	4	3	2	1
8. Doing the work required of students provides many chances for me to figure out how well I am doing.	1	2	3	4	5	6	7
9. The work students must do is quite simple and repetitive.	7	6	5	4	3	2	1
10. The work of a student is the type where a lot of other people can be affected by how well the work gets done.	1	2	3	4	5	6	7
11. Student work denies me any chance to use my personal initiative or judgment in carrying out the work.	7	6	5	4	3	2	1
12. Student work provides me the chance to completely finish the pieces of work I begin.	1	2	3	4	5	6	7
13. Doing student work by itself provides very few clues about whether I am performing well.	7	6	5	4	3	2	1
14. As a student, I have considerable opportunity for independence and freedom in how I do the work.	1	2	3	4	5	6	7
15. The work I perform as a student is not very significant or important in the broader scheme of things.	7	6	5	4	3	2	1

Source: Adapted from the Job Diagnostic Survey, developed by J. R. Hackman and G. R. Oldham. The authors have released any copyright ownership of this scale [see J. R. Hackman and G. Oldham, *Work Redesign* (Reading, MA: Addison-Wesley, 1980), p. 275].

Calculating the Motivating-Potential Score

Scoring Core Job Characteristics: Referring to your answers from the Job Diagnostic Survey that you completed above, use the following set of calculations to estimate the motivating-potential score for the job of being a student.

Skill variety (SV) $\dfrac{\text{Question } 3 + 6 + 9}{3} = \_\_\_\_$

Task identity (TI) $\dfrac{\text{Question } 2 + 7 + 12}{3} = \_\_\_\_$

Task significance (TS) $\dfrac{\text{Question } 4 + 10 + 15}{3} = \_\_\_\_$

Autonomy $\dfrac{\text{Question } 1 + 11 + 14}{3} = \_\_\_\_$

Job feedback $\dfrac{\text{Question } 5 + 8 + 13}{3} = \_\_\_\_$

Calculating Motivating-Potential Score (MPS): Use the following formula and the results above to calculate the motivating-potential score. Notice that skill variety, task identity and task significance are averaged before being multiplied by the score for autonomy and job feedback.

$$\left(\frac{SV + TI + TS}{3}\right) \times \text{Autonomy} \times \text{Job feedback}$$

$$\left(\frac{\_\_ + \_\_ + \_\_}{3}\right) \times \_\_ \times \_\_ = \_\_\_\_$$

Skill Builder 6.2

SELF-ASSESSMENT

What Is Your Attitude Toward Money?

Purpose

This exercise is designed to help you understand the types of attitudes toward money and assess your attitude toward money.

Instructions

Read each of the statements below and circle the response that you believe best reflects your position regarding each statement. Then use the scoring key in Appendix B at the end of the book to calculate your results. This exercise should be completed alone so that you can assess yourself honestly without concerns of social comparison. Class discussion will focus on the meaning of money, including the dimensions measured here and other aspects of money that may have an influence on behaviour in the workplace.

Money Attitude Scale

To what extent do you agree or disagree that ...	Strongly agree	Agree	Neutral	Disagree	Strongly disagree
1. I sometimes purchase things because I know they will impress other people.	5	4	3	2	1
2. I regularly put money aside for the future.	5	4	3	2	1
3. I tend to get worried about decisions involving money.	5	4	3	2	1
4. I believe that financial wealth is one of the most important signs of a person's success.	5	4	3	2	1
5. I keep a close watch on how much money I have.	5	4	3	2	1
6. I feel nervous when I don't have enough money.	5	4	3	2	1
7. I tend to show more respect to people who are wealthier than I am.	5	4	3	2	1
8. I follow a careful financial budget.	5	4	3	2	1
9. I worry about being financially secure.	5	4	3	2	1
10. I sometimes boast about my financial wealth or how much money I make.	5	4	3	2	1
11. I keep track of my investments and financial wealth.	5	4	3	2	1
12. I usually say 'I can't afford it', even when I can afford something.	5	4	3	2	1

Sources: Adapted from J. A. Roberts and C. J. Sepulveda, 'Demographics and Money Attitudes: A Test of Yamauchi and Templer's (1982) Money Attitude Scale in Mexico', *Personality and Individual Differences* 27 (July 1999): 19–35; K. Yamauchi and D. Templer, 'The Development of a Money Attitudes Scale', *Journal of Personality Assessment* 46 (1982): 522–528.

SELF-ASSESSMENT

Skill Builder 6.3

Assessing Your Self-Leadership

This exercise is designed to help you understand self-leadership concepts and assess your self-leadership tendencies. Self-leadership is the process of influencing yourself to establish the self-direction and self-motivation needed to perform a task. Indicate the extent to which each statement in this instrument describes you very well or does not describe you at all. Complete each item honestly to get the best estimate of your score on each self-leadership dimension.

SELF-ASSESSMENT

Skill Builder 6.4

Student Empowerment Scale

Empowerment is a concept that applies to people in a variety of situations. This instrument is specifically adapted to your position as a student at this university or college. Indicate the extent to which you agree or disagree with each statement in this instrument, then request the results, which provide an overall score as well as scores on each of the four dimensions of empowerment. Complete each item honestly to get the best estimate of your level of empowerment.

Endnotes

1 E. Clark, 'The Cost of Fun', *The Telegraph (London)*, 26 March 2007; D. Eimer, 'China's Toy Makers Face Bleak Christmas as Factories Shut Down', *The Telegraph (London)*, 2 November 2008, 31; A. Harney, *The China Price: The True Cost of Chinese Competitive Advantage* (London: Penguin, 2008), 154–155.

2 M. C. Bloom and G. T. Milkovich, 'Issues in Managerial Compensation Research', in *Trends in Organizational Behavior*, ed. C. L. Cooper and D. M. Rousseau (Chichester, UK: Wiley, 1996), 23–47.

3 S. E. G. Lea and P. Webley, 'Money as Tool, Money as Drug: The Biological Psychology of a Strong Incentive', *Behavioral and Brain Sciences* 29 (2006): 161–209; D. Valenze, *The Social Life of Money in the English Past* (New York: Cambridge University Press, 2006); G. M. Rose and L. M. Orr, 'Measuring and Exploring Symbolic Money Meanings', *Psychology and Marketing* 24, no. 9 (2007): 743–761.

4 D. W. Krueger, 'Money, Success, and Success Phobia', in *The Last Taboo: Money as Symbol and Reality in Psychotherapy and Psychoanalysis*, ed. D. W. Krueger (New York: Brunner/Mazel, 1986), 3–16.

5 P. F. Wernimont and S. Fitzpatrick, 'The Meaning of Money', *Journal of Applied Psychology* 56, no. 3 (1972): 218–226; T. R. Mitchell and A. E. Mickel, 'The Meaning of Money: An Individual-Difference Perspective', *Academy of Management Review* 24 (1999): 568–578; R. Trachtman, 'The Money Taboo: Its Effects in Everyday Life and in the Practice of Psychotherapy', *Clinical Social Work Journal* 27, no. 3 (1999): 275–288; S. Lea, 'Money: Motivation, Metaphors, and Mores', *Behavioral and Brain Sciences* 29, no. 2 (2006): 196–209; Lea and Webley, 'Money as Tool, Money as Drug'; T. L.-P. Tang *et al.*, 'The Love of Money and Pay Level Satisfaction: Measurement and Functional Equivalence in 29 Geopolitical Entities around the World', *Management and Organization Review* 2, no. 3 (2006): 423–452.

6 A. Furnham and R. Okamura, 'Your Money or Your Life: Behavioral and Emotional Predictors of Money Pathology', *Human Relations* 52 (September 1999): 1157–1177.

7 Tang *et al.*, 'The Love of Money and Pay Level Satisfaction'; T. Tang *et al.*, 'To Help or Not to Help? The Good Samaritan Effect and the Love of Money on Helping Behavior', *Journal of Business Ethics* 82, no. 4 (2008): 865–887; T. Tang and Y.-J. Chen, 'Intelligence Vs. Wisdom: The Love of Money, Machiavellianism, and Unethical Behavior across College Major and Gender', *Journal of Business Ethics* 82, no. 1 (2008): 1–26.

8 R. Lynn, *The Secret of the Miracle Economy* (London: SAE, 1991), cited in Furnham and Okamura, 'Your Money or Your Life'.

9 A. Furnham, B. D. Kirkcaldy and R. Lynn, 'National Attitudes to Competitiveness, Money, and Work among Young People: First, Second, and Third World Differences', *Human Relations* 47 (January 1994): 119–132; S. H. Ang, 'The Power of Money: A Cross-Cultural Analysis of Business-Related Beliefs', *Journal of World Business* 35 (March 2000): 43–60; G. Dell'Orto and K. O. Doyle, 'Poveri Ma Belli: Meanings of Money in Italy and in Switzerland', *American Behavioral Scientist* 45, no. 2 (2001): 257–271; K. O. Doyle, 'Introduction: Ethnicity and Money', *American Behavioral Scientist* 45, no. 2 (2001): 181–190; V. K. G. Lim, 'Money Matters: An Empirical Investigation of Money, Face and Confucian Work Ethic', *Personality and Individual Differences* 35, no. 4 (2003): 953–970; T. L.-P. Tang, A. Furnham and G. M.-T. Davis, 'A Cross-Cultural Comparison of the Money Ethic, the Protestant Work Ethic, and Job Satisfaction: Taiwan, the USA, and the UK', *International Journal of Organization Theory and Behavior* 6, no. 2 (2003): 175–194.

10 D. G. Gardner, V. D. Linn and J. L. Pierce, 'The Effects of Pay Level on Organization-Based Self-Esteem and Performance: A Field Study', *Journal of Occupational and Organizational Psychology* 77, no. 3 (2004): 307–322; S. L. Rynes, B. Gerhart and K. A. Minette, 'The Importance of Pay in Employee Motivation: Discrepancies between What People Say and What They Do', *Human Resource Management* 43, no. 4 (2004): 381–394; B. S. Frey, 'Awards as Compensation', *European Management Journal* 4 (2007): 6–14.

11 J. S. Mill, *Utilitarianism*, 7th edn (London: Longmans, Green and Co., 1879; Project Gutenberg e-book), ch. 4.

12 'Seniority Pay System Seeing Revival', *Kyodo News (Tokyo)*, 29 March 2004; R. J. Palabrica, '13th Month Pay', *Philippine Daily Inquirer*, 30 November 2007; T. Bromley, 'Coal-Miners' Wages Soar with Demand', *Otago Daily Times (New Zealand)*, 15 September 2008.

13 D. M. Figart, 'Equal Pay for Equal Work: The Role of Job Evaluation in an Evolving Social Norm', *Journal of Economic Issues* 34 (March 2000): 1–19.

14 E. E. Lawler III, *Rewarding Excellence: Pay Strategies for the New Economy* (San Francisco: Jossey-Bass, 2000), 30–35, 109–119; R. McNabb and K. Whitfield, 'Job Evaluation and High Performance Work Practices: Compatible or Conflictual?', *Journal of Management Studies* 38 (March 2001): 293–312.

15 P. K. Zingheim and J. R. Schuster, 'Competencies and Rewards: Substance or Just Style?', *Compensation Benefits Review* 35, no. 5 (2003): 40–44.

16 T. Law, 'Keeping Staff Happy Good for Business', *The Press (Christchurch, NZ)*, 23 August 2008, 6.

17 R. J. Long, 'Paying for Knowledge: Does It Pay?', *Canadian HR Reporter*, 28 March 2005, 12–13; J. D. Shaw *et al.*, 'Success and Survival of Skill-Based Pay Plans', *Journal of Management* 31, no. 1 (2005): 28–49; E. C. Dierdorff and E. A. Surface, 'If You Pay for Skills, Will They Learn? Skill Change and Maintenance under a Skill-Based Pay System', *Journal of Management* 34, no. 4 (2008): 721–743.

18 Zingheim and Schuster, 'Competencies and Rewards'; F. Giancola, 'Skill-Based Pay—Issues for Consideration', *Benefits & Compensation Digest* 44, no. 5 (2007): 1–15.

19 E. B. Peach and D. A. Wren, 'Pay for Performance from Antiquity to the 1950s', *Journal of Organizational Behavior Management* (1992): 5–26.

20 H.-H. Pai, '"Our Eyes Have Been Opened to the Abuse"', *The Guardian (London)*, 29 April 2006, 2; K. Patterson, 'Luxury Cars Bonus for Hair Staff', *Courier Mail (Brisbane)*, 30 September 2007, 36.

21 K. Walters, 'Dream Team', *Business Review Weekly*, 13 October 2005, 92.

22 V. L. Parker, 'Org Charts Turn around with Teams', *News & Observer (Raleigh, NC)*, 21 July 2005, D1; N. Byrnes and M. Arndt, 'The Art of Motivation', *BusinessWeek*, 1 May 2006, 56; M. Bolch, 'Rewarding the Team', *HRMagazine*, February 2007, 91–93; P. Glader, 'Nucor Bets on Growth in North America', *Wall Street Journal*, 3 January 2007, A3.

23 G. Hamel, *The Future of Management* (Boston: Harvard Business School Press, 2007), 73–75.

24 J. D. Ketcham and M. F. Furukawa, 'Hospital-Physician Gainsharing in Cardiology', *Health Affairs* 27, no. 3 (2008): 803–812.

25 L. R. Gomez-Mejia, T. M. Welbourne and R. M. Wiseman, 'The Role of Risk Sharing and Risk Taking under Gainsharing', *Academy of Management Review* 25 (2000): 492–507; K. M. Bartol and A. Srivastava, 'Encouraging Knowledge Sharing: The Role of Organizational Reward System', *Journal of Leadership & Organizational Studies* 9 (Summer 2002): 64–76.

26 T. Mitchell, 'Winners of the "ESOP of the Year" for 2005–2006 Announced' (Sydney: Australian Employee Ownership Association, December 2005), www.aeoa.org.au (accessed 3 May 2009); 'Beca CoFounder Receives an Entrepreneurship Award', *Scoop (Auckland)*, 13 October 2005; Australian Government Department of Employment and Workplace Relations, *Employee Share Ownership in Australia: Aligning Interests—Executive Summary* (Canberra: Commonwealth of Australia, 2005), www.workplace.gov.au (accessed 28 May 2009).

27 A. Kittel, 'New Lonsdale Plant to Aim at Export Growth', *The Advertiser (Adelaide)*, 11 October 2005, 32.

28 J. Chelius and R. S. Smith, 'Profit Sharing and Employment Stability', *Industrial and Labor Relations Review* 43, no. 3 (1990): 256–273; S. H. Wagner, C. P. Parkers and N. D. Christiansen, 'Employees That Think and Act Like Owners: Effects of Ownership Beliefs and Behaviors on Organizational Effectiveness', *Personnel Psychology* 56, no. 4 (2003): 847–871; G. Ledford, M. Lucy and P. Leblanc, 'The Effects of Stock Ownership on Employee Attitudes and Behavior: Evidence from the Rewards of Work Studies', *Perspectives (Sibson Consulting)*, January 2004; C. Rosen, J. Case and M. Staubus, 'Every Employee an Owner. Really.', *Harvard Business Review* 83, no. 6 (2005): 122–130.

29 A. J. Maggs, 'Enron, ESOPs, and Fiduciary Duty', *Benefits Law Journal* 16, no. 3 (2003): 42–52; C. Brodzinski, 'ESOP's Fables Can Make Coverage Risky', *National Underwriter: Property & Casualty*, 13 June 2005, 16–17.

30 J. Pfeffer, *The Human Equation* (Boston: Harvard Business School Press, 1998); B. N. Pfau and I. T. Kay, *The Human Capital Edge* (New York: McGraw-Hill, 2002); D. Guest, N. Conway and P. Dewe, 'Using Sequential Tree Analysis to Search for "Bundles" of HR Practices', *Human Resource Management Journal* 14, no. 1 (2004): 79–96. The problems with performance-based pay are discussed in W. C. Hammer, 'How to Ruin Motivation with Pay', *Compensation Review* 7, no. 3 (1975): 17–27; A. Kohn, *Punished by Rewards* (Boston: Houghton Mifflin, 1993); M. O'Donnell and J. O'Brian, 'Performance-Based Pay in the Australian Public Service', *Review of Public Personnel Administration* 20 (Spring 2000): 20–34; M. Beer and M. D. Cannon, 'Promise and Peril of Implementing Pay-for-Performance', *Human Resource Management* 43, no. 1 (2004): 3–48.

31 S. Allen, 'Finding Value in Employee Reviews', *Dominion Post (Wellington)*, 22 July 2005, 4.

32 S. Kerr, 'Organization Rewards: Practical, Cost-Neutral Alternatives That You May Know, but Don't Practice', *Organizational Dynamics* 28 (Summer 1999): 61–70.

33 J. S. DeMatteo, L. T. Eby and E. Sundstrom, 'Team-Based Rewards: Current Empirical Evidence and Directions for Future Research', *Research in Organizational Behavior* 20 (1998): 141–183; S. Rynes, B. Gerhart and L. Parks, 'Personnel Psychology: Performance Evaluation and Pay for Performance', *Annual Review of Psychology* 56 (2005): 571–600.

34 'Dream Teams', *Human Resources Professional* (November 1994): 17–19.

35 D. R. Spitzer, 'Power Rewards: Rewards That Really Motivate', *Management Review* (May 1996): 45–50. For a classic discussion on the unintended consequences of pay, see S. Kerr, 'On the Folly of Rewarding A, While Hoping for B', *Academy of Management Journal* 18 (1975): 769–783.

36 'There's Only One Lesson to Learn from UBS', *Euromoney*, May 2008, 9; *Shareholder Report on UBS's Write-Downs* (Zurich: UBS, 18 April 2008); U. Harnischfeger, 'UBS Says Excess of Ambition Led to Its Miscues on Subprime Loans', *New York Times*, 22 April 2008, C3; S. Reed, 'Behind the Mess at UBS', *BusinessWeek*, 3 March 2008, 30–31.

37 R. M. Johnson, D. Lucking-Reiley and J. C. Munos, *'The War for the Fare': How Driver Compensation Affects Bus System Performance* (Cambridge, MA: National Bureau of Economic Research, 2005).

38 H. Connon, 'Overhyped, Overpaid and Overextended', *The Observer (London)*, 20 March 2005, 4; J. Harris and P. Bromiley, 'Incentives to Cheat: The Influence of Executive Compensation and Firm Performance on Financial Misrepresentation', *Organization Science* 18, no. 3 (2007): 350–367.

39 A. Holecek, 'Griffith, Ind., Native Takes over as Steel Plant Manager', *Northwest Indiana Times (Munster, IN)*, 25 May 2003.

40 F. F. Reichheld, *The Loyalty Effect* (Boston: Harvard Business School Press, 1996), 236.

41 Pretoria Portland Cement, *Annual Report, 2003* (Sandton, South Africa: Pretoria Portland Cement, December 2003).

42 J. R. Edwards, J. A. Scully and M. D. Brtek, 'The Nature and Outcomes of Work: A Replication and Extension of Interdisciplinary Work-Design Research', *Journal of Applied Psychology* 85, no. 6 (2000): 860–868; F. P. Morgeson and M. A. Campion, 'Minimizing Tradeoffs When Redesigning Work: Evidence from a Longitudinal Quasi-Experiment', *Personnel Psychology* 55, no. 3 (2002): 589–612.

43 'Grads Find Job-Hopping Is Not a Career-Stopper', *Shanghai Daily*, 23 June 2008.

44 H. Fayol, *General and Industrial Management*, trans. C. Storrs (London: Pitman, 1949); E. E. Lawler III, *Motivation in Work Organizations* (Monterey, CA: Brooks/Cole, 1973), ch. 7; M. A. Campion, 'Ability Requirement Implications of Job Design: An Interdisciplinary Perspective', *Personnel Psychology* 42 (1989): 1–24.

45 F. C. Lane, *Venice: A Maritime Republic* (Baltimore: Johns Hopkins University Press, 1973), 361–364; R. C. Davis, 'Arsenal and *Arsenalotti*: Workplace and Community in Seventeenth-Century Venice', in *The Workplace before the Factory*, ed. T. M. Safley and L. N. Rosenband (Ithaca, NY: Cornell University Press, 1993), 180–203.

46 A. Smith, *An Inquiry into the Nature and Causes of the Wealth of Nations*, 5th edn (London: Methuen, 1904), 8–9.

47 F. W. Taylor, *The Principles of Scientific Management* (New York: Harper & Row, 1911); R. Kanigel, *The One Best Way: Frederick Winslow Taylor and the Enigma of Efficiency* (New York: Viking, 1997).

48 C. R. Walker and R. H. Guest, *The Man on the Assembly Line* (Cambridge, MA: Harvard University Press, 1952); W. F. Dowling, 'Job Redesign on the Assembly Line: Farewell to Blue-Collar Blues?', *Organizational Dynamics* (Autumn 1973): 51–67; E. E. Lawler III, *High-Involvement Management* (San Francisco: Jossey-Bass, 1986).

49 M. Keller, *Rude Awakening: The Rise, Fall, and Struggle for Recovery of General Motors* (New York: Harper Perennial, 1989), 128.

50 F. Herzberg, B. Mausner and B. B. Snyderman, *The Motivation to Work* (New York: Wiley, 1959).

51 S. K. Parker, T. D. Wall and J. L. Cordery, 'Future Work Design Research and Practice: Towards an Elaborated Model of Work Design', *Journal of Occupational and Organizational Psychology* 74, no. 4 (2001): 413–440. For a decisive critique of motivator-hygiene theory, see N. King, 'Clarification and Evaluation of the Two-Factor Theory of Job Satisfaction', *Psychological Bulletin* 74, no. 1 (1970): 18–31.

52 J. R. Hackman and G. Oldham, *Work Redesign* (Reading, MA: Addison-Wesley, 1980).

53 C. Hosford, 'Flying High', *Incentive* 181, no. 12 (2007): 14–20; C. Hosford, 'Training Programs Benefit Rolls-Royce', *B to B*, 16 July 2007, 14.

54 J. E. Champoux, 'A Multivariate Test of the Job Characteristics Theory of Work Motivation', *Journal of Organizational Behavior* 12, no. 5 (1991): 431–446; R. B. Tiegs, L. E. Tetrick and Y. Fried, 'Growth Need Strength and Context Satisfactions as Moderators of the Relations of the Job Characteristics Model', *Journal of Management* 18, no. 3 (1992): 575–593.

55 'Region Positioned among DCX Leaders in Advanced Manufacturing', *Toledo Business Journal*, August 2004, 1;

M. Connelly, 'Chrysler Boosts Belvidere Flexibility', *Automotive News*, 13 February 2006, 44.

56 M. A. Campion and C. L. McClelland, 'Follow-up and Extension of the Interdisciplinary Costs and Benefits of Enlarged Jobs', *Journal of Applied Psychology* 78, no. 3 (1993): 339–351; N. G. Dodd and D. C. Ganster, 'The Interactive Effects of Variety, Autonomy, and Feedback on Attitudes and Performance', *Journal of Organizational Behavior* 17, no. 4 (1996): 329–347.

57 A. Lawson, 'Outrunning Death in Race for the Future of News', *The Age (Melbourne)*, 15 February 2009, 18.

58 J. R. Hackman *et al.*, 'A New Strategy for Job Enrichment', *California Management Review* 17, no. 4 (1975): 57–71; R. W. Griffin, *Task Design: An Integrative Approach* (Glenview, IL: Scott Foresman, 1982).

59 P. E. Spector and S. M. Jex, 'Relations of Job Characteristics from Multiple Data Sources with Employee Affect, Absence, Turnover Intentions, and Health', *Journal of Applied Psychology* 76, no. 1 (1991): 46–53; P. Osterman, 'How Common Is Workplace Transformation and Who Adopts It?', *Industrial and Labor Relations Review* 47, no. 2 (1994): 173–188; R. Saavedra and S. K. Kwun, 'Affective States in Job Characteristics Theory', *Journal of Organizational Behavior* 21, no. 2 (2000): 131–146.

60 Hackman and Oldham, *Work Redesign*, 137–138.

61 S. Wong, 'Open Communication Gives Better Connection', *South China Morning Post (Hong Kong)*, 19 January 2008, 4.

62 R. Semler, *The Seven-Day Weekend* (London: Century, 2003); L. M. Fisher, 'Ricardo Semler Won't Take Control', *strategy+business*, Winter 2005, 1–11; 'Concept of Managerial Control "Is an Illusion"—Semler', *All Africa (Johannesburg)*, 28 August 2007.

63 This definition is based mostly on G. M. Spreitzer and R. E. Quinn, *A Company of Leaders: Five Disciplines for Unleashing the Power in Your Workforce* (San Francisco: Jossey-Bass, 2001). However, most elements of this definition appear in other discussions of empowerment. See, for example, R. Forrester, 'Empowerment: Rejuvenating a Potent Idea', *Academy of Management Executive* 14 (August 2000): 67–80; W. A. Randolph, 'Re-Thinking Empowerment: Why Is It So Hard to Achieve?', *Organizational Dynamics* 29 (November 2000): 94–107; S. T. Menon, 'Employee Empowerment: An Integrative Psychological Approach', *Applied Psychology: An International Review* 50, no. 1 (2001): 153–180.

64 The positive relationship between these structural empowerment conditions and psychological empowerment is reported in H. K. S. Laschinger *et al.*, 'A Longitudinal Analysis of the Impact of Workplace Empowerment on Work Satisfaction', *Journal of Organizational Behavior* 25, no. 4 (2004): 527–545.

65 C. S. Koberg *et al.*, 'Antecedents and Outcomes of Empowerment: Empirical Evidence From the Health Care Industry', *Group and Organization Management* 24, no. 1 (1999): 71–91; Y. Melhem, 'The Antecedents of Customer-Contact Employees' Empowerment', *Employee Relations* 26, no. 1/2 (2004): 72–93.

66 B. J. Niehoff *et al.*, 'The Influence of Empowerment and Job Enrichment on Employee Loyalty in a Downsizing Environment', *Group and Organization Management* 26, no. 1 (2001): 93–113; J. Yoon, 'The Role of Structure and Motivation for Workplace Empowerment: The Case of Korean Employees', *Social Psychology Quarterly* 64 (June 2001): 195–206; T. D. Wall, J. L. Cordery and C. W. Clegg, 'Empowerment, Performance, and Operational Uncertainty: A Theoretical Integration', *Applied Psychology: An International Review* 51, no. 1 (2002): 146–169.

67 'Running a Business: Managing a Handelsbanken Branch', *A View from the Top (Handelsbanken Maidstone Newsletter)*, Winter 2007, 1; O. Hammarström, 'Handelsbanken, Sweden: Make Work Pay—Make Work Attractive', (Dublin: Eurofound, 22 October 2007), www.eurofound.europa.eu (accessed 4 May 2009); R. M. Lindsay and T. Libby, 'Svenska Handelsbanken: Controlling a Radically Decentralized Organization without Budgets', *Issues in Accounting Education* 22, no. 4 (2007): 625–640; 'The *Sunday Times* 100 Best Companies to Work for 2008' (Chester, UK: Svenska Handelsbanken, 10 March 2008), www.handelsbanken.co.uk (accessed 11 September 2008).

68 G. M. Spreitzer, 'Social Structural Characteristics of Psychological Empowerment', *Academy of Management Journal* 39 (April 1996): 483–504; J. Godard, 'High Performance and the Transformation of Work? The Implications of Alternative Work Practices for the Experience and Outcomes of Work', *Industrial and Labor Relations Review* 54, no. 4 (2001): 776–805; P. A. Miller, P. Goddard and H. K. Spence Laschinger, 'Evaluating Physical Therapists' Perception of Empowerment Using Kanter's Theory of Structural Power in Organizations', *Physical Therapy* 81 (December 2001): 1880–1888.

69 J.-C. Chebat and P. Kollias, 'The Impact of Empowerment on Customer Contact Employees' Role in Service Organizations', *Journal of Service Research* 3 (August 2000): 66–81; H. K. S. Laschinger, J. Finegan and J. Shamian, 'The Impact of Workplace Empowerment, Organizational Trust on Staff Nurses' Work Satisfaction and Organizational Commitment', *Health Care Management Review* 26 (Summer 2001): 7–23.

70 'Bosses Love Team Workers', *Lancashire Evening Post (Preston, UK)*, 25 May 2006; G. Hohmann, 'Bayer to Add

24 Jobs at Institute', *Charleston Gazette (Charleston, WV)*, 6 August 2008, P1A.

71 C. P. Neck and C. C. Manz, 'Thought Self-Leadership: The Impact of Mental Strategies Training on Employee Cognition, Behavior, and Affect', *Journal of Organizational Behavior* 17, no. 5 (1996): 445–467.

72 J. Woods, 'Upwardly Mobile', *Sydney Morning Herald*, 13 April 2005, 9.

73 C. C. Manz, 'Self-Leadership: Toward an Expanded Theory of Self-Influence Processes in Organizations', *Academy of Management Review* 11 (1986): 585–600; C. C. Manz and C. Neck, *Mastering Self-Leadership*, 3rd ed. (Upper Saddle River, NJ: Prentice Hall, 2004); C. P. Neck and J. D. Houghton, 'Two Decades of Self-Leadership Theory and Research', *Journal of Managerial Psychology* 21, no. 4 (2006): 270–295.

74 O. J. Strickland and M. Galimba, 'Managing Time: The Effects of Personal Goal Setting on Resource Allocation Strategy and Task Performance', *Journal of Psychology* 135 (July 2001): 357–367.

75 R. M. Duncan and J. A. Cheyne, 'Incidence and Functions of Self-Reported Private Speech in Young Adults: A Self-Verbalization Questionnaire', *Canadian Journal of Behavioral Science* 31 (April 1999): 133–136.

76 J. E. Driscoll, C. Copper and A. Moran, 'Does Mental Practice Enhance Performance?', *Journal of Applied Psychology* 79, no. 4 (1994): 481–492; C. P. Neck, G. L. Stewart and C. C. Manz, 'Thought Self-Leadership as a Framework for Enhancing the Performance of Performance Appraisers', *Journal of Applied Behavioral Science* 31 (September 1995): 278–302. Some research separates mental imagery from mental practice, whereas most studies combine both into one concept.

77 A. Joyce, 'Office Perks: Re-Energize to Get through the Blahs', *Washington Post*, 28 August 2005, F05.

78 A. Wrzesniewski and J. E. Dutton, 'Crafting a Job: Revisioning Employees as Active Crafters of Their Work', *Academy of Management Review* 26 (2001): 179–201.

79 'Steve Collier Profile', *CCMA Case Study*, January 2008, www.ccma.asn.au (accessed 4 May 2009).

80 M. I. Bopp, S. J. Glynn and R. A. Henning, 'Self-Management of Performance Feedback During Computer-Based Work by Individuals and Two-Person Work Teams', paper presented at the APA-NIOSH Conference: Work, Stress, and Health '99, Baltimore, 12 March 1999.

81 A. W. Logue, *Self-Control: Waiting until Tomorrow for What You Want Today* (Englewood Cliffs, NJ: Prentice Hall, 1995).

82 Neck and Manz, 'Thought Self-Leadership: The Impact of Mental Strategies Training on Employee Cognition, Behavior, and Affect'; A. M. Saks and B. E. Ashforth, 'Proactive Socialization and Behavioral Self-Management', *Journal of Vocational Behavior* 48 (1996): 301–323; L. Morin and G. Latham, 'The Effect of Mental Practice and Goal Setting as a Transfer of Training Intervention on Supervisors' Self-Efficacy and Communication Skills: An Exploratory Study', *Applied Psychology: An International Review* 49 (July 2000): 566–578; J. S. Hickman and E. S. Geller, 'A Safety Self-Management Intervention for Mining Operations', *Journal of Safety Research* 34 (2003): 299–308.

83 S. Ming and G. L. Martin, 'Single-Subject Evaluation of a Self-Talk Package for Improving Figure Skating Performance', *Sport Psychologist* 10 (1996): 227–238; J. Bauman, 'The Gold Medal Mind', *Psychology Today* 33 (May 2000): 62–69; L. J. Rogerson and D. W. Hrycaiko, 'Enhancing Competitive Performance of Ice Hockey Goaltenders Using Centering and Self-Talk', *Journal of Applied Sport Psychology* 14, no. 1 (2002): 14–26; A. Papaioannou *et al.*, 'Combined Effect of Goal Setting and Self-Talk in Performance of a Soccer-Shooting Task', *Perceptual and Motor Skills* 98, no. 1 (2004): 89–99; R. A. Hamilton, D. Scott and M. P. MacDougall, 'Assessing the Effectiveness of Self-Talk Interventions on Endurance Performance', *Journal of Applied Sport Psychology* 19, no. 2 (2007): 226–239. For a review of the self-talk research, including limitations of this self-leadership strategy, see J. Hardy, 'Speaking Clearly: A Critical Review of the Self-Talk Literature', *Psychology of Sport and Exercise* 7 (2006): 81–97.

84 S. Williams, 'Personality and Self-Leadership', *Human Resource Management Review* 7, no. 2 (1997): 139–155; J. D. Houghton *et al.*, 'The Relationship between Self-Leadership and Personality: A Comparison of Hierarchical Factor Structures', *Journal of Managerial Psychology* 19, no. 4 (2004): 427–441; R. W. Renn *et al.*, 'The Roles of Personality and Self-Defeating Behaviors in Self-Management Failure', *Journal of Management* 31, no. 5 (2005): 659–679.

85 J. D. Houghton and S. K. Yoho, 'Toward a Contingency Model of Leadership and Psychological Empowerment: When Should Self-Leadership Be Encouraged?', *Journal of Leadership & Organizational Studies* 11, no. 4 (2005): 65–83; J. D. Houghton and D. L. Jinkerson, 'Constructive Thought Strategies and Job Satisfaction: A Preliminary Examination', *Journal of Business and Psychology* 22 (2007): 45–53.

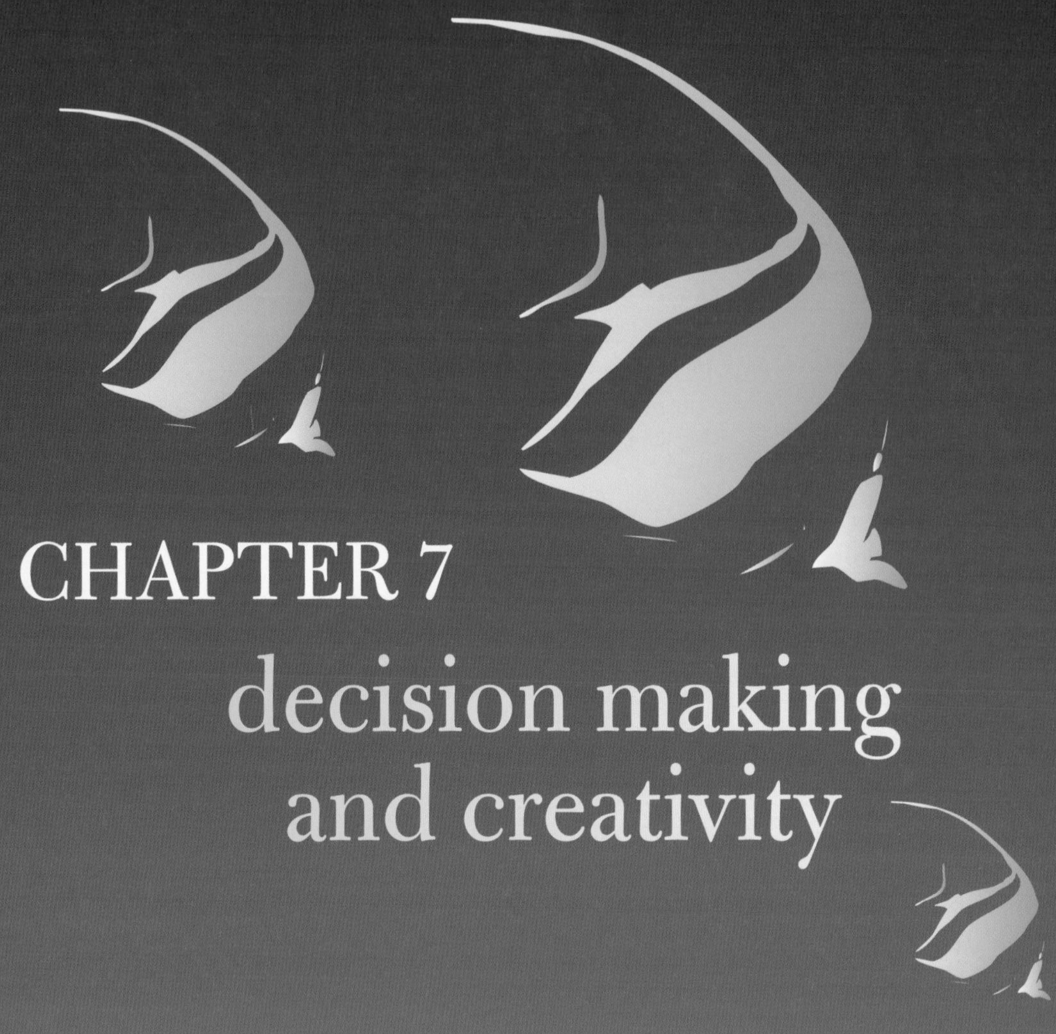

CHAPTER 7

decision making and creativity

LEARNING OBJECTIVES

After reading this chapter, you should be able to:

- describe the six stages in the rational choice decision process
- explain why people have difficulty identifying problems and opportunities
- explain why people do not follow the rational choice model when evaluating alternative choices
- describe three ways in which emotions influence the selection of alternatives
- outline how intuition operates
- describe four causes of escalation of commitment
- describe four benefits of employee involvement in decision making
- identify four contingencies that affect the optimal level of employee involvement
- outline the four steps in the creative process
- describe the characteristics of creative employees and workplaces that support creativity.

Courtesy of Google Australia

Google employees in Sydney, Australia (shown here) and around the world make better decisions by having 20 per cent of their time to work on pet projects, using evidence-based experiments to test ideas and being involved in organisational decisions.

Google is a hotbed of creativity and innovation in an industry already famed for churning out new ideas. The company famously encourages its engineers to use 20 per cent of their time to develop projects of their choosing. 'Almost everything that is interesting which Google does starts out as a 20 per cent time idea,' says Google CEO Eric Schmidt. The company initially allocates limited resources to initiatives, then assigns more people and budget to projects that show progress and viability.

For example, Google Maps began with a small team of engineers in Australia working out of a 'broom closet' in Sydney with a small budget. (Four of these engineers developed an early version of the technology in their private firm, which Google acquired.) 'You have to remember, this stuff [Google Maps] had been put together by only six engineers with chewing gum and safety pins,' says Lars Rasmussen, one of Google Maps' founding engineers. As Google Maps gained popularity, Rasmussen persuaded Google to make the Sydney office an engineering hub. Two hundred people now work in that office, more than half of them in engineering.

Along with encouraging creative thinking, Google relies on razor-sharp analytic decision making. 'We are firm believers in fair, algorithmical approaches [to decision making],' explains Alan Noble, Google Australia's director of engineering. Google's business product management team, for instance, has experimented with the placement, colour and size of ads on Google results pages to decide which characteristics yield the most clicks and the best revenue.

'Employees know that decisions about the business are data-driven,' says Laszlo Bock, Google's top human resource executive. Bock's human resource team carefully analyses two dozen performance variables of current staff to help choose qualified job applicants. Michael Fox can attest to Google's careful decision making when hiring. Fox completed more than a dozen job interviews over six months before being hired as relationship manager at Google Australia.

When a problem or opportunity lacks information, Google tries to fill in the missing pieces through 'prediction markets' in which employees use play money (called Goobles) to cast their bets on strategic and operational questions. Google has conducted hundreds of these markets on issues ranging from whether a particular project will be completed on time to how many people will use Gmail (Google's email system) by the end of the quarter. 'Google uses these bets for its own planning. It helps them make decisions,' says an economist studying Google's prediction markets.[1]

decision making The conscious process of making choices among alternatives with the intention of moving toward some desired state of affairs.

Many Google watchers claim that the company's success is largely driven by its superb decision making. One recent article even 'reverse-engineered' Google's innovation process as a guide for others to follow.[2] **Decision making** is the conscious process of making choices among alternatives with the intention of moving toward some desired state of affairs.[3] This chapter begins by outlining the rational choice paradigm of decision making. Then we examine this perspective more critically by recognising how people identify problems and opportunities, choose among alternatives and evaluate the success of their decisions differently from the rational model. Bounded rationality, intuition and escalation of commitment are three of the more prominent topics in this section. Next, we explore the role of employee involvement in decision making, including the benefits of involvement and the factors that determine the optimal level of involvement. The final section of this chapter examines the factors that support creativity in decision making, including characteristics of creative people, work environments that support creativity and creativity activities.

LEARNING OBJECTIVE 

Describe the six stages in the rational choice decision process.

RATIONAL CHOICE PARADIGM OF DECISION MAKING

How should people make decisions in organisations? Most business leaders would likely answer this question by saying that effective decision making involves identifying, selecting and applying the best possible alternative. In other words, the best decisions use pure logic and all available information to choose the alternative with the highest value—such as highest expected profitability, customer satisfaction, employee wellbeing or some combination of these outcomes. For example, Google relies on careful analysis to choose the best job applicants, the best way to present advertisements on its web pages, the best companies to acquire, the best projects to fund and so on. These decisions sometimes involve complex calculations of data to produce a formula that points to the best choice.

rational choice paradigm The view in decision making that people should—and typically do—use logic and all available information to choose the alternative with the highest value.

In its extreme form, this calculative view of decision making represents the **rational choice paradigm**, which has dominated decision-making philosophy in Western societies for most of written history. It was established 2500 years ago when Plato and his contemporaries in ancient Greece raised logical debate and reasoning to a fine art. A few centuries later, Greek and Roman Stoics insisted that one should always 'follow where reason leads' rather than fall victim to passion and emotions. About 400 years ago, Descartes and other European philosophers emphasised that the ability to make logical decisions is one of the most important accomplishments of human beings. In the 1700s, Scottish philosophers proposed that the best choice is the one that offers the 'greatest good for the greatest number'. This eventually evolved into the ethical principle of utilitarianism (described in Chapter 2), as well as maximisation, which is at the heart of contemporary economics. In the mid-1800s, while working at Australia's Royal Mint, William Stanley Jevons began to develop the first mathematical rational choice model, which scholars later refined for economics, operations research and other decision sciences.[4]

subjective expected utility The probability (expectation) of satisfaction (utility) resulting from choosing a specific alternative in a decision.

The ultimate principle of the rational choice paradigm is to choose the alternative with the highest **subjective expected utility**.[5] Subjective expected utility is the probability (expectation) of satisfaction (utility) for each alternative. Rational choice assumes that decision makers should (and do) select the alternative that offers the greatest level of happiness (i.e. maximisation), such as highest returns for shareholders and highest satisfaction for customers, employees, government and other stakeholders. Subjective expected utility involves calculating (1) the probability that each alternative will cause any of the possible outcomes to occur and (2) the value (or happiness) of those possible outcomes. Consider Google's hiring process, which processes several hundred thousand applications each year to select a few thousand of the applicants. The company wants to hire the best people—those who will provide the greatest value to Google. In other words, it wants to choose applicants with the highest subjective expected utility. Google estimates the potential of each applicant using a selection formula and selects those with the highest scores.

Along with its principle of making decisions around subjective expected utility, the rational choice paradigm assumes that decision makers follow the systematic process illustrated in Exhibit 7.1.[6] The first step is to identify the problem or recognise an opportunity. A *problem* is a deviation between the current and the desired situation—the gap between 'what is' and 'what ought to be'. This deviation is a symptom of more fundamental root causes that need to be corrected.[7] An *opportunity* is a deviation between current expectations and a potentially better situation that was not previously expected. In other words, decision makers realise that some decisions may produce results beyond current goals or expectations.

The second step involves deciding how to process the decision.[8] One issue is whether the decision maker has enough information or needs to involve others in the process. Later in this chapter, we'll examine the contingencies of employee involvement in the decision. Another issue is whether the decision is programmed or nonprogrammed. *Programmed decisions* follow standard operating procedures; they have been resolved in the past, so the optimal solution has already been identified and documented. In contrast, *nonprogrammed decisions* require all steps in the decision model because the problems are new, complex or ill-defined. The third step is to identify and develop a list of possible solutions. This usually begins by searching for ready-made solutions,

Exhibit 7.1 ***Rational Choice Decision-Making Process***

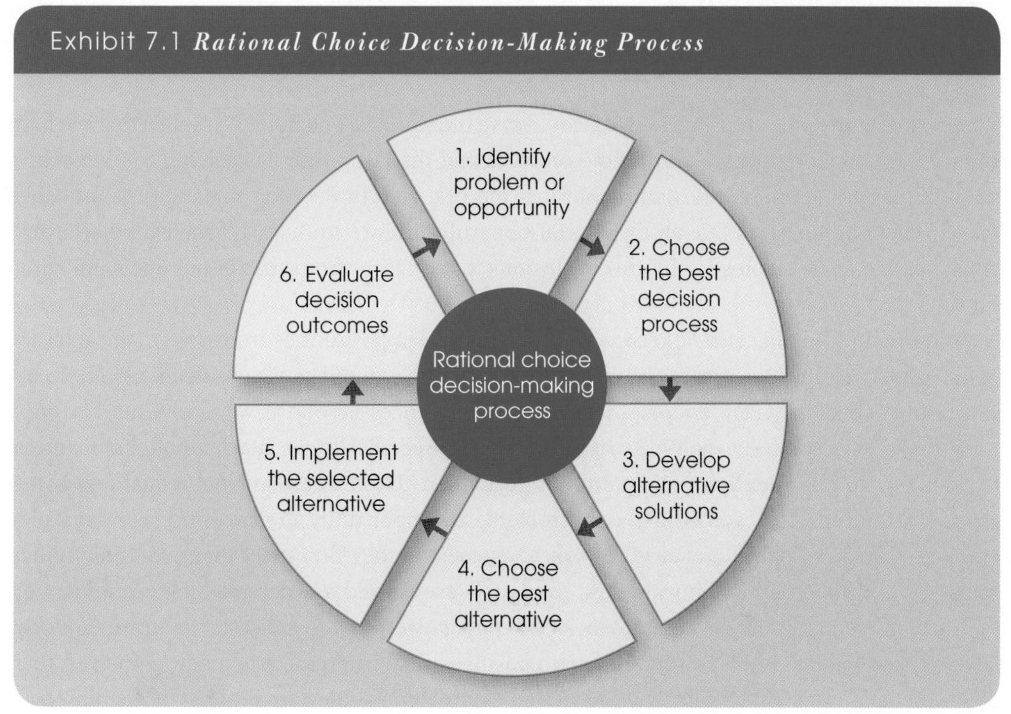

such as practices that have worked well on similar problems. If an acceptable solution cannot be found, then decision makers need to design a custom-made solution or modify an existing one.

The fourth step in the rational choice decision process is to choose the alternative with the highest subjective expected utility. This calls for all possible information about all possible alternatives and their outcomes, but the rational choice paradigm assumes this can be accomplished with ease. The fifth step in the rational choice decision process is to implement the selected alternative. Rational choice experts have little to say about this step because they assume implementation occurs without any problems. This is followed by the sixth step, evaluating whether the gap has narrowed between 'what is' and 'what ought to be'. Ideally, this information should come from systematic benchmarks so that relevant feedback is objective and easily observed.

Problems with the Rational Choice Paradigm

The rational choice paradigm seems so logical, yet it is impossible to apply in reality. One reason is that the model assumes people are efficient and logical information-processing machines. But as we will discuss over the next few pages, people have difficulty recognising problems; they cannot (or will not) simultaneously process the huge volume of information needed to identify the best solution; and they have difficulty recognising when their choices have failed. The second reason why the rational model doesn't fit reality is that it focuses on logical thinking and completely ignores the fact that emotions also influence—perhaps even dominate—the decision-making process. As we shall discover in this chapter, emotions both support and interfere with our quest to make better decisions.[9] With these points in mind, let's look again at each step in the rational choice decision-making process, but with more detail about what really happens.

LEARNING OBJECTIVE

Explain why people have difficulty identifying problems and opportunities.

IDENTIFYING PROBLEMS AND OPPORTUNITIES

When Albert Einstein was asked how he would save the world in one hour, he replied that the first 55 minutes should be spent defining the problem and the last 5 minutes solving it.[10] Einstein's point is that problem identification is not just the first step in decision making; it is arguably the most important step. But problems and opportunities are not clearly labelled objects that appear on our desks. Instead, they are conclusions that we form from ambiguous and conflicting information.

You might think that people recognise problems and opportunities from systematic analysis of the facts. In reality, this process begins much earlier and without conscious deliberation. Recall from earlier chapters (Chapters 3–5) that we form preferences as soon as we receive information, not after we have carefully analysed that information.[11] Specifically, we attach emotional markers (e.g. anger, caution or delight) to incoming information. These automatic emotional responses shape our attitude that something is a problem, an opportunity or irrelevant. For example, employees form an opinion of new coworkers as soon as they first meet them, and this initial impression influences how quickly new employees are viewed as successes (opportunities) or failures (problems). If the new employee is viewed negatively, any instances of failure are quickly labelled as problems. But if coworkers form a positive initial impression of a new employee, that newcomer's failures are less likely to be viewed as problems—they are ignored or dismissed as temporary setbacks.

Problems with Problem Identification

The problem identification stage is, itself, filled with problems. Below are five of the most widely recognised concerns.[12]

Stakeholder Framing

One school of management thought, called the **attention-based theory of the firm**, states that organisational decisions and actions are influenced mainly by what attracts management's attention, rather than by the objective reality of the external or internal environment.[13] This attention process is subject to a variety of cognitive biases, such as the decision maker's perceptual process, specific circumstances and deliberate actions of stakeholders. Suppliers, employees, clients and other stakeholders actively manage information so it becomes more (or less) conspicuous to decision makers. Furthermore, stakeholders present the information in such a way that it triggers the decision maker's emotional response that the information is a problem, an opportunity or inconsequential.

attention-based theory of the firm A school of management thought based on the idea that organisational decisions and actions are influenced mainly by what attracts management's attention, rather than by objective reality.

Mental Models

Even if stakeholders don't frame information, our cognitive structure does it through preconceived mental models. Recall from Chapter 3 that mental models are visual or relational images in our mind of the external world; they fill in information that we don't immediately see, which helps us understand and navigate in our surrounding environment. Many mental images are also prototypes—they represent models of how things should be. Unfortunately, these mental models also blind us from seeing unique problems or opportunities because they produce a negative evaluation of things that are dissimilar to the mental model. If an idea doesn't fit the existing mental model of how things should work, the idea is dismissed as unworkable or undesirable. Reality Check 7.1 describes how narrow mental models are the source of several famous missed or near-missed opportunities.

Decisive Leadership

Studies report that decisive leaders are rated by employees as more effective leaders.[17] Being decisive includes quickly forming an opinion of whether an event signals a problem or opportunity. Consequently, eager to look effective, many leaders quickly announce a problem or opportunity before having a chance to logically assess the situation. The result, according to research, is more often a poorer decision than would result if more time had been devoted to identifying the problem and evaluating the alternatives.

Solution-Focused Problems

Decision makers have a tendency to define problems as veiled solutions.[18] For instance, someone might say: 'The problem is that we need more control over our suppliers.' This statement doesn't describe the problem; it is really a slightly rephrased presentation of a solution to an ill-defined problem. Decision makers engage in solution-focused problem identification because it provides comforting closure to the otherwise ambiguous and uncertain nature of problems. People with a strong need for cognitive closure (those who feel uncomfortable with ambiguity) are particularly prone to solution-focused problems. Some decision makers take this solution focus a step further by seeing all problems as solutions that have worked well for them in the past, even though they were applied under different circumstances. Again, the familiarity of past solutions makes the current problem less ambiguous or uncertain.

Famous Missed Opportunities

The best television commercial in history—the Apple Macintosh 1984 ad—almost never saw the light of day because it was so different from existing mental models of what a good television ad should look like.

MENTAL MODELS CREATE ROAD maps that guide our decisions. Unfortunately, these maps also potentially block our ability to see emerging problems and opportunities. Here are a few famous examples.

- Apple, Inc.'s '1984' television commercial, which launched the Apple Macintosh during the 1984 Superbowl, is considered the best television commercial in history (as rated by *Advertising Age*), yet it almost didn't see the light of day. Unlike traditional commercials, which name the product throughout and illustrate its features, the sixty-second '1984' ad shows a female athlete hurling a sledgehammer at a giant television screen of an Orwellian Big Brother, liberating thousands of subjugated followers. The Macintosh computer isn't shown at all and its name is revealed only during the last eight seconds.

  Apple's external board members loathed the ad because it was so contrary to their mental prototype of what a good ad should look like. Some claimed it was the worst

Perceptual Defence

People sometimes block out bad news as a coping mechanism. Their brain refuses to see information that threatens their self-concept. This phenomenon is not true for everyone. Some people inherently avoid negative information, whereas others are more sensitive to it. Recent studies also report that people are more likely to disregard danger signals when they have limited control over the situation.[19] For example, an investigation of the space shuttle *Columbia* disaster revealed that NASA managers rejected suggestions and evidence that the shuttle and its seven crew members were in trouble.

Identifying Problems and Opportunities More Effectively

Recognising problems and opportunities will always be a challenge, but one way to improve the process is by becoming aware of the five problem identification biases described above. For example, by recognising that mental models restrict a person's perspective of the world, decision makers are more motivated to consider other perspectives of reality. Along with increasing their awareness of problem identification flaws, leaders require considerable willpower to resist the temptation of looking decisive when a more thoughtful examination of the situation should occur. A third way to improve problem identification is for leaders to create a norm of 'divine discontent'. They are never satisfied with the status quo, and this aversion to complacency creates a mindset that more actively searches for problems and opportunities.[21]

Finally, employees can minimise these difficulties with problem identification by discussing the situation with colleagues. The logic here is that blind spots in problem identification are more easily identified by hearing how others perceive certain information and diagnose problems. Opportunities also become apparent when outsiders explore this information from

REALITY CHECK 7.1

commercial in history; others proposed firing Apple's ad agency. On the basis of this reaction, Apple CEO John Sculley asked Jay Chiat (the head of Apple's ad agency, Chiat-Day) to sell the company's only two Superbowl time slots. Instead, Chiat sold the short 30-second space but claimed that he could not find a buyer for the 60-second slot. The single 60-second ad shown during the Superbowl had such a huge effect that it was featured on evening news over the next several days. A month later, Apple's board members applauded the Macintosh team for a successful launch and apologised for their misjudgment of the '1984' commercial.[14]

- Graphical user interfaces, mice, windows, pull-down menus, laser printing, distributed computing and ethernet technologies weren't invented by Apple, Microsoft or IBM. These essential elements of contemporary personal computing originated in the 1970s from researchers at Xerox PARC. Unfortunately, Xerox executives were so focused on their photocopier business that they didn't bother to patent most of these inventions. Xerox has successfully applied some of its laser technology, but the lost value of Xerox PARC's other computing discoveries is much larger than the entire photocopier industry today.[15]
- When the World Wide Web burst onto the cyberspace scene in the early 1990s, Bill Gates wondered what all the fuss was about. Even as late as 1996, the Microsoft founder lampooned investors for their love-in with companies that made internet products. However, Gates eventually realised the error in his mental model of computing. Making up for lost time, Microsoft bought Hotmail and other Web-savvy companies, and added internet support to its Windows operating system.[16]

their different mental models. Google, described at the beginning of this chapter, actively applies this practice. The company deliberately puts employees into teams so that they bounce ideas off each other. In addition, the company has an online 'suggestion box' where employees post their ideas (including perspectives on a problem or opportunity) so that other Google employees can comment on and rate them.[22]

EVALUATING AND CHOOSING ALTERNATIVES

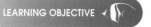

Explain why people do not follow the rational choice model when evaluating alternative choices.

According to the rational choice paradigm of decision making, people rely on logic to evaluate and choose alternatives. This paradigm assumes that decision makers have well-articulated and agreed-on organisational goals, that they efficiently and simultaneously process facts about all alternatives and the consequences of those alternatives, and that they choose the alternative with the highest pay-off.

Nobel Prize–winning organisational scholar Herbert Simon questioned these assumptions more than half a century ago. He argued that people engage in **bounded rationality** because they process limited and imperfect information and rarely select the best choice.[23] Simon and other OB experts demonstrated that how people evaluate and choose alternatives differs from the rational choice paradigm in several ways, as illustrated in Exhibit 7.2. These differences are so significant that many economists are now shifting from rational choice to bounded rationality assumptions in their theories. Let's look at these differences in terms of goals, information processing and maximisation.

bounded rationality The view that people are bounded in their decision-making capabilities, including access to limited information, limited information processing and tendency toward satisficing rather than maximising when making choices.

No Problem, Houston?

In February 2003, the NASA space shuttle *Columbia* disintegrated during re-entry, killing all seven crew members. The disintegration was technically caused by a hole in the left wing, created when a large piece of foam debris struck the wing during lift-off. However, a special accident investigation board concluded that NASA's middle management continually resisted attempts to recognise that the *Columbia* was in trouble and therefore made no attempt to prevent loss of life. For example, when a team of engineers requested that military satellites take photos of Columbia's exterior to determine if any damage was visible, NASA management shot back an email just 26 minutes later, rejecting the request without explanation. Managers also questioned tests suggesting that a chunk of foam debris could cause wing damage, yet they were quick to accept a faulty test showing that the foam could not damage the wing. In addition, the accident board reported that NASA managers criticised those who believed that a problem existed. One engineer was called 'alarmist'. A report submitted by an engineering team concerned about the wing damage was called 'lousy' by NASA's lead flight director. In one meeting, *Columbia*'s lead flight director candidly admitted: 'I don't think there is much we can do, so you know it's not really a factor during the flight because there isn't much we can do about it.'[20]

Courtesy of NASA

Problems with Goals

The rational choice paradigm assumes that organisational goals are clear and agreed-on. In fact, these conditions are necessary to identify 'what ought to be' and, therefore, provide a standard against which each alternative is evaluated. Unfortunately, organisational goals are often ambiguous or in conflict with each other. One survey reported that 25 per cent of managers and employees felt decisions are delayed because of difficulty agreeing on what they want the decision to achieve.[24]

Problems with Information Processing

The rational choice paradigm also makes several assumptions about the human capacity to process information. It assumes that decision makers can process information about all alternatives and their consequences, whereas this is not possible in reality. Instead, people evaluate only a few alternatives and only some of the main outcomes of those alternatives.[25] For example, there may

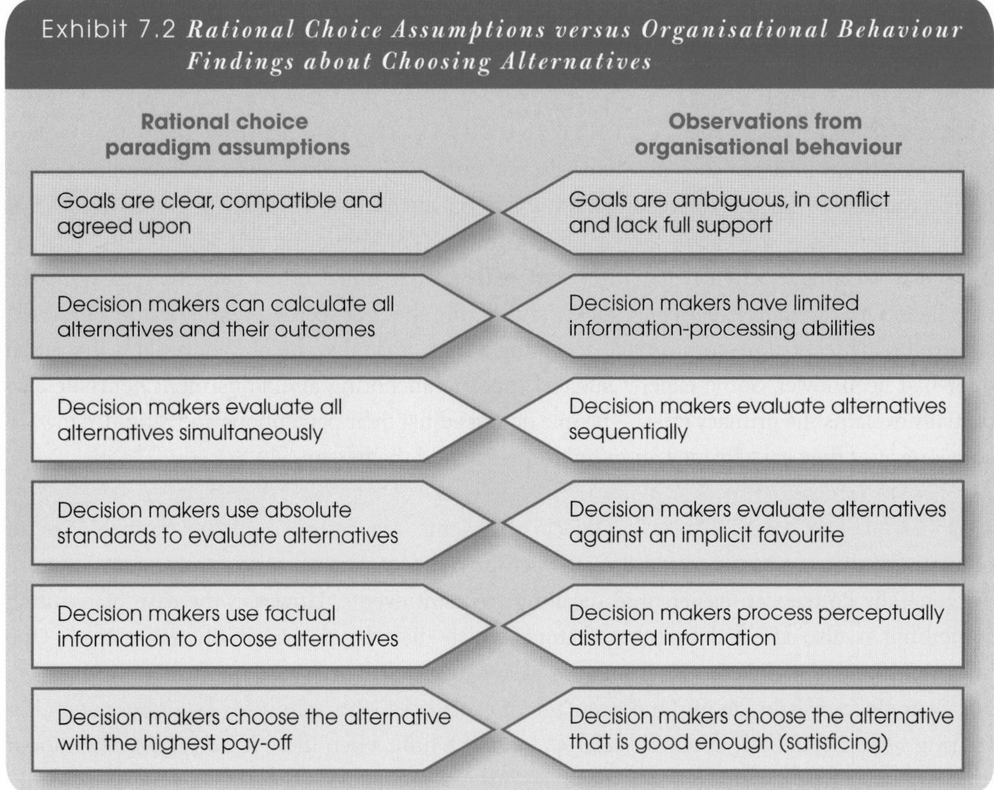

be dozens of computer brands to choose from and dozens of features to consider, yet people typically evaluate only a few brands and a few features.

Exhibit 7.2 Rational Choice Assumptions versus Organisational Behaviour Findings about Choosing Alternatives
Rational choice paradigm assumptions
Observations from organisational behaviour
Goals are clear, compatible and agreed upon
Goals are ambiguous, in conflict and lack full support
Decision makers can calculate all alternatives and their outcomes
Decision makers have limited information-processing abilities
Decision makers evaluate all alternatives simultaneously
Decision makers evaluate alternatives sequentially
Decision makers use absolute standards to evaluate alternatives
Decision makers evaluate alternatives against an implicit favourite
Decision makers use factual information to choose alternatives
Decision makers process perceptually distorted information
Decision makers choose the alternative with the highest pay-off
Decision makers choose the alternative that is good enough (satisficing)

A related problem is that decision makers typically evaluate alternatives sequentially rather than all at the same time. As a new alternative comes along, it is immediately compared to an **implicit favourite**—an alternative that the decision maker prefers and that is used as a comparison with other choices. When choosing a new computer system, for example, people typically have an implicit favourite brand or model in their heads that they use to compare with the others. This sequential process of comparing alternatives with an implicit favourite occurs even when decision makers aren't consciously aware that they are doing this.[26]

implicit favourite A preferred alternative that the decision maker uses repeatedly as a comparison with other choices.

Although the implicit favourite comparison process seems to be hardwired in human decision making (i.e. we naturally compare things), it often undermines effective decision making because people distort information to favour their implicit favourite over the alternative choices. They tend to ignore problems with the implicit favourite and the advantages of the alternative. Decision makers also overweight factors on which the implicit favourite is better and underweight areas in which the alternative is superior.[27]

Biased Decision Heuristics

One of the key ingredients of the rational choice paradigm is that people can estimate the probabilities of outcomes. This estimation of probabilities is, in essence, the 'expected' part of subjective expected utility. However, psychologists Amos Tversky and Daniel Kahneman discovered that human beings have built-in *decision heuristics*—unstructured and often nonconscious modes of reasoning or rules of thumb—that bias an individual's perceived probabilities that specific outcomes will occur. Three of the most widely studied heuristic biases are the anchoring and adjustment heuristic, availability heuristic and representativeness heuristic.[28]

anchoring and adjustment heuristic A natural tendency for people to be influenced by an initial anchor point such that they do not sufficiently move away from that point as new information is provided.

ANCHORING AND ADJUSTMENT HEURISTIC This heuristic states that we are influenced by an initial anchor point and do not sufficiently move away from that point as new information is provided.[29] The result is that the initial anchor point biases our estimate above or below the true value of what we are trying to estimate. The anchoring and adjustment heuristic is used to advantage when negotiators start with a high initial offer. The other party in the negotiation may initially experience 'sticker shock' (the shock of seeing a high price on a product) but eventually feels more comfortable accepting a high price than he or she would if the initial offer had been lower. Some experts suggest that the anchoring and adjustment heuristic also partially explains the primacy effect—people do not adjust their perceptions and attitudes toward someone after they have formed an initial impression of the person.

availability heuristic A natural tendency to assign higher probabilities to objects or events that are easier to recall from memory, even though ease of recall is also affected by nonprobability factors (e.g. emotional response, recent events).

AVAILABILITY HEURISTIC Objects or events are assigned higher probabilities of occurring if they are easier to recall from memory. This makes sense to some extent, because we generally do have an easier time recalling frequent events. However, the ease of recalling something is also affected by other factors, which distort our probability estimates.[30] One biasing influence is that recent events are easier to recall than are events further in the past. For example, our estimate of the percentage of executives who are greedy is higher soon after hearing news about high executive salaries than at a time when there is no recent news about executive salaries. This ease of recall increases our perception that executives are highly paid and greedy. Another influence on our recall is the emotional strength of the event. Shark attacks are an example. These attacks on human beings receive considerable media attention and generate gory images in our minds, so they are easy to recall. Because of this ease of recollection, we think the probability of being bitten by sharks is much higher than it is in reality.

representativeness heuristic A natural tendency to evaluate probabilities of events or objects by the degree to which they resemble (are representative of) other events or objects rather than on objective probability information.

REPRESENTATIVENESS HEURISTIC People tend to evaluate the likelihood that objects have particular characteristics by the degree to which they resemble or represent other objects, rather than on objective probability information.[31] Stereotyping is one form of this bias. Suppose you are asked to identify a student's university course on the basis of only the person's personality profile and the fact that the person is in a population of 25 engineers and 75 social science students. If the personality fits your stereotype of engineers, you would likely identify the student as an engineer even though he or she is three times as likely to be studying social science. Another form of the representativeness heuristic, known as the *clustering illusion*, is the tendency to see patterns from a small sample of events when those events are, in fact, random. For example, most players and coaches believe that players are more likely to have a successful shot on the net when their previous two or three shots have been successful. The representativeness heuristic is at work here because players and coaches believe these sequences are causally connected (representative) when, in reality, they are random events.

Problems with Maximisation

One of the main assumptions of the rational choice paradigm is that people want to (and are able to) choose the alternative with the highest pay-off. This highest pay-off is the 'utility' in subjective expected utility. Yet rather than aiming for maximisation, people engage in

satisficing—they choose an alternative that is satisfactory or 'good enough'.[32] They evaluate alternatives sequentially and select the first one perceived to be above a standard of acceptance for their needs and preferences. One reason why satisficing occurs is that, as mentioned earlier, decision makers have a natural tendency to evaluate alternatives sequentially, not all at the same time. They evaluate each alternative against the implicit favourite and eventually select an option that scores above a subjective minimum point considered to be good enough.

satisficing Selecting an alternative that is satisfactory or 'good enough' rather than the alternative with the highest value (maximisation).

A second reason why people engage in satisficing rather than maximisation is that choosing the best alternative demands more information processing capacity than people possess or are willing to apply. Studies have found that people like to have choices, but when exposed to many alternatives, they become cognitive misers by engaging in less optimal decision making.[33] Such decision-making efficiencies include discarding alternatives that fail a threshold level on one or two factors (such as colour or size), comparing among only a few alternatives rather than all choices, and choosing the first alternative above a preset standard (i.e. satisficing). One study found that, compared to people given few alternatives, those given a large number of alternatives subsequently experienced less physical stamina, had more difficulty performing arithmetic calculations, were less resilient in the face of failure and engaged in more procrastination. In other words, making the best choice among many alternatives can be cognitively and emotionally draining.

One other observation suggests that people lack information-processing capacity to select the best alternative. Research has found that as the number of alternatives increases, people are less likely to make any choice at all. This problem was highlighted in a study of consumer responses to two jam-tasting booths in a grocery store, one displaying 6 types of jam and the other displaying 24 flavours. Thirty per cent of shoppers who stopped at the 6-jam display bought some jam; only 3 per cent of shoppers who stopped by the 24-jam display bought jam. The larger number of choices discouraged customers from making any purchase decision. These results are similar to those in other studies where people made decisions about chocolates, essays and pension plan investment options.[34] Four decades ago, futurist Alvin Toffler warned about the increasing risk of choice overload: 'People of the future may suffer not from an absence of choice, but from a paralysing surfeit of it. They may turn out to be victims of that peculiarly super-industrial dilemma: overchoice.'[35]

Evaluating Opportunities

Opportunities are just as important as problems, but what happens when an opportunity is 'discovered' is quite different from the process of problem solving. According to a recent study of decision failures, decision makers do not evaluate several alternatives when they find an opportunity; after all, the opportunity *is* the solution, so why look for others! An opportunity is usually experienced as an exciting and rare revelation, so decision makers tend to have an emotional attachment to the opportunity. Unfortunately, this emotional preference motivates decision makers to apply the opportunity and short-circuit any detailed evaluation of it.[36]

Emotions and Making Choices

LEARNING OBJECTIVE 

Describe three ways in which emotions influence the selection of alternatives.

Herbert Simon and many other experts have presented plenty of evidence that people do not evaluate alternatives nearly as well as is assumed by the rational choice paradigm. However, they neglected to mention another glaring weakness with rational choice: it completely ignores the effect of emotions in human decision making. Just as both the rational and emotional brain centres alert us to problems, they also influence our choice of alternatives.[37] Emotions affect the evaluation of alternatives in three ways.

Emotions Form Early Preferences

The emotional marker process described earlier in this chapter as well as in previous chapters (Chapters 3–5) determines our preferences for each alternative. Our brain very quickly attaches specific emotions to information about each alternative, and our preferred alternative is strongly influenced by those initial emotional markers. Of course, logical analysis also influences the alternative we choose, but it requires strong logical evidence to change our initial preferences (initial emotional markers). Yet even logical analysis depends on emotions to sway our decision. Specifically, neuroscientific evidence says that information produced from logical analysis is tagged with emotional markers that then motivate us to choose or avoid a particular alternative. Ultimately, emotions, not rational logic, energise us to make the preferred choice. In fact, people with damaged emotional brain centres have difficulty making choices.[38]

Emotions Change the Decision Evaluation Process

A considerable body of literature indicates that moods and specific emotions influence the *process* of evaluating alternatives.[39] For instance, we pay more attention to details when in a negative mood, possibly because a negative mood signals that there is something wrong that requires attention. When in a positive mood, on the other hand, we pay less attention to details and rely on a more programmed decision routine. This phenomenon explains why executive teams in successful companies are often less vigilant about competitors and other environmental threats.[40] Research also suggests that decision makers rely on stereotypes and other shortcuts to speed up the choice process when they experience anger. Anger also makes them more optimistic about the success of risky alternatives, whereas the emotion of fear tends to make them less optimistic. Overall, emotions shape *how* we evaluate information, not just which choice we select.

Emotions Serve as Information When We Evaluate Alternatives

The third way that emotions influence the evaluation of alternatives is through a process called 'emotions as information'. Marketing experts have found that we listen in on our emotions to help guide us when making choices.[41] You might think of this as a temporary improvement in emotional intelligence. Most emotional experiences remain below the level of conscious awareness, but people actively try to be more sensitive to these subtle emotions when making a decision.

When buying a new car, for example, you not only logically evaluate each vehicle's features; you also try to gauge your emotions when visualising what it would be like to own each of the alternative cars on your list of choices. Even if you have solid information about the quality of each vehicle on key features (purchase price, fuel efficiency, maintenance costs, resale value, and so on), you are swayed by your emotional reaction to each vehicle and actively try to sense that emotional response when thinking about it. Some people pay more attention to these gut feelings, and personality tests such as the Myers-Briggs Type Indicator (see Chapter 2) identify individuals who listen in on their emotions more than others.[42] But all of us use our emotions as information to some degree. This phenomenon ties directly into our next topic: intuition.

Intuition and Making Choices

LEARNING OBJECTIVE

Outline how intuition operates.

Greg McDonald felt uneasy about a suspicious-looking crack in the rock face, so the veteran miner warned a coworker to stay away from the area. 'There was no indication there was anything wrong—just a little crack,' McDonald recalled. A few minutes later, the ceiling in the mine shaft more than 900 metres underground caved in. Fortunately, the coworker had heeded McDonald's advice. 'If he had been there, he would be dead,' McDonald said in an interview following a near-sleepless night after the incident.[43]

The gut instinct that helped Greg McDonald save his coworker's life is known as **intuition**—the ability to know when a problem or opportunity exists and to select the best course of action without conscious reasoning.[44] Intuition is both an emotional experience and a rapid, unconscious, analytic process. As mentioned in the previous section, the gut feelings we experience are emotional signals that have enough intensity to make us consciously aware of them. These signals warn us of impending danger, such as a dangerous mine wall, or motivate us to take advantage of an opportunity. Some intuition also directs us to preferred choices relative to other alternatives in the situation.

intuition The ability to know when a problem or opportunity exists and to select the best course of action without conscious reasoning.

All gut feelings are emotional signals, but not all emotional signals are intuition. The key distinction is that intuition involves rapidly comparing our observations with deeply held patterns learned through experience.[45] These templates represent tacit knowledge that has been implicitly acquired over time. They are mental models that help us to understand whether the current situation is good or bad, depending on how well that situation fits our mental model. When a template fits or doesn't fit the current situation, emotions are produced that motivate us to act. Greg McDonald's years of experience produced mental templates of unsafe rock faces that matched what he saw on that fateful day. Studies have also found that chess masters receive emotional signals when they sense an opportunity through quick observation of a chessboard. When given the opportunity to think about the situation, they can explain why they see a favourable move on the chessboard. However, their intuition signals the opportunity long before this rational analysis takes place.

As mentioned, some emotional signals are not intuition, so some experts warn that we should not trust our gut feelings. The problem is that emotional responses are not always based on well-grounded mental models. Instead, they occur when we compare the current situation to more remote templates, which may or may not be relevant. A new employee might feel confident about relations with a supplier, whereas an experienced employee senses potential problems. The difference is that the new employee relies on templates from other experiences or industries that might not work well in this situation. Thus, whether the emotions we experience in a situation represent intuition or not depends largely on our level of experience in that situation.

So far, we have described intuition as an emotional experience (gut feeling) and a process in which we compare the current situation with well-established templates of the mind. Intuition also relies on *action scripts*—programmed decision routines that speed up our response to pattern matches or mismatches.[46] Action scripts effectively shorten the decision-making process by jumping from problem identification to selection of a solution. In other words, action scripting is a form of programmed decision making. Action scripts are generic, so we need to consciously adapt them to the specific situation.

Making Choices More Effectively

It is very difficult to get around the human limitations of making choices, but a few strategies help to minimise these concerns. One important discovery is that decisions tend to have a higher failure rate when leaders are decisive rather than contemplative about the available options. Of course, decisions can also be ineffective when leaders take too long to make a choice, but research indicates that a lack of logical evaluation of alternatives is a greater concern. By systematically assessing alternatives against relevant factors, decision makers minimise the implicit favourite and satisficing problems that occur when they rely on general subjective judgements. This recommendation does not suggest that we ignore intuition; rather, it suggests that we use it in combination with careful analysis of relevant information.[47]

A second piece of advice is that we need to remember that decisions are influenced by both rational and emotional processes. With this awareness, some decision makers deliberately revisit important issues so that they can look at the information in different moods after allowing their initial emotions to subside. For example, if you sense that your team is feeling somewhat too self-confident when making an important competitive decision, you might decide to have the team members revisit the decision a few days later when they are thinking more critically. Another strategy is **scenario planning**, which is a disciplined method for imagining possible futures. It typically involves thinking about what would happen if a significant environmental condition changed and what the organisation should do to anticipate and react to such an outcome.[48] Scenario planning is a useful vehicle for choosing the best solutions within possible scenarios long before they occur, because alternative courses of action are evaluated without the pressure and emotions that occur during real emergencies.

scenario planning A systematic process of thinking about alternative futures and what the organisation should do to anticipate and react to those environments.

IMPLEMENTING DECISIONS

Implementing decisions is often skipped over in most writing about the decision-making process. Yet leading business writers emphasise that execution—translating decisions into action—is one of the most important and challenging tasks of leaders. A survey of 3600 managers identified the 'drive for results' as one of the five most important competencies of effective managers. This evidence is backed up by Larry Bossidy's experience leading thousands of managers. 'When assessing candidates, the first thing I looked for was energy and enthusiasm for execution,' says the former CEO of Honeywell and Allied Signal. The art and science of implementing decisions will be covered more fully in later chapters, particularly those on leadership and organisational change.[49]

EVALUATING DECISION OUTCOMES

Contrary to the rational choice paradigm, decision makers aren't completely honest with themselves when evaluating the effectiveness of their decisions. One problem is *confirmation bias* (also known as *post-decisional justification* in the context of decision evaluation), which is the 'unwitting selectivity in the acquisition and use of evidence'.[50] When evaluating decisions, confirmation bias involves ignoring or downplaying the negative features of the selected alternative and overemphasising its positive features. Research has found that confirmation bias is typically nonconscious and driven by emotions. Confirmation bias gives people an excessively optimistic evaluation of their decisions, but only until they receive very clear and undeniable information to the contrary. Unfortunately, it also inflates the decision maker's initial evaluation of the decision, so reality often comes as a painful shock when objective feedback is finally received.

Escalation of Commitment

LEARNING OBJECTIVE

Describe four causes of escalation of commitment.

In addition to confirmation bias, people poorly evaluate their decision outcomes due to **escalation of commitment**—the tendency to repeat an apparently bad decision or allocate more resources to a failing course of action.[51] Scotland's new parliament building is one example of escalation of commitment. Originally estimated at £50 million, the Holyrood building eventually cost £400 million and took twice as long to construct than originally planned. Another example might be the Sydney Opera House, which cost ten times more than originally proposed, took seventeen years to complete and has never functioned well for its intended purpose. Fortunately, the high cost of the Sydney Opera House has easily been recouped by its reputation as a priceless iconic structure for Sydney and Australia.[52]

escalation of commitment The tendency to repeat an apparently bad decision or allocate more resources to a failing course of action.

A third example of escalation of commitment is the Darlington nuclear power plant in Ontario, Canada, which had an estimated cost of CDN$2 billion (some claim the estimate was $5 billion) and was eventually completed at a cost of more than $14 billion. This huge debacle prompted the Ontario government to deregulate the electricity industry and split Ontario Hydro (now called Hydro One) into two operating companies. Ironically, a former CEO of Ontario Hydro warned that Darlington and other mega-projects invite escalating commitment because 'once you commit to them, there's very little you can do to reverse that commitment'.[53]

Irish Health under re-PPARS

In the mid-1990s, executives at five health boards across Ireland decided to develop a common payroll system, called PPARS (Payroll, Payment and Related Systems). Using well-established enterprise software, the project would be completed in three years at a total estimated cost of US$12 million. Health department officials were enthusiastic about the many benefits of PPARS, but four years later the system was still far from completion even though costs had more than doubled to $25 million. Asked in 2002 to evaluate the project, Hay Associates concluded that PPARS was worth continuing, even if only to recoup the funds spent so far. The catch, however, was that the government needed to fork out another $120 million, which it agreed to do. By 2005, Ireland's finance department was sounding alarm bells that PPARS costs had spiralled out of control and the operational parts of the system were error-prone. The most embarrassing example was a health department employee who received a $1.5 million pay cheque one week. The Irish government halted the rollout of PPARS, yet senior health officials remained confident in its success, ordering staff as late as May 2007 to 'realise the benefits' of the system. PPARS was officially axed in July 2007. The estimated cost of the failed project: somewhere between $250 and $350 million.[54]

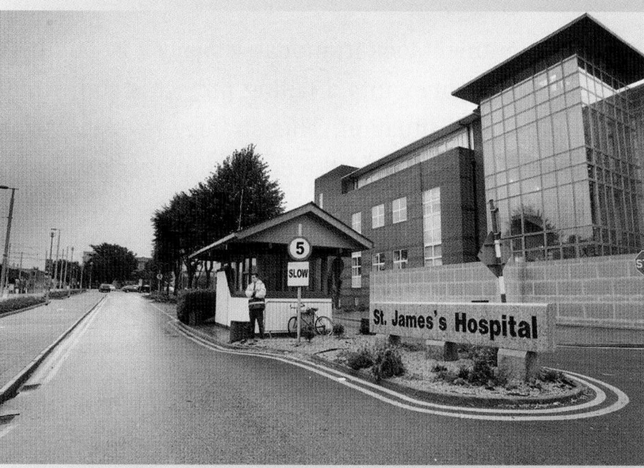

Brenda Fitzsimons/Irish Times LTD

Causes of Escalating Commitment

The four main reasons why people are led deeper and deeper into failing projects are self-justification, prospect theory effect, perceptual blinders and closing costs.

SELF-JUSTIFICATION Individuals are motivated to maintain their course of action when they have a high need to justify their decision. This self-justification is particularly evident when decision makers are personally identified with the project and have staked their reputations to some extent on the project's success.[55] The Irish government's PPARS project mentioned earlier likely experienced escalation to some degree for this reason. The reputations of government politicians and health board officials depended on the success of PPARS, and pouring more money into the project symbolised their continued support and appeared to provide evidence that the decision was a wise one.

PROSPECT THEORY EFFECT You would think that people dislike losing $50 just as much as they like receiving $50, but that isn't true for most of us. The negative emotions we experience when losing a particular amount are stronger than the positive emotions we experience when gaining the same amount. Consequently, we are more motivated to take risks that potentially avoid losses than to take risks that potentially increase our gains. This effect, called **prospect theory**, is a second explanation for escalation of commitment. Stopping a project is a certain loss, which is more painful to most people than the uncertainty of success associated with continuing to fund the project. Given the choice, decision makers choose the less painful option.[56]

prospect theory A natural tendency to feel more dissatisfaction from losing a particular amount than satisfaction from gaining an equal amount.

PERCEPTUAL BLINDERS Escalation of commitment sometimes occurs because decision makers do not see the problems soon enough.[57] They nonconsciously screen out or explain away negative information to protect self-esteem. Serious problems initially look like random errors along the trend line to success. Even when decision makers see that something is wrong, the information is sufficiently ambiguous that it can be misinterpreted or justified.

CLOSING COSTS Even when a project's success is in doubt, decision makers will persist because the costs of ending the project are high or unknown. Stopping a major project before its completion may involve large financial penalties, a bad public image or personal political costs.

These four conditions make escalation of commitment look irrational. Usually it is, but there are exceptions. Studies suggest that throwing more money into a failing project is sometimes a logical attempt to further understand an ambiguous situation. This strategy is essentially a variation of testing unknown waters. By adding more resources, the decision maker gains new information about the effectiveness of these funds, which provides more feedback about the project's future success. This strategy is particularly common where the project has high closing costs.[58]

Evaluating Decision Outcomes More Effectively

One of the most effective ways to minimise escalation of commitment and confirmation bias is to ensure that the people who made the original decision are not the same people who later evaluate that decision. This separation of roles minimises the self-justification effect because the person responsible for evaluating the decision is not connected to the original decision. A second strategy is to publicly establish a preset level at which the decision is abandoned or re-evaluated. This is similar to a stop loss order in the stock market, whereby the shares are sold if it falls below a certain price. The problem with this solution is that it is difficult to identify an appropriate point to abandon a project.[59]

A third strategy is to find a source of systematic and clear feedback.[60] For example, the phenomenally large cost overruns at Scotland's new parliament building might have been smaller if the Scottish government had received less ambiguous or less distorted information from civil servants about the true costs of the project during the first few years. (In fact, civil servants hid some of these costs from elected officials.)[61] A fourth strategy to improve the decision evaluation process is to involve several people in the evaluation. Coworkers continuously monitor each other and might notice problems sooner than someone working alone on the project. Employee involvement offers these and other benefits to the decision-making process, as we discuss next.

EMPLOYEE INVOLVEMENT IN DECISION MAKING

LEARNING OBJECTIVE 

Describe four benefits of employee involvement in decision making.

In this world of rapid change and increasing complexity, leaders rarely have enough information to make the best decision alone, so organisations rely on the knowledge and multiple perspectives of employees to more effectively solve problems or realise opportunities. 'The Information Age has brought us into a democratic age, an age of participation and influence,' says Traci Fenton, founder and CEO of WorldBlu, a consulting firm that specialises in employee involvement and organisational democracy.[62]

Employee involvement (also called *participative management*) refers to the degree to which employees influence how their work is organised and carried out.[63] Every organisation has some form of employee involvement operating at various levels. At the lowest level, participation involves asking employees for information. They do not make recommendations and might not even know what the problem is about. At a moderate level of involvement, employees are told about the problem and provide recommendations to the decision maker. At the highest level of involvement, the entire decision-making process is handed over to employees. They identify the problem, choose the best alternative and implement their choice.

employee involvement The degree to which employees influence how their work is organised and carried out.

Benefits of Employee Involvement

For the past half century, organisational behaviour scholars have advised that employee involvement potentially improves decision-making quality and commitment.[65] Involved employees can help improve decision quality by recognising problems more quickly and defining them more accurately. Employees are, in many respects, the sensors of the organisation's environment. When the organisation's activities misalign with customer expectations, employees are usually the first to know. Employee involvement ensures that everyone in the organisation is quickly alerted to such problems.[66] Employee involvement can also potentially improve the number and quality of solutions generated. In a well-managed meeting, team members create synergy by pooling their knowledge to form new alternatives. In other words, several people working together can potentially generate more and better solutions than the same people working alone.

Employee Involvement Keeps Thai Carbon Black in the Black

Thai Carbon Black, which makes the black colouring agent in tyres, inks and many other products, views all of its employees as problem solvers. 'The "can do" attitude of every employee is important,' says the president of the Thai-Indian joint venture. Each year, the staff submits over 600 productivity improvement suggestions, placing their ideas in one of the little red boxes located around the company's site. Participatory management meetings are held every month, at which employees are encouraged to come up with new ideas on ways to improve day-to-day operations. For instance, the company cut its transport costs by more than 10 per cent after employees developed a special shipping bag allowing packers to stuff more product into the same volume. Thanks in part to its emphasis on employee involvement, Thai Carbon Black is one of the few companies outside Japan to receive the Deming Prize for total quality management. It is also one of a few companies to be recognised by the Stock Exchange of Thailand as a 'Best Performance Management Company'. On multiple occasions, *Forbes* magazine has listed Thai Carbon Black as one of the best-managed companies in the region. Hewitt Associates has ranked it as one of the best employers in Asia and Thailand.[64]

Yvan Cohen/On Asia Images

A third benefit of employee involvement is that, under specific conditions, it improves the evaluation of alternatives. Numerous studies on participative decision making, constructive conflict and team dynamics have found that involvement brings out more diverse perspectives, tests ideas and provides more valuable knowledge, all of which help the decision maker to select the best alternative.[67] A mathematical theorem introduced in 1785 by the Marquis de Condorcet states that the alternative selected by the team's majority is more likely to be correct than is the alternative selected by any team member individually.[68] More recently, scholars and practitioners alike have promoted the 'wisdom of crowds'. Consistent with Condorcet's theorem, these writers explain that a group of people makes better decisions than individuals alone. However, this advantage requires that each person has relevant information about the decision topic, each person's information is unique within the group (i.e. other people don't have the same information), and each person's opinion is not influenced by the opinion of other people.[69] As was described in the opening vignette to this chapter, Google applies the wisdom of crowds in its prediction markets. By encouraging a large number of employees to vote on various alternatives, Google executives typically receive better information about choices or estimates about future events than if individual experts were asked for their predictions.

Along with improving decision quality, employee involvement tends to strengthen employee commitment to the decision. Rather than viewing themselves as agents of someone else's decision, staff members feel personally responsible for its success. Involvement also has positive effects on employee motivation, satisfaction and turnover. A recent study reported that

Exhibit 7.3 *Model of Employee Involvement in Decision Making*

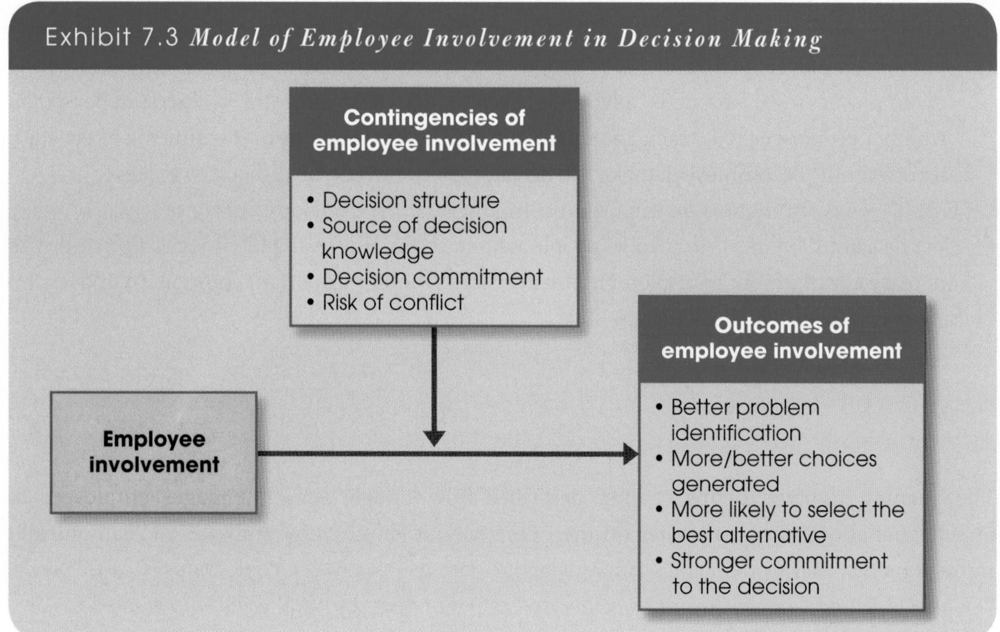

employee involvement increases skill variety, feelings of autonomy and task identity, all of which increase job enrichment and potentially employee motivation. Participation is also a critical practice in organisational change because employees are more motivated to implement the decision and less likely to resist changes resulting from the decision.[70]

Contingencies of Employee Involvement

Identify four contingencies that affect the optimal level of employee involvement.

If employee involvement is so wonderful, why don't leaders leave all decisions to employees? The answer is that the optimal level of employee involvement depends on the situation. The employee involvement model shown in Exhibit 7.3 lists four contingencies: decision structure, source of decision knowledge, decision commitment and risk of conflict in the decision process:

- Decision structure—At the beginning of this chapter, we learned that some decisions are programmed, whereas others are nonprogrammed. Programmed decisions are less likely to need employee involvement because the solutions have already been worked out from past incidents. In other words, the benefits of employee involvement increase with the novelty and complexity of the problem or opportunity.
- Source of decision knowledge—Subordinates should be involved in some level of decision making when the leader lacks sufficient knowledge and subordinates have additional information to improve decision quality. In many cases, employees are closer to customers and production activities, so they often know where the company can save money, improve product or service quality and realise opportunities. This is particularly true for complex decisions where employees are more likely to possess relevant information.
- Decision commitment—Participation tends to improve employee commitment to the decision. If employees are unlikely to accept a decision made without their involvement, some level of participation is usually necessary.

- Risk of conflict—Two types of conflict undermine the benefits of employee involvement. First, if employee goals and norms conflict with the organisation's goals, only a low level of employee involvement is advisable. Second, the degree of involvement depends on whether employees will reach agreement on the preferred solution. If conflict is likely, high involvement (i.e. employees make the decision alone) would be difficult to achieve.

Employee involvement is an important component of the decision-making process. To make the best decisions, we need to involve people who have the most valuable information and who will increase commitment to implement the decision. Another important component of decision making is creativity, which we discuss next.

LEARNING OBJECTIVE 

Outline the four steps in the creative process.

CREATIVITY

The opening vignette to this chapter described how Google actively engages employees in organisational decisions and relies on their creativity to identify new software applications and improvements. Many of Google's runaway achievements—such as Google Maps, Google News, Google Docs, and Google Chrome—originated as pet projects by employees who wanted to solve problems or realise opportunities. The company is also a leader in hardware design with its energy-efficient servers.[71] Google encourages and relies on **creativity**—the development of original ideas that make a socially recognised contribution.[72] Although there are unique conditions for creativity that we discuss over the next few pages, it is really part of the decision-making process described earlier in the chapter. We rely on creativity to find problems, identify alternatives and

creativity The development of original ideas that make a socially recognised contribution.

Animated Creativity

Some of the world's most successful films have their special effects completed by companies in Australia and New Zealand, including Rising Sun Pictures (*Harry Potter, Blood Diamond, X-Men Origins*), Animal Logic (*Happy Feet, Australia, 300*), and Weta Digital/Weta Workshop (*Chronicles of Narnia, The Lord of the Rings, King Kong, Wall-E*). These firms have the world's most powerful computers and latest digital software, yet their success originates much more from the creative strength of their employees. 'The underpinning idea of Animal Logic is about using technology as a tool to express creativity,' explains Bruce Carter, creative director of the Sydney-based company. 'But the key people in the company were, and still are, on the creative side rather than the computer side.' Eileen Moran, visual effects producer at Weta Digital in Wellington, New Zealand, agrees. 'Mainly our strength is our crew, which have been with Weta throughout the delivery of *Lord of the Rings* and *King Kong*,' says Moran. 'They are dedicated to creating great work and always pushing to create new effects.'[73]

Rising Sun Pictures

implement solutions. Creativity is not something saved for special occasions. It is an integral part of decision making.

Exhibit 7.4 illustrates one of the earliest and most influential models of creativity.[74] Although there are other models of the creative process, many of them overlap with the model presented here. The first stage is *preparation*—the person or team's effort to acquire knowledge and skills regarding the problem or opportunity. Preparation involves developing a clear understanding of what you are trying to achieve through a novel solution and then actively studying information seemingly related to the topic.

The second stage, called *incubation*, is the period of reflective thought. We put the problem aside, but our mind is still working on it in the background.[75] The important condition here is to maintain a low-level awareness by frequently revisiting the problem. Incubation does not mean that you forget about the problem or issue. Incubation assists **divergent thinking**—reframing the problem in a unique way and generating different approaches to the issue. This contrasts with *convergent thinking*—calculating the conventionally accepted 'right answer' to a logical problem. Divergent thinking breaks us away from existing mental models so that we can apply concepts or processes from completely different areas of life. Consider the following classic example. Years ago, the experimental light bulbs in Thomas Edison's laboratory kept falling off their fixtures until a technician wondered whether the threaded caps that screwed down tightly on kerosene bottles would work on light bulbs. They did, and the design remains to this day.[76]

divergent thinking Reframing a problem in a unique way and generating different approaches to the issue.

Insight, the third stage of creativity, refers to the experience of suddenly becoming aware of a unique idea.[77] Insight is often visually depicted as a light bulb, but a better image would be a brief flash of light or perhaps a briefly flickering candle because these bits of inspiration are fleeting and can be quickly lost if not documented. For this reason, many creative people keep a journal or notebook nearby so that they can jot down their ideas before they disappear. Also, flickering ideas don't keep a particular schedule; they might come to you at any time of day or night.

Insights are merely rough ideas. Their usefulness still requires verification through detailed logical evaluation, experimentation and further creative insight. Thus, although *verification* is labelled the final stage of creativity, it is really the beginning of a long process of creative decision making that moves toward development of an innovative product or service.

Exhibit 7.4 *The Creative Process Model*

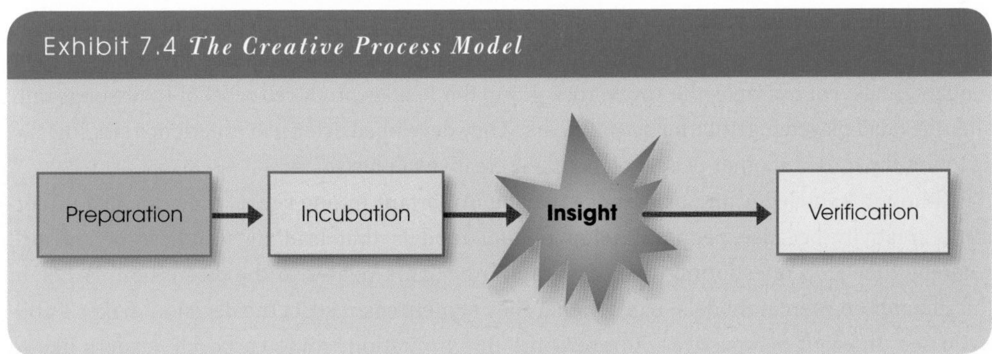

Source: Based on Graham Wallas, *The Art of Thought* (New York: Harcourt Brace Jovanovich, 1926).

LEARNING OBJECTIVE

Describe the characteristics of creative employees and workplaces that support creativity.

Characteristics of Creative People

Everyone is creative, but some people have a higher potential for creativity. Four of the main characteristics that give individuals more creative potential are intelligence, persistence, knowledge and experience, and a cluster of personality traits and values representing independent imagination.

Cognitive and Practical Intelligence

Creative people have above-average intelligence to synthesise information, analyse ideas and apply their ideas.[78] Like the fictional sleuth Sherlock Holmes, creative people recognise the significance of small bits of information and are able to connect them in ways that no one else could imagine. They also have *practical intelligence*—the capacity to evaluate the potential usefulness of their ideas.

Persistence

A second characteristic of creative people is persistence, which includes a higher need for achievement, a strong motivation from the task itself and a moderate or high degree of self-esteem. In support of this, studies report that inventors have higher levels of confidence and optimism than do people in the general population, and these traits motivate inventors to continue working on and investing in a project after receiving diagnostic advice to quit.[79]

Persistence is vital because creative ideas meet with plenty of resistance from other people, as well as failures along the way to success. For example, Australian medical researchers Barry Marshall and Robin Warren faced plenty of doubters when they first proposed that peptic ulcers are caused by specific bacteria. The prevailing belief was that these ulcers were caused by weak stomach linings, gastric acid and unhealthy diets. Even when Marshall and Warren submitted research evidence, journal editors were sceptical of the results. To further convince the doubters, Marshall ingested the bacteria into his healthy stomach and developed ulcer symptoms within a few days. 'It took 10 years and there was a lot of opposition,' recalls one expert. '[But Marshall] had this enormous self-belief that what he'd found was right.' Marshall and Warren were awarded the 2005 Nobel Prize in medicine for their discovery. Fittingly, the Nobel committee acknowledged that through their 'tenacity and a prepared mind' the pair had 'challenged prevailing dogmas'.[80]

Subject Knowledge and Experience

A third feature of creative people is that they possess sufficient knowledge and experience on the subject.[81] Creativity experts explain that discovering new ideas requires knowledge of the fundamentals. For example, the 1960s rock group the Beatles produced most of their songs only after they had played together for several years. They developed extensive experience singing and adapting the music of other people before their creative talents soared.

Although knowledge and experience may be important in one sense, they can also undermine creativity because people develop mental models that lead to 'mindless behaviour', whereby they stop questioning their assumptions.[82] This relates to the discussion earlier in this chapter on mental models, namely, that they sometimes restrict the decision maker's ability to see different perspectives. To overcome this limitation, some corporate leaders like to hire people from other industries and areas of expertise. For instance, Geoffrey Ballard, founder of Ballard Power Systems, hired a chemist to develop a better battery. When the chemist protested that he didn't know anything about batteries, Ballard replied: 'That's fine. I don't want someone who knows batteries. They know what won't work.'[83] Ballard explained that he wanted to hire people who would question and investigate avenues that experts had long ago closed their minds to. The point here is that knowledge and experience is a double-edged sword. It is an important prerequisite for creativity, but too much routinisation of knowledge and experience can cause people to be less investigative.

Independent Imagination

The fourth characteristic of creative people is a cluster of personality traits and values that support an independent imagination: high openness to experience, moderately low need for affiliation, and strong values around self-direction and stimulation. Several studies report that these personal characteristics improve the individual's creative potential under some circumstances.[84] Let's examine each of them:

- High openness to experience—This Big Five personality dimension represents the extent to which a person is imaginative, curious, sensitive, open-minded and original (see Chapter 2).
- Moderately low need for affiliation—People are more creative when they have less need for social approval and have a somewhat high (but not necessarily very high) degree of nonconformity. Because of these characteristics, creative people are less embarrassed when they make mistakes, and they remain motivated to explore ideas even when others criticise them for their persistence.
- High self-direction and stimulation values—Self-direction includes the values of creativity and independent thought; stimulation includes the values of excitement and challenge. Together, these values form openness to change—representing the motivation to pursue innovative ways (see Chapter 2).

Organisational Conditions Supporting Creativity

Intelligence, persistence, knowledge and experience, and independent imagination represent a person's creative potential, but the extent to which this translates into more creative output depends on a work environment that supports the creative process.[85] Several job and workplace characteristics have been identified in the literature, and different combinations of situations can equally support creativity; there isn't one best work environment.[86]

One of the most important conditions that supports creative practice is that the organisation has a *learning orientation*; that is, leaders recognise that employees make reasonable mistakes as part of the creative process. 'Creativity comes from failure,' Samsung Electronics CEO and vice chairman Yun Jong-yong recently advised employees. 'We should reform our corporate culture to forgive failure if workers did their best.'[87] Motivation from the job itself is another important condition for creativity.[88] Employees tend to be more creative when they believe their work benefits the organisation and/or larger society (i.e. task significance) and when they have the freedom to pursue novel ideas without bureaucratic delays (i.e. autonomy). Creativity is about changing things, and change is possible only when employees have the authority to experiment. More generally, jobs encourage creativity when they are challenging and aligned with the employee's competencies.

Along with supporting a learning orientation and creating intrinsically motivating jobs, companies foster creativity through open communication and sufficient resources. They also provide a reasonable level of job security, which explains why creativity suffers during times of downsizing and corporate restructuring.[89] Some companies support the reflection stage of creativity by designing nontraditional workspaces.[90] Google is one example. The internet innovator has funky offices in several countries that include hammocks, gondola- and hive-shaped privacy spaces, slides and brightly painted walls.

To some degree, creativity also improves with support from leaders and coworkers. One study reported that effective product champions provide enthusiastic support for new ideas. Other studies suggest that coworker support can improve creativity in some situations whereas competition among coworkers improves creativity in other situations.[91] Similarly, it isn't clear how much pressure should be exerted on employees to produce creative ideas. Extreme time pressures are well-known creativity inhibitors, but lack of pressure doesn't seem to produce the highest creativity either.

Activities That Encourage Creativity

Hiring people with strong creative potential and providing a work environment that supports creativity are two cornerstones of a creative workplace. The third cornerstone consists of various activities that help employees think more creatively. One set of activities involves redefining the problem. Employees might be encouraged to revisit old projects that have been set aside. After a few months of neglect, these projects might be seen in new ways.[92] Another strategy involves asking people unfamiliar with the issue (preferably with different areas of expertise) to explore the problem with you. You would state the objectives and give some facts, then let the other person ask questions to further understand the situation. By verbalising the problem, listening to questions and hearing what others think, you are more likely to form new perspectives on the issue.[93]

A second set of creativity activities, known as *associative play*, ranges from art classes to impromptu storytelling and acting. For example, British media giant OMD sends employees to two-day retreats in the countryside, where they play grapefruit croquet, chant like medieval monks and pretend to be dog collars. 'Being creative is a bit like an emotion; we need to be stimulated,' explains Harriet Frost, one of OMD's specialists in building creativity. 'The same is true for our imagination and its ability to come up with new ideas. You can't just sit in a room and devise hundreds of ideas.'[94]

Another associative play activity, called *morphological analysis*, involves listing different dimensions of a system and the elements of each dimension and then looking at each combination. This encourages people to carefully examine combinations that initially seem nonsensical. Tyson Foods, the world's largest poultry producer, applied this activity to identify new ways to serve chicken for lunch. The marketing and research team assigned to this task focused on three categories: occasion, packaging and taste. Next, the team worked through numerous combinations of items in the three categories. This created unusual ideas, such as cheese chicken pasta (taste) in pizza boxes (packaging) for food stands at baseball games (occasion). Later, the team looked more closely at the feasibility of these combinations and sent them to customer focus groups for further testing.[95]

A third set of activities that promote creative thinking falls under the category of *cross-pollination*.[96] Cross-pollination occurs when people from different areas of the organisation

Mother's Creative Cross-Pollination

Mother is an unusual creative agency with an equally unusual name, located in a converted warehouse in an artsy district of London. All of this quirkiness fuels creativity, but the ad agency's most creative practice is its workspace arrangement. The company's 100 or so employees perform their daily work around one monster-size table—a 2.5-metre-wide reinforced-concrete slab that extends 100 metres like a skateboard ramp around the entire floor. If that image isn't sufficiently unusual, consider this: every three weeks, employees are asked to relocate their laptop, portable telephone and trolley to another area around the table. 'At the end of every three weeks we have a tidy Friday, which helps keep the mess down, and then we move the following Monday,' explains Stef Calcraft, one of Mother's founding partners. 'One week, you may be sitting next to a finance person and opposite a creative. The next, you'll be sitting between one of the partners and someone from production.' Why the musical-chairs exercise? 'It encourages cross-pollination of ideas,' Calcraft answers. 'You have people working on the same problem from different perspectives. It makes problem-solving much more organic.'[97]

Adrian Wilson

exchange ideas. 'Creativity comes out of people bumping into each other and not knowing where to go,' claims Laszlo Bock, Google's top human resource executive. IDEO, the California-based product design company, engages in cross-pollination by mixing together employees from different past projects so that they share new knowledge with each other.

Cross-pollination highlights the fact that creativity rarely occurs alone. Some creative people may be individualistic, but most creative ideas are generated through teams and informal social interaction. 'This whole thing about the solitary tortured artist is nonsense I think,' says John Collee, the Sydney-based screenwriter, who cowrote such films as *Happy Feet* and *Master and Commander: The Far Side of the World*. 'All the great creative people I know have become great precisely because they know how to get along with people and swim around in the communal unconscious.'[98] The next chapter turns our attention to teams, including team effectiveness, as well as ways to improve team decision making and creativity.

CHAPTER SUMMARY

Decision making is a conscious process of making choices among one or more alternatives with the intention of moving toward some desired state of affairs. The rational choice paradigm of decision making includes identifying problems and opportunities, choosing the best decision style, developing alternative solutions, choosing the best solution, implementing the selected alternative and evaluating decision outcomes.

Stakeholder framing, mental models, decisive leadership, solution-oriented focus and perceptual defence affect our ability to identify problems and opportunities. We can minimise these challenges by being aware of our human limitations and discussing the situation with colleagues.

Evaluating and choosing alternatives is often challenging because organisational goals are ambiguous or in conflict, human information processing is incomplete and subjective, and people tend to satisfice rather than maximise. Decision makers also short-circuit the evaluation process when faced with an opportunity rather than a problem. Emotions shape our preferences for alternatives and the process we follow to evaluate alternatives. We also listen to our emotions for guidance when making decisions. This activity relates to intuition—the ability to know when a problem or opportunity exists and to select the best course of action without conscious reasoning. Intuition is both an emotional experience and a rapid, nonconscious, analytic process that involves both pattern matching and action scripts.

People generally make better choices by systematically evaluating alternatives. Scenario planning can help people make future decisions without the pressure and emotions that occur during real emergencies.

Confirmation bias and escalation of commitment make it difficult to accurately evaluate decision outcomes. Escalation is mainly caused by self-justification, the prospect theory effect, perceptual blinders and closing costs. These problems are minimised by separating decision choosers from decision evaluators, establishing a preset level at which the decision is abandoned or re-evaluated, relying on more systematic and clear feedback about the project's success, and involving several people in decision making.

Employee involvement (or participation) is the degree to which employees influence how their work is organised and carried out. The level of participation may range from low (an employee providing specific information to management without knowing the problem or issue) to high (complete involvement in all phases of the decision process). Employee involvement may lead to higher decision quality and commitment, but several contingencies need to be considered, including the decision structure, source of decision knowledge, decision commitment and risk of conflict.

Creativity is the development of original ideas that make a socially recognised contribution. The four creativity stages are preparation, incubation, insight and verification. Incubation assists divergent thinking, which involves reframing the problem in a unique way and generating different approaches to the issue.

Four of the main features of creative people are intelligence, persistence, knowledge and experience, and personality and values that support independent imagination. Creativity is also strengthened for everyone when the work environment supports a learning orientation; the job has high intrinsic motivation; the organisation provides a reasonable level of job security; and project leaders provide appropriate goals, time pressure and resources. Three types of activities that encourage creativity are redefining the problem, associative play and cross-pollination.

KEY TERMS

anchoring and adjustment heuristic, p. 250
attention-based theory of the firm, p. 245
availability heuristic, p. 250
bounded rationality, p. 247
creativity, p. 260
decision making, p. 242
divergent thinking, p. 261
employee involvement, p. 257
escalation of commitment, p. 255
implicit favourite, p. 249
intuition, p. 253
prospect theory, p. 256
rational choice paradigm, p. 242
representativeness heuristic, p. 250
satisficing, p. 251
scenario planning, p. 254
subjective expected utility, p. 242

Critical Thinking Questions

1. A management consultant is hired by a manufacturing firm to determine the best site for its next production facility. The consultant has had several meetings with the company's senior executives regarding the factors to consider when making the recommendation. Discuss the decision-making problems that might prevent the consultant from choosing the best site location.

2. You have been asked to personally recommend a new travel agency to handle all airfare, accommodation and related travel needs for your organisation of 500 employees. One of your coworkers, who is responsible for the company's economic planning, suggests that the best travel agent could be selected mathematically by inputting the relevant factors for each agency and the weight (importance) of each factor. What decision-making approach is your colleague recommending? Is this recommendation a good idea in this situation? Why or why not?

3. Intuition is both an emotional experience and an unconscious analytic process. One problem, however, is that not all emotions signalling that there is a problem or opportunity represent intuition. Explain how we would know if our 'gut feelings' are intuition or not. If they are not intuition, suggest what might be causing them.

4. A developer received financial backing for a new business financial centre along a derelict section of the waterfront, a few kilometres from the central business district of a large European city. The idea was to build several high-rise structures, attract to those sites prestigious tenants requiring large leases and have the city extend transportation systems out to the new centre. Over the next decade, the developer believed that others would build in the area, thereby attracting the regional or national offices of many financial institutions. Interest from potential tenants was much lower than initially predicted, and the city did not build transportation systems as quickly as expected. Still, the builder proceeded with the original plans. Only after financial support was curtailed did the developer reconsider the project. Using your knowledge of escalation of commitment, discuss three possible reasons why the developer was motivated to continue with the project.

5 Ancient Book Company has a problem with new book projects. Even when others are aware that a book is far behind schedule and may engender little public interest, sponsoring editors are reluctant to terminate contracts with authors whom they have signed. The result is that editors invest more time in these projects than on more fruitful projects. Describe two methods that Ancient Book Company can use to minimise this problem, which is a form of escalation of commitment.

6 Employee involvement applies just as well to the classroom as to the office or factory floor. Explain how student involvement in classroom decisions typically made by the instructor alone might improve decision quality. What potential problems may occur in this process?

7 Think of a time when you experienced the creative process. Maybe you woke up with a brilliant (but usually sketchy and incomplete) idea or you solved a baffling problem while doing something else. Describe the incident to your class and explain how the experience followed the creative process.

8 Two characteristics of creative people are that they have relevant experience and are persistent in their quest. Does this mean that people with the most experience and the highest need for achievement are the most creative? Explain your answer.

Skill Builder 7.1

CLASS EXERCISE

Employee Involvement Scenarios

Scenario 1: The Sugar Substitute Research Decision

You are the head of research and development (R&D) for a major beer company. While working on a new beer product, one of the scientists in your unit seems to have tentatively identified a new chemical compound that has few calories but tastes more like sugar than current sugar substitutes. The company has no foreseeable need for this product, but it could be patented and licensed to manufacturers in the food industry.

The sugar-substitute discovery is in its preliminary stages and would require considerable time and resources before it would be commercially viable. This means that it would necessarily take some resources away from other projects in the lab. The sugar-substitute project is beyond your technical expertise, but some of the R&D lab researchers are familiar with that field of chemistry. As with most forms of research, it is difficult to determine the amount of research required to further identify and perfect the sugar substitute. You do not know how much demand is expected for this product. Your department has a decision process for funding projects that are behind schedule. However, there are no rules or precedents about funding projects that would be licensed but not used by the organisation.

The company's R&D budget is limited, and other scientists in your work group have recently complained that they require more resources and financial support to get their projects completed. Some of these R&D projects hold promise for future beer sales. You believe that most researchers in the R&D unit are committed to ensuring that the company's interests are achieved.

Scenario 2: Coast Guard Cutter Decision Problem

You are the captain of a 42-metre Australian Coastwatch patrol vessel, with a crew of 24, including officers. Your mission is coastal surveillance and at-sea search and rescue. At 2:00 am this morning, while en route to your home port after a routine 28-day patrol, you received word from the nearest Coastwatch station that a small plane has crashed 100 kilometres offshore. You obtained all the available information concerning the location of the crash, informed your crew of the mission, and set a new course at maximum speed for the scene to commence a search for survivors and wreckage.

You have now been searching for 20 hours. Your search operation has been increasingly impaired by rough seas, and there is evidence of a severe storm building. The atmospherics associated with the deteriorating weather have made communications with the Coastwatch station impossible. A decision must be made shortly about whether to abandon the search and place your vessel on a course that would ride out the storm (thereby protecting the vessel and your crew, but relegating any possible survivors to almost certain death from exposure) or to continue a potentially futile search and the risks it would entail.

Before losing communications, you received an update weather advisory concerning the severity and duration of the storm. Although your crew members are extremely conscientious about their responsibility, you believe that they would be divided on the decision of leaving or staying.

Discussion Questions (for both scenarios)

1. To what extent should your subordinates be involved in this decision? Select one of the following levels of involvement:
   - No involvement—You make the decision alone without any participation from subordinates.
   - Low involvement—You ask one or more subordinates for information relating to the problem, but you don't ask for their recommendations and might not mention the problem to them.
   - Medium involvement—You describe the problem to one or more subordinates (alone or in a meeting) and ask for any relevant information as well as their recommendations on the issue. However, you make the final decision, which might or might not reflect their advice.
   - High involvement—You describe the problem to subordinates. They discuss the matter, identify a solution without your involvement (unless they invite your ideas) and implement that solution. You have agreed to support their decision.
2. What factors led you to choose this level of employee involvement rather than the others?
3. What problems might occur if less or more involvement occurred in this case (where possible)?

Sources: The Sugar Substitute Research Decision: © 2002 Steven L. McShane. The Coast Guard cutter case is adapted from V. H. Vroom and A. G. Jago, *The New Leadership: Managing Participation in Organisations* (Englewood Cliffs, NJ: Prentice Hall, 1988), © 1987 V. H. Vroom and A. G. Jago.

Skill Builder 7.2

TEAM EXERCISE

Where in the World Are We?

Purpose

This exercise is designed to help you understand the potential advantages of involving others in decisions rather than making decisions alone.

Materials

The instructor will give you an unmarked copy of a map of Asia with grid marks (Exhibit 1). You are not allowed to look at any other maps or use any other materials. The instructor will provide a list of communities located somewhere on Exhibit 2, and will also provide copies of the answer sheet after you have individually and in teams estimated the locations of communities.

Instructions

STEP 1 Using the table in Exhibit 2, write down the list of communities identified by your instructor. Then, working alone, estimate the location in Exhibit 2 of these communities, all of which are in Asia. For example, mark a small '1' in Exhibit 2 on the spot where you believe the first community is located. Mark a small '2' where you think the second community is located, and so on. Be sure to number each location clearly and with numbers small enough to fit within one grid space.

STEP 2 The instructor will organise students into approximately equal-sized teams (typically five or six people per team). Working with your team members, reach a consensus on the location of each community listed in Exhibit 2. The instructor might provide teams with a separate copy of this map, or each member can identify the team's numbers using a different coloured pen on their individual maps. The team's decision for each location should occur by consensus, not voting or averaging.

STEP 3 The instructor will provide or display an answer sheet, showing the correct locations of the communities. Using this answer sheet, count the minimum number of grid squares between the location you individually marked and the true location of each community. Write the number of grid squares in the second column of Exhibit 2, then add up the total. Next, count the minimum number of grid squares between the location the team marked and the true location of each community. Write the number of grid squares in the third column of Exhibit 2, then add up the total.

STEP 4 The instructor will ask for information about the totals and the class will discuss the implication of these results for employee involvement and decision making.

Exhibit 1: Map Showing Most of Asia

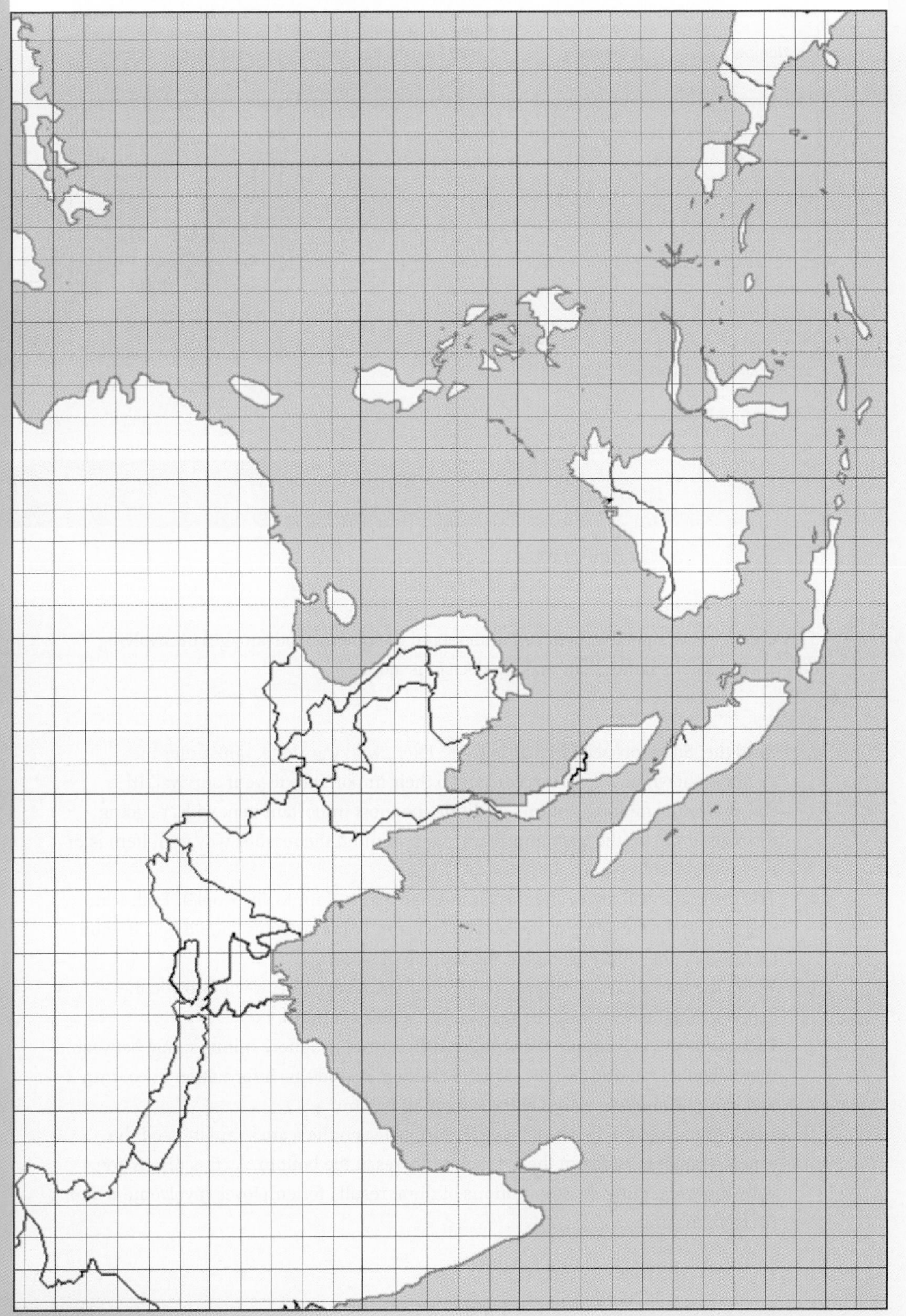

Exhibit 2: List of Selected Communities in Asia

Number	Community	Individual distance in grid units from the true location	Team distance in grid units from the true location
1			
2			
3			
4			
5			
6			
7			
8			
	TOTAL		

Skill Builder 7.3

Winter Survival Exercise

Purpose

This exercise is designed to help you understand the potential advantages of involving others in decisions rather than making decisions alone.

Instructions

1. Read the 'Situation' section that follows. Then, working alone, rank-order the 12 items shown in the chart according to their importance to your survival. In the 'individual ranking' column, indicate the most important item with '1', going through to '12' for the least important. Keep in mind the reasons why each item is or is not important.
2. The instructor will divide the class into small teams (four to six people). Each team will rank-order the items in the second column. Team rankings should be based on consensus, not simply averaging the individual rankings.
3. When the teams have completed their rankings, the instructor will provide the expert's ranking, which can be entered in the third column.
4. Each student will compute the absolute difference (i.e. ignore minus signs) between the individual ranking and the expert's ranking, record this information in column 4 and sum the absolute values at the bottom of column 4.
5. In column 5, record the absolute difference between the team's ranking and the expert's ranking, and sum these absolute scores at the bottom. A class discussion will follow regarding the implications of these results for employee involvement and decision making.

Situation

You have just crash-landed somewhere in the woods of southern Manitoba or possibly northern Minnesota. It is 11.32 am in mid-January. The small plane in which you were travelling crashed on a small lake. The pilot and copilot were killed. Shortly after the crash, the plane sank completely into the lake with the pilot's and copilot's bodies inside. Everyone else on the flight escaped to land dry and without serious injury.

The crash came suddenly; the pilot did not have time to radio for help or inform anyone of your position. Since your pilot was trying to avoid a storm, you know the plane was considerably off course. The pilot announced shortly before the crash that you were 70 kilometres north-west of a small town that is the nearest known habitation.

You are in a wilderness area made up of thick woods broken by many lakes and rivers. The snow depth varies from above the ankles in windswept areas to more than knee-deep where it has drifted. The last weather report indicated that the temperature would reach –15 degrees Celsius in the daytime and –26 degrees at night. There are plenty of dead wood pieces and twigs in the area around the lake. You and the other surviving passengers are dressed in winter clothing appropriate for city wear—suits, pantsuits, street shoes and overcoats. While escaping from the plane, your group salvaged the 12 items listed in the chart below. You may assume that the number of persons in the group is the same as the number in your team, and that you have agreed to stay together.

Winter Survival Tally Sheet

Items	Step 1: Your Individual Ranking	Step 2: Your Team's Ranking	Step 3: Survival Expert's Ranking	Step 4: Difference between Steps 1 and 3	Step 5: Difference between Steps 2 and 3
Ball of steel wool					
Newspaper					
Compass					
Hand axe					
Cigarette lighter					
45-calibre pistol					
Section air map					
Canvas					
Shirt and pants					
Can of shortening (animal fat)					
Whisky					
Chocolate bars					
			Total		
				Your Score	Your Team Score

Source: Adapted from D. Johnson and F. Johnson, 'Winter Survival', in *Joining Together*, 3rd edn (Englewood Cliffs, NJ: Prentice Hall, 1984).

Skill Builder 7.4

CLASS EXERCISE

The Hopping Orange

Purpose

This exercise is designed to help students understand the dynamics of creativity and team problem solving.

Instructions

You will be placed in teams of six students. One student serves as the official timer for the team and must have a watch, preferably with a stopwatch timer. The instructor will give each team an orange (or similar object) with a specific task involving use of the orange. The objective is easy to understand and nonthreatening, and it will be described by the instructor at the beginning of the exercise. Each team will have a few opportunities to achieve the objective more efficiently. To maximise the effectiveness of this exercise, no other information is provided here.

Skill Builder 7.5

CLASS EXERCISE

Creativity Brainbusters

Purpose

This exercise is designed to help you understand the dynamics of creativity and team problem solving.

Instructions (Large or Small Class)

The instructor describes the problem, and you are asked to figure out the solution by working alone. When enough time has passed, the instructor may then ask specific students, who think they have the solution, to describe or demonstrate (using overhead transparency) their answer. The instructor will review the solutions and discuss the implications of this exercise. In particular, be prepared to discuss what you needed to solve these puzzles and what may have prevented you from solving them more quickly

1. **DOUBLE-CIRCLE PROBLEM** Draw two circles, one inside the other, with a single line, and with neither circle touching the other (as shown left). In other words, you must draw both of these circles without lifting your pen (or other writing instrument).

2. **NINE-DOT PROBLEM** To the left are nine dots. Without lifting your pencil, draw no more than four straight lines that pass through all nine dots.

3. **NINE-DOT PROBLEM REVISITED** Referring to the nine-dot exhibit above, describe how, without lifting your pencil, you could pass a pencil line through all dots with three or fewer straight lines.

4. **WORD SEARCH** In the following line of letters, cross out five letters so that the remaining letters, without altering their sequence, spell a familiar English word.

CFRIVEELATETITEVRSE

5. **BURNING ROPES** You have two pieces of rope of unequal lengths and a box of matches. In spite of their different lengths, each piece of rope takes one hour to burn; however, parts of each rope burn at unequal speeds. For example, the first half of one piece might burn in 10 minutes. Use these materials to accurately determine when 45 minutes has elapsed.

CLASS EXERCISE

Skill Builder 7.6

Measuring Your Creative Personality

Purpose

This self-assessment is designed to help you measure the extent to which you have a creative personality.

Instructions

Listed below is an adjective checklist with 30 words that may or may not describe you. Put a mark in the box beside each word that you think accurately describes you. Do *not* mark the boxes for words that do not describe you. When finished, you can score the test using the scoring key in Appendix B at the end of the book. This exercise should be completed alone so that you can assess yourself without concerns of social comparison. Class discussion will focus on how this scale might be applied in organisations and on the limitations of measuring creativity in work settings.

Adjective Checklist

Affected ❑	Honest ❑	Reflective ❑
Capable ❑	Humorous ❑	Resourceful ❑
Cautious ❑	Individualistic ❑	Self-confident ❑
Clever ❑	Informal ❑	Sexy ❑
Commonplace ❑	Insightful ❑	Sincere ❑
Confident ❑	Intelligent ❑	Snobbish ❑
Conservative ❑	Inventive ❑	Submissive ❑
Conventional ❑	Mannerly ❑	Suspicious ❑
Dissatisfied ❑	Narrow interests ❑	Unconventional ❑
Egotistical ❑	Original ❑	Wide interests ❑

Source: Adapted from and based on information in H. G. Gough and A. B. Heilbrun Jr, *The Adjective Check List Manual* (Palo Alto, CA: Consulting Psychologists Press, 1965).

Skill Builder 7.7

Available online

SELF-ASSESSMENT

Testing Your Creative Bench Strength

This self-assessment takes the form of a self-scoring quiz. It consists of 12 questions that require divergent thinking to identify the correct answers. For each question, type in your answer in the space provided. When finished, look at the correct answer for each question, along with the explanation for that answer.

Skill Builder 7.8

Available online

SELF-ASSESSMENT

Decision-Making Style Inventory

People have different styles of decision making that are reflected in how they identify problems or opportunities and make choices. This self-assessment estimates your decision-making style through a series of statements describing how individuals go about making important decisions. Please indicate whether you agree or disagree with each statement. Answer each item as truthfully as possible so that you get an accurate estimate of your decision-making style. This exercise should be completed alone so that you can assess yourself honestly without concerns of social comparison. Class discussion will focus on the decision-making style that people prefer in organisational settings.

Endnotes

1 N. Apostolou, 'Sydney's Role in Google's World View', *Digital Media Australia*, 5 May 2008; N. Cohen, 'Google's Lunchtime Betting Game', *New York Times*, 7 January 2008, 4; R. Dye, 'The Promise of Prediction Markets: A Roundtable', *McKinsey Quarterly* (April 2008): 82–93; A. Fawcett, 'Job Searchers', *Sydney Morning Herald*, 5 April 2008, 5; M. Helft, 'The Human Hands Behind the Google Money Machine', *New York Times*, 2 June 2008, 1; V. Khanna, 'The Voice of Google', *Business Times Singapore*, 12 January 2008; A. Serpo, 'Q&A: Google's Alan Noble on the Future Web', *ZDNet Australia*, 11 March 2008.

2 'Google: Inside the Googleplex', *The Economist*, 10 September 2007, 1; B. Iyer and T. H. Davenport, 'Reverse Engineering Google's Innovation Machine', *Harvard Business Review* 86, no. 4 (2008): 58–68.

3 F. A. Shull Jr, A. L. Delbecq and L. L. Cummings, *Organizational Decision Making* (New York: McGraw-Hill, 1970), 31.

4 M. V. White, 'Jevons in Australia: A Reassessment', *The Economic Record* 58 (1982): 32–45; R. E. Nisbett, *The Geography of Thought: How Asians and Westerners Think Differently—and Why* (New York: Free Press, 2003); R. Hanna, 'Kant's Theory of Judgment' (Stanford: Stanford Encyclopedia of Philosophy, 2009), http://plato.stanford.edu/entries/kant-judgment/ (accessed 5 May 2009); D. Baltzly, 'Stoicism' (Stanford: Stanford Encyclopedia of Philosophy, 2008), http://plato.stanford.edu/entries/stoicism/ (accessed 5 May 2009).

5 J. G. March and H. A. Simon, *Organizations* (New York: Wiley, 1958).

6 This model is adapted from several sources, including H. A. Simon, *The New Science of Management Decision* (New York: Harper & Row, 1960); H. Mintzberg, D. Raisinghani and A. Théorét, 'The Structure of "Unstructured" Decision Processes', *Administrative Science Quarterly* 21 (1976): 246–275; W. C. Wedley and R. H. G. Field, 'A Predecision Support System', *Academy of Management Review* 9 (1984): 696–703.

7 P. F. Drucker, *The Practice of Management* (New York: Harper & Brothers, 1954), 353–357; B. M. Bass,

Organizational Decision Making (Homewood, IL: Irwin, 1983), ch. 3.

8 L. R. Beach and T. R. Mitchell, 'A Contingency Model for the Selection of Decision Strategies', *Academy of Management Review* 3 (1978): 439–449; I. L. Janis, *Crucial Decisions: Leadership in Policymaking and Crisis Management* (New York: Free Press, 1989), 35–37; W. Zhongtuo, 'Meta-Decision Making: Concepts and Paradigm', *Systematic Practice and Action Research* 13, no. 1 (2000): 111–115.

9 N. Schwarz, 'Social Judgment and Attitudes: Warmer, More Social, and Less Conscious', *European Journal of Social Psychology* 30 (2000): 149–176; N. M. Ashkanasy and C. E. J. Härtel, 'Managing Emotions in Decision-Making', in *Managing Emotions in the Workplace,* ed. N. M. Ashkanasy, W. J. Zerbe and C. E. J. Härtel (Armonk, NY: M. E. Sharpe, 2002); S. Maitlis and H. Ozcelik, 'Toxic Decision Processes: A Study of Emotion and Organizational Decision Making', *Organization Science* 15, no. 4 (2004): 375–393.

10 A. Howard, 'Opinion', *Computing*, 8 July 1999, 18.

11 A. R. Damasio, *Descartes' Error: Emotion, Reason, and the Human Brain* (New York: Putnam Sons, 1994); P. Winkielman and K. C. Berridge, 'Unconscious Emotion', *Current Directions in Psychological Science* 13, no. 3 (2004): 120–123; A. Bechara and A. R. Damasio, 'The Somatic Marker Hypothesis: A Neural Theory of Economic Decision', *Games and Economic Behavior* 52, no. 2 (2005): 336–372.

12 T. K. Das and B. S. Teng, 'Cognitive Biases and Strategic Decision Processes: An Integrative Perspective', *Journal of Management Studies* 36, no. 6 (1999): 757–778; P. Bijttebier, H. Vertommen and G. V. Steene, 'Assessment of Cognitive Coping Styles: A Closer Look at Situation-Response Inventories', *Clinical Psychology Review* 21, no. 1 (2001): 85–104; P. C. Nutt, 'Expanding the Search for Alternatives During Strategic Decision-Making', *Academy of Management Executive* 18, no. 4 (2004): 13–28.

13 W. Ocasio, 'Toward an Attention-Based View of the Firm', *Strategic Management Journal* 18, no. S1 (1997): 187–206; S. Kaplan, 'Framing Contests: Strategy Making under Uncertainty', *Organization Science* 19, no. 5 (2008): 729–752; J. S. McMullen, D. A. Shepherd and H. Patzelt, 'Managerial (In)Attention to Competitive Threats', *Journal of Management Studies* 46, no. 2 (2009): 157–181.

14 M. McCarthy, 'Top 20 in 20 Years: Apple Computer—1984' (2003), www.adweek.com (accessed 16 January 2003); O. W. Linzmayer, *Apple Confidential 2.0: The Definitive Story of the World's Most Colorful Company* (San Francisco: No Starch Press, 2004), 109–114.

15 T. Jones, *Innovating at the Edge: How Organizations Evolve and Embed Innovation Capability* (San Francisco: Butterworth-Heinemann, 2002), 59–62; R. K. Sawyer, *Explaining Creativity: The Science of Human Innovation* (New York: Oxford University Press, 2006), ch. 15.

16 T. Abate, 'Meet Bill Gates, Stand-up Comic', *San Francisco Examiner*, 13 March 1996, D1.

17 P. C. Nutt, *Why Decisions Fail* (San Francisco, CA: Berrett-Koehler, 2002); S. Finkelstein, *Why Smart Executives Fail* (New York: Viking, 2003).

18 E. Witte, 'Field Research on Complex Decision-Making Processes—The Phase Theorum', *International Studies of Management and Organization*, no. 56 (1972): 156–182; J. A. Bargh and T. L. Chartrand, 'The Unbearable Automaticity of Being', *American Psychologist* 54, no. 7 (1999): 462–479.

19 J. Brandtstadter, A. Voss and K. Rothermund, 'Perception of Danger Signals: The Role of Control', *Experimental Psychology* 51, no. 1 (2004): 24–32; M. Hock and H. W. Krohne, 'Coping with Threat and Memory for Ambiguous Information: Testing the Repressive Discontinuity Hypothesis', *Emotion* 4, no. 1 (2004): 65–86.

20 Reuters, 'NASA Managers Differed over Shuttle Strike', news release (22 July 2003); Columbia Accident Investigation Board, *Report*, vol. 1 (Washington, D.C.: Government Printing Office, August 2003); C. Gibson, 'Columbia: The Final Mission', *NineMSN* (13 July 2003); S. Jefferson, 'NASA Let Arrogance on Board', *Palm Beach Post (Palm Beach, FL)*, 30 August 2003; R. J. Smith, 'NASA Culture, Columbia Probers Still Miles Apart', *Washington Post*, 22 August 2003, A3.

21 R. Rothenberg, 'Ram Charan: The Thought Leader Interview', *strategy+business*, Fall 2004, 1–6.

22 'Over the Last Ten Years, Google Has Become a Poster Child', *Computer Weekly*, 9 September 2008, 188.

23 H. A. Simon, *Administrative Behavior*, 2nd edn (New York: Free Press, 1957); H. A. Simon, 'Rational Decision Making in Business Organizations', *American Economic Review* 69, no. 4 (1979): 493–513.

24 D. Sandahl and C. Hewes, 'Decision Making at Digital Speed', *Pharmaceutical Executive* 21 (August 2001): 62.

25 Simon, *Administrative Behavior*, xxv, 80–84.

26 P. O. Soelberg, 'Unprogrammed Decision Making', *Industrial Management Review* 8 (1967): 19–29; J. E. Russo, V. H. Medvec and M. G. Meloy, 'The Distortion of Information During Decisions', *Organizational Behavior and Human Decision Processes* 66, no. 1 (1996): 102–110. This is consistent with the observations by Milton Rokeach, who famously stated, 'Life is ipsative, because decisions in everyday life are inherently and phenomenologically ipsative decisions.' M. Rokeach, 'Inducing Changes and Stability in Belief Systems and Personality Structures', *Journal of Social Issues* 41, no. 1 (1985): 153–171.

27 A. L. Brownstein, 'Biased Predecision Processing', *Psychological Bulletin* 129, no. 4 (2003): 545–568.

28 T. Gilovich, D. Griffin and D. Kahneman, *Heuristics and Biases: The Psychology of Intuitive Judgment* (Cambridge: Cambridge University Press, 2002); D. Kahneman, 'Maps of Bounded Rationality: Psychology for Behavioral Economics', *American Economic Review* 93, no. 5 (2003): 1449–1475.

29 A. Tversky and D. Kahneman, 'Judgment under Uncertainty: Heuristics and Biases', *Science* 185, no. 4157 (27 September 1974): 1124–1131; I. Ritov, 'Anchoring in Simulated Competitive Market Negotiation', *Organizational Behavior and Human Decision Processes* 67, no. 1 (1996): 16; D. Ariely, G. Loewenstein and A. Prelec, '"Coherent Arbitrariness": Stable Demand Curves without Stable Preferences', *The Quarterly Journal of Economics* 118 (2003): 73; N. Epley and T. Gilovich, 'Are Adjustments Insufficient?', *Personality and Social Psychology Bulletin* 30, no. 4 (2004): 447–460; J. D. Jasper and S. D. Christman, 'A Neuropsychological Dimension for Anchoring Effects', *Journal of Behavioral Decision Making* 18 (2005): 343–369; S. D. Bond *et al.*, 'Information Distortion in the Evaluation of a Single Option', *Organizational Behavior and Human Decision Processes* 102, no. 2 (2007): 240–254.

30 A. Tversky and D. Kahneman, 'Availability: A Heuristic for Judging Frequency and Probability', *Cognitive Psychology* 5 (1973): 207–232.

31 D. Kahneman and A. Tversky, 'Subjective Probability: A Judgment of Representativeness', *Cognitive Psychology* 3, no. 3 (1972): 430; T. Gilovich, *How We Know What Isn't So: The Fallibility of Human Reason in Everyday Life* (New York: Free Press, 1991); B. D. Burns, 'Heuristics as Beliefs and as Behaviors: The Adaptiveness of the "Hot Hand"', *Cognitive Psychology* 48, no. 3 (2004): 295–331; E. M. Altmann and B. D. Burns, 'Streak Biases in Decision Making: Data and a Memory Model', *Cognitive Systems Research* 6, no. 1 (2005): 5.

32 H. A. Simon, 'Rational Choice and the Structure of Environments', *Psychological Review* 63, no. 2 (1956): 129–138.

33 S. Botti and S. S. Iyengar, 'The Dark Side of Choice: When Choice Impairs Social Welfare', *Journal of Public Policy and Marketing* 25, no. 1 (2006): 24–38; K. D. Vohs *et al.*, 'Making Choices Impairs Subsequent Self-Control: A Limited-Resource Account of Decision Making, Self-Regulation, and Active Initiative', *Journal of Personality and Social Psychology* 94, no. 5 (2008): 883–898.

34 S. S. Iyengar and M. R. Lepper, 'When Choice Is Demotivating: Can One Desire Too Much of a Good Thing?', *Journal of Personality and Social Psychology* 79, no. 6 (2000): 995–1006.

35 A. Toffler, *Future Shock* (New York: Random House, 1970), p. 264.

36 P. C. Nutt, 'Search During Decision Making', *European Journal of Operational Research* 160, no. 3 (2005): 851–876.

37 P. Winkielman *et al.*, 'Affective Influence on Judgments and Decisions: Moving Towards Core Mechanisms', *Review of General Psychology* 11, no. 2 (2007): 179–192.

38 N. Naqvi, B. Shiv and A. Bechara, 'The Role of Emotion in Decision Making: A Cognitive Neuroscience Perspective', *Current Directions in Psychological Science* 15, no. 5 (2006): 260–264; J. D. Wallis, 'Orbitofrontal Cortex and Its Contribution to Decision-Making', *Annual Review of Neuroscience* 30, no. 1 (2007): 31–56.

39 J. P. Forgas, 'Affective Intelligence: Towards Understanding the Role of Affect in Social Thinking and Behavior', in *Emotional Intelligence in Everyday Life*, ed. J. V. Ciarrochi, J. P. Forgas and J. D. Mayer (New York: Psychology Press, 2001), 46–65; J. P. Forgas and J. M. George, 'Affective Influences on Judgments and Behavior in Organizations: An Information Processing Perspective', *Organizational Behavior and Human Decision Processes* 86, no. 1 (2001): 3–34; G. Loewenstein and J. S. Lerner, 'The Role of Affect in Decision Making', in *Handbook of Affective Sciences*, ed. R. J. Davidson, K. R. Scherer and H. H. Goldsmith (New York: Oxford University Press, 2003), 619–642; J. S. Lerner, D. A. Small and G. Loewenstein, 'Heart Strings and Purse Strings: Carryover Effects of Emotions on Economic Decisions', *Psychological Science* 15, no. 5 (2004): 337–341; M. T. Pham, 'Emotion and Rationality: A Critical Review and Interpretation of Empirical Evidence', *Review of General Psychology* 11, no. 2 (2007): 155–178.

40 D. Miller, *The Icarus Paradox* (New York: HarperBusiness, 1990); D. Miller, 'What Happens after Success: The Perils of Excellence', *Journal of Management Studies* 31, no. 3 (1994): 325–368; A. C. Amason and A. C. Mooney, 'The Icarus Paradox Revisited: How Strong Performance Sows the Seeds of Dysfunction in Future Strategic Decision-Making', *Strategic Organization* 6, no. 4 (2008): 407–434.

41 M. T. Pham, 'The Logic of Feeling', *Journal of Consumer Psychology* 14 (September 2004): 360–369; N. Schwarz, 'Metacognitive Experiences in Consumer Judgment and Decision Making', *Journal of Consumer Psychology* 14 (September 2004): 332–349.

42 L. Sjöberg, 'Intuitive vs. Analytical Decision Making: Which Is Preferred?', *Scandinavian Journal of Management* 19 (2003): 17–29.

43 M. Lyons, 'Cave-in Too Close for Comfort, Miner Says', *Saskatoon StarPhoenix*, 6 May 2002.

44 W. H. Agor, 'The Logic of Intuition', *Organizational Dynamics* 14, no. 3 (1986): 5–18; H. A. Simon, 'Making

Management Decisions: The Role of Intuition and Emotion', *Academy of Management Executive* 1 (February 1987): 57–64; O. Behling and N. L. Eckel, 'Making Sense out of Intuition', *Academy of Management Executive* 5 (February 1991): 46–54. This process is also known as *naturalistic decision making*. For a discussion of research on naturalistic decision making, see the special issue in *Organization Studies:* R. Lipshitz, G. Klein and J. S. Carroll, 'Introduction to the Special Issue: Naturalistic Decision Making and Organizational Decision Making: Exploring the Intersections', *Organization Studies* 27, no. 7 (2006): 917–923.

45 M. D. Lieberman, 'Intuition: A Social Cognitive Neuroscience Approach', *Psychological Bulletin* 126, no. 1 (2000): 109–137; G. Klein, *Intuition at Work: Why Developing Your Gut Instincts Will Make You Better at What You Do* (New York: Currency/Doubleday, 2003); E. Dane and M. G. Pratt, 'Exploring Intuition and Its Role in Managerial Decision Making', *Academy of Management Review* 32, no. 1 (2007): 33–54.

46 Klein, *Intuition at Work*, 12–13, 16–17.

47 Y. Ganzach, A. H. Kluger and N. Klayman, 'Making Decisions from an Interview: Expert Measurement and Mechanical Combination', *Personnel Psychology* 53 (Spring 2000): 1–20; A. M. Hayashi, 'When to Trust Your Gut', *Harvard Business Review* 79 (February 2001): 59–65. Evidence of high failure rates from quick decisions is reported in Nutt, *Why Decisions Fail*; Nutt, 'Search During Decision Making'; P. C. Nutt, 'Investigating the Success of Decision Making Processes', *Journal of Management Studies* 45, no. 2 (2008): 425–455.

48 P. Goodwin and G. Wright, 'Enhancing Strategy Evaluation in Scenario Planning: A Role for Decision Analysis', *Journal of Management Studies* 38 (January 2001): 1–16; R. Bradfield *et al.*, 'The Origins and Evolution of Scenario Techniques in Long Range Business Planning', *Futures* 37, no. 8 (2005): 795–812; G. Wright, G. Cairns and P. Goodwin, 'Teaching Scenario Planning: Lessons from Practice in Academe and Business', *European Journal of Operational Research* 194, no. 1 (2009): 323–335.

49 J. Pfeffer and R. I. Sutton, 'Knowing "What" to Do Is Not Enough: Turning Knowledge into Action', *California Management Review* 42, no. 1 (1999): 83–108; R. Charan, C. Burke and L. Bossidy, *Execution: The Discipline of Getting Things Done* (New York: Crown Business, 2002). The survey of managerial competencies is reported in D. Nilsen, B. Kowske and A. Kshanika, 'Managing Globally', *HRMagazine*, August 2005, 111–115.

50 R. N. Taylor, *Behavioral Decision Making* (Glenview, IL: Scott Foresman, 1984), 163–166; R. S. Nickerson, 'Confirmation Bias: A Ubiquitous Phenomenon in Many Guises', *Review of General Psychology* 2, no. 2 (1998): 175–220.

51 G. Whyte, 'Escalating Commitment to a Course of Action: A Reinterpretation', *Academy of Management Review* G. Whyte, 'Escalating Commitment to a Course of Action: A Reinterpretation,' *Academy of Management Review* 11 (1986): 311–321; J. Brockner, 'The Escalation of Commitment to a Failing Course of Action: Toward Theoretical Progress,' *Academy of Management Review* 17, No. 1 (January 1992): 39–61.

52 P. Hall, *Great Planning Disasters* (New York: Penguin Books, 1980), ch. 5; I. Swanson, 'Holyrood Firms Face Grilling over Costs', *Evening News (Edinburgh)*, 6 June 2003, 2; Lord Fraser of Carmyllie QC, *The Holyrood Inquiry* (Edinburgh: Scottish Parliamentary Corporate Body, 2004); P. Murray, *The Saga of Sydney Opera House* (London: Taylor & Francis, 2004). For a somewhat partisan evaluation of the Sydney Opera House cost escalation and other major building projects, see B. Flyvbjerg, 'Design by Deception', *Harvard Design Magazine* (Spring/Summer 2005): 50–59.

53 J. Lorinc, 'Power Failure', *Canadian Business*, November 1992, 50–58; M. Keil and R. Montealegre, 'Cutting Your Losses: Extricating Your Organization When a Big Project Goes Awry', *Sloan Management Review*, no. 41 (Spring 2000): 55–68.

54 D. Collins, 'Senior Officials Tried to Stop Spending', *Irish Examiner*, 5 October 2005; M. Sheehan, 'Throwing Good Money after Bad', *Sunday Independent (Dublin)*, 9 October 2005; 'Computer System Was Budgeted at EUR9m ... It's Cost EUR170m ... Now Health Chiefs Want a New One', *Irish Mirror*, 7 July 2007, 16; E. Kennedy, 'Health Boss Refuses to Ditch Ill-Fated PPARS System', *Irish Independent*, 5 February 2007.

55 F. D. Schoorman and P. J. Holahan, 'Psychological Antecedents of Escalation Behavior: Effects of Choice, Responsibility, and Decision Consequences', *Journal of Applied Psychology* 81 (1996): 786–793.

56 G. Whyte, 'Escalating Commitment in Individual and Group Decision Making: A Prospect Theory Approach', *Organizational Behavior and Human Decision Processes* 54, no. 3 (1993): 430–455; D. J. Sharp and S. B. Salter, 'Project Escalation and Sunk Costs: A Test of the International Generalizability of Agency and Prospect Theories', *Journal of International Business Studies* 28, no. 1 (1997): 101–121.

57 M. Keil, G. Depledge and A. Rai, 'Escalation: The Role of Problem Recognition and Cognitive Bias', *Decision Sciences* 38, no. 3 (2007): 391–421.

58 J. D. Bragger *et al.*, 'When Success Breeds Failure: History, Hysteresis, and Delayed Exit Decisions', *Journal of Applied Psychology* 88, no. 1 (2003): 6–14. A second logical reason for escalation, called the *Martingale strategy*, is described in J. A. Aloysius, 'Rational Escalation of Costs by Playing a Sequence of Unfavorable Gambles: The Martingale',

Journal of Economic Behavior & Organization 51 (2003): 111–129.

59 I. Simonson and B. M. Staw, 'Deescalation Strategies: A Comparison of Techniques for Reducing Commitment to Losing Courses of Action', *Journal of Applied Psychology* 77, no. 4 (1992): 419–426; W. Boulding, R. Morgan and R. Staelin, 'Pulling the Plug to Stop the New Product Drain', *Journal of Marketing Research*, no. 34 (1997): 164–176; B. M. Staw, K. W. Koput and S. G. Barsade, 'Escalation at the Credit Window: A Longitudinal Study of Bank Executives' Recognition and Write-Off of Problem Loans', *Journal of Applied Psychology* 82, no. 1 (1997): 130–142; M. Keil and D. Robey, 'Turning around Troubled Software Projects: An Exploratory Study of the Deescalation of Commitment to Failing Courses of Action', *Journal of Management Information Systems* 15 (Spring 1999): 63–87.

60 D. Ghosh, 'De-Escalation Strategies: Some Experimental Evidence', *Behavioral Research in Accounting*, no. 9 (1997): 88–112.

61 I. Macwhirter, 'Let's Build a Parliament', *The Scotsman* (17 July 1997): 19; Swanson, 'Holyrood Firms Face Grilling over Costs'; Lord Fraser of Carmyllie QC, *The Holyrood Inquiry*.

62 M. Gardner, 'Democratic Principles Making Businesses More Transparent', *Christian Science Monitor*, 19 March 2007, 13.

63 M. Fenton-O'Creevy, 'Employee Involvement and the Middle Manager: Saboteur or Scapegoat?', *Human Resource Management Journal*, no. 11 (2001): 24–40. Also see V. H. Vroom and A. G. Jago, *The New Leadership: Managing Participation in Organizations* (Englewood Cliffs, NJ: Prentice Hall, 1988).

64 S. W. Crispin, 'Workers' Paradise', *Far Eastern Economic Review*, 17 April 2003, 40–41; 'Thai Carbon Black: Worker-Driven Focus Key to Firm's Success', *The Nation (Thailand)*, 3 June 2004; J. Gage, 'The Top 200 in Asia-Pacific', *Forbes Asia*, 29 September 2008, 50.

65 Some of the early OB writing on employee involvement includes C. Argyris, *Personality and Organization* (New York: Harper & Row, 1957); D. McGregor, *The Human Side of Enterprise* (New York: McGraw-Hill, 1960); R. Likert, *New Patterns of Management* (New York: McGraw-Hill, 1961).

66 A. G. Robinson and D. M. Schroeder, *Ideas Are Free: How the Idea Revolution Is Liberating People and Transforming Organizations* (San Francisco: Berrett-Koehler, 2004).

67 R. J. Ely and D. A. Thomas, 'Cultural Diversity at Work: The Effects of Diversity Perspectives on Work Group Processes and Outcomes', *Administrative Science Quarterly* 46 (June 2001): 229–273; E. Mannix and M. A. Neale, 'What Differences Make a Difference? The Promise and Reality of Diverse Teams in Organizations', *Psychological Science in the Public Interest* 6, no. 2 (2005): 31–55.

68 D. Berend and J. Paroush, 'When Is Condorcet's Jury Theorem Valid?', *Social Choice and Welfare* 15, no. 4 (1998): 481–488.

69 J. Surowiecki, *The Wisdom of Crowds* (New York: Anchor, 2005); C. R. Sunstein, *Infotopia: How Many Minds Produce Knowledge* (Oxford: Oxford University Press, 2006), ch. 1.

70 K. T. Dirks, L. L. Cummings and J. L. Pierce, 'Psychological Ownership in Organizations: Conditions under Which Individuals Promote and Resist Change', *Research in Organizational Change and Development* 9 (December 1996): 1–23; J. P. Walsh and S.-F. Tseng, 'The Effects of Job Characteristics on Active Effort at Work', *Work and Occupations* 25, no. 1 (1998): 74–96; B. Scott-Ladd and V. Marshall, 'Participation in Decision Making: A Matter of Context?', *Leadership & Organization Development Journal* 25, no. 8 (2004): 646–662.

71 S. Shankland, 'Google Uncloaks Once-Secret Server', *CNET News*, 1 April 2009.

72 J. Zhou and C. E. Shalley, 'Research on Employee Creativity: A Critical Review and Directions for Future Research', *Research in Personnel and Human Resources Management* 22 (2003): 165–217; M. A. Runco, 'Creativity', *Annual Review of Psychology* 55 (2004): 657–687.

73 J. Beck, 'Weta Evolves into Global Giant', *Variety (Los Angeles)*, 13 November 2006, C1–C3; D. Parker, 'Screen Team Stuns the World', *The Australian*, 26 January 2007, 28; K. Rockwood, '#40 Weta Digital (the Most Innovative Companies)', *Fast Company*, March 2009, 101–105.

74 G. Wallas, *The Art of Thought* (New York: Harcourt Brace Jovanovich, 1926). For recent applications of Wallas' classic model, see T. Kristensen, 'The Physical Context of Creativity', *Creativity and Innovation Management* 13, no. 2 (2004): 89–96; U.-E. Haner, 'Spaces for Creativity and Innovation in Two Established Organizations', *Creativity and Innovation Management* 14, no. 3 (2005): 288–298.

75 R. S. Nickerson, 'Enhancing Creativity', in *Handbook of Creativity*, ed. R. J. Sternberg (New York: Cambridge University Press, 1999), 392–430.

76 R. I. Sutton, *Weird Ideas That Work* (New York: Free Press, 2002), 26.

77 For a thorough discussion of insight, see R. J. Sternberg and J. E. Davidson, *The Nature of Insight* (Cambridge, MA: MIT Press, 1995).

78 R. J. Sternberg and L. A. O' Hara, 'Creativity and Intelligence', in *Handbook of Creativity*, ed. R. J. Sternberg (New York: Cambridge University Press, 1999), 251–272; S. Taggar, 'Individual Creativity and Group Ability to Utilize Individual Creative Resources: A Multilevel Model', *Academy of Management Journal* 45 (April 2002): 315–330.

79 G. J. Feist, 'The Influence of Personality on Artistic and Scientific Creativity', in *Handbook of Creativity*, ed. R. J. Sternberg (New York: Cambridge University Press, 1999), 273–296; Sutton, *Weird Ideas That Work*, 8–9, ch. 10; T. Åsterbro, S. A. Jeffrey and G. K. Adomdza, 'Inventor Perseverance after Being Told to Quit: The Role of Cognitive Biases', *Journal of Behavioral Decision Making* 20, no. 3 (2007): 253–272.

80 V. Laurie, 'Gut Instinct', *The Australian Magazine*, 10 December 2005, 1; The Nobel Foundation, 'The Nobel Prize in Physiology or Medicine 2005', press release (Stockholm: The Nobel Foundation, 3 October 2005), http://nobelprize.org (accessed 28 May 2009); J. Robotham, 'Of Guts and Glory', *Sydney Morning Herald*, 5 October 2005, 16; M. Irving, 'Nobel Deeds, Words of Praise', *West Australian (Perth)*, 14 January 2006, 4.

81 R. W. Weisberg, 'Creativity and Knowledge: A Challenge to Theories', in *Handbook of Creativity*, ed. R. J. Sternberg (New York: Cambridge University Press, 1999), 226–250.

82 Sutton, *Weird Ideas That Work*, 121, 153–154; C. Andriopoulos, 'Six Paradoxes in Managing Creativity: An Embracing Act', *Long Range Planning* 36, no. 4 (2003): 375–388.

83 T. Koppell, *Powering the Future* (New York: Wiley, 1999), 15.

84 R. J. Sternberg and T. I. Lubart, *Defying the Crowd: Cultivating Creativity in a Culture of Conformity* (New York: Free Press, 1995); Feist, 'The Influence of Personality on Artistic and Scientific Creativity'; S. J. Dollinger, K. K. Urban and T. A. James, 'Creativity and Openness to Experience: Validation of Two Creative Product Measures', *Creativity Research Journal* 16, no. 1 (2004): 35–47; C. E. Shalley, J. Zhou and G. R. Oldham, 'The Effects of Personal and Contextual Characteristics on Creativity: Where Should We Go from Here?', *Journal of Management* 30, no. 6 (2004): 933–958; T. S. Schweizer, 'The Psychology of Novelty-Seeking, Creativity and Innovation: Neurocognitive Aspects within a Work-Psychological Perspective', *Creativity and Innovation Management* 15, no. 2 (2006): 164–172.

85 T. M. Amabile *et al.*, 'Leader Behaviors and the Work Environment for Creativity: Perceived Leader Support', *The Leadership Quarterly* 15, no. 1 (2004): 5–32; Shalley, Zhou and Oldham, 'The Effects of Personal and Contextual Characteristics on Creativity'; S. T. Hunter, K. E. Bedell and M. D. Mumford, 'Climate for Creativity: A Quantitative Review', *Creativity Research Journal* 19, no. 1 (2007): 69–90; T. C. DiLiello and J. D. Houghton, 'Creative Potential and Practised Creativity: Identifying Untapped Creativity in Organizations', *Creativity and Innovation Management* 17, no. 1 (2008): 37–46.

86 R. Westwood and D. R. Low, 'The Multicultural Muse: Culture, Creativity and Innovation', *International Journal of Cross Cultural Management* 3, no. 2 (2003): 235–259.

87 'Samsung CEO Yun Picks Google as New Role Model', *Korea Times*, 1 October 2007.

88 T. M. Amabile, 'Motivating Creativity in Organizations: On Doing What You Love and Loving What You Do', *California Management Review* 40 (Fall 1997): 39–58; A. Cummings and G. R. Oldham, 'Enhancing Creativity: Managing Work Contexts for the High Potential Employee', *California Management Review* 40 (Fall 1997): 22–38.

89 T. M. Amabile, 'Changes in the Work Environment for Creativity During Downsizing', *Academy of Management Journal* 42 (December 1999): 630–640.

90 J. Moultrie *et al.*, 'Innovation Spaces: Towards a Framework for Understanding the Role of the Physical Environment in Innovation', *Creativity and Innovation Management* 16, no. 1 (2007): 53–65.

91 J. M. Howell and K. Boies, 'Champions of Technological Innovation: The Influence of Contextual Knowledge, Role Orientation, Idea Generation, and Idea Promotion on Champion Emergence', *The Leadership Quarterly* 15, no. 1 (2004): 123–143; Shalley, Zhou and Oldham, 'The Effects of Personal and Contextual Characteristics on Creativity'; S. Powell, 'The Management and Consumption of Organisational Creativity', *Journal of Consumer Marketing* 25, no. 3 (2008): 158–166.

92 A. Hiam, 'Obstacles to Creativity—And How You Can Remove Them', *Futurist* 32 (October 1998): 30–34.

93 M. A. West, *Developing Creativity in Organizations* (Leicester, UK: BPS Books, 1997), 33–35.

94 S. Hemsley, 'Seeking the Source of Innovation', *Media Week*, 16 August 2005, 22.

95 J. Neff, 'At Eureka Ranch, Execs Doff Wing Tips, Fire up Ideas', *Advertising Age*, 9 March 1998, 28–29.

96 A. Hargadon and R. I. Sutton, 'Building an Innovation Factory', *Harvard Business Review* 78 (May–June 2000): 157–166; T. Kelley, *The Art of Innovation* (New York: Currency Doubleday, 2001), 158–162.

97 M. Burton, 'Open Plan, Open Mind', *Director*, March 2005, 68–72; A. Benady, 'Mothers of Invention', *The Independent (London)*, 27 November 2006; B. Murray, 'Agency Profile: Mother London', *Ihaveanidea*, 28 January 2007, www.ihaveanidea.org (accessed 5 May 2009).

98 'John Collee—Biography', IMDB (Internet Movie Database), 2009, www.imdb.com (accessed 27 April 2009).

1

BUST UP

David Pick, Curtin University of Technology

'We might as well have it out while we're at it!' Wendy stood in the doorway of Tanya's office, hands on hips, shouting angrily. 'I come here and do my job. That's all I need to do.'

Tanya sat impassively.

Wendy continued, her face red and contorted by anger. 'I hate it here because you're here and in this office!'

Wendy spun around on her heels and walked away. Wendy, a clinic nurse, was angry that Tanya had been promoted to nurse manager. Wendy believed that she deserved the job and was venting the anger that had been building up over the three months since Tanya was promoted.

Tanya suddenly realised she was shaking—she was in a state. The clock on the wall ticked over to 8.45 am, and the recently promoted nurse manager had just completed the day's list of patients who were to be seen by the doctors in the hospital clinic. As usual, she had been at work since 6.30 am and would be there until well after her scheduled finish time.

Tanya had no time to dwell on the situation. The clinic was due to open in 15 minutes and there were 100 patients to be seen that day. Tanya also had to coordinate and run a ward round of 50 patients. However, she had to get things off her chest and so called a close colleague for advice. 'Should I take this to the director of nursing, Linda?' Tanya asked. 'But I need to get what happened straight in my head first. I suppose I should write it down, but I'm so busy today ...'

Tanya was rattled by the thought of making a big deal of Wendy's outburst. As she walked quickly across to the clinic with the day's schedule of patients, she thought about how powerless she felt in dealing with the situation. Maybe it was just a misunderstanding, but if Wendy continued her behaviour, it could spread to the whole team in the clinic and that would mean big trouble.

Four months earlier, the previous nurse manager of the clinic retired. Both Tanya and Wendy were nurses in the clinic and both applied for the position. Unknown to Tanya, the retiring nurse manager had been grooming Wendy to take over and virtually assured her that the position was hers if she wanted it. As a result, Wendy was confident of being the successful applicant. However, the selection panel who reviewed the applications decided after interviews that Tanya was more experienced, skilled and qualified for the position. One month later, Tanya took up the nurse manager's job. Wendy became aloof and uncommunicative. She also took a month's leave to, as she put it, 'reconsider her position at the clinic'.

Tanya thought that in spite of the disappointment, Wendy would eventually come around. The staff at the clinic were less optimistic. They pointed out that Wendy was not one to let bygones be bygones.

As Tanya entered the clinic, she felt uneasy. As usual, the day was going to be very busy with many difficult patients and sometimes demanding medical staff. One of the clinic nurses, Freda, greeted her. Despite the bad feeling between Tanya and Wendy, it looked like business as usual.

'How are you?' Freda asked as they checked around the treatment rooms.

'Fine,' Tanya replied. 'Just trying to get my head around how to fit today's patient list and the ward round into the time we have—looks like we are going to have a hectic day.'

'Situation normal then,' joked Freda. They both laughed. Tanya knew that Freda was concerned about Wendy disrupting relationships between staff. Freda had experienced Wendy's anger during the previous few weeks. Tanya also knew that Freda wanted to know more about Wendy's outburst that morning.

'Looks like we're one short today.' Freda piped up. 'I just saw Wendy leaving the clinic—looked like she was worked up about something—gave me a blast on her way out.' Freda hoped that Tanya would take this as an opportunity to discuss what had happened.

Tanya thought about this but decided to focus on the day's business: 'If Wendy is not in today, we'll just need to reorganise a little to make sure all the patients are seen.'

Tanya's approach to running the clinic was simple. It had a reputation for excellence in patient care that she was determined to maintain and develop. The staff she selected since taking over were well-qualified nurses, dedicated to providing a high level of service. Tanya thought that by recruiting the top talent she could build a team that could run the clinic without close supervision, and could also contribute to coordinating the ward round, running seminars and developing strategies for the future. It also meant that leave could easily be covered, roles could be shared and potential leaders identified. This was why Tanya had recruited Freda, and why a number of recently qualified nurses had been asking to join the clinic team. 'Sometimes, though, a positive work environment just isn't enough,' thought Tanya darkly. Her mind returned to the question of what to do about Wendy.

Tanya returned to her office around 11 am and began to think about Wendy. Wendy's behaviour was obviously causing problems in the clinic and word was spreading around the hospital. She could let this incident go. After all, Wendy had good reason to be disappointed after being led to believe that the nurse manager position was hers. 'Am I being too sensitive?' Tanya asked herself. Perhaps she should just take it on the chin and move on. To pursue the matter would mean a formal disciplinary action being brought against Wendy, compulsory mediation and counselling, and bringing the senior departmental and hospital managers into the dispute. It also meant a lot of extra paperwork and stress. Tanya pondered these issues as she sat down to tackle the ever-growing list of emails in her inbox.

Discussion Questions

1. Using the EVLN model of job dissatisfaction, predict and explain Wendy's future actions and recommend a strategy for Tanya.
2. Describe Tanya's causes of stress, and propose a stress management plan for her.
3. Assess the usefulness of four-drive theory and equity theory in suggesting how Tanya might deal with Wendy and keep the clinic staff motivated.

CASE STUDY 2

FRAN HAYDEN JOINS DAIRY ENGINEERING

Glyn Jones, University of Waikato

Background

Dairy Engineering (NZ) Ltd has its headquarters in Hamilton, New Zealand, with manufacturing plants in South Auckland and Christchurch. The company manufactures equipment for the dairy industry. In its early years it focused on the domestic market, but in the last five years it has expanded into the export market. The company employs 450 people, which makes it a large company by New Zealand standards.

The accounting department at the head office is organised into two sections: cost accounting and management information services (MIS). The accounting department is structured as shown in Exhibit 1.

Exhibit 1: Description of Employees in the Case

Name	Position	Description
Rob Poor	Chief accountant	Rob is the accounting department manager. He is 40 years old and is a qualified accountant with a chartered accounting (ACA) qualification. He has been with the company for six years. He is an unassuming person regarded as a bit 'soft' by his staff.
Vernon Moore	Chief cost accountant	Vernon is 30 years old and is a graduate with an ACA qualification. He joined the company 18 months ago. He is considered an easygoing type and is well liked by his staff.
Peter Bruton	Management accountant	Peter is 37 years old and has a science degree in dairy technology. He is also studying part-time for a management degree through Massey University. He is regarded as 'moody' and is not well liked by his staff.

Fran, the New Graduate

Fran Hayden was in the final year of her bachelor of management studies (BMS) degree at the University of Waikato, where she had proved to be a high achiever. Fran was interested in a position with Dairy Engineering because of the opportunity to gain practical experience and the company's higher starting salary compared to the industry average.

Fran sent her curriculum vitae to the company, and two weeks later she was invited to an interview with the chief accountant. She was surprised at the end of the interview to be offered the position of assistant cost accountant. Fran said she would like to think it over. Two weeks later, Fran had still not replied, so Rob telephoned her to ask if she was going to take the position. Although not totally convinced that she would enjoy the job, Fran decided to accept the offer.

The First Day at Work

Like many of her peers, Fran was glad to be leaving university after four years of study. She was looking forward to having money to spend as well as reducing her student debt. In order to 'look the part', she had gone further into debt to buy new corporate clothing. On reporting to the accounting department, she got her first shock in the real world. No one was expecting her! Even worse, she discovered that there was no vacancy for her in cost accounting. Instead, she had been assigned to management information systems (MIS).

Mike, a coworker in MIS, accompanied Fran to the department, where she was introduced to two other colleagues, Tom and Adrian. They seemed to be a friendly bunch, as apparently was her boss, Peter Bruton, who explained that her main duties were to assist with compiling information for the monthly management report known as 'Big Brother'.

After two weeks, the time came to compile Big Brother. Fran found that her part was almost entirely clerical and consisted of photocopying, collating, binding, punching and stamping the pages of the report. She then had to hand-deliver copies of the report to the senior manager at headquarters.

After Big Brother was completed, Fran found that she had little to do. She began to wonder why MIS needed four people.

The Big Opportunity

One afternoon, the chief accountant called Fran to his office to tell her about an upcoming management workshop in Auckland on performance measurement. Rob talked about the importance of staff development and said that he would like to see one of his younger staff members attending the workshop. He then asked Fran if she would be interested. She jumped at the opportunity. Unfortunately, her boss was away on two weeks' leave at the time, but Rob said he would talk with Peter.

Fran enjoyed the workshop, particularly rubbing shoulders with experienced managers, staying in an Auckland hotel and generally acting the management part. Even before returning to Hamilton, she wrote a detailed report on the workshop for the chief accountant. On her return to Hamilton, however, she found all was far from well.

On Sunday evening Fran was telephoned by her colleague Mike with some disturbing news. When Peter had returned to work to find that Fran was in Auckland, he was furious, complaining that he had not been consulted and that his authority was being undermined.

Peter: Fran is no longer employed in this section.

Fran returned to work full of trepidation, only to find that the expected encounter with her boss did not take place because he was in Christchurch. She handed two copies of her report about the workshop to the chief accountant's secretary before taking the opportunity to seek the advice of her colleagues in her boss's absence.

Fran: I am really worried. What do you think I should do?

Adrian: Stop worrying about it. He's just letting off steam. I have seen this all before. He'll get over it.

Fran: Come on, get serious. He is my boss! He can make things very difficult for me.

Mike: I think you should talk with Rob. After all, he's the one who suggested you go. It's not like it was your idea. He has to stick up for you.

The next day Fran managed to get an appointment with the chief accountant. She started by saying that she found the workshop very useful. She then brought up her fears about Peter's displeasure with her attendance at the workshop, to which the chief accountant responded:

Rob: Well, yes, he was a bit upset, but don't worry, I'll sort it out. The report was really good. By the way, I think you should treat it as confidential. Don't show it to anyone or discuss it with anyone. Is that OK? Don't worry about this. I assure you that I will sort it out.

Fran left the meeting feeling reassured but also a bit puzzled, wondering how Rob could have read her report in such a short time.

On Thursday Peter returned to work and just before lunch called Fran into his office, where he proceeded to attack her verbally, saying that she had 'connived' behind his back to attend the workshop and that she had never asked for his permission. He said that he realised she was an intelligent 'girl' but that she was 'sneaky'.

Peter: You better know which side your bread is buttered on—that for better or worse, you are in my section. No other section would want you.

He then called Mike in and spoke to him.

Peter: I don't want Fran wasting any more time—she is not to make any private calls from work.

Later, in 'confidence', he also spoke to Janet, one of the administration assistants.
Peter: Don't go talking with Fran—she has far too much work to catch up on.

Naturally, Janet did tell Fran!

The following week, Vernon happened to pass Fran in the corridor and stopped to talk with her. Fran had met Vernon only briefly during her first week in the company and was surprised when he asked her why she looked so miserable. She explained, and he said that they should talk with the chief accountant; taking Fran with him, he went to Rob's office. Vernon said that they needed a word, and Fran listened as Vernon outlined the situation to Rob. Fran made it clear that if Peter continued to treat her this way, she would have to ask for a transfer. She also said that there was certainly not enough work in MIS to keep her occupied for more than a day or so each week.

The chief accountant listened, and then asked her to give him a written report of what had happened since she had joined the company, including the latest incident with her boss. This, he said, would be brought up at the next senior management meeting. On the weekend Fran wrote the report, which included a request for a transfer out of MIS due to the lack of work and her boss's attitude toward her. On Monday morning she handed her report to the chief accountant's secretary.

Fran expected a reply but by early afternoon had heard nothing. At the end of the day, however, Peter called all his staff into his office. He was obviously in a good mood and told them that he had put his plan for revising Big Brother to the management meeting and had received an enthusiastic response. As he spoke, Fran noticed the colour draining out of Mike's face. On the way out, Mike told her that Peter was describing Mike's revision plans, not his own. Mike resolved never again to give his boss one of his ideas.

Mike: He just uses other people's brains—but that's the last time he uses mine.

Fran drove home from work feeling despondent. She wished she had never joined the company. Her job was boring, almost entirely clerical, and it certainly did not require a degree. She was also taking the stresses home, resulting in quarrels with her boyfriend and housemates.

Fran concluded that she had only two alternatives: a transfer or resignation. But to leave her job after less than five months would hardly impress any future employer. In desperation, she went to talk with Vernon, who she thought would be sympathetic, but she received more unwelcome news. He told her about the outcome of the senior management meeting. Contrary to Fran's expectation, the chief accountant had not confronted Peter. In fact, it appeared that he had been eclipsed by Peter's presentation for the revision of Big Brother and the chief accountant had not attempted to raise the issue.

Vernon was frank—she must either transfer or resign. Then, to Fran's surprise, he suggested she apply for a position in his section that would become vacant in three weeks' time. One of his assistant accountants was leaving to go overseas at short notice, and he did not have a replacement. Vernon cautioned, however, that Fran's only chance was to apply directly to the chief accountant; that would force the issue. With a formal, written application before him, the chief accountant would have to make a decision. Just as certainly, Peter would resist the request. Later Fran drafted a letter to Rob requesting that she be transferred from MIS to the upcoming position in cost accounting.

The Confrontation

The next morning, Fran took her request to the chief accountant. After he read it, she was surprised by his comment.

Rob: You really needn't have done this, you know—I intended dealing with the situation.

Fran left Rob's office wondering what to believe. From her desk she watched as Peter made his way across to the chief accountant's office. The meeting was brief. Five minutes later, he left Rob's office, and as he passed by Fran's desk, he spoke to her in a loud voice.

Peter: Fran—you are finished at this company.

Fran saw her colleagues duck their heads down and pretend to be working. No one envied her position. She wondered how, in such a short time, she had ended up in such a situation.

Discussion Questions

1. Analyse the problems in this case in terms of what you know about workplace emotions and attitudes.
2. What should this organisation do to minimise the problems apparent in this case?

HY DAIRIES, INC.

3 CASE STUDY

Steven L. McShane, The University of Western Australia

Syd Gilman read the latest sales figures with a great deal of satisfaction. The vice president of marketing at Hy Dairies, Inc., a large US milk products manufacturer, was pleased to see that the marketing campaign to improve sagging sales of Hy's gourmet ice-cream brand was working. Sales volume and market share of the product had increased significantly over the past two quarters compared with the previous year.

The improved sales of Hy's gourmet ice-cream could be credited to Rochelle Beauport, who was assigned to the gourmet ice-cream brand last year. Beauport had joined Hy less than two years ago as an assistant brand manager after leaving a similar job at a food products firm. She was one of the few women of colour in marketing management at Hy Dairies and had a promising career with the company. Gilman was pleased with Beauport's work and tried to let her know this in the annual performance reviews. He now had an excellent opportunity to reward her by offering her the recently vacated position of market research coordinator. Although technically only a lateral transfer with a modest salary increase, the marketing research coordinator job would give Beauport broader experience in some high-profile work, which would enhance her career with Hy Dairies. Few people were aware that Gilman's own career had been boosted by working as marketing research coordinator at Hy several years earlier.

Rochelle Beauport had also seen the latest sales figures on Hy's gourmet ice-cream and was expecting Gilman's call to meet with her that morning. Gilman began the conversation by briefly mentioning the favourable sales figures and then explained that he wanted Beauport to take the marketing research coordinator job. Beauport was shocked by the news. She enjoyed brand management and particularly the challenge involved with controlling a product that directly affected the company's profitability. Marketing research coordinator was a technical support position—a 'backroom' job—far removed from the company's bottom-line activities. Marketing research was not the route to top management in most organisations, Beauport thought. She had been sidelined.

After a long silence, Beauport managed a weak 'Thank you, Mr Gilman'. She was too bewildered to protest. She wanted to collect her thoughts and reflect on what she had done wrong. Also, she did not know her boss well enough to be openly critical.

Gilman recognised Beauport's surprise, which he naturally assumed was her positive response to hearing of this wonderful career opportunity. He, too, had been delighted several years earlier about his temporary transfer to marketing research to round out his marketing experience. 'This move will be good for both you and Hy Dairies,' said Gilman as he escorted Beauport from his office.

Beauport was preoccupied with several tasks that afternoon, but she was able to consider the day's events that evening. She was one of the top women and few minorities in brand management at Hy Dairies and feared that she was being sidelined because the company didn't want women or people of colour in top management. Her previous employer had made it quite clear that women 'couldn't take the heat' in marketing management and tended to place women in technical support positions after a brief term in lower brand management jobs. Obviously Syd Gilman and Hy Dairies were following the same game plan. Gilman's comments that the coordinator job would be good for her was just a nice way of saying that Beauport couldn't go any further in brand management at Hy Dairies.

Beauport now faced the difficult decision of whether to confront Gilman and try to change Hy Dairies' sexist and possibly racist practices, or to leave the company.

Discussion Questions

1. What perceptual problems occurred in this case?
2. What can organisations do to minimise misperceptions in these types of situations?

CASE STUDY 4

KEEPING SUZANNE CHALMERS

Steven L. McShane, The University of Western Australia

Thomas Chan hung up the telephone and sighed. The vice president of software engineering at Advanced Photonics Inc. (API) had just spoken to Suzanne Chalmers, who called to arrange a meeting with Chan later that day. She didn't say what the meeting was about, but Chan almost instinctively knew that Chalmers was going to quit after working at API for the past four years. Chalmers was a software engineer in internet protocol (IP), the software that directed fibre optic light through API's routers. It was very specialised work, and Chalmers was one of API's top talents in that area.

Thomas Chan had been through this before. A valued employee would arrange a private meeting. The meeting would begin with a few pleasantries, then the employee would announce that he or she wanted to quit. Some employees said they were leaving because of the long hours and stressful deadlines. They would say they needed to decompress, get to know the kids again, or whatever. But that was not usually the real reason. Almost every organisation in this industry is scrambling to keep up with technological advances and the competition. These employees would just leave one stressful job for another one.

Also, many of the people who left API joined a start-up company a few months later. These start-up firms could be pressure cookers, where everyone worked sixteen hours each day and performed a variety of tasks. For example, engineers in these small firms might have to meet customers or work on venture capital proposals rather than focus on specialised tasks related to their knowledge. API had over 6000 employees, so it was easier to assign people to work that matched their technical competencies.

No, the problem wasn't the stress or long hours, Chan thought. The problem was money—too much money. Most of the people who left were millionaires. Chalmers was one of them. Thanks to generous share options that had skyrocketed on the stock markets, many employees at API had more money than they could use. Most were under 40 years old, so it was too early for them to retire. But their financial independence gave them less reason to remain with API.

The Meeting

The meeting with Suzanne Chalmers took place a few hours after the telephone call. It began like the others, with the initial pleasantries and brief discussion about progress on the latest fibre-optic router project. Then, Chalmers made her well-rehearsed statement: 'Thomas, I've really enjoyed working here, but I'm going to leave Advanced Photonics.' She took a breath, then looked at Chan. When he didn't reply after a few seconds, she continued: 'I need to take time off. You know, get away to recharge my batteries. The project's nearly done and the team can complete it without me. Well, anyway, I'm thinking of leaving.'

Chan spoke in a calm voice. He suggested that Chalmers should take an unpaid leave for two or maybe three months, complete with paid benefits, then return refreshed. Chalmers politely rejected that offer, saying that she needs to get away from work for a while. Thomas then asked Suzanne whether she was unhappy with her work environment—whether she was getting the latest computer technology to do her work and whether there were problems with coworkers. The workplace was fine, Chalmers replied. The job was getting a bit routine, but she had a comfortable workplace with excellent coworkers.

Chan then apologised for the cramped work space, due mainly to the rapid increase in the number of people hired over the past year. He suggested that if Chalmers took a couple of months off, API would give her special treatment, with a larger work space with a better view of the park behind the campus-like building when she returned. She politely thanked Chan for that offer, but it wasn't what she needed. Besides, she suggested, it wouldn't be fair to have a large work space when other team members worked in smaller quarters.

Chan was running out of tactics, so he tried his last hope: money. He asked whether Chalmers had higher offers. She replied that she regularly received calls from other companies, and some of them offered more money. Most were start-up firms that offered a lower salary but higher potential gains in share options. Chan knew from market surveys that Chalmers was already paid well in the industry. He also knew that API couldn't compete on share option potential. Employees working in start-up firms sometimes saw their shares increase by five or ten times their initial value, whereas shares at API and other large firms increased more slowly. However, Chan promised Chalmers that he would recommend that she receive a significant raise—maybe 25 per cent more—and more share options. Chan added that Chalmers was one of API's most valuable employees and that the company would suffer if she left the firm.

The meeting ended with Chalmers promising to consider Chan's offer of higher pay and share options. Two days later, Chan received her resignation in writing. Five months later, Chan learned that after a few months travelling with her husband, Chalmers joined a start-up software firm in the area.

Discussion Questions

1. Why didn't money motivate Suzanne Chalmers to stay with API?
2. Do financial rewards have any value in situations such as this, where employees are relatively wealthy?
3. Analyse this case study using four-drive and expectancy theories.
4. Of what importance is job design in this case?
5. If you were Thomas Chan, what strategy, if any, would you have used to motivate Suzanne Chalmers to stay at Advanced Photonics Inc.?

CASE STUDY 5

THE REGENCY GRAND HOTEL

Elizabeth Ho, Prada Singapore, under the supervision of Steven L. McShane, The University of Western Australia

The Regency Grand Hotel is a five-star hotel in Bangkok, Thailand. The hotel was established fifteen years ago by a local consortium of investors and has been operated by a Thai general manager throughout this time. The hotel is one of Bangkok's most prestigious hotels, and its 700 employees enjoyed the prestige of being associated with the hotel. The hotel provided good welfare benefits, above-market-rate salary and job security. In addition, a good year-end bonus amounting to four months' salary was rewarded to employees regardless of the hotel's overall performance during the year.

Recently, the Regency was sold to a large American hotel chain that was very keen to expand its operations into Thailand. When the acquisition was announced, the general manager decided to take early retirement when the hotel changed ownership. The American hotel chain kept all of the Regency employees, although a few were transferred to other positions. John Becker, an American with ten years of management experience with the hotel chain, was appointed as the new general manager of the Regency Grand Hotel. Becker was selected as the new general manager because of his previous successes in integrating newly acquired hotels in the United

States. In most of the previous acquisitions, Becker took over operations with poor profitability and low morale.

Becker is a strong believer in empowerment. He expects employees to go beyond guidelines and standards to consider guest needs on a case-by-case basis. That is, employees must be guest-oriented at all times to provide excellent customer service. From his US experience, Becker has found that empowerment increases employee motivation, performance and job satisfaction, all of which contribute to the hotel's profitability and customer service ratings. Soon after becoming general manager of the Regency Grand, Becker introduced the practice of empowerment to replicate the successes that he had achieved back home.

The Regency Grand Hotel has always been very profitable, and its employees have always worked according to management's instructions. Their responsibility has been to ensure that the instructions from their managers are carried out diligently and conscientiously. Under the previous management, innovation and creativity were discouraged. Indeed, employees were punished for their mistakes and discouraged from trying out ideas that had not been approved by management. As a result, employees were afraid to be innovative and to take risks.

Becker met with Regency's managers and department heads to explain that empowerment would be introduced in the hotel. He told them that employees must be empowered with decision-making authority so that they could use their initiative, creativity and judgment to satisfy guest needs, and handle problems effectively and efficiently. However, he stressed that the more complex issues and decisions were to be referred to superiors, who were to coach and assist rather than provide direct orders. Furthermore, Becker stressed that mistakes were allowed but that making the same mistakes more than twice would not be tolerated. He advised his managers and department heads not to discuss with him minor issues or problems and not to consult with him about minor decisions. Nevertheless, he told them that they were to discuss important, major issues and decisions with him. He concluded the meeting by asking for feedback. Several managers and department heads told him that they liked the idea and would support it, while others simply nodded their heads. Becker was pleased with the response and was eager to have his plan implemented.

In the past, the Regency Grand had emphasised administrative control, resulting in many bureaucratic procedures throughout the organisation. For example, the front-counter employees needed to seek approval from their manager before they could upgrade guests to another category of room. The front-counter manager would then have to write and submit a report to the general manager justifying the upgrade. Soon after his meeting with the managers, Becker reduced the number of bureaucratic rules at the hotel and allocated more decision-making authority to front-line employees. This action upset those who previously had decision-making power over these issues. As a result, several of these employees left the hotel.

Becker also began spending a large portion of his time observing and interacting with the employees at the front desk, lobby, restaurants and various departments. This direct interaction with Becker helped many employees to understand what he wanted and expected of them. However, the employees had much difficulty trying to distinguish between a major and a minor issue or decision. More often than not, supervisors would reverse employee decisions by stating that they were major issues requiring management approval. Employees who displayed initiative and made good decisions in satisfying the needs of the guests rarely received any positive feedback from their supervisors. Eventually, most of these employees lost confidence in making decisions and reverted back to relying on their superiors for decision making.

Not long after the implementation of the practice of empowerment, Becker realised that his subordinates were consulting him more frequently than before. Most of them came to him with minor issues and consulted with him about minor decisions. He had to spend most of his time attending to his subordinates. Soon he began to feel highly frustrated and exhausted, and very often he would tell his secretary that 'unless the hotel is on fire, don't let anyone disturb me'.

Becker thought that the practice of empowerment would benefit the overall performance of the hotel. However, contrary to his expectation, the business and overall performance of the hotel began to deteriorate. There was an increasing number of guest complaints. In the past, the hotel had minimal guest complaints. Now there was a significant number of formal written complaints every month. Many other guests voiced their dissatisfaction to hotel employees. The number of mistakes made by employees was on the increase. Becker was very upset when he realised that two of the local newspapers and an overseas newspaper had published negative feedback on the hotel in terms of service standards. He was most distressed when an international travel magazine voted the hotel 'one of Asia's nightmare hotels'.

The stress levels of the employees were continuously mounting since the introduction of the practice of empowerment. Absenteeism due to illness was increasing at an alarming rate. In addition, the employee turnover rate reached an all-time high. The good working relationships that were established under the old management had been severely strained. The employees were no longer united and supportive of each other. They were quick to 'point fingers' at or to 'backstab' one another when mistakes were made and when problems occurred.

Discussion Questions

1. Identify the symptoms indicating that problems exist in this case.
2. Diagnose the problems in this case using organisational behaviour concepts.
3. Recommend solutions that overcome or minimise the problems and symptoms in this case.

CASE STUDY 6 SK TELECOM GOES EGALITARIAN

Until recently, Hur Jae-hoon could end debate with junior staff members just by declaring that the discussion was over. Employed at the fourth tier in SK Telecom Co.'s five-tier management/professional hierarchy, the 33-year-old strategist held the corresponding title of 'Hur Daeri' and received plenty of respect from people in lower positions. No one below Hur was allowed to question his decisions, and Hur was expected to silently comply with requests from above. South Korea's culture of deferring to people in higher positions was deeply ingrained in the telecommunications company. In some South Korean companies, such as Samsung, junior staff members weren't even allowed to initiate conversations with anyone above their boss.

Now, in spite of South Korea's strong hierarchical culture, SK Telecom wants to support more egalitarian values. It has already removed its five management ranks and their differentiated titles and status. The English word 'manager' is now used to address anyone employed throughout the five former ranks. (Hur Jae-hoon's title has changed from Hur Daeri to 'Hur Manager').

Only vice presidents and above retain their previous status titles. Those in charge of projects or people are also called 'team leader'. Furthermore, the company is assigning project leadership responsibilities to employees in their twenties, whereas these roles were previously held only by people with much more seniority. As an added change, the company is allowing a more casual dress code at work.

Through this dramatic shift in values and practices, SK Telecom's senior executives hope that junior staff will speak up more freely, thereby improving creativity and decision making. They particularly want to avoid incidents such as one that occurred several years ago in which an excellent idea from younger employees was initially shot down by their bosses. The junior staff suggested that allowing customers to change their mobile phone ringtones to music chosen by the friend they've phoned would generate revenue through music licensing. Fortunately, the idea was introduced several months later, after a few persistent employees proposed the idea again.

SK Telecom's initiative is not completely new to South Korea. Small high-tech companies have already embraced egalitarian values and flatter corporate structures. But SK Telecom is among the first large firms in the country to attempt this culture shift, and has met with resistance along the way. SK Telecom executives were initially divided over how quickly and to what extent the company should distance itself from South Korea's traditional hierarchical culture. 'There were ideas for gradual versus all-out reforms,' recalls chief executive Kim Shin-bae. 'But the word "gradually" means "not now" to some people. So we decided to go all-out.'

According to a company survey, 80 per cent of employees support the changes. However, even with the changes in titles, many still look for subtle evidence of who has higher status and, therefore, should receive more deference. Some also rely on what positions managers held under the old five-tier hierarchy. 'I know what the old titles were,' says an LG Electronics Co. manager who supplies cell phones to SK Telecom. 'So unconsciously, I keep that in mind.'

Hur Jae-hoon admits there are times when he prefers a more hierarchical culture, but he believes that SK Telecom's more egalitarian values and practices are already showing favourable results. In one recent meeting, a younger colleague sparred with Hur over the better way to complete a strategy project. 'For a moment, I wished it was back in the old days when I could have shut that guy down,' Hur recalls. 'But I had to admit his opinion was better than mine, and I adjusted. So the system worked.'

Discussion Questions

1. SK Telecom is attempting to distant itself from which South Korean cultural value? What indicators of this value are identified in this case study? What other artefacts of this cultural value would you notice while visiting a South Korean company that upheld this national culture?
2. In your opinion, why is this hierarchical value so strong in South Korea? What are the advantages and disadvantages of this value in societies?
3. Do you think SK Telecom will be successful in integrating a more egalitarian culture, even though it contrasts with South Korea's culture? What are some of the issues that may complicate or support this transition?

Source: Adapted from E. Ramstad, 'Pulling Rank Gets Harder at One Korean Company,' *Wall Street Journal*, 20 August 2007, p. B1.

7 CASE STUDY

VÊTEMENTS LTÉE

Steven L. McShane, The University of Western Australia

Vêtements Ltée is a chain of men's retail clothing stores located throughout the province of Quebec, Canada. Two years ago, the company introduced new incentive systems for both store managers and sales employees. Store managers in each store receive a salary with annual merit increases based on sales above targeted goals, store appearance, store inventory management, customer complaints and several other performance measures. Some of this information (e.g. store appearance) is gathered during visits by senior management, while other information is based on company records (e.g. sales volume).

Sales employees are paid a fixed salary plus a commission based on the percentage of sales credited to that employee over the pay period. The commission represents about 30 per cent of a typical pay cheque, and is intended to encourage employees to actively serve customers and increase sales volume. Because returned merchandise is discounted from commissions, sales employees are discouraged from selling products that customers do not really want.

Soon after the new incentive systems were introduced, senior management began to receive complaints from store managers regarding the performance of their sales staff. They observed that sales employees tended to stand near the store entrance waiting to 'tag' customers as their own. Occasionally, sales staff would argue over 'ownership' of the customer. Managers were concerned that this aggressive behaviour intimidated some customers. It also tended to leave some parts of the store unattended by staff.

Many managers also became concerned about inventory duties. Previously, sales staff would share responsibility for restocking inventory and completing inventory reorder forms. Under the new compensation system, however, few employees were willing to do these essential tasks. On several occasions, stores have faced stock shortages because merchandise was not stocked or reorder forms were not completed in a timely manner. Potential sales have suffered from empty shelves when plenty of merchandise was available in the back storeroom or at the warehouse. The company's new automatic inventory system could reduce some of these problems, but employees must still stock shelves and assist in other aspects of inventory management.

Store managers have tried to correct the inventory problem by assigning employees to inventory duty, but this has created resentment among the employees selected. Other managers have threatened sales staff with dismissals if they do not do their share of inventory management. This strategy has been somewhat effective when the manager is in the store, but staff members sneak back onto the floor when the manager is away. It has also hurt staff morale, particularly relations with the store manager.

To reduce the tendency of sales staff to hoard customers at the store entrance, some managers have assigned employees to specific areas of the store. This has also created some resentment among employees stationed in areas with less traffic or lower-priced merchandise. Some staff have openly complained of lower pay cheques because they have been placed in a slow area of the store or have been given more than their share of inventory duties.

Discussion Questions

1. What symptom(s) in this case suggest that something has gone wrong?
2. What are the main causes of these symptoms?
3. What actions should Vêtements executives take to correct these problems?

8 CASE STUDY

YAKKATECH PTY LTD

Steven L. McShane, The University of Western Australia

YakkaTech Pty Ltd is an information technology services firm employing 1500 people throughout Australia and New Zealand. YakkaTech has a consulting division, which mainly installs and upgrades enterprise software systems and related hardware on the client's site. YakkaTech also has a customer service division which consists of four customer contact centres serving clients within each region.

Each customer service centre consists of a half-dozen departments representing functional specialisations (computer systems, intranet infrastructure, storage systems, enterprise software systems, customer billing, etc.). These centres typically have more than two dozen employees in each department. When a client submits a problem to the centre by email or telephone, the message or call is directed to the department where the issue best applies. The query is given a 'ticket' number and is assigned to the next available employee in that department. Individual employees are solely responsible for the tickets assigned to them. The employee investigates and corrects the issue, and the ticket is 'closed' when the problem has been resolved.

If the client experiences the same problem again, even a few days later, a new ticket is issued and sent to whichever employee is available to receive the ticket. A client's problems are almost always handled by different employees each time, even when the issue is sent to the same department. Furthermore, when a customer centre department is heavily backlogged, clients are redirected to the same department at another regional centre where their problem can be addressed more quickly.

At one time, YakkaTech operated more than a dozen small customer contact centres in each city because client problems had to be diagnosed and resolved on-site. Today, employees can investigate most software and hardware system faults from the centre through remote monitoring systems, rather than personally visit the client. Consequently, eight years ago, YakkaTech amalgamated its customer service operations into four large regional centres. Customer service staff work entirely within the centre. When a client visit is required, the ticket is transferred to an individual or team in the consulting business, who then visits the client.

YakkaTech's customer service business has nearly doubled over the past five years, but with this growth has come increasing customer complaints regarding poor quality service. Many say that employees seem indifferent to the client's problems. Others have commented on the slow response to their problems where the issue requires the involvement of more than one department. Several clients have also complained that they are continually educating YakkaTech's customer service employees about details of their unique IT systems infrastructure.

Another concern is that until eighteen months ago, the number of employee resignations in YakkaTech's contact centres had risen above the industry average. This increased labour costs due to the cost of recruiting new technical staff as well as lower productivity of new employees. According to results of an employee survey two years ago (as well as informal comments since then), many employees felt that their work was monotonous. Some also said that they felt disconnected from the consequences of their work. A few also complained about ongoing conflicts with people in other departments and the stress of serving dissatisfied clients.

Eighteen months ago, YakkaTech's executive team decided to raise pay rates for its customer service staff to become among the highest in the industry. The assumption was that the high pay rates would improve morale and reduce turnover, thereby reducing hiring costs and improving productivity. In addition, YakkaTech introduced a vested profit-sharing plan, in which employees received the profit-sharing bonus only if they remained with the company for two years after the bonus was awarded. Employees who resigned or were fired for just cause before the vesting period forfeited the bonus.

Employee turnover rates dropped dramatically, so the executive team concluded that customer service quality and productivity would improve. Instead, customer complaints and productivity remain below expectations and, in some cases, have worsened. Experienced employees continue to complain about the work. There have been a few disturbing incidents where employees have been careless at solving client problems or have not bothered to forward tickets that belonged in another department. Employee referrals (where staff recommend friends to join the company) have become rare events, whereas at one time they represented a significant source of qualified job applicants. Furthermore, a few executives have recently overheard employees say that they would like to work elsewhere but can't afford to leave YakkaTech.

Discussion Questions

1. What symptom(s) in this case suggest that something has gone wrong?
2. What are the main causes of these symptoms?
3. What actions should YakkaTech executives take to correct these problems?

PART 3

team processes

CHAPTER 8
team dynamics

LEARNING OBJECTIVES

After reading this chapter, you should be able to:

- define *teams*, and discuss their benefits and limitations
- explain why people are motivated to join informal groups
- diagram the team effectiveness model
- discuss how task characteristics, team size and team composition influence team effectiveness
- summarise the team development process.
- discuss how team norms develop and how they may be altered
- list six factors that influence team cohesion
- describe the three foundations of trust in teams and other interpersonal relationships
- discuss the characteristics and factors required for success of self-directed teams and virtual teams
- identify four constraints on team decision making
- discuss the advantages and disadvantages of four structures that potentially improve team decision making.

Courtesy of Ergon Energy

Ergon Energy relies on teams to more effectively serve customers.

Ray Hobbs, an Ergon Energy employee in Hervey Bay, Queensland, had just returned from holidays when he received a call from team leader Alan Melville. Brisbane had been hit with one of the worst storms in two decades, and Melville was organising a crew of Hervey Bay staff to help restore electrical service to their city neighbours further south. Hobbs happily agreed to join six fellow employees to the site—a scene of 'sheer devastation' where power to 140 000 homes had been cut. 'It was very hazardous work,' says Melville, adding that the various teams from across the state worked long hours to repair the damage. 'The teams ... weren't knocking off until 10 or 11pm.' Two days later, power had been restored to 120 000 of those homes.

At Ergon Energy, teamwork is a critical operational practice for achieving excellent customer service. The state government–owned corporation that distributes electricity to approximately 600 000 homes across regional Queensland organises its employees into teams, each led by a team leader. Teamwork is one of Ergon's six core values. This emphasis on teams is even evident in the recruitment literature. 'Teamwork is a way of life, and it's something you can feel from your first day on the job,' says Ergon's careers website.

Teamwork is also reinforced through company rewards. For example, Ergon Energy has a unique safety behaviour rewards program (called Power Aid) in which work teams accrue points when they demonstrate positive and proactive health and safety behaviours, and report any incidents that could affect workplace safety. Points are converted to cash, and each team nominates a local charity to which the funds are donated. Almost $1 million has been distributed to charities through this team-based reward program.

'Our employees really value teamwork,' says Lucie Bennett, manager of Ergon Energy's careers. 'It is a real key to our success and there's a real family culture, a sort of feeling that everyone is your mate.'[1]

Ergon Energy's emphasis on teamwork is one of the reasons why it was able to successfully integrate six regional Queensland electricity distributors a decade ago to become one of the state's most respected companies. Other organisations around the Pacific Rim and globally have also embraced teamwork as their operational model. New Zealand Post's largest delivery branch in Marua Road, Auckland, was the poorest performing branch in the country until employees were reorganised into teams. Now, it is the company's model operation in terms of performance and morale. Hong Kong–based Regal Printing relies on advanced technology to print up to 40 000 softcover books per day, but it also created a special team of 20 staff members to handle urgent jobs. Rackspace Hosting, Inc. physically organises most of its 1900 employees into teams of 14 to 20 people. The world's largest provider of enterprise-level Web infrastructure assigns every customer to one of these dedicated teams, which provides around-the-clock service.[2]

This chapter begins by defining *teams* and examining the reasons why organisations rely on teams, and why people join informal groups in organisational settings. A large segment of this chapter examines a model of team effectiveness, which includes organisational and team environment; team design; and the team processes of development, norms, cohesion and trust. We then turn our attention to two specific types of teams: self-directed and virtual teams. The final section of this chapter looks at the challenges of team decision making and strategies for making better decisions in teams.

TEAMS AND INFORMAL GROUPS

LEARNING OBJECTIVE 

Define *teams*, and discuss their benefits and limitations.

teams Groups of two or more people who interact and influence each other, are mutually accountable for achieving common goals associated with organisational objectives and perceive themselves as a social entity within an organisation.

Teams are groups of two or more people who interact with and influence each other, are mutually accountable for achieving common goals associated with organisational objectives and perceive themselves as a social entity within an organisation.[3] This definition has a few important components worth repeating. First, all teams exist to fulfil some purpose, such as repairing electric powerlines, assembling a product, designing a new social welfare program or making an important decision. Second, team members are held together by their interdependence and need for collaboration to achieve common goals. All teams require some form of communication so that members can coordinate and share common objectives. Third, team members influence each other, although some members may be more influential than others regarding the team's goals and activities. Finally, a team exists when its members perceive themselves to be a team.

Exhibit 8.1 briefly describes various types of teams in organisations. Some teams are permanent, while others are temporary; some are responsible for making products or providing services, while others exist to make decisions or share knowledge. Each type of team has been created deliberately to serve an organisational purpose. Some teams, such as skunkworks teams, are not initially sanctioned by management, yet are called 'teams' because members work toward an organisational objective.

Informal Groups

LEARNING OBJECTIVE 

Explain why people are motivated to join informal groups.

Although most of our attention in this chapter is on formal teams, employees also belong to informal groups. All teams are groups, but many groups do not satisfy our definition of teams. Groups include people assembled together, whether or not they have any interdependence or organisationally focused objective. The friends you meet for lunch are an *informal group*, but they wouldn't be called a team because they have little or no interdependence (each person could just

Exhibit 8.1 *Types of Teams in Organisations*

Team type	Description
Departmental teams	Teams that consist of employees who have similar or complementary skills and are located in the same unit of a functional structure; usually minimal task interdependence because each person works with employees in other departments.
Production/service/leadership teams	Typically multiskilled (employees have diverse competencies), team members collectively produce a common product/service or make ongoing decisions; production/service teams typically have an assembly-line type of interdependence, whereas leadership teams tend to have tight interactive (reciprocal) interdependence.
Self-directed teams	Similar to production/service teams except (1) they are organised around work processes that complete an entire piece of work requiring several interdependent tasks, and (2) they have substantial autonomy over the execution of those tasks (i.e. they usually control inputs, flow and outputs with little or no supervision).
Advisory teams	Teams that provide recommendations to decision makers; include committees, advisory councils, work councils and review panels; may be temporary, but often permanent, some with frequent rotation of members.
Task force (project) teams	Usually multiskilled, temporary teams whose assignment is to solve a problem, realise an opportunity, or design a product or service.
Skunkworks	Multiskilled teams that are usually located away from the organisation and are relatively free of its hierarchy; often initiated by an entrepreneurial team leader who borrows people and resources (*bootlegging*) to design a product or service.
Virtual teams	Teams whose members operate across space, time and organisational boundaries, and are linked through information technologies to achieve organisational tasks; may be a temporary task force or permanent service team.
Communities of practice	Teams (but often informal groups) bound together by shared expertise and passion for a particular activity or interest; main purpose is to share information; often rely on information technologies as the main source of interaction.

as easily eat lunch alone) and no organisationally mandated purpose. Instead, they exist primarily for the benefit of their members. Although the terms are used interchangeably, *teams* has largely replaced *groups* in the language of business when referring to employees who work together to complete organisational tasks.[5]

Why do informal groups exist? One reason is that human beings are social animals. Our drive to bond is hardwired through evolutionary development, creating a need to belong to informal groups.[6] This is evident in the way that people invest considerable time and effort forming and maintaining social relationships without any special circumstances or ulterior motives. A second explanation is provided by social identity theory, which states that individuals define themselves by their group affiliations. Thus, we join groups—particularly those that are viewed favourably by others and that have values similar to our own—because they shape and reinforce our self-concept.[7]

A third reason why people are motivated to form informal groups is that such groups accomplish tasks that cannot be achieved by individuals working alone. For example, employees will sometimes create a group to oppose organisational changes because the

GM Holden's Secret Skunkworks

In the late 1990s, eight designers at GM Holden's small development centre in Australia secretly worked on a souped-up coupé, something that was missing from General Motors' line-up. 'It had to stay quiet,' recalls Michael Simcoe (shown in this photo), who led the clandestine skunkworks group. 'It wasn't an official Holden project and management hadn't asked us to produce a coupé. It was all after hours work; people stayed on at the office instead of going straight home at night and they even came in on weekends to make it happen.' The project was so secret that the family room wall at one team member's home was used to complete the first full-sized line drawings. When GM Holden executives were notified, they excitedly supported the project, which eventually became the Monaro in Australia and the Pontiac GTO in North America. Members of the skunkworks team are now working with their US colleagues on a new version of the Camaro; Simcoe has since been promoted as executive director for body frame design at General Motors headquarters in Detroit.[4]

Joe Armao/The Age

group collectively has more power than individuals complaining alone. A fourth explanation for informal groups is that in stressful situations we are comforted by the mere presence of other people and are therefore motivated to be near them. When in danger, people congregate near each other even though doing so serves no protective purpose. Similarly, employees tend to mingle more often after hearing rumours that the company might be acquired by a competitor. As you learned in Chapter 4, this social support minimises stress by providing emotional and/or informational support to buffer the stress experience.[8]

Informal Groups and Organisational Outcomes

Although informal groups are not created to serve organisational objectives, they have a profound influence on organisations and individual employees. Informal groups are the backbone of *social networks,* which are important sources of trust building, information sharing, power, influence and employee wellbeing in the workplace.[9] Chapter 9 describes how some companies have established social networking sites similar to Facebook and MySpace to encourage the formation of informal groups and associated communication. These companies recognise that informal groups build trust and mutual understanding, which improve the transfer of tacit knowledge through these informal networks more than through formal reporting relationships.

Social networks also play an important role in employee power and influence. As Chapter 10 describes, informal groups tend to increase an employee's **social capital**—the knowledge and other resources available to people from a durable network that connects them to others. Employees with strong informal networks tend to have more power and influence because they receive better information and preferential treatment from others, and because their talent is more visible to key decision makers. Finally, informal groups potentially minimise employee stress because, as mentioned above, group members provide emotional and informational social support. This stress-reducing capability of informal groups improves employee wellbeing, thereby improving organisational effectiveness.

social capital The knowledge and other resources available to people or social units (teams, organisations) from a durable network that connects them to others.

ADVANTAGES AND DISADVANTAGES OF TEAMS

When 1760 professionals were recently asked about their work, 86 per cent agreed that working in teams is more important to business success today than it was five years ago. This is certainly true in scientific research. A study of almost 20 million research publications reported that the percentage of journal articles written by teams rather than individuals has increased substantially over the past five decades. Furthermore, team-based articles had a much higher number of subsequent citations, which indicates that journal-article quality is higher when articles are written by teams rather than individuals.[10] 'I always remind people that team achievements, not individual ones, count most in a company like Nokia,' says Bruce Lam, who oversees Nokia Mobile Phone's operations in Hong Kong and Macau.[11]

Why are teams so important at Ergon Energy in Queensland and in other organisations around the world? The answer to this question has a long history, dating back to research on British coal mining in the 1940s and highly regarded Japanese managemet practices of the 1970s.[12] These early studies and a huge number of investigations since then have revealed that *under the right conditions*, teams make better decisions, develop better products and services, and create a more engaged workforce than do employees working alone.[13] Similarly, team members can quickly share information and coordinate tasks, whereas these processes are slower and prone to more errors in traditional departments led by supervisors. Teams typically provide superior customer service because they provide more breadth of knowledge and expertise to customers than individual 'stars' can offer.

In many situations, people are potentially more motivated when working in teams than when working alone.[14] One reason for this motivation is that, as we mentioned a few paragraphs ago, employees have a drive to bond and are motivated to fulfil the goals of groups to which they belong. This motivation is particularly strong when the team is part of the employee's social identity. Second, people are more motivated in teams because they are accountable to fellow team members, who monitor performance more closely than a traditional supervisor. This is particularly true where the team's performance depends on the worst performer, such as on an assembly line, where how fast the product is assembled depends on the speed of the slowest employee. Third, under some circumstances, performance improves when employees work near others because coworkers become benchmarks of comparison. Employees are also motivated to work harder because of apprehension that their performance will be compared to others' performance.

The Challenges of Teams

In spite of the many benefits of teams, they are not always as effective as individuals working alone.[15] Teams are usually better suited to complex work, such as designing a building or auditing a company's financial records. Under these circumstances, one person rarely has all the necessary knowledge and skills. Instead, tasks are performed better when the work is divided into more specialised roles, with people in those specialised jobs coordinating with each other. In contrast, work is typically performed more effectively by individuals alone when they have all the necessary knowledge, and skills, and it is difficult to divide the work between two or more people. Even where the work can and should be specialised, a team structure might not be necessary if the tasks performed by several people require minimal coordination.

process losses Resources (including time and energy) expended toward team development and maintenance rather than the task.

The main problem with teams is that they have additional costs called **process losses**—resources (including time and energy) expended toward team development and maintenance rather than the task.[16] It is much more efficient for an individual to work out an issue alone than to resolve differences of opinion with other people. For a team to perform well, team members need to agree and have mutual understanding of their goals, the strategy for accomplishing those goals, their specific roles and informal rules of conduct.[17] Developing and maintaining these team requirements divert time and energy away from performing the work. The process-loss problem is particularly apparent when more staff are added or replace others on the team. Team performance suffers when a team adds members, because those employees need to learn how the team operates and how to coordinate efficiently with other team members. When people are added, process losses also occur in redistributing the workload, sometimes with the result that tasks are duplicated or accidentally forgotten.

Brooks' law The principle that adding more people to a late software project only makes it later. Also called the *mythical man-month*.

The software industry even has a name for this phenomenon: **Brooks' law** (also called the 'mythical man-month') says that adding more people to a late software project only makes it later! According to some sources, Apple may have fallen into this trap in the recent development of its professional photography software program, called Aperture. When the project started to fall behind schedule, the manager in charge of the Aperture project increased the size of the team—some sources say it ballooned from 20 to almost 150 engineers and quality assurance staff within a few weeks. Unfortunately, adding so many people further bogged down the project. The result? When Aperture was finally released, it was nine months late and considered one of Apple's buggier software offerings.[18]

Social Loafing

social loafing The problem that occurs when people exert less effort (and usually perform at a lower level) when working in teams than when working alone.

Perhaps the best known limitation of teams is the risk of productivity loss due to **social loafing**. Social loafing occurs when people exert less effort (and usually perform at a lower level) when working in teams than when working alone.[19] Social loafing tends to be more serious when the individual's performance is less likely to be noticed, such as when people work together in very large teams. The individual's output is also less noticeable where the team produces a single output (rather than each team member producing output), such as finding a single solution to a customer's problem. There is less social loafing when each team member's contribution is more noticeable; this can be achieved by reducing the size of the team or measuring each team member's performance.

Social loafing also depends on the employee's motivation to perform the work. Social loafing is less prevalent when the task is interesting, because individuals are more motivated by the work itself to perform their duties. For example, one recent study revealed that student apathy explains some of the social loafing that occurs in university student teams. Social loafing is also less common when the team's objective is important, possibly because individuals experience more pressure from coworkers to perform well. Finally, social loafing occurs less frequently among members who value team membership and believe in working toward the team's objectives.[20]

In summary, teams can be very powerful forces for competitive advantage, or they can be much more trouble than they are worth, so much so that job performance and morale may decline when employees are placed in teams. To understand when teams are better than individuals working alone, we need to more closely examine the conditions that make teams effective or ineffective. The next few sections of this chapter discuss the model of team effectiveness.

A MODEL OF TEAM EFFECTIVENESS

LEARNING OBJECTIVE

Diagram the team effectiveness model.

Why are some teams effective while others fail? Before answering this question, let's clarify the meaning of team effectiveness. A team is effective when it benefits the organisation, its members and its own survival.[21] First, most teams exist to serve some organisational purpose, so effectiveness is partly measured by the achievement of those objectives. Second, a team's effectiveness relies on the satisfaction and wellbeing of its members. People join groups to fulfil their personal needs, so effectiveness is partly measured by this need fulfilment. Finally, team effectiveness includes the team's viability—its ability to survive. It must be able to maintain the commitment of its members, particularly during the turbulence of the team's development. Without this commitment, people leave and the team will fall apart. The team must also secure sufficient resources and find a benevolent environment in which to operate.

Researchers have developed several models over the years to identify the features or conditions that make some teams more effective than others.[22] Exhibit 8.2 integrates the main components

Exhibit 8.2 *Team Effectiveness Model*

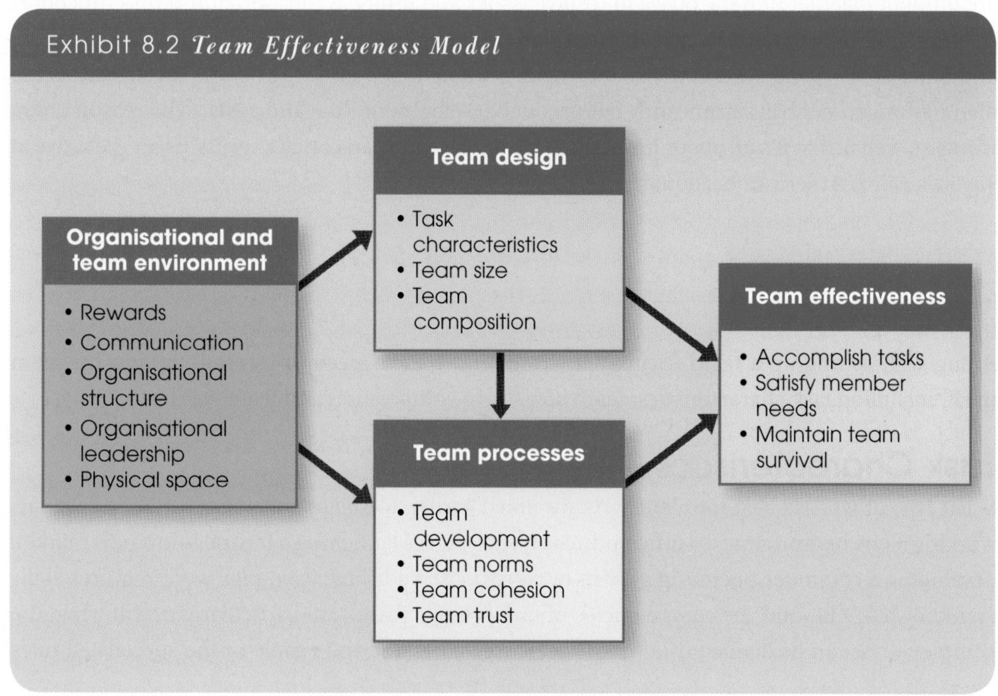

of these team effectiveness models. We will closely examine each component over the next several pages. This model is best viewed as a template of several theories because each component (team development, team cohesion, and so on) includes its own set of theories and models to explain how that component operates.

ORGANISATIONAL AND TEAM ENVIRONMENT

The organisational and team environment represents all conditions beyond the team's boundaries that influence its effectiveness. Team members tend to work together more effectively when they are at least partly rewarded for team performance.[23] For instance, the opening vignette to this chapter described how Ergon Energy rewards teams for the safe behaviours of members within those teams. Communication systems can influence team effectiveness, particularly in virtual teams, which are highly dependent on information technologies to coordinate work. Another environmental factor is the organisational structure; teams flourish when organised around work processes because this structure increases interaction and interdependence among team members and reduces interaction with people outside the team. High-performance teams also depend on organisational leaders who provide support and strategic direction while team members focus on operational efficiency and flexibility.[24]

The physical layout of the team's work space can also make a difference. For instance, Medibank executives say that teamwork improved dramatically when the Melbourne-based health insurer moved employees from several headquarters buildings and 150 offices into a single headquarters building and just 14 offices.[25] The Toyota Motor Company also recognises the importance of physical layout in team effectiveness by congregating people in a large open-space room (called an *obeya*). In some projects, such as development of the Prius hybrid vehicle, department managers are brought together into the obeya to resolve issues and improve collaboration across functions. In other projects, a few dozen development staff from engineering, design, production, marketing and other areas spend several weeks or longer working together in the obeya. Toyota claims the obeya arrangement has significantly cut product development time and costs. 'The reason obeya works so well is that it's all about immediate face-to-face human contact,' explains an executive at Toyota's North American headquarters.[26]

Discuss how task characteristics, team size and team composition influence team effectiveness.

TEAM DESIGN ELEMENTS

Along with setting up a team-friendly environment, leaders need to carefully design the team itself, including task characteristics, team size, team composition and team roles.

Task Characteristics

What type of work is best for teams? As we noted earlier, teams operate better than individuals working alone on work that is sufficiently complex, such as launching a business in a new market, developing a computer operating system or constructing a bridge. Complex work requires skills and knowledge beyond the competencies of one person. Teams are particularly useful when the complex work can be divided into more specialised roles and the people in the specialised roles require frequent coordination with each other. Some evidence also suggests that teams work best with well-structured tasks because it is easier to coordinate such work among several people.[27]

Furniture construction seems to be suited to teams because it is both complex and well structured. Constructing a sofa or chair is fairly complex because it requires knowledge from diverse trades (carpentry, sewing and so on). At the same time, the work is structured enough that these tradespeople can coordinate efficiently to build several pieces of furniture. Consider recent production developments at La-Z-Boy Inc. The American furniture company previously organised production staff around their respective trades. 'You would have a group of upholsterers in one place, the sewing people in another section, the framing people in another area, and everyone would just work in the same place all day,' recalls Jovie Dabu, general manager of La-Z-Boy's manufacturing facility in Redlands, California. Now, the company organises one or two people from each trade into teams of five to seven employees who work side by side to build an entire piece of furniture. La-Z-Boy executives say the new team structure has improved coordination, communication and team bonding. 'The idea is to help make workers accountable, but also to give them a sense of ownership of what they do,' said Greg Bachman, Redlands' production manager.[28]

One task characteristic that is particularly important for teams is **task interdependence**—the extent to which team members must share materials, information or expertise to perform their jobs.[29] Aside from complete independence, there are three levels of task interdependence, as illustrated in Exhibit 8.3. The lowest level of interdependence, called *pooled interdependence*, occurs when an employee or work unit shares a common resource, such as machinery, administrative support or a budget, with other employees or work units. This would occur in a team setting where each member works alone but shares raw materials or machinery to perform her or his otherwise independent tasks. Interdependence is higher under *sequential interdependence*, in

task interdependence The extent to which team members must share materials, information or expertise in order to perform their jobs.

Exhibit 8.3 *Levels of Task Interdependence*

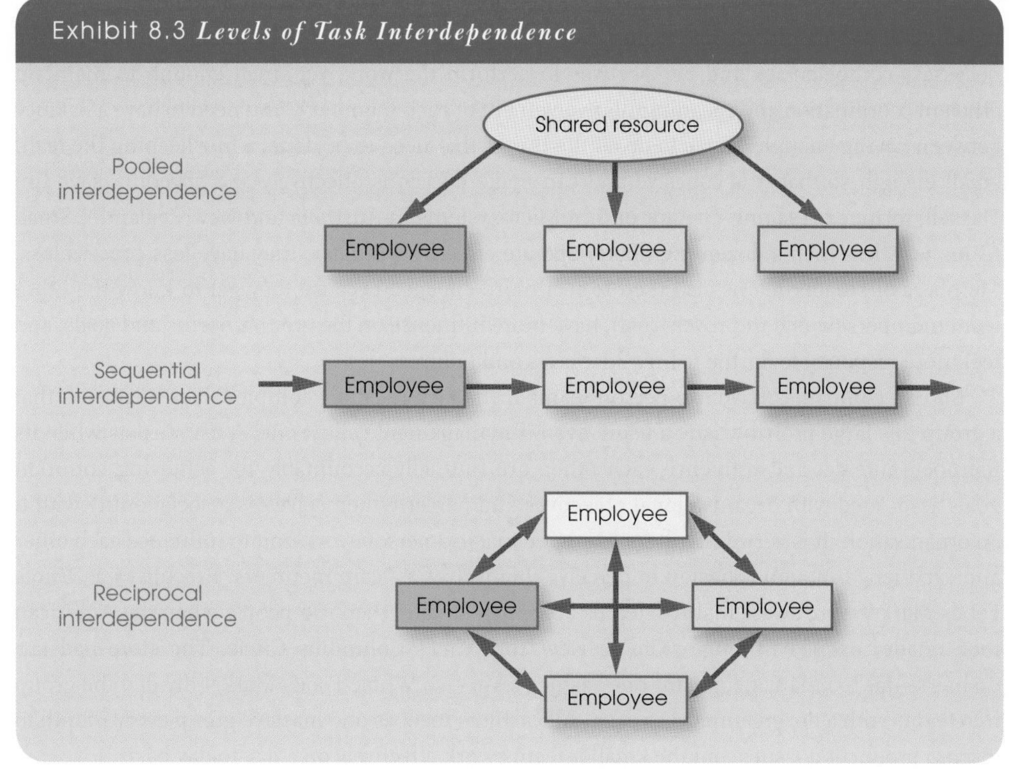

which the output of one person becomes the direct input for another person or unit. Sequential interdependence occurs where team members are organised in an assembly line.

Reciprocal interdependence, in which work output is exchanged back and forth among individuals, produces the highest degree of interdependence. People who design a new product or service would typically have reciprocal interdependence because their design decisions affect others involved in the design process. Any decision made by the design engineers would influence the work of the manufacturing engineer and purchasing specialist, and vice versa. Employees with reciprocal interdependence should be organised into teams to facilitate coordination in their interwoven relationship.

As a rule, the higher the level of task interdependence, the greater the need to organise people into teams rather than have them work alone. A team structure improves interpersonal communication and thus results in better coordination. High task interdependence also motivates most people to be part of the team. However, the rule that a team should be formed when employees have high interdependence generally applies when team members have the same task goals, such as serving the same clients or collectively assembling the same product. When team members have different goals (such as serving different clients) but must depend on other team members to achieve those unique goals, teamwork might create excessive conflict. Under these circumstances, the company should try to reduce the level of interdependence, or rely on supervision as a buffer or mediator among employees.

Team Size

What is the ideal size for a team? One popular (but untested) rule is that the optimal team size is between five and seven people. However, some observers have recently argued that tasks are getting so complex that many teams need to have more than 100 members.[30] Unfortunately, the former piece of advice is excessively simplistic, and the latter seems to have lost sight of the meaning and dynamics of real teams. Generally, teams should be large enough to provide the necessary competencies and perspectives to perform the work, yet small enough to maintain efficient coordination and meaningful involvement of each member.[31] 'You need to have a balance between having enough people to do all the things that need to be done, while keeping the team small enough so that it is cohesive and can make decisions effectively and speedily,' says Jim Hassell, former managing director of Sun Microsystems in Australia and New Zealand.[32] Small teams (say, less than a dozen members) operate effectively because they have less process loss. Members of smaller teams also tend to feel more engaged because they get to know the other team members (which improves trust), have more influence on the group's norms and goals, and feel more responsible for the team's successes and failures.

Should companies have 100-person teams if the task is highly complex? The answer is that a group this large probably isn't a team, even if management calls it one. A team exists when its members interact and influence each other, are mutually accountable for achieving common goals associated with organisational objectives and perceive themselves as a social entity within an organisation. It is very difficult for everyone in a 100-person work unit to influence each other and experience enough cohesion to perceive themselves as team members. Executives at Whole Foods Market were aware that real teams are much smaller than 100 people when the American food retailer opened its huge store in New York City's Columbus Circle. The store had 140 cashiers—far too many people for one cashier team—so Whole Foods Market divided the group into teams with a dozen employees each. All cashiers meet as one massive group every month to discuss production issues, but the smaller teams work effectively on a day-to-day basis.[33]

Team Composition

When the Hewlett-Packard Company (HP) hires new talent, it doesn't just look for technical skills and knowledge. The high-tech computer manufacturer looks for job applicants who fit into a team environment. 'It's important for candidates to prove to us that they can work well with others,' explains business development manager Bill Avey. 'We're looking for people who value the different perspectives that each individual brings to a team.' Avey describes how HP recruiters will ask applicants to recall a time they worked in a group to solve a problem. 'Successful candidates tend to show how they got differences out in the open and reached a resolution as a team,' says Avey.[34]

To support its strong team orientation, Hewlett-Packard carefully selects people with the necessary motivation and competencies for teamwork. Royal Dutch/Shell is also serious about selecting job applicants who have excellent team skills. As Reality Check 8.1 describes, the global energy giant hosts a special five-day exercise in Europe, North America, Asia and the Middle East to observe how well participants work under pressure with others from diverse backgrounds.

To work effectively in a team, employees must have more than technical skills and self-leadership to perform their own work; they must also be able and willing to perform that work in a team environment. The most frequently mentioned characteristics or behaviours of effective team members are the 'five Cs' illustrated in Exhibit 8.4: cooperating, coordinating,

Exhibit 8.4 *The Five Cs of Team-member Competency*

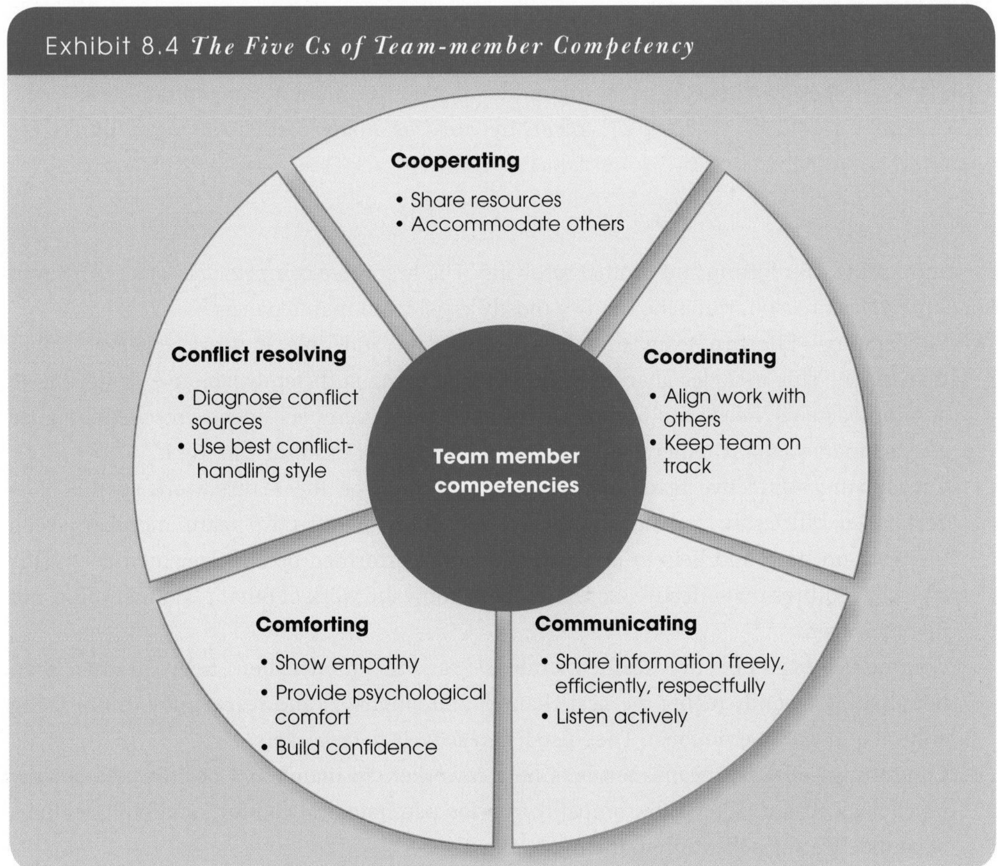

Sources: Based on information in V. Rousseau, C. Aubé and A. Savoie, 'Teamwork Behaviours: A Review and an Integration of Frameworks', *Small Group Research* 37, no. 5 (2006): 540–570; M. L. Loughry, M. W. Ohland and D. D. Moore, 'Development of a Theory-Based Assessment of Team Member Effectiveness', *Educational and Psychological Measurement* 67, no. 3 (2007): 505–524.

Royal Dutch/Shell Finds Team Players in Gourami

Courtesy of Royal Dutch/Shell

Royal Dutch/Shell has found a better way to identify the team skills of prospective job applicants by observing business and engineering students in the Shell Gourami Business Challenge.

ROYAL DUTCH/SHELL (SHELL) DISCOVERED long ago that a job interview isn't the best way to determine a job applicant's technical skills, or how well he or she works in a team environment. That's why the global energy company launched the Shell Gourami Business Challenge a decade ago in Europe and very recently in the United States, Asia and the Middle East. The five-day event involves up to 50 engineering and business university students who are split into several teams representing different departments (exploration, refining, manufacturing, finance and so on). Teams initially develop a business plan for their own department; later, they must merge the departmental plans into an organisation-wide business strategy. On the final day, the multiteam's strategy is presented to Gourami's board of directors, which consists of several Shell senior executives.

Shell leaders emphasise that the Gourami event is more like an audition than a competition because the company hires as many participants as it thinks are

communicating, comforting and conflict resolving. The first three competencies are mainly (but not entirely) task-related, while the last two mostly assist team maintenance:[36]

- Cooperating—Effective team members are willing and able to work together rather than alone. This includes sharing resources and being sufficiently adaptive or flexible to accommodate the needs and preferences of other team members, such as rescheduling use of machinery so that another team member with a tighter deadline can use it.
- Coordinating—Effective team members actively manage the team's work so that it is performed efficiently and harmoniously. For example, effective team members keep the team on track and help to integrate the work performed by different members. This typically requires that effective team members know the work of other team members, not just their own.
- Communicating—Effective team members transmit information freely (rather than hoarding), efficiently (using the best channel and language) and respectfully (minimising arousal of negative emotions). They also listen actively to coworkers.
- Comforting—Effective team members help coworkers to maintain a positive and healthy psychological state. They show empathy, provide psychological comfort, and build feelings of confidence and self-worth in their coworkers.
- Conflict resolving—Conflict is inevitable in social settings, so effective team members have the skills and motivation to resolve dysfunctional disagreements among team members.

This requires effective use of various conflict-handling styles as well as diagnostic skills to identify and resolve the structural sources of conflict.

REALITY CHECK 8.1

qualified. Throughout the event, Shell assessors evaluate students' technical knowledge and skills, but they equally observe how effectively the students work in diverse teams. The need for team skills is quickly apparent to most participants. 'Working with people from all sorts of disciplines and cultures has taught me the importance of expanding my knowledge to beyond my field,' acknowledges a geology student at Universiti Malaysia Sabah. 'You need to be able to combine your expertise with everyone else's in order to make a project work.'

A University of Texas finance student who attended the Gourami exercise in the United States also recognised that team skills were vital to help him work with people from different specialisations. 'Coming from a business background, it's most difficult to understand the engineering aspect of the oil industry,' he says. 'We have to work together so that both sides understand each other.'

Team cooperation isn't easy, however, due to the challenges created in the Gourami exercise. 'Having to come up with the proposal then integrate all our ideas into one plan was definitely not easy,' admits a mechanical engineering student at Universiti Teknologi Malaysia. 'Initially, we did have conflict. But we soon realised that everyone operates differently and, if we are to function well as a whole, we have to understand how others work.'

A mechanical engineering student at Imperial College, London, who attended the European event, also noticed the challenges and potential of teamwork with people from other disciplines. 'Dealing with the "real-life" challenges of Gourami made us all aware of the value of other skills and aptitudes and the need to work as a team,' she says.[35]

These characteristics of effective team members are associated with conscientiousness and extroversion personality traits, as well as with emotional intelligence. Furthermore, the old saying 'One bad apple spoils the barrel' seems to apply to teams; one team member who lacks these teamwork competencies may undermine the dynamics of the entire team.[37]

Team Diversity

Another important dimension of team composition is diversity. There are two distinct and sometimes opposing effects of diversity of team effectiveness.[38] One effect is that diverse teams make better decisions under some circumstances, for three reasons. One reason is that people from different backgrounds tend to see a problem or opportunity from different angles. Team members have different mental models, so they are more likely to identify viable solutions to difficult problems.

A second reason why diverse teams tend to make better decisions is that they have a broader pool of technical competencies. For example, each team at Rackspace Hosting consists of more than a dozen people with diverse skills such as account management, systems engineering, technical support, billing expertise and data centre support. The American-based provider of enterprise-level Web infrastructure requires these diverse technical competencies within each team to serve the needs of customers assigned to the team. A third reason favouring teams with diverse members is that they provide better representation of the team's constituents, such as other departments or clients from similarly diverse backgrounds. A team responsible for designing and launching a new service, for instance, should have representation from the organisation's various specialisations so that people in those work units will support the team's decisions.

So far, we have outlined the reasons why membership diversity potentially improves team effectiveness. However, diversity also has a potentially opposing influence on the internal functioning of the team.[39] Specifically, groups of diverse employees take longer to become high-performing teams. This partly occurs because team members take longer to bond with people who are different from them, particularly when others hold different perspectives and values (i.e. deep diversity). Diverse teams are susceptible to 'fault lines'—hypothetical dividing lines that may split a team into subgroups along gender, ethnic, professional or other dimensions. These fault lines hamper team effectiveness by reducing the motivation to communicate and coordinate with teammates on the other side of the invisible divisions. In contrast, members of homogeneous teams experience higher satisfaction, less conflict and better interpersonal relations. Consequently, homogeneous teams tend to be more effective on tasks requiring a high degree of cooperation and coordination, such as emergency response activities.

LEARNING OBJECTIVE

Summarise the team development process.

TEAM PROCESSES

The third set of elements in the team effectiveness model, collectively known as *team processes*, includes team development, norms, cohesion and trust. These elements represent characteristics of the team that continuously evolve.

Team Development

The National Transportation Safety Board (NTSB) in the United States studied the circumstances under which aeroplane cockpit crews were most likely to have accidents and related problems. What the NTSB discovered was startling: 73 per cent of all incidents took place on the crew's first day, and 44 per cent occurred on the crew's very first flight together. This isn't an isolated example. NASA studied fatigue of pilots after returning from multiple-day trips. Fatigued pilots made more errors in the NASA flight simulator, as one would expect. What the NASA researchers didn't expect, however, was evidence that fatigued crews who had worked together made *fewer* errors than did rested crews who had not yet flown together.[40]

The NTSB and NASA studies reveal that team members must resolve several issues and pass through several stages of development before emerging as an effective work unit. They need to get to know and trust each other, understand and agree on their respective roles, discover appropriate and inappropriate behaviours, and learn how to coordinate with each other. The longer that team members work together, the better they develop common or complementary mental models, mutual understanding and effective performance routines to complete the work.

A popular model that captures many team development activities is shown in Exhibit 8.5.[41] The model shows teams moving systematically from one stage to the next, while the dashed lines illustrate that teams might fall back to an earlier stage of development as new members join or other conditions disrupt the team's maturity. *Forming*, the first stage of team development, is a period of testing and orientation in which members learn about each other and evaluate the benefits and costs of continued membership. People tend to be polite, will defer to authority, and try to find out what is expected of them and how they will fit into the team. The *storming*

Exhibit 8.5 *Stages of Team Development*

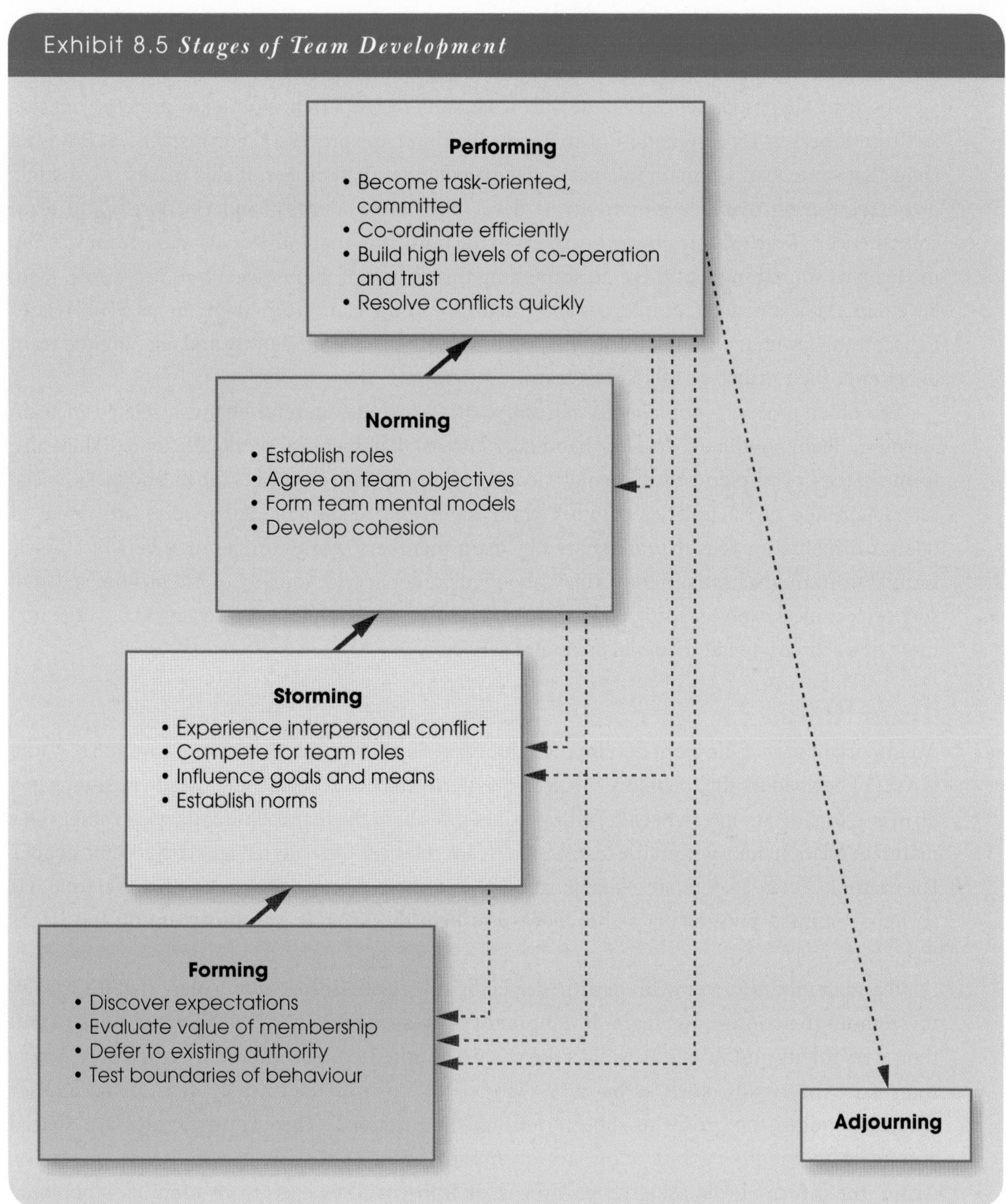

stage is marked by interpersonal conflict as members become more proactive and compete for various team roles. Members try to establish norms of appropriate behaviour and performance standards.

During the *norming* stage, the team develops its first real sense of cohesion as roles are established, and a consensus forms around group objectives and a common or complementary team-based mental model. By the *performing* stage, team members have learned to efficiently coordinate and resolve conflicts. In high-performance teams, members are highly cooperative, have a high level of trust in each other, are committed to group objectives and identify with the team. Finally, the *adjourning* stage occurs when the team is about to disband. Team members shift their attention away from task orientation to a relationship focus.

The five-stage model is consistent with what students experience on team projects, but it is far from a perfect representation of the team development process.[42] For instance, it does not show that some teams remain in a particular stage longer than others. It also masks two distinct processes during team development: (1) developing team identity, and (2) developing team competence.[43] *Developing team identity* refers to the transition that individuals make from viewing the team as something 'out there' to something that is part of themselves. In other words, team development occurs when employees shift their view of the team from 'them' to 'us'. This relates to becoming familiar with the team, making it part of their social identity and shaping the team to better fit their prototype of an ideal team.

The other process—*developing team competence*—includes several changes related to team learning. Team members develop habitual routines that increase work efficiency. They also form shared or complementary mental models regarding team resources, goals and tasks, social interaction and characteristics of other team members.[44] Team mental models are visual or relational mental images that are shared by team members. For example, members of a newly formed team might have different views about customer service (quality of interaction, speed of service, technical expertise provided and so on). As the team develops, these views converge into more of a shared mental model of customer service.

Team Roles

role A set of behaviours that people are expected to perform because of the positions they hold in a team and organisation.

An important part of the team development process is forming and reinforcing team roles. A **role** is a set of behaviours that people are expected to perform because they hold certain positions in a team and organisation.[45] In a team setting, some roles help the team achieve its goals; other roles maintain relationships within the team. Some team roles are formally assigned to specific people. For example, team leaders are usually expected to initiate discussion, ensure that everyone has an opportunity to present his or her views and help the team reach agreement on the issues discussed.

Team members are typically assigned specific roles as their formal job responsibilities. Yet, throughout the continuous team development process, people vary their formal roles to suit their personality and values as well as the wishes of other team members. Furthermore, many roles exist informally, such as being a cheerleader, an initiator of new ideas, or an adviser who encourages the group to soberly rethink their actions. The informal roles are shared among team members, but many are eventually associated with specific team members. Again, the informal role assignment process is influenced by each team member's personal preferences (personality and values) as well as through negotiated dynamics with other team members.[46]

Accelerating Team Development through Team Building

team building A process that consists of formal activities intended to improve the development and functioning of a work team.

Team development, including sorting out team roles, takes time, so many companies try to speed up the process through team-building activities. **Team building** consists of formal activities intended to improve the development and functioning of a work team.[47] It can help new teams, but it is more commonly applied to existing teams that have regressed to earlier stages of team development due to membership turnover or loss of focus.

Sounds Like Team Building

Some companies try to build stronger teams by sending staff into the bush. Others have them collectively prepare fancy meals, fight paintball wars, or play board games. An emerging team-building practice is far more creative: team members visit a sound studio where they write and record an original song. Coca-Cola Amatil is one of many companies that has used song recording to improve team dynamics. Two departments at the Sydney-based drinks company were forced to merge into one work unit. Working with Song Division, an Australian company that specialises in this type of team building, management of the new group penned and sang a Johnny Cash-styled tune about the 'arranged marriage'. 'The merged management team was now closer as a unit, had worked through an issue together, and as a result was much more upbeat and efficient in the planning session that followed,' says Song Division founder and managing director Andy Sharpe. 'Our experience is that the successful companies are the ones that know the value in good team-building activities and use them as part of a culture of creativity and effective communication.'[48]

Louie Douvis/*Australian Financial Review*

Some team-building interventions clarify the team's performance goals, increase the team's motivation to accomplish these goals and establish a mechanism for systematic feedback on the team's goal performance. Others try to improve the team's problem-solving skills. A third category of team building clarifies and reconstructs each member's perceptions of her or his role as well as the role expectations that member has of other team members. Role-definition team building also helps the team to develop shared mental models—common internal representations of the external world, such as how to interact with clients, maintain machinery and engage in meetings. Research studies indicate that team processes and performance depend on how well teammates share common mental models about how they should work together.[49]

A popular form of team building is aimed at improving relations among team members. This includes activities that help team members learn more about each other, build trust in each other and develop ways to manage conflict within the team. Popular interventions such as wilderness team activities, paintball wars and obstacle-course challenges are typically offered to build trust. 'If two colleagues hold the rope for you while you're climbing 10 metres up, that is truly team-building,' suggests a partner in a German communications consulting firm who participated in that team-building event.[50]

Although team-building activities are popular, their success is less certain than many claim.[51] One problem is that team-building activities are used as general solutions to general team problems. A better approach is to begin with a sound diagnosis of the team's health and then select team-building interventions that address weaknesses.[52] Another problem occurs when team building is applied as a one-shot medical inoculation that every team should receive when it is formed. In truth, team building is an ongoing process, not a three-day jump-start.[53] Finally, we must remember that team building occurs on the job, not just on an obstacle course or in a national park. Organisations should encourage team members to reflect on their work experiences and to experiment with just-in-time learning for team development.

LEARNING OBJECTIVE

Discuss how team norms develop and how they may be altered.

norms The informal rules and shared expectations that groups establish to regulate the behaviour of their members.

Team Norms

Norms are the informal rules and shared expectations that groups establish to regulate the behaviour of their members. Norms apply only to behaviour, not to private thoughts or feelings. Furthermore, team norms exist only for behaviours that are important to the team.[54] Norms are enforced in various ways. Coworkers grimace if we are late for a meeting, or they make sarcastic comments if we don't have our part of the project completed on time. Norms are also directly reinforced through praise from high-status members, more access to valued resources, or other rewards available to the team. But team members often conform to prevailing norms without direct reinforcement or punishment because they identify with the group and want to align their behaviour with the team's values. The more closely the person's social identity is connected to the group, the more the individual is motivated to avoid negative sanctions from that group.[55]

How Team Norms Develop

Norms develop as soon as teams form because people need to anticipate or predict how others will act. Even subtle events during the team's formation, such as how team members initially greet each other and where they sit in the first meetings, can initiate norms that are later difficult to change. Norms also form as team members discover behaviours that help them function more effectively (such as the need to respond quickly to email). In particular, a critical event in the team's history can trigger formation of a norm or sharpen a previously vague one. A third influence on team norms is the past experiences and values that members bring to the team. If members of a new team value work–life balance, they are likely to develop norms that discourage long hours and work overload.[56]

Preventing and Changing Dysfunctional Team Norms

Team norms often become deeply anchored, so the best way to avoid norms that undermine organisational success or employee wellbeing is to establish desirable norms when the team is first formed. One way to do this is to clearly state desirable norms when the team is created. Another approach is to select people with appropriate values. If organisational leaders want their teams to have strong safety norms, they should hire people who already value safety and who clearly identify the importance of safety when the team is formed.

The suggestions so far refer to new teams, but how can organisational leaders maintain desirable norms in older teams? First, as one recent study affirmed, leaders often have the capacity to alter existing norms.[57] By speaking up or actively coaching the team, they can often subdue dysfunctional norms while developing useful norms. Team-based reward systems can also weaken counterproductive norms; however, studies report that employees might continue to adhere to a dysfunctional team norm (such as limiting output) even though this behaviour reduces their pay cheque. Finally, if dysfunctional norms are deeply ingrained and the previous solutions don't work, it may be necessary to disband the group and replace it with people who adhere to more favourable norms.

Team Cohesion

Team cohesion refers to the degree of attraction people feel toward the team and their motivation to remain members. It is a characteristic of the team, and includes the extent to which its members are attracted to the team and are committed to the team's goals or tasks. A collective sense of team pride is also a key component of team cohesion.[58] Thus, team cohesion is an emotional experience, not just a calculation of whether to stay or leave the team. It exists when team members make the team part of their social identity. Team cohesion is therefore associated with the team development process because, as mentioned earlier, team members form a team identity as part of this process.

team cohesion The degree of attraction people feel toward the team and their motivation to remain members.

Influences on Team Cohesion

List six factors that influence team cohesion.

Several factors influence team cohesion: member similarity, team size, member interaction, difficult entry, team success and external competition or challenges. For the most part, these factors reflect the individual's social identity with the group and beliefs about how team membership will fulfil personal needs:

- Member similarity—For more than 2000 years, philosophers and researchers have observed that people with similar backgrounds and values are more comfortable with and attractied to each other. In team settings, this similarity-attraction effect means that teams have higher cohesion—or become cohesive more quickly—when members are similar to each other. Diversity tends to undermine cohesion, but this depends on the type of diversity. For example, teams consisting of people from different job groups seem to gel together just as well as teams of people who do the same job.[59]
- Team size—Smaller teams tend to have more cohesion than larger teams because it is easier for a few people to agree on goals and coordinate work activities. However, small teams have less cohesion when they lack enough members to perform the required tasks.
- Member interaction—Teams tend to have more cohesion when team members interact with each other fairly regularly. This occurs when team members perform highly interdependent tasks and work in the same physical area.
- Difficult entry—Teams tend to have more cohesion when entry to the team is restricted. The more elite the team, the more prestige it confers on its members, and the more they tend to value their membership in the unit. At the same time, research suggests that severe initiations can weaken team cohesion because of the adverse effects of humiliation, even for those who successfully endure the initiation.[60]
- Team success—Cohesion is both emotional and instrumental, with the latter referring to the notion that people feel more cohesion to teams that fulfil their needs and goals. Consequently, cohesion increases with the team's level of success.[61] Furthermore, individuals are more likely to attach their social identity to successful teams than to those with a string of failures. For example, Mobil New Zealand successfully acquired a group of service stations before the main competitor (BP) could buy them. The quick action not only boosted Mobil's market position; this decisive battle victory in 'the BP Wars' also boosted the management team's cohesion and confidence in their collective abilities.[62]

- External competition or challenges—Team cohesion tends to increase when members face external competition or a valued objective that is challenging. This might include a threat from an external competitor or friendly competition from other teams. Employees value their membership on the team because of its ability to overcome the threat or competition and as a form of social support. However, cohesion can dissipate when external threats are severe because these threats are stressful and cause teams to make less effective decisions.[63]

Consequences of Team Cohesion

Every team must have some minimal level of cohesion to maintain its existence. People who belong to high-cohesion teams are motivated to maintain their membership and to help the team perform effectively. Compared to low-cohesion teams, high-cohesion team members spend more time together, share information more frequently and are more satisfied with each other. They provide each other with better social support in stressful situations.[64]

Members of high-cohesion teams are generally more sensitive to each other's needs and develop better interpersonal relationships, thereby reducing dysfunctional conflict. When conflict does arise, members tend to resolve their differences swiftly and effectively. With better cooperation and more conformity to norms, high-cohesion teams usually perform better than low-cohesion teams.[65] However, as Exhibit 8.6 illustrates, this relationship holds true only when team norms are compatible with organisational values and objectives. Cohesion motivates employees to perform at a level more consistent with team norms. When those norms conflict with the organisation's success (such as when norms support high absenteeism or acting unethically), high cohesion will reduce team performance.[66]

Exhibit 8.6 ***Effect of Team Cohesion on Task Performance***

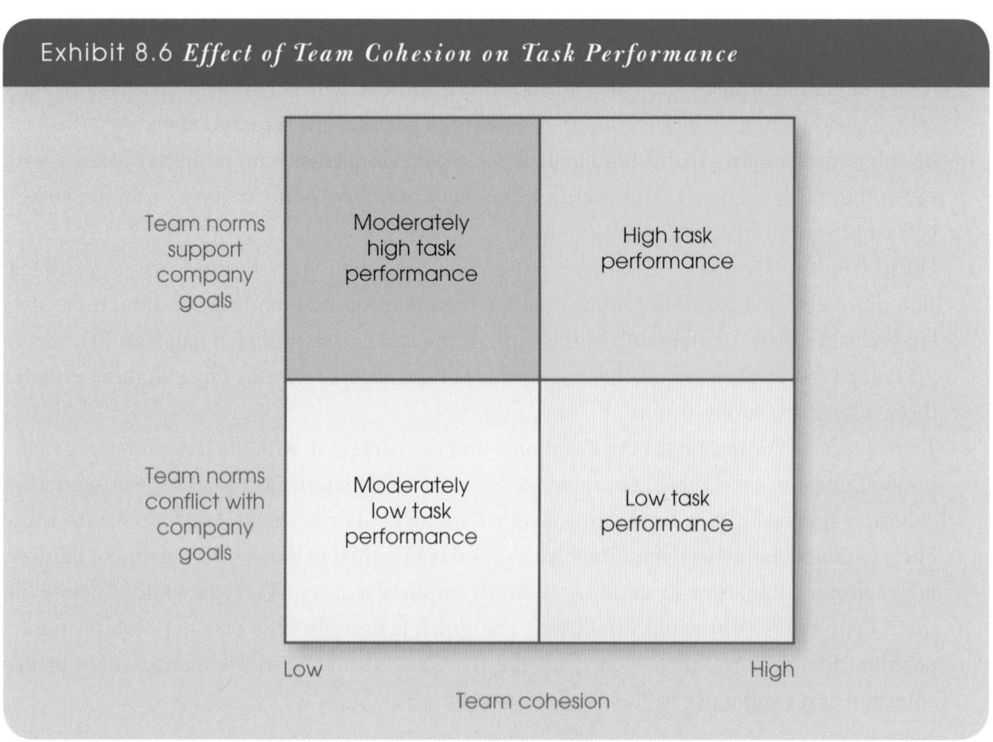

Team Trust

Any relationship—including the relationship among team members—depends on a certain degree of trust.[67] **Trust** refers to positive expectations one person has toward another person or group in situations involving risk. A high level of trust occurs when others affect you in situations where you are at risk but you believe they will not harm you. Trust includes both your beliefs and conscious feelings about the relationship with other team members. In other words, a person both logically evaluates the situation as trustworthy and feels that it is trustworthy.[68] Trust can also be understood in terms of the foundation of the trust. From this perspective, people trust others on the basis of three foundations: calculus, knowledge and identification (see Exhibit 8.7).

LEARNING OBJECTIVE 

Describe the three foundations of trust in teams and other interpersonal relationships.

trust positive expectations one person has toward another person or group in situations involving risk.

Calculus-based trust represents a logical calculation that other team members will act appropriately because they face sanctions if their actions violate reasonable expectations.[69] It offers the lowest potential trust and is easily broken by a violation of expectations. Generally, calculus-based trust alone cannot sustain a team's relationship, because it relies on deterrence. *Knowledge-based trust* is based on the predictability of another team member's behaviour. Even if we don't agree with a particular team member's actions, his or her consistency generates some level of trust. Knowledge-based trust also relates to confidence in the other person's ability or competence, such as the confidence that exists when we trust a medical practitioner.[70] Knowledge-based trust offers a higher potential level of trust and is more stable because it develops over time.

Identification-based trust is based on mutual understanding and an emotional bond among team members. It occurs when team members think, feel and act like each other. High-performance teams exhibit this level of trust because they share the same values and mental models. Identification-based trust is potentially the strongest and most robust of all three types of trust. The individual's self-concept is based partly on membership of the team, and he or she believes the members' values highly overlap, so any transgressions by other team members are quickly forgiven. People are more reluctant to acknowledge a violation of this high-level trust because it strikes at the heart of their self-concept.

Exhibit 8.7 *Three Foundations of Trust in Teams*

Potential level of trust	Type of trust	Description
High	Identification-based trust	• Based on common mental models and values • Increases with person's social identity with team
	Knowledge-based trust	• Based on predictability and competence • Fairly robust
Low	Calculus-based trust	• Based on deterrence • Fragile and limited potential because dependent on punishment

Dynamics of Team Trust

Employees typically join a team with a moderate or high level—not a low level—of trust in their new coworkers. The main explanation for the initially high trust (called *swift trust*) in organisational settings is that people usually believe fellow team members are reasonably competent (knowledge-based trust) and they tend to develop some degree of social identity with the team (identification-based trust). Even when working with strangers, most of us display some level of trust, if only because it supports our self-concept of being a good person.[71] However, trust is fragile in new relationships because it is based on assumptions rather than well-established experience. Consequently, recent studies report that trust tends to decrease rather than increase over time. This is unfortunate because employees become less forgiving and less cooperative toward others as their level of trust decreases, and this undermines team and organisational effectiveness.[72]

The team effectiveness model is a useful template for understanding how teams work—and don't work—in organisations. With this knowledge in hand, let's briefly investigate two types of teams that have received considerable attention among OB experts and practitioners: self-directed teams and virtual teams.

LEARNING OBJECTIVE

Discuss the characteristics and factors required for success of self-directed teams and virtual teams.

SELF-DIRECTED TEAMS

When Whole Foods Market opens new stores, the organic food retailer isn't just looking for employees with good customer service skills. It is looking for people who also work well in self-directed teams. Every Whole Foods Market store in the United States, United Kingdom and Canada is divided into about 10 teams, such as the prepared-foods team, the cashier/front-end team and the seafood team. Teams are 'self-directed' because team members make the decisions about their work unit with minimal interference from management. 'Each team is ... responsible for managing its own business,' explains Whole Foods Market cofounder John Mackey. 'It gets a profit-and-loss statement, it's responsible for managing inventory, labour productivity, gross margins; and its members are responsible for many of the product-placement decisions.'[73]

self-directed team (SDT) A cross-functional work group that is organised around work processes, completes an entire piece of work requiring several interdependent tasks and has substantial autonomy over the execution of those tasks.

Whole Foods Market operates with self-directed teams. A **self-directed team (SDT)** is defined by two distinctive features.[74] First, the team completes an entire piece of work requiring several interdependent tasks. This type of work arrangement clusters the team members together while minimising their interdependence and interaction with employees outside the team. The result is a close-knit group of employees who depend on each other to accomplish their individual tasks. For example, Whole Foods Market employees responsible for a store's fish department would naturally work more closely with each other than with members of other teams. La-Z-Boy also recently shifted from a traditional assembly line to self-directed teams. As described earlier in this chapter, the furniture manufacturer reorganised production employees into teams responsible for constructing an entire product. Members of each team work closely with each other and much less with members of other teams.

The second distinctive feature of SDTs is that they have substantial autonomy over the execution of their tasks. In particular, these teams plan, organise and control work activities with little or no direct involvement of a higher status supervisor. The teams at Whole Foods Market are considered self-directed because of their autonomy. Every team is responsible for its work area, including managing inventory, profitability, scheduling and hiring.

Self-directed teams are found in many industries, ranging from petrochemical plants to manufacturers of aircraft parts. Almost all the top-rated manufacturing firms in North America rely on SDTs.[75] The popularity of SDTs is consistent with research indicating that they potentially increase both productivity and job satisfaction. For instance, one study found that car dealership service shops that organise employees into SDTs are significantly more profitable than shops where employees work without a team structure. Another study reported that both short- and long-term measures of customer satisfaction increased after street cleaners in a German city were organised into SDTs.[76]

Success Factors for Self-Directed Teams

Although they receive less fanfare in this region than in the United States and Europe, self-directed work teams have been successfully implemented at ALCOA Australia, Davao Light & Power Co. in the Philippines, Work and Income New Zealand, the Western Australian State Revenue department and Aztec Software in Mumbai, India, among many others.[77] At the same time, many companies in Australia and other countries have introduced self-directed teams, only to see them fail to improve productivity or morale.[78]

Whether self-directed teams succeed or fail depends on several factors.[79] In addition to managing the team dynamics issues described earlier in this chapter, SDTs should be responsible for an entire work process, such as making an entire product or providing a service. Organisation around a work process keeps each team sufficiently independent from other teams, yet it demands a relatively high degree of interdependence among employees within the team.[80] SDTs should also have sufficient autonomy to organise and coordinate their work. Autonomy allows them to respond more quickly and effectively to client and stakeholder demands. It also motivates

Reckitt Benckiser's Prescription for Productivity: Self-Directed Teams

Through teamwork and lean manufacturing practices, Reckitt Benckiser Healthcare has become one of the most productive pharmaceutical operations in Europe. In fact, teamwork is one of the company's four core values. At its facility in Hull, United Kingdom, for example, every line is operated by a dedicated self-directed team. 'The people on the lines decide how they are going to run over the next three to four weeks,' says Lisa Adams, team leader of the area that packages products in sachets and tubes. Mark Smith, a crew leader of one line, proudly notes that his team has become 'one of the most efficient in northern Europe' because 'we were given the opportunity to take ownership of the line'. The benefits of self-directed teams were apparent when the team responsible for producing Gaviscon antacid tablets tackled a problem with the delivery of tablets in the production process. The team changed the tablet-feed angle and, after a few trials, found a solution. That production line hasn't experienced any tablet-feed problems, and this has significantly reduced costs and improved efficiency due to reduced downtime and less wasted product.[82]

www.worksmanagement.co.uk

team members through feelings of empowerment. Finally, SDTs are more successful when the work site and technology support coordination and communication among team members and increase job enrichment.[81] Too often, management calls a group of employees a 'team', yet the work layout, assembly-line structure and/or other technologies isolate the employees from each other.

VIRTUAL TEAMS

Agilent Technologies is on the cutting edge of major trends in digital electronics and optical and wireless communications. It is also on the cutting edge of a globally distributed organisational structure where most employees work in virtual teams. The company closed its 48 US sales offices a few years ago and instructed its employees on how to work from home. In Australia, more than half of Agilent's 170 employees report to a manager located in another country. For example, Australian employees work with human resources staff in Malaysia, IT and finance staff in Singapore, and accounts payable/receivable staff in India.[83]

virtual teams Teams whose members operate across space, time and organisational boundaries, and are linked through information technologies to achieve organisational tasks.

Agilent Technologies employees in Australia and elsewhere perform much of their work in **virtual teams.** Virtual teams are teams whose members operate across space, time and organisational boundaries and are linked through information technologies to achieve organisational tasks.[84] Virtual teams differ from traditional teams in two ways: (1) They are not usually colocated (do not work in the same physical area), and (2) due to their lack of colocation, members of virtual teams depend primarily on information technologies rather than face-to-face interaction to communicate and coordinate their work effort.

According to one estimate, more than 60 per cent of employees in professions are members of a virtual team at some point during the year. In global companies such as IBM and Accenture, almost everyone in knowledge-based work is part of a virtual team. One reason why virtual teams have become so widespread is that information technologies have made it easier than ever before to communicate and coordinate with people at a distance.[85] The shift from production-based to knowledge-based work is a second reason why virtual teamwork is feasible. It isn't yet possible to make a product when team members are located apart, but most of us are now in jobs that mainly process knowledge.

Information technologies and knowledge-based work make virtual teams *possible*, but organisational learning and globalisation are two reasons why they are increasingly *necessary*. Virtual teams represent a natural part of the organisational learning process because they encourage employees to share and use knowledge where geography limits more direct forms of collaboration. Globalisation makes virtual teams increasingly necessary because employees are spread around the planet rather than around one city. Thus, global businesses depend on virtual teamwork to leverage their human capital.

Success Factors for Virtual Teams

Virtual teams have all the challenges of traditional teams, along with the complications of distance and time. Fortunately, OB researchers have been keenly interested in virtual teams, and their studies are now yielding ways to improve virtual-team effectiveness.[86] First, along with having the team competencies described earlier in this chapter, members of successful virtual teams must have good communication technology skills, strong self-leadership skills to motivate and guide their behaviour without peers or bosses nearby, and higher emotional intelligence so that they can decipher the feelings of other team members from email and other limited communication media.

A second recommendation is that virtual teams should have a toolkit of communication channels (email, virtual whiteboards, video conferencing and so on) as well as the freedom to choose the channels that work best for them. This may sound obvious, but unfortunately senior management tends to impose technology on virtual teams, often based on advice from external consultants, and expects team members to use the same communication technology throughout their work. In contrast, research suggests that communication channels gain and lose importance over time, depending on the task and level of trust.

Third, virtual teams need plenty of structure. In one recent review of effective virtual teams, many of the principles for successful virtual teams related mostly to creating these structures, such as clear operational objectives, documented work processes, and agreed-on roles and responsibilities.[87] Agilent Australia's country manager explains the importance of structure for successful virtual teams. 'When you have everyone in the same place, you can get people in a room to talk through issues—at least things seem to be easier! When the team is virtual, you have to be much more structured in how you communicate with your team.'[88]

The final recommendation is that virtual-team members should meet face-to-face fairly early in the team development process. This idea may seem contradictory to the entire notion of virtual teams, but so far, no technology has replaced face-to-face interaction for high-level bonding and mutual understanding. 'I always try to do the kick-off meeting face-to-face,' says Scott Patterson, PricewaterhouseCooper's e-learning manager in Atlanta. 'We also try to bring the group back together for major milestones in a project.' Similarly, when IBM formed a virtual team to build an electronic customer-access system for Shell, employees from both firms began with an 'all hands' face-to-face gathering to assist the team development process. The two firms also made a rule that the dispersed team members (most of whom were located in the same city) should have face-to-face contact at least once every six weeks throughout the project. Without this, 'after about five or six weeks we found some of that communication would start to break down,' says the IBM comanager for the project.[89]

TEAM DECISION MAKING

Identify four constraints on team decision making.

Self-directed teams, virtual teams and practically all other groups are expected to make decisions. Under certain conditions, teams are more effective than individuals at identifying problems, choosing alternatives and evaluating their decisions. To leverage these benefits, however, we first need to understand the constraints on effective team decision making. Then, we look at specific team structures that try to overcome these constraints.

Constraints on Team Decision Making

Anyone who has spent enough time in the workplace can recall several ways in which teams stumble in decision making. The four most common problems are time constraints, evaluation apprehension, pressure to conform and groupthink.

Time Constraints

There's a saying that 'committees keep minutes and waste hours'. This reflects the fact that teams take longer than individuals to make decisions.[90] Unlike individuals, teams require extra time to organise, coordinate and maintain relationships. The larger the group, the more time is required to make a decision. Team members need time to learn about each other and build rapport. They need to manage an imperfect communication process so that there is sufficient understanding of each other's ideas. They also need to coordinate roles and rules of order within the decision process.

production blocking A time constraint in team decision making due to the procedural requirement that only one person may speak at a time.

Another time-related constraint found in most team structures is that only one person can speak at a time.[91] This problem, known as **production blocking**, undermines idea generation in several ways. First, team members need to listen in on the conversation to find an opportune time to speak up, and this monitoring makes it difficult for them to concentrate on their own ideas. Second, ideas are fleeting, so the longer they wait to speak up, the more likely these flickering ideas will die out. Third, team members might remember their fleeting thoughts by concentrating on them, but this causes them to pay less attention to the conversation. By ignoring what others are saying, team members miss other potentially good ideas as well as the opportunity to convey their ideas to others in the group.

Evaluation Apprehension

evaluation apprehension A decision-making problem that occurs when individuals are reluctant to mention ideas that seem silly because they believe (often correctly) that other team members are silently evaluating them.

Individuals are reluctant to mention ideas that seem silly because they believe (often correctly) that other team members are silently evaluating them.[92] This **evaluation apprehension** is based on the individual's desire to create a favourable self-presentation and need to protect self-esteem. It is most common when meetings are attended by people with different levels of status or expertise, or when members formally evaluate each other's performance throughout the year (as in 360-degree feedback). Creative ideas often sound bizarre or illogical when first presented, so evaluation apprehension tends to discourage employees from mentioning them in front of coworkers.

Pressure to Conform

Team cohesion leads employees to conform to the team's norms. This control keeps the group organised around common goals, but it may also cause team members to suppress their dissenting opinions, particularly when a strong team norm is related to the issue. When someone does state a point of view that violates the majority opinion, other members might punish the violator or try to persuade him or her that the opinion is incorrect. Conformity can also be subtle. To some extent, we depend on the opinions that others hold to validate our own views. If coworkers don't agree with us, we begin to question our own opinions even without overt peer pressure.

Groupthink

groupthink The tendency of highly cohesive groups to value consensus at the price of decision quality.

Groupthink is the tendency of highly cohesive groups to value consensus at the price of decision quality.[93] The concept includes the dysfunctional effects of conformity on team decision making, which was described above. It also includes the dysfunctional consequences of trying to maintain harmony within the team. This desire for harmony exists as a group norm and is most apparent when team members have a strong social identity with the group. Groupthink supposedly occurs most often when the team is isolated from outsiders, the team leader is opinionated (rather than impartial), the team is under stress due to an external threat, the team has experienced recent failures or other decision-making problems, and the team lacks clear guidance from corporate policies or procedures.

The term *groupthink* is now part of everyday language, so much so that some experts worry that it commonly refers to almost any problem in team decision making. Meanwhile, scholarly studies have found that the symptoms of groupthink do not cluster together as the concept assumes; some groupthink characteristics actually improve rather than undermine decision making in some situations. Although many cases of groupthink have been documented, one study found that this evidence is illusory because observers retrospectively make sense of bad decisions by incorrectly perceiving evidence of groupthink.[94]

In spite of the problems with the groupthink concept, some of its specific elements continue to be relevant because they explain specific problems with team decision making. One of these elements, conformity, was described above as a concern. Another important element is the team's overconfidence. Studies consistently report that highly confident teams have a false sense of invulnerability, which makes them less attentive in decision making than are moderately confident teams.[95]

Team Structures to Improve Decision Making

LEARNING OBJECTIVE 

Discuss the advantages and disadvantages of four structures that potentially improve team decision making.

There is plenty of research revealing problems with team decision making, but several solutions also emerge from these bad-news studies. Team members need to be confident in their decision making but not so confident that they collectively feel invulnerable. This calls for team norms that encourage critical thinking as well as team membership with sufficient diversity. Checks and balances need to be in place to prevent one or two people from dominating the discussion. The team should also be large enough to possess the collective knowledge to resolve the problem yet small enough that the team doesn't consume too much time or restrict individual input. One recent perspective is that executives typically face messy problems (i.e. ill-defined problems, or those with incomplete information) and that members of the executive team represent their constituents (divisions, departments, regions and so on). Therefore, the best strategy is to get everyone's preferences out in the open quickly, have them vigorously debated, create a few plausible options and, in most cases, acknowledge that the CEO needs to make the final decision because consensus is rarely possible.[96]

Team structures also help to minimise the problems described over the previous few pages. Four structures potentially improve team decision making in team settings: constructive conflict, brainstorming, electronic brainstorming and nominal group technique.

Constructive Conflict

A popular way to improve team decision making at Corning Inc. is to assign promising ideas to two-person teams, who spend up to four months analysing the feasibility of their assigned idea. The unique feature of this process is that the team is deliberately designed so that one person is from marketing and the other has technical expertise. This oil-and-water combination sometimes ruffles feathers, but it seems to generate better ideas and evaluations. 'We find great constructive conflict this way,' says Deborah Mills, who leads Corning's early-stage marketing team.[97]

Constructive conflict occurs when people focus their discussion on the issue while maintaining respect for people who hold other points of view. This conflict is called 'constructive' because different viewpoints are encouraged so that ideas and recommendations can be clarified, redesigned and tested for logical soundness. The main advantage of this debate is that it presents different points of view and thus encourages all participants to re-examine their assumptions

constructive conflict A type of conflict in which people focus their discussion on the issue while maintaining respect for people having other points of view.

and logic. The main challenge with constructive conflict is that healthy debate too often slides into personal attacks, a problem that may explain why constructive conflict does not always have a positive effect on team decision making.[98] We explore this issue further in Chapter 11, along with specific strategies for minimising the emotional effects of conflict while maintaining constructive debate.

Brainstorming

brainstorming A freewheeling, face-to-face meeting where team members aren't allowed to criticise but are encouraged to speak freely, generate as many ideas as possible and build on the ideas of others.

Brainstorming tries to leverage the creative potential of teams by establishing four simple rules: (1) speak freely—describe even the craziest ideas; (2) don't criticise others or their ideas; (3) provide as many ideas as possible—the quality of ideas increases with the quantity of ideas; and (4) build on the ideas that others have presented. These rules are supposed to encourage divergent thinking while minimising evaluation apprehension and other team dynamics problems. Lab studies using university students concluded many years ago that brainstorming isn't very effective, largely because production blocking and evaluation apprehension still interfere with team dynamics.[100]

However, brainstorming may be more beneficial than these earlier studies indicated.[101] The earlier lab studies measured the number of ideas generated, whereas recent investigations within companies using brainstorming indicate that this team structure results in more *creative* ideas, which is the main reason why companies use brainstorming. Also, evaluation apprehension is less of a problem in high-performing teams that embrace a learning orientation culture than it is for students brainstorming in lab experiments. Another overlooked advantage of brainstorming is that participants interact and participate directly, thereby increasing decision acceptance and team cohesion. Finally, brainstorming sessions often spread enthusiasm, which tends to generate more creativity. Overall, while brainstorming might not always be the best team structure, it seems to be more valuable than some of the earlier research studies indicated.

NASA's Constructive Conflict Room

The ill-fated flight of the space shuttle *Columbia* in 2003 was a wake-up call for NASA's mission management team, specifically how it makes decisions. The *Columbia* accident investigation team concluded that concerns raised by engineers were either deflected or watered down because the mission management team appeared to be 'immersed in a culture of invincibility' and hierarchical authority discouraged constructive debate. If top decision makers had more fully considered the extent of damage during take-off, they might have been able to save *Columbia*'s seven crew members. To foster more open communications and constructive conflict, the mission management team's assigned-seating rectangular table has been replaced by a C-shaped arrangement where people sit wherever they want (shown in photo). None of the 24 members stands out above the others in the new set-up. Around the walls of the room are pearls of wisdom reminding everyone of the pitfalls of team decision making. 'People in groups tend to agree on courses of action which, as individuals, they know are stupid,' warns one poster.[99]

NASA

Electronic Brainstorming

Electronic brainstorming is a more recent form of brainstorming that relies on networked computers for submitting and sharing creative ideas. After receiving the question or issue, participants enter their ideas using special computer software. The ideas are distributed anonymously to other participants, who are encouraged to piggyback on those ideas. Team members eventually vote electronically on the ideas presented. Face-to-face discussion usually follows. Electronic brainstorming can be quite effective at generating creative ideas with minimal production blocking, evaluation apprehension or conformity problems.[102] Despite these numerous advantages, electronic brainstorming seems to be too structured and technology-bound for some executives. Some leaders may also feel threatened by the honesty of statements generated through this process and by their limited ability to control the discussion.

electronic brainstorming A form of brainstorming that relies on networked computers for submitting and sharing creative ideas.

Nominal Group Technique

Nominal group technique is a variation of traditional brainstorming that tries to combine the benefits of team decision making without the problems mentioned earlier.[103] The method is called 'nominal' because participants form a group in name only during two of its three stages. After the problem is described, team members silently and independently write down as many solutions as they can. In the second stage, participants describe their solutions to the other team members, usually in a round-robin format. As with brainstorming, there is no criticism or debate, although members are encouraged to ask for clarification of the ideas presented. In the third stage, participants silently and independently rank-order or vote on each proposed solution. Nominal group technique tends to generate a higher number of ideas, and better quality ideas, than do traditional interacting and possibly brainstorming groups.[104] Due to its high degree of structure, nominal group technique usually maintains a high task orientation and relatively low potential for conflict within the team. However, production blocking and evaluation apprehension still occur to some extent.

nominal group technique A variation of brainstorming consisting of three stages: participants (1) silently and independently document their ideas, (2) collectively describe these ideas to the other team members without critique, and (3) silently and independently evaluate the ideas presented.

CHAPTER SUMMARY

Teams are groups of two or more people who interact and influence each other, are mutually accountable for achieving common goals associated with organisational objectives, and perceive themselves as a social entity within an organisation. All teams are groups, because they consist of people with a unifying relationship; not all groups are teams, because some groups do not exist to serve organisational objectives.

People join informal groups (and are motivated to be on formal teams) for four reasons: (1) people have an innate drive to bond; (2) group membership is an inherent ingredient in a person's self-concept; (3) some personal goals are accomplished better in groups; and (4) individuals are comforted in stressful situations by the mere presence of other people. Teams have become popular because they tend to make better decisions, support the knowledge management process and provide superior customer service. People also tend to be more motivated working in teams. However, teams are not always as effective as individuals working alone. Process losses and social loafing are two particular concerns that drag down team performance.

Team effectiveness includes the team's ability to achieve its objectives, fulfil the needs of its members and maintain its survival. The model of team effectiveness considers the organisational and team environment, team design and team processes. Three team design elements are task characteristics, team size and team composition. Teams tend to be better suited for situations in which the work is complex and the tasks among employees have high interdependence. Teams should be large enough to perform the work yet small enough for efficient coordination and meaningful involvement. Effective teams are composed of people with the competencies and motivation to perform tasks in a team environment. Team member diversity has advantages and disadvantages for team performance.

Teams develop through the stages of forming, storming, norming, performing and eventually adjourning. Within these stages are two distinct team development processes: developing team identity and developing team competence. Team development can be accelerated through team building—any formal activity intended to improve the development and functioning of a work team. Teams develop norms to regulate and guide member behaviour. These norms may be influenced by initial experiences, critical events, and the values and experiences that team members bring to the group.

Team cohesion—the degree of attraction people feel toward the team and their motivation to remain members—increases with member similarity, smaller team size, higher degree of interaction, difficult entry, team success and external challenges. Cohesion increases team performance when the team's norms are congruent with organisational goals. Trust is a psychological state comprising the intention to accept vulnerability on the basis of positive expectations of the intent or behaviour of another person. People trust others on the basis of three foundations: calculus, knowledge and identification.

Self-directed teams (SDTs) complete an entire piece of work requiring several interdependent tasks, and they have substantial autonomy over the execution of their tasks. Members of virtual teams operate across space, time and organisational boundaries, and are linked through information technologies, to achieve organisational tasks. Virtual teams are more effective when the team members have certain competencies, the team has the freedom to choose the preferred communication channels, and the members meet face-to-face fairly early in the team development process.

Team decisions are impeded by time constraints, evaluation apprehension, the pressure to conform and groupthink (specifically overconfidence). Four structures potentially improve decision making in team settings: constructive conflict, brainstorming, electronic brainstorming and nominal group technique.

KEY TERMS

brainstorming, p. 326
Brooks' law, p. 304
constructive conflict, p. 325
electronic brainstorming, p. 327
evaluation apprehension, p. 324
groupthink, p. 324
nominal group technique, p. 327
norms, p. 316
process losses, p. 304
production blocking, p. 324
role, p. 314
self-directed team (SDT), p. 320
social capital, p. 303
social loafing, p. 304
task interdependence, p. 307
team building, p. 314
team cohesion, p. 317
teams, p. 300
trust, p. 319
virtual teams, p. 322

Critical Thinking Questions

1 Informal groups exist in almost every form of social organisation. What types of informal groups exist in your classroom? Why are students motivated to belong to these informal groups?

2 The late management guru Peter Drucker said: 'The now-fashionable team in which everybody works with everybody on everything from the beginning rapidly is becoming a disappointment.' Discuss three problems associated with teams.

3 You have been put in charge of a cross-functional task force that will develop enhanced internet banking services for retail customers. The team includes representatives from marketing, information services, customer service and accounting, all of whom will move to the same location at headquarters for three months. Describe the behaviours you might observe during each stage of the team's development.

4 You have just been transferred from the Christchurch office to the Wellington office of your company, a New Zealand-wide sales organisation of electrical products for developers and contractors. In Christchurch, team members regularly called customers after a sale to ask whether the products arrived on time and whether they were satisfied. But when you

moved to the Wellington office, no one seemed to make these follow-up calls. A recently hired coworker explained that other coworkers discouraged her from making those calls. Later, another coworker suggested that your follow-up calls were making everyone else look lazy. Give three possible reasons why the norms in Christchurch might be different from those in the Wellington office, even though the customers, products, sales commissions and other characteristics of the workplace are almost identical.

5 You have been assigned to a class project with five other students, none of whom you have met before. To what extent would team cohesion improve your team's performance on this project? What actions would you recommend to build team cohesion among student team members in this situation?

6 Suppose that you are put in charge of a virtual team whose members are located in different cities around the country or region. What tactics could you use to build and maintain team trust, as well as minimise the decline in trust that often occurs in teams?

7 You are responsible for convening a major event in which senior officials from several state governments will try to come to an agreement on environmental issues. It is well known that some officials posture so that they appear superior, whereas others are highly motivated to solve the environmental problems that cross adjacent states. What team decision-making problems are likely to be apparent in this government forum, and what actions can you take to minimise these problems?

8 Bangalore Technologies wants to use brainstorming with its employees and customers to identify new uses for its technology. Advise Bangalore's president about the potential benefits of brainstorming, as well as its potential limitations.

Skill Builder 8.1

TEAM EXERCISE

Team Tower Power

Purpose

This exercise is designed to help you understand team roles, team development, and other issues in the development and maintenance of effective teams.

Materials

The instructor will provide enough Lego pieces or similar materials for each team to complete the assigned task. All teams should have identical (or very similar) amounts and types of pieces. The instructor will need a measuring tape and stopwatch. Students may use writing materials during the design stage (step 2, page 331). The instructor will distribute a 'Team Objectives Sheet' and 'Tower Specifications Effectiveness Sheet' to all teams.

Instructions

STEP 1 The instructor will divide the class into teams. Depending on class size and space availability, teams may have between four and seven members, but all should be around the same size.

STEP 2 Each team is given 20 minutes to design a tower that uses only the materials provided, is freestanding and provides an optimal return on investment. Team members may wish to draw their tower on paper or a flipchart to facilitate the tower's design. Teams are free to practise building their tower during this stage. Preferably, teams are assigned to their own rooms so that the design can be created privately. During this stage, each team will complete the Team Objectives Sheet distributed by the instructor. This sheet requires the Tower Specifications Effectiveness Sheet, also distributed by the instructor.

STEP 3 Each team will show the instructor that it has completed its Team Objectives Sheet. Then, with all teams in the same room, the instructor will announce the start of the construction phase. The time allowed for construction will be closely monitored, and the instructor will occasionally call out the time elapsed (particularly if there is no clock in the room).

STEP 4 Each team will advise the instructor as soon as it has completed its tower. The team will write down the time elapsed that the instructor has determined. It may be asked to assist the instructor by counting the number of blocks used and measuring the height of the tower. This information is also written on the Team Objectives Sheet. Then the team calculates its profit.

STEP 5 After presenting the results, the class will discuss the elements of team dynamics that contribute to team effectiveness. Team members will discuss their strategy, division of labour (team roles), expertise within the team and other elements of team dynamics.

Source: Several published and online sources describe variations of this exercise, but there is no known origin of this activity.

SELF-ASSESSMENT

Skill Builder 8.2

What Team Roles Do You Prefer?

Purpose

This self-assessment is designed to help you identify your preferred roles in meetings and similar team activities.

Instructions

Read each of the statements on page 332 and circle the response that you believe best reflects your position regarding each statement. Then use the scoring key in Appendix B at the end of the book to calculate your results for each team role. This exercise should be completed alone so that you can assess yourself honestly without concerns of social comparison. Class discussion will focus on the roles that people assume in team settings. This scale assesses only a few team roles.

Team Roles Preferences Scale

Circle the number that best reflects your position regarding each of these statements.	Does not describe me at all	Does not describe me very well	Describes me somewhat	Describes me well	Describes me very well
1. I usually take responsibility for getting the team to agree on what the meeting should accomplish.	1	2	3	4	5
2. I tend to summarise to other team members what the team has accomplished so far.	1	2	3	4	5
3. I'm usually the person who helps other team members overcome their disagreements.	1	2	3	4	5
4. I try to ensure that everyone gets heard on issues.	1	2	3	4	5
5. I'm usually the person who helps the team determine how to organise the discussion.	1	2	3	4	5
6. I praise other team members for their ideas more than do others in the meetings.	1	2	3	4	5
7. People tend to rely on me to keep track of what has been said in meetings.	1	2	3	4	5
8. The team typically counts on me to prevent debates from getting out of hand.	1	2	3	4	5
9. I tend to say things that make the group feel optimistic about its accomplishments.	1	2	3	4	5
10. Team members usually count on me to give everyone a chance to speak.	1	2	3	4	5
11. In most meetings, I am less likely than others to criticise the ideas of teammates.	1	2	3	4	5
12. I actively help teammates to resolve their differences in meetings.	1	2	3	4	5
13. I actively encourage quiet team members to describe their ideas about each issue.	1	2	3	4	5
14. People tend to rely on me to clarify the purpose of the meeting.	1	2	3	4	5
15. I like to be the person who takes notes or minutes of the meeting.	1	2	3	4	5

Skill Builder 8.3

SELF-ASSESSMENT

Are You a Team Player?

How much do you like working in teams? Some of us avoid teams whenever possible; others tolerate teamwork; still others thrive in team environments. This exercise is designed to help you estimate the extent to which you are positively predisposed to work in teams. Read each statement in the scale and indicate the extent to which you agree or disagree with the statement.

This exercise should be completed alone so that you can assess yourself honestly without concerns of social comparison. Class discussion will focus on the characteristics of individuals who are more or less compatible with working in teams.

SELF-ASSESSMENT

Skill Builder 8.4

How Trusting Are You?

Trust refers to positive expectations one person has toward another person or group in situations involving risk. While trust varies from one situation to the next, some people have a higher or lower propensity to trust. In other words, some people are highly trusting of others, even when first meeting them, whereas others have difficulty trusting anyone, even over a long time. This self-assessment provides an estimate of your propensity to trust. Indicate your preferred response to each statement, being honest with yourself for each item. This self-assessment should be completed alone. Class discussion will focus on the meaning of propensity to trust, why it varies from one person to the next and how it affects teamwork.

Endnotes

1 'Safe Hands a Boost for Blue Care', *Northern Miner (Charters Towers, Queensland)*, 11 July 2008, 5; 'Powerhouse Team Switched on by Pride', *The Australian*, 23 August 2008, 4; C. Walker, 'Call Answered with Vigour', *Fraser Coast Chronicle (Hervey Bay, Queensland)*, 20 November 2008, 7.

2 'Interview: David Bryce—Part 3 of 3', *Service Untitled*, 13 October 2006, www.serviceuntitled.com (accessed 6 May 2009); T. Tan, 'Playing to Win', *Publishers Weekly*, 28 July 2008; Mediacom, 'Transformational Business Project and Top Professionals among HR Awards Winners', news release (Auckland, 3 March 2009).

3 M. E. Shaw, *Group Dynamics*, 3rd edn (New York: McGraw-Hill, 1981), 8; S. A. Mohrman, S. G. Cohen and A. M. Mohrman Jr, *Designing Team-Based Organizations: New Forms for Knowledge Work* (San Francisco: Jossey-Bass, 1995), 39–40; E. Sundstrom, 'The Challenges of Supporting Work Team Effectiveness', in *Supporting Work Team Effectiveness*, ed. E. Sundstrom and Associates (San Francisco: Jossey-Bass, 1999), 6–9.

4 A. Doak, 'New-Age Style, Old-Fashioned Grunt, but How Will It Look with Fluffy Dice?', *The Age (Melbourne)*, 16 October 1998, 4; W. Webster, 'How a Star Was Born', *Daily Telegraph (Sydney)*, 17 October 1998, 11; R. Edgar, 'Designers Front up to World Stage', *The Age (Melbourne)*, 11 February 2004, 6; P. Gover, 'The Camaro Commandos', *Herald-Sun (Melbourne)*, 7 April 2006, G07.

5 R. A. Guzzo and M. W. Dickson, 'Teams in Organizations: Recent Research on Performance and Effectiveness', *Annual Review of Psychology* 47 (1996): 307–338; D. A. Nadler, 'From Ritual to Real Work: The Board as a Team', *Directors & Boards*, June 1998, 28–31; L. R. Offerman and R. K. Spiros, 'The Science and Practice of Team Development: Improving the Link', *Academy of Management Journal* 44, no. 2 (2001): 376–392.

6 B. D. Pierce and R. White, 'The Evolution of Social Structure: Why Biology Matters', *Academy of Management Review* 24 (October 1999): 843–853; P. R. Lawrence and N. Nohria, *Driven: How Human Nature Shapes Our Choices* (San Francisco: Jossey-Bass, 2002); J. R. Spoor and J. R. Kelly, 'The Evolutionary Significance of Affect in Groups: Communication and Group Bonding', *Group Processes & Intergroup Relations* 7, no. 4 (2004): 398–412. For a critique of this view, see G. Sewell, 'What Goes Around, Comes Around', *Journal of Applied Behavioral Science* 37, no. 1 (2001): 70–91.

7 M. A. Hogg *et al.*, 'The Social Identity Perspective: Intergroup Relations, Self-Conception, and Small Groups', *Small Group Research* 35, no. 3 (2004): 246–276; N. Michinov, E. Michinov and M.-C. Toczek-Capelle,

'Social Identity, Group Processes, and Performance in Synchronous Computer-Mediated Communication', *Group Dynamics: Theory, Research, and Practice* 8, no. 1 (2004): 27–39; M. Van Vugt and C. M. Hart, 'Social Identity as Social Glue: The Origins of Group Loyalty', *Journal of Personality and Social Psychology* 86, no. 4 (2004): 585–598.

8 S. Schacter, *The Psychology of Affiliation* (Stanford: Stanford University Press, 1959), 12–19; R. Eisler and D. S. Levine, 'Nurture, Nature, and Caring: We Are Not Prisoners of Our Genes', *Brain and Mind* 3 (2002): 9–52; A. C. DeVries, E. R. Glasper and C. E. Detillion, 'Social Modulation of Stress Responses', *Physiology & Behavior* 79, no. 3 (2003): 399–407; S. Cohen, 'The Pittsburgh Common Cold Studies: Psychosocial Predictors of Susceptibility to Respiratory Infectious Illness', *International Journal of Behavioral Medicine* 12, no. 3 (2005): 123–131.

9 Cohen, 'The Pittsburgh Common Cold Studies'; M. T. Hansen, M. L. Mors and B. Løvås, 'Knowledge Sharing in Organizations: Multiple Networks, Multiple Phases', *Academy of Management Journal* 48, no. 5 (2005): 776–793; R. Cross *et al.*, 'Using Social Network Analysis to Improve Communities of Practice', *California Management Review* 49, no. 1 (2006): 32–60; P. Balkundi *et al.*, 'Demographic Antecedents and Performance Consequences of Structural Holes in Work Teams', *Journal of Organizational Behavior* 28, no. 2 (2007): 241–260; W. Verbeke and S. Wuyts, 'Moving in Social Circles: Social Circle Membership and Performance Implications', *Journal of Organizational Behavior* 28, no. 4 (2007): 357–379.

10 'Teamwork and Collaboration Major Workplace Trends', *Ottawa Business Journal*, 18 April 2006; S. Wuchty, B. F. Jones and B. Uzzi, 'The Increasing Dominance of Teams in Production of Knowledge', *Science* 316, no. 5827 (18 May 2007): 1036–1039.

11 J. Cremer, 'Nokia Sets the Tone for Teamwork', *South China Morning Post (Hong Kong)*, 18 December 2004, 4.

12 M. Moldaschl and W. Weber, 'The "Three Waves" of Industrial Group Work: Historical Reflections on Current Research on Group Work', *Human Relations* 51 (March 1998): 347–388. Several popular books in the 1980s encouraged teamwork, based on the Japanese economic miracle. These books include W. Ouchi, *Theory Z: How American Management Can Meet the Japanese Challenge* (Reading, MA: Addison-Wesley, 1981); R. T. Pascale and A. G. Athos, *Art of Japanese Management* (New York: Simon and Schuster, 1982).

13 C. R. Emery and L. D. Fredenhall, 'The Effect of Teams on Firm Profitability and Customer Satisfaction', *Journal of Service Research* 4 (February 2002): 217–229; G. S. Van der Vegt and O. Janssen, 'Joint Impact of Interdependence and Group Diversity on Innovation', *Journal of Management* 29, no. 5 (2003): 729–751.

14 R. E. Baumeister and M. R. Leary, 'The Need to Belong: Desire for Interpersonal Attachments as a Fundamental Human Motivation', *Psychological Bulletin* 117, no. 3 (1995): 497–529; S. Chen, H. C. Boucher and M. P. Tapias, 'The Relational Self Revealed: Integrative Conceptualization and Implications for Interpersonal Life', *Psychological Bulletin* 132, no. 2 (2006): 151–179; J. M. Feinberg and J. R. Aiello, 'Social Facilitation: A Test of Competing Theories', *Journal of Applied Social Psychology* 36, no. 5 (2006): 1087–1109; A. M. Grant, 'Relational Job Design and the Motivation to Make a Prosocial Difference', *Academy of Management Review* 32, no. 2 (2007): 393–417; N. L. Kerr *et al.*, 'Psychological Mechanisms Underlying the Kohler Motivation Gain', *Personality and Social Psychology Bulletin* 33, no. 6 (2007): 828–841.

15 E. A. Locke *et al.*, 'The Importance of the Individual in an Age of Groupism', in *Groups at Work: Theory and Research*, ed. M. E. Turner (Mahwah, NJ: Lawrence Erlbaum, 2001), 501–528; N. J. Allen and T. D. Hecht, 'The "Romance of Teams": Toward an Understanding of Its Psychological Underpinnings and Implications', *Journal of Occupational and Organizational Psychology* 77, no. 4 (2004): 439–461.

16 I. D. Steiner, *Group Process and Productivity* (New York: Academic Press, 1972); N. L. Kerr and S. R. Tindale, 'Group Performance and Decision Making', *Annual Review of Psychology* 55 (2004): 623–655.

17 D. Dunphy and B. Bryant, 'Teams: Panaceas or Prescriptions for Improved Performance?', *Human Relations* 49 (May 1996): 677–699. For a discussion of Brooks' Law, see F. P. Brooks, ed., *The Mythical Man-Month: Essays on Software Engineering*, 2nd edn (Reading, MA: Addison-Wesley, 1995).

18 J. Gruber, 'More Aperture Dirt', Daring Fireball, 4 May 2006, http://daringfireball.net (accessed 6 May 2009); J. Gruber, 'Aperture Dirt', Daring Fireball, 28 April 2006, http://daringfireball.net (accessed 6 May 2009).

19 S. J. Karau and K. D. Williams, 'Social Loafing: A Meta-Analytic Review and Theoretical Integration', *Journal of Personality and Social Psychology* 65, no. 4 (1993): 681–706; R. C. Liden *et al.*, 'Social Loafing: A Field Investigation', *Journal of Management* 30, no. 2 (2004): 285–304; L. L. Chidambaram, 'Is out of Sight, out of Mind? An Empirical Study of Social Loafing in Technology-Supported Groups', *Information Systems Research* 16, no. 2 (2005): 149–168; U.-C. Klehe and N. Anderson, 'The Moderating Influence of Personality and Culture on Social Loafing in Typical Versus Maximum Performance Situations', *International Journal of Selection and Assessment* 15, no. 2 (2007): 250–262.

20 M. Erez and A. Somech, 'Is Group Productivity Loss the Rule or the Exception? Effects of Culture and Group-Based

Motivation', *Academy of Management Journal* 39, no. 6 (1996): 1513–1537; Kerr and Tindale, 'Group Performance and Decision Making'; A. Jassawalla, H. Sashittal and A. Malshe, 'Students' Perceptions of Social Loafing: Its Antecedents and Consequences in Undergraduate Business Classroom Teams', *Academy of Management Learning and Education* 8, no. 1 (2009): 42–54.

21 G. P. Shea and R. A. Guzzo, 'Group Effectiveness: What Really Matters?', *Sloan Management Review* 27 (1987): 33–46; J. R. Hackman *et al.*, 'Team Effectiveness in Theory and in Practice', in *Industrial and Organizational Psychology: Linking Theory with Practice*, ed. C. L. Cooper and E. A. Locke (Oxford: Blackwell, 2000), 109–129.

22 M. A. West, C. S. Borrill and K. L. Unsworth, 'Team Effectiveness in Organizations', *International Review of Industrial and Organizational Psychology* 13 (February 1998): 1–48; R. Forrester and A. B. Drexler, 'A Model for Team-Based Organization Performance', *Academy of Management Executive* 13 (August 1999): 36–49; J. E. McGrath, H. Arrow and J. L. Berdahl, 'The Study of Groups: Past, Present, and Future', *Personality and Social Psychology Review* 4, no. 1 (2000): 95–105; M. A. Marks, J. E. Mathieu and S. J. Zaccaro, 'A Temporally Based Framework and Taxonomy of Team Processes', *Academy of Management Review* 26, no. 3 (2001): 356–376.

23 J. S. DeMatteo, L. T. Eby and E. Sundstrom, 'Team-Based Rewards: Current Empirical Evidence and Directions for Future Research', *Research in Organizational Behavior* 20 (1998): 141–183; E. E. Lawler III, *Rewarding Excellence: Pay Strategies for the New Economy* (San Francisco: Jossey-Bass, 2000), 207–214; G. Hertel, S. Geister and U. Konradt, 'Managing Virtual Teams: A Review of Current Empirical Research', *Human Resource Management Review* 15, no. 1 (2005): 69–95.

24 These and other environmental conditions for effective teams are discussed in R. Wageman, 'Case Study: Critical Success Factors for Creating Superb Self-Managing Teams at Xerox', *Compensation and Benefits Review* 29 (September–October 1997): 31–41; Sundstrom, 'The Challenges of Supporting Work Team Effectiveness'; J. N. Choi, 'External Activities and Team Effectiveness: Review and Theoretical Development', *Small Group Research* 33 (April 2002): 181–208; T. L. Doolen, M. E. Hacker and E. M. Van Aken, 'The Impact of Organizational Context on Work Team Effectiveness: A Study of Production Team', *IEEE Transactions on Engineering Management* 50, no. 3 (2003): 285–296; S. D. Dionne *et al.*, 'Transformational Leadership and Team Performance', *Journal of Organizational Change Management* 17, no. 2 (2004): 177–193.

25 S. Dabkowski, 'Healthy Diagnosis Deems Medibank Might Be Fit to Float', *The Age (Melbourne)*, 3 October 2005, 1.

26 A. Niimi, 'The Slow and Steady Climb toward True North', Toyota Motor Manufacturing North America, news release (Traverse City, MI, 7 August 2003); L. Adams, 'Medrad Works and Wins as a Team', *Quality Magazine*, October 2004, 42; J. Teresko, 'Toyota's Real Secret', *Industry Week*, 1 February 2007.

27 M. A. Campion, E. M. Papper and G. J. Medsker, 'Relations between Work Team Characteristics and Effectiveness: A Replication and Extension', *Personnel Psychology* 49, no. 2 (1996): 429–452; D. C. Man and S. S. K. Lam, 'The Effects of Job Complexity and Autonomy on Cohesiveness in Collectivistic and Individualistic Work Groups: A Cross-Cultural Analysis', *Journal of Organizational Behavior* 24, no. 8 (2003): 979–1001.

28 L. Hirsh, 'Manufacturing in Action', *Press-Enterprise (Riverside, CA)*, 21 June 2008, E01.

29 G. S. Van der Vegt, J. M. Emans and E. Van de Vliert, 'Patterns of Interdependence in Work Teams: A Two-Level Investigation of the Relations with Job and Team Satisfaction', *Personnel Psychology* 54, no. 1 (2001): 51–69; R. Wageman, 'The Meaning of Interdependence', in *Groups at Work: Theory and Research*, ed. M. E. Turner (Mahwah, NJ: Lawrence Erlbaum, 2001), 197–217; S. M. Gully *et al.*, 'A Meta-Analysis of Team-Efficacy, Potency, and Performance: Interdependence and Level of Analysis as Moderators of Observed Relationships', *Journal of Applied Psychology* 87, no. 5 (2002): 819–832; M. R. Barrick *et al.*, 'The Moderating Role of Top Management Team Interdependence: Implications for Real Teams and Working Groups', *Academy of Management Journal* 50, no. 3 (2007): 544–557.

30 L. Gratton and T. J. Erickson, 'Eight Ways to Build Collaborative Teams', *Harvard Business Review* (November 2007): 100–109.

31 G. Stasser, 'Pooling of Unshared Information During Group Discussion', in *Group Process and Productivity*, ed. S. Worchel, W. Wood and J. A. Simpson (Newbury Park, CA: Sage, 1992); J. R. Katzenbach and D. K. Smith, *The Wisdom of Teams: Creating the High-Performance Organization* (Boston: Harvard University Press, 1993), 45–47.

32 J. O'Toole, 'The Power of Many: Building a High-Performance Management Team' (Melbourne/Sydney: CEO Forum Group, March 2003), http://ceoforum.com.au (accessed 6 May 2009).

33 C. Fishman, 'The Anarchist's Cookbook', *Fast Company*, July 2004, 70.

34 S. E. Nedleman, 'Recruiters Reveal Their Top Interview Questions', *Financial News Online*, 16 February 2005.

35 P. Wise, 'How Shell Finds Student World's Brightest Sparks', *Financial Times (London)*, 8 January 2004, 12; University of Texas at Austin, 'Shell Oil Introduces Undergrads to Gourami Business Challenge', news release,

(Austin, 15 August 2005); S. Ganesan, 'Talent Quest', *Malaysia Star*, 28 January 2007; J. Porretto, 'Wanted: Engineers', *The Commercial Appeal*, 4 September 2007, B3.

36 F. P. Morgenson, M. H. Reider and M. A. Campion, 'Selecting Individuals in Team Setting: The Importance of Social Skills, Personality Characteristics, and Teamwork Knowledge', *Personnel Psychology* 58, no. 3 (2005): 583–611; V. Rousseau, C. Aubé and A. Savoie, 'Teamwork Behaviors: A Review and an Integration of Frameworks', *Small Group Research* 37, no. 5 (2006): 540–570. For a detailed examination of the characteristics of effective team members, see M. L. Loughry, M. W. Ohland and D. D. Moore, 'Development of a Theory-Based Assessment of Team Member Effectiveness', *Educational and Psychological Measurement* 67, no. 3 (June 2007): 505–524.

37 C. O. L. H. Porter *et al.*, 'Backing up Behaviors in Teams: The Role of Personality and Legitimacy of Need', *Journal of Applied Psychology* 88, no. 3 (2003): 391–403; C. E. J. Härtel and D. Panipucci, 'How "Bad Apples" Spoil the Bunch: Faultlines, Emotional Levers, and Exclusion in the Workplace', *Research on Emotion in Organizations* 3 (2007): 287–310. The bad apple phenomenon is also identified in executive team 'derailers': see R. Wageman *et al.*, *Senior Leadership Teams: What it Takes to Make Them Great* (Boston: Harvard Business School Press, 2008), 97–102.

38 D. van Knippenberg, C. K. W. De Dreu and A. C. Homan, 'Work Group Diversity and Group Performance: An Integrative Model and Research Agenda', *Journal of Applied Psychology* 89, no. 6 (2004): 1008–1022; E. Mannix and M. A. Neale, 'What Differences Make a Difference?: The Promise and Reality of Diverse Teams in Organizations', *Psychological Science in the Public Interest* 6, no. 2 (2005): 31–55.

39 D. C. Lau and J. K. Murnighan, 'Interactions within Groups and Subgroups: The Effects of Demographic Faultlines', *Academy of Management Journal* 48, no. 4 (2005): 645–659; R. Rico *et al.*, 'The Effects of Diversity Faultlines and Team Task Autonomy on Decision Quality and Social Integration', *Journal of Management* 33, no. 1 (2007): 111–132.

40 The NTSB and NASA studies are summarised in J. R. Hackman, 'New Rules for Team Building', *Optimize* (July 2002): 50–62.

41 B. W. Tuckman and M. A. C. Jensen, 'Stages of Small-Group Development Revisited', *Group and Organization Studies* 2, no. 4 (1977): 419–442; B. W. Tuckman, 'Developmental Sequence in Small Groups', *Group Facilitation*, no. 3 (2001): 66–81.

42 D. L. Miller, 'The Stages of Group Development: A Retrospective Study of Dynamic Team Processes', *Canadian Journal of Administrative Sciences* 20, no. 2 (2003): 121–134.

43 G. R. Bushe and G. H. Coetzer, 'Group Development and Team Effectiveness: Using Cognitive Representations to Measure Group Development and Predict Task Performance and Group Viability', *Journal of Applied Behavioral Science* 43, no. 2 (2007): 184–212.

44 J. E. Mathieu and G. F. Goodwin, 'The Influence of Shared Mental Models on Team Process and Performance', *Journal of Applied Psychology* 85, no. 2 (2000): 273–284; J. Langan-Fox and J. Anglim, 'Mental Models, Team Mental Models, and Performance: Process, Development, and Future Directions', *Human Factors and Ergonomics in Manufacturing* 14, no. 4 (2004): 331–352; B.-C. Lim and K. J. Klein, 'Team Mental Models and Team Performance: A Field Study of the Effects of Team Mental Model Similarity and Accuracy', *Journal of Organizational Behavior* 27, no. 4 (2006): 403–418; R. Rico, M. Sánchez-Manzanares and C. Gibson, 'Team Implicit Coordination Processes: A Team Knowledge-Based Approach', *Academy of Management Review* 33, no. 1 (2008): 163–184.

45 A. P. Hare, 'Types of Roles in Small Groups: A Bit of History and a Current Perspective', *Small Group Research* 25 (1994): 443–448; A. Aritzeta, S. Swailes and B. Senior, 'Belbin's Team Role Model: Development, Validity and Applications for Team Building', *Journal of Management Studies* 44, no. 1 (2007): 96–118.

46 S. H. N. Leung, J. W. K. Chan and W. B. Lee, 'The Dynamic Team Role Behavior: The Approaches of Investigation', *Team Performance Management* 9 (2003): 84–90; G. L. Stewart, I. S. Fulmer and M. R. Barrick, 'An Exploration of Member Roles as a Multilevel Linking Mechanism for Individual Traits and Team Outcomes', *Personnel Psychology* 58, no. 2 (2005): 343–365.

47 W. G. Dyer, *Team Building: Current Issues and New Alternatives*, 3rd edn (Reading, MA: Addison-Wesley, 1995); C. A. Beatty and B. A. Barker, *Building Smart Teams: Roadmap to High Performance* (Thousand Oaks, CA: Sage, 2004).

48 M. Laff, 'The Sound of Teamwork', *T & D*, February 2008, 16; A. Sharpe, 'Music Fosters Innovation and Strengthens Teams', HR.com, 25 February 2008, http://hr.com (accessed 6 May 2009); S. Toomey, 'Teams Turn to New Tunes', *The Australian*, 2 February 2008, C1.

49 Langan-Fox and Anglim, 'Mental Models, Team Mental Models, and Performance'; J. E. Mathieu *et al.*, 'Scaling the Quality of Teammates' Mental Models: Equifinality and Normative Comparisons', *Journal of Organizational Behavior* 26, no. 1 (2005): 37–56.

50 Reuters, 'German Businesswoman Demands End to Fun at Work', news release (9 July 2003).

51 R. W. Woodman and J. J. Sherwood, 'The Role of Team Development in Organizational Effectiveness: A Critical Review', *Psychological Bulletin* 88, no. 1 (1980): 166–186.

52 L. Mealiea and R. Baltazar, 'A Strategic Guide for Building Effective Teams', *Personnel Management* 34, no. 2 (2005): 141–160.

53 G. E. Huszczo, 'Training for Team Building', *Training and Development Journal* 44 (February 1990): 37–43; P. McGraw, 'Back from the Mountain: Outdoor Management Development Programs and How to Ensure the Transfer of Skills to the Workplace', *Asia Pacific Journal of Human Resources* 31 (Spring 1993): 52–61.

54 D. C. Feldman, 'The Development and Enforcement of Group Norms', *Academy of Management Review* 9 (1984): 47–53; E. Fehr and U. Fischbacher, 'Social Norms and Human Cooperation', *Trends in Cognitive Sciences* 8, no. 4 (2004): 185–190.

55 N. Ellemers and F. Rink, 'Identity in Work Groups: The Beneficial and Detrimental Consequences of Multiple Identities and Group Norms for Collaboration and Group Performance', *Advances in Group Processes* 22 (2005): 1–41.

56 J. J. Dose and R. J. Klimoski, 'The Diversity of Diversity: Work Values Effects on Formative Team Processes', *Human Resource Management Review* 9, no. 1 (1999): 83–108.

57 S. Taggar and R. Ellis, 'The Role of Leaders in Shaping Formal Team Norms', *Leadership Quarterly* 18, no. 2 (2007): 105–120.

58 D. J. Beal *et al.*, 'Cohesion and Performance in Groups: A Meta-Analytic Clarification of Construct Relations', *Journal of Applied Psychology* 88, no. 6 (2003): 989–1004; S. W. J. Kozlowski and D. R. Ilgen, 'Enhancing the Effectiveness of Work Groups and Teams', *Psychological Science in the Public Interest* 7, no. 3 (2006): 77–124.

59 K. A. Jehn, G. B. Northcraft and M. A. Neale, 'Why Differences Make a Difference: A Field Study of Diversity, Conflict, and Performance in Workgroups', *Administrative Science Quarterly* 44 (1999): 741–763; van Knippenberg, De Dreu and Homan, 'Work Group Diversity and Group Performance: An Integrative Model and Research Agenda'. For evidence that diversity/similarity does not always influence cohesion, see S. S. Webber and L. M. Donahue, 'Impact of Highly and Less Job-Related Diversity on Work Group Cohesion and Performance: A Meta-Analysis', *Journal of Management* 27, no. 2 (2001): 141–162.

60 E. Aronson and J. Mills, 'The Effects of Severity of Initiation on Liking for a Group', *Journal of Abnormal and Social Psychology* 59 (1959): 177–181; J. E. Hautaluoma and R. S. Enge, 'Early Socialization into a Work Group: Severity of Initiations Revisited', *Journal of Social Behavior and Personality* 6 (1991): 725–748.

61 B. Mullen and C. Copper, 'The Relation between Group Cohesiveness and Performance: An Integration', *Psychological Bulletin* 115, no. 2 (1994): 210–227.

62 Wageman *et al.*, *Senior Leadership Teams*, 69–70.

63 M. Rempel and R. J. Fisher, 'Perceived Threat, Cohesion, and Group Problem Solving in Intergroup Conflict', *International Journal of Conflict Management* 8 (1997): 216–234; M. E. Turner and T. Horvitz, 'The Dilemma of Threat: Group Effectiveness and Ineffectiveness under Adversity', in *Groups at Work: Theory and Research*, ed. M. E. Turner (Mahwah, NJ: Lawrence Erlbaum, 2001), 445–470.

64 W. Piper *et al.*, 'Cohesion as a Basic Bond in Groups', *Human Relations* 36 (1983): 93–108; C. A. O'Reilly, D. E. Caldwell and W. P. Barnett, 'Work Group Demography, Social Integration, and Turnover', *Administrative Science Quarterly* 34 (1989): 21–37.

65 Mullen and Copper, 'The Relation between Group Cohesiveness and Performance'; A. V. Carron *et al.*, 'Cohesion and Performance in Sport: A Meta-Analysis', *Journal of Sport and Exercise Psychology* 24 (2002): 168–188; Beal *et al.*, 'Cohesion and Performance in Groups'.

66 C. Langfred, 'Is Group Cohesiveness a Double-Edged Sword? An Investigation of the Effects of Cohesiveness on Performance', *Small Group Research* 29 (1998): 124–143; K. L. Gammage, A. V. Carron and P. A. Estabrooks, 'Team Cohesion and Individual Productivity: The Influence of the Norm for Productivity and the Identifiablity of Individual Effort', *Small Group Research* 32 (February 2001): 3–18.

67 S. L. Robinson, 'Trust and Breach of the Psychological Contract', *Administrative Science Quarterly* 41 (1996): 574–599; D. M. Rousseau *et al.*, 'Not So Different after All: A Cross-Discipline View of Trust', *Academy of Management Review* 23 (1998): 393–404; D. L. Duarte and N. T. Snyder, *Mastering Virtual Teams: Strategies, Tools, and Techniques That Succeed*, 2nd edn (San Francisco: Jossey-Bass, 2000), 139–155. For the importance of trust in virtual teams, see L. M. Peters and C. C. Manz, 'Getting Virtual Teams Right the First Time', in *The Handbook of High-Performance Virtual Teams: A Toolkit for Collaborating across Boundaries*, ed. J. Nemiro and M. M. Beyerlein (San Francisco: Jossey Bass, 2008), 105–130.

68 D. J. McAllister, 'Affect- and Cognition-Based Trust as Foundations for Interpersonal Cooperation in Organizations', *Academy of Management Journal* 38, no. 1 (1995): 24–59; M. Williams, 'In Whom We Trust: Group Membership as an Affective Context for Trust Development', *Academy of Management Review* 26, no. 3 (2001): 377–396.

69 O. E. Williamson, 'Calculativeness, Trust, and Economic Organization', *Journal of Law and Economics* 36, no. 1 (1993): 453–486.

70 E. M. Whitener *et al.*, 'Managers as Initiators of Trust: An Exchange Relationship Framework for Understanding Managerial Trustworthy Behavior', *Academy of Management Review* 23 (July 1998): 513–530; J. M. Kouzes and B. Z. Posner, *The Leadership Challenge*, 3rd edn (San Francisco: Jossey-Bass, 2002), ch. 2; T. Simons, 'Behavioral Integrity: The Perceived Alignment between Managers' Words and Deeds as a Research Focus', *Organization Science* 13, no. 1 (2002): 18–35.

71 S. L. Jarvenpaa and D. E. Leidner, 'Communication and Trust in Global Virtual Teams', *Organization Science* 10, no. 6 (1999): 791–815; M. M. Pillutla, D. Malhotra and J. K. Murnighan, 'Attributions of Trust and the Calculus of Reciprocity', *Journal of Experimental Social Psychology* 39, no. 5 (2003): 448–455.

72 K. T. Dirks and D. L. Ferrin, 'The Role of Trust in Organizations', *Organization Science* 12, no. 4 (2004): 450–467.

73 Fishman, 'The Anarchist's Cookbook'; J. Mackey, 'Open Book Company', *Newsweek*, 28 November 2005, 42; D. Jacobson, 'Best-Kept Secrets of the World's Best Companies: Gainsharing', *Business 2.0*, April 2006, 82; A. Kimball-Stanley, 'Bucking the Trend in Benefits', *Providence Journal (Rhode Island)*, 14 May 2006, H01; K. Zimbalist, 'Green Giant', *Time*, 24 April 2006, 24.

74 Mohrman, Cohen and Mohrman Jr, *Designing Team-Based Organizations*; D. E. Yeatts and C. Hyten, *High-Performing Self-Managed Work Teams: A Comparison of Theory and Practice* (Thousand Oaks, CA: Sage, 1998); E. E. Lawler, *Organizing for High Performance* (San Francisco: Jossey-Bass, 2001); R. J. Torraco, 'Work Design Theory: A Review and Critique with Implications for Human Resource Development', *Human Resource Development Quarterly* 16, no. 1 (2005): 85–109.

75 P. Panchak, 'Production Workers Can Be Your Competitive Edge', *Industry Week*, October 2004, 11; S. K. Muthusamy, J. V. Wheeler and B. L. Simmons, 'Self-Managing Work Teams: Enhancing Organizational Innovativeness', *Organization Development Journal* 23, no. 3 (2005): 53–66.

76 Emery and Fredenhall, 'The Effect of Teams on Firm Profitability and Customer Satisfaction'; A. Krause and H. Dunckel, 'Work Design and Customer Satisfaction: Effects of the Implementation of Semi-Autonomous Group Work on Customer Satisfaction Considering Employee Satisfaction and Group Performance (Translated Abstract)', *Zeitschrift Fur Arbeits-Und Organisationspsychologie* 47, no. 4 (2003): 182–193; H. van Mierlo *et al.*, 'Self-Managing Teamwork and Psychological Well-Being: Review of a Multilevel Research Domain', *Group & Organization Management* 30, no. 2 (April 2005): 211–235.

77 P. McDonald and A. Sharma, 'Toward Work Teams within a New Zealand Public Service Organization' in *Annual Conference of the Center for the Study of Work Teams* (Fort Worth: Center for the Study of Work Teams, 1994); C. Q. Francisco, 'Making a Company Grow', *BusinessWorld (Manila)*, 16 January 2004, 27; 'Aztec Software Ranked 11th in Top 25 Great Places to Work in India', *Hindustan Times (Mumbai)*, 4 February 2006.

78 The historical developments of self-directed teams in Australia are described in J. Cordery, 'Work Teams in Australia', in *Work Teams: Past, Present, and Future*, ed. M. M. Beyerlein (Amsterdam: Kluwer, 2000), 183–192.

79 Moldaschl and Weber, 'The "Three Waves" of Industrial Group Work'; W. Niepce and E. Molleman, 'Work Design Issues in Lean Production from Sociotechnical System Perspective: Neo-Taylorism or the Next Step in Sociotechnical Design?', *Human Relations* 51, no. 3 (1998): 259–287.

80 E. Ulich and W. G. Weber, 'Dimensions, Criteria, and Evaluation of Work Group Autonomy', in *Handbook of Work Group Psychology*, ed. M. A. West (Chichester, UK: Wiley, 1996), 247–282.

81 K. P. Carson and G. L. Stewart, 'Job Analysis and the Sociotechnical Approach to Quality: A Critical Examination', *Journal of Quality Management* 1 (1996): 49–65; C. C. Manz and G. L. Stewart, 'Attaining Flexible Stability by Integrating Total Quality Management and Socio-Technical Systems Theory', *Organization Science* 8, no. 1 (1997): 59–70.

82 'Medical Marvel', *Works Management (Best Factory Awards Supplement)*, October 2007, 21–22.

83 G. Marshall, 'Leading the Virtual Team: Agilent's Grant Marshall' (Melbourne/Sydney: CEO Forum Group, March 2005), http://ceoforum.com (accessed 7 May 2009); 'Supporting Australian Innovation', *Electronics News*, 11 January 2005; M. Conlin, 'The Easiest Commute of All', *Business Week*, 12 December 2005, 78.

84 J. Lipnack and J. Stamps, *Virtual Teams: People Working across Boundaries with Technology* (New York: Wiley, 2001); B. S. Bell and W. J. Kozlowski, 'A Typology of Virtual Teams: Implications for Effective Leadership', *Group & Organization Management* 27, no. 1 (2002): 14–49; Hertel, Geister and Konradt, 'Managing Virtual Teams'.

85 G. Gilder, *Telecosm: How Infinite Bandwidth Will Revolutionize Our World* (New York: Free Press, 2001); L. L. Martins, L. L. Gilson and M. T. Maynard, 'Virtual Teams: What Do We Know and Where Do We Go From Here?', *Journal of Management* 30, no. 6 (2004): 805–835.

86 Martins, Gilson and Maynard, 'Virtual Teams'; G. Hertel, U. Konradt and K. Voss, 'Competencies for Virtual Teamwork: Development and Validation of a Web-Based Selection Tool for Members of Distributed Teams', *European*

Journal of Work and Organizational Psychology 15, no. 4 (2006): 477–504.

87 G. G. Harwood, 'Design Principles for Successful Virtual Teams', in *The Handbook of High-Performance Virtual Teams: A Toolkit for Collaborating across Boundaries*, ed. J. Nemiro and M. M. Beyerlein (San Francisco: Jossey-Bass, 2008), 59–84.

88 Marshall, 'Leading the Virtual Team'.

89 J. Gordon, 'Do Your Virtual Teams Deliver Only Virtual Performance?', *Training*, June 2005, 20–24.

90 V. H. Vroom and A. G. Jago, *The New Leadership* (Englewood Cliffs, NJ: Prentice Hall, 1988), 28–29.

91 M. Diehl and W. Stroebe, 'Productivity Loss in Idea-Generating Groups: Tracking Down the Blocking Effects', *Journal of Personality and Social Psychology* 61, no. 3 (1991): 392–403; R. B. Gallupe *et al.*, 'Blocking Electronic Brainstorms', *Journal of Applied Psychology* 79, no. 1 (1994): 77–86; B. A. Nijstad, W. Stroebe and H. F. M. Lodewijkx, 'Production Blocking and Idea Generation: Does Blocking Interfere with Cognitive Processes?', *Journal of Experimental Social Psychology* 39, no. 6 (2003): 531–548; B. A. Nijstad and W. Stroebe, 'How the Group Affects the Mind: A Cognitive Model of Idea Generation in Groups', *Personality and Social Psychology Review* 10, no. 3 (2006): 186–213.

92 B. E. Irmer, P. Bordia and D. Abusah, 'Evaluation Apprehension and Perceived Benefits in Interpersonal and Database Knowledge Sharing', *Academy of Management Proceedings* (2002): B1–B6.

93 I. L. Janis, *Groupthink: Psychological Studies of Policy Decisions and Fiascoes*, 2nd edn (Boston: Houghton Mifflin, 1982); J. K. Esser, 'Alive and Well after 25 Years: A Review of Groupthink Research', *Organizational Behavior and Human Decision Processes* 73, no. 2/3 (1998): 116–141.

94 J. N. Choi and M. U. Kim, 'The Organizational Application of Groupthink and Its Limitations in Organizations', *Journal of Applied Psychology* 84, no. 2 (1999): 297–306; W.-W. Park, 'A Comprehensive Empirical Investigation of the Relationships among Variables of the Groupthink Model', *Journal of Organizational Behavior* 21, no. 8 (2000): 873–887; D. D. Henningsen *et al.*, 'Examining the Symptoms of Groupthink and Retrospective Sensemaking', *Small Group Research* 37, no. 1 (2006): 36–64.

95 D. Miller, *The Icarus Paradox: How Exceptional Companies Bring about Their Own Downfall* (New York: HarperBusiness, 1990); S. Finkelstein, *Why Smart Executives Fail* (New York: Viking, 2003); K. Tasa and G. Whyte, 'Collective Efficacy and Vigilant Problem Solving in Group Decision Making: A Non-Linear Model', *Organizational Behavior and Human Decision Processes* 96, no. 2 (2005): 119–129.

96 B. Frisch, 'When Teams Can't Decide', *Harvard Business Review* 86, no. 11 (2008): 121–126.

97 H. Collingwood, 'Best-Kept Secrets of the World's Best Companies: Outside-in R & D', *Business 2.0*, April 2006, 82.

98 K. M. Eisenhardt, J. L. Kahwajy and L. J. Bourgeois III, 'Conflict and Strategic Choice: How Top Management Teams Disagree', *California Management Review* 39 (1997): 42–62; R. Sutton, *Weird Ideas That Work* (New York: Free Press, 2002); C. J. Nemeth *et al.*, 'The Liberating Role of Conflict in Group Creativity: A Study in Two Countries', *European Journal of Social Psychology* 34, no. 4 (2004): 365–374. For discussion on how all conflict is potentially detrimental to teams, see C. K. W. De Dreu and L. R. Weingart, 'Task Versus Relationship Conflict, Team Performance, and Team Member Satisfaction: A Meta-Analysis', *Journal of Applied Psychology* 88, no. 4 (2003): 741–749; P. Hinds and D. E. Bailey, 'Out of Sight, out of Sync: Understanding Conflict in Distributed Teams', *Organization Science* 14, no. 6 (2003): 615–632.

99 K. Darce, 'Ground Control: NASA Attempts a Cultural Shift', *Seattle Times*, 24 April 2005, A3; R. Shelton, 'NASA Attempts to Change Mindset in Wake of Columbia Tragedy', *Macon Telegraph (Macon, GA)*, 7 July 2005.

100 B. Mullen, C. Johnson and E. Salas, 'Productivity Loss in Brainstorming Groups: A Meta-Analytic Integration', *Basic and Applied Social Psychology* 12, no. 1 (1991): 2–23. The original description of brainstorming appeared in A. F. Osborn, *Applied Imagination* (New York: Scribner, 1957).

101 R. I. Sutton and A. Hargadon, 'Brainstorming Groups in Context: Effectiveness in a Product Design Firm', *Administrative Science Quarterly* 41 (1996): 685–718; T. Kelley, *The Art of Innovation* (New York: Currency/ Doubleday, 2001); V. R. Brown and P. B. Paulus, 'Making Group Brainstorming More Effective: Recommendations from an Associative Memory Perspective', *Current Directions in Psychological Science* 11, no. 6 (2002): 208–212; K. Leggett Dugosh and P. B. Paulus, 'Cognitive and Social Comparison Processes in Brainstorming', *Journal of Experimental Social Psychology* 41, no. 3 (2005): 313–320.

102 R. B. Gallupe, L. M. Bastianutti and W. H. Cooper, 'Unblocking Brainstorms', *Journal of Applied Psychology* 76, no. 1 (1991): 137–142; W. H. Cooper *et al.*, 'Some Liberating Effects of Anonymous Electronic Brainstorming', *Small Group Research* 29, no. 2 (1998): 147–178; A. R. Dennis, B. H. Wixom and R. J. Vandenberg, 'Understanding Fit and Appropriation Effects in Group Support Systems Via Meta-Analysis', *MIS Quarterly* 25, no. 2 (2001): 167–193; D. M. DeRosa, C. L. Smith and D. A. Hantula, 'The Medium Matters: Mining the Long-Promised Merit of Group Interaction in Creative Idea

Generation Tasks in a Meta-Analysis of the Electronic Group Brainstorming Literature', *Computers in Human Behavior* 23, no. 3 (2007): 1549–1581.

103 A. L. Delbecq, A. H. Van de Ven and D. H. Gustafson, *Group Techniques for Program Planning: A Guide to Nominal Group and Delphi Processes* (Middleton, WI: Green Briar Press, 1986).

104 S. Frankel, 'NGT + MDS: An Adaptation of the Nominal Group Technique for Ill-Structured Problems', *Journal of Applied Behavioral Science* 23, no. 4 (1987): 543–551; H. Barki and A. Pinsonneault, 'Small Group Brainstorming and Idea Quality: Is Electronic Brainstorming the Most Effective Approach?', *Small Group Research* 32, no. 2 (2001): 158–205.

CHAPTER 9

communicating in teams and organisations

LEARNING OBJECTIVES

After reading this chapter, you should be able to:

- explain why communication is important in organisations
- diagram the communication process and identify four ways to improve this process
- discuss problems with communicating through electronic mail
- identify two ways in which nonverbal communication differs from verbal communication
- appraise the appropriateness of a communication medium for a particular situation based on social acceptance and media richness factors
- identify four common communication barriers
- discuss the degree to which men and women communicate differently
- outline the key strategies for getting your message across and engaging in active listening
- summarise three communication strategies in organisational hierarchies
- debate the benefits and limitations of the organisational grapevine.

Shutterstock

Social networking sites are the new tool for businesses recruiting staff.

It has never been easier to communicate. With the growth of social networking sites such as Facebook and MySpace, not to mention blogs, we can reach hundreds if not thousands of people instantaneously. A recent Nielsen survey showed that, in a 12-month period, 51 per cent of internet users accessed social networking sites, and 28 per cent spent more than five hours a week on these sites. What does this mean in the workplace? According to RMIT University's John Lenarcic, 'these sites are really a way of promoting yourself and it was only a matter of time before the business world would take it up'.

Lenarcic was right. Around one-quarter of managers believe that social networking sites have a place in the Australian workforce. And in the United Kingdom, about two-thirds of managers reported that their organisations allowed access to social networking sites. The perceived advantages include building new relationships, learning about new trends and providing information about organisational culture. Taking the idea of building new relationships further, KPMG reported that 14 per cent of its new employees were recruited from Facebook. REA Group used Facebook to track down a former employee and rehire her. And one networking site, SkyLounge, was created specifically to help business people meet each other while they are travelling.

Should organisations increase their use of social networking sites? According to REA's Asia-Pacific general manager, Shaun Di Gregorio, REA Group increased its use of social networking sites because they are so popular with younger employees. 'As we try to understand the needs of Gen Y... we realise they are not watching television or reading the paper, but they are spending an inordinate amount of time on these social networking sites.'

The use of social networking sites also has its dangers. Users place their reputations online—and, potentially, on the line. Organisations are at risk of sites being openly critical of them. As Di Gregorio says, 'You are subject to criticism, without barrier, by anyone who cares to [criticise].' But the biggest risk may be to individual reputations. If users don't restrict access, employers can check out job candidates: *Personnel Today* reports that about 17 per cent of UK companies routinely check these sites to screen job candidates. Organisations also monitor their existing employees. The British Transport Police recently sacked an employee who posted sexually explicit photos of himself—wearing his uniform. And the Alberta Public Service (Canada) dismissed an employee when she posted derogatory comments about her coworkers, calling them 'imbeciles' and 'idiot savants', on her blog.[1]

Information technologies have transformed how we communicate in organisations, yet we may still be at the beginning of this revolution. Wire cablegrams and telephones introduced a century ago are giving way to email, instant messaging, weblogs, podcasting and virtual-reality social networking. Each of these inventions creates fascinating changes in how people communicate with each other in the workplace, as well as new opportunities to improve organisational effectiveness and employee wellbeing.

communication The process by which information is transmitted and understood between two or more people.

Communication refers to the process by which information is transmitted and *understood* between two or more people. We emphasise the word 'understood' because transmitting the sender's intended meaning is the essence of good communication. This chapter begins by discussing the importance of effective communication and outlining a model of the communication process. Next, we identify types of communication channels, including computer-mediated communication, followed by factors to consider when choosing a communication medium. We then identify barriers to effective communication, and explore cross-cultural and gender differences in communication. This is followed by an overview of improving interpersonal and workplace communication, and of the pervasive organisational grapevine.

THE IMPORTANCE OF COMMUNICATION

LEARNING OBJECTIVE

Explain why communication is important in organisations.

Effective communication is vital to all organisations, so much so that no company could exist without it. The reason? In Chapter 1 we defined organisations as groups of people who work interdependently toward some purpose. People can only work interdependently if they communicate effectively. Communication is the vehicle through which people clarify their expectations and coordinate work, which allows them to achieve organisational objectives more efficiently and effectively. Chester Barnard, a telecommunications CEO and a respected pioneer in organisational behaviour theory, stated this point back in 1938: 'An organisation is born when there are individuals who are able to communicate.'[2]

Communication is also an important instrument for organisational learning and decision making. Chapter 1 explained that one perspective of organisational effectiveness is organisational learning, which refers to the firm's capacity to acquire, share, use and store valuable knowledge. These processes depend on various forms of communication. Effective communication minimises 'silos of knowledge', the situation whereby knowledge is cloistered or hoarded rather than distributed to others throughout the organisation.[3] IBM improves organisational learning through various informal and computer-mediated communication media. For instance, when IBM employees need to find expertise for a client, they tap into the company's 'Small Blue' search engine, which quickly identifies people with various forms of expertise throughout the company.[4]

Communication also aids employee wellbeing.[5] Information communicated from coworkers helps employees to manage their work environment, such as how to complete work procedures correctly or handle difficult customers. Equally important, employee wellbeing benefits from the communication experience itself, so much so that people who experience social isolation are much more susceptible to colds, cardiovascular disease, and other physical and mental illnesses.[6] Why? As we learned in Chapter 5, people have an inherent drive to bond, and communication is the means through which that drive is fulfilled. Communicating with others is an important means through which individuals validate their self-worth and maintain their social identity. This occurs even in the online virtual world of Second Life. 'In Second Life we

Speaking Gen Y

Tanya Constantine/Corbis

Just as the work habits of Gen Y-ers differ from those of baby boomers, so do their preferred communication styles. A recent global survey found that, for Generation Y, 'faster' and 'more often' are the keys to successful communication. Communication should avoid jargon: Generation Y prefers 'authentic' communication and opportunities to offer feedback. An Australian respondent to this survey wrote that 'by engaging them (Generation Y) in crafting key messages we've seen them become advocates for both messages and the process'. Trust emerges as a key issue, as a respondent from Hong Kong observed: 'One of the great challenges ... is that younger professionals do not think it is safe or have ways to share (valuable) information with senior management.'[8]

gather and mingle before the meeting, and when it finishes, some people stop and talk again,' explains Ian Hughes, an IBM employee who attends these virtual meetings as a pudgy avatar with spiky green hair. 'We start to form social networks and the kinds of bonds you make in real life.'[7]

A MODEL OF COMMUNICATION

LEARNING OBJECTIVE 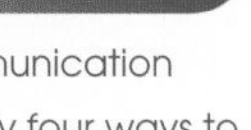

Diagram the communication process and identify four ways to improve this process.

The communication process model presented in Exhibit 9.1 provides a useful 'conduit' metaphor for thinking about the communication process.[9] According to this model, communication flows through channels between the sender and receiver. The sender forms a message and encodes it into words, gestures, voice intonations and other symbols or signs. Next, the encoded message is transmitted to the intended receiver through one or more communication channels (media). The receiver senses the incoming message and decodes it into something meaningful. Ideally, the decoded meaning is what the sender had intended.

In most situations, the sender looks for evidence that the other person received and understood the transmitted message. This feedback may be a formal acknowledgment, such as 'Yes, I know what you mean', or indirect evidence from the receiver's subsequent actions. Notice that feedback repeats the communication process. Intended feedback is encoded, transmitted, received and decoded from the receiver to the sender of the original message. This model recognises that communication is not a free-flowing conduit. Rather, the transmission of meaning from one person to another is hampered by *noise*—the psychological, social and structural barriers that distort and obscure the sender's intended message. If any part of the communication process is distorted or broken, the sender and receiver will not have a common understanding of the message.

Exhibit 9.1 *The Communication Process Model*

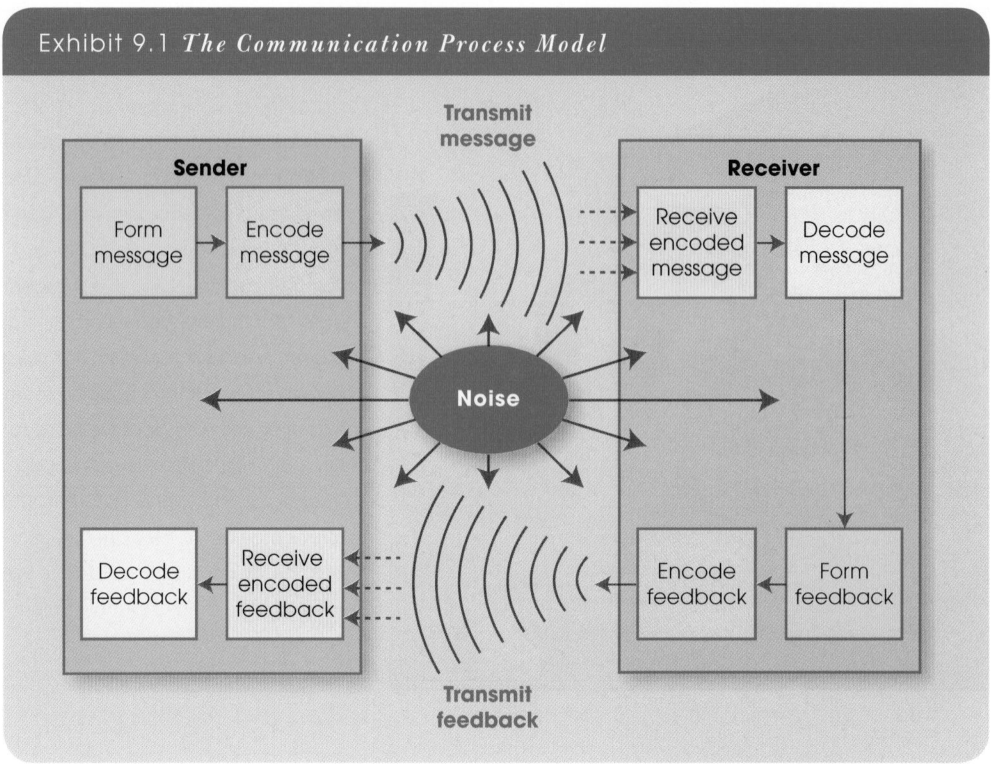

Influences on Effective Encoding and Decoding

The communication process model suggests that communication effectiveness depends on the ability of sender and receiver to efficiently and accurately encode and decode information. Experts have identified four factors that influence the effectiveness of the encoding–decoding process.[10] One factor is the sender's and receiver's ability and motivation to communicate through the communication channel. Some people communicate better through face-to-face conversation and prefer using this communication channel. Others are awkward in conversations, yet are quite good at communicating via BlackBerry or similar text message technologies. Generally, the encoding–decoding process is more effective when both parties are skilled at using the selected communication channel and enjoy using that channel.[11]

A second factor is the extent to which both parties have similar 'codebooks'—dictionaries of symbols, language, gestures, idioms and other tools used to convey information. With similar codebooks, the communication participants are able to encode and decode more accurately because they both have the same or similar meaning. Communication efficiency also improves because there is less need for redundancy (such as saying the same thing in different ways) and less need for confirmation feedback ('So, you are saying that ... ?').

A third factor that influences the effectiveness of the encoding–decoding process is the extent to which both parties have shared mental models about the topic's context. Mental models are internal representations of the external world that allow us to visualise elements of a setting and relationships among those elements (see Chapter 3). When sender and receiver have shared mental models, they have a common understanding of the environment relating to the information, so less communication is necessary to clarify meaning about that context.

Notice that sharing the same codebook differs from sharing the same mental models of the topic context. Codebooks contain symbols used to convey message content, whereas mental models are knowledge structures of the communication topic's setting. For example, a Russian cosmonaut and American astronaut might have excellent knowledge (i.e. shared mental models) about the International Space Station, yet they experience poor communication because of language differences (i.e. different codebooks).

A fourth factor influencing encoding–decoding process effectiveness is the sender's experience at communicating the message. As people become more familiar with the subject matter, they develop more efficient or colourful language to describe the subject. In other words, they become more proficient at using the codebook of symbols to convey the message. This is similar to the effect of job training or sports practice. The more experience and practice gained at communicating a subject, the more people learn how to effectively transmit that information to others.

COMMUNICATION CHANNELS

A critical part of the communication model is the channel or medium through which information is transmitted. There are two main types of channels: verbal and nonverbal. Verbal communication uses words, and occurs through either spoken or written channels. Nonverbal communication is any part of communication that does not use words. Although spoken and written communication are both verbal (i.e. they both use words), we will learn in this section that they are quite different from each other, and have different strengths and weaknesses in communication effectiveness. Also, written communication has traditionally been much slower than spoken communication at transmitting messages, but email, weblogs and other computer-mediated communication channels have significantly improved the efficiency of written communication.

Computer-Mediated Communication

LEARNING OBJECTIVE 

Discuss problems with communicating through electronic mail.

Two decades ago, computer-mediated communication was a novel development. Today, it seems that many of us rely more on these channels than the old-fashioned options. By far the most widely used of these is electronic mail (email), which has revolutionised the way we communicate in organisational settings. Email has become the medium of choice in most workplaces because messages are quickly written, edited and transmitted. Information can be appended and conveyed to many people with a simple click of a mouse. Email is asynchronous (i.e. messages are sent and received at different times), so there is no need to coordinate a communication session. Email software has also become an efficient filing cabinet.[12] Employees increasingly rely on email to filter, store, sort and search messages and attachments far more quickly than is possible with paper-based memos.

Email tends to be the preferred medium for coordinating work (e.g. confirming deadlines against a coworker's schedule) and for sending well-defined information for decision making. It often increases the volume of communication and significantly alters the flow of that information within groups and throughout the organisation.[13] Specifically, it reduces some face-to-face and telephone communication but increases communication with people further up the hierarchy. Some social and organisational status differences still exist with email,[14] but they are somewhat less apparent than in face-to-face communication. By hiding age, race and other features, email

Safe to Check your Email? Cyber-bullying in the Workplace

Jose Luis Pelaez, Inc./Blend Images/Corbis

Mobile phones and email have become the weapons of choice for workplace harassment.

COMMUNICATING HAS NEVER BEEN easier. Mobile phones, email, BlackBerrys and blogs mean that we are in constant and immediate contact with the world. The downside of this constant stream of communication is that bullying—threatening other people—has never been easier. Now that people are more accessible to each other via technology, cyber-bullying is on the rise—and is making its way into the workplace. Matt Witheridge of the the Andrea Adams Trust (UK) suggests that cyber-bullying 'is a natural human behaviour when individuals are forced into high-pressure situations... The big thing with cyber-bullying, particularly email, is it's very hard to gauge tone, and a lot of confusion arises.'

reduces stereotype biases. However, it also tends to increase reliance on stereotypes when we are already aware of the other person's personal characteristics.[15]

Problems with Email

In spite of the wonders of email, anyone who has used this communication medium knows that it has its limitations. Here are the top four complaints:

POOR MEDIUM FOR COMMUNICATING EMOTIONS People rely on facial expressions and other nonverbal cues to interpret the emotional meaning of words; email lacks this parallel communication channel. Senders try to clarify the emotional tone of their messages by using expressive language ('Wonderful to hear from you!'), highlighting phrases in bold face or quotation marks and inserting graphic faces (called emoticons or 'smileys') to represent the desired emotion. These actions help, but do not replace the full complexity of real facial expressions, voice intonation and hand movements.[16]

REDUCES POLITENESS AND RESPECT As we learn in Reality Check 9.1, email messages are often less diplomatic than written letters because individuals can post email messages before their emotions subside. Also, email has low social presence (it's more impersonal), so people are more likely to write things that would never be spoken in face-to-face conversation. 'It is much easier to have a row by email than it is face to face, and people are often ruder as a result,' says Justin Beddows, a spokesperson at Welsh-based Admiral Insurance. 'Orders can be

REALITY CHECK 9.1

As mentioned earlier, email and other remote forms of communication disinhibit people—we say things we would not say in face-to-face communications. Ninety per cent of the time, threats arrive via email. As Gary Cooper at Lancaster University's Management School says, 'With technology and the internet, it's much easier and less constraining for the bully ... They don't have to look at the other person and the technology is instant.' What's more, the lines between home and work become blurred, so cyber-bullies can continue to threaten their coworkers after they leave the office.

Just how common is cyber-bullying? A survey by the Samaritans shows that 80 per cent of employees report bullying at work. And, according to Dignity at Work, about 20 per cent of employees report being bullied via email. Not only do employers need to be concerned about the legal consequences for them, but should consider the costs to their organisations as cyber-bullied staff take sick leave, work less effectively or leave the organisation altogether.

To tackle cyber-bullying, employers need to update their communication policies, train managers and offer mediation services to help resolve conflicts. At the same time, Ellen Pinnell of Capital Law says that employees should ask themselves if they would actually say the message they are emailing directly to the recipient in a face-to-face situation. 'Where email is sensitive and the topic is difficult, go back to it a couple of hours later before sending it,' she advises.[21]

issued out and people can be quite abrupt because they feel protected by the distance the email provides.'[17] These 'flaming' emails are aggravated by misinterpretation of the emotional tone of the message. Fortunately, research has found that flaming decreases as teams move to later stages of development, and when explicit norms and rules of communication are established.[18]

POOR MEDIUM FOR AMBIGUOUS, COMPLEX AND NOVEL SITUATIONS

Email is usually fine for well-defined situations, such as giving basic instructions or presenting a meeting agenda, but it can be cumbersome in ambiguous, complex and novel situations. As we will describe later in this section, these circumstances require communication channels that transmit a larger volume of information with more rapid feedback. 'I've stopped using email volleys where you just keep going back and forth and back and forth and nothing is going in the right direction,' says a manager at an oil refinery. By talking face-to-face or by telephone in these complex situations, the manager has discovered that he is 'coming up with much better outcomes and a much better understanding of an issue'.[19] In other words, when the issue gets messy, stop emailing and start talking, preferably face to face.

CONTRIBUTES TO INFORMATION OVERLOAD Email contributes to information overload.[20] More than 22 trillion emails are estimated to be transmitted annually, up from just 1.1 trillion in 1998. According to one survey, professionals spend an average of two hours per day processing email. The email glut occurs because messages are created and copied to many people without much effort. The number of email messages will probably decrease as people become more familiar with it, but to date email volume continues to rise. To reduce email overload and encourage more face-to-face interaction, Welsh-based Admiral Insurance holds no-email Wednesdays.

Social Networking Communication

The opening story to this chapter described how organisations are experimenting with innovative forms of computer-mediated communication, including technologies that support *social networking*.[22] Social networking websites such as Facebook, MySpace and LinkedIn are rapidly becoming part of popular culture. Recently, university students rated Facebook as the second most 'in' thing (iPods were number one). [23] These technologies allow people to form communities around friendships, common interests, expertise and other themes, resulting in closer interaction in the co mmunication experience. Indeed, many social networking technologies, from Facebook to online forums, gain value as more people participate in the technology.[24]

Yet just as corporate leaders stumbled their way through Web 1.0 (the internet's first stage) over the past two decades, many are fighting rather than leveraging the potential of the more socially interactive second stage (called Web 2.0). A large number of companies have banned employee access to social networking sites after discovering that staff spend too much work time using these sites. Yet recognising the popularity of this social networking technology, a few organisational leaders are experimenting with ways to use it as a conduit for employees to communicate productively with each other, and with customers and other external stakeholders. Procter & Gamble employees use Facebook to keep in touch with summer intern students. Serena Software has even made Facebook its new corporate intranet. The California-based company introduced 'Facebook Fridays' sessions in which teenagers are hired to teach older

Watching Everything You Post

Colin Anderson/Corbis

It has never been easier to monitor what employees do in the workplace. Employers have unprecedented access to employees' emails. Graham Sewell from the University of Melbourne surveyed 100 companies, and found that approximately one-third of companies read their employees' emails, and 40 per cent did so in secret. At Marks and Spencer, staff say they live in a 'culture of fear' because of the level of electronic surveillance. And the dangers do not end with email. According to Australian Privacy Commissioner, Karen Curtis, many Facebook users don't realise that employers can see the information that they post. This was certainly the case when Swimming Australia asked its swim team to remove potentially damaging photos that showed the team drinking and partying.[27]

staff how to use Facebook. IBM developed Beehive, a corporate version of Facebook, where employees can post their profiles, photos, interests and comments about work or other aspects of their lives.[25]

IBM has also been at the forefront of another form of social networking communication, called **wikis**. Wikis are collaborative web spaces in which anyone in a group can write, edit or remove material from the website. Wikipedia, the popular online encyclopedia, is a massive public example of a wiki. Wikis hold considerable promise for communicating in organisational settings because they are democratic, collaborative social networking spaces that rapidly document new knowledge. IBM introduced wiki technology a few years ago in the form of WikiCentral, which now hosts more than 20 000 wiki projects involving 100 000 employees. One of IBM's many wiki projects involved gathering staff ideas and issues about a new patent policy within IBM. 'Wikis are good for project management, for to dos, status reports, creating an issues log—you're always up to date,' explains Brad Kasell, an IBM manager for emerging technologies. 'There's no collating reports from everyone at the end of the week for an update.' The accuracy of wikis depends on the quality of participants, but Kasell says that errors are quickly identified by IBM's online community.[26]

wikis Collaborative Web spaces at which anyone in a group can write, edit or remove material from the website.

Nonverbal Communication

Identify two ways in which nonverbal communication differs from verbal communication.

Nonverbal communication includes facial gestures, voice intonation, physical distance and even silence. This communication channel is necessary where noise or physical distance prevents effective verbal exchanges and the need for immediate feedback precludes written communication. But even in quiet face-to-face meetings, most information is communicated nonverbally. Rather like a parallel conversation, nonverbal cues signal subtle information to both parties, such as reinforcing their interest in the verbal conversation or demonstrating their relative status in the relationship.[28]

Nonverbal communication differs from verbal (i.e. written and spoken) communication in a couple of ways. First, it is less rule-bound than verbal communication. We receive plenty of formal training on how to understand spoken words, but very little on understanding the nonverbal signals that accompany those words. Consequently, nonverbal cues are generally more ambiguous and susceptible to misinterpretation. At the same time, many facial expressions (such as smiling) are hardwired and universal, thereby providing the only reliable means of communicating across cultures.

The other difference between verbal and nonverbal communication is that the former is typically conscious, whereas most nonverbal communication is automatic and nonconscious. We normally plan the words we say or write, but we rarely plan every blink, smile or other gesture during a conversation. Indeed, as we just mentioned, many of these facial expressions communicate the same meaning across cultures because they are hardwired, nonconscious responses to human emotions.[29] For example, pleasant emotions cause the brain centre to widen the mouth, whereas negative emotions produce constricted facial expressions (squinting eyes, pursed lips, etc.).

Decoding Hidden Meanings

The words we choose, how we sound and how we look when we speak all convey important information to the other person. Two important messages that we convey are about *status*, or how we perceive our own and others' power, and *affiliation*, or the degree to which we set ourselves apart from others. Others use our communication style to infer how we perceive the relationship.

We signal status when we use language that distances us from others. This can include use of the first person singular pronoun ('I'), the present tense, judgmental adjectives and vocalised pauses. Expressing certainty, correcting the other person, telling the other what to do ('should', 'ought'), interrupting others or changing the topic of conversation also signals greater power. Conversely, we leave the impression that we have little power when we use tag questions ('... isn't it?'), disclaimers ('I'm not really sure, but I think ...') and qualifiers ('possibly'), and when we make indirect requests. Interestingly, the same speech styles that convey powerlessness also build relationships because they reduce the level of interpersonal conflict. We can further reduce interpersonal conflict and build affiliation by highlighting common goals and values, signalling that we are similar, and engaging in gossip and small talk. As we will see in the next section, the speech styles that reflect status and affiliation are also associated with men and women, respectively.[30]

Nonverbal cues also provide important information to our listeners. Others may also scan our communication for its truthfulness. Although there are many popular beliefs about how to tell if others are lying, not all of them are accurate. Do liars speak more quickly, squirm more or avoid eye contact? No. But they do blink more rapidly, give shorter answers to your questions, are more hesitant when they speak and tell less compelling stories. What is important to remember is that many of the nonverbal cues we associate with deception are not absolute—to read these cues, we need to know how people behave in normal circumstances. Once we have this baseline, signs of anxiety, such as higher vocal tone, can alert us to deception.[31]

Emotional Contagion

emotional contagion The nonconscious process of 'catching' or sharing another person's emotions by mimicking that person's facial expressions and other nonverbal behaviour.

One of the most fascinating effects of emotions on nonverbal communication is the phenomenon called **emotional contagion**, which is the automatic process of 'catching' or sharing another person's emotions by mimicking that person's facial expressions and other nonverbal behaviour. Consider what happens when you see a coworker accidentally bang his or her head against a filing cabinet. Chances are, you wince and put your hand on your own head as if you had hit the cabinet. Similarly, while listening to someone describe a positive event, you tend to smile and exhibit other emotional displays of happiness. While some of our nonverbal communication is planned, emotional contagion represents nonconscious behaviour—we automatically mimic and synchronise our nonverbal behaviours with those of other people.[32]

Emotional contagion serves three purposes. First, mimicry provides continuous feedback, communicating that we understand and empathise with the sender. To consider the significance of this, imagine employees remaining expressionless after watching a coworker bang his or her head! The lack of parallel behaviour conveys a lack of understanding or caring. Second, mimicking the nonverbal behaviours of other people seems to be a way of receiving emotional meaning from those people. If a coworker is angry with a client, your tendency to frown and show anger while listening helps you share that emotion more fully. In other words, we receive meaning by expressing the sender's emotions as well as by listening to the sender's words.

The third function of emotional contagion is to fulfill the drive to bond that was described in Chapter 5. Social solidarity in a team is built out of each member's awareness of a collective sentiment. Through nonverbal expressions of emotional contagion, people see others share the same emotions that they feel. This strengthens relations among team members, as well as between leaders and followers, by providing evidence of their similarity.[33]

CHOOSING THE BEST COMMUNICATION CHANNEL

LEARNING OBJECTIVE 

Appraise the appropriateness of a communication medium for a particular situation based on social acceptance and media richness factors.

Which communication channel is most appropriate in a particular situation? Two important sets of factors to consider are (a) social acceptance, and (b) media richness.

Social Acceptance

Social acceptance refers to how well the communication medium is approved and supported by the organisation, teams and individuals.[34] One factor in social acceptance is the organisation's and team's norms regarding the use of specific communication channels. Norms partly explain why telephone conversations are more common among staff in some firms, whereas email or instant messaging is the medium of choice in other organisations. Some companies expect employees to meet face to face, whereas meetings and similar conversations are rare events elsewhere. Norms also shape the use of communication media for people in specific positions. For instance, front-line employees are more likely to write an email and less likely to telephone or personally visit the company's CEO.

A second social acceptance factor is individual preferences for specific communication channels.[35] You may have discovered that a coworker prefers email rather than voicemail, or wants to meet in person more than you think is necessary. These preferences are due to personality traits, as well as previous experience and reinforcement with particular channels. A third social acceptance factor to consider is the symbolic meaning of a channel. Some communication channels are viewed as impersonal whereas others are more personal; some are considered professional whereas others are casual; some are 'cool' whereas others are not. To illustrate the importance of a channel's symbolic meaning, consider stories about corporate leaders who use emails or mobile phone text messages to tell employees that they have been fired or laid off. These actions make front-page headlines because email and text messages are considered inappropriate (too impersonal) for transmission of that particular information.[36]

Media Richness

Along with social acceptance, people select communication media based on their **media richness**. Media richness refers to the medium's data-carrying capacity—the volume and variety of information that can be transmitted during a specific time.[37] Exhibit 9.2 illustrates various communication channels arranged in a hierarchy of richness, with face-to-face interaction at the top and lean data-only reports at the bottom. A communication channel has high richness when it is able to convey multiple cues (such as both verbal and nonverbal information), allows timely feedback from receiver to sender, allows the sender to customise the message to the receiver and makes use of complex symbols (such as words and phrases with multiple meanings). Face-to-face communication is at the top of the media richness hierarchy because it allows us to communicate both verbally and nonverbally at the same time, to receive feedback almost immediately from the receiver, to quickly adjust our message and style, and to use complex language such as metaphors and idioms (e.g. 'spilling the beans').

media richness A medium's data-carrying capacity, that is, the volume and variety of information that can be transmitted during a specific time.

According to media richness theory, rich media are better than lean media when the communication situation is nonroutine and ambiguous. In nonroutine situations (such as an unexpected and unusual emergency), the sender and receiver have little common experience, so

Exhibit 9.2 *Media Richness Hierarchy*

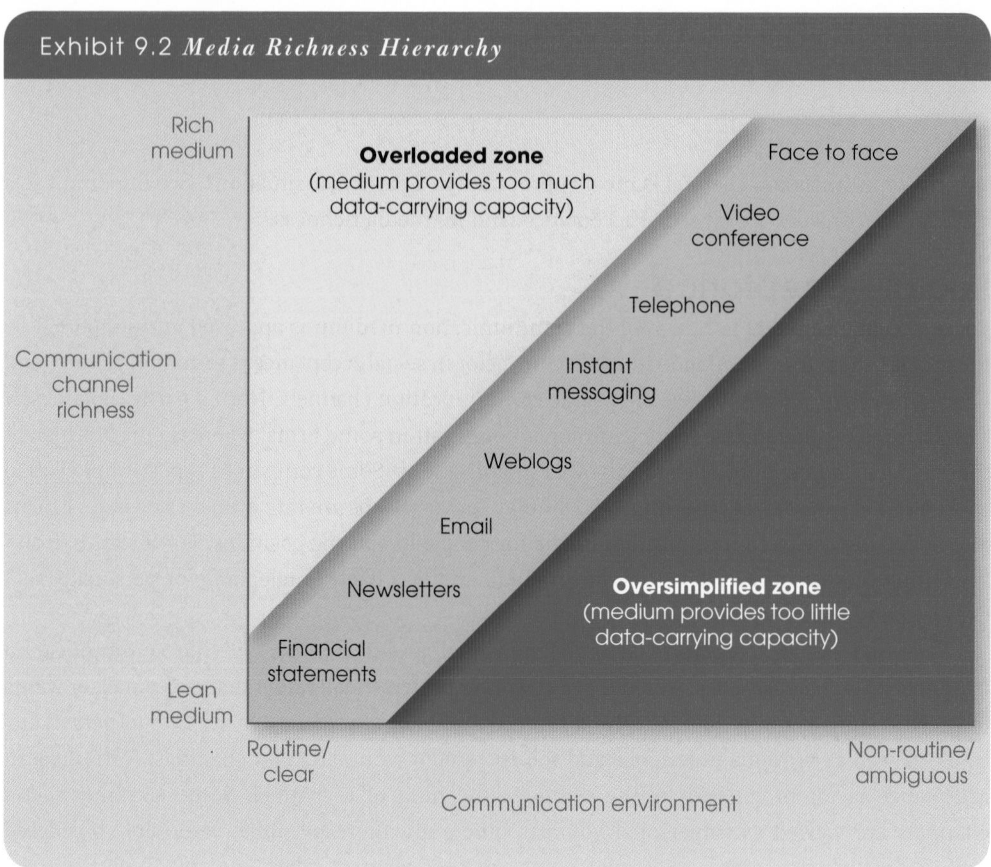

Source: Based on R. Lengel and R. Daft, 'The Selection of Communication Media as an Executive Skill,' *Academy of Management Executive* 2, no. 3 (1988): 226; R. L. Daft and R. H. Lengel, 'Information Richness: A New Approach to Managerial Behavior and Organization Design,' *Research in Organizational Behavior* 6 (1984): 199.

they need to transmit a large volume of information with immediate feedback. Lean media work well in routine situations because the sender and receiver have common expectations through shared mental models. Ambiguous situations also require rich media because the parties must share large amounts of information with immediate feedback to resolve multiple and conflicting interpretations of their observations and experiences.[38] Choosing the wrong medium reduces communication effectiveness. When the situation is routine or clear, using a rich medium—such as holding a special meeting—would seem like a waste of time. On the other hand, if a unique and ambiguous issue is handled through email or another lean medium, then issues take longer to resolve and misunderstandings are more likely to occur.

Evaluating Media Richness Theory

Research generally supports the relevance of media richness for traditional channels (face-to-face meetings, written memos, etc.). However, the evidence is mixed when computer-mediated communication channels are studied. Three factors seem to override or blur the medium's richness:

THE ABILITY TO MULTICOMMUNICATE It is usually difficult (as well as rude) to communicate face to face with someone while simultaneously transmitting messages to someone else using another medium. Most computer-mediated technologies, on the other hand, require less sensory demand, so employees can easily engage in two or more communication events at the same time. In other words, they can multicommunicate.[39] For example, people routinely scan web pages while carrying on telephone conversations. Some write text messages to a client while simultaneously listening to a discussion at a large meeting. Although people do not multitask as efficiently as is often believed, some employees have become good enough at multicommunicating that they likely exchange as much information through two or more lean media as through one high media-richness channel during the same time period.

MORE VARIED PROFICIENCY LEVELS Earlier in this chapter we explained that communication effectiveness is partially determined by the sender's competency with the communication channel. Those with higher proficiency can 'push' more information through the channel, thereby increasing the channel's information flow. Experienced BlackBerry users, for instance, can whip through messages in a flash, whereas new users struggle to type notes and organise incoming messages. In contrast, there is less variation in the ability to communicate through casual conversation and other natural channels because most of us develop good levels of proficiency throughout life and possibly through hardwired evolutionary development.[40]

SOCIAL DISTRACTIONS OF RICH CHANNELS Channels with high media richness tend to involve more direct social interaction. However, this social presence sensitises both parties to their relative status and self-presentation, which diverts their attention from the message.[41] In other words, the benefits of media richness channels such as face-to-face communication may be offset by social distractions from the message content, whereas lean media have much less social presence.

Communication Channels and Persuasion

Media richness as well as social issues lay the foundation for understanding which communication channels are more effective for **persuasion**, that is, changing another person's beliefs and attitudes. Recent studies support the long-held view that spoken communication, particularly face-to-face interaction, is more persuasive than emails, websites and other forms of written communication. There are three main reasons for this persuasive effect.[42] First, spoken communication is typically accompanied by nonverbal communication. People are often persuaded more when they receive both emotional and logical messages, and the combination of spoken with nonverbal communication provides this dual punch. A lengthy pause, raised voice tone and (in face-to-face interaction) animated hand gestures can amplify the emotional tone of the message, thereby signaling the vitality of the issue.

persuasion The use of facts, logical arguments and emotional appeals to change another person's beliefs and attitudes, usually for the purpose of changing the person's behaviour.

Second, spoken communication offers the sender high-quality, immediate feedback about whether the receiver understands and accepts the message (i.e. is being persuaded). This feedback allows the sender to adjust the content and emotional tone of the message more quickly than with written communication. Third, people are persuaded more under conditions of high social presence than low social presence. In face-to-face conversations (high social presence), people are more sensitive to how they are perceived by others in that social setting, so they pay attention to the sender's message and are more willing to actively consider that viewpoint. This is particularly true when the sender is a member of the receiver's social identity group. However, when people receive persuasion attempts through a website, email or another source of written communication, they experience a higher degree of anonymity and psychological distance from the persuader. These conditions reduce the motivation to think about and accept the persuasive message.

Although spoken communication tends to be more persuasive, written communication can also persuade others to some extent. Written messages have the advantage of presenting more technical detail than can occur through conversation. This factual information is valuable when the issue is important to the receiver. Also, people experience a moderate degree of social presence in written communication when they are exchanging messages with close associates, so messages from friends and coworkers can be persuasive.

LEARNING OBJECTIVE 

Identify four common communication barriers.

COMMUNICATION BARRIERS (NOISE)

In spite of the best intentions of sender and receiver to communicate, several barriers (called 'noise' earlier in Exhibit 9.1) inhibit the effective exchange of information. As author George Bernard Shaw wrote, 'The greatest problem with communication is the illusion that it has been accomplished.' One barrier is the imperfect perceptual process of both sender and receiver. As receivers, we don't listen as well as senders assume, and our needs and expectations influence the signals we notice and ignore. We aren't any better as senders, either. Some studies suggest that we have difficulty stepping out of our own perspectives and stepping into the perspectives of others, so we overestimate how well other people understand the message we are communicating.[43]

Even if the perceptual process is well tuned, messages sometimes get filtered on their way up or down the corporate hierarchy. Filtering may involve deleting or delaying negative information or using less harsh words so the message sounds more favourable.[44] Filtering is most common where the organisation rewards employees who communicate mainly positive information and among employees with strong career mobility aspirations.

A different kind of filtering occurs because of the expectations we have about others' behaviour. If one of our coworkers usually communicates aggressively, we are likely to interpret everything this person says through this filter. Although many factors shape our expectations, some of our strongest expectations are created by stereotypes. Gender stereotypes, for example, establish strong expectations about how men and women will communicate: while we expect men to communicate in an assertive way, we expect women to be more relationship-oriented in their communication style. Violating these stereotypes is especially problematic for women, and can trigger backlash: they are less influential when they communicate in an assertive way and their performance is appraised more negatively.[45]

Language differences represent a third source of communication noise. But even if two people speak the same language, they might have different meanings for particular words and phrases. For example, a French executive might call an event a 'catastrophe' as a casual exaggeration, whereas someone in Germany usually interprets this word literally as an earth-shaking event.[46]

Jargon, which includes specialised words and phrases for specific occupations or groups, is designed to improve communication efficiency. However, it has the opposite effect when senders transmit jargon to people who do not possess the jargon codebook. Furthermore, people who use jargon to excess put themselves in an unflattering light. For example, soon after Robert Nardelli became Chrysler's new CEO, he proudly announced: 'I'm blessed to have individuals with me who can take areas of responsibility and do vertical dives to really get the granularity and make sure that we're coupling horizontally across those functions so that we have a pure line of sight toward the customer.' Business journalists weren't impressed, even if they did figure out what Nardelli meant.[47]

No matter how well we know a language, words and phrases have enough ambiguity to create confusion. Consider the question 'Can you close the door?' You might assume the sender is asking whether shutting the door is permitted. But the question might be asking whether you are physically able to shut the door or whether the door is designed so that it can be shut. In fact, this question might not be a question at all; the person could be politely *telling* you to shut the door.[48]

The ambiguity of language isn't always dysfunctional noise.[49] Corporate leaders sometimes rely on metaphors and other vague language to describe ill-defined or complex ideas. Ambiguity is also used to avoid conveying or creating undesirable emotions. For example, one study reported that people rely on more ambiguous language when communicating with people who have different values and beliefs. In these situations, ambiguity minimises the risk of conflict.

Information Overload

Start with a daily avalanche of email, then add in voicemail, mobile phone text messages, PDF file downloads, web pages, hard copy documents, instant messages, blogs, wikis and other sources of incoming information. You have created a perfect recipe for **information overload.**[50] As Exhibit 9.3 illustrates, information overload occurs whenever the job's information load

information overload A condition in which the volume of information received exceeds the person's capacity to process it.

Exhibit 9.3 *Dynamics of Information Overload*

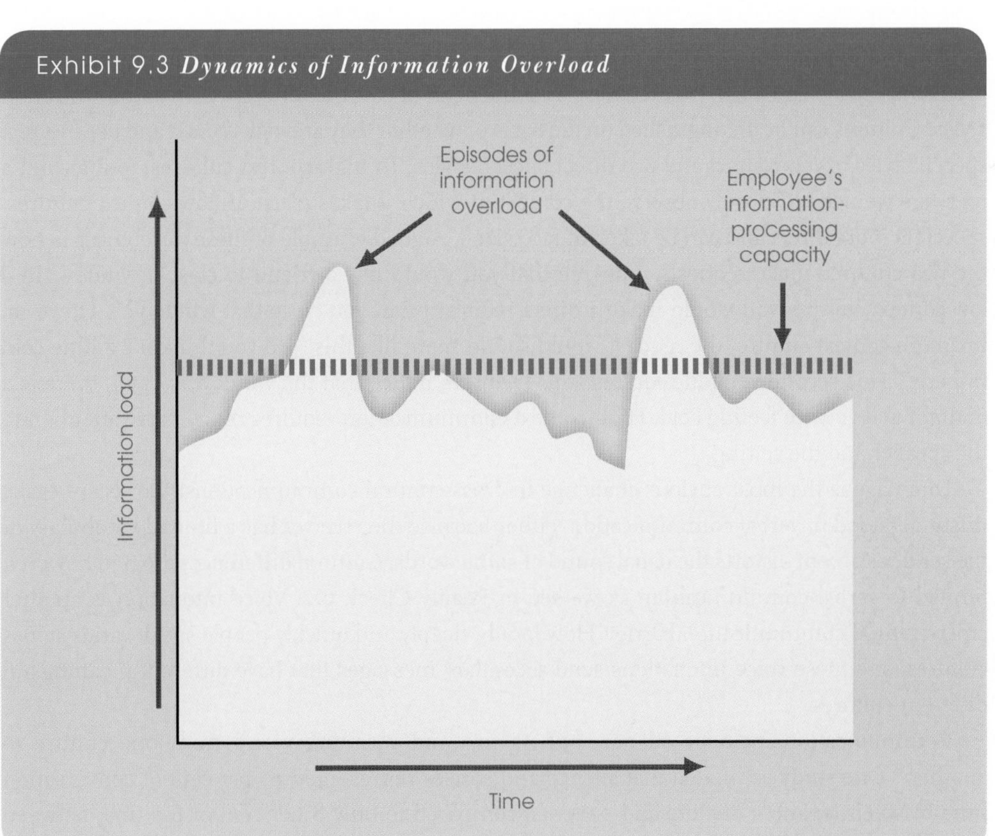

exceeds the individual's capacity to get through it. Employees have a certain *information-processing capacity*—the amount of information that they are able to process in a fixed unit of time. At the same time, jobs have a varying *information load*—the amount of information to be processed per unit of time. Information overload creates noise in the communication system because information gets overlooked or misinterpreted when people can't process it fast enough. The result is poorer quality decisions as well as higher stress.[51]

Information overload problems can be minimised by increasing our information-processing capacity, reducing the job's information load, or through a combination of both. Studies suggest that employees often increase their information-processing capacity by temporarily reading faster, scanning through documents more efficiently, and removing distractions that slow information-processing speed. Time management also increases information-processing capacity. When information overload is temporary, information-processing capacity can increase by working longer hours. Information load can be reduced by buffering, omitting and summarising. Buffering involves having incoming communication filtered, usually by an assistant. Omitting occurs when we decide to overlook messages, such as using software rules to redirect emails from distribution lists to folders that we never look at. An example of summarising would be where we read an executive summary rather than the full report.

CROSS-CULTURAL DIFFERENCES IN COMMUNICATION

As globalisation and cultural diversity increase, you can be sure that cross-cultural communication problems will also increase.[52] 'Directness' is at the heart of cultural differences in communication styles. Cultures can be distinguished on the basis of whether they are *high-context* and use indirect speech styles or *low-context* and use direct speech styles. In high-context cultures, to interpret a message we need to closely observe the context in which it takes place. In low-context cultures, speech is more direct and can be taken at face value. A good example of these differences is how the two cultures make requests. Imagine that you would like a friend to close a window. In a low-context culture, you would make a direct request ('Can you close that window?'). However, in a high-context culture, the request would sound more like this: 'Do you think it's a little cold in here?' This second version requires your friend to notice that the window is open, there is a draught and you are feeling cold. High-context communication requires much more attention to the speaker and the setting.

Language is the most obvious challenge in cross-cultural communications. Words are easily misunderstood in verbal communication, either because the receiver has a limited vocabulary or the sender's accent distorts the usual sound of some words. Cultural differences are not, however, limited to verbal communication, as we see in Reality Check 9.2. Voice intonation is another cross-cultural communication barrier. How loudly, deeply and quickly people speak varies across cultures, and these voice intonations send secondary messages that have different meanings in different cultures.

Communication includes silence, but its use and meaning varies from one culture to another.[53] One study estimated that silence and pauses represented 30 per cent of conversation time between Japanese doctors and patients, compared to only 8 per cent of the time between American doctors and patients. Why is there more silence in Japanese conversations? In Japan, silence symbolises respect and indicates that the listener is thoughtfully contemplating what has just been said.[54] Empathy is very important in Japan, and this shared understanding is demonstrated without using words. In contrast, most people in the United States and many other cultures view silence as a *lack* of communication and often interpret long breaks as a sign of disagreement.

Conversational overlaps also send different messages in different cultures. Japanese people usually stop talking when they are interrupted, whereas talking over the other person's speech is more common in Brazil, France and some other countries. The difference in communication behaviour is, again, due to interpretations. Talking while someone is speaking to you is considered quite rude in Japan, whereas Brazilians and French are more likely to interpret this as the person's interest and involvement in the conversation.

Nonverbal communication represents another potential area for misunderstanding across cultures. Many nonconscious or involuntary nonverbal cues (such as smiling) have the same meaning around the world, but deliberate gestures often have different interpretations. For example, most of us shake our head from side to side to say 'No', but a variation of head shaking means 'I understand' to many people in India. Filipinos raise their eyebrows to give an affirmative answer, yet Arabs interpret this expression (along with clicking one's tongue) as a negative response. Most Americans are taught to maintain eye contact with the speaker to show interest and respect, whereas some North American native groups and Australian Aboriginal people learn at an early age to show respect by looking down when an older or more senior person is talking to them.[56]

GENDER DIFFERENCES IN COMMUNICATION

LEARNING OBJECTIVE

Discuss the degree to which men and women communicate differently.

Men and women have similar communication practices, but there are subtle distinctions that can occasionally lead to misunderstanding and conflict.[57] The key difference is in how men and women perceive the functions of language. Men are more likely than women to view conversations as negotiations of relative power and status. Women are more likely than men to view conversations as opportunities to strengthen social bonds. These differences come into play when men and women interact with each other. Not only do women and men increase the use of gender-linked language styles when they talk with each other, but differences in how language is interpreted pave the way for miscommunication.[58]

Like culture, gender affects directness. This difference is most apparent in the use of the powerful and powerless speech styles we described earlier. Men are more likely to use a powerful speech style. They assert their power by directly giving advice to others (e.g. 'You should do ...') and using combative language. There is also evidence that men dominate the talk time in conversations with women, as well as interrupt more and adjust their speaking style less than do women. Women, in comparison, use a powerless speech style: they make more use of indirect requests ('Do you think you should ...'), are more likely to qualify what they say ('kind of', 'sort of') and ask tag questions ('... isn't it?'). Like high-context communication, a 'powerless' speech style protects relationships. Difficulties arise when men interpret this speech style as indicating deference and low power. For example, a woman might say 'What do you think?' as a way of engaging the other person in conversation. Men, however, are likely to interpret this question as a request for advice.[59]

Global Communication

Christine Schneider/Corbis

The art of exchanging business cards is critical in many cultures.

WE ALL KNOW THAT culture affects how we communicate. As we have learned in this chapter, what we say and how we say is important, but it's not safe to assume that the strategies that lead to effective communication in our culture will be equally effective in other cultures. When we head to Asian countries, for example, much of our communication efforts need to be directed toward ensuring that relationships are preserved and that we speak in a face-saving way. Charles Wigley, chairman of Bartle Bogle Hegarty Singapore, offers some tips for businesspeople travelling to Asia: 'Talk less, listen more. You have to coax more out of people... relationships take time. A quick trip to "fix" a relationship by someone the client is never likely to see again won't work.' Here are some more tips for more effective communication:

BUSINESS CARDS ARE SACROSANCT They rapidly communicate our rank and status; in short, they represent 'us'. Treat business cards with respect:

Men's use of language is also more task-oriented. They engage in more 'report talk', in which the primary function of the conversation is impersonal and efficient information exchange. Women also do report talk, particularly when conversing with men, but conversations among women have a higher incidence of relationship building through 'rapport talk'. This is because women place greater emphasis on maintaining social bonds. Women apologise more often and seek advice from others more quickly than do men. Finally, research fairly consistently indicates that women are more sensitive than men to nonverbal cues in face-to-face meetings.[60] Together, these conditions can create communication conflicts. Women who describe problems get frustrated that men offer advice rather than rapport, whereas men become frustrated because they can't understand why women don't appreciate their advice.

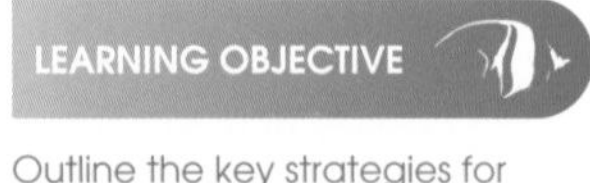

Outline the key strategies for getting your message across and engaging in active listening.

IMPROVING INTERPERSONAL COMMUNICATION

Effective interpersonal communication depends on the sender's ability to get the message across and the receiver's performance as an active listener. In this section, we outline these two essential features of effective interpersonal communication.

REALITY CHECK 9.2

present them with two hands; keep them in a card wallet; in Indonesia, give your business card with your right hand. Take the advice of Michelle Kristula-Green, the Asia-Pacific president of Leo Burnett, who says of Japan: 'If you drop [a business card] on the floor and step on it, you're stepping on the person.'

TIME IS ELASTIC Don't take offence if you are kept waiting. Whereas in Western cultures such a delay may signal perceived power differences, in Asian countries it reflects a different (and more relaxed) attitude to time. In India, you can expect meetings to start late and run long. Sam Balsara of Madison Communications observes that meetings can be long and without an obvious conclusion.

ADAPT YOUR LANGUAGE Indonesian experts advise that you should first apologise for not speaking Bahasa and ask if it is acceptable to speak in English. Avoid the jargon that comes naturally and, if possible, use a local person to translate for you.

MANAGE THE RELATIONSHIP Because face is important, many Asian cultures adopt an indirect communication style, as Alex Thompson of Kinetic Asia-Pacific (Thailand) discovered. When one of his staff members wanted to leave for another job, the employee tried to help Thompson save face by saying he needed to help his father in a family business. One British company's joint venture in China ended when the manager of the Chinese partner said that his Western partner possessed 'no manners, no upbringing and no culture'. Finally, remember that in Japan, indirection means that Japanese avoid tough topics, and their reluctance to cause embarrassment may mean that you miss the early signs of potential difficulties.[55]

Getting Your Message Across

Effective communication occurs when a receiver is able to receive and understand a message. To accomplish this difficult task, the sender must learn to empathise with the receiver, repeat the message, choose an appropriate time for the conversation and be descriptive rather than evaluative.

EMPATHISE Recall from earlier chapters that empathy is a person's ability to understand and be sensitive to the feelings, thoughts and situation of others. In conversations, this involves putting yourself in the receiver's shoes when encoding the message. For instance, be sensitive to words that may be ambiguous or trigger the wrong emotional response.

REPEAT THE MESSAGE Rephrase the key points a couple of times. The saying 'Tell them what you're going to tell them; tell them; then tell them what you've told them' reflects this need for redundancy.

USE MULTIPLE COMMUNICATION CHANNELS People differ in how they like to receive information. While some people prefer to 'see' communication, others prefer to hear it. Using more than one communication channel means you have a better chance of getting your message across.

USE TIMING EFFECTIVELY Your message competes with other messages and noise, so find a time when the receiver is less likely to be distracted by other matters.

BE DESCRIPTIVE Focus on the problem, not the person, if you have negative information to convey. People stop listening when the information attacks their self-esteem. Also, suggest things the listener can do to improve, rather than point to him or her as a problem.

Active Listening

'Nature gave people two ears but only one tongue, which is a gentle hint that they should listen more than they talk.'[61] To follow this advice, we need to recognise that listening is a process of actively sensing the sender's signals, evaluating them accurately and responding appropriately. These three components of listening—sensing, evaluating and responding—reflect the receiver's side of the communication model described at the beginning of this chapter. Listeners receive the sender's signals, decode them as intended, and provide appropriate and timely feedback to the sender (see Exhibit 9.4). Active listeners constantly cycle through sensing, evaluating and responding during the conversation, and engage in various activities to improve these processes.[62]

Sensing

Sensing is the process of receiving signals from the sender and paying attention to them. Active listeners improve sensing in three ways. First, they postpone evaluation by not forming an opinion until the speaker has finished. Second, they avoid interrupting the speaker's conversation. Third, they remain motivated to listen to the speaker.

Exhibit 9.4 *Active Listening Process and Strategies*

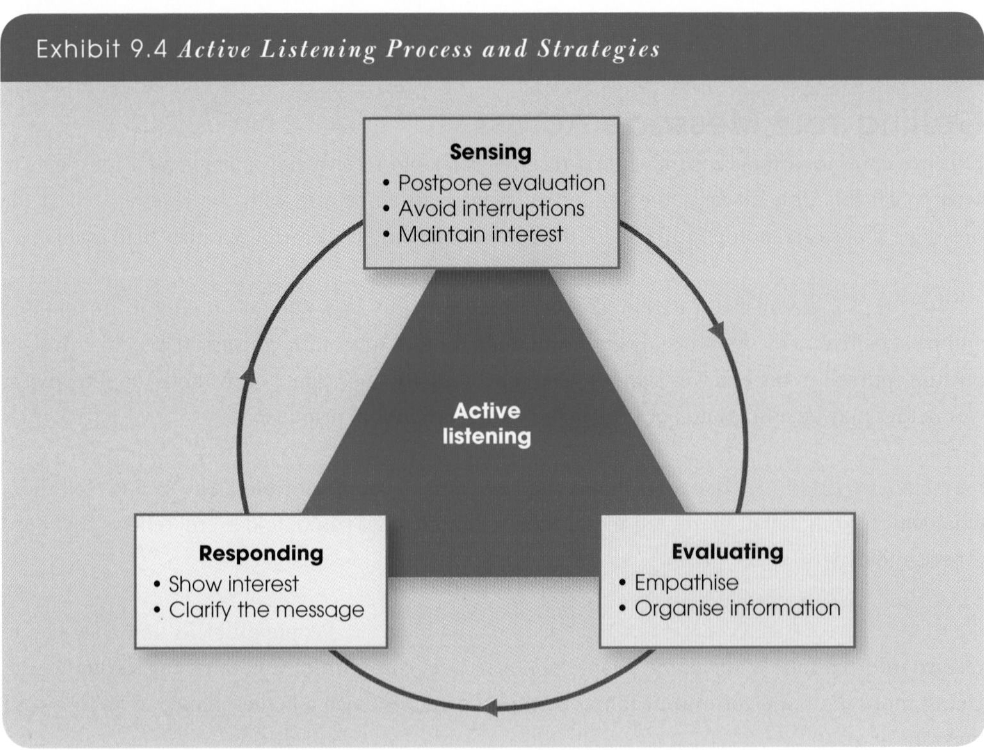

Evaluating

This component of listening includes understanding the message meaning, evaluating the message and remembering the message. To improve their evaluation of the conversation, active listeners empathise with the speaker—they try to understand and be sensitive to the speaker's feelings, thoughts and situation. Evaluation also improves when the listener organises the speaker's ideas into key points while they are being communicated.

Responding

Responding, the third component of listening, is feedback to the sender, which motivates and directs the speaker's communication. Active listeners accomplish this by maintaining sufficient eye contact and sending back channel signals (e.g. 'I see'), both of which show interest. They also respond by clarifying the message and rephrasing the speaker's ideas at appropriate breaks ('So you're saying that ... ?').

IMPROVING WORKPLACE COMMUNICATION

Summarise three communication strategies in organisational hierarchies.

So far, we have focused on 'micro-level' issues in the communication process, namely, the dynamics of sending and receiving information between two employees or the informal exchanges of information across several people. But in this era where knowledge is a competitive advantage, corporate leaders also need to maintain an open flow of communication up, down and across the organisation. In this section, we discuss three communication strategies for use in organisational hierarchies: work space design, web-based communication and direct communication with top management.

Work Space Design

Executives at Japan Airlines recently decided that knocking down a few walls might improve the airline's performance. The airline's board members and senior executive team moved out of individual offices into a single large room where it is easier for them to spontaneously share information. The new space also includes an elliptical conference table where they can hold meetings.[63] Japan Airlines' executives have discovered that people communicate more with each other when there are no walls between them.[64] The location and design of hallways, offices, cubicles and communal areas (e.g. cafeterias, lifts) all shape whom we speak to as well as the frequency of that communication.

Japan Airlines has applied a widely adopted work space strategy of replacing traditional offices with an open space where all employees (including management) work together. One recent convert to open space is Continuum, the Boston-based design and innovation firm. 'We do not have doors,' explains a Continuum executive. 'It's structured that way to stimulate conversation and to allow people to work collaboratively. Anyone from the chief operating officer to our interns shares space and sits next to each other. You can stop in and have a conversation with anyone, anytime you want.'[65] Although these open space arrangements increase communication, they also potentially increase noise, distractions and loss of privacy.[66] The challenge is to increase social interaction without these stressors.

Another work space strategy is to cloister employees into team spaces, but also encourage sufficient interaction with people from other teams. Pixar Animation Studios constructed its campus in Emeryville, California, with these principles in mind. The buildings encourage communication

Communicating without Walls

Courtesy the bookseller.com

When Penguin Books in London moved to their new offices, the walls were missing. A little further along the Thames, publishers Little, Brown have also converted their office space to an open-plan design. Will it help or hurt creativity and work flow? There is opposition to open-plan offices because they are noisy and distracting. Some publishers are concerned that they will limit creativity. Ursula Mackenzie, Little, Brown's CEO, disagrees. She says that 'publishing is essentially a very collaborative business' and that creativity will be enhanced by open-plan offices. She also believes that it will reduce the need for time-consuming meetings because individuals will 'naturally pick up on relevant information, and have informal conversations about projects'. However, both companies have also ensured that private spaces are available in library rooms.[68]

among team members. At the same time, the campus encourages happenstance interactions with people on other teams. Pixar executives call this the 'bathroom effect', because team members must leave their isolated pods to fetch their mail, have lunch or visit the bathroom.[67]

Web-based Organisational Communication

For decades, employees received official company news through hard copy newsletters and magazines. Many firms still use these communication devices, but most have supplemented or replaced them completely with web-based sources of information. The traditional company magazine is now typically published on web pages or distributed in PDF format. The advantage of these *e-zines* is that company news can be prepared and distributed quickly.

However, employees are increasingly sceptical of information that has been screened and packaged by management. In response, Children's Hospital and Regional Medical Center in Seattle keeps employees up to date through staff who volunteer to write news about their departments on the hospital's central weblog site. 'The distributed authorship of people from different departments means the content is fresher' than in the hospital's previous newsletter or e-zine, says the Children's Hospital manager responsible for the website. IBM relies on e-zines, but employees increasingly rely on BlogCentral, an inward-facing (i.e. for IBM employees' eyes only) blog-hosting service where several thousand employees write about their own news of the week. A search engine helps staff find important information on any of the blogs.[69]

Direct Communication with Top Management

'The best fertiliser in any field is that of the farmer's footsteps!' This old Chinese saying suggests that farmers will be more successful if they spend more time in the fields directly observing the crop's development. Translated into an organisational context, this means that senior executives will understand their business better if they meet directly with employees and other stakeholders. Nearly 40 years ago, people at Hewlett-Packard coined a phrase for this communication strategy: **management by walking around (MBWA)**. Brian Scudamore, founder and CEO of 1-800-Got-Junk?, takes this practice further. 'I don't have my own office, and I very often move around to different departments for a day at a time,' says Scudamore.[70]

management by walking around (MBWA) A communication practice in which executives get out of their offices and learn from others in the organisation through face-to-face dialogue.

Along with MBWA, executives communicate more directly with employees through 'town hall meetings'. For example, soon after becoming chief executive of McDonald's in the UK, Peter Beresford instituted a monthly online town hall event where board members answered questions from any McDonald's staff member.[71] Some executives also conduct employee roundtable forums to hear opinions from a small representation of staff about various issues. At the departmental level, some companies hold daily or weekly 'huddles'—brief stand-up meetings in which staff and their manager discuss goals and hear good-news stories. These direct communication strategies potentially minimise filtering because executives listen directly to employees. They also help executives to understand organisational problems more quickly and thoroughly. A third benefit of direct communication is that employees might have more empathy for decisions made further up the corporate hierarchy.

COMMUNICATING THROUGH THE GRAPEVINE

LEARNING OBJECTIVE 

Debate the benefits and limitations of the organisational grapevine.

No matter how much corporate leaders try to communicate through e-zines, blogs, wikis, MBWA and other means, employees will still rely on the oldest communication channel: the corporate **grapevine**. The grapevine is an unstructured and informal network founded on social relationships rather than organisational charts or job descriptions. What do employees think about the grapevine? Surveys of employees in two firms—one in Florida, the other in California—found that almost all employees use the grapevine, but very few of them prefer this source of information. The Californian survey also reported that only one-third of employees believe grapevine information is credible. In other words, employees turn to the grapevine when they have few other options.[72]

grapevine An unstructured and informal network founded on social relationships rather than organisational charts or job descriptions.

Grapevine Characteristics

Research conducted several decades ago reported that the grapevine transmits information very rapidly in all directions throughout the organisation. The typical pattern is a cluster chain, whereby a few people actively transmit rumours to many others. The grapevine works through informal social networks, so it is more active where employees have similar backgrounds and are able to communicate easily. Many rumours seem to have at least a kernel of truth, possibly because they are transmitted through media-rich communication channels (e.g. face to face) and employees are motivated to communicate effectively. Nevertheless, the grapevine distorts information by deleting fine details and exaggerating key points of the story.[73]

Some of these characteristics might still be true, but other features of the grapevine almost certainly have changed as email, social networking sites and blogs have replaced the traditional water cooler discussion as sources of gossip. For example, several Facebook sites are themed around specific companies, allowing employees and customers to vent their complaints about particular organisations. Along with altering the speed and network of corporate grapevines, information technologies have expanded these networks around the globe, not just around the next cubicle.

Grapevine Benefits and Limitations

Should the grapevine be encouraged, tolerated or quashed? The difficulty in answering this question is that the grapevine has both benefits and limitations.[74] One benefit, as mentioned earlier, is that employees rely on the grapevine when information is not available through formal channels. It is also the main conduit through which organisational stories and other symbols of the organisation's culture are communicated. A third benefit of the grapevine is that this social interaction relieves anxiety. This explains why rumour mills are most active during times of uncertainty.[75] Finally, the grapevine is associated with the drive to bond. Being a recipient of gossip is a sign of inclusion, according to evolutionary psychologists. Trying to quash the grapevine is, in some respects, an attempt to undermine the natural human drive for social interaction.[76]

While the grapevine offers these benefits, it is not a preferred communication medium. Grapevine information is sometimes so distorted that it escalates rather than reduces employee anxiety. Furthermore, employees develop more negative attitudes toward the organisation when management is slower than the grapevine in communicating information. What should corporate leaders do with the grapevine? The best advice seems to be to listen to the grapevine as a signal of employee anxiety, then correct the cause of this anxiety. Some companies also listen to the grapevine and step in to correct blatant errors and fabrications. Most important, corporate leaders need to view the grapevine as a competitor, and meet this challenge by directly informing employees of news before it spreads throughout the grapevine.

CHAPTER SUMMARY

Communication refers to the process by which information is transmitted and *understood* between two or more people. Communication supports work coordination, organisational learning, decision making and employee wellbeing. The communication process involves forming, encoding and transmitting the intended message to a receiver, who then decodes the message and provides feedback to the sender. Effective communication occurs when the sender's thoughts are transmitted to and understood by the intended receiver. Four ways to improve this process is for both sender and receiver to have common codebooks, to share common mental models, to be familiar with the message topic and to be proficient with the communication channel.

The two main types of communication channels are verbal and nonverbal. Various forms of computer-mediated communication are widely used in organisations, with email the most popular. Although efficient and a useful filing cabinet, email is relatively poor at communicating emotions; it tends to reduce politeness and respect; it is an inefficient medium for communicating in ambiguous, complex and novel situations; and it contributes to information overload. Facebook-like websites, wikis, virtual reality platforms and other forms of virtual social networking are also gaining popularity as forms of communication. Nonverbal communication includes facial gestures, voice intonation, physical distance and even silence. It is less rule-bound than verbal communication, and is mostly automatic and nonconscious.

The message is more than the literal meaning of the words that we use. Listeners use our language to make judgments about status and affiliation. Language that signals status also distances us from others. In contrast, language that signals strong affiliation can be interpreted as signalling powerlessness. Another watchpoint is the level of anxiety that we convey both verbally and nonverbally: listeners use anxiety as an indicator of deception.

The most appropriate communication medium partly depends on social acceptance factors, including organisation and team norms, individual preferences for specific communication channels and the symbolic meaning of a channel. A communication medium should also be chosen for its data-carrying capacity (media richness). Nonroutine and ambiguous situations require rich media. However, we also need to recognise that lean media allow people to multicommunicate, that the capacity of computer-mediated communication is varied due to the proficiency of individual users and that social distractions can reduce the efficient processing of information in high media-richness channels.

Several barriers create noise in the communication process. People misinterpret messages because of perceptual biases. Some information is filtered out as it gets passed up the hierarchy. Jargon and ambiguous language are barriers when the sender and receiver have different interpretations of the words and symbols used. People also screen out or misinterpret messages due to information overload. These problems are often amplified in cross-cultural settings because of language barriers and differences in meaning of nonverbal cues. There are also some communication differences between men and women, such as the tendency for men to exert status and engage in report talk in conversations. Women tend to use more rapport talk and are more sensitive than are men to nonverbal cues.

To get a message across, the sender must learn to empathise with the receiver, repeat the message, use multiple communication channels, choose an appropriate time for the conversation and be descriptive rather than evaluative. Listening includes sensing, evaluating and responding. Active listeners support these processes by postponing evaluation, avoiding interruptions, maintaining interest, empathising, organising information, showing interest and clarifying the message.

Some companies try to encourage communication through work space design, as well as through web-based communication devices. Some executives also meet directly with employees, such as through the strategy of 'management by walking around' (MBWA), to facilitate communication across the organisation.

In any organisation, employees rely on the grapevine, particularly during times of uncertainty. The grapevine is an unstructured and informal network founded on social relationships rather than organisational charts or job descriptions. Although early research identified several unique features of the grapevine, some of these features may be changing as the internet plays an increasing role in grapevine communication.

KEY TERMS

communication, p. 344
emotional contagion, p. 352
grapevine, p. 365
information overload, p. 357
management by walking around (MBWA), p. 365
media richness, p. 353
persuasion, p. 355
wikis, p. 349

Critical Thinking Questions

1 You have been hired as a consultant to improve communication between engineering and marketing staff in a large high-technology company. Use the communication model and the four ways to improve that process to devise strategies to improve communication effectiveness among employees between these two work units.

2 A company in a country that is just entering the information age intends to introduce email for office staff at its three buildings located throughout the city. Describe two benefits as well as two potential problems that employees will likely experience with this medium.

3 Senior management at a consumer goods company wants you to investigate the feasibility of using a virtual-reality platform (such as Second Life) for monthly online meetings involving its three dozen sales managers located in several cities and countries. Use the social acceptance and media richness factors described in this chapter to identify information you need to consider when conducting this evaluation.

4 Wikis are collaborative websites where anyone in the group can post, edit or delete any information. Where might this communication technology be most useful in organisations?

5 Under what conditions, if any, do you think it is appropriate to use email to notify an employee that he or she has been laid off or fired? Why is email usually considered an inappropriate channel to convey this information?

6 Suppose that you are part of a virtual team and must persuade other team members on an important matter (such as switching suppliers or altering a project deadline). Assuming that you cannot visit these people in person, what can you do to maximise your persuasiveness?

7 Explain why men and women are sometimes frustrated with each other's communication behaviours.

8 In your opinion, has the introduction of email and other information technologies increased or decreased the amount of information flowing through the corporate grapevine? Explain your answer.

TEAM EXERCISE

Skill Builder 9.1

Analysing the Blogosphere

Purpose

This exercise is designed to help you understand the dynamics of corporate blogs as a way to communicate around organisations.

Instructions

This activity is usually conducted in between classes as a homework assignment. The instructor will divide the class into teams, although this can also be conducted as an individual exercise). Each team will identify a corporate blog, written by a company or government executive and aimed at customers, employees or the wider community. Each team will analyse content on their selected blog and answer the following questions for class (preferably with brief samples where applicable).

1. Who is the main intended audience of the selected blog?
2. To what extent do you think this blog attracts the interest of its intended audience? Explain.
3. What are the main topics in recent postings on this blog? Do they mostly contain good or bad news? Why?

Skill Builder 9.2

TEAM EXERCISE

Active Listening Exercise

Mary Gander, Winona State University

Purpose

This exercise is designed to help you understand the dynamics of active listening in conversations and to develop active listening skills.

Instructions

For each of the four vignettes presented here, student teams (or students working individually) will compose three statements that demonstrate active listening. Specifically, one statement will indicate that you show empathy for the situation, the second will ask for clarification and detail in a nonjudgmental way, and the third statement will provide nonevaluative feedback to the speaker. Here are details about each of these three types of responses:

SHOWING EMPATHY: ACKNOWLEDGE FEELINGS Sometimes it sounds like a speaker wants you to agree with him or her, but in reality the speaker mainly wants you to understand how he or she feels. 'Acknowledging feelings' involves taking in the speaker's statements while looking at the 'whole message' including body language, tone of voice and level of arousal, and trying to determine what emotion the speaker is conveying. Then you let the speaker know that you realise what he or she is feeling by acknowledging it in a sentence.

ASKING FOR CLARIFICATION AND DETAIL WHILE WITHHOLDING YOUR JUDGMENT AND OPINIONS This conveys that you are trying to understand and not just trying to push your opinions onto the speaker. To formulate a relevant question in asking for more clarification, you will have to listen carefully to what the speaker says. Frame your question as someone trying to understand in more detail; often asking for a specific example is useful. This also helps the speaker evaluate his or her own opinions and perspective.

PROVIDING NONEVALUATIVE FEEDBACK: FEEDING BACK THE MESSAGE YOU HEARD This will allow the speaker to determine if he or she conveyed the message to you and will help prevent troublesome miscommunication. It will also help the speaker become more aware of how he or she is coming across to another person (self-evaluation). Just think about what the speaker is conveying; paraphrase it in your own words and say it back to the speaker (without judging the correctness or merit of what was said), then ask him or her if that is what was meant.

After teams (or individual students) have prepared the three statements for each vignette, the instructor will ask them to present their statements and explain how these statements satisfy the active listening criteria.

VIGNETTE 1

A colleague stops by your desk and says, 'I am tired of the lack of leadership around here. The boss is so wishy-washy, he can't get tough with some of the slackers around here. They just keep milking the company, living off the rest of us. Why doesn't management do something about these guys? And you are always so supportive of the boss; he's not as good as you make him out to be.'

Develop three statements that respond to the speaker in this vignette by (a) showing empathy, (b) seeking clarification, and (c) providing nonevaluative feedback.

VIGNETTE 2

Your coworker stops by your cubicle; her voice and body language show stress, frustration and even some fear. You know she has been working hard and has a strong need to get her work done on time and done well. You are trying to concentrate on some work and have had a number of interruptions already. She abruptly interrupts you and says, 'This project is turning out to be a mess. Why can't the other three people on my team quit fighting with each other?'

Develop three statements that respond to the speaker in this vignette by (a) showing empathy, (b) seeking clarification, and (c) providing nonevaluative feedback.

VIGNETTE 3

One of your subordinates is working on an important project. He is an engineer who has good technical skills and knowledge and was selected for the project team because of that. He stops by your office and appears to be quite agitated: his voice is loud and strained, and his face has a look of bewilderment. He says, 'I'm supposed to be working with four other people from four other departments on this new project, but they never listen to my ideas and seem to hardly know I'm at the meeting!'

Develop three statements that respond to the speaker in this vignette by (a) showing empathy, (b) seeking clarification, and (c) providing nonevaluative feedback.

VIGNETTE 4

Your subordinate comes into your office in a state of agitation, asking if she can talk to you. She is polite and sits down. She seems calm and does not have an angry look on her face. However, she says, 'It seems like you consistently make up lousy schedules; you are unfair and unrealistic in the kinds of assignments you give certain people, me included. Everyone else is so intimidated they don't complain, but I think you need to know that this isn't right and it's got to change.'

Develop three statements that respond to the speaker in this vignette by (a) showing empathy, (b) seeking clarification, and (c) providing nonevaluative feedback.

Skill Builder 9.3

TEAM EXERCISE

Cross-Cultural Communication Game

Purpose

This exercise is designed to develop and test your knowledge of cross-cultural differences in communication and etiquette.

Materials

The instructor will provide one set of question/answer cards to each pair of teams.

Instructions

STEP 1 The class is divided into an even number of teams. Ideally, each team would have three students. (Two- or four-student teams are possible if matched with an equal-sized team.) Each team is then paired with another team and the paired teams (Team 'A' and Team 'B') are assigned a private space away from other matched teams.

STEP 2 The instructor will hand each pair of teams a stack of cards with the multiple choice questions face down. These cards have questions and answers about cross-cultural differences in communication and etiquette. No books or other aids are allowed.

STEP 3 The exercise begins with a member of Team A picking up one card from the top of the pile and asking the question on that card to the members of Team B. The information given to Team B includes the question and all alternatives listed on the card. Team B has 30 seconds after the question and alternatives have been read to give an answer. Team B earns one point if the correct answer is given. If Team B's answer is incorrect, however, Team A earns that point. Correct answers to each question are indicated on the card and, of course, should not be revealed until the question is correctly answered or time is up. Whether or not Team B answers correctly, it picks up the next card on the pile and reads it to members of Team A. In other words, cards are read alternatively to each team. This procedure is repeated until all of the cards have been read or time has expired. The team receiving the most points wins.

IMPORTANT NOTE The textbook provides very little information pertaining to the questions in this exercise. Rather, you must rely on past learning, logic and luck to win.

Skill Builder 9.4

SELF-ASSESSMENT

Are You an Active Listener?

Purpose

This self-assessment is designed to help you estimate your strengths and weaknesses on various dimensions of active listening.

Instructions

Think back to face-to-face conversations you have had with a coworker or client in the office, hallway, factory floor or other setting. Indicate the extent that each item below describes your behaviour during those conversations. Answer each item as truthfully as possible so that you get an accurate estimate of where your active listening skills need improvement. Then use the scoring key in Appendix B to calculate your results for each scale. This exercise is completed alone so you can assess yourself honestly without concerns of social comparison. However, class discussion will focus on the important elements of active listening.

Active Listening Skills Inventory

Tick the best response to the right that indicates the extent to which each statement describes you when listening to others.	Not at all	A little	Somewhat	Very much
1. I keep an open mind about the speaker's point of view until he/she has finished talking.	❑	❑	❑	❑
2. While listening, I mentally sort out the speaker's ideas in a way that makes sense to me.	❑	❑	❑	❑
3. I stop the speaker and give my opinion when I disagree with something he/she has said.	❑	❑	❑	❑
4. People can often tell when I'm not concentrating on what they are saying.	❑	❑	❑	❑
5. I don't evaluate what a person is saying until he/she has finished talking.	❑	❑	❑	❑
6. When someone takes a long time to present a simple idea, I let my mind wander to other things.	❑	❑	❑	❑
7. I jump into conversations to present my views rather than wait and risk forgetting what I wanted to say.	❑	❑	❑	❑
8. I nod my head and make other gestures to show I'm interested in the conversation.	❑	❑	❑	❑
9. I can usually keep focused on what people are saying to me even when they don't sound interesting.	❑	❑	❑	❑
10. Rather than organising the speaker's ideas, I usually expect the person to summarise them for me.	❑	❑	❑	❑
11. I always say things like 'I see' or 'Uh-huh' so people know that I'm really listening to them.	❑	❑	❑	❑
12. While listening, I concentrate on what is being said and regularly organise the information.	❑	❑	❑	❑
13. While the speaker is talking, I quickly determine whether I like or dislike his/her ideas.	❑	❑	❑	❑
14. I pay close attention to what people are saying even when they are explaining something I already know.	❑	❑	❑	❑
15. I don't give my opinion until I'm sure the other person has finished talking.	❑	❑	❑	❑

Endnotes

1 G. Bennett, 'You Have Been Poked, High-Fived and Had a Ninja Sent after You—Facebook, Privacy and the Workplace', *Information Law Insights (Clayton Utz)*, 25 July 2008; G. Cain and J. Jones, 'Employment Law: The Dangers of Social Networking Sites', *New Zealand Management*, November 2008, 59; L. D'Angelo, 'Social Opportunities at Work', *BRW Management Update*, June 2008; F. Fadaghi, 'Job Networks', *Business Review Weekly*, 28 February 2008, 38; F. Fadaghi, 'Global Moaning', *Business Review Weekly*, 14 August 2008, 55; R. Woolnough, 'Get Out of My Facebook', *Employer's Law*, May 2008, 14.

2 C. Barnard, *The Functions of the Executive* (Cambridge, MA: Harvard University Press, 1938).

3 M. T. Hansen, M. L. Mors and B. Lovås, 'Knowledge Sharing in Organizations: Multiple Networks, Multiple Phases', *Academy of Management Journal* 48, no. 5 (2005): 776–793; R. Du, S. Ai and Y. Ren, 'Relationship between Knowledge Sharing and Performance: A Survey in Xu'an, China', *Expert Systems with Applications* 32 (2007): 38–46; S. R. Murray and J. Peyrefitte, 'Knowledge Type and Communication Media Choice in the Knowledge Transfer Process', *Journal of Managerial Issues* 19, no. 1 (2007): 111–133.

4 S. Hamm, 'International Isn't Just IBM's First Name', *BusinessWeek*, 28 January 2008.

5 N. Ellemers, R. Spears and B. Doosje, 'Self and Social Identity', *Annual Review of Psychology* 53 (2002): 161–186; S. A. Haslam and S. Reicher, 'Stressing the Group: Social Identity and the Unfolding Dynamics of Responses to Stress', *Journal of Applied Psychology* 91, no. 5 (2006): 1037–1052; M. T. Gailliot and R. F. Baumeister, 'Self-Esteem, Belongingness, and Worldview Validation: Does Belongingness Exert a Unique Influence Upon Self-Esteem?', *Journal of Research in Personality* 41, no. 2 (2007): 327–345.

6 S. Cohen, 'The Pittsburgh Common Cold Studies: Psychosocial Predictors of Susceptibility to Respiratory Infectious Illness', *International Journal of Behavioral Medicine* 12, no. 3 (2005): 123–131; B. N. Uchino, 'Social Support and Health: A Review of Physiological Processes Potentially Underlying Links to Disease Outcomes', *Journal of Behavioral Medicine* 29, no. 4 (2006): 377–387.

7 D. Kirkpatrick, 'It's Not a Game', *Fortune*, 5 February 2007, 34–38.

8 L. Reynolds, E. C. Bush and R. Geist, 'The Gen Y Imperative', *Communication World*, March–April 2008, 19–22.

9 C. E. Shannon and W. Weaver, *The Mathematical Theory of Communication* (Urbana, IL: University of Illinois Press, 1949); R. M. Krauss and S. R. Fussell, 'Social Psychological Models of Interpersonal Communication', in *Social Psychology: Handbook of Basic Principles*, ed. E. T. Higgins and A. Kruglanski (New York: Guilford Press, 1996), 655–701.

10 J. R. Carlson and R. W. Zmud, 'Channel Expansion Theory and the Experiential Nature of Media Richness Perceptions', *Academy of Management Journal* 42 (April 1999): 153–170.

11 P. Shachaf and N. Hara, 'Behavioral Complexity Theory of Media Selection: A Proposed Theory for Global Virtual Teams', *Journal of Information Science* 33, no .1 (2007): 63–75.

12 N. B. Ducheneaut and L. A. Watts, 'In Search of Coherence: A Review of E-Mail Research', *Human-Computer Interaction* 20, no. 1/2 (2005): 11–48.

13 W. Lucas, 'Effects of E-Mail on the Organization', *European Management Journal* 16, no. 1 (1998): 18–30; D. A. Owens, M. A. Neale and R. I. Sutton, 'Technologies of Status Management Status Dynamics in E-Mail Communications', *Research on Managing Groups and Teams* 3 (2000): 205–230; N. B. Ducheneaut, 'Ceci N'est Pas Un Objet? Talking about Objects in E-Mail', *Human-Computer Interaction* 18, no. 1/2 (2003): 85–110.

14 N. B. Ducheneaut, 'The Social Impacts of Electronic Mail in Organizations: A Case Study of Electronic Power Games Using Communication Genres', *Information, Communication & Society* 5, no. 2 (2002): 153–188; N. Panteli, 'Richness, Power Cues and Email Text', *Information & Management* 40, no. 2 (2002): 75–86.

15 N. Epley and J. Kruger, 'When What You Type Isn't What They Read: The Perseverance of Stereotypes and Expectancies over E-Mail', *Journal of Experimental Social Psychology* 41, no. 4 (2005): 414–422.

16 J. B. Walther, 'Language and Communication Technology: Introduction to the Special Issue', *Journal of Language and Social Psychology* 23, no. 4 (2004): 384–396; J. B. Walther, T. Loh and L. Granka, 'Let Me Count the Ways: The Interchange of Verbal and Nonverbal Cues in Computer-Mediated and Face-to-Face Affinity', *Journal of Language and Social Psychology* 24, no. 1 (2005): 36–65; K. Byron, 'Carrying Too Heavy a Load? The Communication and Miscommunication of Emotion by Email', *Academy of Management Review* 33, no. 2 (2008): 309–327.

17 S. Williams, 'Apologies and Rows by Email Are a New Sin for Hi-Tech Cowards', *Western Mail (Cardiff, Wales)*, 1 April 2006, 11.

18 G. Hertel, S. Geister and U. Konradt, 'Managing Virtual Teams: A Review of Current Empirical Research', *Human*

Resource Management Review 15, no. 1 (2005): 69–95; H. Lee, 'Behavioral Strategies for Dealing with Flaming in an Online Forum', *The Sociological Quarterly* 46, no. 2 (2005): 385–403.

19 K. Cox, 'Irving Oil Fuels Its Leaders', *Globe & Mail (Toronto)*, 21 April 2004, C1.

20 D. D. Dawley and W. P. Anthony, 'User Perceptions of E-Mail at Work', *Journal of Business and Technical Communication* 17, no. 2 (2003): 170–200; 'Email Brings Costs and Fatigue', *Western News (University of Western Ontario) (London, Ontario)*, 9 July 2004; G. F. Thomas and C. L. King, 'Reconceptualizing E-Mail Overload', *Journal of Business and Technical Communication* 20, no. 3 (2006): 252–287; S. Carr, 'Email Overload Menace Growing', *Silicon.com*, 12 July 2007.

21 H. Jewitt, 'Tackling Tormentors', *Employer's Law*, November 2007, 14–15; M. Kubicek, 'Virtual Fighters', *Personnel Today*, December 2008, 18–20.

22 W. M. Bulkeley, 'Playing Well with Others: How IBM's Employees Have Taken Social Networking to an Unusual Level', *Wall Street Journal*, 18 June 2007, R10; M. Rauch, 'Virtual Reality', *Sales & Marketing Management* 159, no. 1 (2007): 18–23.

23 K. Brewis, 'Who's Pressing Your Buttons?', *Sunday Times Magazine (UK)*, 3 February 2008, 14.

24 A. F. Cameron and J. Webster, 'Unintended Consequences of Emerging Communication Technologies: Instant Messaging in the Workplace', *Computers in Human Behavior* 21, no. 1 (2005): 85–103.

25 H. Green, 'The Water Cooler Is Now on the Web', *BusinessWeek*, 1 October 2007, 78; N. J. Hoover, 'Social Experiment', *InformationWeek*, 24 September 2007, 40; C. Boulton, 'IBM's Social Beehive and Discovery Search', *eWeek.com*, 21 January 2008.

26 C. Wagner and A. Majchrzak, 'Enabling Customer-Centricity Using Wikis and the Wiki Way', *Journal of Management Information Systems* 23, no. 3 (2006): 17–43; R. B. Ferguson, 'Build a Web 2.0 Platform and Employees Will Use It', *eWeek*, 20 June 2007; C. Karena, 'Working the Wiki Way', *Sydney Morning Herald*, 6 March 2007.

27 Bennett, 'You Have Been Poked, High-Fived and Had a Ninja Sent after You'; R. Ottley, 'Office Surveillance', *Mondaq Business Briefing*, 12 August 2008; R. Hewitt , 'Oh Brother, Some Bosses Are So Nosy', *MX (Melbourne)*, 28 July 2008, 6; P. Barclay, 'Privacy Laws', *Australia Talks*, radio program, 19 August 2008 (Canberra: ABC Radio National).

28 L. Z. Tiedens and A. R. Fragale, 'Power Moves: Complementarity in Dominant and Submissive Nonverbal Behavior', *Journal of Personality and Social Psychology* 84, no. 3 (2003): 558–568.

29 P. Ekman and E. Rosenberg, *What the Face Reveals: Basic and Applied Studies of Spontaneous Expression Using the Facial Action Coding System* (Oxford: Oxford University Press, 1997); P. Winkielman and K. C. Berridge, 'Unconscious Emotion', *Current Directions in Psychological Science* 13, no. 3 (2004): 120–123.

30 J. J. Bradac, 'Language Attitudes and Impression Formation', in *Handbook of Language and Social Psychology*, ed. H. Giles and W. P. Robinson (Chichester, UK: Wiley, 1990), 387–412; P. Brown and S. C. Levinson, *Politeness: Some Universals in Language Usage* (Cambridge: Cambridge University Press, 1987); A. Donellon, 'Team Work: Linguistic Models of Negotiating Differences', *Research on Negotiation in Organizations* 4 (1994): 71–124; D. Tannen, *Gender and Discourse* (New York: Oxford University Press, 1994).

31 P. Ekman, *Telling Lies: Clues to Deceit in the Marketplace, Politics and Marriage* (New York: W.W. Norton & Co, 2001); B. M. DePaulo *et al.*, 'Cues to Deception', *Psychological Bulletin* 129, no. 1 (2003): 74–118.

32 E. Hatfield, J. T. Cacioppo and R. L. Rapson, *Emotional Contagion* (Cambridge, UK: Cambridge University Press, 1993); S. G. Barsade, 'The Ripple Effect: Emotional Contagion and Its Influence on Group Behavior', *Administrative Science Quarterly* 47, no. 4 (2002): 644–675; M. Sonnby-Borgstrom, P. Jonsson and O. Svensson, 'Emotional Empathy as Related to Mimicry Reactions at Different Levels of Information Processing', *Journal of Nonverbal Behavior* 27 (Spring 2003): 3–23; S. G. Barsade and D. E. Gibson, 'Why Does Affect Matter in Organizations?', *Academy of Management Perspectives* (February 2007): 36–59; S. K. Johnson, 'I Second That Emotion: Effects of Emotional Contagion and Affect at Work on Leader and Follower Outcomes', *Leadership Quarterly* 19, no. 1 (2008): 1–19.

33 J. R. Kelly and S. G. Barsade, 'Mood and Emotions in Small Groups and Work Teams', *Organizational Behavior and Human Decision Processes* 86, no. 1 (2001): 99–130.

34 L. K. Treviño, J. Webster and E. W. Stein, 'Making Connections: Complementary Influences on Communication Media Choices, Attitudes, and Use', *Organization Science* 11, no. 2 (2000): 163–182; B. Barry and I. S. Fulmer, 'The Medium Is the Message: The Adaptive Use of Communication Media in Dyadic Influence', *Academy of Management Review* 29, no. 2 (2004): 272–292; J. W. Turner *et al.*, 'Exploring the Dominant Media: How Does Media Use Reflect Organizational Norms and Affect Performance?', *Journal of Business Communication* 43, no. 3 (2006): 220–250; M. B. Watson-Manheim and F. Bélanger, 'Communication Media Repertoires: Dealing with the Multiplicity of Media Choices', *MIS Quarterly* 31, no. 2 (2007): 267–293.

35 R. C. King, 'Media Appropriateness: Effects of Experience on Communication Media Choice', *Decision Sciences* 28, no. 4 (1997): 877–910.

36 K. Griffiths, 'KPMG Sacks 670 Employees by E-Mail', *The Independent (London)*, 5 November 2002, 19; 'Shop Worker Sacked by Text Message', *The Post (Perth, Western Australia)*, 28 July 2007, 1, 78.

37 R. L. Daft and R. H. Lengel, 'Information Richness: A New Approach to Managerial Behavior and Organization Design', *Research in Organizational Behavior* 6 (1984): 191–233; R. H. Lengel and R. L. Daft, 'The Selection of Communication Media as an Executive Skill', *Academy of Management Executive* 2 (1988): 225–232.

38 R. E. Rice, 'Task Analyzability, Use of New Media, and Effectiveness: A Multi-Site Exploration of Media Richness', *Organization Science* 3, no. 4 (1992): 475–500.

39 J. W. Turner and N. L. Reinsch Jr, 'The Business Communicator as Presence Allocator', *Journal of Business Communication* 44, no. 1 (2007): 36–58; N. L. Reinsch, J. W. Turner and C. H. Tinsley, 'Multicommunicating: A Practice Whose Time Has Come?', *Academy of Management Review* 33, no. 2 (2008): 391–403.

40 Carlson and Zmud, 'Channel Expansion Theory and the Experiential Nature of Media Richness Perceptions'; N. Kock, 'Media Richness or Media Naturalness? The Evolution of Our Biological Communication Apparatus and Its Influence on Our Behavior toward E-Communication Tools', *IEEE Transactions on Professional Communication* 48, no. 2 (2005): 117–130.

41 D. Muller, T. Atzeni and F. Butera, 'Coaction and Upward Social Comparison Reduce the Illusory Conjunction Effect: Support for Distraction-Conflict Theory', *Journal of Experimental Social Psychology* 40, no. 5 (2004): 659–665; L. P. Robert and A. R. Dennis, 'Paradox of Richness: A Cognitive Model of Media Choice', *IEEE Transactions on Professional Communication* 48, no. 1 (2005): 10–21.

42 E. V. Wilson, 'Perceived Effectiveness of Interpersonal Persuasion Strategies in Computer-Mediated Communication', *Computers in Human Behavior* 19, no. 5 (2003): 537–552; K. Sassenberg, M. Boos and S. Rabung, 'Attitude Change in Face-to-Face and Computer-Mediated Communication: Private Self-Awareness as Mediator and Moderator', *European Journal of Social Psychology* 35, no. 3 (2005): 361–374; P. Di Blasio and L. Milani, 'Computer-Mediated Communication and Persuasion: Peripheral vs. Central Route to Opinion Shift', *Computers in Human Behavior* 24, no. 3 (2008): 798–815.

43 J. Kruger *et al.*, 'Egocentrism over E-Mail: Can We Communicate as Well as We Think?', *Journal of Personality and Social Psychology* 89, no. 6 (2005): 925–936.

44 D. Goleman, R. Boyatzis and A. McKee, *Primal Leaders* (Boston: Harvard Business School Press, 2002), 92–95.

45 M. C. Bolino and W. H. Turnley, 'Counternormative Impression Management, Likeability, and Performance Ratings: The Use of Intimidation in an Organizational Setting', *Journal of Organizational Behavior* 24, no. 2 (2003): 237–250; L. L. Carli, 'Gender Differences in Interaction Style and Influence', *Journal of Personality and Social Psychology* 56, no. 4 (1989): 565–576; S. T. Fiske and S. E. Taylor, *Social Cognition*, 2nd edn (New York: McGraw-Hill, 1991); L. A. Rudman and J. E. Phelan, 'Backlash Effects for Disconfirming Gender Stereotypes in Organizations', *Research in Organizational Behavior* 28 (2008): 61–79.

46 D. Woodruff, 'Crossing Culture Divide Early Clears Merger Paths', *Asian Wall Street Journal*, 28 May 2001, 9.

47 T. Walsh, 'Nardelli Brags on VIP Recruits, Game Plan', *Detroit Free Press*, 8 September 2007.

48 R. M. Krauss, 'The Psychology of Verbal Communication', in *International Encyclopedia of the Social and Behavioral Sciences*, ed. N. Smelser and P. Baltes (London: Elsevier, 2002), 16161–16165.

49 L. L. Putnam, N. Phillips and P. Chapman, 'Metaphors of Communication and Organization', in *Handbook of Organization Studies*, ed. S. R. Clegg, C. Hardy and W. R. Nord (London: Sage, 1996), 373–408; G. Morgan, *Images of Organization*, 2nd edn (Thousand Oaks, CA: Sage, 1997); M. Rubini and H. Sigall, 'Taking the Edge Off of Disagreement: Linguistic Abstractness and Self-Presentation to a Heterogeneous Audience', *European Journal of Social Psychology* 32, no. 3 (2002): 343–351.

50 T. Koski, 'Reflections on Information Glut and Other Issues in Knowledge Productivity', *Futures* 33 (August 2001): 483–495.

51 A. G. Schick, L. A. Gordon and S. Haka, 'Information Overload: A Temporal Approach', *Accounting, Organizations and Society* 15, no. 3 (1990): 199–220; A. Edmunds and A. Morris, 'The Problem of Information Overload in Business Organisations: A Review of the Literature', *International Journal of Information Management* 20, no. 1 (2000): 17–28; R. Pennington, 'The Effects of Information Overload on Software Project Risk Assessment', *Decision Sciences* 38, no. 3 (2007): 489–526.

52 D. C. Thomas and K. Inkson, *Cultural Intelligence: People Skills for Global Business* (San Francisco: Berrett-Koehler, 2004), ch. 6; D. Welch, L. Welch and R. Piekkari, 'Speaking in Tongues', *International Studies of Management & Organization* 35, no. 1 (2005): 10–27.

53 S. T. Ohtaki and M. D. Fetters, 'Doctor-Patient Communication: A Comparison of the USA and Japan', *Family Practice* 20 (June 2003): 276–282; M. Fujio, 'Silence

During Intercultural Communication: A Case Study', *Corporate Communications* 9, no. 4 (2004): 331–339.

54 D. C. Barnlund, *Communication Styles of Japanese and Americans: Images and Realities* (Belmont, CA: Wadsworth, 1988); H. Yamada, *American and Japanese Business Discourse: A Comparison of Interaction Styles* (Norwood, NJ: Ablex, 1992), ch. 2; H. Yamada, *Different Games, Different Rules* (New York: Oxford University Press, 1997), 76–79.

55 R. Hicks, 'Asia: A Rough Guide to Asian Business Etiquette', *Campaign*, 2 November 2007, 24–25.

56 P. Harris and R. Moran, *Managing Cultural Differences* (Houston: Gulf, 1987); H. Blagg, 'A Just Measure of Shame?', *British Journal of Criminology* 37 (Autumn 1997): 481–501; R. E. Axtell, *Gestures: The Do's and Taboos of Body Language around the World*, revised edn (New York: Wiley, 1998).

57 D. Tannen, *You Just Don't Understand: Men and Women in Conversation* (New York: Ballentine Books, 1990); D. Tannen, *Talking from 9 to 5* (New York: Avon, 1994); M. Crawford, *Talking Difference: On Gender and Language* (Thousand Oaks, CA: Sage, 1995), 41–44; L. L. Namy, L. C. Nygaard and D. Sauerteig, 'Gender Differences in Vocal Accommodation: The Role of Perception', *Journal of Language and Social Psychology* 21, no. 4 (2002): 422–432; H. Itakura and A. B. M. Tsui, 'Gender and Conversational Dominance in Japanese Conversation', *Language in Society* 33, no. 2 (2004): 223–248.

58 E. Aries, *Men and Women in Interaction: Reconsidering the Differences* (New York: Oxford University Press, 1996); Carli, 'Gender Differences in Interaction Style and Influence'; L. L. Carli, 'Gender, Language, and Influence', *Journal of Personality and Social Psychology* 59, no. 5 (1990): 941–951.

59 Bradac, 'Language Attitudes and Impression Formation'; J. J. Bradac, A. Mulac and S. A. Thompson, 'Men's and Women's Use of Intensifiers and Hedges in Problem-Solving Interaction: Molar and Molecular Analyses', *Research on Language and Social Interaction* 28, no. 2 (1995): 93–116; A. Mulac and J. J. Bradac, 'Women's Style in Problem-Solving Interaction: Powerless, or Simply Feminine?', in *Gender, Power, and Communication in Human Relationships*, ed. P. J. Kalbfleisch and M. J. Cody (Hillsdale, NJ: Lawrence Erlbaum, 1995); D. Tannen, *Gender and Discourse* (New York: Oxford University Press, 1994), 83–104.

60 A. Mulac *et al.*, '"Uh-Huh. What's That All About?" Differing Interpretations of Conversational Backchannels and Questions as Sources of Miscommunication across Gender Boundaries', *Communication Research* 25 (December 1998): 641–668; N. M. Sussman and D. H. Tyson, 'Sex and Power: Gender Differences in Computer-Mediated Interactions', *Computers in Human Behavior* 16 (2000): 381–394; D. R. Caruso and P. Salovey, *The Emotionally Intelligent Manager* (San Francisco: Jossey-Bass, 2004), 23; D. Fallows, *How Women and Men Use the Internet*, (Washington, D.C.: Pew Internet and American Life Project, 28 December 2005).

61 K. Davis and J. W. Newstrom, *Human Behavior at Work: Organizational Behavior*, 7th edn (New York: McGraw–Hill, 1985), 413.

62 The three components of listening discussed here are based on several studies in the field of marketing, including: S. B. Castleberry, C. D. Shepherd and R. Ridnour, 'Effective Interpersonal Listening in the Personal Selling Environment: Conceptualization, Measurement, and Nomological Validity', *Journal of Marketing Theory and Practice* 7 (Winter 1999): 30–38; L. B. Comer and T. Drollinger, 'Active Empathetic Listening and Selling Success: A Conceptual Framework', *Journal of Personal Selling & Sales Management* 19 (Winter 1999): 15–29; K. de Ruyter and M. G. M. Wetzels, 'The Impact of Perceived Listening Behavior in Voice-to-Voice Service Encounters', *Journal of Service Research* 2 (February 2000): 276–284.

63 'Jal Reform Step Ejects Execs from Private Rooms', *Japan Times*, 17 May 2007.

64 A. Leaman and B. Bordass, 'Productivity in Buildings: The Killer Variables', *Building Research & Information* 27, no. 1 (1999): 4–19; T. J. Allen, 'Architecture and Communication among Product Development Engineers', *California Management Review* 49, no. 2 (2007): 23–41; F. Becker, 'Organizational Ecology and Knowledge Networks', *California Management Review* 49, no. 2 (2007): 42–61.

65 M. Gardner, 'Democratic Principles Make Businesses More Transparent', *Christian Science Monitor*, 19 March 2007, 13.

66 G. Evans and D. Johnson, 'Stress and Open-Office Noise', *Journal of Applied Psychology* 85, no. 5 (2000): 779–783; F. Russo, 'My Kingdom for a Door', *Time Magazine*, 23 October 2000, B1.

67 S. P. Means, 'Playing at Pixar', *Salt Lake Tribune (Utah)*, 30 May 2003, D1; G. Whipp, 'Swimming against the Tide', *Daily News of Los Angeles*, 30 May 2003, U6.

68 J. Rickett, 'Open-Plan Office Politics', *The Bookseller*, no. 5307 (2007), 34–35.

69 E. Cone, 'Rise of the Blog', *CIO Insight*, April 2005, 54; M. Delio, 'The Enterprise Blogosphere', *InfoWorld*, 28 March 2005, 42–47.

70 T. Fenton, 'Inside the WorldBlu List: 1-800-Got-Junk?'s CEO on Why "Being Democratic Is Extremely Important to Maintaining Our Competitive Advantage"' (Atlanta: WorldBlu, 3 January 2008). The original term is 'management by *wandering* around', but this has been

replaced with 'walking around' over the years. See W. Ouchi, *Theory Z* (New York: Avon Books, 1981), 176–177; T. Peters and R. Waterman, *In Search of Excellence* (New York: Harper & Row, 1982), 122.

71 D. Thomas, 'HR Challenges ... I'm Lovin' It', *Personnel Today*, 6 September 2005, 11.

72 R. Rousos, 'Trust in Leaders Lacking at Utility', *The Ledger (Lakeland, FL)*, 29 July 2003, B1; B. Whitworth and B. Riccomini, 'Management Communication: Unlocking Higher Employee Performance', *Communication World*, March/April 2005, 18–21.

73 K. Davis, 'Management Communication and the Grapevine', *Harvard Business Review* 31 (September–October 1953): 43–49; W. L. Davis and J. R. O'Connor, 'Serial Transmission of Information: A Study of the Grapevine', *Journal of Applied Communication Research* 5 (1977): 61–72.

74 H. Mintzberg, *The Structuring of Organizations* (Englewood Cliffs, NJ: Prentice Hall, 1979), 46–53; D. Krackhardt and J. R. Hanson, 'Informal Networks: The Company Behind the Chart', *Harvard Business Review* 71 (July–August 1993): 104–111.

75 C. J. Walker and C. A. Beckerle, 'The Effect of State Anxiety on Rumor Transmission', *Journal of Social Behaviour and Personality* 2 (August 1987): 353–360; R. L. Rosnow, 'Inside Rumor: A Personal Journey', *American Psychologist* 46 (May 1991): 484–496; M. Noon and R. Delbridge, 'News from Behind My Hand: Gossip in Organizations', *Organization Studies* 14, no. 1 (1993): 23–36.

76 N. Nicholson, 'Evolutionary Psychology: Toward a New View of Human Nature and Organizational Society', *Human Relations* 50, no. 9 (1997): 1053–1078; R. F. Baumeister, L. Zhang and K. D. Vohs, 'Gossip as Cultural Learning', *Review of General Psychology* 8, no. 2 (2004): 111–121; E. K. Foster, 'Research on Gossip: Taxonomy, Methods, and Future Directions', *Review of General Psychology* 8, no. 2 (2004): 78–99.

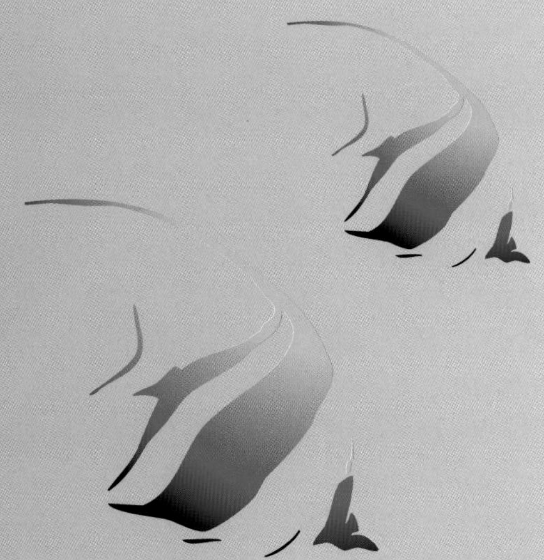

CHAPTER 10

power and influence in the workplace

LEARNING OBJECTIVES

After reading this chapter, you should be able to:

- define power and countervailing power
- describe the five sources of power in organisations
- explain how information relates to power in organisations
- discuss the four contingencies of power
- summarise the effects of power on the powerholder's own performance and wellbeing
- summarise the eight types of influence tactics
- discuss three contingencies to consider when deciding which influence tactic to use
- describe the key elements of social networks
- distinguish influence from organisational politics
- describe the organisational conditions and personal characteristics that support organisational politics
- identify ways to minimise organisational politics.

Andersen Ross/Getty

Workplace bullying isn't always this overt.

When her manager called her 'the dragon', 'useless' and threatened to 'plant her one', Sandra McCullough took her employer, Otago Sheetmetal, to court. Recognising that she was being bullied, the court awarded her compensation as a result of her workplace experiences. In another case, junior doctors at Auckland's City Hospital made the headlines when they claimed they were subjected to a range of bullying behaviours.

Bullying is an abuse of either formal or informal power in the workplace. Estimates put the cost of workplace bullying at up to $13 billion per year, once absenteeism, lower productivity, decreased performance and turnover are accounted for.

The image of bullies is one of the powerful tyrannising the powerless. However, this need not always be the case. Susan, a manager in an Australian organisation, discovered this after giving performance feedback to one of her staff members. Her employee became emotional, criticised Susan and looked to other team members for support. Over time, Susan's team started to exclude her from their social activities. She was being bullied by her staff. What happened to Susan occurs in workplaces around the world.

What we see is that increased power can lessen the constraints that individuals place on their behaviour. Unjustified criticism, having the value of your work undermined, humiliation and verbal threats are all examples of the use of coercive power. These actions punish individuals by undermining their self-esteem, socially isolating them and creating a climate of fear in which the bully can control behaviour. As competition increases in the workplace, some managers look for scapegoats who can be blamed for errors or poor organisational performance. Power harassment, which involves attacking the self-esteem of employees, often targets vulnerable employees, such as part-time female workers and temporary employees. The number of harassment cases, including power harassment, dealt with by the Tokyo Metropolitan Labour Consultation Centre increased from 2852 in the 2003 financial year to 5258 in 2007.

There are also more subtle forms of bullying, such as the social exclusion experienced by Susan. According to Caroline Dean, who works with Tasmanian businesses to manage bullying, gossip and rumours can aid bullying. 'Men are more likely to bully directly by abusing staff, putting people down, making inappropriate comments and using offensive language ... Women are a bit more covert and are more likely to start rumours or deliberately ostracise people.'[1]

Criticism, rumours, ridicule and unwanted jokes all contribute to creating a hostile work climate. This situation arises when individuals with power feel there are no constraints on their behaviour. As we saw in the opening story, the behaviour of bullies in the workplace has negative consequences not only for the targets of bullying but also the organisation. To victims of bullying, the workplace feels increasingly unwelcome, so they work less effectively, are absent more often and may ultimately leave. In the worst cases, they may seek compensation from the organisations that failed to protect them. Although this story illustrates the dark side of power and influence, these concepts are equally relevant to ethical conduct and organisational performance. In fact, some OB experts point out that power and influence are inherent in all organisations. They exist in every business, and in every decision and action.

This chapter unfolds as follows: first, we define power and present a basic model depicting the dynamics of power in organisational settings. The chapter then discusses the five sources of power, as well as information as a power base. Next, we look at the contingencies necessary to translate those sources into meaningful power. The latter part of this chapter examines the various types of influence in organisational settings as well as the contingencies of effective influence strategies. We then look at one powerful tool for increasing power and influence—the social network. The final section of this chapter looks at situations in which influence becomes organisational politics, as well as ways of minimising dysfunctional politics.

Define power and countervailing power.

THE MEANING OF POWER

power The capacity of a person, team or organisation to influence others.

Power is the capacity of a person, team or organisation to influence others.[2] Power is not the act of changing someone's attitudes or behaviour; it is only the potential to do so. People frequently have power they do not use; they might not even know they have power. Also, power is not a personal feeling of power. You might feel powerful or think you have power over someone else, but this is not power unless you truly have the capacity to influence that person. The most basic prerequisite of power is that one person or group believes it is dependent on another person or group for a resource of value.[3] This relationship, shown in Exhibit 10.1, occurs where Person A has power over Person B by controlling something that Person B wants. You might have power over others by controlling a desired job assignment, useful information, important resources or even the privilege of being associated with you! However, power requires the *perception* of dependence, so people might gain power by convincing others that they have something of value, whether or not they actually control that resource. Thus, power exists when others believe that you control resources they want.

countervailing power The capacity of a person, team or organisation to keep a more powerful person or group in the exchange relationship.

Although dependence is a key element of power relationships, it is really more accurate to say that the parties are *interdependent*.[4] In Exhibit 10.1, Person A dominates in the power relationship, but Person B also has some **countervailing power**—enough power to keep Person A in the exchange relationship and ensure that they use their dominant power judiciously. For example, executives have power over subordinates by controlling their job security and promotional opportunities. At the same time, employees have countervailing power by possessing skills and knowledge to keep production humming and customers happy, something that executives can't accomplish alone. Finally, the power relationship depends on some minimum level of trust. Trust indicates a level of expectation that the more powerful party will deliver the resource. For example, you trust your employer to give you a pay cheque at the end of each pay period. Even

Exhibit 10.1 *Dependence in the Power Relationship*

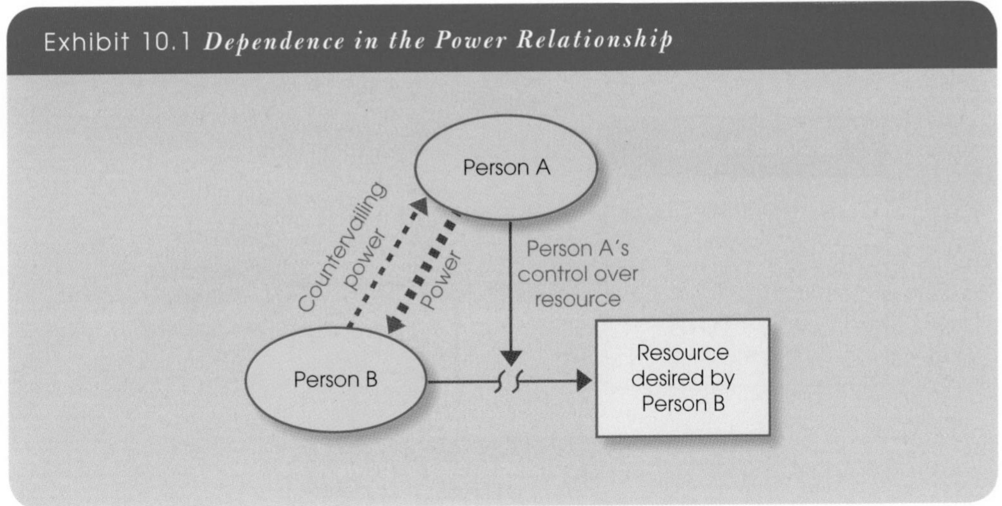

those in extremely dependent situations will usually walk away from the relationship if they lack a minimum level of trust in the more powerful party.

A Model of Power in Organisations

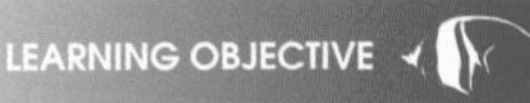

Describe the five sources of power in organisations.

Power involves more than just dependence or interdependence. As Exhibit 10.2 illustrates, power is derived from five sources: legitimate, reward, coercive, expert and referent. The model also indicates that these sources yield power only under certain conditions. The four contingencies of power include the employee's or department's substitutability, centrality, discretion and visibility. Finally, as you will read later in this chapter, the type of power applied affects the type of influence the powerholder has over the other person or work unit.

SOURCES OF POWER IN ORGANISATIONS

Power derives from several sources and a few contingencies that determine the potential of those power sources.[5] Three sources of power—legitimate, reward and coercive—originate mostly from the powerholder's formal position or informal role. In other words, the person is granted these sources of power formally by the organisation or informally by coworkers. Two other sources of power—expert and referent—originate from the powerholder's own characteristics; that is, they bring these power bases to the organisation. Sources of power are resources that help the dependent person directly or indirectly achieve his or her goals. For example, your expertise is a source of power when others need that expertise to accomplish their objectives.

Legitimate Power

legitimate power An agreement among organisational members that people in certain roles can request certain behaviours of others.

Legitimate power is an agreement among organisational members that people in certain roles can request certain behaviours of others. This perceived right originates from formal job descriptions as well as informal rules of conduct. This legitimate power extends to employees, not just managers. For example, an organisation might give employees the right to request customer

Exhibit 10.2 *A Model of Power Within Organisations*

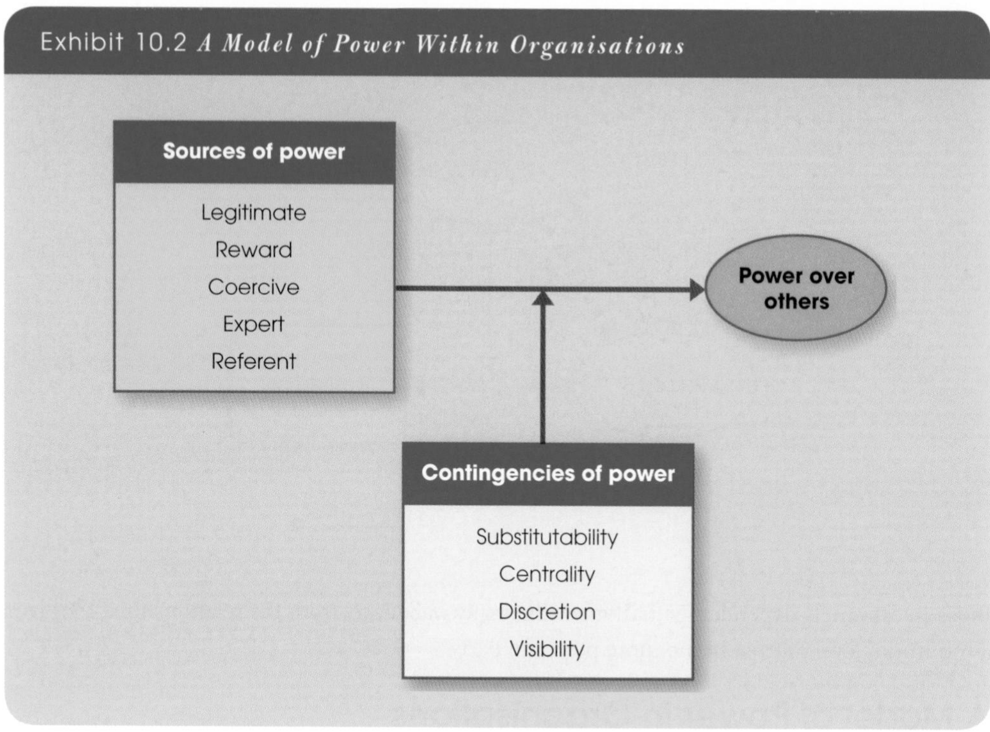

files if this information is required for their job. Legitimate power depends on more than job descriptions. It also depends on mutual agreement from those expected to abide by this authority. Your boss's power to make you work overtime partly depends on your agreement to this authority. Thus, legitimate power operates within a 'zone of indifference'—the range within which people are willing to accept someone else's authority.[6]

The size of this zone of indifference (and, consequently, the magnitude of legitimate power) increases with the extent that the powerholder is trusted and makes fair decisions. Some people are also more obedient than others to authority, particularly those who value conformity and tradition. People in high power-distance cultures (i.e. those who accept an unequal distribution of power) also tend to have higher obedience to authority compared with people in low power-distance cultures. The organisation's culture represents a third factor. A 3M scientist might continue to work on a project after being told by superiors to stop working on it because the 3M culture supports an entrepreneurial spirit, which includes ignoring your boss's authority from time to time.[7]

Reward Power

Reward power is derived from the person's ability to control the allocation of rewards valued by others and to remove negative sanctions (i.e. negative reinforcement). Managers have formal authority that gives them power over the distribution of organisational rewards such as pay, promotions, time off, vacation schedules and work assignments. Employees also have reward power over their bosses through the use of 360-degree feedback systems. Employee feedback affects supervisors' promotions and other rewards, so they tend to behave differently toward employees after 360-degree feedback is introduced.

DeCourcy's Trendspotting Power

Colleen DeCourcy has seen the future of digital marketing—and we're definitely not there yet. 'I think we have a long way to go before we're really using technology in marketing,' says the chief digital officer at advertising agency TBWA. 'We're all in this very sophomoric stage, trying to figure out a new medium.' Digital media may be new, but many people in the creative business say DeCourcy is better than most people at predicting digital trends and helping clients to benefit from them. 'Her knowledge of the digital landscape, grounded in creativity, make her an invaluable additional to TBWA,' says Decourcy's boss, TBWA Worldwide CEO Tom Carroll. Ty Montague, copresident of JWT in New York and DeCourcy's former employer, agrees: 'It's hard to overstate the impact she's had.' For example, DeCourcy was an early adopter of marketing to the younger generation through mobile phone ringtones and social network media (e.g. Facebook). Her ability to predict and manage the volatile digital marketing landscape has given her considerable expert and informational power in the industry. She uses her skills to reduce uncertainty for others. For example, when sportswear company Adidas recently picked TBWA to handle its global digital marketing work, TBWA put DeCourcy in charge of a new company in Amsterdam (called Riot) to exclusively handle this account. Also, DeCourcy was selected as president of the jury that picks the best digital advertising entries at the Cannes Lions International Advertising Festival.[13]

Erwin Brown

Coercive Power

Coercive power is the ability to apply punishment. The opening story to this chapter described how coercive power can be used to bully and intimidate employees. Employees also have coercive power, ranging from sarcasm to ostracism, to ensure that coworkers conform to team norms. Many firms rely on this coercive power to control coworker behaviour in team settings. Nucor is one such example: 'If you're not contributing with the team, they certainly will let you know about it,' says Dan Krug, manager of HR and organisational development at the steelmaker in Charlotte, North Carolina. 'The few poor players get weeded out by their peers.' Similarly, when asked how AirAsia maintained attendance and productivity after the Malaysian discount airline removed the time clocks, chief executive Tony Fernandes replied: 'Simple. Peer pressure sees to that. The fellow employees, who are putting their shoulders to the wheel, will see to that.'[8]

Expert Power

For the most part, legitimate, reward and coercive power originate from the position.[9] In contrast, expert power originates from within the person. It is an individual's or work unit's capacity to influence others by possessing knowledge or skills that they value. Employees are gaining expert power as our society moves from an industrial to a knowledge-based economy.[10] The reason is that employee knowledge becomes the means of production and is ultimately outside the control of those who own the company. And without this control over production, owners are more dependent on employees to achieve their corporate objectives.

The power of expertise is most apparent when observing how people respond to authority figures.[11] In one classic study, a researcher posing as a hospital physician telephoned on-duty nurses to prescribe a specific dosage of medicine to a hospitalised patient. None of the nurses knew the person calling, and hospital policy prohibited them from accepting treatment by telephone. Furthermore, the medication was unauthorised and the prescription was twice the maximum daily dose. Yet almost all 22 nurses who received the telephone call followed the 'doctor's' orders until stopped by researchers.[12]

Referent Power

referent power The capacity to influence others on the basis of an identification with and respect for the powerholder.

People have **referent power** when others identify with them, like them or otherwise respect them. Like expert power, referent power comes from within the person. It is largely a function of the person's interpersonal skills and tends to develop slowly. Referent power is usually associated with charismatic leadership. Experts have difficulty agreeing on the meaning of *charisma*, but it is most often described as a form of interpersonal attraction whereby followers ascribe almost magical powers to the charismatic individual.[14] Some experts describe charisma is a special 'gift' or trait within the charismatic person, while others say it is mainly in the eyes of the beholder. However, all agree that charisma produces a high degree of trust, respect and devotion towards the charismatic individual.

Explain how information relates to power in organisations.

Information and Power

Information is power.[15] In one form, people gain information power when they control (through legitimate power) the flow of information to others. Employees are ultimately dependent on these information gatekeepers to release the information required to perform their jobs. Furthermore, by deciding what information is distributed to whom, those who control information flow also control perceptions of the situation by releasing information favouring one perspective more than another.[16] This right to control information flow is a form of legitimate power and is most common in highly bureaucratic firms. The wheel formation in Exhibit 10.3 depicts this highly centralised control over information flow. The all-channels structure, on the other hand, depicts a situation where no one has control over the flow of information. The former would occur when information must flow through your boss to you, whereas the latter occurs when information is distributed to many people, such as coworkers in a self-directed team.

The other form of information power occurs when a person or work unit has the ability—or is believed to have the ability—to manage environmental uncertainties. This capability, which is a derivative of expert power, is valued because organisations are more effective when they can operate in predictable environments. A groundbreaking study of breweries and container companies identified three general strategies to help organisations cope with uncertainty. These coping strategies are arranged in a hierarchy of importance, with the first being the most powerful:[17]

PREVENTION The most effective strategy is to prevent environmental changes from occurring. For example, financial experts acquire power by preventing the organisation from experiencing a cash shortage or defaulting on loans.

FORECASTING The next best strategy is to predict environmental changes or variations. In this respect, trendspotters and other marketing specialists gain power by predicting changes in consumer preferences.

Exhibit 10.3 *Power Through the Control of Information*

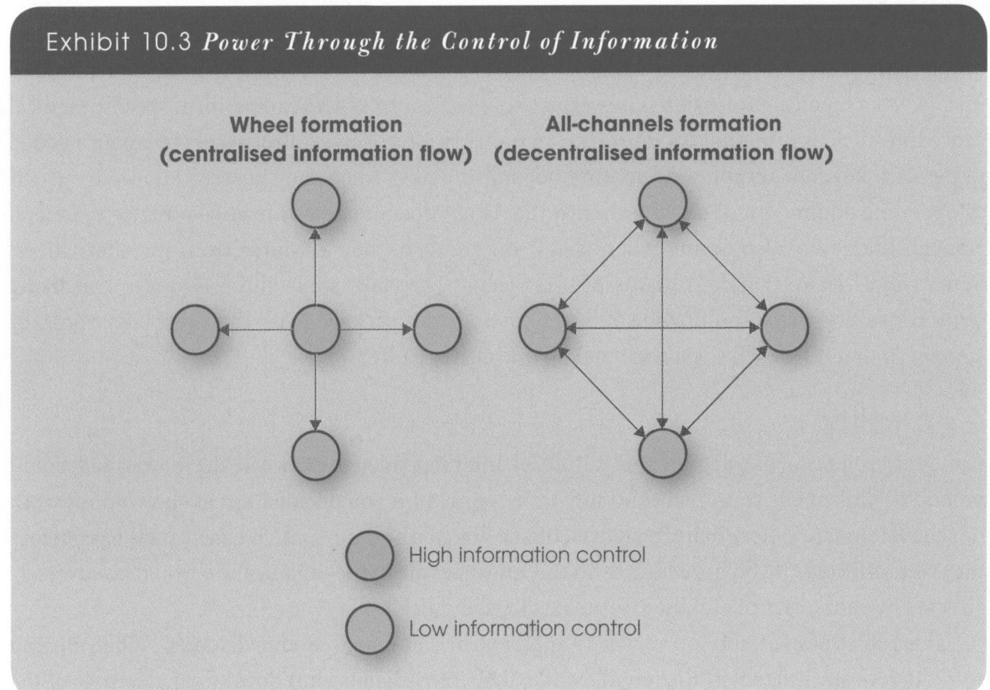

ABSORPTION People and work units also gain power by absorbing or neutralising the impact of environmental shifts as they occur. An example is the ability of maintenance crews to come to the rescue when machines break down and the production process stops.

CONTINGENCIES OF POWER

Discuss the four contingencies of power.

Let's say that you have expert power because of your ability to forecast and possibly even prevent dramatic changes in the organisation's environment. Does this expertise mean that you are influential? Not necessarily. As we saw earlier in Exhibit 10.2, sources of power generate power only under certain conditions. Four important contingencies of power are substitutability, centrality, discretion and visibility.[18]

Substitutability

Substitutability refers to the availability of alternatives. Power is strongest when someone has a monopoly over a valued resource. Conversely, power decreases as the number of alternative sources of the critical resource increases. If you—and no one else—has expertise across the organisation on an important issue, you would be more powerful than if several people in your company possess this valued knowledge. Substitutability refers not only to other sources that offer the resource, but also to substitutions of the resource itself. For instance, labour unions are weakened when companies introduce technologies that replace the need for union members. Technology is a substitute for employees and, consequently, reduces union power.

substitutability A contingency of power pertaining to the availability of alternatives.

Controlling access to valued resources increases nonsubstitutability. Professions and labour unions gain power by controlling knowledge, tasks or labour to perform important activities. For instance, the medical profession is powerful because it controls who can perform specific medical procedures. Labour unions that dominate an industry effectively control access to labour needed to perform key jobs. Employees become nonsubstitutable when they possess knowledge (such as operating equipment or serving clients) that is not documented or readily available to others. Nonsubstitutability also occurs when people differentiate their resource from the alternatives. Some people claim that consultants use this tactic. They take skills and knowledge that many other consulting firms can provide and wrap them into a package (with the latest buzzwords, of course) so that it looks like a service that no one else can offer.

Centrality

centrality A contingency of power pertaining to the degree and nature of interdependence between the powerholder and others.

Centrality refers to the degree and nature of interdependence between the powerholder and others.[19] Think about your own centrality for a moment: if you decided not to show up for work or school tomorrow, how many people would be affected and how much time would pass before they were affected? If you have high centrality, most people in the organisation would be adversely affected by your absence and they would be affected quickly.

This effect of centrality on power is apparent in well-timed labour disputes. When Boeing workers recently walked off the job in Seattle, they immediately shut down final assembly of the aerospace company's commercial jets. Analysts estimate that the resulting delivery delays cost Boeing $2.8 billion in revenue for every month that the strike continued.[20] The New York City transit strike during the busy Christmas shopping season a few years ago also displayed centrality. The illegal three-day work stoppage immediately clogged roads and prevented most city workers from showing up to work on time or at all. '[The Metropolitan Transit Authority] told us we got no power, but we got power,' said one striking transit worker. 'We got the power to stop the city.'[21]

Discretion

The freedom to exercise judgment—to make decisions without referring to a specific rule or receiving permission from someone else—is another important contingency of power in organisations. Consider the plight of first-line supervisors. It may seem that they have legitimate, reward and coercive power over employees, but this power is often curtailed by specific rules. The lack of discretion makes supervisors less powerful than their positions would indicate. 'Middle managers are very much "piggy-in-the-middle,"' complains a middle manager at Britain's National Health System. 'They have little power, only what senior managers are allowed to give them.'[22] More generally, research indicates that managerial discretion varies considerably across industries, and that managers with an internal locus of control are viewed as more powerful because they don't act like they lack discretion in their job.[23]

Visibility

Several years ago, a junior copywriter at advertising agency Chiat/Day, Mimi Cook, submitted an idea for a potential client to her boss, who then presented it to cofounder Jay Chiat. Chiat was thrilled with the concept, but Cook's boss 'never mentioned the idea came from me', recalls Cook. She confronted her boss, who claimed the oversight was unintentional. But when a similar incident occurred a few months later, Cook left the agency for another firm.[24]

Mimi Cook, who went on to become associate creative director at another ad agency, knows that power does not flow to unknown people in the organisation. Those who control valued resources or knowledge will yield power only when others are aware of these sources of power—in other words, when it is visible. One way to increase visibility is to take people-oriented jobs and work on projects that require frequent interaction with senior executives. 'You can take visibility in steps,' advises a pharmaceutical industry executive. 'You can start by making yourself visible in a small group, such as a staff meeting. Then when you're comfortable with that, seek out larger arenas.'[25]

Employees also gain visibility by being, quite literally, visible. Some people strategically locate themselves in more visible offices, such as those closest to the lifts or staff tearoom. People often use public symbols as subtle (and not-so-subtle) cues to make their power sources known to others. Many professionals display their educational diplomas and awards on office walls to remind visitors of their expertise. Medical professionals wear white coats and carry stethoscopes around their necks to symbolise their legitimate and expert power in hospital settings. Other people play the game of 'face time'—spending more time at work and showing that they are working productively.

Consequences of Power

LEARNING OBJECTIVE

Summarise the effects of power on the powerholder's own performance and wellbeing.

How does power affect the powerholder? We partly answered this question in Chapter 6 when describing empowerment—an individual's feelings of self-determination, meaning, competence and impact in the organisation. Under the right conditions, employees who receive more power feel more empowered, which tends to increase their motivation, job satisfaction, organisational commitment and job performance. More broadly, having (or not having) power influences whether individuals choose to take action. Not surprisingly, high-power people are more likely to take action, whereas low-power people are more cautious and reluctant to act.[26] This, in turn, has far-reaching consequences for how we relate to others.

Research suggests that as people become more powerful, they are more goal-directed and tend to act on their environment rather than hide from it. Having power reduces the perceived constraints on individuals' behaviour and they are more willing to take action, independent of whether that action has positive or negative outcomes.[27] One consequence of this approach orientation is that increased power can potentially undermine an individual's effectiveness and interpersonal relations. Some studies have found that people who have (or believe they have) power engage in more automatic than mindful thinking. This has important implications for employees during the performance appraisal process. It is likely that managers' evaluations will be based on their overall stereotype of individuals, meaning they are less likely to be aware of unique information. This information, as we will see in the next section, is an important source of influence on people.

Organisational relationships are also likely to be affected by the exercise of power because high-power individuals show less empathy. Their orientation to social rewards rather than social punishments means that they are much better at recognising positive reactions from others. Research shows that high-power individuals are better able to recognise rewards (e.g. others like me) than to recognise punishments (e.g. others are angry with me). Finally, relationships may be undermined because high-power individuals approach others in an instrumental way, assessing their value based on their usefulness to the high-power person.[28]

Power also has consequences for organisational processes. Not only do high-power individuals neglect individuating information, they have greater difficulty in taking others' perspectives. One consequence is that they fail to pass on crucial information because they fail to take into consideration their privileged access to information. They just don't realise that not everyone has access to the information that they have by virtue of their position. High-power individuals can also increase organisational risk. Because they are more optimistic than low-power individuals, they are more willing to take risks. In addition, they are unlikely to be challenged by low-power individuals, because low power not only inhibits action but also impairs executive decision-making functions such as monitoring for new and relevant goal-related information, inhibiting any actions that are not goal-relevant, and planning—that is, switching between the main goal and subgoals.[29]

LEARNING OBJECTIVE

Summarise the eight types of influence tactics.

INFLUENCING OTHERS

influence Any behaviour that attempts to alter someone's attitudes or behaviour.

Up to this point, we have focused on the sources and contingencies of power. But power is only the capacity to influence others. It represents the potential to change someone's attitudes and behaviour. **Influence**, on the other hand, refers to any behaviour that attempts to alter someone's attitudes or behaviour.[30] Influence is power in motion. It applies one or more sources of power to get people to alter their beliefs, feelings and activities. Consequently, our interest in the remainder of this chapter is on how people use power to influence others.

Influence tactics are woven throughout the social fabric of all organisations. This is because influence is an essential process through which people coordinate their effort and act in concert to achieve organisational objectives. Indeed, influence is central to the definition of leadership. Influence operates down, across and up the corporate hierarchy. Executives ensure that subordinates complete required tasks. Employees influence coworkers to help them with their job assignments. Subordinates engage in upward influence tactics so corporate leaders make decisions compatible with subordinates' needs and expectations.

Types of Influence Tactics

Organisational behaviour researchers have devoted considerable attention to the various types of influence tactics found in organisational settings. They do not agree on a definitive list of influence tactics, but the most commonly identified are listed in Exhibit 10.4 and described over the next few pages.[31] The first five are known as 'hard' influence tactics because they force behaviour change through position power (legitimate, reward and coercion). The latter three—ingratiation and impression management, persuasion and exchange—are called 'soft' tactics because they rely more on personal sources of power (referent, expert) and appeal to the target person's attitudes and needs.

Silent Authority

The silent application of authority occurs where someone complies with a request because of the requester's legitimate power as well as the target person's role expectations. This condition is known as *deference to authority*.[32] This deference occurs when you comply with your boss's request to complete a particular task. If the task is within your job scope and your boss has the right to make this request, then this influence strategy operates without negotiation, threats, persuasion or other tactics. Silent authority is the most common form of influence in high power-distance cultures.[33]

Exhibit 10.4 *Types of Influence Tactics in Organisations*

Influence tactic	Description
Silent authority	Influencing behaviour through legitimate power without explicitly referring to that power base
Assertiveness	Actively applying legitimate and coercive power by applying pressure or threats
Information control	Explicitly manipulating someone else's access to information for the purpose of changing their attitudes and/or behaviour
Coalition formation	Forming a group that attempts to influence others by pooling the resources and power of its members
Upward appeal	Gaining support from one or more people with higher authority or expertise
Persuasion	Using logical arguments, factual evidence and emotional appeals to convince people of the value of a request
Ingratiation/impression management	Attempting to increase liking by, or perceived similarity to, some targeted person
Exchange	Promising benefits or resources in exchange for the target person's compliance

Assertiveness

In contrast to silent authority, assertiveness might be called 'vocal authority' because it involves actively applying legitimate and coercive power to influence others. Assertiveness includes persistently reminding the target of his or her obligations, frequently checking the target's work, confronting the target and using threats of sanctions to force compliance. Assertiveness typically applies or threatens to apply punishment if the target does not comply. Explicit or implicit threats range from job loss to losing face by letting down the team. Extreme forms of assertiveness include blackmailing colleagues, such as by threatening to reveal the other person's previously unknown failures unless he or she complies with your request.

Information Control

Information control involves explicitly manipulating others' access to information for the purpose of changing their attitudes and/or behaviour. With limited access to potentially valuable information, others are at a disadvantage. According to one major survey, almost half of employees believe coworkers keep others in the dark about work issues if it helps their own cause. Employees also influence executive decisions by screening out (filtering) information flowing up the hierarchy. One study found that CEOs influence their board of directors by selectively feeding and withholding information.[34]

Coalition Formation

When people lack sufficient power alone to influence others in the organisation, they might form a **coalition** of people who support the proposed change. A coalition is influential in three ways.[35] First, it pools the power and resources of many people, so the coalition potentially has more influence than any number of people operating alone. Second, the coalition's mere existence

coalition A group that attempts to influence people outside the group by pooling the resources and power of its members.

can be a source of power by symbolising the legitimacy of the issue. In other words, a coalition creates a sense that the issue deserves attention because it has broad support. Third, coalitions tap into the power of the social identity process introduced in Chapter 2. A coalition is essentially an informal group that advocates a new set of norms and behaviours. If the coalition has a broad-based membership (i.e. its members come from various parts of the organisation), then other employees are more likely to identify with that group and, consequently, accept the ideas the coalition is proposing.

Upward Appeal

upward appeal A type of influence in which someone with higher authority or expertise is called on (in reality or symbolically) to support the influencer's position.

The tactic of **upward appeal** involves calling upon higher authority or expertise, or symbolically relying on these sources to support the influencer's position. Along with seeking out support from higher sources, upward appeal occurs when relying on the authority of the firm's policies or values. By reminding others that your request is consistent with the organisation's overarching goals, you are implying support from senior executives without formally involving them.

Persuasion

persuasion The use of facts, logical arguments and emotional appeals to change another person's beliefs and attitudes, usually for the purpose of changing the person's behaviour.

Persuasion is one of the most effective influence strategies for career success. The ability to present facts, logical arguments and emotional appeals to change another person's attitudes and behaviour is not just an acceptable way to influence others; in many societies, it is a noble art and a quality of effective leaders. The effectiveness of persuasion as an influence tactic depends on characteristics of the persuader, message content, communication medium and the audience being persuaded.[36] People are more persuasive when listeners believe they have expertise and credibility, such as when the persuader does not seem to profit from the persuasion attempt and states a few points against the position.

The message is more important than the messenger when the issue is important to the audience. Persuasive message content acknowledges several points of view so the audience does not feel cornered by the speaker. The message should also be limited to a few strong arguments, which are repeated a few times, but not too frequently. The message should use emotional appeals (such as graphically showing the unfortunate consequences of a bad decision), but only in combination with logical arguments and specific recommendations to overcome the threat. Finally, message content is more persuasive when the audience is warned about opposing arguments. This **inoculation effect** causes listeners to generate counterarguments to the anticipated persuasion attempts, which makes the opponent's subsequent persuasion attempts less effective.[37]

inoculation effect A persuasive communication strategy of warning listeners that others will try to influence them in the future and that they should be wary about the opponent's arguments.

Two other considerations when persuading people are the medium of communication and characteristics of the audience. Generally, persuasion works best in face-to-face conversations and through other media-rich communication channels. The personal nature of face-to-face communication increases the persuader's credibility, and the richness of this channel provides faster feedback that the influence strategy is working. With respect to audience characteristics, it is more difficult to persuade people who have high self-esteem and intelligence, as well as those whose targeted attitudes are strongly connected to their self-identity.[38]

Ingratiation and Impression Management

Silent authority, assertiveness, information control, coalitions and upward appeals are somewhat (or very!) forceful ways to influence other people. In contrast, a very 'soft' influence tactic is

ingratiation—any attempt to increase liking by, or perceived similarity to, some targeted person.[39] Ingratiation comes in several flavours. Employees might flatter their boss in front of others, demonstrate that they have similar attitudes as their boss (e.g. agreeing with the boss's proposal) and ask their boss for advice. Ingratiation is one of the more effective influence tactics for boosting a person's career success (i.e. performance appraisal feedback, salaries and promotions).[40] However, people who engage in high levels of ingratiation are less (not more) influential and less likely to get promoted.[41] The explanation for the contrasting evidence is that those who engage in too much ingratiation are viewed as insincere and self-serving. The terms 'apple polishing' and 'brown-nosing' are applied to those who ingratiate to excess or in ways that suggest selfish motives for the ingratiation.

ingratiation Any attempt to increase liking by, or perceived similarity to, some targeted person.

Ingratiation is part of a larger influence tactic known as impression management. **Impression management** is the practice of actively shaping our public images. Individuals differ in whether they focus mainly on positive impression management techniques (ingratiation, self-promotion and exemplification) or are less selective in how they approach impression management, adding supplication (appearing needy) and intimidation to these more positive techniques.[42] Which set of techniques individuals choose is affected by their impression management goals: to be liked, to be seen as competent, to convey status or to gain compliance. Recent research demonstrating gender differences in impression management styles suggests that women use strategies associated with a 'likeability' goal whereas men use tactics associated with a 'competence' goal.[43]

impression management The practice of actively shaping our public images.

For the most part, employees routinely engage in pleasant impression management behaviours to satisfy the basic norms of social behaviour, such as the way they dress and how they behave toward colleagues and customers. Impression management is a common strategy for people trying to get ahead in the workplace. In fact, career professionals encourage people to develop a personal 'brand'; that is, to demonstrate and symbolise a distinctive competitive advantage.[44] Just as running shoes and soft drinks have brand images that represent an expectation, successful individuals build a personal brand in which they deliver valued knowledge or skills. Furthermore, people who are adept at personal branding rely on impression management through distinctive personal characteristics. You can more easily recall people who wear distinctive clothing or accoutrements.

Unfortunately, a few individuals carry impression management beyond ethical boundaries by exaggerating their credentials and accomplishments on their résumé. For instance, a Lucent Technologies executive lied about having a PhD from Stanford University and hid his criminal past involving forgery and embezzlement. Ironically, the executive was Lucent's director of recruiting![45] One of the most elaborate misrepresentations occurred a few years ago when a Singaporean entrepreneur sent out news releases claiming to be a renowned artificial intelligence researcher, the author of several books, and the recipient of numerous awards from MIT and Stanford University (one of the awards was illustrated on his website). These falsehoods were so convincing that the entrepreneur almost received a real award, the 'Internet Visionary of the Year' at the Internet World Asia Industry Awards.[46]

Exchange

Exchange activities involve the promise of benefits or resources in exchange for the target person's compliance with your request. This tactic also includes reminding the target of past benefits or favours with the expectation that the target will now make up for that debt. The norm of reciprocity is a central and explicit theme in exchange strategies. According to the norm of reciprocity, individuals are expected to help those who have helped them.[47] Negotiation is also an integral part of exchange influence activities. For instance, you might negotiate with your boss for a day off in return for working a less desirable shift at a future date.

What can we exchange to influence others in our organisations? Our negotiation example suggests that exchanges involve concrete resources such as money or time. However, there are many different resources that we can trade. Although some, such as money and information, are concrete, others, such as liking, status and esteem, are intangible. Researchers have identified five organisational currencies that can be used in the exchange process. *Task-related* currencies describe resources that focus on task completion, such as larger budgets, organisational information, contributing effort in order to complete a project or providing organisational information. When individuals offer others the possibility of promotion, recognise their achievements and skills, increase their visibility or provide contacts, they are offering *position-related* currencies. These currencies are at the heart of the social networks we discuss in the next section.

In addition, individuals can offer others the opportunity to behave ethically, to contribute to a greater good or to display excellence (*inspiration-related* currencies). They may also use personal concerns such as the need for acceptance and growth by offering friendship, personal support and empathy (*relationship-related* currencies), or they may offer challenges, the opportunity to influence others and appreciation (*personal-related* currencies) in their exchanges with others. And, as we can see in the following story about business–charity relationships, when organisations and charities enter into an exchange relationship, organisations offer task-related currencies in exchange for inspirational and personal-related currencies.[48]

Networking is another form of exchange as an influence strategy. Active networkers build up 'exchange credits' by helping colleagues in the short term for reciprocal benefits in the long term. Networking as an influence strategy is a deeply ingrained practice in several cultures. The

Money Can Buy Love

The increasing social awareness of corporations and their investors has paid off for charities. The business–charity alliances that have formed demonstrate how the principle of exchange works. Charities benefit from large corporate donations, but to get those they need to offer organisations valuable 'resources' in return. What rewards can charities offer? One of the benefits that organisations receive is respect and an enhanced reputation among their employees and the broader community. According to Michael Browne, CEO of Datacom (Australasia), employees expect organisations to be involved with the community: 'It makes for a more rewarding environment to work in … It's good for our people and it's good for the community.' However, organisations expect more tangible returns as well: they expect charities to show greater transparency, accountability and better management practices. When organisations and charities start an exchange relationship, they trade economic currencies for socioemotional currencies such as status and esteem.[49]

Courtesy of RSPCA

Chinese term *guanxi* refers to special relationships and active interpersonal connectedness. It is based on traditional Confucian values of helping others without expecting future repayment. However, some writers suggest that the original interpretation and practice of guanxi has shifted to include implicit long-term reciprocity, which can slip into cronyism. As a result, some Asian governments are discouraging guanxi-based decisions, preferring more arms-length transactions in business and government decisions.[50]

Consequences and Contingencies of Influence Tactics

LEARNING OBJECTIVE

Discuss three contingencies to consider when deciding which influence tactic to use.

Now that the main influence strategies have been described, you are probably asking: 'Which ones are best?' The best way to answer this question is to identify the three ways that people react when others try to influence them: resistance, compliance or commitment.[51] *Resistance* occurs when people or work units oppose the behaviour desired by the influencer, and consequently refuse, argue or delay engaging in the behaviour. *Compliance* occurs when people are motivated to implement the influencer's request at a minimal level of effort and for purely instrumental reasons. Without external sources to prompt the desired behaviour, it would not occur. *Commitment* is the strongest form of influence, whereby people identify with the influencer's request and are highly motivated to implement it even when extrinsic sources of motivation are no longer present.

Generally, people react more favourably to 'soft' tactics than to 'hard' tactics (see Exhibit 10.5). Soft influence tactics rely on personal sources of power (expert and referent power), which tend to build commitment to the influencer's request. In contrast, hard tactics rely on position power

Exhibit 10.5 *Consequences of Hard and Soft Influence Tactics*

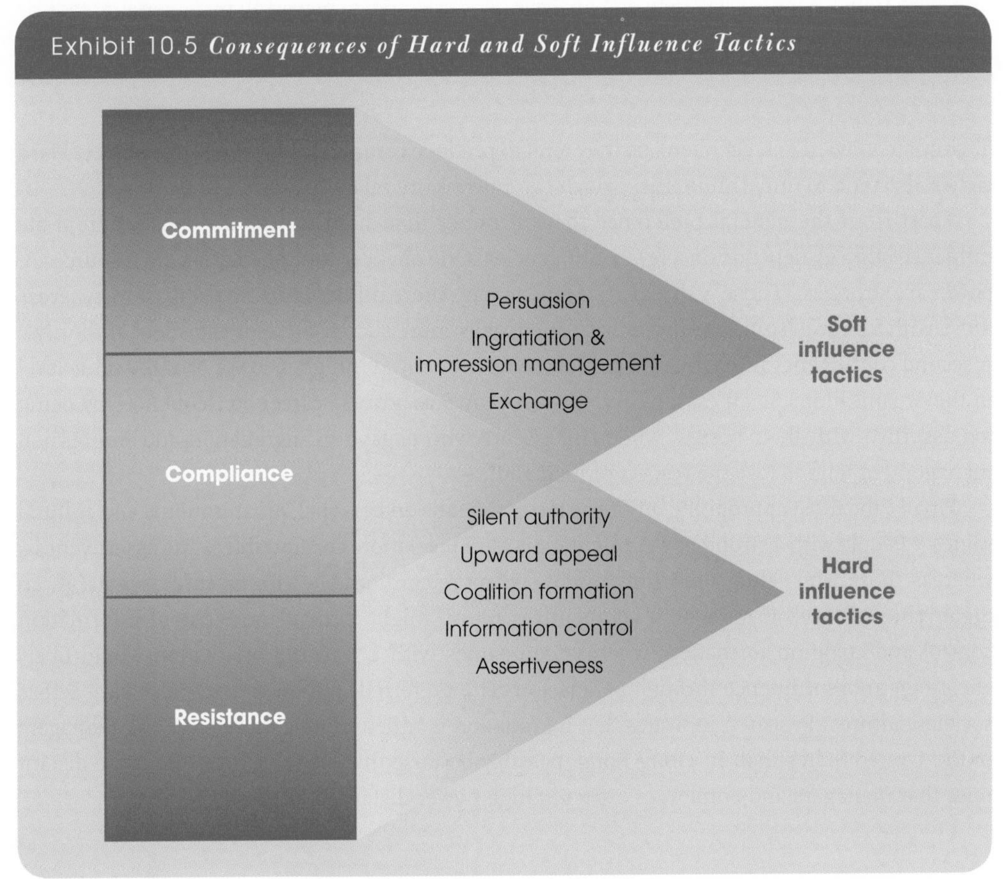

Powered by the Social Network

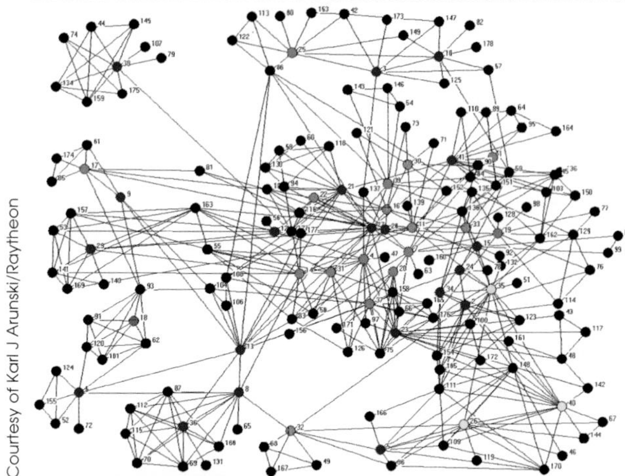

Courtesy of Karl J Arunski/Raytheon

This is one of several social network analysis diagrams that helped Raytheon engineering director Karl Arunski determine who has the most social network power.

ENGINEERING AND ENVIRONMENTAL CONSULTING firm MWH Global reorganised its information technology (IT) operations into a single global division and located its main service centre in New Zealand. Ken Loughridge was transferred from England to manage the new service centre, but he didn't know who the key players in his New Zealand team were. 'By and large, the staff I'd adopted were strangers,' he says. Fortunately, Loughridge was able to consult a report displaying the informal social network of relationships among his staff. MWH Global had surveyed its IT employees a few months earlier about who they communicated with most often for information. These data produced a web-like diagram of nodes (people) connected by a maze of lines (relationships). From this picture, Loughridge could identify the 'go-to' people in the work unit. 'It's as if you took the top off an ant hill and could see where there's a hive of activity,' he says of the map. 'It really helped me understand who the players were.'

For the past half-century, sociologists have mapped informal power relationships in organisations. Now, social network analysis is becoming a powerful management tool as practitioners discover that visual displays of relationships and information flows can help them

(legitimate, reward and coercion), so they tend to produce compliance or, worse, resistance. Hard tactics also tend to undermine trust, which can hurt future relationships.

Apart from the general preference for soft rather than hard tactics, the most appropriate influence strategy depends on a few contingencies. One obvious contingency is which sources of power are strongest. Those with expertise tend to have more influence using persuasion, whereas those with a strong legitimate power base are usually more successful applying silent authority.[52] A second contingency is whether the person being influenced is higher, lower or at the same level in the organisation. As an example, employees may face adverse career consequences by being too assertive with their bosses, while supervisors who engage in ingratiation and impression management tend to lose the respect of their staff.

Finally, the most appropriate influence tactic depends on personal, organisational and cultural values.[53] People with a strong power orientation might feel more comfortable using assertiveness, whereas those who value conformity might feel more comfortable with upward appeals. At an organisational level, firms with a competitive culture might foment more use of information control and coalition formation, whereas companies with a learning orientation would likely encourage more influence through persuasion. The preferred influence tactics also vary across societal cultures. Research indicates that ingratiation is much more common among managers in the United States than in Hong Kong, possibly because this tactic disrupts the more distant roles that managers and employees expect in high power-distance cultures.

REALITY CHECK 10.1

to tap into employees with expertise and influence. 'You look at an [organisational] chart within a company and you see the distribution of power that should be,' says Eran Barak, global head of marketing strategies at Thomson Reuters. 'You look at the dynamics in the social networks [to] see the distribution of power that is. It reflects where information is flowing—who is really driving things.'

Karl Arunski, director of Raytheon's engineering centre in Colorado, can appreciate these words. The defence and technology company's organisational chart didn't show how mission management specialists influenced people across departmental boundaries. So Arunski asked two executives to name up to ten experts who didn't fit squarely in a particular department, then he conducted social network analysis to see how these people collaborated with engineers throughout the organisation.

The resulting maps (one of which is shown here) showed Arunski the influence and knowledge flow of various experts. It also highlighted problems, such as where a cluster of employees was almost completely disconnected from the rest of the engineering group (such as the top left side of this diagram). One team's isolation was worrisome because its members were experts in systems architecture, an important growth area for Raytheon. To increase the team's network power, Arunski encouraged the team leader to hold meetings where engineers could share information about systems architecture. The number of people attending eventually grew to seventy-five, reducing the team's isolation from others. 'Social Network Analysis helped Rocky Mountain Engineering understand how organisations develop architectures, and it enabled us to know how engineers become architects,' says Arunski.[58]

POWER AND INFLUENCE THROUGH SOCIAL NETWORKS

Describe the key elements of social networks.

'It's not what you know, but who you know that counts!' This often-heard statement reflects the idea that employees get ahead not just by developing their competencies, but by *social networking*—cultivating social relationships with others to accomplish one's goals. Networking increases a person's power in three ways. First, as we noted in Chapter 8, networks represent a critical component of *social capital*—the knowledge and other resources available to people or social units (teams, organisations) due to a durable network that connects them to others. Networks consist of people who trust each other, which increases the flow of knowledge among those within the network. The more you network, the more likely it is that you will receive valuable information that increases your expert power in the organisation.[54] Social networks are important foundations of power for individuals, but as Reality Check 10.1 describes, companies are applying social network analysis tools to discover who has this power. By identifying who is the most connected, leaders know who to approach for information, who might be the most influential over other employees and who would be most costly when they leave the company.

Although social networks are natural elements of all organisations, they can create a formidable barrier for those who are not actively connected to them.[55] Women are often excluded from informal management networks because they do not participate in golf games and other male-dominated social events. Nina Smith, who leads Sage Software's Business Management Division, has had several conversations with female executives about these power dynamics. 'I'm still trying to knock down the Boys Club and I still have women at Sage coming to me and saying, "Nina, that's the boys' network and I can't get in."'[56] Several years ago, executives at Deloitte Touche Tohmatsu discovered that inaccessibility to powerful social networks partly explained why many junior female employees left the accounting and consulting firm before reaching partnership level. The Swiss-based company now relies on mentoring, formal women's network groups and measurement of career progress to ensure that female staff members have the same career development opportunities as their male colleagues.[57]

Understanding and Analysing Networks

Social networks apply many of the principles we have described in this chapter. In well-developed networks, individuals increase their social power because they obtain important information from their network contacts. As we discussed in the last section, information is an important organisational currency and one that can be exchanged for other favours. In terms of information, there are three ways that a network can benefit individuals: through access, timing and referral.[59] *Access* and *timing* help build power because they give individuals information that is unavailable to others: if you can obtain information more easily than other people in your network (access) and if you get it before anyone else (timing), you increase your power. Another source of power and influence is position-related currencies such as visibility: others in your network think of you when recommending someone for key positions or promotions, either internally or externally. These *referrals* from network contacts build power because they increase visibility and give greater access to people. To use networks strategically, you need to consider whether network contacts will give you access to information and people who would be otherwise inaccessible.

What makes an effective network? To understand networks, we need to understand three related concepts: breadth, depth and centrality. *Breadth* refers to the number of people in a network, and the kinds of relationships shared by those people. The more people and the more diverse the range of people, the more breadth a network has. A benefit of breadth is that each member adds value to the network and helps members connect with a greater range of people. This, in turn, increases visibility.[60] The second characteristic of networks is the *depth* of their relationships. How often the people in the network meet, how strongly attached they are and whether people serve more than one function (e.g. a friend who is also a colleague) determine the strength of network relationships. Typically, people operate within a core network defined by strong ties and an extended network defined by weak ties. Both have their benefits. While strong ties lead to greater trust and more immediate help for members when they need it, weak ties offer access to different groups of people.

The third dimension, *centrality*, is key in building power. Centrality refers to a person's importance in a particular network. Networkers increase their power when they place themselves in strategic positions in the network, thereby gaining centrality.[61] For example, an individual might be regarded as the main person who distributes information in the network or who keeps the network connected through informal gatherings. One way of thinking about the issue of centrality is to ask yourself, 'If I left the network, would the remaining individuals still have access to each other?' If the answer is 'Yes', you are not central to the network.

A person's centrality in a network is determined by three factors: the number of people that the person can access directly, whether the person is the shortest path between others in the network, and whether the person can reach everyone else in the network through the shortest path. When you are the shortest path between two others people in a network, your power increases because you control their interactions; when you can easily access everyone else, your power increases because you do not need to rely on others for access. One way to gain centrality is to occupy a *structural hole*.[62] A structural hole is a gap between two networks that would benefit from being in touch with each other. If you can bridge this gap, you become a broker—someone who connects two independent networks and controls information flow between them. The 'business angels' described in Reality Check 10.2 act as brokers between young entrepreneurs and venture capitalists. Not surprisingly, research shows that brokers gain career benefits. The more brokering relationships you have, the more likely you are to get early promotions, higher pay and bonuses.

Building and Maintaining Networks

When first starting to build networks, people tend to follow the *self-similarity principle*. Often, their first relationships are with people similar to them. One benefit of following this principle is that it is easier to establish relationships. We have greater trust in those who are similar to ourselves, we are more willing to cooperate with them and we share a common language. Similarly, we often develop the strongest ties with people we see most frequently, for example the people we work with (*proximity principle*).

However, neither strategy is likely to deliver the full range of benefits associated with networks. Building networks with like-minded others or those we frequently interact with means we restrict our opportunities for accessing new information or new contacts.[63] As a result, following the *shared activities principle* will build more effective networks. According to this principle, the benefits of networking are maximised when networks are built around important activities that create contact with a diverse group of people. This reasoning has led Opera Australia to encourage enthusiastic networkers to subscribe to opening-night packages. By doing this, they gain access to a wide variety of influential people, including leading business figures, diplomats and politicians.[64]

When we start to develop networks, we need to think strategically. A key benefit of networks is the contacts they provide and the access they offer to new groups of people, so our activities need to add to the breadth of our networks—meaning that we should look for people who can create new opportunities for us. We also need to assess our networks to identify redundancies (too many people with overlapping contacts) and obvious missing links. As part of our analysis, we need to consider whether there are key people missing from our network. Finally, it pays to think ahead. It's not just about who can help us now, given our career aspirations, but who can help us in the future. As we build our networks, it is also important to ensure that our existing ties are not neglected. Reality Check 10.2 provides examples of how these networking principles are applied to receive knowledge, assistance and investment support.

Need Help? Dial-an-Angel

Courtesy of S-Central

S Central is one of the companies that has benefited from a business angel.

BUSINESS ANGELS ARE EXPERIENCED, wealthy executives who are willing to finance innovative start-up companies. Angels offer these start-ups more than money. They offer critical but intangible sources of power—their knowledge and their contacts. In network terms, they are brokers who connect otherwise independent people or groups of people.

'Angel group capital comes with a lot of expertise,' says John Ballard, who chairs BioAngels (Australia). 'Whoever leads

Distinguish influence from organisational politics.

INFLUENCE TACTICS AND ORGANISATIONAL POLITICS

You might have noticed that organisational politics has not been mentioned yet, even though some of the practices or examples described over the past few pages are usually considered political tactics. The phrase was carefully avoided because, for the most part, organisational politics is in the eye of the beholder. You might perceive a coworker's attempt to influence the boss as normal behaviour, whereas someone else might perceive the tactic as brazen organisational politics.

This perceptual issue explains why OB experts increasingly discuss influence tactics as *behaviours* and organisational politics as *perceptions*.[66] The influence tactics described earlier are perceived as **organisational politics** when observers view the tactics as self-serving behaviours at the expense of others and sometimes contrary to the interests of the entire organisation or work unit. Of course, some tactics are so blatantly selfish that almost everyone views them as political. But in most situations, there is no consensus that a person is engaging in organisational politics. When employees perceive many incidents of organisational politics, the result is lower job satisfaction, organisational commitment and organisational citizenship, as well as high levels of work-related stress.[67] And because political tactics serve individuals rather than organisations, they potentially divert resources away from the organisation's effective functioning and potentially threaten its survival.

organisational politics Behaviours that others perceive as self-serving tactics for personal gain at the expense of other people and possibly the organisation.

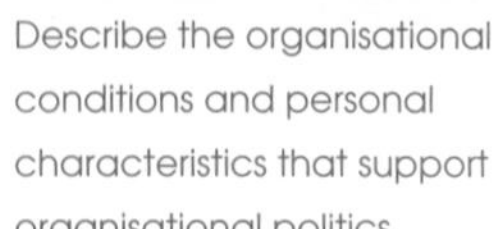

Describe the organisational conditions and personal characteristics that support organisational politics.

Conditions Supporting Organisational Politics

Organisational politics flourish under the right conditions.[68] One of those conditions is scarce resources. When budgets are slashed, people rely on political tactics to safeguard their resources and maintain the status quo. Office politics also flourish when resource allocation decisions are ambiguous, complex or lack formal rules. This occurs because decision makers are given more discretion over resource allocation, so potential recipients of those resources use political tactics to influence the factors that should be considered in the decision. Organisational change encourages political behaviours for this reason. Change creates uncertainty and ambiguity as the it comes back to the group and gets more information ... from our broader networks. The mentoring is the reason why we do it.'

When Peter Mavridis, now a successful business entrepreneur named on *Business Review Weekly*'s Young Rich list, needed an angel to start his company S Central, he applied the principle of self-similarity to nurture a relationship. Like Mavridis, his chosen angel—Polly Mazaris—had family connections in northern Greece, and Mavridis recognised that Mazaris could offer important skills and support. After meeting her when she judged an entrepreneurship award, Mavridis implemented a key principle of network-building by maintaining regular contact with Mazaris. He started to seek out her advice, eventually asking her to join his company's board. Only then did he raise the issue of investing in his company.[65]

REALITY CHECK 10.2

company moves from an old set of rules and practices to a new set. During these times, employees apply political strategies to protect their valued resources, position and self-concept.[69]

Personal Characteristics

Several personal characteristics affect a person's motivation to engage in self-serving behaviour.[70] This includes a strong need for personal as opposed to socialised power. Those with a need for personal power seek power for its own sake and try to acquire more power. Some individuals have strong **Machiavellian values**. Machiavellianism is named after Niccolò Machiavelli, the sixteenth-century Italian philosopher who wrote *The Prince*, a famous treatise about political behaviour. People with high Machiavellian values are comfortable with getting more than they deserve, and they believe that deceit is a natural and acceptable way to achieve this goal. They seldom trust coworkers and tend to use cruder influence tactics, such as bypassing one's boss or being assertive, to get their own way.[71]

Machiavellian values The beliefs that deceit is a natural and acceptable way to influence others and that getting more than one deserves is acceptable.

Minimising Organisational Politics and its Consequences

LEARNING OBJECTIVE

Identify ways to minimise organisational politics.

The conditions that fuel organisational politics also give us some clues about how to control dysfunctional political activities.[72] One strategy to keep organisational politics in check is to introduce clear rules and regulations to specify the use of scarce resources. Organisational politics can become a problem during times of organisational change, so politics can be minimised through effective organisational change practices. Leaders also need to actively manage group norms to curtail self-serving influence activities. In particular, they can support organisational values that oppose political tactics, such as altruism and customer focus. One of the most important strategies is for leaders to become role models of organisational citizenship rather than symbols of successful organisational politicians.

Along with minimising organisational politics, companies can limit the adverse effects of political perceptions by giving employees more control over their work and keeping them informed of organisational events. Research has found that employees who are kept informed of what is going on in the organisation and who are involved in organisational decisions are less likely to experience organisational politics, which results in less stress, job dissatisfaction and absenteeism.

CHAPTER SUMMARY

Power is the capacity to influence others. It exists when one party perceives that he or she is dependent on the other for something of value. However, the dependent person must also have countervailing power—some power over the dominant party—to maintain the relationship.

There are five sources of power. Legitimate power is an agreement among organisational members that people in certain roles can request certain behaviours of others. Reward power is derived from the ability to control the allocation of rewards valued by others and to remove negative sanctions. Coercive power is the ability to apply punishment. Expert power is the capacity to influence others by possessing knowledge or skills that they value. People have referent power when others identify with them, like them or otherwise respect them. Information plays an important role in organisational power. Employees gain power by controlling the flow of information that others need and by being able to cope with uncertainties related to important organisational goals.

Four contingencies determine whether these sources of power translate into real power. Individuals and work units are more powerful when they are non-substitutable, that is, there is a lack of alternatives. Employees, work units and organisations reduce substitutability by controlling tasks, knowledge and labour, and by differentiating themselves from competitors. A second contingency is centrality. People have more power when they have high centrality, that is, when the number of people affected is large and people are quickly affected by their actions. Discretion, the third contingency of power, refers to the freedom to exercise judgment. Power increases when people have freedom to use their power. The fourth contingency, visibility, refers to the idea that power increases to the extent that a person's or work unit's competencies are known to others. Power has both beneficial and adverse consequences for individuals. On the positive side, empowerment strengthens their wellbeing and effectiveness. On the negative side, research indicates that when people become more powerful, their perceptual and decision making skills can suffer.

Influence refers to any behaviour that attempts to alter someone's attitudes or behaviour. The most widely studied influence tactics are silent authority, assertiveness, information control, coalition formation, upward appeal, persuasion, ingratiation and impression management, and exchange. 'Soft' influence tactics such as friendly persuasion and subtle ingratiation are more acceptable than 'hard' tactics such as upward appeal and assertiveness. However, the most appropriate influence tactic also depends on the influencer's power base; whether the person being influenced is higher, lower or at the same level in the organisation; and personal, organisational and cultural values regarding influence behaviour.

Social networking involves cultivating social relationships with others to accomplish one's goals. This activity increases an individual's social capital, which strengthens expert power, referent power, visibility and possibly centrality.

Organisational politics refers to influence tactics that others perceive to be self-serving behaviours at the expense of others and sometimes contrary to the interests of the entire organisation or work unit. Organisational politics are more prevalent when scarce resources are allocated using complex and ambiguous decisions, and when the organisation tolerates or rewards political behaviour. Individuals with a high need for personal power and strong Machiavellian values have a higher propensity to use political tactics.

Organisational politics can be minimised by providing clear rules for resource allocation, establishing a free flow of information, using education and involvement during organisational change, supporting team norms and a corporate culture that discourage dysfunctional politics, and having leaders who role model organisational citizenship rather than political savvy.

KEY TERMS

centrality, p. 388
coalition, p. 391
countervailing power, p. 382
impression management, p. 393
influence, p. 390
ingratiation, p. 393
inoculation effect, p. 392
legitimate power, p. 383
Machiavellian values, p. 401
organisational politics, p. 400
persuasion, p. 392
power, p. 382
referent power, p. 386
substitutability, p. 387
upward appeal, p. 392

Critical Thinking Questions

1. What role does countervailing power play in the power relationship? Give an example of your own encounter with countervailing power at school or work.

2. Several years ago, the Major League Baseball Players Association in the US went on strike in September, just before the World Series started. The players' contracts expired at the beginning of the season (May), but they held off the strike until September when they would lose only one-sixth of their salaries. In contrast, a September strike would hurt the owners financially, because they earn a larger portion of their revenue during the play-offs. As one player explained: 'If we strike next spring, there's nothing stopping [the club owners] from letting us go until next June or July because they don't have that much at stake.' Use your knowledge of the sources and contingencies of power to explain why the baseball players had more power in negotiations by walking out in September rather than March.

3. You have just been hired as a brand manager of toothpaste for a large consumer products company. Your job mainly involves encouraging the advertising and production groups to promote and manufacture your product more effectively. These departments aren't under your direct authority, although company procedures indicate that they must complete certain tasks requested by brand managers. Describe the sources of power you can use

to ensure that the advertising and production departments will help you make and sell toothpaste more effectively.

4 How does social networking increase a person's power? What social networking strategies could you initiate now to potentially enhance your future career success?

5 List the eight influence tactics described in this chapter in terms of how they are used by students to influence their course instructors. Which influence tactic is applied most often? Which is applied least often, in your opinion? To what extent is each influence tactic considered legitimate behaviour or organisational politics?

6 How do cultural differences affect the following influence factors: (a) silent authority, and (b) upward appeal?

7 A few years ago, the CEO of Apple Computer invited Steve Jobs (who was not associated with the company at the time) to serve as a special adviser and raise morale among Apple employees and customers. While doing this, Jobs spent more time advising the CEO on how to cut costs, redraw the organisation chart and hire new people. Before long, most of the top people at Apple were Jobs' colleagues, who began to systematically evaluate and weed out teams of Apple employees. While publicly supporting Apple's CEO, Jobs privately criticised him and, in a show of nonconfidence, sold 1.5 million shares of Apple stock he had received. This action caught the attention of Apple's board of directors, who soon after decided to replace the CEO with Steve Jobs. The CEO claimed Jobs was a conniving back-stabber who used political tactics to get his way. Others suggest that Apple would be out of business today if he hadn't taken over the company. In your opinion, were Steve Jobs' actions examples of organisational politics? Justify your answer.

8 This book frequently emphasises that successful companies engage in organisational learning. How do political tactics interfere with organisational learning objectives?

Skill Builder 10.1

TEAM EXERCISE

Budget Deliberations

Sharon Card

Purpose

This exercise is designed to help you understand some of the power dynamics and influence tactics that occur across hierarchical levels in organisations.

Materials

This activity works best using one small room that leads to a larger room, which in turn leads to a larger area.

Instructions

These exercise instructions are based on a class size of about 30 students, but the instructor may adjust the size of the first two groups slightly for larger classes. The instructor will organise students as follows: a few (3–4) students are assigned the position of executives.

They are preferably located in a secluded office or corner of a large classroom. Another six to eight students are assigned positions as middle managers. These people will ideally be located in an adjoining room or space, allowing privacy for the executives. The remaining students represent the nonmanagement employees in the organisation. They are located in an open area outside the executive and management rooms.

Rules

Members of the executive group are free to enter the space of either the middle management or nonmanagement groups and to communicate whatever they wish, whenever they wish. Members of the middle management group may enter the space of the nonmanagement group whenever they wish, but must request permission to enter the executive group's space. The executive group can refuse the middle management group's request. Members of the nonmanagement group are not allowed to disturb the top group in any way unless specifically invited by members of the executive group. The nonmanagement group does have the right to request permission to communicate with the middle management group. The middle management group can refuse the lower group's request.

Task

Your organisation is in the process of preparing a budget. The challenge is to balance needs with the financial resources. Of course, the needs are greater than the resources. The instructor will distribute a budget sheet showing a list of budget requests and their costs. Each group has control over a portion of the budget and must decide how to spend the money over which they have control. Nonmanagement has discretion over a relatively small portion and the executive group has discretion over the greatest portion. The exercise is finished when the organisation has negotiated a satisfactory budget, or until the instructor calls time out. The class will then debrief with the following questions and others the instructor might ask.

Discussion Questions

1. What can we learn from this exercise about power in organisational hierarchies?
2. How is this exercise similar to relations in real organisations?
3. How did students in each group feel about the amount of power they held?
4. How did they exercise their power in relations with the other groups?

SELF-ASSESSMENT

Skill Builder 10.2

Coworker Influence Scale

Purpose

This exercise is designed to help you understand different forms of influence when working with coworkers (i.e. people at the same organisational level), as well as estimate your preference for each influence tactic in this context.

Instructions

Think about the occasions when a coworker disagreed with you, opposed your preference or was reluctant to actively support your point of view about something at work. These conflicts might have been about company policy, assignment of job duties, distribution of resources or any other matter. What did you do to try to get the coworker to support your preference?

The statements below describe ways that people try to influence coworkers. Thinking about your own behaviour *over the past six months*, how often did you engage in each of these behaviours to influence coworkers, that is, people at a similar level in the organisation? (If you have not been in the workforce recently, complete this instrument thinking about influencing another student instead of a coworker.) Circle the most accurate number for each statement.

When you have completed the self-assessment, use the scoring key in Appendix B to calculate your results. This exercise is completed alone so you can assess yourself honestly without concerns of social comparison. However, class discussion will focus on the types of influence in organisations, and which influence tactics are most and least successful or popular when influencing coworkers.

Coworker Influence Scale

Over the past six months, how often did you use the following tactics to influence coworkers?	Rarely/ Never	Seldom	Sometimes	Often	Almost always
1. Presented the coworker with logical reasons why the matter should be decided in my favour.	1	2	3	4	5
2. Made my authority or expertise regarding the issue known without being obvious about it.	1	2	3	4	5
3. Tried to negotiate a solution, where I would offer something in return for the coworker's support.	1	2	3	4	5
4. Demanded that the decision or matter should be resolved in my favour.	1	2	3	4	5
5. Avoided showing the coworker information that opposed my preference.	1	2	3	4	5
6. Enlisted the support of other employees so the coworker would see that I had the more popular preference.	1	2	3	4	5
7. Claimed or demonstrated that my preference had the support of managers or others with higher authority.	1	2	3	4	5
8. Deliberately said something positive about the coworker in the hope that he/she would be more supportive of my preference.	1	2	3	4	5

Over the past six months, how often did you use the following tactics to influence coworkers?	Rarely/ Never	Seldom	Sometimes	Often	Almost always
9. Tried to convince the coworker using factual information and logic.	1	2	3	4	5
10. Subtly let the coworker know about my expertise on the matter.	1	2	3	4	5
11. Offered to support or assist the coworker on something if he/she would agree with me on this matter.	1	2	3	4	5
12. Showed impatience or frustration with the coworker's opposition to my preference.	1	2	3	4	5
13. Presented information in a way that more clearly supported my preference.	1	2	3	4	5
14. Claimed that other coworkers or subordinates supported my position on this matter.	1	2	3	4	5
15. Suggested or threatened to have the issue resolved by higher management.	1	2	3	4	5
16. Became more friendly towards the coworker, hoping this would create a more favourable opinion of me and my point of view.	1	2	3	4	5
17. Helped the coworker to visualise the positive outcomes of my preference and/or the negative outcomes of other choices.	1	2	3	4	5
18. Quietly or indirectly showed the coworker my authority, expertise or right to have this matter decided in my favour.	1	2	3	4	5
19. Reminded the coworker that I had helped him/her in the past, hoping that he/she would reciprocate by supporting me now.	1	2	3	4	5
20. Let the coworker know that I would be disagreeable or punish him/her in some other way if the coworker did not support me on this matter.	1	2	3	4	5
21. Ensured that the coworker only received information that mainly agreed with (rather than opposed) my preference.	1	2	3	4	5
22. Made sure that at least a few other coworkers or subordinates were on my side of this issue.	1	2	3	4	5
23. Argued that my preference was consistent with the company's values or policies.	1	2	3	4	5
24. Showed a great deal of respect toward the coworker in the hope that this would encourage him/her to see my point of view and agree with me.	1	2	3	4	5

Endnotes

1 L. Ahwan , 'Bullying Bosses', *The Advertiser (Adelaide)*, 29 November 2008; M. Johnston, 'Junior Doctors Report Bullying', *New Zealand Herald*, 19 September 2008; N. Sakakibara, 'Power Harassment on Rise/Female Part-timers, Temps Seen as Particularly Vulnerable', *Daily Yomiuri (Japan)*, 8 November 2008; A. Scott-Howman, 'Sticks and Stones: Workplace Bullying', *The Independent Financial Review (NZ)*, 13 November 2008; K. Warren, 'Workplace Bullying Hidden', *Sunshine Coast Daily (Maroochydore, Qld)*, 27 September 2008; M. Worley, 'Bullies Make a Job Just Misery', *Sunday Tasmanian*, 14 September 2008.

2 J. R. P. French and B. Raven, 'The Bases of Social Power', in *Studies in Social Power*, ed. D. Cartwright (Ann Arbor, MI: University of Michigan Press, 1959), 150–167; A. D. Galinsky *et al.*, 'Power and Perspectives Not Taken', *Psychological Science* 17, no. 12 (2006): 1068–1074. Also see H. Mintzberg, *Power in and around Organizations* (Englewood Cliffs, NJ: Prentice Hall, 1983), ch. 1; J. Pfeffer, *Managing with Power* (Boston: Harvard Business University Press, 1992), 17, 30.

3 R. A. Dahl, 'The Concept of Power', *Behavioral Science* 2 (1957): 201–218; R. M. Emerson, 'Power-Dependence Relations', *American Sociological Review* 27 (1962): 31–41; A. M. Pettigrew, *The Politics of Organizational Decision-Making* (London: Tavistock, 1973).

4 R. Gulati and M. Sytch, 'Dependence Asymmetry and Joint Dependence in Interorganizational Relationships: Effects of Embeddedness on a Manufacturer's Performance in Procurement Relationships', *Administrative Science Quarterly* 52, no. 1 (2007): 32–69.

5 French and Raven, 'The Bases of Social Power'; P. Podsakoff and C. Schreisheim, 'Field Studies of French and Raven's Bases of Power: Critique, Analysis, and Suggestions for Future Research', *Psychological Bulletin* 97, no. 3 (1985): 387–411; P. P. Carson and K. D. Carson, 'Social Power Bases: A Meta-Analytic Examination of Interrelationships and Outcomes', *Journal of Applied Social Psychology* 23, no. 14 (1993): 1150–1169.

6 C. Barnard, *The Function of the Executive* (Cambridge, MA: Harvard University Press, 1938); C. Hardy and S. R. Clegg, 'Some Dare Call It Power', in *Handbook of Organization Studies*, ed. S. R. Clegg, C. Hardy and W. R. Nord (London: Sage, 1996), 622–641.

7 A. I. Shahin and P. L. Wright, 'Leadership in the Context of Culture: An Egyptian Perspective', *Leadership & Organization Development Journal* 25, no. 5/6 (2004): 499–511; Y. J. Huo *et al.*, 'Leadership and the Management of Conflicts in Diverse Groups: Why Acknowledging Versus Neglecting Subgroup Identity Matters', *European Journal of Social Psychology* 35, no. 2 (2005): 237–254.

8 L. S. Sya, 'Flying to Greater Heights', *New Sunday Times (Kuala Lumpur)*, 31 July 2005, 14; M. Bolch, 'Rewarding the Team', *HRMagazine*, February 2007, 91–93.

9 J. M. Peiro and J. L. Melia, 'Formal and Informal Interpersonal Power in Organisations: Testing a Bifactorial Model of Power in Role-Sets', *Applied Psychology* 52, no. 1 (2003): 14–35.

10 P. F. Drucker, 'The New Workforce', *The Economist*, 3 November 2001, 8–12.

11 R. B. Cialdini and N. J. Goldstein, 'Social Influence: Compliance and Conformity', *Annual Review of Psychology* 55 (2004): 591–621.

12 C. K. Hofling *et al.*, 'An Experimental Study in Nurse-Physician Relationships', *Journal of Nervous and Mental Disease* 143, no. 2 (1966): 171–180.

13 D. Brady, 'The It Girl', *Canadian Business*, 5 November 2007, 43–46; A. McMains, 'TBWA Confirms DeCourcy Hire', *AdWeek*, 21 August 2007; 'The Judges', *Advertising Age's Creativity*, May 2008, 100; N. Bussey, 'TBWA Forms Digital Agency for Adidas', *Campaign*, 26 September 2008, 2; D. Kaplan, 'Interview: Colleen DeCourcy, CDO, TBWA', *paidcontent.org*, 1 June 2008; D. Long, 'Digital Thinkers: Judge and Jury', *New Media Age*, 27 March 2008, 29.

14 K. Miyahara, 'Charisma: From Weber to Contemporary Sociology', *Sociological Inquiry* 53, no. 4 (1983): 368–388; J. D. Kudisch and M. L. Poteet, 'Expert Power, Referent Power, and Charisma: Toward the Resolution of a Theoretical Debate', *Journal of Business and Psychology* 10, no. 2 (1995): 177–195; D. Ladkin, 'The Enchantment of the Charismatic Leader: Charisma Reconsidered as Aesthetic Encounter', *Leadership* 2, no. 2 (2006): 165–179.

15 G. Yukl and C. M. Falbe, 'Importance of Different Power Sources in Downward and Lateral Relations', *Journal of Applied Psychology* 76, no. 3 (1991): 416–423; B. H. Raven, 'Kurt Lewin Address: Influence, Power, Religion, and the Mechanisms of Social Control', *Journal of Social Issues* 55 (Spring 1999): 161–186.

16 P. L. Dawes, D. Y. Lee and G. R. Dowling, 'Information Control and Influence in Emergent Buying Centers', *Journal of Marketing* 62, no. 3 (1998): 55–68; D. Willer, 'Power-at-a-Distance', *Social Forces* 81, no. 4 (2003): 1295–1334; D. J. Brass *et al.*, 'Taking Stock of Networks and Organizations: A Multilevel Perspective', *Academy of Management Journal* 47, no. 6 (2004): 795–817.

17 C. R. Hinings *et al.*, 'Structural Conditions of Intraorganizational Power', *Administrative Science Quarterly* 19, no. 1 (1974): 22–44. Also see C. S. Saunders, 'The Strategic Contingencies Theory of Power: Multiple Perspectives', *Journal of Management Studies* 27, no. 1 (1990): 1–18.

18 D. J. Hickson *et al.*, 'A Strategic Contingencies' Theory of Intraorganizational Power', *Administrative Science Quarterly* 16, no. 2 (1971): 216–227; Hinings *et al.*, 'Structural Conditions of Intraorganizational Power'; R. M. Kanter, 'Power Failure in Management Circuits', *Harvard Business Review* (July–August 1979): 65–75.

19 Hickson *et al.*, 'A Strategic Contingencies' Theory of Intraorganizational Power'; J. D. Hackman, 'Power and Centrality in the Allocation of Resources in Colleges and Universities', *Administrative Science Quarterly* 30, no. 1 (1985): 61–77; D. J. Brass and M. E. Burkhardt, 'Potential Power and Power Use: An Investigation of Structure and Behavior', *Academy of Management Journal* 36 (1993): 441–470.

20 D. Gates, 'Simmering Strike Scorching Both Sides', *Seattle Times*, 29 September 2008, A1; J. Wallace and A. James, 'Strike Time', *Seattle Post-Intelligencer*, 6 September 2008, A1.

21 S. D. Harrington and B. Ivry, 'For Commuters, a Day to Adapt', *The Record (Bergen, NJ)*, 21 December 2005, A1; S. McCarthy, 'Transit Strike Cripples New York', *Globe & Mail (Toronto)*, 21 December 2005, A17.

22 Kanter, 'Power Failure in Management Circuits'; B. E. Ashforth, 'The Experience of Powerlessness in Organizations', *Organizational Behavior and Human Decision Processes* 43, no. 2 (1989): 207–242; L. Holden, 'European Managers: HRM and an Evolving Role', *European Business Review* 12 (2000).

23 D. C. Hambrick and E. Abrahamson, 'Assessing Managerial Discretion across Industries: A Multimethod Approach', *Academy of Management Journal* 38, no. 5 (1995): 1427–1441; M. A. Carpenter and B. R. Golden, 'Perceived Managerial Discretion: A Study of Cause and Effect', *Strategic Management Journal* 18, no. 3 (1997): 187–206.

24 J. Voight, 'When Credit Is Not Due', *Adweek*, 1 March 2004, 24.

25 R. Madell, 'Ground Floor', *Pharmaceutical Executive (Women in Pharma Supplement)*, June 2000, 24–31.

26 D. Keltner, D. Gruenfeld and C. Anderson, 'Power, Approach, and Inhibition', *Psychological Review* 110, no. 2 (2003): 265–284; C. Anderson and J. Berdahl , 'The Experience of Power: Examining the Effects of Power on Approach and Inhibition Tendencies', *Journal of Personality and Social Psychology* 83, no. 6 (2002): 1362–1377.

27 C. Anderson and J. Berdahl , 'The Experience of Power: Examining the Effects of Power on Approach and Inhibition Tendencies'; A. Galinsky, D. Gruenfeld and J. Magee, 'From Power to Action', *Journal of Personality and Social Psychology* 85, no. 3 (2003): 453–466; D. Gruenfeld, D. Keltner and C. Anderson, 'The Effects of Power on Those Who Possess It: How Social Structure Can Affect Social Cognition', in *Foundations of Social Cognition: A Festschrift in Honor of Robert S. Wyer, Jr*, ed. G. V. Bodenhausen and A. J. Lambert (Mahwah, NJ: Lawrence Erlbaum, 2003), 237–261.

28 D. Gruenfeld *et al.*, 'Power and the Objectification of Social Targets', *Journal of Personality and Social Psychology* 95, no. 1 (2008): 111–127; A. Galinsky *et al.*, 'Power and Perspectives Not Taken', *Psychological Science* 17, no. 12 (2006): 1068–1074.

29 C. Anderson and A. Galinsky, 'Power, Optimism, and Risk-taking', *European Journal of Social Psychology* 36, no. 5 (2006): 511–536; P. K. Smith *et al.*, 'Lacking Power Impairs Executive Functions', *Psychological Science* 19, no. 5 (2008): 441–447.

30 K. Atuahene-Gima and H. Li, 'Marketing's Influence Tactics in New Product Development: A Study of High Technology Firms in China', *Journal of Product Innovation Management* 17 (2000): 451–470; A. Somech and A. Drach-Zahavy, 'Relative Power and Influence Strategy: The Effects of Agent/Target Organizational Power on Superiors' Choices of Influence Strategies', *Journal of Organizational Behavior* 23, no. 2 (2002): 167–179.

31 D. Kipnis, S. M. Schmidt and I. Wilkinson, 'Intraorganizational Influence Tactics: Explorations in Getting One's Way', *Journal of Applied Psychology* 65, no. 4 (1980): 440–452; A. Rao and K. Hashimoto, 'Universal and Culturally Specific Aspects of Managerial Influence: A Study of Japanese Managers', *Leadership Quarterly* 8, no. 3 (1997): 295–312; L. A. McFarland, A. M. Ryan and S. D. Kriska, 'Field Study Investigation of Applicant Use of Influence Tactics in a Selection Interview', *Journal of Psychology* 136 (July 2002): 383–398.

32 Cialdini and Goldstein, 'Social Influence: Compliance and Conformity'.

33 Rao and Hashimoto, 'Universal and Culturally Specific Aspects of Managerial Influence'. Silent authority as an influence tactic in non-Western cultures is also discussed in S. F. Pasa, 'Leadership Influence in a High Power Distance and Collectivist Culture', *Leadership & Organization Development Journal* 21, no. 8 (2000): 414–426.

34 'Be Part of the Team If You Want to Catch the Eye', *Birmingham Post (UK)*, 31 August 2000, 14; S. Maitlis, 'Taking It from the Top: How CEOs Influence (and Fail to Influence) Their Boards', *Organization Studies* 25, no. 8 (2004): 1275–1311.

35 A. T. Cobb, 'Toward the Study of Organizational Coalitions: Participant Concerns and Activities in a Simulated Organizational Setting', *Human Relations* 44, no. 10 (1991): 1057–1079; E. A. Mannix, 'Organizations as Resource Dilemmas: The Effects of Power Balance on Coalition Formation in Small Groups', *Organizational Behavior and Human Decision Processes* 55, no. 1 (1993): 1–22; D. J. Terry, M. A. Hogg and K. M. White, 'The Theory of Planned Behavior: Self-Identity, Social Identity and Group Norms', *British Journal of Social Psychology* 38 (September 1999): 225–244.

36 A. P. Brief, *Attitudes in and around Organizations* (Thousand Oaks, CA: Sage, 1998), 69–84; D. J. O'Keefe, *Persuasion: Theory and Research* (Thousand Oaks, CA: Sage, 2002).

37 These and other features of message content in persuasion are detailed in: R. Petty and J. Cacioppo, *Attitudes and Persuasion: Classic and Contemporary Approaches* (Dubuque, IA: W. C. Brown, 1981); M. Pfau, E. A. Szabo and J. Anderson, 'The Role and Impact of Affect in the Process of Resistance to Persuasion', *Human Communication Research* 27 (April 2001): 216–252; O'Keefe, *Persuasion: Theory and Research*, ch. 9; R. Buck *et al.*, 'Emotion and Reason in Persuasion: Applying the Ari Model and the Casc Scale', *Journal of Business Research* 57, no. 6 (2004): 647–656; W. D. Crano and R. Prislin, 'Attitudes and Persuasion', *Annual Review of Psychology* 57 (2006): 345–374.

38 N. Rhodes and W. Wood, 'Self-Esteem and Intelligence Affect Influenceability: The Mediating Role of Message Reception', *Psychological Bulletin* 111, no. 1 (1992): 156–171.

39 D. Strutton and L. E. Pelton, 'Effects of Ingratiation on Lateral Relationship Quality within Sales Team Settings', *Journal of Business Research* 43, no. 1 (1998): 1–12; R. Vonk, 'Self-Serving Interpretations of Flattery: Why Ingratiation Works', *Journal of Personality and Social Psychology* 82, no. 4 (2002): 515–526.

40 C. A. Higgins, T. A. Judge and G. R. Ferris, 'Influence Tactics and Work Outcomes: A Meta-Analysis', *Journal of Organizational Behavior* 24, no. 1 (2003): 89–106.

41 D. Strutton, L. E. Pelton and J. Tanner, J. F., 'Shall We Gather in the Garden: The Effect of Ingratiatory Behaviors on Buyer Trust in Salespeople', *Industrial Marketing Management* 25 (1996): 151–162; J. O' Neil, 'An Investigation of the Sources of Influence of Corporate Public Relations Practitioners', *Public Relations Review* 29 (June 2003): 159–169.

42 M. C. Bolino and W. H. Tunley, 'More Than One Way to Make an Impression: Exploring Profiles of Impression Management', *Journal of Management* 29, no. 2 (2003): 141–160.

43 R. E. Guadagno and R. Cialdini, 'Gender Differences in Impression Management in Organizations: A Qualitative Review', *Sex Roles* 56 (2007): 483–494.

44 T. Peters, 'The Brand Called You', *Fast Company*, August 1997, www.fastcompany.com (accessed 18 May 2009); J. Sills, 'Becoming Your Own Brand', *Psychology Today* 41, no. 1 (2008): 62–63.

45 S. L. McShane, 'Applicant Misrepresentations in Résumés and Interviews in Canada', *Labor Law Journal* (January 1994): 15–24; S. Romero and M. Richtel, 'Second Chance', *New York Times*, 5 March 2001, C1; P. Sabatini, 'Fibs on Résumés Commonplace', *Pittsburgh Post-Gazette*, 24 February 2006.

46 J. Laucius, 'Internet Guru's Credentials a True Work of Fiction', *Ottawa Citizen*, 12 June 2001.

47 A. W. Gouldner, 'The Norm of Reciprocity: A Preliminary Statement', *American Sociological Review* 25 (1960): 161–178.

48 A. R. Cohen and D. L. Bradford, *Influence without Authority* (New York: Wiley, 1990).

49 L. D'Angelo, 'Charity Wars', *Business Review Weekly*, 13 November 2008; K. Burgess, 'Mean Spirits', *Business Review Weekly*, 11 December 2008.

50 Y. Fan, 'Questioning Guanxi: Definition, Classification, and Implications', *International Business Review* 11, no. 5 (2002): 543–561; D. Tan and R. S. Snell, 'The Third Eye: Exploring Guanxi and Relational Morality in the Workplace', *Journal of Business Ethics* 41, no. 4 (2002): 361–384; W. R. Vanhonacker, 'When Good Guanxi Turns Bad', *Harvard Business Review* 82, no. 4 (2004): 18–19.

51 C. M. Falbe and G. Yukl, 'Consequences for Managers of Using Single Influence Tactics and Combinations of Tactics', *Academy of Management Journal* 35 (1992): 638–652.

52 R. C. Ringer and R. W. Boss, 'Hospital Professionals' Use of Upward Influence Tactics', *Journal of Managerial Issues* 12, no. 1 (2000): 92–108.

53 G. Blickle, 'Do Work Values Predict the Use of Intraorganizational Influence Strategies?', *Journal of Applied Social Psychology* 30, no. 1 (2000): 196–205; P. P. Fu *et al.*, 'The Impact of Societal Cultural Values and Individual Social Beliefs on the Perceived Effectiveness of Managerial Influence Strategies: A Meso Approach', *Journal of International Business Studies* 35, no. 4 (2004): 284–305.

54 D. Krackhardt and J. R. Hanson, 'Informal Networks: The Company Behind the Chart', *Harvard Business Review* 71 (July–August 1993): 104–111; P. S. Adler and S.-W. Kwon, 'Social Capital: Prospects for a New Concept', *Academy of Management Review* 27, no. 1 (2002): 17–40.

55 B. R. Ragins and E. Sundstrom, 'Gender and Power in Organizations: A Longitudinal Perspective', *Psychological Bulletin* 105, no. 1 (1989): 51–88; M. Linehan, 'Barriers to Women's Participation in International Management', *European Business Review* 13, no. 1 (2001): 10–19.

56 A. DeFelice, 'Climbing to the Top', *Accounting Technology*, 1 January 2008, 12–18.

57 D. M. McCracken, 'Winning the Talent War for Women: Sometimes It Takes a Revolution', *Harvard Business Review* 78 (November–December 2000): 159–167.

58 D. Bushey and M. Joll, 'Social Network Analysis Comes to Raytheon', *The Monitor (Raytheon)* (2006); J. McGregor, 'The Office Chart That Really Counts', *BusinessWeek*, 27 February 2006, 48; J. Reingold and J. L. Yang, 'The Hidden Workplace: What's Your OQ?', *Fortune*, 23 July 2007, 98–106; T. Cox, 'Map Quest', *Quality Progress*, May 2008, 44.

59 R. Burt, *Structural Holes: The Social Structure of Competition* (Cambridge, MA: Harvard University Press, 1992).

60 M. Granovetter, 'The Strength of Weak Ties', *American Journal of Sociology* 78, no. 6 (1973): 1360–1380; M. Granovetter, *Getting a Job: A Study of Contacts and Careers* (Cambridge, MA: Harvard University Press, 1974).

61 A. Mehra, M. Kilduff and D. J. Brass, 'The Social Networks of High and Low Self-Monitors: Implications for Workplace Performance', *Administrative Science Quarterly* 46 (March 2001): 121–146.

62 Burt, *Structural Holes: The Social Structure of Competition*.

63 B. Uzzi and S. Dunlap, 'How to Build Your Network', *Harvard Business Review* 83, no. 12 (2005): 53–60.

64 J. -V. Douglas, 'Just the Ticket', *Business Review Weekly*, 28 August 2008.

65 K. Walters, 'Heaven Help Them', *Business Review Weekly*, 25 September 2008.

66 This definition of organisational politics has become the dominant perspective over the past 15 years. See G. R. Ferris and K. M. Kacmar, 'Perceptions of Organizational Politics', *Journal of Management* 18, no. 1 (1992): 93–116; R. Cropanzano *et al.*, 'The Relationship of Organizational Politics and Support to Work Behaviors, Attitudes, and Stress', *Journal of Organizational Behavior* 18, no. 2 (1997): 159–180; E. Vigoda, 'Stress-Related Aftermaths to Workplace Politics: The Relationships among Politics, Job Distress, and Aggressive Behavior in Organizations', *Journal of Organizational Behavior* 23, no. 5 (2002): 571–591. However, organisational politics was previously viewed as influence tactics outside the formal role that could be either selfish or altruistic. This older definition is less common today, possibly because it is incongruent with popular views of politics and because it overlaps too much with the concept of influence. For the older perspective of organisational politics, see J. Pfeffer, *Power in Organizations* (Boston: Pitman, 1981); Mintzberg, *Power in and around Organizations*.

67 K. M. Kacmar and R. A. Baron, 'Organizational Politics: The State of the Field, Links to Related Processes, and an Agenda for Future Research', in *Research in Personnel and Human Resources Management*, ed. G. R. Ferris (Greenwich, CT: JAI Press, 1999), 1–39; L. A. Witt, T. F. Hilton and W. A. Hochwarter, 'Addressing Politics in Matrix Teams', *Group & Organization Management* 26 (June 2001): 230–247; Vigoda, 'Stress-Related Aftermaths to Workplace Politics'.

68 C. Hardy, *Strategies for Retrenchment and Turnaround: The Politics of Survival* (Berlin: Walter de Gruyter, 1990), ch. 14; M. C. Andrews and K. M. Kacmar, 'Discriminating among Organizational Politics, Justice, and Support', *Journal of Organizational Behavior* 22, no. 4 (2001): 347–366.

69 S. Blazejewski and W. Dorow, 'Managing Organizational Politics for Radical Change: The Case of Beiersdorf-Lechia S.A., Poznan', *Journal of World Business* 38 (August 2003): 204–223.

70 L. W. Porter, R. W. Allen and H. L. Angle, 'The Politics of Upward Influence in Organizations', *Research in Organizational Behavior* 3 (1981): 120–122; R. J. House, 'Power and Personality in Complex Organizations', *Research in Organizational Behavior* 10 (1988): 305–357.

71 R. Christie and F. Geis, *Studies in Machiavellianism* (New York: Academic Press, 1970); S. M. Farmer *et al.*, 'Putting Upward Influence Strategies in Context', *Journal of Organizational Behavior* 18 (1997): 17–42; K. S. Sauleya and A. G. Bedeian, 'Equity Sensitivity: Construction of a Measure and Examination of Its Psychometric Properties', *Journal of Management* 26 (September 2000): 885–910.

72 G. R. Ferris *et al.*, 'Perceptions of Organizational Politics: Prediction, Stress-Related Implications, and Outcomes', *Human Relations* 49, no. 2 (1996): 233–263.

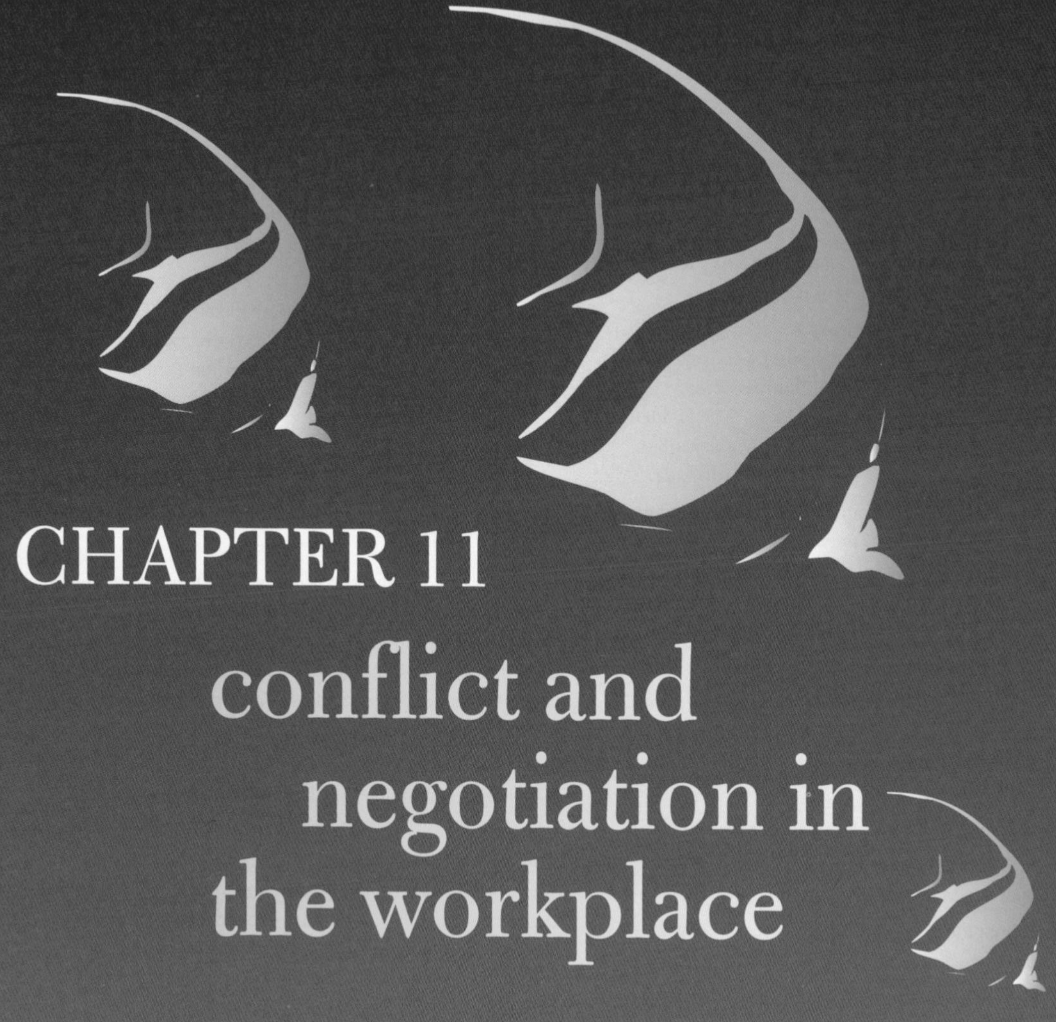

CHAPTER 11

conflict and negotiation in the workplace

LEARNING OBJECTIVES

After reading this chapter, you should be able to:

- debate the positive and negative consequences of conflict in the workplace
- diagram the conflict process model
- describe three conflict frames and their consequences
- identify six structural sources of conflict in organisations
- outline the five strategic approaches to conflict or negotiation and discuss the circumstances in which each would be most appropriate
- describe effective negotiation skills
- outline four contextual influences on negotiations
- describe how cultural and gender differences influence approaches to conflict and negotiation
- compare and contrast the three types of third-party dispute resolution
- outline the seven actions that organisations can take to reduce dysfunctional conflicts.

Alan Levenson/Corbis

Even business tycoon Rupert Murdoch is sometimes challenged by the delicate nuances and consequences of conflict management and negotiation.

Negotiations move through predictable stages. They start with offers and counteroffers, then move to information sharing and problem solving before negotiators start to haggle. When negotiators reach the endgame, their goal is to claim as much value as possible, and brinkmanship becomes a key strategy.

When Rupert Murdoch made his bid for Dow Jones, which owns *The Wall Street Journal*, he had to play hardball to keep the deal on track. One of the blocks to the deal was his reputation in the industry. Despite an offer worth $5 billion, the Bancrofts—who controlled Dow Jones—were reluctant to sell. Their key concern was that Murdoch would take away the *Journal*'s independence, so early negotiations involved a lot of haggling designed to protect the *Journal* from interference by Murdoch.

With these assurances in place, the deal should have gone through. However, when the final proposal arrived from the Bancrofts, it gave the Bancrofts more control than they currently had. Murdoch responded: 'They're taking five billion dollars out of me ... They can't sell their company and still control it—that's not how it works. I'm sorry!' Because the print-media industry was in crisis, and the Bancrofts were having trouble selling their paper, Murdoch had considerable power. To make that power clear, he realised that he had to convince the Bancrofts he was willing to walk away from the deal. How could he signal this intention? First, he told Dow Jones CEO Richard Zannino that he was rejecting the deal. Then, to make his intention clear, he talked to other key players in the negotiation and threatened to pull his offer, an action that would have dramatically lowered Dow Jones' stock price. But the costs of such a move were far greater to Dow Jones and the Bancrofts than to Murdoch. The threat of walking was enough for the parties to reach a compromise: the creation of an independent editorial-oversight committee, with the expectation that a majority of the Bancroft family would agree to this suggestion.

However, the quest for the deal was not without social consequences. The press has been filled with stories about Murdoch's perceived misuse of the press for personal ends. As Murdoch himself says, 'The price of the *Journal* is $60 plus vitriol.'[1]

One of the facts of life is that people hold different points of view. They have unique values hierarchies, develop unique perceptions of reality and establish different norms about how to act in social settings. At the same time, organisations are living systems that demand dynamic rather than static relationships among employees. In other words, employees and managers need to frequently agree on new work arrangements, revise the company's strategic direction and renegotiate the allocation of scarce resources required to perform their jobs.

conflict A process in which one party perceives that its interests are being opposed or negatively affected by another party.

Without identical viewpoints, and with the need to frequently adjust to change, conflict is bound to occur. **Conflict** is a process in which one party perceives that its interests are being opposed or negatively affected by another party.[2] It may occur when one party obstructs or plans to obstruct another's goals in some way. For example, baby boomer managers experience conflict with Gen X or Gen Y employees who spend time text messaging, believing that this interferes with the manager's goal of completing departmental deadlines on time. Text-messaging employees experience conflict with their bosses because they view this form of communication as a valuable way to network, keep informed and (contrary to the boss's opinion) achieve departmental objectives. Conflict is ultimately based on perceptions; it exists whenever one party *believes* that another might obstruct its efforts, whether or not the other party actually intends to do so.

This chapter investigates the dynamics of conflict in organisational settings. We begin by considering the age-old question: is conflict good or bad? Next, we describe the conflict process and examine in detail the main factors that cause or amplify conflict. We then focus on three groups of strategies that can help manage conflicts. Starting with the individual, we discuss the five ways in which people approach conflicts. We also consider how gender and culture might shape preferred conflict resolution styles. We then describe two processes, negotiation and mediation, that are frequently used for conflict resolution. Finally, we discuss what organisations can do to minimise dysfunctional conflicts.

LEARNING OBJECTIVE

Debate the positive and negative consequences of conflict in the workplace.

IS CONFLICT GOOD OR BAD?

For at least the past century, and likely much longer, experts have been debating whether conflict is good or bad for organisational effectiveness. The 'conflict-is-bad' perspective has prevailed for most of that time.[3] According to this perspective, even moderately low levels of disagreement tatter the fabric of workplace relations and sap energy away from productive activities. Conflict with one's supervisor not only wastes productive time; it violates the hierarchy of command and questions the efficient assignment of authority (where managers make the decisions and employees follow them).

Although the 'conflict-is-bad' perspective is now considered oversimplistic, numerous studies report that conflict can potentially undermine team cohesion, information sharing, decision making and employee wellbeing (i.e. through increased stress and lower job satisfaction). It also seems to distort perceptions and increase organisational politics.[4] Conflict distracts employees from their work and, in some cases, motivates them to withhold valuable knowledge and other resources. People who experience conflict are less motivated to communicate or try to understand the other party, which further escalates conflict as each side relies increasingly on distorted perceptions and stereotypes. One survey estimates that 42 per cent of a manager's time is spent dealing with workplace conflict, and that conflict triggers most voluntary and involuntary employee turnover.[5]

More than 80 years ago, social worker and political science scholar Mary Parker Follett proposed the then-radical notion that conflict can be beneficial.[6] Her ideas were slow to gain support. By the 1970s, however, the 'conflict-is-bad' perspective had been replaced by the 'optimal conflict' perspective, namely that organisations are most effective when employees experience some level of conflict in discussions, but become less effective when they have high levels of conflict.

Why is this so? Conflict energises people to debate issues and evaluate alternatives more thoroughly. The debate tests the logic of arguments and encourages participants to re-examine their basic assumptions about the problem and its possible solution. It prevents individuals and groups from making decisions that are suboptimal. As individuals and teams strive to reach agreement, they learn more about each other and come to understand the underlying issues that need to be addressed. This helps them to develop more creative solutions that reflect the needs of multiple stakeholders.

CONFLICT PROCESS MODEL

Diagram the conflict process model.

Now that we have outlined the history and current knowledge about conflict and its outcomes, let's look at the model of the conflict process, shown in Exhibit 11.1.[7] This model begins with the sources of conflict, which we will describe in more detail in the next section. At some point, the sources of conflict lead one or both parties to perceive that conflict exists. They become aware that one party's statements and actions are incompatible with their own goals. These perceptions usually interact with emotions experienced about the conflict.[8] Conflict perceptions and emotions manifest themselves in the decisions and behaviours of one party toward the other. These *conflict episodes* may range from subtle nonverbal behaviours to warlike aggression. Particularly when people experience high levels of conflict emotions, they have difficulty finding the words and

Exhibit 11.1 ***Model of the Conflict Process***

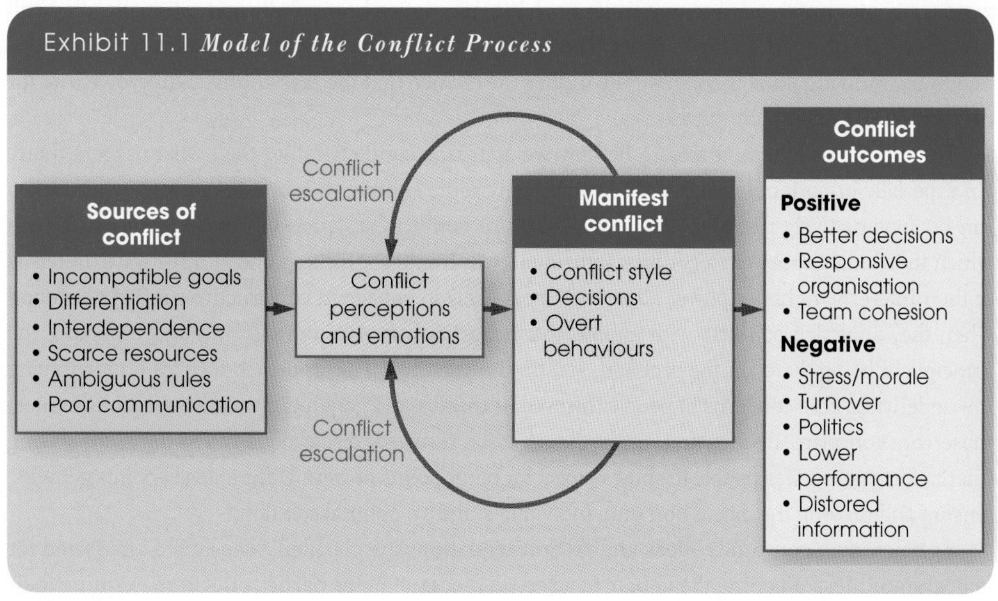

expressions to communicate effectively without further irritating the relationship.[9] Conflict is also manifested by the style each side uses to resolve the conflict. Some people tend to avoid the conflict whereas others try to defeat those with opposing views.

Exhibit 11.1 shows arrows looping back from manifest conflict to conflict perceptions and emotions. These arrows illustrate that the conflict process is really a series of episodes that potentially cycle into conflict escalation.[10] It doesn't take much to start this conflict cycle—just an inappropriate comment, a misunderstanding or an action that lacks diplomacy. These behaviours cause the other party to perceive that conflict exists. Even if the first party did not intend to demonstrate conflict, the second party's response may create that perception.

WHERE CONFLICTS START

LEARNING OBJECTIVE

Describe three conflict frames and their consequences.

To understand where conflicts start, we need to understand both what triggers conflicts and how individuals approach those conflicts. Even relatively minor conflicts can escalate rapidly if individuals focus on attacking and undermining each other rather than working together.

Task conflicts Disagreements among group members about how a task should be accomplished.

Relationship conflicts Types of conflict in which people focus on the characteristics of other individuals, rather than on the issues, as the source of conflict.

Broadly, conflicts can be either task- or relationship-focused. **Task conflicts** are disagreements among group members about how a task should be accomplished. **Relationship conflicts** are not task-related, focusing instead on personal values, gossip, individuals' styles or personality and personal taste. Until recently, there has been a strong belief that whereas relationship conflicts are always dysfunctional, task conflicts can stimulate high levels of performance. The emerging picture, however, is more complex. A recent overview of research shows that although relationship conflict has a bigger impact on performance than task conflict, team satisfaction and performance decrease as *either* kind of conflict increases. When we look at task conflict, the biggest impact on performance occurs when individuals are working in an uncertain environment, for example, in decision-making or project teams.[11]

As these findings suggest, separating task and relationship conflicts isn't easy. Most of us experience some degree of relationship conflict during and after any task conflict.[12] In other words, any attempt to engage in problem solving, no matter how calmly and rationally, may still sow the seeds of relationship conflict. The stronger the level of debate and the more the issue is tied to the individual's self-concept, the higher the chance that the task conflict will evolve into (or mix with) relationship conflict.

The critical issue may therefore be how we approach conflicts rather than what triggers them. An especially important issue is to understand why some conflicts become all-out wars while others can be constructively resolved. One explanation for conflict escalation lies in the perspective with which individuals approach a conflict. Individuals can frame conflicts in one of three ways: in terms of their interests, rights or power.[13] They are most likely to engage in constructive conflict resolution when they approach conflicts with an **interests-based frame**. An *interest-based frame* embodies the principle of being 'hard on the problem, soft on the person'.[14] This approach focuses on identifying the underlying, core concerns of people involved in conflict and generating creative solutions to meet those core concerns. By focusing on the issues to be resolved, discussions have a problem-solving orientation that enables people to show respect for other points of view. Different viewpoints generate tension and prolong the discussion until individuals find an optimal solution.

interests-based frame An approach to conflict that emphasises disputants' underlying needs and interests.

As discussion continues, ideas and recommendations are clarified, redesigned and tested for logical soundness. Keeping the debate focused on the issue helps participants to re-examine their assumptions and beliefs without triggering the drive to defend, along with its associated negative emotions and ego-defence mechanism behaviours. Teams and organisations with very low levels of constructive conflict are less effective, but there is also likely to be an upper limit to the level of intensity of constructive conflict.[15]

Conflicts escalate rapidly and are likely to become personal when individuals adopt a **rights-based frame** or **power-based frame**. A *rights-based frame* focuses on contractual obligations, legal rights or precedents. Disputants who adopt this perspective focus on what is 'fair' or what they are entitled to. Often, disputants have different legal opinions about the interpretation of contract clauses with the result that parties end up in court to resolve their differences. A *power-based frame* focuses on who has more power. Individuals invoke their status and use threats in order to intimidate others and to enforce their preferred solution. Because power is subjective, the conflict will escalate as individuals attempt to demonstrate their power while eroding others' power.

rights-based frame An approach to conflict that focuses on contractual obligations, legal rights or precedents.

power-based frame An approach to conflict that focuses on who has more power in the dispute.

Conflicts often start with individuals asserting their rights and power. A rights- or power-based frame often leads to attacks on the other person. As individuals attempt to gain more power or to apportion blame to the other person, they try to undermine the other person's argument by questioning their competency. Attacking a person's credibility or displaying an aggressive response triggers defence mechanisms and a competitive orientation from that person. The subjects of those verbal attacks become less motivated to communicate and share information, making it more difficult for the parties to discover common ground and ultimately resolve the conflict. Instead, they rely more on distorted perceptions and stereotypes which, as we noted earlier, tend to further escalate the conflict.

SOURCES OF CONFLICT IN ORGANISATIONS

Identify six structural sources of conflict in organisations.

In the following section, we discuss how task and relationship conflicts develop. The six main conditions that cause conflict in organisational settings are incompatible goals, value differences, interdependence, scarce resources, ambiguous rules and communication problems. We then go on to consider the options that team members and organisations have for resolving these conflicts.

Incompatible Goals

Microsoft has been highly successful with its host of products and services, yet various sources conclude that the company suffers from vicious infighting across product groups. 'Pretty much across the board people are saying that Microsoft is dysfunctional,' concludes one industry analyst. 'They are not cooperating across business groups.' One of the major sources of this conflict is that some work units have incompatible goals with other units. For example, the MSN group developed desktop search software which would compete against Google Desktop. However, Microsoft's Windows group opposed release of the MSN software because the Windows group had developed similar software for its Vista operating system. The MSN group also fought against the Office group over MSN's desire to connect their online calendar with the calendar in Office. The Office group baulked because 'then MSN could cannibalise Office', says an employee who recently left Microsoft. 'Windows and Office would never let MSN have more budget or more control.'[16]

The battles between Microsoft MSN and Windows work units illustrates how goal incompatibility—where the goals of one person or department seem to interfere with another person's or department's goals—can be a source of conflict in organisations.[17] MSN's goal of competing against Google with desktop search software threatened the Windows group's goals of launching new features in Microsoft Vista. MSN's goal of providing users with better calendar integration threatened the Microsoft Office group's product territory, which might undermine its profitability or control over the calendar feature.

Differentiation

Another source of conflict is differentiation—differences among people, departments and other entities regarding their training, values, beliefs and experiences. Differentiation can be distinguished from goal incompatibility because two people or departments may agree on a common goal but have profound differences in how to achieve that goal. Consider the classic tension between employees from two companies brought together through a merger. Employees in each organisation fight over the 'right way' to do things because of their unique experiences in the separate companies. This source of conflict is apparent as Porsche AG takes control of Volkswagen Group. As Reality Check 11.1 describes, VW chairman Ferdinand Piëch and his allies are battling Porsche CEO Wendelin Wiedeking and his executive team because they have substantially different views on how Europe's largest car manufacturer should be run.

Intergenerational conflicts are also mainly caused by differentiation. Younger and older employees have different needs, different expectations and different workplace practices, which sometimes produces conflicting preferences and actions. Recent studies suggest that intergenerational differences occur because people develop social identities around technological developments and other pivotal social events.[19] Information technology also maintains differentiation because without face-to-face experiences, employees have more difficulty forming common mental models and norms. For instance, recent investigations indicate that virtual teams have a high incidence of conflict because technology makes it difficult for them to form common experiences and perspectives.[20]

Interdependence

Conflict tends to increase with the level of interdependence. Interdependence exists when team members must share common inputs to their individual tasks, need to interact in the process of executing their work, or receive outcomes (such as rewards) that are partly determined by the performance of others.[21] Higher interdependence increases the risk of conflict because there is a greater chance that each side will disrupt or interfere with the other side's goals.[22]

Other than complete independence, employees tend to have the lowest risk of conflict when working with others in a pooled interdependence relationship. Pooled interdependence occurs where individuals operate independently except for reliance on a common resource or authority (see Chapter 8). The potential for conflict is higher in sequential interdependence work relationships, such as an assembly line. The highest risk of conflict tends to occur in reciprocal interdependence situations. With reciprocal interdependence, employees are highly dependent on each other and, consequently, have a higher probability of interfering with each other's work and personal goals.

Scarce Resources

Resource scarcity generates conflict because each person or unit requiring the same resource necessarily undermines others who also need that resource to fulfil their goals. These conflict episodes occur partly because there aren't enough financial, human capital and other resources for everyone to accomplish their goals, so employees need to justify why they should receive the resources. The more resources one project receives, the fewer resources another project will have available to accomplish its goals.

Ambiguous Rules

Ambiguous rules—or the complete lack of rules—breed conflict. This occurs because uncertainty increases the risk that one party intends to interfere with the other party's goals. Ambiguity also encourages political tactics and, in some cases, employees enter a free-for-all battle to win decisions in their favour. This explains why conflict is more common during mergers and acquisitions. Employees from both companies have conflicting practices and values, and few rules have developed to minimise the manoeuvring for power and resources.[23] When clear rules exist, on the other hand, employees know what to expect from each other and have agreed to abide by those rules.

Communication Problems

Conflict often occurs due to the lack of opportunity, ability or motivation to communicate effectively. Let's look at each of these causes. First, when two parties lack the opportunity to communicate, they tend to rely more on stereotypes to understand the other party in the conflict. Unfortunately, stereotypes are sufficiently subjective that emotions can negatively distort the meaning of an opponent's actions, thereby escalating perceptions of conflict. Second, some people lack the necessary skills to communicate in a diplomatic, nonconfrontational manner. When one party communicates its disagreement arrogantly, opponents are more likely to heighten their perception of the conflict. This may lead the other party to reciprocate with a similar response, which further escalates the conflict.[24]

A third problem is that the perception of conflict reduces motivation to communicate. Relationship conflict is uncomfortable, so people avoid interacting with others in a conflicting relationship. Unfortunately, less communication can further escalate the conflict because there is less opportunity to empathise with the opponent's situation and opponents are more likely to rely on distorted stereotypes of the other party. In fact, conflict tends to further distort these stereotypes through the process of social identity (see Chapter 3). We begin to see competitors less favourably so our self-concept remains positive during these uncertain times.[25]

INDIVIDUAL DIFFERENCES IN CONFLICT RESOLUTION

Outline the five strategic approaches to conflict or negotiation and discuss the circumstances in which each would be most appropriate.

Individual differences play an important role in how we manage conflicts. Emotional intelligence, for example, has a strong impact on whether relationship conflicts develop and, if they do, whether they escalate. Relationship conflict is less likely to occur, or is less likely to escalate, when team members have high levels of emotional intelligence. Emotionally intelligent employees are better

Conflict in Overdrive at VW and Porsche

AFP/Getty Images

Behind these smiling faces of Volkswagen Group chairman Ferdinand Piëch (left) and Porsche CEO Wendelin Wiedeking (right) is a deep conflict that poisoned relations between the car companies and nearly sent Porsche into bankruptcy.

Volkswagen Group (VW) became a den of internal conflict over the past decade as it acquired several fiefdoms—Audi, Lamborghini, Bentley, Bugatti, Skoda and SEAT—that jealously guarded their brand and continuously rebelled against sharing knowledge. One member of VW's supervisory board (German equivalent of a board of directors) commented that managing the company is 'like trying to ride a chariot with four or five horses, each of which pulls in a different direction'. These internal skirmishes, however, paled against the battle VW recently fought with luxury sports car company Porsche AG.

Through an unswerving drive for efficient production and astute marketing, Porsche CEO Wendelin Wiedeking and his executive team transformed Porsche into the world's most profitable and prestigious car company. As confidence in their management skills increased, Porsche executives wanted to apply those practices at VW, Europe's largest car company and a significant provider of Porsche production work. Porsche started buying shares of VW a few years ago and eventually achieved a controlling interest.

Several car industry experts warned that there would be major conflicts ahead as Porsche executives attempted to streamline VW by closing down inefficient operations and money-losing car lines. 'Wiedeking is a Porsche CEO from another corporate culture,' says German auto analyst Christoph Stuermer. 'He's out to maximize profits by cutting costs. He snubbed everyone, telling off VW management, interfering with their way of doing business.'

able to regulate their emotions during debate, which reduces the risk of escalating perceptions of interpersonal hostility. People with high emotional intelligence are also more likely to view a coworker's emotional reaction as valuable information about that person's needs and expectations, rather than as a personal attack.

Our personal preferences also affect the way that we approach a conflict. In any conflict or negotiation, we need to select an approach that will help us to achieve our goals. Which goals we emphasise are shaped by the relative importance that we, personally, place on two factors: maximising our outcomes and preserving the relationship with the other person. Combined, these two factors yield five distinct conflict-handling styles.

It is important to remember that, whatever our personal preferences, these same questions arise when we analyse the context in which a negotiation or conflict is occurring. Whether we are thinking about how to manage a conflict or start a negotiation, we need to assess our priorities. The starting point for our interaction should always be careful consideration of the importance of our personal outcomes relative to the value that we place on maintaining our relationship with the other person. This analysis helps people to decide which approach best meets their needs in any given situation.

The number of conflict-handling styles identified by conflict experts has varied over the years, but most common are variations of the five-category model shown in Exhibit 11.2 and described

REALITY CHECK 11.1

Ferdinand Dudenhoeffer, director of the Germany's Centre of Automotive Research (CAR), agrees, 'Porsche is very successful in being lean and profitable. It's not going to be harmonious.'

Particularly offended by Wiedeking's plans was VW chairman Ferdinand Piëch, who has a different vision for Europe's largest automaker. Piëch, whose grandfather developed the VW Beetle, places more emphasis on spectacular engineering than exceptional profits. For example, he continues to support the money-losing Bugatti brand, which VW acquired several years ago when Piëch was CEO. More recently, Piëch championed the Phaeton, VW's luxury car that broke new ground in innovation (it boasts 100 patents), but has not been a commercial success.

Wiedeking, on the other hand, believed that VW could be more profitable if it stopped producing the Phaeton and Bugatti. 'Piech sees his vision endangered by Wiedeking,' says Dudenhoeffer. 'Wiedeking said that there are no holy cows at VW, no more Phaetons, no more Bugattis.' These ideas make Piëch's blood boil, 'Anyone who says that VW should pull the Phaeton doesn't understand the world,' grumbles Piëch, explaining that luxury cars represent the only segment with double-digit growth.

There are two ironies in this tale of corporate conflict. The first is that Piëch is a member of the Porsche family. He is a cousin of Porsche chairman Wolfgang Porsche and owns a 10 per cent share of the Porsche company. Piëch began his career at Porsche and was their chief engineer before moving to Audi and later VW. Furthermore, Piëch supported Porsche's initial investment in VW, mainly to ensure that Porsche remained a loyal customer.

The second irony is that, just when Porsche had acquired 50 per cent of VW shares, the tables turned. The VW share purchases and the taxes due from options received from those shares drained Porsche's cash resources just as the world's financial markets went into a tailspin. Banks that gladly lent Porsche USD$15 billion at other times to purchase VW shares now wanted to call in those loans. Suddenly, Porsche needed a friendly investor to avoid bankruptcy. VW, the company Porsche was acquiring, came to the rescue, initially by lending cash to Porsche and later by acquiring the company. Wiedeking stepped down as Porsche's CEO 'to make an important contribution to the pacification of the situation.'[18]

below.[26] Each style has both advantages and disadvantages that we need to take into consideration before selecting an approach. However, once we have selected a style, there are some key actions that help us to implement it effectively.[27]

PROBLEM SOLVING Problem solving tries to find a mutually beneficial solution for both parties. This is known as the **win–win orientation** because people using this style believe the resources at stake are expandable rather than fixed if the parties work together to find a creative solution. Information sharing is an important feature of this style because both parties collaborate to identify common ground and potential solutions that satisfy everyone involved. Two actions help us to implement problem solving effectively. The first action is the display of *firm flexibility*, where we remain firm in meeting our most important needs while being flexible about how this is accomplished. The second action, described in more detail in the section on negotiation, is the use of trade-offs to ensure that both parties' needs are met.

win–win orientation The belief that the parties will find a mutually beneficial solution to their disagreement.

FORCING Forcing tries to win the conflict at the other's expense. People who use this style typically have a **win–lose orientation**—they believe the parties are drawing from a fixed pie, so the more one party receives, the less the other party will receive. Consequently, this style relies on some of the 'hard' influence tactics described in Chapter 10, particularly

win–lose orientation The belief that conflicting parties are drawing from a fixed pie, so the more one party receives, the less the other party will receive.

Exhibit 11.2 *Interpersonal Conflict-Handling Styles*

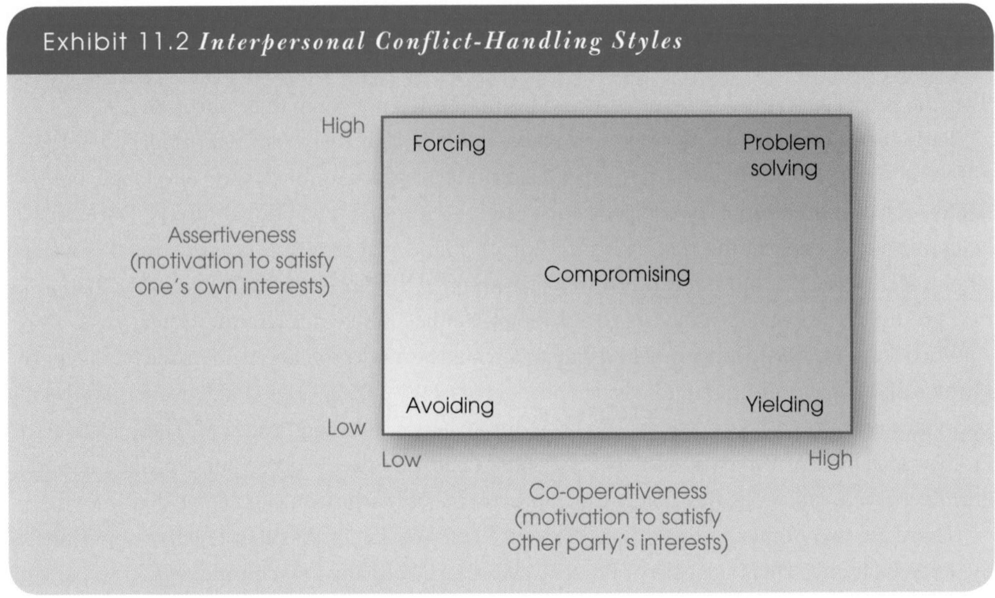

Sources: C. K. W. De Dreu *et al.*, 'A Theory-Based Measure of Conflict Management Strategies in the Workplace', *Journal of Organizational Behavior* 22, no. 6 (2001): 645–668. For other variations of this model, see T. L. Ruble and K. Thomas, 'Support For a Two-Dimensional Model of Conflict Behavior', *Organizational Behavior and Human Performance* 16, no. 1 (1976): 145; R. R. Blake, H. A. Shepard and J. S. Mouton, *Managing Intergroup Conflict in Industry* (Houston: Gulf Publishing, 1964); M. A. Rahim, 'Toward a Theory of Managing Organizational Conflict', *International Journal of Conflict Management* 13, no. 3 (2002): 206–235.

assertiveness, to get one's own way. In selecting a forcing style, two actions help a person to implement it effectively. The first action is to ensure that good alternatives are developed, which increase the person's power. The second action is to develop a small number of strong arguments and then keep repeating them. Research shows that this is what effective negotiators do.[28]

AVOIDING Avoiding tries to smooth over or avoid conflict situations altogether. It represents a low concern for both self and the other party; in other words, avoiders try to suppress thinking about the conflict. For example, some employees will rearrange their work area or tasks to minimise interaction with certain coworkers.[29]

YIELDING Yielding involves giving in completely to the other side's wishes, or at least cooperating with little or no attention to one's own interests. This style involves making unilateral concessions and unconditional promises, as well as offering help with no expectation of reciprocal help. Negotiators who implement this style effectively also treat the other party with respect and avoid triggering escalatory cycles of anger and retaliation.[30]

COMPROMISING Compromising involves looking for a position in which your losses are offset by equally valued gains. It involves matching the other party's concessions, making conditional promises or threats, and actively searching for a middle ground between the interests of the two parties.

Choosing the Best Conflict-Handling Style

Chances are that you have a preferred conflict handling style. You might have a tendency toward avoiding or yielding because disagreement makes you feel uncomfortable and is inconsistent with your self-concept as someone who likes to get along with everyone. Or, perhaps you prefer the compromising and forcing strategies because they reflect your strong need for achievement and to control your environment. In general, people gravitate toward one or two preferred conflict-handling styles that match their personality, personal and cultural values, and past experience. However, most people recognise that they should use different conflict-handling styles in different situations.[31] In other words, the best style varies with the situation.[32]

Exhibit 11.3 summarises the main contingencies, as well as problems with using each conflict-handling style. Problem solving has long been identified as the preferred conflict-handling style where possible because dialogue and clever thinking helps people to break out of the limited boundaries of their opposing alternatives to find an integrated solution where both gain value. In addition, recent studies report that problem solving improves long-term relationships, reduces

Exhibit 11.3 *Conflict Handling Style Contingencies and Problems*

Conflict-handling style	Preferred style when ...	Problems with this style
Problem solving	• Interests are not perfectly opposing (i.e. not pure win–lose) • Parties have trust, openness and time to share information • The issues are complex	• Sharing information that the other party might use to their advantage
Forcing	• You have a deep conviction about your position (e.g. believe other person's behaviour is unethical) • Dispute requires a quick solution • The other party would take advantage of more cooperative strategies	• Highest risk of relationship conflict • High risk of escalation or impasse if other employs a forcing style • May damage long-term relations, reducing future problem solving
Avoiding	• Conflict has become too emotionally charged • Cost of trying to resolve the conflict outweighs the benefits	• Doesn't usually resolve the conflict • May increase other party's frustration
Yielding	• Other party has substantially more power • Issue is much less important to you than to the other party • The value and logic of your position isn't as clear	• Increases other party's expectations in future conflict episodes • High risk of suboptimal outcome if other also yields
Compromising	• Parties have equal power • Time pressure to resolve the conflict • Parties lack trust/openness for problem solving	• Suboptimal solution where mutual gains are possible

stress, and minimises emotional defensiveness and other indications of relationship conflict.[33] However, problem solving is the best choice of conflict handling only when there is some potential for mutual gains, which is more likely to occur when the issue is complex, and when the parties have enough trust, openness and time to share information. If problem solving is used under the wrong conditions, there is an increased risk that the other party will take advantage of the information you have openly shared.

You might think that avoiding is an ineffective conflict management strategy, but it is actually the best approach where conflict has become emotionally charged or where negotiating has a higher cost than the benefits of conflict resolution.[34] At the same time, conflict avoidance is often ineffective because it doesn't resolve the conflict and may increase the other party's frustration. The forcing style of conflict resolution is usually inappropriate because research indicates that it generates relationship conflict more quickly or intensely than other conflict-handling styles. However, forcing may be necessary where you know you are correct (e.g. the other party's position is unethical or based on obviously flawed logic), the dispute requires a quick solution or the other party would take advantage of a more cooperative conflict handling style.

The yielding style may be appropriate when the other party has substantially more power, the issue is not as important to you as to the other party and you aren't confident that your position has the best value or logical consistency. On the other hand, yielding behaviours may give the other side unrealistically high expectations, thereby motivating them to seek more from you in the future. In the long run, yielding may produce more conflict rather than resolve it. The compromising style may be best when there is little hope for mutual gain through problem solving, both parties have equal power and both are under time pressure to settle their differences. However, we rarely know for certain that mutual gains are not available, so entering a conflict with the compromising style may cause the parties to overlook better solutions.

Describe effective negotiation skills.

RESOLVING CONFLICT THROUGH NEGOTIATION

Think back through yesterday's events. Maybe you had to work out an agreement with other students about what tasks to complete for a team project. Chances are that you shared transportation with someone, so you had to clarify the timing of the ride. Then perhaps there was the question of who made dinner. Each of these daily events created potential conflict, and they were resolved through negotiation. **Negotiation** occurs whenever two or more conflicting parties attempt to resolve their divergent goals by redefining the terms of their interdependence. In other words, people negotiate when they think that discussion can produce a more satisfactory arrangement (at least for them) in their exchange of goods or services.

negotiation The process whereby two or more conflicting parties attempt to resolve their divergent goals by redefining the terms of their interdependence.

As you can see, negotiation is not an obscure practice reserved for labour and management bosses when hammering out a collective agreement. Everyone negotiates, every day. Most of the time, you don't even realise that you are in negotiations. Negotiation is particularly evident in the workplace because employees work interdependently with each other. They negotiate with their supervisors over next month's work assignments, with customers over the sale and delivery schedules of their product and with coworkers over when to have lunch. And yes, they occasionally negotiate with each other in labour disputes and workplace agreements.

Although the interpersonal styles we described in the previous section will shape how negotiators approach a negotiation, to be effective they need to balance collaborative and competitive behaviours. Collaboration is important because it helps negotiators to *create value,* that is, to identify ways to maximise both negotiators' outcomes and develop mutually satisfactory outcomes. Competition is equally important because it helps negotiators to *claim value,* that is, to get the best possible outcomes. The reason that negotiators need to balance these two processes is that we can rarely get everything we want in a negotiation. To reach a deal we must satisfy both our own and the other negotiator's needs.[35]

Key Skills for Value Claiming

The goal of value claiming is to obtain the best possible outcomes for yourself. To do this, you need to persuade the other negotiator to give you what you want. This is usually done by presenting strong arguments to support your claims while rejecting the arguments made by the other negotiator. A clear danger in this approach is that the discussion will become increasingly heated and you will fail to reach agreement. Despite this potential pitfall, value claiming is a critical strategy for protecting our outcomes. There are four skills that help us to effectively claim value.

Identify Limits

Research consistently reports that people have more favourable negotiation results when they prepare for the negotiation and set goals.[36] One important goal is a negotiator's **target point**, which identifies the best possible outcome for that person. It's the outcome we aspire to. Negotiators who set high, specific target points obtain better outcomes than those with low or vague target points. A second important goal is a negotiator's **resistance point,** or the very worst outcome that is acceptable. Resistance points are important because they tell us when we should stop making concessions and consider negotiating with someone else.

target point The best possible outcome that an individual hopes to achieve in a negotiation.

resistance point The worst outcome that an individual is prepared to accept before walking away from a negotiation.

Identify Power

Having alternatives is a key source of power in negotiation. Negotiation writers often talk about BATNA (Best Alternative To Negotiated Agreement)—this means knowing what happens if you fail to reach agreement in a specific negotiation. Can you walk away and start the negotiation with someone else? For example, when you are negotiating with dealers for a price for your new car, you have more power if several dealers have the model you want. Consequently, identifying as many possible alternatives to a negotiation as you can increases your power. Power also increases when the skills or goods that you have are in scarce supply and the other person has few alternatives. Good alternatives tell you when to walk away from a negotiation.

Manage Time

Deadlines can help to improve outcomes. Research shows that as negotiators get closer to their deadlines, they make more concessions. This means that if you can increase the time pressure on the other person by creating a deadline, you can improve your outcomes. Reality Check 11.2 shows us an extreme use of time pressure: going on strike. The 'exploding offer'—a contract with a very short deadline—is another example of how time can be used to a negotiator's advantage. An extreme example is the use of strike action by labour unions—unions anticipate a greater chance of gaining concessions because, as time passes, the cost of the strike to management

Time to Get Tough

AAP

In Bihar, India, state government workers went on an indefinite strike in their quest for pay entitlements they believed had been unjustly withheld.

When negotiations are competitive, a key goal for negotiators is to pressure the other parties to accept agreement. There are many ways to do this, including increasing the costs involved in a failure to reach agreement. In labour management negotiations, this can involve strike action.

Recently, state government employees in Bihar, India, decided to go on indefinite strike in a protest about the government's perceived failure to meet their core demands. Employees called on the Bihar government to implement both the 'letter and the spirit' of the Sixth Pay Commission's recommendations by backdating all benefits to 1 January 2006. The employees attacked both the government's reputation and bottom line.

increases. What happens when the other side imposes a deadline on you? Rather than focusing on the deadline, remind yourself that when you get to the deadline the negotiation ends for both of you.[38] This will help you focus on negotiating effectively rather than conceding in order to get a deal before the deadline.

Manage First Offers and Concessions

Two critical decisions centre on first offers and concessions. Negotiators often ask, 'Who should make the first offer?' One reason for making the first offer is to ensure you anchor the negotiation. Imagine that you are hoping to sell your car for $10 000. One potential buyer offers you $5000. You notice there is a big difference between these two starting positions, and worry that you might not sell the car. So you respond to the buyer by saying, '$5000 seems a little low. I was hoping for $7500.' The buyer has effectively obtained a big concession from you by anchoring what you thought was possible. However, you may also experience the 'winner's curse' by accepting the offer, because your rapid acceptance means that you were expecting the buyer to offer even less, and the buyer's offer is above your target point.

Whether or not you make the first offer depends on how much information you have. If you are well informed about the price of a car or starting salaries in your profession, you will benefit from making the first offer. However, in the absence of information, getting the other person to make the first offer provides a vital clue to the kind of outcome they were expecting: it tells you about their target point.

REALITY CHECK 11.2

By going public, they eroded the state government's reputation. Striking workers accused the government of adopting a rigid stance that signalled unwillingness to end the deadlock. Going further, the general secretary of the Bihar State Non-Gazetted Employees Federation (Gope faction), Rambali Prasad Singh, said, 'The state government was misleading the people by claiming that recommendations of the Sixth Pay Commission had been implemented with effect from January 1, 2006, as only national benefits [i.e. retirement pensions] were being given to employees while financial benefits [i.e. salary increases for current workers] were being given from April 1, 2007.' He went on to describe the government's appeal for the strike to end as a 'bundle of lies'.

At the same time, the government was counting the costs of its inability to deliver services. Not only were most government offices empty, but hospitals were unable to deliver treatments, appropriates tests and medicine to their patients. Galleries at the Patna Museum were closed, leading to large revenue losses. Teachers were also on strike and government engineers announced their intention to join the strike. As the inconvenience experienced by the general public mounted, the government experienced growing pressure to restore services as quickly as possible, increasing the need for them to make concessions to striking workers. The workers themselves, who ignored the state government's 'no work no pay' warning, signalled that they would not succumb to time pressure. Manjul Kumar Das, general secretary of the Bihar State Non-Gazetted Employees Federation, stated that 'We will not end our strike unless our demands are accepted by the government.'[37]

Once the first offers are on the table, negotiators start to make concessions. Concessions are important because they (1) enable the parties to move toward the area of potential agreement, (2) they symbolise each party's motivation to bargain in good faith, and (3) they tell the other party of the relative importance of the negotiating items.[39] However, concessions move the parties toward agreement only under certain conditions.[40] First, concessions need to be labelled—the other party needs to be aware that your action is a concession, that this concession is costly to you and that it is beneficial to the other party. Second, the concessions should be accompanied by an expectation that the other party will reciprocate. In fact, when there is a lack of trust, the concession should be contingent on a specific reciprocal action by the other party.

Finally, concessions should be given in instalments, not all at once. The rationale is that people experience more positive emotions from two smaller concessions than one larger concession—even if the larger concession simply combines the two smaller ones. For example, rather than making one concession to complete the project a month earlier than initially offered, you might first offer to finish the work three weeks earlier, then later make a concession to complete it an additional week earlier. Generally, the best strategy is to be moderately tough and give just enough concessions to communicate sincerity and motivation to resolve the conflict.[41] Being too tough can undermine relations between the parties; giving too many concessions implies weakness and encourages the other party to use power and resistance.

Key Skills for Value Creation

The goal of value creation is to ensure that both negotiators obtain the best possible outcomes. To do this means negotiators need to become problem solvers. A key element of this approach is information exchange. A potential pitfall is that, because information is power, information sharing gives the other party more power to leverage a better deal if the opportunity occurs. Skilled negotiators often adopt a cautious problem-solving style at the outset by sharing information slowly and determining whether the other side will reciprocate. In this way, they try to establish trust with the other party. Several strategies ensure that negotiators will reap the benefits of problem solving and value creation.

Manage Information

Information is the cornerstone of effective value creation. Negotiators would do well to embrace the principle from management guru Stephen Covey: 'Seek to understand before you seek to be understood.' But what does it mean to understand? When we focus on value creation, the emphasis shifts from understanding the other person's justifications to understanding *why* they are making particular claims. By doing this, we gather information about the other person's needs and begin to understand how they arrived at their claims. This is important because there are usually many options for meeting someone's needs. The more information we gather, the easier it is for us to discover low-cost concessions or proposals that will satisfy the other side.

Manage Offers and Concessions

Not all offers and concessions are equally effective in creating value. The key to value creation is the ability to identify issues that are weighted differently by the negotiators. For example, when negotiating an employment contract, getting a large signing bonus might be more important than your starting salary. Through information sharing, you might discover that your employer is not concerned about the size of your signing bonus but does want to keep salary costs low. You can create value by agreeing on a large signing bonus (important to you) and a lower starting salary (important to your employer).

Two strategies help a negotiator discover these potential trade-offs. The first strategy is to make multi-issue proposals. Rather than making an offer on a single item (for example, a signing bonus), you might propose a package that includes a mix of high-value and low-value items. This gives the other negotiator flexibility to make concessions on her or his low-value items. The second strategy is to ensure that you concede on your low-value items while getting concessions on your high-value items.[42]

Build the Relationship

Because the strategies associated with value creation are risky, the relationship between the two negotiators increases in importance. Before negotiators are willing to share information and engage in problem solving, they need to be sure that they will not be exploited by the other party. There are several straightforward techniques that help negotiators build stronger relationships with each other.

First, it is important to remember that we form first impressions very quickly—literally, in the blink of an eye.[43] So, building a relationship starts as soon as the negotiators meet. It is easier to build trust when there are obvious similarities between negotiators, such as gender, age, culture or socioeconomic background. This is because we assume people who are similar to us will also behave as we do. When there are no obvious similarities, it is important to spend time 'schmoozing' to identify ways in which we are similar. Signalling trustworthiness also helps strengthen the relationship. Negotiators can do this by demonstrating that they are reliable and will keep their promises, or by identifying shared goals and values. Finally, they can improve the relationship by putting the other person in a good mood. Flattery and humour improve the other person's mood, strengthen the relationship and encourage greater creativity.[44]

Manage the Process

An important part of value creation is ensuring the negotiation does not enter into an escalating cycle of attack and counterattack. These cycles occur when negotiators start with the power-based or rights-based frames we described earlier. Faced with power and rights tactics, negotiators need to reframe the negotiation. To do this, they need to exercise self-control and avoid being pulled into attack mode. To redirect a negotiation, we need to ignore personal attacks and refocus on the substantive problem. We can explicitly suggest that we try a different process and we can ask the other party to explain what is behind their point of view. An effective way to disrupt attacks is to take a break—simply pause and take a deep breath, suggest a coffee break or even suggest coming back to the negotiation at another time.[45]

Contextual Influences on Negotiation

Outline four contextual influences on negotiations.

We have seen that negotiators should carefully think through their initial offer, target and resistance points. They need to consider alternative strategies in case the negotiation fails. Negotiators also need to check their underlying assumptions, as well as goals and values. Equally important is the need to research what the other party wants from the negotiation. 'You have to be prepared every which way about the people, the subject, and your fallback position,' advises Paul Tellier, the former president of Bombardier, Inc.[46] The final part of preparing for a negotiation is to assess the context in which we are negotiating. Four contextual influences need to be considered: characteristics of the other negotiator, distribution of power, constraints on negotiators and physical setting.

Characteristics of the Other Negotiator

Negotiators need to be flexible and responsive to the other party. As each negotiator gathers information about how the other party is approaching the negotiation, they need to adapt their strategies. In preparing for negotiations, we should consider the possibility that the other negotiator will have different goals or a different strategic approach. For example, we might plan to adopt a collaborative approach only to discover that the other negotiator is highly competitive. Anticipating such differences helps us to 'expect the unexpected' and to respond in a planned way.[47] To help in this process, we should gather as much information as possible about the other negotiator, including his or her reputation, relevant organisational or national culture, and other factors that shape the person's goals and strategies.

Distribution of Power

Another factor that we need to consider is the other person's power. We have already discussed the role that alternatives play in giving negotiators power. We now also need to think about how power is distributed in the negotiation.[48] Power is much more likely to affect negotiators' strategies and outcomes when it is unevenly distributed—that is, when one negotiator has more power than the other. Under these circumstances, the high-power negotiator is able to gain more concessions than the low-power negotiator, and has little motivation to engage in value creation. For negotiators in the less powerful position, it is even more important to develop good alternatives.

Constraints on Negotiators

Most negotiators have audiences—anyone with a vested interest in the negotiation outcomes, such as executives, other team members, or the general public. Negotiators tend to act differently when their audience observes the negotiation or has detailed information about the process, compared to situations in which the audience sees only the end results.[49] When the audience has direct surveillance over the proceedings, negotiators tend to be more competitive, less willing to make concessions and more likely to engage in political tactics against the other party. This 'hardline' behaviour shows the audience that the negotiator is working for their interests. With their audience watching, negotiators also have more interest in saving face.

Physical Setting

It is easier to negotiate on your own turf because you are familiar with the negotiating environment and are able to maintain comfortable routines.[50] Also, there is no need to cope with travel-related stress or depend on others for resources during the negotiation. Of course, you can't walk out of negotiations as easily when on your own turf, but this is usually a minor issue. Considering these strategic benefits of home turf, many negotiators agree to neutral territory. Phone calls, videoconferences and other forms of information technology potentially avoid territorial issues, but skilled negotiators usually prefer the media richness of face-to-face meetings. Frank Lowy, cofounder of retail property giant Westfield Group, says that telephones are 'too cold' for negotiating. 'From a voice I don't get all the cues I need. I go by touch and feel and I need to see the other person.'[51]

The physical distance between the parties and formality of the setting can influence their orientation toward each other and the disputed issues. So can the seating arrangements. People who sit face to face are more likely to develop a win–lose orientation toward the conflict situation. In contrast, some negotiation groups deliberately intersperse participants around the table to convey a win–win orientation. Others arrange the seating so that both parties face a whiteboard, reflecting the notion that both parties face the same problem or issue.

LEARNING OBJECTIVE 

Describe how cultural and gender differences influence approaches to conflict and negotiation.

CULTURE AND CONFLICT

While individual preferences will influence which of the five conflict-handling styles a person uses, these preferences are modified by culture. For example, cultures that place a strong emphasis on interpersonal harmony are more likely to use avoiding strategies than cultures that are less concerned with preserving relationships.[53] Cultural differences shape how individuals approach both negotiations and conflicts.[54] Three cultural dimensions are especially important in determining how people manage disagreements: individualism and collectivism, power distance and high–low context communication styles.[55]

INDIVIDUALISM AND COLLECTIVISM As we discussed in Chapter 2, individualism and collectivism are distinct dimensions that shape our behaviour. In negotiation, they affect the kinds of outcomes that people value. Cultures that are high on the collectivism dimension emphasise group goals and harmonious relationships within groups. This means that they are more attuned to social capital in negotiation, placing greater emphasis on how the negotiation

Time Is Not of the Essence

Global negotiations are complex and require highly skilled negotiators. Often they involve negotiations with governments, who bring both social and economic interests to the negotiation table. Task-oriented and time-pressured Westerners also need to remember the importance of relationship building, not to mention the very different time frames over which agreement is reached. A key skill for the Walt Disney Company, who have been negotiating with the Shanghai Municipal Government about the construction of the first Disneyland in mainland China, has been patience. When Shanghai's mayor Han Zheng announced that agreement had been reached, he added that 'the government has been in talks with Disney for more than ten years, and the two sides have kept smooth communication'.[52]

Atlantide Phototravel/Corbis

process affects factors such as interpersonal liking and trust. In comparison, cultures that are high on the individualism dimension emphasise personal goals. They are more attuned to economic capital and focus on deal making—the processes of creating and claiming value.

POWER DISTANCE This describes the importance that people place on status and authority. Cultures that are classified as hierarchical have highly differentiated social structures, and power comes from social status. In contrast, egalitarian cultures have flat social structures, and power comes from sources other than status. This dimension affects negotiations in several ways. Negotiators from hierarchical cultures are likely to start negotiations by talking about their company and products—an indirect way of signalling status and one that is often not recognised by negotiators from egalitarian cultures. Conversely, while multiple alternatives are a source of power in egalitarian cultures, the social obligations that underlie hierarchical structures mean that alternatives are not seen as a source of power in these cultures.

HIGH–LOW CONTEXT COMMUNICATION STYLE As we learned in Chapter 9, people from high-context cultures are more indirect in their speech styles and expect the listener to infer meaning from context. Those from low-context cultures are more direct, and context plays a limited role in clarifying meaning. In negotiation, individuals from high-context cultures are unlikely to share direct information, such as what is important to them. Instead they will present many offers, making modifications that reflect what is more and less important to them. Those from high-context cultures are also more likely to use formal communication channels and appeals to general principles and emotion strengthen their case. Negotiators from low-context cultures, by comparison, will be more informal in their communication style and use logic and reason to build a case for their demands.

It is important to remember that people from collectivist and high power-distance cultures are less comfortable with the practice of resolving differences through direct and open communication.[56] People in Confucian cultures prefer an avoidance conflict management style because it is the most consistent with harmony and face saving. Direct communication is a high-risk strategy because it easily threatens the need to save face and maintain harmony.

GENDER AND CONFLICT

Many of the factors that differentiate cultures also differentiate men and women.[57] Like people from collectivist cultures, women are more oriented toward preserving relationships. They see any conflict or negotiation episode as embedded in a relationship that stretches from the past into

Still Struggling for Wage Equality

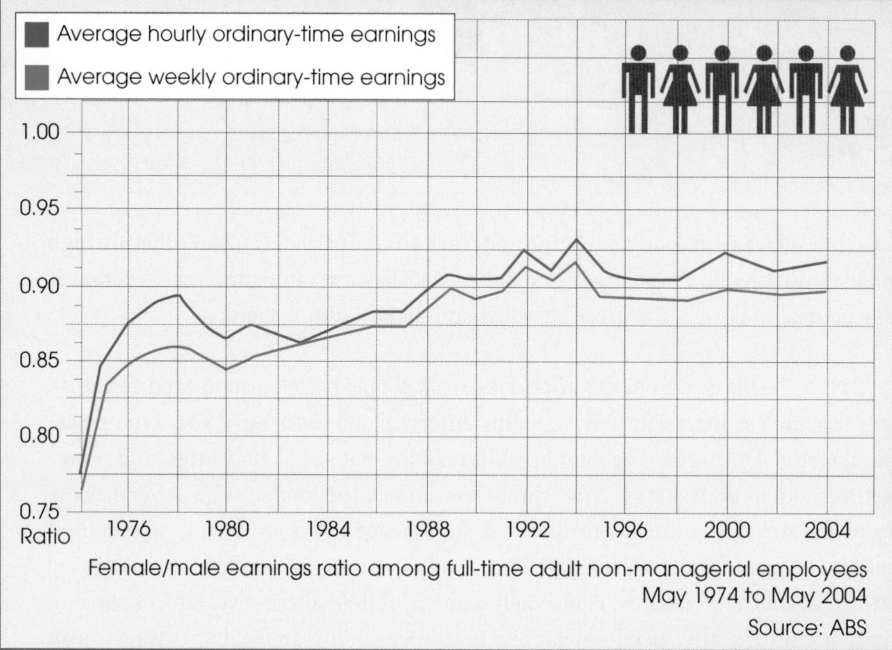

Female/male earnings ratio among full-time adult non-managerial employees
May 1974 to May 2004
Source: ABS

Being a woman is costly. Evidence from around the world shows that the gender wage gap is alive and well: women still earn less than their male counterparts. A recent survey in New Zealand demonstrated that even women in the highest wage brackets earn progressively less than men as they get older. While the wage gap is $64–$179 per week for those aged under 25, it widens to $380–$429 per week in the over-25 age group. According to a recent survey, women around the world earn less than men. In Korea, the average wage for women is 60 per cent that of men, rising to 75 per cent in Portugal and 80 per cent in Lithuania, Germany and Holland. In Australia, women earn, on average, about $196 per week less than their male colleagues. This flows on to their retirement savings: for every $3 women have in their superannuation accounts, men have $10. Some of these differences can be attributed to the ways in which men and women negotiate. Two strategies that help women improve their outcomes are collective bargaining and greater transparency in salary levels. As Andy Rogerson, chief executive of Hudson UK, says: 'British employees are ready to break one of the biggest taboos in the workplace—revealing salaries—in order to ensure true equality of pay. The gender pay gap persists, and businesses that neglect to address it are risking alienating half their workforce.'[62]

the future. As a result, they are more likely to consider how their behaviour in *this* negotiation or conflict will affect their future relationship with the other person. Men, on the other hand, are more focused on the present and—in general—less likely to consider how actions taken in *this* negotiation or conflict will affect future interactions with the other person. And, as we saw in Chapter 9, women's speech style is very similar to the style used by individuals from high-context cultures.

There is now a substantial amount of evidence that women obtain poorer personal outcomes than men in negotiation.[58] There are several factors that affect women's outcomes.[59] Thinking back to our list of key skills for effective value claiming, important differences emerge between men and women. Research shows that women typically set themselves lower target points than men, and are more likely to accept offers just above their resistance points. By comparison, men set high target points and push to get a deal as close to their target point as possible. Women are also less likely than men to use alternatives to improve their outcomes. However, the differences in men's and women's outcomes are not just the result of what women do in negotiations. They are also a consequence of how others treat women. Research shows that women receive less generous offers than men. In one study, men and women went into a used-car yard and asked about the price of one of the cars. The car dealer quoted a lower price to men than to women—for the same car.[60]

Research also shows that many of these differences occur because women see the negotiation process as necessarily competitive, and that women perform most poorly when they are told that their outcome is an indication of their effectiveness as a negotiator.[61] This may be because the traditional view of an effective negotiator is of someone who is assertive, rational and strong—all traits that are usually ascribed to men. In fact, when men and women are told that these traits are characteristic of effective negotiators, women perform more poorly than men. However, when effective negotiation is linked to problem solving, women obtain better outcomes than men. This suggests that women can improve their outcomes by ensuring that a negotiation or conflict is approached collaboratively.

RESOLVING CONFLICT THROUGH THIRD-PARTY INTERVENTION

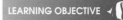

Compare and contrast the three types of third-party dispute resolution.

Most of this chapter has focused on people directly involved in a conflict, yet many disputes in organisational settings are resolved with the assistance of the manager responsible for the feuding parties, or some other third party. **Third-party conflict resolution** is any attempt by a relatively neutral person to help the parties resolve their differences. There are generally three types of third-party dispute resolution activities: arbitration, inquisition and mediation. These activities can be classified by their level of control over the process and control over the decision (see Exhibit 11.4).[63]

third-party conflict resolution Any attempt by a relatively neutral person to help conflicting parties resolve their differences.

ARBITRATION Arbitrators have high control over the final decision, but low control over the process. Executives engage in this strategy by following previously agreed rules of due process, listening to arguments from the disputing employees and making a binding decision. Arbitration is applied as the final stage of grievances by unionised employees in many countries, but it is also becoming more common in nonunion conflicts.

INQUISITION Inquisitors control all discussion about the conflict. Like arbitrators, they have high decision control because they choose the form of conflict resolution. However, they also have high process control because they choose which information to examine and how to examine it, and they generally decide how the conflict resolution process will be handled.

MEDIATION Mediators have high control over the intervention process. In fact, their main purpose is to manage the process and context of interaction between the disputing parties. However, the parties make the final decision about how to resolve their differences. Thus, mediators have little or no control over the conflict resolution decision.

Choosing the Best Third-Party Intervention Strategy

Team leaders, executives and coworkers regularly intervene in disputes between employees and departments. Sometimes they adopt a mediator role; other times they serve as arbitrators. Occasionally, they begin with one approach then switch to another. However, research suggests that people in positions of authority (e.g. managers) usually adopt an inquisitional approach whereby they dominate the intervention process as well as make a binding decision.[64] Managers prefer the inquisition approach because it is consistent with the decision-oriented nature of managerial jobs, gives them control over the conflict process and outcome, and tends to resolve disputes efficiently.

However, the inquisitional approach to third-party conflict resolution is usually the least effective in organisational settings.[65] One problem is that leaders who take an inquisitional role tend to collect limited information about the problem, so their imposed decision may produce an ineffective solution to the conflict. Another problem is that employees often view inquisitional procedures and outcomes as unfair because they have little control over this approach. In particular, the inquisitional approach potentially violates several practices required to support procedural justice (see Chapter 5).

Which third-party intervention is most appropriate in organisations? The answer partly depends on the situation, such as the type of dispute, the relationship between the manager and

Exhibit 11.4 *Types of Third-Party Intervention*

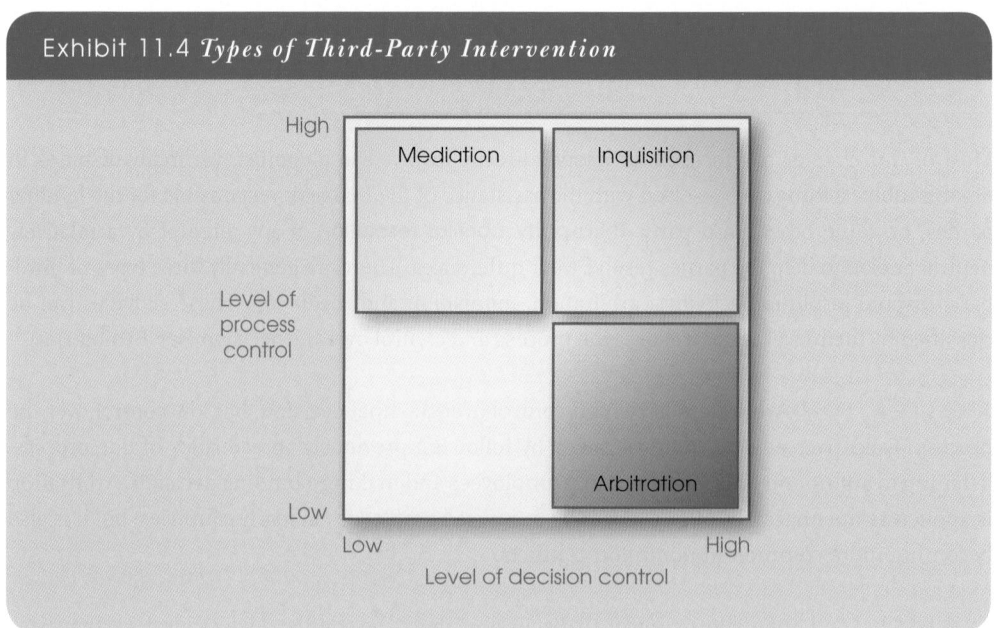

employees, and cultural values such as power distance.[66] But generally speaking, for everyday disagreements between two employees, the mediation approach is usually best because this gives employees more responsibility for resolving their own disputes. The third-party representative merely establishes an appropriate context for conflict resolution. Although not as efficient as other strategies, mediation potentially offers the highest level of employee satisfaction with the conflict process and outcomes.[67] When employees cannot resolve their differences through mediation, arbitration seems to work best because the predetermined rules of evidence and other processes create a higher sense of procedural fairness.[68] Moreover, arbitration is preferred where the organisation's goals should take priority over individual goals.

Alternative Dispute Resolution

Rather than battle each other in court or external arbitration, the US Air Force and its civilian staff have resolved most workplace conflicts quickly and with improved mutual understanding through alternative dispute resolution (ADR). 'The parties, in essence, maintain control over the [ADR] process and its outcome,' explains Air Mobility Command civilian programs branch chief Diana Hendrix. Some Air Force bases retain a mediator to identify issues and explore options with the parties without imposing a solution. Other bases use peer review panels, consisting of four or six union and nonunion employees who examine facts, listen to the parties and make a final binding decision. But even with these formal third-party systems in place, Hendrix explains that supervisors are the first line of defence in resolving workplace conflict. 'Ultimately, it's about Air Force employees and supervisors resolving conflicts in an efficient and effective manner so they can continue performing the Air Force mission of supporting and defending the United States of America,' she says.[69]

Mediate, Don't Litigate

Disputes are costly. Disputants start with power- and rights-based frames that limit their ability to solve problems. When Multiplex and Cleveland Bridge went to court to settle a dispute over the building of Wembley Stadium, the final legal bill was £22 million.

John Harper/Corbis

At the end of the case, Multiplex was award £6 million in damages and only 20 per cent of its costs, leaving the presiding judge to observe that 'the result of the litigation is that neither party has gained any significant financial benefit'. So it's not surprising that alternative forms of dispute resolution are increasing in popularity. Dispute resolution processes such as mediation are faster, less costly and less damaging to relationships than lengthy court cases, and may reduce the costs to disputants by up to 75 percent. This is significant when we realise just how many disputes end in court: in 2007, Beijing courts processed 23 055 cases involving loan contract disputes. Anticipating an increase in disputes as the economic crisis takes hold, China recently passed legislation to manage land contract disputes in order to preserve 'rural harmony and stability'.[71]

alternative dispute resolution (ADR) An orderly process of third-party dispute resolution, typically including mediation followed by arbitration.

The US Air Force has joined a growing list of organisations that have taken third-party resolution one step further through an **alternative dispute resolution (ADR)** process (for employees only, also called *internal dispute resolution* or *employee dispute resolution*). ADR combines third-party dispute resolution in an orderly sequence. ADR typically begins with a meeting between the employee and employer to clarify and negotiate their differences. If this fails, a mediator is brought in to help the parties reach a mutually agreeable solution. If mediation fails, the parties submit their case to an arbitrator whose decision may be either binding or voluntarily accepted by the employer. Although most ADR systems rely on professional arbitrators, some firms, such as Eastman Kodak and some US Air Force bases, prefer peer arbitration, which includes a panel of coworkers and managers who are not involved in the dispute.[70]

Whether resolving conflict through third-party dispute resolution or direct dialogue, we need to recognise that many solutions come from the sources of conflict that were identified earlier in this chapter. This may seem obvious, but in the heat of conflict, people often focus on each other rather than the underlying causes. Recognising these conflict sources is the role of effective leadership, which is discussed in the next chapter.

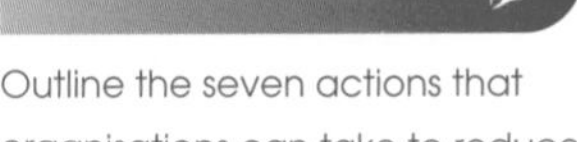

Outline the seven actions that organisations can take to reduce dysfunctional conflicts.

ORGANISATIONAL APPROACHES TO CONFLICT MANAGEMENT

So far, we have focused on how individuals manage conflicts. Individuals, because of their conflict management, differ in how they approach the other party in a conflict situation. No matter which approach they adopt, they may choose to negotiate in order to resolve conflicts of interest. If negotiations fail, they may use a third party to help them re-establish communication. However, organisations also have a role to play in managing conflicts. They can do this by implementing policies and organisational structures that remove the underlying causes of potential conflict. The main organisational approaches are emphasising superordinate goals, reducing value differences, improving communication and understanding, reducing task interdependence, increasing resources, clarifying rules and procedures, and establishing a positive climate.

Emphasising Superordinate Goals

superordinate goals A broad goal that all parties to a dispute value and agree is important.

One of the oldest recommendations for resolving conflict is to seek out and find common goals.[72] In organisational settings, this typically takes the form of a **superordinate goal**, which is any goal that both conflicting parties value and whose attainment is beyond the resources and effort of either party alone.[73] By increasing commitment to corporate-wide goals, employees pay less attention to competing individual or departmental-level goals, which reduces their perceived conflict with coworkers. They also potentially reduce the problem of value differences by establishing a common frame of reference. For example, research indicates that the most effective executive teams frame their decisions as superordinate goals that rise above each executive's departmental or divisional goals.[74]

Reducing Value Differences

Another way to minimise dysfunctional conflict is to reduce the differences that produce the conflict in the first place. The more employees think they have common backgrounds or experiences with coworkers, the more motivated they are to coordinate their activities and resolve conflict through constructive discussion with those coworkers.[75] One way to increase this commonality is by creating common experiences. SAP, the German enterprise software company, applied this strategy when it recently acquired Business Objects, a French company with a strong US presence. Conflict is common following many acquisitions because employees at each company have different cultures, experiences and loyalties. SAP minimised this differentiation by immediately intermingling people from the two organisations. 'In the first six months after the acquisition, more than 35 per cent of senior m anagers transferred from SAP while all of the original Business Objects corporate services people are now a part of a global shared services team,' says Business Objects CEO John Schwarz. 'We also encourage cross-border, cross-functional teamwork on projects such as major product releases. In this way team members come to depend on each other.'[76]

Improving Communication and Understanding

A third way to resolve dysfunctional conflict is to give the conflicting parties more opportunities to communicate and understand each other. This recommendation relates back to the contact hypothesis described in Chapter 3. Specifically, the more meaningful interaction we have with someone, the less we rely on stereotypes to understand that person.[77] However, communication and understanding interventions should be applied only *after* differentiation between the two sides has been reduced, or where differentiation is already sufficiently low. If perceived differentiation remains high, attempts to manage conflict through dialogue might escalate rather than reduce relationship conflict. The reason is that when forced to interact with people who we believe are quite different and in conflict with us, we tend to select information that reinforces that view.[78] Thus, communication and understanding interventions are effective only when differentiation is sufficiently low.

Reducing Interdependence

Conflict increases with the level of interdependence, so minimising dysfunctional conflict might involve reducing the level of interdependence between the parties. If cost-effective, this can occur by dividing the shared resource so that each party has exclusive use at different times. Sequentially or reciprocally interdependent jobs might be combined so that they form a pooled interdependence. For example, rather than having one employee serve customers and another operate the cash register, each employee could handle both customer activities alone. Buffers also help to reduce interdependence between people. Buffers include resources, such as adding more inventory between people who perform sequential tasks. Organisations also use human buffers—people who serve as intermediaries between interdependent people or work units who do not get along through direct interaction.

Increasing Resources

An obvious way to reduce conflict caused by resource scarcity is to increase the amount of resources available. Corporate decision makers might quickly dismiss this solution because of the costs involved. However, they need to carefully compare these costs with the costs of dysfunctional conflict arising out of resource scarcity.

Clarifying Rules and Procedures

Conflicts that arise from ambiguous rules can be minimised by establishing rules and procedures. Armstrong World Industries, Inc., applied this strategy when consultants and information systems employees clashed while working together on development of a client–server network. Information systems employees at the flooring and building materials company thought they should be in charge, whereas consultants believed they had the senior role. Also, the consultants wanted to work long hours and take Friday off to fly home, whereas Armstrong employees wanted to work regular hours. The company reduced these conflicts by having both parties agree on specific responsibilities and roles. The agreement also assigned two senior executives at the companies to establish rules if future disagreements arose.[79]

Rules establish changes to the terms of interdependence, such as an employee's hours of work or a supplier's fulfilment of an order. In most cases, the parties affected by these rules are involved in the process of deciding these terms of interdependence. Thus, by redefining the terms of interdependence, the strategy of clarifying rules involves negotiation, which we discussed earlier in this chapter.

Establishing a Positive Climate

Establishing norms that encourage openness can help reduce conflict. When team norms encourage openness, team members learn to appreciate honest dialogue without personally reacting to any emotional display during the disagreements.[80] Other norms might discourage team members from displaying negative emotions toward coworkers. Organisational norms also encourage tactics that diffuse relationship conflict when it first appears. For instance, research has found that teams with low relationship conflict use humour to maintain positive group emotions, which offsets the negative feelings that team members might develop toward some coworkers during debate.

Openness will be encouraged when teams are cohesive. The longer people work together, get to know each other and develop mutual trust, the more latitude they give to each other to show emotions without being personally offended. Strong cohesion also allows each person to know about and anticipate the behaviours and emotions of their teammates. Another benefit is that cohesion produces a stronger social identity with the group, so team members are motivated to avoid escalating relationship conflict during otherwise emotionally turbulent discussions.

CHAPTER SUMMARY

Conflict is the process in which one party perceives that its interests are being opposed or negatively affected by another party. For many years, conflict was viewed as undesirable and counterproductive. There is evidence that conflict can produce undesirable outcomes such as lower job satisfaction, team cohesion and knowledge sharing, as well as higher levels of organisational politics and turnover. However, experts later formed the opinion that organisations suffer from too little as well as too much conflict. Research indicates that a moderate level of conflict can improve decision making, organisational responsiveness to the environment and team cohesion (when conflict is with sources outside the team).

The conflict process model begins with the five structural sources of conflict: incompatible goals, differentiation (different values and beliefs), interdependence, scarce resources, ambiguous rules and communication problems. These sources lead one or more parties to perceive a conflict and to experience conflict emotions. This, in turn, produces manifest conflict, such as behaviours toward the other side. The conflict process often escalates through a series of episodes.

The current perspective on conflict involves distinguishing task from relationship conflict. The former focuses on issues and a logical evaluation of ideas, whereas the latter pays attention to interpersonal incompatibilities and flaws. Although the ideal would be to encourage constructive conflict and minimise relationship conflict, relationship conflict tends to emerge in most constructive conflict episodes.

Both task- and relationship-based conflicts can spiral out control. This is most likely to happen when we approach conflict with a power-based (who has more power?) or rights-based (what are your contractual obligations?) frame. We are more likely to manage conflicts in a constructive, problem-solving way when we approach them with an interests-based (what are our most important needs?) frame.

Organisational behaviour experts have identified several conflict-handling styles: problem solving, forcing, avoiding, yielding and compromising. People who use problem solving have a win–win orientation. Others, particularly forcing, assume a win–lose orientation. In general, people gravitate toward one or two preferred conflict-handling styles that match their personality, personal and cultural values, and past experience. However, the best style depends on various characteristics of the situation.

Negotiation occurs whenever two or more conflicting parties attempt to resolve their divergent goals by redefining the terms of their interdependence. Effective negotiators need to engage in both collaboration and competition in order to obtain outcomes. Key skills include managing information, managing concessions, understanding the role of time and power, and building relationships. How negotiators do this is affected by the context of the negotiation. Conflict and negotiation are also influenced by cultural and gender differences.

Third-party conflict resolution is any attempt by a relatively neutral person to help the parties resolve their differences. The three main forms of third-party dispute resolution are arbitration, inquisition and mediation. Managers tend to use an inquisition approach, although mediation and arbitration are often more appropriate, depending on the situation.

Organisational approaches to conflict management include emphasising superordinate goals, reducing value differences, improving communication and understanding, reducing interdependence, increasing resources, clarifying rules and procedures, and establishing a positive climate.

KEY TERMS

alternative dispute resolution (ADR), p. 436
conflict, p. 414
interests-based frame, p. 416
negotiation, p. 424
power-based frame, p. 417
relationship conflicts, p. 416
resistance point, p. 425
rights-based frame, p. 417
superordinate goal, p. 436
target point, p. 425
task conflicts, p. 416
third-party conflict resolution, p. 434
win–win orientation, p. 421
win–lose orientation, p. 421

Critical Thinking Questions

1 Distinguish task conflict from relationship conflict and explain how to engage in the former with minimal levels of the latter.

2 The chief executive officer of Creative Toys, Inc. read about cooperation in Japanese companies and vowed to bring this same philosophy to the company. The goal was to avoid all conflict, so that employees would work cooperatively and be happier at Creative Toys. Discuss the merits and limitations of the CEO's policy in reducing conflict.

3 Conflict among managers emerged soon after a French company acquired a Swedish firm. The Swedes perceived the French management as hierarchical and arrogant, whereas the French thought the Swedes were naive, cautious and lacking an achievement orientation. Describe ways to reduce dysfunctional conflict in this situation.

4 Three levels of interdependence (pooled, sequential, reciprocal) exist in interpersonal and intergroup relationships (see Chapter 8 for more details). Identify examples of these three levels in your work or school activities. How might these three levels of interdependence create conflict for you?

5 Jane has just been appointed as purchasing manager of Tacoma Technologies Corp. The previous purchasing manager, who recently retired, was known for his 'winner-take-all' approach to suppliers. He continually fought for more discounts and was sceptical about any special deals that suppliers would propose. A few suppliers refused to do business with Tacoma Technologies, but senior management was confident that the former purchasing manager's approach minimised the company's costs. Jane wants to try a more collaborative approach to working with suppliers. How could she adopt a more collaborative approach in future negotiations with suppliers? Will her approach work?

6 You are a special assistant to the commander-in-chief of a peacekeeping mission to a war-torn part of the world. The unit consists of a few thousand peacekeeping troops from Australia, France, India and four other countries. The troops will work together for approximately one year. What strategies would you recommend to improve mutual understanding and minimise conflict among these troops?

7 The chief operating officer (COO) has noticed that production employees in the company's Mexican manufacturing operations are unhappy with some of the production engineering decisions made in the company's headquarters in Chicago. At the same time, the engineers complain that production employees aren't applying their engineering specifications correctly and don't understand why those specifications were put in place. The COO believes that the best way to resolve this conflict is to have a frank and open discussion between some of the engineers and a group of employees representing the Mexican production crew. This open dialogue approach worked well recently among managers in the company's Chicago headquarters, so the COO believes it should work equally well between the engineers and production staff. Based on your knowledge of communication and mutual understanding as a way to resolve conflict, discuss the COO's proposal.

8 Describe the inquisitional approach to resolving disputes between employees or work units. Discuss its appropriateness in organisational settings, including the suitability of its use with a multigenerational workforce.

CLASS EXERCISE

Skill Builder 11.1

The Contingencies of Conflict Handling

Gerard A. Callanan and David F. Perri, West Chester University of Pennsylvania

Purpose

This exercise is designed to help you understand the contingencies of applying conflict-handling styles in organisational settings.

Instructions

STEP 1 Read each of the five scenarios presented below and select the most appropriate response from among the five alternatives. Each scenario has a correct response for that situation.

STEP 2 (OPTIONAL) The instructor may ask you to complete the Dutch Test for conflict-handling self-assessment (Skill Builder 11.3) or a similar instrument. This instrument will provide an estimate of your preferred conflict-handling style.

STEP 3 As a class, you will give feedback on your responses to each of the scenarios, with the instructor guiding discussion on the contextual factors embodied in each scenario. For each scenario, the class should identify the response selected by the majority. In addition, class members will discuss how they decided on the choices they made and the contextual factors they took into account in making their selections.

STEP 4 Compare your responses to the five scenarios with your results from the conflict-handling self-assessment. Discussion will focus on the extent to which each person's preferred conflict-handling style influenced their alternatives in this activity, and the implications of this style preference for managing conflict in organisations.

Scenario 1

Setting

You are a manager of a division in the accounting department of a large bank. Nine analysts and six administrative staff report to you. Recently, one of your analysts, Jane Wilson, has sought the bank's approval for tuition reimbursement for the cost of an evening MBA program specialising in organisational behaviour. The bank normally encourages employees to seek advanced degrees on a part-time basis. Indeed, through your encouragement, nearly all of the members of your staff are pursuing additional study. You consult the bank's policy manual and discover that two approvals are necessary for reimbursement—yours and that of the manager of training and development, Kathy Gordon. Further, the manual states that approval for reimbursement will only be granted if the coursework is 'reasonably job-related'. Based on your review of the matter, you decide to approve Jane's request for reimbursement. However, Kathy Gordon rejects it outright by claiming that coursework in organisational behaviour is not related to an accounting analyst position. She states that the bank will only reimburse the analyst for a degree in either accounting or finance. In your opinion, however, the interpersonal skills and insights to be gained from a degree in organisational behaviour are job-related and can also benefit Jane in future assignments. The analyst job requires interaction with a variety of individuals at different levels in the organisation, and it is important that interpersonal and communication skills be strong.

After further discussion it becomes clear that you and Kathy Gordon have opposite views on the matter. Since both of you are at the same organisation level and have equal status, it appears that you are at an impasse. Although the goal of reimbursement is important, you are faced with other pressing demands on your time. In addition, the conflict has diverted the attention of your work group away from its primary responsibilities. Because the university semester is about to begin, it is essential that you and Kathy Gordon reach a timely agreement to enable Jane to pursue her studies.

Action Alternatives for Scenario 1

Please indicate your first (1) and second (2) choices from among the following alternatives by writing the appropriate number in the space provided.

Action alternative	Ranking (1st and 2nd)
1. You go along with Kathy Gordon's view and advise Jane Wilson to select either accounting or finance as a major for her MBA.	________
2. You decide to withdraw from the situation completely, and tell Jane to work it out with Kathy Gordon on her own.	________
3. You decide to take the matter to those in higher management levels and argue forcefully for your point of view. You do everything in your power to ensure that a decision will be made in your favour.	________
4. You decide to meet Kathy Gordon halfway in order to reach an agreement. You advise Jane to pursue her MBA in accounting or finance, but also recommend she minor in organisational behaviour by taking electives in that field.	________
5. You decide to work more closely with Kathy Gordon by attempting to get a clear as well as flexible policy written that reflects both of your views. Of course, this will require a significant amount of your time.	________

Scenario 2

Setting

You are the vice president of a relatively large division (80 employees) in a medium-sized consumer products company. Due to the recent turnover of minority staff, your division has fallen behind in meeting the company's goal for Equal Employment Opportunity (EEO) hiring. Because of a scarcity of qualified minority candidates, it appears that you may fall further behind in achieving stated EEO goals.

Although you are aware of the problem, you believe that the low level of minority hiring is due to increased attrition in minority staff as well as the lack of viable replacement candidates. However, the EEO officer believes that your hiring criteria are too stringent, resulting in the rejection of minority candidates with the basic qualifications to do the job. You support the goals and principles of EEO; however, you are concerned that the hiring of less qualified candidates will weaken the performance of your division. The EEO officer believes that your failure to hire minority employees is damaging to the company in the short term because corporate goals will not be met, and in the long term because it will restrict the pool of minority candidates available for upward mobility. Both of you regard your concerns as important. Further, you recognise that both of you have the company's best interests in mind and that you have a mutual interest in resolving the conflict.

Action Alternatives for Scenario 2

Please indicate your first (1) and second (2) choices from among the following alternatives by writing the appropriate number in the space provided.

Action alternative	Ranking (1st and 2nd)
1. You conclude that the whole problem is too complex an issue for you to handle right now. You put it on the 'backburner' and decide to reconsider the problem at a later date.	________
2. You believe that your view outweighs the perspective of the EEO officer. You decide to argue your position more vigorously and hope that your stance will sway the EEO officer to agree with your view.	________
3. You decide to accept the EEO officer's view. You agree to use less stringent selection criteria and thereby hire more minority employees.	________
4. You give in to the EEO officer somewhat by agreeing to relax your standards a little bit. This would allow slightly more minority hiring (but not enough to satisfy the EEO goal) and could cause a small reduction in the overall performance of your division.	________
5. You try to reach a consensus that addresses each of your concerns. You agree to work harder at hiring more minority applicants and request that the EEO officer agree to help find the most qualified minority candidates available.	________

Scenario 3

Setting

You are the manager in charge of the financial reporting section of a large insurance company. It is the responsibility of your group to make periodic written and oral reports to senior management regarding the company's financial performance. The company's senior management has come to rely on your quick and accurate dissemination of financial data as a way to make vital decisions in a timely fashion. This has given you a relatively high degree of organisational influence. You rely on various operating departments to supply you with financial information according to a pre-established reporting schedule.

In two days, you must make your quarterly presentation to the company's board of directors. However, the claims department has failed to supply you with several key pieces of information that are critical to your presentation. You check the reporting schedule and realise that you should have had the information two days ago. When you call Bill Jones, the claims department manager, he informs you that he cannot possibly have the data to you within the next two days. He states that other pressing work has a higher priority. Although you explain the critical need for this data, he is unwilling to change his position. You believe that your presentation is vital to the company's welfare and explain this to Bill Jones. Although Bill has less status than you, he has been known to take advantage of individuals who are unwilling or unable to push their point of view. With your presentation less than two days away, it is critical that you receive information from the claims department within the next twenty-four hours.

Action Alternatives for Scenario 3

Please indicate your first (1) and second (2) choices from among the following alternatives by writing the appropriate number in the space provided.

Action alternative	Ranking (1st and 2nd)
1. Accept the explanation from Bill Jones and try to get by without the figures by using your best judgment as to what they would be.	______
2. Tell Bill Jones that unless you have the data from his department on your desk by tomorrow morning, you will be forced to go over his head to compel him to give you the numbers.	______
3. Meet Bill Jones halfway by agreeing to receive part of the needed figures and using your own judgment on the others.	______
4. Try to get your presentation postponed until a later date, if possible.	______
5. Forget about the short-term need for information and try to achieve a longer term solution, such as adjusting the reporting schedule to better accommodate your mutual needs.	______

Scenario 4

Setting

You are the production manager of a medium-sized building products company. You control a production line that runs on a three-shift basis. Recently, Ted Smith, the materials handling manager, requested you to accept a different packaging of the raw materials for the production process than what has been customary. He states that new machinery he has installed makes it much easier to provide the material in 50-kilogram sacks instead of the 25-kilogram bags that you currently receive. Ted further explains that the provision of the material in the 25-kilogram bags would put an immense strain on his operation, and he therefore has a critical need for you to accept the change. You know that accepting materials in the new packaging will cause some minor disruption in your production process, but should not cause long-term problems for any of the three shifts. However, you are a little annoyed by the proposed change because Ted did not consult with you before he installed the new equipment. In the past, you and he have been open in your communication. You do not think that this failure to consult you represents a change in your relationship.

Because you work closely with Ted, it is essential that you maintain the harmonious and stable working relationship that you have built over the past few years. In addition, you may need some help from him in the future, since you already know that your operation will have special material requirements in about two months. You also know that Ted has influence at higher levels of the organisation.

Action Alternatives for Scenario 4

Please indicate your first (1) and second (2) choices from among the following alternatives by writing the appropriate number in the space provided.

Action alternative	Ranking (1st and 2nd)
1. Agree to accept the raw material in the different format.	______
2. Refuse to accept the material in the new format because it would cause a disruption in your operation.	______
3. Propose a solution where you accept material in the new format during the first shift, but not during the second and third.	______
4. Tell Ted Smith that you do not wish to deal with the issue at this time, but that you will consider his request and get back to him at a later date.	______
5. You decide to tell Ted Smith of your concern regarding his failure to consult with you before installing new equipment. You inform him that you wish to find longer term solutions to the conflict between you.	______

Scenario 5

Setting

You are employed as supervisor of the compensation and benefits section in the human resources department of a medium-sized pharmaceutical company. Your staff of three clerks is responsible for maintaining contacts with the various benefits providers and answering related questions from the company's employees. Your section shares secretarial, word processing and copier resources with the training and development section of the department. Recently, a disagreement has arisen between you and Beth Hanson, the training and development supervisor, over when the secretarial staff should take their lunches. Beth would like the secretarial staff to take their lunches an hour later to coincide with the time most of her people go to lunch. You know that the secretaries do not want to change their lunch times. Further, the current time is more convenient for your staff.

At this time, you are hard-pressed to deal with the situation. You have an important meeting with the provider of dental insurance in two days. It is critical that you are well prepared for this meeting, and these other tasks are a distraction.

Action Alternatives for Scenario 5

Please indicate your first (1) and second (2) choices from among the following alternatives by writing the appropriate number in the space provided.

Action alternative	Ranking (1st and 2nd)
1. Take some time over the next day and propose a solution whereby three days a week the secretaries take their lunch at the earlier time and two days at the later.	______
2. Tell Beth Hanson you will deal with the matter in a few days, after you have addressed the more pressing issues.	______
3. Let Beth Hanson have her way by agreeing to a later lunch hour for the secretarial staff.	______
4. Flat out tell Beth Hanson that you will not agree to a change in the secretaries' lunchtime.	______
5. Devote more time to the issue. Attempt to achieve a broad-based consensus with Beth Hanson that meets her needs as well as yours and those of the secretaries.	______

Sources: G. A. Callanan and D. F. Perri, 'Teaching Conflict Management Using a Scenario-Based Approach', *Journal of Education for Business* 81, no. 3 (2006): 131–139.

Skill Builder 11.2

TEAM EXERCISE

Ugli Orange Role Play

Purpose

This exercise is designed to help you understand the dynamics of interpersonal and intergroup conflict as well as the effectiveness of negotiation strategies under specific conditions.

Materials

The instructor will distribute roles for Dr Roland, Dr Jones and a few observers. Ideally, each negotiation should occur in a private area away from other negotiations.

Instructions

STEP 1 The instructor will divide the class into an even number of teams of three people each, with one participant left over for each team formed (e.g. six observers if there are six teams). One-half of the teams will take the role of Dr Roland and the other half will be Dr Jones. The instructor will distribute roles after these teams have been formed.

STEP 2 Members within each team are given 10 minutes (or other time limit stated by the instructor) to learn their roles and decide negotiating strategy.

STEP 3 After reading their roles and discussing strategy, each Dr Jones team is matched with a Dr Roland team to conduct negotiations. Observers will receive observation forms from the instructor, and two observers will be assigned to watch the paired teams during prenegotiations and subsequent negotiations.

STEP 4 As soon as Roland and Jones reach agreement, or at the end of the time allotted for the negotiation (whichever comes first), the Roland and Jones teams report to the instructor for further instruction.

STEP 5 At the end of the exercise, the class will congregate to discuss the negotiations. Observers, negotiators and instructors will then discuss their observations and experiences and the implications for conflict management and negotiation.

Note: This exercise was developed by Robert J. House, Wharton Business School, University of Pennsylvania. A similar activity is also attributed to earlier writing by R. R. Blake and J. S. Mouton.

SELF-ASSESSMENT

Skill Builder 11.3

The Dutch Test for Conflict Handling

Purpose

This self-assessment is designed to help you to identify your preferred conflict-management style.

Instructions

Read each of the statements below and circle the response that you believe best reflects your position regarding each statement. Then use the scoring key in Appendix B to calculate your results for each conflict-management style. This exercise is completed alone so you can assess yourself honestly without concerns of social comparison. However, class discussion will focus on the different conflict-management styles and the situations in which each is most appropriate.

Dutch Test for Conflict Handling

When I have a conflict at work, I do the following:	Not at all				Very much
1. I give in to the wishes of the other party.	1	2	3	4	5
2. I try to realise a middle-of-the-road solution.	1	2	3	4	5
3. I push my own point of view.	1	2	3	4	5
4. I examine issues until I find a solution that really satisfies me and the other party.	1	2	3	4	5
5. I avoid confrontation about our differences.	1	2	3	4	5
6. I concur with the other party.	1	2	3	4	5
7. I emphasise that we have to find a compromise solution.	1	2	3	4	5
8. I search for gains.	1	2	3	4	5
9. I stand for my own and other's goals and interests.	1	2	3	4	5
10. I avoid differences of opinion as much as possible.	1	2	3	4	5
11. I try to accommodate the other party.	1	2	3	4	5
12. I insist we both give in a little.	1	2	3	4	5
13. I fight for a good outcome for myself.	1	2	3	4	5
14. I examine ideas from both sides to find a mutually optimal solution.	1	2	3	4	5
15. I try to make differences loom less severe.	1	2	3	4	5
16. I adapt to the parties' goals and interests.	1	2	3	4	5
17. I strive whenever possible towards a fifty-fifty compromise.	1	2	3	4	5
18. I do everything to win.	1	2	3	4	5
19. I work out a solution that serves my own as well as others' interests as much as possible.	1	2	3	4	5
20. I try to avoid a confrontation with the other.	1	2	3	4	5

Endnotes

Sources: C. K. W. de Dreu *et al.*, 'A Theory-based Measure of Conflict Management Strategies in the Workplace', *Journal of Organizational Behavior* 22, no. 6 (2001): 645–668.

1 E. Pooley, 'The Fox in the Henhouse', *Time*, 9 July 2007, 32–38.

2 D. Tjosvold, *Working Together to Get Things Done* (Lexington, MA: Lexington, 1986), 114–115; J. A. Wall and R. R. Callister, 'Conflict and Its Management', *Journal of Management* 21, no. 3 (1995): 515–558; M. A. Rahim, 'Toward a Theory of Managing Organizational Conflict', *International Journal of Conflict Management* 13, no. 3 (2002): 206–235; D. Tjosvold, 'Defining Conflict and Making Choices about Its Management', *International Journal of Conflict Management* 17, no. 2 (2006): 87–95.

3 For example, see L. Urwick, *The Elements of Administration*, 2nd edn (London: Pitman, 1947); C. Argyris, 'The Individual and Organization: Some Problems of Mutual Adjustment', *Administrative Science Quarterly* 2, no. 1 (1957): 1–24; K. E. Boulding, 'Organization and Conflict', *Conflict Resolution* 1, no. 2 (1957): 122–134; R. R. Blake, H. A. Shepard and J. S. Mouton, *Managing Intergroup Conflict in Industry* (Houston: Gulf Publishing, 1964).

4 C. K. W. De Dreu and L. R. Weingart, 'A Contingency Theory of Task Conflict and Performance in Groups and Organizational Teams', in *International Handbook of Organizational Teamwork and Cooperative Working*, ed. M. A. West, D. Tjosvold and K. G. Smith (Chichester, UK: Wiley, 2003), 151–166; K. A. Jehn and C. Bendersky, 'Intragroup Conflict in Organizations: A Contingency Perspective on the Conflict-Outcome Relationship', *Research in Organizational Behavior* 25 (2003): 187–242.

5 N. Oudeh, 'Functional Harmony—Assessing the Impact of Conflict on Organizational Health', paper presented at the Workplace Health in a Tight Labour Market Conference, Toronto, 7 March 2007.

6 M. P. Follett, 'Constructive Conflict', in *Dynamic Administration: The Collected Papers of Mary Parker Follett*, ed. H. C. Metcalf and L. Urwick (New York: Harper & Brothers, 1942), 30–37.

7 L. Pondy, 'Organizational Conflict: Concepts and Models', *Administrative Science Quarterly* 2 (1967): 296–320; K. W. Thomas, 'Conflict and Negotiation Processes in Organizations', in *Handbook of Industrial and Organizational Psychology*, ed. M. D. Dunnette and L. M. Hough, 2nd edn (Palo Alto, CA: Consulting Psychologists Press, 1992), 651–718.

8 H. Barki and J. Hartwick, 'Conceptualizing the Construct of Interpersonal Conflict', *International Journal of Conflict Management* 15, no. 3 (2004): 216–244.

9 M. A. Von Glinow, D. L. Shapiro and J. M. Brett, 'Can We Talk, and Should We? Managing Emotional Conflict in Multicultural Teams', *Academy of Management Review* 29, no. 4 (2004): 578–592.

10 G. E. Martin and T. J. Bergman, 'The Dynamics of Behavioral Response to Conflict in the Workplace', *Journal of Occupational and Organizational Psychology* 69 (December 1996): 377–387; J. M. Brett, D. L. Shapiro and A. L. Lytle, 'Breaking the Bonds of Reciprocity in Negotiations', *Academy of Management Journal* 41 (August 1998): 410–424.

11 C. K. W. De Dreu and L. R. Weingart, 'Task Versus Relationship Conflict, Team Performance, and Team Member Satisfaction: A Meta-Analysis', *Journal of Applied Psychology*, 88, no. 4 (2003): 741–749.

12 De Dreu and Weingart, 'Task Versus Relationship Conflict, Team Performance, and Team Member Satisfaction'; A. C. Mooney, P. J. Holahan and A. C. Amason, 'Don't Take It Personally: Exploring Cognitive Conflict as a Mediator of Affective Conflict', *Journal of Management Studies* 44, no. 5 (2007): 733–758.

13 W. L. Ury, J. M. Brett and S. B. Goldberg, *Getting Disputes Resolved: Designing Systems to Cut the Costs of Conflict* (San Francisco: Jossey-Bass, 1988).

14 R. Fisher and W. Ury, *Getting to Yes: Negotiating an Agreement Without Giving In*, 2nd edn (London: Century Business, 1992).

15 C. K. W. De Dreu, 'When Too Little or Too Much Hurts: Evidence for a Curvilinear Relationship between Task Conflict and Innovation in Teams', *Journal of Management* 32, no. 1 (2006): 83–107.

16 B. Dudley, 'Bring Back the Dazzle', *Seattle Times*, 23 September 2005; J. Greene, 'Troubling Exits at Microsoft', *BusinessWeek*, 26 September 2005, 98; A. Linn, 'Microsoft Reorganizes to Compete Better with Google, Yahoo', *Associated Press Newswires*, 21 September 2005; V. Murphy, 'Microsoft's Midlife Crisis', *Forbes*, 3 October 2005, 88; L. Vaas, 'Microsoft Expands Bureaucracy, Crowns MSN King', *eWeek*, 20 September 2005; J. L. Yang, 'Microsoft's New Brain', *Fortune*, 1 May 2006, 56.

17 R. E. Walton and J. M. Dutton, 'The Management of Interdepartmental Conflict: A Model and Review', *Administrative Science Quarterly* 14, no. 1 (1969): 73–84;

S. M. Schmidt and T. A. Kochan, 'Conflict: Toward Conceptual Clarity', *Administrative Science Quarterly* 17, no. 3 (1972): 359–370.

18 M. Landler, 'Twist in the intrigue at VW may help chief keep his job,' *New York Times*, 21 April 2006, 5; R. Hutton, 'Porsche ready to swallow VW,' *Aurocar*, 7 November 2007; 'German carmaker family feud plays out in VW boardroom,' *Deutsche Welle*, 18 September 2008; D. Hawranek, 'Clans, Executives sharpen knives backstage at Porsche and VW,' *Spiegel Online*, 11 March 2008; N. D. Schwartz, 'Porsche takes a controlling interest in VW,' *New York Times*, 17 September 2008; D. Hawranek, 'German carmaker narrowly averts bankruptcy,' *Spiegel Online*, 25 May 2009; 'Porsche CEO Wiedeking resigns,' *Spiegel Online*, 23 July 2009.

19 J. A. McMullin, T. Duerden Comeau and E. Jovic, 'Generational Affinities and Discourses of Difference: A Case Study of Highly Skilled Information Technology Workers', *British Journal of Sociology* 58, no. 2 (2007): 297–316.

20 P. Hinds and D. E. Bailey, 'Out of Sight, out of Sync: Understanding Conflict in Distributed Teams', *Organization Science* 14, no. 6 (2003): 615–632; P. Hinds and M. Mortensen, 'Understanding Conflict in Geographically Distributed Teams: The Moderating Effects of Shared Identity, Shared Context, and Spontaneous Communication', *Organization Science* 16, no. 3 (2005): 290–307.

21 R. Wageman and G. Baker, 'Incentives and Cooperation: The Joint Effects of Task and Reward Interdependence on Group Performance', *Journal of Organizational Behavior* 18, no. 2 (1997): 139–158; G. S. van der Vegt, B. J. M. Emans and E. van der Vliert, 'Patterns of Interdependence in Work Teams: A Two-Level Investigation of the Relations with Job and Team Satisfaction', *Personnel Psychology* 54, no. 1 (2001): 51–69.

22 P. C. Earley and G. B. Northcraft, 'Goal Setting, Resource Interdependence, and Conflict Management', in *Managing Conflict: An Interdisciplinary Approach*, ed. M. A. Rahim (New York: Praeger, 1989), 161–170; K. Jehn, 'A Multimethod Examination of the Benefits and Detriments of Intragroup Conflict', *Administrative Science Quarterly* 40, no. 2 (1995): 245–282.

23 A. Risberg, 'Employee Experiences of Acquisition Processes', *Journal of World Business* 36 (March 2001): 58–84.

24 Jehn and Bendersky, 'Intragroup Conflict in Organizations'.

25 M. Hewstone, M. Rubin and H. Willis, 'Intergroup Bias', *Annual Review of Psychology* 53 (2002): 575–604; J. Jetten, R. Spears and T. Postmes, 'Intergroup Distinctiveness and Differentiation: A Meta-Analytic Integration', *Journal of Personality and Social Psychology* 86, no. 6 (2004): 862–879.

26 Follett, 'Constructive Conflict'; Blake, Shepard and Mouton, *Managing Intergroup Conflict in Industry*; T. Ruble and K. Thomas, 'Support for a Two-Dimensional Model of Conflict Behavior', *Organizational Behavior and Human Performance* 16 (1976): 143–155; C. K. W. De Dreu *et al.*, 'A Theory-Based Measure of Conflict Management Strategies in the Workplace', *Journal of Organizational Behavior* 22, no. 6 (2001): 645–668; Rahim, 'Toward a Theory of Managing Organizational Conflict'.

27 K. G. Allred, 'Distinguishing Best and Strategic Practices: A Framework for Managing the Dilemma Between Creating and Claiming Value', *Negotiation Journal* 16, no. 4 (2000): 387–398.

28 N. Rackham, 'The Behaviour of Successful Negotiators', in *Negotiation: Readings, Exercises, and Cases*, ed. R. Lewicki, D. Saunders and J. Minton, 3rd edn (Homewood, IL: McGraw-Hill, 1999), 341–353.

29 Jehn, 'A Multimethod Examination of the Benefits and Detriments of Intragroup Conflict'.

30 Allred, 'Distinguishing Best and Strategic Practices'.

31 G. A. Callanan, C. D. Benzing and D. F. Perri, 'Chcoie of Conflict-Handling Strategy: A Matter of Context', *Journal of Psychology* 140, no. 3 (2006): 269–288.

32 D. W. Johnson *et al.*, 'Effects of Cooperative, Competitive, and Individualistic Goal Structures on Achievement: A Meta-Analysis', *Psychological Bulletin* 89, no. 1 (1981): 47–62; Rahim, 'Toward a Theory of Managing Organizational Conflict'.

33 R. A. Friedman *et al.*, 'What Goes around Comes around: The Impact of Personal Conflict Style on Work Conflict and Stress', *International Journal of Conflict Management* 11, no. 1 (2000): 32–55; X. M. Song, J. Xile and B. Dyer, 'Antecedents and Consequences of Marketing Managers' Conflict-Handling Behaviors', *Journal of Marketing* 64 (January 2000): 50–66; M. Song, B. Dyer and R. J. Thieme, 'Conflict Management and Innovation Performance: An Integrated Contingency Perspective', *Academy of Marketing Science* 34, no. 3 (2006): 341–356; L. A. DeChurch, K. L. Hamilton and C. Haas, 'Effects of Conflict Management Strategies on Perceptions of Intragroup Conflict', *Group Dynamics* 11, no. 1 (2007): 66–78

34 C. K. W. De Dreu and A. E. M. Van Vianen, 'Managing Relationship Conflict and the Effectiveness of Organizational Teams', *Journal of Organizational Behavior* 22, no. 3 (2001): 309–328; R. J. Lewicki, D. M. Saunders and B. Barry, eds., *Negotiation: Readings, Exercises, and Cases*, 4th edn (Burr Ridge, IL.: McGraw-Hill/Irwin, 2003), 35–36.

35 D. Lax and J. Sebenius, *The Manager As Negotiator* (New York: Free Press, 1986).

36 S. Doctoroff, 'Reengineering Negotiations', *MIT Sloan Management Review* 39, no. 3 (1998): 63–71; D. C. Zetik and A. F. Stuhlmacher, 'Goal Setting and Negotiation Performance: A Meta-Analysis', *Group Processes & Intergroup Relations* 5 (January 2002): 35–52.

37 UNI (United News of India), 'Stalemate Between Govt and Employees Continues', news release, 16 January 2009; M. Chatterjee, 'Strike Hits Functioning of Government Offices in Bihar', *Indo-Asian News Service*, 13 January 2009; UNI (United News of India), 'Indefinite Strike by Govt Employees in Bihar Paralyses Work', news release, 12 January 2009; UNI (United News of India), 'Indefinite Strike of Bihar Govt Employees Continues on 4th Day', news release, 10 January 2009; UNI (United News of India), 'Modi Reappeals Govt Employees Not to Go on Strike', news release, 7 January 2009.

38 D. A. Moore, 'Myopic Prediction, Self-Destructive Secrecy, and the Unexpected Benefits of Revealing Final Deadlines in Negotiation', *Organizational Behavior and Human Decision Processes* 94, no. 2 (2004): 125–139; D. A. Moore, 'Myopic Biases in Strategic Social Prediction: Why Deadlines Put Everyone under More Pressure Than Everyone Else', *Personality and Social Psychology Bulletin* 31, no. 5 (2005): 668–679.

39 Lewicki, Saunders and Barry, *Negotiation: Readings, Exercises, and Cases*, 90–96; S. Kwon and L. R. Weingart, 'Unilateral Concessions from the Other Party: Concession Behavior, Attributions, and Negotiation Judgments', *Journal of Applied Psychology* 89, no. 2 (2004): 263–278.

40 D. Malhotra, 'The Fine Art of Making Concessions', *Negotiation (Harvard Law School)* 9, no. 1 (2006): 3–5.

41 J. Z. Rubin and B. R. Brown, *The Social Psychology of Bargaining and Negotiation* (New York: Academic Press, 1976), ch. 9.

42 Lewicki, Saunders and Barry, *Negotiation: Readings, Exercises, and Cases.*

43 M. Gladwell, *Blink: The Power of Thinking Without Thinking* (New York: Little, Brown, 2005).

44 P. J. Carnevale and A. M. Isen, 'The Influence of Positive Affect and Visual Access on the Discovery of Integrative Solutions on Bilateral Negotiation', *Organizational Behavior and Human Decision Processes*, 37, no. 1 (1986): 1–13; L. Thompson, *The Mind and Heart of the Negotiator*, 3rd edn (Upper Saddle River, NJ: Prentice Hall, 2005).

45 J. M. Brett, D. L. Shapiro and A. L. Lytle, 'Refocusing Rights- and Power-Oriented Negotiators toward Integrative Negotiations: Process and Outcome Effects', *Academy of Management Journal*, 15 (1998): 31–49; D. M. Kolb, 'Staying in the Game or Changing It: An Analysis of Moves and Turns in Negotiation', *Negotiation Journal*, 20, no. 2 (2004): 253–267.

46 B. McRae, *The Seven Strategies of Master Negotiators* (Toronto: McGraw-Hill Ryerson, 2002), 7–11.

47 M. Watkins, 'Negotiating in a Complex World', *Negotiation Journal* 15, no. 3 (1999): 245–270.

48 J. Z. Rubin and I. W. Zartman, 'Asymmetrical Negotiations: Some Survey Results That May Surprise', *Negotiation Journal*, 11, no. 4 (1995): 349–364.

49 Lewicki, Saunders and Barry, *Negotiation: Readings, Exercises, and Cases*, 4th edn, 298–322.

50 J. W. Salacuse and J. Z. Rubin, 'Your Place or Mine? Site Location and Negotiation', *Negotiation Journal* 6, no. 1 (1990): 5–10; J. Mayfield *et al.*, 'How Location Impacts International Business Negotiations', *Review of Business* 19 (December 1998): 21–24.

51 J. Margo, 'The Persuaders', *Boss Magazine*, 29 December 2000, 38. For a full discussion of the advantages and disadvantages of face-to-face and alternative negotiations situations, see M. H. Bazerman *et al.*, 'Negotiation', *Annual Review of Psychology* 51 (2000): 279–314.

52 Xinhua's China Economic Information Service, 'Shanghai, Disney Reach Agreement to Build Theme Park: Mayor', news release, 19 January 2009.

53 M. Olekalns, 'Negotiating With Australia: The Individualist Among Us', in *Conflict Management in the Pacific Rim*, ed. K. Leung and D. Tjosvold (New York: Wiley, 1998): 277–302.

54 M. W. Morris and H.-Y. Fu, 'How Does Culture Influence Conflict Resolution? Dynamic Constructivist Analysis', *Social Cognition* 19 (June 2001): 324–349; C. H. Tinsley, 'How Negotiators Get to Yes: Predicting the Constellation of Strategies Used across Cultures to Negotiate Conflict', *Journal of Applied Psychology* 86, no. 4 (2001): 583–593; J. L. Holt and C. J. DeVore, 'Culture, Gender, Organizational Role, and Styles of Conflict Resolution: A Meta-Analysis', *International Journal of Intercultural Relations* 29, no. 2 (2005): 165–196.

55 J. M. Brett, *Negotiating Globally: How to Negotiate Deals, Resolve Disputes, and Make Decisions across Cultural Boundaries*, 2nd edn (San Francisco: Jossey-Bass, 2007).

56 Von Glinow, Shapiro and Brett, 'Can We Talk, and Should We?'.

57 N. Brewer, P. Mitchell and N. Weber, 'Gender Role, Organizational Status, and Conflict Management Styles', *International Journal of Conflict Management* 13, no. 1 (2002): 78–95; N. B. Florea *et al.*, 'Negotiating from Mars to Venus: Gender in Simulated International Negotiations',

Simulation & Gaming 34 (June 2003): 226–248; Holt and DeVore, 'Culture, Gender, Organizational Role, and Styles of Conflict Resolution'.

58 L. Kray and L. Thompson, 'Gender Stereotypes and Negotiation Performance: An Examination of Theory and Research', *Research in Organizational Behavior* 26 (2005): 102–182.

59 L. Babcock and S. Laschever, *Ask For It: How Women Can Use the Power of Negotiation to Get What They Really Want* (New York: Bantam Books, 2007); L. Babcock and S. Laschever, *Women Don't Ask: Negotiation and the Gender Divide* (Princeton: Princeton University Press, 2003).

60 I. Ayres and P. Siegelman, 'Race and Gender Discrimination in Bargaining for a New Car', *American Economic Review* 83, no 3 (1995): 304–321.

61 L. Kray and C. Locke, 'To Flirt or Not to Flirt? Sexual Power at the Bargaining Table', *Negotiation Journal* 24, no. 4 (2008): 483–494; L. Kray, A. Galinsky and L. Thompson, 'Reversing the Gender Gap in Negotiations: An Exploration of Stereotype Regeneration', *Organizational Behavior and Human Decision Processes* 87, no. 2 (2002): 386–409; L. Kray, L. Thompson and A. Galinsky, 'Battle of the Sexes: Gender Stereotype Confirmation and Reactance in Negotiations', *Journal of Personality and Social Psychology* 80, no. 6 (2001): 942–958.

62 'Lithuania: Gender Wage Gap Remains Unchanged', *Baltic Business News*, 30 November 2008; N. Smith, 'Gender Wage Gap Widening Again', *The Independent Financial Review (NZ)*, 30 October 2008; 'Women Still Earn Less Than Men in Europe', *Waterford News & Star (Waterford City, Ireland)*, 29 August 2008; AAP Bulletins, 'Women Still Being Paid Less: ACTU', news release, 27 August 2008; S. Dunlevy, 'Women Losing the Fight For Equal Pay', *Daily Telegraph (Sydney)*, 27 August 2008; 'Females Earn Only 61% of What Males Earn', *Korea Times*, 30 June 2008; F. Felgueroso, M. Pérez-Villadóniga and J. Prieto-Rodriguez, 'The Effect of the Collective Bargaining Level on the Gender Wage Gap: Evidence From Spain', *The Manchester School* 76, no. 3 (2008): 301–319; 'It May Pay to Talk Wages', *The Western Mail (Cardiff, Wales)*, 3 May 2008.

63 L. L. Putnam, 'Beyond Third Party Role: Disputes and Managerial Intervention', *Employee Responsibilities and Rights Journal* 7 (1994): 23–36; A. R. Elangovan, 'The Manager as the Third Party: Deciding How to Intervene in Employee Disputes', in *Negotiation: Readings, Exercises, and Cases*, ed. R. J. Lewicki, J. A. Litterer and D. Saunders, 3rd edn (New York: McGraw-Hill, 1999), 458–469. For a somewhat different taxonomy of managerial conflict intervention, see P. G. Irving and J. P. Meyer, 'A Multidimensional Scaling Analysis of Managerial Third-Party Conflict Intervention Strategies', *Canadian Journal of Behavioural Science* 29, no. 1 (1997): 7–18. A more recent review describes ten species of third-party intervention, but these consist of variations of the three types described here. See D. E. Conlon *et al.*, 'Third Party Interventions across Cultures: No "One Best Choice"', in *Research in Personnel and Human Resources Management* (JAI, 2007), 309–349.

64 B. H. Sheppard, 'Managers as Inquisitors: Lessons from the Law', in *Bargaining inside Organizations*, ed. M. H. Bazerman and R. J. Lewicki (Beverly Hills, CA: Sage, 1983); N. H. Kim, D. W. Sohn and J. A. Wall, 'Korean Leaders' (and Subordinates') Conflict Management', *International Journal of Conflict Management* 10, no. 2 (1999): 130–153; D. J. Moberg, 'Managers as Judges in Employee Disputes: An Occasion for Moral Imagination', *Business Ethics Quarterly* 13, no. 4 (2003): 453–477.

65 R. Karambayya and J. M. Brett, 'Managers Handling Disputes: Third Party Roles and Perceptions of Fairness', *Academy of Management Journal* 32 (1989): 687–704; R. Cropanzano *et al.*, 'Disputant Reactions to Managerial Conflict Resolution Tactics', *Group & Organization Management* 24, no. 2 (1999): 124–153.

66 A. R. Elangovan, 'Managerial Intervention in Organizational Disputes: Testing a Prescriptive Model of Strategy Selection', *International Journal of Conflict Management* 9, no. 4 (1998): 301–335; P. S. Nugent, 'Managing Conflict: Third-Party Interventions for Managers', *Academy of Management Executive* 16, no. 1 (2002): 139–154.

67 J. P. Meyer, J. M. Gemmell and P. G. Irving, 'Evaluating the Management of Interpersonal Conflict in Organizations: A Factor-Analytic Study of Outcome Criteria', *Canadian Journal of Administrative Sciences* 14 (1997): 1–13; L. B. Bingham, 'Employment Dispute Resolution: The Case for Mediation', *Conflict Resolution Quarterly* 22, no. 1–2 (2004): 145–174; M. Hyde *et al.*, 'Workplace Conflict Resolution and the Health of Employees in the Swedish and Finnish Units of an Industrial Company', *Social Science & Medicine* 63, no. 8 (2006): 2218–2227.

68 W. H. Ross and D. E. Conlon, 'Hybrid Forms of Third-Party Dispute Resolution: Theoretical Implications of Combining Mediation and Arbitration', *Academy of Management Review* 25, no. 2 (2000): 416–427; W. H. Ross, C. Brantmeier and T. Ciriacks, 'The Impact of Hybrid Dispute-Resolution Procedures on Constituent Fairness Judgments', *Journal of Applied Social Psychology* 32, no. 6 (2002): 1151–1188.

69 Department of Defense, US Air Force, 'AMC Uses Alternative Dispute Resolution to Solve Workplace Conflicts', news release (Scott Air Force Base, IL, 13 July 2005).

70 S. L. Hayford, 'Alternative Dispute Resolution', *Business Horizons* 43 (January–February 2000): 2–4; O. Rabinovich-Einy, 'Beyond IDR: Resolving Hospital Disputes and Healing Ailing Organizations through ITR', *St. John's Law Review* 81, no. 1 (2007): 173–202; T. M. Marcum and E. A. Campbell, 'Peer Review in Employment Disputes: An Employee Right or an Employee Wrong?', *Journal of Workplace Rights* 13, no. 1 (2008): 41–58.

71 China Daily Information Company, 'Busy Year on Cards For Courts', news release, 6 January 2009; 'Land Disputes Headed For Arbitration under China Draft Law', *Xinhua Business Weekly*, 29 December 2008; P. Perry, 'The Current Landscape For Construction Disputes', *Mondaq Business Briefing*, 12 November 2008; G. Dent, 'Fight Paths', *Business Review Weekly*, 8 January 2009.

72 K. Lewin, *Resolving Social Conflicts* (New York: Harper, 1948).

73 J. D. Hunger and L. W. Stern, 'An Assessment of the Functionality of the Superordinate Goal in Reducing Conflict', *Academy of Management Journal* 19, no. 4 (1976): 591–605; M. Sherif, 'Superordinate Goals in the Reduction of Intergroup Conflict', *The American Journal of Sociology* 63, no. 4 (1958): 349–356.

74 Sherif, 'Superordinate Goals in the Reduction of Intergroup Conflict'; K. Eisenhardt, J. Kahwajy and L. Bourgeois III, 'How Management Teams Can Have a Good Fight', *Harvard Business Review* 75, no 4 (1997): 77–84; Song, Xile and Dyer, 'Antecedents and Consequences of Marketing Managers' Conflict-Handling Behaviors'.

75 H. C. Triandis, 'The Future of Workforce Diversity in International Organisations: A Commentary', *Applied Psychology: An International Journal* 52, no. 3 (2003): 486–495.

76 'Can the New CEO End a Culture Clash after a Merger?', *Financial Times (UK)*, 10 September 2008, 16.

77 T. F. Pettigrew, 'Intergroup Contact Theory', *Annual Review of Psychology* 49 (1998): 65–85; S. Brickson, 'The Impact of Identity Orientation on Individual and Organizational Outcomes in Demographically Diverse Settings', *Academy of Management Review* 25 (January 2000): 82–101; J. Dixon and K. Durrheim, 'Contact and the Ecology of Racial Division: Some Varieties of Informal Segregation', *British Journal of Social Psychology* 42, no. 1 (2003): 1–23.

78 Triandis, 'The Future of Workforce Diversity in International Organisations'.

79 E. Horwitt, 'Knowledge, Knowledge, Who's Got the Knowledge', *Computerworld*, 8 April 1996, 80, 81, 84.

80 A. C. Amason and H. J. Sapienza, 'The Effects of Top Management Team Size and Interaction Norms on Cognitive and Affective Conflict', *Journal of Management* 23, no. 4 (1997): 495–516.

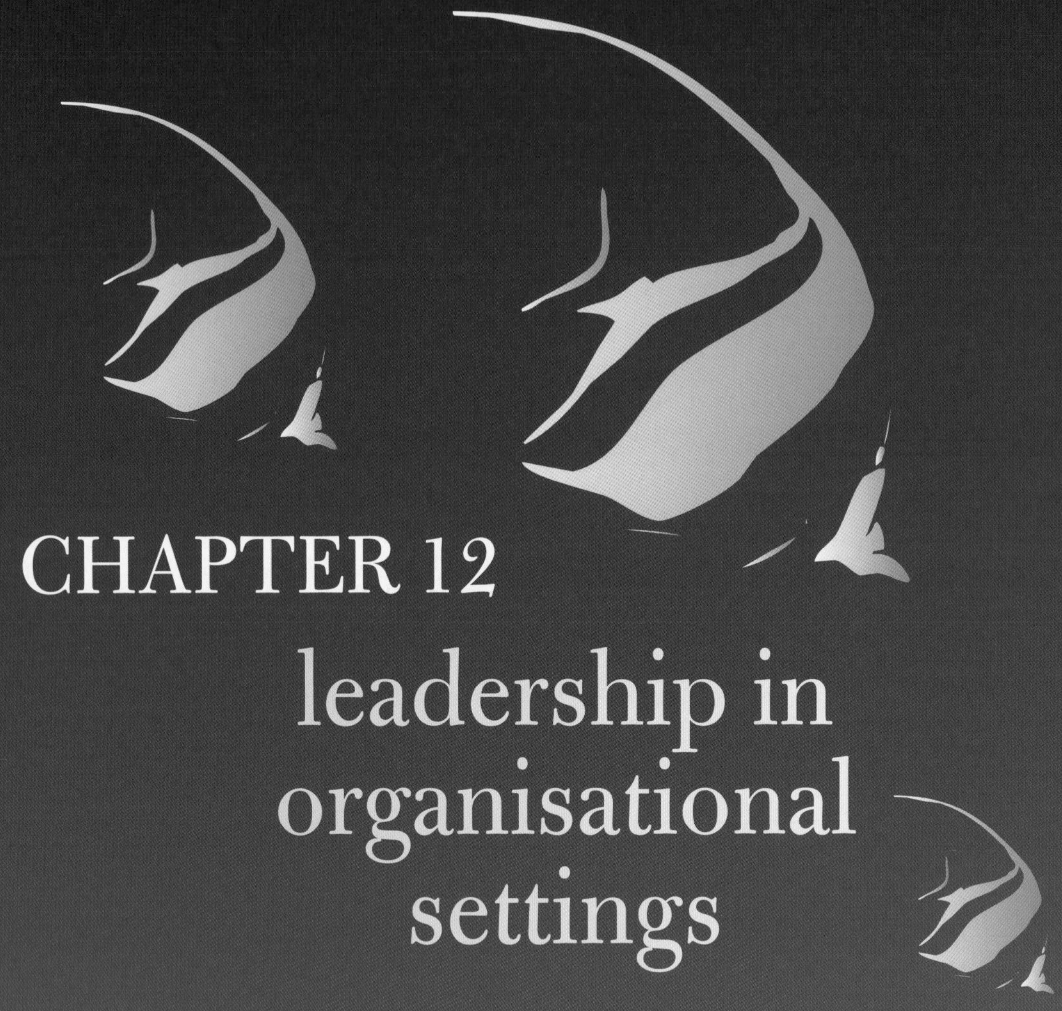

CHAPTER 12
leadership in organisational settings

LEARNING OBJECTIVES

After reading this chapter, you should be able to:

- define *leadership* and *shared leadership*
- list the main competencies of effective leaders and discuss the limitations of the competency perspective of leadership
- describe the people-oriented and task-oriented leadership styles
- outline the path–goal theory of leadership
- summarise leadership substitutes theory
- distinguish transformational leadership from transactional and charismatic leadership
- describe the four elements of transformational leadership
- describe the implicit leadership perspective
- discuss similarities and differences in the leadership styles of women and men.

New Zealand Post CEO John Allen demonstrates both the competencies and transformational behaviours of an effective leader.

In a country that produces its fair share of notable business leaders, New Zealand Post CEO John Allen is among the best. One leadership awards group recently described him as an 'inspirational leader' with a 'transparent, innovative and people-focused leadership style'. Others describe him as an enthusiastic optimist about NZ Post and 'an energetic yet methodical speaker ... with the tenacity of a seasoned politician'.

For Allen, leadership begins with personal values aligned with the organisation's objectives. 'It is not hard [to represent New Zealand Post] because the business values and objectives are very aligned to my personal value set,' says Allen. 'I am, like New Zealand Post, ambitious for New Zealand.'

Allen's enthusiasm for NZ Post's future is driven by a 'world-class customer-centric' vision of the company's future. 'We need to rethink the model and build it around customers, value and competitive advantage,' says Allen with characteristic enthusiasm. 'We need to understand those things.' Embarking on any vision requires an 'intellectual curiosity', says Allen, because leaders need to foster continual adaptation for the company to reach that overarching objective.

Allen also points out that leaders play a vital role in communicating the company's vision and brand, both internally and externally. At the same time, he warns against supporting the myth of the heroic leader, in which the company's success is overly attributed to the leader. 'The company's story needs to be told both internally and externally and the CEO is one of the people who can communicate that message,' Allen says. 'However I am very resistant to the cult of personality which surrounds many CEOs. In my assessment, their personal brand is substituted for that of the company.'[1]

Leadership is one of the most researched, and possibly the most complex, topics in organisational behaviour. This has resulted in an enormous volume of leadership literature, most of which can be organised into five perspectives: competency, behavioural, contingency, transformational and implicit.[2] Although some of these perspectives are currently more popular than others, each helps us to more fully understand the complex issue of leadership. This chapter explores each of these five perspectives of leadership. In the final section, we also consider cross-cultural and gender issues in organisational leadership.

Define *leadership* and *shared leadership*.

WHAT IS LEADERSHIP?

What makes someone an effective leader? This question has challenged great thinkers for most of written history, and it is the focus of this chapter. The opening vignette, which describes the leadership of John Allen, CEO of New Zealand Post, offers a few clues. Allen's leadership is viewed from several perspectives, all of which are important. For example, Allen exhibits several competencies found in successful leaders, such as drive, emotional intelligence, conscientiousness and a self-concept aligned with his leadership roles. The opening vignette also reveals that the idea of leadership no longer conforms to yesteryear's image of the command-and-control boss. Although Allen is front-and-centre when the situation requires, he emphasises that leaders should not be seen as the company's heroes. Instead, he focuses on a visionary strategy, communicating that strategy and being a cheerleader for the people who bring NZ Post closer to that vision.

leadership Influencing, motivating and enabling others to contribute toward the effectiveness and success of the organisations of which they are members.

A decade ago, fifty-four leadership experts from thirty-eight countries reached a consensus that **leadership** is about influencing, motivating and enabling others to contribute to the effectiveness and success of the organisations of which they are members.[3] Leaders apply various forms of influence—from subtle persuasion to direct application of power—to ensure that followers have the motivation and role clarity to achieve specified goals. Leaders also arrange the work environment, such as allocating resources and altering communication patterns, so that employees can achieve organisational objectives more easily.

Shared Leadership

Several decades ago in a public forum on leadership, activist and author Ralph Nader contended that leaders need to do a better job of redistributing power: 'I start with the premise that the function of leadership is to produce more leaders, not more followers,' he suggested. Another participant in that forum, Time Inc. editor-in-chief Hedley Donovan, added that people demonstrate leadership in many aspects of their lives, even though they may not hold formal leadership positions. 'You get a more intelligent, responsible followership if the followers themselves have experience with leadership,' Donovan concluded.[4]

shared leadership The view that leadership is broadly distributed, rather than assigned to one person, such that people within the team and organisation lead each other.

Ralph Nader and Hedley Donovan were making the point that leadership isn't restricted to the executive suite. Anyone in the organisation may be a leader in various ways and at various times.[5] This view is known as **shared leadership** or the *leaderful organisation*. Shared leadership suggests that *leadership* is plural, not singular. It doesn't operate out of one formally assigned position or role. Instead, a team or work unit may have several leaders at the same time. One team member might champion the introduction of new technology, while a coworker keeps the work unit focused on key performance indicators. Some organisations, such as Semco SA and W. L. Gore & Associates, depend entirely on shared leadership because there are no formal leaders.[6] Anyone

Shared Leadership at Rolls-Royce Engine Services

Rolls-Royce Plc 2009

As part of its employee engagement initiative, Rolls-Royce Engine Services involved employees directly with clients, encouraged weekly huddles for information sharing and accepted employee requests for less micromanagement. Employees not only experienced higher levels of engagement and empowerment; they also accepted more leadership responsibilities. 'I saw people around me, all front-line employees, who were leaders,' says a machine programmer at the Rolls-Royce Oakland plant. 'They weren't actually leading the company, but they were people you would listen to and follow. We didn't have titles, but people had respect for what we did.'[8]

can be a leader, if he or she has an idea or vision that other employees are eager to follow. In fact, when Gore employees are asked in annual surveys 'Are you a leader?' more than 50 per cent of them answer 'Yes'.[7]

Shared leadership flourishes in organisations where the formal leaders are willing to delegate power, and encourage employees to take initiative and risks without fear of failure (i.e. a learning orientation culture). Shared leadership also calls for a collaborative rather than an internally competitive culture because employees take on shared leadership roles when coworkers support them for their initiative. Furthermore, shared leadership lacks formal authority, so it operates best when employees learn to influence others through their enthusiasm, logical analysis and involvement of coworkers in their idea or vision.

COMPETENCY PERSPECTIVE OF LEADERSHIP

LEARNING OBJECTIVE 

List the main competencies of effective leaders and discuss the limitations of the competency perspective of leadership.

Since the beginning of recorded civilisation, people have been interested in the personal characteristics that distinguish great leaders from the rest of us.[9] In the sixth century BC, the Chinese philosopher Lao-tzu described effective leaders as selfless, honest, fair and hardworking. The Greek philosopher Plato claimed that great leaders have wisdom and a superior capacity for logical thinking. During the past century, hundreds of leadership studies have tried to empirically identify the traits of effective leaders. However, a major review in the late 1940s concluded that no consistent list of traits could be distilled from this research. This conclusion was revised a decade later, suggesting that a few traits are associated with effective leaders.[10] These paltry findings caused many scholars to give up their search for personal characteristics that distinguish effective leaders.

Over the past two decades, leadership researchers and consultants have returned to the notion that effective leaders possess specific personal characteristics.[11] The earlier research was apparently plagued by methodological problems, lack of theoretical foundation and inconsistent definitions of leadership. The emerging work has identified several leadership *competencies*, that is, skills, knowledge, aptitudes and other personal characteristics that lead to superior performance (see Chapter 2). The main categories of leadership competencies are listed in Exhibit 12.1 and described below:[12]

- Personality—Most of the Big Five personality dimensions (see Chapter 2) are associated with effective leadership to some extent, but the strongest predictors are high levels of extroversion (outgoing, talkative, sociable and assertive) and conscientiousness (careful, dependable and self-disciplined). With high extroversion, effective leaders are comfortable having an influential role in social settings. With higher conscientiousness, effective leaders set higher goals for themselves (and others) and are more motivated to pursue those goals.
- Self-concept—Successful leaders have a positive self-evaluation, including high self-esteem, self-efficacy and internal locus of control (see Chapter 2).[13] They are confident in their leadership skills and ability to achieve objectives. These leaders also have a complex, internally consistent and clear self-concept. They know themselves and act consistently with that self-concept. These characteristics are essential for *authentic leadership*, which refers to how well leaders know themselves (have a clear self-concept) and act consistently with that self-concept, such as being consistent with their personal values.[14]
- Drive—Related to their high conscientiousness and positive self-concept, successful leaders have a high need for achievement (see Chapter 5). This drive represents the inner motivation that leaders possess to pursue their goals and encourage others to move forward with theirs. Drive inspires inquisitiveness, an action orientation and boldness to take the organisation or

Exhibit 12.1 *Competencies of Effective Leaders*

Leadership competency	Description
Personality	The leader's higher levels of extroversion (outgoing, talkative, sociable and assertive) and conscientiousness (careful, dependable and self-disciplined).
Self-concept	The leader's self-beliefs and positive self-evaluation about his or her own leadership skills and ability to achieve objectives.
Drive	The leader's inner motivation to pursue goals.
Integrity	The leader's truthfulness and tendency to translate words into deeds.
Leadership motivation	The leader's need for socialised power to accomplish team or organisational goals.
Knowledge of the business	The leader's tacit and explicit knowledge about the company's environment, enabling the leader to make more intuitive decisions.
Cognitive and practical intelligence	The leader's above-average cognitive ability to process information (cognitive intelligence) and ability to solve real-world problems by adapting to, shaping or selecting appropriate environments (practical intelligence).
Emotional intelligence	The leader's ability to monitor his or her own and others' emotions, discriminate among them, and use the information to guide his or her thoughts and actions.

team into uncharted waters. In fact, Larry Bossidy, the former CEO of Honeywell and Allied Signal, says that drive is so important for leadership that 'if you have to choose between someone with a staggering IQ ... and someone with a lower IQ who is absolutely determined to succeed, you'll always do better with the second person'.[15]

- Integrity—Integrity involves truthfulness and consistency of words and actions, qualities that are related to honesty and ethical conduct. Leaders have a high moral capacity to judge dilemmas on the basis of sound values and to act accordingly. Notice that integrity is ultimately based on the leader's values, which provide an anchor for consistency. Several large-scale studies have reported that integrity and honesty are the most important characteristics of effective leaders.[16] Unfortunately, numerous surveys report that employees don't trust their leaders and don't think they have integrity. For example, only 48 per cent of employees in UK/Ireland and 53 per cent in North America trust senior management. This global survey reported somewhat higher trust in senior management among employees in South-East Asia (56 per cent) and Australia/New Zealand (64 per cent) and much higher in India (75 per cent). Another survey reported that only 2 per cent of Americans have a great deal of trust in the people who run big companies; 30 per cent say they don't trust these leaders at all![17]
- Leadership motivation—Effective leaders are motivated to lead others. They have a strong need for socialised power, meaning that they want power as a means to accomplish organisational objectives and similar good deeds. This contrasts with a need for *personalised power*, which is the desire to have power for personal gain or for the thrill one might experience from wielding power over others (see Chapter 5).[18] Leadership motivation is also necessary because, even in collegial firms, leaders are in contests for positions further up the hierarchy. Effective leaders thrive rather than wither in the face of this competition.[19]
- Knowledge of the business—Effective leaders possess tacit and explicit knowledge of the business environment in which they operate.
- Cognitive and practical intelligence—Leaders have above-average cognitive ability to process enormous amounts of information. Leaders aren't necessarily geniuses; rather, they have a superior ability to analyse a variety of complex alternatives and opportunities. Furthermore, leaders have practical intelligence; they are able to use their knowledge of the business to solve real-world problems by adapting to, shaping or selecting appropriate environments. Unlike cognitive intelligence, which is assessed by performance on clearly defined problems with sufficient information and usually one best answer, practical intelligence is assessed by performance in real-world settings, where problems are poorly defined, information is missing and more than one solution may be plausible.[20]
- Emotional intelligence—Effective leaders have a high level of emotional intelligence.[21] They are able to perceive and express emotion, assimilate emotion in thought, understand and reason with emotion, and regulate emotion in themselves and others (see Chapter 4).

Limitations and Practical Implications of the Competency Perspective

Although the competency perspective is gaining popularity (again), it has a few limitations.[22] First, it assumes that all effective leaders have the same personal characteristics that are equally important in all situations. This is probably a false assumption; leadership is far too complex to have a universal list of traits that apply to every condition. Some competencies might not be important all the time. Second, alternative combinations of competencies may be equally successful; two people with different sets of competencies might be equally good leaders. Third, the competency perspective views leadership as something within a person, yet experts emphasise that leadership is relational. People are effective leaders because of their favourable relationships with followers, so effective leaders cannot be identified without considering the quality of these relationships.[23]

One concern, which we will expand on later in this chapter, is that some personal characteristics might influence only our perception that someone is a leader, not whether the individual really makes a difference to the organisation's success. People who exhibit self-confidence, extroversion and other traits are called leaders because they fit our prototype of an effective leader. Alternatively, we might see a successful person, call that person a leader, and then attribute to that person unobservable traits that we consider essential for great leaders.

The competency perspective of leadership does not necessarily imply that leadership is a talent acquired at birth rather than developed throughout life. On the contrary, competencies indicate only leadership *potential*, not leadership performance. People with these characteristics become effective leaders only after they have developed and mastered the necessary leadership behaviours. People with somewhat lower leadership competencies may become very effective leaders because they have leveraged their potential more fully.

LEARNING OBJECTIVE

Describe the people-oriented and task-oriented leadership styles.

BEHAVIOURAL PERSPECTIVE OF LEADERSHIP

In the 1940s and 1950s, leadership experts at several universities launched an intensive research investigation to answer the question 'What behaviours make leaders effective?' Questionnaires were administered to subordinates, asking them to rate their supervisors on a large number of behaviours. These studies distilled two clusters of leadership behaviours from literally thousands of leadership behaviour items.[24]

One cluster represents people-oriented behaviours. This cluster includes behaviours such as showing mutual trust and respect for subordinates, demonstrating a genuine concern for their needs and having a desire to look out for their welfare. Leaders with a strong people-oriented style listen to employee suggestions, do personal favours for employees, support employee interests when required and treat employees as equals. The other cluster represents a task-oriented leadership style and includes behaviours that define and structure work roles. Task-oriented leaders assign employees to specific tasks, clarify their work duties and procedures, ensure that they follow company rules and push them to reach their performance capacity. They establish stretch goals and challenge employees to push themselves beyond those high standards.

Choosing Task- versus People-Oriented Leadership

Should leaders be task-oriented or people-oriented? This is a difficult question to answer because each style has its advantages and disadvantages. Recent evidence suggests that both styles are positively associated with leader effectiveness, but differences are often apparent only in very high or very low levels of each style. Generally, absenteeism, grievances, turnover and job dissatisfaction are higher among employees who work with supervisors with very low levels of people-oriented leadership. Job performance is lower among employees who work for supervisors with low levels of task-oriented leadership.[25] Research suggests that university students value task-oriented instructors because they want clear objectives and well-prepared lectures that abide by the unit's objectives.[26] Effective leaders clearly require both styles in their repertoire, but also need to know how much to apply each style, and when to apply it. As Reality Check 12.1 describes, Disney/ABC executive Anne Sweeney seems to have the uncanny ability to apply both styles simultaneously, which has resulted in tremendous success for the television network.

One problem with the behavioural leadership perspective is that the two categories are broad generalisations that mask specific behaviours within each category. For instance, task-oriented leadership includes planning work activities, clarifying roles, and monitoring operations and performance. Each of these clusters of activities are fairly distinct and likely have different effects on employee wellbeing and performance. A second concern is that the behavioural approach assumes that high levels of both styles are best in all situations. In reality, the best leadership style depends on the situation.[28] On a positive note, the behavioural perspective lays the foundation for two of the main leadership styles—people-oriented and task-oriented—found in many contemporary leadership theories. These contemporary theories adopt a contingency perspective, which is described next.

CONTINGENCY PERSPECTIVE OF LEADERSHIP

The contingency perspective of leadership is based on the idea that the most appropriate leadership style depends on the situation. Most (although not all) contingency leadership theories assume that effective leaders must be both insightful and flexible.[29] They must be able to adapt their behaviours and styles to the immediate situation. This isn't easy to do, however. Leaders typically have a preferred style. It takes considerable effort for leaders to choose and enact different styles to match the situation. As we noted earlier, leaders must have high emotional intelligence so that they can diagnose the circumstances and match their behaviours accordingly.

LEARNING OBJECTIVE 

Outline the path–goal theory of leadership.

Path–Goal Theory of Leadership

Several contingency theories have been proposed over the years, but **path–goal leadership theory** has withstood scientific critique better than the others. Indeed, one recent study found that the path–goal theory explained more about effective leadership than did another popular perspective of leadership (transformational, which we describe later in this chapter).[30] Path–goal leadership theory has its roots in the expectancy theory of motivation (see Chapter 5).[31] Early research incorporated expectancy theory into the study of how leader behaviours influence employee perceptions of expectancies (paths) between employee effort and performance (goals). Out of this early work, path–goal theory was born as a contingency leadership model.

path–goal leadership theory A contingency theory of leadership based on the expectancy theory of motivation that relates several leadership styles to specific employee and situational contingencies.

servant leadership The view that leaders serve followers, rather than vice versa; leaders help employees fulfil their needs and are coaches, stewards and facilitators of employee performance.

Path–goal theory states that effective leaders ensure that employees who perform their jobs well receive more valued rewards than those who perform poorly. Effective leaders also provide the information, support and other resources necessary to help employees complete their tasks.[32] In other words, path–goal theory advocates **servant leadership**.[33] Servant leaders do not view leadership as a position of power; rather, they are coaches, stewards and facilitators. Leadership

Leading With a Steel Fist in a Velvet Glove

AP Images

LEADERSHIP EXPERTS HAVE LONG debated whether great leaders are people-oriented or task-oriented. Their conclusion? Great leaders apply one style or the other, depending on the situation. Even so, some of the world's most respected leaders have the knack of keeping employees focused on the task while simultaneously being supportive. Anne Sweeney, co-chair of Disney Media Networks and president of Disney/ABC Television Group, is a case in point. News Corporation founder Rupert Murdoch was once quoted as saying that Sweeney has 'a steel fist in a velvet glove'.

Sweeney is renowned for her empathy and consideration. 'She has been incredibly supportive through all the ups and downs of rebuilding a network schedule, which made it possible for us to achieve so much so fast,' says ABC Entertainment president Stephen McPherson. Albert Cheng echoes this view: 'Anne makes it a point to engage with

Disney/ABC executive Anne Sweeney is renowned for applying both task-oriented and people-oriented leadership styles to help staff reach their potential.

is an obligation to understand employee needs and to facilitate their work performance. Servant leaders ask, 'How can I help you?' rather than expect employees to serve them. 'The role of the leader is to create environments where others can do great work—and then to get out of the way,' suggests Steve Vamos, president of the Society for Knowledge Economics—an Australian think tank—and former international vice president of Microsoft's online services group. Similarly, when Financial Planning Association president Jim Barnash was asked about his leadership style, he replied: 'I try to live a servant-leader's life, which means being more interested in your needs than my needs.'[34]

Path–Goal Leadership Styles

Exhibit 12.2 presents the path–goal theory of leadership. This model specifically highlights four leadership styles and several contingency factors leading to three indicators of leader effectiveness. The four leadership styles are described below:[35]

- Directive—This leadership style consists of clarifying behaviours that provide a psychological structure for subordinates. The leader clarifies performance goals, the means to reach those goals and the standards against which performance will be judged. It also includes judicious use of rewards and disciplinary actions. Directive leadership is the same as task-oriented leadership, described earlier, and echoes our discussion in Chapter 2 on the importance of clear role perceptions in employee performance. One study reported that the Australian managers interviewed dislike using the directive style because it sets them apart as 'the boss' and is generally tedious.[36]

REALITY CHECK 12.1

everyone,' says the Disney Digital Media executive vice president. 'She's very concerned about the people who work for her.'

At the same time, Sweeney maintains a sharp focus on the future and ensures that her staff reach their potential. Disney Channel Entertainment president Rich Ross notes that Sweeney avoids micromanaging her staff but applies her analytic skill to challenge managers to think through their ideas. '[She] asks the tough questions ... It trains you to anticipate it,' says Ross. According to ABC News president David Westin, 'Anne draws upon her optimism and her grace in keeping her focus firmly on the future.' He adds: 'None of us could wish for a better leader, through whatever may come our way.'

Anne Sweeney's combination of task- and people-oriented leadership has undoubtedly been a factor in the company's success. For example, the American television network ABC was floundering in fourth place and employee morale was low before Sweeney took the reins. Yet less than four years later, ABC was competing for the top spot with popular programs such as *Desperate Housewives*, *Lost* and *Grey's Anatomy*. Similar achievements occurred earlier when Sweeney was head of the Disney, Nickelodeon and FX cable networks.[27]

Exhibit 12.2 *Path-Goal Leadership Theory*

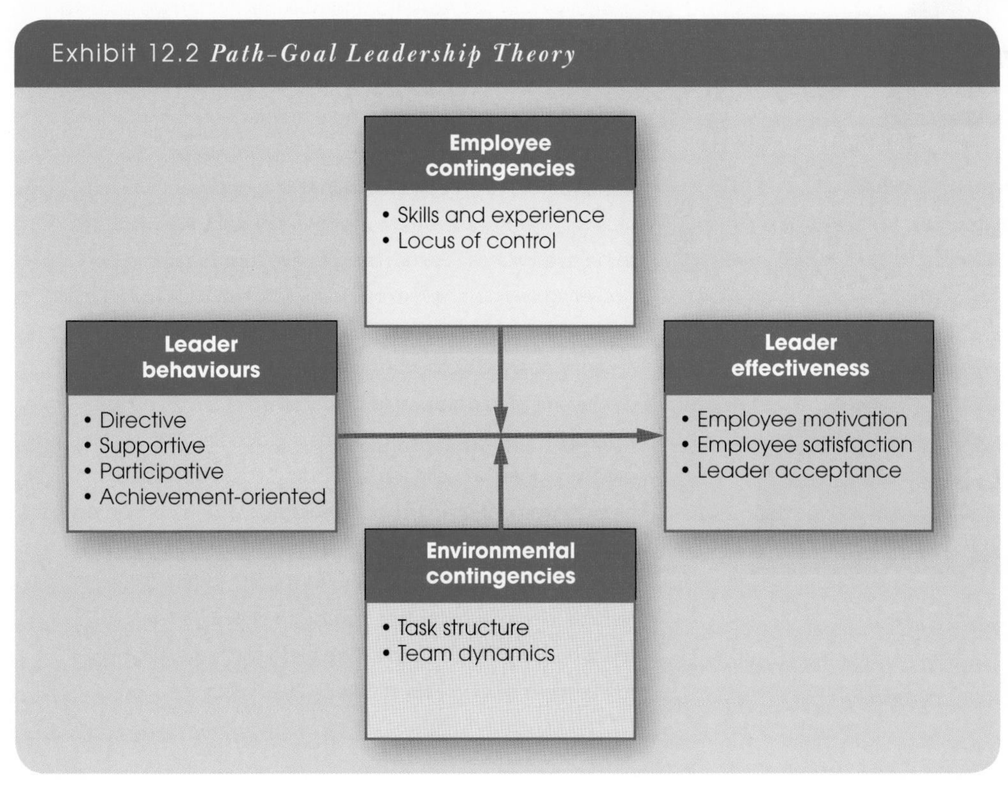

- Supportive—In this style, the leader's behaviours provide psychological support for subordinates. The leader is friendly and approachable; makes the work more pleasant; treats employees with equal respect; and shows concern for the status, needs and wellbeing of employees. Supportive leadership is the same as people-oriented leadership, described earlier, and reflects the benefits of social support to help employees cope with stressful situations.
- Participative—Participative leadership behaviours encourage and facilitate the involvement of subordinates in decisions beyond their normal work activities. The leader consults with employees, asks for their suggestions and takes these ideas into serious consideration before making a decision. Participative leadership relates to involving employees in decisions.
- Achievement-oriented—This leadership style emphasises behaviours that encourage employees to reach their peak performance. The leader sets challenging goals, expects employees to perform at their highest level, continuously seeks improvement in employee performance, and shows a high degree of confidence that employees will assume responsibility and accomplish challenging goals. Achievement-oriented leadership applies goal-setting theory, as well as positive expectations in self-fulfilling prophecy.

The path–goal model contends that effective leaders are capable of selecting the most appropriate behavioural style (or styles) for each situation. Leaders might simultaneously use two or more styles. For example, as was presented earlier in Reality Check 12.1, Disney/ABC

Striving to Become the Starbucks of Sushi

Theresa Barraclough/AFP/Getty Images

Douglas Foo has high expectations of himself and of his executive team at Apex-Pal International. 'When we opened our first Sakae Sushi restaurant, we didn't want it to be just another restaurant, we wanted it to be a global brand,' says the award-winning Singaporean entrepreneur who launched the Sakae Sushi chain of restaurants a decade ago. Foo's achievement-oriented leadership style is apparent when he says: 'We want to be the Starbucks of sushi. We want to be everywhere.' So far, his executive team seems to be delivering on Foo's high expectations. Sakae Sushi now boasts more than 80 outlets across seven countries in Asia, and it recently opened restaurants in New York City. 'My proudest achievement to date would be my team of driven people. They are the reason why my business is accelerating and they are the biggest value in the company,' says Foo. Along with his achievement-oriented leadership style, Foo is considered a supportive boss. He emphasises family values, holds Family Days and hands out vouchers so that staff can bring their families to the restaurants to celebrate birthdays. 'He's a great boss and treats us more like his family,' says Apex-Pal's marketing executive, Joyce Lee.[37]

executive Anne Sweeney is applauded for being simultaneously supportive *and* directive or achievement-oriented.

Contingencies of Path–Goal Theory

As a contingency theory, path–goal theory states that each of the four leadership styles will be effective in some situations but not in others. The path–goal leadership model specifies two sets of situational variables that moderate the relationship between a leader's style and effectiveness: (1) employee characteristics, and (2) characteristics of the employee's work environment. Several contingencies have already been studied within the path–goal framework, and the model is open for more variables in the future.[38] However, only four contingencies are reviewed here (see Exhibit 12.3) and described below:

- Skill and experience—A combination of directive and supportive leadership is best for employees who are (or perceive themselves to be) inexperienced and unskilled.[39] Directive leadership gives subordinates information about how to accomplish the task, whereas supportive leadership helps them cope with the uncertainties of unfamiliar work situations. Directive leadership is detrimental when employees are skilled and experienced because it introduces too much supervisory control.
- Locus of control—Recall from Chapter 2 that people with an internal locus of control believe that they have control over their work environment. Consequently, these employees prefer participative and achievement-oriented leadership styles and may become frustrated with a directive style. In contrast, people with an external locus of control believe that their performance is due more to luck and fate, so they tend to be more satisfied with directive and supportive leadership.
- Task structure—Leaders should adopt the directive style when the task is nonroutine, because this style minimises role ambiguity that tends to occur in complex work situations (particularly for inexperienced employees).[40] The directive style is ineffective when employees have routine and simple tasks because the manager's guidance serves no purpose and may be viewed as unnecessarily close control. Employees in highly routine and simple jobs may require supportive leadership to help them cope with the tedious nature of the work and lack of control over the pace of work. Participative leadership is preferred for employees

Exhibit 12.3 ***Selected Contingencies of Path-goal Theory***

	Directive	**Supportive**	**Participative**	**Achievement-oriented**
Employee contingencies				
Skill and experience	Low	Low	High	High
Locus of control	External	External	Internal	Internal
Environmental contingencies				
Task structure	Nonroutine	Routine	Nonroutine	?
Team dynamics	Negative norms	Low cohesion	Positive norms	?

performing nonroutine tasks because the lack of rules and procedures gives them more discretion to achieve challenging goals. The participative style is ineffective for employees in routine tasks because they lack discretion over their work.

- Team dynamics—Cohesive teams with performance-oriented norms act as a substitute for most leader interventions. High team cohesion substitutes for supportive leadership, whereas performance-oriented team norms substitute for directive and possibly achievement-oriented leadership. Thus, when team cohesion is low, leaders should use the supportive style. Leaders should apply a directive style to counteract team norms that oppose the team's formal objectives. For example, the team leader may need to use legitimate power if team members have developed a norm to 'take it easy' rather than get a project completed on time.

Path–goal theory has received more research support than other contingency leadership models, but the evidence is far from complete. A few contingencies (e.g. task structure) have limited research support. Other contingencies and leadership styles in the path–goal leadership model haven't been investigated at all (as noted by the question marks in Exhibit 12.3).[41] Another concern is that as path–goal theory expands, the model may become too complex for practical use. Few people would be able to remember all the contingencies and the appropriate leadership styles for those contingencies. In spite of these limitations, path–goal theory remains a relatively robust contingency leadership theory.

Other Contingency Theories

At the beginning of this chapter we noted that numerous leadership theories have developed over the years. Most of them are found in the contingency perspective of leadership. Some overlap with the path–goal model in terms of leadership styles, but most use simpler and more abstract contingencies. We will very briefly mention only two here because of their popularity and historical significance to the field.

Situational Leadership Theory

situational leadership theory (SLT) A commercially popular but poorly supported leadership model stating that effective leaders vary their style (telling, selling, participating, delegating) with the 'readiness' of followers.

One of the most popular contingency theories among practitioners is the **situational leadership theory (SLT)**, also called the *life-cycle theory* of leadership, developed by Paul Hersey and Ken Blanchard.[42] SLT suggests that effective leaders vary their style with the 'readiness' of followers. (An earlier version of the model called this 'maturity'.) *Readiness* refers to the employee's or work team's ability and willingness to accomplish a specific task. *Ability* refers to the extent to which the follower has the skills and knowledge to perform the task without the leader's guidance. *Willingness* refers to the follower's motivation and commitment to perform the assigned task. The model compresses these distinct concepts into a single situational condition.

The situational leadership model also identifies four leadership styles—telling, selling, participating and delegating—that Hersey and Blanchard distinguish in terms of the amount of directive and supportive behaviour provided. For example, 'telling' has high task behaviour and low supportive behaviour. The situational leadership model has four quadrants, with each quadrant showing the leadership style that is most appropriate under different circumstances.

In spite of its popularity, several studies and at least three reviews have concluded that the situational leadership model lacks empirical support.[43] Only one part of the model apparently works, namely, that leaders should use 'telling' (i.e. directive style) when employees lack motivation and ability. (Recall that this is also documented in path–goal theory.) The model's elegant simplicity is attractive and entertaining, but most parts don't represent reality very well.

Fiedler's Contingency Model

Fiedler's contingency model, developed by Fred Fiedler and his associates, was the earliest contingency theory of leadership to be developed.[44] According to this model, leader effectiveness depends on whether the person's natural leadership style is appropriately matched to the situation. The theory examines two leadership styles that essentially correspond to the previously described people-oriented and task-oriented styles. Unfortunately, Fiedler's model relies on a questionnaire that does not measure either leadership style very well.

Fiedler's contingency model An early contingency leadership model, developed by Fred Fiedler, that suggests that leader effectiveness depends on whether the person's natural leadership style is appropriately matched to the situation.

Fiedler's model suggests that the best leadership style depends on the level of *situational control*, that is, the degree of power and influence that the leader possesses in a particular situation. Situational control is affected by three factors in the following order of importance: leader–member relations, task structure and position power.[45] *Leader–member relations* refers to how much employees trust and respect the leader and are willing to follow his or her guidance. *Task structure* refers to the clarity or ambiguity of operating procedures. *Position power* is the extent to which the leader possesses legitimate, reward and coercive power over subordinates. These three contingencies form the eight possible combinations of *situation favourableness* from the leader's viewpoint. Good leader–member relations, high task structure and strong position power create the most favourable situation for the leader because he or she has the most power and influence under these conditions.

Fiedler has gained considerable respect for pioneering the first contingency theory of leadership. However, his theory has fared less well. As mentioned, the leadership-style scale used by Fiedler has been widely criticised. There is also no scientific justification for placing the three situational control factors in a hierarchy. Moreover, the concept of leader–member relations is really an indicator of leader effectiveness (as in path–goal theory) rather than a situational factor. Finally, the theory considers only two leadership styles, whereas other models present a more complex and realistic array of behaviour options. These concerns explain why the theory has limited empirical support.[46]

Changing the Situation to Match the Leader's Natural Style

Fiedler's contingency model may have become a historical footnote, but it does make an important and lasting contribution by suggesting that leadership style is related to the individual's personality and, consequently, is relatively stable over time. Leaders might be able to alter their style temporarily, but they tend to use a preferred style in the long term. More recent scholars have also proposed that leadership styles are 'hardwired' more than most contingency leadership theories assume.[47]

If leadership style is influenced by a person's personality, organisations should engineer the situation to fit the leader's dominant style, rather than expect leaders to change their style with the situation. A directive leader might be assigned inexperienced employees who need direction rather than seasoned people who work less effectively under a directive style. Alternatively, companies might transfer supervisors to workplaces where their dominant style fits best. For instance, directive leaders might be parachuted into work teams with counterproductive norms, whereas leaders who prefer a supportive style should be sent to departments in which employees face work pressures and other stressors.

Summarise leadership substitutes theory.

leadership substitutes A theory identifying contingencies that either limit a leader's ability to influence subordinates or make a particular leadership style unnecessary.

Leadership Substitutes

So far, we have looked at theories that recommend using different leadership styles in various situations. But one theory, called **leadership substitutes**, identifies conditions that either limit the leader's ability to influence subordinates or make a particular leadership style unnecessary. The literature identifies several conditions that possibly substitute for task-oriented or people-oriented leadership. For example, performance-based reward systems keep employees directed toward organisational goals, so they might replace or reduce the need for task-oriented leadership. Task-oriented leadership is also less important when employees are skilled and experienced. These propositions are similar to path–goal leadership theory; namely, directive leadership is unnecessary—and may be detrimental—when employees are skilled or experienced.[48]

Some research suggests that effective leaders help team members learn to lead themselves through leadership substitutes; in other words, coworkers substitute for leadership in high-involvement team structures.[49] Coworkers instruct new employees, thereby providing directive leadership. They also provide social support, which reduces stress among fellow employees. Teams with norms that support organisational goals may substitute for achievement-oriented leadership, because employees encourage (or pressure) coworkers to stretch their performance levels.[50]

Self-leadership—the process of influencing oneself to establish the self-direction and self-motivation needed to perform a task (see Chapter 6)—is another possible leadership substitute.[51] Employees with high self-leadership set their own goals, reinforce their own behaviour, maintain positive thought processes and monitor their own performance, thereby managing both personal motivation and abilities. As employees become more proficient in self-leadership, they presumably require less supervision; self-leadership alone keeps employees focused and energised toward their objectives.

The leadership substitutes model has intuitive appeal, but the evidence so far is mixed. Some studies show that a few substitutes do replace the need for task- or people-oriented leadership, but others do not. The difficulties of statistically testing for leadership substitutes may account for some problems, but a few writers contend that the limited support is evidence that leadership plays a critical role regardless of the situation.[52] At this point, we can conclude that a few conditions such as self-directed work teams, self-leadership and reward systems might reduce the importance of task- or people-oriented leadership but probably won't completely replace leaders in these roles.

LEARNING OBJECTIVE

Distinguish transformational leadership from transactional and charismatic leadership.

TRANSFORMATIONAL PERSPECTIVE OF LEADERSHIP

The opening vignette to this chapter described New Zealand CEO John Allen as an excellent leader because he focuses on an appealing vision of the company's future. He is considered an eternal optimist and an engaging speaker who transports listeners to a positive image of that vision. Through his vision, communication and actions, John Allen practices **transformational leadership.** Transformational leaders such as John Allen, Gail Kelly (Westpac), Nandan Nilekani (Infosys), A. G. Lafley (Procter & Gamble), Anne Sweeney (Disney/ABC) and Richard Branson (Virgin) dot the corporate landscape. These leaders are agents of change. They create, communicate and model a shared vision for the team or organisation, and they inspire followers to strive for that vision.[53]

transformational leadership A leadership perspective that explains how leaders change teams or organisations by creating, communicating and modelling a vision for the organisation or work unit, and inspiring employees to strive for that vision.

Transformational versus Transactional Leadership

A popular mantra among scholars devoted to this subject is that transformational leadership differs from **transactional leadership.**[54] Unfortunately, the literature offers a confusing and sometimes conflicting array of definitions and measures for transactional leadership. Political scholar James McGregor Burns, who coined both terms four decades ago, describes transactional leaders as people in positions of power who exchange resources with others.[55] Transactional leaders mainly gain compliance by using rewards and penalties as well as by negotiating or 'brokering' services from employees. Transformational leadership, on the other hand, engages employees by appealing to their values and aspirations. Yet Burns acknowledges that transactional leadership may also appeal to follower wants and convictions about morality and justice, and that it is inherently more ethical because transactional relations have reciprocity, trustworthiness and promise keeping.[56] Meanwhile, contemporary organisational behaviour writers sometimes equate transactional leadership with the contingency theories described earlier.

transactional leadership Leadership that helps organisations achieve their current objectives more efficiently, such as by linking job performance to valued rewards and ensuring that employees have the resources needed to get the job done.

We will avoid the 'transactional leadership' phrase, focusing instead on the elements of transformational leadership because the two are not opposites. Meanwhile, it may be more appropriate to distinguish transformational leadership in the context of 'leading' versus 'managing'. Transformational leadership is about 'leading'—changing the organisation's strategies and culture so that they have a better fit with the surrounding environment. Transformational leaders are change agents who energise and direct employees to a new vision and corresponding behaviours. 'Managing', on the other hand, refers to helping employees become more proficient and satisfied in the current situation.[57] To a large degree, the contingency and behavioural theories of leadership described earlier refer to managing employees because they focus on leader behaviours that improve employee performance and wellbeing rather than on behaviours that move the organisation and work unit to a new direction.

Organisations require leaders who both 'manage' employees and transform the work unit or organisation.[58] Managing improves organisational efficiency, whereas transformational leadership steers companies onto a better course of action. Transformational leadership is particularly important in organisations that require significant alignment with the external environment. Unfortunately, too many leaders get trapped in the daily activities that represent managerial leadership.[59] They lose touch with the transformational aspect of effective leadership. Without transformational leaders, organisations stagnate and eventually become seriously misaligned with their environments.

Transformational versus Charismatic Leadership

Another topic that has generated some confusion and controversy is the distinction between *transformational* and *charismatic* leadership.[60] Many researchers either use the words interchangeably, as if they have the same meaning, or view charismatic leadership as an essential ingredient of transformational leadership. Others take this view further by suggesting that charismatic leadership is the highest degree of transformational leadership.

Leading without Charisma

Charisma is not a word that comes to mind when seeing Alan George Lafley in action as a leader. Various sources say that the Procter & Gamble (P&G) CEO is distinctly 'unassuming', with 'a humble demeanour that belies his status'. Lafley is so soft-spoken that colleagues have to bend forward to hear him. One industry observer declared that 'if there were 15 people sitting around the conference table, it wouldn't be obvious that he was the CEO'. Lafley may lack charisma, but that hasn't stopped him from transforming the household products company where his charismatic predecessor had failed (and was ousted after just 18 months). Lafley's consistent vision, as well as symbolic and strategic actions toward a more customer-friendly and innovative organisation, have provided the direction and clarity that P&G lacked. Importantly, Lafley also walks the talk; for 10 to 15 days each year, he personally interviews and observes customers using P&G products in their homes, from Germany to Venezuela. The result: P&G has become the industry's hotspot for innovation, and its market share and profitability have experienced sustained growth.[61]

AP Images

However, the emerging view, which this book adopts, comes from a third group of experts who contend that charisma is distinct from transformational leadership. These scholars point out that charisma is a personal trait or relational quality that provides referent power over followers, whereas transformational leadership is a set of behaviours that people use to lead the change process.[62] Charismatic leaders might be transformational leaders; indeed, their personal power through charisma is a tool to change the behaviour of followers. However, some research points out that charismatic or 'heroic' leaders easily build allegiance in followers but do not necessarily change the organisation. Other research suggests that charismatic leaders produce dependent followers, whereas transformational leaders have the opposite effect—they build follower empowerment, which tends to reduce dependence on the leader. For example, one study reported a negative relationship between charismatic leadership and the self-efficacy of followers.[63]

The main point here is that effective transformational leaders are not necessarily charismatic. Alan Lafley, the CEO of Proctor & Gamble, is not known for being charismatic, but he has transformed the household goods company like no leader in recent memory. Similarly, IBM CEO Sam Palmisano speaks with humility yet continues to drive IBM's success. 'I don't have much curb appeal,' Palmisano says of his minimal charisma, adding that IBM has more than 300 000 brilliant people to drive the organisation. 'I just try to lead them and get them to come together around a common point of view,' he explains.[64] In other words, Palmisano and Lafley lead by applying transformational leadership behaviours.

LEARNING OBJECTIVE

Describe the four elements of transformational leadership.

Elements of Transformational Leadership

There are several descriptions and models of transformational leadership, but most include the following four elements: create a strategic vision, communicate the vision, model the vision and

Exhibit 12.4 *Elements of Transformational Leadership*

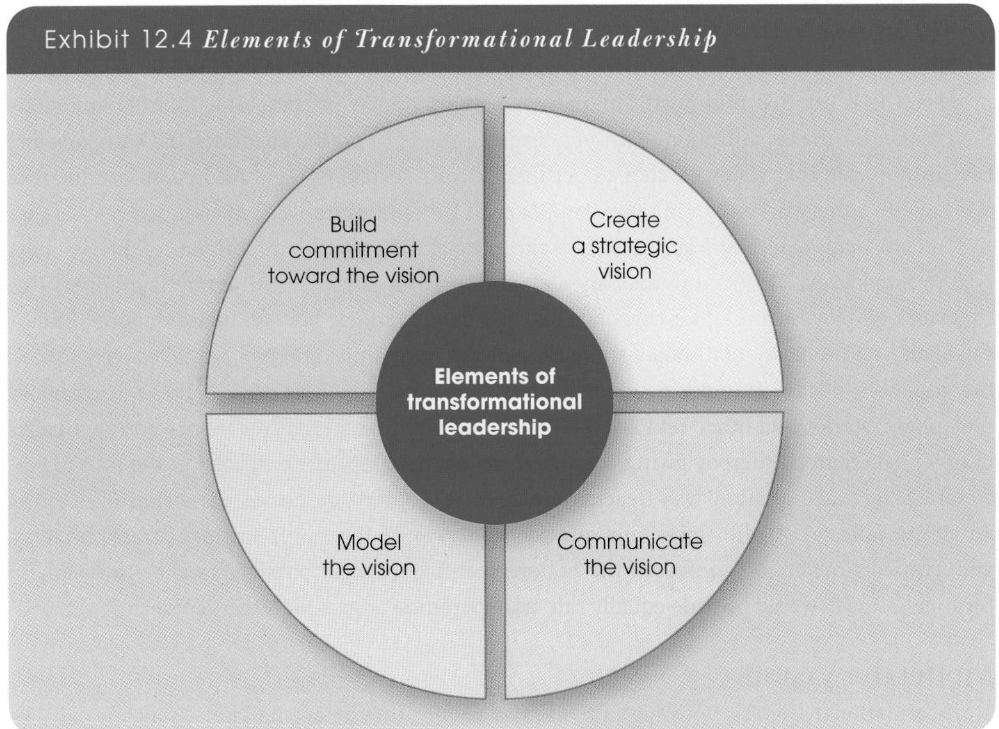

build commitment toward the vision (see Exhibit 12.4). The important feature of these elements is that they refer to the leader's behaviours and decisions. The importance of this observation will become apparent when we discuss limitations with the transformational perspective of leadership.

Create a Strategic Vision

Transformational leaders establish a vision of the company's future state that engages employees with objectives they didn't think possible. These leaders shape a strategic vision of a realistic and attractive future that bonds employees together and focuses their energy toward a superordinate organisational goal.[65] For example, New Zealand Post CEO John Allen has formed a compelling vision of his organisation as a customer-centric business. This shared strategic vision represents the substance of transformational leadership. It reflects a future for the company or work unit that is ultimately accepted and valued by organisational members. 'In essence, leadership is about dreaming the impossible and helping followers achieve the same,' says Nandan Nilekani, former CEO of India's information technology giant, Infosys. 'Moreover, the dream has to be built on sound and context-invariant values to sustain the enthusiasm and energy of people over a long time.'[66]

Strategic vision creates a 'higher purpose' or superordinate goal that energises and unifies employees.[67] A strategic vision might originate with the leader, but it is just as likely to emerge from employees, clients, suppliers or other stakeholders. A shared strategic vision plays an important role in organisational effectiveness.[68] Visions offer the motivational benefits of goal setting, but they are compelling future states that bond employees and motivate them to strive for those objectives. Visions are typically described in a way that distinguishes them from the current situation yet makes the goal both appealing and achievable.

Communicate the Vision

If vision is the substance of transformational leadership, communicating that vision is the process. CEOs say that the most important leadership quality is being able to build and share their vision for the organisation. 'Part of a leader's role is to set the vision for the company and to communicate that vision to staff to get their buy-in,' explains Dave Anderson, president of WorkSafeBC (the Workers' Compensation Board of British Columbia, Canada).[69]

Transformational leaders communicate meaning and elevate the importance of the visionary goal to employees. They frame messages around a grand purpose with emotional appeal that captivates employees and other corporate stakeholders. Framing helps transformational leaders establish a common mental model so that the group or organisation will act collectively toward the desirable goal.[70] Transformational leaders bring their visions to life through symbols, metaphors, stories and other vehicles that transcend plain language. Metaphors borrow images of other experiences, thereby giving the vision richer meaning. For example, in the mid-1800s, when ocean transportation was treacherous, Samuel Cunard described his vision of creating an 'ocean railway'. At the time, railroads provided one of the safest forms of transportation, and Cunard's metaphor reinforced the notion to employees and passengers alike that Cunard Steamship Lines would provide equally safe transportation across the Atlantic Ocean.[71]

Model the Vision

Transformational leaders not only talk about a vision; they enact it. They 'walk the talk' by stepping outside the executive suite and doing things that symbolise the vision.[72] Leaders walk the talk through significant events such as visiting customers, moving their offices closer to employees and holding ceremonies to destroy outdated policy manuals. However, they also alter mundane activities—meeting agendas, dress codes, executive schedules—so that the activities are more consistent with the vision and its underlying values. Modelling the vision is important because doing so legitimises and demonstrates what the vision looks like in practice. 'As an executive, you're always being watched by employees, and everything you say gets magnified—so you teach a lot by how you conduct yourself,' advises Carl Bass, CEO of California software company Autodesk.[73]

Modelling the vision is also important because it builds employee trust in the leader. The greater the consistency between the leader's words and actions, the more employees will believe in and be willing to follow the leader. In fact, one survey reported that leading by example is the most important characteristic of a leader. Unfortunately, other surveys suggest that leaders don't live up to expectations. A recent survey of Taiwanese employees estimated that only 28 per cent believe senior management behaves in accordance with the company's core values. A global survey reported that only 53 per cent of employees in Australia and 63 per cent of Singaporean employees believe leaders in their company make decisions that are consistent with company values. 'There are lots of people who talk a good story, but very few deliver one,' warns Peter Farrell, the Australian founder and chairman of ResMed, which leads the world in technology that corrects sleep disorders. 'You've got to mean what you say, say what you mean, and be consistent.'[74]

Build Commitment toward the Vision

Transforming a vision into reality requires employee commitment. Transformational leaders build this commitment in several ways. Their words, symbols and stories build a contagious enthusiasm that energises people to adopt the vision as their own. Leaders demonstrate a can-do attitude by enacting their vision and staying on course. Their persistence and consistency reflect an image of honesty, trust and integrity. Finally, leaders build commitment by involving employees in the process of shaping the organisation's vision.

Evaluating the Transformational Leadership Perspective

Transformational leaders do make a difference. Subordinates are more satisfied and have higher affective organisational commitment under transformational leaders. They also perform their jobs better, engage in more organisational citizenship behaviours and make better or more creative decisions. One study of bank branches reported that organisational commitment and financial performance seem to increase where the branch manager completed a transformational leadership training program.[75]

Transformational leadership is currently the most popular leadership perspective, but it faces a number of challenges. One serious problem is that some writers engage in circular logic by defining transformational leadership by the leader's success.[76] They suggest that leaders are transformational when they *successfully* change the organisation, rather than whether they engage in specific *behaviours* that identify them as transformational leaders. For example, one popular model says that transformational leaders inspire followers, and create enthusiasm and optimism, yet these are outcomes of successful leaders. This circular definition makes it impossible to determine whether transformational leadership is effective because, by definition, all transformational leaders are effective. Circular logic also undermines the predictive value of these models; we can't determine whether someone is a transformational leader until we find whether they are successful! This problem explains why we noted earlier that the four elements of transformational leadership discussed earlier are actually behaviours.

Another concern is that transformational leadership is usually described as a universal rather than contingency-oriented model. Only very recently have writers begun to explore the idea that transformational leadership is more valuable in some situations than others.[77] For instance, transformational leadership is probably more appropriate when organisations need to adapt than when environmental conditions are stable. Preliminary evidence suggests that the transformational leadership perspective is relevant across cultures. However, there may be specific elements of transformational leadership, such as the way visions are formed and communicated, that are more appropriate in some cultures than others.

IMPLICIT LEADERSHIP PERSPECTIVE

LEARNING OBJECTIVE 

Describe the implicit leadership perspective.

The competency, behaviour, contingency and transformational leadership perspectives make the basic assumption that leaders 'make a difference'. Certainly, there is evidence that senior executives do influence organisational performance. However, leadership also involves followers' perceptions about the characteristics and influence of people they call leaders. This perceptual perspective of leadership is collectively called **implicit leadership theory**.[78]

implicit leadership theory A theory stating that people evaluate a leader's effectiveness in terms of how well that person fits preconceived beliefs about the features and behaviours of effective leaders (leadership prototypes) and that people tend to inflate the influence of leaders on organisational events.

Prototypes of Effective Leaders

Implicit leadership theory consists of two related concepts. The main part of this theory states that everyone has *leadership prototypes*—preconceived beliefs about the features and behaviours of effective leaders. These prototypes, which develop through socialisation within the family and society,[79] shape our expectations and acceptance of others as leaders, and this in turn affects our willingness to serve as followers. In other words, we are more willing to allow someone to influence us as a leader if that person looks and acts like our prototype of a leader. For example, one recent study established that inherited personality characteristics significantly influence the perception that someone is a leader in a leaderless situation.[80] Such leadership prototypes not only support a person's role as leader; they also form or influence our perception of the leader's effectiveness. If the leader looks like and acts consistently with our prototype, we are more likely to believe that the leader is effective.[81] This prototype comparison process occurs because people have an inherent need to quickly evaluate individuals as leaders, yet leadership effectiveness is often ambiguous and might not be apparent for a long time.

The Romance of Leadership

Along with relying on implicit prototypes of effective leaders, followers tend to distort their perception of the influence that leaders have on the environment. This 'romance of leadership' effect exists because in most cultures people want to believe that leaders make a difference. Consider the experience of Ricardo Semler, the charismatic CEO of Brazilian conglomerate Semco SA:

> *'At the company, no matter what you do, people will naturally create and nurture a charismatic figure. The charismatic figure, on the other hand, feeds this; it doesn't just happen and it is very difficult to check your ego at the door. The people at Semco don't look and act like me. They are not yes-men by any means. What is left, however, is a certain feeling that has to do with the cult of personality. They credit me with successes that are not my own and they don't debit me my mistakes. They give undue importance to what I say and I think that doesn't go away.'*[82]

There are two main reasons why people inflate their perceptions of the leader's influence over the environment.[83] First, leadership is a useful way for us to simplify life events. It is easier to explain organisational successes and failures in terms of the leader's ability than by analysing a complex array of other forces. Second, there is a strong tendency in Australia, New Zealand and other Western cultures to believe that life events are generated more from people than from uncontrollable natural forces.[84] This illusion of control is satisfied by believing that events result from the rational actions of leaders. In other words, employees feel better believing that leaders make a difference, so they actively look for evidence that this is so.

One way that followers support their perceptions that leaders make a difference is through fundamental attribution error (see Chapter 3). Research has found that (at least in Western cultures) leaders are given credit or blame for the company's success or failure because employees do not readily see the external forces that also influence these events. Leaders reinforce this belief by taking credit for organisational successes.[85]

The implicit leadership perspective provides valuable advice to improve leadership acceptance. It highlights the fact that leadership is a perception of followers as much as the actual behaviours and formal roles of people calling themselves leaders. Potential leaders must be sensitive to this fact, understand what followers expect and act accordingly. Individuals who do not make an effort to fit leadership prototypes will have more difficulty bringing about necessary organisational change.

CROSS-CULTURAL AND GENDER ISSUES IN LEADERSHIP

Discuss similarities and differences in the leadership styles of women and men.

Along with the five perspectives of leadership presented throughout this chapter, cultural values and practices affect what leaders do. Culture shapes the leader's values and norms, which influence his or her decisions and actions. Cultural values also shape the expectations that followers have of their leaders. An executive who acts inconsistently with cultural expectations is more likely to be perceived as an ineffective leader. Furthermore, leaders who deviate from those values may experience various forms of influence to get them to conform to the leadership norms and expectations of the society. In other words, implicit leadership theory, described in the previous section, explains differences in leadership practices across cultures.

Over the past few years, 150 researchers from dozens of countries have worked together on Project GLOBE (Global Leadership and Organizational Behavior Effectiveness) to identify the effects of cultural values on leadership.[86] The project organised countries into 10 regional clusters. (Australia and New Zealand are grouped in the 'Anglo' cluster with the United States, Great Britain and Canada.) The results of this massive investigation suggest that some features of leadership are universal and some differ across cultures. Specifically, the GLOBE project reports that 'charismatic visionary' is a universally recognised concept, and that middle managers

Microsoft Germany's Gender Leadership Boom

Europe's population is shrinking and ageing, two trends that worried Achim Berg (far right, below) when he was recently hired as CEO of Microsoft Germany. Fortunately, in a country where men still overwhelmingly dominate the executive suite, the former Deutsche Telekom executive has a straightforward solution: hire more female managers and create a work

Courtesy Microsoft

environment that motivates them to stay. Berg now has 5 women on the 12-person management board and a growing pool of junior female staff members working their way into leadership positions. Berg also welcomes the gender balance because it brings more diverse leadership styles. 'Women have a different management style,' Berg claims. Dorothee Belz (2nd from left), Microsoft Germany's director of legal and corporate affairs, agrees. Women, she suggests, look at issues differently and are more willing than men to discuss problems. Berg says that working with more female colleagues has also altered his own leadership style; it has become more consultative, with less emphasis on 'speed and quick results'. He has also noticed less politics in executive meetings. 'It seems that there is a noticeable decline in territorial behaviour. But perhaps we'd be better off consulting a zoologist,' Berg suggests, humorously.[90]

around the world believe that it is characteristic of effective leaders. Charismatic visionary represents a cluster of concepts including visionary qualities, the ability to inspire, performance orientation, integrity and decisiveness.[87] In contrast, participative leadership is perceived as characteristic of effective leadership in low power-distance cultures but less so in high power-distance cultures. For instance, one study reported that Mexican employees expect managers to make decisions affecting their work. Mexico has a high power-distance culture, so followers expect leaders to apply their authority rather than delegate their power most of the time.[88] In summary, there are similarities and differences in the concept and preferred practice of leadership across cultures.

With respect to gender, studies in field settings have generally found that male and female leaders do not differ in their levels of task-oriented or people-oriented leadership. The main explanation is that real-world jobs require similar behaviour from male and female job incumbents.[89] However, women do adopt a participative leadership style more readily than their male counterparts. One possible reason is that, compared to boys, girls are often raised to be more egalitarian and less status-oriented, which is consistent with being participative. There is also some evidence that women have somewhat better interpersonal skills than men, and this translates into their relatively greater use of the participative leadership style. A third explanation is that subordinates, on the basis of their own gender stereotypes, expect female leaders to be more participative, so female leaders comply with follower expectations to some extent.

Several recent surveys report that women rate higher than men in the emerging leadership qualities of coaching, teamwork and empowering employees.[91] Yet research also suggests that women are evaluated negatively when they try to apply the full range of leadership styles, particularly more directive and autocratic approaches. Thus, ironically, women may be well suited to contemporary leadership roles, yet they often continue to face limitations of leadership through the gender stereotypes and prototypes of leaders that are held by followers.[92] Overall, both male and female leaders must be sensitive to the fact that followers have expectations about how leaders should act, and negative evaluations may go to leaders who deviate from those expectations.

CHAPTER SUMMARY

Leadership is defined as the ability to influence, motivate and enable others to contribute toward the effectiveness and success of the organisations of which they are members. Leaders use influence to motivate followers and arrange the work environment so that they do the job more effectively. Leaders exist throughout the organisation, not just in the executive suite.

The competency perspective tries to identify the characteristics of effective leaders. Recent writing suggests that leaders have specific personality characteristics, positive self-concept, drive, integrity, leadership motivation, knowledge of the business, cognitive and practical intelligence, and emotional intelligence. The behavioural perspective of leadership identifies two clusters of leader behaviour: people-oriented and task-oriented. People-oriented behaviours include showing mutual trust and respect for subordinates, demonstrating a genuine concern for their needs and having a desire to look out for their welfare. Task-oriented behaviours include assigning employees to specific tasks, clarifying their work duties and procedures, ensuring they follow company rules and pushing them to reach their performance capacity.

The contingency perspective of leadership takes the view that effective leaders diagnose the situation and adapt their style to fit that situation. The path–goal model is the prominent contingency theory that identifies four leadership styles—directive, supportive, participative and achievement-oriented—and several contingencies relating to the characteristics of the employee and of the situation.

Two other contingency leadership theories include the situational leadership theory and Fiedler's contingency theory. Research support is quite weak for both theories. However, a lasting element of Fiedler's theory is the idea that leaders have natural styles and, consequently, organisations need to change the leaders' environments to suit their style. Leadership substitutes theory identifies contingencies that either limit the leader's ability to influence subordinates or make a particular leadership style unnecessary.

Transformational leaders create a strategic vision, communicate that vision through framing and use of metaphors, model the vision by 'walking the talk' and acting consistently, and build commitment toward the vision. This contrasts with transactional leadership, which has ambiguous meaning, but is usually viewed as involving an exchange relationship with followers. Transformational leadership is also distinguished from 'managing', which relates to the contingency theories of leadership.

According to the implicit leadership perspective, people have leadership prototypes, which they use to evaluate the leader's effectiveness. Furthermore, people form a romance of leadership; they want to believe that leaders make a difference, so they engage in fundamental attribution error and other perceptual distortions to support this belief that leaders influence the company's success.

Cultural values also influence the leader's personal values, which in turn influence his or her leadership practices. Women generally do not differ from men in the degree of people-oriented or task-oriented leadership. However, female leaders more often adopt a participative style. Research also suggests that people evaluate female leaders on the basis of gender stereotypes, which may result in higher or lower ratings.

KEY TERMS

Fiedler's contingency model, p. 467
implicit leadership theory, p. 473
leadership, p. 456
leadership substitutes, p. 468
path–goal leadership theory, p. 461
servant leadership, p. 462
shared leadership, p. 456
situational leadership theory (SLT), p. 466
transactional leadership, p. 469
transformational leadership, p. 469

Critical Thinking Questions

1 Why is it important for top executives to value and support leadership at all levels of the organisation?

2 Find two newspaper advertisements for management or executive positions. What leadership competencies are mentioned in these ads? If you were on the selection panel, what methods would you use to identify these competencies in job applicants?

3 Consider your favourite lecturer. What people-oriented and task-oriented leadership behaviours did he or she use effectively? In general, do you think students prefer an instructor who is more people-oriented or task-oriented? Explain your preference.

4 Your employees are skilled and experienced customer service representatives who perform nonroutine tasks, such as solving unique customer problems or meeting special needs with the company's equipment. Use path–goal theory to identify the most appropriate leadership style(s) you should use in this situation. Be sure to fully explain your answer, and discuss why other styles are inappropriate.

5 Transformational leadership is the most popular perspective of leadership. However, it is far from perfect. Discuss the limitations of transformational leadership.

6 This chapter distinguished charismatic leadership from transformational leadership. Yet charisma is identified by most employees and managers as a characteristic of effective leaders. Why is charisma commonly related to leadership? In your opinion, are the best leaders charismatic? Why or why not?

7 Identify a current political leader (e.g. president, prime minister, state premier, mayor) and his or her recent accomplishments. Now, using the implicit leadership perspective, think of ways that these accomplishments of the leader may be overstated. In other words, explain why they may be due to factors other than the leader.

8 You hear two people debating the merits of women as leaders. One person claims that women make better leaders than do men because women are more sensitive to their employees' needs and involve them in organisational decisions. The other person counters that although these leadership styles may be increasingly important, most women have trouble gaining acceptance as leaders when they face tough situations in which a more autocratic style is required. Discuss the accuracy of the comments made in this discussion.

TEAM EXERCISE

Skill Builder 12.1

Leadership Diagnostic Analysis

Purpose

To help you learn about the different path–goal leadership styles and understand when to apply each style.

Instructions

1. On your own, write down two incidents in which someone was an effective manager or leader over you. The leader and situation can be from work, a sports team, a student work group or any other setting where leadership might emerge. For example, you might describe how your supervisor in a part-time job helped you to reach higher performance goals than you would have done otherwise. Each incident should state the actual behaviours that the leader used, (e.g. 'My boss sat down with me and we agreed on specific targets and deadlines; then he said several times over the next few weeks that I was capable of reaching those goals.') Each incident requires only two or three sentences.
2. After everyone has written his or her two incidents, the instructor will form small groups (typically, four or five students). In your team, answer the following questions for each incident presented by the team's members:
   a. Which path–goal theory leadership style(s)—directive, supportive, participative or achievement-oriented—did the leader apply in this incident?
   b. Ask the person who wrote the incident about the conditions that made this leadership style (or these styles, if more than one was used) appropriate in this situation. Your team should list these contingency factors clearly and, where possible, connect them to the contingencies described in path–goal theory. (*Note*: Your team might identify path–goal leadership contingencies that are not described in the book. These, too, should be noted and discussed.)
3. After all teams have diagnosed the incidents, each team will describe to the entire class the most interesting incident, as well as the team's diagnosis of that incident. Other teams will critique the diagnosis. Any leadership contingencies not mentioned in the textbook should also be presented and discussed.

SELF-ASSESSMENT

Skill Builder 12.2

What Is Your Boss's Preferred Leadership Style?

Purpose

This assessment is designed to help you understand two important dimensions of leadership and identify which of these dimensions is more prominent in your supervisor, team leader or coach, or in another person to whom you are accountable.

Instructions

Read each of the statements below and circle the response that you believe best describes your supervisor. You may substitute for 'supervisor' anyone else to whom you are accountable, such as a team leader, CEO, course instructor or sports coach. Then use the scoring key in Appendix B at the end of the book to calculate the results for each leadership dimension. After completing this assessment, be prepared to discuss in class the distinctions between these leadership dimensions.

Leadership Dimensions Instrument

My supervisor ...	Strongly agree	Agree	Neutral	Disagree	Strongly disagree
1. Focuses attention on irregularities, mistakes, exceptions and deviations from what is expected of me.	5	4	3	2	1
2. Engages in words and deeds that enhance his or her image of competence.	5	4	3	2	1
3. Monitors performance for errors needing correction.	5	4	3	2	1
4. Serves as a role model for me.	5	4	3	2	1
5. Points out what I will receive if I do what is required.	5	4	3	2	1
6. Instils pride in being associated with him or her.	5	4	3	2	1
7. Keeps careful track of mistakes.	5	4	3	2	1
8. Can be trusted to help me overcome any obstacle.	5	4	3	2	1
9. Tells me what to do to be rewarded for my efforts.	5	4	3	2	1
10. Makes me aware of strongly held values, ideals and aspirations that are shared in common.	5	4	3	2	1
11. Is alert for failure to meet standards.	5	4	3	2	1
12. Mobilises a collective sense of mission.	5	4	3	2	1
13. Works out agreements with me on what I will receive if I do what needs to be done.	5	4	3	2	1
14. Articulates a vision of future opportunities.	5	4	3	2	1
15. Talks about special rewards for good work.	5	4	3	2	1
16. Talks optimistically about the future.	5	4	3	2	1

Source: Items and dimensions are adapted from D. N. Den Hartog, J. J. Van Muijen and P. L. Koopman, 'Transactional versus Transformational Leadership: An Analysis of the MLQ', *Journal of Occupational and Organizational Psychology* 70, no. 1 (1997): 19–34. Den Hartog and colleagues label transactional leadership as 'rational-objective leadership' and transformational leadership as 'inspirational leadership'.

Endnotes

1 J. Robinson, 'Leader of the Brand', *New Zealand Management*, June 2005, 26; A. Bennett, 'Slick Talker with a Message to Deliver', *New Zealand Herald*, 18 November 2006; 'Deloitte/Management Magazine Executive of the Year', *New Zealand Management*, December 2007, 42; V. Jayne, 'Championing Diversity—Minds Wide Open', *New Zealand Management*, November 2008, 26–30.

2 Many of these perspectives are summarised in R. N. Kanungo, 'Leadership in Organizations: Looking Ahead to the 21st Century', *Canadian Psychology* 39 (Spring 1998): 71–82; G. A. Yukl, *Leadership in Organizations*, 6th edn (Upper Saddle River, NJ: Pearson Education, 2006).

3 R. House, M. Javidan and P. Dorfman, 'Project GLOBE: An Introduction', *Applied Psychology: An International Review* 50, no. 4 (2001): 489–505; R. House *et al.*, 'Understanding Cultures and Implicit Leadership Theories across the Globe: An Introduction to Project GLOBE', *Journal of World Business* 37, no. 1 (2002): 3–10.

4 'Leadership: The Biggest Issue', *Time*, 8 November 1976.

5 R. G. Isaac, W. J. Zerbe and D. C. Pitt, 'Leadership and Motivation: The Effective Application of Expectancy Theory', *Journal of Managerial Issues* 13 (Summer 2001): 212–226; C. L. Pearce and J. A. Conger, eds., *Shared Leadership: Reframing the Hows and Whys of Leadership* (Thousand Oaks, CA: Sage, 2003); J. S. Nielson, *The Myth of Leadership* (Palo Alto, CA.: Davies-Black, 2004); J. A. Raelin, 'We the Leaders: In Order to Form a Leaderful Organization', *Journal of Leadership & Organizational Studies* 12, no. 2 (2005): 18–30.

6 J. A. Raelin, *Creating Leaderful Organizations: How to Bring out Leadership in Everyone* (San Francisco: Berrett-Koehler, 2003).

7 A. Deutschman, 'The Fabric of Creativity', *Fast Company*, December 2004, 54–62; P. J. Kiger, 'Power to the Individual', *Workforce Management*, 27 February 2006, 1–7; G. Hamel, *The Future of Management* (Boston: Harvard Business School Press, 2007), ch. 5.

8 'Powered by Frontline People', *Employee Engagement Today*, September 2007; C. Hosford, 'Flying High', *Incentive* 181, no. 12 (2007): 14–20.

9 The history of the trait perspective of leadership, as well as current research on this topic, is nicely summarised in S. J. Zaccaro, C. Kemp and P. Bader, 'Leader Traits and Attributes', in *The Nature of Leadership*, ed. J. Antonakis, A. T. Cianciolo and R. J. Sternberg (Thousand Oaks, CA: Sage, 2004), 101–124.

10 R. M. Stogdill, *Handbook of Leadership* (New York: The Free Press, 1974), ch. 5.

11 J. Intagliata, D. Ulrich and N. Smallwood, 'Leveraging Leadership Competencies to Produce Leadership Brand: Creating Distinctiveness by Focusing on Strategy and Results', *Human Resources Planning* 23, no. 4 (2000): 12–23; J. A. Conger and D. A. Ready, 'Rethinking Leadership Competencies', *Leader to* Leader, no. 32 (Spring 2004): 41–47; Zaccaro, Kemp and Bader, 'Leader Traits and Attributes'.

12 This list is based on several sources, including: S. A. Kirkpatrick and E. A. Locke, 'Leadership: Do Traits Matter?', *Academy of Management Executive* 5 (May 1991): 48–60; R. M. Aditya, R. J. House and S. Kerr, 'Theory and Practice of Leadership: Into the New Millennium', in *Industrial and Organizational Psychology: Linking Theory with Practice*, ed. C. L. Cooper and E. A. Locke (Oxford: Blackwell, 2000), 130–165; D. Goleman, R. Boyatzis and A. McKee, *Primal Leadership: Realizing the Power of Emotional Intelligence* (Boston: Harvard Business School Press, 2002); T. A. Judge *et al.*, 'Personality and Leadership: A Qualitative and Quantitative Review', *Journal of Applied Psychology* 87, no. 4 (2002): 765–780; T. A. Judge, A. E. Colbert and R. Ilies, 'Intelligence and Leadership: A Quantitative Review and Test of Theoretical Propositions', *Journal of Applied Psychology* 89, no. 3 (2004): 542–552; Zaccaro, Kemp and Bader, 'Leader Traits and Attributes'.

13 M. Popper *et al.*, 'The Capacity to Lead: Major Psychological Differences between Leaders and Nonleaders', *Military Psychology* 16, no. 4 (2004): 245–263.

14 B. George, *Authentic Leadership* (San Francisco: Jossey-Bass, 2004); W. L. Gardner *et al.*, '"Can You See the Real Me?" A Self-Based Model of Authentic Leader and Follower Development', *Leadership Quarterly* 16, no. 3 (2005): 343–372; B. George, *True North: Discover Your Authentic Leadership* (San Francisco: Jossey-Bass, 2007), ch. 4; M. E. Palanski and F. J. Yammarino, 'Integrity and Leadership: Clearing the Conceptual Confusion', *European Management Journal* 25, no. 3 (2007): 171–184.

15 R. Charan, C. Burke and L. Bossidy, *Execution: The Discipline of Getting Things Done* (New York: Crown Business, 2002); D. Nilsen, B. Kowske and A. Kshanika, 'Managing Globally', *HRMagazine*, August 2005, 111–115.

16 The large-scale studies are reported in C. Savoye, 'Workers Say Honesty Is Best Company Policy', *Christian Science Monitor*, 15 June 2000; J. M. Kouzes and B. Z. Posner, *The Leadership Challenge*, 3rd edn (San Francisco: Jossey-Bass, 2002), ch. 2; J. Schettler, 'Leadership in Corporate America', *Training & Development*, September 2002, 66–73.

17 M. Dolliver, 'Deflating a Myth', *Brandweek*, 12 May 2008, 30–32; BlessingWhite, *The State of Employee Engagement 2008: Asia Pacific Overview* (Princeton, NJ: BlessingWhite, 3 March 2009). For other surveys on low perceived integrity of business leaders, see Watson Wyatt Worldwide, 'Asia-Pacific Workers Satisfied with Jobs Despite Some

Misgivings with Management and Pay', news release (Singapore, 16 November 2004); J. Cremer, 'Asian Workers Give Low Marks to Leaders', *South China Morning Post (Hong Kong)*, 30 July 2005, 8; D. Jones, 'Optimism Puts Rose-Colored Tint in Glasses of Top Execs', *USA Today*, 16 December 2005, B1; E. Pondel, 'Friends & Bosses?', *Seattle Post-Intelligencer*, 10 April 2006, C1.

18 R. Davidovitz *et al.*, 'Leaders as Attachment Figures: Leaders' Attachment Orientations Predict Leadership-Related Mental Representations and Followers' Performance and Mental Health', *Journal of Personality and Social Psychology* 93, no. 4 (2007): 632–650.

19 J. B. Miner, 'Twenty Years of Research on Role-Motivation Theory of Managerial Effectiveness', *Personnel Psychology* 31, no. 4 (1978): 739–760; R. J. House and R. N. Aditya, 'The Social Scientific Study of Leadership: Quo Vadis?', *Journal of Management* 23, no. 3 (1997): 409–473.

20 J. Hedlund *et al.*, 'Identifying and Assessing Tacit Knowledge: Understanding the Practical Intelligence of Military Leaders', *Leadership Quarterly* 14, no. 2 (2003): 117–140; R. J. Sternberg, 'A Systems Model of Leadership: WICS', *American Psychologist* 62, no. 1 (2007): 34–42.

21 J. George, 'Emotions and Leadership: The Role of Emotional Intelligence', *Human Relations* 53 (August 2000): 1027–1055; Goleman, Boyatzis and McKee, *Primal Leadership*; R. G. Lord and R. J. Hall, 'Identity, Deep Structure and the Development of Leadership Skill', *Leadership Quarterly* 16, no. 4 (2005): 591–615; C. Skinner and P. Spurgeon, 'Valuing Empathy and Emotional Intelligence in Health Leadership: A Study of Empathy, Leadership Behaviour and Outcome Effectiveness', *Health Services Management Research* 18, no. 1 (2005): 1–12.

22 R. Jacobs, 'Using Human Resource Functions to Enhance Emotional Intelligence', in *The Emotionally Intelligent Workplace*, ed. C. Cherniss and D. Goleman (San Francisco: Jossey-Bass, 2001), 161–163; Conger and Ready, 'Rethinking Leadership Competencies'.

23 R. G. Lord and D. J. Brown, *Leadership Processes and Self-Identity: A Follower-Centered Approach to Leadership* (Mahwah, NJ: Lawrence Erlbaum, 2004); R. Bolden and J. Gosling, 'Leadership Competencies: Time to Change the Tune?', *Leadership* 2, no. 2 (2006): 147–163.

24 P. G. Northouse, *Leadership: Theory and Practice*, 3rd edn (Thousand Oaks, CA: Sage, 2004), ch. 4; Yukl, *Leadership in Organizations*, ch. 3.

25 A. K. Korman, '"Consideration", "Initiating Structure", and Organizational Criteria—A Review', *Personnel Psychology* 19, no. 4 (1966): 349–362; E. A. Fleishman, 'Twenty Years of Consideration and Structure', in *Current Developments in the Study of Leadership*, ed. E. A. Fleishman and J. C. Hunt (Carbondale, IL: Southern Illinois University Press, 1973), 1–40; T. A. Judge, R. F. Piccolo and R. Ilies, 'The Forgotten Ones? The Validity of Consideration and Initiating Structure in Leadership Research', *Journal of Applied Psychology* 89, no. 1 (2004): 36–51; Yukl, *Leadership in Organizations*, 62–75.

26 V. V. Baba, 'Serendipity in Leadership: Initiating Structure and Consideration in the Classroom', *Human Relations* 42, no. 6 (1989): 509–525.

27 'Driving the Engine', *Broadcasting & Cable*, 21 April 2003, 6A; S. Pappu, 'The Queen of Tween', *Atlantic Monthly*, November 2004, 118–125; A. Becker, 'The Wonderful World of Sweeney', *Broadcasting & Cable*, 25 February 2008, 19; J. R. Littlejohn, 'Distinguished Vanguard Award for Leadership', *Multichannel News*, 19 May 2008.

28 S. Kerr *et al.*, 'Towards a Contingency Theory of Leadership Based Upon the Consideration and Initiating Structure Literature', *Organizational Behavior and Human Performance* 12, no. 1 (1974): 62–82; L. L. Larson, J. G. Hunt and R. N. Osbom, 'The Great Hi-Hi Leader Behavior Myth: A Lesson from Occam's Razor', *Academy of Management Journal* 19 (1976): 628–641.

29 R. Tannenbaum and W. H. Schmidt, 'How to Choose a Leadership Pattern', *Harvard Business Review* (May–June 1973): 162–180.

30 R. P. Vecchio, J. E. Justin and C. L. Pearce, 'The Utility of Transactional and Transformational Leadership for Predicting Performance and Satisfaction within a Path-Goal Theory Framework', *Journal of Occupational and Organizational Psychology* 81, no. 1 (2008): 71–82.

31 For a thorough study of how expectancy theory of motivation relates to leadership, see Isaac, Zerbe and Pitt, 'Leadership and Motivation'.

32 R. J. House, 'A Path-Goal Theory of Leader Effectiveness', *Administrative Science Quarterly* 16 (1971): 321–338; M. G. Evans, 'Extensions of a Path-Goal Theory of Motivation', *Journal of Applied Psychology* 59, no. 2 (1974): 172–178; R. J. House and T. R. Mitchell, 'Path-Goal Theory of Leadership', *Journal of Contemporary Business* (Autumn 1974): 81–97; M. G. Evans, 'Path Goal Theory of Leadership', in *Leadership*, ed. L. L. Neider and C. A. Schriesheim (Greenwich, CT: Information Age Publishing, 2002), 115–138.

33 Various thoughts on servant leadership are presented in L. C. Spears and M. Lawrence, eds., *Focus on Leadership: Servant-Leadership* (New York: Wiley, 2002).

34 D. Tarrant, 'The Leading Edge', *The Bulletin*, 15 November 2005; '2006 Movers & Shakers', *Financial Planning*, January 2006, 1.

35 R. J. House, 'Path-Goal Theory of Leadership: Lessons, Legacy, and a Reformulated Theory', *Leadership Quarterly* 7, no. 3 (1996): 323–352.

36 G. Avery and J. Ryan, 'Applying Situational Leadership in Australia', *Journal of Management Development* 21, no. 3/4 (2002): 242–262.

37 M. Bong, 'You, Me, and Suchi', *Tiger Tales (Tiger Airways Magazine)*, November 2006; 'Apex-Pal Unveils New Growth Strategies for the Year', *Channel NewsAsia*, 2 April 2008; C. Prystay, 'Sushi for All', *Forbes Asia*, 10 March 2008; N. Theresianto, 'Apex-Pal Expands Its Sakae Sushi Empire', *Edge Singapore*, 11 February 2008; L. Wei, 'Tête À Tête with Mr Douglas Foo', *Newsmag F&B*, April 2008.

38 J. Indvik, 'Path-Goal Theory of Leadership: A Meta-Analysis', *Academy of Management Proceedings* (1986): 189–192; J. C. Wofford and L. Z. Liska, 'Path-Goal Theories of Leadership: A Meta-Analysis', *Journal of Management* 19, no. 4 (1993): 857–876.

39 J. D. Houghton and S. K. Yoho, 'Toward a Contingency Model of Leadership and Psychological Empowerment: When Should Self-Leadership Be Encouraged?', *Journal of Leadership & Organizational Studies* 11, no. 4 (2005): 65–83.

40 R. T. Keller, 'A Test of the Path-Goal Theory of Leadership with Need for Clarity as a Moderator in Research and Development Organizations', *Journal of Applied Psychology* 74, no. 2 (1989): 208–212.

41 C. A. Schriesheim and L. L. Neider, 'Path-Goal Leadership Theory: The Long and Winding Road', *Leadership Quarterly* 7, no. 3 (1996): 317–321.

42 P. Hersey and K. H. Blanchard, *Management of Organizational Behavior: Utilizing Human Resources*, 5th edn (Englewood Cliffs, NJ: Prentice Hall, 1988).

43 R. P. Vecchio, 'Situational Leadership Theory: An Examination of a Prescriptive Theory', *Journal of Applied Psychology* 72, no. 3 (1987): 444–451; W. Blank, J. R. Weitzel and S. G. Green, 'A Test of the Situational Leadership Theory', *Personnel Psychology* 43, no. 3 (1990): 579–597; C. L. Graeff, 'Evolution of Situational Leadership Theory: A Critical Review', *Leadership Quarterly* 8, no. 2 (1997): 153–170.

44 F. E. Fiedler, *A Theory of Leadership Effectiveness* (New York: McGraw-Hill, 1967); F. E. Fiedler and M. M. Chemers, *Leadership and Effective Management* (Glenview, IL: Scott Foresman, 1974).

45 F. E. Fiedler, 'Engineer the Job to Fit the Manager', *Harvard Business Review* 43, no. 5 (1965): 115–122.

46 For a summary of criticisms, see Yukl, *Leadership in Organizations*, 217–218.

47 N. Nicholson, *Executive Instinct: Managing the Human Animal in the Information Age* (New York: Crown, 2000).

48 This observation has also been made by C. A. Schriesheim, 'Substitutes-for-Leadership Theory: Development and Basic Concepts', *Leadership Quarterly* 8, no. 2 (1997): 103–108.

49 D. F. Elloy and A. Randolph, 'The Effect of Superleader Behavior on Autonomous Work Groups in a Government Operated Railway Service', *Public Personnel Management* 26 (Summer 1997): 257–272; C. C. Manz and H. Sims Jr., *The New SuperLeadership: Leading Others to Lead Themselves* (San Francisco: Berrett-Koehler, 2001).

50 M. L. Loughry, 'Coworkers Are Watching: Performance Implications of Peer Monitoring', *Academy of Management Proceedings* (2002): O1–O6.

51 C. C. Manz and C. Neck, *Mastering Self-Leadership*, 3rd edn (Upper Saddle River, NJ: Prentice Hall, 2004).

52 P. M. Podsakoff and S. B. MacKenzie, 'Kerr and Jermier's Substitutes for Leadership Model: Background, Empirical Assessment, and Suggestions for Future Research', *Leadership Quarterly* 8, no. 2 (1997): 117–132; S. D. Dionne *et al.*, 'Neutralizing Substitutes for Leadership Theory: Leadership Effects and Common-Source Bias', *Journal of Applied Psychology* 87, no. 3 (2002): 454–464; J. R. Villa *et al.*, 'Problems with Detecting Moderators in Leadership Research Using Moderated Multiple Regression', *Leadership Quarterly* 14, no. 1 (2003): 3–23; S. D. Dionne *et al.*, 'Substitutes for Leadership, or Not', *Leadership Quarterly* 16, no. 1 (2005): 169–193.

53 J. M. Burns, *Leadership* (New York: Harper & Row, 1978); B. J. Avolio and F. J. Yammarino, eds., *Transformational and Charismatic Leadership: The Road Ahead* (Greenwich, CT: JAI Press, 2002); B. M. Bass and R. E. Riggio, *Transformational Leadership*, 2nd edn (Mahwah, NJ: Lawrence Erlbaum, 2006).

54 V. L. Goodwin, J. C. Wofford and J. L. Whittington, 'A Theoretical and Empirical Extension to the Transformational Leadership Construct', *Journal of Organizational Behaviour*, 22, no. 7 (2001): 759–774.

55 Burns, *Leadership*, 19–20. Burns also describes transactional and 'transforming leadership' in his more recent book: J. M. Burns, *Transforming Leadership* (New York: Grove Press, 2004).

56 For Burns' discussion on the ethics of transactional leadership, see Burns, *Transforming Leadership*, 28. Regarding transactional leadership and appealing to needs, justice, and morality, see Burns, *Leadership*, 258.

57 A. Zaleznik, 'Managers and Leaders: Are They Different?', *Harvard Business Review* 55, no. 5 (1977): 67–78; W. Bennis and B. Nanus, *Leaders: The Strategies for Taking Charge* (New York: Harper & Row, 1985). For a recent discussion regarding managing versus leading, see G. Yukl and R. Lepsinger, 'Why Integrating the Leading and Managing Roles Is Essential for Organizational Effectiveness', *Organizational Dynamics* 34, no. 4 (2005): 361–375.

58 B. M. Bass *et al.*, 'Predicting Unit Performance by Assessing Transformational and Transactional Leadership', *Journal of Applied Psychology* 88, no. 2 (2003): 207–218; Yukl and Lepsinger, 'Why Integrating the Leading and Managing Roles Is Essential for Organizational Effectiveness'.

59 For a discussion on the tendency to slide from transformational to managerial leadership, see W. Bennis, *An Invented Life: Reflections on Leadership and Change* (Reading, MA: Addison-Wesley, 1993).

60 R. J. House, 'A 1976 Theory of Charismatic Leadership', in *Leadership: The Cutting Edge*, ed. J. G. Hunt and L. L. Larson (Carbondale, IL: Southern Illinois University Press, 1977), 189–207; J. A. Conger, 'Charismatic and Transformational Leadership in Organizations: An Insider's Perspective on These Developing Streams of Research', *Leadership Quarterly* 10, no. 2 (1999): 145–179.

61 K. Brooker and J. Schlosser, 'The Un-CEO', *Fortune*, 16 September 2002, 88–93; B. Nussbaum, 'The Power of Design', *BusinessWeek*, 17 May 2004, 86; N. Buckley, 'The Calm Reinventor', *Financial Times (London)*, 29 January 2005, 11; S. Ellison, 'Women's Touch Guides P&G Chief's Firm Hand in Company Turnaround', *Wall Street Journal Europe*, 1 June 2005, A1; S. Hill Jr, 'P&G's Turnaround Proves Listening to Customer Pays', *Manufacturing Business Technology*, July 2005, 64; J. Tylee, 'Procter's Creative Gamble', *Campaign*, 18 March 2005, 24–26.

62 J. E. Barbuto Jr, 'Taking the Charisma out of Transformational Leadership', *Journal of Social Behavior and Personality* 12, no. 3 (1997): 689–697; Y. A. Nur, 'Charisma and Managerial Leadership: The Gift That Never Was', *Business Horizons* 41 (July 1998): 19–26; M. D. Mumford and J. R. Van Doorn, 'The Leadership of Pragmatism—Reconsidering Franklin in the Age of Charisma', *Leadership Quarterly* 12, no. 3 (2001): 279–309; A. Fanelli, 'Bringing out Charisma: CEO Charisma and External Stakeholders', *The Academy of Management Review* 31, no. 4 (2006): 1049–1061; M. J. Platow *et al.*, 'A Special Gift We Bestow on You for Being Representative of Us: Considering Leader Charisma from a Self-Categorization Perspective', *British Journal of Social Psychology* 45, no. 2 (2006): 303–320.

63 B. Shamir *et al.*, 'Correlates of Charismatic Leader Behavior in Military Units: Subordinates' Attitudes, Unit Characteristics, and Superiors' Appraisals of Leader Performance', *Academy of Management Journal* 41, no. 4 (1998): 387–409; R. E. De Vries, R. A. Roe and T. C. B. Taillieu, 'On Charisma and Need for Leadership', *European Journal of Work and Organizational Psychology* 8, no. 1 (1999): 109–133; R. Khurana, *Searching for a Corporate Savior: The Irrational Quest for Charismatic CEOs* (Princeton, NJ: Princeton University Press, 2002).

64 D. Olive, 'The 7 Deadly Chief Executive Sins', *Toronto Star*, 17 February 2004, D01.

65 Y. Berson *et al.*, 'The Relationship between Vision Strength, Leadership Style, and Context', *Leadership Quarterly* 12, no. 1 (2001): 53–73.

66 N. Nilekani, 'How Do I Develop Next Generation Leaders', *Economic Times (India)*, 25 November 2005.

67 Bennis and Nanus, *Leaders*, 27–33, 89; I. M. Levin, 'Vision Revisited', *Journal of Applied Behavioral Science* 36, no. 1 (2000): 91–107; R. E. Quinn, *Building the Bridge as You Walk on It: A Guide for Leading Change* (San Francisco: Jossey-Bass, 2004), ch. 11; J. M. Strange and M. D. Mumford, 'The Origins of Vision: Effects of Reflection, Models, and Analysis', *Leadership Quarterly* 16, no. 1 (2005): 121–148.

68 J. R. Baum, E. A. Locke and S. A. Kirkpatrick, 'A Longitudinal Study of the Relation of Vision and Vision Communication to Venture Growth in Entrepreneurial Firms', *Journal of Applied Psychology* 83, no. 1 (1998): 43–54; S. L. Hoe and S. L. McShane, 'Leadership Antecedents of Informal Knowledge Acquisition and Dissemination', *International Journal of Organisational Behaviour* 5 (January–June 2002): 282–291.

69 Canada Newswire, 'Canadian CEOs Give Themselves Top Marks for Leadership!', news release (9 September 1999); L. Manfield, 'Creating a Safety Culture from Top to Bottom', *WorkSafe Magazine*, February 2005, 8–9.

70 J. A. Conger, 'Inspiring Others: The Language of Leadership', *Academy of Management Executive* 5 (February 1991): 31–45; G. T. Fairhurst and R. A. Sarr, *The Art of Framing: Managing the Language of Leadership* (San Francisco: Jossey-Bass, 1996); A. E. Rafferty and M. A. Griffin, 'Dimensions of Transformational Leadership: Conceptual and Empirical Extensions', *Leadership Quarterly* 15, no. 3 (2004): 329–354; S. Denning, 'How Leaders Can Use Powerful Narratives as Change Catalysts', *Strategy and Leadership* 36, no. 2 (2008): 11–15.

71 S. Franklin, *The Heroes: A Saga of Canadian Inspiration* (Toronto: McClelland and Stewart, 1967).

72 D. E. Berlew, 'Leadership and Organizational Excitement', *California Management Review* 17, no. 2 (1974): 21–30; Bennis and Nanus, *Leaders*, 43–55; T. Simons, 'Behavioral Integrity: The Perceived Alignment between Managers' Words and Deeds as a Research Focus', *Organization Science* 13, no. 1 (2002): 18–35.

73 C. Hymowitz, 'Today's Bosses Find Mentoring Isn't Worth the Time and Risks', *Wall Street Journal*, 13 March 2006, B1.

74 M. Webb, 'Executive Profile: Peter C. Farrell', *San Diego Business Journal*, 24 March 2003, 32; P. Benesh, 'He Likes Them Breathing Easy', *Investor's Business Daily*, 13 September 2005, A04. The three surveys are described in ISR, 'Driving an Innovative Culture: Insights from Global Research and Implications for Businesses in Hong Kong' (2004), www.isrsurveys.com.au/pdf/insight/IHRM%20Show-18Nov04.pdf (accessed 22 December 2005); Watson Wyatt Worldwide, 'WorkTaiwan: Key Findings' (Singapore: Watson Wyatt Worldwide, 2004), www.watsonwyatt.com/asia-pacific/research/workasia/worktw_keyfindings.asp (accessed 2 December 2005); J. C. Maxwell, 'People Do What People See', *BusinessWeek*, 19 November 2007, 32. For a discussion of trust in leadership, see C. S. Burke *et al.*, 'Trust in Leadership: A Multi-Level Review and Integration', *Leadership Quarterly* 18, no. 6 (2007): 606–632.

75 J. Barling, T. Weber and E. K. Kelloway, 'Effects of Transformational Leadership Training on Attitudinal and Financial Outcomes: A Field Experiment', *Journal of Applied Psychology* 81, no. 6 (1996): 827–832.

76 A. Bryman, 'Leadership in Organizations', in *Handbook of Organization Studies*, ed. S. R. Clegg, C. Hardy and W. R. Nord (Thousand Oaks, CA: Sage, 1996), 276–292.

77 B. S. Pawar and K. K. Eastman, 'The Nature and Implications of Contextual Influences on Transformational Leadership: A Conceptual Examination', *Academy of Management Review* 22 (1997): 80–109; C. P. Egri and S. Herman, 'Leadership in the North American Environmental Sector: Values, Leadership Styles, and Contexts of Environmental Leaders and Their Organizations', *Academy of Management Journal* 43, no. 4 (2000): 571–604.

78 J. R. Meindl, 'On Leadership: An Alternative to the Conventional Wisdom', *Research in Organizational Behavior* 12 (1990): 159–203; L. R. Offermann, J. J. K. Kennedy and P. W. Wirtz, 'Implicit Leadership Theories: Content, Structure, and Generalizability', *Leadership Quarterly* 5, no. 1 (1994): 43–58; R. J. Hall and R. G. Lord, 'Multi-Level Information-Processing Explanations of Followers' Leadership Perceptions', *Leadership Quarterly* 6, no. 3 (1995): 265–287; O. Epitropaki and R. Martin, 'Implicit Leadership Theories in Applied Settings: Factor Structure, Generalizability, and Stability over Time', *Journal of Applied Psychology* 89, no. 2 (2004): 293–310.

79 R. G. Lord *et al.*, 'Contextual Constraints on Prototype Generation and Their Multilevel Consequences for Leadership Perceptions', *Leadership Quarterly* 12, no. 3 (2001): 311–338; T. Keller, 'Parental Images as a Guide to Leadership Sensemaking: An Attachment Perspective on Implicit Leadership Theories', *Leadership Quarterly* 14, no. 2 (2003): 141–160; K. A. Scott and D. J. Brown, 'Female First, Leader Second? Gender Bias in the Encoding of Leadership Behavior', *Organizational Behavior and Human Decision Processes* 101, no. 2 (2006): 230–242.

80 R. Ilies, M. W. Gerhardt and H. Le, 'Individual Differences in Leadership Emergence: Integrating Meta-Analytic Findings and Behavioral Genetics Estimates', *International Journal of Selection and Assessment* 12, no. 3 (2004): 207–219.

81 S. F. Cronshaw and R. G. Lord, 'Effects of Categorization, Attribution, and Encoding Processes on Leadership Perceptions', *Journal of Applied Psychology* 72, no. 1 (1987): 97–106; J. L. Nye and D. R. Forsyth, 'The Effects of Prototype-Based Biases on Leadership Appraisals: A Test of Leadership Categorization Theory', *Small Group Research* 22 (1991): 360–379.

82 L. M. Fisher, 'Ricardo Semler Won't Take Control', *strategy+business*, no. 41 (Winter 2005): 1–11.

83 Meindl, 'On Leadership: An Alternative to the Conventional Wisdom'; J. Felfe and L.-E. Petersen, 'Romance of Leadership and Management Decision Making', *European Journal of Work and Organizational Psychology* 16, no. 1 (2007): 1–24; B. Schyns, J. R. Meindl and M. A. Croon, 'The Romance of Leadership Scale: Cross-Cultural Testing and Refinement', *Leadership* 3, no. 1 (2007): 29–46.

84 J. Pfeffer, 'The Ambiguity of Leadership', *Academy of Management Review* 2 (1977): 102–112.

85 R. Weber *et al.*, 'The Illusion of Leadership: Misattribution of Cause in Coordination Games', *Organization Science* 12, no. 5 (2001): 582–598; N. Ensari and S. E. Murphy, 'Cross-Cultural Variations in Leadership Perceptions and Attribution of Charisma to the Leader', *Organizational Behavior and Human Decision Processes* 92, no. 1/2 (2003): 52–66; M. L. A. Hayward, V. P. Rindova and T. G. Pollock, 'Believing One's Own Press: The Causes and Consequences of CEO Celebrity', *Strategic Management Journal* 25, no. 7 (July 2004): 637–653.

86 Six of the Project GLOBE clusters are described in a special issue of the *Journal of World Business* 37, no. 1 (2000). For an overview of Project GLOBE, see House, Javidan and Dorfman, 'Project GLOBE: An Introduction'; R. House *et al.*, 'Understanding Cultures and Implicit Leadership Theories across the Globe: An Introduction to Project GLOBE', *Journal of World Business* 37, no. 1 (2002): 3–10.

87 J. C. Jesiuno, 'Latin Europe Cluster: From South to North', *Journal of World Business* 37, no. 1 (2002): 88. Another GLOBE study, of Iranian managers, also reported that 'charismatic visionary' stands out as a primary leadership dimension. See A. Dastmalchian, M. Javidan and K. Alam, 'Effective Leadership and Culture in Iran: An Empirical Study', *Applied Psychology: An International Review* 50, no. 4 (2001): 532–558.

88 D. N. Den Hartog *et al.*, 'Culture Specific and Cross-Cultural Generalizable Implicit Leadership Theories: Are Attributes of Charismatic/Transformational Leadership Universally Endorsed?', *Leadership Quarterly* 10, no. 2 (1999): 219–256; F. C. Brodbeck *et al.*, 'Cultural Variation of Leadership Prototypes across 22 European Countries', *Journal of Occupational and Organizational Psychology* 73, no. 1 (2000): 1–29; E. Szabo *et al.*, 'The Germanic Europe Cluster: Where Employees Have a Voice', *Journal of World Business* 37, no. 1 (2002): 55–68. The Mexican study is reported in C. E. Nicholls, H. W. Lane and M. B. Brechu, 'Taking Self-Managed Teams to Mexico', *Academy of Management Executive* 13 (August 1999): 15–25.

89 G. N. Powell, 'One More Time: Do Female and Male Managers Differ?', *Academy of Management Executive* 4 (1990): 68–75; M. L. van Engen and T. M. Willemsen, 'Sex and Leadership Styles: A Meta-Analysis of Research Published in the 1990s', *Psychological Reports* 94, no. 1 (2004): 3–18.

90 R. Fend, 'Wir Sind Die Firma (We Are the Company)', *Financial Times Deutschland*, 2 October 2008, 31; N. Klawitter *et al.*, 'Die Natur Der Macht (The Nature of Power)', *Der Spiegel*, 22 September 2008, 52; M. Schiessl, 'Microsoft Reaps the Rewards of Female Managers', *Spiegel Online*, 8 February 2008, www.spiegel.de/international/business/0,1518,533852,00.html (accessed 12 May 2009).

91 R. Sharpe, 'As Leaders, Women Rule', *BusinessWeek*, 20 November 2000, 74; M. Sappenfield, 'Women, It Seems, Are Better Bosses', *Christian Science Monitor*, 16 January 2001; A. H. Eagly and L. L. Carli, 'The Female Leadership Advantage: An Evaluation of the Evidence', *Leadership Quarterly* 14, no. 6 (2003): 807–834; A. H. Eagly, M. C. Johannesen-Schmidt and M. L. van Engen, 'Transformational, Transactional, and Laissez-Faire Leadership Styles: A Meta-Analysis Comparing Women and Men', *Psychological Bulletin* 129, no. 4 (2003): 569–591.

92 A. H. Eagly, S. J. Karau and M. G. Makhijani, 'Gender and the Effectiveness of Leaders: A Meta-Analysis', *Psychological Bulletin* 117, no. 1 (1995): 125–145; J. G. Oakley, 'Gender-Based Barriers to Senior Management Positions: Understanding the Scarcity of Female CEOs', *Journal of Business Ethics* 27, no. 4 (2000): 821–834; N. Z. Stelter, 'Gender Differences in Leadership: Current Social Issues and Future Organizational Implications', *Journal of Leadership Studies* 8 (2002): 88–99; M. E. Heilman *et al.*, 'Penalties for Success: Reactions to Women Who Succeed at Male Gender-Typed Tasks', *Journal of Applied Psychology* 89, no. 3 (2004): 416–427; A. H. Eagly, 'Achieving Relational Authenticity in Leadership: Does Gender Matter?', *Leadership Quarterly* 16, no. 3 (2005): 459–474.

BRIDGING THE TWO WORLDS—THE ORGANISATIONAL DILEMMA

1

Part 3 CASE STUDY

William Todorovic, Indiana-Purdue University, Fort Wayne

I had been hired by Aluminium Elements Corp. (AEC), and it was my first day of work. I was 26 years old, and I was now the manager of AEC's customer service group which looked after customers, logistics and some of the raw material purchasing. My superior, George, was the vice president of the company. AEC manufactured most of its products, a majority of which were destined for the construction industry, from aluminium.

As I walked around the shop floor, the employees appeared to be concentrating on their jobs, barely noticing me. Management held daily meetings, in which various production issues were discussed. No one from the shop floor was invited to the meeting, unless there was a specific problem. Later I also learned that management had separate bathrooms, separate lunch rooms, and other perks that floor employees did not have. Most of the floor employees felt that management, although polite on the surface, did not really feel they had anything to learn from the floor employees.

John, who worked on the aluminium slitter—a crucial operation required before any other operations could commence—had experienced a number of unpleasant encounters with George. As a result, George usually sent written memos to the floor in order to avoid a direct confrontation with John. Because the directions in the memos were complex, these memos were often more than two pages in length.

One morning, as I was walking around, I noticed that John was very upset. Feeling that perhaps there was something I could do, I approached John and asked him if I could help. He indicated that everything was just fine. From the looks of the situation, and John's body language, I felt that he was willing to talk, but John knew that this was not the way things were done at AEC. Tony, who worked at the machine next to John's, swore and said that the office guys only cared about schedules, not about the people down on the floor. I just looked at him and said that I only began working here last week and thought that I could address some of their issues. Tony gave me a strange look, shook his head and went back to his machine. I could hear him still swearing as I left. Later I realised that most of the office staff were also offended by Tony's language.

On the way back to my office, Lesley, a recently hired engineer from Russia, approached me and pointed out that the employees were not accustomed to the managers talking to them. Management only issued orders, and made demands. As we discussed the different perceptions between office and floor staff, we were interrupted by a very loud lunch bell, which startled me. I was happy to join Lesley for lunch, but she asked me why I was not eating in the office lunch room. I replied that if I was going to understand how AEC worked, I had to get to know all the people better. I realised that this was not how things were done and wondered about the nature of this apparent division between the management and the floor. In the lunch room, the other workers were amazed to see me there, commenting that I was just new and had not learned the ropes yet.

After lunch, when I asked George, my supervisor, about his recent confrontation with John, George was surprised that John got upset, and exclaimed, 'I just wanted John to know that he did a great job and, as a result, we will be able to ship on time one large order to the West Coast. In fact, I thought I was complimenting him.'

Earlier, Lesley had indicated that certain behaviour was expected from management, and therefore from me. I reasoned that I did not think that this behaviour works, and besides it is not what I believe or how I care to behave. For the next couple of months, I simply walked around the floor and took every opportunity to talk to the shop-floor employees. Often when the employees related specific information about their workplaces, I felt that it went over my head. Frequently I had to write down the information and revisit it later. I made a point of listening to them, identifying where they were coming from, and trying to understand them. I needed to keep my mind open to new ideas. Because the shop employees expected me to make requests and demands, I made a point of not doing any of that. Soon enough, the employees became friendly, and started to accept me as one of their own, or at least as a different type of management person.

During my third month of work, the employees showed me how to improve the scheduling of jobs, especially those on the aluminium slitter. In fact, the greatest contribution was made by John, who demonstrated better ways to combine the most common slitting sizes, and reduce waste by retaining some of the 'common-sized' material for new orders. Seeing the opportunity, I programmed a spreadsheet to calculate and track inventory. This, in addition to better planning and forecasting, allowed us to reduce our new order turnarounds from four to five weeks to a single day—in by 10 am, out by 5 pm.

By the time I was employed for four months, I realised that members of other departments had started coming to me and asking me to relay messages to the shop employees. When I asked why they were delegating this task to me, they stated that I spoke the same language as the shop employees. Increasingly, I became the messenger for the office-to-shop-floor communications.

One morning, George called me into his office and complimented me on the levels of customer service and the improvements that had been achieved. As we talked, I mentioned that we could not have done it without John's help. 'He really knows his stuff and he is good,' I said. I suggested that we consider him for some type of promotion. Also, I hoped that this would be a positive gesture that would improve the communication between the office and shop floor.

George turned and pulled a flyer out of his desk. 'Here's a management skills seminar. Do you think we should send John to it?'

'That's a great idea,' I exclaimed. 'Perhaps it would be good if he were to receive the news from you directly, George.' George agreed, and after discussing some other issues, we parted company.

That afternoon, John came into my office, upset and ready to quit. 'After all my effort and work, you guys are sending me for training seminars. So, am I not good enough for you?'

Discussion Questions

1. What barriers to effective communication existed in Aluminium Elements Corp.?
2. How did the author, William, try to address these communication barriers? What would you do differently?
3. Identify and discuss why John was upset at the end of the case.
4. What actions could William take in response to John's reaction?

JOSH MARTIN

2

CASE STUDY

Joseph C. Santora, Essex County College and TSTDCG, Inc., and James C. Sarros, Monash University

Josh Martin is a 41-year-old administrator at the Centre Street Settlement House, a nonprofit social service agency with seventy employees and more than $6 million in assets. One morning he sat pensively at his desk outside the executive suite, and thought to himself, 'No, it can't be. I can't have been working here for twenty years. Where did the time go?'

Martin has spent his entire adult life working at the Centre Settlement House. He began his career there immediately after graduating from university with a degree in economics, and very slowly climbed the narrow administrative ladder from his initial position as the director of a government-funded project to his current position as the deputy agency administrator. In addition, for the past five years, he has been serving as the president of the agency's for-profit construction company. He reports directly to Tom Saunders, the autocratic executive director of the agency.

Martin, a competent administrator, often gets things done through his participative leadership style. In the last few years, Martin's job responsibilities have increased exponentially. He fills many informational, decisional and interpersonal managerial roles for the agency. Six months ago, he was given the added responsibility of processing invoices for agency vendors and consultants, authority he shares with Saunders and the agency's accountant.

Martin is rewarded handsomely for his role in the non-profit agency. Last year, he earned $110 000, plus a liberal fringe benefits package that included an agency car, a generous superannuation plan, a month's paid leave and unlimited sick time. Although he has received an annual cost-of-living allowance (COLA), Martin has no written contractual agreement and essentially serves at the pleasure of Saunders.

Martin pays a high personal price for his attractive compensation package. He is on call twenty-four hours a day, complete with a beeper. Each Sunday morning, Martin attends a mandatory agency strategy meeting required of all agency managers.

Over the years, Martin has tolerated Saunders' erratic mood swings and his inattentiveness to agency details, but tension between the two men has reached a high point in recent months. For example, two months ago, Martin called in sick because he was suffering from a severe bout of the flu. Martin's absence forced Saunders to cancel an important meeting to supervise an agency fiscal audit. Saunders responded to Martin's absence in an irrational fashion by focusing on a small piece of tile missing from the cafeteria floor. He screamed at two employees who were eating lunch in the cafeteria.

'You see,' he said, 'Martin doesn't give a damn about anything in this agency. I always have to make sure things get done around here. Just look at the floor! There's a piece of tile missing!' Mary Thompson and Elizabeth Duncan, two veteran employees, seemed shocked by Saunders' reaction to the missing piece of tile. As Saunders stormed out of the cafeteria, throwing his hands in the air, Mary turned to Elizabeth and whispered, 'Saunders is really going off the deep end. Without Josh nothing would get done around here. I don't see how Saunders can blame Josh for every little problem. I wonder how long Josh can take this unfair treatment.' Elizabeth nodded her head in agreement.

A month after this incident, Martin recommended pay increases for two employees who had received excellent performance appraisals by their supervisors. Martin believed that a 2 per cent raise, admittedly only a symbolic amount, would provide motivation and increase morale, and would not seriously jeopardise the agency's budget. When Martin proposed the raises to Saunders at the Thursday weekly fiscal meeting, Saunders vehemently rejected Martin's proposal and countered it by ranting: 'Everybody wants a raise around here. It's about time people started doing more work and stopped whining about money. Let's move on to the next agenda item.'

Saunders closed the weekly staff meeting by saying 'I'm the leader of this agency. I have to manage everything for this agency to run effectively.' Phil Jones, the director of field operations, turned to Paul Lindstrom, the fiscal officer, and whispered, 'Sure, Saunders is the director of this agency all right, but he couldn't manage his way out of a paper bag. Without Josh, this place would be in total chaos. Besides, at least Josh listens to us and tries to implement some of our ideas to make life simpler around here.'

Martin has often contemplated resigning from the agency to seek other public-sector employment. However, he believes such opportunities are rare. Besides, Saunders knows just about every agency CEO in the public sector, and Martin believes that Saunders would find out that he applied for a job as soon as his résumé reached another agency's personnel department. Moreover, Martin feels that his long tenure with the agency may be detrimental to his chances of securing another position; most prospective employers would be suspicious of his motives for leaving the settlement house after some two decades of service. 'Perhaps I stayed too long at the dance,' Martin mused. Finally, given the troubled economic conditions, Martin knows that many public-sector agencies would be reluctant to match his salary and benefits package—at least not in his first few years of service.

Martin is uncertain of his options at this point. Although his wife is also employed full-time and possesses good technical skills and experience in the printing industry, Martin still needs to maintain his present salary to support his family (including two teenaged daughters), a $100 000 mortgage on his home and other financial obligations. He has significant nonprofit and for-profit experience, and excellent managerial and leadership skills. Yet he wonders if there is any way out of his current situation.

Discussion questions

1. Describe the two different leadership styles used by Josh Martin and Tom Saunders. Do these two different styles tell you anything about leadership traits?
2. Do you think there is any resolution to the organisational problems resulting from the conflicting leadership styles?
3. What are the characteristics/elements of an effective leader? Do you think Saunders is an effective leader? Why or why not? Is Martin an effective leader? Why or why not?
4. Does Martin have any way out of his current situation? What would you do if you were Josh Martin?

NELSON MANDELA

Kandy Dayaram, Curtin University of Technology

I have taken a moment here to rest, to steal a view of the glorious vista that surrounds me, to look back on the distance I have come. But I can rest only for a moment, for with freedom comes responsibilities, and I dare not linger, for my long walk is not yet ended.

— Nelson Mandela, *Long Walk to Freedom.*

Nelson Mandela grew up in the Transkei area of South Africa as a member of royalty within the Xhosa tribe. He was groomed to counsel the rulers of the tribe. After his father died, he was formally adopted by Chief Dalindyebo, acting regent of the Thembu people, and had many first-hand opportunities to observe the chief's leadership skills in action as he led tribal councils in the community. But Mandela chose not to follow his predetermined path; instead, he left the Transkei after completing his second year of studies at Fort Hare University and moved to Johannesburg where he joined the African National Congress (ANC). His education continued, and his struggle for freedom began.

Nelson Mandela remains one of the world's most revered statesmen, and led the struggle to replace the apartheid regime of South Africa with a multiracial democracy. He has spent his entire life, including 27 years in prison, fighting for social justice. He discovered the importance of education as a tool for understanding the history and culture of his own people, and of other groups. Retaining a lifelong thirst for education and knowledge, he completed his law degree while in jail, and continuing to study through his years of imprisonment on Robben Island. Mandela was also instrumental in encouraging fellow political prisoners to continue their education, so much so that warders would sometimes refer to his prison block as 'Mandela University'. Despite many years in jail, he emerged to become South Africa's first black president and to play a leading role in the drive for peace in other spheres of conflict. He showed true statesmanship by reaching out a reconciliatory hand to his oppressors. In 1993, together with his presidential predecessor, F. W. de Klerk, he won the Nobel Peace Prize.

From his early days observing tribal politics, Nelson Mandela learned that listening is often more important than talking. Having learned this skill, he gained a reputation as someone who could hear and be open to differing points of view, but at the same time maintain an unwavering commitment to his beliefs. 'Often, my own opinion will simply represent a consensus of what I heard in the discussion … a leader is like a shepherd. He stays behind the flock, letting the most nimble go out ahead, whereupon the others follow, not realising that all along they are being directed from behind.'

Mandela stepped down as president after the ANC's landslide victory in 1999, and Thabo Mbeki became the second democratically elected president of South Africa. Since then, Mandela has become South Africa's highest profile ambassador, campaigning for HIV/AIDS initiatives and securing his country's right to host the 2010 soccer World Cup. Former US president Bill Clinton is one of his many admirers, stating, 'Every time Nelson Mandela walks into a room we all feel a little bigger, we all want to stand up, we all want to cheer, because we'd like to be him on our best day.'

Discussion Questions

1. Identify whether Nelson Mandela displays a leadership style that is congruent with charismatic or transformational leadership.
2. How did Nelson Mandela's leadership role change as his circumstances changed?
3. What can we learn about leadership from Nelson Mandela?
4. Why is Nelson Mandela so admired as a leader? How is he similar or different from other world leaders?
5. What personality dimensions, values and attitudes might be particularly useful to an individual who wants to act as a transformational leader? Do you believe anyone can develop them? Discuss.

Sources: N. Mandela, *Long Walk to Freedom: The Autobiography of Nelson Mandela* (Randburg, South Africa: Macdonald Purnell, 1994); R. Stengel, 'The Making of a Leader', *Time*, 9 May 1994; J. Gregory, *Goodbye Bafana: Nelson Mandela, My Prisoner, My Friend* (London: Headline, 1995); M. Maharaj and A. Kathrada, eds., *Mandela: The Authorised Portrait* (Melbourne: Five Mile Press/PQ Blackwell, 2006).

CASE STUDY 4

PROFITEL INC.

Steven L. McShane, The University of Western Australia

As a formerly government-owned telephone monopoly, Profitel enjoyed many decades of minimal competition. Even today, as a publicly traded enterprise, the company's almost exclusive control over telephone copper wiring across the country keeps its profit margins above 40 per cent. Competitors in telephone and DSL broadband continue to rely on Profitel's wholesale business, which generates substantially more profit than similar wholesale services in many other countries. However, Profitel has stiff competition in the mobile telephone business, and other emerging technologies (e.g. voice over internet protocol, or VOIP) threaten Profitel's dominance. Because of these threats, Profitel's board of directors decided to hire an outsider as the new chief executive.

Although several qualified candidates expressed an interest in Profitel's top job, the board selected Lars Peeters, who had been CEO of a publicly-traded European telephone company for six years. This was followed by a brief stint as CEO of a mobile telephone company in the United States until it was acquired by a larger firm. Profitel's board couldn't believe its good fortune; Peeters brought extensive industry knowledge and global experience, a high-octane energy level, self-confidence, decisiveness and a congenial yet strongly persuasive interpersonal style. He also had a unique 'presence', which caused people to pay attention and respect his leadership.

The board was also impressed with Peeters' strategy to bolster Profitel's profit margins. This included investing heavily in the latest wireless broadband technology (for both mobile telephone and computer internet services) before competitors could gain a foothold, cutting costs through lay-offs and reduction of peripheral services, and putting pressure on the government to deregulate Profitel's traditional and emerging businesses. When Peeters described his strategy to the board, one board member commented that this was the same strategy Peeters had used in his previous two CEO postings. Peeters dismissed the comment, saying that each situation is unique.

Peeters lived up to his reputation as a decisive executive. Almost immediately after taking the CEO job at Profitel, he hired two executives from the European company where he had previously worked. Together, over the next two years, they cut the workforce by 5 per cent and rolled out the new wireless broadband technology for mobile phones and the internet. Costs increased somewhat due to downsizing expenses and the wireless technology rollout. Profitel's wireless broadband subscriber list grew quickly because, in spite of its very high prices, the technology faced limited competition and Profitel was pushing customers off the older technology to the new network.

In the meantime, however, Profitel's customer satisfaction ratings fell. A national consumer research group reported that Profitel's broadband offered the country's worst value. Employee morale also declined due to lay-offs and the company's public image problems. Some industry experts also noted that Profitel selected its wireless technology without evaluating the alternative emerging wireless technologies, which had been gaining ground in other countries. Peeters' aggressive campaign against government regulation also had unintended consequences. Rather than achieving less regulation, criticising the government and its telecommunications regulator made Profitel look even more arrogant in the eyes of both customers and government leaders.

Profitel's board was troubled by the company's lacklustre share price, which had declined 20 per cent since Peeters was hired. Some board members also worried that the company had bet on the wrong wireless technology and that subscription levels would stall far below the number necessary to achieve the profits projected in Peeters' strategic plan. This concern came closer to reality when a foreign-owned competitor won a $1 billion government contract to improve broadband services in regional areas of the country. Profitel's proposal for that regional broadband upgrade had specified high prices and limited corporate investment, but Peeters had been confident Profitel would be awarded the contract because of its market dominance and existing infrastructure with the new wireless network. When the government decided otherwise, Profitel's board fired Peeters, along with the two executives he had hired from the European company. Now, the board had to figure out what went wrong and how to avoid this problem in the future.

Discussion Questions

1. Which perspective of leadership best explains the problems experienced in this case? Analyse the case using concepts discussed in that leadership perspective.
2. What can organisations do to minimise the leadership problems discussed above?

CASE STUDY 5

TAMARACK INDUSTRIES

David J. Cherrington, Brigham Young University

Tamarack Industries manufactures motor boats that are primarily used for water skiing. During the summer months, a third production line is normally created to help meet the heavy summer demand. This third line is usually created by assigning the experienced workers to all three lines, and hiring university students on their three-month summer holidays to complete the crews. In the past, however, experienced workers resented having to break up their teams to form a third line. They also resented having to work with a bunch of uni students and complained that the 'kids' were slow and arrogant.

The supervisor, Dan Jensen, has decided to try a different strategy this summer and have all the university students work on the new line. He asked Mark Allen to supervise the new crew because Allen claimed that he knew everything about boats and could perform every job 'with my eyes closed'. Allen was happy to accept the new job and participated in selecting his own crew. Allen's crew was called 'The Geek Team' because the university students were always talking about computer technology.

Allen spent many hours in training to get his group running at full production. The students learned quickly, and by the end of the first month their production rate was up to standard, with an error rate that was only slightly above normal. To simplify the learning process, Dan Jensen assigned The Geek Team long production runs that generally consisted of 30 to 40 identical units. Thus the training period was shortened and errors were reduced. Shorter production runs were assigned to the experienced teams.

Within six weeks, a substantial rivalry had been created between The Geek Team and the older workers. At first, the rivalry was good-natured. But after a few weeks, the older workers became resentful of the remarks made by the students. The Geek Team often met its production schedules with time to spare at the end of the day for goofing around. It wasn't uncommon for someone from The Geek Team to go to another line pretending to look for materials, just to make demeaning comments. The experienced workers resented having to perform all the shorter production runs and began to retaliate with sabotage. They would sneak over during breaks and hide tools, dent materials, install something crooked and in other small ways do something that would slow production for The Geek Team.

Jensen felt good about his decision to form a separate crew of university students, but when he heard reports of sabotage and rivalry, he became very concerned. Because of complaints from the experienced workers, Dan equalised the production so that all of the crews had similar production runs. The rivalry, however, did not stop. The Geek Team continued to finish early and flaunt their performance in front of the other crews.

One day The Geek Team suspected that one of their assemblies was going to be sabotaged during the lunch break by one of the experienced crews. By skilful deception, they were able to substitute an assembly from the other experienced line for theirs. By the end of the lunch period, The Geek Team was laughing wildly because of their deception, while one experienced crew was very angry with the other one.

Dan Jensen decided that the situation had to be changed and announced that the job assignments between the different crews would be shuffled. The employees were told that when they appeared for work the next morning, the names of the workers assigned to each crew would be posted on the bulletin board. The announcement was not greeted with much enthusiasm, and Mark Allen decided to stay late to try to talk Jensen out of his idea. Allen didn't believe the rivalry was serious enough for this type of action, and he suspected that many of the university students would quit if their team was broken up.

Discussion Questions

1. Use the conflict model to (a) identify the structural causes of conflict, and (b) discuss the escalation of conflict described in this case. Your answer should also identify the signs (symptoms) of conflict in this case.
2. Analyse this case using relevant theories on team dynamics.
3. If you were Dan Jensen, what action would you take in this situation?

TREETOP FOREST PRODUCTS

6

CASE STUDY

Steven L. McShane, The University of Western Australia, and David Lebeter

Treetop Forest Products Ltd is a sawmill operation in British Columbia, Canada, that is owned by a major forest products company but operates independently of headquarters. It was built thirty years ago and was completely updated with new machinery five years ago. Treetop receives raw logs from the area for cutting and planing into building-grade timber, mostly 2-by-4 and 2-by-6 pieces of standard lengths. Higher grade logs leave Treetop's sawmill department in finished form and are sent directly to the packaging department. The remaining 40 per cent of sawmill output is made up of cuts from lower grade logs, requiring further work by the planing department.

Treetop has one general manager, 16 supervisors and support staff, and 180 unionised employees. The unionised employees are paid an hourly rate specified in the collective agreement, whereas management and support staff are paid a monthly salary. The mill is divided into six operating departments: boom, sawmill, planer, packaging, shipping and maintenance. The sawmill, boom and packaging departments operate a morning shift starting at 6 am and an afternoon shift starting at 2 pm. Employees in these departments rotate shifts every two weeks. The planer and shipping departments operate only morning shifts. Maintenance employees work the night shift (starting at 10 pm).

Each department, except for packaging, has a supervisor on every work shift. The planer supervisor is responsible for the packaging department on the morning shift and the sawmill supervisor is responsible for the packaging department on the afternoon shift. However, the packaging operation is housed in a separate building from the other departments, so supervisors seldom visit the packaging department. This is particularly true for the afternoon shift, because the sawmill supervisor is the furthest distance from the packaging building.

Packaging Quality

Ninety per cent of Treetop's product is sold on the international market through Westboard Co., a large marketing agency. Westboard represents all forest-products mills owned by Treetop's parent company as well as several other clients in the region. The market for building-grade timber is very price-competitive, because there are numerous mills selling a relatively undifferentiated product. However, some differentiation does occur in product packaging and presentation. Buyers will look closely at the packaging when deciding whether to buy from Treetop or another mill.

To encourage its clients to package their products better, Westboard sponsors a monthly package quality award. The marketing agency samples and rates its clients' packages daily, and the sawmill with the highest score at the end of the month is awarded a plaque. Package quality is a combination of how the timber is piled (e.g. defects turned in), where the bands and dunnage (packing material) are placed, how neatly the stencil and seal are applied, the stencil's accuracy, and how neatly and tightly the plastic wrap is attached.

Treetop Forest Products has won Westboard's packaging quality award several times over the past five years, and received high ratings in the months that it didn't win. However, the mill's ratings have started to decline over the past year or two, and several clients have complained about the appearance of the finished product. A few large customers switched to competitors' timber, saying that the decision was based on the substandard appearance of Treetop's packaging when it arrived in their yards.

Bottleneck in Packaging

The planing and sawmilling departments have significantly increased productivity over the past couple of years. The sawmill operation recently set a new productivity record on a single day. The planer operation has increased productivity to the point where last year it reduced operations to just one (rather than two) shifts per day. These productivity improvements are due to better operator training, fewer machine breakdowns and better selection of raw logs. (Sawmill cuts from high-quality logs usually do not require planing work.)

Productivity levels in the boom, shipping and maintenance departments have remained constant. However, the packaging department has recorded decreasing productivity over the past couple of years, with the result that a large backlog of finished product is typically stockpiled outside the packaging building. The morning shift of the packaging department is unable to keep up with the combined production of the sawmill and planer departments, so the unpackaged output is left for the afternoon shift. Unfortunately, the afternoon shift packages even less product than the morning shift, so the backlog continues to build. The backlog adds to Treetop's inventory costs and increases the risk of damaged stock.

Treetop has added Saturday overtime shifts as well as extra hours before and after the regular shifts for the packaging department employees to process this backlog. Last month, the packaging department employed 10 per cent of the workforce but accounted for 85 per cent of the overtime. This is frustrating to Treetop's management, because time and motion studies recently confirmed that the packaging department is capable of processing all of the daily sawmill and planer production without overtime. Moreover, with employees earning one and a half or two times their regular pay on overtime, Treetop's cost competitiveness suffers.

Employees and supervisors at Treetop are aware that people in the packaging department tend to extend lunch by ten minutes and coffee breaks by five minutes. They also typically leave work a few minutes before the end of shift. This abuse has worsened recently, particularly on the afternoon shift. Employees who are temporarily assigned to the packaging department also seem to participate in this time-loss pattern after a few days. Although they are punctual and productive in other departments, these temporary employees soon adopt the packaging crew's informal schedule when assigned to that department.

Discussion Questions

1. What symptom(s) in this case suggest that something has gone wrong?
2. What are the main causes of these symptoms?
3. What actions should Treetop Forest Products executives take to correct these problems?

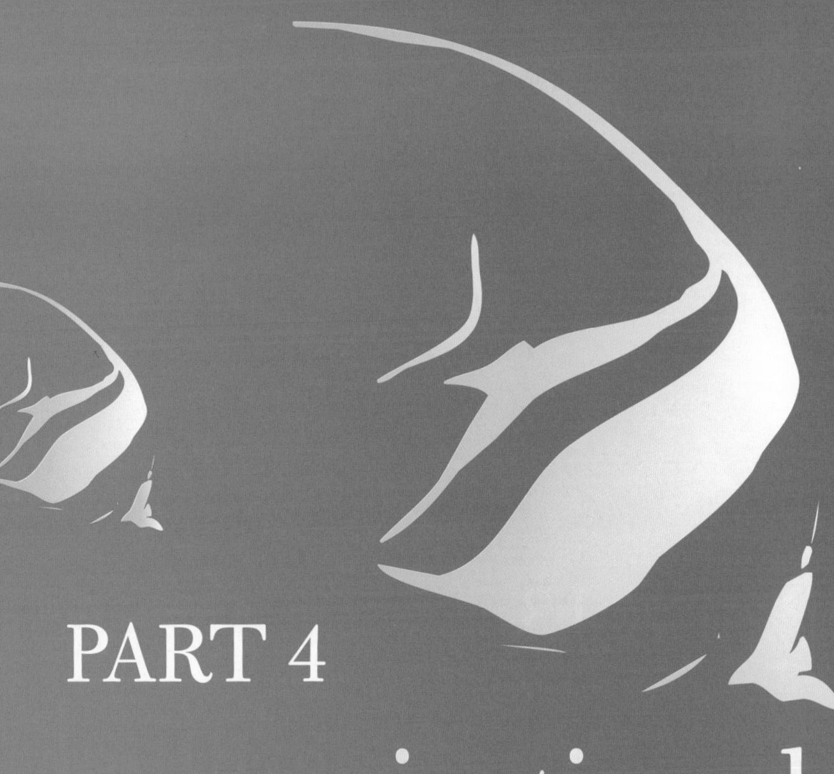

PART 4

organisational processes

CHAPTER 13

organisational structure

LEARNING OBJECTIVES

After reading this chapter, you should be able to:

- describe three types of coordination in organisational structures
- justify the optimal span of control in a given situation
- discuss the advantages and disadvantages of centralisation and formalisation
- distinguish organic from mechanistic organisational structures
- identify and evaluate the six pure types of departmentalisation
- describe three variations of divisional structure and explain which one should be adopted in a particular situation
- diagram the matrix structure, and discuss its advantages and disadvantages
- compare and contrast network structures with other forms of departmentalisation
- identify four characteristics of external environments and discuss the preferred organisational structure for each environment
- summarise the influences of organisational size, technology and strategy on organisational structure.

SapientNitro

SapientNitro, including its Australian business shown in this photo, has established a global organisational structure that retains the flexibility of a boutique agency.

Globalisation and technological change are playing havoc with the organisational structures of advertising agencies. Some multinational firms need creative agencies that have a global footprint. Other companies (such as Nike and Mars) position their advertising decisions regionally, so agencies serving these clients need to offer both regional and global expertise. Meanwhile, technology has dramatically expanded the ways in which a company's products and brand can be marketed.

Australian executive Chris Clarke launched creative agency Nitro Group (now SapientNitro) in Shanghai, China, with an organisational structure that attempts to satisfy this mishmash of client needs. Nitro's structure is designed to provide the relationship building of a local boutique operation but also offer the strength and 'scale' of a global business. 'What we are about is trying to create a new style network ... a micro-global network that has a unique product offering under one roof,' says Clarke, whose company is now part of Sapient, but retains its global boutique structure.

After its successful launch in China, Nitro formed additional hubs in New York, London, Australia, Brazil (Santa Clara Nitro) and Russia, thereby providing clients with a truly global reach. The hubs are creative engines of expertise, which support smaller satellite operations. These hubs also have strong regional leaders to drive growth. One of Nitro's regional leaders is Sean Cummins, head of SapientNitro in Australia, the agency that created the wildly successful Great Barrier Reef 'dream job' campaign for Tourism Queensland.

Clarke also wanted to avoid the highly specialised organisational structures found at most global creative agencies. 'Agency holding companies have a collection of specialist companies that they try to force together for clients,' Clarke explains. 'But clients are tired of being integration directors. They don't want to have to corral different companies.' In contrast, SapientNitro is designed as a one-stop agency; specialisations are located under one roof and the company maintains a culture that minimises departmentalisation.

'Chris had a compelling vision for a new kind of creative group, one that brought advertising, digital and innovation under one roof across five continents, to drive growth for global businesses,' says Tom Adams, cofounder of London-based Mook, which Nitro acquired a few years ago as the company's source of digital content expertise.[1]

organisational structure The division of labour as well as the patterns of coordination, communication, work flow and formal power that direct organisational activities.

There is something of a revolution occurring in how organisations are structured. Nitro and many companies are trying out new organisational structures that they hope will more effectively achieve corporate objectives. **Organisational structure** refers to the division of labour as well as the patterns of coordination, communication, workflow and formal power that direct organisational activities. The chapter begins by introducing the two fundamental processes in organisational structure: division of labour and coordination. This is followed by a detailed investigation of the four main elements of organisational structure: span of control, centralisation, formalisation and departmentalisation. The latter part of this chapter examines the contingencies of organisational design, including external environment, organisational size, technology and strategy.

Throughout this chapter, we hope to show that an organisation's structure is much more than an organisational chart diagramming which employees report to which managers. Organisational structure includes reporting relationships, but it also relates to job design, information flow, work standards and rules, team dynamics and power relationships. Organisational structures are frequently used as tools for organisational change because they establish new communication patterns and align employee behaviour with the corporate vision.[2] Consider the following: when Charles Schwab Co. experienced financial trouble not long ago, founder Charles Schwab (who returned as CEO) held a two-day marathon session in which the company's top executives were asked to redraw the organisational chart in a way that would make the company simpler, more decentralised and refocused on the customer. Every executive in the room, including those whose jobs would be erased from the new structure, was asked for his or her input.[3] The point we want to emphasise here is that organisational structure reconfigures power, communication patterns and sometimes the company's culture in the long term. As such, altering the organisation's structure is an important component of an executive's toolkit for organisational change.[4]

DIVISION OF LABOUR AND COORDINATION

All organisational structures include two fundamental requirements: the division of labour into distinct tasks, and the coordination of that labour so that employees are able to accomplish common goals.[5] Organisations are made up of groups of people who work interdependently toward some purpose. To efficiently accomplish their goals, these groups typically divide the work into manageable chunks, particularly when there are many different tasks to perform. They also introduce various coordinating mechanisms to ensure that everyone is working effectively toward the same objectives.

Division of Labour

Division of labour refers to the subdivision of work into separate jobs assigned to different people. Subdivided work leads to job specialisation, because each job now includes a narrow subset of the tasks necessary to complete the product or service. To serve clients, Nitro Group organises employees into specific jobs, such as project manager, web/Flash designer, art director and business strategist. Some projects are so sophisticated that they may extend for more than a year and involve several dozen people with highly specialised expertise. As companies get larger, this horizontal division of labour is usually accompanied by vertical division of labour. Some people are assigned the task of supervising employees, others are responsible for managing those supervisors and so on.

Why do companies divide their work into several jobs? As you learned earlier in this book, job specialisation increases work efficiency.[6] Job incumbents can master their tasks quickly because work cycles are very short. Less time is wasted changing from one task to another. Training costs are reduced because employees require fewer physical and mental skills to accomplish the assigned work. Finally, job specialisation makes it easier to match people with specific aptitudes or skills to the jobs for which they are best suited. Although one person working alone might be able to design an advertising campaign, doing so would take much longer than having the campaign designed by a team of specialists. Also, an employee who thinks up clever advertising scripts might deliver only mediocre web designs, whereas a highly skilled team of people would have higher quality across all areas of work.

Coordinating Work Activities

LEARNING OBJECTIVE

Describe three types of coordination in organisational structures.

When people divide work among themselves, they require coordinating mechanisms to ensure that everyone works in concert. Coordination is so closely connected to division of labour that the optimal level of specialisation is limited by the feasibility of coordinating the work. In other words, an organisation should divide work among many people only to the extent that those people can coordinate with each other. Otherwise, individual effort is wasted due to misalignment, duplication and mistiming of tasks. Coordination also tends to become more expensive and difficult as the division of labour increases, so companies specialise jobs only to the point where it isn't too costly or challenging to coordinate the people in those jobs.[7]

Every organisation—from the two-person corner convenience store to the largest corporate entity—uses one or more of the following coordinating mechanisms:[8] informal communication, formal hierarchy and standardisation (see Exhibit 13.1). These forms of coordination align the

Exhibit 13.1 *Coordinating Mechanisms in Organisations*

Coordinating mechanism	Description	Subtypes/strategies
Informal communication	Sharing information on mutual tasks; forming common mental models to synchronise work activities	• Direct communication • Liaison roles • Integrator roles • Temporary teams
Formal hierarchy	Assigning legitimate power to individuals who then use this power to direct work processes and allocate resources	• Direct supervision • Formal communication channels
Standardisation	Creating routine patterns of behaviour or output	• Standardised skills • Standardised processes • Standardised output

Sources: Based on information in J. R. Galbraith, *Designing Complex Organizations* (Reading, MA: Addison-Wesley, 1973), 8–19; H. Mintzberg, *The Structuring of Organizations* (Englewood Cliffs, NJ: Prentice Hall, 1979), ch. 1; D. A. Nadler and M. L. Tushman, *Competing by Design: The Power of Organizational Architecture* (New York: Oxford University Press, 1997), ch. 6.

work of staff within the same department as well as across work units. These coordinating mechanisms are also critical when several organisations work together, such as in joint ventures and humanitarian aid programs.[9]

Coordination through Informal Communication

Informal communication is a coordinating mechanism in all organisations. It includes sharing information on mutual tasks as well as forming common mental models so that employees synchronise work activities using the same mental road map.[10] Informal communication is vital in nonroutine and ambiguous situations because employees can exchange a large volume of information through face-to-face communication and other media-rich channels.

Coordination through informal communication is easiest in small firms, such as Nitro when it was a start-up firm in Shanghai. However, information technologies have further leveraged this coordinating mechanism in large organisations.[11] Companies employing thousands of people also support informal communication by keeping each production site small. Brisbane-based Flight Centre travel agency supports informal communication by limiting the number of staff working at each store. Magna International, the global automotive systems manufacturer, keeps most of its plants to a maximum size of around 200 employees. Magna's leaders believe that employees have difficulty remembering each other's names in plants that are any larger, a situation that makes informal communication more difficult as a coordinating mechanism.[12]

Larger organisations also encourage coordination through informal communication by assigning *liaison roles* to employees, who are expected to communicate and share information with coworkers in other work units. Where coordination is required among several work units, companies create *integrator roles*. These people are responsible for coordinating a work process by encouraging employees in each work unit to share information and informally coordinate work activities. Integrators do not have authority over the people involved in that process, so they must rely on persuasion and commitment. Brand managers at Procter & Gamble have integrator roles because they coordinate work among marketing, production and design groups.[13]

concurrent engineering The organisation of employees from several departments into a temporary team for the purpose of developing a product or service.

Another way that larger organisations encourage coordination through informal communication is by organising employees from several departments into temporary teams. This strategy occurs through **concurrent engineering** in the product or service development process. Traditional product development is a sequential arrangement. For example, the marketing department might develop a product strategy, which is passed 'over the wall' to design engineers, whose design work is then passed on to manufacturing engineers to figure out a cost-efficient production process and to the purchasing department to source raw materials. This serial process can be cumbersome because its main coordinating mechanism is formal hierarchical communication.

In contrast, concurrent engineering involves forming a cross-functional project team of people from these specialised departments to engage in product development simultaneously. By being assigned to a team, rather than working within their usual specialised departments, employees are given the mandate and opportunity to coordinate with each other using informal communication. As soon as the design engineer begins to form the product specifications, representatives from manufacturing, engineering, marketing, purchasing and other departments can offer feedback as well as begin their contribution to the process. These teams are often colocated (assigned to the same physical area), which allows more media-rich face-to-face communication. The result: Chrysler, Toyota, Harley-Davidson and many other organisations have found that the concurrent-engineering process tends to produce higher quality products with dramatically less development time than does the traditional arrangement.[14]

Coordination through Formal Hierarchy

Informal communication is the most flexible form of coordination, but it can become chaotic as the number of interdependencies among employees increases. Consequently a second coordinating mechanism—formal hierarchy—gains importance as organisations grow.[15] Hierarchy assigns legitimate power to individuals, who then use this power to direct work processes and allocate resources. In other words, work is coordinated through direct supervision—the chain of command.

The formal hierarchy has traditionally been applauded as the optimal coordinating mechanism for large organisations. A century ago, administrative management scholars argued that organisations are most effective when managers exercise their authority and employees receive orders from only one supervisor. Coordination should occur through the chain of command; that is, up the hierarchy and across to the other work unit. Any organisation with a formal structure coordinates work to some extent through this arrangement. For instance, project leaders at Nitro Group are responsible for ensuring that employees on their team remain on schedule and that their respective tasks are compatible with tasks completed by other team members.

The formal hierarchy also coordinates work among executives through the division of organisational activities. If the organisation is divided into geographic areas, the structure gives the regional group leaders legitimate power over executives responsible for production, customer service and other activities in those areas. If the organisation is divided into product groups, the heads of those groups have the right to coordinate work across regions.

The formal hierarchy can be efficient for simple and routine situations, but it is not as agile for coordination in complex and novel situations. Communicating through the chain of command is rarely as fast or accurate as direct communication between employees. For this reason, the product development process described earlier tends to be more effective when people are organised into concurrent engineering teams and, preferably, located in the same work area. Product development is typically a complex and novel activity, so employees need to rely on informal communication rather than formal hierarchy to coordinate more quickly and ultimately create better products and services.

Cost is another concern with formal hierarchy. Managers are not directly involved in the production process—they are overhead costs—and their ability to closely supervise employees is limited. As the business grows, the number of supervisors and layers of management must increase, resulting in a costly bureaucracy. Finally, today's workforce is less tolerant of rigid structures. Employees demand more autonomy over their work and more involvement in company decisions. When traditional supervision is used as the coordinating mechanism, it tends to conflict with employee autonomy and involvement. For instance, Pretoria Portland Cement is considered one of South Africa's best places to work, partly because it minimises formal hierarchy as a coordinating mechanism.

Coordination through Standardisation

Standardisation, the third means of coordination, involves creating routine patterns of behaviour or output. This coordinating mechanism takes three distinct forms:

- Standardised Processes—Quality and consistency of a product or service can often be improved by standardising work activities through job descriptions and procedures.[16] This coordinating mechanism is feasible when the work is routine (such as mass production) or simple (such as making pizzas), but it is less effective in nonroutine and complex work such as product design.
- Standardised Outputs—This form of standardisation involves ensuring that individuals and work units have clearly defined goals and output measures (e.g. customer satisfaction, production efficiency). For instance, to coordinate the work of salespeople, companies assign sales targets rather than specific behaviours.
- Standardised Skills—When work activities are too complex to standardise through processes or goals, companies often coordinate work effort by extensively training employees or hiring people who have learned precise role behaviours from educational programs. This form of coordination is used in hospital operating rooms. Surgeons, nurses and other operating-room professionals coordinate their work more through training than through goals or company rules.

Division of labour and coordination of work represent the two fundamental ingredients of all organisations. But how work is divided, which coordinating mechanisms are emphasised, who makes decisions and other issues are related to the four elements of organisational structure, which we will discuss next.

ELEMENTS OF ORGANISATIONAL STRUCTURE

Every company is configured in terms of four basic elements of organisational structure. This section introduces three of them: span of control, centralisation and formalisation. The fourth element—departmentalisation—is presented in the next section.

LEARNING OBJECTIVE

Justify the optimal span of control in a given situation.

span of control The number of people directly reporting to the next level in the hierarchy.

Span of Control

Span of control (also called *span of management*) refers to the number of people directly reporting to the next level in the hierarchy. A narrow span of control exists when very few people report directly to a manager, whereas a wide span exists when a manager has many direct reports.[17] A century ago, French engineer and management scholar Henri Fayol strongly recommended a relatively narrow span of control, typically no more than twenty employees per supervisor and six supervisors per manager. Fayol championed formal hierarchy as the primary coordinating mechanism, so he believed that supervisors should closely monitor and coach employees. His views were similar to those of Napoleon Bonaparte and other military leaders, who declared that somewhere between three and ten subordinates is the optimal span of control. These prescriptions were based on the belief that managers could not effectively monitor and control any more subordinates.[18]

Today, we know better. The best-performing manufacturing plants currently have an average of thirty-eight production employees per supervisor.[19] What's the secret here? Did Fayol, Napoleon and others miscalculate the optimal span of control? The answer is that those sympathetic to hierarchical control believed that employees should perform the physical tasks, whereas supervisors and other management personnel should make the decisions and monitor employees to make sure they performed their tasks. In contrast, the best performing manufacturing operations today rely on self-directed teams, so direct supervision (formal hierarchy) is supplemented with other coordinating mechanisms. Self-directed teams coordinate mainly through informal communication and specialised knowledge, so formal hierarchy plays a minor role.

Similarly, many firms that employ doctors, lawyers and other professionals have a larger span of control because these staff members coordinate their work mainly through standardised skills. For example, more than two dozen people report directly to Cindy Zollinger, president of litigation-consulting firm Cornerstone Research. Zollinger explains that this large number of direct reports is possible because she leads professional staff who don't require close supervision. 'They largely run themselves,' Zollinger explains. 'I help them in dealing with obstacles they face, or in making the most of opportunities that they find.'[20]

A second factor influencing the best span of control is whether employees perform routine tasks. A wider span of control is possible when employees perform routine jobs, because there is less frequent need for direction or advice from supervisors. A narrow span of control is necessary when employees perform novel or complex tasks, because these employees tend to require more supervisory decisions and coaching. This principle is illustrated in a survey of American property and casualty insurers. The average span of control in commercial-policy processing departments is around 15 employees per supervisor, whereas the span of control is 6.1 in claims service and 5.5 in commercial underwriting. Staff members in the latter two departments perform more technical work, so they have more novel and complex tasks. Commercial-policy processing, on the other hand, is like production work, where tasks are routine and have few exceptions.[21]

A third influence on span of control is the degree of interdependence among employees within the department or team.[22] Generally, a narrow span of control is necessary where employees perform highly interdependent work with others. More supervision is required for highly interdependent jobs because employees tend to experience more conflict with each other, which requires more of a manager's time to resolve. Also, employees are less clear on their personal work performance in highly interdependent tasks, so supervisors spend more time providing coaching and feedback.

Tall versus Flat Structures

Span of control is interconnected with organisational size (number of employees) and the number of layers in the organisational hierarchy. Consider two companies with the same number of employees. If Company A has a wider span of control (more direct reports per manager) than Company B, then Company A necessarily has fewer layers of management (i.e. a flatter structure) than does Company B. The reason for this relationship is that a company with a wider span of control has more employees per supervisor, more supervisors for each middle manager and so on. This larger number of direct reports, compared to a company with a narrower span of control, is possible only by removing layers of management. The interconnection of span of control, organisational size (number of employees) and number of management layers also means that as companies employ more people, they must widen the span of control, build a taller hierarchy, or both. Most companies end up building taller structures because they rely on direct supervision to some extent as a coordinating mechanism and there are limits to how many people each manager can coordinate.

The Struggle to Stay Flat

When Ken Iverson became CEO of Nucor Corporation in the mid-1960s, he insisted that the American steelmaker have only three layers of management below him. Crew supervisors reported to their functional manager (production, shipping, maintenance), who reported to the plant manager, who reported to Iverson. By allowing each plant to operate as an independent business, this flat structure was manageable even as Nucor grew to more than two dozen plants. But today Nucor is America's largest steelmaker, employing 20 000 people at more than four dozen facilities worldwide (including one steel smelter in Western Australia). Managing 50 or more direct reports would itself be a full-time job, so Nucor's chair and CEO, Dan DiMicco, reluctantly added five executive vice presidents, creating another layer of management. 'I needed to be free to make decisions on trade battles,' says DiMicco, adding that he continues to stay involved by checking his own email and meeting with staff at every opportunity. Even with five layers of hierarchy, Nucor is incredibly lean. Many other companies the same size have twice as many levels of management.[23]

AP Images

Unfortunately, building a taller hierarchy (more layers of management) creates problems. First, tall structures have higher overhead costs because most layers of hierarchy consist of managers rather than employees who make the product or supply the service. Second, senior managers in tall structures often receive lower quality and less timely information from the external environment because information from front-line employees is transmitted slowly or not at all up the hierarchy. Also, the more layers of management through which information must pass, the higher the probability that managers will filter out information that does not present them in a positive light. Finally, tall hierarchies tend to undermine employee empowerment and engagement because they focus power around managers rather than employees.[24]

These problems have prompted leaders to 'delayer'—remove one or more levels in the organisational hierarchy.[25] Soon after Mark Hurd was hired as CEO of Hewlett-Packard (HP), he stripped the high-technology company's eleven layers of hierarchy down to eight layers. He argued that this action reduced costs and would make HP more nimble. BASF's European Seal Sands plant went even further when it was dramatically restructured around self-directed teams. 'Seven levels of management have been cut basically to two,' said a BASF executive.[26]

Although many companies enjoy reduced costs and more empowered employees when they delayer the organisational hierarchy, some organisational experts warn that there are also negative long-term consequences of cutting out too much middle management.[27] These include undermining necessary managerial functions, increasing workload and stress among management, and restricting managerial career development:

- Undermining Managerial Functions—Critics of delayering point out that all companies need managers to guide work activities, coach subordinates and manage company growth. Furthermore, managers are needed to make quick decisions and represent a source of appeal over conflicts. These valuable functions are underserved when the span of control becomes too wide.
- Increasing Workload and Stress—Delayering increases the number of direct reports per manager and thus significantly increases management workload and corresponding levels of stress. Managers partly reduce the workload by learning to give subordinates more autonomy rather than micromanaging them. However, this role adjustment itself is stressful (same responsibility, but less authority or control), and many companies increase the span of control beyond the point at which many managers are capable of coaching or leading their direct reports.
- Restricting Managerial Career Development—Delayering results in fewer managerial jobs, so companies have less manoeuvrability to develop managerial skills. Promotions are also riskier in flatter hierarchies because they involve a larger jump in responsibility than occurs in taller hierarchies. Furthermore, having fewer promotion opportunities means that managers experience more career plateauing, which reduces their motivation and loyalty. Chopping back managerial career structures also sends a signal that managers are no longer valued. 'Delayering has had an adverse effect on morale, productivity and performance,' argues a senior executive in the Australian federal government. 'Disenfranchising middle management creates negative perceptions and lower commitment to the organisation with consequent reluctance to accept responsibility.'[28]

Centralisation and Decentralisation

LEARNING OBJECTIVE 

Discuss the advantages and disadvantages of centralisation and formalisation.

centralisation The degree to which formal decision authority is held by a small group of people, typically those at the top of the organisational hierarchy.

A second element to consider when designing an organisational structure is the degree of centralisation or decentralisation. **Centralisation** means that formal decision-making authority is held by a small group of people, typically those at the top of the organisational hierarchy. Most organisations begin with centralised structures, as the founder makes most of the decisions and tries to direct the business toward his or her vision. As organisations grow, however, they diversify and their environments become more complex. Senior executives aren't able to process all the decisions that significantly influence the business. Consequently, larger organisations typically *decentralise*; that is, they disperse decision authority and power throughout the organisation.

The optimal level of centralisation or decentralisation depends on several contingencies that we will examine later in this chapter. However, we also need to keep in mind that different degrees of decentralisation can occur simultaneously in different parts of an organisation. Nestlé, the Swiss-based food company, has decentralised marketing decisions to remain responsive to local markets, but has centralised production, logistics and supply-chain management activities to improve cost efficiencies and avoid having too much complexity across the organisation. 'If you are too decentralised, you can become too complicated—you get too much complexity in your production system,' explains a Nestlé executive.[29]

Likewise, 7-Eleven relies on both centralisation and decentralisation in different parts of the organisation. The convenience-store chain is able to leverage its buying power and efficiencies by centralising decisions about information technology and supplier purchasing. At the same time, it decentralises local inventory decisions to store managers so that they

Malaysian Government Decentralises for Better Service

The Malaysian government recently concluded that most government departments are too centralised. Department heads make most of the decisions, which results in long queues, slow service and frustrated clients. To improve this situation, the government advised department heads to delegate more decision-making authority to lower level staff. 'Department heads who are responsible for decision making should empower their subordinates and allow them to make decisions in their absence so that the public will not be inconvenienced,' said the Malaysian government's chief secretary. The government also encourages departments to set up 'centres for decision making' as part of the decentralisation process. Along with improving customer service, the government believes decentralisation will reduce the incidence of corruption. 'If there is no proper delegation of authority and there are no centres for decision making, then there are a lot of opportunities to do negative things,' explains a senior government official.[31]

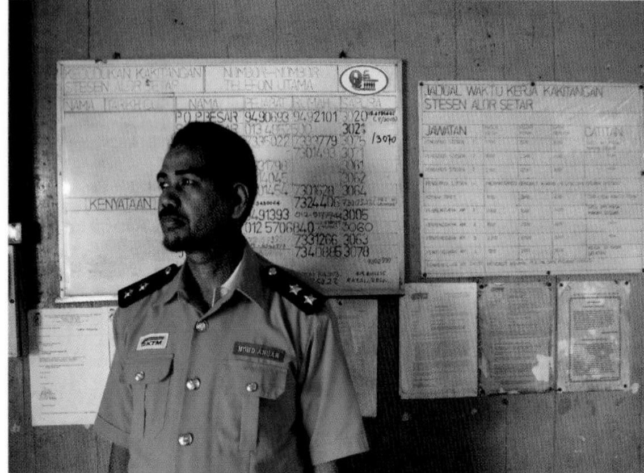

Picture Media

can adapt quickly to changing circumstances at the local level. Along with receiving ongoing product training and guidance from regional consultants, store managers have the best information about their customers and can respond quickly to local market needs. 'We could never predict a busload of football players on a Friday night, but the store manager can,' explains a 7-Eleven executive.[30]

Formalisation

formalisation The degree to which organisations standardise behaviour through rules, procedures, formal training and related mechanisms.

Formalisation is the degree to which organisations standardise behaviour through rules, procedures, formal training and related mechanisms.[32] In other words, companies become more formalised as they increasingly rely on various forms of standardisation to coordinate work. McDonald's Restaurants and most other efficient fast-food chains typically have a high degree of formalisation because they rely on standardisation of work processes as a coordinating mechanism. Employees have precisely defined roles, right down to how much mustard should be dispensed, how many pickles should be added and how long each hamburger should be cooked.

Older companies tend to become more formalised because work activities become routinised, making them easier to document into standardised practices. Larger companies also tend to have more formalisation because direct supervision and informal communication among employees do not operate as easily when large numbers of people are involved. External influences, such as government safety legislation and strict accounting rules, also encourage formalisation.

Formalisation may increase efficiency and compliance, but it can also create problems.[33] Rules and procedures reduce organisational flexibility, so employees are likely to follow prescribed behaviours even when the situation clearly calls for a customised response. High levels of formalisation tend to undermine organisational learning and creativity. Some work rules become so convoluted that organisational efficiency would decline if they were actually followed as prescribed. Formalisation is also a source of job dissatisfaction and work stress. Finally, rules and procedures have been known to take on a life of their own in some organisations. They become the focus of attention rather than the organisation's ultimate objectives of producing a product or service and serving its dominant stakeholders.

The challenge that companies face as they get larger and older is to avoid too much formalisation. Yahoo! Inc. seems to be a case in point. A decade ago, Yahoo! owned the world's most popular Web portal site and was a creative hotspot in the internet industry. Through strategic acquisitions (Flickr, del.icio.us, Yahoo! 360, etc.), the company continues to launch new services, but observers and former staff say that internal innovations have been hampered by creeping bureaucracy. 'In a small company [the attitude] is, "Hey, let's launch it and let's see if the users like it,"' says a senior Yahoo staffer who recently moved to a smaller firm. 'There was a time a few years ago where Yahoo had more of that mentality. But as companies get bigger and bigger, many of them reach a point where they can't do that as quickly.' Another former Yahoo employee is more blunt: 'If you are on the internet, you have to be fast and you have to take risks. The organisational structure that Yahoo has is completely antithetical to the industry they are in.'[34]

Mechanistic versus Organic Structures

LEARNING OBJECTIVE 

Distinguish organic from mechanistic organisational structures.

We discussed span of control, centralisation and formalisation together because they cluster around two broader organisational forms: mechanistic and organic structures.[35] A **mechanistic structure** is characterised by a narrow span of control and high degree of formalisation and centralisation. Mechanistic structures have many rules and procedures, limited decision making at lower levels, tall hierarchies of people in specialised roles and vertical rather than horizontal communication flows. Tasks are rigidly defined and are altered only when sanctioned by higher authorities. Companies with an **organic structure** have the opposite characteristics. They operate with a wide span of control, decentralised decision making and little formalisation. Tasks are fluid, adjusting to new situations and organisational needs.

mechanistic structure An organisational structure with a narrow span of control, and a high degree of formalisation and centralisation.

organic structure An organisational structure with a wide span of control, little formalisation and decentralised decision making.

As a rule, mechanistic structures operate better in stable environments because they rely on efficiency and routine behaviours, whereas organic structures work better in rapidly changing (i.e. dynamic) environments because they are more flexible and responsive to the changes. Organic structures are also more compatible with organisational learning, high-performance workplaces and quality management because they emphasise information sharing and an empowered workforce rather than hierarchy and status.[36] Nitro Group, which was described at the beginning of this chapter, has an organic structure because it operates in a rapidly changing environment and depends on organisational learning to remain competitive.

Organic structures are superior to mechanistic structures in dynamic environments only when employees have developed well-established roles and expertise.[37] Without these conditions, employees are unable to coordinate effectively with each other, resulting in errors and gross inefficiencies. Start-up companies often face this problem, known as the *liability of newness.* Newness makes start-up firms more organic—they tend to be smaller organisations with few rules and considerable delegation of authority. However, employees in new organisations often lack industry experience, and their teams have not developed sufficiently for peak performance. As a result, the organic structures of new companies cannot compensate for the poorer coordination and significantly lower efficiencies caused by the lack of structure from experience and team mental models.

Fortunately, companies can minimise the liability of newness by launching businesses with existing teams of people or with industry veterans guiding the novices. Nitro Group is an example. Each of Nitro's offices is highly organic, with fairly young staff, yet each local office is able to draw on the expertise of several experienced executives—such as Sean Cummins in Australia and Jennifer Tan in Shanghai—to guide the less experienced staff members. Thus, Nitro enjoys an organic structure yet has the foundations of well-established roles and expertise to deliver the service.[38]

Identify and evaluate the six pure types of departmentalisation.

FORMS OF DEPARTMENTALISATION

Span of control, centralisation and formalisation are important elements of organisational structure, but most people think about organisational charts when the discussion of organisational structure arises. The organisational chart represents the fourth element in the structuring of organisations, called *departmentalisation*. Departmentalisation specifies how employees and their activities are grouped together. Organisational charts are a fundamental strategy for coordinating organisational activities because they influence organisational behaviour in the following ways:[39]

- Departmentalisation—establishes the chain of command—the system of common supervision among positions and units within the organisation. It frames the membership of formal work teams and typically determines which positions and units must share resources. Thus, departmentalisation establishes interdependencies among employees and subunits.
- Departmentalisation—focuses people around common mental models or ways of thinking, such as serving clients, developing products or supporting a particular skill set. This focus is typically anchored around the common budgets and measures of performance assigned to employees within each departmental unit.
- Departmentalisation—encourages coordination through informal communication among people and subunits. With common supervision and resources, members within each configuration typically work near each other, so they can use frequent and informal interaction to get the work done.

There are almost as many organisational charts as there are businesses, but the six most common pure types of departmentalisation are simple, functional, divisional, team-based, matrix and network.

Simple Structure

Most companies begin with a *simple structure*.[40] They employ only a few people and typically offer only one distinct product or service. There is minimal hierarchy—usually just employees reporting to the owners. Employees perform broadly defined roles because there are insufficient economies of scale to assign them to specialised jobs. The simple structure is highly flexible and minimises the walls that form between employees in other structures. However, the simple

Boost Juice Outgrows its Simple Structure

Boost Juice Pty Ltd

When Janine Allis opened her first Boost Juice store in Adelaide, she didn't employ many staff to fill in the organisational chart. 'I've had to do everything from painting the floor to doing the dishes, to typing up the million email addresses to put in the databases,' she recalls. The simple organisational structure consisted of Allis, a few employees, and her husband who assisted with marketing and franchising. Boost Juice grew to five stores within the first year, then mushroomed through franchising to more than 200 stores employing 2000 people. Along the way, the company hired people for marketing, information technology, franchising, human resources, training and other functions. As these departments developed, Boost Juice's simple structure morphed into a functional structure. And as the company expands into Asia, Europe and South America, Allis and her corporate board may soon need to revise the organisational structure again.[41]

structure usually depends on the owner's direct supervision to coordinate work activities, so it is very difficult to maintain this structure as the company grows and becomes more complex.

Functional Structure

Growing organisations usually introduce a functional structure at some level of the hierarchy or at some time in their history. A **functional structure** organises employees around specific knowledge or other resources. Employees with marketing expertise are grouped into a marketing unit, those with production skills are located in manufacturing, engineers are found in product development and so on. Organisations with functional structures are typically centralised to coordinate their activities effectively. Standardisation of work processes is the most common form of coordination used in a functional structure.

functional structure
An organisational structure in which employees are organised around specific knowledge or other resources.

Evaluating the Functional Structure

The functional structure creates specialised pools of talent that typically serve everyone in the organisation. This provides more economies of scale than are possible if functional specialists are spread over different parts of the organisation. It increases employee identity with the specialisation or profession. Direct supervision is easier in functional structures because managers oversee people with common issues and expertise.[42]

The functional structure also has limitations.[43] Grouping employees around their skills tends to focus attention on those skills and related professional needs rather than on the company's product, service or client needs. Unless people are transferred from one function to the next, they might not develop a broader understanding of the business. Compared with other structures, the functional structure usually produces higher dysfunctional conflict and poorer coordination in serving clients or developing products. These problems occur because employees need to work with coworkers in other departments to complete organisational tasks, yet they have different subgoals and mental models of ideal work. Together, these problems require substantial formal controls and coordination if a functional structure is imposed.

LEARNING OBJECTIVE

Describe three variations of divisional structure and explain which one should be adopted in a particular situation.

divisional structure An organisational structure in which employees are organised around geographic areas, outputs (products or services) or clients.

Divisional Structure

The **divisional structure** (sometimes called the *multidivisional* or *M-form* structure) groups employees around geographic areas, outputs (products or services) or clients. Exhibit 13.2 illustrates these three variations of divisional structure. The *geographic divisional structure* organises employees around distinct regions of the country or world. Exhibit 13.2 (*a*) illustrates a geographic divisional structure recently adopted by Barrick Gold Corporation, the world's largest gold-mining company. The *product/service divisional structure* organises employees around distinct outputs. Exhibit 13.2 (*b*) illustrates a simplified version of this type of structure at Philips. The Dutch electronics company divides its workforce mainly into three divisions: health care products, lighting products and consumer products. The *client divisional structure* organises employees around specific customer groups. Exhibit 13.2 (*c*) illustrates a customer-focused divisional structure similar to one adopted by the US Internal Revenue Service.[44]

Which form of divisional structure should large organisations adopt? The answer depends mainly on the primary source of environmental diversity or uncertainty.[45] Suppose an organisation has one type of product sold to people across the country. If customer needs vary across regions, or if state governments impose different regulations on the product, then a geographic structure would be best to be more vigilant of this diversity. On the other hand, if the company sells several types of products across the country and customer preferences and government regulations are similar everywhere, then a product structure would likely work best.

Coca-Cola, Nestlé, and many other food and beverage companies are organised mainly around geographic regions because consumer tastes and preferred marketing strategies vary considerably around the world. Even though McDonald's makes the same Big Mac throughout the world, the company has more fish products in Hong Kong and more vegetarian products in India, in line with traditional diets in those countries. Philips, on the other hand, is organised around products because consumer preferences around the world are similar within each product group. Hospitals from Geneva, Switzerland, to Santiago, Chile, buy similar medical equipment from Philips, whereas the manufacturing and marketing of these products are quite different from Philips' consumer electronics business.

The Globally Integrated Enterprise

Many companies are moving away from structures that organise people around geographic clusters.[46] One reason is that clients can purchase products online and communicate with businesses from almost anywhere in the world, so local representation is less critical. Reduced geographic variation is another reason for the shift away from geographic structures; freer trade has reduced government intervention, and consumer preferences for many products and services are becoming more similar (converging) around the world. The third reason is that large companies increasingly have global business customers who demand one global point of purchase, not one in every country or region.

globally integrated enterprise An organisational structure in which work processes and executive functions are distributed around the world through global centres, rather than developed in a home country and replicated in satellite countries or regions.

This shift away from geographic and toward product or client-based divisional structures reflects the trend toward the **globally integrated enterprise.**[47] As the label implies, a globally integrated enterprise connects work processes around the world, rather than replicating them

Exhibit 13.2 *Three Types of Divisional Structure*

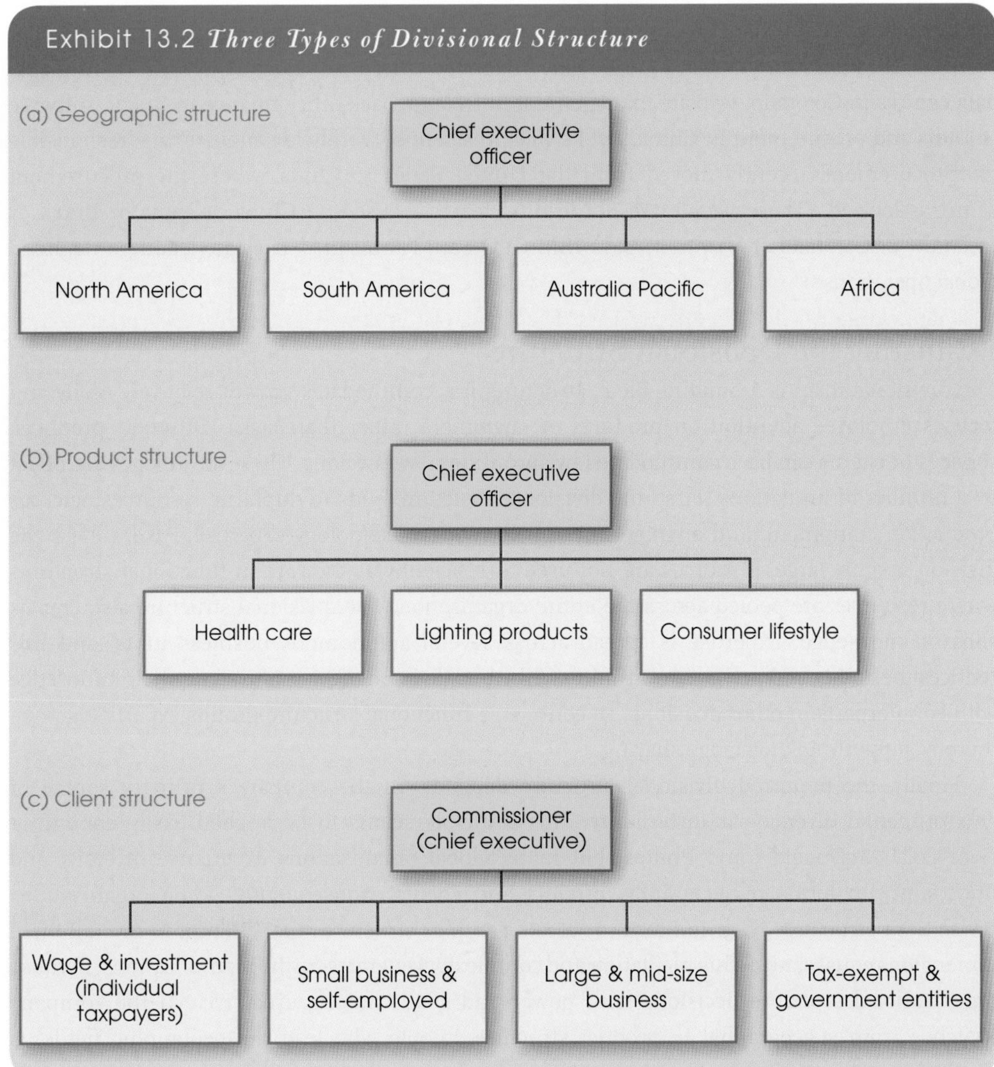

Note: Diagram (*a*) shows the global geographic divisional structure of Barrick Gold Corporation; diagram (*b*) is similar to the product divisions at Philips; diagram (*c*) is similar to the customer-focused structure at the US Internal Revenue Service.

within each country or region. This type of organisation typically organises people around product or client divisions. Even functional units—production, marketing, design, human resources and so on—serve the company worldwide rather than within specific geographic clusters. These functions are sensitive to cultural and market differences, and have local representation to support that sensitivity, but local representatives are associates of a global function rather than a local subsidiary copied across several regions. Indeed, a globally integrated enterprise is marked by a dramatic increase in virtual teamwork, because employees are assigned global projects and ongoing responsibilities for work units that transcend geographic boundaries.

The globally integrated enterprise no longer orchestrates its business from a single headquarters in one 'home' country. Instead, its divisional and functional operations are led from where the work is concentrated, and this concentration depends on economics (cost of labour, infrastructure, etc.), expertise and openness (trade, capital flow, knowledge sharing, etc.). For example, IBM has moved toward the globally integrated enterprise structure by locating its global data centres in Colorado, website management in Ireland, back-office finance in Brazil, software in India and procurement in China. IBM's vice president of worldwide engineering, responsible for procurement, recently moved from the United States to China, where the procurement centre is located. 'These people are not leading teams focused on China or India or Brazil or Ireland—or Colorado or Vermont,' says IBM CEO Sam Palmisano. 'They are leading integrated global operations.'[48]

Evaluating the Divisional Structure

The divisional form is a building-block structure; it accommodates growth relatively easily and focuses employee attention on products or customers rather than tasks. Different products, services or clients can be accommodated by sprouting new divisions. These advantages are offset by a number of limitations. First, the divisional structure tends to duplicate resources, such as production equipment, and engineering or information technology expertise. Also, unless the division is quite large, resources are not used as efficiently as they are in functional structures where resources are pooled across the entire organisation. The divisional structure also creates silos of knowledge. Expertise is spread across several autonomous business units, and this reduces the ability and perhaps motivation of the people in one division to share their knowledge with counterparts in other divisions. In contrast, a functional structure groups experts together, thereby supporting knowledge sharing.

Finally, the preferred divisional structure depends on the company's primary source of environmental diversity or uncertainty. This principle seems to be applied easily enough at Coca-Cola, McDonald's and Philips, but many global organisations experience diversity and uncertainty in terms of geography, product and clients. Consequently, some organisations revise their structures back and forth or create complex structures that attempt to give all three dimensions equal status. This vacillation and complexity generates further complications, because organisational structure decisions shift power and status among executives. If the company switches from a geographic to product structure, people who lead the geographic fiefdoms suddenly get demoted under the product chiefs. In short, leaders of global organisations struggle to find the best divisional structure, often with the result that some executives leave and those who remain experience frustration with the process.

Team-Based Structure

Several years ago, Criterion Group Ltd adopted a team-based organisation to improve quality and efficiency. The New Zealand manufacturer of ready-to-assemble furniture organises its 150 production employees into self-directed work teams with their own performance indicators and activity-based costing systems. Criterion now has just one layer of managers between the managing director and production staff.[49]

team-based structure An organisational structure built around self-directed teams that complete an entire piece of work.

The Criterion Group has adopted a **team-based structure** in its production operations. The team-based structure has a few distinguishing features from other organisational forms. First, it is built around self-directed teams that complete an entire piece of work, such as manufacturing a product or developing an electronic game (see Chapter 8). This type of structure is usually organic. There is a wide span of control because teams operate with minimal supervision. In extreme situations, there is no formal leader, just someone selected by other team members to help coordinate the work and liaise with top management. Team structures are highly decentralised because almost all day-to-day decisions are made by team members rather than someone further up the organisational hierarchy. Finally, many team-based structures have low formalisation because teams are given relatively few rules about how to organise their work. Instead, executives assign quality and quantity output targets and often productivity improvement goals to each team. Teams are then encouraged to use available resources and their own initiative to achieve those objectives.

Team-based structures are usually found within the manufacturing or service operations of larger divisional structures. For example, several GE Aircraft Engines plants are organised as team-based structures, but these plants operate within GE's larger divisional structure. However, a small number of firms apply the team-based structure from top to bottom, including W. L. Gore & Associates, and Semco SA, where almost all associates work in teams.

Evaluating the Team-Based Structure

The team-based organisation represents an increasingly popular structure because it is usually more flexible and responsive to the environment.[50] It tends to reduce costs because teams have less reliance on formal hierarchy (direct supervision). A cross-functional team structure improves communication and cooperation across traditional boundaries. With greater autonomy, this structure also allows quicker and more informed decision making.[51] For this reason, some hospitals have restructured several functional departments into cross-functional teams. Teams composed of nurses, radiologists, anaesthetists, a pharmacology representative, possibly social workers, a rehabilitation therapist and other specialists communicate and coordinate more efficiently, thereby reducing delays and errors.[52]

Against these benefits, the team-based structure can be costly to maintain due to the need for ongoing interpersonal skill training. Teamwork potentially takes more time to coordinate than formal hierarchy during the early stages of team development. Employees may experience more stress due to increased ambiguity in their roles. Team leaders also experience more stress due to increased conflict, loss of functional power and unclear career progression ladders. In addition, team structures suffer from duplication of resources and potential competition (and lack of resource sharing) across teams.[53]

Matrix Structure

Diagram the matrix structure, and discuss its advantages and disadvantages.

When medical doctors Ray Muzyka and Greg Zeschuk and a third partner (who later returned to medical practice) founded BioWare Corp., they initially organised employees at the electronic games company into a simple structure in which everyone worked together on the first game, *Shattered Steel*. Soon after, Muzyka and Zeschuk formed ideas about a second game (*Baldur's Gate*), but they weren't sure what organisational structure would be best. Simply creating a second team might duplicate resources, undermine information sharing among people with the same expertise across teams and weaken employee loyalty to the overall company. Alternatively, the game developer could adopt a functional structure by assigning employees to specialised departments such as art, programming, audio, quality assurance and design. A functional structure would encourage employees within each specialisation to share information, but it might undermine team dynamics on game projects and reduce employee commitment to the game they were developing.[54]

matrix structure An organisational structure that overlays two structures (such as a geographic divisional and a functional structure) in order to leverage the benefits of both.

After carefully weighing the various options, Muzyka and Zeschuk adopted a **matrix structure** to gain the benefits of both a functional structure and a project-based (team) structure. BioWare's matrix structure, which is similar to the diagram in Exhibit 13.3, is organised around functions (art, audio, programming and so on) as well as team-based game development projects. Employees are assigned to a cross-functional team responsible for a specific game project, yet they also belong to a permanent functional unit from which they are reassigned when their work is completed on a particular project.[55]

Muzyka and Zeschuk claim that the matrix structure encourages employees to think in terms of the final product yet keeps them organised around their expertise to encourage knowledge sharing. 'The matrix structure also supports our overall company culture where BioWare is the team, and everyone is always willing to help each other whether they are on the same project or not,' they add. BioWare's matrix structure has proved to be a good choice, particularly as the company (which recently became an independent division of Electronic Arts) has grown to almost 400 employees working on more than half a dozen game projects.

Exhibit 13.3 ***Project-Based Matrix Structure (Similar to BioWare's Structure)***

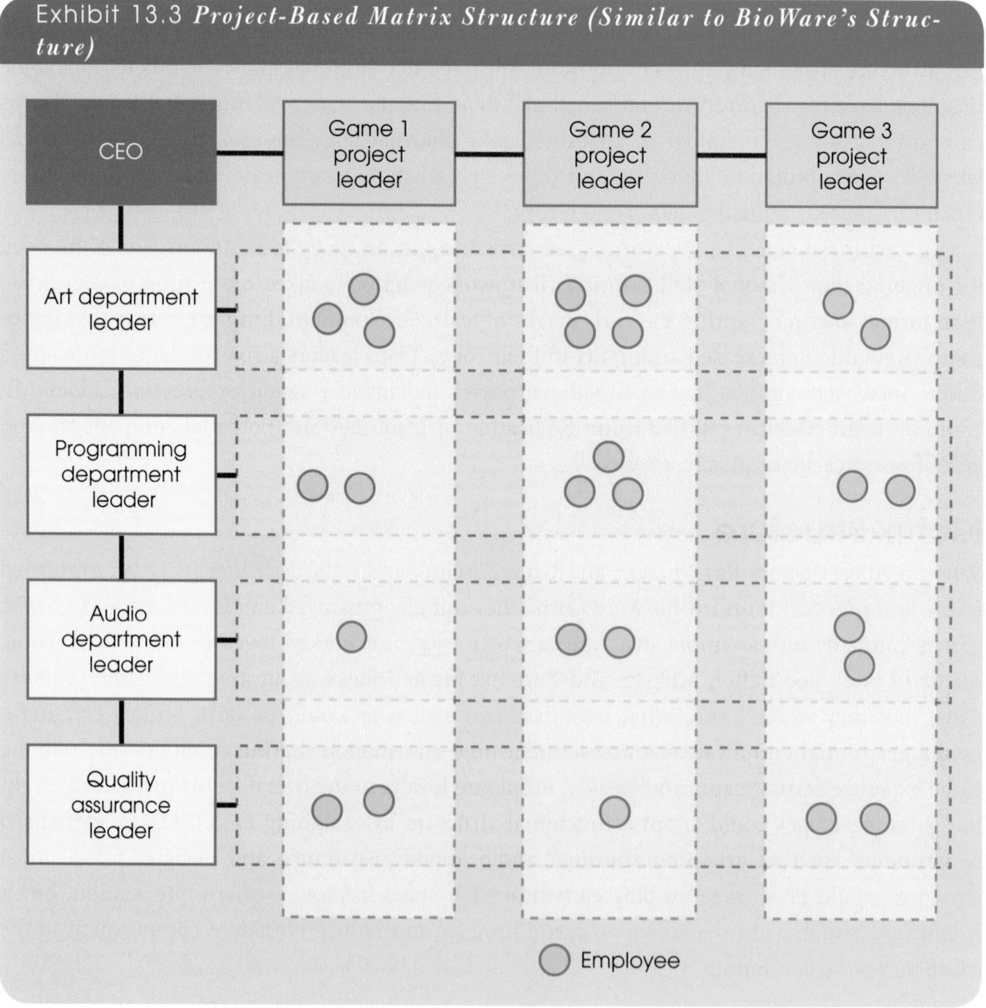

Losing Data in the Matrix

Soon after Britain's Inland Revenue and Customs/ Excise departments merged to become HM Revenue & Customs (HMRC), the combined department experienced a series of errors that violated individual privacy rights. The most serious of these incidents occurred when HMRC staff somehow lost two computer discs containing confidential details of 25 million child welfare claimants. The UK government's investigation into the security lapse concluded that along with resulting from poor security procedures, the error was partly due to 'muddled accountabilities' created by the matrix organisational structure under which the new department operated. The investigator's initial briefing stated that the matrix structure and numerous departments made it 'difficult to relate roles and responsibilities amongst senior management to accountability'. In fact, responsibility for data security was assigned to no less than five departments, each of which reported to different director generals. The final report concluded that '(HMRC) is not suited to the so-called "constructive friction" matrix type organisation (that was) in place at the time of the data loss.' HMRC has since changed to a more traditional, single-command organisational structure.[57]

Kevin Foy/Alamy

BioWare's structure, in which project teams overlap with functional departments, is just one form of matrix structure. Another variation, which is common in large global firms, is to have geography on one axis and products/services or client groups on the other. Procter & Gamble (P&G) recently moved toward this type of global matrix structure with geographic divisions (called 'market development organisations') on one axis and 'global business units', representing global brands, on the other axis. Previously, P&G had a geographic divisional structure, which gave too much power to country managers and not enough power or priority to globalising its major brands (e.g. Pantene, Tide, Pringles). P&G's leaders believe that the matrix structure will balance this power, thereby supporting its philosophy of thinking globally and acting locally.[56]

Evaluating the Matrix Structure

The matrix structure usually makes very good use of resources and expertise, making it ideal for project-based organisations with fluctuating workloads. When properly managed, it improves communication efficiency, project flexibility and innovation when compared to purely functional or divisional designs. It focuses employees on serving clients or creating products yet keeps people organised around their specialisation, so knowledge sharing improves and resources are used more efficiently. The matrix structure is also a logical choice when, as in the case of Procter & Gamble, two different dimensions (regions and products) are equally important. Structures determine executive power and what is important; the matrix structure works when two different dimensions deserve equal attention.

In spite of these advantages, the matrix structure has several well-known problems.[58] One concern is that it increases conflict among managers who equally share power. Employees working at the matrix level have two bosses and, consequently, two sets of priorities that aren't always aligned with each other. Project leaders might squabble with functional leaders regarding the assignment of specific employees to projects, and disagree about the employee's technical competence. For example, Citigroup, Inc. recently adopted a geographic-product matrix structure and apparently is already experiencing dysfunctional conflict between the regional and product group executives.[59] Aware of these potential conflicts, BioWare holds several 'synchronisation meetings' each year involving all department directors (i.e. art, design, audio, etc.), producers (i.e. game project leaders) and the human resource manager. These meetings sort out differences and ensure that staff members are properly assigned to each game project.

Another challenge is that the existence of two bosses can dilute accountability. In a functional or divisional structure, one manager is responsible for everything, even the most unexpected issues. But in a matrix structure, the unusual problems don't get resolved because neither manager takes ownership of them.[60] Mark Hurd was so concerned about accountability that he replaced Hewlett-Packard's matrix structure soon after becoming CEO. 'The more accountable I can make you, the easier it is for you to show you're a great performer,' Hurd declared. 'The more I use a matrix, the easier I make it to blame someone else.'[61] The combination of dysfunctional conflict and ambiguous accountability in matrix structures also explains why some employees experience more stress and some managers are less satisfied with their work arrangements within this structure.

Compare and contrast network structures with other forms of departmentalisation.

Network Structure

BMW and Daimler AG aren't eager to let you know this, but some of their vehicles designed and constructed with Germanic precision are neither designed nor constructed by them or in Germany. Much of BMW's X3, for example, was designed by Magna Steyr in Austria. Magna also manufactured the vehicle in Austria until BMW transferred this work to its manufacturing plant in the United States. The contract manufacturer also builds Daimler's off-road G-class Mercedes. Both BMW and Daimler are hub organisations that own and market their respective brands, whereas Magna and other suppliers are spokes around the hub that provide production, engineering and other services that get the firms' luxury products to customers.[62]

network structure An alliance of several organisations for the purpose of creating a product or serving a client.

BMW, Daimler AG and many other organisations are moving toward a **network structure** as they design and build a product or serve a client through an alliance of several organisations.[63] As Exhibit 13.4 illustrates, this collaborative structure typically consists of several satellite organisations beehived around a hub or core firm. The core firm orchestrates the network process and provides one or two other core competencies, such as marketing or product development. In our example, BMW or Daimler is the hub that provides marketing and management, whereas other firms perform many other functions. The core firm might be the main contact with customers, but most of the product or service delivery and support activities are farmed out to satellite organisations located anywhere in the world. Extranets (Web-based networks with partners) and other technologies ensure that information flows easily and openly between the core firm and its array of satellites.[64]

One of the main forces pushing toward a network structure is the recognition that an organisation has only a few *core competencies*. A core competency is a knowledge base that resides throughout the organisation and provides a strategic advantage. As companies discover their core competency, they 'unbundle' noncritical tasks to other organisations that have a core competency in performing those tasks. For instance, BMW decided long ago that its core competency is not facilities management, so it outsourced this function at its British engine plant to Dalkia, which specialises in facility maintenance and energy management.[65]

Companies are also more likely to form network structures when technology is changing quickly and production processes are complex or varied.[66] Many firms cannot keep up with the hyperfast changes in information technology, so they have outsourced their entire information system departments to IBM, EDS and other firms that specialise in information system services. Similarly, many high-technology firms create networks with Flextronics, Celestica and other electronic equipment manufacturers that have expertise in diverse production processes.

Evaluating the Network Structure

For several years, organisational behaviour theorists have argued that organisational leaders must develop a metaphor of organisations as plasma-like organisms rather than rigid machines.[67] Network structures come close to the organism metaphor because they offer the flexibility for an

Exhibit 13.4 *A Network Structure*

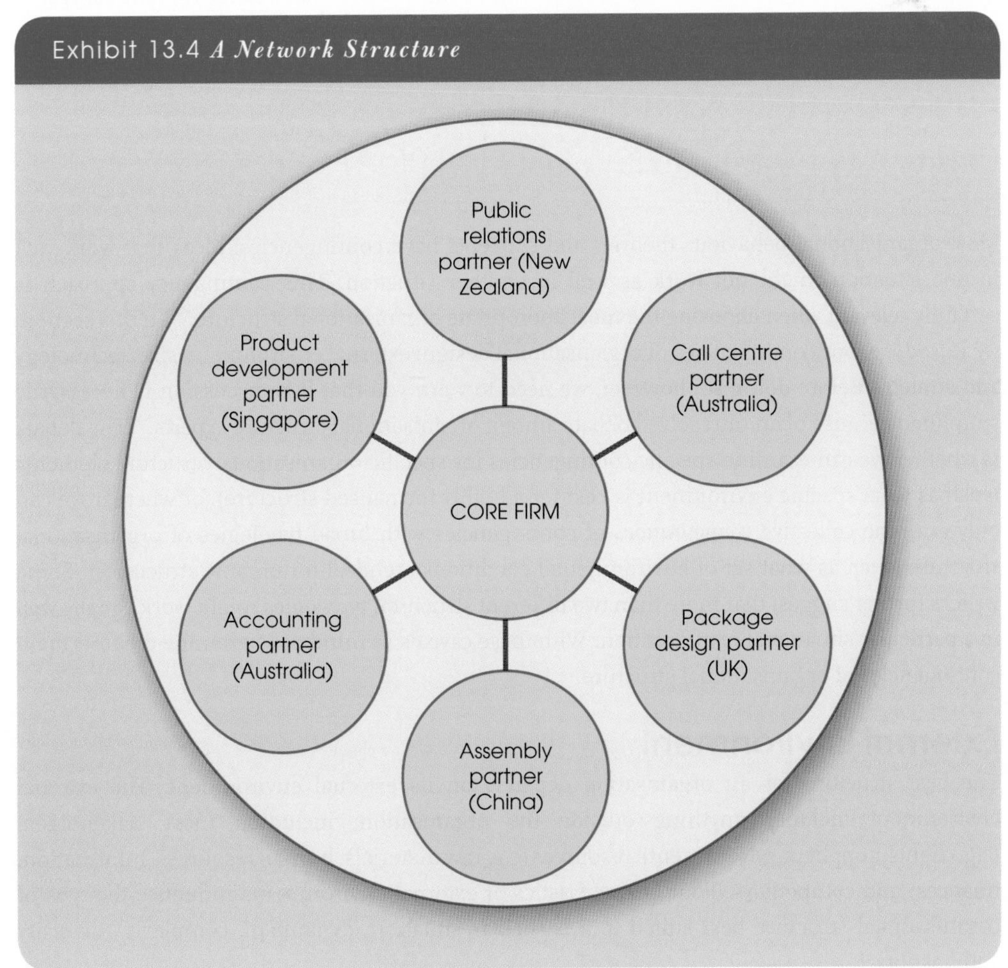

organisation to realign its structure with changing environmental requirements. If customers demand a new product or service, the core firm creates new alliances with other firms offering the appropriate resources. For example, by working with Magna International, BMW was probably able to develop and launch the X3 vehicle much sooner than if it had performed these tasks on its own. When BMW needs a different type of manufacturing, it isn't saddled with nonessential facilities and resources. Network structures also offer efficiencies because the core firm becomes globally competitive as it shops worldwide for subcontractors with the best people and the best technology at the best price. Indeed, the pressures of global competition have made network structures more vital, and computer-based information technology has made them possible.[68]

A potential disadvantage of network structures is that they expose the core firm to market forces. Other companies may bid up the price for subcontractors, whereas the short-term cost would be lower if the company hired its own employees to perform the same function. Another problem is that although information technology makes worldwide communication much easier, it will never replace the degree of control organisations have when manufacturing, marketing and other functions are in-house. The core firm can use arm's-length incentives and contract provisions to maintain the subcontractor's quality, but these actions are relatively crude compared to maintaining the quality of work performed by in-house employees.

Identify four characteristics of external environments and discuss the preferred organisational structure for each environment.

CONTINGENCIES OF ORGANISATIONAL DESIGN

Most organisational behaviour theories and concepts have contingencies: ideas that work well in one situation might not work as well in another situation. This contingency approach is certainly relevant when choosing the most appropriate organisational structure.[69] In this section, we introduce four contingencies of organisational design: external environment, size, technology and strategy. Before doing so, however, we need to warn you that this discussion is necessarily simplified because of an unresolved debate among organisational structure experts.[70] The debate is whether we can examine specific contingencies for specific organisational structure elements (such as what specific environment is best for a highly formalised structure), or whether we can only examine collective *configurations* of contingencies with broad typologies of organisational structure (such as what set of environmental conditions are ideal for organic structures). Some writers further suggest that more than two different structural typologies might work equally well in a particular situational configuration. With these caveats in mind, let's examine the four main contingencies of organisational structure.

External Environment

The best structure for an organisation depends on its external environment. The external environment includes anything outside the organisation, including most stakeholders (e.g. clients, suppliers, government), resources (e.g. raw materials, human resources, information, finances) and competitors. Four characteristics of external environments influence the type of organisational structure best suited to a particular situation: dynamism, complexity, diversity and hostility.[71]

Being Big and Small All at Once

Johnson & Johnson (J&J) may be best known for Band-Aids and baby powder, but the company is really a conglomerate of 250 businesses in 57 countries that manufacture and/or market prescription medicines (accounting for 40 per cent of its total business), medical devices and diagnostics (the largest such business in the world), and personal care products (toothbrushes, skin creams, shampoos, etc.). Successful companies decentralise when operating in complex and diversified environments, and J&J is no exception. 'J&J is probably the reference company for being decentralised,' says William Weldon, J&J's chairman and CEO. Weldon points out that the company's decentralised structure allows it to be more sensitive and responsive to each unique culture and business setting. 'The men and women who run our businesses around the world usually are people who grew up in those markets, understand those markets, and develop themselves in those markets,' Weldon explains. Decentralisation of a large organisation has other advantages. 'We are big and we are small all at once,' says J&J's website. 'Each of our operating companies functions as its own small business ... (yet) they also have access to the know-how and resources of a Fortune 50 company. It's like having dozens of strategic partners at their fingertips.'[73]

AP Images

Dynamic versus Stable Environments

Dynamic environments have a high rate of change, leading to novel situations and a lack of identifiable patterns. Organic structures are better suited to this type of environment so that the organisation can adapt more quickly to changes, but only if employees are experienced and coordinate well in teamwork.[72] In contrast, stable environments are characterised by regular cycles of activity, and steady changes in supply and demand for inputs and outputs. Events are more predictable, enabling the firm to apply rules and procedures. Mechanistic structures are more efficient when the environment is predictable, so they tend to work better than organic structures.

Complex versus Simple Environments

Complex environments have many elements, whereas simple environments have few things to monitor. As an example, a large university library operates in a more complex environment than a rural public library. The university library's clients require several types of services—book borrowing, online full-text databases, research centres, course reserve collections and so on. A rural public library has fewer of these demands placed on it. The more complex the environment, the more decentralised the organisation should become. Decentralisation is a logical response to complexity because decisions are pushed down to people and subunits with the necessary information to make informed choices.

Diverse versus Integrated Environments

Organisations located in diverse environments have a greater variety of products or services, clients and regions. In contrast, an integrated environment has only one client, product and geographic area. The more diversified the environment, the more the firm needs to use a divisional structure aligned with that diversity. If it sells a single product around the world, a geographic divisional structure would align best with the firm's geographic diversity, for example.

Hostile versus Munificent Environments

Firms located in a hostile environment face resource scarcity and more competition in the marketplace, whereas firms in a munificent environment have enough resources for their needs. Hostile environments are typically dynamic ones because they make access to resources and demand for outputs less predictable. Munificent environments, on the other hand, tend to be relatively stable and predictable. Mechanistic structures operate better in munificent environments, whereas organic structures are better for hostile environments. However, when the environment is extremely hostile—such as a severe shortage of supplies or lower market share—organisations tend to temporarily centralise so that decisions can be made more quickly and executives feel more comfortable being in control.[74] Ironically, centralisation may result in lower quality decisions during organisational crises, because top management has less information, particularly when the environment is complex.

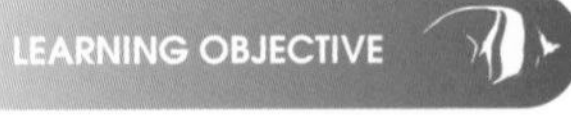

Summarise the influences of organisational size, technology and strategy on organisational structure.

Organisational Size

Larger organisations should have different structures from smaller organisations.[75] As the number of employees increases, job specialisation increases due to a greater division of labour. The greater division of labour requires more elaborate coordinating mechanisms. Thus, larger firms make greater use of standardisation (particularly work processes and outcomes) to coordinate work activities. This creates an administrative hierarchy and greater formalisation. Historically, larger organisations made less use of informal communication as a coordinating mechanism. However, emerging information technologies and an increased emphasis on empowerment have caused informal communication to regain its importance in large firms.[76]

Larger organisations also tend to be more decentralised. Executives have neither sufficient time nor expertise to process all the decisions that significantly influence the business as it grows. Therefore, decision-making authority is pushed down to lower levels, where incumbents are able to cope with the narrower range of issues under their control.

Technology

Technology is another factor to consider when designing the best organisational structure for the situation.[77] *Technology* refers to the mechanisms or processes by which an organisation turns out its product or service. One technological contingency is *variability*—the number of exceptions to standard procedure that tend to occur. In work processes with low variability, jobs are routine and follow standard operating procedures. Another contingency is *analysability*—the predictability or difficulty of the required work. The less analysable the work, the more it requires experts with sufficient discretion to address the work challenges. An organic, rather than a mechanistic, structure should be introduced where employees perform tasks with high variability and low analysability, such as in a research setting. The reason is that employees face unique situations with little opportunity for repetition. In contrast, a mechanistic structure is preferred where the technology has low variability and high analysability, such as an assembly line. The work is routine and highly predictable, an ideal situation for a mechanistic structure to operate efficiently.

Organisational Strategy

Organisational strategy refers to the way the organisation positions itself in its setting in relation to its stakeholders, given the organisation's resources, capabilities and mission.[78] In other words, strategy represents the decisions and actions applied to achieve the organisation's goals. Although the contingencies of size, technology and environment influence the optimal organisational structure, they do not necessarily determine structure. Instead, corporate leaders formulate and implement strategies that shape the characteristics of these contingencies as well as the organisation's resulting structure.

organisational strategy The way the organisation positions itself in its setting in relation to its stakeholders, given the organisation's resources, capabilities and mission.

This concept is summed up with the simple phrase 'Structure follows strategy'.[79] Organisational leaders decide how large their organisation will grow and which technologies to use. They take steps to alter their environments and move into more hospitable environments, rather than let the organisation's fate be entirely determined by external influences. Furthermore, organisational structures don't evolve as a natural response to these contingencies. Instead, they result from organisational decisions. Thus, organisational strategy influences both the contingencies of structure and the structure itself. If a company's strategy is to compete through innovation, a more organic structure would be preferred because it creates the conditions for employees to share knowledge and be creative. If a company chooses a low-cost strategy, a mechanistic structure is preferred because it maximises production and service efficiency.[80] Overall, it is now apparent that organisational structure is influenced by size, technology and environment, but the organisation's strategy may reshape these elements and loosen their connection to organisational structure.

CHAPTER SUMMARY

Organisational structure is the division of labour as well as the patterns of coordination, communication, workflow and formal power that direct organisational activities. All organisational structures divide labour into distinct tasks and coordinate that labour to accomplish common goals. The primary means of coordination are informal communication, formal hierarchy and standardisation.

The four basic elements of organisational structure are span of control, centralisation, formalisation and departmentalisation. The optimal span of control—the number of people directly reporting to the next level in the hierarchy—depends on the presence of coordinating mechanisms other than formal hierarchy, as well as on whether employees perform routine tasks and how much interdependence there is among employees within the department.

Centralisation occurs when formal decision authority is held by a small group of people, typically senior executives. Many companies decentralise as they become larger and more complex, but some sections of the company may remain centralised while other sections decentralise. Formalisation is the degree to which organisations standardise behaviour through rules, procedures, formal training and related mechanisms. Companies become more formalised as they get older and larger. Formalisation tends to reduce organisational flexibility, organisational learning, creativity and job satisfaction.

Span of control, centralisation and formalisation cluster into mechanistic and organic structures. Mechanistic structures are characterised by a narrow span of control and a high degree of formalisation and centralisation. Companies with an organic structure have the opposite characteristics.

Departmentalisation specifies how employees and their activities are grouped together. It establishes the chain of command, focuses people around common mental models, and encourages coordination through informal communication among people and subunits. Most companies begin with a simple structure in which there is minimal hierarchy and employees are grouped into broadly defined roles. A functional structure organises employees around specific knowledge or other resources. This fosters greater specialisation and improves direct supervision, but it weakens the focus on serving clients or developing products.

A divisional structure groups employees around geographic areas, clients or outputs. This structure accommodates growth and focuses employee attention on products or customers rather than tasks. However, this structure duplicates resources and creates silos of knowledge. Team-based structures are very flat, with low formalisation, and organise self-directed teams around work processes rather than functional specialities. The matrix structure combines two structures to leverage the benefits of both types of structure. However, this approach requires more coordination than functional or pure divisional structures, may dilute accountability and increases conflict. A network structure is an alliance of several organisations for the purpose of creating a product or serving a client.

The best organisational structure depends on the firm's external environment, size, technology and strategy. The optimal structure depends on whether the environment is dynamic or stable, complex or simple, diverse or integrated, and hostile or munificent. As organisations increase in size, they become more decentralised and more formalised.

The work unit's technology—including variability of work and analysability of problems—influences whether to adopt an organic or mechanistic structure. These contingencies influence but do not necessarily determine structure. Instead, corporate leaders formulate and implement strategies that shape both the characteristics of these contingencies as well as the organisation's resulting structure.

KEY TERMS

centralisation, p. 509
concurrent engineering, p. 504
divisional structure, p. 514
formalisation, p. 510
functional structure, p. 513
globally integrated enterprise, p. 514
matrix structure, p. 518
mechanistic structure, p. 511
network structure, p. 520
organic structure, p. 511
organisational strategy, p. 525
organisational structure, p. 502
span of control, p. 506
team-based structure, p. 516

Critical Thinking Questions

1 Nitro Group, the creative advertising company described at the beginning of this chapter, has an organic, team-based structure. What coordinating mechanism likely dominates in this type of organisational structure? Describe the extent and form in which the other two types of coordination might be apparent at Nitro Group.

2 Think about the university or other organisation whose classes you currently attend. What is the dominant coordinating mechanism used to guide or control your instructor? Why is this coordinating mechanism used the most here?

3 Administrative theorists concluded many decades ago that the most effective organisations have a narrow span of control. Yet today's top-performing manufacturing firms have a wide span of control. Why is this possible? Under what circumstances, if any, should manufacturing firms have a narrow span of control?

4 Leaders of large organisations struggle to identify the best level and types of centralisation and decentralisation. What should companies consider when determining the degree of decentralisation?

5 Diversified Technologies Ltd (DTL) makes four types of products, each type to be sold to different types of clients. For example, one product is sold exclusively to motor vehicle

repairers, whereas another is used mainly in hospitals. Customer expectations and needs are surprisingly similar throughout the world. The company has separate marketing, product design and manufacturing facilities in Asia, North America, Europe and South America because, until recently, each jurisdiction had unique regulations governing the production and sales of these products. However, several governments have begun the process of deregulating the products that DTL designs and manufactures, and trade agreements have opened several markets to foreign-made products. Which form of departmentalisation might be best for DTL if deregulation and trade agreements occur?

6 IBM is becoming a globally integrated enterprise. What does this organisation look like in terms of its departmentalisation? What challenges might face companies that try to adopt the globally integrated enterprise model?

7 From an employee perspective, what are the advantages and disadvantages of working in a matrix structure?

8 Suppose that you have been hired as a consultant to diagnose the environmental characteristics of your university. How would you describe the school's external environment? Is the school's existing structure appropriate for this environment?

Skill Builder 13.1

TEAM EXERCISE

The Club Ed Exercise

Cheryl Harvey and Kim Morouney, Wilfred Laurier University

Purpose

This exercise is designed to help you understand the issues to consider when designing organisations at various stages of growth.

Materials

Each student team should have enough overhead transparencies or flip-chart sheets to display several organisational charts.

Instructions

Each team discusses the scenario presented below. The instructor will facilitate discussion and notify teams when to begin the next step. The exercise and debriefing require approximately 90 minutes, although fewer scenarios can reduce the time.

1. Your instructor will place your class into teams (typically four or five people).
2. In your team, read Scenario 1, on page 529. Design an organisational chart (departmentalisation) that is most appropriate for the situation. You should be able to describe the type of structure drawn and explain why it is appropriate. The structure should be drawn on an overhead transparency or flip chart for others to see during later class discussion. The instructor will set a fixed time (e.g. 15 minutes) to complete this task.

SCENARIO 1: Determined never to endure another cold, rainy Melbourne winter, you decide to establish a new resort business on a South Pacific island accessible to air travellers. The resort is under construction and is scheduled to open one year from now. You decide it is time to draw up an organisational chart for this new venture, called Club Ed.

3. At the end of the time allowed, the instructor will present Scenario 2, and teams will be asked to draw another organisational chart to suit that situation. Again, you should be able to describe the type of structure drawn and explain why it is appropriate.

4. At the end of the time allowed, the instructor will present Scenario 3, and teams will be asked to draw another organisational chart to suit that situation.

5. Depending on the time available, the instructor might present a fourth scenario. The class will gather to present their designs for each scenario. During each presentation, teams should describe the type of structure drawn and explain why it is appropriate.

Source: Adapted from C. Harvey and K. Morouney, 'Organization Structure and Design: The Club ED Exercise', *Journal of Management Education* 22, no. 3 (1998): 425–429. Used with permission of the authors.

SELF-ASSESSMENT

Skill Builder 13.2

What Organisational Structure Do You Prefer?

Purpose

This exercise is designed to help you understand how an organisation's structure influences the personal needs and values of people working in that structure.

Instructions

Personal values influence how comfortable you are working in different organisational structures. You might prefer an organisation with clearly defined rules or no rules at all. You might prefer a firm where almost any employee can make important decisions or one where important decisions are screened by senior executives. Read each statement below and indicate the extent to which you would like to work in an organisation with that characteristic. When finished, use the scoring key in Appendix B at the end of the book to calculate your results. This self-assessment should be completed alone so that you can assess yourself honestly without concerns of social comparison. Class discussion will focus on the elements of organisational design and their relationship to personal needs and values.

Organisational Structure Preference Scale

I would like to work in an organisation where …	Not at all	A little	Somewhat	Very much	Score
1. A person's career ladder has several steps toward higher status and responsibility.	❑	❑	❑	❑	___
2. Employees perform their work with few rules to limit their discretion.	❑	❑	❑	❑	___
3. Responsibility is pushed down to employees who perform the work.	❑	❑	❑	❑	___
4. Supervisors have few employees, so they work closely with each person.	❑	❑	❑	❑	___
5. Senior executives make most decisions to ensure that the company is consistent in its actions.	❑	❑	❑	❑	___
6. Jobs are clearly defined so that there is no confusion over who is responsible for various tasks.	❑	❑	❑	❑	___
7. Employees have their say on issues, but senior executives make most of the decisions.	❑	❑	❑	❑	___
8. Job descriptions are broadly stated or nonexistent.	❑	❑	❑	❑	___
9. Everyone's work is tightly synchronised around top-management operating plans.	❑	❑	❑	❑	___
10. Most work is performed in teams without close supervision.	❑	❑	❑	❑	___
11. Work gets done through informal discussion with coworkers rather than through formal rules.	❑	❑	❑	❑	___
12. Supervisors have so many employees that they can't watch anyone very closely.	❑	❑	❑	❑	___
13. Everyone has clearly understood goals, expectations and job duties.	❑	❑	❑	❑	___
14. Senior executives assign overall goals, but leave daily decisions to front-line teams.	❑	❑	❑	❑	___
15. Even in a large company, the CEO is only three or four levels above the lowest position.	❑	❑	❑	❑	___

Endnotes

1 S. Elliott, 'Watch out, Giant Agencies. Boutique Shops Like Nitro Are Winning Some Big Clients', *New York Times*, 4 April 2005, 6; S. Russell, 'Global Ambitions', *B&T*, 8 June 2007, 17; D. Blecken, 'Nitro Pins Growth Plans on Collaborative Model', *Media*, 17 April 2008; N. Madden, 'Nitro's Chris Clarke', *AdAgeChina*, 17 April 2008; N. Shoebridge, 'Nitro in Ignition Mode Despite Meltdown', *Australian Financial Review*, 10 November 2008, 56; T. Adams, 'Opt in When You Earn Out', *Design Week*, 12 March 2009, 21. Also see the company's website: www.nitrogroup.com

2 S. Ranson, R. Hinings and R. Greenwood, 'The Structuring of Organizational Structure', *Administrative Science Quarterly* 25, no. 1 (1980): 1–14; K. Walsh, 'Interpreting

the Impact of Culture on Structure', *Journal of Applied Behavioral Science* 40, no. 3 (2004): 302–322.

3 B. Morris, 'Charles Schwab's Big Challenge', *Fortune*, 30 May 2005, 60–69.

4 J.-E. Johanson, 'Intraorganizational Influence', *Management Communication Quarterly* 13 (February 2000): 393–435.

5 H. Mintzberg, *The Structuring of Organizations* (Englewood Cliffs, NJ: Prentice Hall, 1979), 2–3.

6 E. E. Lawler III, *Motivation in Work Organizations* (Monterey, CA: Brooks/Cole, 1973); M. A. Campion, 'Ability Requirement Implications of Job Design: An Interdisciplinary Perspective', *Personnel Psychology* 42, no. 1 (1989): 1–24.

7 G. S. Becker and K. M. Murphy, 'The Division-of-Labor, Coordination Costs and Knowledge', *Quarterly Journal of Economics* 107, no. 4 (1992): 1137–1160; L. Borghans and B. Weel, 'The Division of Labour, Worker Organisation, and Technological Change', *The Economic Journal* 116, no. 509 (2006): F45–F72.

8 Mintzberg, *The Structuring of Organizations*, ch. 1; D. A. Nadler and M. L. Tushman, *Competing by Design: The Power of Organizational Architecture* (New York: Oxford University Press, 1997), ch. 6; J. R. Galbraith, *Designing Organizations: An Executive Guide to Strategy, Structure, and Process* (San Francisco: Jossey-Bass, 2002), ch. 4.

9 J. Stephenson, Jr., 'Making Humanitarian Relief Networks More Effective: Operational Coordination, Trust and Sense Making', *Disasters* 29, no. 4 (2005): 337.

10 A. Willem, M. Buelens and H. Scarbrough, 'The Role of Inter-Unit Coordination Mechanisms in Knowledge Sharing: A Case Study of a British MNC', *Journal of Information Science* 32, no. 6 (2006): 539–561; R. R. Gulati, 'Silo Busting', *Harvard Business Review* 85, no. 5 (2007): 98–108.

11 Borghans and Weel, 'The Division of Labour, Worker Organisation, and Technological Change'.

12 T. Van Alphen, 'Magna in Overdrive', *Toronto Star*, 24 July 2006.

13 For a discussion of the role of brand manager at Proctor & Gamble, see C. Peale, 'Branded for Success', *Cincinnati Enquirer*, 20 May 2001, A1. Details about how to design integrator roles in organisational structures are presented in Galbraith, *Designing Organizations* , 66–72.

14 M. Hoque, M. Akter and Y. Monden, 'Concurrent Engineering: A Compromise Approach to Develop a Feasible and Customer-Pleasing Product', *International Journal of Production Research* 43, no. 8 (2005): 1607–1624; S. M. Sapuan, M. R. Osman and Y. Nukman, 'State of the Art of the Concurrent Engineering Technique in the Automotive Industry', *Journal of Engineering Design* 17, no. 2 (2006): 143–157; D. H. Kincade, C. Regan and F. Y. Gibson, 'Concurrent Engineering for Product Development in Mass Customization for the Apparel Industry', *International Journal of Operations & Production Management* 27, no. 6 (2007): 627–649.

15 A. H. Van De Ven, A. L. Delbecq and R. J. Koenig Jr, 'Determinants of Coordination Modes within Organizations', *American Sociological Review* 41, no. 2 (1976): 322–338.

16 Y.-M. Hsieh and A. Tien-Hsieh, 'Enhancement of Service Quality with Job Standardisation', *Service Industries Journal* 21 (July 2001): 147–166.

17 For recent discussion of span of control, see N. A. Theobald and S. Nicholson-Crotty, 'The Many Faces of Span of Control: Organizational Structure across Multiple Goals', *Administration & Society* 36, no. 6 (2005): 648–660; R. M. Meyer, 'Span of Management: Concept Analysis', *Journal of Advanced Nursing* 63, no. 1 (2008): 104–112.

18 H. Fayol, *General and Industrial Management*, trans. C. Storrs (London: Pitman, 1949); D. D. Van Fleet and A. G. Bedeian, 'A History of the Span of Management', *Academy of Management Review* 2 (1977): 356–372; D. A. Wren, A. G. Bedeian and J. D. Breeze, 'The Foundations of Henri Fayol's Administrative Theory', *Management Decision* 40, no. 9 (2002): 906–918.

19 D. Drickhamer, 'Lessons from the Leading Edge', *Industry Week*, 21 February 2000, 23–26.

20 G. Anders, 'Overseeing More Employees with Fewer Managers—Consultants Are Urging Companies to Loosen Their Supervising Views', *Wall Street Journal*, 24 March 2008, B6.

21 J. Greenwald, 'Ward Compares the Best with the Rest', *Business Insurance*, 26 August 2002, 16.

22 J. H. Gittell, 'Supervisory Span, Relational Coordination and Flight Departure Performance: A Reassessment of Postbureaucracy Theory', *Organization Science* 12, no. 4 (2001): 468–483.

23 P. Glader, 'It's Not Easy Being Lean', *Wall Street Journal*, 19 June 2006, B1; Nucor Corporation, 'About Us', Nucor Steel, n.d., www.nucor.com (accessed 13 May 2009).

24 T. D. Wall, J. L. Cordery and C. W. Clegg, 'Empowerment, Performance, and Operational Uncertainty: A Theoretical Integration', *Applied Psychology: An International Review* 51, no. 1 (2002): 146–169.

25 J. Morris, J. Hassard and L. McCann, 'New Organizational Forms, Human Resource Management and Structural Convergence? A Study of Japanese Organizations', *Organization Studies* 27, no. 10 (2006): 1485–1511.

26 'BASF Culling Saves (GBP) 4m', *Personnel Today*, 19 February 2002, 3; A. Lashinsky, 'The Hurt Way', *Fortune*, 17 April 2006, 92.

27 Q. N. Huy, 'In Praise of Middle Managers', *Harvard Business Review* 79 (September 2001): 72–79; C. R. Littler,

R. Wiesner and R. Dunford, 'The Dynamics of Delayering: Changing Management Structures in Three Countries', *Journal of Management Studies* 40, no. 2 (2003): 225–256; H. J. Leavitt, *Top Down: Why Hierarchies Are Here to Stay and How to Manage Them More Effectively* (Cambridge, MA: Harvard Business School Press, 2005); L. McCann, J. Morris and J. Hassard, 'Normalized Intensity: The New Labour Process of Middle Management', *Journal of Management Studies* 45, no. 2 (2008): 343–371.

28 Littler, Wiesner and Dunford, 'The Dynamics of Delayering: Changing Management Structures in Three Countries'.

29 S. Wetlaufer, 'The Business Case against Revolution: An Interview with Nestle's Peter Brabeck', *Harvard Business Review* 79, no. 2 (February 2001): 112–119; H. A. Richardson *et al.*, 'Does Decentralization Make a Difference for the Organization? An Examination of the Boundary Conditions Circumscribing Decentralized Decision-Making and Organizational Financial Performance', *Journal of Management* 28, no. 2 (2002): 217–244; G. Masada, 'To Centralize or Decentralize?', *Optimize*, May 2005, 58–61.

30 J. G. Kelley, 'Slurpees and Sausages: 7-Eleven Holds School', *Richmond Times-Dispatch (Richmond, VA)*, 12 March 2004, C1; S. Marling, 'The 24-Hour Supply Chain', *InformationWeek*, 26 January 2004, 43.

31 'Set up Decision-Making Centres to Speed up Approvals—CUEPACS', *Bernama Daily Malaysian News*, 30 June 2005; S. Singh and M. Kaur, 'Who Can I Speak To? Sorry, Officer Not In', *New Straits Times (Kuala Lumpur)*, 28 December 2005; N. A. Siddiquee, 'Public Management Reform in Malaysia: Recent Initiatives and Experiences', *International Journal of Public Sector Management* 19, no. 4 (2006): 339–358.

32 Mintzberg, *The Structuring of* Organizations, ch. 5.

33 W. Dessein and T. Santos, 'Adaptive Organizations', *Journal of Political Economy* 114, no. 5 (2006): 956–995; A. A. M. Nasurdin *et al.*, 'Organizational Structure and Organizational Climate as Potential Predictors of Job Stress: Evidence from Malaysia', *International Journal of Commerce and Management* 16, no. 2 (2006): 116–129; C.-J. Chen and J.-W. Huang, 'How Organizational Climate and Structure Affect Knowledge Management—The Social Interaction Perspective', *International Journal of Information Management* 27, no. 2 (2007): 104–118.

34 C. Holahan, 'Bidding Yahoo Adieu', *BusinessWeek*, 23 June 2008, 23.

35 T. Burns and G. Stalker, *The Management of Innovation* (London: Tavistock, 1961).

36 J. Tata, S. Prasad and R. Thom, 'The Influence of Organizational Structure on the Effectiveness of TQM Programs', *Journal of Managerial Issues* 11, no. 4 (1999): 440–453; A. Lam, 'Tacit Knowledge, Organizational Learning and Societal Institutions: An Integrated Framework', *Organization Studies* 21, no. 3 (2000): 487–513.

37 W. D. Sine, H. Mitsuhashi and D. A. Kirsch, 'Revisiting Burns and Stalker: Formal Structure and New Venture Performance in Emerging Economic Sectors', *Academy of Management Journal* 49, no. 1 (2006): 121–132.

38 R. Gardner, 'Charismatic Clarke Brings His Client Service Approach to UK', *Campaign*, 8 October 2004, 18; N. O'Leary, 'Chris Clarke Is Coming for Your Business', *Adweek*, 9 April 2007, 8, 39; Russell, 'Global Ambitions'.

39 Mintzberg, *The Structuring of Organizations*, 106.

40 Mintzberg, *The Structuring of Organizations*, ch. 17.

41 J. Hall, 'Liquid Assets', *Voyeur Magazine (VirginBlue)*, January 2004; R. O'Neill, 'Small Tricks, Big Business', *The Age (Melbourne)*, 14 December 2004, 1; C. Cooper, 'The Wizards of Biz', *The Bulletin*, 8 November 2005. Some information also originates from Boost Juice's website: www.boostjuice.com

42 Galbraith, *Designing* Organizations, 23–25.

43 E. E. Lawler III, *Rewarding Excellence: Pay Strategies for the New Economy* (San Francisco: Jossey-Bass, 2000), 31–34.

44 These structures were identified from corporate websites and annual reports. These organisations typically rely on a mixture of other structures, so the charts shown have been adapted for learning purposes.

45 M. Goold and A. Campbell, 'Do You Have a Well-Designed Organization?', *Harvard Business Review* 80 (March 2002): 117–124.

46 J. R. Galbraith, 'Structuring Global Organizations', in *Tomorrow's Organization: Crafting Winning Capabilities in a Dynamic World*, ed. S. A. Mohrman *et al.* (San Francisco: Jossey-Bass, 1998), 103–129; C. Homburg, J. P. Workman Jr and O. Jensen, 'Fundamental Changes in Marketing Organization: The Movement toward a Customer-Focused Organizational Structure', *Academy of Marketing Science Journal* 28 (Fall 2000): 459–478; T. H. Davenport, J. G. Harris and A. K. Kohli, 'How Do They Know Their Customers So Well?', *MIT Sloan Management Review*, Winter 2001, 63–73; J. R. Galbraith, 'Organizing to Deliver Solutions', *Organizational Dynamics* 31, no. 2 (2002): 194–207.

47 S. J. Palmisano, 'The Globally Integrated Enterprise', *Foreign Affairs* 85, no. 3 (2006): 127–136; S. J. Palmisano, 'The Globally Integrated Enterprise: A New Model', *Vital Speeches of the Day* 73, no. 10 (2007): 449–453.

48 'IBM Moves Engineering VP to China as Part of Global Focus', *Manufacturing Business Technology*, September 2007, 13; J. Bonasia, 'Globalization: Learning to Close the Continental Divide', *Investor's Business Daily*, 7 September 2007.

49 C. Campbell-Hunt *et al.*, *World Famous in New Zealand: How New Zealand's Leading Firms Became World-Class Competitors* (Auckland: University of Auckland Press, 2001), 89.

50 J. R. Galbraith, E. E. Lawler III and Associates, *Organizing for the Future: The New Logic for Managing Complex Organizations* (San Francisco: Jossey-Bass, 1993); R. Bettis and M. Hitt, 'The New Competitive Landscape', *Strategic Management Journal* 16, no. S1 (1995): 7–19.

51 P. C. Ensign, 'Interdependence, Coordination, and Structure in Complex Organizations: Implications for Organization Design', *Mid-Atlantic Journal of Business* 34 (March 1998): 5–22.

52 M. M. Fanning, 'A Circular Organization Chart Promotes a Hospital-Wide Focus on Teams', *Hospital & Health Services Administration* 42 (June 1997): 243–254; L. Y. Chan and B. E. Lynn, 'Operating in Turbulent Times: How Ontario's Hospitals Are Meeting the Current Funding Crisis', *Health Care Management Review* 23 (June 1998): 7–18.

53 R. Cross, 'Looking before You Leap: Assessing the Jump to Teams in Knowledge-Based Work', *Business Horizons*, 43, no. 5 (2000): 29–36; M. Fenton-O'Creevy, 'Employee Involvement and the Middle Manager: Saboteur or Scapegoat?', *Human Resource Management Journal* 11, no. 1 (2001): 24–40; G. Garda, K. Lindstrom and M. Dallnera, 'Towards a Learning Organization: The Introduction of a Client-Centered Team-Based Organization in Administrative Surveying Work', *Applied Ergonomics* 34, no. 2 (2003): 97–105; C. Douglas and W. L. Gardner, 'Transition to Self-Directed Work Teams: Implications of Transition Time and Self-Monitoring for Managers' Use of Influence Tactics', *Journal of Organizational Behavior* 25, no. 1 (2004): 47–65.

54 R. Muzyka and G. Zeschuk, 'Managing Multiple Projects', *Game Developer*, March 2003, 34–42; M. Saltzman, 'The Ex-Doctors Are In', *National Post*, 24 March 2004, AL4; R. McConnell, 'For Edmonton's Bioware, Today's the Big Day', *Edmonton Journal*, 14 April 2005, C1; D. Gladstone and S. Molloy, 'Doctors & Dragons', *Computer Gaming World*, December 2006.

55 R. C. Ford and W. A. Randolph, 'Cross-Functional Structures: A Review and Integration of Matrix Organization and Project Management', *Journal of Management* 18, no. 2 (1992): 267–294.

56 N. Buckley, 'P&G Shakes up Its Global Units', *Financial Times (London)*, 19 May 2004; 'Merely Splitting Hairs', *Marketing Week*, 17 February 2005, 26. Procter & Gamble's structure is actually more complex than we have described here. Its 'four pillars' also include global business services and corporate functions. See Proctor & Gamble, 'Corporate Info— Structure—Four Pillars', PG.com, 2009, www.pg.com/jobs/corporate_structure/four_pillars.jhtml (accessed 13 May 2009).

57 K. Poynter, *Data Security at HMRC*, Poynter Review Initial Report (London: HM Treasury, Government of the United Kingdom, 14 December 2007); V. Houlder, 'The Merger That Exposed a Taxing Problem for Managers', *Financial Times*, 11 July 2008, 12; K. Poynter, *Review of Information Security at HM Revenue and Customs*, Poynter Review Final Report (London: HM Treasury, Government of the United Kingdom, 25 June 2008).

58 G. Calabrese, 'Communication and Cooperation in Product Development: A Case Study of a European Car Producer', *R & D Management* 27 (July 1997): 239–252; T. Sy and L. S. D'Annunzio, 'Challenges and Strategies of Matrix Organizations: Top-Level and Mid-Level Managers' Perspectives', *Human Resource Planning* 28, no. 1 (2005): 39–48.

59 D. Enrich, 'Citigroup Will Revamp Capital-Markets Group', *Wall Street Journal*, 23 August 2008, B7.

60 Nadler and Tushman, *Competing by Design*, ch. 6; M. Goold and A. Campbell, 'Structured Networks: Towards the Well-Designed Matrix', *Long Range Planning* 36, no. 5 (2003): 427–439.

61 D. Ciampa and M. Watkins, 'Rx for New CEOs', *Chief Executive*, January–February 2008.

62 P. Siekman, 'This Is Not a BMW Plant', *Fortune*, 18 April 2005, 208; 'Magna's Austria Plant to Lose Production of BMW X3', *Reuters*, 16 May 2007.

63 R. F. Miles and C. C. Snow, 'The New Network Firm: A Spherical Structure Built on a Human Investment Philosophy', *Organizational Dynamics* 23, no. 4 (1995): 5–18; C. Baldwin and K. Clark, 'Managing in an Age of Modularity', *Harvard Business Review* 75 (September–October 1997): 84–93.

64 J. Hagel III and M. Singer, 'Unbundling the Corporation', *Harvard Business Review* 77 (March–April 1999): 133–141; R. Hacki and J. Lighton, 'The Future of the Networked Company', *McKinsey Quarterly* (August 2001): 26–39.

65 J. Dwyer, 'Mind How You Go', *Facilities Management*, May 2008, 22–25.

66 M. A. Schilling and H. K. Steensma, 'The Use of Modular Organizational Forms: An Industry-Level Analysis', *Academy of Management Journal* 44 (December 2001): 1149–1168.

67 G. Morgan, *Images of Organization*, 2nd edn (Newbury Park, CA: Sage, 1996); G. Morgan, *Imagin-I-Zation: New Mindsets for Seeing, Organizing and Managing* (Thousand Oaks, CA: Sage, 1997).

68 H. Chesbrough and D. J. Teece, 'When Is Virtual Virtuous? Organizing for Innovation', *Harvard Business Review* 74 (January–February 1996): 65–73; P. M. J. Christie and R. Levary, 'Virtual Corporations: Recipe for Success', *Industrial Management* 40 (July 1998): 7–11.

69 L. Donaldson, *The Contingency Theory of Organizations* (Thousand Oaks, CA: Sage, 2001); J. Birkenshaw, R. Nobel and J. Ridderstråle, 'Knowledge as a Contingency Variable: Do the Characteristics of Knowledge Predict Organizational Structure?', *Organization Science* 13, no. 3 (2002): 274–289.

70 A. D. Meyer, A. S. Tsui and C. R. Hinings, 'Configurational Approaches to Organizational Analysis', *Academy of Management Journal* 36, no. 6 (1993): 1175–1195; K. K. Sinha and A. H. Van De Ven, 'Designing Work within and between Organizations', *Organization Science* 16, no. 4 (2005): 389–408.

71 P. R. Lawrence and J. W. Lorsch, *Organization and Environment* (Homewood, IL: Irwin, 1967); Mintzberg, *The Structuring of Organizations*, ch. 15.

72 T. Burns and G. Stalker, *The Management of Innovation* (London: Tavistock, 1961); Lawrence and Lorsch, *Organization and Environment.*

73 S. Warner, 'From Band-Aids to Biotech', *New York Times*, 10 April 2005, 1; 'Johnson & Johnson CEO William Weldon: Leadership in a Decentralized Company', *Knowledge@ Wharton*, 25 June 2008; Johnson & Johnson, 'Our Management Approach', Johnson & Johnson, 2009, www.jnj.com/connect/about-jnj/ (accessed 13 May 2009).

74 Mintzberg, *The Structuring of Organizations*, 282.

75 D. S. Pugh and C. R. Hinings, *Organizational Structure: Extensions and Replications* (Farnborough, UK: Lexington Books, 1976); Mintzberg, *The Structuring of Organizations*, ch. 13.

76 Galbraith, *Designing Organizations*, 52–55; G. Hertel, S. Geister and U. Konradt, 'Managing Virtual Teams: A Review of Current Empirical Research', *Human Resource Management Review* 15, no. 1 (2005): 69–95.

77 C. Perrow, 'A Framework for the Comparative Analysis of Organizations', *American Sociological Review* 32, no. 2 (1967): 194–208; D. Gerwin, 'The Comparative Analysis of Structure and Technology: A Critical Appraisal', *Academy of Management Review* 4, no. 1 (1979): 41–51; C. C. Miller *et al.*, 'Understanding Technology-Structure Relationships: Theory Development and Meta-Analytic Theory Testing', *Academy of Management Journal* 34, no. 2 (1991): 370–399.

78 R. H. Kilmann, *Beyond the Quick Fix* (San Francisco: Jossey-Bass, 1984), 38.

79 A. D. Chandler, *Strategy and Structure* (Cambridge, MA: MIT Press, 1962).

80 D. Miller, 'Configurations of Strategy and Structure', *Strategic Management Journal* 7, no. 3 (1986): 233–249.

CHAPTER 14

organisational culture

LEARNING OBJECTIVES

After reading this chapter, you should be able to:

- describe the elements of organisational culture
- discuss the importance of organisational subcultures
- list four categories of artefacts through which corporate culture is deciphered
- identify three functions of organisational culture
- discuss the conditions under which organisational culture strength improves organisational performance
- compare and contrast four strategies for merging organisational cultures
- identify the four strategies for changing or strengthening an organisation's culture
- apply attraction-selection-attrition theory to explain how organisational culture strengthens
- describe the stages of organisational socialisation
- explain how realistic job previews assist the socialisation process.

Picture Media/Reuters

National Australia Bank has taken a long journey to transform its inward-looking, profit motivated and 'good-news' culture to one that supports transparent and ethical conduct.

National Australia Bank (NAB) was battered a few years ago by a trading scandal that caused $360 million in trading losses. NAB staff were sentenced for trading violations and both the bank's chief executive and chairperson resigned. The Australian government's bank industry regulator (APRA) found that rogue trading occurred at NAB because the bank's control system broke down. However, the report concluded that the underlying culprit was NAB's dysfunctional organisational culture.

'The culture that exists within NAB contributed to many of the control breakdowns that led to the currency options losses,' said the APRA report. The report concluded that NAB was plagued by a 'profit motive' culture that encouraged employees to achieve financial gains without due consideration of risk or ethical conduct. NAB also had a 'close management' culture, in which employees were discouraged from communicating problems to higher management. 'One of the worst aspects of the bank was its good-news culture,' says John Stewart, who became NAB's chief executive following the scandal. 'People did not like to talk about their problems and senior people were reluctant to address those problems.'

Ironically, NAB's executive team had documented the company's shared values during the year before the trading scandal unfolded. The problem was that executives neither lived nor reinforced those values. 'We had major gaps in our cultural framework,' says Elizabeth Hunter, NAB's executive general manager of people and culture. 'While we had a set of values, people were not held accountable and values were not reflected in the way people were assessed.'

Over the next few years, NAB established a 'cultural transformation program' that articulated a set of guiding principles aligned with the company's core values. The bank's board of directors participated in a workshop to discuss these principles. New leaders who practised the company's desired values were installed throughout the company. Employees received training and coaching to enact behaviours consistent with the company's values. A performance management plan was introduced that rewarded employees who applied the company's values.

Elizabeth Hunter acknowledges that NAB's cultural transformation has been slow. 'NAB has a long history of almost 150 years in Australia, and culture in an institution of that age takes a lot of hard work and commitment to change.' However, she also notes that changing the bank's culture remains a top priority. 'Cultural transformation is seen by all parts of the business as integral to delivering on the organisation's strategy and mitigating business risk,' says Hunter.[1]

organisational culture The values and assumptions shared within an organisation.

National Australia Bank's challenges illustrate the perils of ignoring organisational culture. This opening story also shows how important organisational culture is to organisational leaders. **Organisational culture** consists of the values and assumptions shared within an organisation.[2] It defines what is important and unimportant in the company and, consequently, directs everyone in the organisation toward the 'right way' of doing things. You might think of organisational culture as the company's DNA—invisible to the naked eye, yet a powerful template that shapes what happens in the workplace.

This chapter begins by identifying the elements of organisational culture and then describing how culture is deciphered through artefacts. This is followed by a discussion of the relationship between organisational culture and performance, including the effects of cultural strength, fit and adaptability. Then we turn our attention to the challenges of and solutions to merging organisational cultures. Next, this chapter examines ways to change or strengthen organisational culture. The final section provides an overview of organisational socialisation, which is an important way to strengthen organisational culture.

LEARNING OBJECTIVE

Describe the elements of organisational culture.

ELEMENTS OF ORGANISATIONAL CULTURE

Exhibit 14.1 illustrates how the shared values and assumptions of an organisation's culture relate to each other and are associated with artefacts, which are discussed later in this chapter. *Values,* which were described in Chapters 1 and 2, are stable, evaluative beliefs that guide our preferences for outcomes or courses of action in a variety of situations.[3] They are conscious perceptions about what is good or bad, right or wrong. In the context of organisational culture, values are discussed as *shared values,* which are values that people within the organisation or work unit have in common and place near the top of their hierarchy of values.[4] At the time of the trading scandal, many National Australia Bank employees embraced the values of power and self-protection, whereas other values (such as information sharing and risk aversion) took a lower priority.

Organisational culture also consists of *shared assumptions*—a deeper element that some experts believe is the essence of corporate culture. Shared assumptions are nonconscious, taken-for-granted perceptions or ideal prototypes of behaviour that are considered the correct way to think and act toward problems and opportunities. Shared assumptions are so deeply ingrained that you probably wouldn't discover them by surveying employees. Only by observing the employees, analysing their decisions and debriefing them on their actions would these assumptions rise to the surface.

It has become a popular practice for leaders to identify and publicly state their organisation's culture or, more precisely, their shared values. Yahoo, the online portal company, is no exception. Its website proudly says that six values represent 'what makes it tick': excellence, innovation, customer fixation, teamwork, community and fun. Korean steelmaker POSCO, which is one of Asia's most admired companies and rated by senior university students as the most desired company to work for in Korea, also proudly describes its five core values: customer focus, execution (achieving goals), integrity, recognising the value of people and challenge (an indomitable spirit of transforming the impossible into reality).

Do these values really represent the cultural content of Yahoo and POSCO? Possibly, to some extent. However, these value proclamations represent *espoused values*—the values that leaders say

Exhibit 14.1 *Organisational Culture Assumptions, Values and Artefacts*

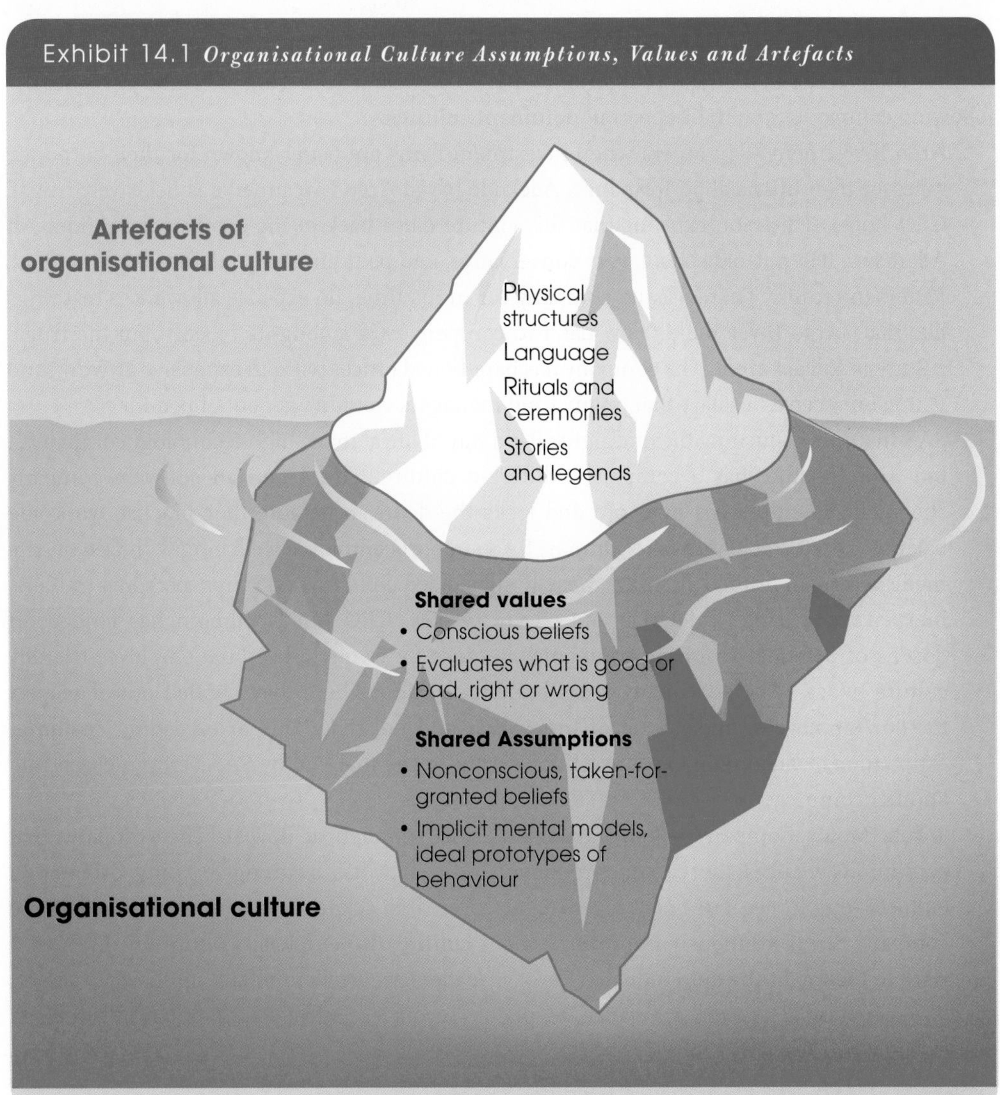

they and their staff rely on to guide their decisions and actions.[5] Organisational leaders construct a positive public image by claiming to believe in values that are socially desirable, even when they are not applied (see Chapter 2). Even if leaders abide by the espoused values, lower level employees might not share these values. In contrast, organisational culture consists of shared *enacted values*—the values that leaders and employees truly rely on to guide their decisions and actions. These 'values-in-use' are apparent by watching people in action.

The distinction between espoused and enacted values was illustrated in the opening story to this chapter. National Australia Bank's executive team identified and publicly proclaimed a set of core values, yet these were espoused values because they were not enacted by employees until the cultural transformation program supported and reinforced them. 'We distilled them and we ended up with five values,' says NAB's former CEO John Stewart. 'Then what had happened—this happens in most companies—we popped it on the shelf and it gathered dust.'

Content of Organisational Culture

Organisations differ in their cultural content, that is, the relative ordering of values. Consider the following companies and their apparent dominant cultures:

- Argo Investments—In an era when investment firms are better known for their corporate excesses than financial performance, Adelaide-based Argo Investments is decisively frugal. CEO Robert Patterson explains that this culture dates back to the company's founder Alf Adamson. 'He was old school, very conservative, and paid himself a pittance, and me, too!' Patterson recalls. 'There was no company car in his time, no expense allowances or things like that.' Argo Investments now has two company cars among its 15 staff, but the frugal culture is still apparent. The company has bare-boned offices without expensive artwork, and Patterson receives a salary that 'many fund managers wouldn't get out of bed for'.[6]
- SAS Institute—Burning the midnight oil is a way of life at many high-technology companies, but SAS Institute has a completely different culture. The American software company shoos out its employees by 6 pm and locks the doors to be sure they practise work–life balance. Located on a 200-acre campus, SAS supports employee wellbeing with free on-site medical care, unlimited sick days, heavily subsidised child care, ski trips, personal trainers, inexpensive gourmet cafeterias and tai chi classes. CEO Jim Goodnight has fended off dozens of potential acquiring companies because he wants to keep the employee-friendly culture intact. 'We spent many years building a culture here that's honed out of respect for our employees, and is one of innovation and creativity, one of exceeding customer expectations,' Goodnight explains. 'I don't want to see that end by SAS being merged into another company.'[7]
- Toyota Motor Company—Being good isn't good enough at Toyota. The company that continuously raises the bar on production efficiency has a strong learning orientation culture—employees are encouraged to discover and acknowledge mistakes so that the company can continuously improve. Toyota's culture also emphasises humility. Even as it rises to the top of the auto industry, Toyota's leaders are hesitant to talk up their successes. 'We're paranoid against arrogance,' explains Toyota executive Ray Tanguay. '"Not good enough" are key words for us.'[8]

Frugal. Employee-friendly and creative. Efficient and humble. How many corporate cultures are there? Several experts have tried to classify corporate culture into a few easy-to-remember categories. One of the most popular and respected models identifies seven corporate cultures (see Exhibit 14.2). Another popular model identifies four coporate cultures organised in a two-by-two table representing internal versus external focus and flexibility versus control. Other models organise cultures around a circle with eight or twelve categories. These circumplex models suggest that some cultures are opposite to others, such as an avoidance culture versus a self-actualisation culture or a power culture versus a collegial culture.[9]

These organisational culture models and surveys are popular with corporate leaders faced with the messy business of diagnosing their company's culture and identifying what kind of culture they want to develop. Unfortunately, they also present a distorted view of organisational culture. First, these models oversimplify the diversity of cultural values in organisations. The fact is, there are dozens of individual values, and many more combinations of values, so the number of organisational cultures that these models describe likely falls considerably short of the full set. Second, we must remember that organisational culture includes shared assumptions about the

Exhibit 14.2 *Organisational Culture Profile Dimensions and Characteristics*

Organisational culture dimension	Characteristics of the dimension
Innovation	Experimentation, opportunity seeking, risk taking, few rules, low cautiousness
Stability	Predictability, security, rule orientation
Respect for people	Fairness, tolerance
Outcome orientation	Action orientation, high expectations, results orientation
Attention to detail	Precision, analysis
Team orientation	Collaboration, people orientation
Aggressiveness	Competitiveness, low emphasis on social responsibility

Source: Based on information in C. A. O'Reilly III, J. Chatman and D. F. Caldwell, 'People and Organisational Culture: A Profile Comparison Approach to Assessing Person-Organisation Fit', *Academy of Management Journal* 34, no. 3 (1991): 487–518.

right way to do things, not just shared values. Few models take this more subterranean aspect of culture into account.

A third concern is that these organisational culture models and measures typically adopt an 'integration' perspective; they assume that most organisations have a fairly clear, unified culture that is easily decipherable.[10] They assert that an organisation's culture is inherently measurable because any ambiguity is outside the domain of the culture. The integration perspective further assumes that when an organisation's culture changes, it shifts from one unified condition to a new unified condition with only temporary ambiguity or weakness during the transition. These assumptions are probably incorrect or, at best, oversimplified. An organisation's culture is usually quite blurry, so much so that it cannot be estimated through employee surveys alone. As we discuss next, organisations consist of diverse subcultures that preclude any potential consensus or consistency in values and assumptions across the organisation. Indeed, even these subcultural clusters can be ill-defined because values and assumptions are ultimately unique to every individual.

We are not suggesting here that organisational culture is nonexistent; some degree of shared values and assumptions does exist in many organisations. Instead, we warn that popular organisational culture models and measures oversimplify the variety of organisational cultures and falsely presume that organisations can easily be identified within these categories.

Organisational Subcultures

Discuss the importance of organisational subcultures.

When discussing organisational culture, we are really referring to the *dominant culture*, that is, the values and assumptions shared most consistently and widely by the organisation's members. The dominant culture is usually understood and internalised by senior management, but it sometimes exists in spite of senior management's desire for another culture. Furthermore, as mentioned in the previous section, an organisation's dominant culture is not as unified or clear as many consultants and business leaders assume. Instead, organisations are composed of *subcultures* located throughout their various divisions, geographic regions and occupational groups.[11] Some subcultures enhance the dominant culture by espousing parallel assumptions and values; others differ from but do not oppose the dominant culture; still others are called *countercultures* because they embrace values or assumptions that directly oppose the organisation's dominant culture. It is also possible that some organisations (including some universities, according to one study) operate with subcultures and no decipherable dominant culture at all.[12]

Subcultures, particularly countercultures, potentially create conflict and dissension among employees, but they also serve two important functions.[13] First, they maintain the organisation's standards of performance and ethical behaviour. Employees who hold countercultural values are an important source of surveillance and critical review of the dominant order. They encourage constructive conflict and more creative thinking about how the organisation should interact with its environment. Subcultures prevent employees from blindly following one set of values and thereby help the organisation to abide by society's ethical values.

The second function of subcultures is that they are the spawning grounds for emerging values that keep the firm aligned with the needs of customers, suppliers, society and other stakeholders. Companies eventually need to replace their dominant values with ones that are more appropriate for the changing environment. If subcultures are suppressed, the organisation may take longer to discover and adopt values aligned with the emerging environment.

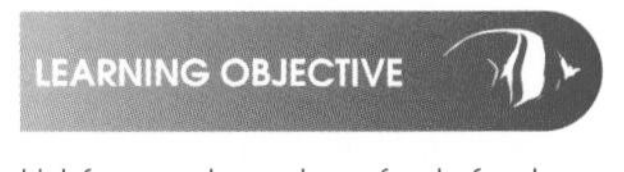

List four categories of artefacts through which corporate culture is deciphered.

DECIPHERING ORGANISATIONAL CULTURE THROUGH ARTEFACTS

artefacts The observable symbols and signs of an organisation's culture.

We can't directly see an organisation's cultural assumptions and values. Instead, as Exhibit 14.1 illustrated earlier, we decipher organisational culture indirectly through artefacts. **Artefacts** are the observable symbols and signs of an organisation's culture, such as the way visitors are greeted, the organisation's physical layout and how employees are rewarded.[14] A few experts suggest that artefacts are the essence of organisational culture, whereas most others (including the authors of this book) view artefacts as symbols or indicators of culture. Either way, artefacts are important because they reinforce and potentially support changes to an organisation's culture.

Artefacts provide valuable evidence about a company's culture.[15] An organisation's culture is usually too ambiguous and complex and its cultural assumptions too deeply ingrained to be measured through surveys. Instead, we need to observe workplace behaviour, listen to everyday conversations among staff and with customers, study written documents and emails, note physical structures and settings, and interview staff about corporate stories. In other words, we need to sample information from a range of organisational artefacts. For example, the Mayo Clinic conducted an assessment of its culture by hiring an anthropologist to decipher the medical organisation's culture at its headquarters in Minnesota, and to identify ways of transferring that culture to its two newer sites in Florida and Arizona. For six weeks, the anthropologist shadowed employees, posed as a patient in waiting rooms, did countless interviews and accompanied doctors on patient visits. The final report outlined Mayo's dominant culture and how its satellite operations varied from that culture.[16]

In this section, we review the four broad categories of artefacts: organisational stories and legends, rituals and ceremonies, language, and physical structures and symbols.

Organisational Stories and Legends

David Ogilvy is a legend in the advertising industry, but equally significant are the stories about him that have continued to reinforce the values that he instilled. For example, Ogilvy's board of directors arrived at one meeting to discover a Russian matryoshka doll at each of their seats. The directors opened each doll, one nested inside the other, until they discovered this message inside the tiniest doll: 'If you hire people who are smaller than you are, we shall become a company of dwarfs. If you hire people who are bigger than you are, we shall become a company of giants.' The Russian dolls became part of Ogilvy's culture, which demands hiring the very best talent.[17]

Stories such as Ogilvy's Russian dolls permeate strong organisational cultures. Some tales recount heroic deeds, whereas others ridicule past events that deviate from the firm's core values. Organisational stories and legends serve as powerful social prescriptions of the way things should (or should not) be done. They add human realism to corporate expectations, individual performance standards and the criteria for getting fired. Stories also produce emotions in listeners, and this tends to improve listeners' memory of the lesson within the story.[18] Stories have the greatest effect on communicating corporate culture when they describe real people, are assumed to be true and are known by employees throughout the organisation. Stories are also prescriptive—they advise people what to do or not to do.[19]

Stories of Cirque du Soleil's Daring Culture

Cirque du Soleil, the troupe that combines circus with theatre, thrives on a culture of daring and creativity. This is apparent in stories about how the troupe was started. In 1980, Gilles Ste-Croix asked the Quebec government for funding to start a street theatre group in Baie-Saint-Paul, north-west of Quebec City. When the government rejected the application, Ste-Croix walked 90 kilometres from Baie-Saint-Paul to Quebec City ... on stilts!

The Canadian Press

The gruelling 22-hour trip got the government's attention and financial support. 'If you're crazy enough to walk all this way on stilts, we'll give you some money to create jobs,' a Quebec government representative apparently said. Without that daring event, Cirque du Soleil probably wouldn't exist today, because Ste-Criox's band of 15 performers included Guy Laliberté, who founded Cirque du Soleil in 1984 with Ste-Croix and others. In 1987, Cirque du Soleil was invited to perform at the Los Angeles Arts Festival, but the festival could not provide funds in advance to cover Cirque du Soleil's costs. Laliberté took a gamble by literally emptying the troupe's bank account to transport the performers and equipment to California. 'I bet everything on that one night (at the Los Angeles Arts Festival),' Laliberté recalls. 'If we failed, there was no cash for gas to come home.' Fortunately, the gamble paid off. Cirque du Soleil was a huge success, which led to more opportunities and successes in the following years.[20]

Rituals and Ceremonies

rituals The programmed routines of daily organisational life that dramatise the organisation's culture.

ceremonies Planned displays of organisational culture, conducted specifically for the benefit of an audience.

Rituals are the programmed routines of daily organisational life that dramatise an organisation's culture. They include how visitors are greeted, how often senior executives visit subordinates, how people communicate with each other, how much time employees take for lunch and so on. For instance, BMW's fast-paced culture is quite literally apparent in the way employees walk around the German car maker's offices. 'When you move through the corridors and hallways of other companies' buildings, people kind of crawl, they walk slowly,' observes a BMW executive. 'But BMW people tend to move faster.'[21] **Ceremonies** are more formal artefacts than rituals. Ceremonies are planned activities conducted specifically for the benefit of an audience. This would include publicly rewarding (or punishing) employees, or celebrating the launch of a new product or newly won contract.

Organisational Language

The language of the workplace speaks volumes about the company's culture. How employees address coworkers, describe customers, express anger and greet stakeholders are all verbal symbols of cultural values. Employees at American retailer The Container Store compliment each other about 'being Gumby', meaning that they are being as flexible as the once-popular green toy to help a customer or another employee.[22] Language also highlights values held by organisational subcultures. For instance, consultants working at Whirlpool kept hearing employees talk about the appliance company's 'PowerPoint culture'. This phrase, which names Microsoft's presentation software, was a critique of Whirlpool's hierarchical culture in which communication is one-way (from executives to employees).[23]

Physical Structures and Symbols

Winston Churchill once said, 'We shape our buildings; thereafter, they shape us.'[24] The former British prime minister was reminding us that buildings both reflect and influence an organisation's culture. The size, shape, location and age of buildings might suggest a company's emphasis on teamwork, environmental friendliness, flexibility or any other set of values.[25] Even if the building doesn't make much of a statement, there is a treasure trove of physical artefacts inside. Desks, chairs, office space and wall hangings (or lack of them) are just a few of the items that might convey cultural meaning.[26]

Consider the physical artefacts that you might notice when visiting the headquarters of Mother. Housed in a converted warehouse in an artsy district of London, the creative agency has a large reception hall with an adjoining casual lounge on one side and a large cafeteria on the other, where staff can get free fruit, cereals, toast and similar snacks any time they want. A wide staircase leads from reception to the next floor, which has meeting rooms separated only by dividers made of hanging strips of opaque plastic. The top floor of Mother's offices is one room dominated by a large rectangular concrete table around which dozens of staff work. Each of these physical artefacts alone might not say much, but put enough of them together and you can see how they symbolise Mother's edgy creative culture with a strong team orientation.[27]

Buildings and their décor have such a strong influence on organisational culture that some leaders are designing offices to reflect what they want the company's culture to become, rather than its current culture. National Australia Bank's (NAB) National@Docklands, a low-rise campus-like building in Melbourne's docklands area, is a case in point. The building's open design and colourful décor are symbolic of a more open, egalitarian and creative culture, compared to the closed hierarchical culture that NAB executives are trying to shed. The docklands building project was initiated when executives realised that MLC, a financial services firm that NAB had acquired a few years earlier, was able to change its culture after moving into its funky headquarters in Sydney. 'There's no doubt that MLC has moved its culture over the last few years to a more open and transparent style which is a good example for the rest of the group to follow,' admits a NAB executive.[28]

IS ORGANISATIONAL CULTURE IMPORTANT?

LEARNING OBJECTIVE

Identify three functions of organisational culture.

Does organisational culture improve organisational effectiveness? Leaders at National Australia Bank think so. 'If you get the people right, and the culture right, you will get the success,' says John Stewart, who served as NAB's chief executive soon after the company discovered violations in its currency trading practices. Herb Kelleher, founder of Southwest Airlines, agrees. 'Culture is one of the most precious things a company has, so you must work harder on it than anything else,' says Kelleher.[29] Many writers of popular-press management books also assert that the most successful companies have strong cultures. In fact, one popular management book, *Built to Last*, suggests that successful companies are 'cultlike' (although not actually cults, the authors are careful to point out).[30]

So, does organisational culture make a difference? The research evidence suggests that companies with strong cultures tend to be more successful, but only under a particular set of conditions.[31] Before discussing these contingencies, let's examine organisational culture *strength* and its potential benefits.

Corporate culture strength refers to how widely and deeply employees hold the company's dominant values and assumptions. In a strong organisational culture, most employees across

Lee Kum Kee's Secret Sauce to Success

AP Images

Guangdong Nanfang Lee Kum Kee Health Products Co., Ltd., a subsidiary of food products company Lee Kum Kee, has a secret sauce that makes it one of the best places to work in Asia. 'Two words explain why we are a Best Employer: corporate culture,' says human resource vice president Raymond Lo. 'Our unique culture is our competitive edge. It plays a major role in the success of our organisation.' Lee Kum Kee's core values include pragmatism, integrity, constant entrepreneurship and sharing benefits with the community. Lo explains that cultural values are so important that leaders must believe in and live them. 'The corporate culture must have a soul,' he says. 'Many companies try to model themselves on successful companies, but unless the chief executive and management truly believe in the culture, it won't work.' Lo adds that his company actively works to ensure everyone understands and believes in the company's culture. 'We also spend a lot of time in team building in order to nourish our corporate culture.'[32]

all subunits understand and embrace the dominant values. These values and assumptions are also institutionalised through well-established artefacts, thereby making it difficult to change the culture. Furthermore, strong cultures tend to be long-lasting; some can be traced back to the values and assumptions established by the company's founder. In contrast, companies have weak cultures when the dominant values are held mainly by a few people at the top of the organisation, are barely discernible and are in flux. A strong corporate culture potentially increases the company's success by serving three important functions (see Exhibit 14.3):

- Control system—Organisational culture is a deeply embedded form of social control that influences employee decisions and behaviour.[33] Culture is pervasive and operates unconsciously. You might think of it as an automatic pilot, directing employees in ways that are consistent with organisational expectations. 'If you have the right culture in place, you can have a lot more confidence that people will deliver on the expectations about risk,' says Michael Ullmer, deputy CEO of National Australia Bank.[34]
- Social glue—Organisational culture is the 'social glue' that bonds people together and makes them feel part of the organisational experience.[35] Employees are motivated to internalise the organisation's dominant culture because it fulfils their need for social identity. This social glue is increasingly important as a way to attract new staff and retain top performers. It also becomes the common thread that holds together employees in global organisations. 'If you're managing a company which has a global footprint, diverse nationalities, diverse clients, diverse all over the place, the values of the company are really the bedrock—the glue which holds the firm together,' explains Nandan Nilekani, CEO of Infosys in India.[36]
- Sense making—Organisational culture assists the sense-making process.[37] It helps employees to understand what goes on and why things happen in the company. Corporate culture also makes it easier for them to understand what is expected of them and to interact with other employees who know the culture and believe in it. For instance, one recent study reported that organisational culture strength increases role clarity, which reduces stress among sales staff.[38]

Exhibit 14.3 *Potential Benefits and Contingencies of Culture Strength*

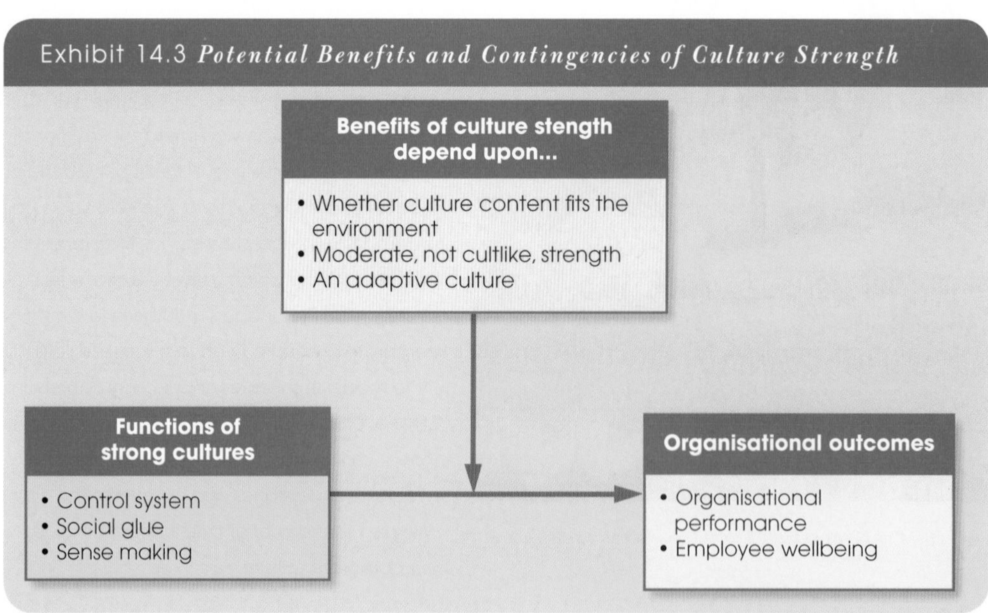

Contingencies of Organisational Culture and Effectiveness

LEARNING OBJECTIVE 

Discuss the conditions under which organisational culture strength improves organisational performance.

Studies have found only a modestly positive relationship between culture strength and organisational effectiveness because three contingencies need to be considered: (1) whether the culture content is aligned with the environment, (2) whether the culture is not so strong that it becomes cultlike, and (3) whether the culture incorporates an adaptive culture (see Exhibit 14.3).

Aligning Culture Content with Environment

One contingency is whether the organisation's culture content—its dominant values and assumptions—is aligned with the external environment. Consider the situation that Dell recently faced. As described in Reality Check 14.1, Dell's culture gave the highest priority to cost efficiency and competitiveness, yet these values and assumptions are no longer ideal for the marketplace. Low-cost computers are still popular, but consumers increasingly demand computers that are innovative and look 'cool'. Dell had a strong culture, but it was no longer the best culture for the external environment.

Avoiding a Corporate Cult

A second contingency is the degree of culture strength. Various experts suggest that companies with very strong cultures (i.e. corporate 'cults') may be less effective than companies with moderately strong cultures.[40] One reason why corporate cults may undermine organisational effectiveness is that they lock decision makers into mental models, which can blind them to new opportunities and unique problems. They overlook or incorrectly define subtle misalignments between the organisation's activities and the changing environment. Dell faced this problem. Kevin Rollins and Michael Dell sensed that the company's culture tolerated competitive staff members even if they didn't collaborate, and it emphasised financial performance far too much (staff even had stock tickers on their computer screens). Yet these leaders never thought about changing this culture. Instead, the program they created a few years ago (called the 'Soul of Dell') merely supplemented the company's core values and assumptions. 'It's not that we didn't have a culture with the qualities that drive business success,' explained a Dell executive at the time. 'We just aspired to do better.'[41]

The other reason why very strong cultures may be dysfunctional is that they suppress dissenting subcultural values. At Dell, for instance, anyone who questioned the company's almost sacred values and assumptions was quickly silenced, even though the dissenting values could have helped Dell shift more quickly to a better aligned culture. The challenge for organisational leaders is to maintain not only a strong culture but one that allows subcultural diversity. Subcultures encourage constructive conflict, which improves creative thinking and offers some level of ethical vigilance over the dominant culture. In the long run, a subculture's nascent values could become important dominant values as the environment changes. Corporate cults suppress subcultures, thereby undermining these benefits.

Encouraging an Adaptive Culture

A third contingency between cultural strength and organisational effectiveness is whether the culture content includes an **adaptive culture**.[42] An adaptive culture exists when employees are receptive to change—they assume that the organisation needs to continuously adapt to its external environment and that they need to be flexible in their roles within the organisation. Employees in an adaptive culture embrace an open-systems perspective, in which the organisation's survival and success require ongoing adaptation to the external environment, which itself is continuously changing. They assume that their future depends on monitoring the external environment and

adaptive culture An organisational culture in which employees are receptive to change, including the ongoing alignment of the organisation to its environment and continuous improvement of internal processes.

Losing Ground with a 'Winning' Culture

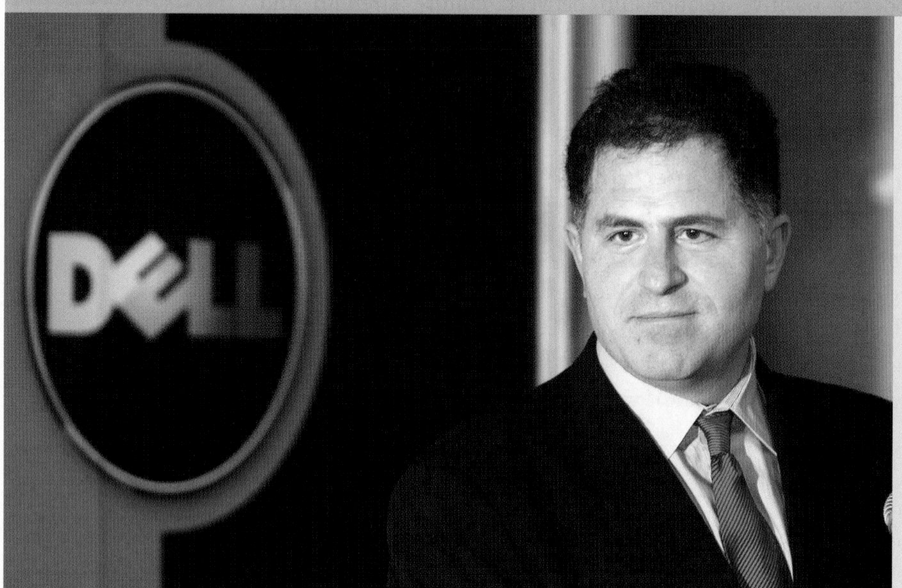

Getty Images

Dell's competitive and efficiency-focused culture is now becoming a liability to the computer-maker's future.

PROPELLED BY A CULTURE of cost efficiency and competitiveness, Dell, Inc., was the unstoppable leader in the computer industry for more than a decade. Experts praised its low-cost, responsive manufacturing and direct-marketing sales model. Founder Michael Dell championed short-term objectives, while Kevin Rollins (until recently Dell CEO) was the architect of efficiency-oriented processes and measures. Dell culture emphasised 'winning', meaning that it focused on beating the competition and staying on top through low prices. 'There are

serving stakeholders with the resources available. Thus, employees in adaptive cultures have a strong sense of ownership. They take responsibility for the organisation's performance and alignment with the external environment.

In an adaptive culture, receptivity to change extends to internal processes and roles. Employees recognise that satisfying stakeholder needs requires continuous improvement of internal work processes. Toyota's culture, described earlier in this chapter, illustrates this aspect of an adaptive culture because it values the continuous improvement of the production process as well as of its products and services. Furthermore, employee support for changing internal work processes involves flexibility in their own work roles. The phrase 'That's not my job' is found in nonadaptive cultures. Finally, an adaptive culture has a strong learning orientation because receptivity to change and improvement logically involves support for action-oriented discovery. With a learning orientation, employees welcome new learning opportunities, actively experiment with new ideas and practices, view reasonable mistakes as a natural part of the learning process and continuously question past practices.[43]

Organisational Culture and Business Ethics

As the opening story in this chapter illustrated, an organisation's culture influences the ethical conduct of the organisation's employees. This makes sense because good behaviour is driven by ethical values, and ethical values can become embedded into an organisation's dominant culture. Several employees at National Australia Bank engaged in illegal activities because the culture reinforced this focus on profit at any price and discouraged employees from bringing bad news about this wrongdoing to management's attention.

Michael Dell and former CEO Kevin Rollins also saw this connection between culture and ethics when they launched the 'Soul of Dell' a few years ago. Concerned about employee obsession

REALITY CHECK 14.1

some organisations where people think they're a hero if they invent a new thing,' Rollins said a few years ago. 'Being a hero at Dell means saving money.'

Although still an efficient manufacturer of low-cost computers, Dell's spectacular success has stalled while HP and other competitors are moving ahead. The reason? Dell's strong culture blinded leaders and most staff to anything other than building low-cost computers, yet the market was shifting toward a preference for style and innovation. 'Dell's culture is not inspirational or aspirational,' suggests one industry expert. '[Its] culture only wants to talk about execution.' A few staff warned that Dell's culture needed to change, but those who dared to criticise the company's deeply ingrained values and assumptions were quickly silenced. 'A lot of red flags got waved—but only once,' recalls a former Dell manager.

Meanwhile, Dell's fortunes—including public ratings of its culture—were falling. A few years ago, Dell ranked number one on *Fortune* magazine's list of most admired companies in America; two years later, it was off the top 20 list. These and other concerns motivated founder Michael Dell to return as CEO, replacing Kevin Rollins. Other senior executives have also left the company. 'The company was too focused on the short term,' Dell admits. He apparently also repeatedly emphasises to staff that Dell's past culture 'is not a religion'. Dell is convinced he can turn the company around, and there is some indication his new vision is working, but a few critics believe that changing Dell's culture will be a mammoth task. 'It's not an easy transition,' warns a technology analyst. 'You've got to change your mindset and your culture.'[39]

with the company's stock price, the executives tried to shift the company's winning culture into one that emphasises 'winning with integrity'.[44] For example, one of the computer maker's revised values was defined as 'behaving ethically in every interaction and in every aspect of how we conduct business'. Unfortunately, the Soul of Dell initiative probably didn't change the company's culture. Two years after the Soul of Dell cultural change program was launched, the company reported that some executives had manipulated the company books to reach performance targets that would give them a larger bonus.[45]

MERGING ORGANISATIONAL CULTURES

Compare and contrast four strategies for merging organisational cultures.

4C Corporate Culture Clash and Chemistry is a company with an unusual name and mandate. The Dutch consulting firm helps clients to determine whether their culture is aligned ('chemistry') or incompatible with ('clash') a potential acquisition or merger partner. The firm also analyses the company's culture with its strategy. There should be plenty of demand for 4C's expertise. According to various studies, most corporate mergers and acquisitions fail in terms of subsequent performance of the merged organisation. Evidence suggests that such failures occur partly because corporate leaders are so focused on the financial or marketing logistics of a merger that they fail to conduct due-diligence audits on their respective corporate cultures.[46] Some forms of integration (which we discuss later in this section) may allow successful mergers between companies with different cultures. However, research concludes that mergers typically suffer when organisations with significantly divergent corporate cultures merge into a single entity with a high degree of integration.[47]

IBM's acquisition of PricewaterhouseCooper's (PwC) consulting business turned into a well-publicised culture clash in Australia and elsewhere. IBM-ers tend to be cost-conscious and flexible, whereas PwC staff are accustomed to flying business class and having a large, personal office (IBMers tend to 'hot-desk'). PwC staff are also much more conservative than their IBM counterparts. At one event in Melbourne, a senior IBM executive was dressed as American tennis star Andre Agassi. 'The IBM-ers went mad that time—nuts, standing and cheering. They loved it,' recalls one onlooker. 'The PwC folk were stunned. Silent.' Less than two years after IBM had acquired PwC's consulting business, up to one quarter of PwC's partners had apparently quit.[48]

Bicultural Audit

bicultural audit A process of diagnosing cultural relations between companies and determining the extent to which cultural clashes will likely occur.

Organisational leaders can minimise these cultural collisions and fulfil their duty of due diligence by conducting a bicultural audit.[49] A **bicultural audit** diagnoses cultural relations between the companies and determines the extent to which cultural clashes are likely to occur. The bicultural audit process begins by identifying cultural differences between the merging companies. Next, the bicultural audit data are analysed to determine which differences between the two firms will result in conflict and which cultural values provide common ground on which to build a cultural foundation in the merged organisation. The final stage involves identifying strategies and preparing action plans to bridge the two organisations' cultures.

Several years ago, pulp-and-paper conglomerate Abitibi-Price applied a bicultural audit before it agreed to merge with rival Stone Consolidated. Specifically, Abitibi developed the Merging Cultures Evaluation Index (MCEI), an evaluation system that helped Abitibi executives compare its culture with other companies in the industry. The MCEI examined several dimensions of corporate culture, such as concentration of power versus diffusion of power, innovation versus tradition, wide versus narrow flow of information and consensus versus authoritative decision making. Abitibi and Stone executives completed the questionnaire to assess their own culture, and then they compared the results. The MCEI results, along with financial and infrastructural information, served as the basis for Abitibi-Price to merge with Stone Consolidated to become Abitibi-Consolidated (now AbitibiBowater), the world's largest pulp-and-paper firm.[50]

Strategies for Merging Different Organisational Cultures

In some cases, the bicultural audit results in a decision to end merger talks because the two cultures are too different to merge effectively. However, even with substantially different cultures, two companies may form a workable union if they apply the appropriate merger strategy. The four main strategies for merging different corporate cultures are assimilation, deculturation, integration and separation (see Exhibit 14.4).[51]

Assimilation

Assimilation occurs when employees at the acquired company willingly embrace the cultural values of the acquiring organisation. Typically, this strategy works best when the acquired company has a weak, dysfunctional culture and the acquiring company's culture is strong and aligned with the external environment. Culture clash is rare with assimilation because the acquired firm's culture is weak and employees are looking for better cultural alternatives. Research in Motion (RIM), the BlackBerry wireless device maker, applies the assimilation strategy by deliberately

Exhibit 14.4 ***Strategies for Merging Different Organisational Cultures***

Merger strategy	Description	Works best when ...
Assimilation	Acquired company embraces acquiring firm's culture	Acquired firm has a weak culture
Deculturation	Acquiring firm imposes its culture on unwilling acquired firm	Rarely works—may be necessary only when acquired firm's culture doesn't work but employees don't realise it
Integration	Merging companies combine the two or more cultures into a new composite culture	Existing cultures can be improved
Separation	Merging companies remain distinct entities with minimal exchange of culture or organisational practices	Firms operate successfully in different businesses requiring different culture

Sources: Based on ideas in A. R. Malekazedeh and A. Nahavandi, 'Making Mergers Work by Managing Cultures,' *Journal of Business Strategy* 11, no. 3 (1990): 55–57; K. W. Smith, 'A Brand-New Culture for the Merged Firm,' *Mergers & Acquisitions* 35 (June 2000): 45–50.

acquiring only small start-up firms. 'Small companies ... don't have cultural issues,' says RIM co-CEO Jim Balsillie, adding that they are typically absorbed into RIM's culture with little fuss or attention.[52]

Deculturation

Assimilation is rare. Employees usually resist organisational change, particularly when they are asked to throw away personal and cultural values. Under these conditions, some acquiring companies apply a *deculturation* strategy by imposing their culture and business practices on the acquired organisation. The acquiring firm strips away artefacts and reward systems that support the old culture. People who cannot adopt the acquiring company's culture often have their employment terminated. Deculturation may be necessary when the acquired firm's culture doesn't work but employees aren't convinced of this. However, this strategy is difficult to apply effectively because the acquired firm's employees resist the cultural intrusions from the buying firm, thereby delaying or undermining the merger process.

Integration

A third strategy is to combine the two or more cultures into a new composite culture that preserves the best features of the previous cultures. Integration is slow and potentially risky because there are many forces preserving the existing cultures. Still, this strategy should be considered when the companies have relatively weak cultures or when their cultures include several overlapping values. Integration also works best when people realise that their existing cultures are ineffective and, therefore, the people are motivated to adopt a new set of dominant values.

Separation

A separation strategy occurs when the merging companies agree to remain distinct entities with minimal exchange of culture or organisational practices. This strategy is most appropriate when the two merging companies are in unrelated industries or operate in different countries, because

A Marriage of Cultural Separation

A decade ago, McDonald's Restaurants took a controlling interest in Chipotle Mexican Grill, a young start-up restaurant chain with a considerably different approach to doing business. While McDonald's epitomises fast food, Chipotle is a model of freshly prepared Mexican-style meals. Recognising that McDonald's culture and practices wouldn't work at Chipotle, founder and CEO Steve Ells (shown at left) convinced the global food giant to keep a distance from the younger restaurant chain's culture. 'Chipotle structured the agreement so that McDonald's would essentially become the "banker" without changing recipes, ingredients or culture—all the elements to which Chipotle fans and team members are loyal,' says Ells. For the most part, McDonald's executives kept to their word, but Ells did have to explain to them on several occasions why the restaurant doesn't offer what it can't make better than anyone else. 'They probably did give me grief,' Ells admitted. Eventually, McDonald's sold its stake in Chipotle for a tidy profit. 'We learned from each other,' Ells says of the partnership, 'but we use different kinds of food, and we aim for a different kind of experience and culture altogether. So we ended up going our separate ways.'[55]

AP Images

the most appropriate cultural values tend to differ by industry and national culture. This strategy is also relevant for the corporate cultures of diversified conglomerates.

For example, Wesfarmers has a strong performance and employee ownership culture across all of its businesses, but each business also has a distinct culture in many respects. 'We do have a couple of common principles across all our business,' says Richard Goyder, CEO of the Australian conglomerate, which includes Coles and Bunnings retailers. 'However each individual business has been encouraged to develop its own culture, as long as, of course, it is a healthy culture ... we don't necessarily want exactly the same culture in all our individual businesses, as retail is different from industrial distribution, which is different again from mining and so on.'[53] Wesfarmers' cultural separation approach is rare, however. Executives in acquiring firms usually have difficulty keeping their hands off the acquired firm. It's not surprising, therefore, that only 15 per cent of mergers leave the acquired company as a stand-alone unit.[54]

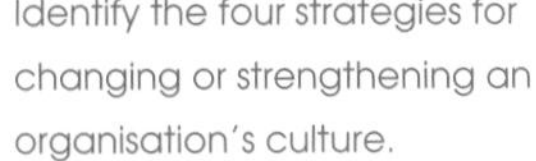

Identify the four strategies for changing or strengthening an organisation's culture.

CHANGING AND STRENGTHENING ORGANISATIONAL CULTURE

Is it possible to change an organisation's culture? Yes, but doing so isn't easy, the change rarely occurs quickly and often the culture ends up changing (or replacing) corporate leaders. For example, although National Australia Bank's leaders have put an enormous focus on transforming its corporate culture, some observers claim the transformation has been slow. They point to the fact that NAB wrote off more than $1 billion during the recent financial crisis because of its exposure to high-risk collateralised debt obligations.[56]

A few experts argue that an organisation's culture 'cannot be managed', so attempting to change the company's values and assumptions is a waste of time.[57] This view is more extreme than most, but organisational culture experts generally agree that changing an organisation's culture is a considerable challenge. At the same time, under the right conditions, the company's values and assumptions can have a powerful influence on the company's success. Over the next few pages, we will highlight four strategies that have had some success at altering corporate cultures. This list, outlined in Exhibit 14.5, is not exhaustive, but each activity seems to work well under the right circumstances.

Actions of Founders and Leaders

An organisation's culture begins with its founders.[58] You can see this at retail giant Harvey Norman, where company chairman and cofounder Gerry Harvey has established a culture that is aggressive, demanding and frugal, yet pays attention to the development of its franchisees. Founders are often visionaries who provide a powerful role model for others to follow. The company's culture sometimes reflects the founder's personality, and this cultural imprint can remain with the organisation for decades.

In spite of the founder's cultural imprint, subsequent leaders are sometimes able to reshape that culture by applying transformational leadership and organisational change practices.[59] The opening story in this chapter describes how National Australia Bank is slowly changing

Exhibit 14.5 *Strategies for Changing and Strengthening Organisational Culture*

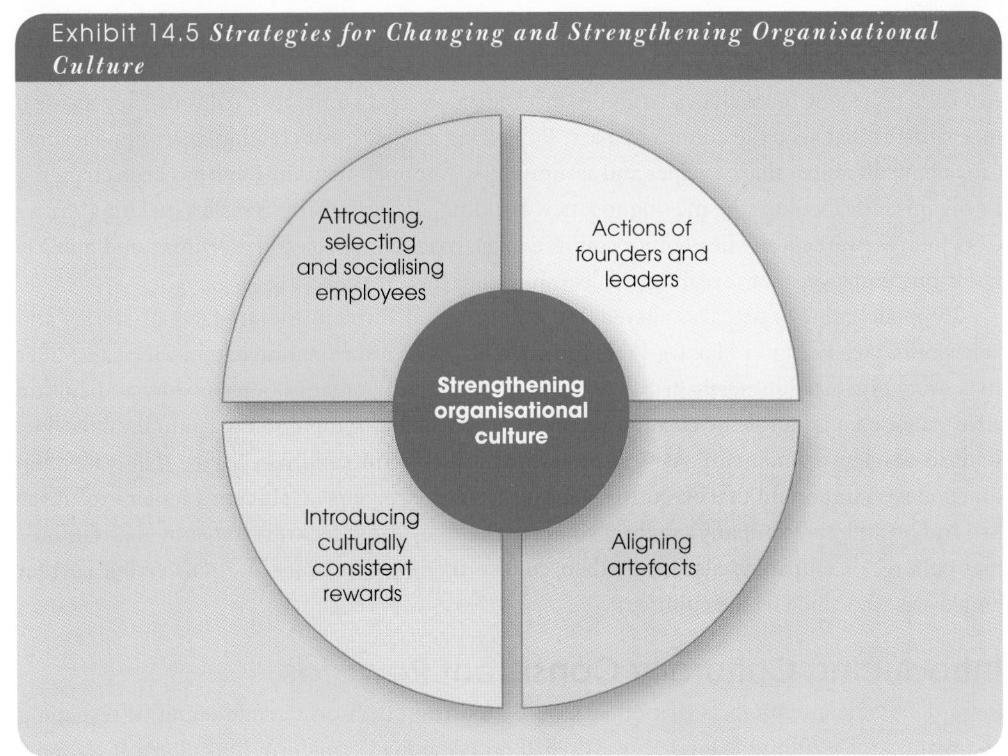

Crafting an Oxygen-Rich Culture

Courtesy Oxygen for Business

Auckland-based Oxygen Business Solutions changed its organisational culture to become more aligned with its environment and employee values.

New Zealand forest products company Carter Holt Harvey spun off its information technology group into an independent consulting business because information technology was not its core competency. Carter executives felt that employees in this group would be more efficient and customer-focused if they competed in the open market. The new company, Oxygen Business Solutions, has since excelled in customer service and competitiveness, recently becoming the largest dedicated SAP (a popular enterprise software) solutions company in New Zealand and Australia.

One of the key factors in Oxygen's success has been its organisational culture. 'We've recognised that our people and the way they deliver to customers is an extension of our culture and brand,' explains CEO Mike Smith. However, Oxygen's culture was neither strong nor focused on customers or competitiveness when the company was launched. Instead, Smith and his

its organisational culture through the dedicated focus of former CEO John Stewart (and his successor, Cameron Clyne). Similarly, Reality Check 14.2 describes how Mike Smith and others at New Zealand-based Oxygen Business Solutions changed the company's organisational culture when the information technology group was spun off as a consulting business from parent company Carter Holt Harvey.

Aligning Artefacts

Artefacts represent more than just the visible indicators of a company's culture. They are also mechanisms that keep the culture in place. By altering artefacts—or creating new ones—leaders can potentially adjust shared values and assumptions. National Australia Bank has been changing its organisational culture by moving to a new building, decentralising decision making (former CEO John Stewart cut the head office count in half), coaching upcoming executives and publicly rewarding employees for revealing and learning from their mistakes.[61]

Corporate cultures are also altered and strengthened through the artefacts of stories and behaviours. According to Max De Pree, former CEO of furniture manufacturer Herman Miller Inc., every organisation needs 'tribal storytellers' to keep the organisation's history and culture alive.[62] Leaders play a role by creating memorable events that symbolise the cultural values they want to develop or maintain. At Wall Street investment firm Goldman Sachs, this leadership function is so important that executives are called 'culture carriers'. Goldman's senior executives live and breathe the company's culture so much that they can effectively transmit and reinforce that culture.[63] Companies also strengthen culture in new operations by transferring current employees who abide by the culture.

Introducing Culturally Consistent Rewards

Reward systems are artefacts that often have a powerful effect on strengthening or reshaping an organisation's culture.[64] John Stewart relied on rewards to transform the culture at National

REALITY CHECK 14.2

executive team had to replace the parent company's production-focused culture with a set of values more aligned with the external environment.

Oxygen began the transformation process by identifying the values by which it wanted to work. 'We ran focus groups with staff, did an e-survey and got feedback on the values they thought would be important if they owned the business,' says Smith. 'The staff came up with seven new values: real, grow, support, fun, zest, imagine and shine.'

Next, groups of Oxygen employees participated in off-site seminars where they were asked to identify their personal values, then compare those values with the ideal culture identified in the earlier focus groups and surveys. 'That [event] was an eye-opener for people,' Smith recalls. 'It is too easy to get caught up in day-to-day things and not see what is important in your own life.'

These events reshaped Oxygen's culture, but Oxygen's executives acknowledge that changing an organisation's culture is a lengthy process. 'We are making our values overt, but over time they will become subconscious and inherent in the organisation,' explains Oxygen's general manager of people. 'I see this as a journey. It is not something where we put a big tick in a column and say it is done.'[60]

Australia Bank. ING Bank Australia has a monthly recognition program in which employees who live the company's values are rewarded with the chance to drive a prestige car for a month. Ergon Energy reinforces the company's values of safety, teamwork and community spirit with a reward system called Power Aid. 'Power Aid is linked to health and safety in our workplace and is administered by local workplace health and safety committees,' explains an executive at the Queensland government-owned corporation that distributes electricity to regional parts of the state. 'Workgroups are recognised and rewarded for their safe work practices by having funds made available to donate to a local charity of their choice.'[65]

Attracting, Selecting and Socialising Employees

LEARNING OBJECTIVE

Apply attraction-selection-attrition theory to explain how organisational culture strengthens.

Organisational culture is strengthened by attracting and hiring people who already embrace the cultural values. This process, along with weeding out people who don't fit the culture, is explained by **attraction-selection-attrition (ASA) theory**.[66] ASA theory states that organisations have a natural tendency to attract, select and retain people with values and personality characteristics that are consistent with the organisation's character, resulting in a more homogeneous organisation and a stronger culture:

attraction-selection-attrition (ASA) theory A theory which states that organisations have a natural tendency to attract, select and retain people with values and personality characteristics that are consistent with the organisation's character, resulting in a more homogeneous organisation and a stronger culture.

- Attraction—Job applicants engage in self-selection by avoiding employment in companies whose values seem incompatible with their own values.[67] Companies often encourage this self-selection by actively describing their cultures, but applicants will look for evidence of the company's culture even when it is not advertised. Applicants also inspect organisational artefacts when visiting the company.
- Selection—How well the person 'fits' in with the company's culture is often a factor in deciding which job applicants to hire. Companies with strong cultures often put applicants through several interviews and other selection tests, in part to better gauge the applicant's values and their congruence with the company's values.[68] Consider Park Place Dealerships. As one of the top-rated luxury-car dealerships in the United States, the Dallas–Fort Worth

company relies on interviews and selection tests to carefully screen applicants for their culture fit. 'Testing is one piece of our hiring process that enables us to find people who will not only be successful in our culture, but thrive and enjoy our culture,' says Park Place chairman Ken Schnitzer. When Park Place recently acquired a Lexus dealership in California, several people left when they realised they did not fit Park Place's culture. 'We've had some turnover,' Schnitzer acknowledges in reference to the Lexus dealership. 'We're looking for people to fit into our culture. It's not easy to get hired by Park Place.'[69]

- Attrition—People are motivated to seek environments that are sufficiently congruent with their personal values and to leave environments that are a poor fit. This occurs because person–organisation value congruence supports their social identity and minimises internal role conflict. Even if employees aren't forced out, many quit when value incongruence is sufficiently high. This likely occurred when Park Place Dealerships acquired the Lexus dealership in California—some staff members left voluntarily or otherwise because they did not fit Park Place's unique culture.[70]

organisational socialisation The process by which individuals learn the values, expected behaviours and social knowledge necessary to assume their roles in the organisation.

Along with their use of attraction, selection and attrition, organisations rely on organisational socialisation to strengthen their cultures. **Organisational socialisation** is the process by which individuals learn the values, expected behaviours and social knowledge necessary to assume their roles in the organisation.[71] When a company clearly communicates its culture, job candidates and new hires are more likely to internalise its values quickly and deeply. Socialisation is an important process for absorbing corporate culture as well as helping newcomers adjust to coworkers, work procedures and other corporate realities. Thus, the final section of this chapter looks more closely at the organisational socialisation process.

ORGANISATIONAL SOCIALISATION

Lindblad Expeditions can't afford to have crew members jump ship soon after starting the job. To minimise reality shock, the 500-employee adventure cruise company gives applicants a DVD showing a realistic picture of what it's like to work on board. The program shows not one but two scenes in which staff members are cleaning toilets. One scene reveals the cramped quarters for crew members. In another scene, a dishwasher talks about washing 5000 dishes in one day. The video is meant to scare off applicants who cannot adjust easily to the challenges of working on a ship. The realistic job preview video does have this effect, says Lindblad human resource manager Kris Thompson, but the attrition is well worth it if it reduces turnover soon after staff are hired. 'If [new hires] get on board and say, "This is not what I expected," then shame on us,' says Thompson.[72]

Lindblad Expeditions successfully brings employees into the organisation through pre-employment information (such as its realistic job preview DVD) and other organisational socialisation practices. An important part of this process is helping newcomers become familiar with, and believe in, the organisation's culture. Research indicates that when employees are effectively socialised into the organisation, they tend to perform better, have higher job satisfaction and remain longer with the organisation.[73]

Socialisation as a Learning and Adjustment Process

Organisational socialisation is a process of both learning and adjustment. It is a learning process because newcomers try to make sense of the company's physical workplace, social dynamics,

Socialising Newcomers into Flight Centre's Culture

New Zealand Herald

Flight Centre relies on a unique culture to retain its leadership in the Australian travel industry. Part of this success comes from the company's unique culture, which it carefully maintains through the selection and socialisation of new staff. 'Through our induction, the first thing that people learn when they come into our organisation is what our culture and what our philosophies are and what that means to them,' says chief executive and cofounder Graham Turner. 'We have a very comprehensive system to make sure that we employ the right people.' Louise Mullane (shown in this photo) describes how Flight Centre made sure that she fit in with the travel agency's culture. 'I had a couple of interviews and then spent a day at the 277 store to see how I fitted in,' says Mullane, who now works at a Flight Centre store in New Zealand. 'I got a real feel for the job, the people and what was expected of me.'[74]

and strategic and cultural environment. They learn about the organisation's performance expectations, power dynamics, corporate culture, company history and jargon. They also need to form successful and satisfying relationships with other people from whom they can learn the ropes.[75] Thus, effective socialisation enables new recruits to form a cognitive map of the physical, social, strategic and cultural dynamics of the organisation without information overload.

Organisational socialisation is also a process of adjustment, because individuals need to adapt to their new work environment. They develop new work roles that reconfigure their social identity, adopt new team norms and practise new behaviours.[76] Research indicates that the adjustment process is fairly rapid for many people, usually occurring within a few months. However, newcomers with diverse work experience seem to adjust better than those with limited previous experience, possibly because they have a larger toolkit of knowledge and skills to make the adjustment possible.[77]

Stages of Organisational Socialisation

LEARNING OBJECTIVE 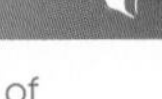

Describe the stages of organisational socialisation.

Socialisation is a continuous process, beginning long before the first day of employment and continuing throughout one's career within the company. However, it is most intense when people move across organisational boundaries, such as when they first join a company or get transferred to an international assignment. Each of these transitions is a process that can be divided into three stages. Our focus here is on the socialisation of new employees, so the three stages are called pre-employment socialisation, encounter and role management (see Exhibit 14.6). These stages parallel the individual's transition from outsider to newcomer and then to insider.[78]

Stage 1: Pre-employment Socialisation

Think back to the months and weeks before you began working in a new job (or attending a new university or college). You actively searched for information about the organisation, formed expectations about working there and felt some anticipation about fitting into that environment. The pre-employment socialisation stage encompasses all the learning and adjustment that occurs before the first day of work. In fact, a large part of the socialisation adjustment process occurs during this stage.[79]

The main problem with pre-employment socialisation is that outsiders rely on indirect information about what it is like to work in the organisation. This information is often distorted by inherent conflicts during the mating dance between employer and applicant.[80] One conflict occurs between the employer's need to attract qualified applicants and the applicant's need for complete information to make accurate employment decisions. Many firms use a 'flypaper' approach by describing only positive aspects of the job and company, causing applicants to accept job offers on the basis of incomplete or false expectations. Another conflict that prevents accurate exchange of information occurs when applicants avoid asking important questions about the company because they don't want to convey an unfavourable image to their prospective employer. For instance, applicants usually don't like to ask about starting salaries and promotion opportunities because it makes them sound greedy or overaggressive. Yet, unless the employer provides this information, applicants might fill in the missing information with false assumptions that produce an inaccurate psychological contract.

Two other types of conflict tend to distort pre-employment information for employers. Applicants engage in impression management when seeking employment, and this tends to motivate them to hide negative information, act out of character and occasionally embellish information about their past accomplishments. At the same time, employers are sometimes reluctant to ask certain questions or use potentially valuable selection devices because they might scare off applicants. Unfortunately, exaggerated résumés from applicants and reluctance to ask for some information causes employers to form a less accurate opinion of the job candidate's potential as an employee.

Stage 2: Encounter

The first day on the job typically marks the beginning of the encounter stage of organisational socialisation. This is the stage in which newcomers test their prior expectations with the

Exhibit 14.6 *Stages of Organisational Socialisation*

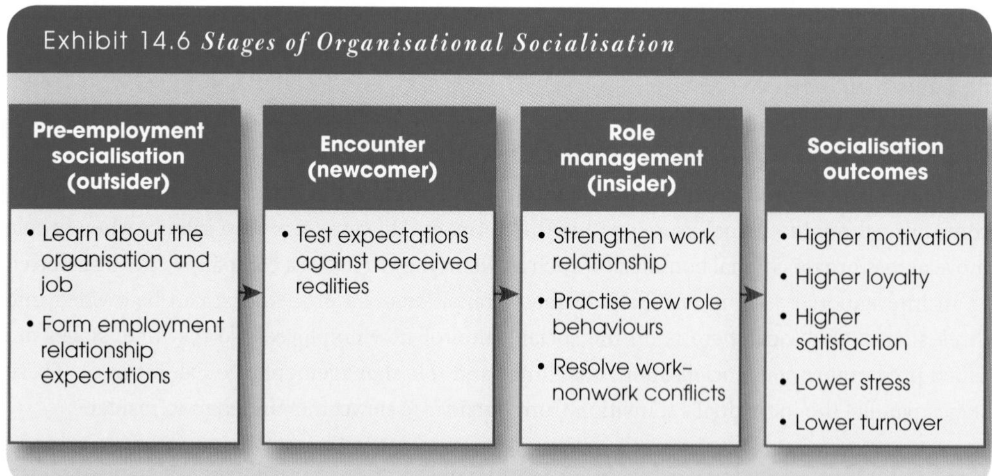

perceived realities. Many companies fail the test, resulting in **reality shock**—the stress that results when employees perceive discrepancies between their pre-employment expectations and on-the-job reality.[81] Reality shock doesn't necessarily occur on the first day; it might develop over several weeks or even months as newcomers form a better understanding of their new work environment.

reality shock The stress that results when employees perceive discrepancies between their pre-employment expectations and on-the-job reality.

Reality shock is common in many organisations.[82] Unmet expectations sometimes occur because the employer is unable to live up to its promises, such as failing to provide challenging projects or the resources to get the work done. Reality shock also occurs because new hires develop distorted work expectations through the information exchange conflicts described above. Whatever the cause, reality shock impedes the socialisation process because the newcomer's energy is directed toward managing the stress rather than learning and accepting organisational knowledge and roles.[83]

Stage 3: Role Management

Role management, the third stage of organisational socialisation, really begins during pre-employment socialisation, but it is most active as employees make the transition from newcomers to insiders. They strengthen relationships with coworkers and supervisors, practise new role behaviours, and adopt attitudes and values consistent with their new positions and the organisation. Role management also involves resolving the conflicts between work and nonwork activities, including resolving discrepancies between an employee's existing values and those emphasised by the organisational culture.

Improving the Socialisation Process

LEARNING OBJECTIVE

Explain how realistic job previews assist the socialisation process.

One potentially effective way to improve the socialisation process is through a **realistic job preview (RJP)**—a balance of positive and negative information about the job and work context.[84] Unfortunately, as mentioned earlier, many companies overpromise. They often exaggerate positive features of the job and neglect to mention the undesirable elements in the hope that the best applicants will get 'stuck' on the organisation.

realistic job preview (RJP) A method of improving organisational socialisation in which job applicants are given a balance of positive and negative information about the job and work context.

In contrast, an RJP helps job applicants to decide for themselves whether their skills, needs and values are compatible with the job and organisation. As was described at the beginning of this section on organisational socialisation, Lindblad Expeditions relies on an RJP to minimise the reality shock employees might otherwise experience from their first job on board a ship. The Royal Australian Navy Submarine Service has also introduced a form of RJP in which junior sailors can take a week-long training course on board the HMAS *Stirling* submarine to determine their suitability for this type of work. A recent review of Australia's submarine service concluded that working on a submarine is '*very* tough' due to the limited space, almost total lack of privacy and isolation from family.[85]

RJPs scare away some applicants, but they also tend to reduce turnover and increase job performance.[86] This occurs because RJPs help applicants develop more accurate pre-employment expectations, which, in turn, minimise reality shock. RJPs represent a type of vaccination by preparing employees for the more challenging and troublesome aspects of work life. There is also some evidence that RJPs increase organisational loyalty. A possible explanation for this is that companies providing candid information are easier to trust. They also show respect for the psychological contract and concern for employee welfare.[87]

Socialisation Agents

Ask new employees what most helped them to adjust to their jobs and chances are they will mention helpful coworkers, bosses or maybe even friends who work for the company. The fact is, much organisational socialisation occurs informally through these socialisation agents.[88] Supervisors tend to provide technical information, performance feedback and information about job duties. They also improve the socialisation process by giving newcomers reasonably challenging first assignments, buffering them from excessive demands and helping them form social ties with coworkers.

Coworkers are important socialisation agents because they are easily accessible, can answer questions when problems arise and serve as role models for appropriate behaviour. New employees tend to receive this information and support when coworkers integrate them into the work team. Coworkers also aid the socialisation process by being flexible and tolerant in their interactions with new hires. When a company opens a new store where most employees are new to the company, however, it can be challenging for newcomers to learn about the company's culture. At Whole Foods Market, the solution is yoghurt. 'One of our secrets is what I refer to as our "yoghurt culture,"' explains John McKey, cofounder of the American health-focused food retailer. This strategy involves transferring employees who carry Whole Foods Market's unique culture to new stores so that recently hired employees learn and embrace that culture more quickly. 'For example, in our Columbus Circle store in New York, about 25 per cent of the team members transferred from existing stores,' McKey recalls. 'They were the starting culture for the fermentation that turned Columbus Circle into a true Whole Foods store.'[89]

Several organisations rely on a 'buddy system', whereby newcomers are assigned to coworkers for sources of information and social support. Meridian Technology Centre relies on a buddy system in the socialisation of new staff members. Buddies introduce new hires to other employees, give them campus tours and generally familiarise them with the physical layout of the workplace. They have lunch with employees on their first day and meet weekly with them for their first two months. Cxtec, the networking and voice technology company in Syracuse, New York, helps new staff meet other employees through food. On the first Friday of each month, new staff members take charge of the doughnut cart, introducing themselves as they distribute the morning snack to the company's 350 employees.[90] Collectively, these practices help newcomers to form social networks, which, as you learned in Chapter 10, are powerful means of gaining information and influence in the organisation.

CHAPTER SUMMARY

Organisational culture consists of the values and assumptions shared within an organisation. Shared assumptions are unconscious, taken-for-granted perceptions or beliefs that have worked so well in the past that they are considered the correct way to think and act toward problems and opportunities. Values are stable, evaluative beliefs that guide our preferences for outcomes or courses of action in a variety of situations.

Organisations differ in their cultural content, that is, the relative ordering of values. There are several classifications of organisational culture, but they tend to oversimplify the wide variety of cultures and completely ignore the underlying assumptions of culture. Organisations have subcultures as well as the dominant culture. Subcultures maintain the organisation's standards of performance and ethical behaviour. They are also the source of emerging values that replace ageing core values.

Artefacts are the observable symbols and signs of an organisation's culture. Four broad categories of artefacts include organisational stories and legends, rituals and ceremonies, language, and physical structures and symbols. Understanding an organisation's culture requires assessment of many artefacts because they are subtle and often ambiguous.

Organisational culture has three main functions: a form of social control, the 'social glue' that bonds people together, and a way to help employees make sense of the workplace. Companies with strong cultures generally perform better than those with weak cultures, but only when the cultural content is appropriate for the organisation's environment. Also, the culture should not be so strong that it drives out dissenting values, which may form emerging values for the future. Organisations should have adaptive cultures so that employees support ongoing change in the organisation and their own roles.

Organisational culture clashes are common in mergers and acquisitions. This problem can be minimised by performing a bicultural audit to diagnose the compatibility of the organisational cultures. The four main strategies for merging different corporate cultures are integration, deculturation, assimilation and separation.

Organisational culture is very difficult to change, but culture change is possible and sometimes necessary for a company's continued survival. Four strategies for changing and strengthening an organisation's culture are the actions of founders and leaders, aligning artefacts with the desired culture, introducing culturally consistent rewards, and attracting, selecting and socialising employees.

Attraction-selection-attrition (ASA) theory states that organisations have a natural tendency to attract, select and retain people with values and personality characteristics that are consistent with the organisation's character, resulting in a more homogeneous organisation and a stronger culture. Organisational socialisation is the process by which individuals learn the values, expected behaviours and social knowledge necessary to assume their roles in the organisation. It is a process of both learning about the work context and adjusting to new work roles, team norms and behaviours.

Employees typically pass through three socialisation stages: pre-employment, encounter and role management. To manage the socialisation process, organisations should introduce realistic job previews (RJPs) and recognise the value of socialisation agents in the process. RJPs give job applicants a realistic balance of positive and negative information about the job and work context. Socialisation agents provide information and social support during the socialisation process.

KEY TERMS

adaptive culture, p. 547
artefacts, p. 542
attraction-selection-attrition (ASA) theory, p. 555
bicultural audit, p. 550
ceremonies, p. 544
organisational culture, p. 538
organisational socialisation, p. 556
realistic job preview (RJP), p. 559
reality shock, p. 559
rituals, p. 544

Critical Thinking Questions

1 Superb Consultants has submitted a proposal to analyse the cultural values of your organisation. The proposal states that Superb has developed a revolutionary new survey to tap the company's true culture. The survey takes just ten minutes to complete, and the consultants say results can be based on a small sample of employees. Discuss the merits and limitations of this proposal.

2 Some people suggest that the most effective organisations have the strongest cultures. What do we mean by the 'strength' of organisational culture, and what possible problems are there with a strong organisational culture?

3 The CEO of a manufacturing firm wants everyone to support the organisation's dominant culture of lean efficiency and hard work. The CEO has introduced a new reward system to reinforce this culture and personally interviews all professional and managerial applicants to ensure that they bring similar values to the organisation. Some employees who criticised these values had their careers sidelined until they left. Two mid-level managers were fired for supporting contrary values, such as work–life balance. Based on your knowledge of organisational subcultures, what potential problems is the CEO creating?

4 Identify at least two artefacts you have observed in your department or university/college from each of the four broad categories: (a) organisational stories and legends (b) rituals and ceremonies (c) language, and (d) physical structures and symbols.

5 'Organisations are more likely to succeed when they have an adaptive culture.' What can an organisation do to foster an adaptive culture?

6 Suppose you are asked by senior officers of a city government to identify ways to reinforce a new culture of teamwork and collaboration. The senior executive group clearly supports these values, but it wants everyone in the organisation to embrace them. Identify four types of activities that would strengthen these cultural values.

7 Socialisation is most intense when people pass through organisational boundaries. One example is your entry into the university you now attend. What learning and adjustment occurred as you moved from outsider to newcomer to insider as a student here?

8 Acme Corporation is planning to acquire Beta Corporation, which operates in a different industry. Acme's culture is entrepreneurial and fast-paced, whereas Beta employees value slow, deliberate decision making by consensus. Which merger strategy would you recommend to minimise culture shock when Acme acquires Beta? Explain your answer.

CLASS EXERCISE

Skill Builder 14.1

Diagnosing Corporate Culture Proclamations

Purpose

This exercise is designed to help you understand the importance and context in which corporate culture is identified and discussed in organisations.

Instructions

This exercise is a take-home activity, although it can be completed in classes where computers and internet connections are available. The instructor will divide the class into small teams (typically four or five people per team). Each team is assigned a specific industry—such as energy, biotechnology or computer hardware.

With your team, search the websites of several companies in the selected industry for company statements about their corporate cultures. Use company website search engines (if they exist) to find documents with key phrases such as 'corporate culture' or 'company values'.

In the next class, or at the end of the time allotted in the current class, report on your observations by answering the following three discussion questions.

Discussion Questions

1. What values seem to dominate the corporate cultures of the companies you searched? Are these values similar or diverse across companies in the industry?
2. What was the broader content of the web pages on which these companies described or mentioned their corporate cultures?
3. Do companies in this industry refer to their corporate cultures on their websites more or less than companies in other industries searched by teams in your class?

SELF-ASSESSMENT

Skill Builder 14.2

What Are Your Corporate Culture Preferences?

Purpose

This self-assessment is designed to help you identify the corporate culture that fits most closely with your personal values and assumptions.

Instructions

Read each pair of statements in the Corporate Culture Preference Scale and circle the statement that describes the organisation you would prefer to work in. Then use the scoring key in Appendix B at the end of the book to calculate your results for each subscale. The scale does not attempt to measure your preference for every corporate culture—just a few of the more common varieties. Also, keep in mind that none of these corporate cultures is inherently good or bad. The focus here is on how well you fit within each of them. This exercise should be completed alone so that you can assess yourself honestly without concerns of social comparison. Class discussion will focus on the importance of matching job applicants to the organisation's dominant values.

Corporate Culture Preference Scale

I would prefer to work in an organisation:

1a. Where employees work well together in teams.	**OR**	1b. That produces highly respected products or services.
2a. Where top management maintains a sense of order in the workplace.	**OR**	2b. Where the organisation listens to customers and responds quickly to their needs.
3a. Where employees are treated fairly.	**OR**	3b. Where employees continuously search for ways to work more efficiently.
4a. Where employees adapt quickly to new work requirements.	**OR**	4b. Where corporate leaders work hard to keep employees happy.
5a. Where senior executives receive special benefits not available to other employees.	**OR**	5b. Where employees are proud when the organisation achieves its performance goals.
6a. Where employees who perform the best get paid the most.	**OR**	6b. Where senior executives are respected.
7a. Where everyone gets her or his job done like clockwork.	**OR**	7b. That is on top of innovations in the industry.
8a. Where employees receive assistance to overcome any personal problems.	**OR**	8b. Where employees abide by company rules.
9a. That is always experimenting with new ideas in the marketplace.	**OR**	9b. That expects everyone to put in 110 per cent for peak performance.
10a. That quickly benefits from market opportunities.	**OR**	10b. Where employees are always kept informed about what's happening in the organisation.
11a. That can quickly respond to competitive threats.	**OR**	11b. Where most decisions are made by the top executives.
12a. Where management keeps everything under control.	**OR**	12b. Where employees care for each other.

Endnotes

1 Australia Prudential Regulation Authority (APRA), *Report into Irregular Currency Options Trading at the National Australia Bank* (Sydney: APRA, March 2004); J. Kavanagh, 'National Emergency', *Business Review Weekly*, 3 November 2005, 32; M. Finch, 'NAB and the Art of Corporate Renewal', *Human Resources Leader*, 16 May 2006; L. Carapiet, 'NAB's John Stewart Knows His ABCs', *Australian Banking & Finance*, December 2007, 6; S. Dellaportas, B. J. Cooper and P. Braica, 'Leadership, Culture and Employee Deceit: The Case of the National Australia Bank', *Corporate Governance: An International Review* 15, no. 6 (2007): 1442–1452.

2 A. Williams, P. Dobson and M. Walters, *Changing Culture: New Organizational Approaches* (London: Institute of Personnel Management, 1989); E. H. Schein, 'What Is Culture?', in *Reframing Organizational Culture*, ed. P. J. Frost *et al.* (Newbury Park, CA: Sage, 1991), 243–253.

3 B. M. Meglino and E. C. Ravlin, 'Individual Values in Organizations: Concepts, Controversies, and Research', *Journal of Management* 24, no. 3 (1998): 351–389; B. R. Agle and C. B. Caldwell, 'Understanding Research on Values in Business', *Business and Society* 38, no. 3 (1999): 326–387; S. Hitlin and J. A. Pilavin, 'Values: Reviving a Dormant Concept', *Annual Review of Sociology* 30 (2004): 359–393.

4 N. M. Ashkanasy, 'The Case for Culture', in *Debating Organization*, ed. R. Westwood and S. Clegg (Malden, MA: Blackwell, 2003), 300–310.

5 B. Kabanoff and J. Daly, 'Espoused Values in Organisations', *Australian Journal of Management* 27, special issue (2002): 89–104.

6 C. Webb, 'Argo Still Aims to Shake out the Golden Fleece', *The Age (Melbourne)*, 24 May 2008, 4.

7 B. Darrow, 'James Goodnight, Founder and CEO, SAS Institute', *Computer Reseller News*, 12 December 2005, 23; 'Doing Well by Being Rather Nice', *Economist*, 1 December 2007, 84; 'SAS Turned Down "Numerous" Acquisition Inquiries This Year, Says CEO', *CMP TechWeb*, 17 December 2007.

8 C. Vander Doelen, 'Toyota Hiring in Woodstock', *Windsor Star*, 30 November 2007; D. Welch, 'Staying Paranoid at Toyota', *BusinessWeek*, 2 July 2007, 80; H. Takeuchi, E. Osono and N. Shimizu, 'The Contradictions That Drive Toyota's Success', *Harvard Business Review* 86, no. 6 (2008): 96–104.

9 C. A. O'Reilly III, J. Chatman and D. F. Caldwell, 'People and Organizational Culture: A Profile Comparison Approach to Assessing Person–Organization Fit', *Academy of Management Journal* 34, no. 3 (1991): 487–516; J. J. van Muijen, 'Organizational Culture', in *A Handbook of Work and Organizational Psychology: Organizational Psychology*, ed. P. J. D. Drenth, H. Thierry and C. J. de Wolff, 2nd edn (East Sussex, UK: Psychology Press, 1998), 113–132; P. A. Balthazard, R. A. Cooke and R. E. Potter, 'Dysfunctional Culture, Dysfunctional Organization: Capturing the Behavioral Norms That Form Organizational Culture and Drive Performance', *Journal of Managerial Psychology* 21, no. 8 (2006): 709–732; C. Helfrich *et al.*, 'Assessing an Organizational Culture Instrument Based on the Competing Values Framework: Exploratory and Confirmatory Factor Analyses', *Implementation Science* 2, no. 1 (2007): 13. For recent reviews of organisational culture survey instruments, see T. Scott *et al.*, 'The Quantitative Measurement of Organizational Culture in Health Care: A Review of the Available Instruments', *Health Services Research* 38, no. 3 (2003): 923–945; D. E. Leidner and T. Kayworth, 'A Review of Culture in Information Systems Research: Toward a Theory of Information Technology Culture Conflict', *MIS Quarterly* 30, no. 2 (2006): 357–399; S. Scott-Findlay and C. A. Estabrooks, 'Mapping the Organizational Culture Research in Nursing: A Literature Review', *Journal of Advanced Nursing* 56, no. 5 (2006): 498–513.

10 J. Martin, P. J. Frost and O. A. O'Neill, 'Organizational Culture: Beyond Struggles for Intellectual Dominance', in *Handbook of Organization Studies*, ed. S. Clegg *et al.*, 2nd edn (London: Sage, 2006), 725–753; N. E. Fenton and S. Inglis, 'A Critical Perspective on Organizational Values', *Nonprofit Management and Leadership* 17, no. 3 (2007): 335–347; K. Haukelid, 'Theories of (Safety) Culture Revisited—An Anthropological Approach', *Safety Science* 46, no. 3 (2008): 413–426.

11 J. Martin and C. Siehl, 'Organizational Culture and Counterculture: An Uneasy Symbiosis', *Organizational Dynamics* 12, no. 2 (1983): 52–64; G. Hofstede, 'Identifying Organizational Subcultures: An Empirical Approach', *Journal of Management Studies* 35, no. 1 (1990): 1–12; E. Ogbonna and L. C. Harris, 'Organisational Culture in the Age of the Internet: An Exploratory Study', *New Technology, Work and Employment* 21, no. 2 (2006): 162–175.

12 H. Silver, 'Does a University Have a Culture?', *Studies in Higher Education* 28, no. 2 (2003): 157–169.

13 A. Sinclair, 'Approaches to Organizational Culture and Ethics', *Journal of Business Ethics* 12, no. 1 (1993): 63–73; A. Boisnier and J. Chatman, 'The Role of Subcultures in Agile Organizations', in *Leading and Managing People in Dynamic Organizations*, ed. R. Petersen and E. Mannix (Mahwah, NJ: Lawrence Erlbaum, 2003), 87–112; C. Morrill, M. N. Zald and H. Rao, 'Covert Political Conflict in Organizations: Challenges from Below', *Annual Review of Sociology* 29 (2003): 391–415.

14 J. S. Ott, *The Organizational Culture Perspective* (Pacific Grove, CA: Brooks/Cole, 1989), ch. 2; J. S. Pederson and J. S. Sorensen, *Organizational Cultures in Theory and Practice* (Aldershot, UK: Gower, 1989), 27–29; M. O. Jones, *Studying Organizational Symbolism: What, How, Why?* (Thousand Oaks, CA: Sage, 1996).

15 E. H. Schein, 'Organizational Culture', *American Psychologist* 45, no. 2 (1990): 109–119; A. Furnham and B. Gunter, 'Corporate Culture: Definition, Diagnosis, and Change', *International Review of Industrial and Organizational Psychology* 8 (1993): 233–261; E. H. Schein, *The Corporate Culture Survival Guide* (San Francisco: Jossey-Bass, 1999), ch. 4.

16 M. Doehrman, 'Anthropologists—Deep in the Corporate Bush', *Daily Record (Kansas City, MO)*, 19 July 2005, 1.

17 K. Roman, 'The House That Ogilvy Built', *strategy+business*, 29 April 2009, 1–5.

18 C. J. Boudens, 'The Story of Work: A Narrative Analysis of Workplace Emotion', *Organization Studies* 26, no. 9 (2005): 1285–1306; S. Denning, *The Leader's Guide to Storytelling* (San Francisco: Jossey-Bass, 2005).

19 A. L. Wilkins, 'Organizational Stories as Symbols Which Control the Organization', in *Organizational Symbolism*, ed. L. R. Pondy *et al.* (Greenwich, CT: JAI Press, 1984), 81–92; R. Zemke, 'Storytelling: Back to a Basic', *Training* 27 (March 1990): 44–50; J. C. Meyer, 'Tell Me a Story: Eliciting Organizational Values from Narratives', *Communication Quarterly* 43, no. 2 (1995): 210–224; W. Swap *et al.*, 'Using Mentoring and Storytelling to Transfer Knowledge in the Workplace', *Journal of Management Information Systems* 18, no. 1 (2001): 95–114.

20 M. Miller, 'The Acrobat', *Forbes*, 15 March 2004, 100–103; R. Ouzounian, 'Cirque's Dream Factory', *Toronto Star*, 1 August 2004.

21 'The Ultimate Chairman', *Business Times Singapore*, 3 September 2005.

22 D. Roth, 'My Job at the Container Store', *Fortune*, 10 January 2000, 74–78.

23 R. E. Quinn and N. T. Snyder, 'Advance Change Theory: Culture Change at Whirlpool Corporation', in *The Leader's Change Handbook*, ed. J. A. Conger, G. M. Spreitzer and E. E. Lawler III (San Francisco: Jossey-Bass, 1999), 162–193.

24 Churchill apparently made this statement on 28 October 1943, in the British House of Commons, when London, damaged by bombings in World War II, was about to be rebuilt.

25 G. Turner and J. Myerson, *New Workspace New Culture: Office Design as a Catalyst for Change* (Aldershot, UK: Gower, 1998).

26 K. D. Elsbach and B. A. Bechky, 'It's More Than a Desk: Working Smarter through Leveraged Office Design', *California Management Review* 49, no. 2 (2007): 80–101.

27 M. Burton, 'Open Plan, Open Mind', *Director*, March 2005, 68–72; B. Murray, 'Agency Profile: Mother London', *Ihaveanidea*, 28 January 2007, www.ihaveanidea.org (accessed 21 May 2009).

28 J. Hewett, 'Office Politics', *Australian Financial Review*, 27 September 2003, 29.

29 Carapiet, 'NAB's John Stewart Knows His ABCs'; J. H. Want, *Corporate Culture: Key Strategies of High-Performing Business Cultures* (New York: St. Martin's Press, 2007), 38.

30 J. C. Collins and J. I. Porras, *Built to Last: Successful Habits of Visionary Companies* (London: Century, 1994); T. E. Deal and A. A. Kennedy, *The New Corporate Cultures* (Cambridge, MA: Perseus Books, 1999); R. Barrett, *Building a Values-Driven Organization: A Whole System Approach to Cultural Transformation* (Burlington, MA: Butterworth-Heinemann, 2006); J. M. Kouzes and B. Z. Posner, *The Leadership Challenge*, 4th edn (San Francisco: Jossey-Bass, 2007), ch. 3.

31 C. Siehl and J. Martin, 'Organizational Culture: A Key to Financial Performance?', in *Organizational Climate and Culture*, ed. B. Schneider (San Francisco, CA: Jossey-Bass, 1990), 241–281; G. G. Gordon and N. DiTomasco, 'Predicting Corporate Performance from Organizational Culture', *Journal of Management Studies* 29, no. 6 (1992): 783–798; J. P. Kotter and J. L. Heskett, *Corporate Culture and Performance* (New York: Free Press, 1992); C. P. M. Wilderom, U. Glunk and R. Maslowski, 'Organizational Culture as a Predictor of Organizational Performance', in *Handbook of Organizational Culture and Climate*, ed. N. M. Ashkanasy, C. P. M. Wilderom and M. F. Peterson (Thousand Oaks, CA: Sage, 2000), 193–210; A. Carmeli and A. Tishler, 'The Relationships between Intangible Organizational Elements and Organizational Performance', *Strategic Management Journal* 25, no. 13 (2004): 1257–1278; S. Teerikangas and P. Very, 'The Culture-Performance Relationship in M&A: From Yes/No to How', *British Journal of Management* 17, no. S1 (2006): S31–S48.

32 A. Krishnan, 'CEOs from the Best Provide Insights Gained from Hewitt Best Employers Study', *The Edge (Malaysia)*, 21 July 2008.

33 J. C. Helms Mills and A. J. Mills, 'Rules, Sensemaking, Formative Contexts, and Discourse in the Gendering of Organizational Culture', in *International Handbook of Organizational Climate and Culture*, ed. N. Ashkanasy, C. Wilderom and M. Peterson (Thousand Oaks, CA: Sage, 2000), 55–70; J. A. Chatman and S. E. Cha, 'Leading by Leveraging Culture', *California Management Review* 45 (Summer 2003): 20–34.

34 M. Fahrer, 'Culture, Strategy, and Risk Management—A New Perspective', *InFinsia*, September 2006, 6–9.

35 B. Ashforth and F. Mael, 'Social Identity Theory and the Organization', *Academy of Management Review* 14 (1989): 20–39.

36 Heidrick & Struggles, *Leadership Challenges Emerge as Asia Pacific Companies Go Global* (Melbourne: Heidrick & Struggles, August 2008).

37 M. R. Louis, 'Surprise and Sensemaking: What Newcomers Experience in Entering Unfamiliar Organizational Settings', *Administrative Science Quarterly* 25 (1980): 226–251; S. G. Harris, 'Organizational Culture and Individual Sensemaking: A Schema-Based Perspective', *Organization Science* 5, no. 3 (1994): 309–321.

38 J. W. Barnes *et al.*, 'The Role of Culture Strength in Shaping Sales Force Outcomes', *Journal of Personal Selling & Sales Management* 26, no. 3 (2006): 255–270.

39 L. M. Fisher, 'How Dell Got Soul', *strategy+business*, 9 July 2004, 1–14; N. Byrnes, P. Burrows and L. Lee, 'Dark Days at Dell', *BusinessWeek*, 4 September 2006, 26; M. Kessler, 'Dell Reverses, Steps into Wal-Mart', *USA Today*, 25 May 2007, B1; S. Lohr, 'Can Michael Dell Refocus His Namesake?', *New York Times*, 9 September 2007, 1; D. Zehr, 'Dell Challenge: New Ideas and Less Red Tape', *Austin American-Statesman*, 4 February 2007, A1; Waterstone Human Capital and National Post, *Canada's 10 Most Admired Corporate Cultures, 2007* (Toronto: Waterstone Human Capital and National Post, February 2008).

40 C. A. O'Reilly III and J. A. Chatman, 'Culture as Social Control: Corporations, Cults, and Commitment', *Research in Organizational Behavior* 18 (1996): 157–200; B. Spector and H. Lane, 'Exploring the Distinctions between a High Performance Culture and a Cult', *Strategy & Leadership* 35, no. 3 (2007): 18–24.

41 Fisher, 'How Dell Got Soul', 6.

42 Kotter and Heskett, *Corporate Culture and Performance*; J. P. Kotter, 'Cultures and Coalitions', *Executive Excellence* 15 (March 1998): 14–15; B. M. Bass and R. E. Riggio, *Transformational Leadership*, 2nd edn (New York: Routledge, 2006), ch. 7. The term *adaptive culture* has a different meaning in organisational behaviour than it has in cultural anthropology, where it refers to nonmaterial cultural conditions (such as ways of thinking) that lag behind the material culture (physical artefacts). For the anthropological perspective, see W. Griswold, *Cultures and Societies in a Changing World*, 3rd edn (Thousand Oaks, CA: Pine Forge Press (Sage), 2008), 66.

43 W. E. Baker and J. M. Sinkula, 'The Synergistic Effect of Market Orientation and Learning Orientation on Organizational Performance', *Academy of Marketing Science Journal* 27, no. 4 (1999): 411–427; Z. Emden, A. Yaprak and S. T. Cavusgil, 'Learning from Experience in International Alliances: Antecedents and Firm Performance Implications', *Journal of Business Research* 58, no. 7 (2005): 883–892.

44 A. Maitland and K. Rollins, 'The Two-in-a-Box World of Dell', *Financial Times (London)*, 20 March 2003, 14.

45 D. Ho, 'Michael Dell Says He Had No Role in Accounting Scandal', *Cox News Service*, 6 September 2007.

46 M. L. Marks, 'Adding Cultural Fit to Your Diligence Checklist', *Mergers & Acquisitions* 34, no. 3 (1999): 14–20; Schein, *The Corporate Culture Survival*, ch. 8; M. L. Marks, 'Mixed Signals', *Across the Board*, May 2000, 21–26; J. P. Daly, R. W. Pouder and B. Kabanoff, 'The Effects of Initial Differences in Firms' Espoused Values on Their Postmerger Performance', *Journal of Applied Behavioral Science* 40, no. 3 (2004): 323–343.

47 Teerikangas and Very, 'The Culture-Performance Relationship in M&A'; G. K. Stahl and A. Voigt, 'Do Cultural Differences Matter in Mergers and Acquisitions? A Tentative Model and Examination', *Organization Science* 19, no. 1 (2008): 160–176.

48 E. Connors, 'Not Drowning, Dancing', *Australian Financial Review*, 12 November 2004, 22.

49 C. A. Schorg, C. A. Raiborn and M. F. Massoud, 'Using a "Cultural Audit" to Pick M&A Winners', *Journal of Corporate Accounting & Finance* 15, no. 4 (2004): 47–55; W. Locke, 'Higher Education Mergers: Integrating Organisational Cultures and Developing Appropriate Management Styles', *Higher Education Quarterly* 61, no. 1 (2007): 83–102.

50 S. Greengard, 'Due Diligence: The Devil in the Details', *Workforce*, October 1999, 68; Marks, 'Adding Cultural Fit to Your Diligence Checklist'.

51 A. R. Malekazedeh and A. Nahavandi, 'Making Mergers Work by Managing Cultures', *Journal of Business Strategy* 11, no. 3 (1990): 55–57; K. W. Smith, 'A Brand-New Culture for the Merged Firm', *Mergers & Acquisitions* 35 (June 2000): 45–50.

52 T. Hamilton, 'RIM on a Roll', *Toronto Star*, 22 February 2004, C01.

53 R. Goyder, 'Sustaining High Performance', CEOForum (Melbourne/Sydney: CEO Forum Group, September 2006), http://ceoforum.com.au (accessed 21 May 2009).

54 Hewitt Associates, 'Mergers and Acquisitions May Be Driven by Business Strategy—But Often Stumble over People and Culture Issues', news release (Lincolnshire, IL, 3 August 1998).

55 R. Brand, 'Chipotle Founder Had Big Dreams', *Rocky Mountain News (Denver)*, 23 December 2006, 1C; M. Heffernan, 'Dreamers: Chipotle Founder Steve Ells', *Reader's Digest*, 15 September 2008; B. Krummert, 'There Will Be Lines', *Restaurant Hospitality*, August 2008, 42.

56 E. Johnson, 'NAB Focus Switches Back to Core Home Business', *Sydney Morning Herald*, 13 March 2009, 21.

57 J. Martin, 'Can Organizational Culture Be Managed?', in *Organizational Culture*, ed. P. J. Frost *et al.* (Beverly Hills, CA: Sage, 1985), 95–98.

58 E. H. Schein, 'The Role of the Founder in Creating Organizational Culture', *Organizational Dynamics* 12, no. 1 (1983): 13–28; R. House, M. Javidan and P. Dorfman, 'Project GLOBE: An Introduction', *Applied Psychology: An International Review* 50, no. 4 (2001): 489–505; R. House *et al.*, 'Understanding Cultures and Implicit Leadership Theories across the Globe: An Introduction to Project GLOBE', *Journal of World Business* 37, no. 1 (2002): 3–10.

59 A. S. Tsui *et al.*, 'Unpacking the Relationship between CEO Leadership Behavior and Organizational Culture', *Leadership Quarterly* 17, no. 2 (2006): 113–137; Y. Berson, S. Oreg and T. Dvir, 'CEO Values, Organizational Culture and Firm Outcomes', *Journal of Organizational Behavior* 29, no. 5 (2008): 615–633.

60 'Oxygen Is a Breath of Fresh Air', *New Zealand Herald*, 11 August 2004, E32; 'Oxygen Gives the Kiss of Life (Outsourcing: A Special Advertising Report)', *The Australian*, 21 January 2005, 23; P. Broekhuyse, 'Eyes on Asia for Oxygen Culture Vulture Dickinson', *The Australian*, 3 May 2005, 36; K. McLaughlin, 'Sales Looms for Carter's High-Flyer', *National Business Review (NZ)*, 20 May 2005.

61 R. Gluyas, 'Back to Grass Roots: Stewart's Culture Shock', *The Australian*, 4 November 2006, 33; Carapiet, 'NAB's John Stewart Knows His ABCs'; Dellaportas, Cooper and Braica, 'Leadership, Culture and Employee Deceit'; M. Stevens, 'Success and Succession: Stewart Bloodied but Unbowed', *The Australian*, 31 July 2008, 19.

62 M. De Pree, *Leadership Is an Art* (East Lansing, MI: Michigan State University Press, 1987).

63 B. McLean, 'Inside the Money Machine', *Fortune*, 6 September 2004, 84.

64 J. Kerr and J. W. Slocum Jr, 'Managing Corporate Culture through Reward Systems', *Academy of Management Executive* 1 (May 1987): 99–107; J. M. Higgins *et al.*, 'Using Cultural Artifacts to Change and Perpetuate Strategy', *Journal of Change Management* 6, no. 4 (2006): 397–415.

65 'Clear Company Values Foster Healthy Attitude', *Independent Financial Review*, 7 May 2008; J. Leslie, 'Powerful Boost for Brigade', *Port Curtis Post (Gladstone, Qld)*, 1 September 2008, 12.

66 B. Schneider, 'The People Make the Place', *Personnel Psychology* 40, no. 3 (1987): 437–453; B. Schneider *et al.*, 'Personality and Organizations: A Test of the Homogeneity of Personality Hypothesis', *Journal of Applied Psychology* 83, no. 3 (1998): 462–470; T. R. Giberson, C. J. Resick and M. W. Dickson, 'Embedding Leader Characteristics: An Examination of Homogeneity of Personality and Values in Organizations', *Journal of Applied Psychology* 90, no. 5 (2005): 1002–1010.

67 T. A. Judge and D. M. Cable, 'Applicant Personality, Organizational Culture, and Organization Attraction', *Personnel Psychology* 50, no. 2 (1997): 359–394; D. S. Chapman *et al.*, 'Applicant Attraction to Organizations and Job Choice: A Meta-Analytic Review of the Correlates of Recruiting Outcomes', *Journal of Applied Psychology* 90, no. 5 (2005): 928–944; A. L. Kristof-Brown, R. D. Zimmerman and E. C. Johnson, 'Consequences of Individuals' Fit at Work: A Meta-Analysis of Person-Job, Person-Organization, Person-Group, and Person-Supervisor Fit', *Personnel Psychology* 58, no. 2 (2005): 281–342; C. Hu, H.-C. Su and C.-I. B. Chen, 'The Effect of Person-Organization Fit Feedback Via Recruitment Web Sites on Applicant Attraction', *Computers in Human Behavior* 23, no. 5 (2007): 2509–2523.

68 A. L. Kristof-Brown, 'Perceived Applicant Fit: Distinguishing between Recruiters' Perceptions of Person-Job and Person-Organization Fit', *Personnel Psychology* 53, no. 3 (2000): 643–671; A. E. M. Van Vianen, 'Person-Organization Fit: The Match between Newcomers' and Recruiters' Preferences for Organizational Cultures', *Personnel Psychology* 53, no. 1 (2000): 113–149.

69 S. Cruz, 'Park Place Lexus Mission Viejo Seeing Improvements', *Orange County Business Journal (Irvine, CA)*, 12 May 2008, 15; C. Hall, '"Emotional Intelligence" Counts in Job Hires', *Dallas Morning News*, 20 August 2008.

70 D. M. Cable and J. R. Edwards, 'Complementary and Supplementary Fit: A Theoretical and Empirical Integration', *Journal of Applied Psychology* 89, no. 5 (2004): 822–834.

71 J. Van Maanen, 'Breaking In: Socialization to Work', in *Handbook of Work, Organization, and Society*, ed. R. Dubin (Chicago: Rand McNally, 1976), 67–130.

72 E. Simon, 'Employers Study Applicants' Personalities', *Associated Press*, 5 November 2007. Also see the Lindblad video at www.expeditions.com/Theater17.asp?Media=475

73 D. G. Allen, 'Do Organizational Socialization Tactics Influence Newcomer Embeddedness and Turnover?', *Journal of Management* 32, no. 2 (2006): 237–256; A. M. Saks, K. L. Uggerslev and N. E. Fassina, 'Socialization Tactics and Newcomer Adjustment: A Meta-Analytic Review and Test of a Model', *Journal of Vocational Behavior* 70, no. 3 (2007): 413–446.

74 E. Johnston, 'Elf Boys', *Boss Magazine*, 8 June 2001, 26; S. Hart, 'Beat the New Job Blues', *New Zealand Herald*, 24 January 2005, D01.

75 G. T. Chao *et al.*, 'Organizational Socialization: Its Content and Consequences', *Journal of Applied Psychology* 79, no. 5

(1994): 730–743; H. D. Cooper-Thomas and N. Anderson, 'Organizational Socialization: A Field Study into Socialization Success and Rate', *International Journal of Selection and Assessment* 13, no. 2 (2005): 116–128.

76 N. Nicholson, 'A Theory of Work Role Transitions', *Administrative Science Quarterly* 29, no. 2 (1984): 172–191; B. E. Ashforth, D. M. Sluss and A. M. Saks, 'Socialization Tactics, Proactive Behavior, and Newcomer Learning: Integrating Socialization Models', *Journal of Vocational Behavior* 70, no. 3 (2007): 447–462; T. N. Bauer, 'Newcomer Adjustment During Organizational Socialization: A Meta-Analytic Review of Antecedents, Outcomes, and Methods', *Journal of Applied Psychology* 92, no. 3 (2007): 707–721; A. Elfering *et al.*, 'First Years in Job: A Three-Wave Analysis of Work Experiences', *Journal of Vocational Behavior* 70, no. 1 (2007): 97–115.

77 J. M. Beyer and D. R. Hannah, 'Building on the Past: Enacting Established Personal Identities in a New Work Setting', *Organization Science* 13, no. 6 (2002): 636–652; H. D. C. Thomas and N. Anderson, 'Newcomer Adjustment: The Relationship between Organizational Socialization Tactics, Information Acquisition and Attitudes', *Journal of Occupational and Organizational Psychology* 75, no. 4 (2002): 423–437.

78 L. W. Porter, E. E. Lawler III and J. R. Hackman, *Behavior in Organizations* (New York: McGraw-Hill, 1975), 163–167; Van Maanen, 'Breaking In: Socialization to Work'; D. C. Feldman, 'The Multiple Socialization of Organization Members', *Academy of Management Review* 6 (1981): 309–318.

79 B. E. Ashforth and A. M. Saks, 'Socialization Tactics: Longitudinal Effects on Newcomer Adjustment', *Academy of Management Journal* 39 (1996): 149–178; J. D. Kammeyer-Mueller and C. R. Wanberg, 'Unwrapping the Organizational Entry Process: Disentangling Multiple Antecedents and Their Pathways to Adjustment', *Journal of Applied Psychology* 88, no. 5 (2003): 779–794.

80 Porter, Lawler III and Hackman, *Behavior in Organizations*, ch. 5.

81 Louis, 'Surprise and Sensemaking'.

82 S. L. Robinson and D. M. Rousseau, 'Violating the Psychological Contract: Not the Exception but the Norm', *Journal of Organizational Behavior* 15, no. 3 (1994): 245–259.

83 D. L. Nelson, 'Organizational Socialization: A Stress Perspective', *Journal of Organizational Behavior* 8 (1987): 311–324; Elfering *et al.*, 'First Years in Job'.

84 J. P. Wanous, *Organizational Entry* (Reading, MA: Addison-Wesley, 1992); J. A. Breaugh and M. Starke, 'Research on Employee Recruitment: So Many Studies, So Many Remaining Questions', *Journal of Management* 26, no. 3 (2000): 405–434.

85 R. A. R. C. Moffitt, *Report of the Review of Submarine Workforce Sustainability* (Canberra: Chief of Navy, Australian Defence Force, 31 October 2008), 12–13; A. D. F. Chief of Navy, *Navy's Response to the Submarine Workforce Sustainability Review* (Canberra: Chief of Navy, Australian Defence Force, 8 April 2009), 6.

86 J. M. Phillips, 'Effects of Realistic Job Previews on Multiple Organizational Outcomes: A Meta-Analysis', *Academy of Management Journal* 41 (December 1998): 673–690.

87 Y. Ganzach *et al.*, 'Social Exchange and Organizational Commitment: Decision-Making Training for Job Choice as an Alternative to the Realistic Job Preview', *Personnel Psychology* 55, no. 3 (2002): 613–637.

88 C. Ostroff and S. W. J. Koslowski, 'Organizational Socialization as a Learning Process: The Role of Information Acquisition', *Personnel Psychology* 45, no. 4 (1992): 849–874; Cooper-Thomas and Anderson, 'Organizational Socialization'; A. Baber and L. Waymon, 'Uncovering the Unconnected Employee', *T&D*, May 2008, 60–66.

89 C. Fishman, 'The Anarchist's Cookbook', *Fast Company*, July 2004, 70; 'World's Finest Food Retailers: Whole Foods, Not Holy Food', *The Grocer*, 12 November 2005, 32.

90 L. Buchanan, 'That's Chief Entertainment Officer', *Inc.*, 1 August 2007, 86–94; P. Burkes Erickson, 'Welcoming Employees: Making That First Day a Great Experience', *Daily Oklahoman*, 15 July 2007.

CHAPTER 15

organisational change

LEARNING OBJECTIVES

After reading this chapter, you should be able to:

- describe the elements of Lewin's force field analysis model
- outline six reasons why people resist organisational change
- discuss six strategies for minimising resistance to change
- outline the conditions for effectively diffusing change from a pilot project
- describe the action research approach to organisational change
- outline the 'Four-D' model of appreciative inquiry and explain how this approach differs from action research
- explain how parallel learning structures assist the change process
- discuss three ethical issues in organisational change.

Kim Kyung Hoon/Reuters

LG Electronics' CEO Nam Yong has introduced several changes to help the company become more of a global organisation.

LG Electronics generates 80 per cent of its revenue, manufactures 60 per cent of its products and employs two-thirds of its 90 000 employees outside Korea. Even with this global footprint, LG (and other Korean firms such as Samsung, Hyundai and SK) remains mainly a Korean company. For example, until recently, all of LG's 84 foreign branches and subsidiaries were led by Koreans.

Nam Yong, chief executive and vice chairman of LG Electronics, aims to transform LG into a 'company with no nationality'. He has hired several American and European executives into key positions and announced that one-third of LG's foreign operations will be led by non-Koreans over the next few years. English is now the required language in emails and at headquarters meetings. 'What we are doing is not just replacing Koreans with foreigners,' Nam explains. 'We want to change the corporate culture. After three or four years, nationality or gender won't be taken into account when hiring top positions. Only performance and capability will be considered.'

Nam is also shifting LG from a engineering-centred culture to one that is more customer- and design-focused. 'The most important part of the change is the customer orientation,' he suggests. Furthermore, in contrast to Korea's high power-distance culture, he is encouraging employees to have more open debate with senior managers. To support a performance culture, Nam introduced performance metrics for employees, including a signal-lighting system (green, yellow, red) so staff know how well they are performing. LG managers are evaluated by the financial return on invested capital (rather than revenue growth) of their business operations. Head office no longer doles out strategic funds and extra staff; instead, these expenses are paid by the local operations.

Nam acknowledges that these changes have not come easily. 'We had at least six months of a chaotic situation,' Nam admits, referring to the managers' new roles and expectations. Some staff also remain sceptical, pointing out that some of Nam's changes in his previous position at LG Telecom were eventually scrapped. Still, LG managers and employees are embracing Nam's vision for a more global enterprise, and one where change will be a regular part of work life.

'This [LG's long-term success through continuous improvement] is possible through effective change management,' explains Daya Prakash, head of information technology at LG Electronics India. 'Thus change management is a very important element of success of an organisation.'[1]

The transformation of LG Electronics from a Korean to a global organisation illustrates many of the strategies and practices necessary to successfully change organisations. It reveals how CEO Nam Yong created an urgency to change, revised systems and structures to support the change, and personally role-modelled the desired changes. Although LG Electronics' transformation sounds as though it was a relatively smooth transition, most organisational change is messy, requiring considerable leadership effort and vigilance. As we will describe throughout this chapter, the challenge of change is not so much in deciding which way to go; the challenge is in the execution of this strategy.

This chapter begins by introducing Lewin's model of change and its component parts. This includes sources of resistance to change, ways to minimise this resistance and ways to stabilise desired behaviours. Next, the chapter examines four approaches to organisational change—action research, appreciative inquiry, large-group interventions and parallel learning structures. The last section of this chapter considers both cross-cultural and ethical issues in organisational change.

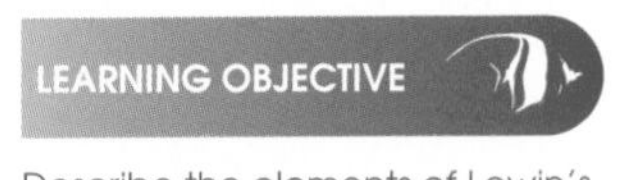

Describe the elements of Lewin's force field analysis model.

LEWIN'S FORCE FIELD ANALYSIS MODEL

force field analysis Kurt Lewin's model of system-wide change that helps change agents diagnose the forces that drive and restrain proposed organisational change.

Social psychologist Kurt Lewin developed the force field analysis model to explain how the change process works (see Exhibit 15.1).[2] Although it was developed more than 50 years ago, recent reviews conclude that Lewin's **force field analysis** model remains one of the most widely respected ways of viewing this process.[3]

One side of the force field model represents the *driving forces* that push organisations toward a new state of affairs. These might include new competitors or technologies, evolving workforce

Exhibit 15.1 *Lewin's Force Field Analysis Model*

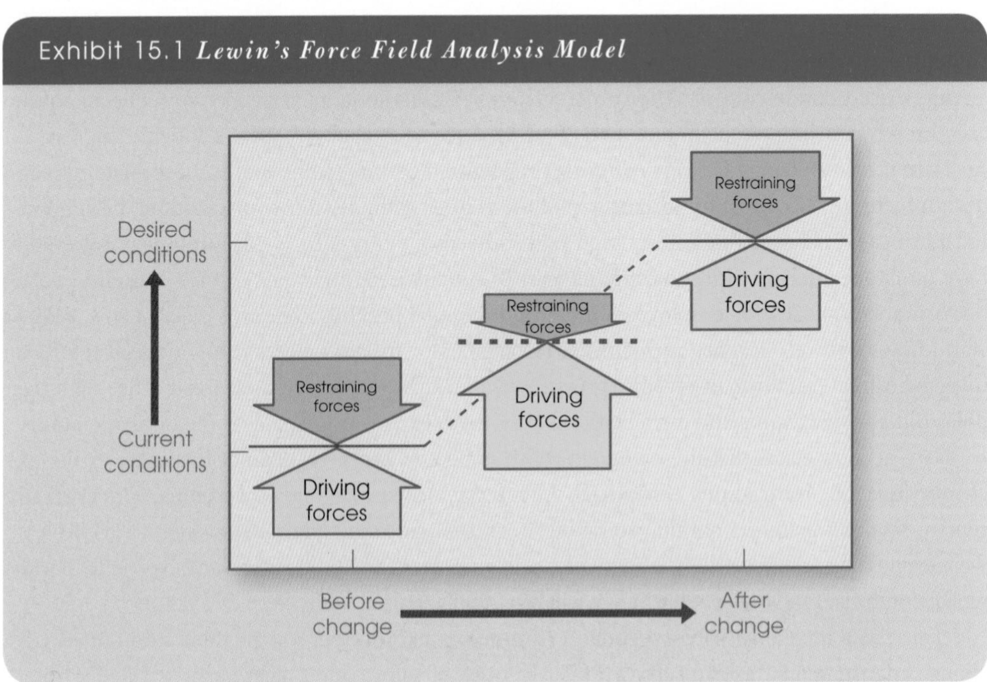

expectations or a host of other environmental changes. Corporate leaders also produce driving forces even when external forces for change aren't apparent. For instance, some experts call for 'divine discontent' as a key feature of successful organisations, meaning that leaders continually urge employees to strive for higher standards or new innovations even when the company outshines the competition.

The other side of Lewin's model represents the *restraining forces* that maintain the status quo. These restraining forces are commonly called 'resistance to change' because they appear as employee behaviours that block the change process. Stability occurs when the driving and restraining forces are roughly in equilibrium, that is, they are of approximately equal strength in opposite directions.

Lewin's force field model emphasises that effective change occurs by **unfreezing** the current situation, moving to a desired condition and then **refreezing** the system so that it remains in the desired state. Unfreezing involves producing disequilibrium between the driving and restraining forces. As we will describe later, this may occur by increasing the driving forces, reducing the restraining forces, or having a combination of both. Refreezing occurs when the organisation's systems and structures are aligned with the desired behaviours. They must support and reinforce the new role patterns and prevent the organisation from slipping back into the old way of doing things. Over the next few pages, we use Lewin's model to understand why change is blocked and how the process can evolve more smoothly.

unfreezing The first part of the organisational change process, in which the change agent produces disequilibrium between the driving and restraining forces.

refreezing The latter part of the organisational change process, in which systems and conditions are introduced that reinforce and maintain the desired behaviours.

Restraining Forces

Robert Nardelli pushed hard to transform Home Depot from a decentralised configuration of entrepreneurial fiefdoms to a more centralised and performance-oriented operation. Change did occur at the world's largest home improvement retailer, but at a price. A large number of talented managers and employees left the company, and some of those remaining continued to resent Nardelli's transformation. Disenchanted staff referred to the company as 'Home Despot' because the changes took away their autonomy. Others named it 'Home GEpot', a cutting reference to the large number of former GE executives that Nardelli hired into top positions. After five years, the Home Depot board decided to replace Nardelli, partly because he made some unsuccessful strategic decisions and partly because of the dysfunctional after-effects of his changes.[4]

Robert Nardelli, who is now CEO of Chrysler, experienced employee *resistance to change* when he transformed Home Depot. Resistance to change takes many forms, ranging from overt work stoppages to subtle attempts to continue the 'old ways'. One recent study of bank employees reported that subtle resistance is much more common than overt resistance. Some employees in that study avoided the desired changes by moving into different jobs. Others continued to perform tasks the old way as long as management didn't notice. Even when employees complied with the planned changes, they engaged in resistance by putting forth less cognitive effort and by communicating nonverbally (and sometimes verbally!) to customers that they disliked the changes forced on them.[5]

Some experts point out that the subtle forms of resistance create the greatest obstacles to change because they are not as visible as overt resistance. In the words of one manager: '[Change efforts] never die because of direct confrontation. Direct confrontation you can work with because it is known. Rather, they die a death of a thousand cuts. People and issues you never confront

Not Hoppy about Change

Hoppy, a carbonated low-alcohol malt-and-hops beverage, was popular around Tokyo after World War II as a cheap alternative to expensive beer, but it fell out of favour as beer became affordable. Mina Ishiwatari (centre in photo), granddaughter of Hoppy Beverage Co.'s founder, was determined to improve Hoppy's image when she joined the company a decade ago.

Yoshiaki Miura/*Japan Times*

Unfortunately, the company's 30 employees—mostly men in their fifties who were family relatives—didn't want to disturb their cosy jobs. 'It was a turbulent decade of eliminating evils from the company and rebuilding a new organisation from scratch,' recalls Ishiwatari, who began as a rank-and-file employee and is now the company's executive vice president. 'I tried to take a new marketing approach to change the image of Hoppy ... but no one would listen to me.' With limited support and budget, Ishiwatari developed a website that informed the public about the product, sold it online and documented Ishiwatari's views in an early weblog. As the contemporary marketing caught the attention of health-conscious young people, Hoppy sales doubled to about US$25 million annually, even though it is sold only around Tokyo. Most employees who opposed Ishiwatari's radical changes have since left the company; almost all of the 43 current staff members were hired by Ishiwatari and support her vision of Hoppy's future.[8]

drain the life out of important [initiatives] and result in solutions that simply do not have the performance impact that they should have.'[6]

John Thompson experienced this subtle resistance to change soon after he became CEO of Symantec Corporation. To reduce costs, Thompson suggested that the computer cable included in all Symantec software packages was an unnecessary expense because most customers already owned these cables. Everyone at the cost-cutting meeting agreed that the cables should no longer be shipped with the software but would be provided free to customers who requested them. Yet several weeks later Thompson discovered that computer cables were still being shipped with the software, so he reminded the executive responsible that the team makes these decisions only once. 'If you've got a disagreement or a point of view, bring it up when we're going through the discussion,' Thompson advised the executive. 'Don't hold back and give me this smiley kind of benign agreement. Go back and get it fixed. We're not shipping cables any more.'[7]

Employee Resistance as a Resource for Change

Although Symantec's CEO was probably frustrated by the executive's passive resistance to change, change agents need to realise that resistance is a common and natural human response. As economist John Kenneth Galbraith once quipped, 'In the choice between changing one's mind and proving there's no need to do so, most people get busy on the proof!'[9] Even when people do support change, they typically assume that it is others—not themselves—who need to change. The problem, however, isn't so much that resistance to change exists. The main problem is that change agents typically view resistance as an unreasonable, dysfunctional and irrational response to a desirable initiative. They often form an 'us versus them' perspective without considering that the causes of resistance may, in fact, be traced back to their own actions or inaction.[10]

The emerging view among change management experts is that resistance to change needs to be seen as a resource to improve the change process. First, resistance incidents are symptoms of deeper problems in the change process. They are signals that the change agent has not sufficiently addressed the underlying conditions that support effective organisational change.[11] In some situations, employees may be worried about the *consequences* of change, such as how the new conditions will take away their power and status. In other situations, employees show resistance because of concerns about the *process* of change itself, such as the effort required to break old habits and learn new skills.

Second, resistance should be recognised as a form of constructive conflict. As was described in Chapter 11, constructive conflict can potentially improve decision making, including identifying better ways to improve the organisation's success. However, constructive conflict is typically accompanied by dysfunctional relationship conflict. This appears to be the case when change agents see resistance to change as an impediment rather than a resource. They describe the *people* who resist as the problem, whereas their focus should be on understanding the *reasons* why these people resist. Thus, by viewing resistance as a form of constructive conflict, change agents may be able to improve the change strategy or change process.

Finally, resistance should be viewed in the context of justice and motivation. Resistance is a form of voice, so it potentially improves procedural justice (see Chapter 5). By redirecting initial forms of resistance into constructive conversations, change agents can increase employee perceptions and feelings of fairness. Furthermore, resistance is motivational; it potentially engages people to think about the change strategy and process. Change agents can harness that motivational force to ultimately strengthen commitment to the change initiative.

Why Employees Resist Change

Outline six reasons why people resist organisational change.

Change management experts have developed a long list of reasons why people do not embrace change.[12] Many of these reasons relate to a lack of motivation. This occurs when employees estimate that the negative consequences the change might impose on them outweigh the positive consequences. Another factor is the inability to change due to inadequate skills and knowledge. Employees also resist change unwittingly because they lack a sufficiently clear understanding of what is expected of them (i.e. lack of role clarity). Six of the most commonly cited reasons why people resist change are summarised below.[13] Reality Check 15.1 describes how some of these sources of resistance existed at the FBI in spite of clear evidence that the law enforcement agency needed to develop a new mandate.

DIRECT COSTS People tend to block actions that result in higher direct costs or lower benefits than those in the existing situation. Reality Check 15.1 describes how some FBI managers likely resisted the bureau's new intelligence mandate because it would necessarily remove some of their resources, personal status and career opportunities.

The FBI Meets Its Own Resistance

AP Images

The FBI experienced many sources of resistance in its mandate of transforming from a reactive law enforcement agency into a proactive domestic intelligence agency.

In 1993, following the first terrorist attack on the World Trade Center, the US Federal Bureau of Investigation (FBI) was given a new mandate: refocus from a reactive law enforcement agency (solving crimes) to a proactive domestic intelligence agency (preventing terrorism). Eight years later, the FBI was still mainly a crime investigation organisation with limited intelligence-gathering capabilities. This failure to change was identified as a factor in the FBI's inability to prevent terrorist attacks on the same buildings, as well as the Pentagon, in 2001. One government report even stated that the FBI and the Central Intelligence Agency (CIA) 'seem to be working harder and harder just to maintain a status quo that is increasingly irrelevant to the new challenges'.

One source of resistance, according to government reports, is that FBI employees and managers are unable or unwilling to change

SAVING FACE Some people resist change as a political strategy to 'prove' that the decision is wrong or that the person encouraging change is incompetent. This 'not-invented-here' syndrome is widespread, according to change experts. Says one consultant, 'Unless they're scared enough to listen, they'll never forgive you for being right and for knowing something they don't.'[15]

FEAR OF THE UNKNOWN People resist change out of worry that they cannot adjust to the new work requirements. This fear of the unknown increases the *risk* of personal loss. For example, even if many FBI managers and professionals recognised that the agency should change its mandate, they likely were reluctant to push the changes forward because it is difficult to anticipate how this mandate would affect them personally.

BREAKING ROUTINES People typically resist initiatives that force them out of their comfort zones and require them to invest time and energy in learning new role patterns. Ray Davis, CEO of Umpqua Bank, calls this the rubber-band effect. 'When you are leading for growth, you know you are going to disrupt comfortable routines and ask for new behaviour, new priorities, new skills,' says Davis, whose bank is regarded as one of America's most

REALITY CHECK 15.1

because solving crimes (rather than intelligence gathering) is burned into their mindset, routines, career paths and decentralised structure. Most FBI field managers were trained in law enforcement, so they continue to give preferential treatment and resources to enforcement rather than terrorist prevention initiatives.

Even if FBI leaders were motivated to become more focused on intelligence gathering, the organisation's systems and structures undermine these initiatives. The FBI has been a decentralised organisation, where field agents operate without much orchestration from headquarters. Until recently, the FBI also lacked a secure centralised information system (in fact, most of its records were still paper-based), which is essential for intelligence work but less important for criminal investigations. Furthermore, information is so closely guarded further down the ranks (called 'close holds') that an information access barrier called 'the wall' isolates FBI intelligence officers from the mainstream criminal investigation staff. Overall, these structural characteristics effectively scuttled any attempt to transform the FBI into an intelligence agency.

Resistance to change was also likely due in part to a historical rivalry between the FBI and the CIA. Raising the profile and legitimacy of intelligence gathering at the FBI would have acknowledged that the CIA's work was valuable, so some FBI leaders and staff were reluctant to move in that direction.

The FBI is now taking concerted steps to address these barriers to change. But John Miller, the FBI's assistant director of the office of public affairs, admits that the FBI continues to face challenges. 'The FBI has no corner on the market of people being resistant to change,' he says. 'We don't recruit people from Planet Perfect; we recruit human beings.'[14]

innovative financial institutions. 'Even when we want to change, and *do* change, we tend to relax and the rubber band snaps us back into our comfort zones.'[16] Indeed, most employees in one Australian survey admitted they don't follow through with organisational changes because they 'like to keep things the way they are' or the changes seem to be too complicated or time wasting.[17]

INCONGRUENT TEAM DYNAMICS Teams develop and enforce conformity to a set of norms that guide behaviour. However, conformity to existing team norms may discourage employees from accepting organisational change. For example, American electronics retailer Best Buy introduced the results-only work environment (ROWE), in which employees were evaluated by their results, not their face time. Yet, even though the program allowed employees to arrive at work at any time, deviations were often met with half-humorous barbs from coworkers, such as 'Forgot to set your alarm clock again?' These rebukes, which were consistent with the team norms that previously governed face-time violations, undermined the ROWE program. Best Buy's consultants eventually set up sessions that warned employees about these taunts, which they called 'sludge'.[18]

INCONGRUENT ORGANISATIONAL SYSTEMS Rewards, information systems, patterns of authority, career paths, selection criteria, and other systems and structures are both friends and foes of organisational change. When properly aligned, they reinforce desired behaviours. When misaligned, they pull people back into their old attitudes and behaviours. Even enthusiastic employees lose momentum after failing to overcome the structural confines of the past.

UNFREEZING, CHANGING AND REFREEZING

According to Lewin's force field analysis model, effective change occurs by unfreezing the current situation, moving to a desired condition and then refreezing the system so that it remains in this desired state. Unfreezing occurs when the driving forces are stronger than the restraining forces. This happens by making the driving forces stronger, weakening or removing the restraining forces, or doing a combination of both.

Regarding the first option, driving forces must increase enough to motivate change. Change rarely occurs by increasing driving forces alone, however, because the restraining forces often adjust to counterbalance the driving forces. This is rather like the coils of a mattress. The harder corporate leaders push for change, the stronger the restraining forces push back. This antagonism threatens the change effort by producing tension and conflict within the organisation. The preferred option is to both increase the driving forces and reduce or remove the restraining forces. Increasing the driving forces creates an urgency for change, whereas reducing the restraining forces minimises resistance to change.

Creating an Urgency for Change

It is almost a cliché to say that organisations today operate in more dynamic, fast-paced environments than they did a few decades ago. These environmental pressures represent the driving forces that push employees out of their comfort zones. They energise people to face the risks that change creates. In many organisations, however, corporate leaders buffer employees from the external environment to such an extent that these driving forces are hardly felt by anyone below the top executive level. The result is that employees don't understand why they need to change and leaders are surprised when their change initiatives do not have much effect.

Simon Kelly discovered this problem when he was hired as chief financial officer of Aristocrat Leisure. The Sydney-based gaming technology firm had suffered significant losses as well as top management problems, but Kelly was surprised to discover that Aristocrat's employees seemed blissfully unaware of the company's woes. 'They managed to divorce themselves very well from the turmoil that was going on at the executive and board levels and in the media,' Kelly recalls. Only when Kelly and the incoming chief executive communicated the company's predicament did staff become more receptive to new attitudes and practices about reducing costs.[19] The point here is that the change process necessarily begins by ensuring that employees develop an urgency for change. This typically occurs by informing employees about competitors, changing consumer trends, impending government regulations and other driving forces in the external environment.[20]

Customer-Driven Change

Some companies fuel the urgency to change by putting employees in direct contact with customers. Dissatisfied customers represent a compelling driving force for change because of the adverse consequences for the organisation's survival and success. Customers also provide a human element that further energises employees to change current behaviour patterns.[21]

Executives at Shell Europe applied customer-driven change when they discovered that middle managers seemed blissfully unaware that Shell wasn't achieving either its financial goals or its customer needs. So, to create an urgency for change, the European managers were loaded onto buses and taken out to talk with customers and employees who work with customers every day. 'We called these "bus rides". The idea was to encourage people to think back from the customer's perspective rather than from the head office,' explains Shell Europe's vice president of retailing. 'The bus rides were difficult for a lot of people who, in their work history, had hardly ever had to talk to a customer and find out what was good and not so good about Shell from the customer's standpoint.'[22]

Creating an Urgency for Change without External Forces

Exposing employees to external forces can strengthen the urgency for change, but leaders often need to begin the change process before problems come knocking at the company's door. The challenge is greatest when companies are successful in their markets. Studies have found that when the organisation is performing well, decision makers become less vigilant of external threats and are more resistant to change. 'The biggest risk is that complacency can also come with that success,' warns Wesfarmers CEO Richard Goyder. 'That complacency may result in risk-aversion, or it may simply show up as a lack of urgency, as people take the foot off the accelerator and just assume that success will come as it always has.'[23]

Creating an urgency for change when the organisation is riding high requires a lot of persuasive influence that helps employees visualise future competitive threats and environmental shifts. 'You want to create a burning platform for change even when there isn't a need for one,' says Steve Bennett, CEO of financial software company Intuit.[24] For instance, Apple Computer's iPod dominates the digital music market, but Steve Jobs wants the company to be its own toughest competitor. Just when sales of the iPod Mini were soaring, Jobs challenged a gathering of 100 top executives and engineers to develop a better product to replace it. 'Playing it safe is the most dangerous thing we can do,' Jobs warned. Nine months later, the company launched the iPod Nano, which replaced the still-popular iPod Mini before competitors could offer a better alternative.[25]

Experts warn, however, that employees may see the burning-platform strategy as manipulative, a view that produces cynicism about change and undermines trust in the change agent.[26] Also, the urgency for change does not always need to be initiated from a problem-oriented perspective. Instead, as we will describe later in this chapter, effective change agents can adopt a positive orientation by championing a vision of a more appealing future state. By creating a future vision of a better organisation, leaders effectively make the current situation less appealing. When the vision connects to employee values and needs, it can be a motivating force for change even when external 'problems' are not strong.

Reducing the Restraining Forces

Discuss six strategies for minimising resistance to change.

Employee resistance should be viewed as a resource, but its underlying causes—the restraining forces—need to be addressed. As we explained earlier using the mattress-coil metaphor, it is not enough to increase the driving forces because employees often push back harder to

Exhibit 15.2 *Strategies for Minimising Resistance to Change*

Strategy	Example	When applied	Problems
Communication	Customer complaint letters are shown to employees.	When employees don't feel an urgency for change or don't know how the change will affect them.	Time-consuming and potentially costly.
Learning	Employees learn how to work in teams as company adopts a team-based structure.	When employees need to break old routines and adopt new role patterns.	Time-consuming and potentially costly.
Employee involvement	Company forms task force to recommend new customer service practices.	When the change effort needs more employee commitment, some employees need to save face and/or employee ideas would improve decisions about the change strategy.	Very time-consuming. Might lead to conflict and poor decisions if employees' interests are incompatible with organisational needs.
Stress management	Employees attend sessions to discuss their worries about the change.	When communication, training and involvement do not sufficiently ease employee worries.	Time-consuming and potentially expensive. Some methods may not reduce stress for all employees.
Negotiation	Employees agree to replace strict job categories with multiskilling in return for increased job security.	When employees will clearly lose something of value from the change and would not otherwise support the new conditions. Also necessary when the company must change quickly.	May be expensive, particularly if other employees want to negotiate their support. Also tends to produce compliance but not commitment to the change.
Coercion	Company president tells managers to 'get on board' the change or leave.	When other strategies are ineffective and the company needs to change quickly.	Can lead to more subtle forms of resistance, as well as long-term antagonism with the change agent.

Sources: Adapted from J. P. Kotter and L. A. Schlesinger, 'Choosing Strategies for Change', *Harvard Business Review* 57, no. 2 (1979): 106–114; P. R. Lawrence, 'How to Deal with Resistance to Change', *Harvard Business Review* 32, no. 3 (1954): 49–57.

offset the opposing force. Exhibit 15.2 summarises six strategies for addressing the sources of employee resistance. If feasible, communication, learning, employee involvement and stress management should be attempted first.[27] However, negotiation and coercion are necessary for people who will clearly lose something from the change, and in cases where the speed of change is critical.

Communication

Communication is the highest priority and first strategy required for any organisational change.[28] According to one recent survey, communication (together with involvement) is considered the top strategy for engaging employees in the change process.[29] Communication improves the change process in at least two ways. First, as mentioned earlier, leaders develop an urgency to change by candidly telling employees about the driving forces for change. Whether through town hall meetings with senior management or by directly meeting with disgruntled customers, employees become energised to change. Second, communication can potentially reduce fear of the unknown. The more corporate leaders communicate their vision of the future, the more easily employees can understand their own role in that future. This effort may also begin the process of adjusting team norms to be more consistent with the new reality.

Consider the situation at the Federal Bureau of Investigation, which was described earlier in Reality Check 15.1. The FBI experienced a high level of resistance to changing into an intelligence-gathering organisation. FBI leaders are now addressing that resistance by communicating in every way possible and to as many audiences as possible that the bureau must change, why it must change and what the new bureau will look like. 'The word is out. Terrorism is the No. 1 priority, and intelligence is what the bureau is about,' says former assistant attorney general Paul R. Corts, who has worked closely with the FBI during the change process. 'You've got to say it, say it, and say it again.'[30]

Learning

Learning is an important process in most change initiatives because employees require new knowledge and skills to fit the organisation's evolving requirements. For example, the opening story to this chapter described the globalisation initiatives at LG Electronics. To help managers adjust to these changes, particularly the new requirement that meetings and correspondence should be in English, the Korean company set up an English language training centre to help Korean managers learn the language.

Learning was also an important strategy for change at CSC. The executive team of the American business and technology consulting and services firm determined that the company's culture required better alignment with its growth strategy. To achieve this transition, CSC launched a leadership development program, which would minimise resistance to the change by equipping managers with the skills to coach employees toward the emerging attitudes and values. CSC's Australian organisational development and learning team was responsible for determining content of the leadership program. They interviewed thirty stakeholders, held twenty focus groups, and reviewed key documents and past employee surveys. This information shaped the leadership workshops, which subsequently produced a stronger customer focus and perceived link between managers' work and business strategy.[31]

Employee Involvement

Unless the change must occur quickly or employee interests are highly incompatible with the organisation's needs, employee involvement is almost an essential part of the change process. Chapter 7 described several potential benefits of employee involvement, all of which are relevant to organisational change. Employees who participate in decisions about the change tend to feel they have more personal responsibility for its successful implementation, rather than being disinterested agents of someone else's decisions.[32] This sense of ownership also minimises the problems of saving face and fear of the unknown. Furthermore, the complexity of today's work environment demands that more people provide ideas regarding the best direction of the change effort. Employee involvement is such an important component of organisational change

Medibank's High-Involvement Change

Medibank Private relied on employee involvement to achieve its dramatic turnaround a few years ago. The Australian private health fund had reported record losses while suffering from low employee morale and high turnover. To improve performance, chief executive George Savvides formed nearly three dozen quality action teams (QATs). Each QAT, which included employees from all levels of the organisation, investigated ways to improve a specific area of the business, then delivered its verdict and recommendations directly to Medibank's board of directors. 'The board took a direct feed from front-line quality action teams,' recalls Derek Linsell, the change agent who Savvides hired to help guide the turnaround. The QAT recommendations saved millions of dollars by identifying better ways to serve customers and complete work processes. Within one year, Medibank was able to eke out a small net profit. Two years later, Medibank Private had the lowest cost structure in the industry and was highly profitable, even with lower premium increases than the industry average.[33]

Medibank Private Limited

that special initiatives have been developed to allow participation in large groups. These change interventions are described later in the chapter.

Stress Management

Organisational change is a stressful experience for many people because it threatens self-esteem and creates uncertainty about the future.[34] Communication, learning and employee involvement can reduce some of the stressors. However, research indicates that companies also need to introduce stress management practices to help employees cope with the changes.[35] In particular, stress management minimises resistance by removing some of the direct costs of the change process, and some of the fear of the unknown. Stress also saps energy, so minimising stress potentially increases employee motivation to support the change process.

Negotiation

As long as people resist change, organisational change strategies will require some influence tactics. Negotiation is a form of influence that involves the promise of benefits or resources in exchange for the target person's compliance with the influencer's request. This strategy potentially activates those who would otherwise lose out from the change. However, it merely gains compliance rather than commitment to the change effort, so it might not be effective in the long term.

Coercion

If all else fails, leaders rely on coercion to change organisations. Coercion can include persistently reminding people of their obligations, frequently monitoring behaviour to ensure compliance, confronting people who do not change and using threats of sanctions to force compliance.

Replacing people who will not support the change is an extreme step, but it is fairly common. For example, within one year after Robert Nardelli was hired as CEO of Home Depot, most of the American home improvement retailer's top management team had voluntarily or involuntarily left the company. Replacing staff is a radical form of organisational unlearning because replacing executives removes knowledge of the organisation's past routines. This potentially opens up opportunities for new practices to take hold.[36] At the same time, coercion is a risky strategy because survivors (employees who do not leave) may have less trust in corporate leaders and engage in more political tactics to protect their own job security.

Refreezing the Desired Conditions

Unfreezing and changing behaviour won't produce lasting change. People are creatures of habit, so they easily slip back into familiar patterns. Therefore, leaders need to refreeze the new behaviours by realigning organisational systems and team dynamics with the desired changes. These 'refreezing' mechanisms include information systems, organisational structures, feedback and rewards. Indeed, change management experts point out that the change process is supported by short-term wins, that is, forms of reward and recognition that reinforce desired behaviours.[37] The opening story to this chapter described how LG Electronics introduced a performance management system that essentially acted as a refreezing mechanism because it reinforced managers' focus on investment returns rather than on increasing market share. Career paths were also changed to support more of a global orientation.

Bank of New Zealand (BNZ) also applied the refreezing strategy by changing the feedback and reward system at its call centres. Previously, call centre employees received feedback and were rewarded for answering and completing calls quickly. However, management concluded that customers wanted efficient calls, not fast talkers. 'What do fast calls have to do with great conversations?' asks Susan Basile, BNZ's managing director of direct sales and service. 'Sure, we don't want to waste the customer's time. But if we were to ask them what they most wanted from our call centre, they might well say they want fast answers, but we'd be wrong to conclude they want fast talkers or hurried conversations.' Now, BNZ provides employee feedback and rewards around 'great conversations', not how quickly the call is completed. Employees are recognised for addressing customer needs rather than on the time it takes to complete the call.[38]

CHANGE AGENTS, STRATEGIC VISIONS AND DIFFUSING CHANGE

Kurt Lewin's force field analysis model is a useful template to explain the dynamics of organisational change. But it overlooks three ingredients in effective change processes: change agents, strategic visions and diffusing change.

Change Agents and Strategic Visions

The opening story to this chapter described how LG Electronics is being transformed into a global organisation. Perhaps the most important aspect of this change process is the transformational leadership of chief executive Nam Yong. He developed an appealing vision of the desired future state, communicated that vision in ways that are meaningful to others, made decisions and acted in ways that were consistent with that vision, and built commitment to that vision.[39] Change agents come in different forms, and more than one person is often required to fulfil these different roles.[40] In most situations, however, formal leaders are the primary agents of change when they engage in transformational leadership.

A key element of leading change is a strategic vision. A leader's vision provides a sense of direction and establishes the critical success factors against which the real changes are evaluated. Furthermore, vision provides an emotional foundation to the change because it links the individual's values and self-concept to the desired change.[41] A strategic vision also minimises employee fear of the unknown and provides a better understanding about what behaviours employees must learn for the desired future.

LEARNING OBJECTIVE

Outline the conditions for effectively diffusing change from a pilot project.

Diffusion of Change

Earlier in this chapter we mentioned that American retailer Best Buy introduced a results-only work environment (ROWE) initiative to support work–life balance and the employment expectations of a younger workforce. ROWE evaluates employees by their results, not their face time. This new arrangement gives employees at the electronics retailer the freedom to come to work when it suits them. ROWE is a significant departure from the traditional employment relationship, so Best Buy wisely introduced an early version of this initiative as a pilot project. Specifically, the program was first tested with a retail division of 320 employees that suffered from low morale and high turnover. The ROWE program expanded to other parts of the organisation only after employee engagement scores increased and turnover fell over several months.[42]

As at Best Buy, change agents often test the transformation process with a pilot project and then diffuse what has been learned from this experience to other parts of the organisation. Unlike centralised, system-wide changes, pilot projects are more flexible and less risky.[43] The pilot project approach also makes it easier to select organisational groups that are most ready for change, thus increasing the pilot project's success.

But how do we ensure that the change process started in the pilot project is adopted by other segments of the organisation? The MARS model introduced in Chapter 2 offers a useful template for organising the answer to this question. First, employees are more likely to adopt the practices of a pilot project when they are motivated to do so.[44] This occurs when they see that the pilot project is successful, and when people in the pilot project receive recognition and rewards for changing their previous work practices. Diffusion also requires supervisor support and reinforcement of the desired behaviours. More generally, change agents need to minimise the sources of resistance to change that we discussed earlier in this chapter.

Second, employees must have the ability—the required skills and knowledge—to adopt the practices introduced in the pilot project. According to innovation diffusion studies, people adopt ideas more readily when they have an opportunity to interact and learn from others who have already applied the new practices.[45] Thus, pilot projects get diffused when employees in the original pilot are dispersed to other work units as role models and knowledge sources.

Third, pilot projects get diffused when employees have clear role perceptions, that is, when they understand how the practices in a pilot project apply to them even though they are in a completely different functional area. For instance, accounting department employees won't easily recognise how they can adopt quality improvement practices developed by employees in the production department. The challenge here is for change agents to provide guidance that is neither too specific, because it might not seem relevant to other areas of the organisation, nor too abstract, because this makes the instructions too vague. Finally, employees require supportive situational factors, including the resources and time necessary to adopt the practices demonstrated in the pilot project.

FOUR APPROACHES TO ORGANISATIONAL CHANGE

So far, this chapter has examined the dynamics of change that occur every day in organisations. However, organisational change agents and consultants also apply various structured approaches to organisational change. This section introduces four of the leading approaches: action research, appreciative inquiry, large-group interventions and parallel learning structures.

Action Research Approach

LEARNING OBJECTIVE 

Describe the action research approach to organisational change.

action research A problem-focused change process that combines action orientation (changing attitudes and behaviour) and research orientation (testing theory through data collection and analysis).

Along with introducing the force field model, Kurt Lewin recommended an **action research** approach to the change process. Action research maintains that meaningful change is a combination of action orientation (changing attitudes and behaviour) and research orientation (testing theory).[46] On the one hand, the change process needs to be action-oriented because the ultimate goal is to bring about change. An action orientation involves diagnosing current problems and applying interventions that resolve those problems. On the other hand, the change process is a research study because change agents apply a conceptual framework (such as team dynamics or organisational culture) to a real situation. As with any good research, the change process involves collecting data to diagnose problems more effectively and to systematically evaluate how well the theory works in practice.[47]

Within this dual framework of action and research, the action research approach adopts an open-systems view. It recognises that organisations have many interdependent parts, so change agents need to anticipate both the intended and the unintended consequences of their interventions. Action research is also a highly participative process because open-systems change requires both the knowledge and the commitment of members within that system. Indeed, employees are essentially coresearchers as well as participants in the intervention. However, a supportive environment is required for employee participation to be meaningful rather than superficial.[48] Overall, action research is a data-based, problem-oriented process that diagnoses the need for change, introduces the intervention, and then evaluates and stabilises the desired changes. The main phases of action research are illustrated in Exhibit 15.3 and described below:[49]

- Form client–consultant relationship. Action research usually assumes that the change agent originates outside the system (such as a consultant), so the process begins by forming the client–consultant relationship. Consultants need to determine the client's readiness for change, including whether people are motivated to participate in the process, are open to meaningful change and possess the abilities to complete the process.
- Diagnose the need for change. Action research is a problem-oriented activity that carefully diagnoses the problem through systematic analysis of the situation. Organisational diagnosis

identifies the appropriate direction for the change effort by gathering and analysing data about an ongoing system, such as through interviews and surveys of employees and other stakeholders. Organisational diagnosis also includes involving employees in agreeing on the appropriate change method, deciding on the schedule for the actions involved and determining the expected standards of successful change.

- Introduce intervention. This stage in the action research model applies one or more actions to correct the problem. It may include any of the prescriptions mentioned throughout this book, such as building more effective teams, managing conflict, building a better organisational structure or changing the corporate culture. An important issue is how quickly the changes should occur.[50] Some experts recommend *incremental change*, in which the organisation finetunes the system and takes small steps toward a desired state. Others claim that *quantum change* is often required, in which the system is overhauled decisively and quickly. Quantum change is usually traumatic to employees and offers little opportunity for correction. But incremental change is also risky when the organisation is seriously misaligned with its environment, thereby facing a threat to its survival.
- Evaluate and stabilise change. Action research recommends evaluating the effectiveness of the intervention against the standards established in the diagnostic stage. Unfortunately, even when these standards are clearly stated, the effectiveness of an intervention might not be apparent for several years or might be difficult to separate from other factors. If the activity has the desired effect, the change agent and participants need to stabilise the new conditions. This refers to the refreezing process that was described earlier. Rewards, information systems, team norms and other conditions are redesigned so that they support the new values and behaviours.

The action research approach has dominated organisational change thinking ever since it was introduced in the 1940s. However, some experts complain that the problem-oriented nature of action research—in which something is wrong that must be fixed—focuses on the negative dynamics of the group or system rather than its positive opportunities and potential. This concern with action research has led to the development of a more positive approach to organisational change, called *appreciative inquiry*.[52]

Exhibit 15.3 *The Action Research Process*

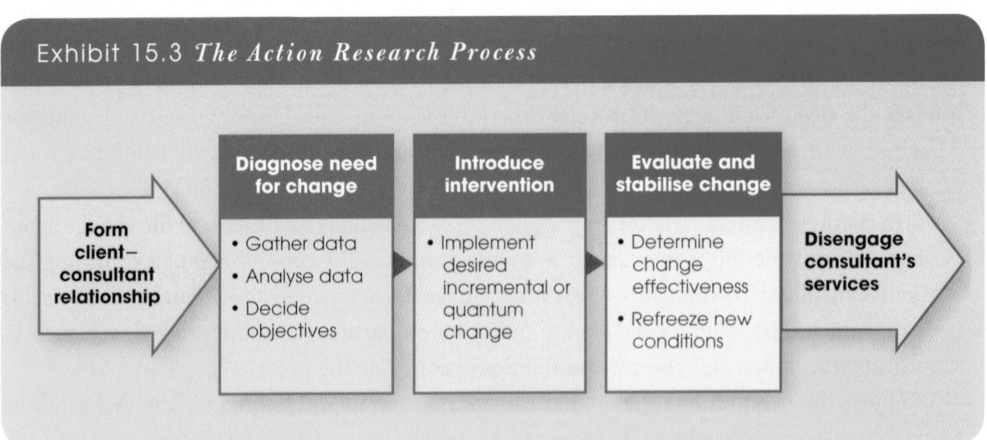

Ergon Energy Goes Incremental For Better Change

When government legislation required companies to upgrade their record-keeping systems, Ergon Energy decided to make the changes incrementally because employees had already experienced constant change over the previous couple of years.

Courtesy of Ergon Energy

'Even resilient staff such as those employed at Ergon Energy have a change tolerance level,' explains Petá Sweeney, a consultant who worked with the Queensland energy company during this transition. 'Consequently this led deliberately to discounting a revolutionary "big bang" approach to record-keeping improvements.' Sweeney reports that the incremental change approach significantly improved employee engagement in the process. 'Staff are more willing to participate in the change journey as well as offering suggestions for improvements. They do so knowing that changes will take place gradually and allow for time to fully bed down new practices and that effective enterprise wide changes require their help.'[51]

Appreciative Inquiry Approach

LEARNING OBJECTIVE 

Outline the 'Four-D' model of appreciative inquiry and explain how this approach differs from action research.

appreciative inquiry An organisational change strategy that directs the group's attention away from its own problems and focuses participants on the group's potential and positive elements.

Appreciative inquiry tries to break out of the problem-solving mentality of traditional change management practices by reframing relationships around the positive and the possible. It searches for organisational (or team) strengths and capabilities and then adapts or applies that knowledge for further success and wellbeing. Appreciative inquiry is therefore deeply grounded in the emerging philosophy of *positive organisational behaviour*, which suggests that focusing on the positive rather than negative aspects of life will improve organisational success and individual wellbeing. In other words, this approach emphasises building on strengths rather than trying to directly correct problems.[53]

Appreciative inquiry typically directs its inquiry toward successful events and successful organisations or work units. This external focus becomes a form of behavioural modelling, but it also increases open dialogue by redirecting the group's attention away from its own problems. Appreciative inquiry is especially useful when participants are aware of their 'problems' or already suffer from negativity in their relationships. The positive orientation of appreciative inquiry enables groups to overcome these negative tensions and build a more hopeful perspective of their future by focusing on what is possible.[54]

The 'Four-D' model of appreciative inquiry (named after its four stages) shown in Exhibit 15.4 begins with *discovery*—identifying the positive elements of the observed events or organisation.[55] This might involve documenting positive customer experiences elsewhere in the organisation. Alternatively, it might include interviewing members of another organisation to discover its fundamental strengths. As participants discuss their findings, they shift into the *dreaming* stage by envisioning what might be possible in an ideal organisation. By referring to a theoretically

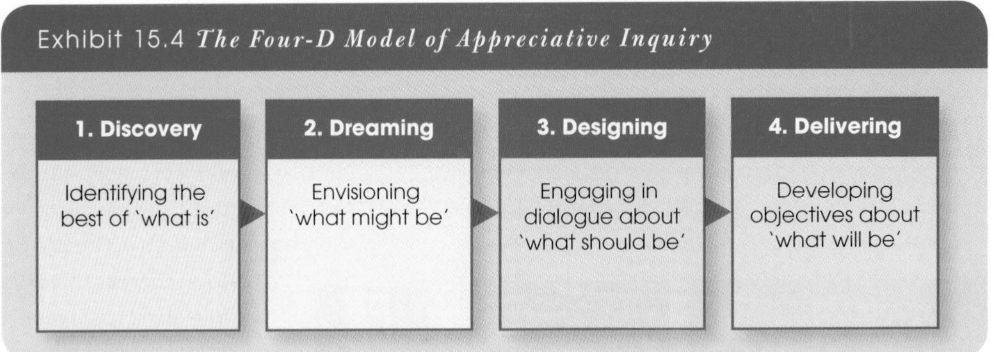

Sources: Based on F. J. Barrett and D. L. Cooperrider, 'Generative Metaphor Intervention: A New Approach for Working with Systems Divided by Conflict and Caught in Defensive Perception', *Journal of Applied Behavioural Science* 26, no. 2 (1990): 229; D. Whitney and C. Schau, 'Appreciative Inquiry: An Innovative Process for Organisation Change', *Employment Relations Today* 25, no. 1 (1998): 11–21; J. M. Watkins and B. J. Mohr, eds., *Appreciative Inquiry: Change at the Speed of Imagination* (San Francisco: Jossey-Bass, 2001): 25, 42–45.

ideal organisation or situation, participants feel safer revealing their hopes and aspirations than they would if they were discussing their own organisation or predicament.

As participants make their private thoughts public to the group, the process shifts into the third stage, called *designing*. Designing involves the process of dialogue, in which participants listen with selfless receptivity to each other's models and assumptions, and eventually form a collective model for thinking within the team. In effect, they create a common image of what should be. As this model takes shape, group members shift the focus back to their own situation. In the final stage of appreciative inquiry, called *delivering* (also known as *destiny*), participants establish specific objectives and direction for their own organisation based on their model of what will be.

Appreciative inquiry was developed twenty years ago, but it really gained popularity only within the past few years. Several success stories of organisational change from appreciative inquiry have emerged in a variety of organisational settings, including British Broadcasting Corporation (BBC), Castrol Marine, Canadian Tire, AVON Mexico, American Express, Green Mountain Coffee Roasters and Hunter Douglas.[56] Although less common in this part of the world, it has been applied in India by Wipro Technologies in the high-technology service firm's team development process, as well as by executives at India's ANZ Information Technology. 'Every organisation has some success factors that have to [be] explored and built upon and we tried to do it at ANZ,' says Shabbir Merchant, the consultant responsible for the appreciative inquiry intervention.[57]

As appreciative inquiry gains popularity, experts warn that this approach to organisational change is not always the best approach and, indeed, has not always been successful. Appreciative inquiry requires participants who are willing to let go of the problem-focused approach and leaders who are willing to accept appreciative inquiry's less structured process.[58] Another concern is that research has not yet examined the contingencies of this approach.[59] In other words, we don't yet know the conditions under which appreciative inquiry is a useful approach to organisational change or the conditions under which it is less effective. Overall, appreciative inquiry has much to offer the organisational change process, but we are just beginning to understand its potential and limitations.

BBC Takes the Appreciative Journey

The British Broadcasting Corporation (BBC) needed more innovative programming to reverse declining audience numbers, but employees complained that the radio, television and internet broadcaster did not provide a creative work environment. To discover how to become more creative, the company sponsored an appreciative inquiry process of employee consultation, called Just Imagine. More than 10 000 employees (about 40 per cent of BBC's workforce) participated in 200 meetings held over six months. At each meeting, employees were paired to ask each other three questions: (1) What has been the most creative/valued experience in your time at the BBC? (2) What were the conditions that made that experience possible? (3) If those experiences were to become the norm, how would the BBC have to change? The pairs then discussed their interview results in teams of ten people, and the most powerful stories were shared with others at the meeting. These meetings produced 98 000 ideas, which boiled down to 15 000 unique suggestions and ultimately 35 concrete initiatives. The BBC's executive publicised the results and immediately implemented several recommendations, such as a job swapping and a newcomer orientation program. Greg Dyke, BBC's respected director-general at the time, commented that the appreciative inquiry process provided valuable guidance. 'It gave me a powerful mandate for change,' he stated. 'I could look staff in the eye and say, "This is what you told us you wanted."'[60]

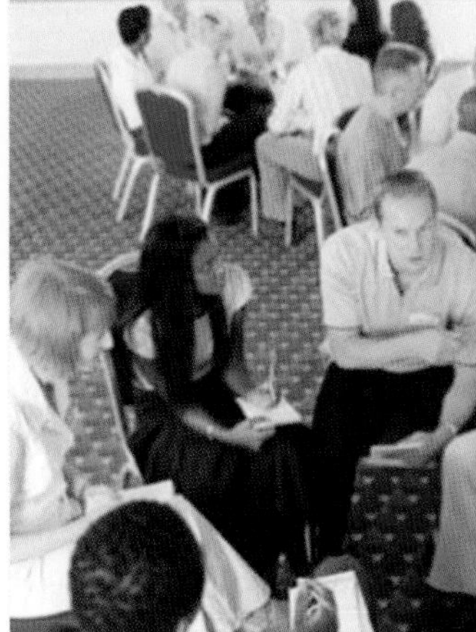

Banana Stock/Picture Quest

Large-Group Intervention Approach

Appreciative inquiry can occur in small teams, but it is often designed to involve a large number of people, such as the 10 000 employees who participated in the process at the BBC. As such, appreciative inquiry is often identified as one of several large-group organisational change interventions. Another large-group intervention, known as **future search** (and its variations—*search conferences* and *open-space technology*), 'puts the entire system in the room', meaning that the process tries to involve as many employees and other stakeholders associated with the organisational system as possible.[61] Future-search conferences were first developed by Australian change expert Fred Emery and his British colleague Eric Trist in 1960 to assist the merger of two British aerospace firms. Most future-search conferences are held over two or three days for the purpose of identifying environmental trends and establishing strategic solutions for those conditions.

future search An organisational change strategy that consists of system-wide group sessions, usually lasting a few days, in which participants identify trends and establish ways to adapt to those changes.

The City of Greater Bendigo held a three-day future-search conference in which various community groups (sport and recreation, the environment, arts, youth, planning and business) met with city councillors to reflect on the Victorian city's development and peer into its future. The city of Cairns held a similar session soon afterwards. Emerson & Cuming's chemical manufacturing facility in the United States relied on a future-search conference in which managers, supervisors and production employees were organised into five stakeholder teams to identify initiatives that would improve the plant's safety, efficiency and cooperation.[62]

IKEA Future Searches for the Perfect Sofa

IKEA held a three-day future-search event involving more than four dozen stakeholders, including the company president, product design staff, sales and distribution staff, information technology, retail managers, suppliers from three countries and six customers. The Swedish furniture company, which was growing rapidly, wanted to 'build a quicker, leaner and simpler' pipeline for its product development and distribution. Focusing on a single product (the Ektorp sofa), participants overcame the immense complexity of the system, the language barriers (for most, English was a second language), and apprehension and suspicions about change to map out a new product development process. One year later, IKEA launched a new sofa line (the Fixhult) based on further iterations of the process designed in the future-search workshop.[64]

Courtesy of IKEA

Future-search meetings and similar large-group change events potentially minimise resistance to change and assist the quality of the change process, but they also have limitations.[63] One problem is that involving so many people invariably limits the opportunity to contribute and increases the risk that a few people will dominate the process. Another concern is that these events focus on finding common ground, and this may prevent the participants from discovering substantive differences that interfere with future progress. A third issue is that these events generate high expectations about an ideal future state that are difficult to satisfy in practice. Employees become even more cynical and resistant to change if they do not see meaningful decisions and actions resulting from these meetings.

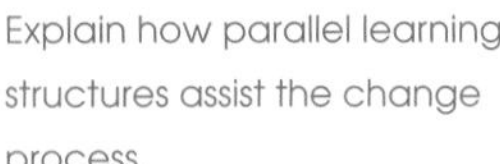
LEARNING OBJECTIVE

Explain how parallel learning structures assist the change process.

parallel learning structures Highly participative arrangements composed of people from most levels of the organisation who follow the action research model to produce meaningful organisational change.

Parallel Learning Structure Approach

Parallel learning structures are highly participative arrangements composed of people from most levels of the organisation who follow the action research model to produce meaningful organisational change. They are social structures developed alongside the formal hierarchy with the purpose of increasing the organisation's learning.[65] Ideally, participants in parallel learning structures are sufficiently free from the constraints of the larger organisation so that they can more effectively solve organisational issues.

Royal Dutch/Shell relied on a parallel learning structure to introduce a more customer-focused organisation.[66] Rather than try to change the entire organisation at once, executives held week-long 'retail boot camps' with six country teams of front-line people (e.g. fuel station managers, truck drivers, marketing professionals). Participants learned about competitive trends in their regions and were taught powerful marketing tools to identify new opportunities. The teams then returned home to study their market and develop proposals for improvement. Four months later, boot camp teams returned for a second workshop, at which each proposal was reviewed by Royal Dutch/Shell executives. Each team had sixty days to put its ideas into action; then the teams returned for a third workshop to analyse what worked and what didn't. This parallel learning process did much more than introduce new marketing ideas. It created enthusiasm in participants that spread contagiously to their coworkers, including managers above them, when they returned to their home countries.

CROSS-CULTURAL AND ETHICAL ISSUES IN ORGANISATIONAL CHANGE

LEARNING OBJECTIVE

Discuss three ethical issues in organisational change.

One significant concern with some organisational change interventions is that they originate in Western countries and may conflict with cultural values in some other cultures.[67] A few experts point out that this Western perspective of change is linear, as is Lewin's force field model discussed earlier. It also assumes that the change process is punctuated by tension and overt conflict, which is incompatible with cultures that view change as a natural cyclical process with harmony and equilibrium as the objectives.[68] This dilemma suggests that we need to develop a more contingency-oriented perspective concerning the cultural values of participants.

Some organisational change practices also face ethical issues. [69] One ethical concern is the risk of violating individual privacy rights. The action research model is built on the idea of collecting information from organisational members, yet this requires that employees provide personal information and emotions that they may not want to divulge.[70] A second ethical concern is that some change activities potentially increase management's power by inducing compliance and conformity in organisational members. For instance, action research is a system-wide activity that requires employee participation rather than allowing individuals to get involved voluntarily. A third concern is that some organisational change interventions undermine the individual's self-esteem. The unfreezing process requires that participants disconfirm their existing beliefs, sometimes including their own competence at certain tasks or interpersonal relations.

Organisational change is usually more difficult than it initially seems. Yet the dilemma is that most organisations operate in hyperfast environments that demand continuous and rapid adaptation. Organisations survive and gain competitive advantage by mastering the complex dynamics of moving people through the continuous process of change as quickly as the external environment is changing.

ORGANISATIONAL BEHAVIOUR: THE JOURNEY CONTINUES

Nearly 100 years ago, American industrialist Andrew Carnegie said: 'Take away my people, but leave my factories, and soon grass will grow on the factory floors. Take away my factories, but leave my people, and soon we will have a new and better factory.' Carnegie's statement reflects the message woven throughout this textbook: organisations are not buildings or machinery or financial assets; rather, they are the people in them. Organisations are human entities—full of life, sometimes fragile, always exciting.

CHAPTER SUMMARY

Lewin's force field analysis model states that all systems have driving and restraining forces. Change occurs through the process of unfreezing, changing and refreezing. Unfreezing produces disequilibrium between the driving and restraining forces. Refreezing realigns the organisation's systems and structures with the desired behaviours.

Restraining forces are manifested as employee resistance to change. Resistance to change should be viewed as a resource, not an inherent obstacle to change. The main reasons why people resist change are direct costs, saving face, fear of the unknown, breaking routines, incongruent team dynamics and incongruent organisational systems. Resistance to change may be minimised by keeping employees informed about what to expect from the change effort (communicating), teaching employees valuable skills for the desired future (learning), involving them in the change process, helping employees cope with the stress of change, negotiating trade-offs with those who will clearly lose from the change effort, and using coercion (sparingly and as a last resort).

Organisational change also requires driving forces. This means that employees need to have an urgency for change by becoming aware of the environmental conditions that demand change in the organisation. The change process also requires refreezing the new behaviours by realigning organisational systems and team dynamics with the desired changes. Every successful change also requires change agents with a clear, well-articulated vision of the desired future state. The change process also often applies a diffusion process in which change begins as a pilot project and eventually spreads to other areas of the organisation.

Action research is a highly participative, open-systems approach to change management that combines an action orientation (changing attitudes and behaviour) with a research orientation (testing theory). It is a data-based, problem-oriented process that diagnoses the need for change, introduces the intervention, and then evaluates and stabilises the desired changes.

Appreciative inquiry embraces the positive organisational behaviour philosophy by focusing participants on the positive and possible. It tries to break out of the problem-solving mentality that dominates organisational change through the action research model. The four stages of appreciative inquiry (the 'Four-D' model) are discovery, dreaming, designing and delivering.

Large-group interventions, such as future-search conferences, are highly participative events that typically try to get the entire system into the room. A fourth organisational change approach, called parallel learning structures, relies on social structures developed alongside the formal hierarchy with the purpose of increasing the organisation's learning. They are highly participative arrangements, composed of people from most levels of the organisation who follow the action research model to produce meaningful organisational change.

One significant concern is that organisational change theories developed with a Western cultural orientation potentially conflict with cultural values in some other countries. Also, organisational change practices can raise one or more ethical concerns, including increasing management's power over employees, threatening individual privacy rights and undermining individual self-esteem.

KEY TERMS

action research, p. 585
appreciative inquiry, p. 587
force field analysis, p.572
future search, p. 589
parallel learning structures, p. 590
refreezing, p. 573
unfreezing, p. 573

Critical Thinking Questions

1. Chances are that the university you attend is currently undergoing some sort of change to adapt more closely with its environment. Discuss the external forces that are driving the change. What internal drivers for change also exist?

2. Use Lewin's force field analysis to describe the dynamics of organisational change at the Federal Bureau of Investigation (Reality Check 15.1 in this chapter).

3. Employee resistance is a symptom, not a problem, in the change process. What are some of the real problems that may underlie employee resistance?

4. Senior management of a large multinational corporation is planning to restructure the organisation. Currently, the organisation is decentralised around geographic areas so that the executive responsible for each area has considerable autonomy over manufacturing and sales. The new structure will transfer power to the executives responsible for different product groups; the executives responsible for each geographic area will no longer be responsible for manufacturing in their area but will retain control over sales activities. Describe two types of resistance senior management might encounter from this organisational change.

5. Discuss the role of reward systems in organisational change. Specifically, identify where reward systems relate to Lewin's force field model and where they undermine the organisational change process.

6. Web Circuits is a Malaysian-based custom manufacturer for high-technology companies. Senior management wants to introduce lean management practices to reduce production costs and remain competitive. A consultant has recommended that the company start with a pilot project in one department and, when successful, diffuse these practices to other areas of the organisation. Discuss the advantages of this recommendation, and identify three ways (other than the pilot project's success) to make diffusion of the change effort more successful.

7. Suppose that you are vice president of branch services at the Bank of Fremantle. You notice that several branches have consistently low customer service ratings even though there are no apparent differences in resources or staff characteristics. Describe an appreciative inquiry process in one of these branches that might help to overcome this problem.

8 This chapter suggests that some organisational change activities face ethical concerns. Yet some change consultants undertake these activities because they believe they benefit the organisation and do less damage to employees than it seems on the surface. For example, some activities try to open up the employee's 'hidden area' (review the Johari Window discussion in Chapter 3) so that there is better mutual understanding with coworkers. Discuss this argument, and identify where you think organisational change interventions should limit this process.

Skill Builder 15.1

TEAM EXERCISE

Strategic Change Incidents

Purpose

This exercise is designed to help you identify strategies for facilitating organisational change in various situations.

Instructions

1. The instructor will divide your class into teams, and each team will be assigned one of the scenarios presented below.
2. Your team will diagnose its assigned scenario to determine the most appropriate set of change management practices. Where appropriate, these practices should (1) create an urgency to change, (2) minimise resistance to change, and (3) refreeze the situation to support the change initiative. Each of these scenarios is based on real events.
3. Each team will present and defend its change management strategy. Class discussion regarding the appropriateness and feasibility of each strategy will occur after all teams assigned the same scenario have presented. The instructor will then describe what the organisations actually did in these situations.

Scenario 1: Greener Telco

The board of directors at a large telephone company wants its executives to make the organisation more environmentally friendly by encouraging employees to reduce waste in the workplace. Government and other stakeholders expect the company to take this action and be publicly successful. Consequently, the managing director wants to significantly reduce paper usage, refuse and other waste throughout the company's many widespread offices. Unfortunately, a survey indicates that employees do not value environmental objectives and do not know how to 'reduce, reuse, recycle'. As the executive responsible for this change, you have been asked to develop a strategy that might bring about meaningful behavioural change toward this environmental goal. What would you do?

Scenario 2: Go Forward Airline

A major airline had experienced a decade of rough turbulence, including two bouts of bankruptcy protection, ten managing directors and morale so low that employees had ripped off company logos from their uniforms out of embarrassment. Service was terrible, and the aeroplanes rarely arrived or left the terminal on time. This was costing the airline significant amounts of money in passenger layovers. Managers were paralysed by anxiety, and many had been with the firm so long that they didn't know how to set strategic goals that worked. One-fifth of all flights were losing money, and the company overall was near financial collapse (just three months away from defaulting on payroll obligations). The newly hired managing director and you must get employees to quickly improve operational efficiency and customer service. What actions would you take to bring about these changes in time?

SELF-ASSESSMENT

Skill Builder 15.2

Are You Tolerant of Change?

Purpose

This exercise is designed to help you understand how people differ in their tolerance of change.

Instructions

Read each of the statements below and circle the response that best fits your personal belief. Then use the scoring key in Appendix B at the end of this book to calculate your results. This self-assessment should be completed alone so that you can rate yourself honestly without concerns of social comparison. Class discussion will focus on the meaning of the concept measured by this scale and its implications for managing change in organisational settings.

Tolerance-of-Change Scale

To what extent do you agree or disagree with each statement? Indicate your level of agreement by marking the appropriate response on the right.	Strongly agree	Moderately agree	Slightly agree	Neutral	Slightly disagree	Moderately disagree	Strongly disagree
1. An expert who doesn't come up with a definite answer probably doesn't know too much.	❑	❑	❑	❑	❑	❑	❑
2. There is really no such thing as a problem that can't be solved.	❑	❑	❑	❑	❑	❑	❑
3. People who fit their lives into a schedule probably miss most of the joy of living.	❑	❑	❑	❑	❑	❑	❑
4. A good job is one where it is always clear what is to be done and how it is to be done.	❑	❑	❑	❑	❑	❑	❑
5. It is more fun to tackle a complicated problem than to solve a simple one.	❑	❑	❑	❑	❑	❑	❑
6. In the long run, it is possible to get more done by tackling small, simple problems rather than large, complicated ones.	❑	❑	❑	❑	❑	❑	❑
7. Often the most interesting and stimulating people are those who don't mind being different and original.	❑	❑	❑	❑	❑	❑	❑

To what extent do you agree or disagree with each statement? Indicate your level of agreement by marking the appropriate response on the right.	Strongly agree	Moderately agree	Slightly agree	Neutral	Slightly disagree	Moderately disagree	Strongly disagree
8. What we are used to is always preferable to what is unfamiliar.	❑	❑	❑	❑	❑	❑	❑
9. People who insist on a yes or no answer just don't know how complicated things really are.	❑	❑	❑	❑	❑	❑	❑
10. A person who leads an even, regular life in which few surprises or unexpected happenings arise really has a lot to be grateful for.	❑	❑	❑	❑	❑	❑	❑
11. Many of our most important decisions are based on insufficient information.	❑	❑	❑	❑	❑	❑	❑
12. I like parties where I know most of the people more than ones where all or most of the people are complete strangers.	❑	❑	❑	❑	❑	❑	❑
13. Teachers or supervisors who hand out vague assignments give people a chance to show initiative and originality.	❑	❑	❑	❑	❑	❑	❑
14. The sooner everyone acquires similar values and ideals, the better.	❑	❑	❑	❑	❑	❑	❑
15. A good teacher is one who makes you wonder about your way of looking at things.	❑	❑	❑	❑	❑	❑	❑

Source: Adapted from S. Budner, 'Intolerance of Ambiguity as a Personality Variable', *Journal of Personality* 30, no. 1 (1962): 29–50.

Endnotes

1 J. A. Song, 'South Korean Bosses Strive for a Global View', *Financial Times (London)*, 13 November 2008, 24; J. S. Cho, 'Can New LG CEO Deliver?', *Korea Times*, 20 December 2006; C. P. Chan, 'Manager@Work: LG Aims to Be No 1', *The Edge Singapore*, 3 November 2008; J. S. Cho, 'LG Goes Multinational', *Korea Times*, 27 May 2008; E. Ramstad, 'Boss Talk: CEO Broadens Vistas at LG', *Wall Street Journal*, 21 May 2008, B1; P. V. Singh, 'Tackling Change Management', *Express Computer*, 25 August 2008. For discussion of LG's evolving customer and design focus, see S. Jang *et al.*, 'Design-Oriented New Product Development', *Research-Technology Management* 52, no. 2 (2009): 36–46.

2 K. Lewin, *Field Theory in Social Science* (New York: Harper & Row, 1951).

3 D. Coghlan and T. Brannick, 'Kurt Lewin: The "Practical Theorist" for the 21st Century', *Irish Journal of Management* 24, no. 2 (2003): 31–37; B. Burnes, 'Kurt Lewin and the Planned Approach to Change: A Re-Appraisal', *Journal of Management Studies* 41, no. 6 (2004): 977–1002.

4 D. Howell, 'Nardelli Nears Five-Year Mark with Riveting Record', *DSN Retailing Today*, 9 May 2005, 1, 38; R. Charan, 'Home Depot's Blueprint for Culture Change', *Harvard Business Review* 84, no. 4 (2006): 61–70; R. DeGross, 'Five Years of Change: Home Depot's Results Mixed under Nardelli', *Atlanta Journal-Constitution*, 1 January 2006, F1; B. Grow, D. Brady and M. Arndt, 'Renovating Home Depot', *BusinessWeek*, 6 March 2006, 50–57; R. Grossman, 'Remodeling HR at Home Depot', *HR Magazine*, November 2008, 66–72.

5 S. Chreim, 'Postscript to Change: Survivors' Retrospective Views of Organizational Changes', *Personnel Review* 35, no. 3 (2006): 315–335.

6 M. Johnson-Cramer, S. Parise and R. Cross, 'Managing Change through Networks and Values', *California Management Review* 49, no. 3 (2007): 85–109.

7 G. L. Neilson, B. A. Pasternack and K. E. Van Nuys, 'The Passive-Aggressive Organization', *Harvard Business Review* 83, no. 10 (2005): 82–92.

8 K. Shimizu, 'Hoppy Enjoying Comeback after Radical Shift in Management', *Japan Times*, 15 August 2007.

9 Variations of this often-cited quotation are found in several books, articles and websites, but unfortunately none cite the original source. This quotation is from D. R. Henderson, 'The New Industrial Economist', *Wall Street Journal*, 2 May 2006.

10 B. J. Tepper *et al.*, 'Subordinates' Resistance and Managers' Evaluations of Subordinates' Performance', *Journal of Management* 32, no. 2 (2006): 185–209; J. D. Ford, L. W. Ford and A. D'Amelio, 'Resistance to Change: The Rest of the Story', *Academy of Management Review* 33, no. 2 (2008): 362–377.

11 E. B. Dent and S. G. Goldberg, 'Challenging "Resistance to Change"', *Journal of Applied Behavioral Science* 35, no. 1 (1999): 25–41; D. B. Fedor, S. Caldwell and D. M. Herold, 'The Effects of Organizational Changes on Employee Commitment: A Multilevel Investigation', *Personnel Psychology* 59, no. 1 (2006): 1–29.

12 For an excellent review of the resistance-to-change literature, see R. R. Sharma, *Change Management: Concepts and Applications* (New Delhi: Tata McGraw-Hill, 2007), ch. 4.

13 D. A. Nadler, 'The Effective Management of Organizational Change', in *Handbook of Organizational Behavior*, ed. J. W. Lorsch (Englewood Cliffs, NJ: Prentice Hall, 1987), 358–369; R. Maurer, *Beyond the Wall of Resistance: Unconventional Strategies to Build Support for Change* (Austin, TX: Bard Books, 1996); P. Strebel, 'Why Do Employees Resist Change?', *Harvard Business Review* 74, no. 3 (1996): 86–92; D. A. Nadler, *Champions of Change* (San Francisco, CA: Jossey-Bass, 1998).

14 D. Eggen, 'FBI Fails to Transform Itself, Panel Says', *Washington Post*, 7 June 2005, A04; C. Ragavan and C. S. Hook, 'Fixing the FBI', *U.S. News & World Report*, 28 March 2005, 18–24, 26, 29–30; The Commission on the Intelligence Capabilities of the United States Regarding Weapons of Mass Destruction, *Report to the President of the United States* (Washington, D.C., 31 March 2005); J. J. Brazil, 'Mission: Impossible?', *Fast Company*, April 2007, 92–97, 108–109.

15 V. Newman, 'The Psychology of Managing for Innovation', *KM Review* 9, no. 6 (2007): 10–15.

16 R. Davis, *Leading for Growth: How Umpqua Bank Got Cool and Created a Culture of Greatness* (San Francisco, CA: Jossey-Bass, 2007), ch. 4

17 Talent2, *Bosses Want Change but Workers Want More of the Same!* (Sydney: Talent2, 29 June 2005).

18 C. Ressler and J. Thompson, *Why Work Sucks and How to Fix It* (New York: Portfolio, 2008), ch. 2.

19 B. Andrews, 'Winning Hand', *Business Review Weekly*, 14 April 2005, 72.

20 T. G. Cummings, 'The Role and Limits of Change Leadership', in *The Leader's Change Handbook*, ed. J. A. Conger, G. M. Spreitzer and E. E. Lawler III (San Francisco: Jossey-Bass, 1999), 301–320; J. P. Kotter and D. S. Cohen, *The Heart of Change* (Boston: Harvard Business School Press, 2002), 15–36; J. P. Kotter, *A Sense of Urgency* (Boston: Harvard Business School Press, 2008).

21 L. D. Goodstein and H. R. Butz, 'Customer Value: The Linchpin of Organizational Change', *Organizational Dynamics* 27 (June 1998): 21–35.

22 I. J. Bozon and P. N. Child, 'Refining Shell's Position in Europe', *McKinsey Quarterly* (June 2003): 42–51.

23 D. Miller, *The Icarus Paradox: How Exceptional Companies Bring about Their Own Downfall* (New York: HarperBusiness, 1990); S. Finkelstein, *Why Smart Executives Fail* (New York: Viking, 2003); A. C. Amason and A. C. Mooney, 'The Icarus Paradox Revisited: How Strong Performance Sows the Seeds of Dysfunction in Future Strategic Decision-Making', *Strategic Organization* 6, no. 4 (2008): 407–434. Richard Goyder's quotation is from R. Goyder, 'Sustaining High Performance', CEOForum (Melbourne/Sydney: CEO Forum Group, September 2006), http://ceoforum.com.au (accessed 21 May 2009).

24 D. Darlin, 'Growing Tomorrow', *Business 2.0*, May 2005, 126.

25 L. Grossman and S. Song, 'Stevie's Little Wonder', *Time*, 19 September 2005, 63; S. Levy, 'Honey, I Shrunk the iPod. A Lot', *Newsweek*, 19 September 2005, 58.

26 T. F. Cawsey and G. Deszca, *Toolkit for Organizational Change* (Los Angeles: Sage, 2007), 104.

27 J. P. Kotter and L. A. Schlesinger, 'Choosing Strategies for Change', *Harvard Business Review* 57, no. 2 (1979): 106–114.

28 J. Allen *et al.*, 'Uncertainty During Organizational Change: Managing Perceptions through Communication', *Journal of Change Management* 7, no. 2 (2007): 187 – 210; T. L. Russ, 'Communicating Change: A Review and Critical Analysis of Programmatic and Participatory Implementation Approaches', *Journal of Change Management* 8, no. 3 (2008): 199 – 211; M. E. Di Virgilio and J. D. Ludema, 'Let's Talk: Creating Energy for Action through Strategic Conversations', *Journal of Change Management* 9, no. 1 (2009): 67–85.

29 M. Meaney and C. Pung, 'Creating Organizational Transformations: McKinsey Global Survey Results', *McKinsey Quarterly* (July 2008): 1–7.

30 J. J. Brazil, 'Mission: Impossible?', *Fast Company*, April 2007, 92–97, 108–109.

31 'A Cornerstone for Learning', *T&D*, October 2008, 66–89.

32 K. T. Dirks, L. L. Cummings and J. L. Pierce, 'Psychological Ownership in Organizations: Conditions under Which Individuals Promote and Resist Change', *Research in Organizational Change and Development* 9 (1996): 1–23; A. Cox, S. Zagelmeyer and M. Marchington, 'Embedding Employee Involvement and Participation at Work', *Human Resource Management Journal* 16, no. 3 (2006): 250–267.

33 J. Bajkowski, 'Users Give Board Execs a Reality Lesson', *Computerworld*, 14 June 2005; A. Tandukar, 'Listen, Learn, Lead', *Business Review Weekly*, 2 June 2005, 66.

34 N. T. Tan, 'Maximising Human Resource Potential in the Midst of Organisational Change', *Singapore Management Review* 27, no. 2 (2005): 25–35.

35 M. McHugh, 'The Stress Factor: Another Item for the Change Management Agenda?', *Journal of Organizational Change Management* 10, no. 4 (1997): 345–362; D. Buchanan, T. Claydon and M. Doyle, 'Organisation Development and Change: The Legacy of the Nineties', *Human Resource Management Journal* 9, no. 1 (1999): 20–37.

36 D. Nicolini and M. B. Meznar, 'The Social Construction of Organizational Learning: Conceptual and Practical Issues in the Field', *Human Relations* 48, no. 7 (1995): 727–746.

37 E. E. Lawler III, 'Pay Can Be a Change Agent', *Compensation & Benefits Management* 16 (Summer 2000): 23–26; P. Kotter and Cohen, *The Heart of Change*, 161–177; M. A. Roberto and L. C. Levesque, 'The Art of Making Change Initiatives Stick', *MIT Sloan Management Review* 46, no. 4 (2005): 53–60.

38 E. G. Brown and J. Lubahn, 'We Need "To Talk"', *ABA Bank Marketing*, September 2007, 32–36.

39 R. E. Quinn, *Building the Bridge as You Walk on It: A Guide for Leading Change* (San Francisco: Jossey-Bass, 2004), ch. 11.

40 R. Caldwell, 'Models of Change Agency: A Fourfold Classification', *British Journal of Management* 14, no. 2 (2003): 131–142.

41 Kotter and Cohen, *The Heart of Change*, 61–82; D. S. Cohen and J. P. Kotter, *The Heart of Change Field Guide* (Boston: Harvard Business School Press, 2005).

42 J. Thottam, 'Reworking Work', *Time*, 25 July 2005, 50; Ressler and Thompson, *Why Work Sucks and How to Fix It*, 20, 45–48.

43 M. Beer, R. A. Eisenstat and B. Spector, *The Critical Path to Corporate Renewal* (Boston: Harvard Business School Press, 1990).

44 R. E. Walton, 'Successful Strategies for Diffusing Work Innovations', *Journal of Contemporary Business* (Spring 1977): 1–22; R. E. Walton, *Innovating to Compete: Lessons for Diffusing and Managing Change in the Workplace* (San Francisco: Jossey-Bass, 1987); Beer, Eisenstat and Spector, *The Critical Path to Corporate Renewal*, ch. 5.

45 E. M. Rogers, *Diffusion of Innovations*, 4th edn (New York: Free Pree, 1995).

46 P. Reason and H. Bradbury, *Handbook of Action Research, London* (Sage: 2001); Coghlan and Brannick, 'Kurt Lewin: The "Practical Theorist" for the 21st Century'; C. Huxham and S. Vangen, 'Researching Organizational Practice through Action Research: Case Studies and Design Choices', *Organizational Research Methods* 6 (July 2003): 383–403.

47 V. J. Marsick and M. A. Gephart, 'Action Research: Building the Capacity for Learning and Change', *Human Resource Planning* 26 (2003): 14–18.

48 L. Twiname, 'Could Action Research Provide the Key to True Workplace Collaboration?', *Journal of Workplace Rights* 13, no. 2 (2008): 147–166.

49 L. Dickens and K. Watkins, 'Action Research: Rethinking Lewin', *Management Learning* 30 (June 1999): 127–140; J. Heron and P. Reason, 'The Practice of Cooperative Inquiry: Research 'with' Rather Than 'on' People', in *Handbook of Action Research*, ed. P. Reason and H. Bradbury (Thousand Oaks, CA: Sage, 2001), 179–188.

50 D. A. Nadler, 'Organizational Frame Bending: Types of Change in the Complex Organization', in *Corporate Transformation: Revitalizing Organizations for a Competitive World*, ed. R. H. Kilmann, T. J. Covin and Associates (San Francisco: Jossey-Bass, 1988), 66–83; K. E. Weick and R. E. Quinn, 'Organizational Change and Development', *Annual Review of Psychology* 50 (1999): 361–386.

51 P. K. Sweeney, 'Corporate Compliance without Burdening the End User: Change Management Lessons from Ergon Energy', *iQ*, November 2006, 24–26.

52 T. M. Egan and C. M. Lancaster, 'Comparing Appreciative Inquiry to Action Research: OD Practitioner Perspectives', *Organization Development Journal* 23, no. 2 (2005): 29–49.

53 F. F. Luthans, 'Positive Organizational Behavior: Developing and Managing Psychological Strengths', *Academy of Management Executive* 16, no. 1 (2002): 57–72; N. Turner, J. Barling and A. Zacharatos, 'Positive Psychology at Work', in *Handbook of Positive Psychology*, ed. C. R. Snyder and S. Lopez (Oxford: Oxford University Press, 2002), 715–730; K. Cameron, J. E. Dutton and R. E. Quinn, eds., *Positive Organizational Scholarship: Foundation of a New Discipline* (San Francisco: Berrett-Koehler, 2003); J. I. Krueger and D. C. Funder, 'Towards a Balanced Social Psychology: Causes, Consequences, and Cures for the Problem-Seeking Approach to Social Behavior and Cognition', *Behavioral and Brain Sciences* 27, no. 3 (2004): 313–327; S. L. Gable and J. Haidt, 'What (and Why) Is

Positive Psychology?', *Review of General Psychology* 9, no. 2 (2005): 103–110; M. E. P. Seligman *et al.*, 'Positive Psychology Progress: Empirical Validation of Interventions', *American Psychologist* 60, no. 5 (2005): 410–421.

54 D. Whitney and D. L. Cooperrider, 'The Appreciative Inquiry Summit: Overview and Applications', *Employment Relations Today* 25, no. 2 (1998): 17–28; J. M. Watkins and B. J. Mohr, eds., *Appreciative Inquiry: Change at the Speed of Imagination* (San Francisco: Jossey-Bass, 2001).

55 F. J. Barrett and D. L. Cooperrider, 'Generative Metaphor Intervention: A New Approach for Working with Systems Divided by Conflict and Caught in Defensive Perception', *Journal of Applied Behavioral Science* 26, no. 2 (1990): 219–239; Whitney and Cooperrider, 'The Appreciative Inquiry Summit'; Watkins and Mohr, *Appreciative Inquiry*, 15–21.

56 M. Schiller, 'Case Study: Avon Mexico', in *Appreciative Inquiry: Change at the Speed of Imagination*, ed. J. M. Watkins and B. J. Mohr (San Francisco: Jossey-Bass, 2001), 123–126; D. Whitney and A. Trosten-Bloom, *The Power of Appreciative Inquiry: A Practical Guide to Positive Change* (San Francisco: Berrett-Koehler, 2003); P. Babcock, 'Seeing a Brighter Future', *HRMagazine*, September 2005, 48; D. S. Bright, D. L. Cooperrider and W. B. Galloway, 'Appreciative Inquiry in the Office of Research and Development: Improving the Collaborative Capacity of Organization', *Public Performance & Management Review* 29, no. 3 (2006): 285; D. Gilmour and A. Radford, 'Using OD to Enhance Shareholder Value: Delivering Business Results in BP Castrol Marine', *Organization Development Journal* 25, no. 3 (2007): P97–P102.

57 T. Narayan, 'Wipro Inducts "Appreciative Inquiry" for Better Team Work', *Financial Express (India)*, 2 December 2002; A. Prayag, 'The Power of Goodness for Corporate Development', *Business Line (The Hindu) (Mumbai)*, 19 May 2004, 5.

58 T. F. Yaeger, P. F. Sorensen and U. Bengtsson, 'Assessment of the State of Appreciative Inquiry: Past, Present, and Future', *Research in Organizational Change and Development* 15 (2004): 297–319; G. R. Bushe and A. F. Kassam, 'When Is Appreciative Inquiry Transformational? A Meta-Case Analysis', *Journal of Applied Behavioral Science* 41, no. 2 (2005): 161–181.

59 G. R. Bushe, 'Five Theories of Change Embedded in Appreciative Inquiry', paper presented at 18th Annual World Congress of Organization Development, Dublin, 14–18 July 1998.

60 S. Berrisford, 'Using Appreciative Inquiry to Drive Change at the BBC', *Strategic Communication Management* 9, no. 3 (2005): 22–25; M.-Y. Cheung-Judge and E. H. Powley, 'Innovation at the BBC', in *The Handbook of Large Group Methods*, ed. B. B. Bunker and B. T. Alban (New York: Wiley, 2006), 45–61.

61 M. Weisbord and S. Janoff, *Future Search: An Action Guide to Finding Common Ground in Organizations and Communities* (San Francisco: Berrett-Koehler, 2000); R. M. Lent, M. T. McCormick and D. S. Pearce, 'Combining Future Search and Open Space to Address Special Situations', *Journal of Applied Behavioral Science* 41, no. 1 (2005): 61–69; S. Janoff and M. Weisbord, 'Future Search as "Real-Time" Action Research', *Futures* 38, no. 6 (2006): 716–722.

62 C. Rance, 'In Bendigo, the People Have Spoken', *The Age (Melbourne)*, 30 April 2005, 24; P. Wex, 'Search for City's Future', *Cairns Post*, 20 December 2005, 16; R. Lent, J. Van Patten and T. Phair, 'Creating a World-Class Manufacturer in Record Time', in *The Handbook of Large Group Methods*, ed. B. B. Bunker and B. T. Alban (New York: Wiley, 2006), 112–124.

63 For a critique of future-search conferences and similar whole-system events, see A. Oels, 'Investigating the Emotional Roller-Coaster Ride: A Case Study-Based Assessment of the Future Search Conference Design', *Systems Research and Behavioral Science* 19 (July–August 2002): 347–355; M. F. D. Polanyi, 'Communicative Action in Practice: Future Search and the Pursuit of an Open, Critical and Non-Coercive Large-Group Process', *Systems Research and Behavioral Science* 19 (July 2002): 357–366; A. De Grassi, 'Envisioning Futures of African Agriculture: Representation, Power, and Socially Constituted Time', *Progress in Development Studies* 7, no. 2 (2007): 79–98.

64 M. Weisbord and S. Janoff, 'Faster, Shorter, Cheaper May Be Simple; It's Never Easy', *Journal of Applied Behavioral Science* 41, no. 1 (2005): 70–82.

65 G. R. Bushe and A. B. Shani, *Parallel Learning Structures* (Reading, MA: Addison-Wesley, 1991); E. M. Van Aken, D. J. Monetta and D. S. Sink, 'Affinity Groups: The Missing Link in Employee Involvement', *Organizational Dynamics* 22, no. 4 (1994): 38–54.

66 D. J. Knight, 'Strategy in Practice: Making It Happen', *Strategy & Leadership* 26, no. 3 (1998): 29–33; R. T. Pascale, 'Grassroots Leadership—Royal Dutch/Shell', *Fast Company*, April–May 1998, 110–120; R. T. Pascale, 'Leading from a Different Place', in *The Leader's Change Handbook*, ed. J. A. Conger, G. M. Spreitzer and E. E. Lawler III (San Francisco: Jossey-Bass, 1999), 301–320; R. Pascale, M. Millemann and L. Gioja, *Surfing on the Edge of Chaos* (London: Texere, 2000).

67 C.-M. Lau, 'A Culture-Based Perspective of Organization Development Implementation', *Research in Organizational Change and Development* 9 (1996): 49–79.

68 T. C. Head and P. F. Sorenson, 'Cultural Values and Organizational Development: A Seven-Country Study',

Leadership and Organization Development Journal 14, no. 2 (1993): 3–7; R. J. Marshak, 'Lewin Meets Confucius: A Review of the OD Model of Change', *Journal of Applied Behavioral Science* 29, no. 4 (1993): 395–415; C.-M. Lau and H. Y. Ngo, 'Organization Development and Firm Performance: A Comparison of Multinational and Local Firms', *Journal of International Business Studies* 32, no. 1 (2001): 95–114.

69 M. McKendall, 'The Tyranny of Change: Organizational Development Revisited', *Journal of Business Ethics* 12, no. 2 (1993): 93–104; C. M. D. Deaner, 'A Model of Organization Development Ethics', *Public Administration Quarterly* 17, no. 4 (1994): 435–446.

70 G. A. Walter, 'Organization Development and Individual Rights', *Journal of Applied Behavioral Science* 20 (1984): 423–439.

1

Part 4 CASE STUDY

GOING TO THE X-STREAM

Roy Smollan, Auckland University of Technology

Gil Reihana is the chief executive officer of X-Stream, an Auckland-based company that assembles personal computers for the New Zealand and Australian markets, and sells them through a number of chain stores and independent retailers. He started the company six years ago, at the age of 25, after graduating from university with a bachelor's degree in information technology and management. To establish the company, Reihana invested $300 000 he had inherited, and persuaded various family members to invest additional money. The company soon developed a reputation for quality hardware, customised products, and excellent delivery times and after-sales service. Six months ago it started a software division, specialising in web design and consulting on various applications for the development of electronic business.

The Key Players

Gil Reihana is driven by a desire to succeed. At the age of 16 he had started working part-time at an electronics retailer, and in his spare time took apart old computers in his garage to see how they were made. He is extroverted, energetic and enthusiastic, often arriving at work before 5 am and seldom leaving before 7 pm. He feels that work should be challenging but fun, too. Initially, he had picked a young senior management team that he thought shared his outlook. A casual, almost irreverent atmosphere developed. However, a poorly organised accounting department led to the resignation of the first accountant after two years.

Reihana believes that major decisions should be made by consensus and that individuals should then be empowered to implement these decisions in their own way. In the beginning, he met with each staff member in January to discuss their level of satisfaction in their jobs, their ambitions, and plans for the coming year in terms of their professional development. As the company grew, this became more difficult, so Reihana had left each member of his senior management team to do this with their own staff, but did not monitor whether they were doing it and how well it worked. Now he tries to keep in touch with staff by having lunch with them in the cafeteria occasionally.

Denise Commins (affectionately known to all staff as 'Dot Com') is X-Stream's chief financial officer. She and Reihana could not be more different. Commins is quiet, methodical and very patient. Her superb interpersonal skills complement a highly analytical mind. At 55, she is considerably older than most of the employees and often shows a strong maternal side. Many of her team (and several from other departments as well) frequently consult her on work issues and personal problems, too. She enjoys the informal relationships she has built up but is now finding that the technical aspects of her role are becoming less rewarding.

Don Head, the marketing manager, is considered to be a rather ruthless operator, often undercutting the competition in terms of price, and, on more than one occasion, by circulating false rumours of defects in their products. He refers to himself as 'a ladies' man' and has been known to flirt with a number of the staff. A case of sexual harassment was dropped after a 22-year-old secretary was paid a sizeable sum of money. Reihana and the members of the senior management team were furious with Head, who had denied any wrongdoing, claiming that the young woman had 'led him on'. Head attended university with Reihana, and over the years they have spent many hours after work at a pub around the corner from the factory. With sales rising year after year, Head's marketing expertise and cunning are regarded as essential to the company's continuing growth. He has a department of eight staff, all ambitious self-starters, whom he carefully selected based on those qualities. They are required to set and achieve their own targets, as long as those targets are 'big hairy ambitious goals'—a phrase Head had heard at a seminar.

Jason Palu, the production manager, is a softly spoken man who started as a supervisor and quickly worked his way to the top position. He sets extremely high standards for the production staff and is considered to be a perfectionist, but is highly regarded by his colleagues for his efficiency and reliability. There are very few occasions when an order cannot be filled on time, and Palu's goal is to have zero defects. He tends to be autocratic, however, and some employees have complained that he never listens to them, allocates work hours that do not suit his staff, and often insists on (paid) overtime at very short notice. When one production worker complained, he tersely remarked, 'We have a job to do and we just have to get on with it. The company depends on us.'

Heather Berkowitz is the chief web designer. She has blue hair and a ring through her nose, and dresses in a variety of exotic clothes that she sources from second-hand shops. She seldom arrives at work much before 11 am and often leaves before 4 pm. She says that she does her best work at home, often at night, so why should she 'punch the clock like the drones on the assembly line'? Reihana and others often receive emails from her that have been sent at all hours of the night. She has established a reputation as a top web designer, and although her physical appearance does not go down too well with some of the company's clients (or staff), the quality and quantity of her work is extremely high.

The Conflict

Every Tuesday at 9 am, X-Stream's senior staff meet to discuss weekly plans and any significant issues that have arisen. All employees are invited to the meeting, an opportunity that some take advantage of by attending. Reihana trusts all staff to keep confidential matters within the company. He believes that if the organisation shares information with employees they are more likely to support management decisions. The meetings lack formality and usually start with some jokes, usually at the expense of particular members of staff. By and large the jokes are meant to be inoffensive, but are not always taken that way. Nicknames are often assigned to staff, mostly by Don Head; although some are quite derogatory, any employee who objects is thought to be a 'wet blanket'. Head seems oblivious to his own unflattering nickname, preferring to call himself 'Braveheart'—sometimes even signing memos in this fashion.

Although employment agreements refer to a 40-hour week, there is an expectation that staff will put in substantially more than that. Only the assembly-line workers have to clock in and out but this, Jason Palu had explained, was due to the overtime that assembly staff were required to work to meet deadlines. The overtime pay was welcomed by some production staff, but resented by some employees in other departments who believed they should be entitled to the same benefits.

Now a conflict has arisen between Jason Palu and Don Head. For some time, X-Stream has been developing a top-of-the-range laptop, the X-MH, which is scheduled for launching in two weeks time. Palu, however, has been urging senior management to delay the introduction of the X-MH until some hitches have been sorted out. A batch of chips acquired from overseas contains some defective features, and Palu wants to postpone the new model until these problems have been ironed out—a process he believes will take another month. Head has found this to be unacceptable. A former All-Blacks captain has already been contracted to attend the launch and market the new model on a roadshow that will travel to all major cities in New Zealand and Australia, but he will not be available at the time Palu is prepared to release the X-MH.

At a heated staff meeting, some of the senior staff backed Head, while others agreed with Palu. Head had urged all of his department to attend the meeting, to present a united front and convey an image of power. Heather Berkowitz arrived halfway through the meeting and, with a mouthful of muffin, proclaimed that there was no rush to get out the 'new toy', because the company had plenty of other issues to which it could devote its energy. She said that she had met the head of information technology of a chain of fast-food restaurants that wanted to revitalise its website, and maintained that she needed three extra staff members to get this up and running. She exited the meeting five minutes later.

Head fumed at the interruption and demanded that Reihana should stick to the original launch date of the X-MH. Reihana calmly replied that he understood Head's frustration but that more consultation was necessary. He said that it would be discussed by the parties concerned during the week and a final decision would be made at the following Tuesday's staff meeting.

Don spent the rest of that day lobbying other senior staff members. He offered Denise Commins the use of his beach cottage if she backed him and promised to support her on the acquisition of expensive new accounting software. She just laughed and said that she was convinced the senior management team would approve the new software. She also informed Head that a member of her staff had seen one of his sales representatives entering a strip club the previous week, at a time when the sales force had been engaged in a staff meeting.

Other Problems

Other problems had also arisen in recent months. Ramesh Patel, the newly recruited head of e-business applications, had—with help from a personal contact—developed a software program that would help hotels and restaurants source products and services over the internet. It was beginning to generate useful revenue. His contact has now billed X-Stream for $25 000 in consultancy fees and development costs. Patel claims that his contact owed him a favour and that no mention of money was ever made. X-Stream has referred the matter to its legal counsel.

Les Kong, the research and development manager (hardware), has also complained to Reihana that he can no longer work under Jason Palu. While he considers him a very pleasant man, and a very capable production manager, he claims that he can no longer tolerate Palu's strict control style. 'You can't do creative work on command!' is his lament. He loves his job and has spent hours over several weekends developing and refining a new product.

There is considerable resentment from Palu and Head about the resources that have been invested in the software division, partly because they do not see the need for the company to diversify, and partly because they claim that money is being diverted from their departments to fund the new ventures. Patel claims that 'a good e-business starts at home—we should open up all our procurement via the internet'. His suggestion does not go down well with Palu and Head.

A Climate of Change

In fact, Reihana has been pondering the structure of X-Stream for some time. He thinks the old functional structure no longer seems appropriate. 'Silo' mentality and departmental interests seemed to predominate, and turf wars were taking place. The company had grown to sixty-four staff in New Zealand and eight in Australia. The ongoing development of new hardware and the introduction of the software side of the business had made management somewhat complicated. He missed the old days when he knew every member of staff. The informal decision making that was characteristic of the business might have to give way to more formal processes. Yet he did not want to lose the creativity that underpinned its success. Despite the open invitation to attend the management meetings, many staff complained that they never knew what was going on. He expected all senior managers to keep their departmental staff informed of developments. Some had done this admirably, while others had virtually ignored his wishes.

A human resources manager, Alkina Bennelong, has now been appointed, reporting to Denise Commins. She has been reviewing the company's loosely worded job descriptions and person specifications, and the recruitment and selection systems, and has suggested more professional but more elaborate approaches. She has also suggested the introduction of a performance management system, including feedback from peers, direct reports and outsiders, such as suppliers and customers. 'Over my dead body!' was the retort of Don Head. 'How can you allow subordinates to tell you how to do your job?' queried Jason Palu. 'Can't see what the fuss is all about,' offered Heather Berkowitz. 'Everybody keeps telling me what to do anyway, even though they don't understand the first thing about my job! But it doesn't worry me.'

Discussion Questions

1. Identify the strengths and weaknesses of X-Stream's organisational culture.
2. Analyse the sources of the resistance to the proposed changes by Gil Reihana and Alkina Bennelong, and discuss how the company could deal with the resistance.
3. Discuss the type of organisational structure you believe the company should adopt and explain why you think this would be the best.

CASE STUDY

2 HILLTON'S TRANSFORMATION

Steven L. McShane, The University of Western Australia

Thirty years ago, Hillton was a small city (about 70 000 residents) that served as an outer suburb to a large metropolitan city. The municipal council of Hillton treated its employees like family and gave them a great deal of autonomy in their work. Everyone in the organisation (including the two labour unions representing employees) implicitly agreed that the leaders and supervisors of the organisation should rise through the ranks on the basis of their experience. Few people were ever hired from the outside into middle or senior positions. The rule of employment at Hillton was to learn the job skills, maintain a reasonably good work record and wait your turn for promotion.

Hillton has grown rapidly over the past three decades. As the population grew, so did the council's workforce to keep pace with the increasing demand for municipal services. This meant that employees were promoted fairly quickly and were almost guaranteed employment. In fact, until recently, Hillton had never laid off any employee. The organisation's culture could be described as one of entitlement and comfort. Neither the elected city councillors nor the city manager bothered the departmental managers about their work. There were few cost controls because the rapid growth placed more emphasis on keeping up with the population expansion. The public became somewhat more critical of the city's poor service, including road construction at inconvenient times and the apparent lack of respect some employees showed toward taxpayers.

During these expansion years, Hillton put most of its money into 'outside' (also called 'hard') municipal services. These included road building, utility construction and maintenance, fire and police protection, recreational facilities and land-use control. This emphasis occurred because an expanding population demanded more of these services and most of Hillton's senior people came from the outside services group. For example, Hillton's city manager for many years was a road development engineer. The 'inside' workers (taxation, community services and so on) tended to have less seniority, and their departments were given less priority.

As commuter and road systems developed, Hillton attracted more upwardly mobile professionals into the community. Some infrastructure demands continued, but now these suburban dwellers wanted more of the 'soft' services, such as libraries, social activities and community services. They also began complaining about the way the municipality was being run. The population had more than tripled over the past three decades, and it was increasingly apparent that the organisation needed more corporate planning, information systems, organisation development and cost-control systems. In various ways, residents voiced their concerns that the municipality was not providing the quality of management that they would expect from a city of Hillton's size.

Three years ago, a new mayor and council replaced most of the previous incumbents, mainly on the platform of improving the municipality's management structure. The new council gave the city manager, along with two other senior managers, an early retirement package. Rather than promoting from the lower ranks, the council decided to fill all three positions with qualified candidates from large municipal corporations in the region. The following year, several long-term managers left Hillton, and at least half of those positions were filled by people from outside the organisation.

In less than two years, Hillton had eight senior or departmental managers hired from other municipalities who played a key role in changing the organisation's value system. These eight managers became known (often with negative connotations) as the 'professionals'. They worked closely with each other to change the way middle and lower-level managers had operated for many years. They brought in a new computer system and emphasised cost controls in areas where managers previously had complete autonomy. Promotions were increasingly based more on merit than seniority.

These managers frequently announced in meetings and newsletters that municipal employees must provide superlative customer service, and that Hillton should become one of the most customer-friendly places for citizens and those who do business with the municipality. To this end, the managers were quick to support the public's increasing demand for more soft services, including expanded library services and recreational activities. Recently, population growth has flattened, so the city manager and other professionals gained council support to lay off a few of the outside workers due to lack of demand for hard services.

One of the most significant changes was that the outside departments no longer held dominant positions in city management. Most of the professional managers had worked exclusively in administrative and related inside jobs. Two had master's degrees in business administration. This led to some tension between the professional managers and the older outside managers.

Even before the lay-offs, managers of outside departments resisted the changes more than others did. These managers complained that their employees with the highest seniority were turned down for promotions. They argued for higher budget allocations, and warned that infrastructure problems would cause liability problems. Informally, these outside managers were supported by the labour union representing outside workers. The union leaders tried to bargain for more job guarantees, whereas the union representing inside workers focused more on improving wages and benefits. Leaders of the outside union made several statements in the local media that the city had 'lost its heart' and that the public would suffer from the actions of the new professionals.

Discussion Questions

1. Contrast Hillton's earlier corporate culture with its emerging set of cultural values.
2. Considering the difficulty in changing organisational culture, why does Hillton's management seem to be successful at this transformation?
3. Identify two other strategies that the city might consider to reinforce the new set of corporate values.

CASE STUDY 3

SHAPING A CULTURE OF COMMITMENT AT LIME INDUSTRIES

Brenda Scott-Ladd, Curtin University of Technology, and Joe Bovell, Optima Agriculture

Joe Bovell was originally engaged to provide marketing consultancy to Lime Industries Pty Ltd, but loved the culture so much he decided to join the company. 'The very first moment I drove into the Lime workplace it struck me that this business had a unique and visible culture. Just walking down the driveway towards the administration office I was faced with large typeface quotes from leaders, some known and others unknown to me, with messages of inspiration, leadership and accountability,' Bovell remembers. Based in Osborne Park, Western Australia, Lime Industries consists of four companies that use lime as their core product. They produce lime for plastering, mining, agricultural, water and soil treatment use. In total, the group employs in excess of sixty people.

As general manager of Optima Agriculture, one of the Lime Industries groups, Bovell has since discovered that many of the leadership quotations he noticed came from Emilio 'Neil' Menchetti, who founded Lime Industries in 1976. 'I never had the opportunity to meet Neil Menchetti, as he passed away in 2002, but his influence on the current owners' values and leadership style have led to a fantastic workplace culture because of the ingrained organisational and personal values,' says Bovell. One particular saying from Neil Menchetti exemplifies the Lime Industries culture: 'I have never let my primary or college schooling interfere with my education, nor does the word failure exist in my vocabulary.'

These days Lime Industries is run by Menchetti's two daughters and son, who have worked hard to preserve their father's legacy. Irene, Peter and Flori, along with Irene's husband Lance, are a close-knit family, yet they keep family life separate from the workplace. They each have very different personalities but still manage to work cohesively and draw on each other's strengths. 'They make a dynamic and strong leadership team,' Bovell adds. Peter and Lance are go-getters; both are highly motivated and have strong, hands-on leadership styles. Peter is responsible for the financial side of the business but also gets involved with innovation projects. Lance is forward-thinking and looks to create new business. Flori is a quiet achiever and manages sales, operations and logistics, whereas Irene, who is very astute, handles all legal aspects of the business and is the chairperson for the group of companies.

Messages of inspiration and innovation from Neil Menchetti and notable leaders, such as Winston Churchill, are displayed around the workplace for all to see—in the boardroom, the workshop and even the staff toilets. These messages are not only positive, but they remind employees of their obligations to the workplace and their need to add value to the business. The environment is mentally challenging for both employees and management as the business is constantly changing, and the companies set their own benchmarks instead of following competitors' standards. Innovation is seen as a prerequisite for success. For example, the water treatment business grew from creating diagnostic equipment which was a market first. There is a strong emphasis on accountability and honesty, and these are part of the daily key performance indicators (KPIs) for employees. Most recruitment is by word of mouth, while merit-based and transparent processes prevent nepotism 'All of this has contributed to a very robust culture,' Bovell says.

The company provides well for its team members and expects their commitment to be shared by employees. They demonstrate this by paying above-award rates, performance bonuses and annual bonuses for each year of service. A high standard of staff amenities are also provided. For example, amenities rooms have espresso coffee machines, there are monthly barbecues, and employees' families are invited to the annual Christmas party—all at no cost to the employees. There is an open-door management policy to support employees through any personal problems they may be experiencing and, where possible, employees have flexibility in working hours to help meet family commitments. Longer term employee commitment is rewarded with other benefits such as interest-free loans. All of this means turnover is low and employees willingly contribute above and beyond what is expected of them in terms of the quality of their work, extra hours and their readiness to take on new tasks. Recognition of this two-way valuing of staff is spelled out in both the company's statements of 'Core Cultural Values' and its 'People Value Proposition'.

Lime Industries Core Cultural Values

At the core of culture there is a commitment to integrity and an ethical way of doing things.

The reliance of supply that our clients expect has created a 'MUST DO ON TIME' attitude in providing services as promised.

Being a family owned company we have an organic culture that creates a two way commitment to all stakeholders.

When we employ an appropriate candidate we see it as a commitment for life.

Our company provides value, useful services and products, not a price, and through transparency and openness with our team an enterprising culture for all has developed.

We believe that the constant improvement of process, systems, safety, and cost containment are the duty of all our team.

We must minimise our impact on the environment in which we work and strive to provide the best work environment for our people.

Like all athletes the time to recover is important, and multi-tasking is encouraged.

Lime Industries People Value Proposition

Our commitment to our team is to apply new technology and innovation wherever possible that will eliminate repetitive tasks and which will provide a workplace environment that is efficient and promotes a learning and team building experience that adds value to ours.

The business is always on the lookout for talented individuals. It will recruit by improving its people value proposition conditions under which they work providing greater flexibility to suit multiple generations.

We endeavour to provide meaningful stakes in the outcomes. To stay at the forefront these people will be challenged to lead and innovate within the business.

Our culture revolves around our people's well being, future security and to provide prosperity for all involved within the business. It is a business where people will want to come to work and enjoy the atmosphere and success of the business and grow with the business.

The challenge facing the company is to maintain and enhance its existing company culture while it manages the complexities of a rapidly growing business in the current booming Western Australian economic environment. Lime Industries is one of the rare companies that still has workers who have been there for more than twenty-five years, although the current average tenure is about seven years. Low unemployment in the state means it is difficult to attract and retain quality staff, particularly support staff, who will fit in with the team of long-serving employees. The skills shortage is placing upward pressure on pay rates. New employees are demanding higher salaries and this means pay rates for current staff need to be increased to maintain harmony. Currently, the company's workforce is mainly a mix of two groups of workers: those aged 40 and over, and those in their mid-twenties. Younger workers do not always fit in easily. If they are honest and hardworking they survive, but if not, their turnover rate is high. Lime Industries rewards those who add value to the business, but those who do not can read the last quote as they head out the gate: 'People do not lack strength, they lack will.'

Discussion Questions

1. Identify the range of strategies that Lime Industries uses to shape its culture.
2. Use two models of organisational culture from this book to diagnose the culture at Lime Industries.
3. What strategies would you recommend Lime Industries adopt to address the issues of an ageing workforce and the current skills shortage?
4. What are the organisational behaviour issues facing Lime Industries and what recommendations would you make to the company to align its values and culture in the future?

SHOWTIME ARABIA RECREATES ITSELF

Julia Connell, University of Technology, Sydney

4 CASE STUDY

Showtime Arabia is the largest pay television company in the Arab world. Located in Dubai, in the United Arab Emirates, Showtime Arabia is the premier subscription television service in the Middle East, North Africa and the Levant territories. With headquarters in Dubai's Media City, Showtime Arabia is a joint venture between KIPCO (79 per cent stake) and the CBS Corporation (21 per cent stake).

On 1 April 2007, the new Showtime Arabia company was launched. This involved rebranding and, in particular, new channels—Showcinema, Showmovies, Showsports and Showseries. The three new Showsports channels replaced the previous Sportsnet channels, and they aimed to provide Showtime with a leap in subscriber numbers just before the soccer season started in August 2007—particularly as Showtime Arabia had won the rights to broadcast the English Premier League.

The network continues to gain market share in spite of the free-to-air challenge of the MBC Group channels, which follow a similar formula in Western entertainment programming. However, the Showtime Arabia management team is not complacent. Their competitors—the free-to-air networks—could pose more of a threat in the future due to the fast-changing nature of the industry. The competition is high as competitors learn from each other very quickly. For example, if Showtime Arabia develops something new, the company frequently sees its competitors doing the same thing one week later!

Prior to the 2007 launch, organisational changes were widespread throughout Showtime Arabia. These began in earnest in 2006. The first high-level change began when the Showtime president and CEO stepped down to pursue other interests. The new CEO and president, Marc-Antoine d'Halluin, stated:

We are fully prepared for the next exciting stage of Showtime—it has so far failed to exploit to its full potential. There are lots of hidden opportunities within the business and we are focusing on revealing them quickly because it's a strong business, a strong company and a great brand but it has lots of areas where it can build on what it already has ... It's not about being short of the things that we need, we have everything we need, its just about doing a better job and packaging it on and off-air. (Bennett, 2007)

How and Why Did Showtime Need to Change?

According to Showtime's organisation development (OD) manager, previously Showtime was in an 'entrepreneurial mode'. It had grown sporadically over the years and, as a result, lacked a clear picture of where it needed to go in the future. The company also needed to 'grow up' in terms of its processes and systems. Lines of decision making needed to be clear, as did lines of accountability. Hence, the OD manager believed that changes were necessary for business survival.

To bring about the necessary changes, the organisation's culture, and the way that employees were operating, needed to be transformed. The first stage in the change process involved a restructure during which the management team was reduced from nine to five people, and sixty job roles were removed (although thirty of these employees were subsequently redeployed into other roles in the company). This brought the number of Showtime employees to 720 people in 2007.

The changes were perceived as non-negotiable, as they were introduced by the new management team in a fairly directive manner. First, the CEO and chief operating officer (COO) came into the organisation and just listened to what employees had to say. This strategy assisted them to make decisions about the restructuring processes that subsequently took place.

Next, the OD manager worked with the leadership team in a coaching role and held development sessions on the management of change. At the same time, he introduced a range of behavioural competencies, and recruitment and development strategies. These included creating assessment centres, developing a leadership program and putting succession planning processes into place.

McKinsey's 'Seven S' principles were adopted as a guide for the change process. One of these 'S' principles—structure—involved large-scale changes. Even though the organisation was previously quite flat in its structure, these new structural changes involved the removal of blockages in decision making and the improvement of interdepartmental communication. Strategies also focused on encouraging new teams to develop, particularly moving to the performing stages of the team development cycle. Project teams also worked within matrix structures, so that team members met together more frequently than previously, and worked on strategies such as advancing 'customer-first' processes.

The Outcome

The OD manager indicated that some of the change processes had been traumatic. Where there was resistance to change, it was often because staff needed to 'let go of the past'. However, it is evident that the new style of leadership has been effective. This was particularly noticed by some employees who left Showtime during the change process, but have since returned and observed that the company now seems like a totally new organisation.

Although the leadership style towards change was directive initially, control and decision-making authority were later delegated. Before the changes took place, decision-making authority went up the hierarchy. Following the change, information was shared more readily internally. For example, employees can now track progress on customer abandonment calls, sales and management reports on the internet.

In attempts to 'bed down' the changes and reward desired behaviour, the OD manager introduced a new reward and recognition policy. Rewards range from having dinner with the CEO to a flight package, and are allocated as a result of performance management processes, line manager suggestions or direct commissions for the sales staff. In addition 'mini-360-degree' feedback meetings were introduced at Showtime. These involve two or three people giving feedback on a particular person.

Employee performance is not all quantitatively focused, however, as there was also an emphasis on behaviours. Competencies such as strategic thinking are encouraged at every level in the organisation. For instance, a person who works in the warehouse may be required to adopt strategic thinking processes to suggest how warehouse space might be utilised more effectively, rather than just working on storage issues.

Moreover, Showtime has a number of what it calls 'business-critical' roles. These are the roles that are central to the organisation: if a person in a business-critical role left Showtime tomorrow, the impact on customer relationships would be significant. That is why there is a need for succession planning and talent management, in addition to the development of knowledge management processes, to be integrated in the organisation.

In summary, the change processes have been very effective so far, but were not without trauma to some employees. The changes won't be stopping, though, and their impact will be measured to some extent through a staff survey conducted every two years. Future surveys will take place more regularly and speedily through online polls, which are likely to be related to specific projects. So, it appears that—at least for the foreseeable future—the only constant at Showtime will be change.

Discussion Questions

1. Identify the type of external environment that established the need for Showtime Arabia to change its structure, processes and systems. Explain how it changed them.
2. The OD manager identified the need for Showtime Arabia to change its culture so it would be more aligned with 'customer-first' processes through an adaptive culture. What are the key features of an adaptive culture, and why would this be relevant to Showtime Arabia?
3. Showtime's top management initially took a directive approach to the change processes. Later, the OD manager implemented strategies to assist with the effective transition and bedding down of the changes. How would these strategies have assisted with the change processes, and how do they link to change concepts and models?

References

J. Bennett, 'It's Showtime!', ArabianBusiness.com, 1 February 2007, www.arabianbusiness.com (accessed 22 May 2009).

TRANSACT INSURANCE CORPORATION

5

CASE STUDY

Steven L. McShane, The University of Western Australia, and Terrance Bogyo, WorkSafeBC

TransAct Insurance Corporation (TIC) provides motor vehicle insurance throughout the south-eastern United States. Last year, a new president was hired by TIC's board of directors to improve the company's competitiveness and customer service. After spending several months assessing the situation, the new president introduced a strategic plan to strengthen TIC's competitive position. He also replaced three vice presidents. Jim Leon was hired as vice president of claims, TIC's largest division, which had 1500 employees, 50 claims centre managers and five regional directors.

Leon immediately met with all claims managers and directors, and he visited employees at TIC's 50 claims centres. As an outsider, this was a formidable task, but his strong interpersonal skills, and uncanny ability to remember names and ideas, helped him through the process. Through these visits and discussions, Leon discovered that the claims division had been managed in a relatively authoritarian, top-down manner. He could also see that morale was very low and employee–management relations were guarded. Heavy workloads and isolation (adjusters work in tiny cubicles) were two other common complaints. Several managers acknowledged that the high turnover among claims adjusters was partly due to these conditions.

Following discussions with TIC's president, Jim Leon decided to make morale and supervisory leadership his top priority. He initiated a divisional newsletter with a tear-off feedback form for employees to register their comments. He announced an open-door policy in which any claims division employee could speak to him directly and confidentially without going first to the immediate supervisor. Leon also fought organisational barriers to initiate a flexitime program so that employees could design work schedules around their needs. This program later became a model for other areas of TIC.

One of Leon's most pronounced symbols of change was the 'Claims Management Credo' outlining the philosophy that every claims manager would follow. At his first meeting with the complete claims management team, Jim presented a list of what he thought were the important philosophies and actions of effective managers. The management group was asked to select and prioritise items from this list. They were told that the resulting list would be the division's management philosophy and all managers would be held accountable for abiding by its principles. Most claims managers were uneasy about this process, but they also understood that the organisation was under competitive pressure and that Leon was using this exercise to demonstrate his leadership.

The claims managers developed a list of ten items, such as encouraging teamwork, fostering a trusting work environment, setting clear and reasonable goals, and so on. The list was circulated to senior management in the organisation for their comments and approval, then sent back to all claims managers for their endorsement. Once this was done, a copy of the final document was sent to every claims division employee. Leon also announced plans to follow up with an annual survey to evaluate each claims manager's performance. This concerned the managers, but most of them believed that the credo exercise was a result of Jim's initial enthusiasm and that he would be too busy to introduce a survey after settling into the job.

One year after the credo had been distributed, Jim announced that the first annual survey would be conducted. All claims employees would complete the survey and return it confidentially to the human resource department where the survey results would be compiled for each claims centre manager. The survey asked the extent to which the manager had lived up to each of the ten items in the credo. Each form also provided space for comments.

Claims centre managers were surprised that a survey would be conducted, but they were even more worried about Leon's statement that the results would be shared with employees. What results would employees see? Who would distribute these results? What happens if a manager received poor ratings from his or her subordinates? 'We'll work out the details later,' said Jim in response to these questions. 'Even if the survey results aren't great, the information will give us a good baseline for next year's survey.'

The claims division survey had a high response rate. In some centres, every employee completed and returned a form. Each report showed the claims centre manager's average score for each of the ten items, as well as how many employees rated the manager at each level of the five-point scale. The reports also included every comment made by employees at that centre.

No one was prepared for the results of the first survey. Most managers received moderate or poor ratings on the ten items. Very few managers averaged above 3.0 (out of the 5 points) on more than a couple of items. This suggested that, at best, employees were ambivalent about whether their claims centre manager had abided by the ten management philosophy items. The comments were even more devastating than the ratings. Comments ranged from mildly disappointed to extremely critical of the claims managers. Employees also described their longstanding frustration with TIC, high workloads and isolated working conditions. Several people bluntly stated that they were sceptical about the changes that Jim had promised. 'We've heard the promises before, but now we've lost faith,' wrote one claims adjuster.

The survey results were sent to each claims manager, the regional director and employees at the claims centre. Jim Leon instructed managers to discuss the survey data and comments with their regional manager and directly with employees. The claims centre managers, who thought employees would see only the average scores, went into shock when they realised that the reports included individual comments. Some managers went to their regional directors, complaining that revealing the personal comments would ruin their careers. Many directors sympathised, but the results were already available to employees.

When Leon heard about these concerns, he agreed that the results were lower than expected and that the comments should not have been shown to employees. After discussing the situation with his directors, he decided that the discussion meetings between claims managers and their employees should proceed as planned. To delay or withdraw the reports would undermine the credibility and trust that Leon was trying to develop with employees. However, the regional director attended the meeting in each claims centre to minimise direct conflict between the claims centre manager and employees.

Although many of these meetings went smoothly, a few created harsh feelings between managers and their employees. The sources of some comments were easily identified by their content, and this created a few delicate moments in several sessions. A few months after the meetings, two claims centre managers quit and three others asked for transfers back to nonmanagement positions in TIC. Meanwhile, Leon wondered how to manage this process more effectively, particularly since employees expected another survey the following year.

Discussion Questions

1. What symptom(s) in this case suggest that something has gone wrong?
2. What are the main causes of these symptoms?
3. What actions should TIC executives take to correct these problems?

additional case studies

A MIR KISS?

1

Additional CASE STUDY

By Steven L. McShane, The University of Western Australia

A team of psychologists at Moscow's Institute for Biomedical Problems (IBMP) wanted to learn more about the dynamics of long-term isolation in space. This knowledge would be applied to the International Space Station, a joint project of several countries that would send people into space for more than six months. It would eventually include a trip to Mars taking up to three years.

IBMP set up a replica of the Mir space station in Moscow. They then arranged for three international researchers from Japan, Canada and Austria to spend 110 days isolated in a chamber the size of a train car. This chamber joined a smaller chamber where four Russian cosmonauts had already completed half of their 240 days of isolation. This was the first time an international crew was involved in the studies. None of the participants spoke English as their first language, yet they communicated throughout their stay in English at varying levels of proficiency.

Judith Lapierre, a French Canadian, was the only female in the experiment. In addition to her PhD in public health and social medicine, Lapierre studied space sociology at the International Space University in France and conducted isolation research in the Antarctic. This was her fourth trip to Russia, and she had already learned the language. The mission was supposed to have a second female participant from the Japanese space program, but she was not selected by IBMP.

The Japanese and Austrian participants viewed the participation of a woman as a favourable factor, says Lapierre. For example, to make the surroundings more comfortable, they rearranged the furniture, hung posters on the wall and put a tablecloth on the kitchen table. 'We adapted our environment, whereas the Russians just viewed it as something to be endured,' she explains. 'We decorated for Christmas, because I'm the kind of person who likes to host people.'

New Year's Eve Turmoil

Ironically, it was at one of those social events, the New Year's Eve party, that events took a turn for the worse. After drinking vodka (allowed by the Russian space agency), two of the Russian cosmonauts got into a fistfight that left blood splattered on the chamber walls. At one point, a colleague hid the knives in the station's kitchen because of fears that the two Russians were about to stab each other. The two cosmonauts, who generally did not get along, had to be restrained by other men. Soon after that brawl, the Russian commander grabbed Lapierre, dragged her out of view of the television monitoring cameras and kissed her aggressively—twice. Lapierre fought him off, but the message didn't register. He tried to kiss her again the next morning.

The next day, the international crew complained to IBMP about the behaviour of the Russian cosmonauts. The Russian institute apparently took no action against any of the aggressors. Instead, the institute's psychologists replied that the incidents were part of the experiment. They wanted crew members to solve their personal problems with mature discussion, without asking for outside help. 'You have to understand that Mir is an autonomous object, far away from anything,' Vadim Gushin, the IBMP psychologist in charge of the project, explained after the experiment had ended in March: 'If the crew can't solve problems among themselves, they can't work together.'

Following IBMP's response, the international crew wrote a scathing letter to the Russian institute and the space agencies involved in the experiment. 'We had never expected such events to take place in a highly controlled scientific experiment where individuals go through a multistep selection process,' they wrote. 'If we had known ... we would not have joined it as subjects.' The letter also complained about IBMP's response to their concerns.

Informed of the New Year's Eve incident, the Japanese space program convened an emergency meeting on 2 January to address the incidents. Soon after, the Japanese team member quit, apparently shocked by IBMP's inaction. He was replaced with a Russian researcher on the international team. Ten days after the fight—a little over a month after the international team began the mission—the doors between the Russian and international crew's chambers were barred at the request of the international research team. Lapierre later emphasised that this action was taken because of concerns about violence, not the incident involving her.

A Stolen Kiss or Sexual Harassment?

By the end of the experiment in March, news of the fistfight between the cosmonauts and the commander's attempts to kiss Lapierre had reached the public. Russian scientists attempted to play down the kissing incident by saying that it was one fleeting kiss, a clash of cultures and a female participant who was too emotional.

'In the West, some kinds of kissing are regarded as sexual harassment. In our culture it's nothing,' said IBMP's Vadim Gushin in one interview. In another interview, he explained: 'The problem of sexual harassment is given a lot of attention in North America but less in Europe. In Russia it is even less of an issue, not because we are more or less moral than the rest of the world; we just have different priorities.'

Judith Lapierre says the kissing incident was tolerable compared to this reaction from the Russian scientists who conducted the experiment. 'They don't get it at all,' she complains. 'They don't think anything is wrong. I'm more frustrated than ever. The worst thing is that they don't realise it was wrong.'

Norbert Kraft, the Austrian scientist on the international team, also disagreed with the Russian interpretation of events. 'They're trying to protect themselves,' he says. 'They're trying to put the fault on others. But this is not a cultural issue. If a woman doesn't want to be kissed, it is not acceptable.'

Sources: G. Sinclair Jr, *'If You Scream in Space, Does Anyone Hear?' Winnipeg Free Press,* 5 May 2000, A4; S. Martin, 'Reining in the Space Cowboys', *Globe & Mail* (Toronto), 19 April 2000, R1; M. Gray, *'A Space Dream Sours',* Maclean's, 17 April 2000, 26; E. Niiler, 'In Search of the Perfect Astronaut', *Boston Globe,* 4 April 2000, E4; J. Tracy, '110-Day Isolation Ends in Sullen ... Isolation', *Moscow Times,* 30 March 2000, 1; M. Warren, 'A Mir Kiss?' *Daily Telegraph* (London), 30 March 2000, 22; G. York, 'Canadian's Harassment Complaint Scorned', *Globe & Mail* (Toronto), 25 March 2000, A2; S. Nolen, 'Lust in Space', *Globe & Mail* (Toronto), 24 March 2000, A3.

CASE STUDY 2

ARCTIC MINING CONSULTANTS

By Steven L. McShane, The University of Western Australia, and Tim Neale

Tom Parker enjoys working outdoors. At various times in the past, he has worked as a ranch hand, high steel rigger, headstone installer, prospector and geological field technician. Now 43, Parker is a geological field technician and field co-ordinator with Arctic Mining Consultants. He has specialised knowledge and experience in all nontechnical aspects of mineral exploration, including claim staking, line cutting and grid installation, soil sampling, prospecting and trenching. He is responsible for hiring, training and supervising field assistants for all of Arctic Mining Consultants' programs. Field assistants are paid a fairly low daily wage (no matter how long they work, which may be up to 12 hours or more) and are provided meals and accommodation. Many of the programs are operated by a project manager who reports to Parker.

Parker sometimes acts as a project manager, as he did on a job that involved staking fifteen claims near Eagle Lake in British Columbia, Canada. He selected John Talbot, Greg Boyce and Brian Millar, all of whom had previously worked with Parker, as the field assistants. To stake a claim, the project team marks a line with flagging tape and blazes along the perimeter of the claim, cutting a claim post every 500 yards (just over 450 metres; called a 'length'). The fifteen claims would require about 95 kilometres of line in total. Parker had budgeted seven days (plus mobilisation and demobilisation) to complete the job. This meant that each of the four stakers (Parker, Talbot, Boyce and Millar) would have to complete a little over seven 'lengths' each day. The following is a chronology of the project.

Day 1

The Arctic Mining Consultants crew assembled in the morning and drove to Eagle Lake, from where they were flown by helicopter to the claim site. On arrival, they set up tents at the edge of the area to be staked, and agreed on a schedule for cooking duties. After supper, they pulled out the maps and discussed the job—how long it would take, the order in which the areas were to be staked, possible helicopter landing spots and areas that might be more difficult to stake.

Parker pointed out that with only a week to complete the job, everyone would have to average seven and a half lengths per day. 'I know that is a lot,' he said, 'but you've all staked claims before and I'm confident that each of you is capable of it. And it's only for a week. If we get the job done in time, there's a $300 bonus for each man.' Two hours later, Parker and his crew members had developed what seemed to be a workable plan.

Day 2

Millar completed six lengths, Boyce six lengths, Talbot eight and Parker eight. Parker was not pleased with Millar's or Boyce's production. However, he didn't make an issue of it, thinking that they would develop their 'rhythm' quickly.

Day 3

Millar completed five and a half lengths, Boyce four and Talbot seven. Parker, who was nearly twice as old as the other three, completed eight lengths. He also had enough time remaining to walk over and check the quality of stakes that Millar and Boyce had completed, then walk back to his own area for helicopter pick-up back to the tent site.

That night Parker exploded with anger. 'I thought I told you that I wanted seven and a half lengths a day!' he shouted at Boyce and Millar. Boyce said that he was slowed down by unusually thick underbrush in his assigned area. Millar said that he had done his best and would try to pick up the pace. Parker did not mention that he had inspected their work. He explained that as far as he was concerned, the field assistants were supposed to finish their assigned area for the day, no matter what.

Talbot, who was sharing a tent with Parker, talked to him later. 'I think that you're being a bit hard on them, you know. I know that it has been more by luck than anything else that I've been able to do my quota. Yesterday I only had five lengths done after the first seven hours and there was only an hour before I was supposed to be picked up. Then I hit a patch of really open bush, and was able to do three lengths in 70 minutes. Why don't I take Millar's area tomorrow and he can have mine? Maybe that will help.'

'Conditions are the same in all of the areas,' replied Parker, rejecting Talbot's suggestion. 'Millar just has to try harder.'

Day 4

Millar did seven lengths and Boyce completed six and a half. When they reported their production that evening, Parker grunted uncommunicatively. Parker and Talbot did eight lengths each.

Day 5

Millar completed six lengths, Boyce six, Talbot seven and a half and Parker eight. Once again Parker blew up, but he concentrated his diatribe on Millar. 'Why don't you do what you say you are going to do? You know that you have to do seven and a half lengths a day. We went over that when we first got here, so why don't you do it? If you aren't willing to do the job then you never should have taken it in the first place!'

Millar replied by saying that he was doing his best, that he hadn't even stopped for lunch, and that he didn't know how he could possibly do any better. Parker launched into him again: 'You have got to work harder! If you put enough effort into it, you will get the area done!'

Later Millar commented to Boyce, 'I hate getting dumped on all the time! I'd quit if it didn't mean that I'd have to walk 80 kilometres to the highway. And besides, I need the bonus money. Why doesn't he pick on you? You don't get any more done than me; in fact, you usually get less. Maybe if you did a bit more he wouldn't be so bothered about me.'

'I only work as hard as I have to,' Boyce replied.

Day 6

Millar raced through breakfast, was the first one to be dropped off by the helicopter, and arranged to be the last one picked up. That evening the production figures were Millar eight and a quarter lengths, Boyce seven and Talbot and Parker eight each. Parker remained silent when the field assistants reported their performance for the day.

Day 7

Millar was again the first out and last in. That night, he collapsed in an exhausted heap at the table, too tired to eat. After a few moments, he announced in an abject tone, 'Six lengths. I worked like a dog all day and I only got a lousy six lengths!' Boyce completed five lengths, Talbot seven and Parker seven and a quarter.

Parker was furious. 'That means we have to do a total of 34 lengths tomorrow if we are to finish this job on time!' With his eyes directed at Millar, he added: 'Why is it that you never finish the job? Don't you realise that you are part of a team, and that you are letting the rest of the team down? I've been checking your lines and you're doing too much blazing and wasting too much time making picture-perfect claim posts! If you worked smarter, you'd get a lot more done!'

Day 8

Parker cooked breakfast in the dark. The helicopter drop-offs began as soon as morning light appeared on the horizon. Parker instructed each assistant to complete eight lengths and, if they finished early, to help the others. Parker said that he would finish the other ten lengths. Helicopter pick-ups were arranged for one hour before dark.

By noon, after working as hard as he could, Millar had only completed three lengths. 'Why bother?' he thought to himself. 'I'll never be able to do another five lengths before the helicopter comes, and I'll catch the same amount of abuse from Parker for doing six lengths as for seven and a half.' So he sat down and had lunch and a rest. 'Boyce won't finish his eight lengths either, so even if I did finish mine, I still wouldn't get the bonus. At least I'll get one more day's pay this way.'

That night, Parker was livid when Millar reported that he had completed five and a half lengths. Parker had done ten and a quarter lengths, and Talbot had completed eight. Boyce proudly announced that he finished seven and a half lengths, but sheepishly added that Talbot had helped him with some of it. All that remained were the two and a half lengths that Millar had not completed.

The job was finished the next morning and the crew demobilised. Millar has never worked for Arctic Mining Consultants again, despite being offered work several times by Parker. Boyce sometimes does staking for Arctic, and Talbot works full-time with the company.

CASE STUDY 3

CHENGDU BUS GROUP

By Runtian Jing, The University of Electronic Science and Technology of China

The Chengdu Bus Group (CBG) is a Chinese, state-owned enterprise with more than 4000 buses and 14 000 employees. A few years ago, CBG encountered serious problems. The primary issue was the company's management systems, but it also faced a considerable financial crisis. Complaints against CBG from its many customers were becoming increasingly common and the operations of the company were in disarray.

At the end of a troubled year, Dr She Chen was appointed as the director (CEO) of CBG. Dr Chen had proven himself in previous positions as a thoughtful and insightful manager. He had accumulated not only a wealth of experience on effective leadership in Chinese society, but also in the field of management theory. Additionally, he had earned a PhD—a very rare achievement in the Chinese business community.

Due to the seriousness of CBG's problems, the mayor of Chengdu gave Dr Chen just three years to reform CBG. This was too short a time to gradually transform the organisation, including the critically flawed management system and financial situation. Therefore, Dr Chen had to implement rapid change and take risks to carry out a successful reform in the required time frame, even though he knew this would be met with great resistance from CBG's employees and many stakeholders.

After taking up his new position, Dr Chen conducted a careful investigation into the functioning of CBG, after which he formulated a series of reform measures. He then discussed his ideas and proposed changes with the mayor and leaders of Chengdu city, obtaining full support in both authorisation and funding before implementing the organisational changes in the company.

Fast-Paced Managerial Reform

Because CBG is an old, state-owned enterprise, very complicated working relationships and politics existed among the 14 000 employees. Dr Chen knew that this would make it very difficult to carry out large-scale organisational reforms within the company. However, after two months of examination, Dr Chen felt he had accurately grasped the important characteristics of the 533 managers in the company. He then carefully designed a reform plan and schedule for the managers and their positions. To avoid the influence of complicated *guanxi* (special relationships) among the managers, and to avoid the managers forming solid opposition to his changes, Dr Chen implemented the reforms with a fast, accurate and ambitious strategy. The changes were made quickly, precisely and without compromise.

This strategy meant that adjustments to the managerial positions were completed before the managers could effectively react to what was happening and potentially disrupt the process. Nonetheless, when they realised what had happened, they began to protest. Dr Chen was very calm and simply said to them: 'After all these events have passed by you will have many different impressions about me and my reforms. Although such an adjustment may bring some loss to you, in the future the commendation from others will be more than the condemnation. All change must face resistance, complaint and even rejection. What I have done is not for myself, but for the company.'

Simplifying the Branch Company Structure

Another notable reform that Dr Chen successfully implemented involved the branch companies of CBG. The organisation had four branch companies; two were wholly state-owned, while the other two were joint ventures with external investors. In addition to operating bus routes, each company owned buses, bus stations, repair workshops, and other facilities and equipment required to run their bus services. However, this created significant problems and inefficiencies as each company ran its operations independently of the other companies, and did not share their stations or repair workshops—essentially, the four companies were in direct competition with each other.

Furthermore, different routes throughout the city had quite different profit rates. Without any formal authority co-ordinating the companies, or implementing policies and rules, there was overcompetition for the desirable high-profit routes, resulting in inefficiencies and losses for all of the companies. To rectify this situation, Dr Chen arranged for CBG to buy back the external equity of the joint ventures, and thereby changed the branch operations to purely state-owned subsidiaries. He then removed the overservicing on the high-profit routes, and redeployed the surplus buses and employees from these routes to develop the potential profitability of other routes under the principle of optimisation.

Additionally, all of the routes were rezoned to fall under the operations of four specific areas of the city, forming the eastern, western, southern and northern bus companies. All of the bus stations were amalgamated into a single station company, and all the repair workshops amalgamated into a single repair company. These reforms made it possible for each of the four bus companies to obtain services from the station company or the repair company anywhere in the city, and thus greatly reduce resource wastage, overcompetition and operating costs.

Salaries and Rewards

Dr Chen also found that the salary system of CBG was questionable in both fairness and efficiency. For example, the front-line staff generally worked very hard, however their salaries were lower than the back-up staff who didn't work as hard. This had resulted in low job satisfaction and high turnover rates among the front-line staff. After careful evaluation of the different jobs' tasks and demands, Dr Chen distinguished the tasks and demands of the front-line and back-up staff. Despite criticism from back-up staff and some managers, he insisted in increasing the wages and bonuses of the front-line staff.

To reduce the frequent accidents by bus drivers, Dr Chen linked the wage system to each driver's 'safe mileage accumulation program'. If accidents were occurring, the amount of 'safe mileage accumulation' decreased and, as a result, the level of wages. Conversely, if a driver had few accidents, or none at all, wages would increase. This meant that a driver who had not been involved in any accidents could earn an even higher wage than the average middle manager! Such a policy quickly improved the safety awareness and practices of the drivers. Furthermore, Dr Chen encouraged managers to use reward instead of punishment to motivate their employees, and abolished more than fifty penalty provisions.

The Results of Reform

After just two years of Dr She Chen's reforms, Chengdu Bus Group achieved remarkable results. The management was greatly improved, the efficiency and profitability of CBG was enhanced, and the employees were performing better and were significantly happier. Through the safe mileage accumulation system, the drivers' safety awareness and quality of service substantially improved, and the rate of accidents decreased greatly. The public attitude toward the company and its social evaluation also improved significantly. CBG was awarded for its successful reform by the State-owned Assets Supervision and Administration Commission (SASAC) of Chengdu city in 2008.

CASE STUDY 4

GLENGARRY MEDICAL REGIONAL CENTRE

Adapted and updated by Steven L. McShane, The University of Western Australia, from a case written by Donald D. White and H. William Vroman*

Glengarry Regional Medical Centre (GlenMed) is an acute-care general hospital located in Scotston, a community of 35 000 in the south-western United States. GlenMed was founded in 1950 with 35 beds and grew to a capacity of 55 beds within three years. Economic growth in the region, along with a rapid influx of people, resulted in additional expansions, and five years ago the hospital reached its present capacity of 166 beds. The hospital was called Glengarry County Hospital until a few years ago.

The population of Glengarry County has grown steadily from approximately 56 800 in 1985 to 86 600 today. However, the hospital size has remained unchanged over this time. Approximately 500 people are employed at the facility. The medical staff consists of 75 doctors and related professionals. A substantial majority of the medical staff members are specialists. Therefore, the hospital offers a wide range of medical services, serving upward of 15 000 inpatients and approximately 19 000 outpatients each year.

Three years ago, GlenMed's board of directors concluded that major expansion of the hospital was necessary to adequately serve residents in Scotston and Glengarry County. The situation had become critical by the time this expansion decision was made. Hospital managers and board members had received numerous complaints concerning the hospital's overcrowded conditions. New patients experienced long waits until beds became available; offices and hallways had become overflow storage space. State health department officials warned GlenMed's administration that if equipment and supplies were not removed from hallways, the hospital would not be licensed for the coming year and therefore could lose its accreditation.

GlenMed would expand from 166 to 248 beds, at an estimated cost of $75 million. To more accurately reflect the services available and the population served by the growing medical complex, the board decided to change the hospital's name from Glengarry County Hospital to Glengarry Regional Medical Centre. A fundraising drive raised $9 million, enough funds to launch the expansion. Tax-exempt revenue bonds would provide most of the remaining funding.

Organisational Background

Glengarry Regional Medical Centre is governed by a seven-member board of directors. State law provided that the board be appointed by the local county judge. As with any political system, appointments are based on a combination of individual qualifications and the political postures of board members. Historically, the board had not provided strong leadership to the hospital. However, recent appointments, together with strong leadership from a new board chairman, had greatly increased the activity and contribution of the board to the operation of the hospital.

All public hospital administrators face ongoing pressure from various groups, including civic political leaders, patients and their families, medical professionals and hospital staff members. These pressures can take a toll on hospital leaders, as has been the case at GlenMed. Over the past decade, the hospital has been led by no less than four chief executives, three of them within the past five years. One administrator was asked to resign after the hospital lost more than $1.6 million in two years. His replacement tried to stem the losses, but she left after eighteen months. Employees complained that she was autocratic and made erratic decisions. It was later discovered that she had been suffering from leukaemia, which may have contributed to these decisions and actions. Her replacement had been the chief financial officer for the previous two years. He lasted three years as CEO before the board asked him to resign. Although never publicly stated, the board concluded that he lacked initiative to develop the hospital and was actually present at the hospital less often than a typical full-time employee.

While searching for a new CEO, the board appointed Donald Dale as acting CEO. Dale had served as second in command (i.e. assistant administrator) under the previous CEO. During this interim period, Dale worked closely with Louise Ogbonna, GlenMed's human resource director. Both managers were acutely aware of employee morale and motivation problems within the medical centre, which they attributed to ineffective leadership over the past few years, and ongoing employee concerns about the hospital's next administrator.

Dale and Ogbonna attended a seminar on improving management competencies for health-care organisations. They were convinced that Glengarry Regional Medical Centre needed to develop management skills, so they contacted Dr Vinkat Chandry, the university professor and management consultant who had conducted the seminar. Over the next month, the two administrators met on four occasions with Chandry to discuss the problems and needs of the hospital.

Dale and Ogbonna were emphatic that they wanted to develop a more employee-oriented culture, and they had taken a few steps in that direction. For example, to enhance two-way communication, they created a nonsupervisory employee council that met once a month to discuss with Dale and Ogbonna problems and conditions throughout the hospital. Each department elected one person to represent it on the council. Initially, most of the communication was from the top down. However, shortly after the council had been created, a core of employees rose to take leadership of the group. They elected a spokesperson and requested that they be permitted to meet once a month without either Dale or Ogbonna present. Thereafter, the employee representatives met twice monthly, once with the administrators and once without them.

Louise Ogbonna also suggested to Chandry that some form of management training should be developed and conducted for department heads and hospital supervisors. Both Dale and Chandry were hesitant about the training program at this time because they didn't want to saddle a new CEO with a program that he or she might not favour. However, Ogbonna felt strongly that the program should be initiated 'as soon as possible'. The program was designed by Chandry, with agreement from Dale and Ogbonna regarding its content. Shortly thereafter, the board announced the selection of Arnold Benson as GlenMed's next CEO. Dale, Ogbonna and Chandry agreed to postpone the management training program until Benson took over the following month, but Dale indicated from his initial meeting with Benson that the new training initiative would be supported.

A New Leader for the 'Troops'

From a pool of seventy applicants, the board selected Arnold Benson as GlenMed's new CEO. At only 36 years old, Benson was one of the youngest applicants, and became the youngest administrator to ever head the hospital. He held bachelor's and master's degrees in business administration and had considerable experience working in hospital organisations. After serving four years in the Marine Corps, Benson began his health-care management career as director of purchasing and human resources in a 78-bed hospital. He then moved to a 156-bed Catholic hospital, where he rose from assistant administrator to associate administrator and finally to CEO, all within three years. Four years ago, Benson accepted the CEO position at a multihospital complex in St Louis, Missouri, which included 144-bed and 134-bed facilities. There, he had overseen a major expansion of the hospital facilities. In Benson's words, 'My objective was to become a professional hospital administrator. I realised that since I did not yet have a master's degree in hospital administration I would have to go with a "back-door approach" by working my way up the ranks.'

Benson accepted the CEO job at GlenMed because he wanted to relocate to a smaller, safer community in the south-western United States. The St Louis hospital where he worked was in a rough part of the city. Also, the hospital had been a prime target for numerous union drives (none of which was successful). Benson's salary expectations were high, given his considerable experience in hospital administration, so he was pleased when the board made him a reasonable offer to lead Glengarry Regional Medical Centre.

Benson was a tall, athletic-looking man whose mild manners and easygoing Texas drawl tended to hide his 'down-to-business' approach to administration. Soon after arriving, he realised that he would be facing many problems inside and outside the hospital in the next few months. He knew that the most pressing of these was the hospital expansion. Moreover, it was clear to him that the primary concern of some board members was the hospital's financial health.

Financial concerns plagued Benson from the moment he arrived at GlenMed. During his first weeks on the job, the building program finances consumed almost half his time. In addition, Benson was advised three weeks after his arrival that employees had been promised a 7 per cent across-the-board pay increase at the beginning of the year (in a few months). The total cost of the increase was more than $1.2 million. Benson felt that the hospital could not afford this amount of payroll increase, so he reduced the increase to 2 per cent.

'When I came aboard, the board charged me with the financial responsibility of the medical centre,' Benson explained to his managers. 'If the troops were to get their pay increase in January, it would throw the entire budget out of kilter. I have only been here three weeks, and quite frankly the current budget didn't get the attention it deserved.'

Benson had his clerical assistant send staff an email announcing the decision to cut the amount of the pay increase. He also stressed that the total financial posture of the hospital would be re-evaluated. Benson's message was also posted on bulletin boards. Over the following week, several of the posted messages were slashed and rude comments were written on them. Soon after, a rumour circulated that the hospital board of directors planned to buy Benson a new luxury car. Pictures of Mercedes and BMWs were emailed around, with suggestions that Benson had expensive taste in cars. (In reality, Benson was given the Mercury Grand Marquis purchased for the previous CEO a year ago.)

Recognising the discontent over his decision, Benson met with members of the employee advisory council to discuss the pay question. Several members of the group quoted statistics showing that, on the average, blue-collar workers throughout the United States were being paid more than were most hospital employees. Benson replied that it was unfair to quote blue-collar statistics because they are in a different industry, adding that hospital employees earn enough to live comfortably. He then asked the members of the advisory council if they would work harder if they had received the full increase. According to Benson, 'When all responded negatively, I told them point blank that it would be foolish to pay people more with no increase in productivity.' He reminded those present that he had approved a smaller pay increase and that he planned to put in effect a new compensation plan in the near future.

The employee council also voiced complaints about other conditions at GlenMed. Over the next few weeks, Benson saw to it that many of the problems were corrected to the group's satisfaction. However, when the last 'demand' was met, Benson announced that the advisory group was no longer necessary. A question was raised by one of the employees concerning whether the group would be permitted to re-form if subsequent problems arose. Benson replied that it would not be permitted to do so.

Benson was confronted by a second important decision not long after the incident involving the pay increase. The hospital had obtained most of its funds for expansion through tax-exempt revenue bonds. However, the building program excluded much-needed parking areas. Benson therefore found it necessary to ask the local banking community for an additional $5.7 million so that parking areas could be built. Although the bankers agreed to underwrite the project, the feasibility study on which their decision was based indicated that the parking areas would have to generate revenue, whereas all hospital parking was currently provided without charge to the medical staff, employees and visitors. Benson was concerned about how employees would react to pay parking so soon after learning that their pay increases had been reduced. The commitment to introduce pay parking had been made to the bankers, but Benson postponed announcement of this news.

Management Development Program

In early January, department heads throughout the hospital attended the management development program that Dr Chandry had developed with the approval of Donald Dale and Louise Ogbonna. The program consisted of seven two-hour sessions held over one month. A similar program would be conducted for supervisors a few months later. The program included many elements of traditional management training, with particular emphasis on interpersonal skill development. Dale and Ogbonna also hoped the program would identify high-potential managers. Attendance in the program was voluntary, but Benson personally recommended that department heads and supervisors should participate. Benson, Dale and Ogbonna received all materials for the program, but they agreed not to attend the sessions due to concerns that their presence might reduce participation.

One event dramatised the high level of distrust among departmental heads throughout the hospital. Participants were asked to complete evaluation forms that were to be used in connection with an exercise known as the Johari Window. The purpose of the exercise was to help the managers see themselves more clearly as others saw them and to help others in the group in a similar manner by providing them with 'image feedback' information. The theory behind the exercise, together with its purpose, was explained to those present. Each manager was asked to write the name of every department head (including himself or herself) and to list at least one asset and one liability of each person listed. Chandry requested that the completed forms be returned to him at the beginning of the next session. The name of the individual providing the 'feedback' information was not to be placed on the sheet itself. Chandry explained that he would facilitate the exchange of feedback at the next session by reading the name of a participant followed by the assets and liabilities that were identified by his or her peers.

Chandry began the next session by asking that all feedback sheets be passed in to him. Much to his surprise, only about half of the sheets were returned and most of them were insufficiently completed. After a short pause, he asked those present to explain why they had failed to complete the assignment. Following a brief discussion, it was evident that the department heads had decided in another meeting that they would not complete the feedback sheet. Some managers explained that they did not know one another well enough. (Prior to the management program many of the department heads did not know one another by name, although a 'get acquainted' exercise was used in the first session.) Others expressed fear that the information assembled on each individual would in some way be used against him or her.

One woman openly expressed concern that other department heads at the meeting might misuse the information. Another head privately suggested that some of those in attendance thought Chandry himself might take the information to the CEO. The discussion that followed had a cathartic effect on the group. For the first time, many of the managers 'opened up' and talked about the lack of communication and trust that existed between the department heads and between the department heads and Benson.

Chandry ended the session by again explaining that the purpose of the exercise was to 'improve our understandings of ourselves as well as of those with whom we associate throughout the hospital'. Participants then agreed to complete and return the feedback sheets at the next session. At the next session, the exercise was completed smoothly. Many of the managers commented afterward that they believed that the exercise had been beneficial and had helped to open up the group. One department head did comment, however, 'To tell you the truth, I think our refusal to complete the feedback sheets helped to break the ice between us. You know, it is the first time we really ever got together and agreed on something.' The remainder of the management development program was well received.

The Retreat

A few days after the department heads' program was completed, Benson asked Chandry to meet with him. He began their conference by stating that he was pleased with what he had heard about the sessions and was anxious to ensure that the momentum that had been created would not be lost. He asked Chandry what he thought of bringing all the department heads together for a weekend retreat at a resort area not far from Scotston. Chandry was pleased with the suggestion, saying that he had considered recommending such an event but was concerned about the hospital's financial situation. Benson replied that the money for the retreat could be found since he anticipated that it would have a positive impact on the hospital's operations.

The following week Benson advised department heads that a retreat had been scheduled for the weekend of 14–15 February. He went on to explain that the department heads would gather on Friday morning at the hospital and would drive directly to the resort. All expenses would be paid by the medical centre. He told them that he hoped that the meeting would permit a free exchange of ideas.

A week before the scheduled retreat, Chandry met alone with the department heads who attended the training program to conduct a brief follow-up session. As he walked into the room, he noticed that many managers were voicing their frustrations to one another. Thinking that the concerns were about this follow-up session, Chandry explained his presence and told them that he was interested in their feedback and application of the management training.

One manager stated that their anger had nothing to do with this meeting or with Chandry. Others then spoke up, most of them about the upcoming retreat. A few department heads stated that they did not want to attend the retreat. One newly married woman stated that it was Valentine's Day and her husband did not want her to go. Two other heads said they already had plans to attend a previously reserved Valentine's Day event at the country club that Friday evening. As discussion continued, it became apparent that the department heads had been told rather than consulted about the retreat. Some expressed displeasure with being 'forced' into going to the retreat and using part of their weekend without first being asked their opinion.

Chandry listened carefully and explained to the managers that he believed the retreat was a good idea. He told them that he had considered such an event but that the CEO suggested the idea on his own. Furthermore, Chandry told them that the department heads should give Benson 'a chance' during the weekend to see what might come out of the retreat. There were a few supportive comments made by one or two department heads and the meeting broke up.

Chandry left the meeting both perplexed and concerned. He had not anticipated the frustration that he witnessed from department heads throughout the hospital. As he walked toward the entrance of the hospital, Dr Chandry asked himself whether he should provide further assistance to Benson before the retreat. He decided to stop in and see the CEO before leaving the hospital.

*Source: The original version of this case was published in Donald D. White and H. William Vroman, *Action in Organisations*. Copyright © 1977 by Holbrook Press, Inc., subsidiary of Allyn and Bacon, Inc., Boston.

CASE STUDY 5

GROWING PAINS AT AUSTRAL TECHNOLOGIES

By Brenda Scott-Ladd, Curtin University of Technology, and Trevor Overton, Austral Technologies

'I wonder if we have encouraged too much employee involvement!' Trevor Overton, the general manager of Austral Technologies was talking to one of his partners, Ross Browne, the evening before he was due to fly to China. Austral was trying to restructure its Perth operations, as a preliminary to expanding operations into China, but changes had been met with considerable resistance from staff.

Austral is a specialised surface engineering company that services the mining, mineral processing and power-generation industries throughout Australia and Asia. It commenced operations in 1993. The company has been through some tough times, though. When Overton and his three partners took over the company's ownership in 2003, Austral had little value other than its equipment and stock, and no regular customers or work in progress.

Since then, Austral has grown through innovation. The company has developed and perfected specialised techniques for refurbishing exotic metals and white irons, and is a leader in its industry. The company has grown at 15–20 per cent each year over the last five years to achieve sales figures of around $2.5 million per annum, and now has a healthy bottom line. Austral employs around thirteen company members, with most being long-term employees. Overton uses the term 'members' deliberately to signify Austral's strong family orientation; for example, employees were retained through the lean times and the company is supportive if personal issues affect employees.

The firm's growth is in part attributable to the Western Australian mining boom, but Overton believes it is also due to Austral's dedication to service and development. Austral places a high value on customer service and enjoys such a strong reputation for excellent service; it is the first choice of customers who are confronted with new and specific 'wear-related' problems. The company enjoys an excellent relationship with its core customers, who appreciate Austral's ability and willingness to innovate when confronted with difficulties, and this has led to significant repeat business. However, the company now faces a dilemma common to many successful small businesses: it needs to grow and expand if it is to maintain its competitive lead in the longer term.

Going Offshore: The Expansion Plan

Austral has almost outgrown its current facilities, and the local market is reaching saturation point. The company has identified that the highest potential for growth comes from emerging markets in Asia, particularly China, so it plans to reproduce their current facilities in China. This planned growth is also fuelling the need to expand staff numbers and competencies within Austral, which is causing employee concerns. Overton wants Austral to double its market in the medium term over the next two years through the Chinese development, but also expects further expansion of services as new opportunities present themselves.

'Currently, employees can actively participate in work procedure and development decisions, and where possible promotions come from within the work teams, but this will have to change as we expand. We will all need to develop new skills—and by that I mean both the management and the production team,' says Overton. Some changes are already happening. Overton has embarked on a Chinese-language course and an MBA, so he can be better equipped to manage the offshore business development program. The next step is for a Chinese production team to be trained in the specialist knowledge that has taken the Australians years to develop. In preparation, a multiskilled workshop supervisor has been appointed, and training programs are being developed in Australia. The new supervisor's current task is to develop procedural manuals, in consultation with production and management. However, it is not all smooth sailing!

Austral needs the Australian workforce to be involved in training and supporting the development of the Chinese workforce. Offshore work is not new at Austral—several employees have already travelled overseas for short periods to service existing contracts. However, despite being informed and reasonably receptive to the plans for expansion, the Australian workers do not want to relocate to China for any length of time. Many of the employees still have school-aged children, and the company acknowledges their concerns about overseas placements. As a compromise, the company wants current employees to take on short-term training assignments in China. Most employees are still not keen to do this, though a few are coming around to the idea. For example, one employee who initially said 'No way am I going there!' has changed his stance to 'Well, it might be interesting for a short visit to train locals.' The downside of rotating Australian staff into China is that it will increase the pressure on the already overloaded Perth facility.

Personnel Changes: A New Supervisor

Another change that has met with resistance is the appointment of the new workshop supervisor from outside the company. The position was created to reduce the load on Overton and Browne, who plan to divide their time between the Chinese and Australian facilities. 'The China growth focus means we need a more strategic and formal management structure,' Trevor says. Initially the company had difficulty finding the right person to fill the supervisor role. The supervisor has responsibility for safety, maintenance, scheduling, procedure and equipment development; however, the pivotal role is to ensure staff training and development, and facilitate change management on the shop floor. Attempts to fill the position internally were unsuccessful but did highlight the need to pay more attention to developing employee skills and putting succession plans in place. Despite not having specific experience in Austral's industry, the new supervisor is considered a good fit for the role because of his general industry experience, dual-trade background, significant remote-site and overseas experience, and experience in developing and delivering training.

Austral is taking a 'double-barrelled approach', tackling the China development and formalising in-house procedure at the same time, and believes this will return the best result for the company. The new supervisor's skills and understanding fit well with management's growth plan; however, the applicant hired for the position comes from a military background and is experiencing some difficulties making the transition. 'Raising money might be no object when defending our country, but funds are only spent here after much discussion as to economic benefit or return on investment and wastage is kept to a minimum,' Overton pointed out to him.

Financial restrictions are not the only difficulty the supervisor is facing. He is attempting to introduce a more hierarchical structure, but has met with resistance from employees. In part, Overton thinks this is because the team and supervisor are still going through the 'forming and storming' processes. Some staff have directly sought support from Overton, while others have disrupted operations with counterproductive work practices. Overton cites an example of one employee admitting he had worked more slowly and with less attention to quality in the hope that he would be given a less demanding job.

Organisational Culture and Management Style

In the past, Austral employees were always involved in making decisions about the company's direction, and the company only engaged in activities employees felt comfortable with. 'This is hardly the best way to run a business,' acknowledges Overton. 'We need a more strategic business focus and to provide employee development, but the challenge is motivating members to support these changes.' He acknowledges that employees are used to working within a low power-distance culture, and have also been accustomed to moderate workloads—although they do work hard when it is needed. The work has plenty of variety, with the opportunity for employees to work on a variety of sites for short periods of time, giving them the opportunity to earn very good money.

The new supervisor admits his is a more directive and centralised style of management, and that his job is to ensure procedures are laid down and followed. Some employees have complained that the supervisor is not very diplomatic when giving guidance or instructions. So far, Overton has thrown his support behind the supervisor because change has to take place, but admits that on occasion he has to smooth the waters and make excuses for him.

From Overton's perspective, the supervisor understands the need for timely performance and its effect on production costs, quality and the effectiveness which is part of Austral's strategic focus. Overton also agrees with the supervisor that some employees have a relaxed attitude and have had it pretty easy, as there have been ongoing problems with some employees' timekeeping. A large part of the problem is that the work is highly specialised and the current employees are very experienced and would be hard to replace, especially given Western Australia's current labour shortage, so some employees know they have significant bargaining power over the management. The counterweight to this is that their specialisation could make it harder for them to find a new position if they left Austral. On the one hand, employees understand the need for growth and

CASE STUDY

change, particularly as the company already has ongoing work with Chinese companies; on the other hand, many are resisting changes initiated by the supervisor.

The fact that the new supervisor lacks specific industry knowledge places him at a disadvantage and has added to the friction in the workshop. Some employees are adjusting, but a few of the long-term employees are refusing to work under the strict conditions and accountability that the supervisor wishes to implement. These employees claim the supervisor would be less autocratic if he learned more about their jobs and really appreciated just how difficult the work can be.

Overton acknowledges that employees may be worried about being forced to accept some time working in China, or concerned that operations might move from Perth to China. 'Their fears are totally unfounded, but it seems a possibility to some of them, though the company has made it clear this is not something we want to do,' explains Overton. 'We have discussed this with employees formally, informally and in group settings. We have reiterated the point a number of times! We are also open to discussing individual concerns. What else can we do?'

6 HIGH NOON AT ALPHA MILL

By Arif Hassan and Thivagar Velayutham, International Islamic University Malaysia

Alpha Plantations Sdn Bhd is an oil palm plantation located in Malaysia. It consists of an oil palm estate and one palm oil mill. It is a wholly owned subsidiary of a British multinational company and was founded with the purpose of supplying crude palm oil for its parent company's detergent manufacturing business. Since its formation, most of the managers have been recruited from the UK, with many British ex-soldiers and police officers joining up. Mr Ang Siow Lee first joined Alpha mill in 1965 at the age of 15 as a labourer, and rose through the ranks to become the most senior nonmanagerial staff member in Alpha. Mr Ang is the senior production supervisor in Alpha's palm oil mill. His immediate superior is the mill manager and he has two junior supervisors to assist him. The mill operates on a three-shift cycle of twenty-five operators each, and each supervisor (including Mr Ang) is in charge of one shift.

Mr Ang is responsible for the smooth operation of the daily palm oil processing. He co-ordinates the activities of all three shifts with the two supervisors, prepares the daily production reports, deals with short-term human resource planning issues and minor discipline issues, and sets and evaluates short-term performance targets for all three shifts. In addition, he acts as the 'gatekeeper', which means that any mill personnel who wish to see the mill manager must first see Mr Ang, who tries to solve the problem first. These problems may be anything from house repairs to a request for an advance on wages. Only in rare cases, when Mr Ang cannot resolve the issue, is the matter brought up with the mill manager. Mr Ang always ran a tight ship, and did not let anyone forget it. His superb technical competency helped him keep the mill in top shape. He became accustomed to receiving the highest appraisal ratings from the mill manager, who appreciated his firm, methodical and almost militarily efficient way of running the mill.

In 1999, the palm oil industry in Malaysia faced many challenges. World oil prices plunged due to oversupply, and palm oil prices hit a fifteen-year low. This cut the profit margins of all palm oil producers and caused Alpha mill to post regular losses. Captain Chubb, the 54-year-old former Royal Engineer and mill manager, was at a loss on how to improve performance. 'We are doing nothing wrong, and have met all our efficiency targets. It's this market that is killing us!' he exasperatedly explained during the annual year-end visit of the directors from London. Very soon Captain Chubb was given his marching orders.

Soon after, a new mill manager was appointed. Mr Ian Davison, a 32-year-old who hailed from Edinburgh, was very different from all his predecessors. He was not a career plantation engineer and had never managed an agricultural product-processing mill before. He was actually an electronics engineer with an Ivy-League MBA on the fast track to a top management position. His previous appointment was as factory manager of a detergent factory in Egypt where he managed to streamline and modernise operations, and increase financial performance drastically. Headquarters in London had high hopes that he would be able to do the same with Alpha mill and return it to profitability.

His first action was to analyse operations at Alpha mill and look for ways to reduce production costs and increase profits. He arrived at the following conclusions:

- Current performance standards allowed too much machine breakdown and changeover time. Better standards were achievable with the latest technology.
- Wastage could be reduced and yield improved drastically by installing machinery based on new technology.
- Personnel numbers were too high—they could be reduced with technology, multitasking and unleashing the full potential of workers.
- Personnel were just 'cruising along'. They were not fully committed to achieving better performance.
- Hygiene needs were not being met.
- The old colonial and hierarchical company culture was not conducive to performance improvement.
- Information was not shared across the mill. Operators only knew about their own little area in the mill and almost nothing about the company as a whole.

Mr Davison proposed to remedy the situation with the following initiatives:

- Empower operators by reorganising the shifts into self-directed production teams where the supervisors would now play the role of 'facilitators' and thereby gain commitment.
- Install new technology and automation.
- Adopt more stringent performance measures.

Mr Davison implemented and executed these initiatives by first organising an excursion to a local picnic spot for the entire factory. After the icebreakers, games and lunch, he held a briefing session on the beach, where he explained the situation Alpha mill was in and the need to make changes. He then unveiled his plan for the first time. The response was enthusiastic, although some operators privately confessed to not understanding some of the terminology Mr Davison used. At the end of the excursion, when there was some time allocated for feedback, Mr Ang expressed his full support for Mr Davison's plan. 'We in Alpha mill have full confidence in you, our new leader and we assure you of our 110 per cent support to make your plan a success!' he said at the end of his speech.

When the new machinery had been installed and each shift had been reorganised into self-directed work teams, the plan was put into motion. Whenever the team faced a problem during processing and tried to find a solution using the techniques that had been taught, Mr Ang would step in after some time, issue instructions and take over the process. 'This is a simple problem, no need to waste time over it. Just do it ...' His instructions were always followed and the immediate problem was always solved. However, the production team reverted to the old ways of working, and none of the expected benefits of teaming were realised. Given the new tighter performance standards and reduced number of staff, the team consistently underperformed. Team meetings were one-way affairs where Mr Ang would tell everyone else what had gone wrong.

Mr Ang's response to this was to push himself harder. He was always the first to arrive and the last to leave. He would spend a lot of time troubleshooting process problems. He pushed his operators even harder, but he felt that he had less of a 'handle' on his operators now that they had direct access to the mill manager and most of their minor needs were seen to by him. Sometimes he became annoyed about his operators' mistakes and would resort to shouting and cursing, which had the immediate effect of moving people in the direction he wanted. This was in contrast to the mere glare that would have sufficed previously.

The continued poor performance of Alpha mill affected Mr Ang's mid-year appraisal rating, which fell down from 'excellent' to merely 'adequate'. During the appraisal interview, an annoyed Mr Davison bluntly told Mr Ang that he needed to understand clearly what the initiatives were all about, and that he had to let the team take some responsibility, make mistakes and learn from them. 'With your knowledge of this mill, you should be able to provide them with all the technical input they need,' he said. Mr Davison also added. 'It might help if you treated our people with a little more respect. We aren't living in the 1940s, anymore you know.' Mr Ang was thunderstruck by the appraisal but did not raise any objections on the spot. He silently deferred to Mr Davison's judgment and promised to do better. He also reiterated his utmost support for Mr Davison and his plan.

After the mid-year appraisal, however, there was a noticeable change in Mr Ang's demeanour. He became very quiet and began to take a less active role in the daily running of the mill. He was superficially polite to the operators and answered most requests for help with 'Get the team together and discuss it amongst yourselves. Show the boss that you can solve it for yourselves.' At first the teams were at a loss and mill performance suffered badly, but within two weeks the team had found its feet and performance began to improve. One of Mr Ang's junior supervisors, Mr Raman, was able to coordinate between production teams to ensure that the performance gains were maintained. The effect on Mr Ang was devastating. He became withdrawn and began to drink more than usual. His presence at team meetings became a mere formality and he contributed next to nothing, taking a back seat to other team members. He spoke very little to mill personnel and became a mere shadow of his former self.

Mr Davison was very aware of the changes taking place on the mill floor. He decided that it was time to have Mr Ang removed from his position. He began to plan for a reshuffle of Alpha mill's organisation chart where Mr Ang would be promoted to the new position of mill executive, a staff position with a small pay raise. His responsibility would be to advise the mill manager on technical, quality and efficiency problems faced by the mill. He would be assigned to carry out minor improvement projects and performance audits from time to time. Mr Raman would be promoted as supervisor and report directly to the mill manager. Mr Ang would no longer have any line authority over the production team. This reorganisation was quickly approved by head office and Mr Davison proceeded to lay the groundwork for the announcements and the necessary paperwork. Little did he foresee what was to follow.

Mr Ang was in the head office one morning when the personnel executive's clerk congratulated him on his imminent promotion. A surprised Mr Ang enquired further and learned of the plans that Mr Davison had in store for him. It was the final straw. He rushed back to Alpha mill just as Mr Davison was about to conduct his noon mill inspection. The confrontation was very loud, acrimonious and public. It ended with Mr Ang being terminated for insubordination and gross misconduct.

After Mr Ang had left, Mr Davison felt that the obstacle to better commitment and morale was gone and that performance would improve greatly. He was very wrong. Team performance began to deteriorate and no amount of pep talks could improve it. He began to wonder what had gone wrong.

CASE STUDY 7

TALENT DEVELOPMENT AND CAPABILITY IN SUNNY OPTICAL

By Peter Lok and Jo Rhodes, University of South Australia

In late 2007, John Wu, CEO of SUNNY Optical in Shanghai, was struggling to retain talent in his firm. He expected that the new policy of 'life employment',* to be introduced by the Labour Department in China over the next few months, would impact negatively on attracting and retaining the right talent for SUNNY. In order to sustain the number-one position in optical retailing in China, Wu took up the challenge to retain and develop human capital as a strategic priority in his firm.

China's Looming Talent Shortage

In 2003, China had roughly 9.6 million graduates with up to seven years' work experience, and an additional 97 million people who would qualify for support-staff positions (Farrell & Grant, 2005). Despite this apparently vast supply of graduates, multinational organisations and top domestic service companies were finding that few local graduates had the necessary skills for service occupations. By 2007, this problem had become even greater. As a result, these firms were confronting many challenges in retaining quality employees. Job-hopping was common among successful managers, and above-average wages and benefits were needed to retain talent.

Company Background

SUNNY Optical originated in 1956 as a small watch and clock retailing store in Taipei. By merging with other similar retail outlets, by 1981 SUNNY had established its name in Taiwan. The company initially entered mainland China in 1997. With only four shops, SUNNY lay its footing in the four 'tier two' cities of Wuhan, Xiamen, Fuzhou and Guanzhou. Once they were consolidated, SUNNY expanded quickly into other cities.

By 2007, SUNNY had become the biggest Chinese retailer for optical products in the world, with 610 optical retail outlets in Taiwan, and 1118 outlets (staffed by 7700 employees) spread across all the major cities of mainland China. Its sales revenue had grown exponentially to 1.8 billion yuan (US$300 billion) per year, and it was projected that SUNNY could be one of the biggest optical retailers in the world within three years.

Leadership Style

Although SUNNY was a family-owned company, it had a flat organisational structure. Senior executives consisted of John Wu (CEO), Lee Chu (CFO) and Ming Chen (COO). There were five other heads of departments responsible for sales, research and development, human resources, operations and finance/accounts. A total of thirty-two other employees were stationed at its Shanghai headquarters. Department heads and executive members were involved in regular weekly meetings, and monthly staff briefings were conducted for all staff.

John Wu maintained an open-door policy and encouraged staff to voice their ideas and complaints directly to him. He 'modelled the way' for his employees. He liked informal exchanges and showed great emotional intelligence. Despite difficulties and setbacks in the past, he had great resilience and the ability to pick himself up and go again; he treated setbacks as lessons to be learned. He had good insight about the business environment and the industry, and identified with his staff, which earned him much respect from his employees. However, one of Wu's weaknesses was his inability to say 'no'. When asked about this aspect of his personality, he simply concluded that he liked new challenges too much!

SUNNY's Philosophy and Value System

From the first day the business started, SUNNY considered product quality, innovation and professional service to be the cornerstones of its business. All the products on its shelves went through a rigorous quality assurance system to ensure the highest technical standards. SUNNY guaranteed that all products it sold were entered into its tracking system, along with all the buyers' information. The buyers, if not satisfied with the products purchased, could exchange them for other products.

The mission of SUNNY was 'to become a world leader in the retailing industry for eye-care optical products and services'. John Wu believed that the key to success was reliable service, high-quality products and superior customer value. Furthermore, he considered that these activities could be enhanced by structured employee learning and development programs to ensure continuous innovation. Continuous innovation would require systematic programs and support from the firm, and Wu realised that learning involved trying new ideas and making mistakes. He made his employees comfortable in working on new ideas by modelling an honest response to failure: 'My idea did not work so well and I have wasted time, energy and resources. I'm sorry for that, but I have learned from this and hope you can do the same.'

Wu found that this approach generated some excellent ideas. One new idea suggested by an employee was enthusiastically received by the firm. The idea was to use information technology and internet interfacing to allow customers to try on different spectacle frames from the firm's online catalogue (different style, sizes, brands, colours and so on), then submit orders to the nearest outlet for fitting and purchase. Although the online experience was still in its developmental stage, this innovation had the potential to expand the firm's market share even more.

SUNNY implemented a structured mentor system; work teams were encouraged to hold informal functions to build up collaboration and support for each other. A special 'collaborator fund' (small seed money) could be used for any of these informal functions to enhance the company's networking capabilities. Overall, the firm had a 'people-first' policy whereby employees who performed well would always be retained by the firm, even when downturns occurred in the industry. The firm had experienced three major downturns in its fifty-year history, and limited its redundancy rate to only 4 per cent in total during these hard times.

Current HR Practices at SUNNY

John Wu was fully aware of the critical importance of the company's employees. He considered them to be strategic assets of the company. From its earliest days, SUNNY focused on employees training and made great efforts to improve employees' professional skills and abilities. The professional skill and competence of SUNNY's optometric technicians ensured the company's competitive position in its markets, and gave it a cutting edge when competing with other firms in the same industry.

Wu always maintained full commitment to developing talent in his firm. His human resource department had fully integrated systems in recruitment, selection, training, mentoring, career development, team reward systems and bonus packages, performance management and leadership development. For example, SUNNY spent 3.9 per cent of its overall payroll on training. Each employee received an average of 224 hours of training per year. Although SUNNY's staff turnover rate was around 16 per cent per annum, this was below the industry average of 22 per cent. Wu was keen to maintain and improve on the level of staff retention and development.

Current Challenges

With the introduction of the new life employment policy, and the continuing shortage of quality managers in the service sector, John Wu wondered what new strategies he could use to sustain his growth and expansion ambitions for SUNNY Optical in China.

References

D. Farrell and A. Grant, 'China's Looming Talent Shortage', *McKinsey Quarterly*, November 2005.

* **The life employment policy** in China requires all companies to provide life-employment contracts to individuals after their second contract renewal (i.e. after two years of continuous full-time employment).

VIDEO CASE STUDIES

To access the video footage refer to: http//: www.mhhe.com/au/mcshane3e

VIDEO CASE STUDIES FOR PART 1

Yahoo!7: Part 1

The four Yahoo!7 video clips for Part 1 present the thoughts and experiences of executives at Yahoo!7 in Australia regarding diversity, globalisation, personal values and work-life balance. Chief operating officer Bruno Fiorentini explains how Yahoo!7 operates in a global environment. In the diversity segment, Fiorentini and HR Director Fiona Cole discuss the benefits of employing a diverse workforce, particularly GenerationX/Y staff. In the third segment, Cole describes Yahoo!7's flexible work arrangements and the benefits to employees and the company of those arrangements. The fourth segment focuses on values, ethics and corporate social responsibility, including the importance of Yahoo!7's values, the types of corporate social responsibility the company engages in and the importance of ethics, as well as how ethics are reinforced.

Discussion Questions

1. *Organisational Behaviour on the Pacific Rim* 3e identifies globalisation, workforce diversity and emerging employment relationships as three contemporary challenges for organisations. How does Yahoo!7 address each of these challenges?
2. Why are values, ethics and corporate social responsibility important at Yahoo!7?

Wal-Mart's Public Image Campaign

After years of criticism from various groups, Wal-Mart is paying more attention to its stakeholders. 'We've talked to environmentalists, we've talked to NGOs; we've talked to people in neighbourhoods. We've really reached out to say: What should we be doing differently?' says Mona Williams, Wal-Mart's VP of corporate communications. In Aurora, Colorado, the world's largest retailer has introduced numerous environmental initiatives, including solar and wind energy and recycled tyres. Wal-Mart also claims that it has removed managers who acted unethically due to pressures to reduce costs. 'We are light years ahead of where we were even two or three years ago,' says Williams. This PBS program details some of the initiatives Wal-Mart has developed to change its relationship with stakeholders. We also hear from critics who explain why Wal-Mart's recent public image campaign doesn't correct the company's underlying problems.

Discussion Questions

1. Which stakeholders does Wal-Mart seem to be serving better than in the past? Why does this shift make a difference to Wal-Mart?
2. Are the ongoing criticisms about Wal-Mart justified? Is it possible to satisfy stakeholders more fully than Wal-Mart is currently attempting?

Good Business Deeds

You might not expect to see British American Tobacco, McDonald's and Microsoft at a meeting on corporate social responsibility but, in their own way, these firms are taking steps to become better employers and citizens in the community. This video program describes how these and other firms are embracing values and corporate social responsibility. It particularly highlights a few firms that serve as role models in this regard. One of these is Greyston Bakery, a multimillion dollar gourmet operation that takes people who need help and turns them into contributing members of the organisation and society. Another is Eileen Fisher Company, which promotes good labour practices both at home and overseas, and helps customers meet their needs. In each case, the company's values are aligned more closely with employee values than at your typical organisation.

Discussion Questions

1. Employees at Greyston Bakery, Eileen Fisher Company, Feed the Children, Green@ Work and other organisations described in this video program seem to have a strong congruence of their personal values with the organisation's values. What are the apparent benefits of this values congruence?
2. Discuss the implications of corporate social responsibility in terms of organisational effectiveness.

VIDEO CASE STUDIES FOR PART 2

To access the video footage refer to: http//: www.mhhe.com/au/mcshane3e

Yahoo!7: Part 2

Five video segments about Yahoo!7 are available for Part 2 of this book. In one segment, several employees describe what they enjoy and what motivates them at Yahoo!7. Another segment refers specifically to employee engagement at the company as well as the application of the Backslappers reward and recognition program. In a third short segment, HR director Fiona Cole and account manager Lani Booth describe Yahoo!7's goal-setting process. Two other segments examine the company's emphasis on employee involvement in company decisions as well as creativity, particularly the creative value of 'hack days'.

Discussion Questions

1. Three Yahoo!7 segments cluster around what employees enjoy about working at Yahoo!7, how they are rewarded through the Backslappers program and how they conduct goal setting. Explain how each of the topics in these three segments relates to employee engagement. Also, based on the interviews in these three segments, identify the aspects of working at Yahoo!7 that employees seem to enjoy the most.
2. What are 'hack days' and how do they encourage creativity at Yahoo!7?
3. Describe how Yahoo!7 involves employees in decision making. Your answer should include some discussion of the 'mash meetings'.

Clockless Office: Best Buy's ROWE Program

Kelly McDevitt has a busy job as online promotions manager for Best Buy. But McDevitt doesn't have to worry about punching a time clock because of the retailer's result-only work environment (ROWE). 'I don't count my hours. I don't have hours,' she says. McDevitt attends office meetings, but even attending those events is optional. 'It's not how many hours somebody puts in face time at the office, it's: are they getting their work done' explains Calli Ressler. This *Business Week* television program describes the ROWE program, explains why it was introduced and outlines its apparent benefits.

Discussion Questions

1. Why would productivity jump at Best Buy under ROWE, compared to the traditional employment arrangement where employees are expected to be at the office?
2. What effect would the ROWE program have on workplace stress? Explain your answer.
3. What are the limitations and risks of the ROWE program? Which jobs and employees would be poorly suited to this work arrangement?

Employee Loyalty

Not so long ago, companies offered secure employment. In return, workers showed their loyalty by remaining with one company for most of their careers. Not any more! This CBC video program illustrates how dramatically times have changed. Joel Baglole received an internship at the *Toronto Star* and later was offered a full-time job. Baglole happily accepted the position, but quit six weeks later when the prestigious *Wall Street Journal* offered him a job. Baglole explains why he had no obligation to be loyal to the *Toronto Star*, whereas the paper's publisher John Honderich believes that loyalty is important and should be expected. This program also examines ways that the *Toronto Star* and other companies try to increase employee loyalty.

Discussion Questions

1. Which, if any, of the five strategies to build organisational commitment would be effective in this situation involving Joel Baglole?
2. Explain how Joel Baglole's psychological contract is influenced by organisational loyalty in this situation.

Johnson & Johnson: (a) Creating a Global Learning Organisation: The Credo; (b) Management Fundamentals Training at Johnson & Johnson

Johnson & Johnson (J&J) is a family-oriented health care and personal products company with about 330 operating units and more than 150,000 employees around the world. The company is well known for 'the Credo', a set of values statements introduced in 1938 to help J&J's executives and employees make better decisions. The Credo helps J&J staff to continuously be aware of and serve the needs of its core stakeholders. It also serves as the glue that holds the company's geographically and industrially diverse operating units together. This program introduces Johnson & Johnson's credo and shows how the company instills those values in its managers.

Discussion Questions

1. Why does Johnson & Johnson place so much importance on The Credo?
2. How does Johnson & Johnson ensure that managers understand and apply The Credo in their daily decisions and actions?

Pike Place Fish Market

Fifteen years ago, Pike Place Fish Market in Seattle had unhappy employees and was in financial trouble. Rather than close shop, owner John Yokoyama sought help from consultant Jim Bergquist to improve his leadership and energise the workforce. Rather than rule as a tyrant, Yokoyama learned how to actively involve employees in the business. Soon, staff felt more empowered and gained more enjoyment from their work. They also began to actively have fun at work, including setting goals as a game, throwing fish to each other as sport and pretending they are 'world famous'. Today, thanks to these and other strategies described in this video case, Pike Place *is* world famous. The little shop has become a tourist attraction and customers from California to New York call in orders.

Discussion Questions

1. Based on the model of emotions and attitudes in Chapter 4, explain how the changes at Pike Place Fish Market improved job satisfaction and reduced turnover. How did these attitude changes affect customer satisfaction?
2. Goal setting is discussed as an important activity at Pike Place. Evaluate the effectiveness of this goal setting process in the context of the characteristics of effective goals described in Chapter 5 of this textbook.
3. How is coaching applied at Pike Place and how does this coaching influence employee performance?

Stress in Japan

Stress from overwork has become an epidemic in Japan. This video program consists of two segments that illustrate the degree to which some Japanese employees are overworked, as well as the consequences of their overwork. The first segment follows a typical day of a Japanese manager, from his two-hour morning commute to his late night working hours. The program also shows how he is under constant pressure to improve efficiency, and experiences a heavy burden and responsibility to do better. The second segment describes how *karoshi*—death from overwork—took the life of 23-year-old Yoshika. It reconstructs Yoshiko's work life as a graphic artist up to the time when she died suddenly on the job due to a brain haemorrhage.

Discussion Questions

1. Identify the various sources of stress (i.e. stressors) that the Japanese manager in the first segment is likely to experience each day. Does he do anything to try to manage his stress?
2. What conditions led up to the *karoshi* death of Yoshika? Are these conditions commonly found in the country where you live?

VIDEO CASE STUDIES

VIDEO CASE STUDIES FOR PART 3

Yahoo!7: Part 3

Part 3 of this book includes four video segments about Yahoo!7. In the segment on teams, client services executive Joanna Holcombe, search engineering manager Sebastian Urban and account manager Lani Booth discuss the importance of teamwork at Yahoo!7, as well as ways

To access the video footage refer to: http//: www.mhhe.com/au/mcshane3e

that the company supports a positive team-oriented environment. In the conflict segment, those interviewed discuss the reality of conflict in organisations as well as the conditions and methods through which conflict is resolved at Yahoo!7. In the segment on workplace design and communication, employees describe Yahoo!7's physical workspace as well as how it encourages communication. In the leadership segment, chief operating officer Bruno Fiorentini explains the key characteristics, goals and approaches to effective leadership at Yahoo!7.

Discussion Questions

1. Based on the two video segments on teamwork and workplace design and communication, how does Yahoo!7 support a positive, team-oriented environment?
2. How do managers at Yahoo!7 view and resolve conflict? In your opinion, is this an effective approach to viewing and managing conflict?
3. According to Yahoo!7 chief operating officer Bruno Fiorentini, what are the important goals or approaches to effective leadership in this organisation?

Generation Next Changes the Face of the Workplace

Jo Muse is baffled. The CEO of Muse Communications received requests from younger staff for holiday time after just two months on the job. 'Why do you think that you can work places for a couple months and then get a holiday,' Muse asks his Generation X and Y staff. 'And unpaid! You don't care if you get paid. What's up with that?'

Baby boomer managers, such as Jo Muse, face the challenge of figuring out the needs and expectations of young employees. The differences—which range from subtle to stark—also produce conflict in the workplace. 'There is a clash,' suggests 24-year-old X-Ray technician Doan Phan. Phan points to differences in technology skills as one source of conflict. Another is the urgency to change the workplace. 'We want to bring in new ideas. We want to change things,' Phan says. This PBS program peeks into several organisations to see how younger and older generation employees are getting along. The program examines how Gen X/Y employees view their employment differently from baby boomers. It also describes the actions of those companies who are addressing these conflicts and changing expectations.

Discussion Questions

1. In this program, how are Generation X and Y employees depicted differently from baby boomer employees? Are these differences a reasonably accurate representation of generational differences in the workplace today?
2. What steps have Deloitte and other companies taken to adjust to the expectations of younger employees and to reduce potential generational conflict in the workplace?

Celebrity CEO Charisma

Does the cult of CEO charisma really make a difference to company profits? This NBC program takes a brief look at chief executives who acted like super-heroes but failed to deliver, as well as a few low-key executives who really made a difference. The program hears from Harvard business school professor Rakesh Khurana, author of *Searching for a Corporate Savior*, a book warning that charismatic leaders are not necessarily effective leaders.

Discussion Questions

1. Why do company boards tend to hire charismatic CEOs?
2. What can corporate boards do to minimise the charisma effect when filling chief executive officer and other senior executive positions?

Southwest CEO: Get to Know Gary Kelly

Southwest Airlines remains one of the most successful airlines in the United States. What is its secret to success? They treat customers as kings and queens—and treat their employees even better. This video program shows how Southwest Airlines CEO, Gary Kelly, keeps in touch with day-to-day activities at the airline. It also describes some of the challenges that Kelly and his executive team have ahead of them.

Discussion Questions

1. Discuss the transactional and transformational leadership of Gary Kelly.
2. How does Gary Kelly's leadership reinforce Southwest Airlines' organisational culture?

Team Work: Team Activities for Co-Workers

Companies have more ways than ever before to help employees with teambuilding. Cooking classes, hula-hoops, human-sized Chinese checkers or horse riding are just a few of the activities that can help employees work more effectively together. This NBC program reveals three teambuilding activities: rodeos, field games and cooking classes. We also hear the opinions of participants in these activities.

Discussion Questions

1. This program shows employees in three teambuilding activities: rodeo, field games and cooking classes. Which of these three appeals to you the most as a teambuilding activity? Explain why.
2. Which individual and teambuilding skills do participants believe will be improved from the cooking classes?
3. To what extent would each of these activities influence team dynamics back on the job? What conditions might further improve the transfer of team dynamics from these activities to the workplace?

VIDEO CASE STUDIES

VIDEO CASE STUDIES FOR PART 4

To access the video footage refer to: http//: www.mhhe.com/au/mcshane3e

Yahoo!7: Part 4

Three Yahoo!7 video programs are provided in Part 4 of this book. In one segment, chief operating officer Bruno Fiorentini and other managers discuss Yahoo!7's organisational structure, including its fit with the company's needs and Australian culture. The segment on organisational culture refers to the role of employees in the company's culture, how employees are selected and the socialisation processes used to help them learn about and adjust to Yahoo!7's work environment. In the segment on organisational change, Bruno Fiorentini discusses the merger of Yahoo! Australia and New Zealand with Channel Seven, as well as the conditions that help to support the change process.

Discussion Questions

1. Determine whether Yahoo!7 is more of a mechanical or an organic structure and justify your conclusion. Evaluate whether this structural configuration is well suited to the company's environment.
2. Describe the selection and socialisation of employees at Yahoo!7 and explain why the company pays so much attention to these processes.
3. The video segment on organisational change refers to the merger of Yahoo! Australia and New Zealand with Channel Seven to form Yahoo!7. What factors are mentioned that supported the change process?

Lindblad Expeditions: Under the Surface

Travelling around the world for six months as a crew member of an expedition ship is a dream job in many respects. But as this recruitment video from Lindblad Expeditions describes, working on the *National Geographic Sea Bird* and other cruise ships requires a dedicated crew, and that means a real working day. This video program provides viewers with a realistic picture of what it is like to work on board one of these vessels. Crew members offer their candid thoughts about why they joined and what they experienced, including the most exciting and most arduous aspects of the job.

Discussion Questions

1. In your opinion, is this program effective in providing a realistic job preview of working life on board an expedition cruise ship? Why or why not?
2. Discuss the effectiveness of this video program in terms of the learning and adjustment of new employees. Are the risks of discouraging some job applicants offset by the positive effects on those who apply and are hired?
3. If you were responsible for the hiring and induction of new employees at Lindblad Expeditions or a similar organisation, what other means would you apply to ensure that employees experience an effective socialisation process?

Ricardo Semler—Brazil's Caring Capitalist

This video program gives the viewer a rare glimpse inside the fabled operations of the Brazilian conglomerate, SEMCO SA. Two decades ago, Ricardo Semler transformed his father's rigidly hierarchical shipbuilding supplies business into an organisation that embraces egalitarianism and worker autonomy. Today, almost all of SEMCO's 3000 employees set their own work schedules. They are encouraged to move around to different workstations, partly so that supervisors have difficulty knowing who is at work and who has gone home. Employees are also key decision makers, choosing everything from the office furniture to how much they should be paid. SEMCO, however, is not a laid-back country club. Employees are rewarded for how well their work unit performs, so co-workers will not tolerate those who fail to pull their weight. Also, although employees can set their own salaries, those who ask for too much can find themselves without a team willing to keep them on the payroll. This video program also describes Ricardo Semler's recent initiatives: education and eco-tourism, both of which also give employees more authority and responsibility.

Discussion Questions

1. Describe SEMCO's organisational culture. What artefacts are mentioned in this program that represent and reinforce this culture? What strategies or practices does SEMCO apply to specifically support its culture?
2. SEMCO is apparently a very successful company. Which of the four perspectives of organisational effectiveness described in Chapter 1 best explains this organisation's success?
3. SEMCO SA is also an example of shared leadership. What information in this video program indicates that SEMCO encourages shared leadership?

Wendy's Restaurants of Canada

Employees at Wendy's Restaurants of Canada are about to be swept up in a tide of extraordinary change. To boost profits, Wendy's wanted to break down the military style of management and create a culture of vulnerability and trust in its place. To launch this process, Wendy's brought together 160 restaurant managers from across Canada to an Ontario resort where New Mexico-based Pecos River guided them to a new way of working with their employees. This classic CBC video program takes the viewer through the Pecos River program, then transports us to Winnipeg where district manager Craig Stapon is responsible for bringing his managers on board the change process. Although this program was filmed in the early 1990s, it remains one of the best video programs to illustrate the challenges of introducing change in the workplace.

Discussion Questions

1. What changes did the restaurant executives expect to result from the Pecos River program? Did these changes occur in the Winnipeg restaurants?
2. Was there any resistance to change among the Winnipeg restaurant managers? If so, what form did the resistance take?
3. What change in management strategies did Craig Stapon use among the Winnipeg managers? Were these strategies effective? Why or why not?

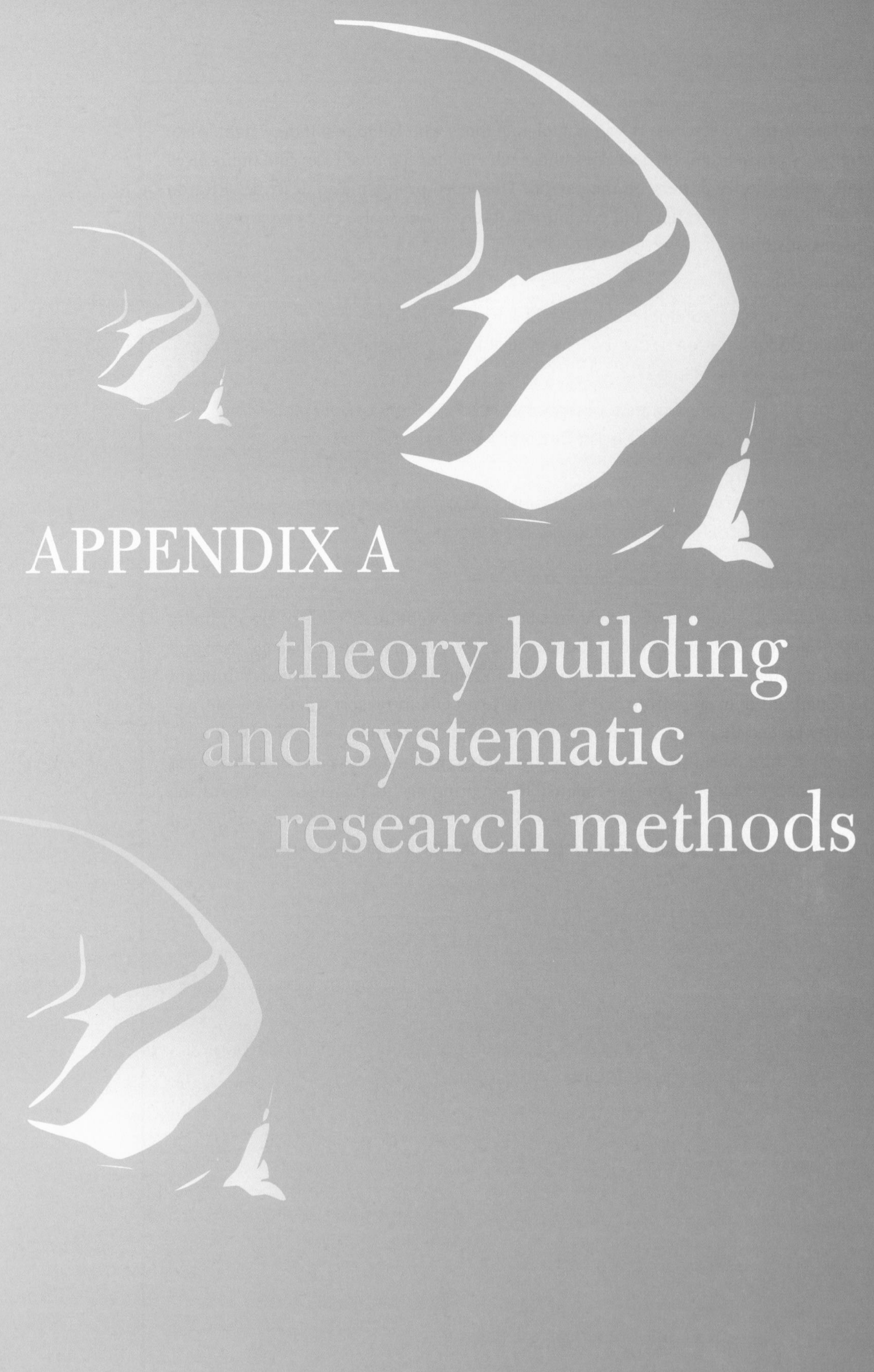

APPENDIX A

theory building and systematic research methods

THEORY BUILDING

People need to make sense of their world, so they form theories about the way the world operates. A **theory** is a general set of propositions that describes interrelationships among several concepts. We form theories for the purpose of predicting and explaining the world around us.[1] What does a good theory look like? First, it should be stated as clearly and simply as possible so that the concepts can be measured and there is no ambiguity regarding the theory's propositions. Second, the elements of the theory must be logically consistent with each other, because we cannot test anything that doesn't make sense. Third, a good theory provides value to society; it helps people understand their world better than they would without the theory.[2]

theory A general set of propositions that describes interrelationships among several concepts.

Theory building is a continuous process that typically includes the inductive and deductive stages shown in Exhibit A.1.[3] The inductive stage draws on personal experience to form a preliminary theory, whereas the deductive stage uses the scientific method to test the theory.

The inductive stage of theory building involves observing the world around us, identifying a pattern of relationships and then forming a theory from these personal observations. For example, you might casually notice that new employees want their supervisor to give direction, whereas this leadership style irritates long-service employees. From these observations, you form a theory about the effectiveness of directive leadership. (See Chapter 12 for a discussion of this leadership style.)

Positivism versus Interpretivism

Research requires an interpretation of reality, and researchers tend to perceive reality in one of two ways. A common view, called **positivism**, is that reality exists independent of people. It is 'out there' to be discovered and tested. Positivism is the foundation for most quantitative research (statistical analysis). It assumes that we can measure variables and that those variables have fixed relationships with other variables. For example, the positivist perspective says that we could study whether a supportive style of leadership reduces stress. If we find evidence that it does, then someone else studying leadership and stress would 'discover' the same relationship.

positivism A view held in quantitative research in which reality exists independent of the perceptions and interpretations of people.

Exhibit A.1 *Theory Building and Theory Testing*

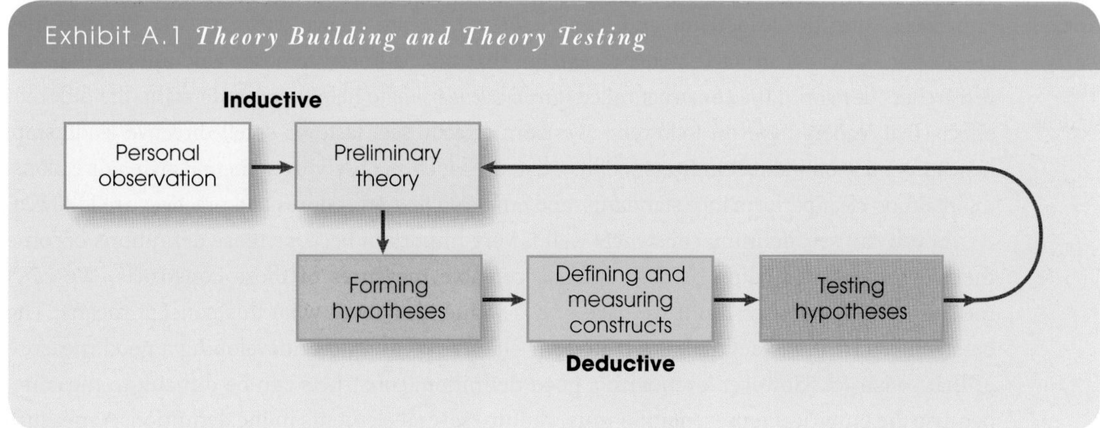

interpretivism The view held in many qualitative studies that reality comes from shared meaning among people in that environment.

Interpretivism takes a different view of reality. It suggests that reality comes from shared meaning among people in a particular environment. For example, supportive leadership is a personal interpretation of reality, not something that can be measured across time and people. Interpretivists rely mainly on qualitative data, such as observation and nondirective interviews. To understand the common meaning that people share in relation to various events or phenomena, interpretivists particularly listen to the language people use. For example, they might argue that you need to experience and observe supportive leadership to effectively study it. Moreover, you can't really predict relationships because the specific situation shapes reality.[4]

Most scholars in the field of organisational behaviour identify themselves somewhere between the extreme views of positivism and interpretivism. Many believe that inductive research should begin with an interpretivist angle. We should consider a new topic with an open mind and search for shared meaning among people in the situation being studied. In other words, researchers should let the participants define reality rather than let the researcher's preconceived notions shape that reality. This process involves gathering qualitative information and letting this information shape their theory.[5] After the theory emerges, researchers shift to the positivist perspective by quantitatively testing relationships in that theory.

Theory Testing: The Deductive Process

Once a theory has been formed, we shift into the deductive stage of theory building. This process includes forming hypotheses, defining and measuring constructs, and testing hypotheses (see Exhibit A.1). **Hypotheses** make empirically testable declarations that certain variables and their corresponding measures are related in a specific way proposed by the theory. For instance, to find support for the directive leadership theory described earlier, we need to form and then test a specific hypothesis from that theory. One such hypothesis might be: 'New employees are more satisfied with supervisors who exhibit a directive rather than nondirective leadership style.' Hypotheses are indispensable tools of scientific research, because they provide the vital link between the theory and empirical verification.

hypotheses Statements making empirically testable declarations that certain variables and their corresponding measures are related in a specific way proposed by the theory.

Defining and Measuring Constructs

Hypotheses are testable only if we can define and then form measurable indicators of the concepts stated in those hypotheses. Consider the hypothesis in the previous paragraph about new employees and directive leadership. To test this hypothesis, we first need to define the concepts, such as 'new employees' 'directive leadership' and 'supervisor'. These are known as **constructs**, because they are abstract ideas constructed by the researcher that can be linked to observable information. OB researchers developed the construct called *directive leadership* to help them understand the different effects that leaders have on followers. We can't directly see, taste or smell directive leadership; instead, we rely on indirect indicators of its existence, such as observing someone giving directions, maintaining clear performance standards, and ensuring that procedures and practices are followed.

constructs Abstract ideas constructed by researchers that can be linked to observable information.

As you can see, defining constructs well is very important because these definitions become the foundation for finding or developing acceptable measures of those constructs. We can't measure directive leadership if we have only a vague idea about what this concept means. The better the construct is defined, the better our chances of finding or developing a good measure of that construct. However, even with a good definition, constructs can be difficult to measure, because the empirical representation must capture several elements in the definition. A measure of directive leadership must be able to identify not only people who give directions, but also those who maintain performance standards and ensure that procedures are followed.

Testing Hypotheses

The third step in the deductive process is to collect data for the empirical measures of the variables. Following our directive leadership example, we might conduct a formal survey in which new employees indicate the behaviour of their supervisors and their attitudes toward their supervisors. Alternatively, we might design an experiment in which people work with someone who applies either a directive or a nondirective leadership style. When the data have been collected, we can use various procedures to statistically test our hypotheses.

A major concern in theory building is that some researchers might inadvertently find support for their theory simply because they use the same information used to form the theory during the inductive stage. Consequently, the deductive stage must collect new data that are completely independent of the data used during the inductive stage. For instance, you might decide to test your theory of directive leadership by studying employees in another organisation. Moreover, the inductive process may have relied mainly on personal observation, whereas the deductive process might use survey questionnaires. By studying different samples and using different measurement tools, we minimise the risk of conducting circular research.

USING THE SCIENTIFIC METHOD

Earlier, we said that the deductive stage of theory building follows the scientific method. The **scientific method** is a systematic, controlled, empirical and critical investigation of hypothetical propositions about the presumed relationships among natural phenomena.[6] There are several elements to this definition, so let's look at each one. First, scientific research is *systematic and controlled*, because researchers want to rule out all but one explanation for a set of interrelated events. To rule out alternative explanations, we need to control them in some way, such as by keeping them constant or removing them entirely from the environment.

scientific method A set of principles and procedures that help researchers to systematically understand previously unexplained events and conditions.

Second, we say that scientific research is *empirical* because researchers need to use objective reality—or as close as we can get to it—to test a theory. They measure observable elements of the environment, such as what a person says or does, rather than relying on their own subjective opinion to draw conclusions. Moreover, scientific research analyses these data using acceptable principles of mathematics and logic.

Third, scientific research involves *critical investigation*. This means that the study's hypotheses, data, methods and results are openly described so that other experts in the field can properly evaluate the research. It also means that scholars are encouraged to critique and build on previous research. The scientific method encourages the refinement and eventually the replacement of a particular theory with one that better suits our understanding of the world.

GROUNDED THEORY: AN ALTERNATIVE APPROACH

grounded theory A process of developing theory through the constant interplay between data gathering and the development of theoretical concepts.

The scientific method dominates the quantitative approach to systematic research, but another approach, called **grounded theory**, dominates research using qualitative methods.[7] Grounded theory is a process of developing knowledge through the constant interplay of data collection, analysis and theory development. It relies mainly on qualitative methods to form categories and variables, analyse relationships among these concepts, and form a model based on the observations and analysis. Grounded theory combines the inductive stages of theory development by cycling back and forth between data collection and analysis to converge on a robust explanatory model. This ongoing reciprocal process results in theory that is grounded in the data (thus, the name *grounded* theory).

Like the scientific method, grounded theory is a systematic and rigorous process of data collection and analysis. It requires specific steps and documentation, and adopts a positivist view by assuming that the results are generalisable to other settings. However, grounded theory also takes an interpretivist view by building categories and variables from the perceived realities of the subjects rather than from an assumed universal truth.[8] It also recognises that personal biases are not easily removed from the research process.

SELECTED ISSUES IN ORGANISATIONAL BEHAVIOUR RESEARCH

There are many issues to consider in theory building, particularly when we use the deductive process to test hypotheses. Some of the more important issues are sampling, causation and ethical practices in organisational research.

Sampling in Organisational Research

When finding out why things happen in organisations, we typically gather information from a few sources and then draw conclusions about the larger population. If we survey several employees and determine that older employees are more loyal to their company, then we would like to generalise this statement to all older employees in our population, not just those whom we surveyed. Scientific inquiry generally requires that researchers engage in **representative sampling**—that is, sampling a population in such a way that we can extrapolate the results of the sample to the larger population.

representative sampling The process of sampling a population in such a way that one can extrapolate the results of that sample to the larger population.

One factor that influences representativeness is whether the sample is selected in an unbiased way from the larger population. Let's suppose that you want to study organisational commitment among employees in your organisation. A casual procedure might result in sampling too few employees from the head office and too many located elsewhere in the country. If head-office employees actually have higher loyalty than employees located elsewhere, the biased sampling would cause the results to underestimate the true level of loyalty among employees in the company. If you repeat the process again next year but somehow overweight employees from the head office, the results might wrongly suggest that employees have increased their organisational commitment over the past year. In reality, the only change may be the direction of sampling bias.

How do we minimise sampling bias? The answer is to randomly select the sample. A randomly drawn sample gives each member of the population an equal probability of being chosen, so there is less likelihood that a subgroup within that population will dominate the study's results.

The same principle applies to random assignment of subjects to groups in experimental designs. If we want to test the effects of a team development training program, we need to randomly place some employees in the training group and randomly place others in a group that does not receive training. Without this random selection, each group might have different types of employees, so we wouldn't know whether the training explains the differences between the two groups. Moreover, if employees respond differently to the training program, we couldn't be sure that the training program results are representative of the larger population. Of course, random sampling does not necessarily produce a perfectly representative sample, but we do know that it is the best approach to ensure unbiased selection.

The other factor that influences representativeness is sample size. Whenever we select a portion of the population, there will be some error in our estimate of the population values. The larger the sample, the less error will occur in our estimate. Let's suppose that you want to find out how employees in a 500-person firm feel about smoking in the workplace. If you asked 400 of those employees, the information would provide a very good estimate of how the entire workforce in that organisation feels. If you survey only 100 employees, the estimate might deviate more from the true population. If you ask only 10 people, the estimate could be quite different from what all 500 employees feel.

Notice that sample size goes hand in hand with random selection. You must have a sufficiently large sample size for the principle of randomisation to work effectively. In our example of attitudes toward smoking, we would do a poor job of random selection if our sample consisted of only 10 employees from the 500-person organisation. The reason is that these 10 people probably wouldn't capture the diversity of employees throughout the organisation. In fact, the more diverse the population, the larger the sample size should be, to provide adequate representation through random selection.

Causation in Organisational Research

Theories present notions about relationships among constructs. Often, these propositions suggest a causal relationship, namely, that one variable has an effect on another variable. When discussing causation, we refer to variables as being independent or dependent. *Independent variables* are the presumed causes of *dependent variables,* which are the presumed effects. In our earlier example of directive leadership, the main independent variable (there might be others) would be the supervisor's directive or nondirective leadership style, because we presume that it causes the dependent variable (satisfaction with supervision).

In laboratory experiments, described later, the independent variable is always manipulated by the experimenter. In our research on directive leadership, we might have subjects (new employees) work with supervisors who exhibit directive or nondirective leadership behaviours. If subjects are more satisfied under the directive leaders, we would be able to infer an association between the independent and dependent variables.

Researchers must satisfy three conditions to provide sufficient evidence of causality between two variables.[9] The first condition of causality is that the variables are empirically associated with each other. An association exists whenever one measure of a variable changes systematically with a measure of another variable. This condition of causality is the easiest to satisfy, because there are several well-known statistical measures of association. A research study might find, for instance, that heterogeneous groups (in which members come from diverse backgrounds) produce more creative solutions to problems. This might be apparent because the measure of creativity (such as number of creative solutions produced within a fixed time) is higher for teams that have a high score on the measure of group heterogeneity. They are statistically associated or correlated with each other.

The second condition of causality is that the independent variable precedes the dependent variable in time. Sometimes, this condition is satisfied through simple logic. In our group heterogeneity example, it doesn't make sense to say that the number of creative solutions caused the group's heterogeneity, because the group's heterogeneity existed before the group produced the creative solutions. In other situations, however, the temporal relationship among variables is less clear. One example is the ongoing debate about job satisfaction and organisational commitment. Do companies develop more loyal employees by increasing their job satisfaction, or do changes in organisational loyalty cause changes in job satisfaction? Simple logic does not answer these questions; instead, researchers must use sophisticated longitudinal studies to build up evidence of a temporal relationship between these two variables.

The third requirement for evidence of a causal relationship is that the statistical association between two variables cannot be explained by a third variable. There are many associations that we quickly dismiss as being causally related. For example, in some countries there is a statistical association between the number of storks in an area and the birth rate in that area. We know that storks don't bring babies, so something else must cause the association between these two variables. The real explanation is that both storks and birth rates have a higher incidence in rural areas.

In other studies, the third variable effect is less apparent. Many years ago, before polio vaccines were available, a study in the United States reported a surprisingly strong association between consumption of a certain soft drink and the incidence of polio. Was polio caused by drinking this beverage, or did people with polio have a unusual craving for it? Neither. Both polio and consumption of the soft drink were caused by a third variable: climate. There was a higher incidence of polio in the summer months and in warmer climates, and people drink more liquids in these climates.[10] As you can see from this example, researchers have a difficult time supporting causal inferences, because third variable effects are sometimes difficult to detect.

Ethics in Organisational Research

Organisational behaviour researchers need to abide by the ethical standards of the society in which the research is conducted. One of the most important ethical considerations is the individual subject's freedom to participate in the study. For example, it is inappropriate to force employees to fill out a questionnaire or attend an experimental intervention for research purposes only. Moreover, researchers have an obligation to tell potential subjects about any possible risks inherent in the study so that participants can make an informed choice about whether to be involved.

Finally, researchers must be careful to protect the privacy of those who participate in the study. This usually includes letting people know when they are being studied as well as guaranteeing that their individual information will remain confidential (unless publication of identities is otherwise granted). Researchers maintain anonymity through careful security of data. The research results usually aggregate data in numbers large enough that they do not reveal the opinions or characteristics of any specific individual. For example, we would report the average absenteeism of employees in a department rather than state the absence rates of each person. When researchers are sharing data with other researchers, it is usually necessary to specially code each case so that individual identities are not known.

RESEARCH DESIGN STRATEGIES

So far, we have described how to build a theory, including the specific elements of empirically testing the theory within the standards of scientific inquiry. But what are the different ways to design a research study so that we get the data necessary to achieve our research objectives? There are many strategies, but they mainly fall under three headings: laboratory experiments, field surveys and observational research.

Laboratory Experiments

A **laboratory experiment** is any research study in which independent variables and variables outside the researcher's main focus of inquiry can be controlled to some extent. Laboratory experiments are usually located outside the everyday work environment, such as in a classroom, simulation lab or any other artificial setting in which the researcher can manipulate the environment. Organisational behaviour researchers sometimes conduct experiments in the workplace (called *field experiments*) in which the independent variable is manipulated. However, researchers have less control over the effects of extraneous factors in field experiments than they have in laboratory situations.

laboratory experiment
Any research study in which independent variables and variables outside the researcher's main focus of inquiry can be controlled to some extent.

Advantages of Laboratory Experiments

There are many advantages of laboratory experiments. By definition, this research method offers a high degree of control over extraneous variables that would otherwise confound the relationships being studied. Suppose we wanted to test the effects of directive leadership on the satisfaction of new employees. One concern might be that employees are influenced by how much leadership is provided, not just the type of leadership style. An experimental design would allow us to control how often the supervisor exhibited this style so that this extraneous variable does not confound the results.

A second advantage of lab studies is that the independent and dependent variables can be developed more precisely than is possible in a field setting. For example, the researcher can ensure that supervisors in a lab study apply specific directive or nondirective behaviours, whereas real-life supervisors would use a more complex mixture of leadership behaviours. By using more precise measures, we are more certain that we are measuring the intended construct. Thus, if new employees are more satisfied with supervisors in the directive leadership condition, we are more confident that the independent variable was directive leadership rather than some other leadership style.

A third benefit of laboratory experiments is that the independent variable can be distributed more evenly among participants. In our directive leadership study, we can ensure that approximately half of the subjects have a directive supervisor, whereas the other half have a nondirective supervisor. In natural settings, we might have trouble finding people who have worked with a nondirective leader and, consequently, we couldn't determine the effects of this condition.

Disadvantages of Laboratory Experiments

With these powerful advantages, you might wonder why laboratory experiments are the least appreciated form of organisational behaviour research.[11] One obvious limitation of this research method is that it lacks realism, and thus the results might be different in the real world. One argument is that laboratory experiment subjects are less involved than their counterparts in an actual work situation. This is sometimes true, although many lab studies have highly motivated participants. Another criticism is that the extraneous variables controlled in the lab setting might produce a different effect of the independent variable on the dependent variables. This might also be true, but remember that the experimental design will control variables in accordance with the theory and its hypotheses. Consequently, this concern is really a critique of the theory, not the lab study.

Finally, there is the well-known problem that participants are aware they are being studied and this causes them to act differently than they normally would. Some participants try to figure out how the researcher wants them to behave and then deliberately try to act that way. Other participants try to upset the experiment by doing just the opposite of what they believe the researcher expects. Still others might act unnaturally simply because they know they are being observed. Fortunately, experimenters are well aware of these potential problems and are usually (although not always) successful at disguising the study's true intent.

Field Surveys

field surveys Research design strategies that involve collecting and analysing information in a natural environment, such as an office, a factory or other existing location.

Field surveys collect and analyse information in a natural environment—an office, a factory, or some other existing location. The researcher takes a snapshot of reality and tries to determine whether elements of that situation (including the attitudes and behaviours of people in that situation) are associated with each other as hypothesised. Everyone does some sort of field research. You might think that people from some states are better drivers than others, so you 'test' your theory by looking at the driving behaviours of people with numberplates from different states. Although your methods of data collection might not satisfy scientific standards, this is a form of field research because it takes information from a naturally occurring situation.

Advantages and Disadvantages of Field Surveys

One advantage of field surveys is that the variables often have a more powerful effect than they would in a laboratory experiment. Consider the effect of peer pressure on the behaviour of members within the team. In a natural environment, team members would form very strong cohesive bonds over time, whereas a researcher would have difficulty replicating this level of cohesiveness and corresponding peer pressure in a lab setting.

Another advantage of field surveys is that the researcher can study many variables simultaneously, thereby permitting a fuller test of more complex theories. Ironically, this is also a disadvantage of field surveys because it is difficult for the researcher to contain his or her scientific inquiry. There is a tendency to shift from deductive hypothesis testing to more inductive exploratory browsing through the data. If these two activities become mixed together, the researcher can lose sight of the strict covenants of scientific inquiry.

The main weakness with field surveys is that it is very difficult to satisfy the conditions for causal conclusions. One reason is that the data are usually collected at one point in time, so the researcher must rely on logic to decide whether the independent variable really preceded the dependent variable. Contrast this with the lab study in which the researcher can usually be confident that the independent variable was applied before the dependent variable occurred. Increasingly, organisational behaviour studies use longitudinal research to provide a better indicator of temporal relations among variables, but this is still not as precise as the lab setting. Another reason why causal analysis is difficult in field surveys is that extraneous variables are not controlled as they are in lab studies. Without this control, there is a higher chance that a third variable might explain the relationship between the hypothesised independent and dependent variables.

Observational Research

In their study of brainstorming and creativity, Robert Sutton and Andrew Hargadon observed twenty-four brainstorming sessions at IDEO, a product design firm in Palo Alto, California. They also attended a dozen 'Monday morning meetings', conducted sixty semistructured interviews with IDEO executives and designers, held hundreds of informal discussions with these people and read through several dozen magazine articles about the company.[12]

Sutton and Hargadon's use of observational research and other qualitative methods was quite appropriate for their research objective, which was to re-examine the effectiveness of brainstorming beyond the number of ideas generated. Observational research generates a wealth of descriptive accounts about the drama of human existence in organisations. It is a useful vehicle for learning about the complex dynamics of people and their activities, such as brainstorming. (Sutton and Hargadon's study is cited in Chapter 8.)

Participant observation takes the observation method one step further by having the observer take part in the organisation's activities. This experience gives the researcher a fuller understanding of the activities compared to just watching others participate in those activities.

In spite of its intuitive appeal, observational research has a number of weaknesses. The main problem is that the observer is subject to the perceptual screening and organising biases that we discuss in Chapter 3 of this textbook. There is a tendency to overlook the routine aspects of organisational life, even though they may prove to be the most important data for research purposes. Instead, observers tend to focus on unusual information, such as activities that deviate from what the observer expects. Because observational research usually records only what the observer notices, valuable information is often lost.

Another concern with the observation method is that the researcher's presence and involvement may influence the people whom he or she is studying. This can be a problem in short-term observations, but in the long term people tend to return to their usual behaviour patterns. With ongoing observations, such as Sutton and Hargadon's study of brainstorming sessions at IDEO, employees eventually forget that they are being studied.

Finally, observation is usually a qualitative process, so it is more difficult to empirically test hypotheses with the data. Instead, observational research provides rich information for the inductive stages of theory building. It helps us to form ideas about the way things work in organisations. We begin to see relationships that lay the foundation for new perspectives and theory. We must not confuse this inductive process of theory building with the deductive process of theory testing.

KEY TERMS

constructs, p. 646
field surveys, p. 652
grounded theory, p. 647
hypotheses, p. 646
interpretivism, p. 646
laboratory experiment, p. 651
positivism, p. 645
representative sampling, p. 648
scientific method, p. 647
theory, p. 645

Endnotes

1 F. N. Kerlinger, *Foundations of Behavioral Research* (New York: Holt, Rinehart and Winston, 1964), 11.

2 J. B. Miner, *Theories of Organizational Behavior* (Hinsdale, IL: Dryden, 1980), 7–9.

3 Miner, *Theories of Organizational Behavior*, 6–7.

4 J. Mason, *Qualitative Researching* (London: Sage, 1996).

5 A. Strauss and J. Corbin, eds., *Grounded Theory in Practice* (London: Sage, 1997); B. G. Glaser and A. Strauss, *The Discovery of Grounded Theory: Strategies for Qualitative Research* (Chicago: Aldine Publishing Co., 1967).

6 Kerlinger, *Foundations of Behavioral Research*, 13.

7 Strauss and Corbin, *Grounded Theory in Practice*; Glaser and Strauss, *The Discovery of Grounded Theory*.

8 W. A. Hall and P. Callery, 'Enhancing the Rigor of Grounded Theory: Incorporating Reflexivity and Relationality', *Qualitative Health Research* 11, no. 2 (2001): 257–272.

9 P. Lazarsfeld, *Survey Design and Analysis* (New York: The Free Press, 1955).

10 This example is cited in D. W. Organ and T. S. Bateman, *Organizational Behavior*, 4th edn (Homewood, IL: Irwin, 1991), 42.

11 Organ and Bateman, *Organizational Behavior*, 45.

12 R. I. Sutton and A. Hargadon, 'Brainstorming Groups in Context: Effectiveness in a Product Design Firm', *Administrative Science Quarterly* 41 (December 1996): 685–718.

APPENDIX B

scoring keys for self-assessment activities

The following pages provide scoring keys for self-assessments that are fully presented in this textbook. These self-assessments, as well as the self-assessments that are only summarised in this book, can also be scored automatically at the student Online Learning Centre.

CHAPTER 2

Scoring Key for 'Are You Introverted or Extroverted?'

Scoring instructions: Use the table below to assign numbers to each box you checked. For example, if you checked 'Moderately inaccurate' for statement #1 ('I feel comfortable around people'), you would assign a '1' to that statement. After assigning numbers for all ten statements, add up the numbers to estimate your extroversion–introversion personality.

For statement items 1, 2, 6, 8, 9		For statement items 3, 4, 5, 7, 10	
Very accurate description of me	= 4	Very accurate description of me	= 0
Moderately accurate	= 3	Moderately accurate	= 1
Neither accurate nor inaccurate	= 2	Neither accurate nor inaccurate	= 2
Moderately inaccurate	= 1	Moderately inaccurate	= 3
Very inaccurate description of me	= 0	Very inaccurate description of me	= 4

Interpreting your score: Extroversion characterises people who are outgoing, talkative, sociable and assertive. It includes several facets, such as friendliness, gregariousness, assertiveness, activity level, excitement-seeking characteristics and cheerfulness. The opposite of extroversion is introversion, which refers to the personality characteristics of being quiet, shy and cautious. Extroverts get their energy from the outer world (people and things around them), whereas introverts get their energy from the internal world, such as personal reflection on concepts and ideas. Introverts are more inclined to direct their interests to ideas rather than to social events.

This is the short version of the IPIP Introversion–Extroversion Scale, so it estimates overall introversion–extroversion but not specific facets within the personality dimension. Scores range from 0 to 40. Low scores indicate introversion; high scores indicate extroversion. The norms in the following table are estimated from results of early adults (under 30 years old) in Scotland and undergraduate psychology students in the United States. However, introversion–extroversion norms vary from one group to the next; the best norms are likely based on the entire class you are attending or on past students in this course.

IPIP Introversion–Extroversion	Interpretation
35–40	High extroversion
28–34	Moderate extroversion
21–27	In between extroversion and introversion
7–20	Moderate introversion
0–6	High introversion

CHAPTER 3

Scoring Key for 'How Much Perceptual Structure Do You Need?'

Scoring instructions: Use the table below to assign numbers to each box you checked. For example, if you checked 'Moderately disagree' for statement #3 ('I enjoy being spontaneous'), you would assign a '5' to that statement. After assigning numbers for all twelve statements, add up your scores to estimate your personal need for structure.

For statement items 1, 5, 6, 7, 8, 9, 10, 12		**For statement items 2, 3, 4, 11**	
Strongly agree	= 6	Strongly agree	= 1
Moderately agree	= 5	Moderately agree	= 2
Slightly agree	= 4	Slightly agree	= 3
Slightly disagree	= 3	Slightly disagree	= 4
Moderately disagree	= 2	Moderately disagree	= 5
Strongly disagree	= 1	Strongly disagree	= 6

Interpreting your score: Some people need to 'make sense' of things around them more quickly or completely than do other people. This personal need for perceptual structure relates to selective attention as well as perceptual organisation and interpretation. For instance, people with a strong personal need for closure might form first impressions, fill in missing pieces and rely on stereotyping more quickly than people who don't mind incomplete perceptual situations.

This scale, called the Personal Need for Structure (PNS) scale, assesses the degree to which people are motivated to structure their world in a simple and unambiguous way. Scores range from 12 to 72 with higher scores indicating a high personal need for structure. PNS norms vary from one group to the next. For instance, a study of Finnish nurses reported a mean PNS score of 34 whereas a study of 236 male and 303 female undergraduate psychology students in the United States had a mean score of 42. The norms in the following table are based on scores from these undergraduate students.

Personal Need for Structure scale	**Interpretation**
58 to 72	High need for personal structure
47 to 57	Above average need for personal structure
38 to 46	Average need for personal structure
27 to 37	Below average need for personal structure
12 to 26	Low need for personal structure

CHAPTER 4

Scoring Key for 'University Commitment Scale'

Scoring instructions: Use the table below to assign numbers to each box you checked. Insert the number for each statement on the appropriate line below the table. For example, if you checked 'Moderately disagree' for statement #1 ('I would be very happy ...'), you would write a '2' on the line with '(1)' underneath it. After assigning numbers for all twelve statements, add up your scores to estimate your affective and continuance university commitment.

For statement items 1, 2, 3, 4, 6, 8, 10, 11, 12		For statement items 5, 7, 9	
Strongly agree	= 7	Strongly agree	= 1
Moderately agree	= 6	Moderately agree	= 2
Slightly agree	= 5	Slightly agree	= 3
Neutral	= 4	Neutral	= 4
Slightly disagree	= 3	Slightly disagree	= 5
Moderately disagree	= 2	Moderately disagree	= 6
Strongly disagree	= 1	Strongly disagree	= 7

Affective commitment ____ + ____ + ____ + ____ + ____ + ____ = ____
(1) (3) (5) (7) (9) (11)

Continuance commitment ____ + ____ + ____ + ____ + ____ + ____ = ____
(2) (4) (6) (8) (10) (12)

Interpreting your affective commitment score: This scale measures both affective commitment and continuance commitment. Affective commitment refers to a person's emotional attachment to, identification with and involvement in a particular organisation. In this scale, the organisation is the university that you are attending as a student. How high or low is your affective commitment? The ideal would be to compare your score with the collective results of other students in your class. You can also compare your score with the following results, which are based on a sample of employees.

Affective commitment score	Interpretation
37 and above	High level of affective commitment
32 to 36	Above average level of affective commitment
28 to 31	Average level of affective commitment
20 to 27	Below average level of affective commitment
Below 20	Low level of affective commitment

Interpreting your continuance commitment score: Continuance commitment occurs when employees believe it is in their own personal interest to remain with the organisation. People with a high continuance commitment have a strong calculative bond with the organisation. In this scale, the organisation is the university that you are attending as a student. How high or low is your continuance commitment? The ideal would be to compare your score with the collective results of other students in your class. You can also compare your score with the following results, which are based on a sample of employees.

Continuance commitment score	Interpretation
32 and above	High level of continuance commitment
26 to 31	Above average level of continuance commitment
21 to 25	Average level of continuance commitment
13 to 20	Below average level of continuance commitment
Below 12	Low level of continuance commitment

CHAPTER 5

Scoring Key for 'Need-Strength Questionnaire'

Scoring instructions: Use the table below to assign numbers to each box you checked. Insert the number for each statement on the appropriate line below the table. For example, if you checked 'Moderately inaccurate' for statement #1 ('I would rather be myself than be well thought of'), you would write a '3' on the line with '(1)' underneath it. After assigning numbers for all 15 statements, add up your scores to estimate your results for the two learned needs measured by this scale.

For statement items 2, 3, 4, 5, 6, 8, 9, 12, 14, 15		For statement items 1, 7, 10, 11, 13	
Very accurate description of me	= 4	Very accurate description of me	= 0
Moderately accurate	= 3	Moderately accurate	= 1
Neither accurate nor inaccurate	= 2	Neither accurate nor inaccurate	= 2
Moderately inaccurate	= 1	Moderately inaccurate	= 3
Very inaccurate description of me	= 0	Very inaccurate description of me	= 4

Need for achievement ____ + ____ + ____ + ____ + ____ + ____ + ____ = ____
(2) (3) (6) (7) (9) (12) (14)

Need for social approval ____ + ____ + ____ + ____ + ____ + ____ + ____ + ____ = ____
(1) (4) (5) (8) (10) (11) (13) (15)

Although everyone has the same innate drives, our secondary or learned needs vary based on our self-concept. This self-assessment provides an estimate of your need strength on two secondary needs: need for achievement and need for social approval.

Interpreting your need for achievement score: This scale, formally called 'achievement striving', estimates the extent to which you are motivated to take on and achieve challenging personal goals. This includes a desire to perform better than others and to reach your potential. The scale ranges from 0 to 28. How high or low is your need for achievement? The ideal would be to compare your score with the collective results of other students in your class. Otherwise, the following table offers a rough set of norms with which you can compare your score on this scale.

Need for achievement score	Interpretation
24–28	High level of need for achievement
18–23	Above average level of need for achievement
12–17	Average level of need for achievement
6–11	Below average level of need for achievement
0–5	Low level of need for achievement

Interpreting your need for social approval score: The need for social approval scale estimates the extent to which your are motivated to seek favourable evaluation from others. Founded on the drive to bond, the need for social approval is a secondary need in that people vary in this need based on their self-concept, values, personality and possibly socialised social norms. This scale ranges from 0 to 32. How high or low is your need for social approval? The ideal would be to compare your score with the collective results of other students in your class. Otherwise, the following table offers a rough set of norms on which you can compare your score on this scale.

Need for social approval score	Interpretation
28–32	High need for social approval
20–27	Above average need for social approval
12–19	Average need for social approval
6–11	Below average need for social approval
0–5	Low need for social approval

CHAPTER 6

Scoring Key for 'What Is Your Attitude Toward Money?'

Scoring instructions: This instrument presents three dimensions with a smaller set of items from the original Money Attitude Scale. To calculate your score on each dimension, write the number that you circled in the scale to the corresponding item number in the scoring key below. For example, write the number you circled for the scale's first statement ('I sometimes purchase things ...') on the line above 'Item 1'. Then add up the numbers for that dimension. The money attitude total score is calculated by adding up all scores on all dimensions.

Money attitude dimension	Calculation	Your score
Money as power/prestige	____ + ____ + ____ + ____ = Item 1 Item 4 Item 7 Item 10	____
Retention time	____ + ____ + ____ + ____ = Item 2 Item 5 Item 8 Item 11	____
Money anxiety	____ + ____ + ____ + ____ = Item 3 Item 6 Item 9 Item 12	____
Money attitude total	Add up all dimension scores =	____

Interpreting your score:

The three Money Attitude Scale dimensions measured here, as well as the total score, are defined as follows:

Money as power/prestige: People with higher scores on this dimension tend to use money to influence and impress others.

Retention time: People with higher scores on this dimension tend to be careful financial planners.

Money anxiety: People with higher scores on this dimension tend to view money as a source of anxiety.

Money attitude total: This is a general estimate of how much respect and attention you give to money.

The following table shows how a sample of MBA students scored on the Money Attitude Scale. The table shows percentiles, that is, the percentage of people with the same or lower score. For example, the table indicates that a score of '12' on the retention scale is quite low because only 20 per cent of students would have scored at this level or lower (80 per cent scored higher). However, a score of '12' on the prestige scale is quite high because 80 per cent of students scored at or below this number (only 20 per cent scored higher).

Percentile (% with scores at or below this number)	Prestige score	Retention score	Anxiety score	Total money score
Average score	9.89	14.98	12.78	37.64
Highest score	17	20	18	53
90	13	18	16	44
80	12	17	15	42
70	11	17	14	40
60	10	16	14	39
50	10	15	13	38
40	9	14	12	36
30	8	14	11	34
20	7	12	10	32
10	7	11	8	29
Lowest score	4	8	6	23

CHAPTER 7

Scoring Key for 'Measuring Your Creative Personality'

Scoring instructions: Assign a positive point (+1) after each of the following words that you checked off in the self-assessment:

Capable	__________	Inventive	__________
Clever	__________	Original	__________
Confident	__________	Reflective	__________
Egotistical	__________	Resourceful	__________
Humorous	__________	Self-confident	__________
Individualistic	__________	Sexy	__________
Informal	__________	Snobbish	__________
Insightful	__________	Unconventional	__________
Intelligent	__________	Wide interests	__________

Assign a negative point (−1) after each of the following words that you checked off in the self-assessment:

Affected	__________	Honest	__________
Cautious	__________	Mannerly	__________
Commonplace	__________	Narrow interests	__________
Conservative	__________	Sincere	__________
Conventional	__________	Submissive	__________
Dissatisfied	__________	Suspicious	__________

Interpreting your score: This instrument estimates your creative potential as a personal characteristic. The scale recognises that creative people are intelligent and persistent, and possess an inventive thinking style. Creative personality varies somewhat from one occupational group to the next. The table below provides norms based on undergraduate and graduate university students.

Creative disposition score	Interpretation
Above +9	You have a high creative personality.
+1 to +9	You have an average creative personality.
Below +1	You have a low creative personality.

CHAPTER 8

Scoring Key for 'What Team Roles Do You Prefer?'

Scoring instructions: Write the scores circled for each item on the appropriate line below (statement numbers are in parentheses), and add up each scale.

Encourager	____ +	____ +	____ =	____
	(6)	(9)	(11)	
Gatekeeper	____ +	____ +	____ =	____
	(4)	(10)	(13)	
Harmoniser	____ +	____ +	____ =	____
	(3)	(8)	(12)	
Initiator	____ +	____ +	____ =	____
	(1)	(5)	(14)	
Summariser	____ +	____ +	____ =	____
	(2)	(7)	(15)	

Interpreting your score: The five team roles measured here are based on scholarship over the years. The following table defines these five roles and presents the range of scores for high, medium and low levels of each role. These norms are based on results from a sample of MBA students.

Team role and definition	Score interpretation
Encourager: People who score high on this dimension have a strong tendency to praise and support the ideas of other team members, thereby showing warmth and solidarity to the group.	High: 12 and above Medium: 9 to 11 Low: 8 and below
Gatekeeper: People who score high on this dimension have a strong tendency to encourage all team members to participate in the discussion.	High: 12 and above Medium: 9 to 11 Low: 8 and below
Harmoniser: People who score high on this dimension have a strong tendency to mediate intragroup conflicts and reduce tension.	High: 11 and above Medium: 9 to 10 Low: 8 and below
Initiator: People who score high on this dimension have a strong tendency to identify goals for the meeting, including ways to work on those goals.	High: 12 and above Medium: 9 to 11 Low: 8 and below
Summariser: People who score high on this dimension have a strong tendency to keep track of what was said in the meeting (i.e. act as the team's memory).	High: 10 and above Medium: 8 to 9 Low: 7 and below

CHAPTER 9

Scoring Key for 'Are You an Active Listener?'

Scoring instructions: Use the table below to score the response you circled for each statement. Write the score for each item on the appropriate line below the table (statement numbers are in parentheses), and add up each subscale. For example, if you checked 'Very much' for statement #1 ('I keep an open mind ...'), you would write a '3' on the line with '(1)' underneath it. Then calculate the overall Active Listening Inventory score by adding up all subscales.

For statement items 3, 4, 6, 7, 10, 13		For statement items 1, 2, 5, 8, 9, 11, 12, 14, 15	
Not at all	= 3	Not at all	= 0
A little	= 2	A little	= 1
Somewhat	= 1	Somewhat	= 2
Very much	= 0	Very much	= 3

Avoiding interruption (AI)	____ +	____ +	____ =	____
	(3)	(7)	(15)	
Maintaining interest (MI)	____ +	____ +	____ =	____
	(6)	(9)	(14)	
Postponing evaluation (PE)	____ +	____ +	____ =	____
	(1)	(5)	(13)	
Organising information (OI)	____ +	____ +	____ =	____
	(2)	(10)	(12)	
Showing interest (SI)	____ +	____ +	____ =	____
	(4)	(8)	(11)	
Active listening (total score):				____

Interpreting your score: The five active listening dimensions and the overall active listening scale measured here are defined below, along with the range of scores for high, medium and low levels of each dimension based on a sample of MBA students:

Active listening dimension and definition	Score interpretation
Avoiding interruption: People with high scores on this dimension have a strong tendency to let the speaker finish his or her statements before responding.	High: 8 to 9 Medium: 5 to 7 Low: Below 5
Maintaining interest: People with high scores on this dimension have a strong tendency to remain focused and concentrate on what the speaker is saying even when the conversation is boring or the information is well known.	High: 6 to 9 Medium: 3 to 5 Low: Below 3
Postponing evaluation: People with high scores on this dimension have a strong tendency to keep an open mind and avoid evaluating what the speaker is saying until the speaker has finished.	High: 7 to 9 Medium: 4 to 6 Low: Below 4
Organising information: People with high scores on this dimension have a strong tendency to actively organise the speaker's ideas into meaningful categories.	High: 8 to 9 Medium: 5 to 7 Low: Below 5
Showing interest: People with high scores on this dimension have a strong tendency to use nonverbal gestures or brief verbal acknowledgments to demonstrate that they are paying attention to the speaker.	High: 7 to 9 Medium: 5 to 6 Low: Below 5
Active listening (total): People with high scores on the total active listening scale have a strong tendency to actively sense the sender's signals, evaluate them accurately and respond appropriately.	High: Above 31 Medium: 26 to 31 Low: Below 26

Note: The Active Listening Inventory does not explicitly measure two other dimensions of active listening, namely, empathising and providing feedback. Empathising is difficult to measure with behaviours; providing feedback involves similar behaviours as showing interest.

CHAPTER 10

Scoring Key for 'Coworker Influence Scale'

Scoring instructions: Write the scores circled for each item on the appropriate line below (statement numbers are in parentheses), and add up the scores for each subscale.

Persuasion	____ +	____ +	____ =	____
	(1)	(9)	(17)	
Silent authority	____ +	____ +	____ =	____
	(2)	(10)	(18)	
Exchange	____ +	____ +	____ =	____
	(3)	(11)	(19)	
Assertiveness	____ +	____ +	____ =	____
	(4)	(12)	(20)	
Information control	____ +	____ +	____ =	____
	(5)	(13)	(21)	
Coalition formation	____ +	____ +	____ =	____
	(6)	(14)	(22)	
Upward appeal	____ +	____ +	____ =	____
	(7)	(15)	(23)	
Ingratiation	____ +	____ +	____ =	____
	(8)	(16)	(24)	

Interpreting your score: Influence refers to any behaviour that attempts to alter someone's attitudes or behaviour. There are several types of influence, including the eight measured by this instrument: persuasion, silent authority, exchange, assertiveness, information control, coalition formation, upward appeal and ingratiation/impression management. This instrument assesses your preference for using each type of influence on coworkers (people at the same level in the organisation). Each subscale has a potential score ranging from 3 to 15 points. Higher scores indicate that you have a higher preference for that particular tactic. The eight coworker influence strategies measured here are defined below, along with the range of scores for high, medium and low levels of each tactic.

Influence tactic and definition	Score interpretation
Persuasion: Persuasion refers to using logical and emotional appeals to change others' attitudes. According to several studies, it is also the most common upward influence strategy.	High: 13 to 15 Medium: 9 to 12 Low: 3 to 8
Silent authority: The silent application of authority occurs when someone complies with a request because the target person is aware of the requester's legitimate or expert power. This influence tactic is very subtle, such as making the target person aware of the status or expertise of the person making the request.	High: 10 to 15 Medium: 6 to 9 Low: 3 to 5
Exchange: Exchange involves the promise of benefits or resources in exchange for the target person's compliance with your request. This tactic also includes reminding the target of past benefits or favours with the expectation that the target will now make up for that debt. Negotiation is also part of the exchange strategy.	High: 10 to 15 Medium: 6 to 9 Low: 3 to 5
Assertiveness: Assertiveness involves actively applying legitimate and coercive power to influence others. This tactic includes confronting those who oppose your views, showing your displeasure of their opposition and using threats of sanctions to force compliance.	High: 8 to 15 Medium: 5 to 7 Low: 3 to 4
Information control: Information control involves changing attitudes and behaviours by explicitly manipulating others' access to information. By actively shaping or filtering the information, the target person's perceptions of the issue may shift more towards the desired view.	High: 9 to 15 Medium: 6 to 8 Low: 3 to 5
Coalition formation: Coalition formation occurs when a group of people with common interests band together to influence others. It also exists as a perception, such as when you convince someone else that several people are on your side and support your position.	High: 11 to 15 Medium: 7 to 10 Low: 3 to 6

Influence tactic and definition	Score interpretation
Upward appeal: Upward appeal occurs when you rely on support from people higher up the organisational hierarchy. This support may be real (senior management shows support) or logically argued (you explain how your position is consistent with company policy).	High: 9 to 15 Medium: 6 to 8 Low: 3 to 5
Ingratiation/Impression management: Ingratiation is any attempt to increase liking by, or perceived similarity to, the targeted person. Ingratiation is a component of impression management, which is the practice of actively shaping our public images. By increasing the extent that the target person likes or respects you, these practices motivate the target person to support your preferences.	High: 13 to 15 Medium: 9 to 12 Low: 3 to 8

CHAPTER 11

Scoring Key for 'The Dutch Test for Conflict Handling'

Scoring instructions: To calculate your scores, write the number circled for each statement on the appropriate line below (statement numbers are in parentheses), then add up each scale.

Yielding	____ +	____ +	____ +	____ =	____
	(1)	(6)	(11)	(16)	
Compromising	____ +	____ +	____ +	____ =	____
	(2)	(7)	(12)	(17)	
Forcing	____ +	____ +	____ +	____ =	____
	(3)	(8)	(13)	(18)	
Problem solving	____ +	____ +	____ +	____ =	____
	(4)	(9)	(14)	(19)	
Avoiding	____ +	____ +	____ +	____ =	____
	(5)	(10)	(15)	(20)	

Interpreting your score: The five conflict-handling dimensions are defined below, along with the range of scores for high, medium and low levels of each dimension:

Conflict-handling dimension and definition	Score interpretation
Yielding: Yielding involves giving in completely to the other side's wishes, or at least cooperating with little or no attention to your own interests. This style involves making unilateral concessions and unconditional promises, and offering help with no expectation of reciprocal help.	High: 14 to 20 Medium: 9 to 13 Low: 4 to 8
Compromising: Compromising involves looking for a position in which your losses are offset by equally valued gains. It involves matching the other party's concessions, making conditional promises or threats and actively searching for a middle ground between the interests of the two parties.	High: 17 to 20 Medium: 11 to 16 Low: 4 to 10
Forcing: Forcing involves trying to win the conflict at the other's expense. It includes 'hard' influence tactics, particularly assertiveness, to get one's own way.	High: 15 to 20 Medium: 9 to 14 Low: 4 to 8
Problem solving: Problem solving tries to find a mutually beneficial solution for both parties. Information sharing is an important feature of this style because both parties need to identify common ground and potential solutions that satisfy both (or all) of them.	High: 17 to 20 Medium: 11 to 16 Low: 4 to 10

Conflict-handling dimension and definition	Score interpretation
Avoiding: Avoiding tries to smooth over or avoid conflict situations altogether. It represents a low concern for both self and the other party. In other words, avoiders try to suppress thinking about the conflict.	High: 13 to 20 Medium: 8 to 12 Low: 4 to 7

CHAPTER 12

Scoring Key for 'What Is Your Boss's Preferred Leadership Style?'

Transactional Leadership

Scoring instructions: Add up scores for the odd-numbered items (i.e. 1, 3, 5, 7, 9, 11, 13, 15). The maximum score is 40.

Interpreting your score: Transactional leadership is 'managing'—helping organisations to achieve their current objectives more efficiently, such as by linking job performance to valued rewards and ensuring that employees have the resources needed to get the job done. The following table shows the range of scores for high, medium and low levels of transactional leadership.

Transactional leadership score	Interpretation
32 to 40	The person you evaluated seems to be a highly transactional leader.
25 to 31	The person you evaluated seems to be a moderately transactional leader.
Below 25	The person you evaluated seems to display few characteristics of a transactional leader.

Transformational Leadership

Scoring instructions: Add up scores for the even-numbered items (i.e. 2, 4, 6, 8, 10, 12, 14, 16). The maximum score is 40. Higher scores indicate that your supervisor has a strong inclination toward transformational leadership.

Interpreting your score: Transformational leadership involves changing teams or organisations by creating, communicating and modelling a vision for the organisation or work unit, and inspiring employees to strive for that vision. The following table shows the range of scores for high, medium and low levels of transformational leadership.

Transformational leadership score	Interpretation
32 to 40	The person you evaluated seems to be a highly transformational leader.
25 to 31	The person you evaluated seems to be a moderately transformational leader.
Below 25	The person you evaluated seems to display few characteristics of a transformational leader.

CHAPTER 13

Scoring Key for 'What Organisational Structure Do You Prefer?'

Scoring instructions: Use the table below to assign numbers to each response you circled. Insert the number for each statement on the appropriate line below the table. For example, if you checked 'Not at all' for item #1 ('A person's career ladder ...'), you would write a '0' on the line with '(1)' underneath it. After assigning numbers for all 15 statements, add up the scores to estimate your degree of preference for a tall hierarchy, formalisation and centralisation. Then calculate the overall score by summing all scales.

For statement items 2, 3, 8, 10, 11, 12, 14, 15	For statement items 1, 4, 5, 6, 7, 9, 13
Not at all = 3	Not at all = 0
A little = 2	A little = 1
Somewhat = 1	Somewhat = 2
Very much = 0	Very much = 3

Tall hierarchy (H)	____ +	____ +	____ +	____ +	____ =	____
	(1)	(4)	(10)	(12)	(15)	(H)
Formalisation (F)	____ +	____ +	____ +	____ +	____ =	____
	(2)	(6)	(8)	(11)	(13)	(F)
Centralisation (C)	____ +	____ +	____ +	____ +	____ =	____
	(3)	(5)	(7)	(9)	(14)	(C)
Total score (mechanistic)	____ +	____ +	____ =	____		
	(H)	(F)	(C)	Total		

Interpreting your score: The three organisational structure dimensions and the overall score are defined below, along with the range of scores for high, medium and low levels of each dimension based on a sample of MBA students:

Organisational structure dimension and definition	Score interpretation
Tall hierarchy: People with high scores on this dimension prefer to work in organisations with several levels of hierarchy and a narrow span of control (few employees per supervisor).	High: 11 to 15 Medium: 6 to 10 Low: Below 6
Formalisation: People with high scores on this dimension prefer to work in organisations where jobs are clearly defined with limited discretion.	High: 12 to 15 Medium: 9 to 11 Low: Below 9
Centralisation: People with high scores on this dimension prefer to work in organisations where decision making occurs mainly among top management rather than being spread out to lower level staff.	High: 10 to 15 Medium: 7 to 9 Low: Below 7

Organisational structure dimension and definition	Score interpretation
Total score (mechanistic): People with high scores on this dimension prefer to work in mechanistic organisations, whereas those with low scores prefer to work in organic organisational structures. Mechanistic structures are characterised by a narrow span of control and high degree of formalisation and centralisation. Organic structures have a wide span of control, little formalisation and decentralised decision making.	High: 30 to 45 Medium: 22 to 29 Low: Below 22

CHAPTER 14

Scoring Key for 'What Are Your Corporate Culture Preferences?'

Scoring instructions: On each line below, write in a '1' if you circled the statement and a '0' if you did not. Then add up the scores for each subscale.

Control culture ____ + ____ + ____ + ____ + ____ + ____ = ____
(2a) (5a) (6b) (8b) (11b) (12a)

Performance culture ____ + ____ + ____ + ____ + ____ + ____ = ____
(1b) (3b) (5b) (6a) (7a) (9b)

Relationship culture ____ + ____ + ____ + ____ + ____ + ____ = ____
(1a) (3a) (4b) (8a) (10b) (12b)

Responsive culture ____ + ____ + ____ + ____ + ____ + ____ = ____
(2b) (4a) (7b) (9a) (10a) (11a)

Interpreting your score: These corporate cultures may be found in many organisations, but they represent only four of many possible organisational cultures. Also, keep in mind none of these cultures is inherently good or bad. Each is effective in different situations. The four corporate cultures are defined below, along with the range of scores for high, medium and low levels of each dimension based on a sample of MBA students:

Corporate culture dimension and definition	Score interpretation
Control culture: This culture values the role of senior executives to lead the organisation. Its goal is to keep everyone aligned and under control.	High: 3 to 6 Medium: 1 to 2 Low: 0
Performance culture: This culture values individual and organisational performance, and strives for effectiveness and efficiency.	High: 5 to 6 Medium: 3 to 4 Low: 0 to 2
Relationship culture: This culture values nurturing and wellbeing. It considers open communication, fairness, teamwork and sharing to be vital parts of organisational life.	High: 6 Medium: 4 to 5 Low: 0 to 3
Responsive culture: This culture values its ability to keep in tune with the external environment, including being competitive and realising new opportunities.	High: 6 Medium: 4 to 5 Low: 0 to 3

CHAPTER 15

Scoring Key for 'Are You Tolerant of Change?'

Scoring instructions: Use the table below to assign numbers to each box you checked. For example, if you checked 'Moderately disagree' for statement #1 ('An expert who doesn't come up with ...'), you would write a '6' beside that statement. After assigning numbers for all 16 statements, add up your scores to estimate your tolerance for change.

For statement items 2, 4, 6, 8, 10, 12, 14, 16		For statement items 1, 3, 5, 7, 9, 11, 13, 15	
Strongly agree	= 7	Strongly agree	= 1
Moderately agree	= 6	Moderately agree	= 2
Slightly agree	= 5	Slightly agree	= 3
Neutral	= 4	Neutral	= 4
Slightly disagree	= 3	Slightly disagree	= 5
Moderately disagree	= 2	Moderately disagree	= 6
Strongly disagree	= 1	Strongly disagree	= 7

Interpreting your score: This measurement instrument is formally known as the 'tolerance of ambiguity' scale. Although it was developed forty years ago, the instrument is still used today in research. People with a high tolerance of ambiguity are comfortable with uncertainty, sudden change and new situations. These are characteristics of the hyperfast changes occurring in many organisations today. The table below indicates the range of scores for high, medium and low tolerance for change. These norms are based on results for MBA students.

Tolerance-for-change score	Interpretation
81 to 112	You seem to have a high tolerance for change.
63 to 80	You seem to have a moderate level of tolerance for change.
Below 63	You seem to have a low degree of tolerance for change. Instead, you prefer stable work environments.

Glossary

A

ability The natural aptitudes and learned capabilities required to successfully complete a task.

absorptive capacity The ability to recognise the value of new information, assimilate it and use it for value-added activities.

achievement–nurturing orientation A cross-cultural value describing the degree to which people in a culture emphasise competitive versus co-operative relations with other people.

action research A problem-focused change process that combines action orientation (changing attitudes and behaviour) and research orientation (testing theory through data collection and analysis).

adaptive culture An organisational culture in which employees are receptive to change, including the ongoing alignment of the organisation to its environment and continuous improvement of internal processes.

alternative dispute resolution (ADR) An orderly process of third-party dispute resolution, typically including mediation followed by arbitration.

anchoring and adjustment heuristic A natural tendency for people to be influenced by an initial anchor point such that they do not sufficiently move away from that point as new information is provided.

appreciative inquiry An organisational change strategy that directs the group's attention away from its own problems and focuses participants on the group's potential and positive elements.

artefacts The observable symbols and signs of an organisation's culture.

attention-based theory of the firm A school of management thought based on the idea that organisational decisions and actions are influenced mainly by what attracts management's attention, rather than by objective reality.

attitudes The cluster of beliefs, assessed feelings and behavioural intentions toward a person, object or event (called an *attitude object*).

attraction-selection-attrition (ASA) theory A theory which states that organisations have a natural tendency to attract, select and retain people with values and personality characteristics that are consistent with the organisation's character, resulting in a more homogeneous organisation and a stronger culture.

attribution process The perceptual process of deciding whether an observed behaviour or event is caused largely by internal or external factors.

autonomy The degree to which a job gives employees the freedom, independence and discretion to schedule their work, and to determine the procedures used in completing it.

availability heuristic A natural tendency to assign higher probabilities to objects or events that are easier to recall from memory, even though ease of recall is also affected by nonprobability factors (e.g. emotional response, recent events).

B

balanced scorecard (BSC) A goal-setting and reward system that translates the organisation's vision and mission into specific, measurable performance goals related to financial, customer, internal and learning/growth (i.e. human capital) processes.

behaviour modification A theory that explains learning in terms of the antecedents and consequences of behaviour.

bicultural audit A process of diagnosing cultural relations between companies and determining the extent to which cultural clashes will likely occur.

bounded rationality The view that people are bounded in their decision-making capabilities, including access to limited information, limited information processing and tendency toward satisficing rather than maximising when making choices.

brainstorming A freewheeling, face-to-face meeting where team members aren't allowed to criticise but are encouraged to speak freely, generate as many ideas as possible and build on the ideas of others.

Brooks' law The principle that adding more people to a late software project only makes it later. Also called the *mythical man-month.*

C

categorical thinking Organising people and objects into preconceived categories that are stored in our long-term memory.

centralisation The degree to which formal decision authority is held by a small group of people, typically those at the top of the organisational hierarchy.

centrality A contingency of power pertaining to the degree and nature of interdependence between the powerholder and others.

ceremonies Planned displays of organisational culture, conducted specifically for the benefit of an audience.

coalition A group that attempts to influence people outside the group by pooling the resources and power of its members.

cognitive dissonance A condition that occurs when we perceive an inconsistency between our beliefs, feelings and behaviour.

collectivism A cross-cultural value describing the degree to which people in a culture emphasise duty to groups to which people belong and to group harmony.

communication The process by which information is transmitted and understood between two or more people.

competencies Skills, knowledge, aptitudes and other personal characteristics that lead to superior performance.

concurrent engineering The organisation of employees from several departments into a temporary team for the purpose of developing a product or service.

conflict A process in which one party perceives that their interests are being opposed or negatively affected by another party.

conscientiousness A personality dimension describing people who are careful, dependable and self-disciplined.

constructive conflict A type of conflict in which people focus their discussion on the issue while maintaining respect for people having other points of view.

constructs Abstract ideas constructed by researchers that can be linked to observable information.

contact hypothesis A theory stating that the more we interact with someone, the less prejudiced or perceptually biased we will be against that person.

continuance commitment An employee's calculative attachment to the organisation, whereby the employee is motivated to stay only because leaving would be costly.

corporate social responsibility (CSR) Organisational activities intended to benefit society and the environment beyond the firm's immediate financial interests or legal obligations.

counterproductive work behaviours (CWBs) Voluntary behaviours that have the potential to directly or indirectly harm the organisation.

countervailing power The capacity of a person, team or organisation to keep a more powerful person or group in the exchange relationship.

creativity The development of original ideas that make a socially recognised contribution.

D

decision making The conscious process of making choices among alternatives with the intention of moving toward some desired state of affairs.

deep-level diversity Differences in the psychological characteristics of employees, including personalities, beliefs, values and attitudes.

distributive justice Perceived fairness in the individual's ratio of outcomes to contributions compared with a comparison other's ratio of outcomes to contributions.

divergent thinking Reframing a problem in a unique way and generating different approaches to the issue.

divisional structure An organisational structure in which employees are organised around geographic areas, outputs (products or services) or clients.

drives Hardwired characteristics of the brain that correct deficiencies or maintain an internal equilibrium by producing emotions to energise individuals.

E

electronic brainstorming A form of brainstorming that relies on networked computers for submitting and sharing creative ideas.

emotional contagion The nonconscious process of 'catching' or sharing another person's emotions by mimicking that person's facial expressions and other nonverbal behaviour.

emotional dissonance The conflict between required and true emotions.

emotional intelligence (EI) A set of abilities to perceive and express emotion, assimilate emotion in thought, understand and reason with emotion, and regulate emotion in oneself and others.

emotional labour The effort, planning and control needed to express organisationally desired emotions during interpersonal transactions.

emotions Physiological, behavioural and psychological episodes experienced toward an object, person or event that create a state of readiness.

empathy A person's understanding of and sensitivity to the feelings, thoughts and situations of others.

employee engagement The employee's emotional and cognitive motivation, self-efficacy to perform the job, perceived clarity of the organisation's vision and his or her specific role in that vision, and belief that he or she has the resources to get the job done.

employee involvement The degree to which employees influence how their work is organised and carried out.

employee share ownership plans (ESOPs) Reward systems that encourage employees to buy company shares.

empowerment A psychological concept in which people experience more self-determination, meaning, competence and impact regarding their role in the organisation.

equity sensitivity An individual's outcome/input preferences and reaction to various outcome/input ratios.

equity theory A theory explaining how people develop perceptions of fairness in the distribution and exchange of resources.

ERG theory A needs hierarchy theory consisting of three fundamental needs—existence, relatedness and growth.

escalation of commitment The tendency to repeat an apparently bad decision or allocate more resources to a failing course of action.

ethical sensitivity A personal characteristic that enables people to recognise the presence of an ethical issue and determine its relative importance.

ethics The study of moral principles or values that determine whether actions are right or wrong and outcomes are good or bad.

evaluation apprehension A decision-making problem that occurs when individuals are reluctant to mention ideas that seem silly because they believe (often correctly) that other team members are silently evaluating them.

evidence-based management The practice of making decisions and taking actions based on research evidence.

exit-voice-loyalty-neglect (EVLN) model The four ways, as indicated in the name, that employees respond to job dissatisfaction.

expectancy theory A motivation theory based on the idea that work effort is directed toward behaviours that people believe will lead to desired outcomes.

extroversion A personality dimension describing people who are outgoing, talkative, sociable and assertive.

F

false-consensus effect A perceptual error in which we overestimate the extent to which others have beliefs and characteristics similar to our own.

Fiedler's contingency model An early contingency leadership model, developed by Fred Fiedler, that suggests that leader effectiveness depends on whether the person's natural leadership style is appropriately matched to the situation.

field surveys Research design strategies that involve collecting and analysing information in a natural environment, such as an office, a factory or other existing location.

five-factor model (FFM) The five abstract dimensions representing most personality traits: conscientiousness, emotional stability, openness to experience, agreeableness and extroversion.

force field analysis Kurt Lewin's model of system-wide change that helps change agents diagnose the forces that drive and restrain proposed organisational change.

formalisation The degree to which organisations standardise behaviour through rules, procedures, formal training and related mechanisms.

four-drive theory A motivation theory that is based on the innate drives to acquire, bond, learn and defend, and that incorporates both emotions and rationality.

functional structure An organisational structure in which employees are organised around specific knowledge or other resources.

fundamental attribution error The tendency to see the person rather than the situation as the main cause of that person's behaviour.

future search An organisational change strategy that consists of system-wide group sessions, usually lasting a few days, in which participants identify trends and establish ways to adapt to those changes.

G

gainsharing plans Team-based rewards that calculate bonuses from the work unit's cost savings and productivity improvement.

general adaptation syndrome A model of the stress experience, consisting of three stages: alarm reaction, resistance and exhaustion.

global mindset The capacity for complex perceiving and thinking characterised by superior awareness of and openness to different ways that others perceive their environment.

globalisation Economic, social and cultural connectivity with people in other parts of the world.

globally integrated enterprise An organisational structure in which work processes and executive functions are distributed around the world through global centres, rather than developed in a home country and replicated in satellite countries or regions.

goal setting The process of motivating employees and clarifying their role perceptions by establishing performance objectives.

grapevine An unstructured and informal network founded on social relationships rather than organisational charts or job descriptions.

grounded theory A process of developing theory through the constant interplay between data gathering and the development of theoretical concepts.

groupthink The tendency of highly cohesive groups to value consensus at the price of decision quality.

H

halo effect A perceptual error whereby our general impression of a person, usually based on one prominent characteristic, colours our perception of other characteristics of that person.

high-performance work practices (HPWP) A perspective which holds that effective organisations incorporate several workplace practices that leverage the potential of human capital.

human capital The stock of knowledge, skills and abilities among employees that provides economic value to the organisation.

hypotheses Statements making empirically testable declarations that certain variables and their corresponding measures are related in a specific way proposed by the theory.

I

implicit favourite A preferred alternative that the decision maker uses repeatedly as a comparison with other choices.

implicit leadership theory A theory stating that people evaluate a leader's effectiveness in terms of how well that person fits preconceived beliefs about the features and behaviours of effective leaders (leadership prototypes) and that people tend to inflate the influence of leaders on organisational events.

impression management The practice of actively shaping our public images.

individualism A cross-cultural value describing the degree to which people in a culture emphasise independence and personal uniqueness.

influence Any behaviour that attempts to alter someone's attitudes or behaviour.

information overload A condition in which the volume of information received exceeds the person's capacity to process it.

ingratiation Any attempt to increase liking by, or perceived similarity to, some targeted person.

inoculation effect A persuasive communication strategy of warning listeners that others will try to influence them in the future and that they should be wary about the opponent's arguments.

intellectual capital A company's stock of knowledge, including human capital, structural capital and relationship capital.

interests-based frame An approach to conflict that emphasises disputants' underlying needs and interests.

interpretivism The view held in many qualitative studies that reality comes from shared meaning among people in that environment.

intuition The ability to know when a problem or opportunity exists and to select the best course of action without conscious reasoning.

J

job burnout The process of emotional exhaustion, cynicism and reduced personal accomplishment that results from prolonged exposure to stressors.

job characteristics model A job design model that relates the motivational properties of jobs to specific personal and organisational consequences of those properties.

job design The process of assigning tasks to a job, including the interdependency of those tasks with other jobs.

job enlargement The practice of adding more tasks to an existing job.

job enrichment The practice of giving employees more responsibility for scheduling, co-ordinating and planning their own work.

job evaluation Systematically rating the worth of jobs within an organisation by measuring their required skill, effort, responsibility and working conditions.

job rotation The practice of moving employees from one job to another.

job satisfaction A person's evaluation of his or her job and work context.

job specialisation The result of division of labour in which work is subdivided into separate jobs and assigned to different people.

Johari Window A model of mutual understanding that encourages disclosure and feedback to increase our own open area and reduce the blind, hidden and unknown areas.

L

laboratory experiment Any research study in which independent variables and variables outside the researcher's main focus of inquiry can be controlled to some extent.

leadership Influencing, motivating and enabling others to contribute toward the effectiveness and success of the organisations of which they are members.

leadership substitutes A theory identifying contingencies that either limit a leader's ability to influence subordinates or make a particular leadership style unnecessary.

lean management A cluster of practices to improve organisational efficiency by continuously reducing waste, unevenness and overburden in the production process.

learning A relatively permanent change in behaviour (or behavioural tendency) that occurs as a result of a person's interaction with the environment.

learning orientation An individual attitude and organisational culture in which people welcome new learning opportunities, actively experiment with new ideas and practices, view reasonable mistakes as a natural part of the learning process and continuously question past practices.

legitimate power An agreement among organisational members that people in certain roles can request certain behaviours of others.

locus of control A person's general belief about the amount of control he or she has over personal life events.

M

Machiavellian values The beliefs that deceit is a natural and acceptable way to influence others and that getting more than one deserves is acceptable.

management by walking around (MBWA) A communication practice in which executives get out of their offices and learn from others in the organisation through face-to-face dialogue.

Maslow's needs hierarchy theory A motivation theory of needs arranged in a hierarchy, whereby people are motivated to fulfil a higher need as a lower one becomes gratified.

matrix structure An organisational structure that overlays two structures (such as a geographic divisional and a functional structure) in order to leverage the benefits of both.

mechanistic structure An organisational structure with a narrow span of control, and a high degree of formalisation and centralisation.

media richness A medium's data-carrying capacity, that is, the volume and variety of information that can be transmitted during a specific time.

mental imagery The process of mentally practising a task and visualising its successful completion.

mental models Visual or relational images in our mind that represent the external world.

moral intensity The degree to which an issue demands the application of ethical principles.

motivation The forces within a person that affect his or her direction, intensity and persistence of voluntary behaviour.

motivator-hygiene theory Herzberg's theory stating that employees are primarily motivated by growth and esteem needs, not by lower level needs.

multisource (360-degree) feedback Information about an employee's performance collected from a full circle of people, including subordinates, peers, supervisors and customers.

Myers-Briggs Type Indicator (MBTI) An instrument designed to measure the elements of Jungian personality theory, particularly preferences regarding perceiving and judging information.

N

need for achievement (nAch) A need in which people want to accomplish reasonably challenging goals, and desire unambiguous feedback and recognition for their success.

need for affiliation (nAff) A need in which people seek approval from others, conform to their wishes and expectations, and avoid conflict and confrontation.

need for power (nPow) A need in which people want to control their environment, including people and material resources, to benefit either themselves (personalised power) or others (socialised power).

needs Goal-directed forces that people experience.

negotiation The process whereby two or more conflicting parties attempt to resolve their divergent goals by redefining the terms of their interdependence.

network structure An alliance of several organisations for the purpose of creating a product or serving a client.

neuroticism A personality dimension describing people with high levels of anxiety, hostility, depression and self-consciousness.

nominal group technique A variation of brainstorming consisting of three stages: participants (1) silently and independently document their ideas, (2) collectively describe these ideas to the other team members without critique, and (3) silently and independently evaluate the ideas presented.

norms The informal rules and shared expectations that groups establish to regulate the behaviour of their members.

O

open systems A perspective which holds that organisations depend on the external environment for resources, affect that environment through their output and consist of internal subsystems that transform inputs to outputs.

organic structure An organisational structure with a wide span of control, little formalisation and decentralised decision making.

organisational (affective) commitment The employee's emotional attachment to, identification with and involvement in a particular organisation.

organisational behaviour (OB) The study of what people think, feel and do in and around organisations.

organisational citizenship behaviours (OCBs) Various forms of co-operation and helpfulness to others that support the organisation's social and psychological context.

organisational culture The values and assumptions shared within an organisation.

organisational effectiveness A broad concept represented by several perspectives, including the organisation's fit with the external environment, internal-subsystems configuration for high performance, emphasis on organisational learning and ability to satisfy the needs of key stakeholders.

organisational efficiency The amount of outputs relative to inputs in the organisation's transformation process.

organisational learning A perspective which holds that organisational effectiveness depends on the organisation's capacity to acquire, share, use and store valuable knowledge.

organisational memory The storage and preservation of intellectual capital.

organisational politics Behaviours that others perceive as self-serving tactics for personal gain at the expense of other people and possibly the organisation.

organisational socialisation The process by which individuals learn the values, expected behaviours and social knowledge necessary to assume their roles in the organisation.

organisational strategy The way the organisation positions itself in its setting in relation to its stakeholders, given the organisation's resources, capabilities and mission.

organisational structure The division of labour as well as the patterns of co-ordination, communication, work flow and formal power that direct organisational activities.

organisations Groups of people who work interdependently toward some purpose.

P

parallel learning structures Highly participative arrangements composed of people from most levels of the organisation who follow the action research model to produce meaningful organisational change.

path–goal leadership theory A contingency theory of leadership based on the expectancy theory of motivation that relates several leadership styles to specific employee and situational contingencies.

perception The process of receiving information about and making sense of the world around us.

personality The relatively enduring pattern of thoughts, emotions and behaviours that characterise a person, along with the psychological processes behind those characteristics.

persuasion The use of facts, logical arguments and emotional appeals to change another person's beliefs and attitudes, usually for the purpose of changing the person's behaviour.

positive organisational behaviour A perspective of organisational behaviour that focuses on building positive qualities and traits within individuals or institutions as opposed to focusing on what is wrong with them.

positivism A view held in quantitative research in which reality exists independent of the perceptions and interpretations of people.

power The capacity of a person, team or organisation to influence others.

power-based frame An approach to conflict that focuses on who has more power in the dispute.

power distance A cross-cultural value describing the degree to which people in a culture accept unequal distribution of power in a society.

primacy effect A perceptual error in which we quickly form an opinion of people on the basis of the first information we receive about them.

procedural justice Perceived fairness of the procedures used to decide the distribution of resources.

process losses Resources (including time and energy) expended toward team development and maintenance rather than the task.

production blocking A time constraint in team decision making due to the procedural requirement that only one person may speak at a time.

profit-sharing plan A reward system that pays bonuses to employees on the basis of the previous year's level of corporate profits.

prospect theory A natural tendency to feel more dissatisfaction from losing a particular amount than satisfaction from gaining an equal amount.

psychological harassment Repeated and hostile or unwanted conduct, verbal comments, actions or gestures that affect an employee's dignity or psychological or physical integrity and that result in a harmful work environment for the employee.

R

rational choice paradigm The view in decision making that people should—and typically do—use logic and all available information to choose the alternative with the highest value.

realistic job preview (RJP) A method of improving organisational socialisation in which job applicants are given a balance of positive and negative information about the job and work context.

reality shock The stress that results when employees perceive discrepancies between their pre-employment expectations and on-the-job reality.

recency effect A perceptual error in which the most recent information dominates our perception of others.

referent power The capacity to influence others on the basis of an identification with and respect for the powerholder.

refreezing The latter part of the organisational change process, in which systems and conditions are introduced that reinforce and maintain the desired behaviours.

relationship conflicts Types of conflict in which people focus on the characteristics of other individuals, rather than on the issues, as the source of conflict.

representativeness heuristic A natural tendency to evaluate probabilities of events or objects by the degree to which they resemble (are representative of) other events or objects rather than on objective probability information.

representative sampling The process of sampling a population in such a way that one can extrapolate the results of that sample to the larger population.

resilience The capability of individuals to cope successfully in the face of significant change, adversity or risk.

resistance point The worst outcome that an individual is prepared to accept before walking away from a negotiation.

rights-based frame An approach to conflict that focuses on contractual obligations, legal rights or precedents.

rituals The programmed routines of daily organisational life that dramatise the organisation's culture.

role A set of behaviours that people are expected to perform because of the positions they hold in a team and organisation.

role perceptions The extent to which people understand the job duties (roles) assigned to or expected of them.

S

satisficing Selecting an alternative that is satisfactory or 'good enough' rather than the alternative with the highest value (maximisation).

scenario planning A systematic process of thinking about alternative futures and what the organisation should do to anticipate and react to those environments.

scientific management The practice of systematically partitioning work into its smallest elements and standardising tasks to achieve maximum efficiency.

scientific method A set of principles and procedures that help researchers to systematically understand previously unexplained events and conditions.

selective attention The process of attending to some information received by our senses and ignoring other information.

self-concept An individual's self-beliefs and self-evaluations.

self-directed team (SDT) A cross-functional work group that is organised around work processes, completes an entire piece of work requiring several interdependent tasks and has substantial autonomy over the execution of those tasks.

self-efficacy A person's belief that he or she has the ability, motivation, correct role perceptions and favourable situation to complete a task successfully.

self-fulfilling prophecy The perceptual process in which our expectations about another person cause that person to act in a way that is consistent with those expectations.

self-leadership The process of influencing oneself to establish the self-direction and self-motivation needed to perform a task.

self-reinforcement Reinforcement that occurs when an employee has control over a reinforcer but doesn't 'take' it until completing a self-set goal.

self-serving bias The tendency to attribute our favourable outcomes to internal factors and our failures to external factors.

self-talk The process of talking to ourselves about our own thoughts or actions.

servant leadership The view that leaders serve followers, rather than vice versa; leaders help employees fulfil their needs and are coaches, stewards and facilitators of employee performance.

sexual harassment Unwelcome conduct of a sexual nature that detrimentally affects the work environment or leads to adverse job-related consequences for its victims.

shared leadership The view that leadership is broadly distributed, rather than assigned to one person, such that people within the team and organisation lead each other.

share options Reward systems that give employees the right to purchase company shares at a future date at a predetermined price.

situational leadership theory (SLT) A commercially popular but poorly supported leadership model stating that effective leaders vary their style (telling, selling, participating, delegating) with the 'readiness' of followers.

skill variety The extent to which employees must use different skills and talents to perform tasks within their jobs.

social capital The knowledge and other resources available to people or social units (teams, organisations) from a durable network that connects them to others.

social identity theory A theory that explains self-concept in terms of the person's unique characteristics (personal identity) and membership in various social groups (social identity).

social learning theory A theory stating that much learning occurs by observing others, then modelling the behaviours that lead to favourable outcomes and avoiding behaviours that lead to punishing consequences.

social loafing The problem that occurs when people exert less effort (and usually perform at a lower level) when working in teams than when working alone.

span of control The number of people directly reporting to the next level in the hierarchy.

stakeholders Individuals, organisations and other entities who affect, or are affected by, the organisation's objectives and actions.

stereotyping The process of assigning traits to people on the basis of their membership in a social category.

strength-based coaching A positive organisational behaviour approach to coaching and feedback that focuses on building and leveraging the employee's strengths rather than trying to correct his or her weaknesses.

stress An adaptive response to a situation that is perceived as challenging or threatening to a person's wellbeing.

stressors Any environmental conditions that place a physical or emotional demand on a person.

subjective expected utility The probability (expectation) of satisfaction (utility) resulting from choosing a specific alternative in a decision.

substitutability A contingency of power pertaining to the availability of alternatives.

superordinate goal A broad goal that all parties to a dispute value and agree is important.

surface-level diversity The observable demographic or physiological differences in people, such as their race, ethnicity, gender, age and physical disabilities.

T

tacit knowledge Knowledge that is embedded in our actions and ways of thinking, and is transmitted only through observation and experience.

target point The best possible outcome that an individual hopes to achieve in a negotiation.

task conflicts Disagreements among group members about how a task should be accomplished.

task identity The degree to which a job requires completion of a whole or an identifiable piece of work.

task interdependence The extent to which team members must share materials, information or expertise in order to perform their jobs.

task significance The degree to which a job has a substantial impact on the organisation and/or larger society.

team-based structure An organisational structure built around self-directed teams that complete an entire piece of work.

team building A process that consists of formal activities intended to improve the development and functioning of a work team.

team cohesion The degree of attraction people feel toward the team and their motivation to remain members.

teams Groups of two or more people who interact and influence each other, are mutually accountable for achieving common goals associated with organisational objectives and perceive themselves as a social entity within an organisation.

theory A general set of propositions that describes interrelationships among several concepts.

third-party conflict resolution Any attempt by a relatively neutral person to help conflicting parties resolve their differences.

transactional leadership Leadership that helps organisations achieve their current objectives more efficiently, such as by linking job performance to valued rewards and ensuring that employees have the resources needed to get the job done.

transformational leadership A leadership perspective that explains how leaders change teams or organisations by creating, communicating and modelling a vision for the organisation or work unit, and inspiring employees to strive for that vision.

trust refers to positive expectations one person has toward another person or group in situations involving risk.

U

uncertainty avoidance A cross-cultural value describing the degree to which people in a culture tolerate ambiguity (low uncertainty avoidance) or feel threatened by ambiguity and uncertainty (high uncertainty avoidance).

unfreezing The first part of the organisational change process, in which the change agent produces disequilibrium between the driving and restraining forces.

upward appeal A type of influence in which someone with higher authority or expertise is called on (in reality or symbolically) to support the influencer's position.

V

values Relatively stable, evaluative beliefs that guide a person's preferences for outcomes or courses of action in a variety of situations.

virtual teams Teams whose members operate across space, time and organisational boundaries, and are linked through information technologies to achieve organisational tasks.

virtual work Work performed away from the traditional physical workplace by means of information technology.

W

wikis Collaborative Web spaces at which anyone in a group can write, edit or remove material from the website.

win–lose orientation The belief that conflicting parties are drawing from a fixed pie, so the more one party receives, the less the other party will receive.

win–win orientation The belief that the parties will find a mutually beneficial solution to their disagreement.

work–life balance The degree to which a person minimises conflict between work and nonwork demands.

workaholic A person who is highly involved in work, feels compelled to work and has a low enjoyment of work.

Index

D

E

F

G

J

K

L

M

N

O

P

Q

R

S

T

X

Y

Z